COMPUTER SCIENCE
A Structured Approach Using C++
Second Edition

Behrouz A. Forouzan
De Anza College

Richard F. Gilberg
Retired, De Anza College

Australia • Canada • Mexico • Singapore • Spain
United Kingdom • United States

Publisher: *Bill Stenquist*
Acquisitions Editor: *Kallie Swanson*
Editorial Assistant: *Aarti Jayaraman*
Technology Project Manager: *Burke Taft*
Executive Marketing Manager: *Tom Ziolkowski*
Advertising Project Manager: *Vicky Wan*
Marketing Assistant: *Jennifer Gee*
Editorial Production Project Manager: *Kelsey McGee*
Print/Media Buyer: *Kristine Waller*
Permissions Editor: *Sommy Ko*
Cover Designer: *Ross Carron*
Cover Image: *Photodisc/Steve Cole*
Cover Printing, Printing and Binding: *Edwards/Ann Arbor*
Composition and Production: *Carlisle Communications*

Printed in the United States of America

1 2 3 4 5 6 7 06 05 04 03 02

For more information about our products, contact us at:
Thomson Learning Academic Resource Center
1-800-423-0563

For permission to use material from this text, contact us by:
Phone: 1-800-730-2214
Fax: 1-800-730-2215
Web: http://www.thomsonrights.com

Library of Congress Control Number: Service: 2003109925

ISBN 0-534-37480-8

Brooks/Cole–Thomson Learning
10 Davis Drive
Belmont, CA 94002
USA

Asia
Thomson Learning
5 Shenton Way #01-01
UIC Building
Singapore 068808

Australia
Nelson Thomson Learning
102 Dodds Street
South Melbourne, Victoria 3205
Australia

Canada
Nelson Thomson Learning
1120 Birchmount Road
Toronto, Ontario M1K 5G4
Canada

Europe/Middle East/Africa
Thomson Learning
High Holborn House
50/51 Bedford Row
London WC1R 4LR
United Kingdom

Latin America
Thomson Learning
Seneca, 53
Colonia Polanco
11560 Mexico D.F.
Mexico

Spain
Paraninfo Thomson Learning
Calle Magallanes, 25
28015 Madrid, Spain

To Farhad, Homeira, Ryan, and Justin

B. A. F.

To Bryan, Christopher, Amanda, Sarah, Zackery, and Patrick

R. F. G.

Preface

Computer Science: A Structured Approach Using C++ has two primary objectives: to teach the basic principles of programming as outlined in the ACM curriculum for a CS1 class and to teach the basic constructs of the C++ language. Our text puts these objectives in the context of good software engineering concepts that we have developed over thirty years in industry and academia.

USING THE C++ LANGUAGE

While C++ is a complex and professional language, our experience has shown that beginning students can easily understand it. In fact, its input/output and pass-by-reference capabilities make it easier than traditional C. We believe that if the language is put into a perspective that allows the student to understand its design, C++ is not a difficult language.

There are three aspects of C++ that separate it from most other languages: expressions, pointers, and classes. The concept of expressions as used in C and C++ is unique. The first half of our text builds a solid understanding of expressions and the basic structured programming constructs. With a firm grasp of the expressions and basic constructs, much of the mystery of C++ disappears. The second C++ power tool is the pointer. Pointers are discussed in Chapter 9 and then used throughout the rest of the text.

While mentioned lightly earlier, the development of classes begins in Chapter 10 with a discussion of basic class concepts, including defining and accessing class objects, constructors and destructors, class functions, invariants, and complex class functions. Chapter 11 continues the development of classes with discussions of initialization lists, overloading, static members, friend classes, classes and pointers, arrays of objects, and the structures inherited from the C language. Chapters 12 and 13 complete the coverage of class concepts, although they are also discussed in our coverage of exception handlers, advanced I/O, and the linked list chapter, which implements the linked list as a class object.

WHAT'S NEW IN THIS EDITION

Our first tenet in this edition was to keep the basic design concepts that were incorporated in the first edition. Therefore, the basic structure and style of the text has not been changed. We still present programming principles before their implementation in C++. Our visual approach coupled with extensive examples has been expanded. While the programs have a more C++ look and feel, readability and consistence of style are still emphasized.

Nonetheless, the changes, especially in the second half of the text, are extensive. They incorporate two important areas.

1. Changes have been made throughout the text to reflect the standard.
2. Our coverage of classes, especially templates, inheritance, and exception handling, is more extensive. Each of these subjects has been expanded to a full chapter.

In general, every program in the text has been reworked to reflect the style and power of the language and its implementation in the field. Review questions have been added at the end of each chapter and some new exercises, problems, and projects added. A few of the programming applications have been extensively reworked: most notedly, the Morse Code program has been redesigned as a class.

With the exception of Chapter 7, changes in the first half of the book are relatively minor. Starting with Chapter 10, the material has been extensively redesigned and reordered.

- Chapter 10, **Classes**, incorporates the material previously found in Chapter 11. Chapter 10's software engineering section has been changed to cover the basic use of **UML** in the portrayal of classes. In addition, UML is used to pictorially depict class structures starting with Chapter 10. This change causes several of the Software Engineering topics in the second half of the book to be moved.
- Chapter 11, **Advanced Class Features**, incorporates the material previously found in Chapter 12, with the exception of inheritance. In addition, a new section on static members has been included. Also found in Chapter 11 are simplified presentations of structures, enumeration, and unions.
- Chapter 12 covers the concepts of **inheritance**, **polymorphism**, **abstract classes**, and **composition**.
- Chapter 13 discusses **templates** and their implementation.
- The coverage of **strings** has been changed to reflect the new string class found in the standard. It is placed as Chapter 14 because strings are required for the following chapters that follow it.
- Chapter 15 is a new chapter that presents the concepts implemented in the C++ **exception handler**.
- Chapter 16 has been renamed **Advanced I/O Concepts**. Although it still covers binary files, the material has been expanded and reoriented to stream objects. At the end of Chapter 16, the software engineering section discusses file updating concepts using the classic sequential file update model.
- **Linked lists** have been placed at the end of the text as Chapter 17 as an example of a class implementation and as a transition to data structures.
- Many of the appendixes are unchanged except for cosmetic improvements, such as changes in the programming style to make them more C++ oriented. Two new appendixes, **Namespaces** and the **STL Library**, introduce these two features of the languages. A basic coverage of namespaces has also been included in Chapter 2.

FEATURES OF THE BOOK

Several features of this book make it unique and easy for beginning students.

Structure and Style

One of our basic tenets is that good habits are formed early. The corollary is that bad habits are hard to break. Therefore, we consistently emphasize the principles of structured programming and software engineering. Every complete program uses a consistent style. As programs are analyzed, style and standards are further explained. We are not saying that there aren't other good styles, but our experience has shown that if students are exposed to a good style and implement it, they will be better able to adapt to other good styles. On the other hand, unlearning sloppy shortcut habits is very difficult.

Principle before Practice

Whenever possible, we develop the principle of a subject before we introduce the language implementation. For example, in Chapter 5, we first introduce the concept of logical data and selection and then we introduce the *if...else* and *switch* statements. This approach gives the student an understanding of selection before introducing the nuances of the language.

Visual Approach

A brief scan of the book will demonstrate that our approach is visual. There are more than 440 figures, 110 tables, and 325 program examples. While this amount of material tends to create a large book, the visual approach makes it easy for students to follow the material.

Examples

While the programming examples vary in complexity, each uses a consistent style. Our experience working with productional programs that live for 10 to 20 years convinced us that readable and understandable programs are easier to work with than programs written in a terse, cryptic manner. We consistently follow a style that includes documentation through comments and intelligent data names; we also limit declarations, definitions, and statements to one per line. These programs are available to students to allow them not only to run them, but to explore related topics through modification and experimentation.

Coding Techniques

Throughout the text, we include coding techniques that make programs more readable and often more efficient. For example, in the analysis of Program 5-4 on page 195, you will find the following discussion:

> Where do we check for **greater than**? The answer is that we **default** the **greater than** condition to the last *else* (statement 20). When coding a two-way selection statement, try to code the most probable condition first; with nested selection statements, code the most probable first and the least probable last.

Software Engineering

A discussion of software engineering principles concludes each chapter. Our intent is not to replace a separate course in software engineering. Rather, we firmly believe that by incorporating basic software engineering principles early in their studies, students will be better prepared for a formal treatment of the subject. Even more important, by writing well-engineered programs from the beginning, students will not be forced to unlearn and relearn. They will better understand software discussions in subsequent classes.

While the software engineering sections are found at the end of each chapter, they are most successfully taught by introducing them as the chapter unfolds. Then, a short review at the end of the chapter summarizes the principles that have been demonstrated during the lectures. The rest of the book stands on its own, however, without the software engineering sections. You may cover these sections during lectures, as additional reading, or you may decide to exclude them entirely.

Pedagogical End Material

Each chapter contains three sets of pedagogical materials:

Tips and Common Programming Errors points out helpful hints and possible problem areas.

Key Terms provides a list of the boldface terms introduced in the chapter.

Summary contains a concise overview of the key points for students to understand in the chapter.

Practice Sets

The practice sets are divided into four sections of increasing complexity:

Review Questions provide a short true/false and multiple choice questions to test the student's understanding of the material.

Exercises are short questions covering the material in the chapter. The answers to selected questions are available online at the Brooks/Cole site.

Problems are short coding problems generally intended to be run on a computer. They can usually be developed in two to three hours.

Projects are longer, major assignments that may take the average student six to nine hours to develop.

The *Instructor's Solution Manual*, available on line, contains a complete set of solutions to all review questions, exercises and problems.

APPENDIXES AND COVER MATERIAL

The appendixes are intended to provide quick reference material (such as the ANSI Character Set) or a review of material (such as numbering systems) usually covered in a general computer class. We have also included four conceptual appendixes, one on manipulators, one on classes related to input and output, one on namespaces, and one on the Standard Template Library. These appendixes provide insight into these features of C++. Finally, three appendixes flesh out the C++ language: command line arguments, bit-wise operators, and pointers to functions. While beyond the scope of a CS1 class, they provide a handy reference when needed.

We have placed the Precedence Table inside the front cover because this table is so often needed. Inside the back cover we have included a quick reference summary of the C++ input/output class methods, manipulators, and flags.

ACKNOWLEDGMENTS

To anyone who has not been through the process, the value of peer reviews cannot be appreciated enough. Writing a text rapidly becomes a myopic process. The important guidance of reviewers who can stand back and review the text as a whole cannot be measured. To twist an old cliche, "They are not valuable, they are priceless." We would especially like to acknowledge the contributions of the following reviewers: Theresa Beauboeuf of South Eastern Louisiana University, Charlotte Busch of Texas A & M University, Robert Cubert of the University of Florida, Eric Nagler of Lawrence Technological University and ITT, and Ron Schwartz of Florida Atlantic University. Also, the editors and production staff at Brooks/Cole have provided extremely valuable guidance and support in the development of this text. We would especially like to acknowledge the contributions of our editor, Kallie Swanson, and others who worked behind the scenes.

Last, and most obviously not the least, is the support of our families and friends. While the authors suffer through the writing process, families and friends suffer through their absence.

Behrouz A. Forouzan
Richard F. Gilberg

Contents

1 Introduction to Computers

Welcome to computer science! You are about to explore a wonderful and exciting world—a world that offers many challenging and interesting careers.

But you must be aware that computer jobs demand a lot from you. If you are going to succeed in the computing field, you must be a planner: someone who can work precisely with a sometimes overwhelming amount of detail and, at the same time, who can see and understand the environment in which you work.

In this chapter, we introduce you to the concepts of computer science, especially as they pertain to computer programming. You will study the concept of a computer system and learn how it relates to computer hardware and software. We will also present a short history of computer programming languages so that you will understand how they have evolved and how C++ fits into the picture.

We will then describe how to write a program, first with a review of the tools and steps involved, and then with a review of a system development methodology.

1-1 COMPUTER SYSTEMS

Today computer systems are found everywhere. Computers have become almost as common as televisions. But what is a computer? A computer is a system made of two major components: hardware and software. The computer hardware is the physical equipment. The software is the collection of programs (instructions) that allow the hardware to do its job. Figure 1-1 represents a **computer system**.

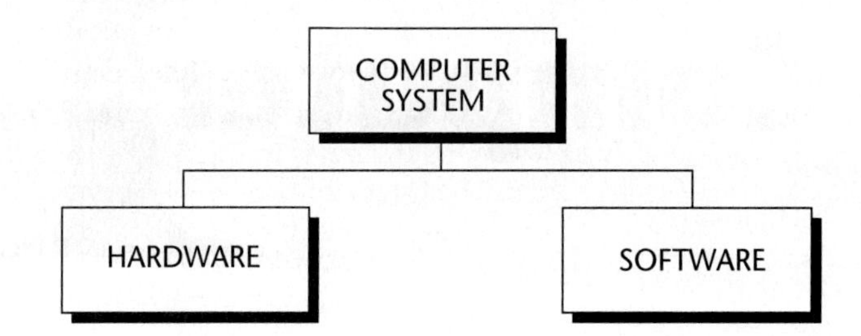

Figure 1-1 A computer system

1-2 COMPUTER HARDWARE

The **hardware** component of the computer system consists of five parts: input devices, central processing unit (CPU), primary storage or main memory, output devices, and auxiliary storage devices (Figure 1-2).

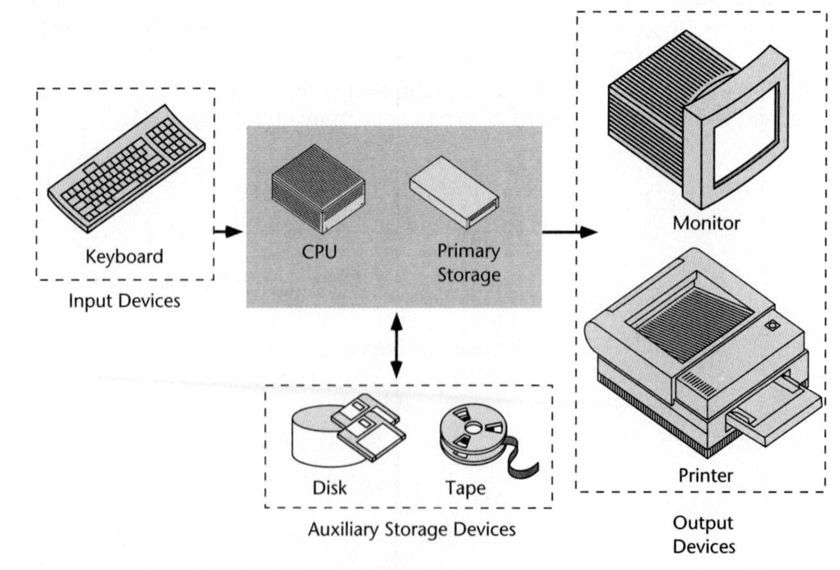

Figure 1-2 Basic hardware components

The **input device** is usually a **keyboard** where programs and data are entered into the computer. Examples of other input devices include a mouse, a pen or stylus, a touch screen, or an audio input unit.

The **central processing unit's (CPU)** function is to execute instructions, such as arithmetic calculations, comparisons among data, and movement of data inside the system. **Primary storage** is a place where the programs and data are stored temporarily during processing. The data in primary storage are erased when you turn off a personal computer or you log off from a time-sharing computer.

The **output device** is usually a monitor or a printer where the output will be shown. If the output is shown on the **monitor**, we say we have a **soft copy**. If it is printed on the **printer**, we say we have a **hard copy**.

Auxiliary or secondary **storage** is used for both input and output. It is the place where the programs and data are stored permanently. When you turn off the computer, your programs and data remain in the secondary storage ready for the next time you need them.

1-3 COMPUTER SOFTWARE

Computer **software** is divided into two broad categories: system software and application software. This is true regardless of the hardware system architecture. System software manages the computer resources. It provides the interface between the hardware and the users, but does nothing to directly serve the users' needs. Application software, on the other hand, is directly responsible for helping users solve their problems. Figure 1-3 shows this breakdown of computer software.

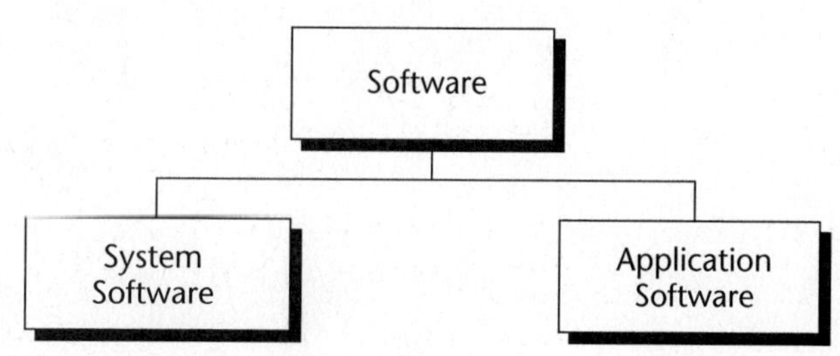

Figure 1-3 Types of software

SYSTEM SOFTWARE

System software consists of programs that manage the hardware resources of a computer and perform required information processing tasks. These programs are divided into three classes: the operating system, system support, and system development.

The **operating system** provides services such as a user interface, file and database access, and interfaces to communication systems. The primary purpose of this software is to keep the system operating in an efficient manner while allowing the users access to the system.

System support software provides system utilities and other operating services. Examples of system utilities are sort programs and disk format programs. Operating services consist of programs that provide performance statistics for the operational staff and security monitors to protect the system and data.

The last system software category, **system development software**, includes the language translators that convert programs into machine language for execution, debugging tools to assure that the programs are error-free, and computer-assisted software engineering (CASE) systems that are beyond the scope of this book.

APPLICATION SOFTWARE

Application software is broken into two classes: general-purpose software and application-specific software. **General-purpose software** is purchased from a software developer and can be used for more than one application. Examples of general-purpose software include word processors, database management systems, and computer-aided design systems. They are called general purpose because they can solve a variety of user computing problems.

Application-specific software can be used only for its intended purpose. A general ledger system used by accountants and a material requirements planning system are examples of application-specific software. They can be used only for the task they were designed for; they cannot be used for other generalized tasks.

The relationship between system and application software is seen in Figure 1-4. In this figure, each circle represents an interface point. The inner core is the hardware. The user is represented by the outer layer. To work with the system, the typical user uses some form of application software. The application software in turn interacts with the operating system, which is a part of the system software layer. The system software provides the direct interaction with the hardware. Note the opening at the bottom of the figure. This is the path followed by the user, who interacts directly with the operating system whenever necessary.

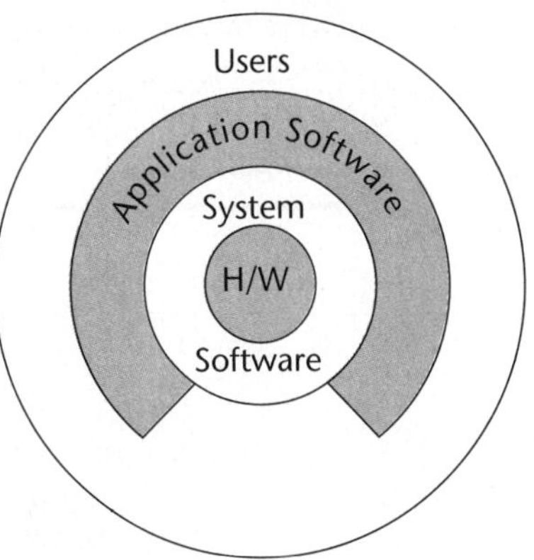

Figure 1-4 Software

If users cannot buy software that supports their needs, then a custom-developed application must be built. In today's computing environment, one of the tools used to develop software is the C++ language that you will be studying in this text.

1-4 COMPUTING ENVIRONMENTS

PERSONAL COMPUTING ENVIRONMENT

In 1971, Marcian E. Hoff, working for Intel, combined the basic elements of the central processing unit into the microprocessor. This first computer on a chip was the Intel 4004 and was the great-great-great grandparent of Intel's Pentium system.

If you are using a personal computer, all of the computer hardware components are tied together in your **personal computer** (or **PC** for short). In this situation, you have the whole computer for yourself; you can do whatever you want to do. A typical personal computer is shown in Figure 1-5.

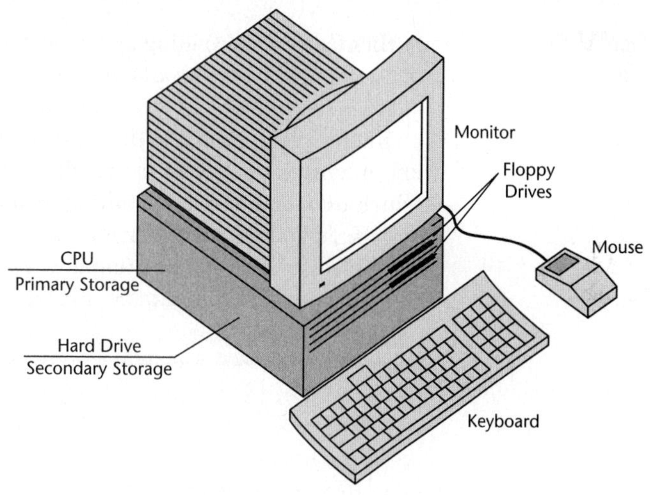

Figure 1-5 Personal computing environment

TIME-SHARING ENVIRONMENT

Employees in large companies often work in what is known as a **time-sharing environment**. In the time-sharing environment, many users are connected to one or more computers. These computers may be minicomputers or central mainframes. The terminals they use are often nonprogrammable, although today we see more and more microcomputers being used to simulate terminals. Also, in the time-sharing environment, the output devices (such as printers) and auxiliary storage devices (such as disks) are shared by all of the users. A typical college lab in which a minicomputer is shared by many students is shown in Figure 1-6.

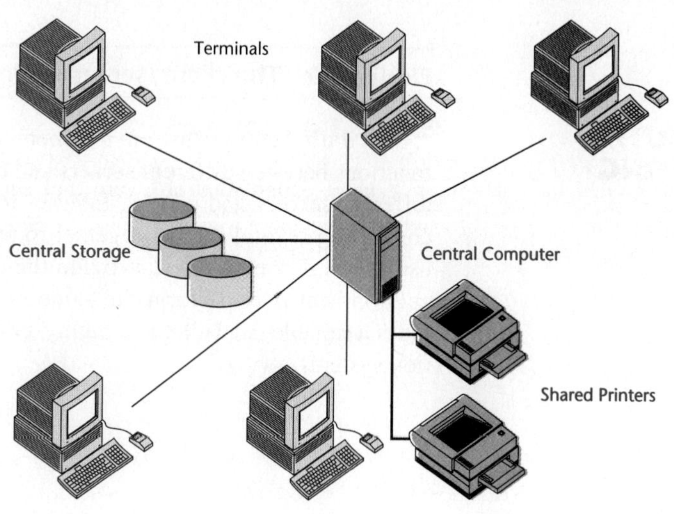

Figure 1-6 Time-sharing environment

In a time-sharing environment, all computing must be done by the central computer. In other words, the central computer has many duties: it must control the shared resources; it must manage the shared data and printing; and, it must also do the computing. All of this work keeps the computer very busy. In fact, it is sometimes so busy that the user becomes frustrated by the computer's slow responses.

CLIENT/SERVER ENVIRONMENT

A **client/server** computing environment splits the computing function between a central computer and users' computers. The users are given personal computers or workstations so that some of the computation responsibility can be moved from the central computer and assigned to the workstations. In the client/server environment, the users' microcomputers or workstations are called the **client**. The central computer, which may be a powerful microcomputer, a minicomputer, or a central mainframe system, is known as the **server**. Because the work is now shared between the users' computers and the central computer, response time and monitor display are faster and the users are more productive. Figure 1-7 shows a typical client/server environment.

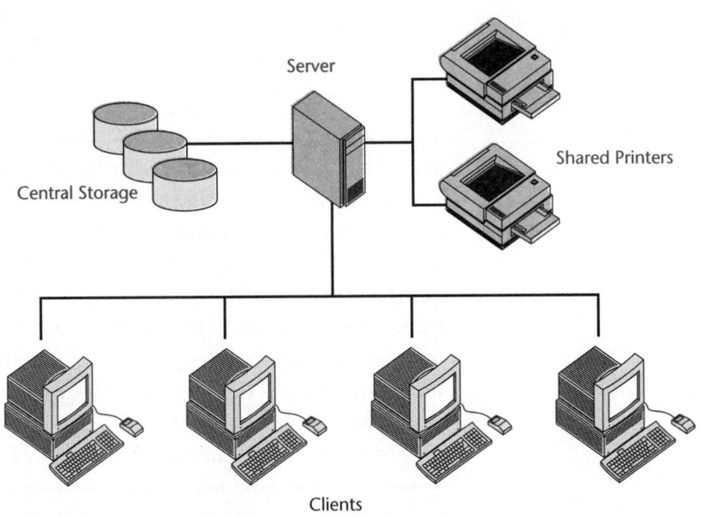

Figure 1-7 The client/server environment

DISTRIBUTED COMPUTING

A **distributed computing** environment provides a seamless integration of computing functions between different servers and clients. The Internet provides connectivity to different servers and clients. Internet today extends to wired and wireless devices connecting several servers together to provide a single service. For example, E-Bay uses several computers to provide the Auction Service. Several computers in this environment may perform the same or different functions. This environment provides a reliable, scalable, and highly available network. Figure 1-8 shows a distribution system.

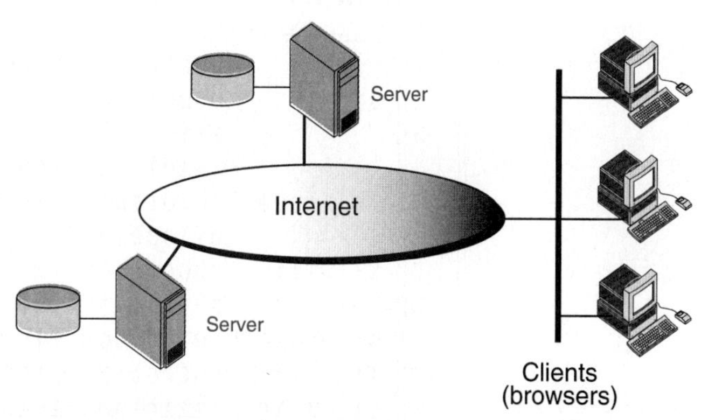

Figure 1-8 Distributed computing

1-5 COMPUTER LANGUAGES

To write a program for a computer, you must use a **computer language**. Over the years, computer languages have evolved from machine language to natural languages. A time line for computer languages is seen in Figure 1-9.

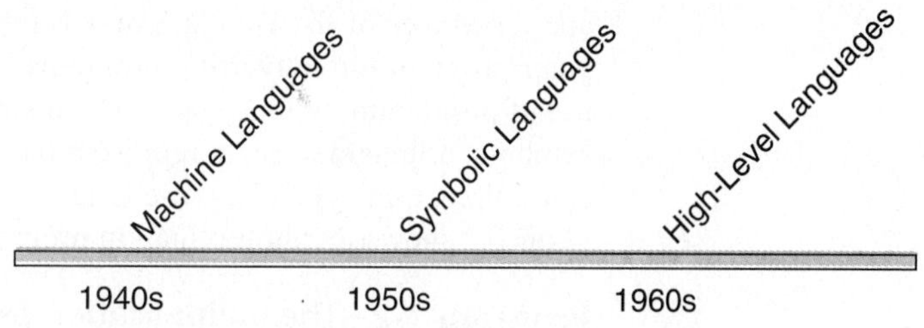

Figure 1-9 Computer language evolution

MACHINE LANGUAGES

In the earliest days of computers, the only programming languages available were **machine languages**. Each computer has its own machine language, which is made of streams of 0s and 1s. Program 1-1 shows an example of a machine language program. This program multiplies two numbers and prints the results.

The instructions in machine language must be in streams of 0s and 1s because the internal circuit of a computer is made of switches, transistors, and other electronic devices that can be in one of two states: off or on. The off state is represented by 0; the on state is represented by 1.

Program 1-1 The multiplication program in machine language

```
         00000000 00000100 0000000000000000
01011110 00001100 11000010 0000000000000010
         11101111 00010110 0000000000000101
         11101111 10011110 0000000000001011
11111000 10101101 11011111 0000000000010010
         01100010 11011111 0000000000010101
11101111 00000010 11111011 0000000000010111
11110100 10101101 11011111 0000000000011110
00000011 10100010 11011111 0000000000100001
11101111 00000010 11111011 0000000000100100
01111110 11110100 10101101
11111000 10101110 11000101 0000000000101011
00000110 10100010 11111011 0000000000110001
11101111 00000010 11111011 0000000000110100
         01010000 11010100 0000000000111011
                  00000100 0000000000111101
```

The only language understood by a computer is machine language.

SYMBOLIC LANGUAGES

It became obvious that not many programs would be written if programmers continued to work in machine language. In the early 1950s, Grace Hopper, a mathematician and a member of the United States Navy, developed the concept of a special computer program for converting programs into machine language. Her work led to the use of programming languages, which simply mirrored the machine languages using symbols, or mnemonics, to represent the various machine language instructions. Because they used symbols, these languages were known as **symbolic languages**. Program 1-2 shows the multiplication program in a symbolic language.

Program 1-2 The multiplication program in a symbolic language

```
entry main,^m<r2>
subl2 #12,sp
jsb   C$MAIN_ARGS
movab $CHAR_STRING_CON

pushal  -8(fp)
pushal  (r2)
calls   #2,read
pushal  -12(fp)
pushal  3(r2)
calls   #2,read
mull3   -8(fp),-12(fp),-
pusha   6(r2)
calls   #2,print
clrl    r0
ret
```

A special program called an **assembler** is used to translate symbolic code into machine language. Because symbolic languages had to be assembled into machine language, they soon became known as **assembly languages**. This name is still used today for symbolic languages that closely represent the machine language of their computer.

HIGH-LEVEL LANGUAGES

Although symbolic languages greatly improved programming efficiency, they still required programmers to concentrate on the hardware they were using. Working with symbolic languages was also very tedious because each machine instruction had to be individually coded. The desire to improve programmer efficiency and to change the focus from the computer to the problem being solved led to the development of **high-level languages**.

High-level languages are portable to many different computers, allowing the programmer to concentrate on the application problem at hand rather than the intricacies of the computer. High-level languages are designed to relieve the programmer from the details of the assembly language. High-level languages share one thing with symbolic languages: They must be converted to machine language. This process is called compilation.

The first widely used high-level language, FORTRAN,[1] was created by John Backus and an IBM team in 1957; it is still widely used today in scientific and engineering applications. Following soon after FORTRAN was COBOL.[2] Admiral Grace Hopper was again a key figure, this time in the development of the COBOL business language.

Over the years, several other languages—most notably BASIC, Pascal, Ada, and C—were developed. Today, one of the more popular high-level languages for system software and new application code is C++. Program 1-3 shows the Program 1-2 multiplication program as it would appear written in the C++ language.

Program 1-3 The multiplication program in C++

```
/* This program reads two integer numbers from the
   keyboard and prints their product.
      Written by:
      Date:
*/
#include <iostream>
using namespace std;

int main ()
{
   int number1;
   int number2;
   int result;

   cin >> number1;
   cin >> number2;
   result = number1 * number2;
   cout << result;
```

[1] FORTRAN is an acronym for FORmula TRANslation.

[2] COBOL is an acronym for COmmon Business-Oriented Language.

Program 1-3 The multiplication program in C++ *(Continued)*

```
    return 0;
} // main
```

NATURAL LANGUAGES

Ideally, we could use our **natural language** (such as English, French, or Chinese), and the computer would understand it and execute our requests immediately. Although this may sound like something out of science fiction, considerable work on natural language is being done in labs today. So far, its use in industry is still quite limited.

1-6 WRITING, EDITING, COMPILING, AND LINKING PROGRAMS

As we learned in the previous section, a computer understands a program only if the program is coded in its machine language. In this section, we explain the procedure for turning a program written in C++ into machine language. The process is presented in a straightforward, linear fashion, but you should recognize that these steps are repeated many times during the development process to correct errors and make improvements to the code.

It is the job of the programmer to write the program and then to turn it into an **executable** (machine language) **file**. There are three steps in this process: (1) writing and editing the program, (2) compiling the program, and (3) linking the program with the required library modules.

WRITING AND EDITING PROGRAMS

The software used to write programs is known as a **text editor**. A text editor helps you enter, change, and store character data. Depending on the editor on your system, you could use it for writing letters, creating reports, or writing programs. The big difference between the other forms of text processing and writing programs is that programs are oriented around lines of code, while most text processing is oriented around characters and lines.

Your text editor could be a generalized word processor, but it is more often a special editor provided by the same company that supplies your compiler. Some of the features you should look for in your editor are search commands to locate and replace statements, copy-and-paste commands that can be used to copy or move statements from one part of your program to another, and formatting commands that allow you to set tabs to align statements.

After you complete a program, you save your file to disk. This file will be input to the compiler; it is known as a **source file**.

COMPILING PROGRAMS

The information in a source file stored on disk must be translated into machine language so the computer can understand it. This is the job of the **compiler**. The C++ compiler is actually two separate programs: the **preprocessor** and the **translator**.

The preprocessor reads the source code and prepares it for the translator. While preparing the code, it scans for special commands known as **preprocessor directives**. These directives tell the preprocessor to look for special code libraries, make substitutions in the code, and in other ways prepare the code for translation into machine language. The result of preprocessing is called the **translation unit**.

After the preprocessor has prepared the code for compilation, the translator does the work of actually converting the program into machine language. The translator reads the translation unit and writes the resulting **object module** to a file that can then be combined with other precompiled units to form the final program. An object module is the code in machine language. Even though the output of the compiler is machine language code, it is not yet ready to run; that is, it is not yet executable because it does not have the required C++ and other functions included.

LINKING PROGRAMS

As we will see later, a C++ program is made up of many functions. Some of these functions are written by you and are a part of your source program. However, there are other functions, such as input/output processes and mathematical library functions, that exist elsewhere and must be attached to your program. The **linker** assembles all of these functions, yours and the system's, into your final **executable program** (Figure 1-10).

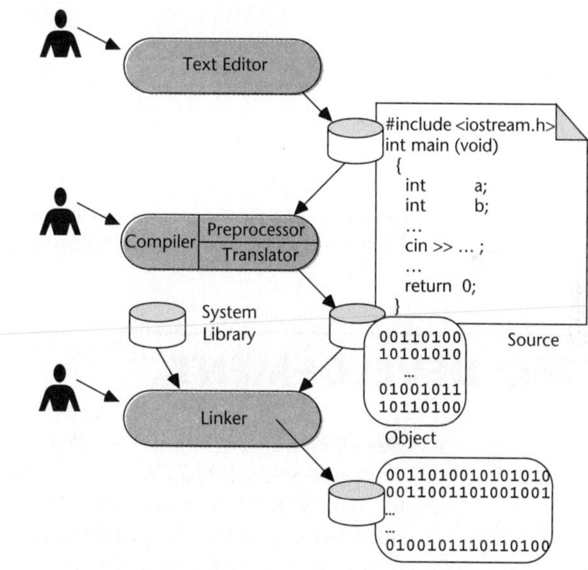

Figure 1-10 Building a C++ program

1-7 PROGRAM EXECUTION

Once your program has been linked, it is ready for execution. To execute your program you use an operating system command, such as *run*, to load your program into primary memory and execute it. Getting the program into memory is the function of an operating system program known as the **loader**. It locates the executable program and reads it into memory. When everything is ready, control is given to the program and it begins execution.

In a typical program execution, the program reads data for processing, either from the user or from a file. After the program processes the data, it prepares the output. Data output can be to the user's monitor or to a file. When the program is finished, it tells the operating system, which removes the program from memory. A program execution in a personal computer environment is seen in Figure 1-11.

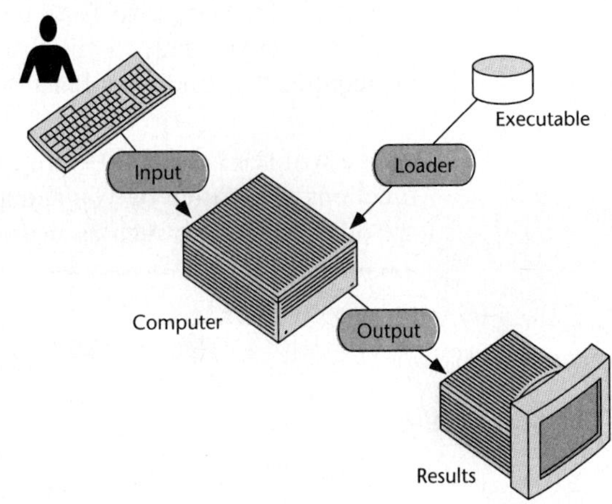

Figure 1-11 Executing programs

1-8 SYSTEM DEVELOPMENT

We've now considered the steps necessary for building your program. In this section, we discuss *how* you go about developing a program. This critical process determines the overall quality and success of your program. If you design each program carefully, using good structured development techniques, your programs will be efficient, error-free,[3] and easy to maintain.

SYSTEM DEVELOPMENT LIFE CYCLE

Today's large-scale, modern programming projects are built using a series of interrelated phases commonly referred to as the **system development life cycle**. Although the exact number and names of the phases differ depending on the environment, there is general agreement as to the steps that must be followed. Whatever the methodology, today's software engineering concepts require a rigorous and systematic approach to software development.[4]

One very popular development life cycle is known as the **waterfall model**. Depending on the company and the type of software being developed, this model has between five and seven phases. Figure 1-12 offers one possible variation on the model.

The waterfall model starts with *systems requirements*. In this phase, the systems analyst defines requirements that specify what the proposed system is to accomplish. The requirements are usually stated in terms that the user understands. The *analysis*

---

[3]Many computer scientists believe that all programs contain at least one *bug* that is just waiting to cause problems given the right set of circumstances. Programs have run for years without problems only to fail when an unusual situation occurs.

[4]For a discussion of various models, see *Software Engineering* by Roger S. Pressman.

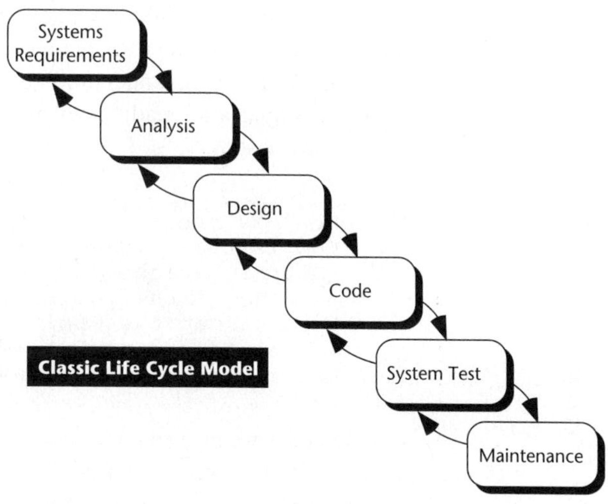

Figure 1-12 System development model

phase looks at different alternatives from a systems point of view, while the *design* phase determines how the system will be built. In the design phase, the functions of the individual programs that will make up the system are determined, and the design of the files and/or the databases is completed. Finally, in the fourth phase, *code*, programs are written. This is the phase that is explained in this book. After the programs have been written and tested to the programmer's satisfaction, the project proceeds to *system test*. All of the programs are tested together to make sure the system works as a whole. The final phase, *maintenance*, focuses on keeping the system working once it has been put into production.

Although the implication of the waterfall approach is that the phases flow in a continuous stream from the first to the last, this is not really the case. Note the iteration as indicated by the backward-flowing arrows in Figure 1-12. As each phase is developed, errors and omissions will often be found in the previous work. When this happens, it is necessary to go back to the previous phase to rework it for consistency and to analyze the impact caused by the changes. Ideally, this is a short rework. We are aware of at least three major projects, however, that were in the code and test phases when it was determined that they could not be implemented and had to be canceled. Thus, millions of dollars and years of development time were lost.

PROGRAM DEVELOPMENT

Program development is a multi-step process that requires you understand the problem, develop a solution, write the program, and then test it. When you are given the assignment to develop a program, you will be given a program requirements statement and the design of any program interfaces. You should also receive an overview of the complete project so that you will understand how your part fits into the whole. Your job is to determine how to take the inputs you are given and convert them into the outputs that have been specified. This is known as *program design*. To give you an idea of how this process works, let's look at a simple problem.

```
Calculate the square footage of your house.
```

How do you go about doing this?

Understand the Problem

The first step in solving any problem is to understand it. Begin by reading the requirements statement carefully. When you think that you fully understand it, review your understanding with the user and the systems analyst. Often this involves asking questions to confirm your understanding.

For example, after reading our simple requirements statement, you should ask several clarifying questions.

```
What is the definition of square footage?
How is the square footage going to be used?
• for insurance purposes?
• to paint the inside or outside of the house?
• to carpet the whole house?
Is the garage included?
Are closets and hallways included?
```

Each of these potential uses for the information requires a different measure. If you don't clarify the exact purpose—that is, if you make assumptions about how the output is going to be used—you may supply the wrong answer.

As this little example shows, even the simplest problem statements may require clarification. Imagine how many questions must be asked for a programmer to write a program that will contain hundreds or thousands of detailed statements.

Develop the Solution

Once you fully understand the problem and have clarified any questions you may have, you must develop your solution. Three tools will help you in this task: (1) structure charts, (2) pseudocode, and (3) flowcharts. Generally, you will use only two of them: a structure chart and either pseudocode or a flowchart.

The structure chart is used to design the whole program. Pseudocode and flowcharts, on the other hand, are used to design the individual parts of the program. These parts are known as modules in pseudocode and as functions in C++.

Structure Chart

A **structure chart**, also known as a hierarchy chart, shows the functional flow through your program. Large programs are complex structures consisting of many interrelated parts; thus, they must be carefully laid out. This task is similar to that of a design engineer who is responsible for the operational design of any complex item. The major difference between the design built by a programmer and the design built by an engineer is that the programmer's product is software, existing only inside the computer, whereas the engineer's product is something that can be seen and touched.

The structure chart shows how you are going to break your program into logical steps; each step will be a separate module. The structure chart shows the interaction between all the parts (modules) of your program.

It is important to realize that the design, as represented by the structure chart, is done *before* you write your program. In this respect, it is like the architect's blueprint. No one would start to build a house without a detailed set of plans, yet one of the most common errors of both experienced and new programmers alike is to start coding a program before the design is complete and fully documented.

This rush to start is partially because programmers think they fully understand the problem and partially because they are excited about getting on with a new problem to solve. In the first case, what they find is that they did not fully understand the problem. By taking the time to design the program, they will raise more questions that must be answered and therefore will gain a better understanding of the problem.

An old programming proverb:
Resist the temptation to code.

The second reason programmers code before completing the design is just human nature. Programming is a tremendously exciting task. To see your design begin to take shape, to see your program creation working for the first time, brings a form of personal satisfaction that is a natural high.

In the business world, when you complete your structure chart, you will convene a review panel for a *structured walk-through* of your program. Such a panel usually consists of a representative from the user community, one or two peer programmers, the system analyst, and possibly a representative from the testing organization. In the review, you will walk your review team through your structure chart to show how you are planning to solve the objectives of your program. The team will then offer constructive suggestions as to how to improve your design.

The primary intent of the review is to increase quality and save time. The earlier a mistake is detected, the easier it is to fix it. If you can eliminate only one or two problems with the structured walk-through, the time will be well spent. Naturally, in a programming class, you will not be able to convene a full panel and conduct a formal walk-through. What you can do, however, is review your design with some of your classmates and with your professor.

Looking at our problem to calculate the square footage of a house, let's assume the following answers to the questions raised in the previous section:

1. The purpose of calculating the square footage is to install new floor covering.
2. Only the living space will be carpeted. The garage and closets will not be considered.
3. The kitchen and bathrooms will be covered with linoleum; the rest of the house is to be carpeted.

With this understanding, we decide to write separate modules for the kitchen, bathroom(s), bedrooms, family room, and living room. We use separate modules because the various rooms may require a different quality of linoleum and carpeting. The structure chart for our design is shown in Figure 1-13.

Whether you use a flowchart or pseudocode to complete the design of your program will depend on your experience, the difficulty of the process you are designing, and the culture and standards of the organization where you are working. We believe that new programmers should first learn program design by flowcharting because a flowchart is a visual tool that is easier to create than pseudocode. On the other hand, pseudocode is more common among professional programmers.

Pseudocode
A precise algorithmic description of program logic.

Pseudocode

Pseudocode is part English, part program logic. Its purpose is to describe, in precise algorithmic detail, what the program being designed is to do. This requires defining the steps to accomplish the task in sufficient detail so that they can be converted into a computer program. Pseudocode excels at this type of precise logic. The pseudocode for determining the linoleum for the bathroom is shown in Program 1-4.

Most of the statements in the pseudocode are easy to understand. A prompt is simply a displayed message telling the user what data are to be entered. The *while* is a loop that

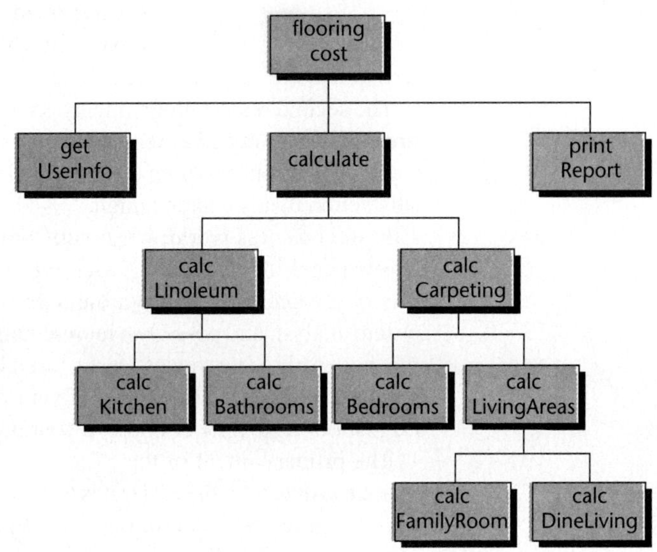

Figure 1-13 Structure chart for calculating square footage

Program 1-4 Pseudocode for calcBathrooms

```
Algorithm Calculate Bathrooms
1  prompt user and read linoleum price
2  prompt user and read number of bathrooms
3  set total bath area and baths processed to zero
4  while ( baths processed < number of bathrooms )
   1   prompt user and read bath length and width
   2   total bath area =
   3   total bath area + bath length * bath width
   4   add 1 to baths processed
5  end while
6  bath cost = total bath area * linoleum price
7  return bath cost
end Algorithm Calculate Bathrooms
```

repeats the three statements that follow it and uses the number of bathrooms read in statement 2 to tell when to stop. Looping is a programming concept that allows you to repeat a block of code. We will study it in Chapter 6. In this case, it allows us to process the information for one or more bathrooms.

Flowchart Appendix C contains complete instructions for creating flowcharts. If you are not familiar with flowcharts, we suggest you read it now.

The flowchart in Figure 1-14 shows the design for obtaining the area and cost for the bathrooms. There are a few points that merit comment.

The **flowchart** is basically the same as the pseudocode. We begin with prompts for the price of the linoleum and the number of bathrooms and read these two pieces of data. (As a general rule, flowcharts do not explicitly show standard concepts such as prompts.) The loop reads the dimensions for each bathroom. Finally, when we know the total area, we calculate the price and return to `calcLinoleum`.

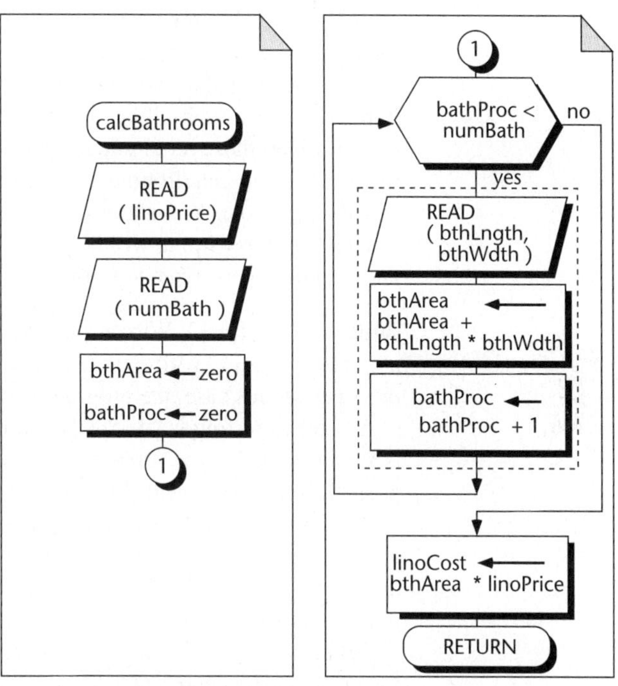

Figure 1-14 Flowchart for calcBathrooms

Write the Program

Now it's time to write the program! But first, let's review the steps that we've used.

1. Understand the problem.
2. Design the program—create the structure chart.
3. Design the algorithms for the program using either flowcharting or pseudocode or both.

When you write a program, you start with the top box on the structure chart and work your way to the bottom. This is known as *top-down* implementation. You will find that it is a very easy and natural way to write programs, especially if you have done a solid job on your design.

For your first few programs, there will be only one module, representing the top box of the structure chart. The first programs are quite simple and do not require subdivision. Once we get to Chapter 4, however, you will begin to write functions, and your structure charts will get larger. At that time, we will point out some more techniques for writing structured programs. In the meantime, concentrate on writing good pseudocode or flowcharts for the main part of your programs.

Test the Program

After you write your program, you must test it. **Program testing** can be a very tedious and time-consuming part of program development. As the programmer, you are responsible for completely testing your program. In large development projects, there are often specialists known as test engineers who are responsible for testing the system as a whole—that is, for testing to make sure all the programs work together.

There are two types of testing: blackbox and whitebox. Blackbox testing is done by the system test engineer and the user. Whitebox testing is the responsibility of the programmer.

Blackbox Testing **Blackbox testing** gets its name from the concept of testing the program without knowing what is inside it—without knowing how it works. In other words, the program is like a black box that you can't see into.

Blackbox test plans are developed by looking only at the requirements statement (this is but one reason why it is so important to have a good set of requirements). The test engineer uses these requirements and his or her knowledge of systems development and the user working environment to create a test plan that will be used when the system is tested as a whole. You should ask to see this test plan before you write your program. The test engineer's plan will help you make sure you fully understand the requirements and also help you create your own test plan.

Whitebox Testing Whereas blackbox testing assumes that the tester knows nothing about the program, **whitebox testing** assumes that the tester knows everything about the program. In this case, the program is like a glass house in which everything is visible.

Whitebox testing is your responsibility. As the programmer, you know exactly what is going on inside the program. You must make sure that every instruction and every possible situation have been tested. That is not a simple task!

Experience will help you design good test data, but one thing you can do from the start is to get in the habit of writing test plans. Start your test plan when you are in the design stage. As you build your structure chart, ask yourself what situations, especially unusual situations, you need to test for, and make a note of them immediately.

When you are writing your flowcharts or pseudocode, review them with an eye toward test cases and make additional notes of the cases you need. Finally, while you are coding, keep paper handy (or a test document open in your word processor) to make additional notes about test cases you need.

Note: If a situation for testing occurs to you at any time during the designing and writing process, jot it down right away, because you may not be able to remember it later.

> **One set of test data**
> **will *never* completely validate a program.**

When it comes time to construct your test cases, review your notes and organize them into logical sets. Except for very simple student programs, one set of test data will never completely validate a program. For large-scale development projects, 20, 30, or even more test cases may need to be run to validate a program.

Finally, while you are testing, you will think of more test cases. Again, write them down and incorporate them into your test plan. After your program is finished and in production, you will need the test plan again when you make modifications to the program.

How do you know when your program is completely tested? In reality, there is no way to know for sure, but there are a few things you can do to help the odds. While some of these concepts will not be clear until you have read other chapters, we include them here for completeness.

1. Verify that every line of code has been executed at least once. Fortunately, there are programming tools on the market today that will help you do this.
2. Verify that every conditional statement in your program has executed both the true and false branches, even if one of them is null.

3. For every condition that has a range, make sure the tests include the first and last items in the range, as well as items below the first and above the last. The most common mistakes in range tests occur at the extremes of the range.
4. If error conditions are being checked, make sure all error logic is tested. This may require you to make temporary modifications to your program to force the errors (for instance, an input/output error usually cannot be created—it must be simulated).

Errors

There are three general classifications of errors: specification errors, code errors, and logic errors. Specification errors occur when the problem definition is either incorrectly stated or misinterpreted. This type of error should be caught during formal blackbox testing.

Code errors usually generate a compiler error message. These errors are the easiest to correct. Some code errors generate what is known as a warning message, which usually means that the compiler has made an assumption about the code and needs to have it verified. It may be right, or it may be wrong. Even though the program may run with a warning message, you should change the code so that all such messages are eliminated.

The most difficult errors to find and correct are logic errors. They can be corrected only by thorough whitebox testing. As you write your program, begin designing the test cases that you will use to test it. And remember, before you run a test case, you should know what the correct answer is. Don't just let the computer tell you the answer; if there's a logic error, the computer's answer will be wrong.

1-9 SOFTWARE ENGINEERING AND PROGRAMMING STYLE

Software engineering is the establishment and use of sound engineering methods and principles to obtain software that is reliable and that works on real machines.[5] This definition, from the first international conference on software engineering in 1969, was proposed 30 years after the first computer was built. During that period, software was more of an art than a science. In fact, one of the most authoritative treatments of programming describes it as an art: *The Art of Computer Programming*. This three-volume series, written by Donald E. Knuth in the late 1960s and early 1970s, offers the most complete discussion of many computer science concepts.

It took time and study to formulate concepts that would be the basis for the creation of reliable and efficient software. To understand the background of structured programming, it is necessary to understand some of the history of computing.

Because there was not yet a science and engineering base upon which to build reliable software, programs written in the 1950s and 1960s were a maze of complexity known as "spaghetti code." It was not until Edsger Dijkstra wrote a letter to the editor of the *Communications of the ACM* (Association of Computing Machinery)[6] in 1968 that the concept of structured programming began to emerge.

Dijkstra was working to develop algorithms that would mathematically prove program accuracy. He proposed that any program could be written with only three constructs or types of instructions: (1) *sequences*, (2) the *if...else* selection statement, and (3) the *while* loop. As we will see, language developers have added constructs, such as the *for* loop and the *switch* in C++. These additional statements are simply enhancements to Dijkstra's basic constructs that make programming easier. Today, virtually all programming languages offer structured programming capabilities. Some older languages, such as FORTRAN, COBOL, and BASIC, have even been reworked to include structured programming capabilities.

Throughout this text we emphasize the concepts of good software engineering. Chief among them is the concept of structured programming and a sound programming style. A section in each chapter will include a discussion of these concepts with specific emphasis on the application of the material in the chapter.

The tools of programming design have also changed over the years. In the first generation of programming, one primary tool was a block diagram. This tool provided boxes, diamonds, and other flowchart symbols to represent different instructions in a program. Each instruction was contained in a separate symbol. This concept allowed programmers to write a program on paper and check its logic flow before they entered it in the computer.

With the advance of symbolic programming, the block diagram gave way to the flowchart. Although the block diagram and flowchart look similar, the flowchart does not contain the detail of the block diagram.

---

[5] F. L. Bauer, Technical University, Munich, Germany (1969).

[6] Edsger W. Dijkstra, "Goto Statement Considered Harmful," *Communications of the ACM* 11, no. 3 (March 1968).

Many instructions are implied by the descriptive names put into the boxes; for example, the READ statements in "Flowchart for calcBathrooms" on page 17 imply the prompt. Flowcharts have largely given way to other techniques in program design, but they are still used today by many programmers when they are working on a difficult logic problem.

Today's programmers are most likely to use a high-level design tool such as tight English or pseudocode. These design tools were made possible by the emergence of structured programming concepts. We will use pseudocode throughout the text to describe many of the algorithms we will be developing.

Finally, the last several years have seen the automation of programming through the use of computer-assisted software engineering (CASE) tools. These tools make it possible to determine requirements, design software, and develop and test software in an automated environment using programming workstations. Much work still must be done on CASE tools, but their use is firmly established in industry. The discussion of the CASE environment is beyond the scope of this text and is left for courses in systems engineering.

1-10 TIPS AND COMMON PROGRAMMING ERRORS

You will find this section at the end of each chapter. It lists some tips to help you program better and some common errors that you should try to avoid. Most of the issues will be specific to the C++ language, although some that concern algorithms or program design may apply to all languages. Not all of the errors we describe in this section will generate compiler syntax messages. We will indicate those that do. It is impossible to specify the exact error message, however, for two reasons. First, there is no standard set of error messages used by all compilers. Second, the error message may vary depending on unrelated factors in your program.

1. Become familiar with the text editor in your system so you will be able to create and edit your programs efficiently. The time spent learning different techniques and shortcuts in a text editor will save time in the future.
2. Also, become familiar with the compiler commands. On most computers, a variety of options are available to be used with the compiler command. Make yourself familiar with all of these options.
3. Read the compiler's error messages. Becoming familiar with the types of error messages and their meanings will be a big help as you learn C++.
4. Remember to save and compile your program each time you make changes or corrections in your source file. When your program has been saved, you won't lose your changes if a program error causes the system to fail during testing.
5. Run your program many times with different sets of data to be sure it does what you want.
6. The most common programming error is not following the old proverb to "resist the urge to code." Make sure you understand the program requirements and take the time to design a solution before you start writing code.

1-11 KEY TERMS

application software
application-specific software
assembler
assembly language
auxiliary storage
blackbox testing
central processing unit (CPU)
client
client/server
compiler
computer language
computer system
distributed computing
executable file
executable program
flowchart
general-purpose software
hard copy
hardware
high-level language
input device
keyboard
linker
loader
machine language
monitor
natural language
object module
operating system
output device
personal computer (PC)
preprocessor
preprocessor directives
primary storage
printer
program development
program testing
pseudocode
server
soft copy
software
source file
structure chart
symbolic language
system development life cycle
system development software
system software
system support software
text editor
time-sharing environment
translation unit
translator
waterfall model
whitebox testing

1-12 SUMMARY

- A computer system consists of hardware and software.
- Computer hardware consists of a central processing unit, primary storage, input devices, output devices, and auxiliary storage.
- Software consists of two broad categories: system software and application software.
- The primary components of system software are system management (operating system), system support, and system development.
- Application software is divided into general-purpose applications and application-specific software.
- Over the years, programming languages have evolved from machine language to symbolic language to high-level languages. Research is currently under way to develop the next generation of programming languages, the natural language.
- The C++ language is considered to be a high-level language.
- The system development life cycle is a series of interrelated steps that provide a rigorous and systematic approach to software development.
- To develop a program, the programmer must complete the following steps:
  - **a.** Understand the problem.
  - **b.** Develop a solution using structure charts and either flowcharts or pseudocode.
  - **c.** Write the program.
  - **d.** Test the program.
- The development of a test plan starts with the design of the program and continues through all steps in program development.
- Blackbox testing consists primarily of testing based on user requirements.
- Testing is one of the most important parts of your programming task. You are responsible for whitebox testing; the systems analyst and user are responsible for blackbox testing.

- Whitebox testing, executed by the programmer, tests the program with full know-ledge of its operational weaknesses.
- Software engineering is the application of sound engineering methods and principles to the design and development of application programs.

1-13 PRACTICE SETS

REVIEW QUESTIONS

1. Computer software is divided into two broad categories: system software and operational software.

   a. True b. False

2. The operating system provides services such as a user interface, file and database access, and interfaces to communications systems.

   a. True b. False

3. The first step in system development is to create a source program.

   a. True b. False

4. The programmer design tool used to design the whole program is the flowchart.

   a. True b. False

5. Blackbox testing gets its name from the concept that the program is being tested without knowing how it works.

   a. True b. False

6. Which of the following is a component(s) of a computer system?

   a. Hardware
   b. Software
   c. Both hardware and software
   d. Pseudocode
   e. System test

7. Which of the following is an example of application software?

   a. Database management system
   b. Language translator
   c. Operating system
   d. Sort
   e. Security monitor

8. Which of the following is not a computer language?

   assembly/symbolic language
   a. Binary language
   b. High-level languages
   c. Machine language
   d. Natural language

9. The computer language that most closely resembles machine language is

   a. Assembly/symbolic
   b. High-level
   c. COBOL
   d. Natural
   e. FORTRAN

10. The tool used by a programmer to convert a source program to a machine language object module is a

    a. Compiler
    b. Preprocessor
    c. Language translator
    d. Text editor
    e. Linker

11. The ________ contains the programmer's original program code.

    a. Application file
    b. Source file
    c. Executable file
    d. Text file
    e. Object file

12. The series of interrelated phases that is used to develop computer software is known as

    a. Program development
    b. Software engineering
    c. system development life cycle
    d. system analysis
    e. system design

13. The ________ is a program design tool that is a visual representation of the logic in a function within a program.

    a. Flowchart

    b. Structure chart

    c. Program map

    d. Waterfall model

    e. Pseudocode

14. The test that validates a program by ensuring that all of its statements have been executed—that is, by knowing exactly how the program is written—is

    a. Blackbox testing

    b. System testing

    c. Destructive testing

    d. Whitebox testing

    e. Nondestructive testing

EXERCISES

15. Describe the two major components of a computer system.
16. Computer hardware is made up of five parts. List and describe them.
17. Describe the major differences between a time-sharing and a client/server environment.
18. Describe the two major categories of software.
19. What is the purpose of an operating system?
20. Identify at least two types of system software that you will use when you write programs.
21. Give at least one example of general-purpose and one example of application-specific software.
22. List the levels of computer languages discussed in the text.
23. What are the primary differences between symbolic and high-level languages?
24. What is the difference between a source program and an object module?
25. Describe the basic steps in the system development life cycle.
26. What documentation should a programmer receive to be able to write a program?
27. List and explain the steps that a programmer follows to develop a program.
28. Describe the three tools that a programmer may use to develop a program solution.
29. What is meant by the old programming proverb, "Resist the temptation to code"?
30. What is the difference between blackbox and whitebox testing?
31. What is software engineering?

PROBLEMS

32. Write pseudocode for "calcLivingAreas" in "Structure chart for calculating square footage" on page 16.
33. Create a flowchart for a routine task, such as calling a friend, that you do on a regular basis.
34. Write pseudocode for the flowchart you created in problem 33 above.

2 Introduction to the C++ Language

In Chapter 1, we looked at the way computer languages evolved, from the original machine languages to the latest language concept, natural language. As mentioned, **C++** (the language used exclusively in this book) is a high-level language. Having read Chapter 1, you now have some idea of C++'s origins and its place in the evolution of computer languages.

In this chapter, we introduce the basics of the C++ language. For your first program, you will write what is known traditionally in C++ as the "Hello" or "Greeting" program. Along the way, you will be introduced to the concepts of data types, constants, and variables, as well as some of the C++ operators that you can use to read and write data. In this chapter, most of these topics are covered only in sufficient detail to enable you to write your first program. You will learn more about these important concepts and operators in future chapters.

2-1 BACKGROUND

C++ is a structured programming language, which is one of the reasons why it is so popular. It is considered a high-level language because it allows the programmer to concentrate on the problem at hand and not worry about the machine that the program will be using. While many languages claim to be machine independent, C++ comes the closest to achieving that goal. That is another reason why it is so popular, especially among software developers whose applications have to run on many different hardware platforms.

C++, like most modern languages, is derived from ALGOL, the first language to use a block structure. ALGOL never gained wide acceptance in the United States, but it was widely used in Europe.

ALGOL's introduction in the early 1960s paved the way for the development of structured programming concepts. Some of the first work was done by two computer scientists, Corrado Bohm and Guiseppe Jacopini, who published a paper in 1966 that defined the concept of structured programming. Another computer scientist, Edsger Dijkstra, popularized the concept. His letter to the editors of the *Communications of the ACM* (Association of Computing Machinery) brought the structured programming concept to the attention of the computer science community.

Several languages preceded the development of C++. In 1967, Martin Richards developed a language he called Basic Combined Programming Language, or BCPL. Ken Thompson followed in 1970 with a similar language he simply called B. B was used to develop the first version of UNIX, one of the most popular network operating systems in use today and the heart of the Internet data superhighway. In 1972, Dennis Ritchie developed C, which took many concepts from ALGOL, BCPL, and B and added the concept of data types. C++ evolved from C over a period of several years starting in 1980. Largely the work of Bjarne Stroustrup, it was in general use in the mid-1980s. This evolutionary path, along with several others, is shown in Figure 2-1.

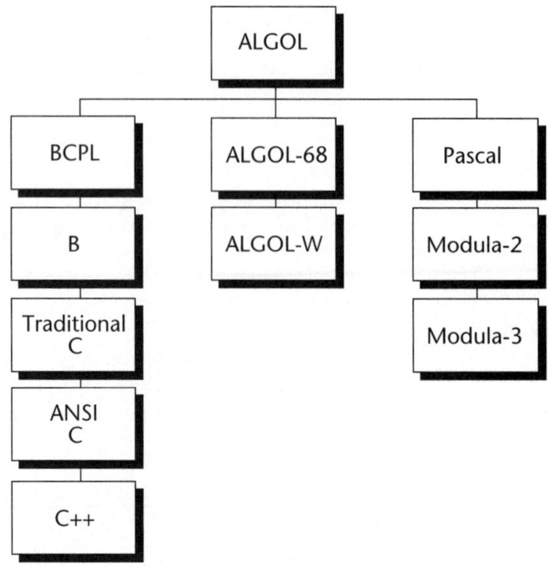

Figure 2-1 Taxonomy of the C++ language

A standard for C++ was jointly developed by the American National Standards Institute (ANSI) and the International Standards Organization (ISO). In March 1995, they released a working draft. In November 1997, the standards were approved. As much as possible, this text incorporates the C++ standard.

The history of C++ is summarized in Table 2-1.

1. In 1960, a block-structured language emerged, which was called ALGOL (ALGOrithmic Language).
2. In 1967, Martin Richards invented BCPL (Basic Combined Programming Language), which was a typeless language. It permitted only one data object (the machine word).
3. In 1970, Ken Thompson invented the typeless system programming language B.
4. In 1972, working at Bell Laboratories, Dennis Ritchie designed C, a combination of BCPL and B but with data types.
5. In 1978, Brian Kernighan and Dennis Ritchie published the ad hoc standard for traditional C.
6. In 1980, Bjarne Stroustrup extended C to include classes.
7. In 1985, after Stroustrup added virtual functions and overloading, the new language became known as C++. Since then it has continued to evolve, adding such features as multiple inheritance and abstract classes.
8. In 1995, the American National Standards Institute (ANSI) and International Standards Organization (ISO) released a working draft of their C++ standard.
9. In November 1997, the ANSI-ISO standard was approved.

Table 2-1 History of C++

2-2 C++ PROGRAMS

Are you ready to write your first C++ program? This section will take you through all the basic parts of a C++ program so that you will be able to write it.

STRUCTURE OF A C++ PROGRAM

Every C++ program is made up of a global definitions section and one or more **functions**. The **global** definitions **section** comes at the beginning of the program. We will talk more about it later, but the basic idea of global definitions is that they are visible to all parts of the program. (The term **global** comes from the concept that your program is a little world. Anything that is global, therefore, pertains to the whole world—to the whole program.)

One, and only one, of the functions in a program must be named **main**. *Main* is the starting point for the program. *Main* and the other functions in a program contain two types of code: definitions and statements. Definitions describe the data that you will be using in the function. Definitions in a function are known as **local definitions** (as opposed to global definitions) because they are visible only to the function that contains them.

Statements are instructions to the computer that cause it to do something, such as add two numbers.

While C++ allows definitions and statements to be intermixed, we believe that functions should be organized for readability. Therefore, we place definitions at the beginning of the function. Beginning in Chapter 4, we will modify this rule for different situations.

A SIMPLE PROGRAM

Figure 2-2 shows the parts of a simple C++ program. In this example, the program is

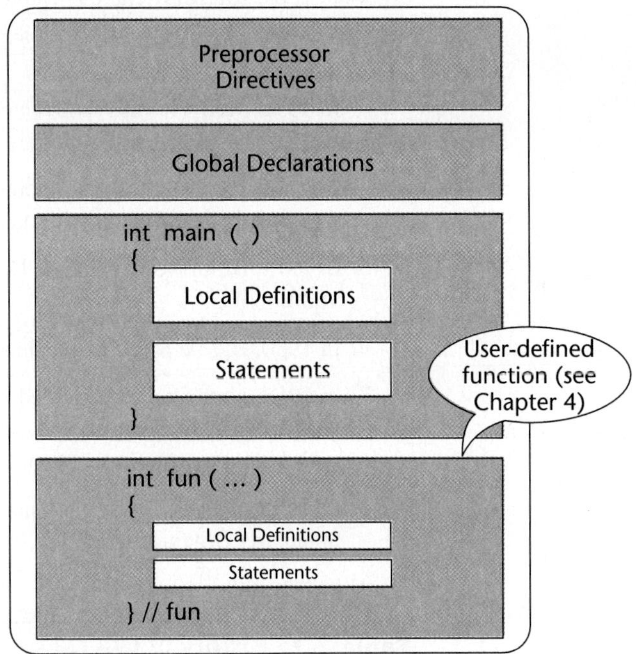

Figure 2-2 Structure of a C++ program

made up of one function, *main,* and another function, `fun`, that is called by *main.* Traditionally, *main* is coded first in the program, and the other functions that it calls, known as **subfunctions**, are coded in the order they are used.

We have explained everything in this program but the **preprocessor directives**. A better name for these statements would be precompiler directives. They are special instructions to the preprocessor that tell it how to prepare your program for compilation. One of the most important of the preprocessor directives, and one that is used in virtually all programs, is ***include***. The *include* command tells the preprocessor that we need information from selected libraries known as **header files**. In today's complex programming environments, it is almost impossible to write even the smallest of programs without at least one system library. In your first program, you will use one *include* command to tell C++ that you need the input and output library to write data to the console screen.

YOUR FIRST PROGRAM

Your first C++ program will be very simple (see Figure 2-3). It will have only one preprocessor command, no global declarations, and no local definitions. Its purpose will be simply to print a greeting to the user. Therefore, its statement section will have only two statements: one that prints a greeting and one that stops the program.

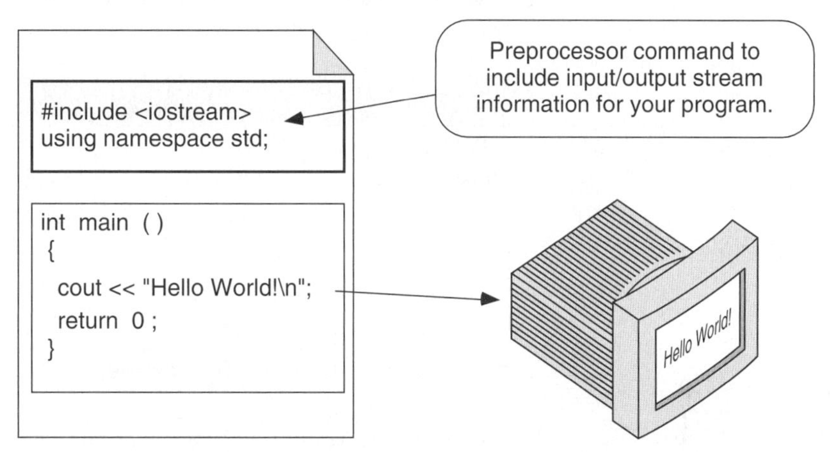

Figure 2-3 The greeting program

Preprocessor Directives

The preprocessor directive comes at the beginning of the program. All preprocessor directives start with a pound sign; this is just one of the rules of C++ known as its **syntax**. Preprocessor directives can start in any column, but they traditionally start in column 1.

Your preprocessor directive tells the compiler to include the **input/output stream** library file in your program. You need this library file because you will be printing a message to the console. (The console is usually your computer's monitor, although it could be a printer or other output device.) Printing is one of the input/output processes identified in this library file. The complete syntax for this directive is shown below.

```
#include <iostream>
```

The format or syntax of this directive must be exact. Since it is a preprocessor directive, it starts with the pound sign. There can be no space between the pound sign and the keyword, *include*. *Include* means just what you would think it does. It tells the preprocessor that you want the library file in the pointed brackets (< >) *included* in your program. The name of the header file is **iostream**. This is an abbreviation for "input/output stream."

Using Directive

In addition to preprocessor directives, we need one more statement, a using directive. This statement tells the compiler where to look for names in the libraries. Briefly, all names used in a program are kept in tables. To make the compiler more efficient, and to make it easier for us to write programs, these names have been organized into areas known as **namespaces**. The namespace for the standard system libraries is standard, abbreviated *std*. We tell the compiler to use it with the following statement. Note the semicolon at the end of the statement. It is required. For a more complete discussion of namespace and its use, refer to Appendix N.

```
using namespace std;
```

C and C++ Library Files

The C Language uses a similar set of library files. Their files all end in ".h," which stands for header file. C++ uses some of these same files. When we use them in C++, however, we add a 'c' before the library name and omit the ".h." Table 2-2 shows the

C and C++ names for the more common libraries. There are others; they all follow the same naming pattern. We will explain their use as the text evolves.

C Library	C++ Library	Usage
ctype.h	cctype	Character type library (Chapter 5)
float.h	cfloat	Floating-point value library (Chapter 3)
limits.h	climits	Integer value library (Chapter 3)
math.h	cmath	Mathematical function library (Chapter 4)
stdlib.h	cstdlib	Standard library (Chapter 4)
string.h	cstring	String library (Chapter 14)

Table 2-2 C and C++ library files

main

The executable part of your program begins with the function *main*, which is identified by the **function header** shown below. We explore the meaning of the function syntax in Chapter 4. For now, all you need to understand is that *int* says that the function will return an integer value to the operating system, that the function's name is *main*, and that it has no parameters (the parameter list is void). Note that there is no punctuation after the function header.

```
int main ()
```

Within *main* there are two statements: one to print your message and one to terminate the program. The print statement uses an operator (<<) to do the actual writing to the console. Known as the *insertion operator*, it places the text string that follows it into an output stream that is written to the console. The output string contains what you want displayed, enclosed in double quote marks ("). The "\n" at the end of the message tells the computer to advance to the next line in the output.

The second statement in your program, *return* 0, terminates the program and returns control to the operating system. The **body** of the function starts with an open brace and terminates with a closed brace. (Braces are those curly brackets that are so hard to write by hand.)

An Operator by Any Other Name

The print statement described in this section uses the insertion operator (<<) to place text data in the output stream. C++ also knows this operator as the bitwise left-shift. Which one is correct?

In C++, the answer is that both are correct. C++ supports a concept known as operator overloading. Simply stated, **overloading** is the definition of more than one process for an operator. When the compiler parses an operator that is overloaded, it examines how it is used and decides which meaning the programmer intended. This is not unlike listening to and evaluating certain words in English. For example, the word *record* can be used as either a noun or a verb. Not only are the meanings different, but the word is even pronounced differently depending on which meaning is intended. The verb (ri kôrd) means to save for future use, such as "I will record your request." The noun (rek´erd) refers to what was saved when we recorded the request.

We will study overloading later. For now, you need simply to remember that some operators are overloaded, and the compiler determines the correct use of an operator by the way it is used.

COMMENTS

Although it is reasonable to expect that a good programmer should be able to read code, sometimes the meaning of a section of code is not entirely clear. This is especially true in C++. Thus, it is helpful if the person who writes the code places some comments in the code to help the reader. Such comments are merely internal **program documentation**. The compiler ignores these comments when it translates the program into executable code.

To identify a comment, C++ uses two different formats. The first is adopted from C and is used when the comment will span several lines. We call this comment format **block comment**. It uses opening and closing comment tokens. A **token** is one or more symbols understood by the compiler that help it interpret code. Each comment token is made of two characters that, taken together, form the token; there can be no space between them. The opening token is /* and the closing token is */. Everything between the opening and closing comment tokens is ignored by the compiler. The tokens can start in any column, and they do not have to be on the same line. The only requirement is that the opening token must precede the closing token.

The second format, the **line comment**, uses two slashes (//) to identify a comment line. This format does not require an end-of-comment token; the end of the line automatically ends the comment. Programmers generally use this format for short comments. The line-comment token can start anywhere on the line. Figure 2-4 shows several examples of comments.

```
// This is a single line comment.

/* This is a comment that
   covers two lines.           */

/*
** It is a very common style to put the opening token
** on a line by itself, followed by the documentation
** and then the closing token on a separate line. Some
** programmers also like to put asterisks at the beginning
** of each line to clearly mark the comment.
*/
```

Figure 2-4 Examples of comments

Comments can appear anywhere in a program. In good programming style, a program starts with a series of comments that document its purpose. Comments are also used wherever it is necessary to explain a point about the code. We will demonstrate the use of comments throughout the text. You should note, however, that many of our comments would not appear in programs written by professional programmers because many of them are intended to explain portions of code to you, the student, that would be obvious to professionals.

Although they can appear anywhere, comments cannot be nested, even with block comments.[1] In other words, you cannot have comments inside comments. Once the compiler sees an opening block-comment token, it ignores everything it sees until it finds the closing token. Therefore, the opening token of the nested comment is not

[1]Some nonstandard compilers provide a nested comment capability. Because they are nonstandard, and therefore nonportable, their nested comments should not be used.

recognized, and the ending token that matches the first opening token is left standing on its own. This error is shown in Figure 2-5.

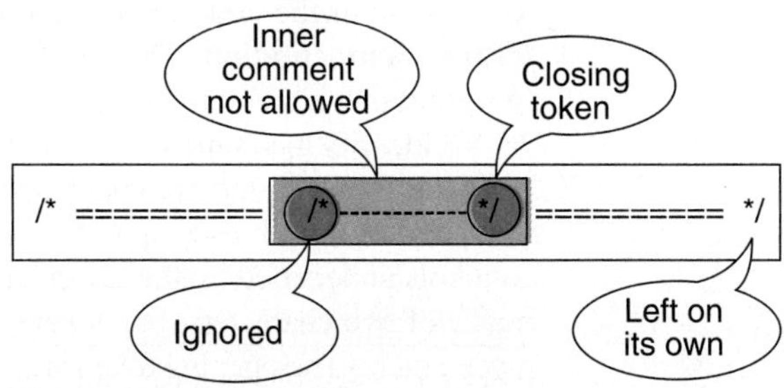

Figure 2-5 Nested block comments are invalid

Program 2-1 shows the greeting program just as you should write it. We have included some comments at the beginning that explain what the program is going to do. Each program you write should begin with documentation explaining the purpose of the program. We have also used comments to identify the declaration and statement sections of your program. Note that the numbers on the left in Program 2-1 and the other programs in the text are for discussion reference. You do not enter them.

Program 2-1 The greeting program

```
/* The greeting program. This program demonstrates
   some of the components of a simple C++ program.
      Written by: your name here
      Date:       date program written
*/
#include <iostream>
using namespace std;

int main ()
{
   cout << "Hello World!\n";
   return 0;
} // main
```

2-3 IDENTIFIERS

One feature present in all computer languages is the **identifier**. Identifiers allow us to name data and other objects in the program. Each piece of data in the computer is stored at a unique address. If we didn't have identifiers that we could use to symbolically represent data locations, we would have to know and use data addresses to manipulate them. Instead, we simply give data identifier names and let the compiler keep track of where they are physically located.

Different programming languages use different rules to form identifiers. In C++, the rules for identifiers are very simple. The only valid name symbols are the capital letters *A* through *Z*, the lowercase letters *a* through *z*, the digits 0 through 9, and the underscore. The first character of the identifier cannot be a digit. By custom, applications do not use the underscore for the first character either, because many of the identifiers in the system libraries that support C++ start with an underscore. In this way, we make sure that our names do not duplicate system names, which could become very confusing. The last rule is that the name you create cannot be any of about 50 special names, known as **reserved words** or **keywords**, that are contained in the language itself. For a list of the reserved words, see Appendix B.

Good identifier names are descriptive but short. To make them short, we often use abbreviations.[2] C++ does not set a limit to the size of an identifier, although some compilers may. Table 2-3 summarizes the rules for identifiers.

1. The first character must be alphabetic character or underscore.
2. The identifier must consist only of alphabetic characters, digits, and underscores.
3. The identifier cannot duplicate a reserved word.

Table 2-3 Rules for identifiers

You might be curious as to why the underscore is included among the possible characters that can be used for an identifier. It is there so that we can separate different parts of an identifier. To make identifiers descriptive, we often combine two or more words. When the names contain multiple words, the underscore makes it easier to read the name. Another way to separate the words in a name is to capitalize the first letter in each word. The traditional method of separation in C++ uses the underscore, but there is a growing group of programmers who prefer to capitalize the first letter of each word. Table 2-4 contains examples of valid and invalid names.

Two more comments about names. Note that the second PI in Table 2-4 is capitalized. By tradition, capitalized names are reserved for preprocessor-defined names. The second comment is that C++ is *case sensitive*. This means that even though two identifiers are spelled the same, if the case of each corresponding letter doesn't match, C++ evaluates them as different names. Under this rule, `PI`, `Pi`, and `pi` are three different identifiers.

Valid names		Invalid names	
`a`	`a1`	`$sum`	`// $ is illegal`
`student_name`	`stdntNm`	`2names`	`// can't start with 2`
`_aSystemName`	`_anthrSysNm`	`stdnt Nmbr`	`// no spaces`
`pi`	`PI`	`int`	`// reserved word`

Table 2-4 Examples of valid and invalid names

2-4 DATA TYPES

A *type* defines a set of **values** and a set of **operations** that can be applied on those values. The set of values for each type is known as the domain for the type. For example, a light switch can be compared to a computer type. It has a set of two values:

[2] One way to abbreviate an identifier is to remove any vowels in the middle of the word. For example, *student* could be abbreviated *stdnt*.

on and off. Since the domain of a light switch consists of only these two values, its size is two. There are only two operations that can be applied to a light switch, turn on and turn off.

Functions also have types. The type of a function is determined by the data it returns. We will talk about the operators and functions later. In this section, we define the different **data types** available in C++ using only the first characteristic, the set of values.

C++ contains five **standard types**: *void, int* (short for integer), *char* (short for character), *float* (short for floating point), and *bool* (short for Boolean). These types are shown in Figure 2-6. Standard types are atomic: They cannot be broken down. They also serve as the basic building blocks for the derived types. **Derived types** are complex structures that are built using the standard types. The derived types are *pointer, enumerated type, union, array, structure,* and *class*. In this chapter, we discuss only the standard types; the derived types appear in later chapters.

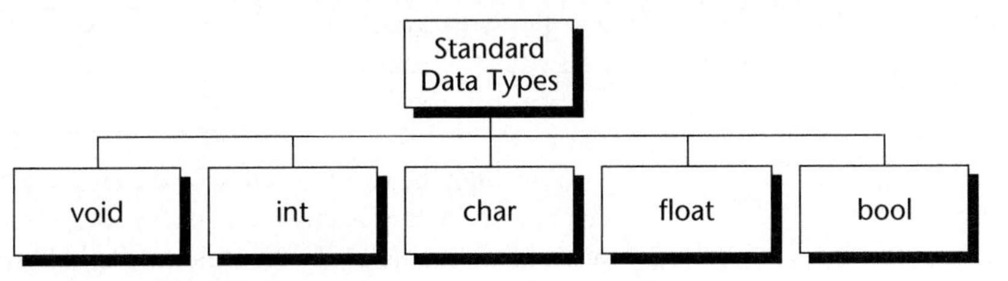

Figure 2-6 Standard data types

VOID

The *void* type has no values and no operations. In other words, both the set of values and the set of operations are empty. Although this might seem unusual, we will see later that it is a very useful data type. For instance, it can play the role of a generic type—that is, a type that can represent any of the other standard types.

INTEGER

An **integer** type is a number without a fraction part. It is also known as an integral number. C++ supports three different sizes of the integer data type: ***short int, int,*** and ***long int***. A ***short int*** can also be referred to as ***short,*** and ***long int*** can be referred to as ***long***. C++ defines these data types so that they can be organized from the smallest to the largest, as shown in Figure 2-7.

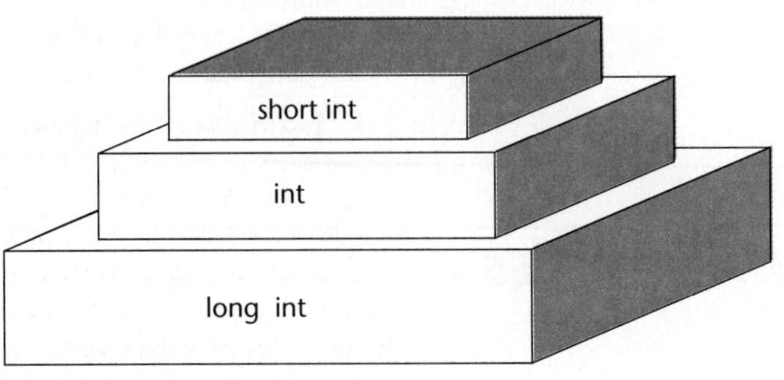

Figure 2-7 Integer types

The type also defines the size of the field in which data can be stored. In C++, this is true even though the size is machine dependent and varies from computer to computer.

Most microcomputers, minicomputers, and mainframes use the integer sizes shown in Table 2-5.

Type	Sign	Byte size	Num of bits	Minimum value	Maximum Value
short int	`signed`	2	16	`-32,768`	`32,767`
	`unsigned`			`0`	`65,535`
int (PC)	`signed`	2	16	`-32,768`	`32,767`
	`unsigned`			`0`	`65,535`
int (main-frame)	`signed`	4	32	`-2,147,483,648`	`2,147,483,647`
	`unsigned`			`0`	`4,294,967,295`
long int	`signed`	4	32[a]	`-2,147,483,648`	`2,147,483,647`
	`unsigned`			`0`	`4,294,967,295`

[a]Some computers use 48, 64, or more bits.

Table 2-5 Typical integer sizes

C++ provides an operator, ***sizeof***, that will tell you the exact size of any data type. We will discuss this operator in detail in Chapter 3. Although size is machine dependent, C++ requires that the following relationship always be true:

```
sizeof (short int) <= sizeof (int) <= sizeof (long int)
```

Each integer data type can be further subdivided into two different subtypes, depending on whether the number stored in the variable is considered as a signed integer or an unsigned integer. If the integer is **signed**, then one bit must be used for the sign (0 is plus, 1 is minus). The **unsigned** integer can store a positive number that is twice as large as the signed integer of the same size (see Table 2-5).[3]

You must be careful about choosing the correct type for integers, especially if you want to run your program on different hardware platforms. Most personal computers use a 16-bit word size for both integer and short integer. By referring to Table 2-5, you can see that the maximum signed value you can store in 16 bits is +32,767. If your numeric value will always be less than this maximum, use *short*. On the other hand, if your value can be larger than 32,767, you should use *long* on a personal computer.

On large computers, most systems use a 32-bit word for both *int* and *long*. To provide maximum flexibility, therefore, we recommend that you also use *int* and *long* when you may be running on large computers.

To provide flexibility across different hardware platforms, C++ has a library, <climits>, that contains size information about integers. For example, the minimum integer value for the computer is defined as INT_MIN, and the maximum value is defined as INT_MAX. See Appendix E, "Standard Libraries," for a complete list of these named values.

CHAR

The third type is **char (character)**. Although we think of characters as the letters of the alphabet, a computer has another definition. To a computer, a character is any value that can be represented in the computer's alphabet. Most computers use the American Standard Code for Information Interchange (**ASCII**—pronounced "ask-key") alphabet.

---

[3] For a complete discussion, see Appendix D, "Numbering Systems."

You do not need to memorize this alphabet as you did when you learned your natural languages, but you will find that you learn many of the special values by using them. The ASCII code is included in Appendix A.

Most of the personal, mini-, and mainframe computers use one byte to store the *char* data types. A byte is eight bits. With eight bits, there are 256 different values in the char set. (Note in Appendix A that ASCII uses only half of these possible values.) Although the size of *char* is machine dependent and varies from computer to computer, normally it is one byte or eight bits.

If you examine the ASCII code carefully, you will notice that there is a pattern to its alphabet that corresponds to the English alphabet. All the lowercase letters are grouped together, as are all the uppercase letters and the digits. Many of the special characters are grouped together, but some are found spread throughout the alphabet.

What makes the letter *a* different from the letter *x*? In English, it is the visual formation of the graphic associated with the letter. In the computer, it is the underlying value of the bit configuration for the letter. The letter *a* is binary 0110 0001; the letter *x* is 0111 1000. The decimal values of these two binary numbers are 97 and 120, respectively. A character is stored in a computer's memory as an integer representing the ASCII code of the corresponding character.[4] For this reason, it is possible—although not necessarily arithmetically consistent—to perform arithmetic operations on characters.[5]

A character in C++ can be interpreted as a small integer (between 0 and 255). For this reason, C++ often treats a character like an integer.

FLOATING POINT

A **floating-point type** is a number with a fractional part, such as 43.32. The C++ language supports three different sizes of floating-point data types: ***float***, ***double***, and ***long double***. As was the case for *int*, *float* types are defined so that they can be organized from smallest to largest. The relationship among the floating-point types is shown in Figure 2-8.

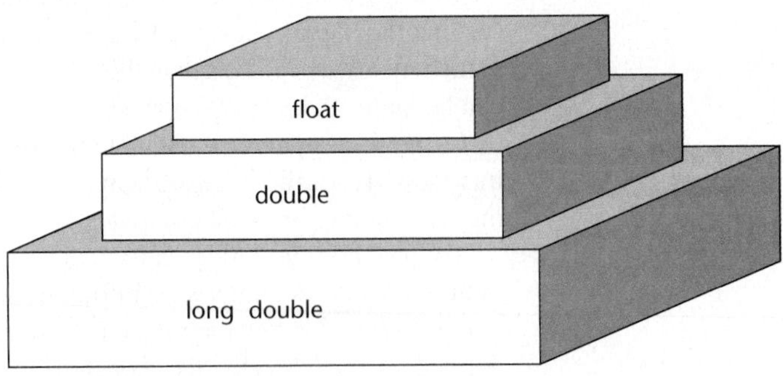

Figure 2-8 Floating-point types

Although the physical size of floating-point types is machine dependent, many computers support the sizes shown in Table 2-6.

[4] For more information, refer to Appendix D, "Numbering Systems."

[5] For example, any arithmetic operation that results in a value less than 0 or greater than 255 is invalid.

Type	Byte size	Number of bits
float	4	32
double	8	64
long double	10	80

Table 2-6 Typical float sizes

Regardless of machine size, C++ requires that the following relationship must be true:

```
sizeof (float) <= sizeof (double) <= sizeof (long double)
```

Another difference between *float* and *int* types is that *float* is always signed. A final point to remember about characters, integers, floats, and any other type we may discuss is that each type has its own internal format.Therefore, when the same number value is stored in different types, the internal bit configuration will be different. For example, the ASCII character plus (+) has a value of 43, but its bit configuration is different from the integer 43, which is also different from the float 43.0. One of your jobs as a programmer is to use these different types consistently in your programs.

A summary of the five standard data types is shown in Table 2-7.

Data type	C++ implementation
void	void
character	char
integer	unsigned short int unsigned int unsigned long int short int int long int
floating point	float double long double
boolean	bool

Table 2-7 Type summary

Like the limits library for integer values, there is a standard library, <cfloat>, for the floating-point values (see Appendix E, "Standard Libraries").

LOGICAL DATA IN C++

Logical, or Boolean, **data**, named after the French mathematician/philosopher George Boole, consists of only two values: true and false. The C++ implementation of logical data is the ***bool*** type. C++ provides two constants to be used with bool: ***true*** and ***false***. The bool type is an integral that, when used with other integral types such as integer values, is converted to the values 1 (true) and 0 (false).

In addition, C++ supports the traditional C logical data type concept through the integer type. In both C++ and C, any nonzero number (positive or negative) can be used to represent true, and zero is used to represent false.

> **In C++ the Boolean constants are *true* and *false*. Additionally, following traditional standards, any nonzero number is considered true, and zero is considered false.**

2-5 VARIABLES

Variables are named memory locations that have a type, such as integer or character, and, consequently, a size, which is inherited from their type. And of course, since variables are types, they have a set of operations that can be used to change or manipulate them.

VARIABLE DECLARATION AND DEFINITION

Each variable in your program must be declared and defined. In C++, a **declaration** is used to name an object, such as a variable. **Definitions** are used to create the object. With a few exceptions, a variable is declared and defined at the same time. The exceptions, which we will see later, declare them first and then define them at a later time. In the common use of the terms, *definition* assumes that the declaration has been done or is being done at the same time. While this distinction is somewhat of an oversimplification, it works in most situations. (We'll discuss the exceptions later.)

When we create variables, the declaration gives them a symbolic name and the definition reserves memory for them. Once defined, variables are used to hold the data that are required by the program for its operation. Generally speaking, where the variable is located in memory is not a programmer's concern; it is a concern only of the compiler. From our perspective, all we are concerned with is being able to access the data through their symbolic names, their identifiers. The concept of variables in memory is illustrated in Figure 2-9.

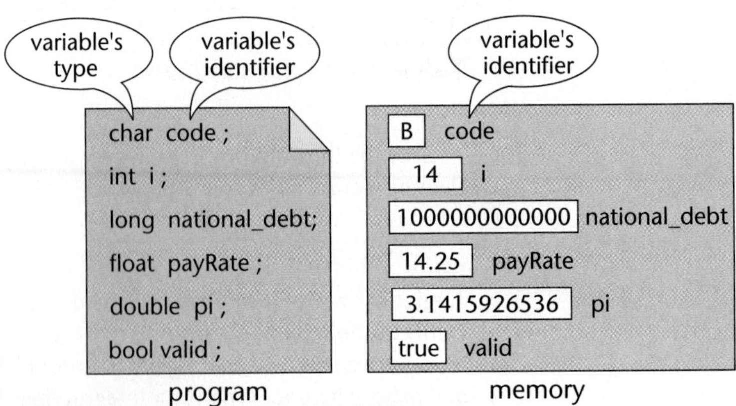

Figure 2-9 Variables in memory

A variable's type can be any of the data types, such as *char*, *int*, and *float*. The one exception to this rule is the type *void*; a variable cannot be type *void*. To create a variable, you first specify the type and then its identifier as shown below in the definition of a floating-point variable named `price`.

```
float price;
```

Table 2-8 gives some examples of variable declarations and definitions. As you study the variable identifiers, note the different styles used to make them readable. You should select a style and use it consistently. We prefer the use of an uppercase letter to identify the beginning of each word after the first one.

```
short int maxItems;          // Word separator: Capital
long int  national_debt;     // Word separator: Underscore
float     payRate;           // Word separator: Capital
double    tax;
char      code;
bool      valid;
int       a, b;             // Poor style—see text
```

Table 2-8 Examples of variable definition

C++ allows multiple variables of the same type to be defined in one statement. The last entry in Table 2-8 uses this format. Even though many professional programmers use it, we do not consider it to be good programming style. It is much easier to find and work with variables if they are defined on separate lines. This makes the compiler work a little harder, but the resulting code is no different. This is one situation in which ease of reading the program and programmer efficiency are more important than the convenience of coding multiple declarations on the same line.

VARIABLE INITIALIZATION

We can initialize a variable at the same time that we declare it by including an initializer. When present, the **initializer** establishes the first value that the variable will contain. To initialize a variable when it is defined, the identifier is followed by the assignment operator (the equal sign) and then the initializer, which is the value the variable is to have when the function starts. This simple initialization format is shown below.

```
int count = 0;
```

Every time the definition statement containing `count` is executed, `count` is set to zero. Now, what will be the result of the following initialization? Are both `count` and `sum` initialized, or is just `sum` initialized?

```
int count, sum = 0;
```

The answer is that the initializer applies only to the variable defined immediately before it. Therefore, only `sum` is initialized. If you wanted both variables initialized, you would have to provide two initializers.

```
int count  = 0, sum = 0;
```

Again, to avoid confusion and error, we prefer using only one variable definition to a line. The preferred code in this case would be

```
int count = 0;
int sum   = 0;
```

It is important to remember that with a few exceptions that we will see later, variables are not initialized automatically. When variables are defined, they usually contain garbage (meaningless values left over from a previous use), so we need to initialize them or store data in them (using run-time statements) before accessing their values.

When a variable is defined, it is not initialized. The programmer must initialize any variable requiring prescribed data when the function starts.

Print Sum

At this point you might like to see what a more complex program looks like. As you read Program 2-2, note the blank lines used to separate different groups of code. This is a good technique for making programs more readable. You should use blank lines in your programs the same way you use them to separate the paragraphs in a report.

Program 2-2 Print the sum of three numbers

```
/* This program calculates and prints the sum of
   three numbers input by the user at the keyboard.
      Written by:
      Date:
*/
#include <iostream>
using namespace std;

int  main ()
{
   cout << "Welcome. This program adds\n";
   cout << "three numbers. Enter three numbers\n";
   cout << "in the form: nnn nnn nnn <return>\n";

   int  a;
   int  b;
   int  c;
   cin >> a >> b >> c;

   // Numbers are now in a, b, and c. Add them.
   int sum = a + b + c;

   cout << "\nThe total is: " << sum << "\n";
   cout << "\nThank you. Have a good day.\n";
   return 0;
}  //  main
```

Program 2-2 Print the sum of three numbers *(continued)*

```
Results:
Welcome. This program adds
three numbers. Enter three numbers
in the form: nnn nnn nnn <return>
11 22 33

The total is: 66

Thank you. Have a good day.
```

2-6 CONSTANTS

Constants are data values that cannot be changed during the execution of a program. Like variables, constants have a type. In this section, we will discuss integer, floating-point, character, string, and Boolean constants.

INTEGER CONSTANTS

Although integers are always stored in their binary form, they are simply coded as you would use them in everyday life. Thus, the value fifteen is simply coded as 15.

If you code the number as a series of digits, its type is signed integer, or long integer if the number is large. You can override this default by specifying unsigned (*u* or *U*) and long (*l* or *L*) after the number. The codes may be combined and may be coded in any order. Note that there is no way to specify a *short int* constant. When you omit the suffix, it defaults to *int*. While both upper- and lowercase codes are allowed, we recommend that you always use uppercase to avoid confusion (especially with the *l*, which in many cases looks like the number 1). Table 2-9 shows several examples of **integer constants**. The default types are typical for a personal computer.

Literal	Value	Type
`+123`	`123`	`int`
`-378`	`-378`	`int`
`-32271L`	`-32,271`	`long int`
`76542LU`	`76,542`	`unsigned long int`

Table 2-9 Examples of integer constants

FLOAT CONSTANTS

Float constants are numbers with decimal parts. They are stored in memory as two parts: the significand and the exponent. The default type for float constants is *double*. If you want the resulting data type to be *float* or *long double*, you must use a code to specify the desired data type. As you might anticipate, *f* and *F* are used for *float* and *l* and *L* are used for *long double*. Do not use the lowercase *l* for *long double*: it is too easily confused with the number 1.

Table 2-10 shows several examples of *float* constants.

Literal	Value	Type
`0.`	`0.0`	`double`
`.0`	`0.0`	`double`
`2.0`	`2.0`	`double`
`3.1416`	`3.1416`	`double`
`-2.0f`	`-2.0`	`float`
`3.1415926536L`	`3.1415926536`	`long double`

Table 2-10 Examples of *float* constants

CHARACTER CONSTANTS

Character constants are enclosed between two single quotes (apostrophes). In addition to the character, there can be a backslash (\) between the quote marks. The backslash is known as the **escape character**. It is used when the character you need to represent does not have any graphic associated with it; that is, when it cannot be printed or when it cannot be entered from the keyboard. The escape character says that what follows is not the normal character but something else. For example, to represent the newline character (line feed), we code (\n). So, even though there may be multiple symbols in the character constant, they always represent only one character.

> A character constant is enclosed in *single quotes.*

ASCII Character Set

The character in the character constant comes from the alphabet supplied by the hardware manufacturer. Most computers use the ASCII alphabet, or as it is more commonly called, the ASCII character set. The ASCII character set is shown in Appendix A. The other common alphabet, usually found only on IBM mainframes and their clones, is the Extended Binary Coded Decimal Interchange Code (EBCDIC—pronounced "ebb-see-dic"). This book uses the ASCII set in all its examples. This is not a major problem if you are working on an EBCDIC computer, however, because C++ has named all the critical values so that we can refer to them symbolically. They are shown in Table 2-11.

ASCII character	Symbolic name
null character	`'\0'`
alert (bell)	`'\a'`
backspace	`'\b'`
horizontal tab	`'\t'`
newline	`'\n'`
vertical tab	`'\v'`
form feed	`'\f'`
carriage return	`'\r'`
single quote	`'\''`
backslash	`'\\'`

Table 2-11 Symbolic names for special characters

STRING CONSTANTS

A **string constant** is a sequence of zero or more characters enclosed in double quotes. You used a string in your first program without even knowing that it was a string. Look at Program 2-1 on page 32 to see if you can identify the string.

Listed in Figure 2-10 are several **strings**, including the one from your first program. The first example, an empty string, is simply two double quotes in succession. The second example, a string containing only the letter *h*, differs from a character constant in that it is enclosed in double quotes. When we study strings, we will see that there is also a big difference in how *h* is stored in memory as a character and as a string.

```
""                                  // A null string
"h"
"Hello World!\n"
"HOW ARE YOU?"
"Good Morning!"
"'Good' Morning!"                   // 'Good' Morning
"\"Good\" Morning!"                 // "Good" Morning
```

Figure 2-10 Some strings

If you want to include a single quote in a string, you simply key the quote mark as seen in 'Good' Morning in Figure 2-10. However, if you want to include double quotes, you must escape each double quote character as shown in the last example in Figure 2-10.

It is important to understand the difference between the null character (see Table 2-11) and an empty string. The null character represents no value. As a character, it is eight 0 bits. An empty string, on the other hand, is a string containing nothing. Figure 2-11 shows the difference between these two constant types.

```
'\0' → Null character
""   → Empty string
```

Figure 2-11 Null characters and null strings

At this point, this is all you need to know about strings. We will explain more about them and how they are stored in the computer after the chapters on arrays and pointers.

> **Use single quotes for character constants.**
> **Use double quotes for string constants.**

BOOLEAN CONSTANTS

The **Boolean** type, *bool*, has two predefined constants associated with it: *true* and *false*. Because these constants are predefined keywords, they cannot be declared or defined by the programmer.

> **The only *bool* types constants are *true*, printed as 1, and *false*, printed as 0.**

2-7 CODING CONSTANTS

In this section we discuss three different ways to code constants in our programs: literal constants, defined constants, and memory constants.

LITERAL CONSTANTS

A **literal** is an unnamed constant used to specify data. If we know that the data cannot be changed, then we can simply code the data value itself in a statement.

The literal is by far the most common form of constant. You used literals in your first program. Table 2-12 shows several examples of literals.

`'A'`	`// a character literal`
`5`	`// numeric literal 5`
`a + 5`	`// another numeric literal (5)`
`3.1416`	`// a float literal`
`"Hello"`	`// a string literal`

Table 2-12 Examples of literals

DEFINED CONSTANTS[6]

Another way to designate a constant is to use the preprocessor command **define**. Like all preprocessor commands, it is prefaced with the pound sign (#). A typical *define* command might be

```
#define  SALES_TAX_RATE .0825
```

Define commands are usually placed at the beginning of the program, although they are legal anywhere. Placing them at the beginning of the program makes them easy to find and change. In the above example, for instance, the sales tax rate changes more often than we would like. By placing it and other similar constants at the beginning of a program, we can find and change them easily.

The way *define* works is that the expression that follows the name (in this case .0825) replaces the name wherever it is found in the source program. This action is just like the search-and-replace command found in your text editor. The preprocessor does not evaluate the code in any way—it just blindly makes the substitution. For a complete discussion of defined constants, see Appendix G, "Preprocessor Directives."

MEMORY CONSTANTS

The third way to use a constant is with memory constants. Memory constants use a C++ **type qualifier** to indicate that the data cannot be changed. We have seen how to define a variable, which does nothing more than give a type and size to a named object in memory. Now let us assume that we want to fix the contents of this memory location so that they cannot be changed. This is exactly the concept of a constant, only now we have stored it in memory and given it a name.

C++ provides the capability to define a named constant. We simply add the type qualifier, *const*, before the definition, as shown in the next example.

---

[6] While the defined constant was heavily used in C programs, today most C++ programmers use memory constants, as described in the next section.

```
const float pi = 3.1416;
```

Note that the type qualifier comes first. There must be an initializer. If we didn't have an initializer, then our named constant would be whatever happened to be in memory at `pi's` location when our program started. Remember that since we have said that `pi` is a constant, we cannot change it.

Program 2-3 demonstrates the three different ways to code `pi` as a constant.

Program 2-3 Memory constants

```
/* This program demonstrates three ways to use constants.
      Written by:
      Date:
*/
#include <iostream>
using namespace std;

#define PI 3.1415926536

int main ()
{
   const double pi = 3.1415926536;

   cout << "Defined constant PI: " << PI << '\n';
   cout << "Memory constant pi:  " << pi << '\n';
   cout << "Literal constant:    " << 3.1415926536 << '\n';
   return 0;
}  // main
```

```
Results:
Defined constant PI: 3.14159
Memory constant pi:  3.14159
Literal constant:    3.14159
```

SUMMARY

Memory constants are preferred for two reasons. First, they conserve memory because they are declared and stored only once. On the other hand, defined constants are actually literals and may be stored wherever they are referenced. Second, programs with memory constants are easier to read. When defined constants are used, the precompiler substitutes the defined constant value wherever it is used, but the program display shows the original code. This creates problems when a compile error occurs because you see your original code rather than the code the compiler sees.

2-8 READING AND WRITING DATA

Every program needs to read and/or write some data. These operations can become quite complex, especially when we read and write large files. As you have already seen, however, C++ provides some relatively simple operators to read data from the keyboard and write data to the console. We introduce them here. Later, in Chapter 7, we fully discuss text input and output, and in Chapter 16, we discuss binary input and output.

DATA SOURCES AND DESTINATIONS

C++ defines one standard source, **standard input**, and two standard destinations, **standard output** and **standard error**. They are called standard because C++ creates them automatically when we need to receive data from the console keyboard or send data to the console monitor. By default, the standard input is associated with the console keyboard and the standard output and error are associated with the console monitor.

The keyboard sends data only as characters; likewise, the monitor receives data only as characters. To receive other types of data, such as integer, we key them as a sequence of characters and C++ converts them to the proper type and stores them. To send noncharacter data types to the monitor, C++ converts the data to a sequence of characters to be displayed.

> **Keyboards and monitors handle data only as a sequence of characters.**

STANDARD STREAMS

A **stream** is an abstract representation of an input data source or output data destination. C++ implements it as an object. Streams can be thought of as a conduit between our programs and the physical devices such as keyboards, monitors, and disks.

C++ automatically defines four **standard streams** called **console input**, **console output**, **console error**, and **console log**. The console input stream is associated with the standard input (keyboard). The console output, console error, and console log are connected to the standard output (monitor). They are named as ***cin***, ***cout***, ***cerr***, and ***clog***, respectively. The difference between the console error and console log is that console log is buffered while the console error is unbuffered. A **buffer** is a temporary storage area that holds data while it is being received (input) or accumulated (output). Because it is buffered, the console log output is held until the system determines that it should be written. On the other hand, the unbuffered console error output is displayed on the console immediately after it is written.

> **The standard streams are created automatically and connected to appropriate devices when a program starts.**

Each of these streams is created by the system automatically when a program that uses them starts. Their corresponding objects are defined in the input/output stream (`<iostream>`) header file. We just need to include this header file at the beginning of our programs. When the program starts, the operating system also automatically associates them with their default devices, the keyboard or the console. Some operating systems allow them to be connected to alternate devices. How this is done is beyond the scope of this text. Figure 2-12 shows the configuration of the standard streams as used in a typical program.

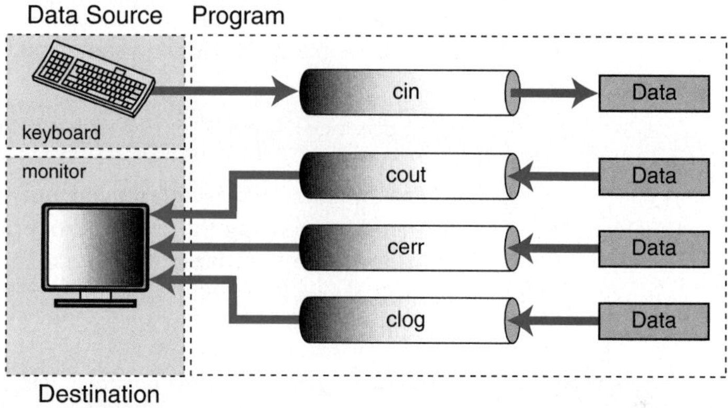

Figure 2-12 Standard streams

Objects

We all know intuitively what an object is. If you were to look in a dictionary, *object* would be defined as something physical that can be seen, touched, and felt. This connotation even carries forward into the computer world. In procedural programming concepts, an object might well be thought of as a file or a report.

In object-oriented programming (OOP), however, *object* takes on a different meaning; it is related to a type. This is especially true in C++, where we can create data objects and tightly couple them with the programming processes that manipulate them. With this in mind, we define an **object** as an entity that defines data and can access a set of processes to manipulate those data.

Earlier in this chapter we wrote a program that sent a message to the console. In the program, we used a C++ object, *cout*, that wrote our message on the console. While our line of code was simple and easy to write, a great deal of work was needed to output our simple message. The *cout* object was responsible for this task.

Since you are just beginning your journey into the programming world, you are not ready to create your own objects. By the end of the book, however, you will be using objects that you create. In the meantime, we will use the many objects that C++ provides for us.

WRITING DATA TO STANDARD OUT (cout)

To send data to standard out, we use the *cout* stream and the **insertion operator** (<<). The data following the insertion operator are inserted into the output stream for display on the system's console. The insertion operator is seen in the following example:

```
cout << "Hello World!\n";
```

Chaining

If we need to print more than one piece of data, we can chain the insertion operator. For example, given three variables—`partNum`, `qtyOnHand`, and `price`—we could write them all with one statement, as shown below.

```
cout << partNum << qtyOnHand << '$' << price;
```

The object, *cout*, is referenced only once. The data to be displayed are then chained by repeating the insertion operator before each piece of data. Note that in addition to the variables, we have also included a character dollar-sign literal so that the user will quickly recognize that the last piece of data represents a dollar amount.

Data Types

One of the advantages of programming in an object-oriented language is that the objects have intelligence built into them. For our output object, *cout*, this means that we only have to supply the data. We don't have to tell it anything about the data, such as the data type. This use of an intelligent object is seen in Program 2-4.

Program 2-4 Printing different types with *cout*

```
/* This program demonstrates the use of the insertion
   operator with several different types
      Written by:
      Date:
*/
#include <iostream>
using namespace std;

int main ()
{
// Statements
   cout << 24      << "\n";          // Print an integer
   cout << 12.3    << "\n";          // Print a float
   cout << 'A'     << "\n";          // Print a character
   cout << "Hello" << "\n";          // Print a string
   return 0;
}  // main
```

```
Results:
24
12.3
A
Hello
```

Program 2-4 Analysis In this simple program, each piece of data is displayed on a separate line. To make them come out on separate lines, we chained each data value with the for the newline character (`"\n"`). Had we not done that, all of the data would have appeared on one line, packed together with no spacing.

If we wanted to print the data on one line, we would still use chaining. In this case, however, we would chain either a tab character (\t) or a string literal containing several spaces.

WRITING ERRORS (cerr and clog)

To send an error message to the console, we use the *cerr* or *clog* stream and the insertion operator (<<). The data following the insertion operator is inserted into the error stream for display on the system's console. The first example in the following code writes buffered data to standard error; the second example writes immediately.

```
cerr << "A buffered error message\n";
clog << "An unbuffered error message\n";
```

FORMATTING OUTPUT

Because intelligence can be included in an object, we can identify functions to perform special tasks. For the input and output objects, these functions have been given a special name: **manipulator.** The manipulator functions format output so that it is presented in a more readable fashion for the user. In Appendix I we show how to write manipulators. For the moment, however, it is enough to know how to use the standard manipulators supplied with the system. The output manipulators are summarized in Table 2-13.

Manipulator	Scope	Use
`endl`	One time	New line
`dec`	Permanent	Formats output as decimal
`oct`	Permanent	Formats output as octal
`hex`	Permanent	Formats output as hexadecimal
`fixed`	Permanent	Sets floating-point decimals
`showpoint`	Permanent	Shows decimal in floating-point values
`setw(...)`	One time	Sets width of output fields
`setprecision(...)`	Permanent	Specifies number of decimals for floating point
`setfill(...)`	Permanent	Specifies fill character

Table 2-13 Output manipulators

The manipulators are found in two different libraries. Those without parameter arguments are found in the basic input/output stream library (<iostream>). Those with parameters arguments, such as set width, set precision, and set fill, are found in a special library known as the input/output manipulator library (<iomanip>).

General Manipulators

There are three general manipulators: newline, set width, and set fill. We call them general manipulators because they can be used with all types of data.

Newline (endl) The newline manipulator terminates the current line and starts a new one. It has the same effect as the newline (`'\n'`) character. The following examples produce identical results:

```
cout << 123 << '\n'         →        cout << 123 << endl
cout << "hello\n"           →        cout << "hello" << end
```

Set Width (setw) **Set width** allows us to set the *minimum* width for an output field. Note that set width sets the minimum space; if the data need more space in the output, *cout* will override the set width request and use whatever space is required.

The set width manipulator also controls the alignment of the output. There are two basic alignment formats: right justification and left justification. **Right justification** places the data in an output area with the data oriented to the right and fill characters on the left. The fill character is generally spaces, although (as we will see) we can control the actual character used. **Left justification** starts the data on the left of an output area and adds trailing fill characters on the right.

Set width uses right justification. This makes sense. When we work with numeric data, we want the data aligned so that we can easily add it or otherwise check the values. When numbers are left-justified, it is very difficult to perceive their values quickly. Character and string data, on the other hand, are more logically justified left. Later we will discover another manipulator to left-justify text data.

Program 2-5 contains a demonstration of the set width rules for several different types of data.

Program 2-5 Demonstrate set width manipulator

```
/* Demonstrate the use of the set width manipulator.
      Written by:
      Date:
*/
#include <iostream>
#include <iomanip>
using namespace std;

int main ()
{
   int    d123   = 123;
   float  f123   = 1.23;
   char   chA    = 'A';

   cout << "Demonstrate set width manipulator\n";

   cout << "0...0....1....1" << endl;
   cout << "1...5....0....5" << endl;
   cout << d123 << f123 << chA << "\t    | no width" << endl;
   cout << setw(1) << d123
        << setw(1) << f123
        << setw(1) << chA
        << "\t     | width too small" << endl;
   cout << setw(5) << d123
        << setw(5) << f123
        << setw(5) << chA
        << "\t | width 5 space each" << endl;
   cout << setw(10) << "Hello"
```

Program 2-5 Demonstrate set width manipulator *(continued)*

```
          << "\t      | string width 10" << endl;
    cout << setw(3) << "Hello"
          << "        \t | string width 3" << endl;

    return 0;
}   // main
```

```
Results:
Demonstrate set width manipulator
0...0....1....1
1...5....0....5
1231.23A            | no width
1231.23A            | width too small
  123 1.23     A    | width 5 space each
     Hello          | string width 10
Hello               | string width 3
```

Program 2-5 Analysis Compare the results carefully with the code to make sure that you understand everything that takes place. The first two lines simply set a scale so that you can count the blank spaces. Next we print the three variables twice. The first time we don't use set width; everything is jammed together. The results are the same on the next line because the width is set too small and is overridden by the insertion operator (<<). On the third line, we provide ample room so that there is space around all of the values.

The first string fits easily into the ten spaces allocated for it. Note that it is also right-justified with five leading spaces. In the last example, however, there is not enough room. C++ therefore overrides the width requested and extends the print area to five spaces to completely print the data. In all cases, C++ ensures that the user will see all of the data even if it is necessary to override the requested formatting.

Set Fill Character (setfill) When the width of a print area is larger than the data values to be placed in it, C++ uses a fill character for the non-data area. The default fill-character value is the space. The space fill is seen in the examples in Program 2-5.

Generally, you will not want to change the fill character. However, one common example of when you may want to is when creating a program that prints checks. To prevent the check amount from being altered, computer-generated check amounts are usually printed with leading asterisks (*). This is done in C++ with the set fill character. Program 2-6 demonstrates this feature.

Program 2-6 Demonstrate fill character manipulator

```
/* Demonstrate fill character.
      Written by:
      Date:
*/
#include <iostream>
#include <iomanip>
using namespace std;

```

Program 2-6 Demonstrate fill character manipulator *(continued)*

```
int main ()
{
   float  amount = 123.45;

   cout << "Demonstrate fill characters\n\n";

   cout << setw(10) << amount
        << "\tAmount with space fill\n";

   cout << setw(10) << setfill('*') << amount
        << "\tAmount with check protection fill\n";

   cout << setw(10) << setfill(' ') << amount
        << "\tand again with space fill\n";

   return 0;
}  // main
```

```
Results:
Demonstrate fill characters

    123.45      Amount with space fill
****123.45      Amount with check protection fill
    123.45      and again with space fill
```

Program 2-6 Analysis Two points must be emphasized concerning fill characters. First, the set width manipulator must be used to set the width of each value being displayed. If the width is not greater than the value, then there is no fill. Second, the fill character is a permanent-until-changed manipulator. To change back to a space fill, it must be reexecuted.

Integer Manipulators (dec, oct, hex)

The **integer manipulators** are used to change the display format for the integer values. The decimal manipulator **(dec)** is the default. It tells the system to print the value in decimal. Similarly, octal **(oct)** tells *cout* to print the value using the octal numbering system, while hexadecimal **(hex)** tells it to print in hexadecimal. Each of these manipulators sets the printing until it is reset by another manipulator. Program 2-7 demonstrates the use of the numeric formats and shows how another manipulator must be used to reset the print format.

Program 2-7 Demonstrate numeric manipulators

```
/* This program demonstrates the use of the numeric
   manipulator.
      Written by:
      Date:
*/
#include <iostream>
#include <iomanip>
using namespace std;

```

Program 2-7 Demonstrate numeric manipulators *(continued)*

```
int main ()
{
   int     d123    = 123;

   cout << "Values in decimal: \t";
   cout << setw(5) << d123 << setw(5) << d123 << endl;

   cout << "Values in hexadecimal: \t";
   cout << hex;
   cout << setw(5) << d123 << setw(5) << d123 << endl;

   cout << "Values in octal: \t";
   cout << oct;
   cout << setw(5) << d123 << setw(5) << d123 << endl;

   cout << "Values in decimal: \t";
   cout << dec;
   cout << setw(5) << d123 << setw(5) << d123 << endl;

   return 0;
}  // main
```

```
Results:
Values in decimal:          123  123
Values in hexadecimal:       7b   7b
Values in octal:            173  173
Values in decimal:          123  123
```

Floating-Point Manipulators

There are three **floating-point manipulators**: fixed, set precision, and showpoint. Generally, if you use one, you will want to use all three.

Fixed The **fixed** manipulator tells *cout* that floating-point numbers are to be displayed with fixed-point rather than floating-point numbers. Floating point numbers are stored in memory in two parts, a mantissa and an exponent (see Appendix D). While small numbers are displayed in the fixed-point format, large numbers are displayed in the floating-point format. When the number to be displayed is very large or very small, the fixed manipulator displays the two parts separated by the exponent token *(e)* as shown in the next example.

```
1.234568e+06
```

This is not a format that most people are used to seeing. Most people understand data much better when they are displayed in a fixed format. The same number in its fixed format is shown below.

```
1234567.875
```

Set Precision **Set precision** is used to control the number of decimal places to be displayed. As a general rule, C++ uses up to six decimal places in its floating-point displays. When the set precision manipulator is used, C++ uses the same precision for all displays (see Program 2-8).

Show Point When we use zero precision with a floating-point number, C++ prints it without a decimal point, which makes it look like an integer. To display the value with a decimal point, we use **showpoint** as shown in the following examples.

All three of these manipulators are seen in Program 2-8.

Program 2-8 Demonstrate fixed-point manipulators

```
/* Demonstrate floating-point manipulators.
      Written by:
      Date:
*/
#include <iostream>
#include <iomanip>
using namespace std;

int main ()
{
   cout << "Demonstrate float manipulators\n\n";

   float  f1         = 1.0;
   float  f1234      = 1.234;
   float  f123456789 = 1234567.875;

   cout << f1 << "\t\t\t\tWith no manipulators\n";
   cout << f1234 << endl;
   cout << f123456789 << endl << endl;

   cout << fixed;
   cout << f1 << "\t\tWith fixed added\n";
   cout << f1234 << endl;
   cout << f123456789 << endl << endl;

   cout << setprecision(2);
   cout << f1 << "\t\t\tWith setprecision added\n";
   cout << f1234 << endl;
   cout << f123456789 << endl << endl;

   cout << setprecision(0);
   cout << f1234 << "\t\t\t\tWith setprecision(0)\n";
   cout << setprecision(0) << showpoint
        << f1234 << "\t\t\t\tWith showpoint\n";
}  // main
```

```
Results:
Demonstrate float manipulators
```

Program 2-8 Demonstrate fixed-point manipulators *(continued)*

```
1                With no manipulators
1.234
1.23457e+06

1.000000         With fixed added
1.234000
1234567.875000

1.00             With setprecision added
1.23
1234567.88

1                With setprecision(0)
1.               With showpoint
```

Program 2-8 Analysis Each example in this small program demonstrates several points. In the first display, when no manipulators are used, we see the integral value 1 with no decimals; the small decimal number that is displayed in a fixed-point format; and the large floating-point number that is displayed in the floating-point format.

The second example sets the format to fixed-point rather than floating-point format. The values are now printed in the fixed-point format with the default of six decimal places. When precision is specified, C++ rounds the number. Thus, in the third example we see that 1.234 rounds down to 1.23 while 1234567.875 rounds up to 1234567.88.

The last example demonstrates the effect of the showpoint manipulator. Because it is used when the precision is zero (no decimal places), we first set the precision and display the value 1.234. It displays as 1 without a decimal. After setting showpoint, we again print 1.234 and this time the value is displayed with a decimal point.

Output Examples

This section contains several output examples. We show the print statement, followed by what would be printed. Cover up the solution and try to predict the results.

1.

```
cout << 23  << 'z'  << 4.1 << endl;
```

```
23z4.1
```

Note that because there are no spaces between the values, the data are formatted without space between them.

2.

```
cout << 23  << " " << 'z'  << " " << 4.1  << endl;
```

```
23 z 4.1
```

This is a repeat of Output Example 1 with spaces between the data.

3. Again, the same example, this time using variables.

```
int   num1 = 23;
char  zee  = 'z';
```

```
float num2 = 4.1;
char space = ' ';

cout << num1 << space << zee << space << num2 << endl;
```

```
23 z 4.1
```

4.

```
cout << fixed;
cout << 23     << '\t'      << 'Z'    << '\t'   << setw(5)
     << setprecision (1) << 14.2   << endl;
cout << 107    << '\t'      << 'A'    << '\t'   << setw(5)
     << setprecision(1)  << 53.6   << endl;
cout << 1754   << '\t'      << 'F'    << '\t'   << setw(5)
     << setprecision (1) << 122.0 << endl;
cout << 3      << '\t'      << 'P'    << '\t'   << setw(5)
     << setprecision (1) << 0.1 << endl;
```

```
23      Z     14.2
107     A     53.6
1754    F    122.0
3       P      0.1
```

In the above code, note the tab character (`\t`) between the first and second, and second and third fields. Since the data are to be printed in separate lines, each format string ends with a newline (`endl`).

5.

```
cout << "The number" << 23
     << "is my favorite number."  << endl;
```

```
The number23is my favorite number.
```

Since there are no spaces before and after the number 23, it runs together with the text before and after it.

6.

```
cout << "The number is " << setw (5) << 23 << endl;
```

```
The number is    23
^^^^^^^^^^^^^^^^^^^^
```

If you count the spaces carefully, you will note that five spaces follow the word `is`. The first space comes from the space after `is` and before the indirection token. The other four come from the width in the `setw` manipulator.

7.

```
cout << "The tax is "
     << setw (6)      << setprecision (6) << 233.12
     << " this year." << endl;
```

```
The tax is 233.12 this year.
```

In this example, the width is six and the precision two. Since the number of digits printed totals five (three for the integral portion and two for the decimal portion), and the decimal point takes one print position, the full width is filled with data. The only spaces are the spaces before and after the conversion code in the format string.

8.

```
cout << "The tax is "
     << setw (8)        << setprecision (6) << 233.12
     << " this year." << endl;
```

```
The tax is   233.12 this year.
^^^^^^^^^^^^^^^^^^^^^^^^^^^^^^
```

9.

```
cout << "The tax is "
     << setw (8) << setprecision (6) << setfill('0')
     << 233.12    << " this year."    << endl;
```

```
The tax is 00233.12 this year.
^^^^^^^^^^^^^^^^^^^^^^^^^^^^^^
```

This example uses the zero flag to print leading zeros. Note that the width is eight positions. Three of these positions are taken up by the precision of two digits and the decimal point. This leaves five positions for the integral portion of the number. Since there are only three digits (233), two leading zeros are inserted.

10.

```
cout << "\"" << 'h' << "    " << 23 << "\"" << endl;
```

```
"h   23"
^^^^^^^^
```

In this example, we want to print the data within quotes. Since quotes are used to identify the format string, we can't use them as print characters. To print them, therefore, we must use the escape character with the quote (\ "), which tells *cout* that what follows is not the end of the string but a character to be printed, in this case, a quote mark.

11.

```
cout << "This line disappears.\r... A New line"  << endl;
cout << "This is the bell character \a" << endl;
cout << "A null (\0) kills the rest of the line" << endl;
cout << "This is 'it' in single quotes" << endl;
cout << "This is \"it\" in double quotes" << endl;
cout << "This is \\ the escape character itself" << endl;
```

```
... A new line
This is the bell character
A null (
This is 'it' in single quotes
This is "it" in double quotes
This is \ the escape character itself
```

These examples use some of the special names found in Table 2-11 on page 42. Two of them give unexpected results. The return character (`\r`) repositions the output at the beginning of the current line without advancing the line. Therefore, the beginning of the line is overlaid. In the third example, the null character effectively kills the rest of the line.

READING DATA FROM STANDARD INPUT (*cin*)

To read data from standard input, we use the ***cin*** (console input) object. The **extraction operator** (>>) reads data from the standard input. It gets its name from the fact that it extracts data from the input stream and stores them in the variable specified after the operator. The format of the extraction operator is shown below.

```
cin >> variable;
```

As with the insertion operator, we do not have to define the type of data being read. The *cin* object has the necessary intelligence to determine the type of data being read and formats it accordingly. While the extraction operator works much like the insertion operator, it does not require the extensive manipulator library. Data are simply formatted to correspond with the variable into which it is being stored.

Chaining is used extensively with the extraction operator. Program 2-9 demonstrates how a program can read several pieces of data and then display them back to the user.

Program 2-9 The extraction operator

```
/* Demonstrate the extraction operator.
      Written by:
      Date:
*/
#include <iostream>
#include <iomanip>
using namespace std;

int main ()
{
   char   aChar;
   int    integer;
   float  dlrAmnt;

   cout << "Please enter an integer, "
        << "a dollar amount and a character.\n";
   cin >> integer >> dlrAmnt >> aChar;

   cout << "\nThank you. You entered:\n";
   cout << setw(6)          << integer << "   "
        << setfill('*')     << setprecision(2) << fixed
        << '$' << setw(10)  << dlrAmnt
        << setfill(' ')     << setw(3) << aChar << endl;

   return 0;
}  // main
```

Program 2-9 The extraction operator *(continued)*

```
Results:
Please enter an integer, a dollar amount and a character.
12 123.45 G

Thank you. You entered:
    12  $****123.45  G
```

Program 2-9 Analysis Once again, a simple program has several important concepts in it. First, note how we prompt the user for exactly what input we want. Had this been a real application rather than a demonstration, we would have prompted with user terminology, such as quantity and price.

While it is not apparent from the example, the user could have entered the data all on one line, as shown in the example, or with each value on a separate line. The program handles either case.

Finally, note that to display the output, we were forced to use many of the manipulators we studied in the previous section.

Input Examples

This section contains several examples. We list the data that will be input first. This allows you to cover up the function and try to formulate your own input statement.

1.
```
214 156 14Z
```

```
cin  >> a >> b >>  c >> d;
```

2.
```
2314  15  2.14
```

```
cin >> a >> b >> c;
```

3.
```
14/26  25/66
```

```
cin >> num1 >> c  >> den1 >> num2 >> c >> den2;
```

We need to remove the fraction token (/). This is easily done by simply providing a variable to read it into and then never using the value.

4.
```
11-25-56
```

```
cin >> month >> c >> day >> c >> year;
```

Again, we see some required user input, this time dashes between the month, day, and year. A better solution for both examples would be to prompt the user separately for the input; the numerators and denominators in example 3 and month, day, and year in example 4.

2-9 PROGRAMMING EXAMPLES

In this section, we write three programs to demonstrate reading and writing data using the extraction and insertion operators.

PRINT "Nothing!"

Program 2-10 is a very simple program that prints "Nothing!"

Program 2-10 A program that prints "Nothing!"

```
/* Prints the message "Nothing!".
      Written by:
      Date:
*/
#include <iostream>
using namespace std;

int main ()
{
   cout << "This program prints\n\n\t\"Nothing!\"\n";
   return 0;
} // main
```

```
Results:
This program prints

     "Nothing!"
```

PRINT CHARACTER VALUES

Program 2-11 demonstrates that all characters are stored in the computer as integers. We define some character variables and initialize them with values, and then we print them as integers. As you study the output, note that the ASCII values of the characters are printed. The program also shows the values of some nonprintable characters. All values can be verified by referring to Appendix A.

Program 2-11 Print value of selected characters

```
/* Display the decimal value of selected characters.
      Written by:
      Date:
*/
#include <iostream>
using namespace std;

int  main ()
{
   char A          = 'A';
   char a          = 'a';
   char B          = 'B';
   char b          = 'b';
   char Zed        = 'Z';
   char zed        = 'z';
```

Program 2-11 Print value of selected characters *(continued)*

```
   char zero       = '0';
   char eight      = '8';
   char NL         = '\n';        // newline
   char HT         = '\t';        // horizontal tab
   char VT         = '\v';        // vertical tab
   char SP         = ' ';         // blank or space
   char BEL        = '\a';        // alert (bell)
   char dblQuote   = '"';         // double quote
   char backSlash  = '\\';        // backslash itself
   char oneQuote   = '\'';        // single quote itself

   cout << "\nASCII char 'A'  is: "  << (int)A;
   cout << "\nASCII char 'a'  is: "  << (int)a;
   cout << "\nASCII char 'B'  is: "  << (int)B;
   cout << "\nASCII char 'b'  is: "  << (int)b;
   cout << "\nASCII char 'Z'  is: "  << (int)Zed;
   cout << "\nASCII char 'z'  is: "  << (int)zed;
   cout << "\nASCII char '0'  is: "  << (int)zero;
   cout << "\nASCII char '8'  is: "  << (int)eight;
   cout << "\nASCII char '\\n' is: " << (int)NL;
   cout << "\nASCII char '\\t' is: " << (int)HT;
   cout << "\nASCII char '\\v' is: " << (int)VT;
   cout << "\nASCII char ' '  is: "  << (int)SP;
   cout << "\nASCII char '\\a' is: " << (int)BEL;
   cout << "\nASCII char '\"'  is: " << (int)dblQuote;
   cout << "\nASCII char '\\'  is: " << (int)backSlash;
   cout << "\nASCII char '''  is: "  << (int)oneQuote;
   return 0;
}  // main
```

```
Results:
ASCII char 'A'  is: 65
ASCII char 'a'  is: 97
ASCII char 'B'  is: 66
ASCII char 'b'  is: 98
ASCII char 'Z'  is: 90
ASCII char 'z'  is: 122
ASCII char '0'  is: 48
ASCII char '8'  is: 56
ASCII char '\n' is: 10
ASCII char '\t' is: 9
ASCII char '\v' is: 11
ASCII char ' '  is: 32
ASCII char '\a' is: 7
ASCII char '"'  is: 34
ASCII char '\'  is: 92
ASCII char '''  is: 39
```

CALCULATE AREA AND CIRCUMFERENCE

In this section, we write a program that calculates the area and circumference of a circle. Although we haven't shown you how to make calculations in C++, if you know algebra you will have no problem reading the code in Program 2-12.

Program 2-12 Calculate a circle's area and circumference

```
/* This program calculates the area and circumference
   of a circle.
      Written by:
      Date:
*/
#include <iostream>
using namespace std;

int main ()
{
   float circ;
   float area;
   float radius;

   cout << "\nPlease enter the value of the radius: ";
   cin  >> radius;

   circ  = 2  * 3.1416 * radius;
   area  = 3.1416 * radius * radius;

   cout << "\nRadius is :          " << radius;
   cout << "\nCircumference is :   " << circ;
   cout << "\nArea is :            " << area;

   return 0;
} // main
```

```
Results:
Please enter the value of the radius: 23
Radius is :                  23
Circumference is :           144.514
Area is:                     1661.91
```

Print a Report

Imagine you are assigned to a new project that is currently being designed. To give the customer an idea of what a proposed report might look like, the project leader has asked you to write a small program to print a sample. The specifications for the report are shown in Figure 2-13, and the code is shown in Program 2-13.

The report contains four fields: a part number, which must be printed with leading zeros; the current quantity on hand; the current quantity on order; and the price of the item, printed to two decimal points. All data are to be aligned in columns with captions indicating the type of data in each column. The report is to be closed with an "End of Report" message.

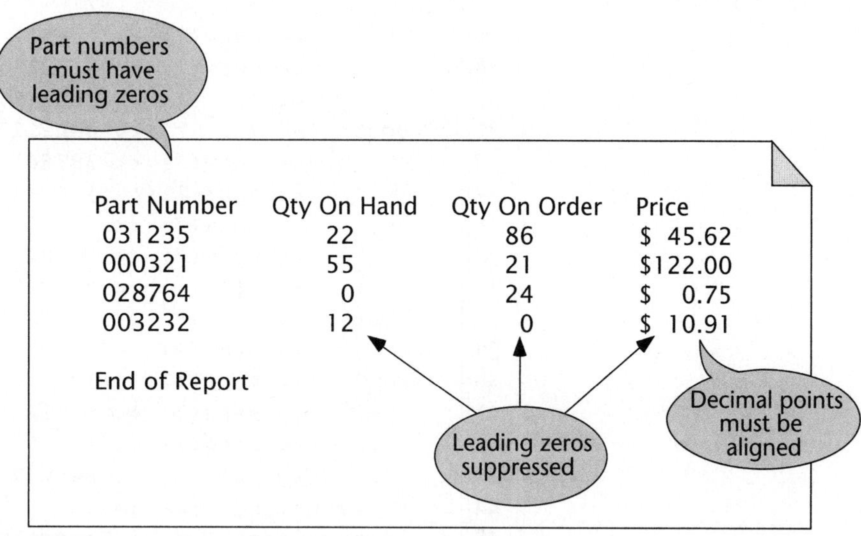

Figure 2-13 Output specifications for inventory report

Program 2-13 A sample inventory report

```
/* This program prints four lines of Inventory data
   on an Inventory report to give the user an idea of
   what a new report will look like. Since this is
   not a real report, no input is required. The data
   are all specified as constants.
      Written by:
      Date:
*/
#include <iostream>
#include <iomanip>
using namespace std;

int main ()
{
   // Print captions
   cout <<  "\tPart Number\tQty On Hand";
   cout <<  "\tQty On Order\tPrice\n";
   // Print data
   cout    << fixed   << setprecision(2);
   cout    << "\t  "  << setfill('0')
           << setw(6) << 31235    << "\t"
           << setfill(' ')
           << setw(7) <<    22    << "\t\t"
           << setw(7) <<    86    << "\t\t"
           << '$'     << setw(7) <<  45.62   << endl;
   cout    << "\t  "  << setfill('0')
           << setw(6) <<   321     << "\t"
           << setfill(' ')
```

Program 2-13 A sample inventory report *(continued)*

```
29              << setw(7) <<     55     << "\t\t"
30              << setw(7) <<     21     << "\t\t"
31              << '$'     << setw(7)  <<  122.    << endl;
32       cout   << "\t  "  << setfill('0')
33              << setw(6) << 28764      << "\t"
34              << setfill(' ')
35              << setw(7) <<      0     << "\t\t"
36              << setw(7) <<     24     << "\t\t"
37              << '$'     << setw(7)  <<  .75     << endl;
38       cout   << "\t  "  << setfill('0')
39              << setw(6) <<  3232      << "\t"
40              << setfill(' ')
41              << setw(7) <<     12     << "\t\t"
42              << setw(7) <<      0     << "\t\t"
43              << '$'     << setw(7)  <<  10.91   << endl;
44       // Print end message
45       cout << "\n\tEnd of Report\n";
46       return 0;
47    }  // main
```

Program 2-13 Analysis There are a few things about Program 2-13 that you should note. First, it is fully documented. Professional programmers often ignore documentation on "one time only" programs, thinking they will throw them away, only to find that they end up using them over and over. It only takes a few minutes to document a program, and it is always time well spent. If nothing else, it helps to clarify the program's purpose in your mind.

Next, look carefully at the formatting for the print statements. Formatting is controlled by a combination of tabs and manipulators. We start in line 19 with the fixed and set precision manipulators to set the formatting for all of the floating-point values. Then, in each statement, we use tabs with set width and endline manipulators to control the spacing on each line.

Finally, note that the program concludes with a *return* statement that informs the operating system that it concluded successfully. Attention to details, even in small programs, is the sign of a good programmer.

2-10 SOFTWARE ENGINEERING AND PROGRAMMING STYLE

Although this chapter introduces only a few programming concepts, there is still much to be said from a software engineering point of view. We will discuss the concepts of program documentation, data naming, and data hiding.

PROGRAM DOCUMENTATION

There are two levels of program documentation. The first is the **general documentation** at the start of the program. The second level is found within each function.

General Documentation

Program 2-14 shows what we recommend for program documentation. Each program should start with a general description of the program. Following the general description is the name of the author and the date the program was written. Following the date is the program's change history, which documents the reason and authority for all changes. For a production program whose use spans several years, the change history can become extensive.

Program 2-14 Sample of general program documentation

```
/* A sample of program documentation. Each program
   starts with a general description of the program.
   Often, this description can be taken from the
   requirements specification given to the programmer.
   Written by: Original Author
   Date:       Date first released to production
   Change History:
      <date> Included in this documentation is a short
             description of each change.
*/
```

Module Documentation

When necessary, you should include a brief comment as **module documentation** for blocks of code. A block of code is much like a paragraph in a report. It contains one thought—that is, one set of statements that accomplish a specific task. Blocks of code in your program should be separated by blank program lines, just as you skip blank lines in your reports between paragraphs.

If the block of code is difficult, or if the logic is especially significant, then you may choose to give the reader a short—one- or two-line—description of the block's purpose and/or operation. We will provide many examples of this type of documentation throughout the text.

Sometimes you will find a textbook suggesting that you document each variable in a program. We disagree with this approach. In the first place, the proper location for variable documentation is in a data dictionary. A data dictionary is a system documentation tool that contains standard names, descriptions, and other information about data used in a system.

Second, good data names eliminate the need for variable comments. In fact, if you think you need to document the purpose of a variable, check your variable name. You will usually find that improving the name eliminates the need for the comment.

DATA NAMES

Another principle of good structured programming is the use of *intelligent* **data names**. This means that the variable name itself should give the reader a good idea about what data it contains and maybe even an idea about how the data are used.

Although there are obvious advantages to keeping names short, the advantage is quickly lost if the names become so cryptic that they are unintelligible. We have seen programmers struggle for hours to find a bug, only to discover that the problem was they were using the wrong variable. The time saved keying short, cryptic names is often lost ten- or a hundredfold in debugging time.

We have formulated several guidelines to help you construct good, intelligent data names.

1. The name should match the terminology of the user as closely as possible.

   Let's suppose that you are writing a program to calculate the area of a rectangle. Mathematicians often label the sides of a rectangle *a* and *b*, but their real names are length and width. Therefore, your program should call the sides of the rectangle *length* and *width.* These would be names that are commonly used by anyone describing a rectangle.

2. When necessary for readability, and to separate similar variables from each other, combine terms to form a variable name.

   Suppose that you are working on a project to compute a payroll. There are many different types of taxes. Each of the different taxes should be clearly distinguished from the others by good data names. Table 2-14 shows both good and bad names for this programming situation. Most of the poor names are either too abbreviated to be meaningful (such as *ftr)* or are generic names (such as *rate*) that could apply to many different pieces of data.

Good names	Poor names
ficaTaxRate fica_tax_rate	rate ftr frate fica
ficaWitholding fica_witholding	fwh ficaw wh
ficaWthldng fica_wthldng	fcwthldng wthldng
ficaMax ficaDlrMax	max fmax

Table 2-14 Examples of good and poor data names

Note the two different concepts used for separating the words in a variable's name. In the first example, we capitalized the first letter of each word. In the second example, we separated the words with an underscore. Both are good techniques for making a compound name readable. If you use capitalization, keep in mind that C++ is case sensitive, so you must be careful to use the same cases for the name each time you use it.

3. Do not create variable names that are different by only one or two letters, especially if the differences are at the end of the word. Names that are too similar create confusion. On the other hand, a naming pattern makes it easier to recall the names. This is especially true when user terminology is being used. Thus, we see that the good names in Table 2-14 all start with *fica*.
4. Abbreviations, when used, should clearly indicate the words being abbreviated.

   Table 2-14 also contains several examples of good abbreviations. Whenever possible, use abbreviations created by the users. They will often have a glossary of abbreviations and acronyms that they use.

   Short words are usually not abbreviated. If they are short in the first place, they don't need to be made shorter.
5. Avoid the use of generic names.

   Generic names are programming or user jargon. For example, *count* and *sum* are both generic names. They tell you their purpose, but don't give you any clue as to the type of data they are associated with. Better names would be *emplyCnt* and *ficaSum*. Programmers are especially fond of using generic names, but they tend to make the program confusing. Several of the poor names in Table 2-14 are generic.
6. Use defined constants for constants that are hard to read or that might change from system to system.

   Some constants are just about impossible to read. We pointed out the space earlier. If you need a space often, create a defined constant for it. Table 2-15 contains several examples of constants that are better when coded as defined constants.

`#define SPACE ' '`	`#define BANG '!'`
`#define DBL_QTE '"'`	`#define QUOTE '''`
`#define COMMA ','`	`#define COLON ':'`

Table 2-15 Examples of named constants

Another advantage of defined constants over literals and memory constants is consistency. Since they are coded only once in the program, they will be the same throughout the program.

DATA HIDING

In "Structure of a C++ Program" on page 27 we discussed the concept of global and local variables. We pointed out that anything placed before *main* was said to be in the global part of the program. With the exception of data that must be visible to other *programs,* no data should be placed in this section.

One of the principles of structured programming states that the data structure should be hidden from view. The two terms you usually hear in connection with this concept are **data hiding** and **data encapsulation**. Both of these principles have as their objective protecting data from accidental destruction by parts of your program that don't require access to the data. In other words, if a part of your program doesn't require data to do its job, it shouldn't be able to *see* or *modify* the data. Until you learn to use functions in Chapter 4, however, you will not be able to provide this data hiding capability.

Nevertheless, you should start your programming with good practices. And since our ultimate objective is good structured programming, we now formulate our first programming standard:

> **Programming Standard**
> **No variables are to be placed in the global area of a program.**

Any variables placed in the global area of your program—that is, before *main*—can be used and changed by every part of your program. This is undesirable and is in direct conflict with the structured programming principles of *data hiding* and *data encapsulation.*

2-11 TIPS AND COMMON PROGRAMMING ERRORS

1. Well-structured programs use global (defined) constants but do not use global variables.
2. The function header for *main* should be complete. We recommend the following format:

```
int main ()
```

   a. If you forget the parentheses after *main*, you will get a compile error.
   b. If you put a semicolon after the parentheses, you will get a compile error.
   c. If you misspell *main* you will not get a compile error, but you will get an error when you try to link the program. All programs must have a function named *main.*
3. Not terminating a comment block with a close token (*/) is a compile error.
4. Not including required libraries, such as <iostream>, at the beginning of your program is a linker error.

5. If you misspell the name of a function, you will get an error when you link the program. For example, if you misspell *cin* or *cout,* your program will compile without errors, but you will get a linker error. Using the wrong case is a form of spelling error. For example, each of the following names is different:

```
cin, Cin, CIN  cout, Cout, COUT
```

2-12 KEY TERMS

ASCII
block comment
body
bool
Boolean
buffered
char
character
cin
console error
console input
console log
console output
constant
cout
data encapsulation
data hiding
data names
data types
dec
declaration
define
definitions
derived types
double
escape character
extraction operator
false
fixed
float
floating-point manipulator
floating-point type
function
function header
general documentation
global definitions section
header file
hex
identifier
include
initializer
input/output stream
insertion operator
int
integer
integer constant
integer manipulators
iostream
keywords
left justification
line comment
literal
local definition
logical data
long
long double
main
manipulator
module documentation
namespace
object
oct
operations
overloading
preprocessor directives
program documentation
reserved words
return
right justification
set precision
set width
short
showpoint
signed
sizeof
standard streams
standard types
statement
stream
string
string constant
subfunctions
syntax
token
true
type qualifier
unsigned
values
variables
void

2-13 SUMMARY

- In 1972, Dennis Ritchie designed C at Bell Laboratories.
- In 1985, Bjarne Stroustrup's extensions to the C language became universally knows as C++.
- The basic processing component of a C++ program is the function.
- Every C++ function is made of declarations and one or more statements.
- One and only one of the functions in a C++ program must be called *main*.
- Identifiers are used in a language to name objects.
- We have two general categories of data types in C++: standard and derived.
- The standard data types are void, character, integer, and floating point.
- The derived data types are arrays, pointers, structures, unions, enumerated, and class.
- Character data represents a character from the alphabet used by the computer, which is normally the ASCII alphabet. In C++, the character data type is called *char*.
- The integer data type represents a number without a fraction. The integer data type in C++ is called *int*. There are three sizes of integer: *short int*, *int*, and *long int*.
- The floating-point data type represents a number with fraction. The floating-point data type in C++ is called *float*. There are three sizes of float: *float*, *double*, and *long double*.
- Logical data are data that evaluate to either true or false. C++ supports logical data in two ways: (1) with the Boolean type (bool), which uses *true* and *false* for its values; and (2) with the integral types, which use nonzero for true and zero for false.
- A constant is a piece of data whose value cannot be changed.
- There are four kinds of constants in C++: integer constant, float constant, character constant, and string constant.
- Constants can be coded in three different ways: as literals, as define commands, and as memory constants.
- Variables are named areas of memory used to hold data.
- Variables must be declared and defined before being used in C++.
- To input data through the keyboard and to output data through the console (or printer), you can use the standard input/output streams.
- *cin* is a standard input stream for inputting data through the keyboard.
- *cout* is a standard output stream for outputting data to the console.
- As necessary, programs should contain comments that provide the reader with in-line documentation for blocks of code.
- Programs that use "intelligent" names are easier to read and understand.

2-14 PRACTICE SETS

REVIEW QUESTIONS

1. The purpose of a library file, such as `iostream`, is to store a program's source code.

   a. True b. False

2. Any valid printable ASCII character can be used in an identifier.

   a. True b. False

3. Logical data in C++ is generally represented by integer values.

   a. True b. False

4. The C++ standard function that receives data from the keyboard is `cout`.

   a. True b. False

5. Which of the following statements about the structure of a C++ program is false?
   a. A C++ program starts with a global declaration section.
   b. Declaration sections contain instructions to the computer.
   c. Every program must have at least one function.
   d. One and only one function may be named `main`.
   e. Each function's local declarations may be coded anywhere within the function block.
6. Which of the following statements about comments is false?
   a. Comments are internal documentation for programmers.
   b. Comments are used by the preprocessor to help format the program.
   c. Comments begin with a `/*` token
   d. Comments cannot be nested.
   e. Comments end with a `*/` token
7. Which of the following identifiers is not valid?
   a. `_option`
   b. `salesAmount`
   c. `amount`
   d. `$salesAmount`
   e. `sales_amount`
8. Which of the following is not a standard data type?
   a. `char`
   b. `int`
   c. `void`
   d. `float`
   e. `logical`
9. Which of the following statements about characters is true?
   a. Each character has a unique binary value.
   b. In C++, characters are normally stored in 2 bytes (16 bits).
   c. Lowercase and uppercase values are organized as value pairs, such as `aAbBcC`.
   d. Most computers use the American Standard Code for Computer Information (ASCCI) for their alphabet.
   e. The special characters are found grouped together between uppercase and lowercase letters.
10. The code that establishes the original value for a variable is known as a(n):
    a. assignment
    b. initializer
    c. value
    d. constant
    e. originator
11. Which of the following statements about a constant is/are true?
    a. Character constants are coded using double quotes (`"`).
    b. It is impossible to tell the computer that a constant should be a *float* or a *long double*.
    c. Like variables, constants have a type and may be named.
    d. Only integer values can be used in a constant.
    e. The value of a constant may be changed during a program's execution.
12. Which of the following statements about files is false?
    a. The keyboard is a file.
    b. The keyboard is usually not buffered.
    c. The standard input file is usually the keyboard.
    d. The standard output file is a text file.
    e. The standard output file is usually the monitor.

EXERCISES

13. Which of the following are *not* character constants in C++?
    a. 'C'   b. 'bb'   c. "C"
    d. '?'   e. ' '
14. Which of the following are *not* integer constants in C++?
    a. -320   b. +45   c. -31.80
    d. 1456   e. 2,456
15. Which of the following are *not* floating-point constants in C++?
    a. 45.6   b. -14.05   c. 'a'
    d. pi   e. 40
16. What is the type of each of the following constants?
    a. 15   b. -14.24   c. 'b'
    d. "1"   e. "16"

17. Which of the following are *not* valid identifiers in C++?

a. A3 b. 4A c. if
d. IF e. tax-rate

18. Find any errors in the following program:

```
// This program does nothing
int main
{
 return 0;
}
```

19. Find any errors in the following program:

```
#include (iostream)
int main ()
{
     cin << "Hello World";
     return 0;
{
```

20. Find any errors in the following program:

```
include <iostream>
using namespace std;
int main ()
{
 cout << 'We are to learn correct';
 cout << 'C++ language here';
 return 0;
}  // main
```

21. Find any errors in the following program:

```
/* This is a program with some errors
     in it to be corrected.
*/
int main ()
{
    integer          a;
    floating-point   b;
    character        c;

    cout << a << b << c;
    return 0;
}  // main
```

22. Find any errors in the following program:

```
/* This is another program with some
errors in it to be corrected.
*/
int main ()
{
    a  int;
    b  float, double;
    c, d char;

    cout << a << b << c;
    return 0;
} // main
```

23. Find any errors in the following program:

```
/* This is the last program to be
     corrected in these exercises.
*/
int main ()
{
     a          int;
     b : c : d char;
     d , e, f   double float;

     cout a;
     cout b, c, d;
     cout e, f;
     return 0;
} // main
```

PROBLEMS

24. Write a program that uses four output statements to print the pattern of asterisks shown below:

```
******
******
******
******
```

25. Write a program that uses four output statements to print the pattern of asterisks shown below:

```
*
**
***
****
```

26. Write a program that uses defined constants for the vowels in the alphabet and memory constants for the even-numbered decimal digits (0, 2, 4, 6, 8) and prints the following three lines using literal constants for the odd digits:

```
a  e  i  o  u
0  2  4  6  8
1  3  5  7  9
```

27. Write a program that defines five integer variables and initializes them to 1, 10, 100, 1000, and 10000 and prints them on a single line separated by spaces.

28. Code the variable definitions for each of the following:

a. a character variable named `option`

b. an integer variable, `sum`, initialized to `0`

c. a floating-point variable, `product`, initialized to 1

29. Code the variable definitions for each of the following:

    a. a short integer variable named code

    b. a constant named salesTax initialized to .0825

    c. a floating-point named sum of size double initialized to 0

30. Write a statement to print the following line. Assume the total value is contained in a variable named cost.

```
The sales total is: $     172.53
^^^^^^^^^^^^^^^^^^^^^^^^^^^^^^^^^
```

31. Write a program that prompts the user to enter a quantity and a cost. The values are to be read into an integer named quantity and a float named unitPrice. Define the variables, and use only *one statement* to read the values. After reading the values, skip one line and print each value, with an appropriate name, on a separate line.

32. Write a program that prompts the user to enter an integer and then prints the integer first as a character, then as a decimal, and finally as a float. Use separate print statements. A sample run is shown below.

```
  The number as a character: K
  The number as a decimal  : 75
  The number as a float    :
0.000000
```

PROJECTS

33. Write a C++ program using output statements to print the three first letters of your first name in big blocks. This program does not read anything from the keyboard. Each letter is formed using seven rows and five columns using the letter itself. For example, the letter B is formed using 17 Bs as shown below as part of the initials BEF.

```
BBB    EEEEE FFFFF
B  B   E     F
B  B   E     F
BBB    EEE   FFF
B  B   E     F
B  B   E     F
BBB    EEEEE F
```

This is just an example. Your program must print the first three letters of your first name. Design your output statements carefully to create enough blank lines at the beginning and end to make your initials readable. Use comments in your program to enhance readability as shown in this chapter.

34. Write a program that reads a character, an integer, and a floating-point number and prints each on a separate line. Be sure to provide complete instructions (prompts) for the user.

35. Write a program that prompts the user to enter three numbers and then prints them vertically (each in one line), first forward and then reversed (the last one first), as shown below.

```
Please enter three numbers: 15 35 72

Your numbers forward:
   15
   35
   72
Your numbers reversed:
   72
   35
   15
```

36. Write a program that reads 10 integers and prints the first and the last on one line, the second and the ninth on the next line, the third and the seventh on the next line, and so forth. Sample input and the results are shown below.

```
Please enter ten numbers: 10 31 2 73
24

65 6 87 18 9

Your numbers are:
   10  9
   31 18
    2 87
   73  6
   24 65
```

37. Write a program that reads nine integers and prints them three in a line separated by commas as shown below.

Input:

```
10 31 2 73 24 65 6 87 18
```

Output

```
10, 31,  2
73, 24, 65
 6, 87, 18
```

3 Structure of a C++ Program

There are three features that set the C++ language apart from many other languages: expressions, pointers, and classes. All of these concepts lie at the very heart of the language, giving it its unique *look* and *feel.*

This chapter explores the first of these concepts: expressions. Expressions are not new to you; you have used them in mathematics. However, the way C++ uses expressions is unique to C++ and its predecessor, C.

Closely tied to the concept of expressions are operators, precedence and associativity, and statements, all of which are discussed in this chapter. The chapter also introduces a concept known as side effects and explains in detail how it affects statements in C++.

3-1 EXPRESSIONS

An **expression** is a sequence of operands and operators that reduces to a single value. For example,

```
2 * 5
```

is an expression whose value is 10. The value can be any type other than *void.*

Expressions always reduce to a single value.

An **operator** is a language-specific syntactical token that requires an action to be taken. The most familiar operators are drawn from mathematics. For example, multiply (*) is an operator. It indicates that two numbers are to be multiplied. Every language has operators, and their use is rigorously specified in the syntax, or rules, of the language.

An **operand** receives an operator's action. For any given operator, there may be one, two, or more operands. In our arithmetic example, the operands of multiply are the multiplier and the multiplicand.

There is no limit to the number of operator and operand sets that can be combined to form an expression. The only rule is that when they have all been evaluated, the result is a single value that represents the expression.

As illustrated in Figure 3-1, C++ implements seven different expression formats. We discuss five of them in this chapter; the ternary and comma expressions will be discussed later. The various types of operands are shown as rectangles; the operators are shown as ovals.

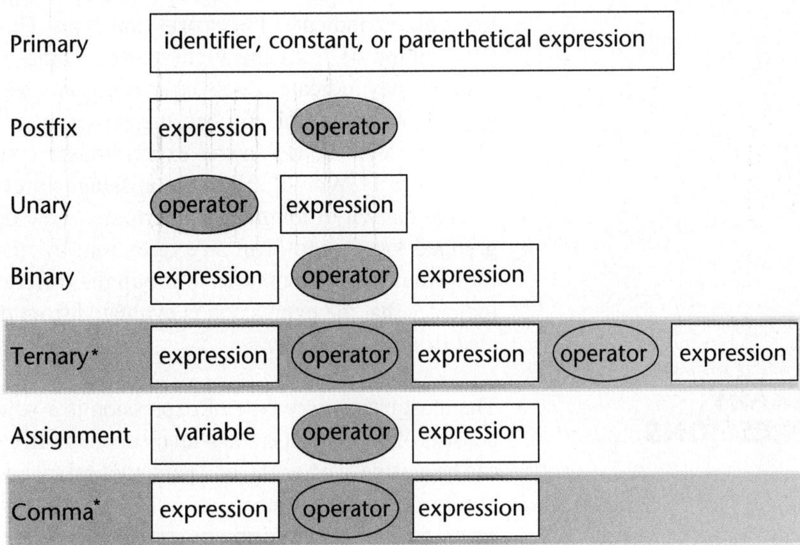

Figure 3-1 C++ expression formats

Now, look at Table 3-1. This is an abbreviated version of the complete precedence table and contains only those expressions we discuss in this chapter. The complete table is found inside the cover. The table groups expressions by the seven formats shown in Table 3-1. By the time you finish this book, you will be quite familiar with all the different expressions, but it will take the whole book to get to that point.

Type	Description		‡	Pr	Assoc
Primary	Identifier Constant Parenthetical Expression		N	18	
Postfix	Function Postfix Increment • Decrement	(...) ++ --	Y Y	17 16	Left
Unary	Prefix Increment • Decrement Size in Bytes Plus • Minus	++ -- sizeof + -	Y N N	15	Right
Binary	Multiply • Divide • Modulus Addition • Subtraction	* / % + -	N N	13 12	Left
Assignment	Assignment	= += -= *= /= %=	Y	2	Right

‡ Side Effects (Yes/No)

Table 3-1 Partial precedence table for C++ expressions

Although the table is easy to use, a brief explanation of its contents is in order. The first column indicates the **expression type**. The expressions are listed in priority order (Pr, column 4) from the highest (18) to the lowest (2). The numbers are important because they indicate which expressions are evaluated first; that is, they indicate **precedence**. The higher the number, the earlier the evaluation. In examining the priority column, you will see that many expressions are missing (the priorities run consecutively from 18 to 1). We will fill in the missing expressions as we progress through the text.

Associativity (column 5) determines how operators with the same precedence are grouped together to form an expression. In other words, associativity determines how C++ would use parentheses to group the different expressions at the same level. "Left" indicates that the expression is evaluated from the left; "right" indicates that it is evaluated from the right.

PRIMARY EXPRESSIONS

The most elementary type of expression is a **primary expression**. A primary expression consists of only one operand with no operator. In C++, the operand in the primary expression can be a name, a constant, or a parenthetical expression. Figure 3-2 contains three examples of primary expressions.

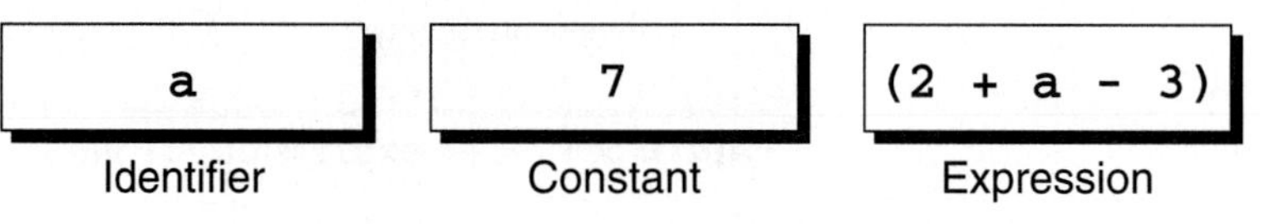

Figure 3-2 Primary expressions

Names

A **name** is any identifier for a variable, a function, or any other object in the language. The following are examples of some names used as primary expressions:

```
a    b12    price    calc    INT_MAX    SIZE
```

Constants

The second type of primary expression is the constant. A constant is data whose value can't change during the execution of the program. The following are examples of constants used as primary expressions:

```
5    123.98    'A'     "Welcome"
```

Parenthetical Expressions

The final type of primary expression is the parenthetical expression. Any value enclosed in parentheses must be reducible to a single value and is therefore a primary expression. This includes any of the complex expression formats when they are enclosed in parentheses. Thus, a complex expression can be enclosed in parentheses to make it a primary expression. The following are primary expressions:

```
( 2  *  3  +  4 )       ( a  =  23  +  b  *  6 )
```

BINARY EXPRESSIONS

Binary expressions are formed by an operand-operator-operand combination. They are perhaps the most common type. Any two numbers added, subtracted, multiplied, or divided are usually written in *infix* (with the operator between its two operands) or algebraic notation, which is a binary expression. There are many binary expressions. We will cover the first two in this chapter. The binary add expression is seen in Figure 3-3.

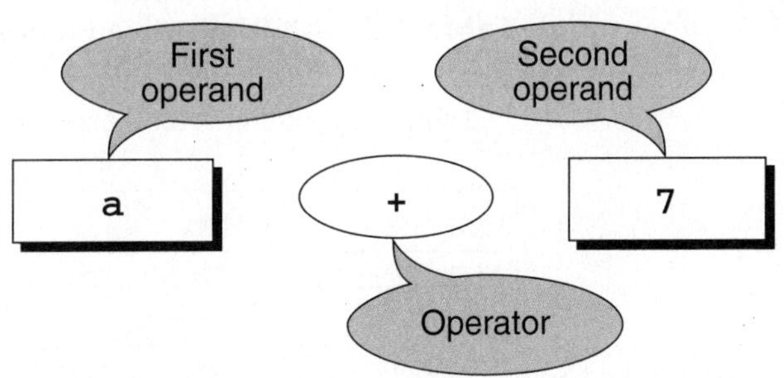

Figure 3-3 Binary expressions

Multiplicative Expressions

The first level of binary expressions, **multiplicative expressions**, takes its name from the first operator, multiply. Multiply, divide, and modulus operators have the highest priority (13) among the binary expressions and are therefore evaluated first among the binary expressions.

The value of a multiply (*) expression is the product of the two operands. The value of a divide (/) expression is a little more complex. If both operands are integers, then the result of the division is the integral value of the quotient, expressed as an integer. If either operand is a floating-point number, then the result of the division is a floating-point number in a type that matches the higher format of the operands (float, double, or long double). The following expression is a binary multiply:

```
10 * 12
```

The multiply and divide operators are well known, but you may not be familiar with the modulus operator (%), more commonly known as *modulo*. This operator divides the first operand by the second and returns the remainder rather than the quotient. For example:

```
5 % 2 evaluates to  1
5 % 3 evaluates to  2
```

Both operands must be integer types, and the operator returns the remainder as an integer type. Because the division and modulus operators are related, they are often confused. Remember: The value of an expression with the division operator is the *quotient*; the value of a modulus operator is the *remainder*. Study the effect of these two operators in the following expressions:

```
3 / 5 evaluates to  0
3 % 5 evaluates to  3
```

The multiplicative expressions are summarized in Table 3-2.

*	Result is algebraic multiplication of two operands.
/	Result is algebraic division of first operand by second operand: • Integer quotient if both operands are integer. • Floating-point quotient if either operand is a floating-point number.
%	Result is integer remainder after first operand is divided by second operand. Both operands must be integer types.

Table 3-2 Multiplicative binary operators

Table 3-3 contains several examples of the multiplicative binary expressions.

Integer		Float	
Multiplication: Value:	3 * 5 15	Multiplication: Value:	3.1 * 5.2 16.12
Division: Value:	20 / 6 3	Division: Value:	20 / 6 3.333333
Modulo: Value:	20% 6 2		

Table 3-3 Examples of multiplicative binary expressions

Additive Expressions

The second level of binary expressions contains the **additive expressions**. The second operand is added to or subtracted from the first operand, depending on the operator used. Additive expressions are evaluated after multiplicative expressions. Their use parallels algebraic notation. Two simple examples are shown below.

```
a + 7          b - 11
```

Before going on, let's look at a little program that uses some of these expressions. Program 3-1 contains several binary expressions.

Program 3-1 Binary expressions

```
/* This program demonstrates binary expressions.
      Written by:
      Date:
*/
#include <iostream>
using namespace std;

int main ()
{
   int a = 17;
   int b = 5;

   cout << a << " + " << b << " = " << a + b << endl;
   cout << a << " - " << b << " = " << a - b << endl;
   cout << a << " * " << b << " = " << a * b << endl;
   cout << a << " / " << b << " = " << a / b << endl;
   cout << a << " % " << b << " = " << a % b << endl;
   cout << "Hope you enjoyed the demonstration.\n";
   return 0;
} // main
```

```
Results:
17 + 5 = 22
17 - 5 = 12
17 * 5 = 85
17 / 5 = 3
17 % 5 = 2
Hope you enjoyed the demonstration.
```

Program 3-1 Analysis This simple program requires only a few comments by way of explanation. First, note that even for a simple program, we include documentation. Second, we do not recommend that you include calculations in your print statements as we have done in this program—it is not a good structured programming technique. We include them in this program because we haven't yet shown you how to save the results of a calculation.

ASSIGNMENT EXPRESSIONS

The **assignment expression** evaluates the operand on the right side of the operator (=) and places its value in the variable on the left. It has a value and a result.

- The value of the total expression is the value of the expression on the right of the assignment operator (=).
- The result places the expression value in the operand on the left of the assignment operator.

There are two forms of assignment: simple and compound. The format of the simple expression is seen in Figure 3-4.

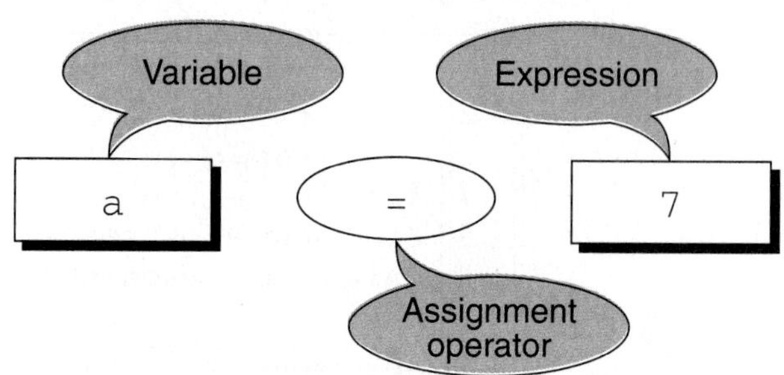

Figure 3-4 Assignment expression

Simple Assignment

Simple assignment is the assignment form found in algebraic expressions. Three examples of simple assignments are shown below.

```
a = 5          b = x + 1          i = i + 1
```

The value of the expression on the right of the assignment operator is evaluated and becomes the value of the total expression. The assignment expression then places the value in the left operand. Of course, for the effect to take place, the left operand must be able to receive it—that is, it must be a variable, not a constant. If the left operand is not able to receive a value and you assign one to it, you will get a compile error.

The left operand in an assignment expression must be a single variable.

Several examples of assignments are shown in Table 3-4.

Expression	Contents of variable *x*	Contents of variable *y*	Value of expression	Result of expression
x = y + 2	10	5	7	x = 7
x = x / y	10	5	2	x = 2
x = y % 4	10	5	1	x = 1

Table 3-4 Examples of assignment expressions

Assignment Expression

The assignment expression has a value and a result.

- The value of the total expression is the value of the expression on the right of the assignment operator (=).
- The result places the expression value in the operator on the left of the assignment operator.

Compound Assignment

A compound assignment is a shorthand notation for a simple assignment. It requires that the left operand be *repeated* as a part of the right expression. There are five compound assignment operators discussed in this chapter: `*=`, `/=`, `%=`, `+=`, and `-=`.

To evaluate a compound assignment expression, first change it to a simple assignment as shown in Table 3-5. Then perform the operation to determine the value of the expression.

Compound expression	Equivalent simple expression
x *= y	x = x * y
x /= y	x = x / y
x %= y	x = x % y
x += y	x = x + y
x -= y	x = x - y

Table 3-5 Expansion of compound expressions

Examples of the five basic compound assignment expressions are seen in Table 3-6. You may find it helpful to convert each expression to its simple form to see how the result is determined.

Expression	Contents of variable *x*	Contents of variable *y*	Value of expression	Result of expression
x *= y	10	5	50	x = 50
x /= y	10	5	2	x = 2
x %= y	10	5	0	x = 0
x += y	10	5	15	x = 15
x -= y	10	5	5	x = 5

Table 3-6 Examples of compound assignment expressions

Program 3-2 demonstrates the first three examples in Table 3-6. You may want to copy it and add the last two.

Program 3-2 Demonstration of compound assignments

```
/* Demonstrate examples of compound assignments.
      Written by:
      Date:
*/
#include <iostream>
using namespace std;

int main ()
{
   int x = 10;
   int y = 5;
   cout << "x: " << x << "  |  " << "y: " << y << "  |  "
        << "x *= y: " << (x *= y);
   cout << "  |  x is now: " << x << endl;

   x = 10;
   cout << "x: " << x << "  |  " << "y: " << y << "  |  "
        << "x /= y:  " <<  (x /= y);
```

Program 3-2 Demonstration of compound assignments *(continued)*

```
    cout << "  |  x is now:  " << x << endl;

    x = 10;
    cout << "x: " << x << "  |  " << "y: " << y << "  |  "
         << "x %= y:  " <<  (x %= y);
    cout << "  |  x is now:  " << x << endl;

    return 0;
}  // main
```

```
Results:
x: 10  |  y:  5   |  x *= y: 50   |  x is now: 50
x: 10  |  y:  5   |  x /= y:  2   |  x is now:  2
x: 10  |  y:  5   |  x %= y:  0   |  x is now:  0
```

Program 3-2 Analysis Note that we have used an assignment statement in the *cout* statements to demonstrate that an assignment expression has a value. As we stated before, this is not good programming style, but we use it here because we haven't yet shown you how to save the results of a calculation. *Do not hide calculations in print statements.* Also, since we are changing the value of x with each assignment, even though it is in a *cout* statement, we need to set it to 10 again for each of the print series.

POSTFIX EXPRESSIONS

The **postfix expression** operates at the second level of the precedence table, immediately after primary expressions. It consists of one operand, which must be a primary expression, followed by one operator (see Figure 3-5).

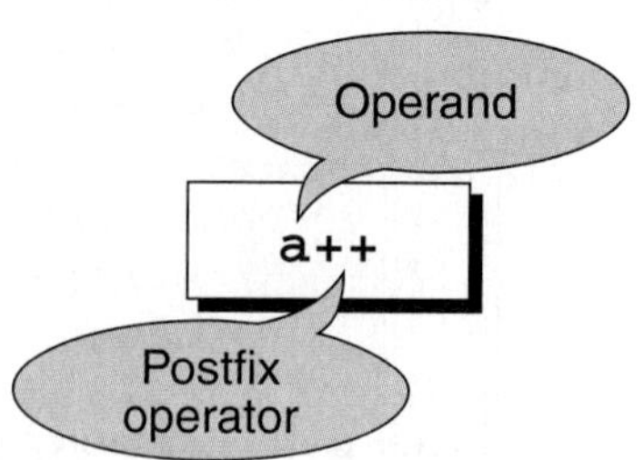

Figure 3-5 Postfix expressions

Function Call

The function call is an integral component of structured programming. We study it in Chapter 4. For now, all you need to recognize is that the function call is actually a postfix expression. The function name is its operand, and the parentheses that follow the name are its operator. What is more important is that, except for void functions,[1] the function call has a value, and therefore can be used in another expression.

Postfix Increment/ Decrement

The **postfix increment** and **postfix decrement** are also postfix operators. Virtually all programs require somewhere in their code that the value 1 be added to a variable. In

[1] As we will see in Chapter 4, void functions do not return a value and therefore can have no value.

most languages, this additive operation can only be represented as a binary expression. C++ provides the same functionality, however, in both the postfix and the unary expressions.

In the postfix increment, the variable is increased by 1. Thus, `i++` results in the variable `i` being increased by 1. This is the same as the assignment expression `i = i + 1`.

```
( i++ ) is identical to ( i  =  i  +  1 )
```

Although the result of both expressions is that `i` is incremented by 1, there is a major difference. The *value* of the postfix increment expression is determined *before* the variable is increased. For instance, if the variable `i` contains 4 before the expression is evaluated, the value of the expression `i++` is 4. As a result of evaluating the expression and its side effect, `i` contains 5. The value and effect of the postfix increment is shown graphically in Figure 3-6.

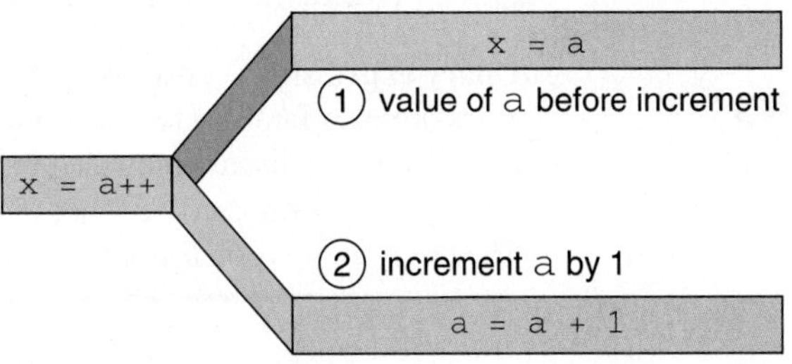

Figure 3-6 Result of postfix a++

The postfix decrement (`i--`) also has a value and a result. In this case, the value is the value of `i` before the expression and results in `i` being decremented by 1. Table 3-7 shows examples of these two expressions.

Expression	Value of *a* before	Value of expression	Value of *a* after
a++	10	10	11
a--	10	10	9

Table 3-7 Examples of postfix expressions

Program 3-3 demonstrates the effect of the postfix increment expression.

Program 3-3 Demonstrate postfix increment

```
/* Example of postfix increment.
      Written by:
      Date:
*/
#include <iostream>
#include <iomanip>
using namespace std;

int main ()
```

Program 3-3 Demonstrate postfix increment (*continued*)

```
{
    int a = 4;

   cout << "value of a      : " << setw(2) << a   << endl;
   cout << "value of a++    : " << setw(2) << a++ << endl;
   cout << "new value of a: " << setw(2) << a   << endl;
   return 0;
} // main
```

```
Results:
value of a     :  4
value of a++   :  4
new value of a:   5
```

UNARY EXPRESSIONS

Unary expressions consist of one operator and one operand. Many of the unary expressions are also familiar to you from mathematics and will require little explanation. In this chapter we discuss only the prefix increment/decrement, the *sizeof* operator, and the plus/minus operators. The other unary expressions will be discussed in later chapters. The unary expression format is seen in Figure 3-7.

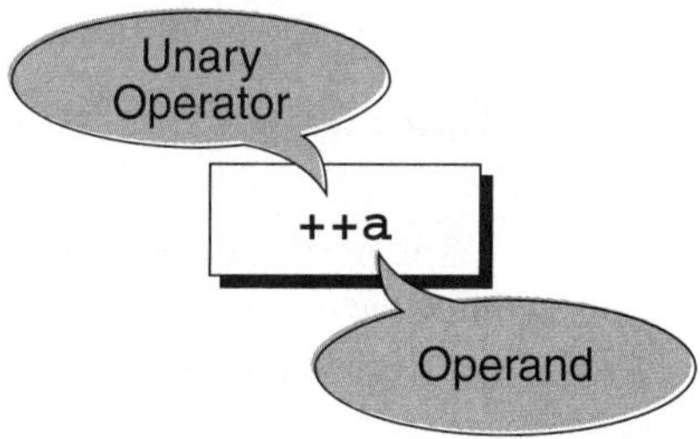

Figure 3-7 Unary expressions

Prefix Increment/ Decrement

Just like the postfix increment and postfix decrement operators, the **prefix increment** and **prefix decrement** operators are shorthand notations for adding or subtracting 1 from a variable. There is one major difference between the postfix and prefix operators, however: With the prefix operators, the effect takes place *before* the expression that contains the operator is evaluated. Note that this is the reverse of the postfix operation. Figure 3-8 shows the operation graphically.

The effect of both the postfix and prefix increment is the same: The variable is increased by 1. If you don't actually require the value of the expression—that is, if all you need is the effect of increasing the value of a variable by 1—then it makes no difference which one you use. You will find that the postfix increment and decrement are used more often, if for no other reason than that the variable is shown first and is therefore easier to read.

> `(++a)` **has the same effect as** `(a = a + 1)`

On the other hand, if you require both the value and the effect, then your application will determine which one you want to use. When you want the value to be the *current*

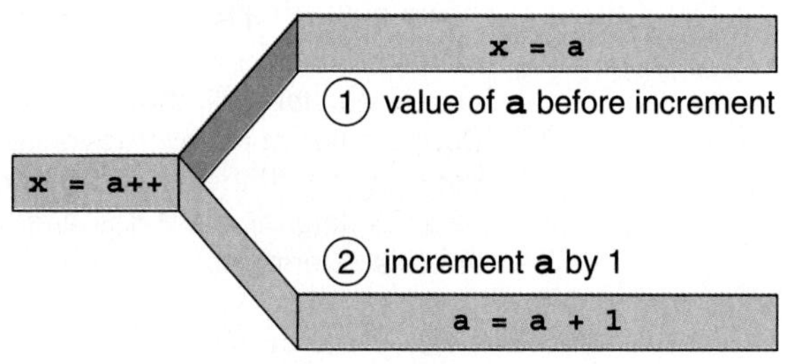

Figure 3-8 Result of prefix ++a

contents of the variable, use the postfix operator; when you want the value to be the *new contents* of the variable (after it has been incremented or decremented), use the prefix operator. Table 3-8 shows examples of the prefix increment and decrement expressions.

Expression	Value of *a* before	Value of *a* after	Value of expression
++a	10	11	11
—a	10	9	9

Table 3-8 Examples of prefix operator expressions

Program 3-4 contains examples of postfix and prefix increment and decrement expressions. Study it carefully, and see if you can predict the results.

Program 3-4 Demonstrate prefix (unary) increment

```
/* Example of postfix/prefix increment and decrement.
      Written by:
      Date:
*/
#include <iostream>
#include <iomanip>
using namespace std;

int main ()
{
   int a = 4;

   cout << "value of a    : " << setw(2) << a   << endl;
   cout << "value of ++a  : " << setw(2) << ++a << endl;
   cout << "new value of a: " << setw(2) << a   << endl;
   return 0;
}  // main
```

```
Results:
value of a    :  4
value of ++a  :  5
new value of a:  5
```

Program 3-4 Analysis The only difference between the printouts in Program 3-3 and Program 3-4 is the use of the increment operators. In Program 3-3, the postfix increment is used; in Program 3-4, the unary prefix increment is used. In both cases, we start with the same value for `a`, and it has the same value at the end. But the value of the expression itself is different. To help remember the difference, use this rule: "If the ++ is *before* the operand, the addition takes place *before* the value is determined; if it is *after* the operand, the addition takes place *after* the value is determined."

Sizeof

The ***sizeof*** operator looks like a function, but it is actually an operator. Its purpose matches its name: It tells you the size, in bytes, of whatever type is specified. By specifying the size of an object during execution, you make your program more portable to other hardware. A simple example will illustrate the point. On most personal computers, the size of the integer type is 2 bytes. On most mainframe computers, it is 4 bytes. On the very large supercomputers, it can be as large as 16 bytes. If it is important to know exactly how large (in bytes) an integer is, you can use the *sizeof* operator as shown below.

```
sizeof (int)
```

Remember that all expressions have a value and that the value can be assigned to a variable. It is therefore possible to save the result of the *sizeof* operator. The following use of the expression saves the value in an integer type:

```
x = sizeof (int)
```

It is also possible to find the size of a primary expression. The value is the size of memory in terms of bytes required to hold the expression. Here are two examples.

```
sizeof (-345.23)          sizeof (x)
```

Unary Plus/Minus

The **unary plus** and **unary minus** operators are what we think of as simply the plus and minus signs. In C++, however, they are actually operators. Because they are operators, they can be used to compute the arithmetic value of an operand.

The plus operator actually does nothing but yield the value of the operand. Its primary purpose is to provide symmetry with the minus operator. The minus operator can be used to change the sign of a value algebraically; that is, to change it from plus to minus or minus to plus. Note, however, that the value of the stored variable is unchanged. The operation of these operators is seen in Table 3-9.

Expression	Contents of a before and after expression	Expression value
+a	3	+3
–a	3	–3
+a	–5	–5
–a	–5	+5

Table 3-9 Examples of unary plus and minus

3-2 PRECEDENCE AND ASSOCIATIVITY

Precedence is used to determine the order in which *different* operators in a complex expression are evaluated. **Associativity** is used to determine the order in which operators *with the same precedence* are evaluated in a complex expression. Another way of stating this is that associativity determines how operators with the same precedence are grouped together to form nested expressions. As its name implies, precedence is applied before associativity to determine the order in which expressions are evaluated. Associativity is then applied, if necessary.

PRECEDENCE

The concept of precedence is well founded in mathematics. For example, in algebra, multiplication and division are performed before addition and subtraction. C++ extends the concept to 18 levels, as shown in the Precedence Table inside the cover of this textbook.

The following expression provides a simple example of precedence:

```
2 + 3 * 4
```

This expression is actually two binary expressions: a binary addition and a binary multiplication. Binary addition has a precedence of 12. Binary multiplication has a precedence of 13. This results in the multiplication's being done first, followed by the addition, as shown below in the same expression with the default parentheses added. The value of the complete expression is 14.

```
( 2 + ( 3 * 4 ) )
```

As another example, consider the expression:

```
-b++
```

There are two different operators in this expression. The first is the unary minus; the second is the postfix increment. The postfix increment has the higher precedence (16), so it is evaluated first. Then the unary minus, with a precedence of 15, is evaluated. To reflect the precedence, we have recoded the expression using parentheses.

```
( -( b++ ) )
```

Assuming that the value of *b* is 5 initially, the expression is evaluated as shown below. What is the value of the expression?

```
( -( 5 ) )
```

Did you get –5? Now another question: What is the value of *b* after the expression is complete? (It is 6, but it was created as an effect that is separate from the value of the expression.)

Program 3-5 Precedence

```
/* Examine the effect of precedence on an expression.
      Written by:
      Date:
*/
```

Program 3-5 Precedence (*continued*)

```
#include <iostream>
using namespace std;

int main ()
{
   int a = 10;
   int b = 20;
   int c = 30;

   cout << "a *  b + c  is: " << a *  b + c  << endl;
   cout << "a * (b + c) is: " << a * (b + c) << endl;
   return 0;
}  // main
```

```
Results:
a *  b + c  is: 230
a * (b + c) is: 500
```

ASSOCIATIVITY

Associativity can be from either the left or the right. **Left associativity** evaluates the expression by starting on the left and moving to the right. Conversely, **right associativity** evaluates the expression by proceeding from the right to the left. Remember, however, that associativity is used only when the operators all have the same precedence (Figure 3-9).

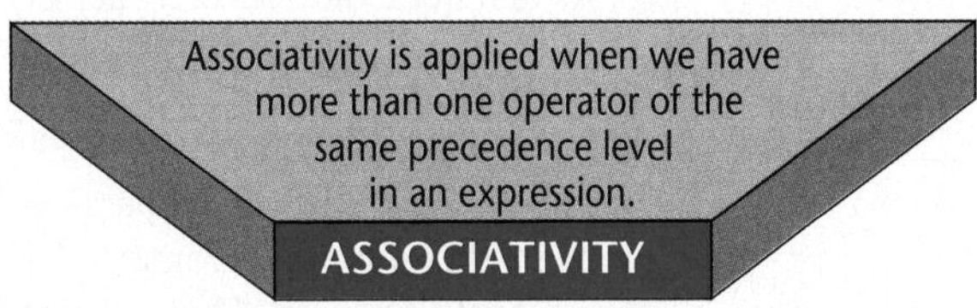

Associativity is applied when we have
more than one operator of the
same precedence level
in an expression.
ASSOCIATIVITY

Figure 3-9 Associativity

Left Associativity

The following shows an example of left-to-right associativity. Here we have four operators of the same precedence `(* / % *)`.

```
3 * 8 / 4 % 4 * 5
```

Associativity determines how the subexpressions are grouped together. All of these operators have the same precedence (13). Their associativity is from left to right, so they are grouped in the following way:

```
( ( ( ( 3 * 8 ) / 4 ) % 4 ) * 5 )
```

What is the value of this expression? Did you get 10? A graphical representation of this expression is seen in Figure 3-10.

Figure 3-10 Left associativity

Right Associativity

There are only three types of expressions that associate from the right: the unary expressions, the conditional ternary expression, and the assignment expressions.

When there is more than one assignment operator in an assignment expression, the assignment operators must be interpreted from right to left. This means that the rightmost expression will be evaluated first; then its value will be assigned to the operand on the left of the assignment operator, and the next expression will be evaluated. Under these rules, the expression

```
a += b *= c -= 5
```

is evaluated as

```
(a += (b *= (c -= 5)))
```

which is expanded to

```
(a = a + (b = b * (c = c - 5)))
```

If a has an initial value of 3, b has an initial value of 5, and c has an initial value of 8, these expressions become

```
(a = 3 + (b = (5 * (c = 8 - 5)))
```

which results in c being assigned a value of 3, b being assigned a value of 15, and a being assigned a value of 18. The value of the complete expression is also 18. A diagram of this expression is seen in Figure 3-11.

a += b *= c -= 5

Figure 3-11 Right associativity

A simple but common form of assignment is shown below. Suppose that you have several variables that all need to be initialized to zero. Rather than initializing each separately, you can form a complex statement to do it.

```
a = b = c = d = 0;
```

3-3 SIDE EFFECTS

A **side effect** is an action that results from the evaluation of an expression. For example, in an assignment expression, C++ first evaluates the expression on the right of the assignment operator and then places its value in the variable on the left of the assignment operator. Changing the value of the variable is a side effect. Consider the following expression:

```
x = 4
```

This simple expression has three parts. First, on the right of the assignment operator is an expression that has the value 4. Second, the whole expression (x = 4) also has a value of 4. And third, as a side effect, x receives the value 4.

Let's modify the expression slightly and see the same three parts.

```
x = x + 4
```

Assuming that x has an initial value of 3, the value of the expression on the right of the assignment operator has a value of 7. The whole expression also has a value of 7. And as a side effect, x receives the value 7. To prove these three steps to yourself, write and run the following block of code:

```
x = 3;
cout << "x is:          " << x            << endl;
cout << "x = x + 4 is:  " << (x = x + 4) << endl;
cout << "x now is:      " << x            << endl;
```

Now, let's consider the side effect in the postfix increment expression. This expression is typically coded as shown below.

```
a++
```

As we saw earlier, the value of this expression is the value of a before the expression is evaluated. As a side effect, however, the value of a is incremented by 1.

There are six different side effects: four pre-effects and two post-effects. The four pre-effect side effects are the unary prefix increment and decrement operators (++a and --a), the function call, and the assignment. The side effect for these expressions takes place *before* the expression is evaluated.

The post-effect operators are the postfix increment and decrement. The side effect takes place after the expression has been evaluated. Therefore, the variable value is not changed until *after* it has been used in the expression. These six operators are shown in Table 3-10.

Type of Side Effect	Expression Type	Example
Pre-effect	Unary prefix increment	`++a`
Pre-effect	Unary prefix decrement	`--a`
Pre-effect	Function call	`doIt( … )`
Pre-effect	Assignment	`a = 1    a += y`
Post-effect	Postfix increment	`a++`
Post-effect	Postfix decrement	`a--`

Table 3-10 Pre- and post-side effects

3-4 EVALUATING EXPRESSIONS

Now that we have introduced the concepts of precedence, associativity, and side effects, let's work through a couple of examples.

EXPRESSIONS WITHOUT SIDE EFFECTS

The first expression is shown below. It has no side effects, so the values of all of its variables are unchanged.

```
a * 4 + b / 2 - c * b
```

For this example, assume that the values of the variables are

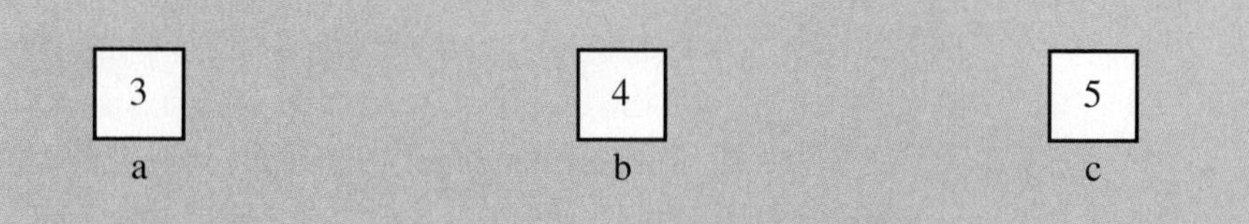

To **evaluate an expression** *without side effects*, follow the simple rules shown below.

1. Replace the variables by their values. This gives us the following expression:

```
3 * 4 + 4 / 2 - 5 * 4
```

2. Evaluate the highest precedence operators, and replace them with the resulting value.

In the above expression, the operators with the highest precedence are the multiply and divide (13). We therefore evaluate them first from the left and replace them with the resulting values. The expression is now

```
(3 * 4) + (4 / 2) - (5 * 4) ⇒ 12 + 2 - 20
```

3. Repeat step 2 until the result is a single value.

In this example, there is only one more precedence, binary addition and subtraction. After they are evaluated, the final value is `-6`. Since this expression had no side effects, all of the variables have the same values after the expression has been evaluated that they had at the beginning.

EXPRESSIONS WITH SIDE EFFECTS

Now let's look at the rules for an expression that has side effects and parenthetical expressions. For this example, consider the expression

```
--a * (3 + b) / 2 - c++ * b
```

Assume that the variables have the values used above, `a = 3`, `b = 4`, `c = 5`. To evaluate this expression, use the following steps:

1. Calculate the value of the parenthetical expression (`3 + b`) first. The expression now reads

   ```
   --a * 7 / 2 - c++ * b
   ```

2. Evaluate the `c++` *postfix* expression next. Remember that as a *postfix* expression, the value of c++ is the same as the value of `c`; the increment takes place after the evaluation. The expression now reads

   ```
   --a * 7 / 2 - 5 * b
   ```

3. Evaluate the `--a` prefix expression next. Remember that as a *prefix* expression, the value of `--a` is the value after the side effect, which means that we first decrement `a` and then use its decremented value. The expression now reads

   ```
   2 * 7 / 2 - 5 * b
   ```

4. The multiplication and division are now evaluated using the associativity rules, left to right, as shown below.

   ```
   14 / 2 - 5 * b ⇒ 7 - 5 * 4 ⇒ 7 - 20
   ```

5. The last step is to evaluate the subtraction. The final expression value is –13 as shown below.

   ```
   7 - 20 ⇒ -13
   ```

After the side effects, the variables are

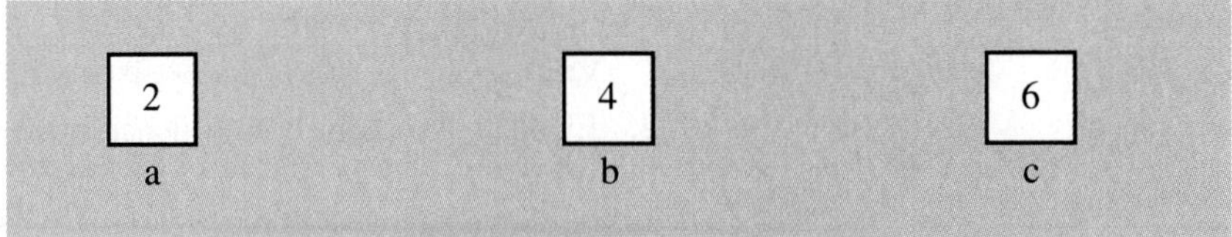

Program 3-6 evaluates these two expressions.

Program 3-6 Evaluating expressions

```
/* Evaluate two complex expressions.
      Written by:
      Date:
*/
#include <iostream>
using namespace std;
```

Program 3-6 Evaluating expressions *(continued)*

```

int main ()
{
   int a = 3;
   int b = 4;
   int c = 5;
   int x;
   int y;

   cout << "Initial values of the variables: \n";
   cout << "a = " << a << "   b = " << b << "   c = "
        << c << endl;
   cout << endl;

   x = a * 4 + b / 2 - c * b;
   cout << "Value of a * 4 + b / 2 - c * b is: "
        << x << endl;

   y = --a * (3 + b) / 2 - c++ * b;
   cout << "Value of --a * (3 + b) / 2 - c++ * b is: "
        << y << endl;

   cout << "\nValues of the variables are now: \n";
   cout << "a = " << a << "   b = " << b << "   c = "
        << c << endl;

   return 0;
} // main
```

```
Results:
Initial values of the variables:
a = 3   b = 4   c = 5

Value of a * 4 + b / 2 - c * b is: -6
Value of --a * (3 + b) / 2 - c++ * b is: -13

Values of the variables are now:
a = 2   b = 4   c = 6
```

WARNING

A warning is in order: In C++, if an expression variable is modified more than once in an expression, the result is undefined. C++ has no specific rule to cover this situation, and compiler writers can implement the expression in different ways. The result is that different compilers will give different expression results. For example, consider the following rather simple expression:

```
(b++  -  b++)
```

In this expression, b is modified twice. There are three possible interpretations of this expression, all of them correct. Given that b is initially 4, one possible evaluation is

```
((4++)  -  (b++))
( 4     -  (5++))
      (-1)
b is 6
```

Two other interpretations are

```
((b++)  -  (4++))                ((4++)  -  (4++))
((5++)  -    4  )                  ((4)  -  (4))
    (5 - 4)                          (4 - 4)
      (+1)                             (0)
b is 6                           b is 6
```

Although the side effect is the same in all cases—b is 6—the value of the expression differs. In the first case, the value is –1; in the second case, the value is +1; and, in the last case, the value is 0. *Never use a variable affected by a side effect more than once in an expression.*

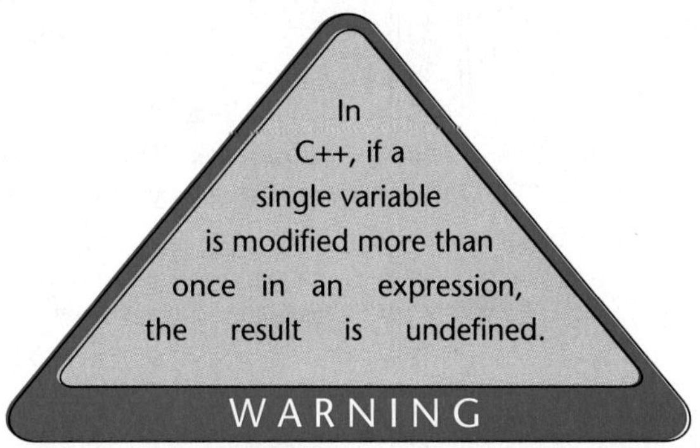
In C++, if a single variable is modified more than once in an expression, the result is undefined.
WARNING

3-5 MIXED TYPE EXPRESSIONS

Up to this point, we have assumed that all of our expressions involved data of the same type. But, what happens when you write an expression that involves two different data types, such as multiplying an integer and a float? These expressions are known as mixed type expressions, and C++ has rules for handling them.

The first, and most important, rule is that in an assignment expression, the final expression value must have the same type as the left operand, the operand that receives the value. This makes sense: You can't store a float in an integer variable.

To handle mixed expressions, the operands must be converted so that they are the same type. Conversion is done either implicitly or explicitly as described in the next two sections.

IMPLICIT TYPE CONVERSION

When we use expressions containing different data types and do not explicitly cast types (see next section), C++ uses two separate sets of rules to convert data to a common type. The first rules concerns the evaluation of expressions; the second rule concerns only the assignment expression.

Evaluating Expressions

The value and type of a mixed expression is determined by the following rules.

1. If the two values are both floating-point types—*float*, *double*, or *long double*—but of different precision, such as *float* and *double*, the type of the value with the lower precision is converted to the type of the value with the higher precision. For example, in an expression containing a *float* plus a *double*, the *float* is implicitly converted to a *double*. Note, however, that only the value is converted; the value and type of the memory variable are unchanged.
2. If one of the values is a floating-point type and the other is an integral type—such as *char*, *short*, *int*, or *long*—the integral type is implicitly converted to the floating-point type. For example, in an expression containing an *int* plus a *double*, the value of the *int* is converted to a *double*.
3. If the two values are both integral types, then the value of the one with the more limited range is converted to the other. For example, in an expression containing a *short* plus an *int*, the *short* is converted to an *int*. Similarly, in an expression containing an *int* plus an *unsigned int*, the *int* is converted to an *unsigned int*.
4. An enumerated type (see Section 11-10, "Enumerated Types" on page 617) is promoted to an appropriate integral type based on the range of the enumerated type.

In all cases, **implicit type conversion** is done according to the precedence and associativity of the operators. For example, in an expression with

```
float + int * double
```

the *int* in the multiply is first converted to a *double*. After the multiply is evaluated, we have

```
float + double
```

which requires that the *float* value be converted to a *double* for the addition. The type of the expression value is therefore a *double*.

Conversion of Assignment Expressions

When an assignment expression contains mixed types, the evaluation of the expression on the right of the assignment operator follows the rules for evaluating expressions covered in the previous section. If, after evaluating the expression, the type of the expression value is not the same as the type on the left of the assignment operator, then the expression value must be implicitly converted to the type of the left-side variable. For example, if a floating-point expression is assigned to an integer variable as shown in the following example, the floating-point expression is converted to an integer before being stored.

```
int x = float-type expression;
```

Assignment of expressions containing mixed types are inherently dangerous. As programmers, it is our responsibility to ensure that the results are always valid. As long as the size of the variable on the left of the assignment operator is the same or larger than the size of the expression value, the conversion is safe. However, if the expression value is larger than can be stored in the variable on the left of the assignment operator, then an invalid result is stored. Similarly, if a floating-point expression value is stored in an integral type, the fractional part is lost even if the integral is large enough to hold the integral part of the floating-point number. Some compilers issue warning messages when the size of the receiving variable is smaller than the size of the expression value type.

Let's look at a small program to see the effect of implicit conversions. In Program 3-7 we add a character, an integer, and a float. We can add characters to integers and floating-point values because all characters have a numeric value.

Program 3-7 Implicit type conversion

```
/* Demonstrate implicit casts of numeric types.
      Written by:
      Date:
*/
#include <iostream>
using namespace std;

int main ()
{
   char   aChar    = 'A';
   int    printChar;
   int    intNum   = 200;
   double fltNum   = 245.3;

   cout << "aChar contains :   " << aChar  << endl;
   printChar = aChar;
   cout << "aChar numeric   :  " << printChar  << endl;
   cout << "intNum contains:   " << intNum << endl;
   cout << "fltNum contains:   " << fltNum << endl;

   intNum = intNum + aChar;   // aChar converted to int
   fltNum = fltNum + aChar;   // aChar converted to float

   cout << "\nAfter additions...\n";
   printChar = aChar;
   cout << "aChar numeric   :  " << printChar  << endl;
   cout << "intNum contains:  " << intNum      << endl;
   cout << "fltNum contains:  " << fltNum      << endl;
   return 0;
} // main
```

```
Results:
aChar contains :  A
aChar numeric  :  65
intNum contains:  200
fltNum contains:  245.3

After additions...
aChar numeric  :  65
intNum contains:  265
fltNum contains:  310.3
```

EXPLICIT TYPE CONVERSION (CAST)

Rather than let the compiler implicitly convert data, you can convert data from one type to another yourself using **explicit type conversion**. C++ provides two types of explicit **casts**: static and dynamic. Explicit type conversions use the cast expression operator found at Priority 14 in the Precedence Table.

Static Cast

The syntax for the static cast is

```
static_cast<type> (expression)
```

In a static cast, the compiler converts the types at compilation time. Once the program is compiled, they cannot be changed. For example, given two integer variables, we can statically cast them to a float as shown in the following code.

```
average = static_cast<float> (totalScores) / numScores;
```

In this statement, there is an explicit conversion of `totalScores` to *float*, and then an implicit conversion of `numScores` so that it will match. The result of the divide is then a floating-point number to be assigned to `average`.

But beware! What would be the result of the following floating-point expression when the value of `a` is 3?

```
static_cast<float> (a / 10)
```

Are you surprised to find that the result is 0.0? Since there is no need to do any conversions to divide integer 3 by integer 10, C++ simply divides with an integer result, 0. The integer 0 is then explicitly converted to the floating-point 0.0.

Dynamic Cast

In a dynamic cast, the conversion is not determined until the program is run. To fully understand dynamic casts requires that we understand classes and dynamic memory allocation. Therefore, we defer its discussion until after we cover these subjects.

C-Style Cast

For compatibility with earlier versions of the language, the C++ compiler still accepts the C-style cast. Its format is shown in the next example.

```
(type) expression
```

The C-style cast should be avoided for two reasons. First, it is not clear whether the cast is static or dynamic. Because of the ambiguity, the determination of the cast type is left to discretion of the compiler. Second, we anticipate that the next release of the C++ standard could deprecate this format, which would require programs using C-style casts to be upgraded before they could be compiled.

One final thought about casts: Even when the compiler could correctly cast for you, it is sometimes better to code the cast explicitly to remind yourself that the cast is taking place. Program 3-8 demonstrates the use of explicit casts. In this program, we divide several mixed types. While the results are nonsense, they demonstrate the effect of casting.

Program 3-8 Explicit casts

```
1  /* Demonstrate casting of numeric types.
2        Written by:
3        Date:
4  */
5  #include <iostream>
6  using namespace std;
7
8  int main ()
9  {
10    int     intNum1  = 100;
11    int     intNum2  =  45;
12    double fltNum3;
13    fltNum3 = static_cast<double> (intNum1 / intNum2);
14    cout << "<double> (intNum1 / intNum2) : "
15         << fltNum3 << endl;
16
17    fltNum3 = static_cast<double> (intNum1) / intNum2;
18    cout << "<double>  intNum1 / intNum2  : "
19         << fltNum3 << endl;
20    return 0;
21 } // main
```

```
Results:
<double> (intNum1 / intNum2) : 2
<double>  intNum1 / intNum2  : 2.22222
```

Program 3-8 Analysis Study the casts carefully. The only difference between Statements 13 and 17 is the use of parentheses around the calculation. In Statement 13, both operands are integers so the result of the division is integer, which is then cast to a *double*. In Statement 17, `intNum1` is cast to a double. The compiler then implicitly casts `intNum2` to a double before the division. The result is therefore a double.

3-6 STATEMENTS

A **statement** causes an action to be performed by the program. It translates directly into one or more executable computer instructions. C++ defines six types of statements, which are shown in Figure 3-12. In this chapter, we will discuss the first two, the **expression statement** and the **compound statement**. The other types—selection, labeled, iterative, and jump—will be covered in later chapters.

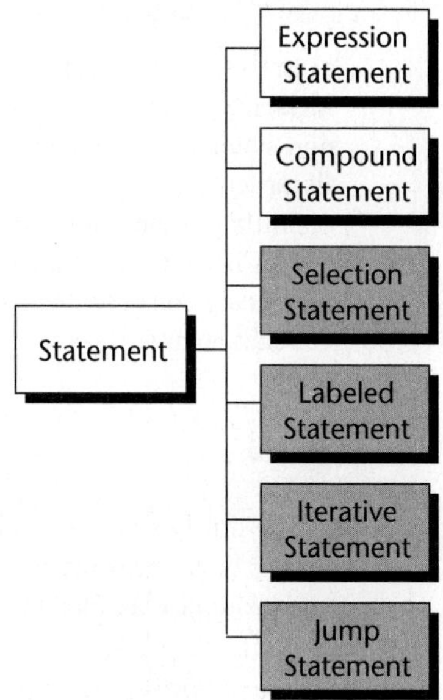

Figure 3-12 Types of statements

EXPRESSION STATEMENTS

An expression is turned into a statement by placing a semicolon (;) after it. When C++ sees the semicolon, it completes any pending side effects and discards the expression value before continuing with the next statement. An expression without side effects does not cause an action. Its value exists and it can be used, but unless a statement has a side effect, it does nothing.

Let us look at some expression statements. First, consider the expression statement

```
a = 2;
```

The effect of the expression statement is to store the value, 2, in the variable a. The value of the expression is 2. After the value has been stored, the expression is terminated (because there is a semicolon) and the value is discarded. C++ then continues with the next statement.

The next expression statement is a little more complex.

```
a = b = 3;
```

There are actually two expressions in this statement. If we put parentheses around them, you will be able to see them clearly.

```
a = ( b = 3 );
```

The parenthetical expression, (b = 3), has a side effect of assigning the value 3 to the variable b. The value of this expression is 3. The expression statement now results in the expression value 3 being assigned to the variable a. Since the expression is terminated, its value, 3, is discarded. The effect of the expression statement, therefore, is that 3 has been stored in both a and b.

Now consider the expression statement at the top of the next page. Assume that a has a value of 5 before the expression is evaluated.

```
a++;
```

In this postfix expression, the value of the expression is 5, which is the value of the variable, a, before it is changed by the side effect. Upon the completion of the expression statement, a is incremented to 6. The value of the expression, which is still 5, is discarded because the expression is now complete.

Although they are useless, the following are also expression statements. They are useless because they have no side effect and their values are not assigned to a variable. We usually don't use them, but it is important to know they are syntactically correct expression statements. C++ will evaluate them, determine their value, and then discard the value.

```
b ;                 3 ;                 ;
```

The third expression above, the semicolon, is an example of a null expression statement. The null expression statement has no side effect and no value, but it is useful in some complex statements.

> **An expression statement is terminated with a semicolon. The semicolon is a terminator, and it tells the compiler that the statement is finished.**

COMPOUND STATEMENTS

A *compound statement* is a unit of code consisting of zero or more statements. It is also known as a **block**. The compound statement allows a group of statements to become one single entity. You used a compound statement in your first program when you formed the body of the function *main*. All C++ functions contain a compound statement known as the function body.

A compound statement consists of an opening brace, optional declarations, definitions, and statements, followed by a closing brace. Although all three are optional, one should be present. If none are present, then we have a null block, which doesn't make much sense. Figure 3-13 shows the makeup of a compound statement.

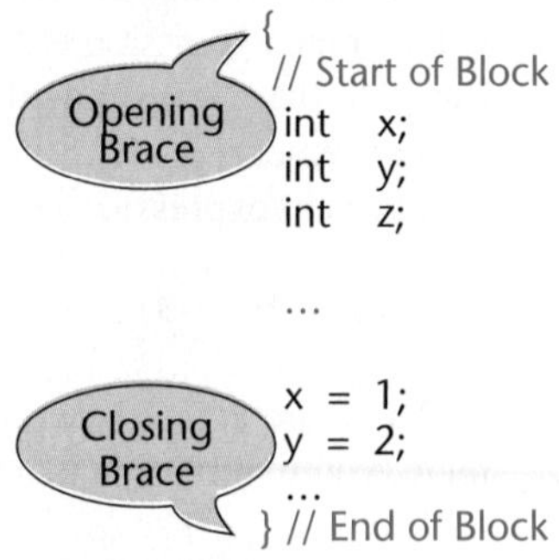

Figure 3-13 Compound statement

One important point to remember is that a compound statement does not need a semicolon. If you put a semicolon after the closing brace, the compiler thinks that you have put an extra null statement after the compound statement. This is poor style, but it does not generate any code or give you a compile error.

STATEMENTS AND DEFINED CONSTANTS

When you use preprocessor-defined commands, you need to be very careful to make sure that you do not create an error. Remember that the define constant is an automatic substitution. This can cause subtle problems. One common mistake is to place a semicolon at the end of the command. Since the preprocessor uses a simple text replacement of the name with whatever expression follows, the compiler will usually generate a compile error if a semicolon was found. This problem is seen in the following example:

```
#define SALES_TAX_RATE  0.0825;
...
salesTax = SALES_TAX_RATE * salesAmount;
```

After the substitution would be the following erroneous code because a semicolon has been coded after the constant value:

```
salesTax = 0.0825; * salesAmount;
```

This can be an extremely difficult compile error to figure out because you see the original statement and not the erroneous substitution error. One of the reasons programmers use UPPERCASE for defined constant identifiers is to provide an automatic warning to readers that they are not looking at the real code.

3-7 SAMPLE PROGRAMS

This section contains several programs that demonstrate recommended programming technique and style. Study them carefully looking for the various programming points you have learned in this textbook so far. Some of the sample programs are followed by an "Analysis" section to help you do this.

EXAMPLE: CALCULATE QUOTIENT AND REMAINDER

Let's write a program that calculates and prints the quotient and remainder of two integer numbers. The code is shown in Program 3-9.

Program 3-9 Calculate quotient and remainder

```
/* Calculate and print quotient and remainder.
      Written by:
      Date:
*/
#include <iostream>
using namespace std;

int main ()
{
   int  intNum1;
   int  intNum2;
   int  intCalc;

   cout << "Enter two integral numbers: ";
   cin  >> intNum1 >> intNum2;
```

Program 3-9 Calculate quotient and remainder (*continued*)

```
16
17      intCalc = intNum1 / intNum2;
18      cout << intNum1 << " / " << intNum2
19           << " is "  << intCalc;
20
21      intCalc = intNum1 % intNum2;
22      cout << " with a remainder of: " << intCalc << endl;
23      return 0;
24   }  // main
```

```
Results:
Enter two integral numbers: 13 2
13 / 2 is 6 with a remainder of: 1
```

Program 3-9 Analysis Using good programming style, the program begins with documentation about what it does, who created it, and when it was created.

Program 3-9 has no global variable declarations, so after including the input/output library, we start immediately with *main*. Following *main* is the opening brace. The matching closing brace is found on line 24.

The most difficult part of this program is figuring out how to get the remainder. Fortunately, C++ has a modulo operator (%) that does the job for us. The rest of the problem is straightforward.

EXAMPLE: PRINT RIGHT DIGIT

Another problem that requires the use of the modulo operator is to print a digit contained in an integer. Program 3-10 prints the least significant (rightmost) digit of an integer.

Program 3-10 Print right digit of integer

```
/* Print rightmost digit of an integer.
      Written by:
      Date:
*/
#include <iostream>
using namespace std;

int main ()
{
   int intNum;
   cout << "Enter an integral numbers: ";
   cin  >> intNum;

   int oneDigit = intNum % 10;
   cout << "\nThe right digit is: " << oneDigit << endl;
   return 0;
}  // main
```

Program 3-10 Print right digit of integer (*continued*)

```
Results:
Enter an integral numbers: 185

The right digit is: 5
```

EXAMPLE: CALCULATE AVERAGE

Program 3-11 reads four integers from the keyboard, calculates their average, and then prints the numbers with their average and the deviation (not the standard deviation, just the difference plus or minus) from the average.

Program 3-11 Calculate average of four numbers

```
/* Calculate the average of four integers and print
   the numbers and their deviation from the average.
      Written by:
      Date:
*/
#include <iostream>
#include <iomanip>
using namespace std;

int main ()
{
   cout << "\nEnter the first number  : ";
   int num1;
   cin  >> num1;
   cout << "Enter the second number : ";
   int num2;
   cin  >> num2;
   cout << "Enter the third  number : ";
   int num3;
   cin  >> num3;
   cout << "Enter the fourth number : ";
   int num4;
   cin  >> num4;

   int   sum      = num1 + num2 + num3 + num4;
   float average = sum / 4.0;
   cout << fixed;
   cout << showpoint;
   cout << setprecision (2);
   cout << "\n ******** average is "
        << average << " ******** \n";
   cout << "\nfirst no:  " << num1 << " -- deviation: "
        << setw(8) << (num1 - average);
   cout << "\nsecond no: " << num2 << " -- deviation: "
        << setw(8) << (num2 - average);
   cout << "\nthird no: " << num3 << " -- deviation: "
        << setw(8) << (num3 - average);
```

Program 3-11 Calculate average of four numbers *(continued)*

```
   cout << "\nfourth no: " << num4 << " -- deviation: "
        << setw(8) << (num4 - average);
   return 0;
} // main
```

```
Results:
Enter the first number  : 23
Enter the second number : 12
Enter the third number  : 45
Enter the fourth number : 23

 ******** average is 25.75 ********

first no:  23 -- deviation:     -2.75
second no: 12 -- deviation:    -13.75
third no:  45 -- deviation:     19.25
fourth no: 23 -- deviation:     -2.75
```

Program 3-11 Analysis Using good programming style, the program begins with documentation about what it does, who created it, and when it was created.

C++ allows variables to be defined anywhere in a block. Using this design, we define each variable before the first statement that uses it.

The statements start by reading the data. Each read is preceded by a display so the user will know what to do. The specific instructions about what to input are known as **user prompts**. You should always tell the user what input is expected from the keyboard. After the user has keyed the data, the program continues by adding the numbers, placing the total in `sum`, and computing the `average`. It then displays the results. Notice that the program displays the results in a format that allows the user to easily verify that the program ran correctly. Not only is the average printed, but each input is repeated with its deviation from the average. After completing its work, the program concludes by returning to the operating system.

Look at the results carefully. Note how each series of numbers is aligned so the numbers can be read easily. Taking the time to align output is one of the things that distinguishes a good programmer from an average programmer. Always pay attention to how your program presents its results to the user. Paying attention to these little details pays off in the long run.

EXAMPLE: DEGREES TO RADIANS

One way to measure an angle in a circle is in degrees. For example, the angle formed by a clock at 3 o'clock is 90°. Another way to measure the angle is in radians. One radian is equal to 57.295779 degrees. In Program 3-12 we ask the user to input an angle in radians, and we convert it to degrees.

Program 3-12 Convert radians to degrees

```
/* This program prompts the user to enter an angle
   in radians and converts it into degrees.
      Written by:
      Date:
```

Program 3-12 Convert radians to degrees (*continued*)

```
*/
#include <iostream>
using namespace std;

const int cDegreeFactor = 57.295779;

int main ()
{
   cout << "Enter the angle in radians: ";
   double  radians;
   cin  >> radians;

   double degrees = radians * cDegreeFactor;

   cout << radians << " radians is "
        << degrees << " degrees\n";
   return 0;
}  // main
```

```
Results:
Enter the angle in radians: 1.578947
1.57895 radians is 90 degrees
```

Program 3-12 Analysis In this short program we introduce the memory constant. Memory constants are an excellent way to document factors in a program. Because factors are usually placed at the beginning of the program where they can easily be found and changed as necessary, they should not be variables. Remember that the area before *main* is global and that variables should be protected in functions.

One more subtle style point. We start the names of memory constants with a "c" for constant followed by a descriptive name beginning with an uppercase alphabetic. Then, when we see it in the code, we know it is a constant.

EXAMPLE: FAHRENHEIT TO CELSIUS

Program 3-13 changes a temperature reading from Fahrenheit to Celsius using the following formula:

```
Celsius = ( 100 / 180 ) * ( Fahrenheit - 32 )
```

Program 3-13 Fahrenheit to Celsius

```
/* This program shows how to change a temperature in
   Fahrenheit to Celsius.
      Written by:
      Date:
*/
#include <iostream>
#include <iomanip>
using namespace std;

```

Program 3-13 Fahrenheit to Celsius *(continued)*

```
const float cConversionFactor = 100.0 / 180.0;

int main ()
{
   cout << "Enter the temperature in Fahrenheit: ";
   float fareh;
   cin  >> fareh;
   float cel =  cConversionFactor * ( fareh - 32 );

   cout << fixed;
   cout << setprecision(1);
   cout << showpoint;
   cout << "Fahrenheit temperature: " << fareh
        << endl;
   cout << "Celsius temperature:    " << cel  << endl;
   return 0;
} // main
```

```
Results:
Enter the temperature in Fahrenheit: 98.6
Fahrenheit temperature: 98.6
Celsius temperature:    37.0
```

EXAMPLE: CALCULATE SALES TOTAL

Program 3-14 calculates a sale given the unit price, quantity, discount rate, and sales tax rate.

Program 3-14 Calculate sales total

```
/* Calculates the total sale given the unit price,
   quantity, discount, and tax rate.
      Written by:
      Date written:
*/
#include <iostream>
#include <iomanip>
using namespace std;

const float cTaxRate = 8.50;

int main ()
{
   cout << "\nEnter number of items sold:         ";
   int  quantity;
   cin  >> quantity;
   cout << "Enter the unit price:               ";
   float unitPrice;
   cin  >> unitPrice;
   cout <<  "Enter the discount rate (percent): ";
   float discountRate;
```

Program 3-14 Calculate sales total *(continued)*

```
   cin  >>  discountRate;

   float subTotal     = quantity    * unitPrice;
   float discountAm   = subTotal    * discountRate
                        /100.0;
   float subTaxable   = subTotal    - discountAm;
   float taxAm        = subTaxable * cTaxRate / 100.0;
   float total        = subTaxable + taxAm;

   cout << fixed;
   cout << setprecision(2);
   cout << showpoint;

   cout << "\nQuantity sold:         "
        << setw(6) << quantity     << endl;
   cout << "Unit Price of items: "
        << setw(9) << unitPrice    << endl;
   cout << "                        --------\n";
   cout << "Subtotal :              "
        << setw(9) << subTotal     << endl;
   cout << "Discount:              -"
        << setw(9) << discountAm << endl;
   cout << "Discounted total:       "
        << setw(9) << subTaxable << endl;
   cout << "Sales tax:             +"
        << setw(9) << taxAm        << endl;
   cout << "Total sale:             "
        << setw(9) << total        << endl;
   return 0;
}  // main
```

```
Results:
Enter number of items sold:        34
Enter the unit price:              12.89
Enter the discount rate (percent): 7

Quantity sold:            34
Unit Price of items:      12.89
                        --------
Subtotal :               438.26
Discount:           -     30.68
Discounted total:        407.58
Sales tax:          +     34.64
Total sale:              442.23
```

Program 3-14 Analysis Look at the results of this program carefully. Do you see any problems? Just because a program runs doesn't mean that it is running correctly. In this case, the total is incorrect (407.58 + 34.64 is not equal to 442.23!). The problem is created by the floating-point arithmetic and rounding errors. If we wanted absolute accuracy, we would have to do the arithmetic in integer (cents) and then divide by 100 to print the report.

EXAMPLE: CALCULATE STUDENT SCORE

Program 3-15 calculates the average score for a student. The class has four quizzes (30%), two midterms (40%), and a final (30%). The maximum score for all quizzes and exams is 100 points.

Program 3-15 Calculate student score

```
/* Calculate a student's average score for a course
   with 4 quizzes, 2 midterms, and a final. The quizzes
   are weighted 30%, the midterms 40%, & the final 30%.
      Written by:
      Date:
*/
#include <iostream>
#include <iomanip>
using namespace std;

const int   cQuizWeight    =  30;
const int   cMidtermWeight =  40;
const int   cFinalWeight   =  30;
const float cQuizMax       = 400.00;
const float cMidtermMax    = 200.00;
const float cFinalMax      = 100.00;

int main ()
{
   cout << "=========== QUIZZES =================\n";
   cout << "Enter the score for the first quiz:  ";
   int  quiz1;
   cin  >> quiz1;
   cout << "Enter the score for the second quiz: ";
   int  quiz2;
   cin  >> quiz2;
   cout << "Enter the score for the third quiz:  ";
   int  quiz3;
   cin  >> quiz3;
   cout << "Enter the score for the fourth quiz: ";
   int  quiz4;
   cin  >> quiz4;
   cout << "============= MIDTERM  =============\n";
   cout << "Enter the score for the first midterm:  ";
   int  midterm1;
   cin  >> midterm1;
   cout << "Enter the score for the second midterm: ";
   int  midterm2;
   cin  >> midterm2;
   cout << "=============== FINAL ==============\n";
   cout << "Enter the score for the final: ";
   int  final;
```

Program 3-15 **Calculate student score *(continued)***

```
   cin  >> final;
   cout << endl;

   int totalQuiz = quiz1 + quiz2 + quiz3 + quiz4;
   int totalMidterm = midterm1 + midterm2;

   float quizPercent    = static_cast<float>
         (totalQuiz * cQuizWeight) / cQuizMax;
   float midtermPercent = static_cast<float>
        (totalMidterm * cMidtermWeight) / cMidtermMax;
   float finalPercent   = static_cast<float>
         (final * cFinalWeight) / cFinalMax;
   float totalPercent =
      quizPercent + midtermPercent + finalPercent;

   cout << fixed;
   cout << showpoint;
   cout << setprecision(1);

   cout << "First Quiz       "
        << setw(3) << quiz1     << endl;
   cout << "Second Quiz      "
        << setw(3) << quiz2     << endl;
   cout << "Third Quiz       "
        << setw(3) << quiz3     << endl;
   cout << "Fourth Quiz      "
        << setw(3) << quiz4     << endl;
   cout << "Quiz Total       "
        << setw(3) << totalQuiz << endl << endl;
   cout << "First Midterm    "
        << setw(3) << midterm1     << endl;
   cout << "Second Midterm   "
        << setw(3) << midterm2     << endl;
   cout << "Total Midterms   "
        << setw(3) << totalMidterm << endl << endl;
   cout << "Final            "
        << setw(3) << final << endl << endl;
   cout << "Quiz    "
        << setw(6) << quizPercent    << "%\n";
   cout << "Midterm "
        << setw(6) << midtermPercent << "%\n";
   cout << "Final   "
        << setw(6) << finalPercent   << "%\n";
   cout << "--------------\n";
   cout << "Total   "
        << setw(6) << totalPercent   << "%\n";
   return 0;
}  // main
```

Program 3-15 Calculate student score *(continued)*

```
Results:
=========== QUIZZES =================
Enter the score for the first quiz:  98
Enter the score for the second quiz: 89
Enter the score for the third quiz:  78
Enter the score for the fourth quiz: 79
============= MIDTERM  =============
Enter the score for the first midterm:  90
Enter the score for the second midterm: 100
=============== FINAL ==============
Enter the score for the final: 92

First Quiz          98
Second Quiz         89
Third Quiz          78
Fourth Quiz         79
Quiz Total         344

First Midterm       90
Second Midterm     100
Total Midterms     190

Final               92

Quiz         25.8%
Midterm      38.0%
Final        27.6%
--------------
Total        91.4%
```

Program 3-15 Analysis There are several points to consider in this rather long program. First, note how the program starts with a series of memory constants. Putting the definitions of constant values at the beginning of the program does two things: (1) it gives them names that we can use in the program, and (2) it makes them easy to change.

Now study the statements. Notice how they are grouped. By putting a blank line between a group of related statements, you separate them visually much as you would separate paragraphs in a report. This makes it easy for the user to follow the program.

Finally, study the input and output. Notice that the user was prompted for all input with clear instructions. We even divided the input with headings.

The output is also divided, making it easy to read. It would be even easier to read if we had aligned all the amounts, but the techniques for doing so will not be introduced until a later chapter.

3-8 SOFTWARE ENGINEERING AND PROGRAMMING STYLE

In this section we are going to discuss three concepts that, although technically not engineering principles, are important to writing clear and understandable programs.

KISS

Keep It Simple and Short (**KISS**)[2] is an old programming principle. Unfortunately, many programmers tend to forget it, especially the simple part. Some programmers tend to think that because they are working on a complex problem, the solution has to be complex too. This is simply not true. Good programmers solve the problem in the simplest possible way; they do not contribute to a complex situation by writing obscure and complex code.

A trivial example will make the point. If you were writing a program that reads floating-point numbers from the keyboard, you would not program it so that the user had to enter the integral portion of the number first and then the fractional part. Although this would work, it is unnecessarily complex (though from a programming standpoint it might be a fun way to solve the problem).

Unfortunately, C++ provides many operators and expression rules that make it easy for a programmer to write obscure and difficult-to-follow code. Your job as a programmer is to make sure that your code is always easy to read. Your code should be unambiguous: It should not be written so that it is easy to misread it.

Another old structured programming principle is that a function should not be larger than one page of code. Updating this principle for online programming in a workstation environment, we would say that a function should be no longer than one screen—about 20 lines of code. The reasoning behind this rule of thumb is that by breaking a problem down into small, easily understood parts, we simplify it, and then we can reassemble the simple components into a simple solution to a complex problem.

> **Blocks of code should be no longer than one screen.**

One element of the C++ language that tends to complicate programs, especially for new programmers, is side effects. We explained in "Evaluating Expressions" on page 91 that side effects can lead to confusing and different results depending on the code. You must fully understand side effects when you write C++ code. If you are unsure of the effects, then simplify your logic until you understand the effects completely.

PARENTHESES

One programming technique is always to use parentheses, even when they are unnecessary. While this approach may lead to a few extra keystrokes, it can save hours of debugging time created by a

---

[2]KISS originally had a different, rather insulting, meaning. We prefer this interpretation.

misunderstanding of the precedence and associativity rules. If a statement contains more than one expression type, use parentheses to ensure that the compiler will interpret it as you intended.

> Computers do what you *tell* them to do, not what you *intended* to tell them to do. Make sure your code is as clear and simple as possible.

USER COMMUNICATION

You should always make sure you communicate with your user from the very first statement in your program to the very last. As mentioned previously, we recommend that you start your program with a message that identifies the program and end with a display that says the program is done.

When you give your user instructions, make sure that they are clear and understandable. In Program 3-14 on page 106, we used three statements to give the user complete and detailed instructions on what we wanted entered. We could have simply said

```
"Enter data"
```

but such an instruction is vague and subject to interpretation. How would the user know what specific data were required? For each input in Program 3-14, we told the users exactly what data we required in terms that they understand. If you don't tell users exactly what data to input, in many cases they will not provide what you want or expect.

One common mistake made by new programmers is to forget to tell the user anything at all. What do you think would be the user's response to Program 3-16 when he or she is confronted with a blank screen and a computer that is doing nothing?

Program 3-16 Program that will confuse the user

```
#include <iostream>
using namespace std;
int main ()
{
   int i;
   int j;
   cin >> i >> j;
   int sum = i + j;
   cout << "The sum of "
        << i << " & " << j
          << " is " << sum << endl;
   return 0;
}
```

We will return to these three concepts from time to time when we introduce new structures that tend to be confusing or misunderstood.

3-9 TIPS AND COMMON PROGRAMMING ERRORS

1. Be aware of expression side effects. They are one of the main sources of confusion and logical errors in a program.
2. Use increment/decrement operators wisely. Understand the difference between postfix and prefix increment/decrement operators before using them.
3. Add parentheses in your program everywhere you feel they will help to make the purpose clear.
4. It is a compile error to use a variable that has not been defined.
5. It is a compile error to forget the semicolon at the end of an expression statement.
6. In most cases it is a compile error to terminate a defined constant (#define) with a semicolon. This is an especially difficult error to decipher because you will not see it in your code—you see the code you wrote, not the code that the preprocessor substituted.
7. It is a compile error when the operand on the left of the assignment operator is not a variable. For example, `a + 3` is not a variable and cannot receive the value of `b * c`.

```
( a + 3 ) = b * c;
```

8. It is a compile error to use the increment or decrement operators with any expression other than a variable identifier. For example, the following code is an error:

```
( a + 3 )++
```

9. It is a compile error to use the modulus operator (%) with anything other than integers.
10. It is a logic error to use a variable before it has been assigned a value.
11. It is a logic error to modify a variable in an expression when the variable appears more than once. For example, the following code compiles and runs but will give inconsistent results:

```
a++ * (a + b)
a = a++ + b
```

3-10 KEY TERMS

additive expression
assignment expression
associativity
binary expression
block
cast
compound statement
explicit type conversion
expression
expression evaluation
expression statement
expression type
implicit type conversion
KISS
left associativity
multiplicative expression
name
operand
operator
postfix decrement
postfix expression
postfix increment
precedence
prefix decrement
prefix increment
primary expression
right associativity
side effect
sizeof
statement
unary expression
unary minus
unary plus
user prompts

3-11 SUMMARY

- An expression is a sequence of operators and operands that reduces to a single value.
- An operator is a language-specific token that requires an action to be taken.
- An operand is the recipient of the action.
- C++ has seven kinds of expressions: primary, postfix, unary, binary, ternary, assignment, and comma.
- The most elementary type of expression is a primary expression. A primary expression is an expression made up of only one operand. It can be a name, a constant, or a parenthetical expression.
- A postfix expression is an expression made up of an operand followed by an operator. There are five different postfix expressions. We studied function call and postfix increment/decrement expressions in this chapter.
- A unary expression is an expression made up of an operator followed by an operand. There are eight kinds of unary expressions. We studied only five in this chapter: prefix increment/decrement, sizeof, and plus/minus expressions.
- A binary expression is an expression made up of two operands with an operator between them. Although we have 10 different categories of binary expressions, we studied only two in this chapter: multiplicative and additive.
- An assignment expression is made up of two operands with the assignment operator (=) between them.
- Precedence is a concept that determines the order in which different operators in a complex expression act upon their operands.
- Associativity defines the order of evaluation when operators have the same precedence.
- The side effect of an expression is one of the unique phenomena in C++. An expression can have a side effect in addition to a value. The side effect can be pre-effect or post-effect.
- To evaluate an expression, we must follow the rules of precedence and associativity.
- A statement causes an action to be performed by the program.
- Although we have six different types of statements, we studied only two types in this chapter: expression and compound statements.
- An expression statement is an expression converted to a statement by keeping the side effect and discarding the value.
- A compound statement is a combination of statements enclosed in two braces.
- KISS means "Keep It Simple and Short."
- One of the important recommendations in software engineering is the use of parentheses when they can help clarify your code.
- Another recommendation in software engineering is to communicate clearly with the user.

3-12 PRACTICE SETS

REVIEW QUESTIONS

1. A unary expression consists of only one operand with no operator.
   a. True
   b. False
2. The left operand in an assignment expression must be a single variable.
   a. True
   b. False
3. Associativity is used to determine which of several different expressions is evaluated first.
   a. True
   b. False
4. Side effect is an action that results from the evaluation of an expression.
   a. True
   b. False
5. An expression statement is terminated with a period.
   a. True
   b. False

6. A(n) __________ is a sequence of operands and operators that reduces to a single value.
   a. Expression
   b. Function
   c. Format
   d. Value
   e. Formula
7. C++ contains seven different expression formats. Which of the following is not an expression format?
   a. Assignment
   b. Conditional
   c. Binary
   d. Primary
8. Which of the following expressions has the highest precedence?
   a. Assignment
   b. Conditional
   c. Binary
   d. Primary
9. Which of the following is a unary expression?
   a. `i + j`
   b. `++a`
   c. `x *= 5`
   d. `c++`
10. The __________ expression evaluates the operand on the right side of the operator and places its value in the variable on the left side of the operator.
   a. Additive
   b. Postfix
   c. Assignment
   d. Primary
   e. Multiplicative
11. __________ is used to determine the order in which different operators in a complex expression are evaluated.
   a. Associativity
   b. Precedence
   c. Evaluation
   d. Side effect
   e. Format
12. __________ is an action that results from the evaluation of an expression.
   a. Associativity
   b. Precedence
   c. Evaluation
   d. Side effect
   e. Format
13. Which of the following statements about mixed expressions is false?
   a. A cast cannot be used to change an assigned value.
   b. An explicit cast can be used to change the expression type.
   c. An explicit cast on a variable changes its type in memory.
   d. An implicit cast is generated by the compiler automatically when necessary.
   e. Constant casting is done by the compiler automatically.
14. A(n) __________ causes an action to be performed by the program.
   a. Expression
   b. Operand
   c. Function
   d. Statement
   e. Operator
15. Which of the following statements about compound statements is false?
   a. A compound statement is also known as a block.
   b. A compound statement is enclosed in a set of braces.
   c. A compound statement must be terminated by a semicolon.
   d. The declarations and definitions in a compound statement are optional.

EXERCISES

16. Which of the following expressions are *not* postfix expressions?
   a. *x*++ b. --*x*
   c. *x* * *y* d. ++*x*
17. Which of the following are *not* unary expressions?
   a. ++*x* b. --*x*
   c. *sizeof* (*x*) d. +5
   e. *x* = 4

18. Which of the following are *not* binary expressions?
a. 3 * 5 b. *x* += 6
c. *y* = 5 +2 d. *z* - 2
e. *y* % *z*

19. Which of the following is *not* a valid assignment expression?
a. *x* = 23 b. 4 = *x*
c. *y* % = 5 d. *x* = 8 = 3
e. *x* = r = 5

20. If originally *x* = 4, what is the value of x after the evaluation of each of the following expressions?
a. *x* = 2 b. *x* += 4
c. *x* + = *x* +3 d. *x* * = 2
e. *x* / = *x* +2

21. If originally x = 3 and y = 5, what are the values of x and y after the evaluation of each of the following expressions?
a. *x*++ + *y* b. ++*x*
c. *x*++ + *y*++ d. ++*x* + 2
e. *x*-- - *y*--

22. What is the value of each of the following expressions?
a. 24 - 6 * 2 b. -15 * 2 + 3
c. 72 / 5 d. 72 % 5
e. 5 * 2 / 6 + 15 % 4

23. What is the value of each of the following expressions?
a. 6.2 + 5.1 * 3.2 b. 2.0 + 3.0 / 1.2
c. 4.0 * (3.0 + 2.0 / 6.0) d. 6.0 / (2.0 + 4.0 * 1.2)
e. 2.7 + 3.2 - 5.3 * 1.1

24. If originally x = 2, y = 3, and z = 2, what is the value of each of the following expressions?
a. *x*++ + *y*++ b. ++*x* - --*z*
c. --*x* + *y*++ d. *x*-- + *x*-- - *y*--
e. *x* + *y* - --*x* + *x*++ - --*y*

25. If originally x = 2, y = 3, and z = 1, what is the value of each of the following expressions?
a. *x* + 2 / 6 + *y* b. *y* - 3 * *z*+2
c. *z* - (*x* + *z*) % 2 + 4 d. *x* - 2 * (3 + *z*) + *y*
e. *y*++ + *z*-- + *x*++

26. If x = 2945, what is the value of each of the following expressions?
a. *x* % 10 b. *x* / 10
c. (*x* / 10) % 10 d. *x* / 100
e. (*x* / 100) % 10

27. What is the output from the following code fragment?

```
int a;
int b;
a = b = 50;
cout << setw(4) << a << setw(4) <<
b << endl;
a = a * 2;
b = b / 2;
cout << setw(4) << a << setw(4) <<
b << endl;
```

PROBLEMS

28. Given the following pseudocode, write a program that executes it. Use floating-point types for all values.

```
read x
read y
compute p = x * y
compute s = x + y
total = s^2 + p * (s - x) * (p + y)
print total
```

29. Write a program that calculates and prints the quotient and remainder of two numbers.

30. Write a program that extracts and prints the rightmost digit of the integral portion of a *float*.

31. Write a program that extracts and prints the second rightmost digit of the integral portion of a *float*.

32. Write a program that calculates the area and perimeter of a rectangle from a user-supplied (*cin*) length and width.

33. We are all familiar with the fact that angles are measured in degrees, minutes, and seconds. Another measure of an angle is a radian. A radian is the angle formed by two radii forming an arc that is equal to the radius of their circle. One radian equals 57.295779 degrees. Write a program that converts degrees into radians. Provide good user prompts. Include the following test data in your run:

```
90° is 1.57080 radians
```

34. The formula for converting centigrade temperatures to Fahrenheit is:

$$F = 32 + \left(C * \frac{180.0}{100.0}\right)$$

Write a program that asks the user to enter a temperature reading in centigrade and then prints the equivalent Fahrenheit value. Be sure to include at least one negative centigrade number in your test cases.

PROJECTS

35. Write a program that converts and prints a user-supplied measurement in inches into
    a. foot (12 inches)
    b. yard (36 inches)
    c. centimeter (2.54/inch)
    d. meter (39.37 inches)

36. Write a program that converts and prints a user-supplied measurement in inches into
    a. foot (12 inches)
    b. yard (36 inches)
    c. centimeter (2.54/inch)
    d. meter (39.37 inches)

37. A Fibonacci number is a member of a set in which each number is the sum of the previous two numbers. (The Fibonacci series describes a form of a spiral.) The series begins

```
0, 1, 1, 2, 3, 5, 8, 13, 21, ...
```

Write a program that calculates and prints the next three numbers in the Fibonacci series. You are to use only three variables: `fib1`, `fib2`, and `fib3`.

38. Write a program that prompts a user for an integer value in the range 0 to 32,767 and then prints the individual digits of the numbers on a line with three spaces between the digits. The first line is to start with the leftmost digit and print all five digits; the second line is to start with the second digit from the left and print four digits, and so forth. For example, if the user enters 1234, your program should print

```
0   1   2   3   4
1   2   3   4
2   3   4
3   4
4
```

39. Write a program to create a customer's bill for a company. The company sells only five different products: TV, VCR, Remote Controller, CD Player, and Tape Recorder. The unit prices are $400.00, $220.00, $35.20, $300.00, and $150.00, respectively. The program must read from the keyboard the quantity of each piece of equipment purchased. It then calculates the cost of each item, the subtotal, and the total cost after an 8.25% sales tax.

The input data consist of a set of integers representing the quantities of each item sold. These integers must be input into the program in a user-friendly way; that is, the program must prompt the user for each quantity as shown below. The numbers in boldface italic show the user's answers.

```
How many TVs were sold?   3
How many VCRs were sold?   5
How many remote controllers
were sold?   1
How many CDs were sold?   2
How many tape recorders
were sold?   4
```

The format for the output from the program is shown below:

```
QTY   DESCRIPTION       UNIT      TOTAL
                        PRICE     PRICE
---   -----------     -------   --------
XX    TV               400.00    XXXX.XX
XX    VCR              220.00    XXXX.XX
XX    REMOTE CTRLR      35.20    XXXX.XX
XX    CD PLAYER        300.00    XXXX.XX
XX    TAPE RECORDER    150.00    XXXX.XX
                                ---------
                SUBTOTAL        XXXXX.XX
                TAX              XXXX.XX
                TOTAL           XXXXX.XX
```

Use constants for the unit prices and the tax rate. Use integer variables to store the quantities for each item. Use floating-point variables to store the total price for each item, the bill subtotal, the tax amount, and the total amount of the bill. Run your program two times with the following data:

```
SET 1  → 2   1   4   1   2
SET 2  → 3   0   2   0   21
```

Functions 4

The programs we have presented thus far have been very simple. They solved problems that could be understood without too much effort. As we consider larger and larger programs, however, you will discover that it is not possible to understand all aspects of such programs without somehow first reducing them to more elementary parts.

Breaking a complex problem into smaller parts is a common practice. For example, suppose that for your vacation this year you decide to drive in a circular route that will allow you to visit as many national parks as possible in two weeks. Your requirements for this problem are very simple: Visit as many parks as possible in two weeks. But how are you going to do it? You might first gather some data about national parks and then calculate the distance between each of them to figure out the travel time. Next, you would estimate how much time it would take to visit each park. Finally, you would put all your data together so you could plan your trip day by day. Once your trip was planned, you would make your motel and camp reservations and any other arrangements that had to be in place in advance.

The planning for large programs involves a similar process. First, you must understand the problem as a whole; then you must break it into simpler parts. We call each of these parts of a program a *module* and the process of subdividing a problem into manageable parts **top-down design**. The implementation of the resulting design using the three basic constructs—sequence (Chapter 3), selection (Chapter 5), and iteration (Chapter 6)—popularized by Edsger Dijkstra[1] is known as *structured programming*.

---

[1]Dijkstra's work was based on earlier research by two Italian computer scientists, Corrado Bohm and Guiseppe Jacopini. They proved that any algorithm could be written with only these three constructs.

4-1 DESIGNING STRUCTURED PROGRAMS

The principles of top-down design and structured programming dictate that a program should be divided into a main module and its related modules.[2] Each module should also be divided into submodules according to software engineering principles that we will discuss in "Software Engineering and Programming Style" on page 159. The division of modules proceeds until the module consists only of elementary processes that are intrinsically clear and cannot be further subdivided. This process is known as *factoring*.

> In top-down design, a program is divided into a main module and its related modules. Each module is in turn divided into submodules until the resulting modules are intrinsic; that is, until they are implicitly understood without further division.

Top-down design is usually done using a visual representation of the modules known as a **structure chart**. The structure chart for a program shows the relation between each module and its submodules. The rules for reading and creating structure charts are covered in "Software Engineering and Programming Style" on page 159, but at this point, a few simple rules are all that are necessary. First, the structure chart is read top-down, left-right. Referring to Figure 4-1, first we read Main Module. In this case, Main Module represents the entire set of code used to solve the problem.

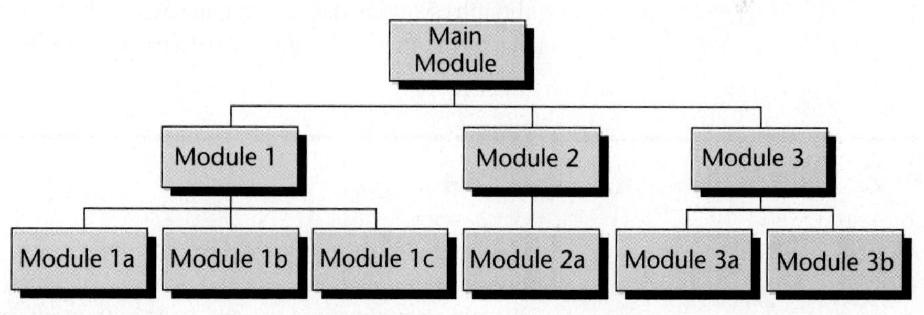

Figure 4-1 **Structure chart**

Going down and left, we then read `Module 1`. On the same level with `Module 1` are `Module 2` and `Module 3`: The main module is decomposed into three submodules. At this point, however, we are looking only at `Module 1`. We now note that `Module 1` is further decomposed into three modules, `Module 1a`, `Module 1b`, and `Module 1c`. To write the code for `Module 1`, therefore, we will have to write code for its three submodules. What does this concept say about writing the code for the `Main Module`?

[2] In C++, modules are implemented as functions.

Now for some more terminology. The `Main Module` is known as a *calling* module because it has submodules. Each of the submodules is known as a *called* module. Because modules 1, 2, and 3 also have submodules, they are also calling modules; thus, they are both called and calling modules.

Communication between modules in a structure chart is allowed only through a calling module. If `Module 1` needs to send data to `Module 2`, the data must be passed through the calling module, which is `Main Module`. No communication can take place directly between modules that do not have a calling-called relationship.

> **In a structure chart, a module can be called by one and only one higher module.**

With this understanding, how can `Module 1a` send data to `Module 3b`? `Module 1a` first sends the data to `Module 1`, which in turn sends it to the `Main Module`, which passes it to `Module 3`, and then on to `Module 3b`. Although this sounds complex, you will find that it is not difficult to arrange.

The technique used to pass data to a function is known as **parameter passing**. The parameters are contained in a list that is a definition of the data passed to the function by the caller. The list serves as the formal declaration of the data types and names.

Data are passed to a function using one of two techniques: **pass by value** or **pass by reference**. In pass by value, a copy of the data is made and the copy is sent to the function. This technique results in the parameters being copied to variables in the called function and also ensures that the original data in the calling function cannot be changed accidentally.

The second technique, pass by reference, sends the address of the data rather than a copy. In this case, the called function can change the original data in the calling function. Although changing data is often necessary, it is one of the common sources of errors and is one of the most difficult errors to trace when it occurs.

4-2 FUNCTIONS IN C++

In C++, the idea of top-down design is done using ***functions***. A C++ program is made of one or more functions, one and only one of which must be called *main*. The execution of the program always starts and ends with *main*, but this function can call other functions to do special tasks. Figure 4-2 shows a C++ program structure chart.

A function in C++ (including *main*) is an independent module that will be called to do a specific task. The function may or may not return a value to the caller. The function *main* is called by the operating system; *main* in turn calls other functions. When *main* is complete, control returns to the operating system.

> **In C++, a program is made of one or more functions, one and only one of which must be named *main*. The execution of the program always starts with *main*, but it can call other functions to do some part of the job.**

In general, the purpose of a function is to receive zero or more pieces of data, operate on them, and return at most one piece of data. At the same time, a function can have a **side effect**. A function side effect is an action that results in a change in the state of the program. If there is a side effect, it occurs while the function is executing and before the

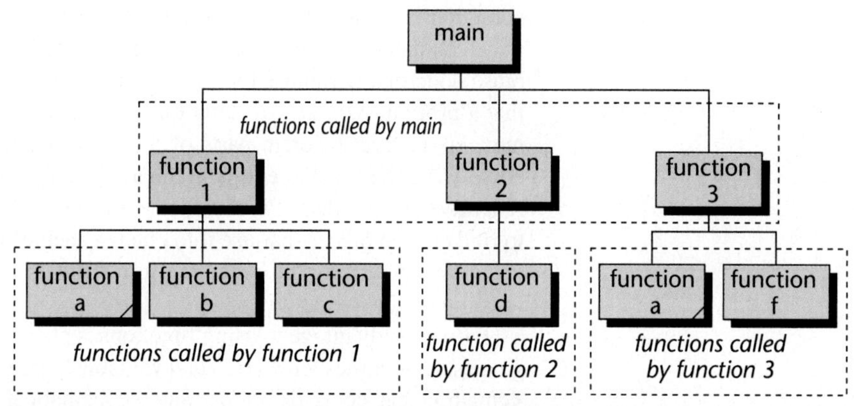

Figure 4-2 Structure chart for a C++ program

function returns. The side effect can involve accepting data from outside the program, sending data out of the program to the monitor or a file, or changing the value of a variable in the calling function. The function concept is shown in Figure 4-3.

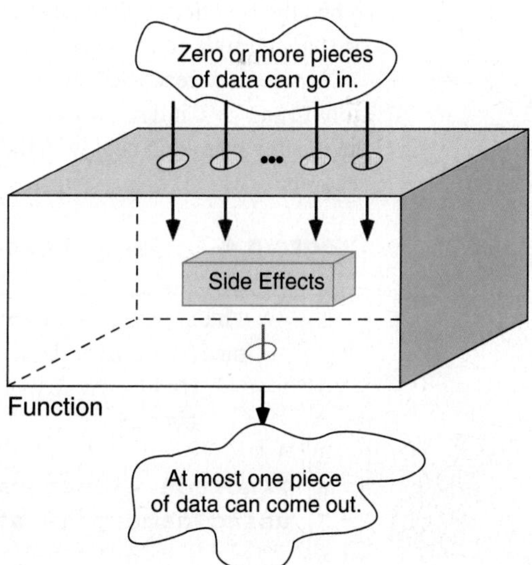

Figure 4-3 Function concept

> A *function* in C++ can have a value, a side effect, or both.
>
> - *The side effect occurs before the value is returned.*
> - *The function's value is the value of the expression in the return statement.*
> - *A function can be called for its value, its side effect, or both.*

There are several advantages associated with using functions in C++ or in any other computer language. The first, as already described, is that problems can be factored into understandable and manageable steps. The second is that functions provide a way to reuse code that is required in more than one place in a program. Assume, for instance, that a program you are working on requires you to compute the average of a series of numbers in five different parts of the program. Each time the data are different. You could write the code to compute the average five times, but this would involve a lot of repetitive effort. Also, if it became necessary to change the calculation, you would have to find all five places that use it to change each of them. Fortunately, you can save time and effort by writing the code once as a function and then calling it whenever you need to compute the average.

The third advantage to using functions is closely tied to reusing code. Like many languages, C++ comes with a rich and valuable library. For example, there is a math library, <cmath>, that contains almost any mathematical or statistical function that you will ever require. These C++ libraries provide standard functions that make your work as a programmer much easier. Appendix F, "Function Prototypes," documents many of the functions included with the C++ language. (Note that you can also create personal and project libraries that make developing systems easier.)

A fourth reason we use functions is to protect data. This rather complex idea centers around the concept of *local* data. Local data consist of data described in a function. These data are available only to the function and only while the function is executing. When the function is done, the data are gone. Data in one function, then, cannot be seen or changed by a function outside of its scope.

We are now ready to look at a program that calls functions. Study Program 4-1 carefully to see how it demonstrates the interaction of the functions. The highlighted portions are the key parts that deal with the functions. They are discussed in detail in the following sections.

Program 4-1 Sample program with subfunction

```
/* This program demonstrates function calls by calling a
   small function to multiply two numbers.
      Written by:
      Date:
*/
#include <iostream>
using namespace std;

// Prototype Declarations
   int multiply (int num1, int num2);

int main ()
{
   int multiplier;
   int multiplicand;
   cout << "Enter two integers: ";
   cin  >> multiplier >> multiplicand;
```

Program 4-1 Sample program with subfunction ***(continued)***

```
   int product = multiply (multiplier, multiplicand);

   cout << "Product of " << multiplier
        << " & "         << multiplicand
        << " is "        << product;
   return 0;
}  // main
/* =================== multiply =====================
   Multiply two numbers and return product.
      Pre  num1 & num2 contain values to be multiplied
      Post product returned
*/
int multiply (int num1, int num2)
{
   return (num1 * num2);
}  // multiply
```

```
Results:
Enter two integers: 17 21
Product of 17 & 21 is 357
```

4-3 USER-DEFINED FUNCTIONS

Like every other object in C++, functions must be both declared and defined. The **function declaration** is done first with a prototype declaration. You use the function by calling it. The **function definition**, which is traditionally coded after the function that makes the call, contains the code required to complete the task. Figure 4-4 shows the interrelationships among these function components. When you study it, note that the function name is used three times: when the function is declared, when it is called, and when it is defined.

Before looking at how we write functions, let's look at examples of the three general function designs: *void* functions with no parameters, *void* functions with parameters, and functions that return values.

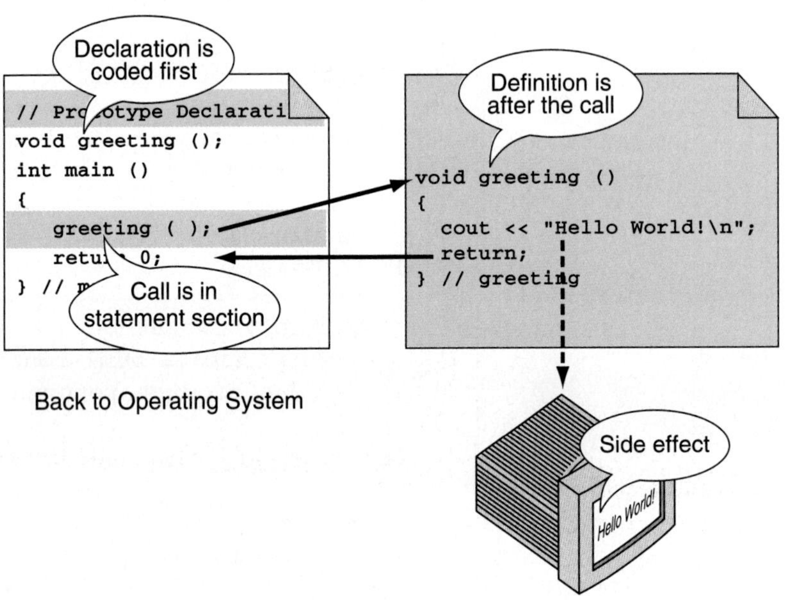

Figure 4-4 Declaring, calling, and defining functions

> The name of a function is used in three ways: for declaration, in a call, and for definition.

VOID FUNCTIONS WITH NO PARAMETERS

A function can be written with no parameters. The `greeting` function in Figure 4-4 receives nothing and returns nothing. It has only a side effect, display the message, and is called only for that side effect.

The call still requires parentheses, however, even when no parameters are present. When you make a call to a function with no parameters, it is tempting to leave the parentheses off the call. Although this is valid syntax, it is not what you intended. Without the parentheses, it is not a function call.

Because a ***void* function** does not have a value, it can be used only as a statement; it cannot be used in an expression. Examine the call to the `greeting` function in Figure 4-4. This call stands alone as a statement. Including this call in an expression, as shown below, would be an error.

```
result = greeting();         // Error. Void function
```

VOID FUNCTIONS WITH PARAMETERS

Now let's call a function that has parameters but still returns *void.* The function `printOne`, as seen in Figure 4-5, receives an integer parameter. Since this function returns nothing to the calling function, *main*, its return type is *void.* As with the greeting function discussed previously, this function must be coded as a stand-alone call because it does not return a value; it cannot be included as part of another expression. Note, however, that while `printOne` returns no values, it does have a side effect: The parameter value is printed to the monitor.

As you study Figure 4-5, note that the name of the variable in *main* (`a`) and the name of parameter in `printOne` (`x`) do not have to be the same. On the other hand, there is no reason why they can't be the same if that makes it easier to understand the code.

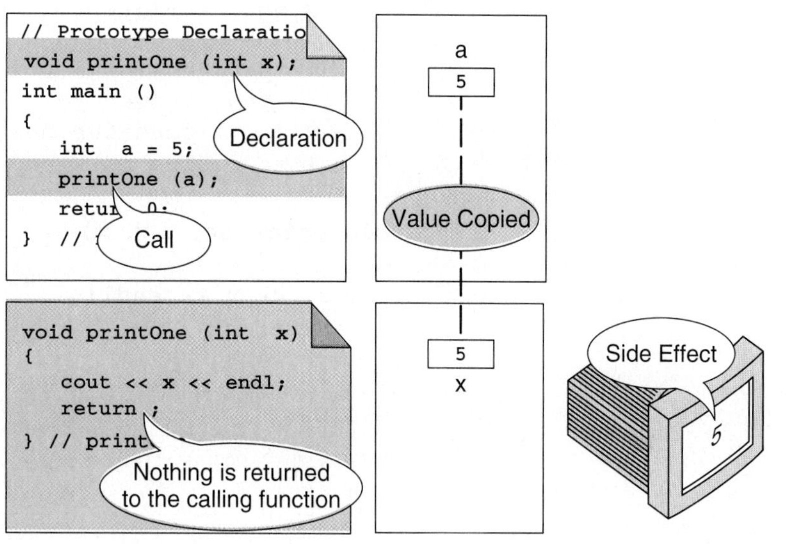

Figure 4-5 ***void*** **function with parameters**

In Program 4-2 we use `printOne` to demonstrate that a function can be called multiple times.

Program 4-2 ***void*** **function with a parameter**

```
/* This program demonstrates that one function can be
   called multiple times.
      Written by:
      Date:
*/
#include <iostream>
using namespace std;

// Prototype Declarations
   void printOne (int x);

int main ()
{
   // First call
   int a = 5;
   printOne (a);

   // Second call
   a = 33;
   printOne (a);

   // Done. Return to operating system.
   return 0;
}  // main
```

Program 4-2 ***void* function with a parameter (*continued*)**

```
/* ================== printOne ==================
   Print one integer value.
      Pre   x contains number to be printed
      Post  value in x printed
*/
void printOne (int x)
{
   cout << x << endl;
   return;
} // printOne
```

```
Results:
5
33
```

FUNCTIONS THAT RETURN VALUES

Figure 4-6 contains a function that passes parameters and returns a value—in this case, the square of the parameter. Note how the returned value is placed in the variable, b. This is not done by the call; it is a result of expression evaluation. Since the call is a postfix expression, it has a value—whatever is returned from the function. After the function has been executed and the value returned, the value on the right side of the assignment expression is the returned value, which is then assigned to b. Thus, again we see the power of expressions in C++. Note that the function, sqr, has no side effect.

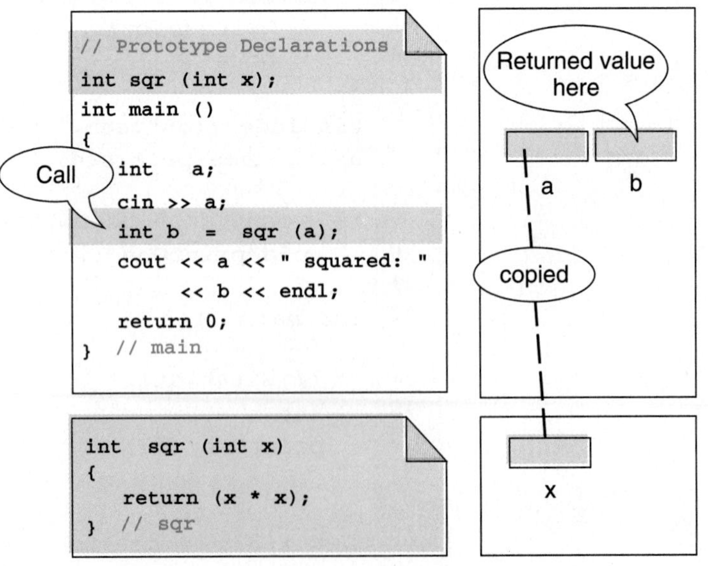

Figure 4-6 Calling a function that returns a value

We saw previously that when a function returns *void*, it cannot be used in an expression. Functions that return values are often found in an expression. In fact, if we didn't assign the return value in Figure 4-6 to the variable b, we would have lost it. C++ would have discarded it, and it would not have been available to be printed.

> ***void* functions cannot be used in an expression; they must be a separate statement.**
>
> **Functions that return a value may be used in an expression or as a separate statement.**

In large programs, *main* is written with only function calls. To demonstrate how this would be done with our simple example, we combine our square and print functions into Program 4-3.

Program 4-3 Read a number and square it

```
/* This program reads a number and prints its square.
      Written by:
      Date:
*/
#include <iostream>
using namespace std;

// Prototype Declarations
int  getNum    (void);
int  sqr       (int x);
void printOne  (int x);

int main ()
{
   // Get number and square it
   int a = getNum ();

   // Square the number just read
   int b = sqr (a);

   // Now print it
   printOne(b);

   // Done. Return to operating system.
   return 0;
}  // main

/* ================== getNum ==================
   Read number from keyboard and return it.
      Pre   nothing
      Post  number read and returned
*/
int getNum (void)
```

Program 4-3 Read a number and square it (*continued*)

```
{
   cout << "Enter a number to be squared: ";
   int numIn;
   cin >>  numIn;
   return numIn;
} // getNum

/* ================== sqr ===================
   Return the square of the parameter.
      Pre   x contains number to be squared
      Post  squared value returned
*/
int sqr (int x)
{
   return (x * x);
} // sqr

/* ================== printOne ===================
   Print one integer value.
      Pre   x contains number to be printed
      Post  value in x printed
*/
void printOne (int x)
{
   cout << "The value is: " << x << endl;
   return;
} // printOne
```

```
Results:
Enter a number to be squared: 81
The value is: 6561
```

Program 4-3 Analysis Our simple program has grown to four functions, including `main`. This is an example of decomposition, the process of breaking a complex problem into simple parts. While our example is not really complex, it still demonstrates the concept.

We made one slight modification to `printOne` in this program. To make the output a little more meaningful, we added `The value is:` to the print statement. As a general principle, the person at the monitor should not have to guess what the output is.

FUNCTION DEFINITION

Now that we have seen examples of the basic function formats, let's look at functions in more detail. We begin with the function definition.

The function definition contains the code for a function. The definition is made up of two parts: the **function header** and the **function body**, which is a compound statement. Remember that a compound statement must have opening and closing braces and it may contain declarations and statements. The function definition format is shown in Figure 4-7.

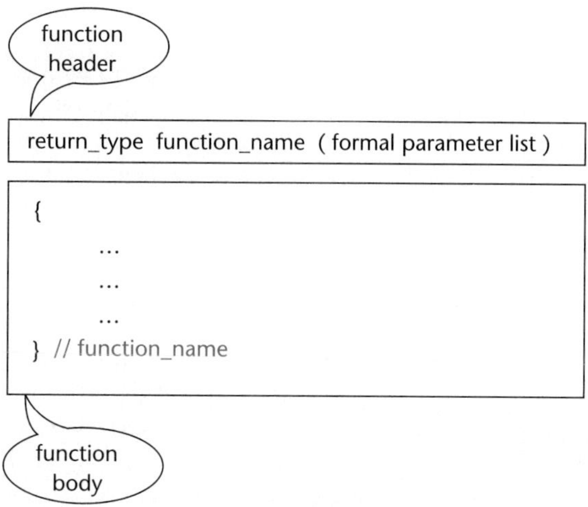

Figure 4-7 Function definition

Function Header

A function header consists of three parts: the return type, the function name, and the formal parameter list. A semicolon is not used at the end of the function definition header.

C++ requires that a return type be specified. If you are returning nothing, you must code the return type as *void.* This differs from earlier versions of C++ that did not require a return type.

Function Body

The function body contains the declarations and statements for the function. The body starts with local definitions that specify the variables required by the function. After the local declarations, the function statements, terminating with a *return* statement, are coded. If a function return type is *void*, it may be written without a *return* statement. However, because we believe that default statements should be explicitly coded for clarity, we strongly recommend that every function, even *void* functions, have a *return* statement.

Figure 4-8 shows two functions: `first` and `second`. The function `first` has been declared to return an integer value. Its *return* statement therefore contains the expression `x + 2`. When the *return* statement is executed, the expression is evaluated and the resulting value is returned. The function `second` returns nothing; its return type is *void*. It therefore needs no *return* statement—the end of the function acts as a *void* return. Again, we strongly recommend that you include a *return* statement even for *void* functions. In this case, the *return* statement has no expression; it is just completed with a semicolon.

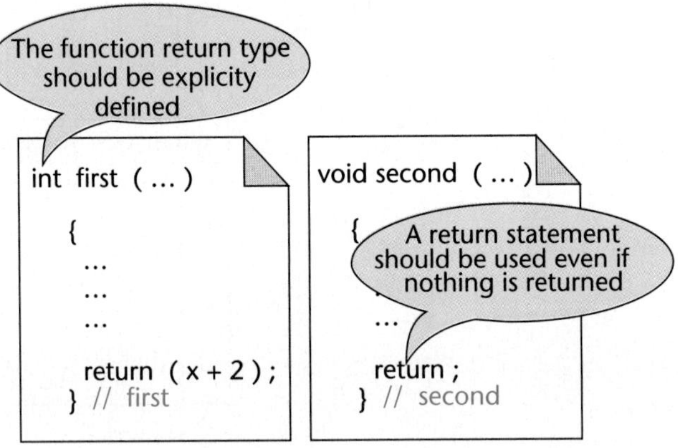

Figure 4-8 Function return statements

> The type of the expression in the return statement must match the return type in the function header.

Formal Parameter List

In the definition of a function, the **parameters** are contained in the **formal parameter list**. This list defines and declares the variables that will contain the data received by the function. The parameter list is always required. If there are no parameters—that is, if the function does not receive any data from the calling function—then the fact that the parameter list is empty may be declared with the keyword *void* or be left empty.

In C++, each variable must be defined and declared fully with multiple parameters separated by commas. In Figure 4-9, the variables `x` and `y` are formal parameters that receive data from the calling function's actual parameters. Since they are value parameters, copies of the values being passed are stored in the called function's memory area. If the function changes either of these values, only the copies will be changed. The original values in the calling function remain unchanged.

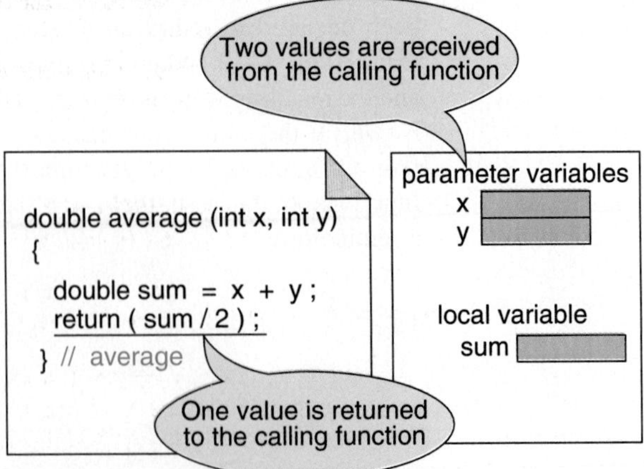

Figure 4-9 Function local variables

Local Variables

A **local variable** is a variable that is defined inside a function and used without having any role in the communication between functions. Referring back to Figure 4-9, it contains an example of a function with both formal parameters and a local variable, `sum`.

PROTOTYPE DECLARATION

Prototype declarations consist only of a function header; they contain no code. Like function definition headers, prototype headers consist of three parts: the return type, the function name, and the formal parameter list. Unlike the header for the function definition, prototype declarations are terminated with a semicolon. Prototype declarations are placed in the global area of the program just before *main* or in a header file.

C++ does not require identifier names for the formal parameters. This does not prevent us from using names in a prototype declaration, however. In fact, readability and understandability are usually improved if names are used. One point to note, however, is that the *names* do not need to be the same in the prototype declaration and the function definition; on the other hand, if the *types* are not the same, you will get a compile error. The compiler checks the types in the prototype declarations with the types in the call to ensure that they are the same or at least compatible.

The major reason to include the identifiers is documentation; thus, their names should be meaningful. Don't include generic identifiers such as `a` or `x`.

- **Formal parameters are variables that are declared in the header of the function definition.**
- **Actual parameters are the expressions in the calling statement.**
- **The formal and actual parameters must match exactly in type, order, and number. Their names, however, do not need to be the same.**

Figure 4-10 demonstrates several of these concepts. The prototype declaration tells *main* that a function named `multiply`, which accepts two integers and returns one integer, will be called. That is all *main* needs; it does not require anything else to make the call.

The illustration in Figure 4-10 also demonstrates that the formal parameter names in the declaration do not have to be the same as the actual parameter names. In this case, the names in the prototype declarations are much more meaningful and for that reason should have been used in the function definition.

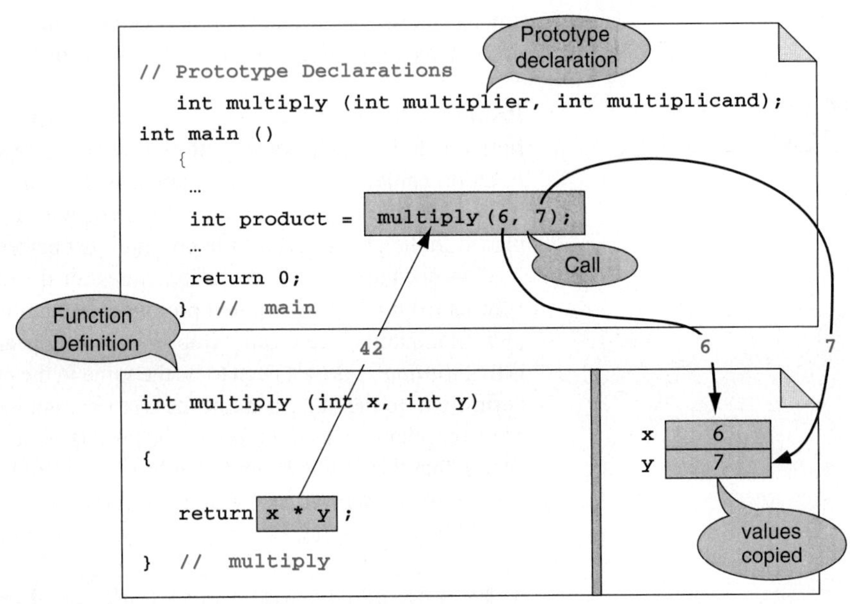

Figure 4-10 Parts of a function call

THE FUNCTION CALL

A **function call** is a postfix expression. The postfix operators are at a very high level (17) in the Precedence Table (see inside cover). In fact, the only thing higher is the primary expression. When a function is used as a part of a larger expression, it will be evaluated first unless parentheses are used to specify a different evaluation order.

The operand in a function call is the function name; the operator is the parentheses set, (...), which contains the **actual parameters**. The actual parameters identify the values that are to be sent to the called function. They match the function's formal parameters in type and order in the parameter list. If there are multiple actual parameters, they are separated by commas.

There are many different ways to call a function. In Figure 4-11, `multiply` is called six different ways. The first three show calls with primary expressions. The fourth uses a binary expression, `a + 6`, as the first parameter value, and the fifth shows the function `multiply (a, b)` as its own first parameter. The last example sums it all up: Any expression that reduces to a single value can be passed as a parameter.

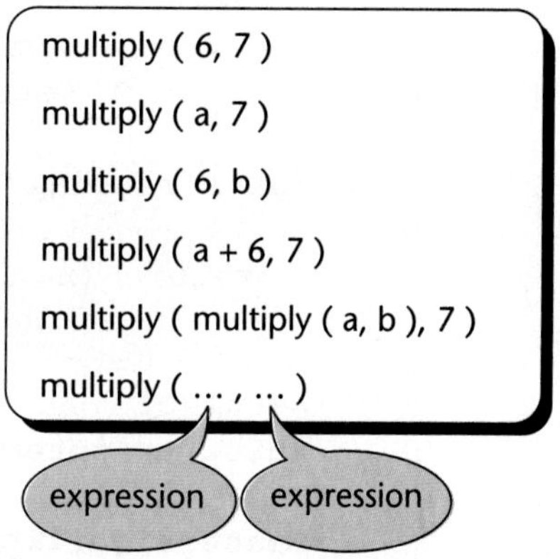

multiply (6, 7)

multiply (a, 7)

multiply (6, b)

multiply (a + 6, 7)

multiply (multiply (a, b), 7)

multiply (... , ...)

expression expression

Figure 4-11 Examples of function calls

FUNCTION EXAMPLES

This section contains four examples of programs in which functions call functions. Look for the points they demonstrate.

Print Least Significant Digit

Program 4-4 prints the least significant (rightmost) digit of any integer read from the keyboard.

Program 4-4 Print least significant digit

```
/* This program prints the first digits of an integer
   read from the keyboard.
      Written by:
      Date:
*/
#include <iostream>
using namespace std;

//  Prototype Declarations
   int firstDigit (int num);

int main ()
{
   cout << "Enter an integer: ";
   int  number;
   cin  >> number;

   int digit = firstDigit (number);
   cout << "Least significant digit is: " << digit << endl;
   return 0;
}  // main

/* ================= firstDigit ==================
   This function extracts the least significant digit
   of an integer.
```

Program 4-4 Print least significant digit *(continued)*

```
      Pre  num contains an integer
      Post Returns least significant digit
*/
int firstDigit (int num)
{
   return (num % 10);
} // firstDigit
```

```
Results:
Enter an integer: 27

Least significant digit is: 7
```

Program 4-4 Analysis This extremely simple program demonstrates how to call a function from *main.* In the sample run, when `firstDigit` was executed it returned 7, which was then put into digit and printed.

Add Two Digits

Write a function that extracts and adds the two least significant digits of any integer number. The design of the program is illustrated in Figure 4-12. (Turn to "Software Engineering and Programming Style" on page 159 if you have trouble understanding the structure charts.)

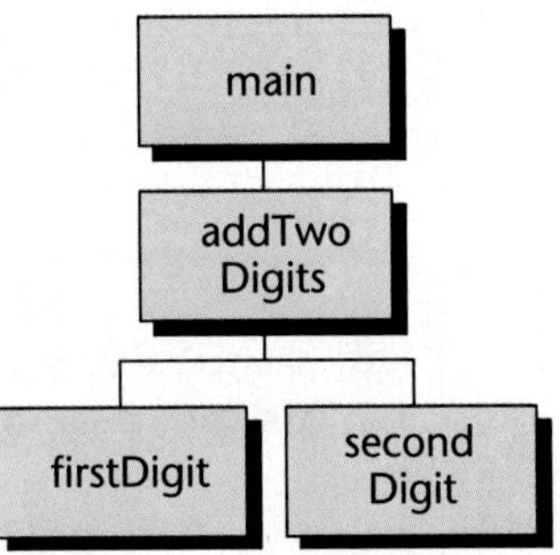

Figure 4-12 Design for addTwoDigits

The implementation in Program 4-5 uses a function called by `addTwoDigits`, which in turn calls two functions.

Program 4-5 Add two digits

```
/* This program extracts and adds the two least
   significant digits of an integer.
      Written by:
      Date:
*/
#include <iostream>
using namespace std;
```

Program 4-5 Add two digits *(continued)*

```
// Prototype Declarations
   int addTwoDigits (int num);
   int firstDigit   (int);
   int secondDigit  (int);
int main ()
{
   cout << "Enter an integer: ";
   int  number;
   cin  >> number;
   int sum  =  addTwoDigits (number);
   cout << "\nSum of last two digits is: " << sum;
   return 0;
}  // main
/* ================== addTwoDigits ==================
   Adds the first two digits of an integer.
      Pre  num contains an integer
      Post Returns sum of two least significant digits
*/
int addTwoDigits (int number)
{
   int result = firstDigit(number) + secondDigit(number);
   return result;
}  // addTwoDigits
/* ================== firstDigit =================
   Extracts the least significant digit of an integer.
      Pre  num contains an integer
      Post Returns least significant digit
*/
int firstDigit (int num)
{
   return (num % 10);
}  // firstDigit
//    ================= secondDigit =================
/* Extracts second least significant (10s) digit.
      Pre  num is an integer
      Post Returns digit in 10s position
*/
int secondDigit (int num)
{
   int result = (num / 10) % 10;
   return result;
}  // secondDigit
```

Program 4-5 Add two digits *(continued)*

```
Results:
Run 1
   Enter an integer: 23

   Sum of last two digits is: 5
Run 2
   Enter an integer: 8

   Sum of last two digits is: 8
```

Program 4-5 Analysis A natural question asked by students when they first read this program is, "Why not put `firstDigit` and `secondDigit` as in-line code in `addTwoDigits`?" This seems to be the obvious way to code the problem. And after all, each of the called functions is *only one statement.*

The answer is that although each function is only one statement, it does a job that can be used in other places. One of the principles of structured programming is that processes should appear in a program in only one place. For example, we have used the same code for `firstDigit` that we used in the first program. If a function is to be reusable in this way, it must do only one thing. The short answer, then, is that it is better structured programming. It is the nature of the task to be performed, not the amount of code, that determines if a function should be used.

An interesting point to note is the way these two different digits were calculated. To get the least significant digit, we took the 10's modulus of the number. But to get the second digit, we had to divide by 10. Can you figure out how to sum the digits in a three-digit number? We will give you a chance to do this in the problems at the end of the chapter.

Note that we tested the program with two different numbers, one containing only one digit. It is good practice to run the program with more than one test case. Another test case that should be run is a negative number. What do you think would happen? As a programmer, not only should you run several tests but you should predict the results before you run the program.

It is the nature of the task to be performed, not the amount of code, that determines if a function should be used.

Format Long Integer

Program 4-6 reads a long integer and prints it with a comma after the first three digits—for example, 123,456. The number should be printed with leading zeros in case the value is less than 100,000.

Program 4-6 Print six digits with comma

```
/* This program reads long integers from the keyboard
   and prints them with leading zeros in the form
   123,456 with a comma between the 3rd & 4th digit.
      Written by:
      Date:
*/
#include <iostream>
#include <iomanip>
```

Program 4-6 Print six digits with comma *(continued)*

```
using namespace std;

// Prototype Declarations
void printWithComma (long num);

int main ()
{
   cout << "Enter a number with up to 6 digits: ";
   long number;
   cin  >> number;
   printWithComma (number);
   return 0;
}  // main
/* ================ printWithComma================
   This function divides num into two three-digit
   numbers and prints them with a comma inserted.
      Pre  num is a six-digit number
      Post num has been printed with a comma inserted
*/
void printWithComma (long num)
{
   float thousands = num / 1000;
   float hundreds  = num % 1000;

   cout << "\nThe number you entered is \t";
   cout << setw(3) << thousands << ",";
   cout << setfill('0');
   cout << setw(3) << hundreds;
   return;
}  // printWithComma
```

```
Results:
Run 1
   Enter a number with up to 6 digits: 123456

   The number you entered is   123,456
Run 2
   Enter a number with up to 6 digits: 1012

   The number you entered is     1,012
```

Program 4-6 Analysis Once again, we have a simple program that has the makings of a very useful function. C++ has no built-in functions that will provide number formatting like commas and dollar signs, so the programmer has to program these details. Since this logic will be used over and over again, it must be in its own function. Note, however, that more work is required to print numbers less than 1,000 correctly; however, we have not yet introduced all the tools required to do the complete job.

As before, we have used two test cases to show that more work must be done. Note how we have used a zero fill character to print the value after the comma. This makes 1012 print correctly as 1,012. However, what would be printed if the number were just 12? An even bigger problem occurs if we try to format a small negative number. Can you see what the problems are? If not, code the problem and run it to see. We will explain how to handle these problems in the next chapter.

Print Tuition for Strange College

For our next example, we write a program that calculates and prints the annual tuition for a student enrolled in "Strange College." In this college, students can take an unlimited number of units each term. Each term, the students will be charged $10 per unit plus a $10 registration fee. To discourage students from overloading their schedules, the college charges $50 extra for each 12 units, or fraction thereof, a student takes after the first 12 units. For example, if a student takes 13 units, the tuition will be $190 ($10 for registration, plus 13 times $10 for units, plus a $50 penalty for the one extra unit). If a student takes 25 units, the tuition will be $360 ($10 for registration, plus 25 times $10 for units, plus $100 for two penalty fees). The design for this problem is shown in Figure 4-13.

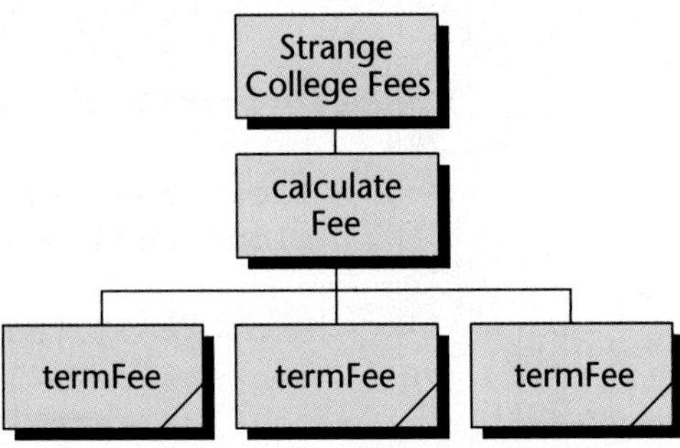

Figure 4-13 **Design for Strange College fees**

The implementation is shown in Program 4-7.

Program 4-7 **Strange College fees**

```
/* This program prints the tuition at Strange College.
   Strange charges $10 for registration, plus $10 per
   unit and a penalty of $50 for each 12 units, or
   fraction of 12, over 12.
      Written by:
      Date:
*/
#include <iostream>
using namespace std;

const int regFee    = 10;
const int unitFee   = 10;
const int excessFee = 50;

```

Program 4-7 **Strange College fees *(continued)***

```
// Prototype Declarations
int calculateFee (int firstTerm,
                  int secondTerm,
                  int thirdTerm);
int termFee (int units);

int main ()
{

   cout << "Enter units for first term:  ";
   int  firstTerm;
   cin  >> firstTerm;

   cout << "Enter units for second term: ";
   int  secondTerm;
   cin  >> secondTerm;

   cout << "Enter units for third term:  ";
   int  thirdTerm;
   cin  >> thirdTerm;

   int  totalFee;
   totalFee = calculateFee
                (firstTerm, secondTerm, thirdTerm);
   cout << "\nThe total tuition is :\t" << totalFee;

   return 0;
} // main
/* =============== calculateFee ================
   Calculate the total fees for the year.
      Pre  The number of units to be taken each term
      Post Returns the annual fees
*/
int calculateFee (int firstTerm,
                  int secondTerm,
                  int thirdTerm)
{
   int fee = termFee (firstTerm)
           + termFee (secondTerm)
           + termFee (thirdTerm);
   return fee;
} // calculateFee

/* ================= termFee =================
   Calculate the tuition for one term.
   Pre units contains units to be taken in the term
   Post The fee is calculated and returned
*/
int termFee (int units)
```

Program 4-7 Strange College fees *(continued)*

```
{
   int totalFees = regFee
            + ((units - 1) / 12 * excessFee)
            +  (units * unitFee);
   return (totalFees);
} // termFee
```

```
Results:
Enter units for first term:  10
Enter units for second term: 20
Enter units for third term:  30

The total tuition is :  780
```

Program 4-7 Analysis The most interesting aspect of this program is how we call `termFee` three different times in one function. Let's look at how it works. The key statement is shown below.

```
fee = termFee (firstTerm)
    + termFee (secondTerm)
    + termFee (thirdTerm);
```

A function call is a postfix expression, so it evaluates from the left. To evaluate the expression (three function calls) on the right of the assignment operator, we first evaluate the first expression, the call to `termFee` with the number of units for the first term. When `termFee` completes the first time, the return value (110) replaces the call. At this point, we have the expression shown below.

```
110 + termFee (secondTerm) + termFee (thirdTerm)
```

When `termFee` is executed a second time, its return value (260) becomes the value of the second expression, and we have

```
110 + 260 + termFee (thirdTerm)
```

After the third call to `termFee`, the expression on the right of the assignment operator is ready for evaluation. Its value is 780, which is assigned to `fee`.

At least two more tests are required to completely evaluate this program. We would run the program with all three terms having zero units and then do another test of 11, 12, and 13 units.

PARAMETER PASSING

Now that you have seen how function parameters work, let's look more closely at how parameters are passed.

Pass by Value

In all the examples up to this point, we have passed data values to the called functions. When you pass by value, a copy of the data is created and placed in a local variable in the called function. This means of passing data ensures that regardless of how the data are manipulated and changed in the called function, the original data in the calling function are safe and unchanged. Because passing the value protects the data in the calling function, it should be used as the general rule when the data are not be to changed. This is demonstrated in Figure 4-14. Even after the call to `fun`, the value of `a` is unchanged.

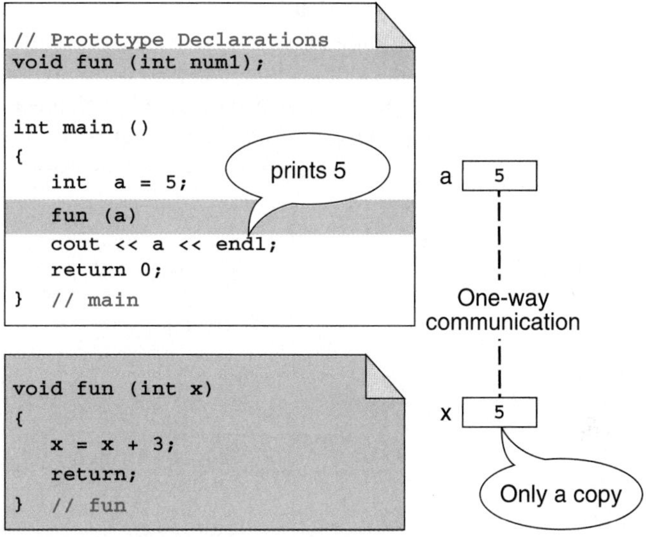

Figure 4-14 Pass by value

Pass by Reference

There are times, however, when it is necessary to pass by reference. Pass by reference sends the address of a variable to the called function rather than sending its value. For example, when we want to change the contents in a variable in the calling function, we must pass by reference.

Consider the case in which we need to write a function that processes two data values and "returns" them to the calling function; that is, it stores their values in the calling function. Since a function can return only one value, we have a problem. The solution is pass by reference. To pass by reference, we use the **address operator** (&) in the parameter definition of the called function. The address operator simply tells the compiler that parameter name is an *alias* for the variable name in the calling function. Any time we refer to the parameter, therefore, we are actually referring to the original variable. The address operator is a unary operator, which has a priority of 15 in the preference table.

Let's look at a program that uses pass by reference. One common process that occurs often in programming is exchanging two pieces of data. We can write a function that, given two integer variables, exchanges them. Since two variables are being changed, we cannot use the return statement. Instead, we use pass by reference.

First, let's make sure we understand how to exchange two variables. You cannot simply assign them to each other as shown below.

```
x = y;          // This won't work.
y = x;          // Result is y in both.
```

If you carefully trace these two statements, you will see that the original value of y ends up in both variables. To exchange variables, you must create a temporary variable to hold the first value while the exchange is being made.

The correct logic is shown next.

```
hold = y;       // value of y saved
y    = x;       // x now in y
x    = hold;    // original y now in x
```

The exchange function and its data flow are shown in Figure 4-15. Examine the prototype declaration in Figure 4-15 carefully. Note that there is an ampersand in the declaration of `num1` and `num2`. The ampersand is used with the type declaration to specify that the function uses pass by reference. Since we will be changing the values of `a` and `b` in *main*, we need to pass by reference. The address operators (&) tell the compiler that the program is passing by reference, not by value.

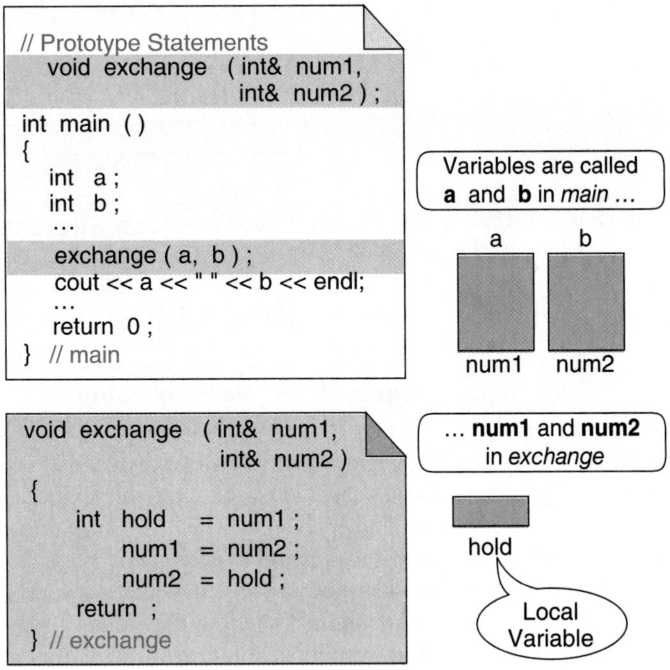

```
// Prototype Statements
   void exchange  ( int& num1,
                          int& num2 ) ;
int main ( )
{
   int  a ;
   int  b ;
   ...
   exchange ( a,  b ) ;
   cout << a << " " << b << endl;
   ...
   return  0 ;
}  // main
```

Variables are called **a** and **b** in *main* ...

a b

num1 num2

```
void exchange  ( int& num1,
                       int& num2 )
{
      int  hold    = num1 ;
           num1  = num2 ;
           num2  = hold ;
      return  ;
} // exchange
```

... **num1** and **num2** in *exchange*

hold

Local Variable

Figure 4-15 Pass by reference

Now, look at the statements in `exchange`. The first thing we do is to copy `num1's` value to `hold`. Hold is a local variable; anything done to it has no effect on the variables in *main*. When we assign `num2` to `num1`, however, the value of the variable in *main* is actually changed. Then, when we assign `hold` to `num2`, the value of the second variable in *main* is also changed, completing the exchange of the two values.

Note that with the exception of `hold`, all of the data movement is being done in the calling program's area. This is the power of pass by reference.

Now, let's look at what happens if you don't pass by reference. This situation is illustrated in Figure 4-16. As you study the figure, note that rather than having one common set of work areas with two sets of names (`a` and `num1`, `b` and `num2`), there are four completely separate variables (`a` and `b` in *main* and `num1` and `num2` in `exchange`). Because in this case we chose to pass by value (there are no address operators in exchange's parameter declarations), copies of the data are sent to `exchange`. Exchange does its job perfectly, but there is no change in the original values in *main*; `a` and `b` are unchanged.

Here is another simple example, one that uses both pass by value and pass by reference parameters. Imagine that we need to write a function that, given two numbers, calculates both the quotient and the remainder. Since we can't return two values, we use pass by reference for the quotient and remainder. Figure 4-17 shows this problem.

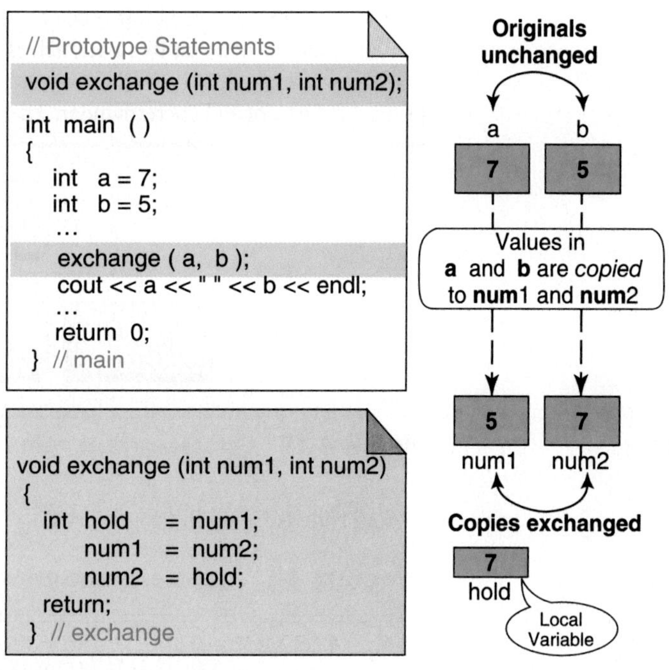

Figure 4-16 A bad exchange

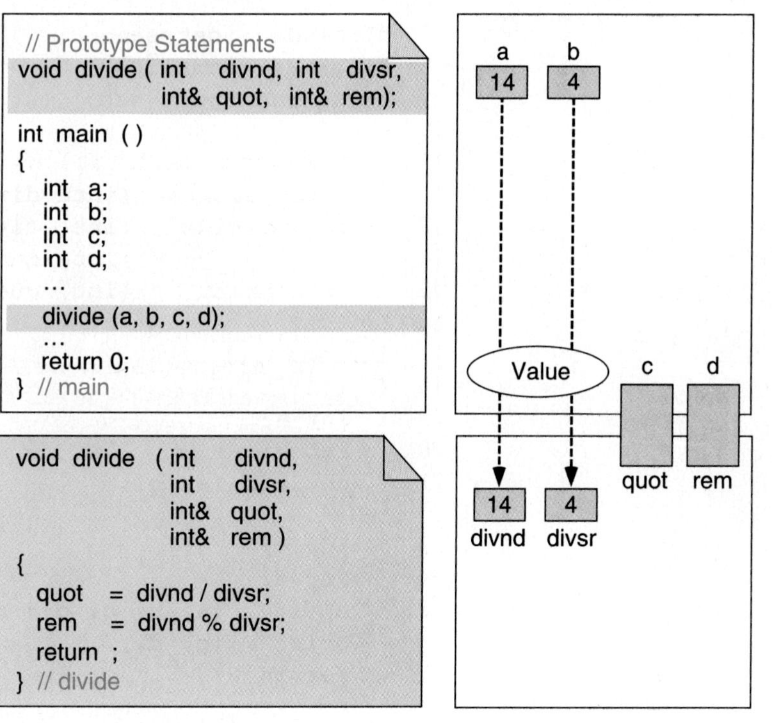

Figure 4-17 Calculate quotient and remainder—concept

Let's examine `divide` first. Note that the first two parameters are pass by value. You can tell this because their types are just *int*; there are no ampersands indicating that they are aliases. The last two parameters are passed by reference.

Now we'll use `divide` in a program that reads two integers, divides them, and then prints the quotient and the remainder. The design for this program is shown in Figure 4-18.

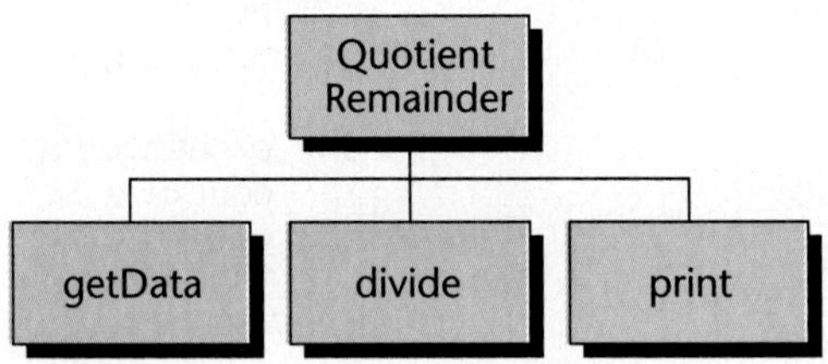

Figure 4-18 Quotient and remainder design

The code is found in Program 4-8.

Program 4-8 Quotient and remainder

```
/* This program reads two integers and then prints the
   quotient and remainder of the first number divided
   by the second.
      Written by:
      Date:
*/
#include <iostream>
#include <iomanip>
using namespace std;

// Prototype Declarations
   void getData   (int& divnd, int& divsr);
   void divide    (int  divnd, int  divsr,
                    int& quot,  int& rem);
   void print     (int  quot,  int  rem);

int main ()
{
   int a;
   int b;
   getData (a, b);

   int c;
   int d;
   divide  (a, b, c, d);
   print   (c, d);
   return 0;
} // main
/* ============== getData ==============
   This function reads two numbers into variables
```

Program 4-8 Quotient and remainder *(continued)*

```
31        specified in the parameter list.
32           Pre     Nothing
33           Post    Data read and placed in calling function
34     */
35     void getData (int& divnd, int& divsr)
36     {
37        cout << "Enter two integers and return: ";
38        cin  >> divnd >> divsr;
39        return;
40     }  // getData
41     /* =============== divide ===============
42        This function divides two integers and places the
43        quotient/remainder in calling program variables.
44           Pre    dividend & divisor contain integer values
45           Post   quotient & remainder calc'd
46     */
47     void divide (int  divnd, int  divsr,
48                  int& quot,  int& rem)
49     {
50        quot    = divnd / divsr;
51        rem     = divnd % divsr;
52        return;
53     }  // divide
54     /* ===================== print =====================
55        This function prints the quotient and the remainder.
56           Pre     quot contains the quotient
57                   rem contains the remainder
58           Post    Quotient and remainder printed
59     */
60     void print (int quot, int rem)
61     {
62        cout << "Quotient : ";
63        cout << setw(3) << quot << endl;
64        cout << "Remainder: ";
65        cout << setw(3) << rem << endl;
66        return;
67     }  // print
```

Program 4-8 Analysis First look at the design of this program. Note how *main* contains only calls to subfunctions. It does no work itself; like a good manager, it delegates all work to lower levels in the program. Keep this principle in mind when you design your own programs.

Study the `getData` function carefully. First note that the parameters identify the variables as aliases; that is, we use pass by reference.

Now study the way we use `quotient` and `remainder` in `divide`. In statement 25, we pass them by reference. Since we are passing by reference, we can change their values in *main.* In the function definition, the formal parameters indicate that `quot` and `rem` are aliases for integer types by coding the type as *int&* (see statement 48). When we refer to `quot` in `divide`, we are therefore actually referring to `c` in *main*. Likewise, when we refer to `rem` in `divide`, we are actually referring to `d` in *main*.

4-4 DEFAULT PARAMETER ARGUMENTS

C++ provides the capability to define **default values** for parameters. When a function with default values is called and one or more default arguments are missing, the default values are used just as though they had been passed. The default values are used just like any other initializer except that they are used only when the parameters are missing.

Default parameters must be declared before the function is called. If they are not, the compiler will not recognize that they are available and will flag the call as a compile error. For this reason, they are coded in the prototype declaration.[3] Also, coding the default parameters in the prototype statement provides more complete documentation for the function.

Program 4-9 demonstrates the use of default parameter arguments.

Program 4-9 Demonstrate default arguments

```
/* Demonstrate use of parameter default.
      Written by:
      Date:
*/
#include <iostream>
using namespace std;

// Prototype Declarations
   void printInt (int num = 0);      //Note default to 0

int main ()
{
   // Demonstrate default parameter
   cout << "Calling with no parameter\n";
   printInt ();

   // Demonstrate parameter value passed
   cout << "\nCalling with parameter 5\n";
   printInt (5);
   return 0;
} // main
/* ============== printInt ==============
   Prints integer value.
      Pre  Nothing
      Post Either 0 or parameter value printed
*/
```

[3] If the function definition is found in the source code before the function call, then the default values can be placed in the function definition. Because we highly recommend that prototype declarations always be used, however, we recommend that the defaults be placed in the prototype declarations.

Program 4-9 Demonstrate default arguments *(continued)*

```
void printInt (int num)
{
   cout << "Parameter value is: " << num << endl;
   return;
} // printInt
```

```
Results
Calling with no parameter
Parameter value is: 0

Calling with parameter 5
Parameter value is: 5
```

There are three rules that you must observe when using default parameters.

1. The default value for the parameters can be given only once, either in the prototype declaration (the preferred method) or in the function definition.
2. If some parameters have defaults and some don't, then the default parameters must be declared last.
3. When calling a function, if a parameter argument is supplied, then all preceding parameters must also have parameters. For example, when using the prototype definition below, you cannot pass a value for `d` unless parameters `a`, `b`, and `c` **all** have values.

```
void fun (int a, int b = 0, int c = 1, int d = 2);
```

4-5 STANDARD LIBRARY FUNCTIONS

There are many standard functions whose definitions have been written and are ready to be used in our programs. To use them, we must include their prototype declarations. The prototypes for these functions are grouped together and collected in several header files. Therefore, instead of adding the individual prototypes of each function in a program, we simply include the header files at the beginning of the program. Appendix F, "Function Prototypes," contains the prototype declarations for most standard library functions.

Figure 4-19 shows how two of the **C++ standard library** functions that we have used several times are brought into the program. The *include* statement causes the library header file for standard input and output (*iostream*) to be copied into the program. In the header file are the declarations for *cin* and *cout.* Then, when the program is linked, the object code for these functions is combined with the application code to build the complete program.

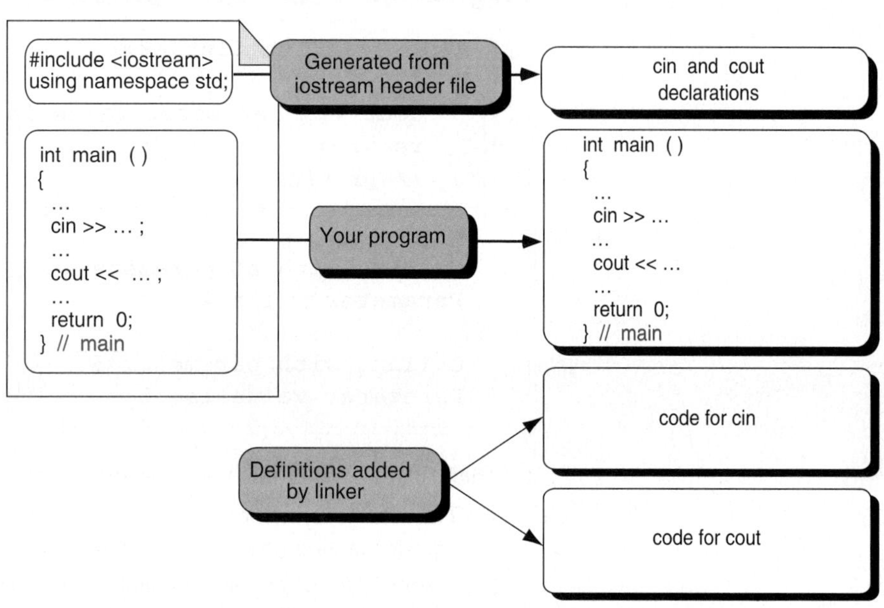

Figure 4-19 Library functions and the linker

STANDARD FUNCTIONS FOR MATHEMATICAL MANIPULATION

Many important library functions are available for mathematical calculations. Most of the prototypes for these functions are in a header file called <*cmath*>. Two of them, *abs* and *labs*, are found in <*cstdlib*>.

abs/fabs/labs

These functions return the absolute value of a number. An absolute value is the positive rendering of the value, regardless of its sign. For ***abs***, the parameter must be an integer, and it returns an integer. For ***labs***, the parameter must be a long integer, and it returns a long integer. For ***fabs***, the parameter is a double, and it returns a double. (The *f* stands for float, even though the type is double.)

The prototype declarations for these three functions are shown below. The *abs* and *labs* functions are found in <*cstdlib*>. The *fabs* function is found in <*cmath*>.

```
int     abs   (int        number);
long    labs  (long       number);
double  fabs  (double     number);
```

Examples:

```
abs  (3)       → returns 3
fabs (-3.4)    → returns 3.4
```

ceil

A **ceiling** is the smallest integral value greater than or equal to a number. For example, the ceiling of 3.0000001 is 4. If we consider all numbers as a continuous range from minus infinity to plus infinity (see Figure 4-20), this function moves the number right to an integer value.

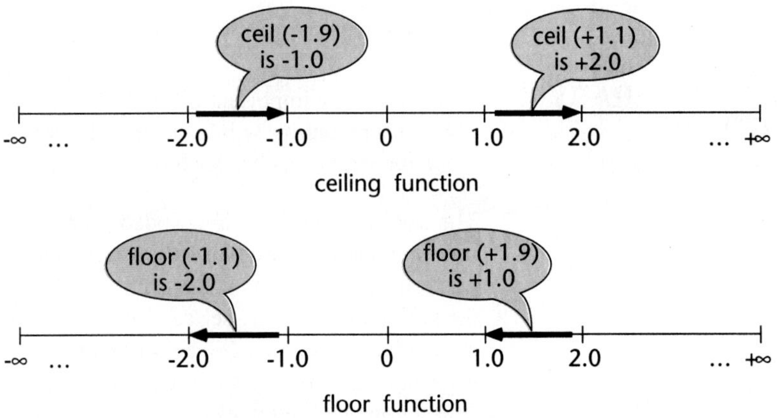

Figure 4-20 Floor and ceiling functions

Although the ceiling function (***ceil***) returns an integral value, note that the return type is *double*. The ceiling prototype is

```
double ceil (double number);
```

Examples:

```
ceil (-1.9)     → returns -1.0
ceil ( 1.1)     → returns  2.0
```

floor

A **floor** is the largest integral value that is equal to or less than a number (see Figure 4-20). For example, the floor of 3.99999 is 3.0. Again, looking at numbers as a continuum, this function moves the number left to an integer value. Its prototype is

```
double floor (double number);
```

Examples:

```
floor (-1.1)    → returns -2.0
floor ( 1.9)    → returns  1.0
```

pow

The ***pow*** function returns the value of the x raised to the power y—that is, x^y. An error occurs if the base (x) is negative and the exponent (y) is not an integer, or if the base is zero and the exponent is not positive. The power prototype is

```
double pow ( double x, double y );
```

Examples:

```
pow (3.0, 4.0)         → returns 81.0
pow (3.4, 2.3)         → returns 16.687893
```

sqrt

The ***sqrt*** function returns the non-negative square root of `number`. An error occurs if `number` is negative. The square root prototype is

```
double sqrt (double number);
```

Example:

```
sqrt (25.0) → returns 5.0
```

GENERAL LIBRARY FUNCTIONS

There are many important general library functions available in C++. We mention two of them here that we will be using in future chapters. The prototypes for these functions are in the <*cstdlib*> header file.

srand

The seed random function, coded ***srand***, creates the first seed for a **pseudorandom number** series. A pseudorandom series is a repeatable series of numbers with random properties. The seed is the variable used by the random number generator to calculate the next number in the series. Each seed produces a different series when the random number generator (*rand*—see following discussion) is called. Note that as each number is generated, it becomes the seed for the next number in the series. Figure 4-21 demonstrates how the seed works.

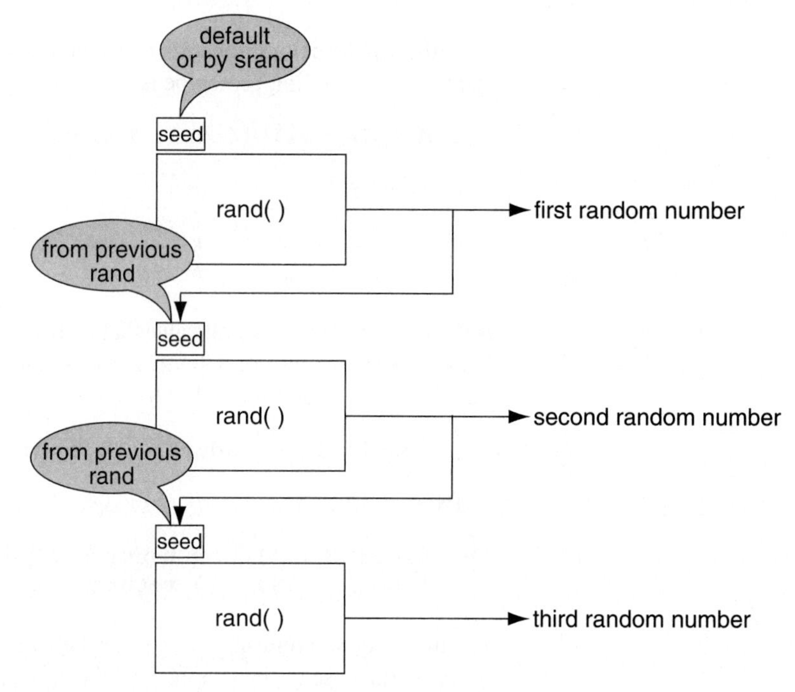

Figure 4-21 The random number seed

To generate a truly random number series, therefore, the seed must be a random number. The most common technique for generating a random number is to use a seed that is a function of the current date or time of day.

The seed random prototype is

```
void srand (unsigned int seed);
```

Example: To generate random numbers, use the call below before your first call to *rand*. (The time requires the <*ctime*> header file.)

```
srand (time (NULL));
```

To generate a pseudorandom number series, seed random is called with a constant, preferably a large prime number.

```
srand (997);
```

Whichever series you want, *srand* should be *called only once* in your program. Program 4-10 uses *srand* to demonstrate three different random number series. (The explanation of the *rand* function that appears after Program 4-8 will help you fully understand the program.)

Program 4-10 Demonstrate random number series

```
/* Demonstrates the use of srand to generate random numbers
    in different series. The user is asked to input a seed,and
   the program then generates four random numbers. The process
   is repeated three times.
       Written by:
       Date:
*/
#include <iostream>
#include <cstdlib>
using namespace std;

int main ()
{
   cout << "Enter random number seed:  ";
   int seed;
   cin  >> seed;
   srand ( seed );

   cout << "Random numbers with seed   " << seed << ": "
         << rand () << " " << rand () << " "
         << rand () << " " << rand ()  << endl << endl;

   cout << "Enter another random seed:  ";
   cin  >> seed;
   srand ( seed );

   cout << "Random numbers with seed   " << seed << ": "
         << rand () << " " << rand () << " "
         << rand () << " " << rand ()  << endl << endl;
```

Program 4-10 Demonstrate random number series *(continued)*

```

    cout << "Enter another random seed:   ";
    cin  >> seed;
    srand ( seed );

    cout << "Random numbers with seed   " << seed << ": "
         << rand () << " " << rand () << " "
         << rand () << " " << rand ()  << endl << endl;

    cout << "Hope you found these numbers interesting.\n";
    return 0;
} // main
```

```
Enter random number seed:  255
Random numbers with seed   255: 28381 9283 13267 1160

Enter another random seed: 511
Random numbers with seed   511: 30044 8703 22126 19158

Enter another random seed: 997
Random numbers with seed   997: 21937 4276 22303 10575

Hope you found these numbers interesting.
```

rand

The ***rand*** function returns a pseudorandom integer between 0 and **RAND_MAX**, which is defined in the standard library as the largest number that *rand* can generate. The C++ standard requires that it be at least 32,767. Each call generates the next number in a random number series.

The random number prototype is

```
int rand (void);
```

If *srand* is not called before the first call to *rand*, the series will be based on the seed 1, and the same series of numbers will always be generated.

SCALING RANDOM NUMBERS

Often you will want to generate a series of numbers in a narrower range than that provided by the standard library. To create your own range, you must scale and shift, if necessary, what is returned from *rand.* The **scaling** is done by the modulus operator. For example, to produce a random number in the range 0 … 50, you simply scale the random number as shown below.

```
rand ( ) % 51
```

Modulus works well when your range starts at 0. But what if you need a different range? In that case, you must shift the result. For example, suppose you want a random number between 3 and 7 (see Figure 4-22). If you call *rand* and then use modulus 8, your range will be 0 through 7. To convert to the correct range, you first determine your modulus factor by subtracting the starting point (3) from the modulus divisor (8) and then adding the starting point to the resulting number. Thus, for our example, we subtract 3 from 8, which makes the modulus divisor 5.

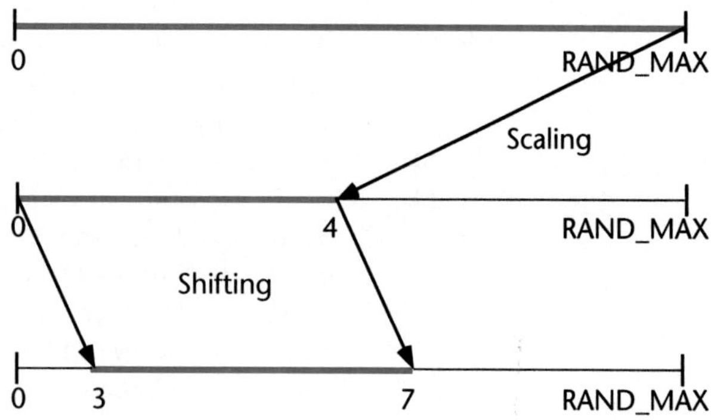

Figure 4-22 Random number scaling for 3-7

Generalizing the algorithm, we get

```
rand ( ) % ( ( max + 1) - min ) + min
```

where *min* is the minimum number and *max* is the maximum number in the desired range. Of course, if a range starting at zero is desired, then the minimum value (min) is zero and therefore ignored. For example, to create a random number in the range 20 to 30, we would use the expression shown below.

```
rand() % ((30 + 1) - 20) + 20 => rand() % 11 + 20
```

Program 4-11 demonstrates the generation of random numbers.

Program 4-11 Scaling for random number generation

```
/* Demonstrates the generation of random numbers in
   three different ranges:
       03 through 07
       20 through 50
       -6 through 15
   After generating three numbers, it prints them.
   The seed for the series is 997, which is set by srand.
      Written by:
      Date:
*/
#include <iostream>
#include <iomanip>
#include <cstdlib>
using namespace std;

int main ()
{
   srand (997);
   // range is 3 through 7
   int a = rand () % 5 + 3;                      // 8 - 3 = 5
```

Program 4-11 Scaling for random number generation *(continued)*

```
    // range is 20 through 50
    int b = rand () % 31 + 20;          // 51 - 20 = 31
    // range is -6 through 15
    int c = rand () % 22 - 6;         // 16 - (-6) = 22

    cout << "Range  3 to  7: ";
    cout << setw(3) << a << endl;
    cout << "Range 20 to 50: ";
    cout << setw(3) << b << endl;
    cout << "Range -6 to 15: ";
    cout << setw(3) << c << endl;

    return 0;
 } // main
```

```
Results:
Range  3 to  7:   5
Range 20 to 50:  27
Range -6 to 15:  -2
```

Program 4-11 Analysis Note that we have used *srand* to generate pseudorandom numbers. The seed we used, 997, is a prime number. Generally speaking, prime numbers generate better random number series than do nonprime numbers. However, the fact that we used a particular seed does not guarantee that we would get the same results if we ran the program on a different computer using that same seed. It only guarantees that when the program is run repetitively on the same computer, the same set of random numbers will be generated. Given the same seed, different compilers may generate different random series depending on each one's random number algorithm.

4-6 SCOPE

GENERAL RULE

Scope determines the region of the program in which a defined object is *visible*; that is, the part of the program in which you can use its name. Scope pertains to any object that can be defined, such as a variable or a function prototype declaration. It does not pertain directly to precompiler directives, such as define statements—they have separate rules. Scope is a source program concept: It has no direct bearing on the run-time program.

To discuss the concept of scope, we need to review two concepts. A **block** is one or more statements enclosed in a set of braces. Recall that a function's body is enclosed in a set of braces; thus, a body is also a block. A block contains declarations and statements. This concept gives us the ability to nest blocks within the body of a function and have each one be an independent group of statements with its own isolated definitions.

The global area of your program consists of all statements that are outside functions. Figure 4-23 provides a graphical representation of the concept of global area and blocks.

An object's scope extends from where it is declared until the end of its block. A variable is said to be in scope if it is visible to the statement being examined. Variables are in scope from their point of declaration until the end of their function or block.

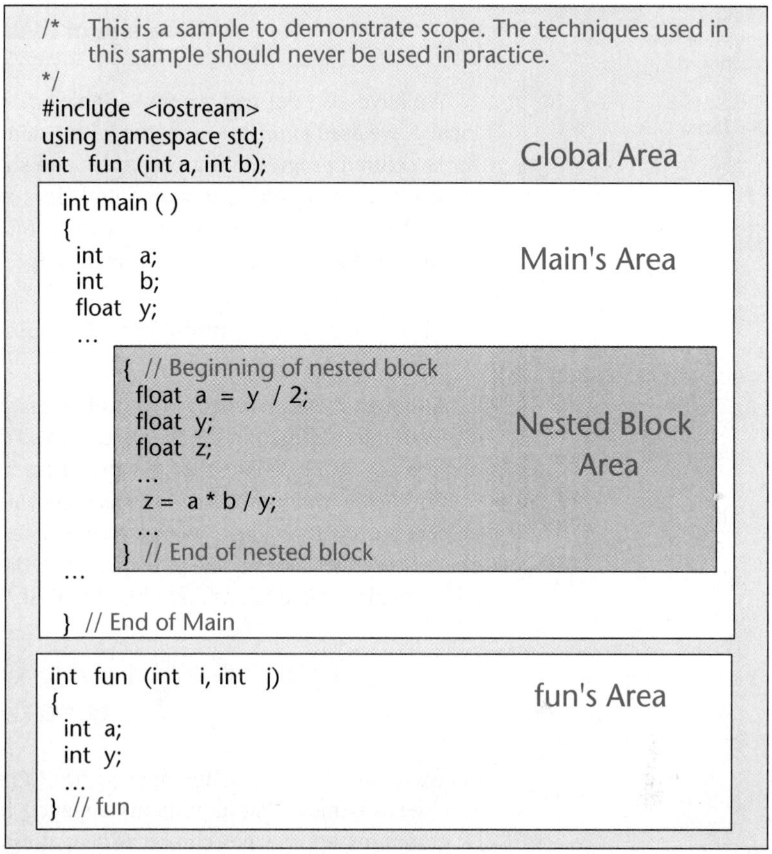

```
/*  This is a sample to demonstrate scope. The techniques used in
    this sample should never be used in practice.
*/
#include <iostream>
using namespace std;
int  fun  (int a, int b);                          Global Area

 int main ( )
 {                                                 Main's Area
  int    a;
  int    b;
  float  y;
  ...
          { // Beginning of nested block
           float  a = y / 2;
           float  y;                               Nested Block
           float  z;                                   Area
           ...
            z =  a * b / y;
           ...
          } // End of nested block
  ...
 } // End of Main

 int  fun  (int   i, int   j)
 {                                                 fun's Area
  int  a;
  int  y;
  ...
 } // fun
```

Figure 4-23 Scope for global and block areas

GLOBAL SCOPE

The global scope is easily defined. Any object defined in the global area of a program is visible from its definition until the end of the program. Referring to Figure 4-23, the prototype declaration for `fun` is a global definition because it is visible everywhere in the program.

LOCAL SCOPE

Variables defined within a block have local scope. They exist only from the point of their declaration until the end of the block (usually a function) in which they are declared. Outside the block they are invisible.

In Figure 4-23, we see two blocks in *main*. The first block is all of *main*. Since the nested block is contained in *main*, all definitions in *main* are visible to the nested block unless local variables with an identical name are defined. In the nested block, a local version of `a` has been defined; its type is float. Under these circumstances, the integer variable `a` in *main* is visible from its declaration until the declaration of the float variable `a` in the nested block. At that point, *main*'s `a` can no longer be referenced in the nested block. Any statement in the block that references `a` will get the float version. At the end of the nested block, the float `a` is no longer in scope and the integer `a` becomes visible again.

Variables are in scope from their point of definition until the end of their function or block.

We have also defined a new variable `y`. Note, however, that before we defined the local `y`, we used *main*'s `y` to set the initial value for `a`. Although this is flagrant disregard for structured programming principles and should never be used in practice, it demonstrates that a variable is in scope until it is redefined. Immediately after using `y`, we defined the local version, so *main*'s version of `y` is no longer available. Since the variable `b` is not redeclared in the block, it is in scope throughout the entire block.

It is poor programming style to reuse identifiers within the same scope.

Although *main*'s variables are visible inside the nested block, the reverse is not true. The variables defined in the block, `a`, `y`, and `z`, exist only for the duration of the block and are no longer visible after the end of the block.

Within the function `fun`, which is coded after *main*, only its variables and any global objects are visible. Thus, we are free to use any names we want. In Figure 4-23, we chose to use the names `a` and `y`, even though they had been used in *main*. This is an acceptable practice; there is nothing wrong with it.

Procedural and Object-Oriented Programming

There are two contrasting approaches to programs in use today: procedural and object-oriented. The arguments engaged in by the advocates of these two programming approaches can be as heated as arguments about religion and politics. Our position is that the differences are more in the approach to the problem than in the solution. Supporting this is the fact that C++ can be used to write either a procedural program or an object-oriented program.

The primary difference between the two approaches is their use of data. In a **procedural program**, the design centers around the rules or procedures for processing the data. The procedures, implemented as functions in C++, are the focus of the design. The data objects are passed to the functions as parameters. The key question is how the functions will transform the data they receive for either storage or further processing. Procedural programming has been the mainstay of computer science since its beginning and is still heavily used today.

In an **object-oriented program**, abbreviated OOP, the design centers around objects that contain (encapsulate) the data and the necessary functions to process the data. In OOP, the objects own the functions that process the data. The key question here is what the characteristics of the object to be processed are. To complicate matters more, OOP refers to the data as the **state** of the object and to the functions as **methods**.

Note the similarities between the implementation of these two approaches. Both use C++. Both build functions to process the data. And, in fact, both can and do use objects in the implementation. As we said above, the primary difference is in the design approach, which either emphasizes the process or the object.

Let's look at two examples to illustrate the difference. In the traditional operating systems, such as UNIX and DOS, the code is procedurally oriented. For example, the program to copy a file looks at the file as external data to be read and written. The procedure is what is important. The UNIX command to invoke the copy is entered as shown below.

```
cp file1  file2
```

The object-oriented environment is typically found in a **graphical user interface** (GUI), as found in a windows-oriented operating system. In our copy file example, the object is a file. To copy the file, we first select it with a mouse and then from a menu select the copy file option. In this case, the file object is what is important.

While the differences between these two examples are subtle, they are critical. The center of the procedural approach is the process—copy. The center of the object-oriented approach is the object—file.

4-7 A PROGRAMMING EXAMPLE—CALCULATOR PROGRAM

We have written a program that asks the user to input two numbers, then calls one function that adds the numbers and another function that subtracts them. The program concludes by displaying the sum and difference of the two numbers. The pseudocode for this program is shown in Algorithm 4-1.

Algorithm 4-1 Pseudocode for calculator program

```
Prompt and Read x and y
sum   = add (x, y)
diff  = subtract (x, y)
print sum, diff
```

The complete code used to implement this program is shown in Program 4-12.

Program 4-12 Calculator program

```
/* This program adds and subtracts two integers read
   from the keyboard.
      Written by:
      Date:
*/
#include <iostream>
#include <iomanip>
using namespace std;

// Prototype Declarations
   int add  (int a, int b);
   int subt (int a, int b);

int main ()
{
```

Program 4-12 Calculator program *(continued)*

```
   // Prompt user for input and get data
   cout << "\nPlease enter two integer numbers: ";

   // Read numbers into a and b
   int a;
   int b;
   cin  >> a >> b;

   // Calculate the sum and difference
   int sum  = add  (a, b);
   int diff = subt (a, b);

   cout << setw(4) << a <<
        " + "  << setw(4) << b <<
        " = "  << setw(4) << sum << endl;


   cout << setw(4) << a
        << " - "  << setw(4) << b
        << " = "  << setw(4) << diff << endl;

   // Close program
   cout << "\nThank you for using my calculator\n";
   return 0;
} // main
/* ===================== add =====================
   This function adds two integers and returns the sum.
      Pre  Parameters a and b
      Post Returns a + b
*/
int add (int a, int b)
{
   return (a + b);
} // add
/* =================== subt ====================
   Return the difference of two integers
      Pre   Parameters a and b
      Post  Returns a - b
*/
int subt (int a, int b)
{
   return (a - b);
} // subt
```

```
Results:
Please enter two integer numbers: 5 10
   5 +   10 =   15
   5 -   10 =   -5

Thank you for using my calculator
```

4-8 SOFTWARE ENGINEERING AND PROGRAMMING STYLE

In this section we discuss three different but related aspects of software engineering design: the structure chart, functional cohesion, and top-down development.

STRUCTURE CHARTS

The structure chart is the primary design tool for a program. As a design tool, it is used before a programmer starts writing a program. An analogy will help you understand the importance of designing before you start coding.

Assume that you have decided to build a house. You will spend a lot of time thinking about exactly what you want. How many rooms will it need? Do you want a family room or a great room? Should the laundry be inside the house or in the garage? To make sure everyone understands what you want, you will prepare formal blueprints that describe everything in detail. Even if you are building something small, like a dollhouse for a child or a toolshed for your backyard, you will make some sketches or plans.

Figuring out what you want in your house is comparable to determining the requirements for a large system. A set of building blueprints parallels the structure chart used in the design of a program. Both require advance planning; only the level of detail changes.

Professionals use the structure chart for another purpose, as mentioned in Chapter 1. In a project team environment, before you start writing your program you must have your design reviewed. This review process is called a structured walk-through. The review team consists of the systems analyst responsible for your area of the project, a representative of the user community, a system test engineer, and one or two programmers from the project.

The design walk-through serves three purposes: First, it ensures that you understand how your program fits into the system by communicating your design to the team. If there are any omissions or communication errors, they should be detected at this point. If you invite programmers who must interface with your program, it will also ensure that the inter-program communication linkages are correct.

Second, it validates your design. In creating your design, you will have considered several alternative approaches to writing your program. The review team will expect to see and understand the different designs you considered and hear why you chose the design you are proposing. They will challenge aspects of the design and suggest approaches you may not have considered. Ideally, the result of the review will be the best possible design.

Finally, it gives the test engineer the opportunity to assess the **testability** of your program. This, in turn, ensures that the final program will be robust and as error-free as possible.

STRUCTURE CHART RULES AND SYMBOLS

Figure 4-24 shows the various symbols that you can use to write a structure chart. All symbols are included here for completeness; however, we will discuss only the two shaded symbols. The others will be discussed in later chapters. In addition to the symbols, we will discuss several rules that you should follow when creating a structure chart.

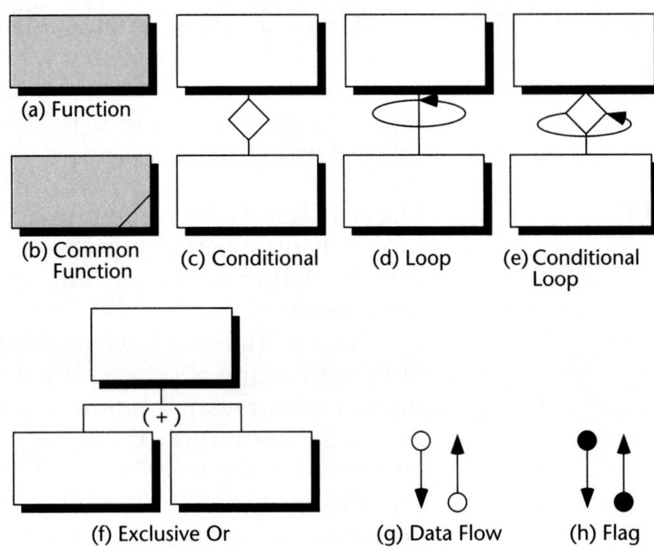

Figure 4-24 Structure chart symbols

Function Symbol

Each rectangle in a structure chart (see Figure 4-25) represents a function *that you write*. Functions found in the standard C++ libraries are not shown. The name in the rectangle is the name you will give to the function when you write the program. It should be meaningful. The software engineering principle known as *intelligent names* states that the names used in a program should be self-documenting; that is, they should convey their intended usage to the reader. Intelligent names should be used both for functions and for data names within your program.

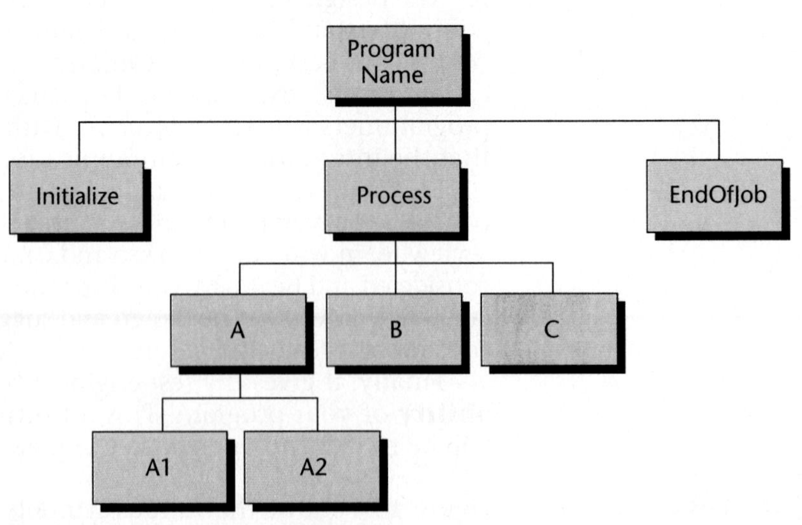

Figure 4-25 Structure chart design

Now that we have explained that all names should be descriptive, we are going to break our own rule because we want to concentrate on the format of a structure chart rather than a particular program. The names in Figure 4-25 have been selected to identify the various modules for discussion.

Reading Structure Charts

Structure charts are read *top-down,* from *left to right.* In Figure 4-25, Program Name *(main)* consists of three subfunctions: `Initialize`, `Process`, and `EndOfJob`. According to the left-right rule, the first call in the program is `Initialize`. After `Initialize` is complete, the program calls `Process`. When `Process` is complete, the program calls `EndOfJob`. In other words, the functions on the same level of a structure chart are called in order from the left to the right.

The concept of top-down is demonstrated by `Process`. When `Process` is called, it calls `A`, `B`, and `C` in turn. Function `B` does not start running, however, until `A` is finished. While `A` is running, it calls `A1` and `A2` in turn. In other words, all functions in a line from `Process` to `A2` must be called before Function `B` can start.

At this point, it is helpful to discuss the next rule of structure charts: No code is contained in a structure chart. A structure chart shows only the function flow through the program. It is not a block diagram or a flowchart. As a map of your program, the structure chart shows only the logical flow of the functions. Exactly how each function does its job is shown by its algorithm design (flowchart or pseudocode). Another way of looking at it is that a structure chart shows the big picture; the details are left to algorithm design.

Structure charts show only function flow; they contain no code.

Often a program will contain several calls to a common function (Figure 4-24b). These calls are usually scattered throughout the program. The structure chart will show the call wherever it logically occurs in the program. A cross-hatch or shading in the lower right corner of a rectangle identifies a common structure. If the common function is complex and contains subfunctions, these subfunctions need to be shown only once. An indication that the incomplete references contain additional structure should be shown. This is usually done with a line below the function rectangle and a cut (~) symbol. This concept is illustrated in Figure 4-26, which uses a common function, `average`, in two different places in the program. Note, however, that you never graphically show a function connected to two calling functions.

It is not necessary to show **data flows** (Figure 4-24g) and **flags** (Figure 4-24h), although it may be helpful in certain circumstances. The data flows represent data passed to or returned from a function. Flags are a special type of data flow that represents events or conditions that have occurred in the program. They are often called **switches**. If they are shown, inputs are on the left of the vertical line, and outputs are on the right. When they are included, the name of the data or flag should also be indicated.

The rules described in this section are summarized in Table 4-1.

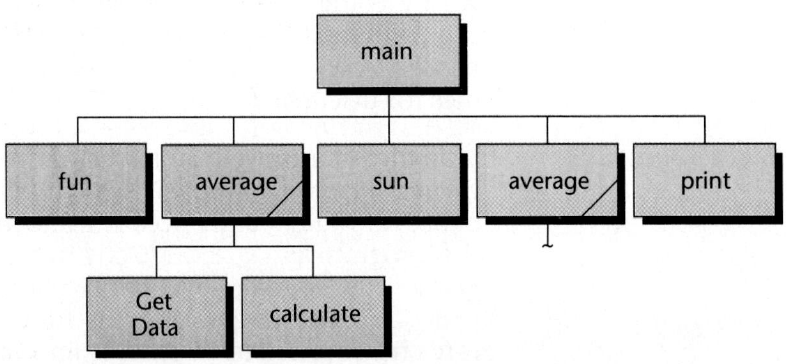

Figure 4-26 Common functions in a structure chart

1. Each rectangle in a structure chart represents a function written by the programmer. Standard C++ functions are not included.
2. The name in the rectangle is an intelligent name that communicates the purpose of the function. It is the name that will be used in the coding of the function.
3. The function chart contains only function flow. No code is indicated.
4. Common functions are indicated by a cross-hatch or shading in the lower right corner of the function rectangle.
5. Common calls are shown in a structure wherever they will be found in the program. If they contain subfunction calls, the complete structure need be shown only once.
6. Data flows and flags are optional. When used, they should be named.
7. Input flows and flags are shown on the left of the vertical line; output flows and flags are shown on the right.

Table 4-1 Structure chart rules

FUNCTIONAL COHESION

One of the most difficult structured programming concepts for new programmers is knowing when and how to create a function.

Functional cohesion is a measure of how closely the processes in a function are related. A function that does one and only one process is said to be "functionally cohesive." A function that contains totally unrelated processes is "coincidentally cohesive." We provide a few rules here to help you write cohesive functions. For a complete discussion of the topic, see Page-Jones.[4]

Before we discuss the rules, however, you should understand why the concept is important. There are three primary reasons for using structurally cohesive functions:

[4]Meilir Page-Jones, *The Practical Guide to Structured Systems Design,* 2nd ed. (Chap. 6). Englewood Cliffs, New Jersey: Prentice Hall, 1988.

1. **Correctness**: If you are concentrating on only one thing as you write a function, you will be less apt to make an error. It is much easier to get a simple task right than it is to complete a complex task error-free.
2. **Maintainability**: Production programs can live for years. The better a program's structuring, the easier it is to change. When programs are not well structured, making a change in one part of the program often leads to errors in other parts.
3. **Reusability**: Some processes are so common that they are found in many programs. Good programmers build libraries of these functions so they don't have to reinvent the function each time they want to use it. This not only leads to quicker program development but also reduces debugging time since the library functions have already been debugged.

Only One Thing

Each function should do only one thing. Furthermore, all of the statements in the function should contribute only to that one thing. For example, assume that you are writing a program that requires the statistical measures of average and standard deviation. The two statistical measures are obviously related, if for no other reason than that they are both measures of the same series of numbers. However, you would not calculate both measures in one function because that would be calculating two things, and each function should do only one thing.

One way to determine if your function is doing more than one thing is to count the number of *objects* that it handles. An object in this sense is anything that exists separately from the other elements of the function. In the previous example, the average and the standard deviation are two different objects.

> **Rule of Thumb**
> When a function has more than four parameters, check its cohesion.

As another example, if you were computing the taxes for a payroll program in the state of California, you would be dealing with FICA taxes, state disability insurance, state unemployment taxes, state withholding taxes, and federal withholding taxes. Each of these is a different object, so your design would group all of these taxes together in a function to calculate taxes and it would call subfunctions to calculate each individual tax. This design is seen in Figure 4-27.

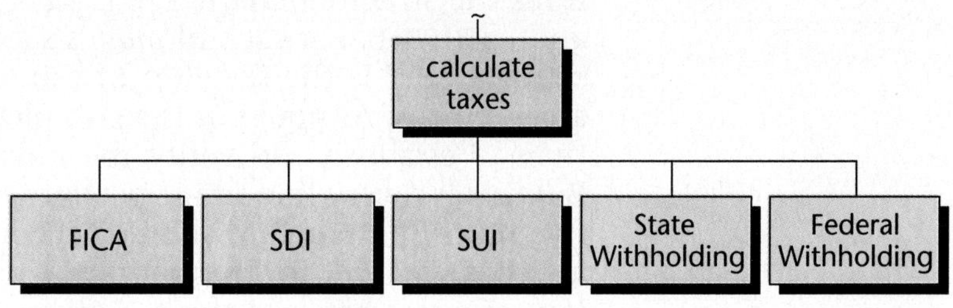

Figure 4-27 Calculate taxes

In One Place

The corollary rule is that the one thing a function does should be done in only one place. If the code for a process is scattered in several different and unrelated parts of the program, it is very difficult to change. Therefore, all the processing for a task should be placed in one function and, if necessary, its subfunctions. This is the reason we created the function `calculate taxes` in Figure 4-27.

A common example of scattered code concerns printing reports. Suppose that we wished to write a program that, among other things, prints a report that includes a heading, some data with a total, and then an end-of-report message. A well-structured solution is shown in Figure 4-28. It is quite common, however, to find the statements for each of these subtasks scattered in *main* and other parts of the program.

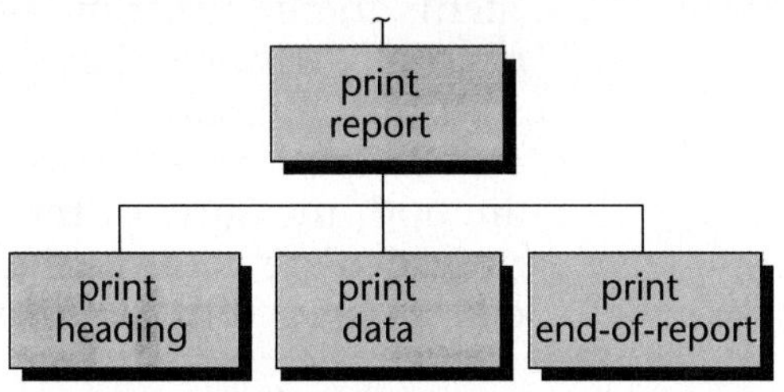

Figure 4-28 Design for print report

Testability

As a final measure of your program's structure, you should be able to test program functions independently. We will discuss a technique for doing this in the next section. Let us simply say here that a well-designed and well-structured program allows each section of the program to be tested separately from the rest of the program.

TOP-DOWN DEVELOPMENT

If you have designed your program using structured programming concepts and a structure chart, you can then proceed to implement it in a top-down fashion.

Referring again to Figure 4-25 on page 160, a top-down implementation starts with the code for *main* only, shown in the structure chart as `Program Name`. The code for the first compile and test is shown in Program 4-13. Note that this program shows only the first four boxes from the structure chart: `ProgramName` (*main*), `initialize`, `process`, and `endOfJob`. For each of *main*'s subfunctions, all that is included is a **stub**. A stub is the skeleton of a function that is called and immediately returns. Although it is a complete function, it does nothing other than to establish and verify the linkage between the caller and itself. But this is a very important part of testing and verifying a program. At this point the program should be compiled, linked, and run. Chances are that you will find some minor problems, such as missing semicolons or errors between the prototype declarations and the function definitions. Before you continue with the program, you should correct these problems.

Program 4-13 Top-down development example

```
/* Sample of top-down development using stubs.
      Written by:
      Date:
*/
#include <iostream>
using namespace std;

//  Prototype Declarations
   int initialize  (void);
   int process     (void);
   int endOfJob    (void);

int main ()
{
   cout << "Begin program \n\n";

   initialize ( );
   process    ( );
   endOfJob   ( );

   return 0;
}  // main
// ================= initialize ==================
int initialize (void)
// Stub for initialize
{
   cout << "In initialize: \n";
   return 0;
}  // initialize
// ================== process ==================
int process (void)
// Stub for process
{
   cout << "In process: \n";
   return 0;
}  // process
// ================== endOfJob ==================
int endOfJob (void)
// Stub for endOfJob
{
   cout << "In endOfJob: \n";
   return 0;
}  // endOfJob
```

The top-down development then continues with the coding of `initialize`, `process`, or `endOfJob`. You would normally develop the functions left to right, but it is not necessary to do so. To develop `process`, you would again stub its subfunctions, `A`, `B`, and `C`, and then test the program. This top-down development continues until the complete program has been coded and tested.

4-9 TIPS AND COMMON PROGRAMMING ERRORS

1. There are several possible errors related to passing parameters.
   a. It is a compile error if the types in the prototype declaration and function definition are incompatible. For example, the types in the following statements are incompatible:

   ```
   double divide (int dividend, int divisor);
   ...
   double divide (float dividend, float divisor)
   {
   ...
   } // divide
   ```

   b. It is a compile error to have a different number of actual parameters in the function call than there are in the prototype declaration.

   c. It is a logic error if you code the parameters in the wrong order. Their meaning will be inconsistent in the called program. For example, in the following statements the types are the same but the meaning of the variables is reversed.

   ```
   double divide (float dividend, float divisor);
   ...
   double divide float divisor, float dividend)
   {
   ...
   } // divide
   ```

2. It is a compile error to define local variables with the same identifiers as formal parameters.

   ```
   double divide (float dividend, float divisor)
   {
      // Local Declarations
      float dividend;
      ...
   } // divide
   ```

3. Using a void return with a function that expects a return value or using a return value with a function that expects a void return is a compile error.

4. Each parameter's type must be individually specified; you cannot use multiple definitions like you can in variables. For example, the following is a compile error because `y` does not have a type:

   ```
   double fun (float x, y);
   ```

5. Forgetting the semicolon at the end of a function prototype declaration is a compile error. Similarly, using a semicolon at the end of the header in a function definition is a compile error.

6. It is most likely a logic error to call a function from within itself or one of its called functions. (This is known as recursion, and its correct use is covered in Chapter 6.)
7. It is a compile error to attempt to define a function within the body of another function.
8. It is a run-time error to code a function call without the parentheses, even when it has no parameters.

```
printHello;                          // Not a call
printHello ( );                      // A valid call
```

9. It is a compile error if the type of data in the return statement does not match the function return type.
10. It is a logic error to call *srand* every time you call *rand*.

4-10 KEY TERMS

actual parameters
address operator
block
ceil
ceiling
C++ standard library
data flow
default values
fabs
flag
floor
formal parameter list
function
function body
function call
function declaration
function definition
function header
graphical user interface
labs
local variables
methods
object-oriented program
object state
parameter passing
parameters
pass by reference
pass by value
pow
procedural program
prototype declaration
pseudorandom numbers
rand
RAND_MAX
random number
scaling (with rand( ))
scope
side effect
sqrt
srand
structure chart
stub
switch
testability
top-down design
void function

4-11 SUMMARY

- In structured programming, a program is divided into modules.
  a. Each module is designed to do a specific task.
  b. Modules in C++ are written as functions.
- Each C++ program must have one and only one function called *main*.
- A function can return only one value.
- A function can be called for its returned value or for its side effect.
- The function call includes the function name and the values of the actual parameters to provide the called function with the data it requires to perform its job.
- Each actual parameter of the function is an expression. The expression must have a value that can be evaluated at the time the function is called.
- A local variable is known only in a function definition. Local variables do not take part in communication between the calling and the called functions.

- The general format for a function definition is

```
return_type  name ( parameter list)
{
    local declarations
    statements
}
```

- If a function returns no value, the return type must be declared as *void*.
- If a function has no parameters, the parameter list must be declared *void*.
- The actual parameters passed to a function must match in number, type, and order with the formal parameters in the function definition.
- When a caller calls a function, control is passed to the called function. The caller "rests" until the called function finishes its job.
- It is highly recommended that every function have a *return* statement. A return statement is required if the return type is anything other than *void*.
- Control returns to the calling function when the *return* statement is encountered.
- A function prototype requires only the return type of the function, the function name, and the number, types, and order of the formal parameters. Parameter identifiers may be added for documentation but are not required.
- The scope of a parameter is the block following the header.
- A local variable is a variable declared inside a block. The scope of a local variable is the block in which it is declared.

4-12 PRACTICE SETS

REVIEW QUESTIONS

1. The principles of topdown design and structured programming dictate that a program should be divided into a main module and its related modules.
   a. True
   b. False
2. The function definition contains the code for a function.
   a. True
   b. False
3. Function calls that return *void* may not be used as a part of an expression.
   a. True
   b. False
4. Variables defined within a block have global scope.
   a. True
   b. False
5. The process of dividing a program into functions—which in turn are divided into functions until they consist of only elementary processing that is intrinsically understood and cannot be further subdivided—is known as
   a. Charting
   b. Factoring
   c. Structuring
   d. Flow charting
   e. Programming
6. Which of the following statements about function declaration and definition is true?
   a. The function call is found in the called function.
   b. The function declaration requires that the parameters be named.
   c. The function definition is done with a prototype statement.
   d. The function definition contains executable statements that perform the function's task.
   e. The function definition header concludes with a semicolon (`;`).

7. Which of the following is not a part of a function header?
   a. Name
   b. Return type
   c. Parameter list
   d. Title
8. Which of the following statements about function parameters is true?
   a. Empty parameter lists may be declared with the keyword *void*.
   b. If there is only one parameter, the function list parentheses are not required.
   c. In the definition of a function, the parameters are known as actual parameters.
   d. Parameters are separated by semicolons.
   e. The parameters in a function definition are defined in the function's body (local declaration section).
9. Which of the following statements about local variables is false?
   a. A local variable's value may be returned through a *return* statement.
   b. Local variables are defined inside a function.
   c. Local variables cannot be referenced through their identifiers outside the function.
   d. Local variables may be initialized with an initializer.
   e. Local variables' names can be the same as the function's parameter names.
10. The function that returns the absolute value of a long integer is
    a. `abs`
    b. `fabs`
    c. `tabs`
    d. `dabs`
    e. `labs`
11. Which of the following statements will generate a random number in the range 30–50?
    a. `rand (33)`
    b. `(rand () % 21) + 30`
    c. `(rand () % 20) + 1`
    d. `(rand () % 51) + 1`
    e. `(rand () % 21) + 20`
12. Which of the following statements about structure charts is false?
    a. Structure charts are a replacement for flowcharts.
    b. Structure charts are the primary design tool for a program.
    c. Structure charts are used in a structured walk-through to validate the design.
    d. Structure charts can be used to assess the testability of a program.
    e. Structure charts should be created before you start writing a program.

EXERCISES

13. Find any errors in the following function definition:

```
void fun (int x, int y)
{
  int z;
  ...
  return z;
} // fun
```

14. Find any errors in the following function definition:

```
int fun (int x, y)
{
    int z;
    ...
    return z;
} // fun
```

15. Find any errors in the following function definition:

```
int fun (int x, int y)
{
  ...
     int sun (int t)
     {
       ...
       return (t + 3);
     }
     ...
       return z;
}    // fun
```

16. Find any errors in the following function definition:

```
void fun (int, x)
{
...
return;
}
```

17. Find any errors in the following prototype declarations:
    a. int sun (int x, y) ;
    b. int sun (int x, int y)
    c. void sun (void, void) ;
    d. void sun (x int, y float) ;
18. Find any errors in the following function calls:
    a. void fun ( ) ;
    b. fun (void) ;
    c. void fun (int x, int y) ;
    d. fun ( ) ;
19. Evaluate the value of the following expressions:
    a. fabs (9.5) b. fabs(–2.4) c. fabs (–3.4)
    d. fabs (–7) e. fabs (7)
20. Evaluate the value of the following expressions:
    a. floor (9.5) b. floor (–2.4) c. floor (–3.4)
    d. ceil (9.5) e. ceil (–2.4) f. ceil (–3.4)
21. Evaluate the value of the following expressions when x is 3.5, 3.45, 3.76, 3.234, and 3.4567:
    a. floor (x * 10 + 0.5) / 10
    b. floor (x * 100 + 0.5) / 100
    c. floor (x * 1000 + 0.5) / 1000
22. Define the range of the random numbers generated by the following expressions:
    a. rand() % 10 b. rand() % 4 c. rand() % 52
    d. rand() % 10 +1 e. rand() % 2 +1
    f. rand() % 52 – 5
23. What would be printed from the following program when run using 3 and 5 as data?

```
#include <iostream>
using namespace std;
// Prototype Declarations
int strange (int, int);

int main ()
{
    int  a;
    int  b;
    cin  >> a >> b;
    int  r  =  strange (a, b);
    int  s  =  strange (b, a);
    cout  << r << "  " << s;
    return 0;
} // main
// ============ strange ==========
int strange (int x, int y)
{
    return (x - y);
} // strange
```

24. What would be printed from the following program when run using 3, 5, 4, and 6 as data?

```
#include <iostream>
using namespace std;
// Prototype Declarations
long strange (long, long);

int main ()
{
   long  a;
   long  b;
   long  c;
   cin >> a >> b >> c >> d;

   long r = strange (a, b);
   long s = strange (r, c);
   long t = strange (strange (s, d),
     strange (4, 2));
   long u = strange (t + 3, s + 2);
   long v = strange (strange (strange
     (u, a), b), c);

   cout << r << "  " << s << "  "
        << t << "  "
        << u << "  " << v;
   return 0;
} // main
// ========= strange ============
long strange (long x, long y)
{
   long t = x + y;
   long  z = x * y;
   return (t + z);
} // strange
```

PROBLEMS

25. Write a function to print your name, as shown below. Write a call as it would be coded in a calling function, such as `main`.

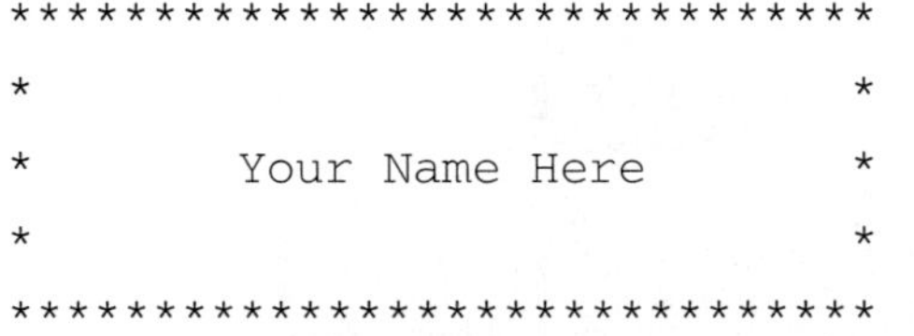

```
*****************************
*                           *
*       Your Name Here      *
*                           *
*****************************
```

26. Write a program that generates a random number from the following set:
`1, 2, 3, 4, 5, 6`

27. Write a program that generates a random number from the following set:
`1, 4, 7, 10, 13, 16`

28. Explain the difference between pass by value and pass by reference.

29. Draw the structure chart for Program 4-12, "Calculator program," on page 157.

30. Explain what is meant by the statement, "A function should do only one thing."

31. Code and run Program 4-13 on page 165 to demonstrate how stubs work.

32. Expand the calculator program on page 157 to calculate the product, quotient, and modulus of the number. Calculate the quotient and modulus in one function using pass by reference.

33. Modify the "Add two digits" program on Page 123 to add the least significant three digits (hundreds, tens, and ones).

34. Write a function that receives a positive floating-point number and rounds it to two decimal places. For example, 127.565031 rounds to 127.570000. Hint: To round, you must convert float to an integer and then back to a float. Print the rounded numbers to six decimal places. Test the function with the following data:
`123.456789   123.499999 123.500001`

35. Write a program that reads a floating-point number and prints the ceiling, floor, and rounded value. For the rounded value, use the function and test data from Problem 34.

36. Write a function to compute the perimeter and area of a right triangle (Figure 4-29) when given the length of the two sides (*a* and *b*).

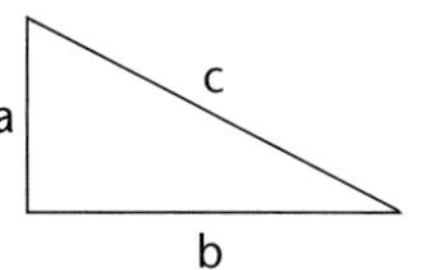

Figure 4-29 Program 11

The following formulas may be helpful:

$$c^2 = a^2 + b^2$$
$$area = 0.5 \times (a \times b)$$

PROJECTS

37. Prepare a payroll earnings statement for the sales force at the Arctic Ice Company. All of Arctic's employees are on a straight commission basis of 12.5% of sales. Each month, they also receive a bonus that varies depending on the profit for the month and their length of service. The sales manager calculates the bonus separately and enters it with the salesperson's total sales for the month. Your program is also to calculate the withholding taxes and retirement for the month based on the following rates:

    a. Federal withholding: 25%

    b. State withholding: 10%

    c. Retirement plan: 8%

    The test data to use for the program are shown in Table 4-2.

SALESPERSON	SALES	BONUS
1	53,500	425
2	41,300	300
3	56,800	350
4	36,200	175

Table 4-2 Test data for Project 24

38. Write a program that, given a beginning balance in your savings account, calculates the balance at the end of one year. The interest is 5.3% compounded quarterly. Show the interest earned and balance at the end of each quarter. Present the data in tabular columns with appropriate headings. Use separate functions to compute the interest and print the balance.

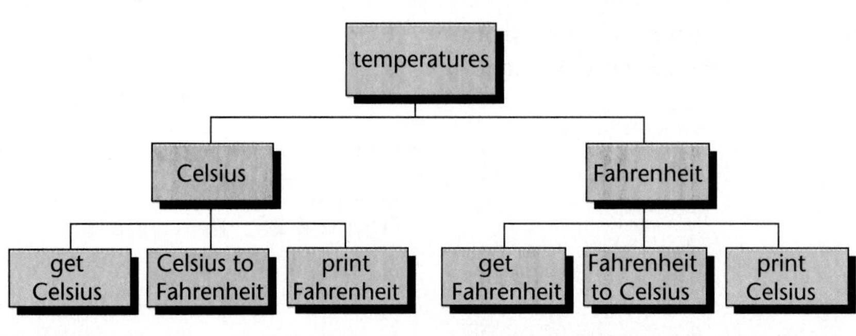

Figure 4-30 A possible design for Project 39

39. The formula for converting centigrade temperatures to Fahrenheit is

$$F = 32 + C \times \left(\frac{180.0}{100.0}\right)$$

Write a program that asks the user to enter a temperature reading in centigrade and then prints the equivalent Fahrenheit value. It then asks the user to enter a Fahrenheit value and prints out the equivalent centigrade value. Run the program several times. Be sure to include at least one negative temperature reading in your test cases. Provide separate functions as required by your design. One possible design is shown in Figure 4-30. (Your *main* function should have only function calls.)

40. Write a program that uses standard functions. The program can be written entirely in main and must follow the pseudocode shown in below. Give displays appropriate captions and align the data.

```
Prompt the user to enter a number.
Read number.
Display number.
Get a random number and scale to range 3...37.
Display random number.
Set product to number * random number.
Display ceiling of product.
Display number raised to power 5.
Display floor of product.
Display number raised to power of modulus
   above.
Display square root of random number.
```

41. Write a C++ program that creates customers' bills for a carpet company when the following information is given:

    a. The length and the width of the carpet in feet.
    b. The carpet price per square foot.
    c. The percent of discount for each customer.

    The labor cost is fixed at $0.35 per square foot. It is to be defined as a constant. The tax rate is 8.5% applied after the discount. It is also to be defined as a constant. The input data consist of a set of three integers and a float, the length and width of the room to be carpeted, the percentage of the discount the owner gives to a customer, and a floating-point number representing the unit price of the carpet. The program is to prompt the user for this input as follows. (Bold numbers are typical responses.)

```
Length of room (feet)? 30
Width of room (feet)? 18
Customer discount (percent)? 9
Cost per square foot (xxx.xx)? 8.23
```

The output is shown below. Be careful to align the decimal points.

```
                MEASUREMENT
Length                    XXX feet
Width                     XXX feet
Area                      XXX square feet
```

```
                  CHARGES

DESCRIPTION   COST/SQ.FT. CHARGE/ROOM
-----------   ----------- -----------
Carpet          XXX.XX        XXXX.XX
Labor             0.35        XXXX.XX
                          -----------
INSTALLED PRICE              $XXXX.XX
Discount          XX.X%       XXXX.XX
                          -----------
SUBTOTAL                     $XXXX.XX
Tax                           XXXX.XX
TOTAL                        $XXXX.XX
```

The program's design should use main and at least the six functions described below:

1. Read data (`getData`) from the keyboard. This function is to use addresses (pass-by-reference concept) to read all data and place it in the calling function's variables.
2. Calculate values (`calculate`). This function calls three subfunctions.
   a. Calculate the installed price (`calcInstall`). The installed price is the cost of the carpet and the cost of the labor.
   b. Calculate the subtotal (`calcSubTotal`).
3. Calculate the total price with discount and tax (`calcTotal`).
4. Print the result (`printResult`). Use two subfunctions to print the results, one to print the measurements and one to print the charges.

Test your program with the three sets of data shown in Table 4-3.

Test	Length	Width	Discount	Price
1	23	13	12	14.20
2	35	8	0	8.00
3	14	11	10	22.25

Table 4-3 Test data sets for Project 41

5 Selection–Making Decisions

In this chapter, we introduce the second of the structured programming constructs: **selection**. Selection allows you to choose between two or more alternatives; that is, it allows you to make decisions.

What a dull world it would be if we didn't have any choices. Vanilla ice cream for everybody. Uniforms all around! And no debates or arguments to keep things interesting. Fortunately, our world is filled with choices. And, since our programs must reflect the world in which they are designed to operate, they too are filled with choices and opportunities for decision making.

How are decisions made by a computer? In this chapter, you will find out. One of the main points to keep in mind is that decisions made by a computer must be very simple since everything in the computer ultimately reduces to either true (1) or false (0). Thus, if complex decisions are required, it is the programmer's job to reduce them to a series of simple decisions that the computer can handle.

5-1 LOGICAL DATA AND OPERATORS

A piece of data is called logical if it conveys the idea of *true* or *false*. **Logical data** is important in real life as well as in programming. In real life, logical data (true or false) are created in answer to a question that requires a yes-no answer. For example, we ask if an item is on sale or not. We ask if a business is open or not. The answer to these questions is a piece of data that is usually yes or no. We can also ask questions like "Is *x* greater than *y*?" The answer is again yes or no. In computer science, we use true or false rather than yes or no.

LOGICAL DATA IN C++

There are two ways to represent logical data in C++. First, we can use the Boolean type (bool) with its constant identifiers, *true* and *false*.[1] Second, we can use other data types (such as *int* and *char*) to represent logical data. If a data item is zero, it is considered false. If it is nonzero, it is considered true. This concept of *true* and *false* on a numeric scale is illustrated in Figure 5-1.

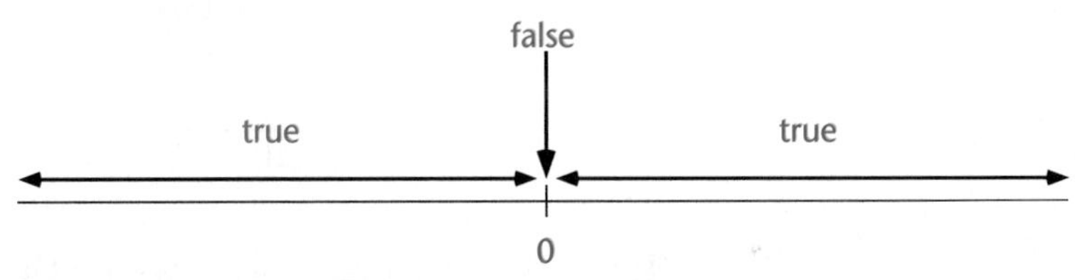

Figure 5-1 True and false on the arithmetic scale

LOGICAL OPERATORS

C++ has three **logical operators** for combining logical values and creating new logical values: *not*, *and*, and *or*. These operators are listed in Table 5-1.

Operator	Meaning	Precedence
!	not	15
&&	Logical and	5
||	Logical or	4

Table 5-1 Logical operators

A common way to show logical relationships is in truth tables. Figure 5-2 contains truth tables that list the values that each operand can assume and the resulting value.

[1]Be aware, however, that bool is an ISO standard implementation and may not be available in older C++ compilers.

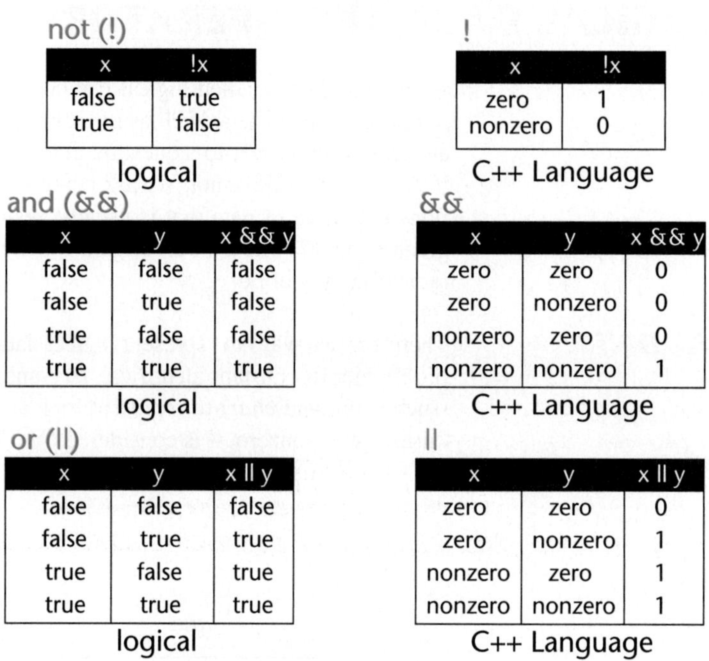

not (!)

x	!x
false	true
true	false

logical

!

x	!x
zero	1
nonzero	0

C++ Language

and (&&)

x	y	x && y
false	false	false
false	true	false
true	false	false
true	true	true

logical

&&

x	y	x && y
zero	zero	0
zero	nonzero	0
nonzero	zero	0
nonzero	nonzero	1

C++ Language

or (||)

x	y	x || y
false	false	false
false	true	true
true	false	true
true	true	true

logical

||

x	y	x || y
zero	zero	0
zero	nonzero	1
nonzero	zero	1
nonzero	nonzero	1

C++ Language

Figure 5-2 Logical operators truth table

> **In C++**
> **If a value is zero, it can be used as the logical value false.**
> **If a value is not zero, it can be used as the logical value true.**
> **ZERO ◄——► FALSE**
> **NONZERO ◄——► TRUE**

not

The ***not* operator (!)** is a unary operator with precedence 15 in Table 5-1. It changes a true value (nonzero) to false (zero), and a false value (zero) to true (one). The truth table for *not* is included in Figure 5-2.

and

The ***and* operator (&&)** is a binary operator with precedence of 5. Since the *and* is a binary operator, there are four distinct possible combinations of values in its operands. The result is *true* only when both operands are true; it is *false* in all other cases. This relationship can be seen in the *and* truth table shown in Figure 5-2.

or

The ***or* operator** (||) is a binary operator with precedence of 4. As with *and*, since *or* is a binary operator, there are four distinct combinations of values in its operands. The result is *false* if both operands are false; it is *true* in all other cases. The *or* truth table is also shown in Figure 5-2.

EVALUATING LOGICAL EXPRESSIONS

Computer languages can use two methods to evaluate the binary logical relationships. The basic difference between the two methods has to do with whether or not a complete expression needs to be evaluated.

In the first method, the expression must be completely evaluated before the result is determined. Thus, the *and* expression must be completely evaluated, even when the first operand is false and it is therefore known that the result *must be* false. Likewise, in the *or* expression, the whole expression must be evaluated, even when the first operand is true and the obvious result of the expression *must be* true. The Pascal language uses this method.

The second method can set the resulting value as soon as it is known, without completing the evaluation. In other words, it operates in a "short-circuit fashion" and stops the evaluation when it knows for sure what the final result will be. Under this method, if the first operand of a logical *and* expression is false, the second half of the expression is not evaluated because it is apparent that the result must be false. Again, with the *or* expression, if the first operand is true, there is no need to evaluate the second half of the expression so the resulting value is set true immediately. C++ uses this short-circuit method, which is graphically shown in Figure 5-3.

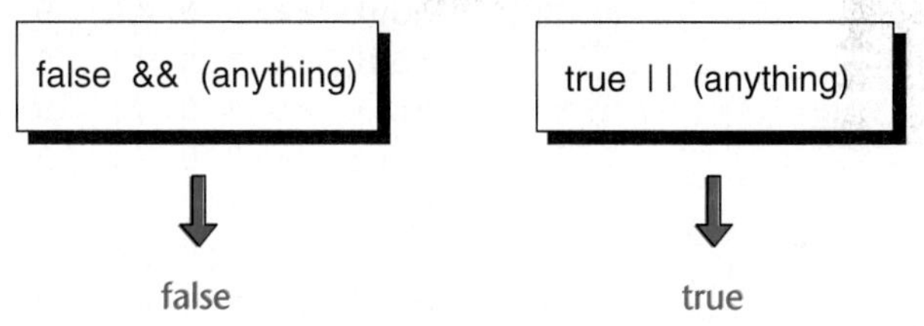

Figure 5-3 Short-circuit methods for *and* and *or*

Although the C++ method is more efficient, it can cause problems when the second operand contains side effects (which is poor programming practice). Consider, for example, the following expression in which a programmer wants to find the value of the logical expression and at the same time wants to increment the value of the second operand:

```
x && y++
```

Everything works fine when the first operand is nonzero. However, if the first operand is zero, the second operand will never be evaluated and therefore will never be incremented. The same thing happens in the next example. If the first operand is nonzero, the second operand will never be incremented.

```
x || y++
```

The obvious conclusion from this discussion is that the order of the expressions in a logical expression is important. In the previous examples, if we always want to increment the variable `y`, then we should code them with the increment first, as shown below.

```
y++ && x                    y++ || x
```

Program 5-1 demonstrates the use of logical data in expressions.

Program 5-1 Logical expressions

```
/* Demonstrate the results of logical operators.
      Written by:
      Date:
*/
#include <iostream>
using namespace std;

int main ()
{
   cout << " 5 && -3 is: " << ( 5 && -3) << endl;
   cout << " 5 &&  0 is: " << ( 5 &&  0) << endl;
   cout << " 0 &&  5 is: " << ( 0 &&  5) << endl;
   cout << " 5 ||  0 is: " << ( 5 ||  0) << endl;
   cout << " 0 ||  5 is: " << ( 0 ||  5) << endl;
   cout << " 0 ||  0 is: " << ( 0 ||  0) << endl;
   cout << "!5 && !0 is: " << (!5 && !0) << endl;
   cout << "!5 && !0 is: " << (!5 && !0) << endl;
   cout << "!5 &&  0 is: " << (!5 &&  0) << endl;
   cout << " 5 && !0 is: " << ( 5 && !0) << endl;
   return 0;
} // main
```

```
Results:
 5 && -3 is: 1
 5 &&  0 is: 0
 0 &&  5 is: 0
 5 ||  0 is: 1
 0 ||  5 is: 1
 0 ||  0 is: 0
!5 && !0 is: 0
!5 && !0 is: 0
!5 &&  0 is: 0
 5 && !0 is: 1
```

Program 5-1 Analysis Each print statement in Program 5-1 contains a logical expression that evaluates either to 1 (true) or 0 (false). The print statements have been written to display the data as an expression and the results. Because the insertion operator (<<) requires only a single value, the expression must be enclosed in parentheses. If you omit the parentheses, you will get a compile error. Make sure you understand why each of the expressions evaluates as shown in the results.

De Morgan's Rule

When we design the logical flow of a program, we often have a situation in which the *not* operator is in front of a logical expression enclosed in the parentheses. Human engineering studies tell us, however, that positive logic is easier to read and understand than negative logic. In these cases, therefore, if we want to make the total expression positive by removing the parentheses, we apply the *not* operator directly to each operand. **De Morgan's rule** governs the complementing of operators in this situation. This rule is defined as follows:

When we remove the parentheses in a logical expression preceded by the *not* operator, we must apply the *not* operator to each expression while complementing the logical operators—that is, changing *and* (&&) to *or* (||) while changing *or* (||) to *and* (&&).

Consider the expression shown below.

```
!(x && y)  ➡  !x || !y
!(x || y)  ➡  !x && !y
```

If the expression has been properly complemented according to De Morgan's rule, then the result of the first expression (true or false) will be the same as the result of the second expression for any given set of values for *x* and *y*. It is important to recognize, however, that in more complex situations, the C++ rules of precedence can affect De Morgan's rule.

RELATIONAL OPERATORS

Six **relational operators** support logical relationships. They are all binary operators that accept two operands and compare them. The result is logical data; that is, it is always *true* (1) or *false* (0). The operators are shown in Figure 5-4.

Operator	Meaning	Precedence
<	less than	10
<=	less than or equal	
>	greater than	
>=	greater than or equal	
==	equal	9
!=	not equal	

Figure 5-4 Relational operators

If you examine Figure 5-4 carefully, you will note that the first four operators—**less than, less than or equal, greater than, greater than or equal**—have a higher priority (10) in the precedence table than do the **equal** and **not equal operators** (9). Thus, the first four operators in Figure 5-4 will be evaluated before the equal operators when they appear together in the same expression.

It is important to recognize that each operator is a complement of another operator in the group. Surprisingly, though, the complement is not the one that you might expect. Figure 5-5 shows each operator and its complement.

In other words, if we want to simplify an expression involving the *not* and the *less than* operator, we use the *greater than or equal* operator. This concept is important for simplifying expressions and coding expressions in good, clear style. Table 5-2 shows an example of each expression and its complement.

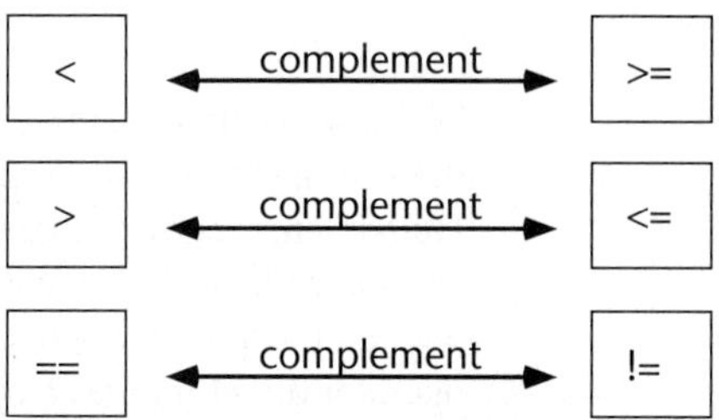

Figure 5-5 Logical operator complements

Original expression	Simplified expression
`! ( x <  y )`	`x >= y`
`! ( x >  y )`	`x <= y`
`! ( x != y )`	`x == y`
`! ( x <= y )`	`x >  y`
`! ( x >= y )`	`x <  y`
`! ( x == y )`	`x != y`

Table 5-2 Examples of relational operator complements

Program 5-2 demonstrates the use of relational operators.

Program 5-2 Relational operators

```
/* Demonstrates the results of relational operators.
      Written by:
      Date written:
*/
#include <iostream>
#include <iomanip>
using namespace std;

int main ( )
{
   int a =  5;
   int b = -3;

   cout << setw(2) <<  a << " <  "
        << setw(2) <<  b << " is "
        << setw(2) << (a < b) << endl;
   cout << setw(2) <<  a << " == "
        << setw(2) <<  b << " is "
        << setw(2) << (a == b) << endl;
   cout << setw(2) <<  a << " != "
        << setw(2) <<  b << " is "
        << setw(2) << (a != b) << endl;
   cout << setw(2) <<  a << " >  "
        << setw(2) <<  b << " is "
```

Program 5-2 Relational operators *(continued)*

```
             << setw(2) << (a > b) << endl;
        cout << setw(2) <<  a << " <= "
             << setw(2) <<  b << " is "
             << setw(2) << (a <= b) << endl;
        cout << setw(2) <<  a << " >= "
             << setw(2) <<  b << " is "
             << setw(2) << (a >= b) << endl;
        return 0;
    } // main
```

```
Results:
  5 <  -3 is 0
  5 == -3 is 0
  5 != -3 is 1
  5 >  -3 is 1
  5 <= -3 is 0
  5 >= -3 is 1
```

Program 5-2 Analysis Program 5-2 follows the same patterns we saw in Program 5-1. Once again, you should make sure that you understand why each of the representations in the results evaluates to true or false.

5-2 TWO-WAY SELECTION

The basic decision statement in the computer is the **two-way selection**. The decision is described to the computer as a selection statement that can be answered either true or false. If the answer is true, one or more action statements are executed. If the answer is false, then a different action or set of actions is executed. Regardless of which set of actions is executed, the program continues with the next statement after the selection statement. The flowchart for two-way decision logic is shown in Figure 5-6.

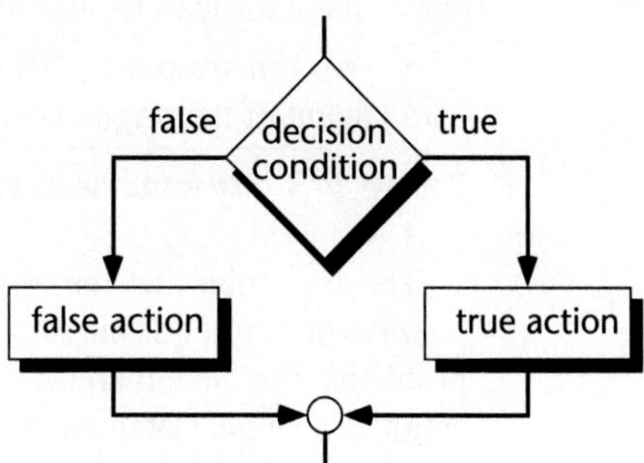

Figure 5-6 Two-way decision logic

if...else STATEMENT

C++ implements two-way selection with the ***if...else*** statement. An *if...else* statement is a composite statement used to make a decision between two alternatives. Figure 5-7 shows the logic flow for an *if...else*. The expression can be any C++ expression. After it has been evaluated, if its value is true (not zero), statement 1 is executed; otherwise, statement 2 is executed. It is impossible for both statements to be executed in the same evaluation.

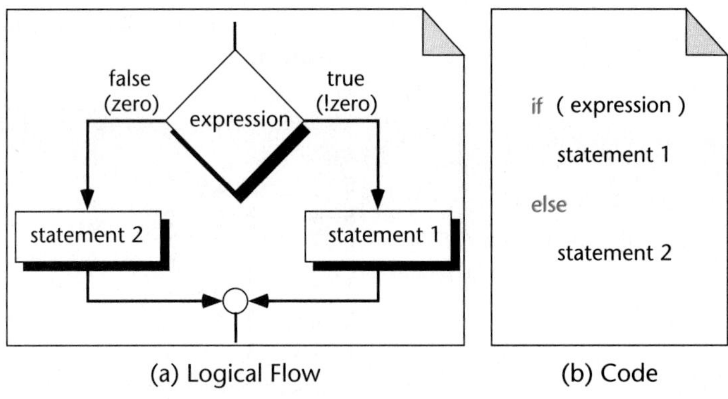

Figure 5-7 *if...else* logic flow

There are some syntactical points you must remember about *if...else* statements. These points are summarized in Table 5-3.

1. The expression must be enclosed in parentheses.
2. No semicolon (;) is needed for an *if...else* statement. Statement 1 and statement 2 (see Figure 5-7) may have a semicolon as required by their types.
3. The expression can have a side effect.
4. Both the true and the false statements can be any statement (even another *if...else* statement) or can be a null statement.
5. Both statement 1 and statement 2 must be one and only one statement. Remember, however, that multiple statements can be combined into a compound statement through the use of braces.
6. We can swap the position of statement 1 and statement 2 if we use the complement of the original expression.

Table 5-3 Syntactical rules for *if...else* statements

The first rule, that the expression must be enclosed in parentheses, is simple and requires no further discussion. The second rule is also simple, but it tends to cause more problems. We have therefore provided an example in Figure 5-8. In this example, each action is a single statement that either adds or subtracts 1 from the variable a. Note that the semicolons belong to the arithmetic statements, not the *if...else*.

The third rule requires more discussion. It is quite common in C++ to code expressions that have side effects. For example, you will find expressions that read data as a side effect. Consider what happens when we are writing a line and we want to go to

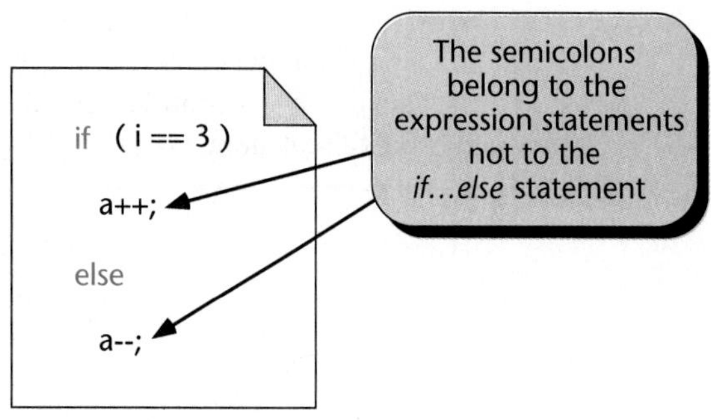

Figure 5-8 A simple *if...else* statement

a new line after we have written 10 numbers. A simple solution increments a line count and tests the limit in the same statement as shown in the next example.

```
if (++lineCnt > 10)
   {
    cout     << "\n";
    lineCnt = 0;
   } // if
```

The fourth and fifth rules are closely related. The fact that any statement can be used in an *if...else* is straightforward, but often new C++ programmers will forget to use a compound statement for complex logic. The use of compound statements is demonstrated in Figure 5-9. The first example shows a compound statement only for the true condition. The second example shows compound statements for both conditions. Note that the compound statements begin with an open brace and end with a close brace.

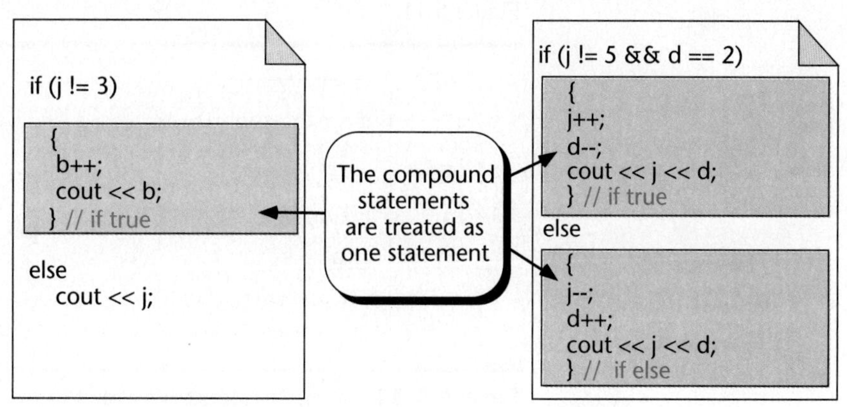

Figure 5-9 Compound statements in an *if...else*

Now let us look at the sixth rule, which states that the true and false statements can be exchanged by complementing the expression. Recall from our discussion of relational operators on page 171 that any expression can be complemented. When we find that we want to make a **complemented *if...else* statement**, all we have to do is to switch the true and false statements. An example of this operation is shown in Figure 5-10.

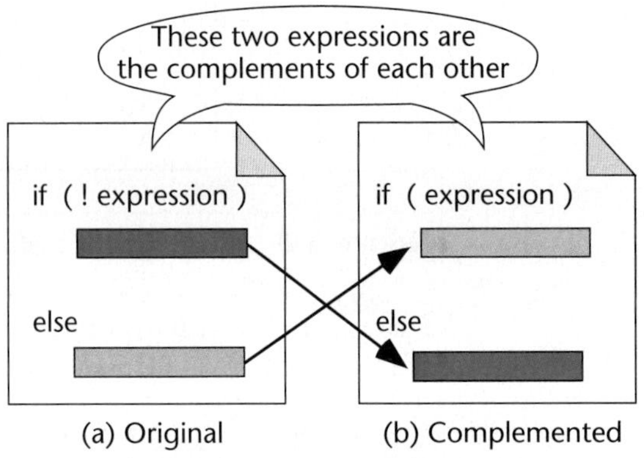

Figure 5-10 Complemented *if...then* statements

NULL *else* STATEMENT

Although there are always two possible actions after a decision, sometimes they are not both relevant. In this case, the false action is usually the one that is left out. For example, assume you are averaging numbers as they are being read. However, for some reason, the logic requires that you average only numbers greater than zero. As you read the number, you test it for greater than zero. If the test is true, you include the number in the average. If it is false, you do nothing.

If the false condition is not required—that is, if it is null—it can be omitted. This omission can be shown as a **null *else*** statement (a null statement consists of only a semicolon); more commonly, the *else* statement is simply omitted entirely, as shown in Figure 5-11.

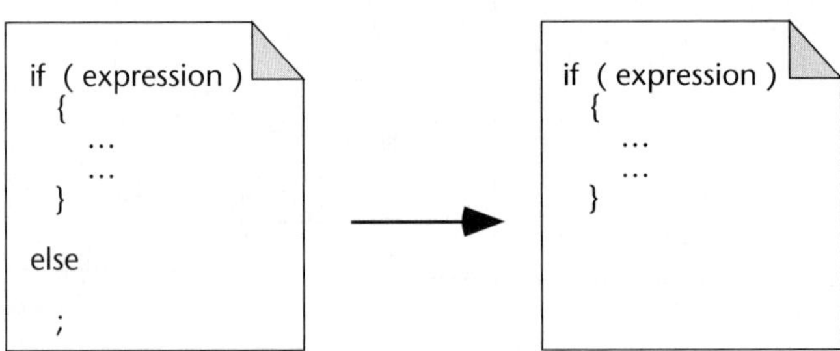

Figure 5-11 A null *else* statement

It is possible to omit the false action, but the true statement cannot be omitted. It can be coded as a null statement; normally, however, we do not use null in the true branch of an *if...else* statement. To eliminate the true statement, we can use rule 6 in Table 5-3, which allows us to complement the expression and swap the two statements. This procedure is shown in Figure 5-12.

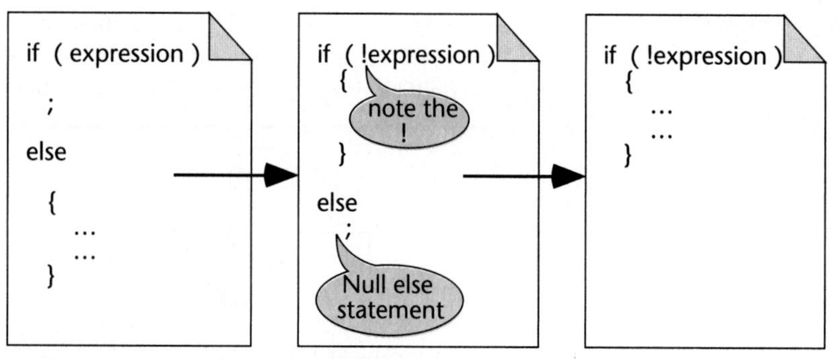

Figure 5-12 A null *if* statement

Program 5–3 contains an example of a simple two-way selection. It displays the relationship between two numbers read from the keyboard.

Program 5-3 Two-way selection

```
/* Two-way selection.
      Written by:
      Date:
*/
#include <iostream>
using namespace std;

int main ()
{
   cout <<"Please enter two integers: ";
   int  a;
   int  b;
   cin  >> a >> b;

   if (a <= b)
       cout << a << " <= " << b << endl;
   else
       cout << a << " > " << b << endl;
   return 0;
} // main
```

```
Results:
Please enter two integers: 10 15
10 <= 15
```

NESTED *if* STATEMENTS

As we stated previously, for the *if...else*, the statement may be any statement, including another *if...else*. When an *if...else* is included within an *if...else*, it is known as a **nested *if***. Figure 5-13 shows a nested *if* statement. There is no limit as to how many levels can be nested, but if there are more than three they can become difficult to read.

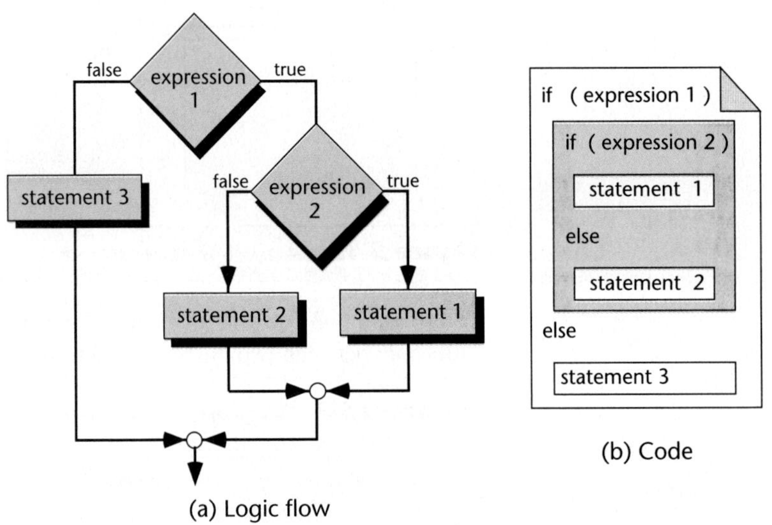

Figure 5-13 Nested *if* statements

Program 5-4 is a modification of Program 5-3. It uses a nested *if* statement to determine if a is less than, equal to, or greater than b.

Program 5-4 Nested *if* statements

```
/* Nested if in two-way selection.
      Written by:
      Date:
*/
#include <iostream>
using namespace std;

int main ()
{
   cout << "Please enter two integers: ";
   int  a;
   int  b;
   cin  >> a >> b;

   if (a <= b)
      if (a < b)
         cout << a << " < " << b << endl;
      else  // equal
         cout << a << " == " << b << endl;
   else  // greater than
```

Program 5-4 Nested *if* statements *(continued)*

```
21          cout << a << " > " << b << endl;
22
23     return 0;
24  }  // main
```

```
Results:
Please enter two integers: 10 5
10 > 5
```

Program 5-4 Analysis You should be able to follow this simple program with relative ease. However, it does contain a subtle software engineering principle. Study the *if* statements (15 and 16) carefully. Where do we check for **greater than**? The answer is that we **default** the **greater than** condition to the last *else* (statement 20). When coding a two-way selection statement, try to code the most probable condition first; with nested selection statements, code the most probable first and the least probable last.

DANGLING *else* PROBLEM

Once you start nesting *if...else* statements, however, you encounter a classic problem known as the **dangling else**. This problem is created when there is no matching *else* for every *if*. C++'s solution to this problem is a simple rule: Always pair an *else* to the closest unpaired *if* in the current block. This rule may result in some *if* statement's being left unpaired. Since such an arbitrary rule often does not match your intent, you must take care to ensure that the resulting code is what you require. Take, for instance, the example shown in Figure 5-14. From the code alignment, we conclude that the programmer intended the *else* statement to be paired with the first *if*. However, the compiler will pair it with the second *if* as shown in the flowchart.

else is always paired with the most recent, unpaired _if_

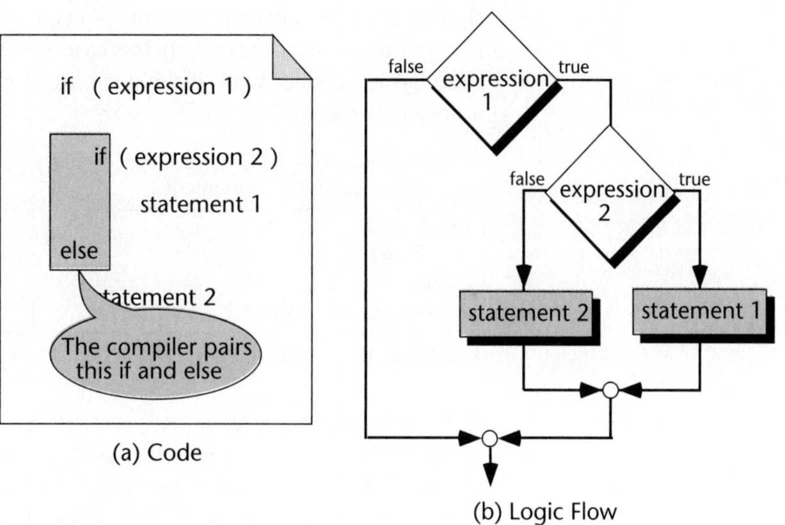

Figure 5-14 Dangling *else*

Figure 5-15 shows a solution to the dangling *else* problem: using a compound statement. In the compound statement, you simply enclose the true actions in braces to make the second *if* a compound statement. Since the closing brace completes the body of the compound statement, the *if* statement is also closed from further consideration, and the *else* is automatically paired with the correct *if.*

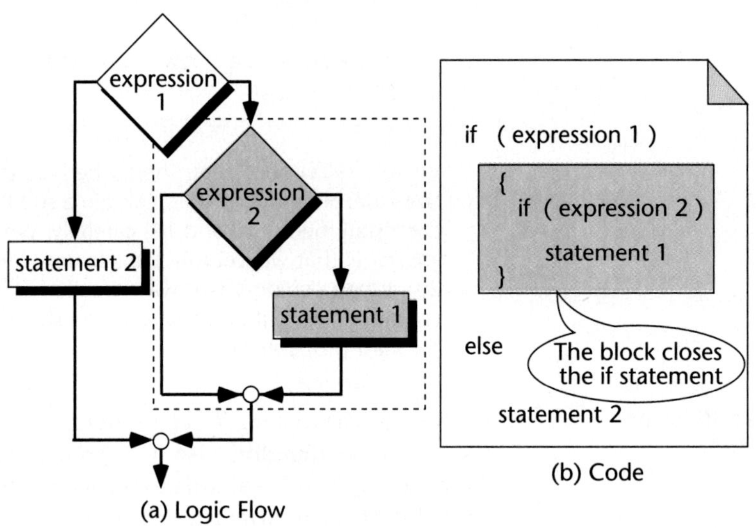

Figure 5-15 Dangling *else* solution

SIMPLIFYING *if* STATEMENTS

By now you should recognize that *if...else* statements can become quite complex. This discussion will give you some ideas on how to simplify such statements. Usually, the purpose of simplification is to provide more readable code.

Another reason for **simplifying *if...else* statements** is to eliminate bad code. For example, look at the code in Table 5-4. Although you would not write this code to begin with, often modifications to your program can result in exactly the same kind of logic shown. The *else* statement in Table 5-4 can never be executed because the constant 5 is always true—so why have it? In this case, simply eliminate the *if...else*. Would the same simplifying concept work if the conditional expression (5) were a variable instead of a constant? (No.)

Original statement	Simplified statement

`if ( 5 )`
`    cout << "Hello";`
`else`
`    cout << "Bye";`
	`cout << "Hello";`

Table 5-4 Eliminating the *else* statement

Sometimes the control expression itself can be simplified. For example, the two statements in Table 5-5 are exactly the same. The simplified statements, however, are much preferred by experienced C++ programmers. When the simplified code becomes a natural way of thinking, you have begun to internalize the C++ concepts; that is, you are beginning to think in C++!

Original statement	Simplified statement
`if ( a!= 0 )` `    statement`	`if ( a )` `    statement`
`if ( a == 0 )` `    statement`	`if ( !a )` `    statement`

Table 5-5 Simplifying the condition

Since the simplified statements in Table 5-5 are new, let's look at them a little more carefully. The expression `a != 0` evaluates to either true or false. If `a` is anything other than zero, then the expression is true and *statement* is executed. However, any integer can be used to represent true or false. In this case, if `a` contains any value other than zero, it is true; otherwise, it is false. Therefore, since we want to execute *statement* whenever `a` is not zero, and since anything other than zero is true, we code the expression as `(a)`—that is, as `a` is true. Similarly, if we want to test for `a` equal to zero, we simply complement the expression, making it `!a`.

The Unintentional Semicolon

One of the most difficult coding errors to detect is the "unintentional semicolon." Consider the following block of code:

```
if (a > b);
    cout << "a > b\a\n";
```

This code will *always* print "a > b" regardless of the values in `a` and `b`. Do you see the error yet?

Because the *if* expression does not require an ending semicolon, the semicolon at the end of the expression is actually a null statement. Therefore, if the expression is true, C++ executes the null statement (does nothing) and then executes the next statement that prints "a > b." By the same token, if the expression is not true, it skips the null statement (does not do nothing) and still prints the message.

Be very careful when you code selection statements not to accidently insert an extra semicolon in the wrong place.

CONDITIONAL EXPRESSIONS

C++ provides a convenient alternative to the traditional *if...else* for two-way selection—the ternary conditional expression found at priority 3 in the Precedence Table (see inside cover).

The conditional expression has three operands and two operators. Each operand is an expression. The first operator, a question mark (?), separates the first two expressions. The second operator, a colon (:), separates the last two expressions. This gives it the following format:

```
expression ? expression1 : expression2
```

To evaluate this expression, C++ first evaluates the leftmost expression. If the expression is true, then the value of the conditional expression is the value of expression1. If the expression is false, then the value of the conditional expression is the value of expression2.

Let's look at an example.

```
a == b ? c-- : c++;
```

In this expression, only one of the two side effects will take place. If `a` is equal to `b`, `c--` will be evaluated and 1 will be subtracted from `c`; expression2 will be ignored. On the other hand, if `a` is not equal to `b`, then `c++` will be evaluated and 1 will be added to `c`; expression1 will be ignored. If this sounds much like a simplified *if...else*, it's because it is! Figure 5-16 shows the flowchart for the expression, which could easily be coded as an *if...else*.

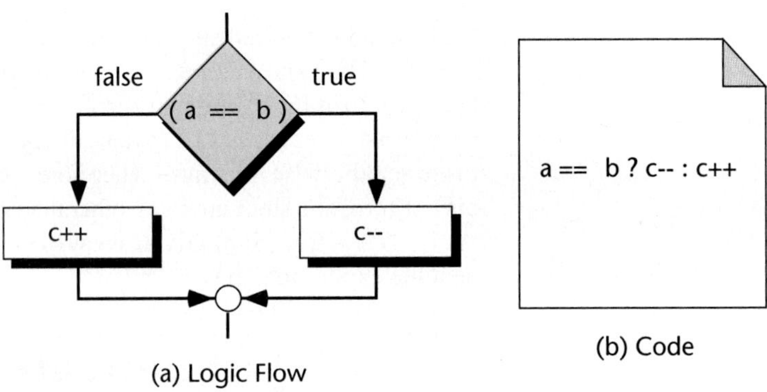

Figure 5-16 Conditional expression

The results of a conditional expression can be assigned. Suppose that we have a program that can write either to a printer or to the system monitor. When we write to the monitor, we can write 10 numbers to a line. When we write to the printer, we can write 15 numbers to a line. Given that `fileFlag` is a variable that indicates either the monitor (M) or printer (P), we could set the numbers per line as shown below. (The parentheses are not necessary but make the statement more readable.)

```
numPerLine = ( fileFlag == 'M' ? 10 : 15 );
```

One final note: Although you can nest conditional expressions, it is not recommended. If the logic begins to get complex, remember the KISS principle and use nested *if* statements.

HANDLING MAJOR ERRORS

One of the better known computer acronyms is GIGO—garbage in, garbage out. In writing programs, we must decide how to handle errors to prevent garbage from corrupting the data. Sometimes, as we will see in the next chapter, we can recover from the error by having the user re-enter it. Other times, there is no way to recover.

When we can't recover, C++ provides two functions that allow us to terminate the functions: *exit* and *abort*. Both functions are found in the standard library (`cstdlib`).

exit

Whereas *return* terminates a function, *exit* terminates the program regardless of where in the program it is executed. While we use it to terminate the program because we detected an error, C++ considers it a normal termination. For this reason, the termination is orderly; any pending file stream writes are first completed and all streams are closed. The exit prototype statement is shown below.

```
void exit (int completionStatus);
```

There is one parameter to the *exit* call, an integer value to be passed to the operating system. While any integer is acceptable, it is usually a nonzero, indicating that the program did not complete successfully. We demonstrate *exit* in the `calc` function in Program 5-10 on page 209.

abort

The *abort* function is used to terminate a program abnormally. It is considered a non-orderly termination because the output streams are not flushed and they are not closed. It is like drawing the "Go to Jail" card in Monopoly—you go directly to jail, you do not pass go, and you do not collect $200. When *abort* is called, the program immediately goes to the operating system.

The abort function has no parameters. Its prototype statement is shown below.

```
void abort ();
```

TWO-WAY SELECTION EXAMPLE

To demonstrate two-way selection, let's look at a program that calculates income taxes. A brief explanation of progressive tax brackets may be helpful. In this system, the higher the income, the higher the tax rate. However, the higher rates are applied only to the income in the bracket level. Thus, if you examine two incomes, they will both require the same taxes on the income at the lower tax brackets. This concept of marginal tax rates is shown in Table 5-6.

Case 1: Total Income 23,000			Case 2: Total Income 18,000		
Income in bracket	**Tax rate**	**Tax**	**Income in bracket**	**Tax rate**	**Tax**
(1) 10,000	2%	200	(1) 10,000	2%	200
(2) 10,000	5%	500	(2) 8,000	5%	400
(3) 3,000	7%	210	(3) none	7%	0
Total Tax		910	Total Tax		600

Table 5-6 Examples of marginal tax rates

The design for the program to calculate taxes is shown in the structure chart in Figure 5-17. There are only four functions besides *main*. The notation for `bracketTax` is somewhat unusual: in the final code, it is called five times in one expression. Therefore, we show it as a set of five calls.

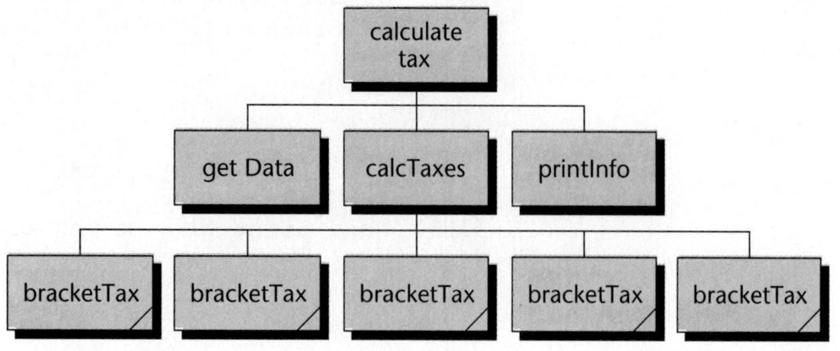

Figure 5-17 Design for calculate taxes

The pseudocode for the program is shown in Algorithm 5-1. Since the logic for reading and printing data is rather straightforward, it is not included in the pseudocode. The logic for calculating the tax information requires three major steps: (1) calculate the taxable income, (2) calculate the taxes, and (3) calculate the taxes due or to be refunded. Note that if more taxes were withheld than are due, the taxes due will be a negative number, indicating a refund.

Algorithm 5-1 Pseudocode for calculate taxes

```
Program Calculate Taxes
Calculate taxes based on marginal tax brackets.

1 Get income data
2 Calculate taxes
3 Print information

End Calculate Taxes
==================== calcTaxes ====================
calcTaxes
4 taxable income = total income - dependent exemptions
5 total tax = tax for bracket 1
                 + tax for bracket 2
                 + tax for bracket 3
                 + tax for bracket 4
                 + tax for bracket 5
6 tax due = total tax - taxes paid

End calcTaxes
```

The coding is seen in Program 5-5.

Program 5-5 Calculate taxes

```
/* Calculate the tax due or the refund for a family based
   on the following imaginary formula.
   1. For each dependent, deduct $1,000 from income.
   2. Determine tax rate from the following brackets:
      bracket taxable income       tax rate
         1          < 10001           2%
         2            10001-20000     5%
         3            20001-30000     7%
         4            30001-50000    10%
         5          > 50001          15%
   Then print the amount of tax or the refund.

      Written by:
      Date:
*/
#include <iostream>
#include <iomanip>
using namespace std;

```

Program 5-5 Calculate taxes *(continued)*

```
const double LOWEST  = 0000000.00;
const double HIGHEST = 1000000.00;

const double LIMIT1  = 10000.00;
const double LIMIT2  = 20000.00;
const double LIMIT3  = 30000.00;
const double LIMIT4  = 50000.00;

const double RATE1   = 02;
const double RATE2   = 05;
const double RATE3   = 07;
const double RATE4   = 10;
const double RATE5   = 15;

const double DEDN_PER_DPNDNT = 1000.00;

void getData   (double& totalIncome,  double& taxPaid,
                int&    numOfDpndnts);

void calcTaxes (double  totalIncome,  double  taxPaid,
                int     numOfDpndnts, double& taxableInc,
                double& totalTax,     double& taxDue);

void printInfo (double totalIncome,  double taxableInc,
                int    numOfDpndnts, double totalTax,
                double taxPaid,      double taxDue);

double bracketTax (double taxableInc, double startLimit,
                   double stopLimit,  int    rate);

int main ()
{
   int    numOfDpndnts;
   double taxDue;
   double taxPaid;
   double totalIncome;
   double taxableInc;
   double totalTax;

   getData   (totalIncome,   taxPaid,  numOfDpndnts);
   calcTaxes (totalIncome,   taxPaid,  numOfDpndnts,
              taxableInc,    totalTax, taxDue);
   printInfo (totalIncome,   taxableInc,
              numOfDpndnts,  totalTax,
              taxPaid,       taxDue);
   return 0;
}  // main
```

Program 5-5 Calculate taxes *(continued)*

```
/* =================== getData ====================
   This function reads tax data from the keyboard.
      Pre    Nothing
      Post   totalIncome, taxPaid, & numOfDpndnts read
*/
void getData (double& totalIncome,  double& taxPaid,
              int&    numOfDpndnts)
{
   cout << "Enter your total income for last year: ";
   cin  >> totalIncome;

   cout << "Enter total of payroll deductions:     ";
   cin  >> taxPaid;

   cout << "Enter the number of dependents:        ";
   cin  >> numOfDpndnts;
   return;
}  // getData
/* ================== calcTaxes ====================
   This function calculates the taxes due.
      Pre    Given-income, numOfDpndnts, & taxPaid
      Post   taxableInc, totTax, taxDue, calculated and
             returned by reference
*/
void calcTaxes (double  totalIncome,  double  taxPaid,
                int     numOfDpndnts, double& taxableInc,
                double& totalTax,     double& taxDue)
{
   taxableInc =
      totalIncome - (numOfDpndnts * DEDN_PER_DPNDNT);

   totalTax =
        bracketTax (taxableInc, LOWEST, LIMIT1, RATE1)
      + bracketTax (taxableInc, LIMIT1, LIMIT2, RATE2)
      + bracketTax (taxableInc, LIMIT2, LIMIT3, RATE3)
      + bracketTax (taxableInc, LIMIT3, LIMIT4, RATE4)
      + bracketTax (taxableInc, LIMIT4, HIGHEST, RATE5);

   taxDue = totalTax - taxPaid;
   return;
}  // calcTaxes
/* =================== printInfo ===================
   This function prints a table showing all information.
      Pre    The parameter list
      Post   Prints the table
*/
```

Program 5-5 Calculate taxes *(continued)*

```
void printInfo (double totalIncome,  double taxableInc,
                int    numOfDpndnts, double totalTax,
                double taxPaid,      double taxDue)
{
   cout << fixed << showpoint << setprecision(2);
   cout << "\nTotal income              : "
        << setw(10) << totalIncome;
   cout << "\nNumber of dependents      : "
        << setw( 7) << numOfDpndnts;
   cout << "\nTaxable income            : "
        << setw(10) << taxableInc;
   cout << "\nTotal tax                 : "
        << setw(10) << totalTax;
   cout << "\nTax already paid          : "
        << setw(10) << taxPaid;

   if (taxDue > 0.0)
       cout << "\nTax due                   : "
            << setw(10) << taxDue;
   else
       cout << "\nRefund                    : "
            << setw(10) << -taxDue;
   return;
} // printInfo
/* ================= bracketTax ==================
   Calculates the tax for a particular bracket.
      Pre    The taxableInc
      Post   Returns the tax for a particular bracket
*/
double bracketTax (double taxableInc, double startLimit,
                   double stopLimit,  int    rate)
{
   double tax;

   if (taxableInc <= startLimit)
      tax = 0.0;
   else
      if (taxableInc > startLimit
          && taxableInc <= stopLimit)
       tax = (taxableInc - startLimit) * rate / 100.00;
      else
       tax = (stopLimit  - startLimit) * rate / 100.00;

   return tax;
} // bracketTax
```

Program 5-5 Analysis Note that Program 5-5 contains extensive internal documentation. This documentation includes a series of comments at the beginning of the program and the global constants used to set some of the key values in the program.

Next examine the structure of the program: *main* contains no detail code, but simply calls three functions to get the job done. Since two of the functions must pass data back to *main*, they use pass by reference. Verify this by examining the prototype statements starting at statement 36. Note that the reference parameters use the address operator (&) to indicate they are pass-by-reference.

Now examine the code for `calcTaxes`. The function header (starting at statement 92) specifies that the first three formal parameters are passed as values and the last three are passed by reference. The last three are reference parameters because they are calculated values that need to be passed back to *main* for later printing.

Finally, and the main point of this example, note how we used the function, `bracketTax`, to calculate the tax. It was designed so that it could calculate the tax for any bracket. This is a much simpler design than writing complex code for different brackets and demonstrates how keeping it simple (KISS) makes for better programs.

5-3 MULTIWAY SELECTION

In addition to two-way selection, most programming languages provide another selection concept known as **multiway selection**. Multiway selection chooses among several alternatives.

There are two different ways to implement multiway selection in C++. The first is by using the ***switch*** statement. The other is by using a programming technique known as the ***else-if*** that provides a convenient style to nest *if* statements. The *switch* statement can be used only when the selection condition reduces to an integral expression. In many cases, however, such as when the selection is based on a range of values, the condition is not an integral. In these cases, we use the *else-if.*

THE *switch* STATEMENT

Switch is a composite statement used to make a decision between many alternatives. The selection condition must be one of the C++ integral types. Although any expression that reduces to an integral value may be used, the most common is a unary expression in the form of an integral identifier. The decision logic for the multiway statement is seen in Figure 5-18.

The *switch* expression contains the condition that is evaluated. For every possible value that can result from the condition, a separate **case** constant is defined. Associated with each possible *case* is one or more statements.

Figure 5-19 shows the *switch* format. There are several syntactical elements evident in this figure. First, there must be at least one *case* statement. Of course, if you had only one value to evaluate, you would not use a *switch* statement; you would use a simple *if...else*.

Second, each *case* expression is associated with a constant. The keyword *case* together with its constant are known as a ***case*-labeled statement**. The label is a syntactical identifier that is used by C++ to determine which statement should be used as the starting point in the *switch* statement. The *case* expression is followed by a colon (:) and then the statement with which it is associated.

There may be one or more statements for each *case*. Everything from a *case*-labeled statement to the next *case* statement is a sequence. The ***case* label** simply provides an entry point to start executing the code.

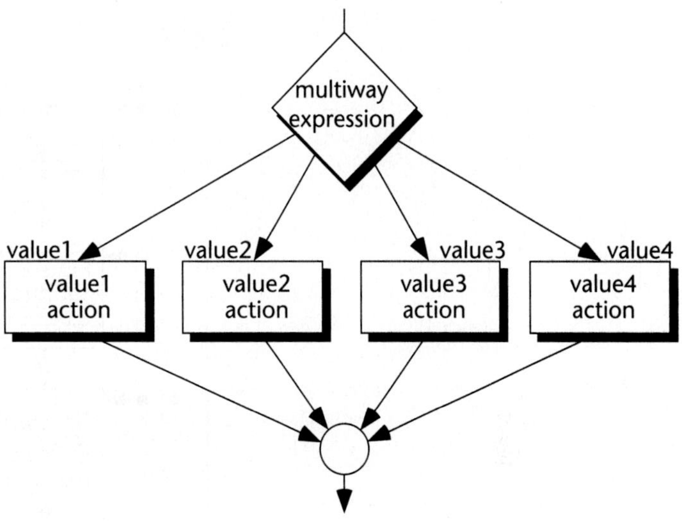

Figure 5-18 ***switch* decision logic**

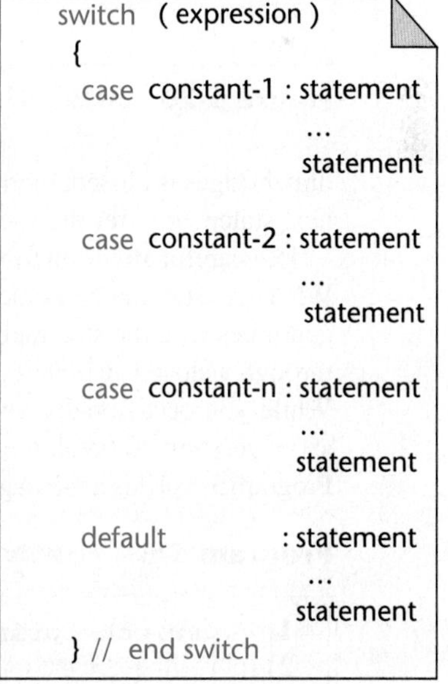

Figure 5-19 ***switch* statement**

The ***default* label** is a special form of the labeled statement. It is executed whenever none of the previous case values matched the value in the *switch* expression. Note, however, that *default* is not required. If you do not provide a *default*, the compiler will simply continue with the statement after the closing brace in the *switch*.

The *switch* statement is a puzzle that must be solved carefully to avoid confusion. Think of the *switch* statement as a series of drawbridges, one for each *case* and one for the *default*. As a result of the *switch* evaluation, one and only one of the drawbridges will be closed so that there will be a path for the program to follow. (If none of the

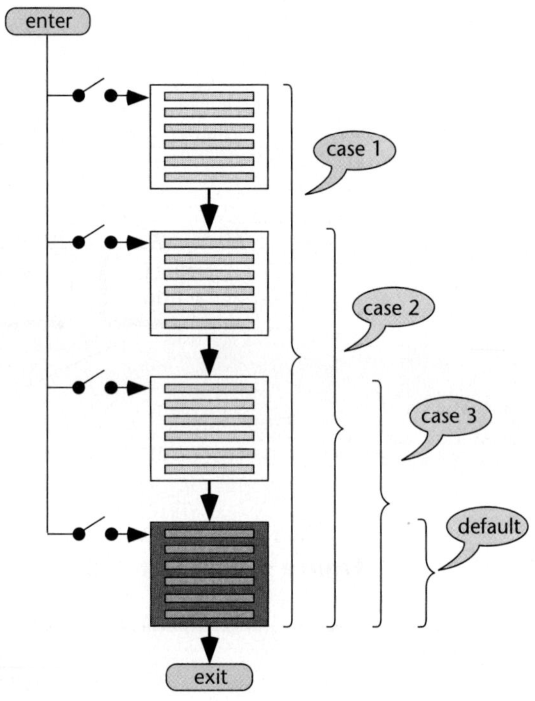

Figure 5-20 ***switch* flow**

drawbridges is closed, then the statement is skipped and the program continues with the next statement after the *switch*.) The *switch* flow is illustrated in Figure 5-20.

Pay careful attention to what happens once the program flow enters a *case* statement. When the statements associated with one *case* have been executed, the program flow continues with the statements for the next *case*. In other words, once the program enters through a closed *switch*, it executes the code for all of the following *cases* until the end. While you occasionally need this flexibility, it is not always what you want. We will show you how to break the flow shortly, but let's look at an example first. Each case in Program 5-6 prints a message and then calls a function. Can you figure out what is printed?

Program 5-6 **A *switch* statement**

```
switch (printFlag)
   {
    case 1:  cout << "do case 1\n";
             doCase1 ();
    case 2:  cout << "do case 2\n";
             doCase2 ();
    default: cout << "do default";
             doDefault ();
   }  // switch
```

There are three different *case*-labeled statements in Program 5-6. The first *case* statement identifies the entry point to be used when `printFlag` is a 1. The second *case* statement identifies the entry point when `printFlag` is a 2. And finally, the third *case* statement identifies the entry point when `printFlag` is neither a 1 nor a 2. While *default* is not a required condition in a *switch* statement, it should be included when all possible situations have not been covered by the *case* statements.

Have you figured out what is printed by Program 5-6? The answers are shown in Figure 5-21. There are three possibilities depending on the value in `printFlag`. If `printFlag` is a 1, then all three print statements are executed. If `printFlag` is a 2, then the first print statement is skipped and the last two are executed. Finally, if `printFlag` is neither a 1 nor a 2, then only *default* is executed. In this case, the first two print statements would be skipped and only the last one would be executed.

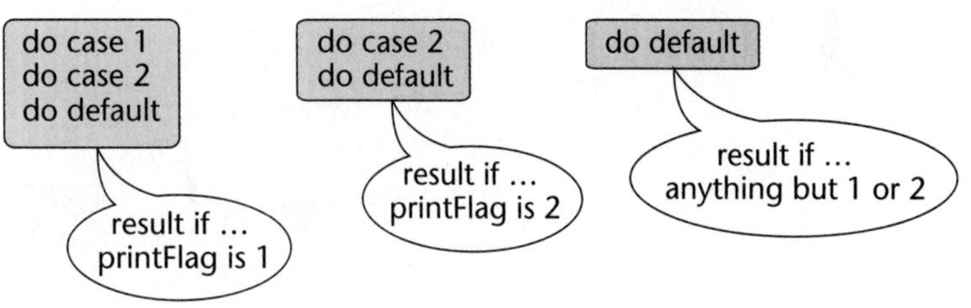

Figure 5-21 ***switch* results**

This use of the multiway selection is useful for accumulations. Consider the situation in which we have three objects, A, B, and C. Each object has a value. We want to accumulate three values: the value of A, the value of A and B, and the value of A, B, and C. The multiway selection for this logic is

```
switch (object)
   {
    case 'C': totalValue += C;
    case 'B': totalValue += B;
    case 'A': totalValue += A;
   } // switch
```

Note that we must list the cases in reverse order to get the correct total.

What if we want to execute only one of the cases? To do so, we must use ***break*** statements. The *break* statement causes the program to jump out of the *switch* statement; that is, to go to the closing brace and continue with the code that follows the *switch*. As shown in Figure 5-22, we can add a *break* as the last statement in each case. Now, only one print statements will be executed regardless of the value of `printFlag`.

Two or more *case* expression values can belong to the same *case* statement. In Program 5-7, for example, we print a message depending on whether `printFlag` is even or odd.

As a matter of style, the last statement in the *switch* does not require a *break*. We recommend, however, that you get in the habit of using it, especially when the last statement is not the default. This good habit will eventually save you hours of debugging time because you will not forget to add it when you add a new *case* to the statement.

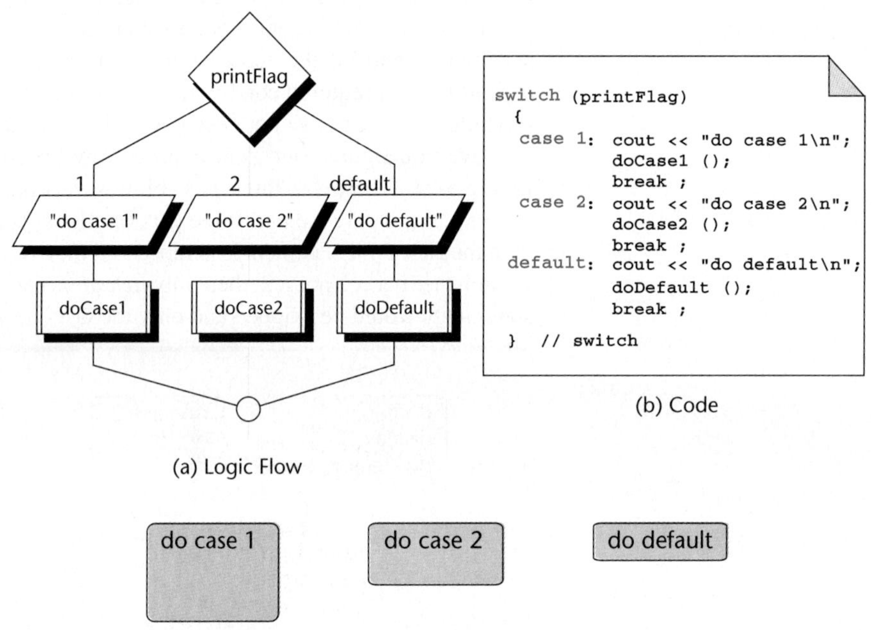

Figure 5-22 A *switch* with *break* statements

Program 5-7 Multivalued *case* statements

```
switch (printFlag)
   {
    case 1:
    case 3:   cout << "Good Day\n";
              cout << "Odds have it!\n";
              break;
    case 2:
    case 4:   cout << "Good Day\n";
              cout << "Evens have it!\n";
              break;
    default:  cout << "Good Day, I'm confused!\n";
              cout << "Bye!\n";
              break;
   } // switch
```

Table 5-7 summarizes some points to remember about the *switch* statement.

1. The control expression that follows the keyword *switch* must be an integral type.
2. The expression followed by each *case* label must be a constant expression. A constant expression is an expression that is evaluated at compilation time, not run time.
3. No two *case* labels may have the same value.
4. Two *case* labels may, however, be associated with the same statements.
5. The *default* **label** is not required. If the value of the expression does not match with any label, the control transfers outside of the *switch* statement.
6. There can be at most one *default* label. It may be coded anywhere, but it is traditionally coded last.

Table 5-7 Summary of *switch* statement rules

switch Example

Program 5-8 converts a numeric score to a letter grade. The grading scale is the rather typical "absolute scale" in which 90% or more is an A, 80 to 90% is a B, 70 to 80% is a C, and 60 to 70% is a D. Anything below 60% is an F.

Program 5-8 Student grading

```
/* This program reads a test score, calculates the letter
   grade for the score, and prints the grade.
      Written by:
      Date:
*/
#include <iostream>
using namespace std;

char scoreToGrade (int score);

int main ()
{
   cout << "Enter the test score (0-100): ";
   int  score;
   cin  >> score;

   char grade = scoreToGrade (score);
   cout << "The grade is: " << grade << endl;

   return 0;
}  // main
/* =============== scoreToGrade ====================
   This function calculates the letter grade for a score.
      Pre    the parameter score
      Post   Returns the grade
*/
char scoreToGrade (int score)
{
   int  temp = score / 10;
```

Program 5-8 Student grading *(continued)*

```
   char grade;
   switch (temp)
      {
       case 10 :
       case  9 : grade = 'A';
                 break;
       case  8 : grade = 'B';
                 break;
       case  7 : grade = 'C';
                 break;
       case  6 : grade = 'D';
                 break;
       default : grade = 'F';
      } // switch
   return grade;
}  // scoreToGrade
```

Program 5-8 Analysis This example shows how we can use the integer division operator (/) to change a range of numbers to individual points to be used by the *switch* statement. The problem requires that if the score is between 80 and 90%, it must be changed to letter grade B. This condition cannot be used in a *switch* statement. However, if we divide the score by 10 (integer division), the entire range (such as 80–89) can be changed to one single number (8), which can then be used as a constant in the *case*-labeled statement.

Note how the *break* statement works. This is an important part of the logic for *switch* statements. Without the *break*, we would have determined and assigned the score, and then proceeded to assign all of the lower scores down to F, with the result that everyone would have received a failing grade. The *break* allows us to leave the body of the *switch* as soon as we have completed the grade assignment.

One word of caution. If the user enters an invalid score, such as 110, this program gives invalid results. We will describe how to prevent this problem in the next chapter.

THE *else-if* STATEMENT

The *switch* statement only works when the *case* values are integral. What if we need to make a multiway decision on the basis of a value that is not integral? The answer is the *else-if.* There is no such C++ construct as the *else-if.* Rather, it is a style of coding that is used when you need a multiway selection based on a value that is not integral.

Suppose we require a selection based on a **range of values**. What we do is code the first *if* condition and its associated statements and then follow it with all other possible values using *else-if.* The last test in the series concludes with an *else.* This is the default condition; that is, it is the condition that is to be executed if all other statements are false. A sample of the *else-if* logic design is provided in Figure 5-23.

What is different about the *else-if* coding? As we said above, it is really nothing more than a style change. Rather than indenting each *if* statement, we code the *else-if* on a single line and align it with the previous *if.* In this way, we simulate the same formatting

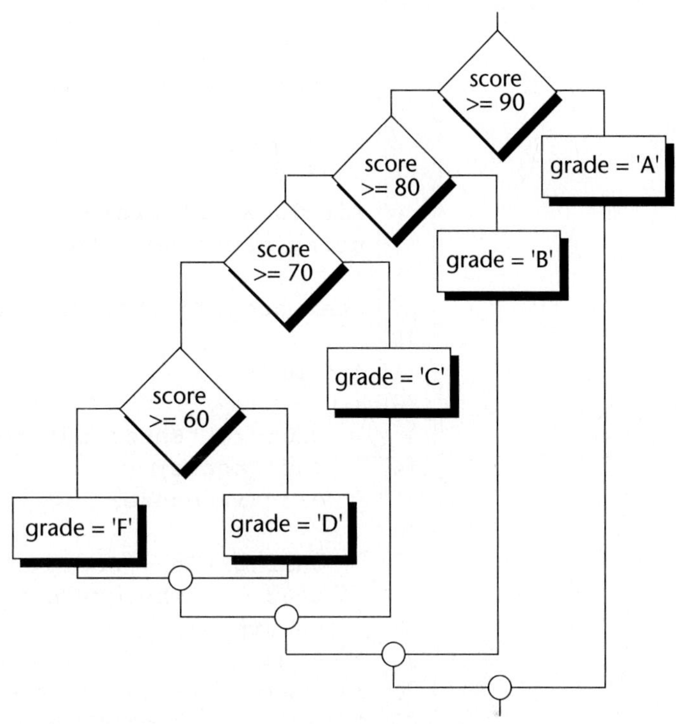

Figure 5-23 The *else...if* for Program 5-9

that you see in the *switch* and its associated *case* expressions. This style format is shown below.

```
if ( score >= 90 )
     grade = 'A';
else if ( score >= 80 )
     grade = 'B';
```

One important point about the *else-if*: It is used *only* when the same basic expression is being evaluated. In Figure 5-23, the expressions are all based on the variable `score`. If different variables were being evaluated, we would use the normal nesting associated with the *if...else* statement. Do not use the *else-if* format with nested *if* statements.

> **The *else-if* is an artificial C++ construct that is only used when**
> **1. The selection variable is not an integral, and**
> **2. The same variable is being tested in the expressions.**

else-if Example

Program 5-9 is the same as the *switch* example on page 201, but this time we use the *else-if* to solve the problem. This example shows how we can use multiway selection and the *else-if* construct to change a numeric score to a letter grade. The rule for the conversion is shown in the program itself.

Program 5-9 Convert score to grade

```
/* This program reads a test score, calculates the letter
   grade based on the absolute scale, and prints it.
      Written by:
      Date:
*/
#include <iostream>
using namespace std;

char scoreToGrade (int score);

int main ()
{
   cout << "Enter the test score (0-100): ";
   int  score;
   cin  >> score;

   char grade = scoreToGrade (score);
   cout << "The grade is: " << grade << endl;
   return 0;
} // main
/* ================ scoreToGrade ==================
This function calculates the letter grade for a score.
      Pre    the parameter score
      Post   Returns the grade
*/
char scoreToGrade (int score)
{
   char grade;
   if (score >= 90)
       grade = 'A';
   else if (score >= 80)
       grade = 'B';
   else if (score >= 70)
       grade = 'C';
   else if (score >= 60)
       grade = 'D';
   else
       grade = 'F';
   return grade;
}  // scoreToGrade
```

Program 5-9 Analysis The *else-if* construct was used because our condition was not an integral; rather, it tested several ranges of the same variable, `score`. Study the code carefully. Note how once the correct range is located, none of the following conditions will be tested. For instance, if a score of 85 is entered, the test against 90% is false, so we execute the *else-if* test for a score greater than 80%. Since this condition is true, we set `grade` to 'B' and skip all the remaining tests.

Also, note how the tests are ordered. In this case, we first eliminate those scores equal to or greater than 90%; then we check 80%, 70%, and 60% in turn. Since we were checking for greater than, we could not have coded it in the reverse, with 60% first. This is an important design concept: When checking a range using greater than, start with the largest value; when checking a range using less than, start with the lowest value.

5-4 MORE STANDARD LIBRARY FUNCTIONS

One of the assets of the C++ language is its rich set of standard functions that make programming much easier. In Chapter 4, we introduced some of these standard functions. Now that we have studied selection, we can discuss two other groups of standard functions that are closely related to selection statements.

STANDARD CHARACTERS FUNCTIONS

There are many important library functions available in C++ for manipulating characters. They are divided into two major groups: classifying functions and converting functions. The prototypes of these functions are in the **<cctype>** header file (character type). Before looking at these functions, let's take a look at the classification of characters that is used by C++. This breakdown of characters is shown in Figure 5-24, which uses a tree to show how characters are classified. You read the tree much like a structure chart, starting at the top and following the branches to the bottom.

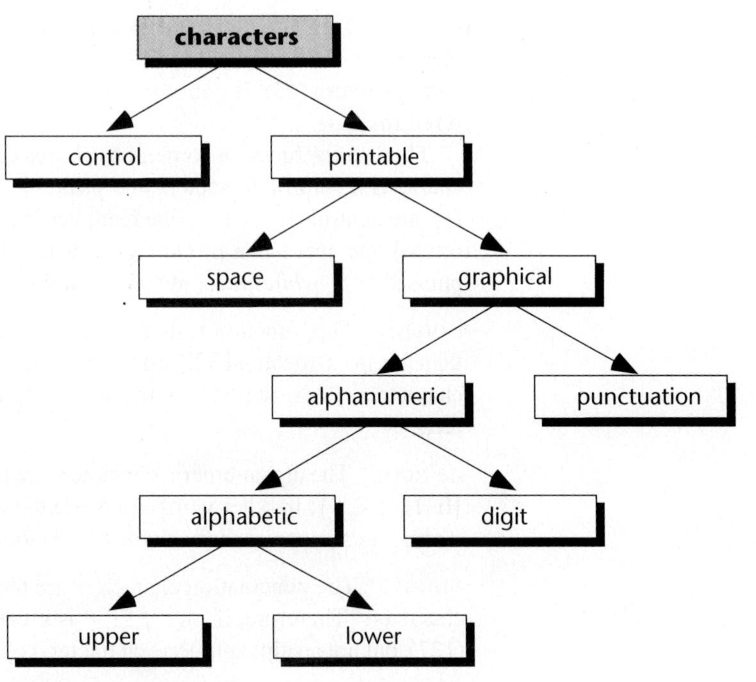

Figure 5-24 Classifications of the character type

Characters are first broken down into control characters, such as carriage return and end of file, or into printable characters. This initial breakdown tells us that control characters are not printable. The printable characters are either a space or the rest of the printable characters, which are classified as graphical. In turn, the graphical characters are broken down into alphanumeric and punctuation characters. Alphanumeric means either an alphabetic character or a digit. Finally, alphabetic characters are either uppercase or lowercase.

Classifying Functions

Classifying functions examine a character and tell if it belongs to a given classification, as described above. They all start with the prefix *is* and return *true* (or integer 1) if the actual parameter is in the specified class and *false* (or 0) if it is not. The prototypes of these functions are found in the *<cctype>* file.

The general form of the prototype function[2] is

```
int is… ( int testChar );
```

where the function name starts with *is*; for example, *iscntrl*, which stands for "is a control character." Listed below is a brief explanation of each function's operation. One final point: Even though the function type is integer, you don't have to concern yourself about it because C++ automatically casts characters to integers and back for you.

iscntrl The ASCII control characters are all the values below space (decimal 32) and the delete character (decimal 127).[3] If `testChar` is one of these values, *iscntrl* returns *true*; otherwise, *iscntrl* returns *false*.

isprint This function is the complement of *iscntrl*. The function *isprint* returns *true* if the value in `testChar` is greater than 31 and less than 127; otherwise, it returns *false*.

isspace This function checks for whitespace. Whitespace consists of the space character (32), horizontal tab (9), line feed (10), vertical tab (11), form feed (12), and carriage return (13). If `testChar` is any of these values, *isspace* returns *true*; otherwise, it returns *false*.

The *isspace* function sometimes causes confusion because it deals with two types of characters: control characters and printable characters. Four of the whitespace characters are control characters (line feed, vertical tab, horizontal tab, form feed, and carriage return); the space is a printable character. The name of this function would be better phrased as *is_whitespace*, but we must live with the name given it long ago.

isgraph This function tests for a graphic character. All of the ASCII values greater than the space (decimal 32) and less than the delete (decimal 127) are considered graphic characters. If `testChar` is in this range, *isgraph* returns *true*; otherwise, it returns *false*.

isalnum The alphanumeric characters are the sets {A, B,…, Y, Z}, {a, b,…, y, z}, and {0, 1,…, 8, 9}; in other words, they are the alphabetic letters and the numeric digits. If `testChar` is one of these characters, *isalnum* returns *true*; otherwise, it returns *false*.

ispunct The punctuation characters are the graphic complement of the alphanumeric characters. Therefore, if `testChar` is greater than a space (32) and less than a delete (127), but not an alphanumeric character, *ispunct* returns *true*; otherwise, it returns *false*.

---

[2]The actual implementation may use macros rather than functions. For an explanation of macros, see Appendix G,"Preprocessor Directives."

[3]Decimal 127 is the last of the standard ASCII character set. Although the values from decimal 128 to 255 can be represented in a byte, they are considered part of the extended ASCII set and are excluded from consideration by these functions.

isalpha The alphabetic set consists of the characters {A, B,..., Y, Z, a, b,..., y, z}. If `testChar` is one of these values, *isalpha* returns *true*; otherwise, it returns *false*.

islower If `testChar` is in the set {a, b,..., y, z}, *islower* returns *true*; otherwise, it returns *false*.

isupper If `testChar` is in the set {A, B,..., Y, Z}, *isupper* returns *true*; otherwise, it returns *false*.

isdigit If `testChar` is a decimal digit, {0, 1,..., 8, 9}, *isdigit* returns *true*; otherwise, it returns *false*.

isxdigit This is a special test for hexadecimal digits. The hexadecimal digits are the decimal digits plus the first six alphabetic characters, both upper- and lowercase {0, 1,..., 8, 9, a,..., f, A,..., F}. If `testChar` is in this set, *isxdigit* returns *true*; otherwise, it returns *false*.

Character Conversion Functions

Two functions in C++ are used to convert a character from one class to another. These functions start with the prefix *to* and return an *integer* that is the value of the converted character.

toupper This function converts the parameter to an uppercase letter {A, B,..., Y, Z} if it is in the lowercase set {a, b,..., y, z}. If it is not in the lowercase set, *toupper* simply returns the parameter.

tolower This function converts the parameter to a lowercase letter {a, b,..., y, z} if it is in the uppercase set {A, B,..., Y, Z}. If it is not, *tolower* simply returns the parameter.

5-5 A MENU PROGRAM

The menu program shown in Program 5-10 uses a somewhat oversimplified example to illustrate how you can communicate with a user through a menu. Figure 5-25 shows the design of the program.

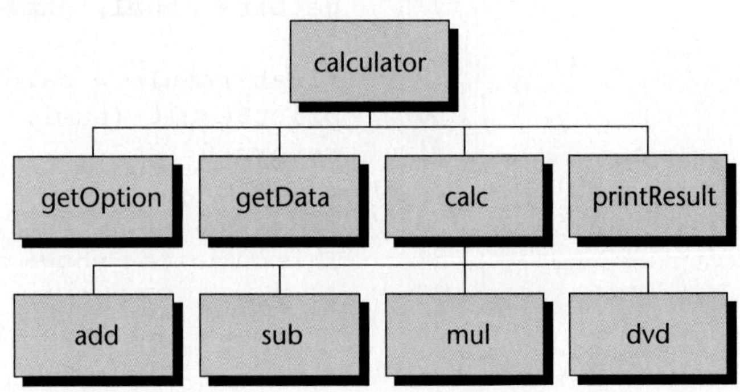

Figure 5-25 Design for menu-driven calculator

In this program, we are doing four different "things." First, we must ask the user what function is desired. Then we need to get the data for the operation, make the calculation, and, finally, print the result. These four processes are seen as called functions in *main*.

In turn, `calc` calls four functions, each one used to perform an arithmetic operation. We could have written one calculate function, but that would have combined four different types of calculations in one function.

Program 5-10 Code for menu-driven calculator

```
/* This program uses a menu to allow the user to add,
   multiply, subtract, or divide two integers.
      Written by:
      Date:
*/
#include <iostream>
#include <cstdlib>
#include <iomanip>
using namespace std;

void  getData     (float &num1,   float &num2);
void  printResult (float  num1,   float  num2,
                   float  result, int    option);
int   getOption   (void);

float calc       (int option, float num1, float num2);
float add          (float num1, float num2);
float sub          (float num1, float num2);
float mul          (float num1, float num2);
float dvd          (float num1, float num2);

int main ()
{
   int option = getOption();

   float   num1;
   float   num2;
   getData (num1, num2);

   float result = calc (option, num1, num2);
   printResult (num1, num2, result, option);
   return 0;
} // main
/* ================== getOption ====================
   This function shows a menu and reads the user option.
      Pre    Nothing
      Post   Returns the option
*/
int getOption()
{
   cout << "\n\n\n";
   cout << "\n\t**********************************";
   cout << "\n\t*              MENU              *";
   cout << "\n\t*                                *";
```

Program 5-10 Code for menu-driven calculator *(continued)*

```
   cout << "\n\t*  1. ADD                          *";
   cout << "\n\t*  2. SUBTRACT                     *";
   cout << "\n\t*  3. MULTIPLY                     *";
   cout << "\n\t*  4. DIVIDE                       *";
   cout << "\n\t*                                  *";
   cout << "\n\t**********************************";

   cout << "\n\nPlease type your choice "
        << "and press the return key : ";
   int  option;
   cin  >> option;
   return option;
} // getOption
/* =================== getData ====================
   This function reads two numbers from the keyboard.
      Pre  Nothing
      Post Two numbers read into variables in main
*/
void getData (float &num1, float &num2)
{
   cout << "\nEnter two numbers separated by a space: ";
   cin  >> num1 >> num2;
   return;
} // getData
/* =================== calc ====================
   This function determines the type of operation
   and calls a function to perform it.
      Pre  option contains the operation
           num1 & num2 contain data
      Post Returns the results
*/
float calc (int option, float num1, float num2)
{
   float result;
   switch (option)
       {
        case 1 : result = add (num1, num2);
                 break;
        case 2 : result = sub (num1, num2);
                 break;
        case 3 : result = mul (num1, num2);
                 break;
        case 4 : if (num2 == 0.0)
                    {
                     cout << "\n\a\aError: ";
                     cout << "division by zero ***\n";
                     exit (1);
                    }
```

Program 5-10 Code for menu-driven calculator *(continued)*

```
                     else
                         result = dvd (num1, num2);
                     break;

/* Better structured programming would validate the
   option in getOption. However, we have not yet
   introduced the technique required to put it there.
*/
          default : cout <<"\aOption not available\n";
                    exit (1);
         } // switch
   return result;
}  // calc
/* ==================== add ====================
   This function adds two numbers.
      Pre  The two numbers are given as parameters
      Post Return the results
*/
float add (float num1, float num2)
{
   return num1 + num2;
}  // add
/* ==================== sub ====================
   This function subtracts two numbers.
      Pre    The two numbers are given as parameters
      Post   Return the results
*/
float sub (float num1, float num2)
{
   return num1 - num2;
}  // sub
/* ==================== mul ====================
   This function multiplies two numbers.
      Pre    The two numbers are given as parameters
      Post   Return the results
*/
float mul (float num1, float num2)
{
   return num1 * num2;
}  // mul
/* ==================== dvd ====================
   This function divides two numbers
      Pre    The two numbers are given as parameters
      Post   Return the results
*/
float dvd (float num1, float num2)
```

Program 5-10 Code for menu-driven calculator *(continued)*

```
{
   return num1 / num2;
} // dvd
/* ================= printResult ==================
   This function prints the result of calculation.
      Pre   The two numbers, result, and option are given
      Post  Prints the numbers and the result
*/
void printResult (float num1, float num2,
                        float res,  int   option)
{
   cout << fixed << setprecision(2);
   cout << "\n\n" << num1;
   switch (option)
      {
       case 1 : cout <<" + ";
                break;
       case 2 : cout <<" - ";
                break;
       case 3 : cout <<" * ";
                break;
       case 4 : cout <<" / ";
                break;
      } // switch option
   cout << num2 << " = " << res << endl;
   return;
} // printResults
```

Program 5-10 Analysis You should spend some time studying this program because it demonstrates several techniques that you will use again and again.

First, study the menu display function, `getOption`. This is a common technique when you have to interact with users. It allows them to select from a set of prescribed options. In the next chapter, we will describe how to validate the options in `getOption`, which will make it a much more powerful function.

Next, note how we give users detailed instructions on how to enter the numbers. We also make sure they know when something has gone wrong, such as when a zero divisor is entered. These are some of the little user communication techniques that make for a user-friendly system.

Finally, study the *switch* statements that are found in `calc` and in `printResults`. Note how they are formatted for readability. Note also that with the exception of the test for divide by zero, we have kept the *case* options as simple as possible. Generally speaking, you want to keep the code in a *case* option simple.

5-6 SOFTWARE ENGINEERING AND PROGRAMMING STYLE

DEPENDENT STATEMENTS

Several statements in the C++ language control other statements that follow them. The *if...else* is the first of these statements that we have presented. When one statement controls or influences statements that follow it, good structured programming style indents the dependent statements to show that the indented code is dependent on the controlling statement. The compiler does not need the **indentation**—it follows its syntactical rules regardless of how a program is formatted—but good style makes for readable programs.

To illustrate the point, consider the two versions of the code for the function in Program 5-11. Both versions accomplish the same task. To make this exercise even more meaningful, cover up the right half of the program and predict the results that will be produced when the ill-formed code executes. Then look at the well-structured code.

Program 5-11 Examples of poor and good nesting styles

Poor Style

```
1  int someFun (int a,
2                int b )
3  {
4  int x;
5
6     if ( a < b )
7     x = a;
8     else
9        x = b;
10       x *= .5f;
11    return x;
12 } // someFun
```

Good Style

```
1  int someFun (int a,
2                int b )
3  {
4     int x;
5
6     if ( a < b )
7        x = a;
8     else
9        x = b;
10    x *= .5f;
11    return x;
12 } // someFun
```

Assume that in this example, a has a value of 10 and b has a value of 20. What value will be returned? First look at statement 7. The assignment of x in this example is dependent on the *if* in statement 6. Since it is not indented, however, the dependency is not readily apparent. Since the value of a (10) is less than the value of b (20), x will be assigned the value 10.

Now, examine statement 10. It is indented and therefore appears to be dependent on the *else* statement. But is it? The answer is no. It just looks that way and is therefore misleading. Statement 10 will therefore execute regardless of the expression in the *if* statement. This relationship is much more clearly seen in the code on the right. The code on the right is properly indented to show the relationships among the statements, and therefore, the chance of misreading the code is minimal.

The **indentation rules** are summarized in Table 5-8.

1. Statements that are dependent on previous statements should be indented at least three spaces from the left end of the controlling statement.
2. Any else statements should be aligned with their corresponding if statement. (See Figure 5-13 on page 188.)
3. The opening brace identifying a body of code should be placed on a separate line. The statements in the body of the code should be indented one space to the right of the opening brace.
4. The closing brace identifying a body of code should be aligned with the opening brace and should be placed on a separate line. Use a comment to identify the block being terminated.
5. All code on the same level, which is dependent on the same control statement, should be aligned to the same point.
6. Nested statements should be further indented according to the above rules.
7. Whitespace should surround operators.
8. Only one variable declaration/definition should be coded on a line.
9. Only one statement should be coded on a line
10. Comments should be meaningful at the block level. They should not simply parrot the code.

Table 5-8 Indentation rules

Negative Logic

In the discussion of Figure 5-12 on page 184 and in the section on simplifying the *if* statement, one technique that we proposed was complementing a conditional statement. This requires making a positive statement negative and a negative statement positive. This can be done by following rule 6 in Table 5-3 on page 182, which states that the positions of the statements in an *else...if* can be swapped if the original control expression is complemented. The concept of complementing the *if* statement was shown in Figure 5-10 on page 184.

One thing to remember, however, is that simple code is the clearest code. This concept has been formulated into an acronym, KISS, which stands for "Keep It Simple and Short!" (See Chapter 4.) Unfortunately, **negative logic** is not always simple. In fact, it can get extremely confusing. We have seen professional programmers work for hours trying to debug negative logic.

Avoid compound negative statements!

When you complement an expression, make sure that the resulting statement is easily readable. Complementing an expression can be more difficult than simply making the condition negative. For example, examine the third statement in Table 5-9 carefully. Note that the complement of the *not* (!) is *not-not* (! !), which in effect cancels the *not*. In general, good programmers try to avoid compound negative statements. In this case, therefore, the complemented statement is greatly preferred.

Original statement	Complemented statement
`if ( x <= 0 )`	`if ( x > 0 )`
`if ( x != 5 )`	`if ( x == 5 )`
`if ( !( x <= 0 || !flag ) )`	`if ( x > 0 && flag )`

Table 5-9 Complementing expressions

Rules for Selection Statements

When it comes to selection statements, three other rules need to be considered. They are shown in Table 5-10. Since these rules are sometimes conflicting, they are listed in their order of importance.

1. Code positive statements whenever possible.
2. Code the normal/expected condition first.
3. Code the most probable conditions first.

Table 5-10 Selection rules

Human engineering studies have shown that people make fewer errors when reading positive statements than when reading negative statements. This is especially true when complex, compound Boolean statements are involved. Therefore, whenever possible, code your selection statements using positive conditions.

The second rule concerns the human expectations about what is to follow. People have a tendency to anticipate things. They will therefore be less confused if what follows is what is expected. In most cases, this means coding the anticipated condition first.

Finally, the third rule concerns the efficiency of the resulting program. Coding the most probable conditions first is especially important in a multiway selection, such as the *else-if.* When you code the most probable test first, then the program can skip the rest of the statements—and the more statements skipped, the more efficient the resulting program.

As we mentioned previously, these rules often conflict with each other. We have listed them in their order of importance from a human engineering point of view. Unless there are overriding circumstances, you should select the higher option (rule 1 before rule 2 before rule 3) in case of conflicts. But remember the most basic principle: KISS—Keep It Simple and Short.

Selection in Structure Charts

We introduced the basic concepts of **structure charts** in Chapter 4. In Figure 4-24 on page 162, there are two symbols for a function that is called by a selection statement: the condition and the exclusive *or*. We repeat them in Figure 5-26 for your convenience.

In Figure 5-26, the function `doIt` contains a conditional call to a sub-function, `fun`. If the condition in the *if* statement is true, we call it. If it is not true, we do not call it. This situation is represented in a structure chart as a small diamond on the vertical line between the two function blocks.

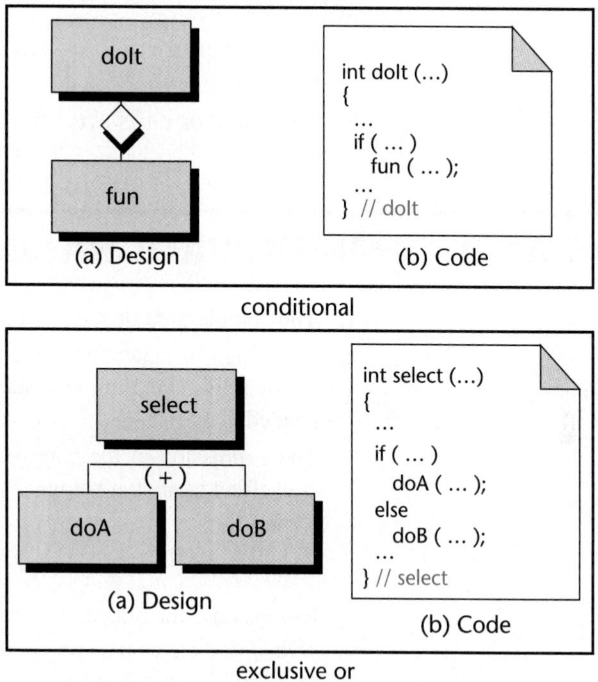

Figure 5-26 Structure chart symbols for selection

Figure 5-26 represents the **selection** between two different functions. In this example, the function `select` chooses between `doA` and `doB`. One and only one of them will be called each time the conditional statement is executed. This is known as an ***exclusive or***; one of the two alternatives is executed to the exclusion of the other. The *exclusive or* is represented by a plus sign between the processes.

Now consider the design used when a series of functions can be called exclusively. This occurs when a multiway selection contains calls to several different functions. Figure 5-27 contains an example of a *switch* statement that calls different functions based on color.

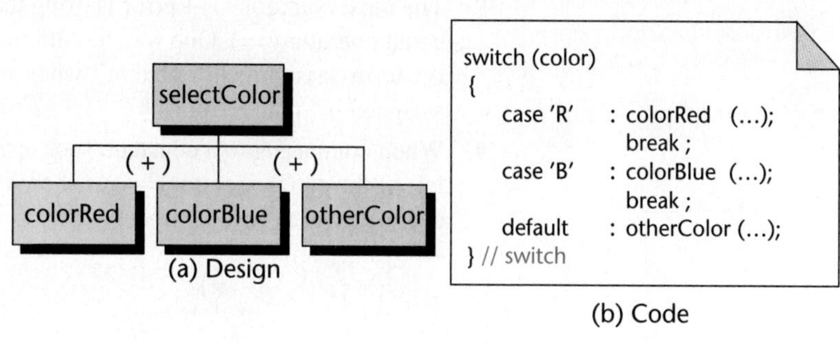

Figure 5-27 Multiway selection in a structure chart

To summarize, the structure chart rules described in this section are as follows:

1. Conditional calls are indicated by a diamond above the function rectangle.
2. *Exclusive or* calls are indicated by a (+) between functions.

5-7 TIPS AND COMMON PROGRAMMING ERRORS

1. The complement of < is >= and the complement of > is <=.
2. Dangling *else* statements are easily created and difficult to debug. One technique for avoiding dangling *else* statements is to use braces, even when they are not needed.
3. The expression in the control expression in the *if...else* statement may have a side effect as shown below.

```
if ( a++ )
```

4. Encapsulate the statements inside braces if you have more than one statement after *if* or *else* in an *if...else* statement.
5. Do not use the equal operator with a floating-point number. Floating-point numbers are seldom exactly equal to a required value. When you need to test for equality, such as a == b, use the expression shown below.

```
if ( fabs ( a - b ) < .0000001 )
```

6. Do not forget to use a *break* statement when the cases in a *switch* statement are exclusive.
7. While not necessarily an error, it is poor programming practice to write a *switch* statement without a *default.* If the logic doesn't require one, code it with an error message to guard against unanticipated conditions. This is shown below.

```
default:  cerr << "\aImpossible default\n";
          exit (100);
```

8. The most common C++ error is using the assignment operator (=) in place of the equal operator (==). One way to minimize this error is to get in the habit of using the term "assignment operator" when reading the code. For example, say "a is assigned b," not "a equals b."
9. When comparing to a constant, such as a literal, always code the constant on the left of the equal operator (==) as shown below. Then, if you make a mistake and accidently use the assignment operator, the compiler will catch the error.

```
if (5 == x)
```

10. For the reasons stated on the next page, it may be an error to place a semicolon after the *if* expression.

a. The semicolon terminates the *if* statement, and any statement that follows it is not part of the *if*.

b. It is a compile error to code an *else* without a matching *if*. This error is usually created by a misplaced semicolon.

```
if ( a == b );              // If terminated here
   cout << … ;
else                        // No matching if
   cout << … ;
```

11. It is a compile error to forget the parentheses in the *if* expression.
12. It is a compile error to put a space between the following relational operators ==, !=, >=, <=. It is also a compile error to reverse them.
13. It is a compile error to use a variable rather than an integral constant as the value in a *case* label.
14. It is a compile error to use the same constant in two *case* labels.
15. The logical operators require two ampersands (&&) or two bars (||). It is a logic error to code them with only one. (Single operators are bitwise operators and are therefore valid code.)
16. It is generally a logic error to use side effects in the second operand in a logical binary expression, as shown below, because the second operand may not be evaluated.

```
( a++ && --b )
```

5-8 KEY TERMS

and operator **(&&)**
break
case
case label
case-labeled statement
complemented *if...else* statement
<cctype>
dangling *else*
De Morgan's rule
default
default label
else-if construct
equal operator (==)
exclusive or
greater than operator (>)
greater than or equal operator (>=)
if...else
indentation
indentation rules
less than operator (<)
less than or equal operator (<=)
logical data
logical operator
multiway selection
negative logic
nested *if* statement
not equal operator (!=)
not operator (!)
null *else*
or operator (||)
range of values
relational operator
selection
selection (in structure chart)
simplifying *if...else* statements
structure chart
switch
two-way selection

5-9 SUMMARY

- Data are called logical if they convey the idea of true or false.
- Logical data in C++ are represented by the Boolean type, *bool*. The type *bool* uses two predefined constants: *true* and *false*.
- C++ also supports the traditional C approach, which uses integral values to represent logical data: If a data item is nonzero, it is considered true; if it is zero, it is considered false.
- C++ has three operators for combining logical values to create new values: *not*, *and*, *or*.
- Six relational operators are used in C++: <, <=, >, >=, ==, and !=.
- Selection in C++ is done using two statements: *if...else* and *switch*.
- The *if...else* construct is used for selection between two alternatives.
- You can swap the statements in the true and false branches if you use the complement of an expression in an *if...else* statement.
- If the false statement is not required in an *if...else*, it is omitted and the keyword *else* is dropped.
- If an *else* is dangling, it will be paired with the last unpaired *if*.
- Multiway selection can be accomplished using either the *switch* statement or an *else-if* format.
- The *switch* statement is used to make a decision between many alternatives when the different conditions can be expressed as integral values.
- The *else-if* format is used to make multiple decisions when the item being tested is not an integral and therefore a *switch* statement cannot be used.
- A *case*-labeled statement is used for selection in a *switch* statement.
- A *default*-labeled statement is used as the last statement in a *switch* statement, to be executed when none of the case alternatives match the tested value.
- Indenting the controlled statements in C++ is good style that enhances the readability of a program.
- Selection is used in a structure chart only when it involves a call to another function.
- The structure chart for selection shows the paths taken by the logic flow. You cannot always tell by looking at the structure chart which selection will be used (two-way or multiway).
  a. A simple *if* is indicated by a diamond below the calling function.
  b. An *if...else* and *switch* are indicated by the *exclusive or* (+).

5-10 PRACTICE SETS

REVIEW QUESTIONS

1. Logical data are data that can be interpreted as true or false.
   a. True
   b. False
2. The expression in a selection statement can have no side effects.
   a. True
   b. False
3. Each case-labeled statement may identify one or more statements.
   a. True
   b. False
4. The character classification functions are found in the standard library (`cstdlib`).
   a. True
   b. False
5. To ensure that a character is uppercase, the *toupper* conversion function is used.
   a. True
   b. False
6. The ___________ logical operator is true only when both operands are true.
   a. and (`&&`)
   b. less than (`<`)
   c. not (`!`)
   d. greater than (`>`)
   e. or (`||`)

7. Which of the following is not a relational operator in C++?
   a. <
   b. =
   c. >=
   d. <=
   e. >
8. Two-way selection is implemented with the ____________ statement.
   a. *case*
   b. *else if*
   c. *switch*
   d. the *if...else* and the *switch*
   e. *if...else*
9. Which of the following is not a syntactical rule for the *if...else* statement?
   a. Any expression can be used for the *if* expression.
   b. Only one statement is allowed for the true and the false actions.
   c. The true and the false statements can be another *if...else* statement.
   d. The expression must be enclosed in parentheses.
   e. The selection expression cannot have a side effect.
10. Which of the following statements creates the "dangling *else* problem"?
    a. A nested *if* statement without a false statement
    b. A nested *if* statement without a true statement
    c. A *switch* statement without a default
    d. An *if* statement without a true or a false statement
    e. Any nested *if* statement
11. There are two different ways to implement a multi-way selection in C++. They are
    a. *if...else* and *switch*
    b. *else-if* and *switch*
    c. *if...else* and *else if*
    d. *switch* and *case*
    e. *else-if* and *case*
12. Which of the following statements about *switch* statements is false?
    a. No two *case* labels can have the same value.
    b. The *switch* control expression must be an integral type.
    c. The *case*-labeled expression can be a constant or a variable.
    d. Two *case* labels can be associated with the same statement series.
    e. A *switch* statement can have at most one *default* statement.
13. Which of the following statements about the *else-if* is false?
    a. Each expression in the *else-if* must test the same variable.
    b. The *else-if* is a coding style rather than a C++ construct.
    c. The *else-if* requires integral values in its expression.
    d. The *else-if* is used for multiway selections.
    e. The last test in the *else-if* series concludes with a single *else*, which is the default condition.
14. Which of the following is not a character classification in the C++ language?
    a. Ascii
    b. Digit
    c. Space
    d. Control
    e. Graphical

EXERCISES

15. If `x = 3`, `y = 0`, and `z = -4`, what is the value of each of the following expressions?
    a. x && y || z
    b. x || y && z
    c. (x && y) || z
    d. (x || y) && z
    e. (x && z) || y

16. Simplify the following expressions by removing the ! operator and the parentheses:
    a. !(x < y)
    b. !(x >= y
    c. !(x == y)
    d. !(x != y
    e. !(! (x > y))
17. If x = −2, y = 5, z = 0, and t = −4, what is the value of each of the following expressions?
    a. x + y < z + t
    b. x − 2 * y + y < z * 2 / 3
    c. 3 * y / 4 % 5 && y
    d. t || z < (y + 5) && y
    e. !(4 + 5 * y >= z − 4) && (z − 2)
18. If originally x = 4, y = 0, and z = 2, what are the values of x, y, and z after executing the following code?

```
if ( x != 0 )
   y = 3;
else
   z = 2;
```

19. If originally x = 4, y = 0, and z = 2, what are the values of x, y, and z after executing the following code?

```
if ( z == 2 )
   y = 1;
else
   x = 3;
```

20. If originally x = 4, y = 0, and z = 2, what are the values of x, y, and z after executing the following code?

```
if ( x && y  )
   x = 3;
else
   y = 2;
```

21. If originally x = 4, y = 0, and z = 2, what are the values of x, y, and z after executing the following code?

```
if ( x || y || z  )
   y = 1;
else
   z = 3;
```

22. If originally x = 0, y = 0, and z = 1, what are the values of x, y, and z after executing the following code?

```
if ( x  )
   if ( y )
      z = 3;
else
   z = 2;
```

23. If originally x = 4, y = 0, and z = 2, what are the values of x, y, and z after executing the following code?

```
if ( z == 0 || x  && !y  )
   if ( !z )
     y = 1;
else
   x = 2;
```

24. If originally x = 0, y = 0, and z = 1, what are the values of x, y, and z after executing the following code?

```
if ( x  )
   if ( y )
      if ( z )
         z = 3;
      else
         z = 2;
```

25. If originally x = 0, y = 0, and z = 1, what are the values of x, y, and z after executing the following code?

```
if ( z < x ||  y >= z && z == 1 )
    if ( z && y )
      y = 1;
else
   x = 1;
```

26. If originally x = 0, y = 0, and z = 1, what are the values of x, y, and z after executing the following code?

```
if ( z = y  )
   {
    y++;
    z--;
   }
else
   --x;
```

27. If originally x = 0, y = 0, and z = 1, what are the values of x, y, and z after executing the following code?

```
if ( z = x < y  )
   {
    x + = 3;
    y - = 1;
   }
else
   x = y++;
```

28. If originally x = 0, y = 0, and z = 1, what are the values of x, y, and z after executing the following code?

```
switch ( x )
{
 case 0 :x = 2;
         y = 3;
 case 1 :x = 4;
 default :y = 3;
         x = 1;
}
```

29. If originally x = 2, y = 1, and z = 1, what are the values of x, y, and z after executing the following code?

```
switch ( x )
{
 case 0 :x = 2;
         y = 3;
 case 1 :x = 4;
         break;

default  :
         y = 3;
         x = 1;
}
```

30. If originally x = 1, y = 3, and z = 0, what are the values of x, y, and z after executing the following code?

```
switch ( x )
   {
    case 0 :x = 2;
            y = 3;
            break;
    case 1 :x = 4;
            break;
    default :y = 3;
            x = 1;
   }
```

31. Evaluate the value of each of the following expressions:
    a. tolower ('C')
    b. tolower ('?')
    c. tolower ('c')
    d. tolower ('5')
32. Evaluate the value of each of the following expressions:
    a. toupper ('c')
    b. toupper ('C')
    c. toupper ('?')
    d. toupper ('7')
33. Use De Morgan's rule to simplify the following expressions:
    a. !(x && y)
    b. !(y || !z)
    c. !(x || y)
    d. !(!(x && y)
34. How many values of the variable num must be used to completely test all branches of the following code fragment?

```
if (num > 0)
   if (value < 25)
      {
       value = 10 * num;
       if (num < 12)
           value = value / 10;
      } /* if sum */
   else
      value = 20 * num;
else
   value = 30 * num;
```

PROBLEMS

35. Write an *if* statement that will assign the value 1 to the variable best if the integer variable score is 90 or greater.
36. Repeat Problem 35 using a conditional expression.
37. Write the code to add 4 to an integer variable, num, if a float variable, amount, is greater than 5.4.
38. Print the value of the integer num if the variable flag is true.
39. Write the code to print either zero or not zero based on the integer variable num.
40. If the variable divisor is not zero, divide the variable dividend by divisor, and store the result in quotient. If divisor is zero, assign it to quotient. Then print all three variables. Assume that dividend and divisor are integers and quotient is a double.

41. If the variable `flag` is true, read the integer variables `a` and `b`. Then calculate and print the sum and average of both inputs.

42. Rewrite the following code using one *if* statement:

```
if (aChar == 'E')
     c++;
if (aChar == 'E')
     printf ("Value is E\n");
```

43. Rewrite the following code fragment using one *switch* statement:

```
if (ch == 'E' || ch == 'e')
   countE++;
else if (ch == 'A' || ch == 'a')
   countA++
else if (ch == 'I' || ch == 'i')
   countI++;
else
print ("Error--Not A, E, or I\a\n");
```

44. Write a code fragment that tests the value of an integer `num1`. If the value is 10, square `num1`. If it is 9, read a new value into `num1`. If it is 2 or 3, multiply `num1` by 99 and print out the result. Implement your code using nested *if* statements, not a *switch.*

45. Rewrite Problem 44 using a *switch* statement.

46. Write a code fragment for the flowchart shown in Figure 5-28. Assume that the variables `x` and `y` are integers and `z` is a float-point number.

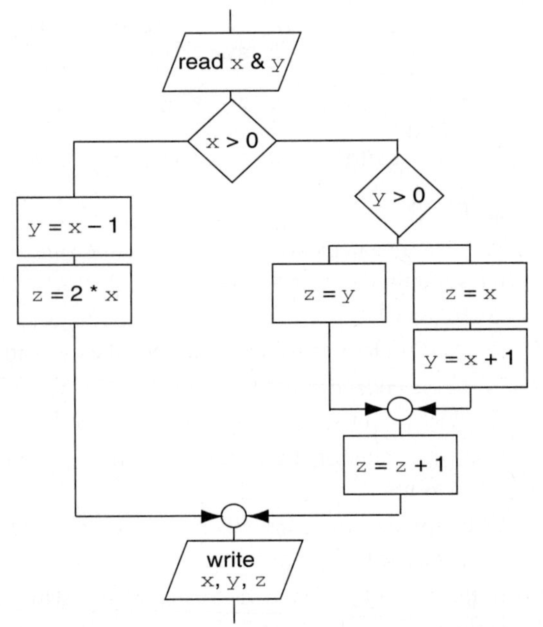

Figure 5-28 Flowchart for problem 46

47. Write a function called `smallest` that, given three integers, returns the smallest one.

48. Write a function called `day_of_week` that, given an integer between 0 and 6, prints the corresponding day of the week. Assume that the first day of the week (0) is Sunday.

49. Write a function called `month_of_year` that, given an integer between 1 and 12, prints the corresponding month of the year.

50. Write a function called `parkingCharge` that, given the type of vehicle ('c' for car, 'b' for bus, 't' for truck) and the hours a vehicle spent in the parking lot, returns the parking charge based on the rates shown below.

```
car   $2 per hour
bus   $3 per hour
truck $4 per hour
```

PROJECTS

51. Write a program that determines a student's grade. It reads three test scores (between 0 and 100) and calls a function that calculates and returns a student's grade based on the following rules:

    a. If the average score is 90% or more, the grade is `'A'`.

    b. If the average score is 70% or more and less than 90%, it checks the third score. If the third score is more than 90%, the grade is `'A'`, otherwise, the grade is `'B'`.

    c. If the average score is 50% or more and less than 70%, it checks the average of the second and third scores. If the average of the two is greater than 70%, the grade is `'C'`, otherwise, it is `'D'`.

    d. If the average score is less than 50 percent, then the grade is `'F'`.

    The program's main is to contain only call statements. At least three subfunctions are required: one to read scores, one to determine the grade, and one to print the results.

52. In Program 4-7, "Strange College fees," page 138, we wrote a program to calculate college fees. Modify this program for Typical College. At Typical College, the students pay a fee of $10 per unit for up to 12 units; once they have paid for 12 units, they have no additional per-unit fee. The registration fee remains $10 but is assessed only if courses are taken in the term.

53. Given a point, a line from the point forms an angle with the horizontal axis to the right of the line. The line is said to terminate in one of four quadrants based on its angle (α) from the horizontal, as shown in Figure 5-29.

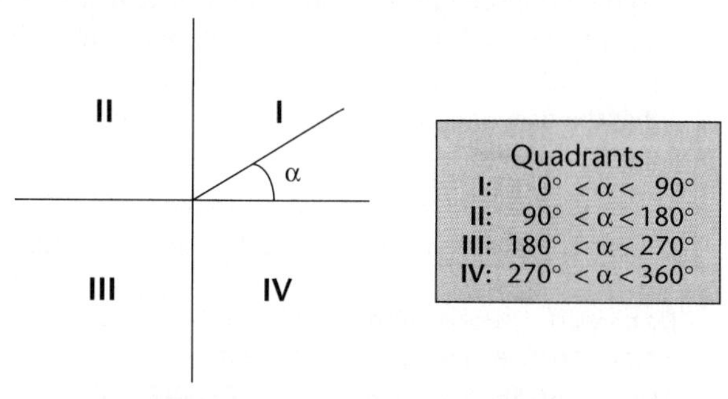

Figure 5-29 Quadrants for Problem 53

Write a program that determines the quadrant, given a user-input angle. Use a function to read and validate the angle. Note: If the angle is exactly 0° it is not in a quadrant but lies on the positive X-axis; if it is exactly 90° it lies on the positive Y-axis; if it is exactly 180° it lies on the negative X-axis; and if it is exactly 270° it lies on the negative Y-axis. Test your program with the following data:

`0°, 48.3°, 90°, 179.8°, 180°, 186°, 270°, 300°, and 360°`

54. Write a program that asks the user to enter the current date and a person's birth date in the form month, day, year. The program then calculates the person's age in integral years. Use separate functions to enter the dates (pass by address), calculate the person's age, and print the results. Test your program with the following dates: 11/14/1957, 5/10/1989, and 1/5/2000.

55. Write a C++ program to calculate the parking fare for customers who park their cars in a parking lot when the following information is given:

    a. A character showing the type of vehicle: 'C' for car, 'B' for bus, 'T' for truck.

    b. An integer between 0 and 24 showing the hour the vehicle entered the lot.

    c. An integer between 0 and 60 showing the minute the vehicle entered the lot.

    d. An integer between 0 and 24 showing the hour the vehicle left the lot.

    e. An integer between 0 and 60 showing the minute the vehicle left the lot.

    This is a public lot. To encourage people to park for a short period of time, the management uses two different rates for each type of vehicle, as shown in Table 5-11.

Type	First rate	Second rate
Car	$0.00/hr. first 3 hr.	$1.50/hr. after the first 3 hr.
Truck	$1.00/hr. first 2 hr.	$2.30/hr. after the first 2 hr.
Bus	$2.00/hr. for first hr.	$3.70/hr. after the first hr.

Table 5-11 Vehicle rates for Project 55

No vehicle is allowed to stay in the parking lot later than midnight; any vehicle that remains past midnight will be towed away.

The input data consist of a character and a set of four integers representing the type of vehicle and the entering and leaving hours and minutes. But these pieces of data must be input into the computer in a user-friendly way. In other words, the computer must prompt the user to enter each piece of data as shown below. (**Bold italic is used below to** indicate typical data.)

```
Type of vehicle? C++
Hour vehicle entered lot (0 - 24)?  14
Minute vehicle entered lot  (0 - 60)?  23
Hour vehicle left lot   (0 - 24)?  18
Minute vehicle left lot (0 - 60)?   8
```

The output format is shown below.

```
        PARKING LOT CHARGE

Type of vehicle:   Car or Bus or Truck
  TIME-IN                      XX : XX
  TIME-OUT                     XX : XX
                              --------
  PARKING TIME                 XX : XX
  ROUNDED TOTAL                  XX
                              --------
  TOTAL CHARGE                 $XX.XX
```

This program must first calculate the actual time spent in the parking lot for each vehicle. This means using *modulo arithmetic* to handle *time calculation*. There are many ways we can handle this type of calculation, one of which is shown below. To calculate the time spent in the parking lot, use the following algorithm:

a. Compare the minute portion of the leaving and the entering time.
   If the first one is smaller than the second,
   - Add 60 to the minute portion of the leaving time.
   - Subtract 1 from the hour portion of the leaving time.
b. Subtract the hour portions.
c. Subtract the minute portions.
d. Since there are no fractional hour charges, the program must also round the parking time up to the next hour before calculating the charge. The program should use the *switch* statement to distinguish between the different types of vehicles.

A well-structured program design is required. A typical solution will use several functions besides *main*. Before you start programming, prepare a structure chart. Run your program six times with the data from Table 5-12:

Test	Type	Hour in	Minute in	Hour out	Minute out
1	C	12	40	14	22
2	B	8	20	8	40
3	T	2	0	3	59
4	C	12	40	16	22
5	B	8	20	14	20
6	T	2	0	12	0

Table 5-12 Data for project 55

56. This program is a simple guessing game. The computer is to generate a random number between 1 and 20. The user is given up to five tries to guess the exact number. After each guess, the computer is to tell the user if the guessed number is greater than, less than, or equal to the random number. If it is equal, no more guesses should be made. If the user hasn't guessed the number after five tries, the program should display the number with a message that the user should know it by now and then terminate the game.

    A typical successful dialog might be:

```
I am thinking of a number between 1 and
20.
Can you guess what it is?         10
Your guess is low. Try again:     15
Your guess is low. Try again:     17
Your guess is high. Try again:    16

Congratulations! You did it.
```

    A typical unsuccessful dialog might be:

```
I am thinking of a number between 1 and
20.
Can you guess what it is?          5
Your guess is low. Try again:     20
Your guess is high. Try again:    10
Your guess is low. Try again:     18
Your guess is high. Try again:    12

Sorry. The number was 15.
You should have gotten it by now.
Better luck next time.
```

    Your design for this program should include a separate function to get the user's guess, a function to print the unsuccessful message, one to print the successful message, and one to print the sorry message.

57. Write a program that, given a person's birth date (or any other date in the Gregorian calendar), will display the day of the week the person was born.

    To determine the day of the week, you will first need to calculate the day of the week for December 31 of the previous year. To calculate the day for December 31, use the formula shown below.

$$\left((\text{year}-1)\times 365+\left\lfloor\frac{(\text{year}-1)}{4}\right\rfloor-\left\lfloor\frac{(\text{year}-1)}{100}\right\rfloor+\left(\left\lfloor\frac{(\text{year}-1)}{400}\right\rfloor\right)\right)\ \%\ 7$$

The formula determines the day based on the values as shown below:

Day_0: Sunday
Day_1: Monday
Day_2: Tuesday
Day_3: Wednesday
Day_4: Thursday
Day_5: Friday
Day_6: Saturday

Once you know the day for December 31, you simply calculate the days in the year before the month in question. Use a *switch* statement to make this calculation. (Hint: Use case 12 first, and then fall into case 11, 10, ..., 2.) If the desired month is 12, add the number of days for November (30). If it is 11, add the number of days for October (31). If it is 3, add the number of days for February (28). If it is 2, add the number of days for January (31). If you do not use a *break* between the months, the *switch* will add the days in each month before the current month.

To this figure, add the day in the current month and then add the result to the day code for December 31. This number modulo seven is the day of the week.

There is one more refinement. If the current year is a leap year, and if the desired date is after February, you need to add one to the day code. The following formula can be used to determine if the year is a leap year.

(!(year % 4) && (year % 100)) || !(year % 400)

Your program should have a function to get data from the user, another to calculate the day of the week, and a third to print the result.

To test your program, run it with the following dates:

a. February 28, 1900 and March 1, 1900
b. February 28, 1955 and March 1, 1955
c. February 28, 1996 and March 1, 1996
d. February 28, 2000 and March 1, 2000
e. December 31, 1996
f. The first and last dates of the current week

58. Write a program that calculates the change due a customer by denomination; that is, how many pennies, nickels, dimes, etc. are needed in change. The input is to be the purchase price and the size of the bill tendered by the customer ($100, $50, $20, $10, $5, $1).

59. Write a menu-driven program that allows a user to enter five numbers and then choose between finding the smallest, largest, sum, or average. The menu and all the choices are to be functions. Use a *switch* statement to determine what action to take. Provide an error message if an invalid choice is entered.

Run the program five times, once with each option and once with an invalid option. Each run is to use the following set of data:

```
18, 21, 7, 54, 9
```

60. Write a program that tests a user-entered character and displays its classification according to the ASCII classifications shown in Figure 5-24 on page 208. Use the *else-if* construct for your solution. The tests should be grouped with the highest probability characters first and the least probable last (see Table 5-10 "Selection rules," on page 216).

61. Write a program to compute the real roots of a quadratic equation ($ax^2 + bx + c = 0$). The roots can be calculated using the following formulas:

$$x1 = \frac{-b + \sqrt{b^2 - 4ac}}{2a}$$

and

$$x2 = \frac{-b - \sqrt{b^2 - 4ac}}{2a}$$

Your program is to prompt the user to enter the constants (*a*, *b*, *c*). It is then to display the roots based on the following rules:

a. If both *a* and *b* are zero, there is no solution.
b. If *a* is zero, there is only one root ($-c / b$).
c. If the discriminate ($b^2 - 4ac$) is negative, there are no real roots.
d. For all other combinations, there are two roots.

Test your program with the data in Table 5-13:

a	b	c
3	8	5
-6	7	8
0	9	-10
0	0	11

Table 5-13 Data for Project 61

6 Repetition

The real power of computers is in their ability to repeat an operation or a series of operations many times. This repetition, called looping, is one of the basic structured programming concepts. In this chapter, we discuss looping and introduce different looping constructs. First we define the basic concepts of loops, including a most important concept: how to stop a loop. We then present the three different loop constructs and take you through the C++ implementation of these three constructs. As part of this discussion, you will see some basic loop applications. The chapter concludes with a section that explores some of the software engineering implications of loops.

6-1 CONCEPT OF A LOOP

The concept of a loop is shown in the flowchart in Figure 6-1. In its most basic form, a loop consists of a loop body, which contains the actions to be performed in each iteration, and a looping mechanism, which causes the loop body to be repeated. In Figure 6-1, the loop body is repeated over and over again. It never stops.

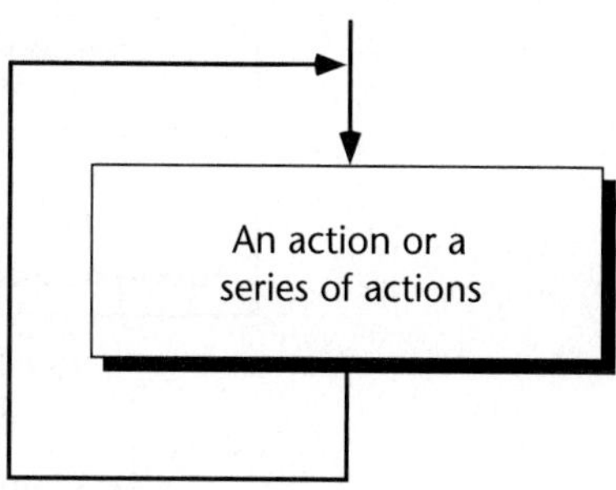

Figure 6-1 The concept of a loop

Since the loop in Figure 6-1 never stops, it is the computer version of the perpetual motion machine. The action (or actions) will be repeated forever. To write meaningful programs, however, we must be able to make a loop end when the work is done. To make sure that the loop ends, we must have a condition that controls it. In other words, the loop must be designed so that before or after each **iteration,** it checks to see if it is done. If it is not done, it repeats one more time; if it is done, it exits the loop. This test is known as a **loop control expression,** or more commonly, as a **loop limit test.**

6-2 PRETEST AND POST-TEST LOOPS

We have established that we must have a loop control test, but where should the test be placed—before or after each iteration? It turns out that programming languages allow us to check the loop control expression either before *or* after each iteration of the loop. In other words, we can have either a pre- or a post-test terminating condition. In a **pretest loop,** the condition is checked before the loop starts and then at the beginning of each iteration after the first. If the test condition is true, the code is executed; if the test condition is false, the loop terminates.

> **Pretest Loop**
> **In each iteration, the loop control expression is tested first. If it is true, the loop action(s) is executed; if it is false, the loop is terminated.**
>
> **Post-test Loop**
> **In each iteration, the loop action(s) are executed. Next, the loop control expression is tested. If it is true, a new iteration is started; otherwise, the loop terminates.**

In the **post-test loop**, the code is always executed at least once. At the completion of the loop code, the loop control expression is tested. If the expression is true, the loop repeats; if it is false, the loop terminates. The flowcharts in Figure 6-2 show these two loop types.

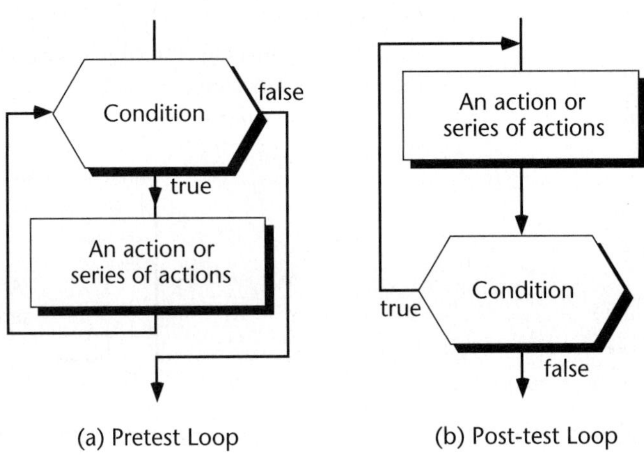

Figure 6-2 Pretest and post-test loops

Here is an example of pretest and post-test looping. Imagine that you are ready to start your daily exercises. Your exercise program requires that you do as many push-ups as possible. You can check your limit using either a pretest or a post-test condition. In the pretest strategy, you first check to see if you have enough energy to start. In the post-test strategy, you do one push-up and then you test to see if you have enough energy to do another one. Note that in both cases the question is phrased so that if the answer is true, you continue the loop. The two strategies are shown in Figure 6-3.

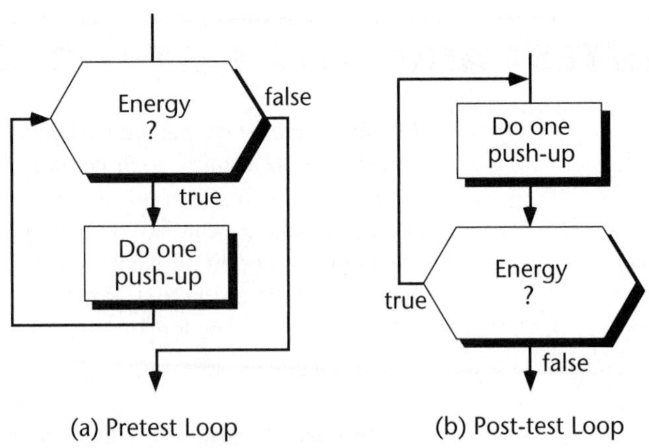

Figure 6-3 Two different strategies for starting exercise

As you can see, if you choose the first strategy, you may not do any push-ups. If you are tired when you start and don't have the energy for at least one push-up, you are done. In the second strategy, you must do at least one push-up. In other words, in a pretest loop, the action may be done zero, one, or more times; in a post-test loop, the action is done one or more times. This major difference between a pretest and a post-test loop, which must be clearly understood, is shown in Figure 6-4.

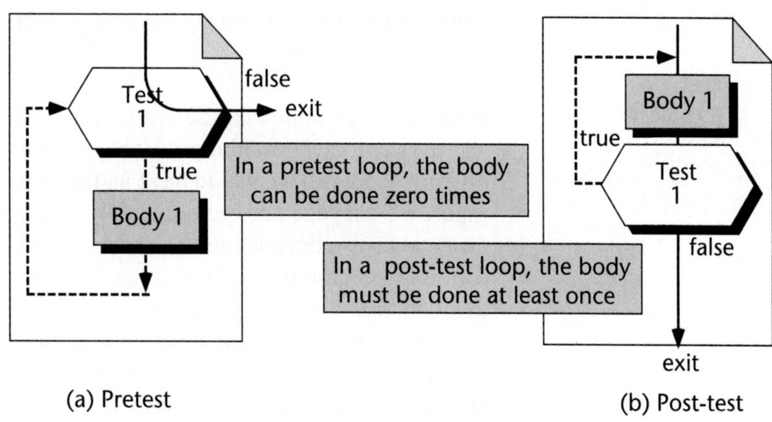

Figure 6-4 Minimum number of iterations in two loops

6-3 INITIALIZATION AND UPDATING

In addition to the loop control expression, there are two other processes associated with almost all loops: initialization and updating.

LOOP INITIALIZATION

Before a loop can start, some preparation is usually required. Such preparation is called **loop initialization.** Initialization must be done before the first execution of the body. It sets the stage for the loop actions. Figure 6-5 shows the initialization as a process box before the loop.

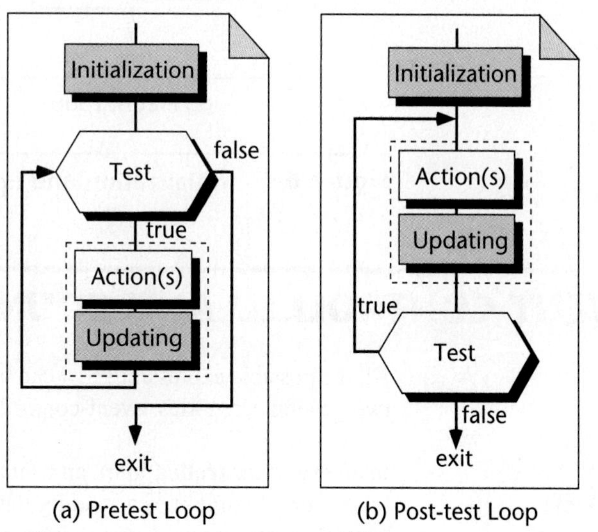

Figure 6-5 Loop initialization and updating

Initialization can be explicit or implicit. Explicit initialization is much more common. When the initialization is explicit, you include code to set the beginning values of key loop variables. Implicit initialization provides no direct code to set the starting values but rather relies on a preexisting situation, such as values passed to the function that controls a loop.

LOOP UPDATE

How can the condition that controls the loop be true for a while and then change to false? The answer is that something must happen inside the body of the loop to change the condition. Otherwise, we would have an **infinite loop.** For example, in the loops shown in Figure 6-3 on page 228, you gradually lose your energy until a point comes when you cannot do one more push-up. This changes the resulting condition from true to false. The actions that cause these changes are known as **loop update.** Updating is done in each iteration, usually as the last action. If the body of the loop is repeated *m* times, then the updating is also done *m* times.

Let's apply the concepts of initialization and updating to our previous push-up example. In this case initialization is created by nutrition, an implicit initialization. During each push-up, some of the initial energy is consumed in the process and your energy is reduced, which updates your energy level. The process is illustrated in Figure 6-6.

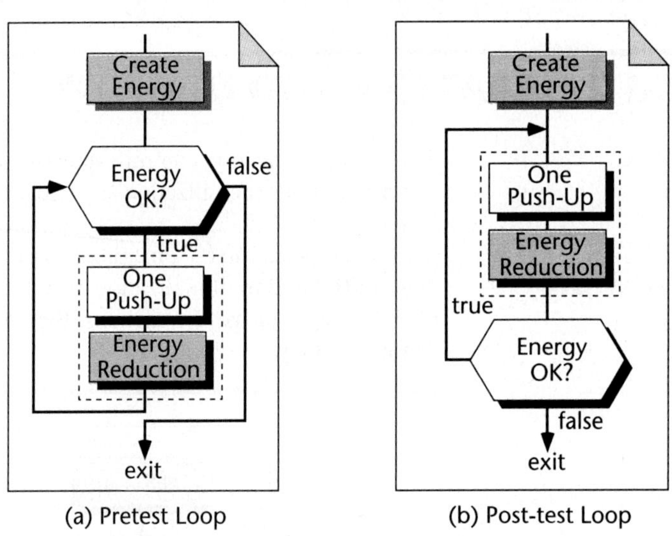

Figure 6-6 Initialization and updating for exercise

6-4 EVENT-CONTROLLED AND COUNTER-CONTROLLED LOOPS

All the possible expressions that can be used in a loop **limit test** can be summarized into two general categories: event-controlled loops and counter-controlled loops.

EVENT-CONTROLLED LOOPS

In an **event-controlled loop,** an event changes the loop control expression from true to false. For example, when reading data, reaching the end of the data changes the loop control expression from true to false. In event-controlled loops, the updating process can be explicit or implicit. If it is explicit, such as finding a specific piece of information, it is controlled by the loop. If it is implicit, such as the temperature of a batch of chemicals reaching a certain point, it is controlled by some external condition. The concept of the event-controlled loop is illustrated in Figure 6-7.

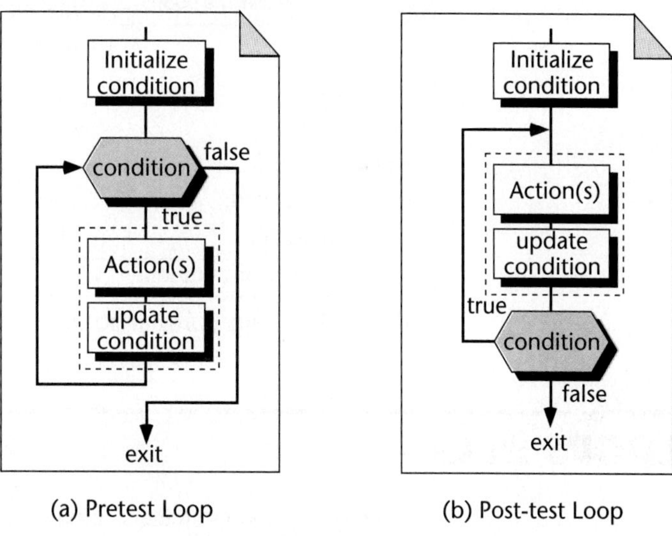

Figure 6-7 Event-controlled loop concept

COUNTER-CONTROLLED LOOPS

If the number of times an action is to be repeated is known, we use a **counter-controlled loop.** We must initialize, update, and test the counter. Although we have to know the number of times we want to execute the loop, the number does not need to be a constant; that is, it can be a variable or a calculated value. The update can be an increment, in which case we are counting up, or a decrement, in which case we are counting down. The concept of counter-controlled loop is illustrated in Figure 6-8.

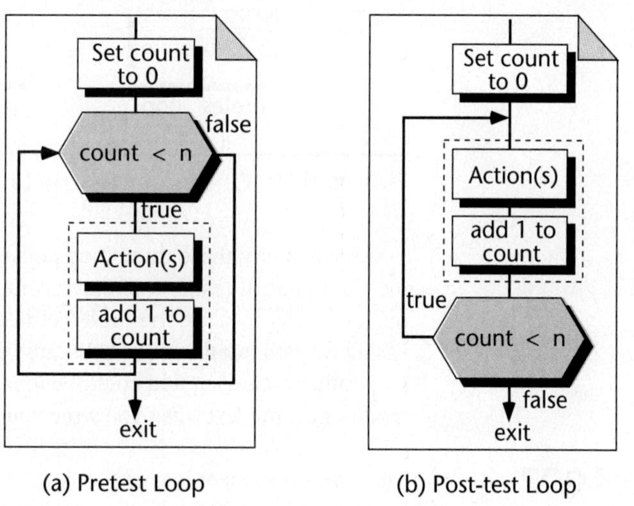

Figure 6-8 Counter-controlled loop concept

LOOP COMPARISON

Note that when we come out of the pretest loop, the limit test has been done $n + 1$ times. In the post-test loop, however, when we come out of the loop, the limit test has been done only n times. Table 6-1 provides a summary of the two different loop concepts.

Pretest loop		Post-test loop	
	Executions		**Executions**
Initialization:	1	Initialization:	1
Number of tests:	$n + 1$	Number of tests:	n
Action executed:	n	Action executed:	n
Updating executed:	n	Updating executed:	n
Minimum iterations:	0	Minimum iterations:	1
n is the number of iterations			

Table 6-1 Loop comparisons

6-5 LOOPS IN C++

There are three loop statements used in C++: the *while*, the *for*, and the *do...while*. The first two are pretest loops, and the *do...while* is a post-test loop. Although all of them can be used for event-controlled and counter-controlled loops, the *while* and *do...while* are most commonly used for event-controlled loops, whereas the *for* is usually used for counter-controlled loops. These loop constructs are shown in Figure 6-9.

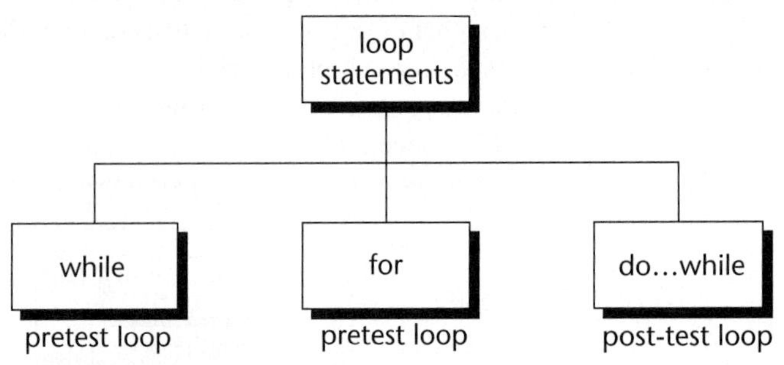

Figure 6-9 C++ loop constructs

As you study these three loop constructs, note that all three of them continue when the limit control test is true and terminate when it is false. This consistency of design makes it easy to write the limit test in C++. On the other hand, general algorithms are usually written just the opposite because analysts tend to think about what will terminate the loop rather than what will continue it. In these cases, you must complement or otherwise modify the limit test when you write your program (see "De Morgan's Rule" on page 179).

THE *while* LOOP

The ***while*** statement is a pretest loop. It uses an expression to control the loop. Since it is a pretest loop, it tests the expression before every iteration of the loop. The basic syntax of the *while* statement is shown in Figure 6-10. No semicolon is required at the end of the *while* statement. If you see a semicolon at the end of the code, it actually belongs to the statement within the *while* statement.

Note that the sample code in Figure 6-10 shows that the loop body is a single statement; that is, the body of the loop must be one, and only one, statement. If we want to include multiple statements in the body, we must put them in a compound statement, as shown in Figure 6-11.

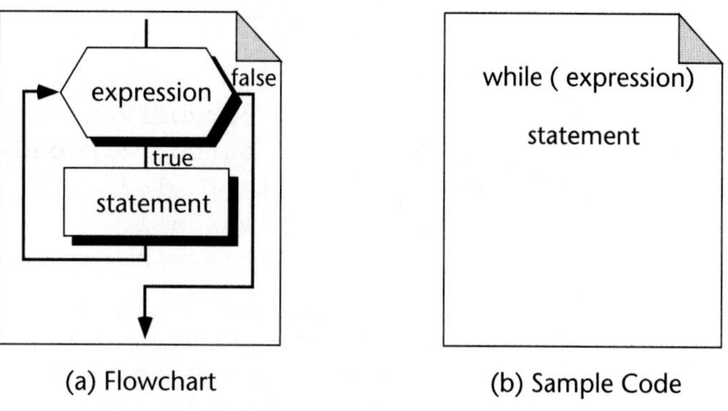

Figure 6-10 The *while* statement

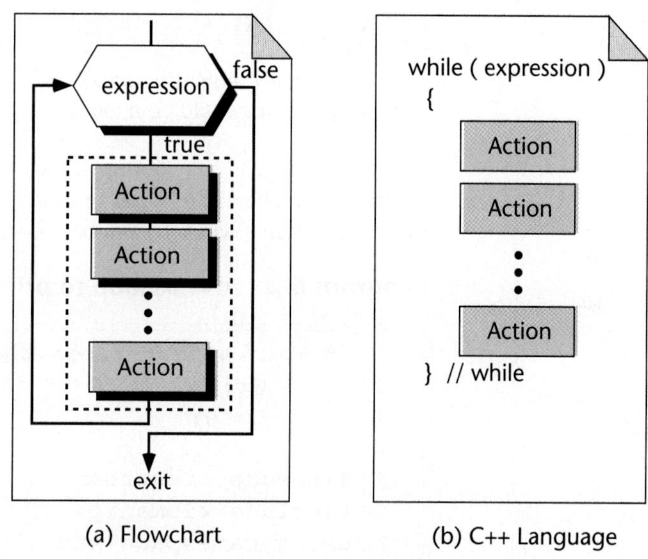

Figure 6-11 Compound *while* statement

Process Control Loops

Perhaps the simplest loop is the loop that never ends. While it is virtually never used in data processing, it is common in **process-control loops** such as network servers, environmental systems, and manufacturing systems. A simple process-control system that might be used to control the temperature in a building is shown in Program 6-1.

Program 6-1 Process-control system example

```
while (1)
   {
    temp = getTemperature();
    if (temp < 68)
         turnOnHeater();
    else if (temp > 78)
         turnOnAirCond();
```

Program 6-1 Process-control system example (*continued*)

```
    else
       {
        turnOffHeater();
        turnOffAirCond();
       } // else
   } // while 1
```

Program 6-1 Analysis The limit test in this simple program is a literal constant. It cannot be changed. Therefore, no update is required. Because the limit test in the *while* statement is always true, it will never stop. We must emphasize, however, that this is not a good construct for anything other than a loop that truly never ends.

As an aside, what would be the effect in Program 6-1 if the following *while* statement was used?

```
while (0)
```

Because the limit condition is a constant false, the loop would never start. Obviously, this would be a logic error.

Print Loops

A more common *while* loop is shown in Program 6-2. In this case we want to print a series of numbers. To keep from running off the end of the line, we have added a test to write a newline when 10 numbers have been written.

Program 6-2 A *while* loop to print numbers

```
/* Simple while loop that prints numbers 10 per line.
      Written by:
      Date:
*/
#include <iostream>
#include <iomanip>
using namespace std;

int main ()
{
   cout << "Enter an integer between 1 and 100: ";
   int num;
   cin  >>  num;

   // Test number
   if (num > 100)
       num = 100;

   int lineCount = 0;
   while (num > 0)
      {
```

Program 6-2 A *while* loop to print numbers (*continued)*

```
22          if (lineCount < 10)
23              lineCount++;
24          else
25             {
26              cout << endl;
27              lineCount = 1;
28             } // else
29          cout << setw(4) << num--;
30         } // while
31      return 0;
32  }  // main
```

```
Results:
Enter an integer between 1 and 100: 15
  15  14  13  12  11  10   9   8   7   6
   5   4   3   2   1
```

Program 6-2 Analysis Find the basic elements of a loop in this program. First, look for loop initialization, then the limit test, and finally the update.

The initialization is done by asking the user to enter `num` in Statement 11. Note how we make sure that the user enters a number that is not too large. If the number is over 100, we simply set it to 100, which is the maximum we told the user to enter. The limit test is in Statement 20. As long as `num` is greater than 0, we continue printing out the number series. The update is hidden in Statement 29; after printing `num`, we subtract 1 from it. Although this is a common C++ programmer trick, the program would have been easier to read if we had put the update (`num--`) on the line after the print. That way it would have been obvious.

File Looping

One of the more common loops in any computer language is reading until all the data have been processed—that is, until the user signals end of data. The question is, "How do we know when the user has signaled end of data?" Fortunately, C++ provides a very simple way to determine when all of the data have been read. When the input stream is read, the extraction operator (>>) returns the status of the input. If the data were read successfully, true is returned; if they were not read successfully, false is returned. We can therefore use the following read statement as the loop limit condition.

```
while (cin >> dataIn)
```

There are three conditions that will cause the extraction to fail: the end of the data—known as end of file—is reached, invalid numeric data is entered, or a read error occurs. We will discuss the determination of read errors in a later chapter. End of file (EOF) occurs automatically when our program reads a disk or any other type of auxiliary storage file. When reading from the keyboard's input stream, however, the user has to signal end of file. How this is done varies by operating system. Table 6-2 summarizes the various techniques.

Operating system	Signal[a]
DOS	^z
UNIX	^d
Macintosh	^d

[a]The carat (^) is used to represent the control key.

Table 6-2 End of file signals

Suppose we want to read and process a list of numbers from the keyboard. We type all the numbers, each one on a separate line. At the end, we type end-of-file as described in Table 6-2. This standard C++ loop for reading and processing data from a file is shown in Program 6-3.

Program 6-3 Adding a list of numbers

```
/* Add a list of integers from the keyboard
      Written by:
      Date:
*/
#include <iostream>
using namespace std;

int main ()
{
   int x;
   int sum = 0;

   cout << "Enter your numbers: <EOF> to stop.\n";
   while (cin >> x)
      sum += x;
   cout << "\nThe total is: " << sum << endl;
   return 0;
} // main
```

```
Results:
Enter your numbers: <EOF> to stop
15
22
3^d
The total is: 40
```

Program 6-3 Analysis Note that a compound statement (block) is not needed in the *while* loop, because the addition can be done in one statement. Another important point is that the statement to print the sum is outside the loop. Since the user can see the input values on the screen, all we need to show is the sum.

THE *for* LOOP

The *for* statement is a pretest loop that uses three expressions. The first expression contains any **initialization statements,** the second contains the **terminating expression,** and the third contains the **updating expression.**

Figure 6-12 shows a flowchart, and an expanded interpretation, for a sample *for* statement. Expression 1 is executed when the *for* starts. Expression 2 is the limit test expression. As shown in the expanded flowchart, it is executed *before* every iteration. Remember that since the *for* is a pretest loop, the body is not executed if the limit condition is false at the start of the loop. Finally, expression 3 is the update expression; it is executed at the end of each loop. Note that the code in the *for* statement must be an expression. This means that you cannot use statements, such as *return*, in the *for* statement itself. Like the *while* statement, the *for* statement does not need a semicolon.

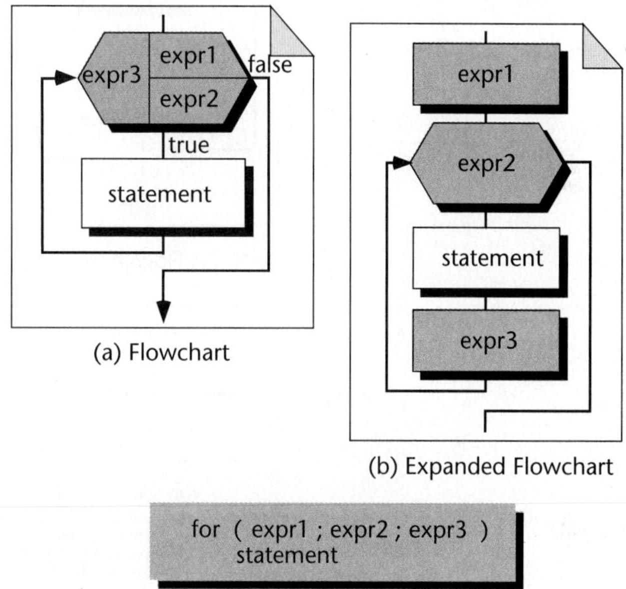


```
for ( expr1 ; expr2 ; expr3 )
    statement
```

Figure 6-12 *for* **statement**

The **body** of the *for* loop must be one, and only one, statement. If we want to include more than one statement in the body, we must code the statements in a compound statement. A *for* statement with a compound statement is shown in Figure 6-13.

Unlike some languages, C++ allows the loop control expression to be controlled inside the *for* statement itself. This means that the updating of the limit condition can also be done in the body of the *for* statement. In fact, expression 3 can be null, and the updating can be controlled entirely within the body of the loop, although this is not a recommended structured programming coding technique.

A *for* loop is used when your loop is to be executed a known number of times. You can do the same thing with a *while* loop, but the *for* loop is easier to read and more natural for counting loops.

Let's compare the *while* and the *for* loops.[1] Figure 6-14 shows a graphical representation of each of these loops side by side. The first thing to note is that the *for* loop contains the initialization, update code, and limit test in one statement. This makes for very readable code. All the control steps, initialization, end-of-loop testing, and updating

[1]This comparison breaks down when the loop contains statements, such as *continue* found on page 258, interrupt the loop execution.

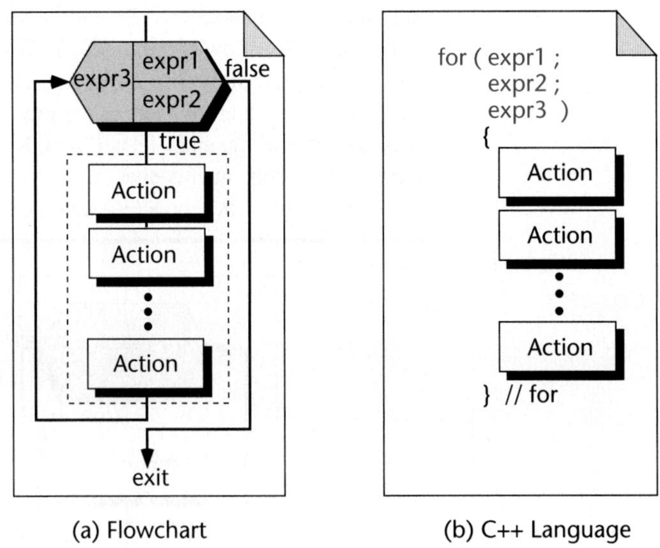

Figure 6-13 Compound *for* statement

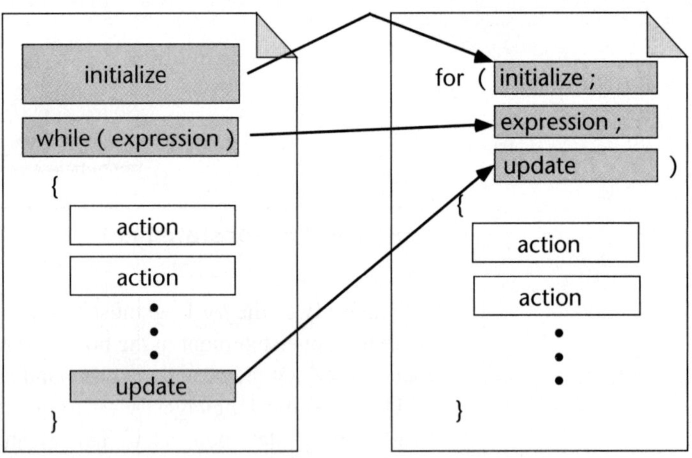

Figure 6-14 Comparing *for* and *while* loops

are done in one place. This is a variation of the structured programming concept of encapsulation, in which all code for a process is placed in one module. Another way of looking at it is that a *for* loop communicates better and is more compact.

Now let's solve the same problem using both a *while* and a *for* loop. The code shown below contains a loop to read 20 numbers from the keyboard and find their sum. This can be done both in a *while* loop and a *for* loop, but as you can see, the *for* loop is more self-documenting.

```
i   = 1;
sum = 0;
while (i <= 20)
   {
    cin >> a;
    sum += a;
    i ++;
   } // while
```

```
sum = 0;
for (int i = 1; i <= 20; i++)
   {
    cin >> a;
    sum += a;

   } // for
```

Example: Print Number Series

To demonstrate the *for* loop, we present Program 6-4, which asks the user for a number and then prints the series of numbers starting at 1 and continuing up to and including the user-entered number.

Program 6-4 Example of a *for* loop

```
/* Print number series from 1 to user limit.
      Written by:
      Date:
*/
#include <iostream>
using namespace std;

int main ()
{
   int limit;

   cout << "\nPlease enter a limit: ";
   cin  >> limit;
   for (int i = 1; i <= limit; i++)
      cout << "\t" << i << endl;
   return 0;
}  // main
```

```
Results:
Please enter the limit: 3
    1
    2
    3
```

Program 6-4 Analysis This simple program is the model for many looping functions. Let's look at three simple modifications to it. First, how would you print only odd numbers? This requires a change only to the update in the *for* statement.

```
for (int i = 1; i <= limit; i += 2)
    cout << "\t" << i << endl;
```

Next, let's have the program print the numbers backward. In this case, all the statements in the *for* statement must be changed, but the rest of the program remains the same.

```
for (int i = limit; i >= 1; i--)
    cout << "\t" << i << endl;
```

For the final example, let's print the numbers in two columns, with the odd numbers in the first column and the even numbers in the second column. This change requires that we modify the update statement in the *for* statement and also the print statement, as shown below.

```
for (int i = 1; i <= limit; i += 2)
     cout << setw(2) << i << setw(2) << i + 1 << endl;
```

We have used width specifications to align the output in columns. Note that the second print value (`i + 1`) is an expression. It does *not* change the value of *i*. There is no side effect, it is just a value.

One last point. This is the first program in which we have placed the local variable definitions within the function statements. This is a common programming style with the loop variables in a *for* statement.

Nested *for* Loops

Any statement, even another *for* loop, can be included in the body of a *for* statement. Using nested loops can create some interesting applications. Let's look at a very simple one here. We will give other examples in "Looping Applications," page 260.

Program 6-5 uses a nested loop to print a series of numbers on multiple lines.

Program 6-5 A simple nested *for* loop

```
/* Print numbers on a line.
      Written by:
      Date:
*/
#include <iostream>
#include <iomanip>
using namespace std;

int main ()
{
   for (int i = 1; i <= 3; i++)
      {
       cout << "Row " << i << ":";
       for (int j = 1; j<= 5; j++)
            cout << setw(3) << j;
       cout << endl;
      } // for i
   return 0;
}  // main
```

```
Results:
Row 1:   1  2  3  4  5
Row 2:   1  2  3  4  5
Row 3:   1  2  3  4  5
```

THE *do...while* LOOP

The ***do...while*** statement is a post-test loop. Like the *while* and *for* loops, it also uses an expression to control the loop, but it tests this expression *after* the execution of the body. The format of the *do...while* statement is shown in Figure 6-15.

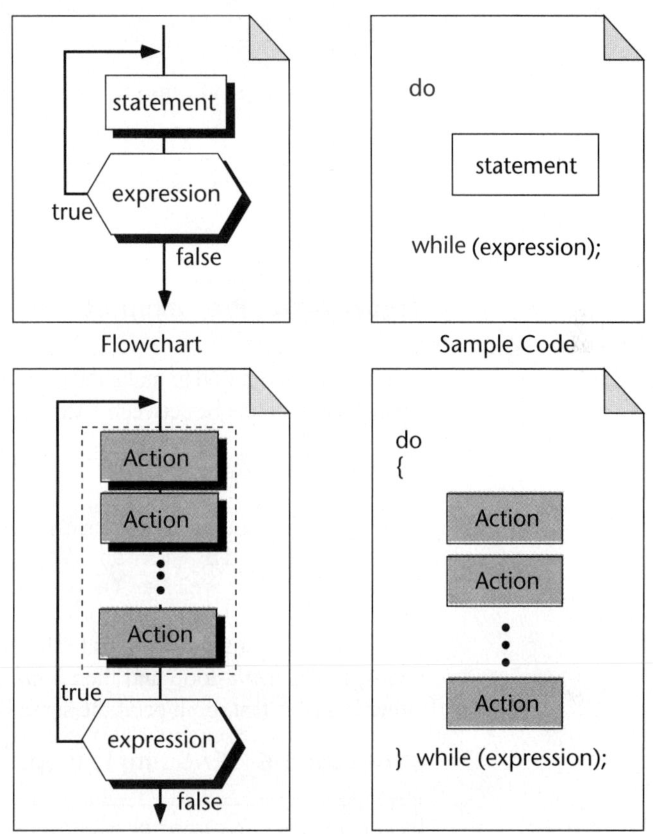

Figure 6-15 **Format of the *do...while* statement**

The body of the *do...while* loop must be one, and only one, statement. If we have to include multiple statements in the body, we must put them in a compound statement. The second example in Figure 6-16 shows the logic flow and code for a *do...while* that uses a compound statement. Look carefully at the code block in the second example. Note that the *do* and the *while* braces are aligned. Note also that the *while* expression follows the brace on the same line. This is a good style because it makes it easy for the reader to see the statement. Finally, note that the *do...while* is concluded with a semicolon. This differs from the other looping constructs that you have seen.

Because the *do...while* limit test isn't done until the end of the loop, we use it when we know that the body of the loop must be done at least once. To demonstrate the impact of the two loops, study the code in Figure 6-16. In the *while* loop, the message is not printed, because the limit condition is tested first. In the *do...while* loop, even though the limit test is false, the message is printed because the message is printed before the limit test.

Since the limit test isn't done until the end of the loop, the *do...while* loop is used when we know that the body of the loop has to be done at least once. It is commonly

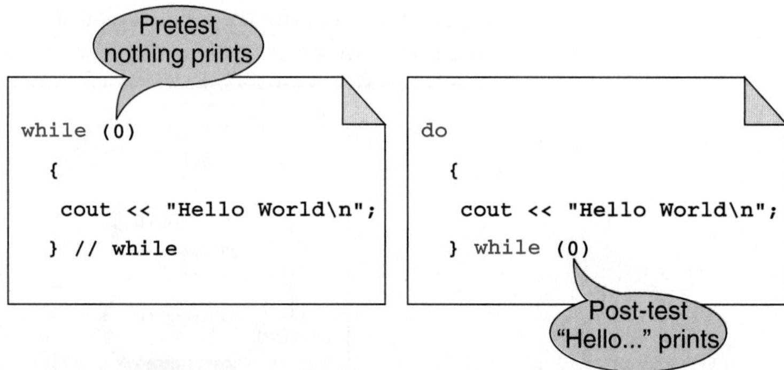

Figure 6-16 Pre- and post-test loops

used in data validation to make the program robust. For example, imagine we want to read an integer that must be between 10 and 20. We can use the *do...while* loop as shown below.

```
do
      {
       cout << "Enter a number between 10 & 20: ";
       cin  >> a;
      }  while (a < 10 || a > 20);
```

Let's look at a simple program that uses a loop to print five numbers. We code two loops, first a *while* loop and then a *do...while*. Although one loop is a pretest and the other is a post-test, both print the same series. The code is seen in Program 6-6.

Program 6-6 Two simple loops

```
/* Demonstrate while and do...while loops.
      Written by:
      Date:
*/
#include <iostream>
#include <iomanip>
using namespace std;

int main ()
{
   int loopCount;

   loopCount = 5;
   cout << "while loop      : ";
   while (loopCount > 0)
      cout << setw(3) << loopCount--;
   cout << "\n\n";

   loopCount = 5;
   cout << "do...while loop: ";
   do
```

Program 6-6 Two simple loops (*continued*)

```
      cout << setw(3) << loopCount--;
    while (loopCount > 0);
    cout << endl;
    return 0;
} // main
```

```
Results
while loop      :   5  4  3  2  1

do...while loop:   5  4  3  2  1
```

do...while Loop Example

To demonstrate the *do...while*, let's rewrite Program 6-3, "Adding a list of numbers." The modified code is shown in Program 6-7.

Program 6-7 Adding a list with the *do...while*

```
/* Adds a list of integers from the keyboard.
      Written by:
      Date:
*/
#include <iostream>
using namespace std;

int main ()
{
   int num;
   int sum;

   num = sum = 0;
   cout << "Enter your numbers: <EOF> to stop.\n";
   cin >> num;
   do
      {
       sum += num;
      } while (cin >> num);
   cout << "Total: " << sum << endl;
   return  0;
}  // main
```

```
Results:
Run 1:
   Enter your numbers: <EOF> to stop.
   10 15 20 25
   ^dTotal: 70

Run 2:
   Enter your numbers: <EOF> to stop.
   ^dTotal: 0
```

Program 6-7 Analysis Since the *do...while* always executes the body of the loop at least once, we had to make some changes. If you compare Program 6-3 and Program 6-7 carefully, you will note that Program 6-3 reads the data once before the loop. This is sometimes known as "priming the stream." We use the same loop limit test as before. The only difference is that now it is at the end of the loop, rather than at the beginning; that is, it is a post-test limit, not a pretest limit.

In the results, we have shown the end-of-file command entered by the user. In an actual run, you would not see it.

THE COMMA EXPRESSION

A **comma expression** is a complex expression made up of two expressions separated by commas. Although it can syntactically be used in many places, it is most commonly used in *for* statements. The expressions are evaluated left to right. The value and type of the expression is the value and type of the right expression; the other expression is included for its side effect. The comma expression has the lowest precedence of all expressions, priority 1.

The following statement is a modification of the *for* statement code shown on page 239. It uses a comma expression to initialize the accumulator, `sum`, and the index, `i`, in the loop. In this example, the value of the *comma* expression is discarded. This is a common use of the **comma operator.**

```
int i;
int sum;
for (i = sum = 0; i <= 20; i++)
        {
         cin >> a;
         sum += a;
        } // for
```

Note however, that the type definitions must precede the loop.

Comma expressions can be nested. When they are, all expression values other than the last are discarded. Figure 6-17 shows the format of a nested *comma* expression.

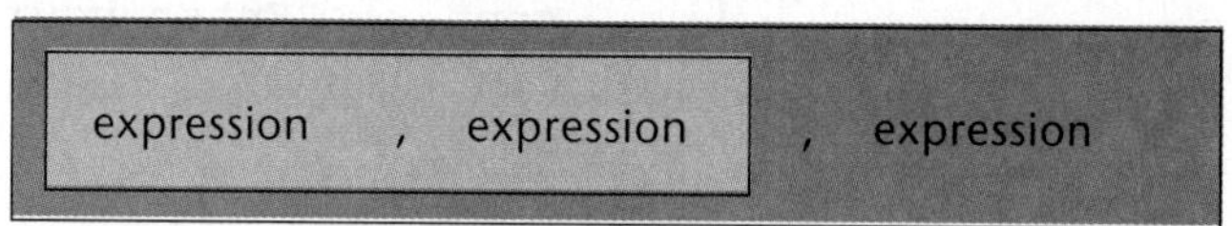

Figure 6-17 Nested comma expression

A final word of caution: Remember that the value of the expression is the value of the rightmost expression. While it is not recommended, if you use a comma expression for the second expression in a *for* loop, make sure that the loop control is the last expression.

Comma Expression Example

Let's use the comma expression to demonstrate the difference between the *while* and the *do...while*. As we saw in Table 6-1, "Loop comparisons," the only difference is the number of limit tests that are made. We also saw in Program 6-7 that the same job can be done by either loop. Program 6-8 uses both loops to count from 1 to 10. It uses the comma expression to count the number of limit tests in each loop.

Program 6-8 Comparison of *while* and *do...while*

```
1  /* Demonstrate while and do ... while loops.
2        Written by:
3        Date:
4  */
5  #include <iostream>
6  #include <iomanip>
7  using namespace std;
8  
9  int main ()
10 {
11    int loopCount = 1;
12    int testCount = 0;
13 
14    cout << "while loop:        ";
15    while (testCount++, loopCount <= 10)
16        cout << setw(3) << loopCount++;
17    cout << "\nLoop Count:       " << loopCount << endl;
18    cout << "Number of tests: "   << testCount << endl;
19 
20    loopCount = 1;
21    testCount = 0;
22    cout << "\ndo...while loop:  ";
23    do
24        cout << setw(3) << loopCount++;
25    while (testCount++, loopCount <= 10);
26    cout  << "\nLoop Count:       " << loopCount << endl;
27    cout  << "Number of tests: "   << testCount << endl;
28 
29    return 0;
30 }  // main
```

```
Results:
while loop:          1  2  3  4  5  6  7  8  9 10
Loop Count:       11
Number of tests: 11
do...while loop:     1  2  3  4  5  6  7  8  9 10
Loop Count:       11
Number of tests: 10
```

Program 6-8 Analysis Look at statements 15 and 25 carefully. Both contain comma expressions. This technique of combining the counter and the limit test in one expression assures that the count will be accurate. Because the value of the whole comma expression is the value of its last expression, however, the limit test must be coded last.

The results demonstrate that both loops count from one to ten. Since they are doing exactly the same job, we expect that the loop bodies would also execute the same number of times. As predicted in Table 6-1 on page 232, the only difference is in the number of tests: The *while* loop control expression was evaluated 11 times; the *do...while* control expression was evaluated only 10 times.

6-6 LOOP EXAMPLES

This section contains several short examples of loop applications. Each program demonstrates one or more programming concepts that you will find helpful in solving other problems.

for LOOPS

Example: Compound Interest

One classic loop problem is calculating the value of an investment. Suppose that we want to know the value of an investment over time, given its initial value and annual interest rate. Program 6-9 displays a compound interest table.

Program 6-9 Compound interest

```
/* Print report showing value of investment.
      Written by:
      Date:
*/
#include <iostream>
#include <iomanip>
using namespace std;

int main ()
{

   cout << "Enter value of investment:   ";
   double presVal;
   cin  >> presVal;
   cout << "Enter rate of return (nn.n): ";
   double rate;
   cin  >> rate;
   cout << "Enter number of years:       ";
   int  years;
   cin  >> years;

   cout << "\nYear\t   Value\n";
   cout <<   "====\t========\n";
   cout << fixed << showpoint << setprecision(2);
   double futureVal =  presVal;
   for (int looper = 1; looper <= years; looper++)
       {
        futureVal = futureVal * (1 + rate/100.0);
        cout << setw(3) << looper    << " \t";
```

Program 6-9 Compound interest *(continued)*

```
        cout << setw(8) << futureVal << endl;
       } // for
   return 0;
}  // main
```

```
Results:
Enter value of investment:   10000
Enter rate of return (nn.n): 7.2
Enter number of years:       5

Year      Value
====    ========
  1     10720.00
  2     11491.84
  3     12319.25
  4     13206.24
  5     14157.09
```

Program 6-9 Analysis This program uses a *for* loop to calculate the value of the investment at the end of each year. Each iteration adds the current year's interest to the investment and then prints its current value.

Note how we prompted the user for input, especially the decimal return rate. Things like percentage rates can be confusing to enter. Is 7.2% entered as 7.2 or .072? Make sure you give the user a sample of how the data should be entered.

Now study the way we created a caption for the reports using equal signs to underscore the captions and tabs with width specifications to align the values in columns. This rather simple technique makes the results quite readable.

Example: Right Triangle

Let's write a program that will print a series of numbers in the form of a right triangle. The user should be asked to enter a one-digit number. Each line, from the first to the limit entered by the user, is to print a number series from one to the current line number. For example, if a user enters 6, the program prints

```
1
12
123
1234
12345
123456
```

The flowchart and pseudocode for the loop is shown in Figure 6-18.

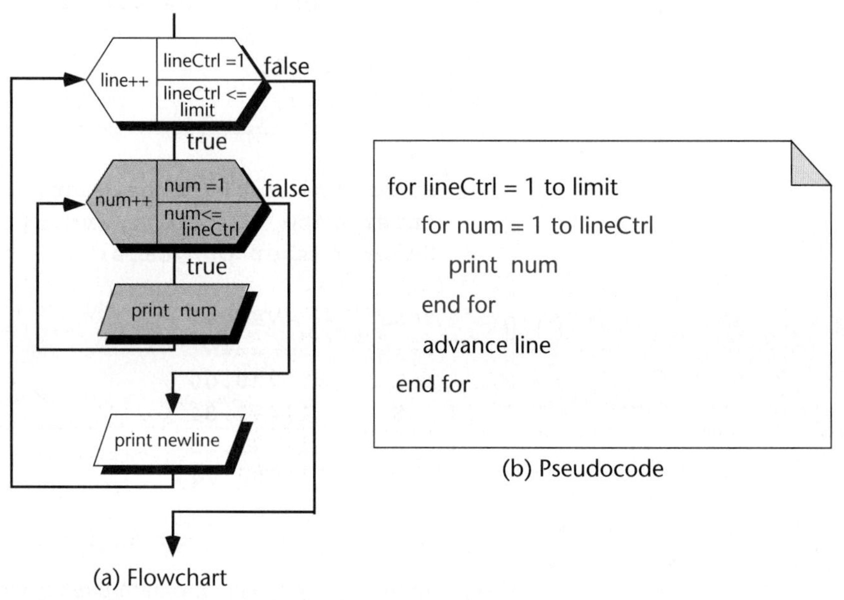

(a) Flowchart

(b) Pseudocode

Figure 6-18 Print triangle flowchart and pseudocode

The completed program is shown in Program 6-10.

Program 6-10 Print right triangle using nested *for* loops

```
/* Print a number series from 1 to a user-specified
   limit in the form of a right triangle.
      Written by:
      Date:
*/
#include <iostream>
using namespace std;

int main ()
{
   int limit;

   // Read limit
   cout << "Please enter a number between 1 and 9: ";
   cin  >> limit;

   for (int lineCtrl = 1; lineCtrl <= limit; lineCtrl++)
       {
        for (int numCtrl = 1;
                  numCtrl <= lineCtrl;
```

Program 6-10 Print right triangle using nested *for* loops *(continued)*

```
                     numCtrl++)
               cout << numCtrl;
            cout << endl;
          } // for lineCtrl
      return 0;
   }  // main
```

Program 6-10 Analysis This program demonstrates the concept of a loop within a loop. Note how we use two *for* loops to print the triangle. The first, or outer, *for* controls how many lines we are going to print. The second, or inner, *for* writes the number series on one line. This concept of nested loops is a very important programming concept.

Another point worth mentioning is the name we used in the loops. Often programmers will use `i` and `j` to control *for* loops. (We often do ourselves.) But notice how much more meaningful the code is when meaningful names are used. By using `lineCtrl` rather than `i` in the outer loop, we make it clear that this *for* is controlling the number of lines we are printing. Likewise, the name `numCtrl` clearly tells the reader that the *for* loop is being used to control the numbers.

Example: Print Rectangle

This time, let's write a program that prints the triangle pattern in the previous example filled out with asterisks to form a rectangle. For example, if a user enters 6, Program 6-11 prints

```
1*****
12****
123***
1234**
12345*
123456
```

Program 6-11 Print rectangle using nested *for* loops

```
/* Print number series 1 to a user-specified limit
   in the form of a rectangle.
      Written by:
      Date:
*/
#include <iostream>
using namespace std;

int main ()
{
   int limit;

   // Read limit
   cout << "\nEnter a number between 1 and 9: ";
   cin  >> limit;

   for (int row = 1; row <= limit; row++)
      {
```

Program 6-11 Print rectangle using nested *for* loops *(continued)*

```
        for (int col = 1; col <= limit; col++)
            if (row >= col)
                cout << col;
            else
                cout << '*';
        cout << endl;
       } // for row ...
    return 0;
} // main
```

Program 6-11 Analysis This program is an interesting variation of the previous program. Compare the inner loop in this program to the inner loop in Program 6-10. This is the only part of the program that is different. The first thing you should note is that the limit test expression is different; it always goes to the maximum number of print positions. Within the inner loop, the program tests the column number (`col`) to determine how many digits to print on the line. If the expression is true, it prints a digit. If it is false, it prints an asterisk.

Example: Print Month

As a final example of a *for* loop, let's print a calendar month. In Program 6-12, the function `printMonth` receives only the start day of the month—Sunday is 0, Monday is 1... Saturday is 6—and the number of days in the month. This is all that the program needs to print any month of the year.

Program 6-12 Print calendar month

```
/* Test driver for function to print a calendar month.
      Written by:
      Date:
*/
#include <iostream>
#include <iomanip>
using namespace std;

void printMonth (int startDay, int days);

int main ()
{
   printMonth (2, 29);              // Day 2 is Tuesday
   return 0;
} // main

/* ================ printMonth ================
   Print one calendar month.
      Pre   startDay is day of week relative
               to Sunday (0)
            days is number of days in month
      Post  Calendar printed
*/
void printMonth (int startDay, int days)
{
```

Program 6-12 Print calendar month (*continued*)

```
    // print day header
    cout << "Sun Mon Tue Wed Thu Fri Sat\n";
    cout << "--- --- --- --- --- --- ---\n";

    // position first day
    for (int skipDay = 0; skipDay < startDay; skipDay++)
        cout << "    ";

    int weekDay = startDay;
    for (int dayCount = 1; dayCount <= days; dayCount++)
        {
         if (weekDay > 6)
            {
             cout << endl;
             weekDay = 1;
            } // if
         else
             weekDay++;
         cout << setw(3) << dayCount << " ";
        } // for
    cout << "\n--- --- --- --- --- --- ---\n";
    return;
} // printMonth
```

```
Results:
Sun Mon Tue Wed Thu Fri Sat
--- --- --- --- --- --- ---
          1   2   3   4   5
  6   7   8   9  10  11  12
 13  14  15  16  17  18  19
 20  21  22  23  24  25  26
 27  28  29
--- --- --- --- --- --- ---
```

Program 6-12 Analysis This program is interesting for two reasons: First, it requires two *for* loops, one to position the printing for the first day of the month and one to print the dates. Second, the logic to control the days of the week is simple yet efficient. In an effort to eliminate one variable (`weekDay`), many programmers would use the modulo statement shown below to determine the day of the week.

```
(dayCount + startDay) % 7
```

Although this logic works, it is inefficient. Using a separate variable to control the days of the week requires simple addition, which is much more efficient.

One more note: We created the loop variables at the beginning of the function because week day is used in both loops. When a variable is used throughout the function, it should be defined at the beginning of the block in which it is used.

while LOOPS

Example: Print Sum of Digits

Program 6-13 accepts an integer from the keyboard and then prints the number of digits in the integer and the sum of the digits.

Program 6-13 Print sum of digits

```
/* Print the number and sum of digits in an integer.
      Written by:
      Date:
*/
#include <iostream>
#include <iomanip>
using namespace std;

int main ()
{
   cout << "Enter an integer: ";
   int number;
   cin  >> number;
   cout << "Your number is:   " << number << endl;

   int count = 0;
   int sum   = 0;
   while (number != 0)
     {
      count++;
      sum +=  number % 10;
      number /= 10;
     }  // while

   cout << "\nThe number of digits is : "
        << setw(3) << count << endl;
   cout << "The sum of the digits is: "
        << setw(3) << sum   << endl;

   return 0;
}  // main
```

```
Results:
Enter an integer: 12345
Your number is:   12345

The number of digits is:   5
The sum of the digits is:  15
```

Program 6-13 Analysis This problem requires that we "peel off" one digit at a time and add it to the total of the previous digits. There are a couple of ways to solve this problem, but by far the most straightforward is to use the modulus operator

(%) to extract the rightmost digit and then to divide the number by 10 to remove the right digit. For example, given the number 123, we first extract the 3 by

```
123 % 10
```

and then eliminate it by dividing by 10 to give 12. Note that since both the dividend and the divisor are integers, the result is an integer. We loop until there is only one digit left, at which time any digit divided by 10 will result in zero and the loop terminates.

Example: Print Number Backward

Now let's look at an example of a loop that prints a number backward. You can solve this problem in several ways. Perhaps the easiest is to simply use modulo division, as shown in Program 6-14.

Program 6-14 Print number backward

```
/* Use a loop to print a number backward.
      Written by:
      Date:
*/
#include <iostream>
using namespace std;

int main ()
{
   long num;

   cout << "Enter a number and I'll print it backward: ";
   cin  >> num;

   while (num > 0)
      {
       int  digit;

       digit = num % 10;
       cout << digit;
       num   = num / 10;
      } // while
   cout << "\nHave a good day.\n";
   return 0;
} // main
```

```
Results:
Enter a number and I'll print it backward: 12345678
87654321
Have a good day.
```

Program 6-14 Analysis In this program, we defined digit in the *while* block because it is used only in the *while* loop. Whenever a variable is used only within a block, it should be defined in that block.

Whenever a variable is used only within a block, it should be defined in that block.

do...while LOOPS

Example: Data Validation

Now we'll write a program that reads an integer consisting of only zeros and ones (a binary number) and converts it to its decimal equivalent. We must provide a function that assures that the number entered is a binary number. The design for this program is shown in Figure 6-19.

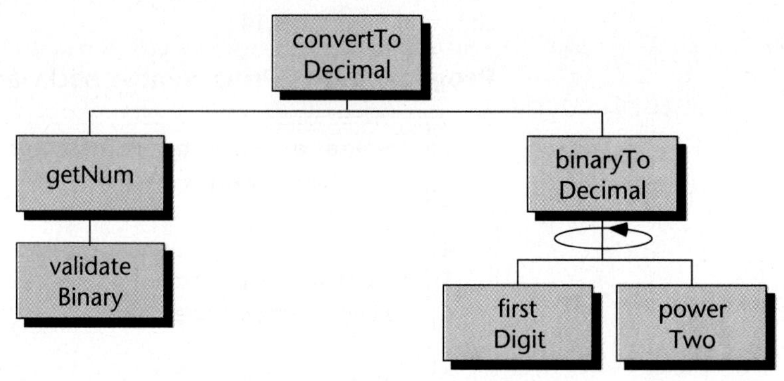

Figure 6-19 Design for binary to decimal

Study the design of `binaryToDecimal`. Note that it uses a loop and calls `firstDigit` and `powerTwo` in turn within the loop. How would you implement this loop? Think about it for a minute and then look at statement 53 in Program 6-15 to see how we did it. If you are not sure of your binary arithmetic and binary conversions, you may want to study Appendix D, "Numbering Systems."

Program 6-15 Convert binary to decimal

```
 1  /* Convert a binary number to a decimal number.
 2        Written by:
 3        Date:
 4  */
 5  #include <iostream>
 6  using namespace std;
 7
 8     long getNum           (void);
 9     long binaryToDecimal  (long binary);
10     bool validateBinary   (long binary);
11     long powerTwo         (long num);
12     long firstDigit       (long num);
13
14  int main ()
15  {
```

Program 6-15 Convert binary to decimal *(continued)*

```
   long binary   =  getNum ();
   long decimal =  binaryToDecimal (binary);
   cout    << "\nThe binary number was: " << binary;
   cout    << "\nThe decimal number is: " << decimal;
   return 0;
} // main

/* ==================== getNum =====================
   This function reads and validates a binary number
   from the keyboard.
      Pre   Nothing
      Post  A valid binary number is returned
*/
long getNum (void)
{
   long  binary;
   bool  isValid;

   do
      {
       cout    << "Enter binary number (0's & 1's): ";
        cin     >> binary;
        isValid =  validateBinary (binary);
        if (!isValid)
           cout << "\a\aNot binary. 0's/1's only.\n\n";
    } while (!isValid);

   return binary;
} // getNum
/* ================ binaryToDecimal ================
   Change a binary number to a decimal number.
      Pre  binary contains number with only 0's & 1's
      Post  Returns the decimal number
*/
long binaryToDecimal (long binary)
{
   long decimal = 0;
   for (int i = 0; binary != 0; i++)
       {
        decimal += firstDigit (binary) * powerTwo (i);
       binary  /= 10;
       }
   return decimal;
} // binaryToDecimal
/* ================= validateBinary ================
   Check the digits in a binary number for only 0 and 1.
      Pre   binary is a number to be validated
      Post  Returns 1 if valid; 0 otherwise
*/
```

Program 6-15 Convert binary to decimal *(continued)*

```
bool validateBinary (long binary)
{
   while (binary != 0)
        {
         if (!(binary % 10 == 0 || binary % 10 == 1))
             return false;
         binary /= 10;
        } // while
   return true;
} // validateBinary
/* =================== powerTwo ==================
   This function raises 2 to the power num
      Pre   num is exponent
      Post  Returns 2 to the power of num
*/
long powerTwo (long num)
{
   long power = 1;
   for (int i = 1; i <= num; i++)
       power *= 2;
   return power;
} // powerTwo
/* ================== firstDigit ==================
   This function returns the rightmost digit of num
      Pre   the integer num
      Post  The right digit of num
*/
long firstDigit (long num)
{
   return (num % 10);
} // first Digit
// ================= End of Program ===============
```

Program 6-15 Analysis There are several aspects to this problem that you should find interesting.

First, note the data validation that we use to ensure that the "binary number" that we read consists of nothing but zeros and ones. This series of modulus and divide statements has been used previously in several examples.

Then note how we enclosed the call to the validation function in a *do...while* that allows us to keep reading input until the user gives us a "binary number." Again, note how we display an error message when the number is not valid. This is a standard data validation technique.

Next, study the `binaryToDecimal` function that converts the binary number to its decimal value. Note that when we extract a digit, it is either a zero or a one. We then multiply the extracted digit by 2 raised to the digit position we are currently evaluating, which gives us the binary value of that digit's position in the binary number. The value is then added to the decimal number. Of course, if the digit is a zero, then the product is zero and the value is unchanged. It is only when the digit is a one that we add to the decimal number.

Finally, note that throughout this program we used *long int* for the binary and decimal number. This is because the decimal representation of a binary number can get very big very fast. On a personal computer, *int* would not be able to hold this representation of a binary number.

6-7 OTHER STATEMENTS RELATED TO LOOPING

Two other C++ statements are related to loops. They belong to a collection of statements known as jump statements (see Figure 6-20). One jump statement, *return*, was discussed in Chapter 4; the *break* and *continue* jump statements are discussed in this section. The last of the jump statements, the *goto*, is not valid for structured programs and therefore is not discussed in this text.

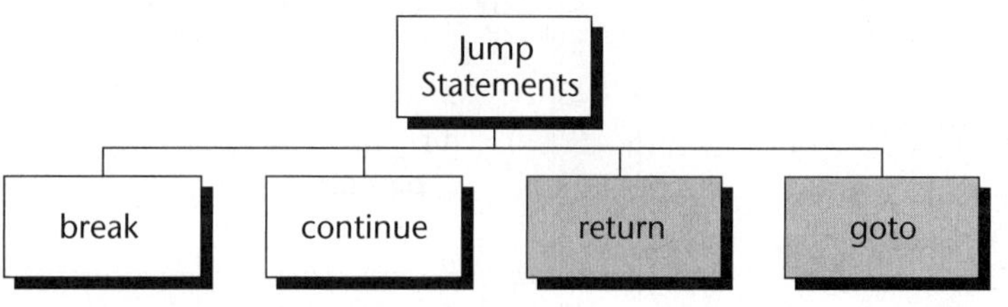

Figure 6-20 Jump statements

break STATEMENT

The first jump statement is ***break***. We previously saw the *break* statement when we discussed *switch* in Chapter 5. In a loop, the *break* statement causes a loop to terminate. It is the same as setting the loop's limit test to false. In a series of nested loops, *break* terminates only the inner loop—the one the program is currently in. Figure 6-21 shows how *break* transfers control out of an inner *for* loop and continues with the next statement in the *while*. Note that *break* needs a semicolon.

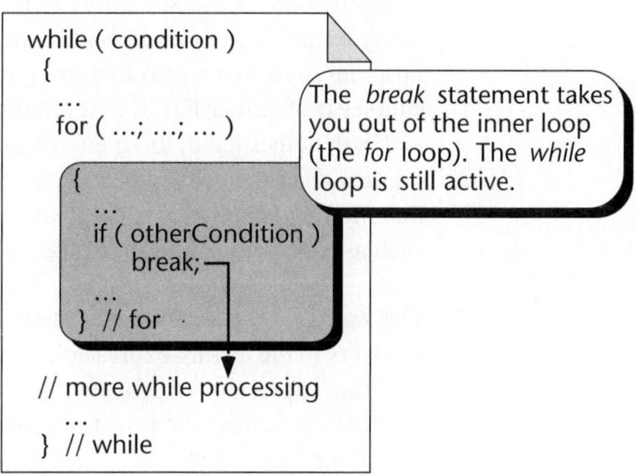

Figure 6-21 *break* and inner loops

The jump statement *break* can be used in any of the loop statements—*while*, *for*, and *do...while*—and in the selection *switch* statement, but good structured programming limits its use to the *switch* statement. It should not be used in any of the looping statements. If you feel you must use *break*, reexamine your design. You will usually find that you have not properly structured your logic.[2]

Program 6-16 shows two examples of poor loop situations and how to restructure them so that the *break* is not needed. In the first example, the *for* statement is a never-ending loop. As coded, there is no way to terminate the loop without the *break*. Although the *break* works, it is better style and provides better documentation to put the limiting condition as the second expression in the *for* statement. After all, that is the use of the limit expression in the first place.

Program 6-16 The *for* and *while* as perpetual loops

```
// The perpetual loop
for ( ; ; )
   {
    ...
    if (condition)
      break ;
   } // for
```

```
// The perpetual loop
for ( ; !condition; )
   {
    ...
   } // for
```

```
while  (x)

   {
    ...
    if (condition)
        break;
    else
        ...
   } // while
```

```
while  (x && !condition)

   {
    ...
    if (!condition)
      ...
   } // while
```

Even if the *break* statement is in the middle of the compound statement, it can be easily removed by complementing the condition test as shown in the second example in Program 6-16. Note also that in both examples, the improved code is also shorter and simpler (remember KISS, first mentioned in Chapter 3).

On the other hand, too many **flags**[3] can make a function overly complex. The use of *break* and flags needs to be tempered with simplicity and clarity of logic. Finally, note that the flag is called `condition`, which is a generic flag. A more descriptive name, such as `accountFlag` or `timeLimitFlag`, would be a much better choice.

continue STATEMENT

The second jump statement is the ***continue.*** It does not terminate the loop, but simply transfers to the testing expression in *while* and *do...while* statements and transfers to the updating expression in a *for* statement (Figure 6-22). Although the transfer is to different positions in pretest and post-test loops, both can be logically thought of as a jump to the end of the loop's body.

---

[2]While this statement is generally true, as you study advanced programming concepts, such as parsing, you will find that *break* and *continue* are used to simplify the code.

[3]Flags are variables used to record the state of a condition in the program. For example, eofFlag could be used to record whether or not the end of a file has been reached.

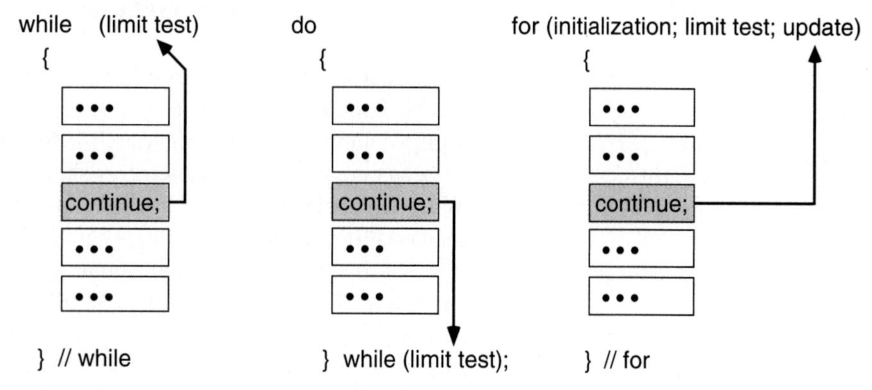

Figure 6-22 The *continue* statement

The use of the *continue* statement is also considered unstructured programming. If you think that you need a *continue*, your algorithm may not be well structured. A little study will show how to eliminate it. Program 6-17 contains a common *continue* example found in many textbooks. In this function, the assignment is to read data and return the average of nonzero numbers read. In other words, the function skips zeros. Note how simply reversing the conditional test eliminates the need for the *continue.*

Program 6-17 *continue* example

```
float readAverage (void)
{
int count = 0;

int    n;
float sum = 0;

while(cin >> n)
   {
    if (n == 0)
        continue;
    sum     += n;
    count ++;

   } // while
return (sum / count);
} // readAverage
```

```
float readAverage (void)
{
  int count = 0;

  int   n;
  float sum = 0;

  while(cin >> n)
     {
      if (n != 0)
         {
          sum += n;
          count++;
         } // if
     } // while
return (sum / count);
} // readAverage
```

Go To Considered Harmful

The concept of structured programming really took off when Edsger Dijkstra wrote his famous letter, "Go To Considered Harmful," to the editor of the ACM in 1968 (Volume 11, Number 3, March 1968, page 147). Since then, programmers have been taught that go to statements should not be used.

While we believe that Nicholas Wirth was correct when he said, and we paraphase, "If you can't write the program without using a *goto*, then you don't understand [C++]," there may be situations in which a *goto* may be necessary. These situations usually occur in complex systems programming applications such as writing a signal handler.

For those situations, and with the admonition that even then they should be avoided, we include the syntax for the *goto* here. First, the target statement of a *goto* must be labeled. To label a statement, code an identifier followed by a colon as shown in the following example.

```
jumpHere: statement
```

The scope of the *goto* label is within the function in which it is defined. Unlike other names, a label can be used before it is declared. The following code fragment demonstrates the concept.

```
while (...)
   {
    ...
    if (error)
       goto out;
    ...
   // while
out: cout << ...
```

Of course, this is a trivial example and could be more easily programmed by using a *break* statement. Even then, however, we would not consider it good program code.

6-8 LOOPING APPLICATIONS

In this section, we examine four common applications for loops: summation, product, smallest or largest, and inquiries. Although the uses for loops are virtually endless, these problems illustrate many common applications. Note that there is a common design running through all looping applications. With few exceptions, each loop contains initialization code, looping code, and disposition code. Disposition code handles the result of the loop, often by printing it, but other times by simply returning it to the calling function.

SUMMATION

As you have seen, we can add two or three numbers very easily, but how can we add many numbers or a variable series of numbers? The solution is simple: Use the add operator in a loop. This concept is graphically shown in Figure 6-23.

A sum function has three logical parts: (1) initialization of any necessary working variables, such as the sum accumulator; (2) the loop, which includes the **summation**

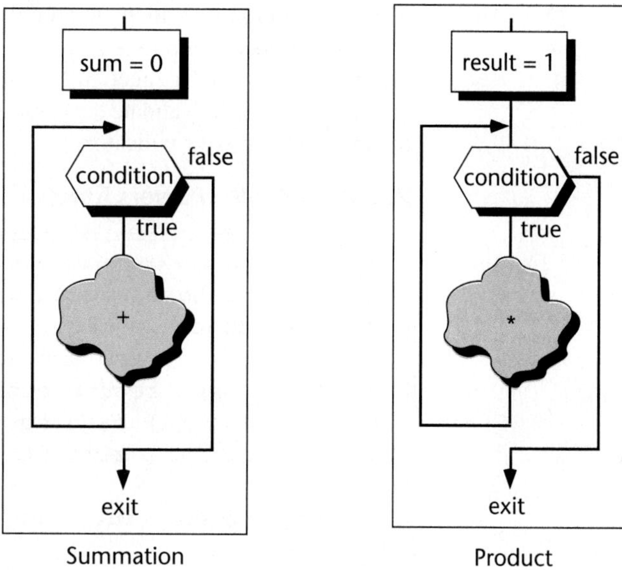

Figure 6-23 Summation and product loops

code and any data validation code (for example, "only nonzero numbers are to be considered"); and (3) the disposition code to print or return the result.

Program 6-18 is a loop function that reads a series of numbers from the keyboard and returns their sum. In each loop, we read the next number and add it to the accumulator, `sum`. A similar application, counting, is a special case of summation in which we add 1 to a counter instead of adding the number we read to an accumulator.

Program 6-18 sumEOF function

```
/* Read a series of numbers, terminated by EOF, and
   return their sum to the calling program.
      Pre   Nothing
      Post  Data read from keyboard and sum returned
*/
int sumEOF (void)
{
   int sum = 0;
   int  nmbr;
   cout << "\nEnter first integer <EOF> to stop: ";
   while (cin >> nmbr)
      {
       sum   += nmbr;
       cout << "Next integer <EOF> to stop: ";
      } // while
   return sum;
} // sumEOF
```

PRODUCT

Just as we were able to add a series of numbers in a loop, we can perform any mathematical operation in a loop. A product loop is useful for two common applications, raising a number to a power and calculating the factorial of a number.[4] For example, Program 6-19 shows a function to return x^n. Notice that this function also includes initialization logic to validate the parameter list. If either of the parameters is invalid, we return zero as an error indicator.

Program 6-19 Powers function

```
/* ================== powers ====================
   Raise base, to an integral power, exp. If the
   exponent is zero, return 1.
      Pre   base and exp are both positive integers
      Post  return either
          (a) base to the exp power
      or  (b) zero if the parameters are invalid
*/
long powers (int base, int exp)
{
   int  i;
   long result;

   if (base < 1 || exp < 0 )
      // Error Condition
      result = 0;
   else
      if (exp > 0)
         for (result = 1, i = 1; i <= exp; i++)
             result *= base;
      else
         result = 1;
   return result;
} // powers
```

SMALLEST AND LARGEST

You will often encounter situations in which you must determine the smallest or largest among a series of data. This is also a natural looping structure.

We can write a statement to find the smaller of two numbers. For example,

```
result = a < b ? a : b;
```

But how can we find the smallest of several numbers? We simply put the same statement inside a loop. Each iteration then tests the current smallest to the next number. If this new number is smaller than the current smallest, it replaces the smallest. In other words, the loop determines the smallest number by looping through a series while remembering the smallest number it has found. This concept is shown in Figure 6-24.

In Program 6-20, the initialization sets the initial value of `smallest` to INT_MAX, which is found in the limits library (<climits>). The loop then proceeds to read a series of numbers and tests each one against the previously stored `smallest` number. Since

[4] In a productional program, we recommend that you use the power function (*pow*) rather than writing your own.

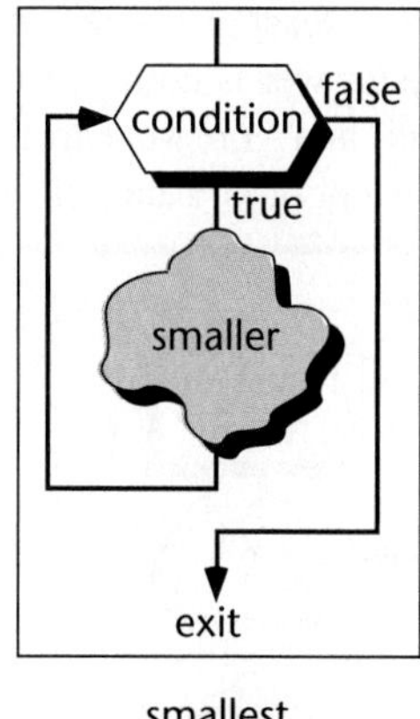

smallest

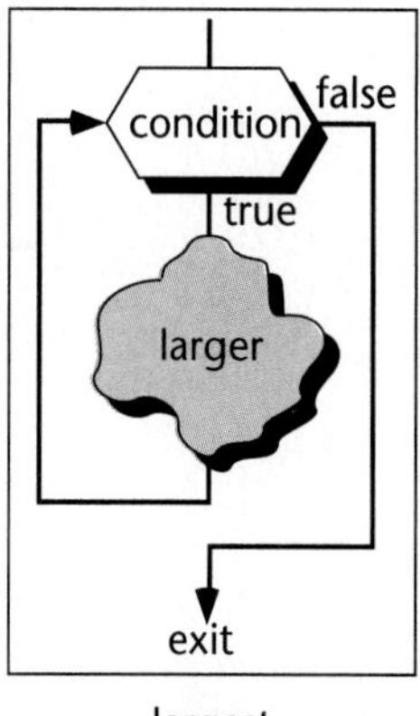

largest

Figure 6-24 Smallest and largest loops

Program 6-20 smallestEOF function

```
/* ================ smallestEOF =================
   Read a series of positive numbers terminated by
   EOF and pass smallest to the calling program
      Pre   Nothing
      Post  Data read and smallest returned
*/
int smallestEOF (void)
{
   int smallest = INT_MAX;        //requires limits lib
   int numIn;
   cout << "\nPlease enter an integer: ";
   while (cin >> numIn)
      {
       if (numIn < smallest)
           smallest = numIn;
       cout << "Enter next integer <EOF> to stop: ";
      } // while
   return smallest;
}  // smallestEOF
```

`smallest` starts with the maximum integer value, the number read first automatically becomes `smallest`. Thereafter, the result will depend entirely on the data being read. The disposition simply returns the `smallest` value found. In this function, no data validation is required.

Of course, the largest number can be found by simply reversing the less than operator in the expression and making it greater than. You will also need to set the variable, renamed `largest`, to INT_MIN.

INQUIRIES

An **inquiry** is simply a question asked of the computer program. In programming, we often encounter one of two basic inquiry types: ***any*** and ***all***. The inquiry type *any* is used when we have a list of data and we want to know if *any* of them meet a given criterion. Here "any" means at least one. The answer to the inquiry is yes if one or more data meet the criterion. The answer is no if none of the data meet the criterion. Use *all* when you have a list of data and you want to make sure that *all* of them meet some specified criterion. The concept of *any* and *all* in an inquiry is shown in Figure 6-25.

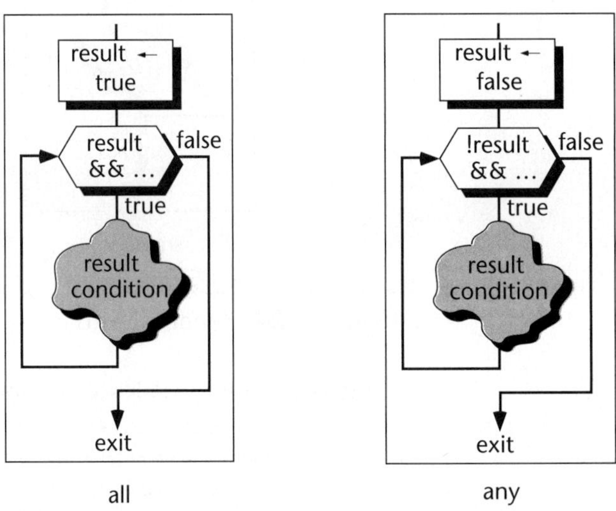

Figure 6-25 *any* **and** *all* **inquiries**

Program 6-21 is an example of an *any* inquiry. It reads a series of numbers and checks to see if any of the numbers in the list is greater than zero. The function terminates and returns *true* as soon as a positive number is read. On the other hand, if all numbers are negative, then the function terminates when the sentinel value is reached. Note that `anyPositive` is a logical variable and is initialized to *false*.

Program 6-21 anyPositiveEOF function

```
/* =============== anyPositiveEOF ================
   Read number series & determine if any are positive.
      Pre   Nothing
      Post  Returns true  if any numbers >  0
            Returns false if all numbers <= 0
*/
bool anyPositiveEOF (void)
{
   bool anyPositive = false;
   int  numIn;
   while ( !anyPositive && (cin >> numIn) )
      anyPositive = (numIn > 0);
   return anyPositive;
} // anyPositiveEOF
```

The *all* function is very similar—it just reverses the logic. For example, suppose that you want to find out if all numbers are positive. In this case, you have the function continue to read as long as all the previous numbers have been greater than zero. This function is used in Program 6-22.

Program 6-22 allPositiveEOF function

```
/* =============== allPositiveEOF ================
   Read number series & determine if all are positive.
      Pre   Nothing
      Post  Returns true  if all numbers >  0
            Returns false if any number  <= 1
*/
bool allPositiveEOF (void)
{
   bool allPositive = true;
   int  numIn;
   while ( allPositive && (cin >> numIn) )
      allPositive = (numIn > 0);
   return allPositive;
} // allPositiveEOF
```

6-9 RECURSION

In general, there are two approaches to writing repetitive algorithms. One uses loops; the other uses recursion. **Recursion** is a repetitive process in which a function calls itself. Both approaches provide repetition, and either can be converted to the other's approach. Some older languages do not support recursion. One major language that does not is COBOL.

ITERATIVE DEFINITION

To study a simple example, let's consider the calculation of a factorial. The factorial of a number is the product of the integral values from 1 to the number. This definition is seen in Formula 6-1.

$$\text{Factorial}(n) = \begin{cases} 1 & \text{if } n == 0 \\ n * (n-1) * (n-2) * \ldots * 3 * 2 * 1 & \text{if } n > 0 \end{cases}$$

Formula 6-1 Iterative function definition

Note that this definition is iterative. A repetitive function is defined iteratively whenever the definition involves only the parameter(s) and not the function itself. We can calculate the value of factorial (4) using Formula 6-1 as follows:

```
factorial (4) = 4 * 3 * 2 * 1 = 24
```

RECURSIVE DEFINITION

A repetitive function is defined recursively whenever the function appears within the definition itself. For example, the factorial function can be defined recursively, as shown in Formula 6-2.

$$\text{Factorial}(n) = \begin{bmatrix} 1 & \text{if } n == 0 \\ n * (\text{Factorial}(n-1)) & \text{if } n > 0 \end{bmatrix}$$

Formula 6-2 Recursive function definition

The decomposition of factorial (3), using Formula 6-2, is shown in Figure 6-26. If you study Figure 6-26 carefully, you will note that the recursive solution for a problem involves a two-way journey. First, we decompose the problem from the top to the bottom, and then we solve it from the bottom to the top.

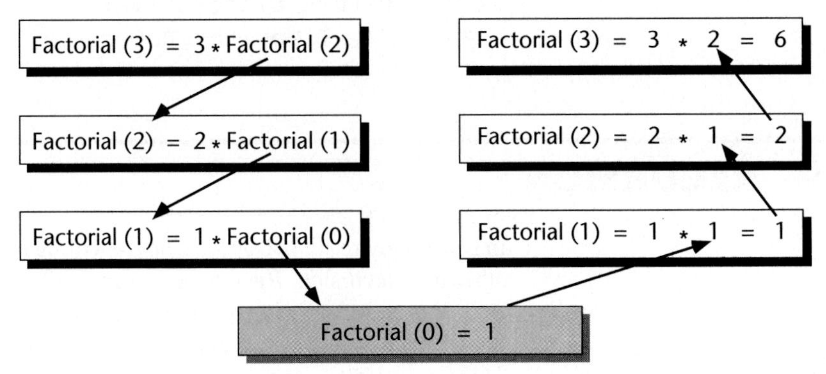

Figure 6-26 Factorial (3) recursively

Judging by the example in Figure 6-26, it looks as if the recursive calculation is much longer and more difficult. So why would we want to use the recursive method? The reason is that the recursive calculation looks more difficult when using paper and pencil, but it is often a much easier and more elegant solution when we use computers. Additionally, it offers a conceptual simplicity to the creator and the reader.

FACTORIAL—ITERATIVE SOLUTION

Let's write a function to solve the factorial problem iteratively. This solution usually involves using a loop, as in Program 6-23.

Program 6-23 Iterative factorial function

```
/* ================== factorial ==================
   Calculates the factorial of a number using a loop.
   There is no test that the result fits in sizeof long
      Pre   num is the number to be raised factorially
      Post  result is returned
*/
long factorial (int num)
```

Program 6-23 Iterative factorial function *(continued)*

```
{
   long  factN = 1;
   for (int i = 1; i <= num; i++)
        factN = factN * i;
   return factN;
} // factorial
```

FACTORIAL—RECURSIVE SOLUTION

Program 6-24 shows the same function written recursively. The recursive solution does not need a loop; the concept itself involves repetition.

Program 6-24 Recursive factorial function

```
1  /* ================= factorial ===================
2     Calculates factorial of a number using recursion.
3     There is no test that the result fits in sizeof long
4        Pre   num is the number being raised factorially
5        Post  result is returned
6  */
7  long factorial (long num)
8  {
9     if (num == 0)
10       return 1;
11    else
12       return (num * factorial (num - 1));
13 } // factorial
```

In the recursive version, we let the function `factorial` call itself, each time with a different set of parameters. Figure 6-27 shows this mechanism with the parameters for each individual call. Note that as is typically the case, the recursive version contains fewer statements than the iterative version.

DESIGNING RECURSIVE FUNCTIONS

Now that we have examined how recursion works, let's turn our attention to the steps for designing a recursive function. If you were to examine all hypothetically possible recursive functions, you would notice that each call used either solves *one* part of the problem or *reduces* the size of the problem. In Program 6-24, statement 10 solves a small piece of the problem—`factorial` (0) is 1. Statement 12, on the other hand, reduces the size of the problem by recursively calling the factorial with $n - 1$. Once the solution to `factorial(n-1)` is known, statement 12 provides part of the solution to the general problem by returning a value to the calling function.

As we see in statement 12, the general part of the solution is the recursive call: Statement 12 calls its own function to solve the problem. We also see this in Figure 6-27. At each recursive call, the size of the problem is reduced from the factorial of 3, to 2, then 1, and finally to factorial 0.

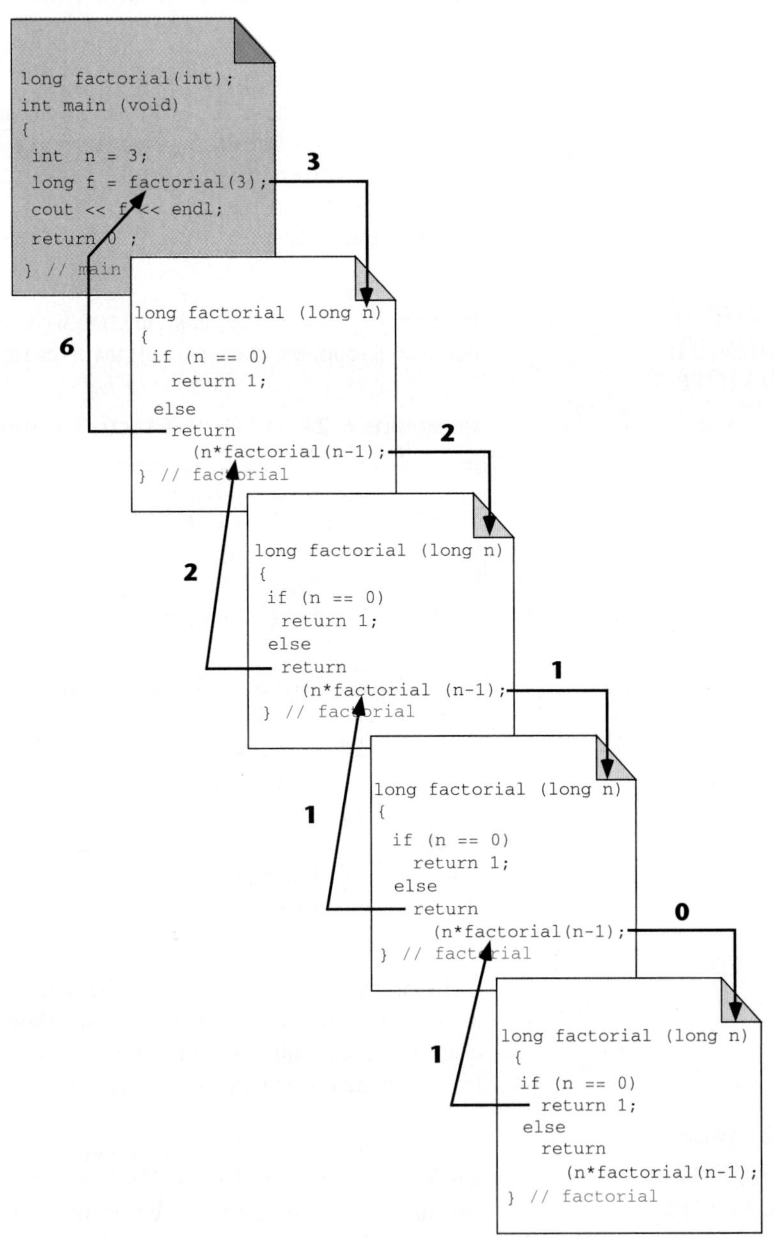

Figure 6-27 Calling a recursive function

The statement that "solves" the problem is known as the **base case.** *Every recursive function must have a base case.* The rest of the function is known as the **general case.** In our factorial example, the base case is `factorial` *(0)*; the general case is `n * factorial (n-1)`. The general case contains the logic needed to reduce the size of the problem.

> **Every recursive call must either solve part of the problem or reduce the size of the problem.**

In the factorial problem, once the base case has been reached, the solution begins. The program has found one part of the answer and can return that part to the next more general statement. Thus, in Program 6-24, once it has been calculated that `factorial (0)` is 1, that value is returned. That leads to solving the next general case,

```
factorial (1) → 1 * factorial (0) → 1 * 1 → 1
```

The value of `factorial` (*1*) is returned to the more general case, `factorial` (*2*), which we know to be

```
factorial (2) → 2 * factorial (1) → 2 * 1 → 2
```

As each general case is solved in turn, the next higher general case can be solved until finally the most general case, the original problem, is solved.

Returning to the purpose of this section, we are now ready to state the rules for designing a recursive function.

1. First determine the base case.
2. Then determine the general case.
3. Combine the base case and general case into a function.

In combining the base and general cases into a function, you must pay careful attention to the logic. Each call must reduce the size of the problem and move it toward the base case. The base case, when reached, must terminate without a call to the recursive function; that is, it must execute a *return*.

FIBONACCI NUMBERS

Now let's look at another example of recursion, a function that generates Fibonacci numbers. Named after an Italian mathematician, Leonardo Fibonacci, who lived in the early 13th century, Fibonacci numbers are a series in which each number is the sum of the previous two numbers. The first few numbers in the Fibonacci series are:

```
0, 1, 1, 2, 3, 5, 8, 13, 21, 34
```

To start the series, we need to know the first two numbers. As you can see from the above series, they are 0 and 1. Since we are discussing recursion, you should recognize these two numbers as the base cases.

We can generalize the Fibonacci series as follows:

Given:

$$Fibonacci_0 = 0$$
$$Fibonacci_1 = 1$$

Then

$$Fibonacci_n = Fibonacci_{n-1} + Fibonacci_{n-2}$$

The generalization of $Fibonacci_4$ is illustrated in Figure 6-28. The left half of the figure shows the components of $Fibonacci_4$ using a general notation. The right half of the figure shows the components as they would be called to generate the numbers in the series.

To determine $Fibonacci_4$, we can start at 0 and move up until we have the number, or we can start at $Fibonacci_4$ and move down to 0. The first technique is used in the iterative solution; the second is used in the recursive solution, which is shown in Program 6-25.

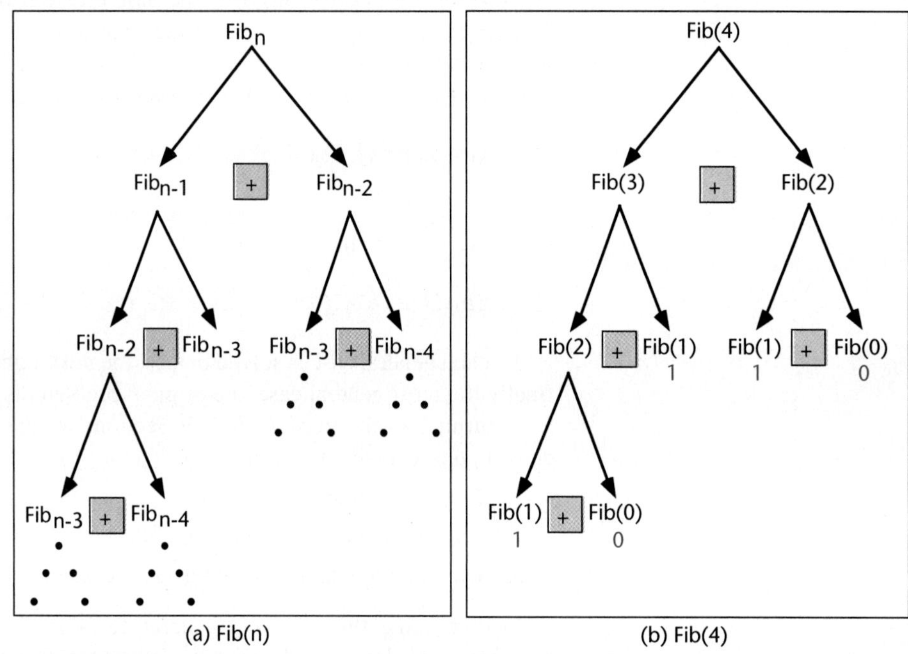

Figure 6-28 Fibonacci numbers

Program 6-25 Recursive Fibonacci

```
/* This program prints out a Fibonacci series.
      Written by:
      Date:
*/
#include <iostream>
#include <iomanip>
using namespace std;

long fib (long num);

int main ()
{
   cout << "This program prints a Fibonacci series.\n";
   cout << "How many numbers do you want? ";
   int seriesSize;
   cin  >> seriesSize;
   if (seriesSize < 2)
      seriesSize = 2;

   cout << "First " << seriesSize
        << " Fibonacci numbers:\n";
   for (int looper = 0; looper < seriesSize; looper++)
      {
       if (looper % 5)
          cout << ", " << setw(8) << fib (looper);
```

Program 6-25 Recursive Fibonacci *(continued)*

```
          else
              cout << endl << setw(8) << fib (looper);
         } // for

    cout << endl;
    return 0;
 }  // main
 /* ================ fib ================
    Calculates the nth Fibonacci number.
       Pre   num identifies Fibonacci number
       Post  returns nth Fibonacci number
 */
 long fib (long num)
 {
    if (num == 0 || num == 1)
       // Base Case
       return num;

    return fib  (num - 1) + fib (num - 2);
 }  // fib
```

```
Results:
This program prints a Fibonacci series.
How many numbers do you want? 33
First 33 Fibonacci numbers:

        0,        1,        1,        2,        3
        5,        8,       13,       21,       34
       55,       89,      144,      233,      377
      610,      987,     1597,     2584,     4181
     6765,    10946,    17711,    28657,    46368
    75025,   121393,   196418,   317811,   514229
   832040,  1346269,  2178309
```

Program 6-25 Analysis Compare `fib` in Program 6-25 with the solution in Figure 6-28. To determine the fourth number in the series, we call `fib` with `num` set to 4. To determine the answer requires that `fib` be called recursively eight times, as shown in Figure 6-28, which with the original call gives us a total of nine calls.

This sounds reasonable. Now, how many calls does it take to determine $Fibonacci_5$? The answer is 15 (see Table 6-3). As you can see from Table 6-3, the number of calls goes up quickly as we increase the size of the Fibonacci number we are calculating.

Table 6-3 leads us to the obvious conclusion that a recursive solution to calculate Fibonacci numbers is not realistic for more than 20 numbers.

No	Calls	No	Calls
1	1	11	287
2	3	12	465
3	5	13	753
4	9	14	1,219
5	15	15	1,973
6	25	20	21,891
7	41	25	242,785
8	67	30	2,692,573
9	109	35	29,860,703
10	177	40	331,160,281

Table 6-3 Fibonacci calls

LIMITATIONS OF RECURSION

We have introduced only the briefest explanation of recursion in this section. No attempt has been made to demonstrate *how* recursion works. To understand how it works, you will need to study data structures and concepts that are beyond the scope of this text.

On the other hand, you should understand the two major limitations of recursion. First, recursive solutions may involve extensive overhead because they use function calls. Second, each time you make a call you use up some of your memory allocation. If the recursion is deep—that is, if there is a large number of recursive calls—then you may run out of memory. Both the factorial and Fibonacci numbers solutions are better developed iteratively.

Does this mean that iterative solutions are always better than recursive functions? The answer is definitely no. Many algorithms are easier to implement recursively and are efficient. When you study data structures you will study many of them. Unfortunately, most of them require data structures beyond the scope of this text, so you will not see them here.

THE TOWERS OF HANOI

There is one classic recursion problem, the Towers of Hanoi, that is relatively easy to follow, is efficient, and uses no complex data structures. Let's look at it.

According to the legend, the monks in a remote mountain monastery knew how to predict when the world would end. They had a set of three diamond needles. Stacked on the first diamond needle were 64 gold disks of decreasing size. The monks moved one disk to another needle each hour, subject to the following rules:

1. Only one disk could be moved at a time.
2. A larger disk must never be stacked above a smaller one.
3. One and only one auxiliary needle could be used for the intermediate storage of disks.

The legend said that when all 64 disks had been transferred to the destination needle, the stars would be extinguished and the world would end. Today we know that it would require $2^{64} - 1$ moves to do this task. Figure 6-29 shows the Towers of Hanoi with only three disks.

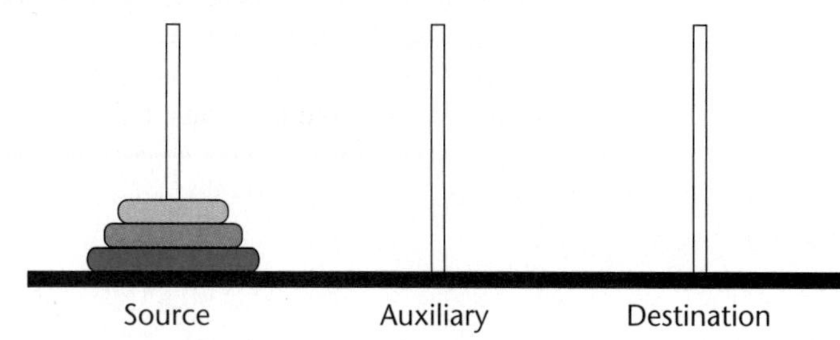

Figure 6-29 Towers of Hanoi—start position

This problem is interesting for two reasons. First, the recursive solution is much easier to code than the iterative solution would be. This is often the case with good recursive solutions. Second, the solution pattern for this problem is different from the simple examples we have been discussing. As you study the Towers solution, note that after each base case, we return to a decomposition of the general case for several steps. In other words, the problem is divided into several subproblems, each of which has a base case of moving one disk.

RECURSIVE SOLUTION OF THE TOWERS OF HANOI

To solve this problem, we must study the moves to see if we can find a pattern. We will use only three disks to simplify the analysis! First, imagine that we have only one disk to move. This is a very simple case, as shown below.

```
Case 1: Move one disk from source to destination
        needle.
```

Now imagine that we have to move two disks. Figure 6-30 traces the steps for two disks. First, the top disk is moved to the auxiliary disk. Next, the second disk is moved to the destination. Finally, the first disk is moved to the top of the second disk on the destination. This gives us Case 2, illustrated in Figure 6-30.

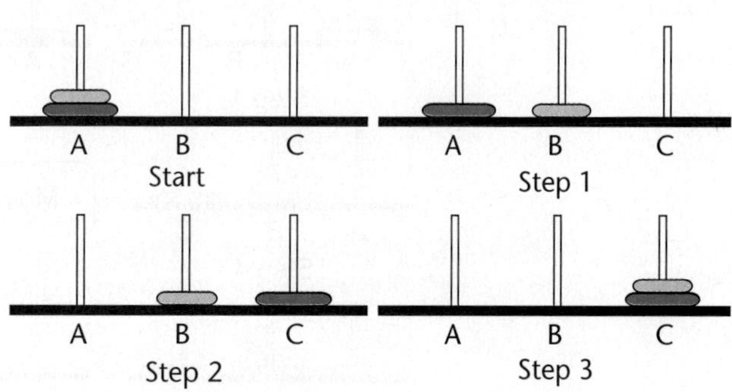

Figure 6-30 Towers solution for two disks

```
Case 2: Move one disk to auxiliary needle.
        Move one disk to destination needle.
        Move one disk from auxiliary to destination.
```

We are now ready to study the case for three disks. Figure 6-31 shows the solution for this case. The first three steps move the top two disks from the source to the auxiliary needle. (To see how to do this, refer to Case 2.) In step 4, we move the bottom disk to the destination. We now have one disk in place. This is an example of Case 1. It then

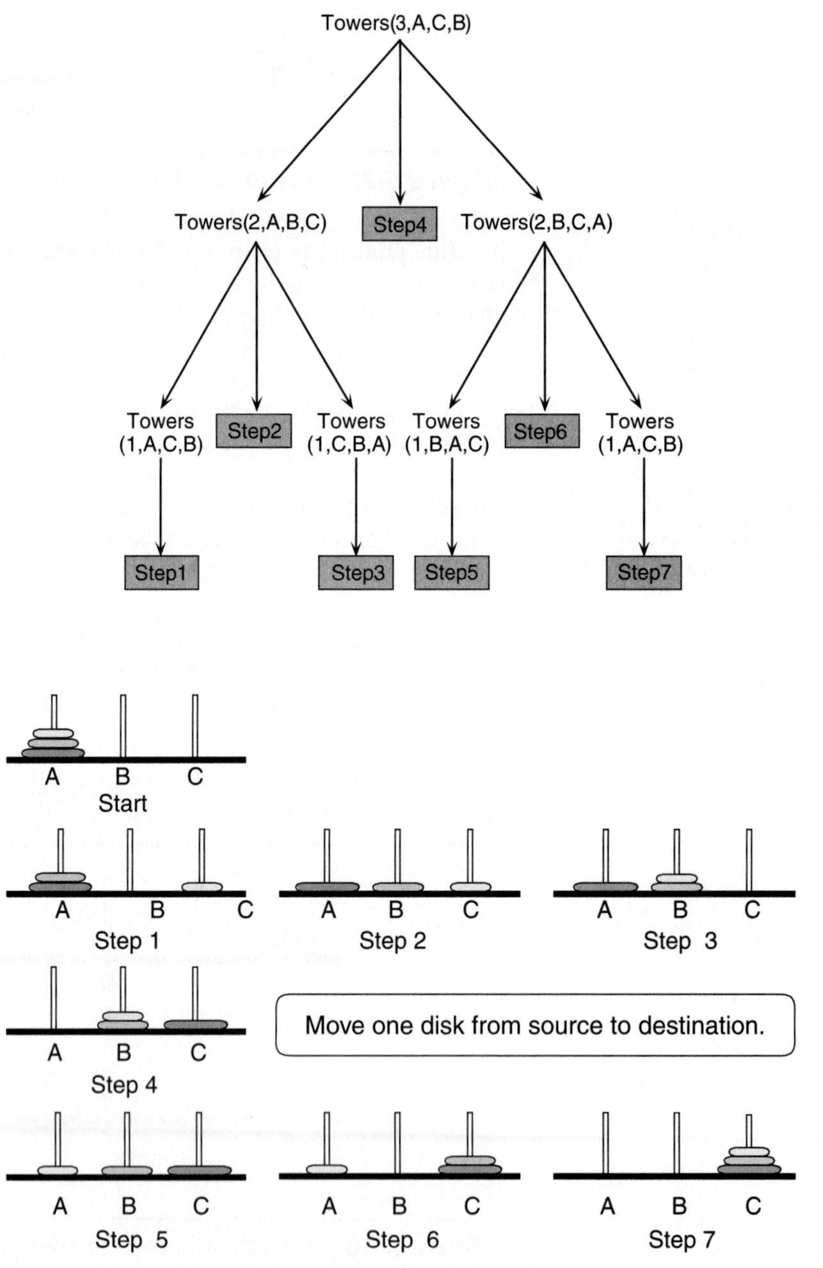

Figure 6-31 Towers solution for three disks

takes three more steps to move the two disks on the auxiliary needle to the destination. These steps are summarized below.

```
Case 3: Move two disks from source to auxiliary needle.
        Move one disk from source to destination needle.
        Move two disks from auxiliary to destination.
```

We are now ready to generalize the problem.

1. Move $n - 1$ disks from source to auxiliary needle. General Case
2. Move one disk from source to destination needle. Base Case
3. Move $n - 1$ disks from auxiliary to destination needle. General Case

Our solution will require a function with four parameters: the number of disks to be moved, the source needle, the destination needle, and the auxiliary needle. Using pseudocode, the three moves in the generalization shown above are then

```
1 Call Towers (n - 1, source, auxiliary, destination)
2 Move one disk from source to destination
3 Call Towers (n - 1, auxiliary, destination, source)
```

Study the third step carefully. After we complete the move of the first disk, the remaining disks are on the auxiliary needle. We must now move them from the auxiliary needle to the destination. In this case, the original source needle becomes the auxiliary needle. (Remember that the positions of the parameters in the *called* function are source, destination, auxiliary. The calling function must remember which of the three needles is the source and which is the destination for each call.)

One final point before we look at the program. In the towers functions, we use a type modifier known as the *static* storage class (see Statement 10). When a variable is defined as *static* in a function, it is initialized only the first time the function is called. After that, its value will be retained between calls. This useful C++ feature reduces the need to pass parameters just to retain a local variable.

We can now put these three calls together with the appropriate print statements to show the moves. The complete function is shown in Program 6-26. The output from the program is shown in Table 6-4.

Program 6-26 Towers of Hanoi

```
1  /* Move one disk from source to destination through
2     the use of recursion.
3     Pre   The tower consists of numDisks disks
4           Source, destination, and auxiliary towers given
5     Post  Steps for moves printed
6  */
7  void towers (int  numDisks, char source,
8                    char dest,     char auxiliary)
9  {
10    static int step = 0;
11
12    cout << "Towers (" << numDisks  << ", "
```

Program 6-26 Towers of Hanoi *(continued)*

```
                                 << source    << ", "
                                 << dest      << ", "
                                 << auxiliary << ")\n";
    if (numDisks == 1)
        cout << "\t\t\t\t\tStep "  << ++step
             << ": Move from "      << source
             << " to "              << dest << endl;
    else
       {
        towers (numDisks - 1, source, auxiliary, dest);
         cout << "\t\t\t\t\tStep " << ++step
              << ": Move from "     << source
              << " to "             << dest << endl;
        towers (numDisks - 1, auxiliary, dest, source);
       } // if ... else
    return;
} // towers
```

Calls	Output
`Towers (3, A, C, B)`	
`Towers (2, A, B, C)`	
`Towers (1, A, C, B)`	
	`Step 1: Move from A to C`
	`Step 2: Move from A to B`
`Towers (1, C, B, A)`	
	`Step 3: Move from C to B`
	`Step 4: Move from A to C`
`Towers (2, B, C, A)`	
`Towers (1, B, A, C)`	
	`Step 5: Move from B to A`
	`Step 6: Move from B to C`
`Towers (1, A, C, B)`	
	`Step 7: Move from A to C`

Table 6-4 Tracing of Program 6-26, Towers of Hanoi

6-10 A PROGRAMMING EXAMPLE—THE CALCULATOR PROGRAM

Let's look at our calculator program one more time. In Chapter 5, we gave the user the capability of selecting one of four options: add, subtract, multiply, or divide. However, if users wished to make two calculations, they had to run the program twice. We now add a loop that allows users to make as many calculations as needed (Program 6-27). We show here only two functions, *main* and `getOption`, since all of the others are the same.

Program 6-27 The complete calculator

```
/* This program adds, subtracts, multiplies, and divides
   two integers.
      Written by:
      Date:
*/
#include <iostream>
#include <iomanip>
using namespace std;

int   getOption   (void);
float add         (float num1,   float num2);
float sub         (float num1,   float num2);
float mul         (float num1,   float num2);
float dvd         (float num1,   float num2);
void printResult  (float num1,   float num2,
                   float result, int   option);

int main ()
{
   int option;

   do
      {
       option = getOption ();
       if (option != 5)
          {
           float num1;
           float num2;
           float result;

           do
              {
               cout << "\n\nEnter two numbers: ";
               cin  >> num1 >> num2;
               if (option == 4 && num2 == 0)
                  {
                   cout << "\a\n *** Error *** Second";
                   cout << " number cannot be 0!\n";
                  } // if
              } while (option == 4 && num2 == 0);

           switch (option)
              {
               case 1   : result = add (num1, num2);
                          break;
               case 2   : result = sub (num1, num2);
                          break;
               case 3   : result = mul (num1, num2);
```

Program 6-27 The complete calculator *(continued)*

```
                            break;
                case 4   : result = dvd (num1, num2);
               } // switch

            printResult (num1, num2, result, option);
           }  // else option != 5
      } while (option != 5);
   cout << "\nThank you for using Calculator.\n";
   return 0;
}  // main
/* ================== getOption ===================
   This function shows a menu and reads user option.
      Pre   Nothing
      Post  Returns a valid option
*/
int getOption (void)
{
   int option;

   do
      {
       cout << "\n******************";
       cout << "\n*       MENU      *";
       cout << "\n*                 *";
       cout << "\n*  1. ADD         *";
       cout << "\n*  2. SUBTRACT    *";
       cout << "\n*  3. MULTIPLY    *";
       cout << "\n*  4. DIVIDE      *";
       cout << "\n*  5. QUIT        *";
       cout << "\n*                 *";
       cout << "\n******************";

       cout << "\n\n\nPlease type your choice ";
       cout << "and press the return key : ";
       cin  >> option;

       if (option < 1 || option > 5)
           cout << "\a\nInvalid option. "
                << "Please re-enter.\n";

      } while (option < 1 || option > 5);
   return option;
}  // getOption
```

Program 6-27 Analysis As you look at the changes in this version of our program, first note the two loops in *main*. The first loop continues the calculator until the user says it's time to quit. The second loop gets and validates the numbers, making sure that the user isn't trying to divide by zero. (Your computer will get very upset if you divide by zero!)

We also modified our `getOption` function to add the quit option and to validate the options. If the user makes a mistake, we correct it in `getOption`. Extending the concept to a general principle, whenever you write a function to get data from a user, the function should handle all data validation. This makes for much simpler code in the rest of the program.

This simplification is also seen in the *switch* statement. Since we have validated the numbers before the *switch*, we no longer need to test for a valid divisor in the fourth *case* option. We also no longer need a *default,* since we know the options are valid. The result is a simpler statement, much more in line with the KISS principle (described in Chapter 3).

6-11 SOFTWARE ENGINEERING AND PROGRAMMING STYLE

LOOPS IN STRUCTURE CHARTS

Now that you understand how to write loops, let's look at how they are shown in a structure chart. The symbols are very simple. Loops go in circles, so the symbol we use is a circle. There are two basic looping symbols. The first is a simple loop, as shown in Figure 6-32a. The other is the conditional loop, shown in Figure 6-32b.

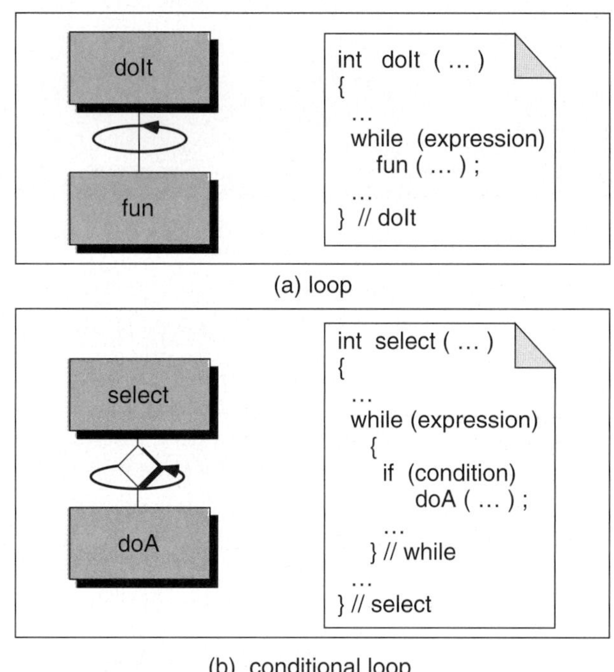

Figure 6-32 Structure chart symbols for loops

When the function is called unconditionally, as in a *while* loop, the circle flows around the line above the called function. On the other hand, if the call is conditional, as in a function called in an *if...else* statement inside a loop, then the circle includes a decision diamond on the line.

Figure 6-33 shows the basic structure for a function called process. The circle is *below* the function that controls the loop. In this example, the looping statement is contained in process, and it calls three functions: A, B, and C. The exact nature of the loop cannot be determined from the structure chart—it could be any of the three basic looping constructs. To help you better visualize the process, however, let's further assume that the loop is a *while* loop that contains a *cin* object that reads until the end of file. Within the *while* loop, there are three calls: the first to A, the second to B, and the third, conditionally, to C.

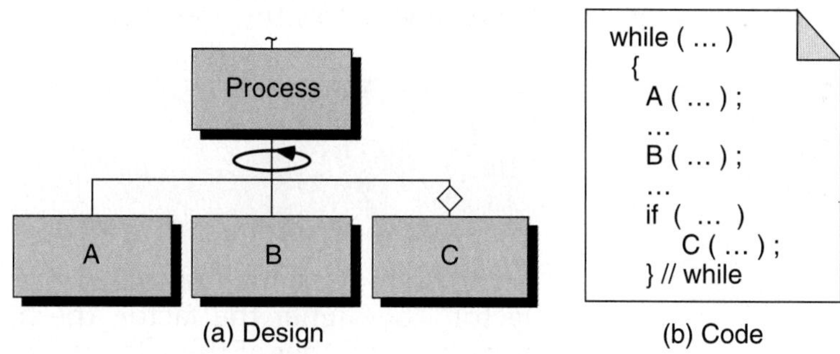

Figure 6-33 Structure chart for process

DETERMINING ALGORITHM EFFICIENCY

There is seldom a single algorithm for any problem. When comparing two different algorithms that solve the same problem, often one will be an order of magnitude more efficient than the other. In this case, it only makes sense that programmers have some way to recognize and choose the more efficient algorithm.

Although there has been much study of algorithms and algorithm efficiency, the field has not been given an official name. Brassard and Bratley coined the term *algorithmics*, which they define as "the systematic study of the fundamental techniques used to design and analyse efficient algorithms."[5] We will also use this term.

If a function is linear—that is, if it contains no loops—then its efficiency is a function of the number of instructions it contains. In this case, its efficiency is dependent on the speed of the computer and is generally not a factor in the overall efficiency in a program. On the other hand, functions that loop will vary widely in their efficiency. The study of algorithm efficiency is therefore largely devoted to the study of loops.

As we study specific examples, we will develop a formula that describes the algorithm's efficiency. We will then generalize the algorithm so that the efficiency can be stated as a function of the number of elements to be processed. The general format is

$$f(n) = \text{efficiency}$$

LINEAR LOOPS

Let us start with a simple loop. We want to know how many times the body of the loop is repeated in the following code.

```
for (int i = 1;  i <= 1000; i++)
  {
   BODY;
  }
```

Assuming `i` is an integer, the answer is 1000 times. But the answer is not always straightforward as it is in the above example. For example,

[5]Gilles Brassard and Paul Bratley. *Algorithmics Theory and Practice.* (Englewood Cliffs, NJ: Prentice Hall, 1988), p. xiii.

consider the loop that follows this paragraph. How many times is the body repeated in this loop? Here the answer is 500 times. Why?[6]

```
for (int i = 1;  i <= 1000;)
   {
    BODY;
    i += 2;
   }
```

In both cases, the number of iterations is directly proportionate to a factor. The higher the factor, the higher the number of loops. If you were to plot either of these loops, you would get a straight line. For that reason, they are known as linear loops.

Since the efficiency is proportionate to the number of iterations, it is

$$f(n) = n$$

LOGARITHMIC LOOPS

Now consider a loop in which the controlling variable is multiplied or divided in each loop. How many times will the body of each loop be repeated in the following program segments?

```
   Multiply loops                        Divide loops
i =  1;                               i =  1000;
while (i < 1000)                      while (i >= 1)
   {                                     {
    BODY;                                 BODY;
    i *= 2;                               i /= 2;
   } // while                         } // while
```

To help you understand this problem, Table 6-5 provides the values of `i` for each iteration.

Multiply		Divide	
Iteration	***i***	**Iteration**	***i***
1	1	1	1,000
2	2	2	500
3	4	3	250
4	8	4	125
5	16	5	62
6	32	6	31
7	64	7	15
8	128	8	7
9	256	9	3
10	512	10	1
(exit)	1024	(exit)	0

Table 6-5 Analysis of multiply/divide loops

[6]Because we start with 1 and add 2 until we get 1,000. 1,000/2 is 500.

As you can see, the number of iterations is 10 in both cases, because in each iteration the value of `i` doubles for the multiplication and is cut in half for the division. This means that the number of iterations is a function of the multiplier or divisor—in this case, 2. That is, the loop continues while the condition shown below is true.

multiply	$2^{\text{Iterations}} < 1{,}000$
divide	$1{,}000/2^{\text{Iterations}} >= 1$

Generalizing the analysis, we can say that iterations in loops that multiply or divide are determined by the following formula.

$$f(n) = ceil(\log_2 n)$$

NESTED LOOPS

When we analyze loops that contain loops, we must determine how many iterations each loop completes. The total is then the product of the number of iterations for the inner loop and the number of iterations in the outer loop.

$$\text{Iterations} = \text{outer loop iterations} * \text{inner loop iterations}$$

We now look at three nested loops: linear logarithmic, dependent quadratic, and quadratic.

Linear Logarithmic

The inner loop in the following code is a loop that multiplies. (To see the multiplication, look at the update expression in the inner *for* statement.)

```
for (int i = 1; i < = 10; i ++)
  for (int j = 1; j <= 10; j *= 2)
      {
       BODY;
      }
```

The number of iterations in the inner loop is therefore

$$ceil(\log_2 10)$$

However, since the inner loop is controlled by an outer loop, the above formula must be multiplied by the number of times the outer loop executes, which is ten. This gives us

$$10(ceil(\log_2 10))$$

which is generalized as

$$f(n) = n(ceil(\log_2 n))$$

Dependent Quadratic

Now consider the nested loop shown below.

```
for (int i = 1; i < = 10; i ++)
     for (int j = 1; j <= i; j ++)
         {
          BODY;
         }
```

The outer loop is the same as for the previous loop. However, the inner loop is executed only once in the first iteration, twice in the second iteration, three times in the third iteration, and so forth. The number of iterations is mathematically stated as

$$1 + 2 + 3 + \ldots + 9 + 10 = 55$$

which is generalized to

$$f(n) = n\frac{n+1}{2}$$

Quadratic

In the final nested loop, each loop executes the same number of times as seen below.

```
for (int i = 1; i <= 10; i ++)
   for (int j = 1; j <= 10; j ++)
       {
        BODY;
       }
```

The outer loop, that is, the loop at the first *for* statement, is executed 10 times. For each iteration, the inner loop is also executed 10 times. The answer, therefore, is 100, which is 10 * 10, the square of the loops. This formula generalizes to

$$f(n) = n^2$$

BIG-O NOTATION

With the speed of computers today, we are not concerned with an exact measurement of an algorithm's efficiency as much as we are with its general magnitude. If the analysis of two algorithms shows that one executes 15 iterations while the other executes 25 iterations, they are both so fast that we don't perceive the difference. On the other hand, if one iterates 15 times and the other iterates 1,500 times, it is clear which algorithm would be preferred.

We have shown that the number of statements executed in the function for n elements of data is a function of the number of elements, expressed as $f(n)$. While the equation derived for a function may be complex, there is usually a dominant factor in the equation that determines the order of magnitude of the result. Therefore, we don't have to determine the complete measure of efficiency, only the factor that determines the magnitude. This factor is the *big-O*, as in On-the-Order-Of. It is expressed as $O(n)$—that is, on-the-order-of n.

This simplification of efficiency is known as **big-O analysis**. For example, if an algorithm is quadratic, we would say its efficiency is

$$O(n^2)$$

or on-the-order of n-squared.

The big-O notation can be derived from $f(n)$ using the following steps:

1. In each term, set the coefficient of the term to 1.
2. Keep the largest term in the function and discard the others. Terms are ranked from lowest to highest, as shown below:

$$\log_2 n \quad n \quad n\log_2 n \quad n^2 \quad n^3 \quad \ldots \quad n^k \quad 2^n \quad n!$$

For example, to calculate the big-O notation for

$$f(n) = n\frac{(n+1)}{2} = \frac{1}{2}n^2 + \frac{1}{2}n$$

we first remove all coefficients. This gives us

$$n^2 + n$$

which after removing the smaller factors gives us

$$n^2$$

which in Big-O notation is stated as

$$O(f(n)) = O(n^2)$$

To consider another example, let's look at the polynomial expression

$$f(n) = a_j n^k + a_{j-1}n^{k-1} + \ldots + a_2 n^2 + an_1 + a_0$$

We first eliminate all of the coefficients, as shown below.

$$f(n) = n^k + n^{k-1} + \ldots + n^2 + n + 1$$

The largest term in this expression is the first one, so we can say that the order of a polynomial expression is

$$O(f(n)) = O(n^k)$$

STANDARD MEASURES OF EFFICIENCY

Computer scientists have defined seven categories of algorithm efficiency. We list them in Table 6-6 in order of decreasing efficiency. Any measure of efficiency presumes that a sufficiently large sample is being considered. If you are only dealing with 10 elements and the time required is a fraction of a second, there will be no meaningful difference between two algorithms. On the other hand, as the number of elements being processed grows, the difference between algorithms can be staggering. In Table 6-6, n is 10,000.

Efficiency	Big-O	Iterations	Est. time[a]
logarithmic	$O(\log_2 n)$	14	microseconds
linear	$O(n)$	10,000	.1 second
linear logarithmic	$O(n(\log_2 n))$	140,000	2 seconds
quadratic	$O(n^2)$	$10{,}000^2$	15–20 min.
polynomial	$O(n^k)$	$10{,}000^k$	hours
exponential	$O(c^n)$	$2^{10{,}000}$	intractable
factorial	$o(n!)$	10,000!	intractable

[a]Assumes instruction speed of 1 microsecond and 10 instructions in a loop.

Table 6-6 Measures of efficiency

Coming back to the question of why we should be concerned about efficiency, consider the situation in which there are three ways to solve a problem: one is linear, another is linear-logarithmic, and the third is quadratic. The order of their efficiency for a problem containing 10,000 elements is shown in Table 6-6, along with the other algorithmics.

Looking at the problem from the other end, if we are using a computer that executes a million instructions per second and the loop contains ten instructions, then we would spend .00001 second for each iteration of the loop. Table 6-6 also contains an estimate of the time required to solve the problem, given different efficiencies. Several of these measures are graphically represented in Figure 6-34.

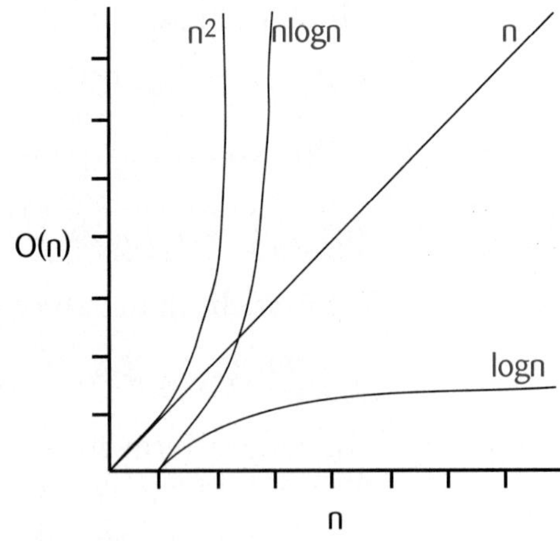

Figure 6-34 Measures of efficiency

6-12 TIPS AND COMMON PROGRAMMING ERRORS

1. Be aware that the *while* and *for* loops are pretest loops. Their body may never be executed. If you want your loop to be executed at least once, use a *do...while*.

2. Do not use equality and inequality for the control expression in loops—use limits that include less than or greater than. You may accidentally create an infinite loop, as shown below.

```
…
i = 0;
  while (i != 13).
     {
      …
      i++;              // sets i to 1,3,5 ..., 13
      …
      i++;              //sets i to 2, 4, 6, ..., 14
      …
     }  //while
```

3. It is a compile error to omit the semicolon after the expression in the *do...while* statement.
4. It is most likely a logic error to place a semicolon after the expression in a *while* or *for* statement.
5. It is a compile error to code a *for* statement with commas rather than semicolons, as shown below.

```
for (int i = 0, i < 10, i++)
```

6. It is a logic error to omit the update statement in the body of a *while* or *do...while* loop. Without an update statement, the loop will never terminate.
7. It is a common logic error to miscode the limit test in *for* statements. The result is usually a loop that executes one extra time or terminates one iteration short. For example, the following statement executes nine times, not ten.

```
for (int i = 1; i < 10; i++)
```

8. It is generally a logic error to update the terminating variable in both the *for* statement and in the body of the loop, as shown below.

```
for (int i = 0; i < 10; i++)
    {
     …
     i += 1;
    }
```

9. A recursive function must have a base case. Therefore, it is most likely an error if a recursive function does not have an *if* statement that prevents the recursive call and allows the function to return. For example, the following code based on Program 6-25 would never terminate.

```
long fib (long num)
{
//     statements
       return (fib (num - 1) + fib (num - 2));
} // fib
```

6-13 KEY TERMS

all inquiry
any inquiry
base case
big-O notation
body (of loop)
break
comma expression
comma operator
continue
counter-controlled loop
do...while
event-controlled loop
flag
for
general case
infinite loop
initialization statement
inquiry
iteration
loop control expression
loop limit test
loop initialization
loop update
post-test loop
pretest loop
process-control loops
recursion
summation
terminating expression
updating expression
while

6-14 SUMMARY

- The real power of computers is in their ability to repeat an operation or a series of operations many times.
- To control the loop, we need a condition to determine if more processing is needed.
- In a pretest loop, in each iteration, we check the condition first. If it is true, we iterate once more; otherwise, we exit the loop.
- In a post-test loop, in each iteration, we do the processing. Then we check the condition. If it is true, we start a new iteration; otherwise, we exit the loop.
- In a pretest loop the processing is done zero or more times.
- In a post-test loop the processing is done one or more times.
- In a pretest loop, if the body is executed n times, the limit test is executed $n + 1$ times.
- In a post-test loop, if the body is executed n times, the limit test is executed n times.
- The control expression in a loop must be explicitly or implicitly initialized.
- If you know exactly the number of times the body must be repeated, use a counter-controlled loop; if an event must occur to terminate a loop, use an event-controlled loop.
- There are three loop statements in C++: *while*, *for*, and *do...while*.
- The *while* loop is a pretest loop. It can be used for a counter-controlled or event-controlled loop, but it is usually used only for event control.
- The *for* loop is a pretest loop. It can be used for both counter-controlled and event-controlled loops, but it is used mostly in the first case.
- The *do...while* loop is a post-test loop. It is usually used when the body must be executed at least once.
- We discussed two C++ statements that are related to looping: *break* and *continue*. They are collectively categorized as jump statements (together with the *return* and *goto* statements).
- The *break* statement is used to terminate a loop prematurely. We strongly recommend that you use the *break* statement only within *switch* statements.
- The *continue* statement is used to skip the rest of the statements in a loop and start a new iteration without terminating the loop. We strongly recommend that you never use the *continue* statement.
- A loop in a structure chart is indicated by a circle on the line connecting it to the called functions. Only loops that call other functions are shown.
- To choose one of the three types of loops in C++ for a specific problem, follow the following strategy:
  1. Check to see if you need a pretest loop or a post-test loop.
  2. If you need a post-test loop, you can use only one loop, *do...while*.
  3. If you need a pretest loop, you can use either a *for* loop or a *while* loop. Although both can be used for counter-controlled and event-controlled loops,

a *for* loop is preferred for a counter-controlled loop and a *while* loop is preferred for an event-controlled loop.

- The best loop for data validation is the *do....while* loop.
- Recursion is a repetitive process in which a function calls itself.
- The statement that solves a recursive problem is known as the base case; the rest of the function is known as the general case.

6-15 PRACTICE SETS

REVIEW QUESTIONS

1. In a pretest loop, the limit test condition is tested first.
   a. True
   b. False
2. The action that causes the loop limit test to change from true to false is the loop update.
   a. True
   b. False
3. The value of a comma expression is the value of the first expression.
   a. True
   b. False
4. Recursion is a repetitive process in which a function calls itself.
   a. True
   b. False
5. Which of the following statements about pretest loops is true?
   a. If a pretest loop limit test is false, the loop executes one more time.
   b. Pretest loop initialization is done first in the loop body.
   c. Pretest loops execute a minimum of one time.
   d. Pretest loops test the limit condition after each execution of the loop body.
   e. The update for a pretest loop must be a part of the loop body.
6. Which of the following statements about loop initialization is false?
   a. Explicit initialization includes code to set the initial values of loop variables.
   b. Implicit initialization relies on preexisting values for loop variables.
   c. Initialization code is explicitly required in all loops.
   d. Initialization is preparation required for proper execution of a loop.
   e. Initialization must be done before the first execution of the loop.
7. Which of the following statements about loop updates is false?
   a. A loop update changes key variable(s) in a loop, thus allowing the loop to terminate.
   b. Loop updates may be made before or after a loop iteration.
   c. Loops may use explicit or implicit updates.
   d. In a *for* loop, updates are generally found in the *for* statement itself.
   e. The number of updates always equals the number of loop iterations.
8. Which of the following statements about counter-controlled loops is false?
   a. Counter-controlled loops are generally pretest loops.
   b. Counter-controlled loops generally increment or decrement a counter.
   c. Counter-controlled loops require a limit test.
   d. The number of times a loop iterates must be a constant.
   e. The update in a counter-controlled loop is generally explicit.

9. Which of the C++ loops is a pretest loop?
   a. *do...while*
   b. both the *do...while* and the *for*
   c. *for*
   d. both the *for* and the *while*
   e. *while*
10. Which of the following statements about the *while* statement is true?
   a. Multiple statements are allowed in a *while* loop.
   b. The limit test in a *while* loop is made before each iteration.
   c. The update in a *while* statement is contained in the *while* statement expression itself.
   d. The *while* statement is a post-test loop.
   e. The *while* statement must be terminated with a semicolon.
11. Which of the following statements about *for* and *while* statements is false?
   a. Both statements allow only one statement in the loop.
   b. Both statements are pretest loops.
   c. Both statements can be used for counter-controlled loops.
   d. Both statements include initialization within the statement.
   e. Both statements require an update statement.
12. Which of the following statements about the *do...while* loop is false?
   a. A *do...while* loop executes one or more iterations.
   b. Any statement may be used as the action in a *do...while*.
   c. The *do...while* is best suited for use as an event-controlled loop.
   d. The *do...while* is the only loop that requires a semicolon.
   e. The limit test in a *do...while* loop is executed at the beginning of each iteration.
13. The __________ is not a jump statement.
   a. *break*
   b. *continue*
   c. *return*
   d. *case*
   e. *goto*
14. Nested loops have a __________ standard measure of efficiency.
   a. exponential
   b. linear
   c. linear logarithmic
   d. quadratic
   e. linear logarithmic or quadratic
15. The __________ standard measure of efficiency is considered the most efficient.
   a. exponential
   b. logarithmic
   c. polynomial
   d. linear
   e. quadratic

EXERCISES

16. What would be printed from each of the following program segments? Compare and contrast your answers to parts a, b, and c.

a.

```
x = 12;
while (x > 7)
     cout << x << endl;
```

b.

```
for (int x = 12; x > 7; )
     cout << x << endl;
```

c.

```
x = 12;
do
   cout << x << endl;
while (x > 7);
```

17. What would be printed from each of the following program segments? Compare and contrast your answers to parts a, b, and c.

a.

```
x = 12;
while (x > 7)
    {
     cout << x << endl;
     x--;
    }
```

b.

```
for (int x = 12; x > 7; x--)
   cout << x << endl;
```

c.

```
x = 12;
do
    {
     cout << x << endl;
     x--;
    } while (x > 7);
```

18. What would be printed from each of the following program segments? Compare and contrast your answers to parts a and b.

a.

```
x = 12;
while (x > 7)
    {
     cout << x << endl;
     x -= 2;
    }
```

b.

```
for (int x = 12; x > 7; x -= 2)
    cout << x << endl;
```

19. What would be printed from each of the following program segments? Compare and contrast your answers to parts a, b, and c.

a.

```
x = 12;
while (x < 7)
    {
     cout << x << endl;
     x--;
    }
```

b.

```
for (int x = 12; x < 7; x--)
     cout << x << endl;
```

c.

```
x = 12;
do
    {
     cout << x << endl;
     x--;
    } while (x < 7);
```

20. Change the following *while* loops to *for* loops.

a.

```
x = 0;
while (x < 10)
    {
     cout << x << endl;
     x++;
    }
```

b.

```
cin >> x;
while (x != 9999)
    {
     cout << x << endl;
     cin  >> x;
    }
```

21. Change the *while* loops in Exercise 20 to *do...while* loops.

22. Change the following *for* loops to *while* loops.

a.

```
for (int x = 1; x < 100; x++)
     cout << x << endl;
```

b.

```
for ( ; cin >> x;)
     cout << x << endl;
```

23. Change the *for* loops in Exercise 22 to *do...while* loops.

24. Change the following *do...while* loops to *while* loops:

a.

```
x = 0;
do
    {
     cout << x++ << endl;
    } while (x < 100);
```

b.

```
do
    {
     cin >> x;
     cout << x << endl;
    } while (cin);
```

25. Change the *do...while* loops in Exercise 24 to *for* loops.

26. A programmer writes the following *for* loop to print the numbers 1 to 10. What is the output? If the output is incorrect, how would you correct it?

```
for (int num = 0; num < 10; num++)
     cout << num;
```

27. Another programmer writes the following for loop to print the numbers 1 to 10. What is the output? If the output is incorrect, how would you correct it?

```
for (int num = 0; num < 10; num++)
    {
     numOut = num + 1;
     cout << numOut;
    } // for
```

28. What will be printed from the following program segments?

a.
```
for (int x = 1; x <= 20; x++)
    cout << x << endl;
```
b.
```
for (int x = 1; x <= 20; x++)
    {
     cout << x << endl;
     x++;
    }
```

29. What will be printed from the following program segments?

a.
```
for (int x = 20; x >= 10; x--)
    cout << x << endl;
```
b.
```
for (int x = 20; x >= 1; x--)
    {
     cout << x << endl;
     x--;
    }
```

30. What will be printed from the following program segments?

a.
```
for (int x = 1; x <= 20; x++)
    {
     for (int y = 1; y <= 5; y++)
         cout << x << endl;
     cout << endl;
    }
```
b.
```
for (int x = 20; x >= 1; x--)
    {
     for (int y = x; y >=1; y--)
         cout << setw(3) << x;
     cout << endl;
    }
```

31. What will be printed from the following program segments?

a.
```
for (int x = 1; x <= 20; x++)
    {
     for (int y = 1; y < x; y++)
         cout << " ";
     cout << x << endl;
    }
```
b.
```
for (int x = 20; x >= 1; x--)
    {
     for (int y = x; y >=1; y--)
       cout << " ";
     cout << x;
    }
```

32. You find the statement shown below in a program you are maintaining.
```
for ( ; ; )
    {
    ...
    }
```
   a. Describe the implications behind the null expressions in the *for* statement.
   b. Since there is no limit condition, how can this statement be exited?
   c. Is this good structured programming style? Explain your answer.

33. Write a program that uses a *for* loop to print a line of 60 asterisks.

34. Write a *for* loop that will produce each of following sequences:
   a. 6, 8, 10, 12, …, 66
   b. 7, 9, 11, 13, …, 67
   c. The sum of the numbers between 1 and 15 inclusive
   d. The sum of the odd numbers between 15 and 45 inclusive
   e. The first 50 numbers in the series 1, 4, 7, 10, … (calculate the total 1 + 4 + 7 + 10 + …)

PROBLEMS

35. Write a program that prompts the user to enter an integer, `n`, and then `n` floating-point numbers. As the numbers are read, the program will calculate the average of the positive numbers.

36. Rewrite Problem 35 to average the negative numbers.

37. Write a program that asks the user to enter a list of integers. The program is to determine the largest value entered and the number of times it was entered. For example, if the following series is entered
```
5 2 15 3 7 15 8 9 5 2 15 3 7
```
it would output the largest value is 15 and it was entered 3 times.

38. Write a program that creates the following pattern:

```
1 2 3 4 5 6 7 8 9
1 2 3 4 5 6 7 8
1 2 3 4 5 6 7
1 2 3 4 5 6
1 2 3 4 5
1 2 3 4
1 2 3
1 2
1
```

39. Write a function that creates the following pattern, given the height (number of rows).

```
*************
*************
*************
*************
*************
```

40. Write a function that creates the following pattern, given the height (number of rows).

```
===========
*         *
*         *
*         *
*         *
*         *
===========
```

41. Write a function that creates the following pattern, given the height (number of rows).

```
*
***
*****
*******
*********
***********
```

42. Write a function that creates the following pattern, given the height (number of rows).

```
***********
*********
*******
*****
***
*
```

43. Write a function that creates the following pattern, given the height (number of rows), which must be even.

```
*
***
*****
*******
*********
*********
*******
*****
***
*
```

44. Modify Program 6-2, "A while loop to print numbers," on page 234 to display the total as each number is entered. The format should be:

```
Enter your numbrs: <EOF> to stop.
5
Total: 5
17
Total:22
8
Total:30
```

45. Write a program that reads integer data from the standard input unit and prints a list of the numbers followed by the minimum integer read, maximum integer read, and the average of the list. Test your program with the data shown below.

```
{ 24 7 31 -5 64 0 57 -23 23 7 63 31
  15 7 -3 2 4 6 }
```

46. In the example on page 242, we demonstrated the use of a *do...while* to validate input. The code fragment contains no message to tell the user that an invalid number has been entered. Write a function that reads only positive even numbers from the keyboard. If a negative or odd number is entered, it should print an error message and ask the user to enter another number. Each call to the function is to read only one number. The valid number read is to be returned to the calling program. Then write a short program to test the function using the data shown below. The valid numbers should be printed, either in a separate function or in *main*.

```
{ 2  18  -18  5  7  100  1  -1 }
```

47. Write a function that reads integers from the keyboard. If any of the numbers are negative, it returns a negative number. If all the numbers are positive, it returns their average. (Hint: See Program 6-21 on page 264.)

48. Program 6-18 on page 261 uses a *while* loop to read a series of numbers from the keyboard. Since you will always have at least one number in this program, rewrite it to use the *do...while*.

49. Program 6-20 on page 263 uses INT_MAX from the <climits> library to initialize the *smallest* variable. Another solution is to read the first number and put its value in *smallest*, then go into the loop to read the rest of the numbers. Modify Program 6-20 to make this change.

50. Euler's number, *e,* is used as the base of natural logarithms. It can be approximated using the following formula.

$$e = 1 + \frac{1}{1!} + \frac{1}{2!} + \frac{1}{3!} + \frac{1}{4!} + \frac{1}{5!} + \frac{1}{6!} + \cdots + \frac{1}{(n-1)!} + \frac{1}{n!}$$

Write a program that approximates e using a loop that terminates when the difference between two successive values of e is less than 0.0000001.

51. Write a program that reads an integer from the keyboard and then calls a recursive function to print it out in reverse. For example, if the user enters 4762, it prints 2674.

52. Rewrite Program 6-25 page 270 using an iterative solution.

PROJECTS

53. Statisticians use many different algorithms in addition to the arithmetic average. Two other averages are the geometric and the harmonic mean. The geometric mean of a set of n numbers, $x_1, x_2, x_3, \ldots, x_{n-1}, x_n$ is defined by the following formula:

$$\sqrt[n]{x_1 \times x_2 \times \ldots \times x_n}$$

The harmonic mean is defined by the following formula:

$$\frac{n}{\frac{1}{x_1} + \frac{1}{x_2} + \ldots + \frac{1}{x_n}}$$

Write a program that reads a series of numbers and calculates the average, geometric mean, and harmonic mean.

54. Write a C++ program that can create four different patterns of different sizes. The size of each pattern is determined by the number of columns or rows. For example, a pattern of size 5 has 5 columns and 5 rows. Each pattern is made of character $ and a digit, which shows the size. The size must be between 2 and 9. The following shows the four patterns in size 5.

Pattern 1	Pattern 2	Pattern 3	Pattern 4
5$$$$	$$$$5	$$$$$	$$$$$
$5$$$	$$$5$	$$$$5	5$$$$
$$5$$	$$5$$	$$$55	55$$$
$$$5$	$5$$$	$$555	555$$
$$$$5	5$$$$	$5555	5555$

Your program displays a menu and asks the user to choose a pattern and size. But note that it must be robust; it must prompt the user to choose an option only between 1 and 5 and a pattern size only between 2 and 9. You are to print the menu and the user's response. The following example shows all user menu responses, including potential errors:

```
        M E N U

      1. Pattern One
      2. Pattern Two
      3. Pattern Three
      4. Pattern Four
      5. Quit

Enter option (1 to 5): 11
Option incorrect. Try again.
Enter option (1 to 5): 3
Enter pattern size (2 to 9): 12
Pattern size incorrect. Try again.
Enter Pattern Size (2 to 9): 4
```

The program must consist of one *main* function and six other functions called `getOption`, `getSize`, `patternOne`, `patternTwo`, `patternThree`, and `patternFour`.

Run your program *once* with the options and sizes shown in Table 6-7. Note that some options and sizes are missing because either the previous option or the size is invalid.

	Option	Size
SET 1	1	2
SET 2	2	3
SET 3	3	4
SET 4	4	5
SET 5	6	6
SET 5	3	
SET 6	2	10
SET 6		7
SET 7	5	

Table 6-7 Text options for Project 54

55. Write a C++ program to create a calendar for a year. The program reads the year from the keyboard. It then calculates which day of the week (SUN, MON, TUE, WED, THU, FRI, SAT) is the first day of the year and prints the calendar for that year. After printing the year, it should ask if the user wants to continue. If the answer is yes, it will print the calendar for another year until the user is done.

The program prompts the user for the input as it is shown below.

```
Enter year for calendar : 1994
```

The output is a calendar for the whole year (12 months). One month is shown below.

```
JANUARY                                   1994
SUN   MON   TUE   WED   THU   FRI   SAT
                                          1
  2     3     4     5     6     7     8
  9    10    11    12    13    14    15
 16    17    18    19    20    21    22
 23    24    25    26    27    28    29
 30    31
```

To obtain the correct calendar for the requested year, you must first find which day of the week is the first day of that year. This can be done with the formula below. (For a complete explanation, see Chapter 5's Project 57 on page 224.

$$\left((\text{year}-1)\times 365+\left\lfloor\frac{(\text{year}-1)}{4}\right\rfloor-\left\lfloor\frac{(\text{year}-1)}{100}\right\rfloor+\left(\left\lfloor\frac{(\text{year}-1)}{400}\right\rfloor\right)+1\right)\ \%\ 7d$$

You will also need to calculate leap years. The formula for this calculation is also found in Chapter 5's Project 59 on page 239.

Run your program once with the following sets of data:[7]

```
SET 1 ===>1993
SET 2 ===>    0
SET 3 ===>2000
SET 4 ===> 123
```

56. Write a C++ program to help a prospective borrower calculate the monthly payment for a loan. The program also prints the amortization (payoff) table to show the balance of the loan after each monthly payment.

The program prompts the user for input as shown in the following example:

```
Loan amount (principal)? 10000.00
Interest per year (percent)? 12
Number of years? 10
```

The program then creates an information summary and amortization table.

Banks and financial institutions use different formulas to calculate the monthly payment of a loan. For the purpose of this assignment, we use the following simple formula:

$$\begin{aligned}NM &= (NY * 12)\\ IM &= (IY / 12) / 100\\ P &= (1 + IM)^{NM}\\ Q &= (P / (P - 1))\\ MP &= (PR * IM * Q)\end{aligned}$$

where

NY: scheduled number of years to amortize the loan

NM: scheduled number of months to amortize the loan

IY: interest rate per year (as a percentage)

IM: interest rate/month (decimal)

PR: principal (the amount of the loan)

P: the value of $(1 + IM)^{NM}$

Q: the value of $P / (P - 1)$

MP: monthly payment (rounded to two decimal places)

[7]The Julian calendar was changed to our current (Gregorian) calendar in 1752. Although calendars prior to this date are valid Gregorian calendars, they do not represent the Julian calendar in use at that time.

The *main* function must call three other functions:

1. `calculateMonthlyPayment`
2. `printInformation`
3. `printAmortizationTable`

Of course, the first function may also call other functions if necessary.

Because of the approximation used in calculation, the value of the new balance at the end of the last month may become nonzero. To prevent this, the last payment must be adjusted. Therefore, we will print the information for every month except the last month. After we exit the loop, we then print the information for the last month. The monthly payment for the last month may be less or greater than the other months. It must be calculated by adding the principal paid to the interest paid for that month. The new balance at the end of the last month must be zero. The following example shows the concept. The program has been run for a loan of $5,000.00 at 11% interest rate for a period of one year. The input was:

```
Loan amount (principal)? 5000.00
Interest per year (percent)? 11
Number of years? 1
```

The output is shown in Figure 6-35.

```
The amount of the loan (principal):      5000.00
Interest rate/year (percent):              11.0
Interest rate/month (decimal):              0.009167
Number of years:                            1
Number of months:                          12
Monthly payment:                          441.91
```

Month	Old Balance	Monthly Payment	Interest Paid	Principal Paid	New Balance
1	5000.00	441.91	45.83	396.08	4603.92
2	4603.92	441.91	42.20	399.71	4204.21
3	4204.21	441.91	38.54	403.37	3800.84
4	3800.84	441.91	34.84	407.07	3393.77
5	3393.77	441.91	31.11	410.80	2982.97
6	2982.97	441.91	27.34	414.57	2568.40
7	2568.40	441.91	23.54	418.37	2150.03
8	2150.03	441.91	19.71	422.20	1727.83
9	1727.83	441.91	15.84	426.07	1301.76
10	1301.76	441.91	11.93	429.98	871.78
11	871.78	441.91	7.99	433.92	437.86
12	437.86	441.87	4.01	437.86	0.00

```
Total amount paid: 5302.88
```

Figure 6-35 Sample output from loan problem

Note: Your answer may look a little different (by a few pennies) because of different precision. Run your program once with the following sets of data:

	Amount	Interest	Years
Set 1	10,000.00	12	1
Set 2	5,000.00	10	2
Set 3	1,000.00	8	3

57. Write a program that reads a list of integers from the keyboard and closes the following:

a. Finds and prints the sum and the average of the integers

b. Finds and prints the largest and the smallest integers

c. Prints a message if some of them are less than 20

d. Prints a message if all of them are between 10 and 90

The input data consist of a list of integers with a sentinel. The program must prompt the user to enter the integers, one by one, and enter the sentinel when the end of the list has been reached. The prompt should look like the following:

```
Enter numbers (99999 to stop).
```

The output should be formatted as shown below using "true" or "false" for the last two outputs:

```
Number of integers:          xxx
Sum of integers:            xxxx
Average:                     xxx.xx
Smallest integer:            xxx
Largest integer:             xxx
Number(s) < 20             false
All in range                true
```

58. The formula for converting Celsius temperatures to Fahrenheit is

$$F = 32 + \left(C * \frac{180.0}{100.0} \right)$$

Write a program that prints out conversion tables for Celsius to Fahrenheit (0° to 100°) and Fahrenheit to Celsius (32° to 212°). Use separate functions to convert Fahrenheit to Celsius and Celsius to Fahrenheit. The output format for each table is to fit on a standard monitor display, 80 columns.

59. Rewrite Program 6-26 on page 275 using an iterative solution.

7 Text I/O

A program is a data processor: It accepts input data, processes data, and creates output data. Although we can write programs with no input/output operations, they do not have practical use. Handling input/output, however, is a complex task. The complexity is due to diversity. Data may come from many different sources and may go to different destinations. For example, data may come from such diverse sources as a keyboard, a file on the disk, or a communication channel; data may also go to many destinations, such as a monitor, a file on the disk, or to a communication channel.

C++ treats each source of data as an input entity and each data destination as an output entity. Although a keyboard is different from a file on a disk, C++ uses the same input operations for each of them. Similarly, the same output operations are applied to a monitor and a file on the disk. In other words, the only difference among a keyboard, an input file, and a communication channel is in the way each is connected to the program. After the connection has been made, the same operations can apply to each.

7-1 INPUT AND OUTPUT ENTITIES

In this text, we concentrate on the keyboard and the files as the input entities and the monitor and the files as the output entities; we do not discuss communication channels.

FILES

A **file** is an external collection of related data treated as a unit. The primary purpose of a file is to keep a record of data. Since the contents of primary memory are lost when the computer is shut down, we need files to store our data in a more permanent form. Additionally, the collection of data is often too large to reside entirely in main memory at one time. Therefore, we must have the ability to read and write portions of the data while the rest remain in the file.

> **A *file* is an external collection of related data treated as a unit.**

There are two broad classes of files: **text files** and **binary files**. In text files, all the data are stored as characters, which must be converted to internal formats when they represent numeric data. Text files are also organized around lines, each of which ends with a newline character (`\n`). Binary files, on the other hand, store data in the internal computer formats, such as integer and floating point. We discuss only text files in this chapter; binary files are handled in Chapter 15.

> **A file on a disk or tape can be a text file or a binary file.**

Files are stored in what are known as **auxiliary** or **secondary storage devices**. The two most common forms of secondary storage are disk (hard disk, CD, and DVD) and tape.

When the computer reads, the data move from the external device to memory; when it writes, the data move from memory to the external device. This data movement often uses a special work area known as a buffer. A **buffer** is a temporary storage area that holds data while they are being transferred to or from memory. The primary purpose of a buffer is to synchronize the physical devices with a program's needs, especially on large storage devices such as disk and tape. Because of the physical requirements of these devices, more data can be inputted at one time than a program can use. The buffer holds the extra data until the program or the user is ready for it. Conversely, the buffer collects data until there are enough to write efficiently. These buffering activities are taken care of by software known as device drivers or access methods provided by the supplier of the computer's operating system.

As a file is being read, there eventually comes a point when all the data have been input. When all of the data have been read, the condition is known as **end of file**. It is the programmer's job to test for end of file. This test is often done in a loop control statement. The end of file in an auxiliary device is detected automatically by the device and passed to the program.

STANDARD INPUT

The keyboard is considered the **standard input** device for a program. When a program needs to read from the keyboard, the program waits for the user to type data on the keyboard. The keyboard behaves like a file that we can only read. It has a problem, however; there is no "end of file" key on the keyboard. When we need to signal end of file, we must enter a special key combination to simulate an end of file found in a file. This combination varies for different operating systems. In the UNIX and Macintosh environments, we use the control (ctrl) and d-key, pressed simultaneously (abbreviated `^d`); in Windows, we use the control key and the z-key (`^z`).

STANDARD OUTPUT

The monitor is considered the **standard output** for a program. It behaves like a file that we can only write to. It also behaves like a text file. We cannot write binary data to a monitor. When we try to write binary data to a monitor, the results are unpredictable.

> **The standard input and output behave like text files.**

STANDARD ERROR

When a program runs, errors may occur. The type and the reason of the error need to be communicated to the user. The normal communication vehicle is the monitor, which is considered as the **standard error** device. This means that the monitor is considered both the standard output and the standard error device.

> **The standard error behaves like a text file.**

7-2 STREAMS

The key to the universal treatment of input and output is the concept of a **stream**. A stream is an abstract representation of an input data source or output data destination. Instead of requiring that a programmer know the operation of each data source or destination that may be attached to a computer, C++ provides the ability to create stream objects that handle it all for us. This means that the details of reading and writing data to and from a source or destination are left to the operating system.

The contents of a stream are a sequence of elements in time. Only one stream element, the current one, is available at a time. Figure 7-1 shows the stream concept. We have shown the streams as data pipes that connect the program to the input/output entities such as a keyboard, a monitor, or a file. The program sends data (or errors) to an output stream and receives data from an input stream.

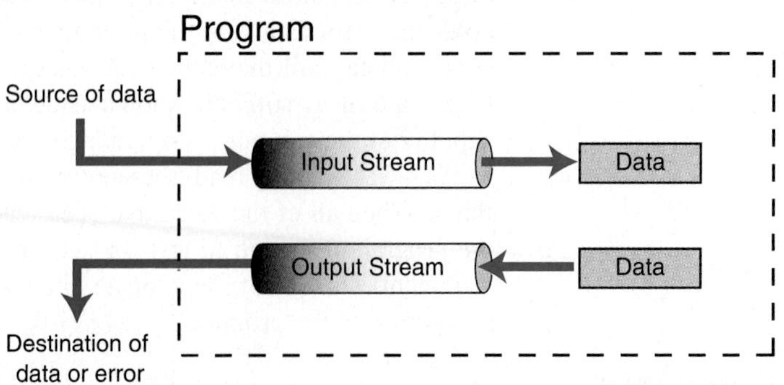

Figure 7-1 The stream concept

Note that we have included the streams inside the program, where they are accessed by the program. In other words, the programmer sees only the stream; the stream sees the data source or destination.

CREATING AND CONNECTING STREAMS

The simplicity of streams comes with a cost. The programmer (or the operating system) has two separate tasks before sending or receiving data: creating streams and connecting them to the data source or destination. When the stream is no longer needed, it should be disconnected.

1. First a stream needs to be created. A stream in C++ is an object that must be instantiated. We discuss classes and objects in Chapter 10; for the moment it suffices to know that streams need to be created before being used. When we create a stream, we need to supply three details about the stream:
   a. Is it an input or an output stream?
   b. What is the input (or output) entity that the stream will send data to (or receive data from)? The stream that receives data from the keyboard is different from the stream that receives data from a file.
   c. What is the transfer mode (text mode or binary mode)?
2. After the stream has been created, it must be connected to a corresponding source or destination.
3. When the source or destination is no longer needed, it should be disconnected from the stream.

STANDARD STREAMS

The C++ language automatically defines four **standard streams** called **console input**, **console output**, **console error**, and **console log**. The console input stream is associated with the standard input (keyboard). The console output, console error, and console log are connected to the standard output (monitor). They are named as ***cin***, ***cout***, ***cerr***, and ***clog***, respectively. The difference between the console error and console log is that console error is unbuffered; that is, the error is displayed on the console immediately after it is written, while the console log is buffered, therefore, it does not display on the console until the buffer is full.

Each of these streams is created by the system automatically when a program that uses them starts. Their corresponding objects are defined in the input/output stream (`<iostream>`) header file. We just need to include this header file at the beginning of our programs. When the program starts, the operating system also automatically associates them with their default devices—the keyboard or the console. Some operating systems allow them to be connected to alternate devices. How this is done is beyond the scope of this text. Figure 7-2 shows the configuration of the standard streams as used in a typical program.

The task of disconnecting standard streams to standard input/output/error entities is also done by the operating system. When a program stops executing, these entities are disconnected from the corresponding streams.

> **Standard streams are created, connected, and disconnected automatically.**

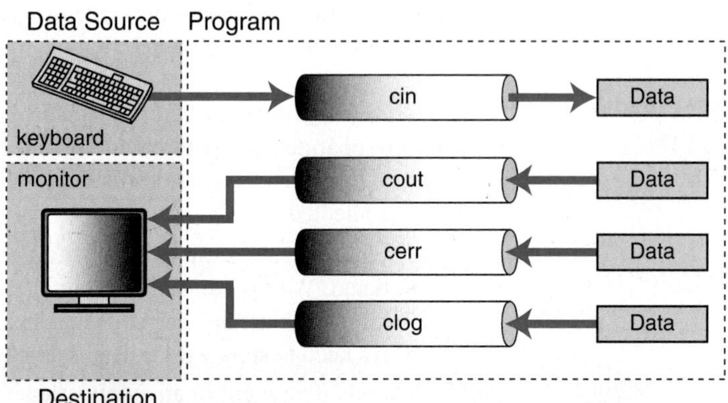

Figure 7-2 Standard streams

FILE STREAMS

To read from a file, we need an input file stream; to write to a file, we need an output file stream. The responsibility of creating a file stream and connecting it to the corresponding source or destination is the responsibility of the programmer.

Creating File Streams

There are three types of streams we can define: an input stream, an output stream, and an input/output stream. We can only read from an input stream; we can only write to an output stream; but we can both read from and write to an input/output stream. C++ defines three classes for this purpose: *ifstream*, *ofstream*, and *fstream*. An *ifstream* object is for input; an *ofstream* object is for output, and an *fstream* object is for input and output. The following example demonstrates how we define these three objects.

```
ifstream fsInput;
ofstream fsOutput;
fstream  fsIO;
```

Connecting File Streams

After we create a file stream, it must be connected to the physical device. This is done by the open function, defined as part of the C++ library. We discuss the open function in the next section. Figure 7-3 depicts the three streams after they have been created and connected.

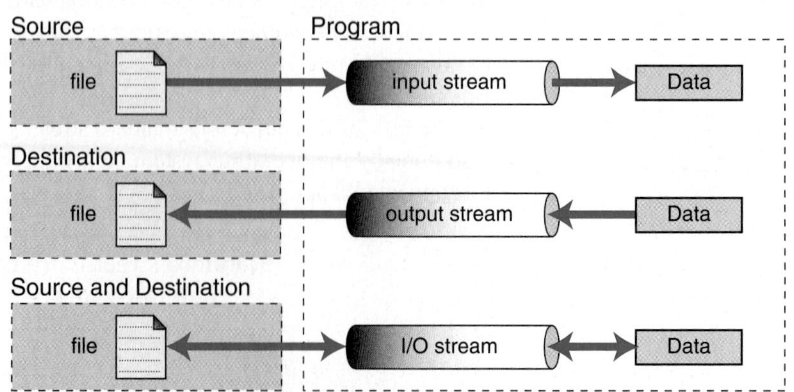

Figure 7-3 Connected file streams

Disconnecting File Streams

When a program does not need a file, the file should be disconnected from the stream. To disconnect a file, we use the close function discussed in the next section.

> **File streams are created, connected to files, and disconnected from files by the programmer.**

7-3 STANDARD LIBRARY INPUT/OUTPUT FUNCTIONS

The C++ input/output library contains several different **input/output functions**. They are grouped into seven different categories, as shown in Figure 7-4. Four of them are discussed here. The functions shown in shaded boxes in the figure will be discussed in Chapters 14 and 16.

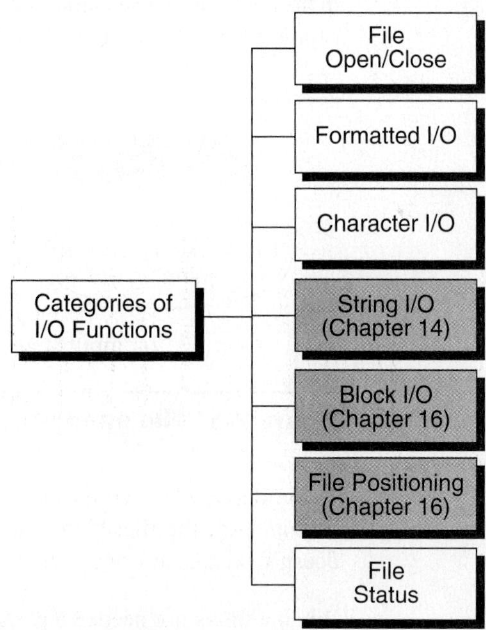

Figure 7-4 Types of standard input/output functions

FILE OPEN AND CLOSE

In this section we discuss how to connect a stream to a physical file (open) and how to disconnect it (close) when we no longer need the file.

File Open

The C++ ***open*** function connects a file to a stream. This requires two steps: First, it makes the connection between the external file and the program. Second, it stores the information required to process the stream in the stream object.

The syntax for opening the file uses a new operator, the member operator (.). We will discuss it fully when we study objects. For now, all we need to know is that to reference a function that is associated with an object we use the member operator. To open the file, therefore, we simply reference the object and its function and pass it the name of the file you wish to open.

To open an input file, we define an *ifstream* object. To open an output file, we define an *ofstream* object. The following example opens an input file that contains temperature readings.

```
ifstream fsDailyTemps;

fsDailyTemps.open ("TEMPS.DAT");
```

A **filename** is a string that supplies the name of a file as it is known to the external world. In our temperatures example, the file on the disk is `TEMPS.DAT`. To open it, we call the open function as a member of `fsDailyTemps` and include as the open parameter the name of the file on the disk. Note that if the file was not in the same directory as our program, we would have to include the full path to the file.[1]

When we open a file, we implicitly define its state by the object type we use—*ifstream* for read state and *ofstream* for write state. We discuss these states in more detail in Chapter 14. For now, it is sufficient for you to understand that when a file is opened in the read state, a file marker positions the stream at the beginning of the data. This concept is illustrated in Figure 7-5a. It is an error to open a file for input when it doesn't exist.

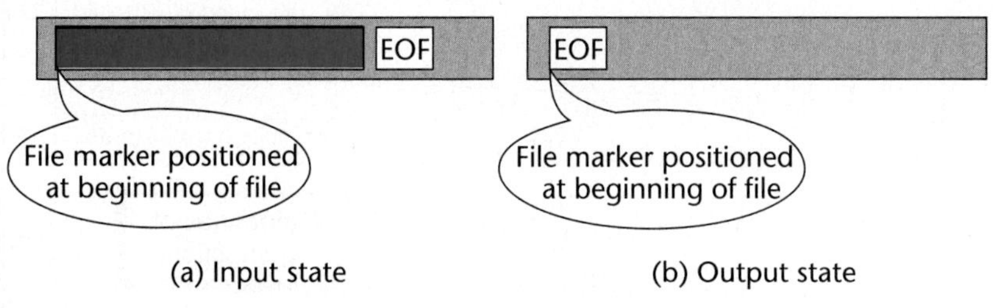

Figure 7-5 File opening states

Similarly, when a file is opened in the write state, the file marker is positioned at the beginning of the file. If the file already exists, then any data in it are lost. If the file doesn't exist, a new one is created. This concept is illustrated in Figure 7-5b.

File Close

When a file is not needed any more, it should be **closed** to free system resources, such as buffer space. Just as each file object has an open function associated with it, there is also a close function, used when the file is no longer required. The following segment of code shows the temperature file definition, open, and close as they would appear in a program.

[1]If you are working in a DOS environment, in which the path uses the backslash, you need to use two backslashes to create one in the filename. Thus, a file found in a weather directory under the root of the C drive would need the following filename:

```
"C:\\weather\\day-temp.dat"
```

```
#include <fstream>
   ...
int main ()
{
   ifstream  fsDailyTemps;
   fsDailyTemps.open ("TEMPS.DAT");

   // process file

   fsDailyTemps.close();
   return 0;
}  // main
```

Open and Close Errors

What if the open or close fails? Open and close errors can occur for a number of reasons. One of the most common errors occurs when the external filename in the open function call does not match a name on the disk. When you are creating a new file, the open can fail if there isn't enough room on the disk.

> **File Disposition Warning**
>
> The operating system controls what happens when you open an existing file for writing. The one consistent thing is that a new file is created. If you are in a UNIX or an MS/DOS environment, the existing file is deleted when the program completes. In other environments, the existing file still exists, but it is no longer the current file. To read it, you would have to use special job control statements that refer to the older version. Check with the documentation for your operating system to make sure you understand what will happen.

Always check to make sure that a file has opened successfully. There are several ways to test for a successful open. By far, the easiest is to simply test the state of the stream in a conditional expression using the not operator (`!`). If the file opened successfully, then the stream's state, as determined by its identifier, is true. If it did not open successfully, then the stream's state is false.

To test for a successful close, we use a function called ***fail*** right after we close the file. These tests are shown in Program 7-1.

Program 7-1 Testing for open and close errors

```
/* Test for open and close errors.
      Written by:
      Date:
*/
#include <iostream>
#include <fstream>
#include <cstdlib>
using namespace std;
int main ()
{
   cout << "Start open/close error test\n";
   ifstream fsDailyTemps;
```

Program 7-1 Testing for open and close errors *(continued)*

```
     fsDailyTemps.open ("ch7TEMPS.DAT");
     if (!fsDailyTemps)
        {
         cerr << "\aERROR 100 opening ch7TEMPS.DAT\n";
         exit (100);
        } // if open
      ...
     fsDailyTemps.close();
     if (fsDailyTemps.fail())
        {
         cerr << "\aERROR 102 closing ch7TEMPS.DAT\n";
         exit (102);
        } // if close
     cout << "End open/close error test\n";
     return 0;
  } // main
```

Program 7-1 Analysis Testing our program is quite simple. If we are opening a read file, we simply change the name of the file slightly so that it can't be found. For example, we can change "TEMPS.DAT" in Program 7-1 to "TEMPXXX.DAT." The other tests require a little more work. To test the code for an output file, we temporarily change it to an input file by changing the file type from *ofstream* to *ifstream* and then use a file name that doesn't exist.

The easiest way to test the close logic is to close a file that is not open. This is easily done by temporarily adding an extra close statement to the program. Then, when it is closed a second time, the close should fail.

7-4 FORMATTING INPUT AND OUTPUT

We first introduced formatted input/output in Chapter 2. At that time we introduced only the basic capabilities for the keyboard and the monitor display. It is now time to discuss them more fully.

INPUT/OUTPUT OPERATORS

We read formatted data from a stream using the **extraction operator** (>>). Writing to a stream uses the **insertion operator** (<<). These operators are overloaded to read and write all standard data types, such as *char*, *int*, and *double*.

Reading Standard Input

The operating system automatically creates the *cin* object and connects it to the keyboard. Therefore, we don't need to open or close it. We simply use the extraction operator to extract (read) data from the stream as shown in the next example.

```
cin >> x;                    // x can be any standard type
```

Writing Standard Output

Similarly, the operating system automatically creates the *cout* stream and connects it to the monitor. To insert (write) data, we simply use the insertion operator as shown below.

```
cout << x;                    // x can be any standard type
```

Reading a File

The extraction operator is also used to read data from a stream connected to a file. Once the file has been defined and opened as described in "File Open" on page 303, we can use the extraction operator just like with standard input. The only difference is that we must use the stream object name, not *cin*. To read the `fsDailyTemps` stream, we would use the following code

```
ifstream fsDailyTemps;
fsDailyTemps.open ("TEMPS.DAT");
...
fsDailyTemps >> inTemp;
```

where `inTemp` matches the type of data stored on the file.

Writing a File

Similarly, we can write to any open file using the insertion operator. The next example writes to an output file, `fsDataOut`, which is defined as an *ofstream*.

```
ofstream fsDataOut;                 // Define output stream
fsDataOut.open("DATA.TXT");         // Open file
...
fsDataOut << anyData;               // Write some data
```

FORMATTING DATA

The first thing to understand about formatting input and output is that the basic type of the data determines how it is formatted. For example, integer data are formatted as digits without decimals. Floating-point numbers, on the other hand, are digits with a decimal point and a fractional part. In both cases, if the number is negative, a minus sign is displayed.

C++ provides two formatting capabilities that allow us to specify exactly how we want data displayed:

1. A set of control variables that provide format-specific detail. For example, there is a precision control variable that specifies how many decimal positions should print in a floating-point number.
2. A set of flags that can be set (turned on) or unset (turned off). A **flag** is an indicator used to designate the presence or absence of a condition. For example, if we want to display a number in hexadecimal, there is a flag to tell the system to do this.

A control variable differs from a flag in that a flag is a binary (on or off) condition, whereas a control variable specifies a value.

Control Variables

Control variables contain formatting information for text output. The three most important control variables are:

1. **width:** determines how many display positions are to be used to display the data.
2. **fill:** determines the nondata character that is to print when the print width is greater than the data width. The most common fill character is space.
3. **precision:** determines the number of digits to be displayed after the decimal point.

Each of these variables must be set with a number (width and precision) or a character (fill). Because they are hidden in the stream class and we cannot access them directly, C++ provides functions to change them.

Width Setting the width control variable is temporary; it is reset to 0 after the next value is output. We set it as shown below. Note that we need to use the member operator (`.`) to specify which stream is being modified.

```
cout.width (10);     or     fsDataOut.width(10)
```

Set Fill The fill character is used whenever the data to be output occupies less space than the output width. Therefore, it must be used in conjunction with the set width control variable. If the output width is zero, then the fill character is not used. The code to set the fill character control variable to an asterisk is shown below.

```
cout.fill ('*');     or     fsDataOut.fill('*');
```

The default fill character is the space. We can set it to any other printable character with the fill control variable. Unlike the set width, however, the fill character is permanently set. We should therefore reset it after we output the data.

Set Precision The precision control variable specifies the *minimum* number of significant digits after the decimal point when a floating-point number is displayed. If it is set to 4, then only four decimal digits are displayed. Like the fill control variable, the precision variable is permanent. One other very important point: Precision is effective only if the fixed flag is on; if the scientific flag is on, precision is ignored (see "Fixed-Point and Scientific Notation" on page 317.) Typical code for setting the precision is shown in the following examples.

```
cout.precision(2);     or     fsDataOut.precision(2);
```

Program 7-2 contains examples of all three control variables and their output.

Program 7-2 Demonstrate control variables

```
/* Demonstrate three control variables.
      Written by:
      Date:
*/
#include <iostream>
using namespace std;

int main ()
{
   cout << "Test control variables\n";
   cout << "Print with default settings\n";
   cout << 'a' << 'B' << 'c' << endl;

   cout << "Print with width 10\n";
   cout.width (10);
   cout << 'a' << 'B' << 'c' << endl;

```

Program 7-2 Demonstrate control variables *(continued)*

```
   cout << "\nTest fill character with * char\n";
   cout.width(5); cout.fill ('*');
   cout << 'a';
   cout.width(5); cout << 'B';
   cout.width(5); cout << 'c';

   cout << "\nResetting default fill char\n";
   cout.fill (' ');
   cout.width(5);
   cout << 'a' << 'B' << 'c' << endl;

   cout << "\nTest precision\n";
   cout.setf (ios::fixed, ios: floatfield);
   cout << "Print without precision\n";
   cout  << 123.45678 << endl;

   cout << "Print with precision 0\n";
   cout.precision(0);
   cout  << 123.45678 << endl;

   cout << "Print with precision 3\n";
   cout.precision(3);
   cout  << 123.45678 << endl;

   cout << "Print without precision\n";
   cout  << 123.45678 << endl;
   return 0;
} // main
```

```
Results
Test control variables
Print with default settings
aBc
Print with width 10
         aBc

Test fill character with * char
****a****B****c
Resetting default fill char
    aBc

Test precision
Print without precision
123.456780
Print with precision
123
Print with precision 3
123.457
Print without precision
123.457
```

Program 7-2 Analysis Study the output carefully. Note that to demonstrate the width and fill control variables, we are printing three characters. With the default settings, they print with no spaces between them. When the width is 10, the first seven print positions are spaces followed by the output values, `aBc`.

Now examine the fill character output. Note that the fill character needs to be set only once. However, the width needs to be set for every field, even if they are in the same output statement. You can verify this by examining the output after the default fill character was set to a space. Note that the width for the first output (a) is five characters, but the width for the next two fields is zero. This is true even though all three fields were printed in one output statement (statement 27).

To demonstrate precision, we need to use the *fixed* I/O flag and its companion *floatfield* flag (see statement 30), which we haven't discussed. They set the formatting to fixed-point decimal. We discuss them in the next section.

The last precision print demonstrates that the precision is permanently set. Even though we used no precision, only three places printed because the precision was set to 3 in statement 39 and is still in effect.

Input/Output Stream Flags

The flags used by C++ are known as **input/output stream (ios) flags**. They use a special C++ object operator that we haven't discussed yet: the scope resolution operator. Until we discuss objects and classes, we won't show you how to create these flags, but we can easily show how to use them.

The different flags used to format input and output in C++ are shown in Table 7-1. Each flag is one bit. If the flag is on, the bit is set to a 1. If the flag is off, the bit is set to a 0. Using bits is a very common flag concept. The purpose of each of the flags is given in the table. We discuss their usage in the sections that follow.

Flag	Description
adjustfield	Used in conjunction with left and right to ensure only one of them is set
boolalpha	Show logical values as *true* or *false*
basefield	Used in conjuncion with dec, oct, hex to ensure only one of them is set at a time
dec	Read input or write output in decimal
fixed	Display floating point with fixed-point decimal
floatfield	Used in conjunction with fixed and scientific to ensure only one of them is set at a time
hex	Read input or write output in hexadecimal
internal	Add fill between sign and number
left	Left-justify output in width area
oct	Read input or write output in octal
right	Right-justify output in width area
scientific	Display floating point in exponent format[a]
showbase	Show octal (`0`) or hexadecimal (`0x`) indicator
showpoint	Show decimal point for floating point when precision is zero
showpos	Show leading plus sign for positive numbers

Table 7-1 Stream flags and their description

Flag	Description
skipws	Skip leading whitespace on input
unitbuf	Write output stream immediately
uppercase	Display A to E and X in hexadecimal, and E in scientific using uppercase

[a]The exponent format is used only for very large and very small numbers.

Table 7-1 Stream flags and their description (*continued*)

Each of these flags can be set or unset by using its *ios* flag. The general format for setting a flag—that is, turning it on—uses the set flag (*setf*) function as shown below. Its parameter is the name of the flag that we are modifying. Note that once again we use the member operator with the stream identifier to specify which stream's flags are being modified.

```
stream.setf (ios::flagName)
```

For example, to unset a flag, that is to turn it off, we use the unset flag (*unsetf*) function as shown below.

```
stream.unsetf (ios::flagName)
```

For example, to turn off the "skip leading whitespace" flag for the standard input stream, we would write the statement shown below.

```
stream.unsetf (ios::skipws);
```

Skip White Space You should not need to use the ***skipws*** flag because it is set on as the standard default. When it is on, C++ skips leading whitespace when reading. The only time you must change it is if you want to read one of the whitespace characters. A fragment of code to demonstrate the concept is shown in Program 7-3.

Program 7-3 Demonstration of skipws

```
/* Deomonstrate use of skip white space
      Written by:
      Date:
*/
#include <iostream>
using namespace std;

int main ()
{
   char aChar;

   // Read Characters
   cout << "Enter <space z>      : ";
   cin  >> aChar;
```

Program 7-3 Demonstration of skipws (*continued*)

```
15     cout << "Character read is     : " << aChar;
16     cin.unsetf (ios::skipws);
17     cin  >> aChar;                              // read \n
18     cout << "\nCharacter read is    : " << (int)aChar;
19     cout << "\nEnter <space z> again: ";
20     cin  >> aChar;
21     cout << "Character read is     : " << (int)aChar;
22     cin  >> aChar;
23     cout << "\nCharacter read is    : " << (int)aChar;
24     cin  >> aChar;
25     cout << "\nCharacter read is    : " << (int)aChar;
26     return 0;
27  } // main
```

```
Results:
Enter <space z>       :  z
Character read is     : z
Character read is     : 10
Enter <space z> again:  z
Character read is     : 32
Character read is     : 122
Character read is     : 10
```

Program 7-3 Analysis When we start this block of code, the *skipws* flag is set to the default: on. When we enter space z, therefore, the space character is thrown away and the `z` is read. This is verified in the first two lines of the results. Note that the `z` in the second line is below the space in the first line.

To understand the next line of output, you must understand a little more about how the input stream works. Whenever we read an integer from the input stream, the character that stops the read remains in the input stream. This could be a whitespace character or any nondigit character. Similarly, when we read a character, the data after the character is left in the input stream. In this case, the character in the input stream is the return character (\n) entered by the user to terminate the input. It is still sitting there waiting to be processed. When the *skipws* flag is on, C++ throws it away. When we turn the flag off, as we did in line 16, the newline character will be read. We therefore must read it to get to the space character and z entered by the user. To prove that the newline is sitting in the input stream, we read it and then print its decimal value by casting the character to an integer. Verify that decimal 10 is the value of the newline character by referring to the ASCII table in Appendix A.

Now that we've gotten by the newline, we can read the next character. This time, since the *skipws* flag is off, we read leading whitespace. The next character read, therefore, is the space. We verify that the space character was read by printing its decimal value, 32. After reading the space, we read the letter z and print its decimal value, 122. Finally, to demonstrate that there is still a newline character in the input stream, we read and display it.

Left and Right Justification **Justification** is the orientation of data in a field whose width is larger than the data. If the data are oriented on the left, with empty space on the right, then the data are left-justified; if the data are oriented on the right, with empty space on the left, then the data are right-justified. To ensure that only one of these flags is set, we use the *adjustfield* flag separated from the justification by a comma.

> Always use the *adjustfield* flag with the *left* and *right* flags.

To demonstrate justification, we display 12345 with default, left, and right justification in Program 7-4. It also demonstrates the adjustfield flag.

Program 7-4 Demonstrate left and right justification

```
1  /* Demonstrate left and right justification
2        Written by:
3        Date:
4  */
5  #include <iostream>
6  using namespace std;
7
8  int main ()
9  {
10    cout << "Default justification: |";
11    cout.width(10);
12    cout << 12345 << "|\n";
13    cout.setf (ios::left, ios::adjustfield);
14    cout << "Left justification    : |";
15    cout.width(10);
16    cout << 12345 << "|\n";
17
18    cout.setf (ios::right, ios::adjustfield);
19    cout << "Right justification   : |";
20    cout.width(10);
21    cout << 12345 << "|\n";
22    return 0;
23 } // main
```

```
Results:
   Default justification: |     12345|
   Left justification   : |12345     |
   Right justification  : |     12345|
```

Program 7-4 Analysis To demonstrate justification, we use vertical bars at the beginning and end of an output area. We also use set width to create an output area that is greater than the data being displayed. The first display uses the default justification, which is right. We then change the justification to left at statement 13 and display the output. Finally, we change the justification back to right at statement 18 and display again.

Internal The ***internal* flag** places a fill character between the sign and the numeric data. When it is not set, the fill character displays before any sign. The fill character can be set to any desired character. For this demonstration, we have set it to an asterisk. We demonstrate the use of the internal flag in Program 7-5.

Program 7-5 Demonstrate internal flag

```
1  /* Demonstrate internal flag.
2        Written by:
3        Date:
4  */
5  #include <iostream>
6  using namespace std;
7
8  int main ()
9  {
10    cout.fill ('*');
11    cout << "Internal default    : |";
12    cout.width(10);
13    cout << -12345 << "|\n";
14    cout.setf (ios::internal);
15    cout << "Internal set on     : |";
16    cout.width(10);
17    cout << -12345 << "|\n";
18    cout << "Display w/o width   : |"
19         << -12345 << "|\n";
20    cout.unsetf (ios::internal);
21    return 0;
22 }  // main
```

```
Results:
   Internal default    : |****-12345|
   Internal set on     : |-****12345|
   Display w/o width   : |-12345|
```

Program 7-5 Analysis To see the fill character, the width must be set larger than the data to be displayed. We begin by displaying –12345 with the internal flag set at the default, which is off. Note that the fill character (*) displays before the minus sign. When we turn the internal flag on at statement 14, the fill character displays between the minus sign and the number. To show its effect when the width is not used, we again display –12345, this time without any width set: The result is –12345 with no fill characters shown.

The internal flag also works with the plus sign when it is displayed. We will see how to display plus signs shortly. It also works when we are displaying numbers in octal and hexadecimal, which we will see in the next section.

Decimal, Octal, and Hexadecimal The decimal (**dec**), octal (**oct**), and hexadecimal (**hex**) flags control the formatting of integer numbers. The default is decimal. In decimal, numbers display as normal decimal values. When the octal flag is set, the numbers display using their octal value. When the hexadecimal flag is set, the numbers display in hexadecimal.

It is possible to use the numeric flags to enter octal and hexadecimal values. When the decimal flag is turned off, the user can enter data in any of the three formats: decimal, octal, and hexadecimal. Decimal data are entered as any value that does not start with a 0. (The value 0 is the same value in all three formats.) To enter an octal number, the user must start with a 0. To enter an hexadecimal number, the user must enter a value starting with 0x or 0X. Thus, to enter the value 93 in the three formats, we must first turn the decimal flag off and then enter the number as shown below.

```
Enter a number: 93                  // Decimal for 93
Enter a number: 0135                // Octal for 93
Enter a number: 0x5d                // Hex for 93
```

To enter octal or hexadecimal values, the octal or hexadecimal flag does not need to be turned on. As long as the decimal flag is turned off, or either the octal or hexadecimal flag is turned on, then the user can enter data in any of the three formats by using the rules described above. Naturally, these options can be very dangerous, and we recommend that you always leave the decimal flag on and the other two flags off when you design a program.

To ensure that only one of these flags is set, we add the *basefield* flag at the end of the set statement. We demonstrate it in the next program.

> **Always use the *basefield* flag with the *dec, oct,* and *hex* flags.**

Showbase and Uppercase Before we demonstrate the numeric base displays, we need to mention two other flags: showbase and uppercase. **showbase** is used to display the base of the number, `0` (zero) for octal and `0x` for hexadecimal, so that it won't be confused with a decimal number. **uppercase** displays the hexadecimal values 10 through 15, the hexadecimal symbol (`0X`), and the scientific symbol (`E`) as uppercase characters rather than the default lowercase.

To demonstrate these formats, we use Program 7-6.

Program 7-6 Demonstrate numeric flags

```
/* Demonstrate numeric flags.
      Written by:
      Date:
*/
#include <iostream>
using namespace std;

int main ()
{
   cout << "\nNumbers with showbase and uppercase off\n";
   cout.setf (ios::dec, ios::basefield);
   cout << "93 as decimal     :";
   cout.width(5);
   cout << 93 << endl;
   cout.setf (ios::oct, ios::basefield);
   cout << "93 as octal       :";
   cout.width(5);
   cout << 93 << endl;
   cout.setf (ios::hex, ios::basefield);
   cout << "93 as hexadecimal :";
   cout.width(5);
   cout << 93 << endl;
```

Program 7-6 Demonstrate numeric flags *(continued)*

```

   cout << "\nNumbers with showbase and uppercase on\n";
   cout.setf (ios::showbase);
   cout.setf (ios::dec, ios::basefield);
   cout << "93 as decimal      :";
   cout.width(5);
   cout << 93 << endl;
   cout.setf (ios::oct, ios::basefield);
   cout << "93 as octal        :" ;
   cout.width(5);
   cout << 93 << endl;
   cout.setf (ios::hex, ios::basefield);
   cout.setf (ios::uppercase);
   cout << "93 as upper hex    :";
   cout.width(5);
   cout << 93 << endl;
   cout.unsetf (ios::hex);          // reset to default
   cout.unsetf (ios::uppercase);    // reset to default
   cout.setf (ios::dec);            // reset to default
   return 0;
} // main
```

```
Results:
Numbers with showbase and uppercase off
93 as decimal     :   93
93 as octal       :  135
93 as hexadecimal :   5d

Numbers with showbase and uppercase on
93 as decimal     :   93
93 as octal       : 0135
93 as upper hex   : 0X5D
```

Program 7-6 Analysis All displays in this demonstration use the decimal value 93. We begin by displaying 93 as decimal, then as octal, and finally as hexadecimal. In these displays, we use the default flag settings for *showbase* (off) and *uppercase* (off). We also set the width to 5 so that the numbers align for readability.

In the first display, the octal value for 93 displays as 135. A casual reader would be completely justified in assuming that the value is decimal 135, since there is no indication otherwise. The hexadecimal number is better, because the value 93 displays as 5d, which should alert an informed reader that the number is hexadecimal.

The next set of displays uses *showbase* and *uppercase* to demonstrate the difference. In this set, we see that the octal value displays with a leading 0. This would alert an informed reader that the number is octal, but a casual reader might still assume that the value is 135. The hexadecimal value is even more explicit; it prefixes the value with a 0X. Had the value been displayed in lowercase, the prefix would be 0x.

Because we are using *basefield*, we don't need to unset the flags when we set a new one. To demonstrate unset flag, however, we use it at the end of the program to set the decimal flags to their default settings.

Show Point If a floating-point number is an integral value, that is the fraction is zero, the precision is set to zero, and **showpoint** is off, then the number displays as though it were an integer. This can be confusing at times. To print floating-point numbers with decimal points, we turn showpoint on.

Show Positive The show positive flag (**showpos**) simply tells the system to display a plus sign when the number is positive and a minus system when it is negative. If this flag is off, then only the minus sign for negative numbers is displayed.

Fixed-Point and Scientific Notation When we use scientific notation, the significand and exponent are specified separately. The significand part is a floating-point number that contains as many significant digits as possible. For example, if it contains six digits, then the number is significant only to six digits; if it has 12 digits, then it is significant to 12 digits. The larger the significance, the greater the precision. Therefore, *long double* may be more precise than *double*, which may be more precise than *float*. Once again, to ensure that only one of the two flags is set, we add *floatfield* after the set.

Always use the *floatfield* flag with the *fixed* and *scientific* flags.

The exponent specifies the magnitude of the number. It may be either positive or negative. If it is positive, then the number is the significand times 10 to the power of the exponent, which may be a very large number. If it is negative, then the number is the significand times the reciprocal of 10 to the absolute value of the exponent, which may be a very small number. These forms are shown below.

123e03 → $123*10^{3}$ 123e-03 → $123*10^{-3}$

All of the following numbers are in scientific notation. The number before e is the significand; the number after the e is the exponent. The default display is lowercase *e*. To make it uppercase, set the *uppercase* flag on.

```
3e      -1.0e-3      0.1+e1      2E2      1.3E-2
```

When the fixed-point flag is on, the numbers are displayed in our normal decimal point format. When the scientific notation flag is on, they are displayed in significand and exponent format. Note that the results when *both* are set may be unpredictable, so you should set them carefully. Program 7-7 demonstrates their use.

Program 7-7 Scientific and fixed-point flags

```
/* Scientific and fixed point flags
      Written by:
      Date:
*/
#include <iostream>
using namespace std;

```

Program 7-7 Scientific and fixed-point flags *(continued)*

```
int main ()
{
   cout.setf  (ios::scientific, ios::floatfield);
   cout << "...scientific format  : " << 3141.59 << endl;

   cout.setf (ios::fixed, ios::floatfield);
   cout << "...with fixed point   : " << 3141.59 << endl;
   return 0;
} // main
```

```
Results
...scientific format  : 3.141590e+03
...with fixed point   : 3141.590000
```

Unit Buffer The ***unitbuf*** flag is used to ensure that all output has been written before we terminate a program. Generally, this is not a concern. However, if we are about to abort a program—because we have an unrecoverable file error, for example—then we want to be sure that any pending output has been written. When the *unitbuf* flag is set, all output is written immediately.

Manipulators

In practice, flags and control variables are seldom used, primarily because they are not as convenient as manipulators. **Manipulators** are special input/output functions that can be used in conjunction with the input (>>) and output (<<) operators to set a flag or a control variable. You have been using the set width and endline manipulators since Chapter 2.

Manipulators with no parameters are used to set flags. Note, however, that some compilers support only a subset of the manipulators described in this section. The following example demonstrates setting the hexadecimal flag on and off with the insertion operator:

```
cout << hex << hexNumber << dec;
```

An interesting flag manipulator is **flush**. It is used to force data to be output immediately and corresponds to the *unitbuf* flag. For example, to print an error message and exit a program, we could write the code shown below.

```
cout << "\aERROR 100\n" << flush;
exit (100);
```

Manipulators with one argument are used to store values in the control variables. An example of each is shown below.

```
cout << setw (10);
cout << setprecision (8);
cout << setfill ('*');
```

SUMMARY

A summary of the control variables and their corresponding manipulators is shown in Table 7-2. When these manipulators are used in a program, the `<iomanip>` library file is required.

Control variable	Set with function/operator[a]	Set with manipulator
width	stream.width(n)	setw(n)
fill	stream.fill(c)	setfill(c)
precision	stream.precision(n)	setprecision(n)

[a]stream: stream name—Parameters: c = character; n = number.

Table 7-2 Stream control variables and manipulators

A summary of the flags and their corresponding manipulators is shown in Table 7-3.

Stream Flag	Set/Unset Flag	Input	Output	Manipulator
			✓	endl
Boolean alpha	stream.setf(ios::boolalpha) stream.unsetf(ios::boolalpha)	✓ ✓	✓ ✓	boolalpha noboolalpha
Decimal	stream.setf(ios::dec)	✓	✓	dec
Fixed Point	stream.setf(ios::fixed)	✓	✓	fixed
Hexadecimal	stream.setf(ios::hex)	✓	✓	hex
Internal	stream.setf(ios::internal)		✓	internal
Left Justify	stream.setf(ios::left)		✓	left
Octal	stream.setf(ios::oct)	✓	✓	oct
Right Justify	stream.setf(ios::right)		✓	right
Scientific	stream.setf(ios::scientific)	✓	✓	scientific
Show Base	stream.setf(ios::showbase) stream.unsetf(ios::showbase)		✓ ✓	showbase noshowbase
Show Point	stream.setf(ios::showpoint) stream.unsetf(ios::showpoint)		✓ ✓	showpoint noshowpoint
Show Position	stream.setf(ios::showpos) stream.unsetf(ios::showpos)		✓ ✓	showpos noshowpos
Skip Whitespace	stream.setf(ios::skipws) stream.unsetf(ios::skipws)	✓ ✓		skipws noskipws
Unit Buffer	stream.setf(ios::unitbuf)		✓	flush
Upper Case	stream.setf(ios::uppercase) stream.unsetf(ios::uppercase)		✓ ✓	uppercase nouppercase

Table 7-3 Stream flags and manipulators

7-5 FILE EXAMPLE

Let's write a program that reads and writes a file of student grades. The program reads a student file and writes a grades file to be turned in at the end of the term. The problem is shown in Figure 7-6.

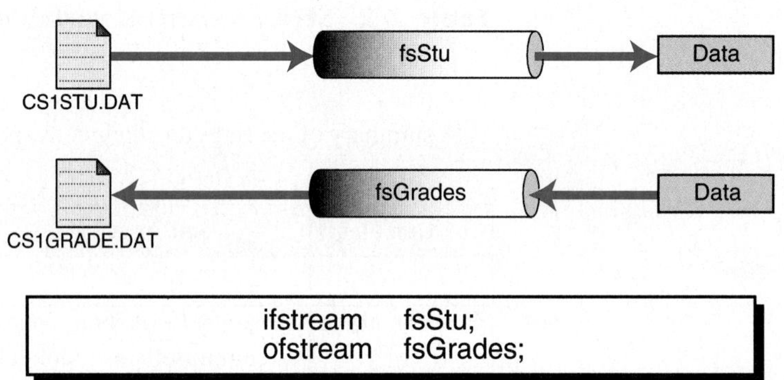

Figure 7-6 Create student grades

The code is shown in Program 7-8.

Program 7-8 Student grades

```
/* Create a grades file for transmission to Registrar.
      Written by:
      Date:
*/
#include <iostream>
#include <fstream>
#include <iomanip>
#include <cstdlib>
using namespace std;
   bool getStu     (ifstream& stuFile,
                    int&      stuID, int& exam1,
                    int&      exam2, int& final);
   void writeStu   (ofstream& gradesFile, int  stuID,
                   int      avrg,        char grade);
   void calcGrade (int  exam1, int  exam2, int final,
                    int&  avrg,   char& grade);

int main ()
{
   ifstream stuFile;
   cout << "Begin student grades\n";
   stuFile.open ("ch7STUFL.DAT");
   if (!stuFile)
       {
        cerr << "\aError opening student file\n";
        exit (100);
```

Program 7-8 Student grades *(continued)*

```
      }  // if open fail

   ofstream gradesFile;
   gradesFile.open ("ch7STUGR.DAT");
   if (!gradesFile)
      {
       cerr << "\aError opening grades file\n";
       exit (102);
      }  // if open fail

   int  stuID;
   int  exam1;
   int  exam2;
   int  final;
   int  avrg;
   char grade;
   while (getStu (stuFile, stuID, exam1,
                  exam2, final))
   {
       calcGrade (exam1, exam2, final, avrg, grade);
       writeStu  (gradesFile,   stuID, avrg, grade);
     } // while

   stuFile.close ();
   gradesFile.close();
   cout << "End student grades\n";
   return 0;
} // main
/* ==================== getStu ===================
   Reads data from student file.

      Pre  stuFile is an open file
           stuID, exam1, exam2, final-ref's to int
      Post reads student ID and exam scores into
           parameter references
      Return  true  if data read
              -- false if end of file
*/
bool getStu (ifstream& stuFile, int& stuID,
             int&      exam1,   int& exam2,
             int&      final)
{
   // !stuFile is either eof or bad file
   stuFile >> stuID >> exam1 >> exam2 >> final;
   if (!stuFile)
       // Read problem or at end of file
       return false;
   return true;
} // getStu
```

Program 7-8 Student grades *(continued)*

```
/* ================= calcGrade ================
   Determine student grade based on absolute scale.
      Pre  exam1, exam2, and final contain scores
           avrg and grade are references to variables
      Post Average and grade copied to references
*/
void calcGrade (int  exam1, int   exam2, int final,
                int& avrg,  char& grade)
{
   avrg = (exam1 + exam2 + final ) / 3;
   if (avrg >= 90)
      grade = 'A';
   else if (avrg >= 80)
      grade = 'B';
   else if (avrg >= 70)
      grade = 'C';
   else if (avrg >= 60)
      grade = 'D';
   else
      grade = 'F';
   return;
} // calcGrade
/* ================= writeStu =================
   Writes student grade data to output file.
      Pre  gradesFile is an open file
           stuID, avrg, and grade have values to write
      Post Data written to file
*/
void writeStu (ofstream& gradesFile, int  stuID,
               int       avrg,        char grade)
{
   gradesFile.fill ('0');
   gradesFile << setw (4) << stuID;
   gradesFile.fill (' ');
   gradesFile << setw (3) << avrg;
   gradesFile << ' ' << grade << endl;
   return;
} // writeStu
```

```
Results:
Input--------
   0090 90 90 90
   0089 88 90 89
   0081 80 82 81
   0079 79 79 79
   0070 70 70 70
   0069 69 69 69
   0060 60 60 60
   0059 59 59 59
```

Program 7-8 Student grades *(continued)*

```
Output----
   0090 90 A
   0089 89 B
   0081 81 B
   0079 79 C
   0070 70 C
   0069 69 D
   0060 60 D
   0059 59 F
```

Program 7-8 Analysis There are several points to study in this program. Let's start at the top. We open and close the files in *main.* Often programmers will write subfunctions for program initialization and conclusion, but in this case we decided to write them in *main.* The processing loop uses the return value from `getStu` to control the loop (see statement 43). If data are read, then the return value is *true* (1); if all data have been read, the return value is *false* (0). This design results in a very simple *while* loop.

Within the loop there are three calls, one to read the student data (in the *while* limit test), one to calculate the grade, and one to write the grades file. Study the parameters carefully. We have used a combination of data values and references. Note especially the file parameters. Since the file status is updated with each read or write, we must pass files as reference parameters (see statements 43 and 47 and their corresponding function definitions at statements 65 and 104).

Now study the results. The student ID is printed as four digits with leading zeros because it is really a code, not a number. To do this we set the fill character to 0 before we wrote the student ID and reset it to space afterward. The rest of the formatting is straightforward.

You should also study the test data. We carefully designed it to verify that all of the boundaries in our multiway selection worked correctly. To make it easy to verify, we made the student ID the same as the average. With these clues to the expected output, it only takes a quick review of the results to tell that the program ran successfully.

7-6 CHARACTER INPUT/OUTPUT FUNCTIONS

Character input functions read one character at a time from a text stream. **Character output functions** write one character at a time to a text stream. In this section, we discuss two basic character functions: *get* and *put.*

get

The ***get*** function reads the next character from the input stream and returns its value through a reference parameter. It can read any character, including whitespace and control characters. This is the big difference between it and the extraction operator; the extraction operator does not read whitespace.

We can use *get* with the standard input stream (*cin*) or with a stream we define. In each of the following examples, the next character in the input stream is placed in the character variable `aChar`.

```
cin.get(aChar);

sfIn.get(aChar);
```

There are two events that prevent *get* from completing its mission to read a character: (1) no more data are available to be read (that is, we have reached end of file), and (2) a physical transmission error occurs. These events are discussed in the section on handling errors starting on page 329.

put

The ***put*** function is the opposite of the *get* function; it writes one character, specified as a parameter, to an output stream. As with *get,* we may put the character to the standard output stream (*cout*) or to our own file, as shown below.

```
cout.put(aChar);

sfOut.put(aChar);
```

7-7 CHARACTER INPUT/OUTPUT EXAMPLES

This section contains several programs that use common text file applications.

CREATE TEXT FILE

Program 7-9 will read text from the standard input unit (keyboard) and create a text file. All data are stored in text format with newlines only where input by the user.

Program 7-9 Create text file

```
/* This program creates a text file.
      Written by:
      Date:
*/
#include <iostream>
#include <fstream>
#include <cstdlib>
using namespace std;
int main ()
{
   ofstream sfTextFile;
   cout << "Begin file creation\n";
   sfTextFile.open ("ch7FILE9.DAT");
   if (!sfTextFile)
      {
       cerr << "Error 100 opening output FILE9.DAT";
       exit (100);
      } // if

   char aChar;
   while (cin.get(aChar))
      sfTextFile.put (aChar);

```

Program 7-9 Create text file *(continued)*

```
   sfTextFile.close ();
   cout << "\nEnd file creation\n";

   return 0;
}  // main
```

Program 7-9 Analysis This simple program is the beginning of a text editor. The biggest element missing is what is known as "word wrap." Word wrap prevents a word from being split between two lines on a page.

COPY TEXT FILE

Program 7-10 is a program for copying one text file to another text file.

Program 7-10 Copy text file

```
/* This program copies one text file into another.
      Written by:
      Date:
*/
#include <iostream>
#include <fstream>
#include <cstdlib>
using namespace std;

int main ()
{
   ifstream fsInFile;
   ofstream fsOutFile;
   cout << "Begin file copy\n";

   fsInFile.open ("ch7FILE9.DAT");
   if (!fsInFile)
      {
        cerr << "\aError 100 opening ch7FILE9.DAT\n";
        exit (100);
       }  // if
   fsOutFile.open ("ch7FILE10.DAT");
   if (!fsOutFile)
       {
         cerr << "\aError 102 opening ch7FILE10.DAT\n";
         exit (102);
       }  // if

   char aChar;
   while (fsInFile.get  (aChar))
           fsOutFile.put (aChar);

   fsInFile.close  ();
   fsOutFile.close ();
```

Program 7-10 Copy text file *(continued)*

```

   cout << "\nEnd file copy\n";
   return 0;
} // main
```

Program 7-10 Analysis This program contains three style points that require some commentary. First, we have used generic names for the streams, `fsInFile` and `fsOutFile`. Since this program simply copies and creates text files, it is not possible to give the files names that reflect their data.

Second, there are two potential file open errors in the program. We give them different error codes for those operating systems whose job control can distinguish between different completion codes.

The third point is a subtle one. Note that we coded the two file definitions at the beginning of *main*. Coding them at the beginning reflects their importance and makes them easy to see. On the other hand, we deferred the definition of `a char` until it was needed, which is the normal C++ style.

COUNT CHARACTERS AND LINES

Program 7-11 counts the number of characters and lines in a file. All ASCII characters, excluding the newline, are counted. Lines are designated by a newline. Note that we guard against a file that ends without a newline for the last line.

Program 7-11 Count characters and lines

```
/* This program counts the number of characters and
   lines in a text file.
      Written by:
      Date:
*/
#include <iostream>
#include <fstream>
#include <iomanip>
#include <cstdlib>
using namespace std;
int main ()
{
   ifstream fsInFile;
   fsInFile.open ("ch7FILE9.DAT");
   if (!fsInFile)
      {
       cerr << "Error 100 opening ch7FILE9.DAT";
       exit (100);
      } // if

   char curCh;
   char preCh;
   int  countLn = 0;
   int  countCh = 0;
   while (fsInFile.get (curCh))
```

Program 7-11 Count characters and lines *(continued)*

```
      {
       if (curCh != '\n')
           countCh++;
       else
           countLn++;
       preCh = curCh;
      } // while

   if (preCh != '\n')
      countLn++;

   cout << "\nNumber of characters: "
        << setw(4) << countCh;
   cout << "\nNumber of lines     : "
        << setw(4) << countLn;

   fsInFile.close ();

   return 0;
} // main
```

Program 7-11 Analysis This program is rather straightforward. The only real problem is in making sure that the last line is counted even if there is no newline. We can check this at the end of the file by making sure that the last character we read, stored in `preCh`, is a newline. If it isn't, we add one to the line count.

In this program we use a slightly different style for the placement of variable definitions. Examine the program carefully and see if you can determine the new style rule.

Each variable is defined just before the statement that first uses it. Some programmers prefer this close association of variables and code. Others prefer to see all variables at the beginning of the block. Try both styles and see which you prefer.

COUNT WORDS IN FILE

Program 7-12 counts the number of words in a file. A word is defined as one or more characters separated by one or more whitespace characters; that is, by a space, a tab, or a newline.

Program 7-12 Count words

```
/* Count number of words in file. Words are separated by
   whitespace characters: space, tab, and newline.
      Written by:
      Date:
*/
#include <iostream>
#include <fstream>
#include <cstdlib>
using namespace std;
```

Program 7-12 Count words *(continued)*

```
#define WHT_SPC (cur == ' ' || cur == '\n' || cur == '\t')

int main ()
{
   ifstream fsInFile;
   fsInFile.open ("ch7FILE9.DAT");
   if (!fsInFile)
      {
       cerr << "Error 100 opening ch7FILE9.DAT";
       exit (100);
      } // if

   char cur;
   char word     = 'O';        // O out of word: I in word
   int  countWd = 0;
   while (fsInFile.get (cur))
      {
      if (WHT_SPC)
         word = 'O';
      else
         if (word == 'O')
            {
             countWd++;
             word = 'I';
            } // if
      } // while

   cout << "\nThe number of words is " << countWd;
   fsInFile.close ();
   return 0;
}  // main
```

Program 7-12 Analysis The selection logic for this problem is similar to that in the previous program. We must determine when we are in a word and when we are between words. We are between words when we start the program and whenever we are at whitespace. To keep track of where we are, we use a flag, `word`. When `word` contains the letter *I*, we are in a word; when it contains the letter *O*, we are out of a word. We increment the counter only at the beginning of a word, when we set the word flag to *I*.

Note that the problem handles multiple whitespace characters in a row by simply setting the word flag to *O*. Note also how we use a preprocessor *define* statement to define whitespace. This has no effect on the efficiency of the program, but it makes it easier to read. The preprocessor substitutes the parenthetical expression for the identifier `WHT_SPC` before sending the source code to the C++ translator. For more discussion, refer to Appendix G, "Preprocessor Directives."

7-8 DETECTING FILE ERRORS

When reading data, whether from the keyboard or from a file, errors happen. Good programmers anticipate errors and provide recovery—or in extreme cases, fail soft procedures.[2] A recovery procedure is generally incorporated in a *do...while* loop that tests for an error and prompts the user to reenter the data when they fail the validation rules. A fail soft procedure determines that the program must be terminated and displays an appropriate message to the user along with any appropriate status information before exiting the program.

Whenever we read data, the read may be successful or unsuccessful. If the read is successful, the program continues its processing in a normal fashion. If the read is not successful, one or more of four different events may have occurred. First, the read may have detected an end of file. This is a normal event, but we must ensure that when it occurs the program takes the correct action.

Second, the user may have entered invalid data. We need to detect invalid data and recover from it. Invalid user input occurs when the user enters data that do not conform to the application or system rules. To understand these errors, consider the situation of a program that processes payroll data. One of the application rules states that the user may not enter a salary below the minimum wage. Whenever the program reads a salary, therefore, it tests the salary to make sure that it is equal to or larger than the minimum wage. If it is not, it displays an error message and asks the user to reenter the correct salary.

To understand the concept of system errors, consider the processing required when a user enters a numeric value from the keyboard. Numeric data have well-known rules. An integer may start with a plus or minus sign, and its characters may consist of only the ten digits. If the skip whitespace flag is on, leading whitespace is read and discarded. If a nondigit character is read before any valid digits, then the read fails. If a nondigit character is read after at least one valid digit has been read, then the read is considered successful and the nondigit character is left in the input stream for later processing. If the first character a user enters is invalid, the read function will set an error flag that we must test and recover from.

Third, an invalid operation may have occurred. Invalid operations are program errors, and when they occur the program must be terminated. An example of an invalid operation is trying to read a file opened for output.

Finally, an unrecoverable error may have occurred. Fortunately, these types of errors occur seldomly. They result when the data cannot be physically read from the disk or tape on which they are stored. In this case, the program must be terminated and the input file recreated before the program can continue.

STREAM STATUS

C++ provides three status flags and four functions to determine the state of a file stream. The three flags, *eof*, *fail*, and *bad* are explained below.

1. The flag *eof* is set on when the file pointer is at the end of the file.
2. The flag ***fail*** indicates that the previous stream operation, which can be anything from open to close, failed. The two most common reasons for an input file operation to fail are miskeyed input from the user, such as an alphabetic character rather than a digit, and end of file. The most common (although still rare) output failure is "out of disk space."

[2]*Fail soft* is a term used to indicate that the program is aborted under the control of the application program rather than the operating system.

3. The flag ***bad*** usually indicates that the data were not properly read or written because of a hardware problem.

The four functions are shown in Table 7-4.

Status	Function	In/out	Example	Action
Success	good()	Both	if (cin.good( ))	Continue
End of file	eof()	Input	if (cin.eof( ))	Terminate reading
Invalid data	fail()	Input	if (cin.fail( ))	Prompt user to reenter
Hardware failure	bad()	Both	if (cin.bad( ))	Gracefully terminate

Table 7-4 File stream status

Testing for Success

Each of the functions listed in the table returns either *true* or *false*. The first function, ***good()***, returns *true* if none of the error flags is set. In practice, however, this function is seldom used because there are simpler ways to test for success.

In Chapter 3 we learned that all expressions have a value. Since the input and output operations are either an operator or a function, they have values. We use these values to check the status of our input and output. Program 7-13 demonstrates how to test the results of an input operation. While we would normally code the input test as shown below,

```
if (cin >> dataIn)
```

statement 13 stores the value of the expression in `status` so that we could display it after the operation was complete.

Program 7-13 Demonstrate I/O status

```
1  /* Demonstrate testing I/O status
2        Written by:
3        Date:
4  */
5  #include <iostream>
6  using namespace std;
7
8  int main ()
9  {
10    cout << "Enter a number: ";
11    bool status;
12    int  dataIn = -2;
13    status = (cin >> dataIn);
14
15    cout << "status: " << boolalpha << status << endl
16         << "dataIn: " << dataIn << endl;
17
18    if (cin.fail())
19        cout << "Input fail flag set.\n";
20    else if (cin.bad())
21        cout << "Input bad flag set.\n";
22    return 0;
23 } // main
```

Program 7-13 Demonstrate I/O status *(continued)*

```
Results:
First run:
   Enter a number: 7
   status: true
   dataIn: 7

Second Run:
   Enter a number: x
   status: false
   dataIn: -2
   Input fail flag set.
```

Program 7-13 Analysis To show the results clearly, we initialize the two variables to –1 and –2. When we successfully input the values, `status` is *true* and `dataIn` contains a value (7 in the first test run). On the other hand, when we miskey a letter as the input, the operation fails. In this case, `status` is *false*, meaning that the operation failed, and `dataIn` contains its original value (–2). Note that we used the ***boolalpha*** manipulator in statement 15 to print the boolean results as true and false rather than 1 and 0.

Testing Failure Status

When the stream input or output operation fails, we must determine the cause of the failure. That's when the other three functions are used. Generally used only for input, the *eof()* function returns *true* if an end of file has been detected successfully. It should always be used when all of the data in an input file are being processed.

Of the two error functions, *fail()* is the more common. If a keyboard operation was not successful because of user operator error, we should prompt the user to reenter the data. This concept is fully demonstrated in the section on error recovery, which follows this section.

The final function, *bad()*, indicates a hardware failure. A hardware failure simply means that the data could not be transmitted correctly. If the data are being read from a file, then the file medium (disk or tape) is bad and needs to be regenerated. If the data are being read from a keyboard, the function *bad()* indicates that there is something physically wrong with the keyboard.

ERROR RECOVERY

If an error occurs while a program is reading a file, as opposed to reading the keyboard, we must generally abort the program, have the error corrected, and then restart the program. When an error is detected from the keyboard, we can ask the user to input the data again. To ask the user to reinput the data, we must reset the file so that it can be read. When a file error is detected, the file is in the **error state**. A file that is in the error state cannot be read. To clear the error and return the file to a read state, we must execute a clear function, ***clear()***, to reset the stream status (see statement 37 in Program 7-14).

Each of the functions described above is shown in Program 7-14. The program shows how a numeric variable, such as the number of units sold, could be validated when the user keys the data.

Program 7-14 Checking for input errors

```
/* Test handling errors
      Written by:
      Date:
*/
#include <iostream>
#include <cstdlib>
using namespace std;

int main ()
{
   int badRead;
   int unitsSold;
   cout << "\nPlease enter Number of Units Sold: ";
   do
       {
        badRead = 0;
        cin >> unitsSold;
        if ( !(cin.good() ) )
            {
             // number not read correctly
             cerr << "\a\nInvalid number. ";
             cerr << "Error status is " << hex
                  << cin.rdstate() << dec << endl;
             if (cin.eof())
                {
                 cerr << "End of file detected.\n"
                      << "You must restart program\n";
                 exit (200);
                } // if eof
             else if (cin.fail())
                {
                 cerr << "Only digits (0..9) allowed\n"
                      << "Please try again: ";
                 badRead = 1;

               // Clear error & Flush invalid characters
                 cin.clear();
                 char aCh;
                 while ( (aCh = cin.get ()) != '\n' )
                     ;
                } // if fail
             else if (cin.bad())
                {
                 cerr << "Keyboard is not working.\n";
                 exit (201);
                } // bad transmission
             else
                {
```

Program 7-14 Checking for input errors *(continued)*

```
49                cerr << "Hard Error. Call programmer.\n";
50                exit (202);
51               } // Program error
52           }  // if
53       } while (badRead);
54
55    cout << "You entered " << unitsSold << endl;
56
57    return 0;
58 } // main
```

```
Results:
Please enter Number of Units Sold: a12

Invalid number. Error status is 4
Only digits (0..9) allowed
Please try again: ^d
Invalid number. Error status is 6
End of file detected.
You must restart program
```

Program 7-14 Analysis The first thing to note in this program is the extensive data validation. We begin by prompting the user to enter the number of units sold. Since units sold must be an integer, in statement 18 we verify that the user entered the value correctly. If an error occurred, then we print a message alerting the user to the error and begin an analysis of what type of error occurred. To help us determine the exact nature of the error, we print the error status in statement 23 using a special function developed for just this purpose, ***rdstate( )***.

If the user accidently entered an end of file (see statement 24), then the program must be restarted. Note that we therefore display a message explaining exactly what happened and what to do about it.

If the user entered an incorrect value (see statement 30)—that is, a non-numeric value—then again, we tell the user exactly what happened and ask that the data be reentered. In this case, however, we must first clear the error and return the program to the read state. This is done in statement 37. Then we must remove the previous entry, which we know to be bad. We do this with a loop that reads characters until it finds a newline. This loop effectively flushes the input stream of the bad input and readies it to read the correct data.

Why is this logic necessary? Recall that when an input encounters an error, it leaves the invalid data in the input stream. If we simply print the error messages and then return to the input statement, the invalid data are still there.

When it is necessary to test several conditions, you should test the most probable condition first. In this case, the most probable error is that the user accidently entered an invalid character. However, the end of file also sets the fail flag, so we must test for end of file before we test for bad user input.

The last two errors, program error and hardware error, both abort the program by calling the system exit function. Note, however, that each error condition uses a different error code. If an invalid end of file is detected, we exit with code 200. If an invalid operation is detected, we exit with code 201. Finally, if a hardware error occurs, we exit with error code 202. Assigning unique error codes helps programmers debug programs when problems occur.

Another point to note is how the error messages tell the user exactly what went wrong rather than giving a general "The numbers entered are incorrect" type of message. Whenever possible, you should tell the user exactly what went wrong and provide good corrective action messages.

Finally, as stated above, there is an easier and more common way to code the input statement. Because the input/output functions return *false* when they have a problem, we can check success as we read the data. The code is shown below.

```
if (!(cin >> unitsSold))
```

7-9 SOFTWARE ENGINEERING AND PROGRAMMING STYLE

TESTING FILES

Testing files can be a very difficult task. There are two reasons for this difficulty. First, many errors cannot be created through normal means. Among these types of errors are those created by bad physical media—for example, disks and tapes, which often become unreadable. Good programs test for these types of errors, but such errors are difficult to simulate.

The second reason testing files can be difficult is that there are so many ways things can go wrong. Your test plan therefore needs to ensure that all possibilities have been tested. Chief among them is the case where a user enters a non-numeric character while trying to enter a number. If you don't provide for this situation, your program will not work properly. In fact, there are situations in which it will not work at all.

Testing for Invalid User Input

Consider the following code to read an integer value. If the user miskeys the data, the program will go into an infinite loop.

```
cout( "\nPlease enter Number of Units Sold: " ) ;
while ( !(cin >> unitsSold) )
        // returns false if number not read
        cout << "\nInvalid units. Re-enter.\n";
```

In this example, it looks as if the programmer has done everything correctly. The program checks for valid data being returned. There is a user prompt that shows what data should be entered, the program checks for valid data being read, and if there was none the program provides the user with a good error message and repeats the input. What is wrong then?

There are two problems. The first problem lies in what the extraction operator does when it finds an invalid first digit. If the number is entirely wrong, it leaves the data pending in the input stream. This means that while the user sees the error message, the invalid data are still in the input stream waiting for an input that will properly read and process them. The extraction operator thinks that these "invalid data" are the beginning of the next field. It is your job as a programmer to get rid of the "bad data."

The second problem is that once an error has been detected and an error flag has been set by *cin*, the flag must be turned off. This can be done with a small piece of code that is commonly coded as a macro named FLUSH.[3] Its purpose is to read through the input stream looking for the end of a line. When it finds the end of the line, it terminates. Before it can read any data, however, it must first clear the error. The code to clear the error and flush the data is seen below.

```
cin.clear();
while (cin.get(aCh) && aCh != '\n');
```

[3]For more information on macros, see Appendix G, "Preprocessor Directives."

Examine the *while* statement carefully. All it does is get a character and then throw it away. That is, the character it reads is not saved. Now examine the expression that is controlling the *while.* If *get* successfully reads a character, then we go to the second half of the test. If it is not a newline, then the loop continues and the data that was read is discarded (flushed). On the other hand, if *get* fails, such as with end of file, then we have finished flushing the input stream and may continue. Similarly, if `aCh` contains a newline character, then the second half of the expression fails and the loop is also terminated. In other words, it *flushes* the input stream to a newline character. This is exactly what we want to do when the user accidentally keys the wrong character when the program is expecting a digit.

Value Errors In Chapter 6, we discussed some of the techniques for data validation. But the subtleties of data validation can be quite complex. Consider another type of human error, the partially correct input. In our example above, we assumed that the user erred on the first digit of the number. What if the error occurs on the second or third digit? Then the input operation is "happy," for the time being anyway, and sets the success condition indicating that it read one number successfully. How do you guard against this?

The best way is to echo the input to the user and ask for verification that it is correct. Although this greatly slows down the input process, for critical data it is necessary. The code for this situation is shown in Program 7-15. Here we present it as a complete function.

Program 7-15 Handling errors with explanations

```
/* This function reads the units sold from the keyboard
   and verifies it with the user.
      Pre  Nothing
      Post Units Sold read, verified, and returned
*/
int getUnitsSold ()
{
   int  unitsSold;
   bool valid;
   char aCh;

   do
      {
       cout << "\nPlease enter Number of Units Sold: ";
       while (!(cin >> unitsSold))
          {
           cin.clear();
           while (cin.get(aCh) && aCh != '\n')  //flush
              ;
```

Program 7-15 Handling errors with explanations *(continued)*

```
20           cout << "\aInvalid units. Re-enter: ";
21          } // while
22       cout << "\nVerify Units Sold: " << unitsSold;
23       cout << "\n<Y> for correct: <N> for wrong: ";
24
25       while (cin.get(aCh) && aCh != '\n')       //flush
26              ;
27       cin.get(aCh);
28       if (toupper(aCh) ==  'Y')
29          valid = true;
30       else
31          {
32           while (cin.get(aCh) && aCh != '\n') //flush
33             ;
34           cout << "\nYou responded 'no.' ";
35           cout << "Please re-enter Units Sold\n";
36           valid = false;
37          } // else
38      } while (!valid);
39    return unitsSold;
40 } // getUnitsSold
```

Program 7-15 Analysis This function merits some discussion. First, note that there is good user communication throughout the function. It begins with a complete prompt and provides clear error messages whenever problems are detected.

We have implemented this logic with a *do...while* statement, which always loops at least once, since we know that there will always be input. This is the standard loop for validating user input. Within the loop there are two different validation steps. The first tests for totally invalid input, and the second asks the user to verify the input. If either test indicates a problem, the input is flushed. Note that the user messages are different depending on the circumstances.

The function cannot end unless the `valid` flag is *true*. The *if* statement in the loop will set it *true* if the user replies positively. Otherwise, it is set *false* and the input is flushed. This code again demonstrates two principles of good human engineering: The *if* statement is coded in a positive manner, and the expected event, good input, is checked first.

You might wonder why we have a flush at statement 25. Remember that when we read a character with the *get* function, it does not discard whitespace. Therefore, we must ensure that there is no whitespace in the input stream before the user enters yes or no.

Many other things can go wrong when you are reading a file, but these two examples cover most of them.

Data Terminology

Computer specialists who deal with data use a set of specific terms to describe their data. These terms deal with data that are stored in files. What we call a variable in our program, they call a *field* or a *data item*. A field is the smallest named unit of data in a file. If we were working with data about the 10 western states in the continental United States, we would have data like Name, Capital, Number, Square Miles, Population in 1990, and Number of Counties. The first two fields are strings (delimited arrays of characters, which we will study in Chapter 13), and the last four are integers.

These six fields grouped together make up a state record. A *record* is a collection of related data, in this case state data, treated as a unit. Each record has a *key*—that is, one or more fields that uniquely identify the record. In our states record, the key could be the name. Names normally do not make good keys because they are not guaranteed to be unique. Although in this case we know that the names are unique, it is good practice to select a field that is guaranteed to be unique, so from that perspective, a better choice for the key would be the state number, which represents the order in which the states entered the union.

A record cannot be created with text files; you must wait until we introduce binary files and structures to do that. However, we can simulate a record by grouping these data on the same line, with each field separated from the next by whitespace. The data for the 10 western states are shown in Table 7-5.

State	Capital	No.	Sq. miles	Population	No. cnty
Arizona	Phoenix	48	113,508	3,665,228	15
California	Sacramento	31	156,299	29,760,021	58
Colorado	Denver	38	103,595	3,294,394	63
Idaho	Boise	43	82,412	1,006,451	44
Montana	Helena	41	145,388	799,065	56
Nevada	Carson City	36	109,894	1,201,833	16
New Mexico	Santa Fe	47	121,335	1,515,069	33
Oregon	Salem	33	96,184	2,842,321	36
Washington	Olympia	42	66,511	4,866,692	39
Wyoming	Cheyenne	44	96,989	453,588	23

Table 7-5 Ten western states

What we have been demonstrating here is that data can be logically organized to provide more meaning. Although computer scientists normally store this type of data using binary files, there is no reason why it can't be stored in a text file as well. We will return to the discussion again when we talk about strings and when we discuss binary files.

7-10 TIPS AND COMMON PROGRAMMING ERRORS

1. After you have finished working with a file, you should close it.
2. If you open a file for writing, a new file will be created. This means that if you already have an existing file with the same name, it could be deleted.

3. C++ output is normally right-justified. If you want your data to be left-justified, use the left-justify flag (`ios::left`) explicitly.
4. It is a run-time error to attempt to open a file that is already opened.
5. It is a run-time error to attempt to read a file opened in the write mode or to write a file opened in the read mode.

7-11 KEY TERMS

auxiliary storage devices
bad()
binary file
boolalpha/noboolalpha
buffer
cerr
character input/output functions
cin
clear()
clog
close file
console error
console input
console log
console output
control variables
cout
dec
end of file
eof( )
error state
extraction operator
fail( )
file
filename
fill character
fixed
flag
flush
get(...)
good( )
hex
input/output functions
input/output stream (ios) flags
insertion operator
internal flag
justification
manipulator
oct
open file
precision
put(...)
rdstate( )
scientific
secondary storage devices
showbase/noshowbase
showpoint/noshowpoint
showpos/noshowpos
skipws/noskipws
standard stream
standard error
standard input
standard output
stream
text file
unitbuf
uppercase/nouppercase
width

7-12 SUMMARY

- A file is a collection of related data treated as a unit.
- Data in a text file are stored as human-readable characters. The data in a text file are usually divided into lines separated by a newline character.
- A stream is a sequence of elements in time.
- A stream is associated with the source or the destination of data.
- There are four standard file stream objects in C++: *cin*, *cout*, *cerr*, and *clog*.
- The standard input is associated with the keyboard. The standard output and the standard error are associated with the monitor.
- To manipulate and access files, there are different types of input/output functions.
- The open (`stream.open(...)`) and close (`stream.close()`) functions are used to open and close external files, and to connect them to and disconnect them from their corresponding streams.
- When a file is opened in read mode, the file marker is positioned at the beginning of the existing file. The file is then ready to be read.
- When a file is opened for writing, the file marker is positioned at the beginning of a newly created empty

file, before the end of file character. The file is then ready to be written.

- Formatted input/output functions allow us to read data from and write data to files character by character while formatting them to the desired data types such as *char*, *int*, and *float*. The operator >> is used for reading formatted data. The operator << is used for writing formatted data.
- Character input/output functions allow us to read or write files character by character. The function *stream.get(...)* is used for reading a character. The function *stream.put(...)* is used for writing a character.
- When we are reading data from files, we should validate the data.

7-13 PRACTICE SETS

REVIEW QUESTIONS

1. Which of the following is considered auxiliary storage?
   a. Disk
   b. Random access memory (RAM)
   c. Read only memory (ROM)
   d. Tape
   e. Both disk and tape
2. A file can be associated with more than one stream.
   a. True
   b. False
3. The four standard streams in C++ are
   a. *stdin*, *stdout*, *stderr*, and *stdlog*
   b. *cin*, *cout*, *cerr*, and *clog*
   c. *STDIN*, *STDOUT*, *STDERR*, and *STDLOG*
4. To open a file for input, we need to use an object of type _______.
   a. *istream*
   b. *ostream*
   c. *ifstream*
   d. *ofstream*
5. To open a file for output, we need to use an object of type _______.
   a. *istream*
   b. *ostream*
   c. *ifstream*
   d. *ofstream*
6. The scope resolution operator that is used to set or unset a flag is ________.
   a. :
   b. ::
   c. ->
   d. *
7. The showbase flag prints the data in octal or hexadecimal.
   a. True
   b. False
8. To read or write data in octal, we need to use the __________ flag in association with the basefield flag.
   a. Showbase
   b. Showpoint
   c. Oct
   d. Hex
9. The default fill character in C++ is __________.
   a. a space
   b. an asterisk
   c. a hyphen
10. If manipulators are not supported by the system, we can use _______ instead of setw (n).
    a. width (n)
    b. stream.width(n)
    c. stream << width(n)
11. All systems provide manipulators for all flags and control variables.
    a. True
    b. False

12. Write the corresponding manipulator for each of the following control variables.

    a. stream.width (10)

    b. stream.fill ('*')

    c. stream.precision (5)

13. Find the error (if any) in each of the following statements.

    a. cin << get (c)

    b. cin >> get (c)

    c. cin.get (c)

    d. cout.get (c)

14. Find the error (in any) in each of the following statements.

    a. cout << put (c)

    b. cout >> put (c)

    c. cin.put (c)

    d. cout.put (c)

EXERCISES

15. Given the following declaration

```
int   i1 ;
int   i2 ;
float f1 ;
char  c1 ;
char  c2 ;
char  c3 ;
```

and the following line of data

```
14    23    76    CD
```

what would be the value of i1, i2, f1, c1, c2, and c3 after the following statement?

```
cin >> i1 >> i2 >> f1 >> c1 >>
c2 >> c3;
```

16. Given the following declaration

```
int   i1 ;
int   i2 ;
float f1 ;
char  c1 ;
char  c2 ;
```

and the following line of data

```
14.2    C*   K   67       67.9
```

what would be the value of i1, i2, f1, c1, and c2 after the following statement?

```
cin >> i1 >> c1 >> c2 >> i2 >> f1;
```

17. Given the following declaration

```
int   i1 ;
int   i2 ;
int   i3 ;
char  c1 ;
char  c2 ;
char  c3 ;
```

and the following line of data

```
c145d123 34.7
```

what would be the value of i1, i2, i3, c1, c2, and c3 after the following statement?

```
cin >> c1 >> c2 >> i1 >>
c3 >> i2 >> i3;
```

18. What would be printed from the following program segment?

```
int   i1 = 123 ;
int   i2 = - 234 ;
int   i3 = -7 ;
float f1 = 23.5 ;
float f2 = 12.09 ;
float f3 = 98.34 ;
char  c1 = 65 ;
char  c2 = '\n' ;
char  c3 = 'E' ;

cout << setw(6) << i1 << setw(6) << i2
        << setw(6) << i3 << c2;
cout.setf(ios::fixed
ios::floatfield);
cout << setprecision(1);
cout.setf(ios::left,
ios::adjustfield);
cout << f3;
cout << "%";
cout << setf(ios::right,
ios::adjustfield);
cout << f1;
cout << c1 << c2;
cout << (c1 + 32) << " "
        << (c3 + 3)  << c2;
```

PROBLEMS

For the problems and projects in this chapter, you will need to create a test file using your text editor. End each line with a newline character; do not write in paragraph format. The "Gettysburg Address" is suggested as a suitable subject for these files.

Fourscore and seven years ago our fathers brought forth on this continent a new nation, conceived in liberty, and dedicated to the proposition that all men are created equal. Now we are engaged in a great civil war, testing whether that nation, or any nation so conceived and so dedicated, can long endure. We are met on a great battlefield of that war. We have come to dedicate a portion of that field as a final resting-place for those who here gave their lives that that nation might live. It is altogether fitting and proper that we should do this. But in a larger sense, we cannot dedicate, we cannot consecrate, we cannot hallow, this ground. The brave men, living and dead, who struggled here have consecrated it far above our poor power to add or detract. The world will little note, nor long remember what we say here, but it can never forget what they did here. It is for us the living, rather to be dedicated here to the unfinished work which they who fought here have thus far so nobly advanced. It is rather for us, to be here dedicated to the great task remaining before us, that from these honored dead we take increased devotion to that cause for which they gave the last full measure of devotion; that we here highly resolve that these dead shall not have died in vain; that this nation, under God, shall have a new birth of freedom, and that government of the people, by the people, for the people, shall not perish from the earth.

19. Write a function that appends one file at the end of the other.
20. Write a function that appends a file to itself. The result is to be a separate file.
21. Write a function that accepts a file of varying-length lines and changes it to a formatted file with 60 characters in each line.
22. Write a function that calculates the average number of characters per line in a file.
23. Write a function that deletes the last line of any file by copying all but the last line to a new file.
24. Write a function that deletes the blank lines in a file. A blank line is a line with only one single character in it: newline. The result is to be a new file.
25. Write a program that prints itself.
26. Write a program to copy only lines beginning with a user-specified character.
27. Write a program to parse words onto separate lines; that is, locate and write each word to its own line. Words are defined as one or more characters separated by whitespace.
28. When *cin* encounters an error, the invalid data are left in the input stream, sometimes making it impossible to continue. Write a function that reads three pieces of numeric data. If an error is detected, flush the erroneous data (see page 335 for details on how to validate user input) and prompt the user to reenter. Test the function by entering the following data:

```
a  1  2
3  b  4
5  6  c
7  8  9
```

29. Write a program to insert a blank line after the seventh line in a file.
30. Write a program to delete the sixth line in a file. Do not change the sixth line to a blank line; delete it completely.
31. Write a program to insert a blank line after each line in a file. In other words, double-space the text.
32. Write a program to duplicate the fourth line in a file.
33. Write a program to copy a file, deleting the first two characters of each line. (Do not replace the characters with blanks.)
34. Write a program to copy a file, inserting two space characters at the beginning of each line. In other words, each line will be shifted two characters to the right.

PROJECTS

35. Write a program that copies the 21st character of each line in a file to a new file. All extracted characters are to be on the same line. If a line in the input file has fewer than 21 characters, write the last character. If a line is blank, that is, if it consists of only whitespace, then copy nothing. At the end of file, write a newline to the new file and close it.
36. Write a program that will read a text file and count the number of alphabetic characters (*isalpha*), digits (*isdigit*), punctuation characters (*ispunct*), and whitespace characters (*isspace*) in the file. At the end of the file, the program is to display an appropriate report. (The classifying functions are discussed in Chapter 5.)

37. Write a text analyzer program that will read any text file. The program is to print a menu that gives the user the options of counting lines, words, characters, sentences (one or more words ending in a period), or all of the above. Provide a separate function for each option. At the end of the analysis, write an appropriate report.

38. Write a menu-driven text utility program. This program is to have the capability of (a) copying a user-named file to a new file, (b) appending a user-named file to another user-named file, (c) changing the file format to double-spaced, (d) removing all blank lines (changing a double-spaced file to single-spaced), or (e) displaying the contents of the file as a series of 60 character lines with no words split between lines.

39. Using an editor, create an inventory file using the data shown in Table 7-6 (do not include the column captions, just the data).

Part no.	Price	Quantity on hand	Reorder point	Minimum order
0123	1.23	23	20	20
0234	2.34	34	50	25
3456	34.56	56	50	10
4567	45.67	7	10	5
5678	6.78	75	75	25

Table 7-6 Data for Project 25

Write a program to read the inventory file and create an inventory report. The report is to contain the part number, price, quantity on hand, reorder point, minimum order, and order amount. The order amount is to be calculated when the quantity on hand falls below the reorder point. It is calculated as the sum of the reorder point and the minimum order less the quantity on hand. Provide a report heading, such as "Inventory Report," captions for each column, and an "End of Report" message at the end of the report. The part number is to be printed with leading zeros.

40. Using an editor, create the employee file shown in Table 7-7.

Employee no.	Department	Pay rate	Exempt	Hours worked
101	41	8.11	Y	49
722	32	7.22	N	40
1273	23	5.43	Y	39
2584	14	6.74	N	45

Table 7-7 Data for Project 26

Write a program to read the employee file and create a payroll register. The register is to contain the following data:

a. Employee number (print left-justified)
b. Department
c. Pay rate
d. Exempt
e. Hours worked
f. Base pay (pay rate * hours worked)
g. Overtime pay

Overtime pay is calculated only for nonexempt employees. An employee is exempt if 'Y' appears in the exempt column. Overtime is paid at time-and-a-half for all hours worked over 40.

h. Total pay

Arrays

So far in this text we have been using only the standard data types: character, integer, floating-point number, and boolean. While these types are very useful, they can handle only limited amounts of data. To learn how to handle more data in your programs, you must study the derived data types. We will begin our presentation of these data types with the array structure, which is the topic of this chapter.

With the introduction of arrays, we also begin the study of **data structures**. While a complete discussion of data structures is well beyond the scope of this text, it is important that you understand some of the basic concepts of data structures. Structured data are data organized to show the relationships among the individual elements. In most cases, a collecting mechanism is required to organize the data. The use of arrays is a common organizing technique that allows us to process data as a group and also as individual elements.

Figure 8-1 contains a summary of the derived types.

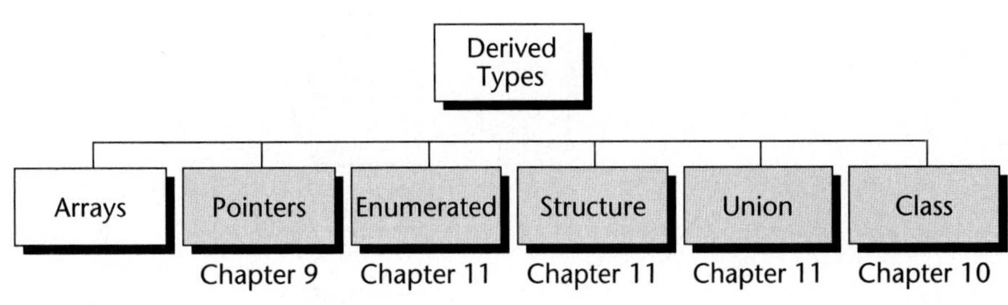

Figure 8-1 Derived types

8-1 CONCEPTS

Let's imagine we have a problem that requires us to read, process, and print 10 integers. We must also keep the integers in memory for the duration of the program. To begin, we can declare and define 10 variables, each with a different name, as shown in Figure 8-2.

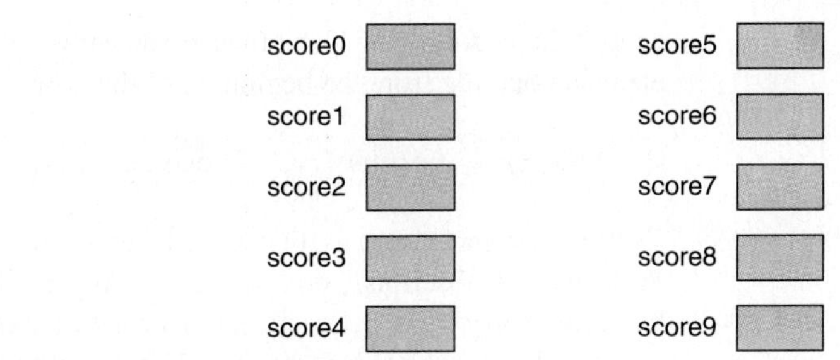

Figure 8-2 Ten variables

Having 10 different names, however, creates a problem: How can we read 10 integers from the keyboard and store them? To read 10 integers from the keyboard, we need 10 read statements, each to a different variable. Furthermore, once we have them in memory, how can we print them? To print them, we need 10 write statements. The flowchart in Figure 8-3 shows a design for reading, processing, and printing these 10 integers.

Although this approach may be acceptable for 10 variables, it is definitely not acceptable for 100 or 1,000 or 10,000. To process large amounts of data we need a powerful data structure, the array. An **array** is a sequenced collection of elements of the same data type.

Since an array is a sequenced collection, we can refer to the elements in the array as the first element, the second element, and so forth until we get to the last element. Thus, when we put the 10 integers of our problem into an array, the address of the first element is 0 as shown below.

$$\texttt{scores}_0$$

In a similar fashion, we refer to the second score as scores_1 and the third score as scores_2. Continuing the series, the last score would be scores_9. We can generalize this

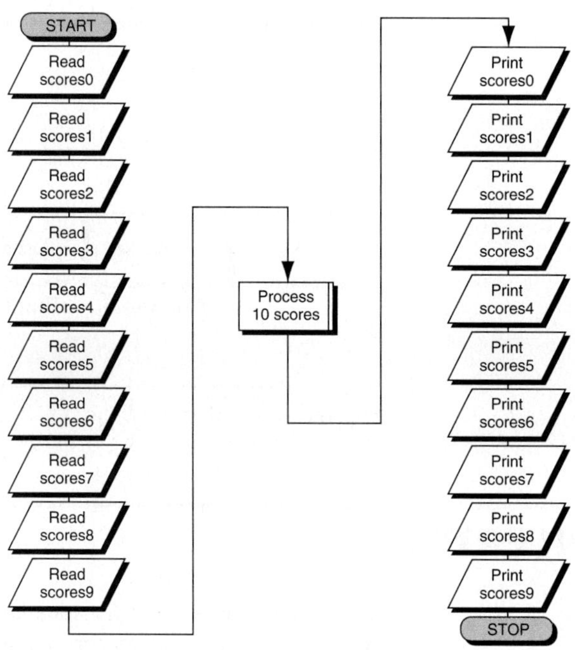

Figure 8-3 Process 10 variables

concept in the following fashion where the **subscripts** indicate the ordinal number of the element counting from the beginning of the array:

$$\texttt{scores}_0\texttt{, scores}_1\texttt{, ..., scores}_{n-1}\texttt{.}$$

What we have seen is that the elements of the array are individually addressed through their subscripts, a concept shown graphically in Figure 8-4. The array as a whole has a name, `scores`, but each member can be accessed individually using its subscript.

The advantages of the array would be limited if we didn't also have programming constructs that would allow us to process the data more conveniently. Fortunately, there is a powerful set of programming constructs—**loops**—that makes array processing easy.

We can use loops to read and write the elements in an array; to add, subtract, multiply, and divide the elements; and even for more complex processing such as calculating averages, searching, or sorting. Now it does not matter if there are 1, 10, 100, 1,000, or 10,000 elements to be processed, because loops make it easy to handle them all.

One question remains: How can we write an instruction so that one time it refers to the first element of an array and the next time it refers to another element? The answer is really quite simple: We simply borrow from the subscript concept we have been using. Rather than using subscripts, however, we will place the subscript value in **brackets**. This format is known as *indexing*. Using the index notation, we would refer to scores_0 as

```
scores[0].
```

Following the convention, scores_1 becomes scores[1] and scores_{19} becomes scores[19]. Using a typical reference, we now refer to our array using the variable *i*.

```
scores[i]
```

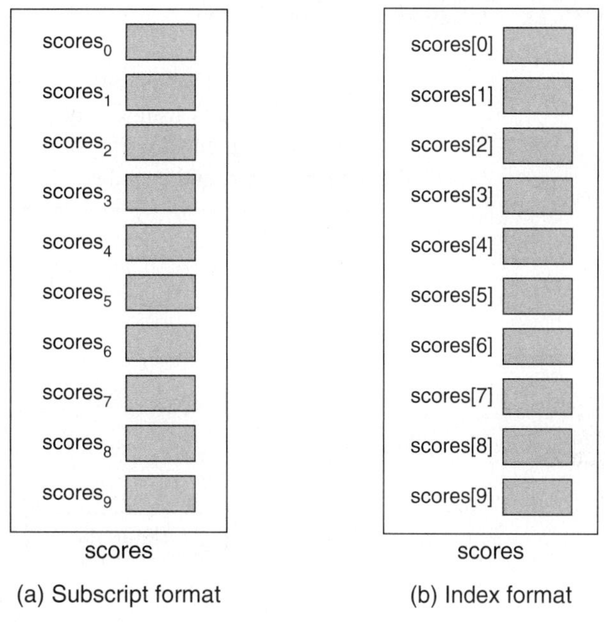

Figure 8-4 An array of *scores*

The flowchart showing the loop used to process our 10 scores using an array is seen in Figure 8-5.

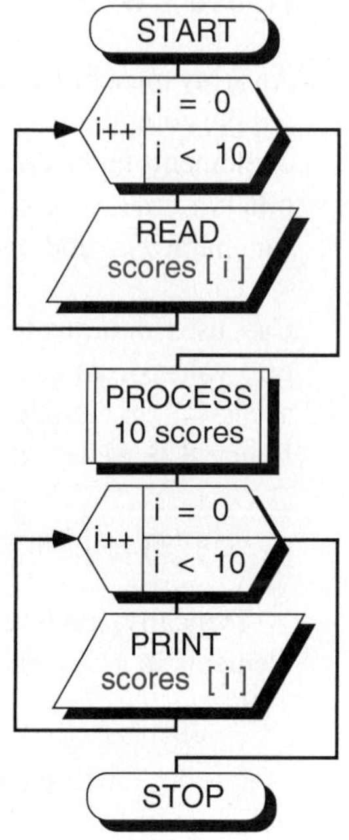

Figure 8-5 Loop for 10 scores

8-2 USING ARRAYS IN C++

In this section, we first show how to declare and define arrays and then look at several typical applications using arrays, including reading values into arrays, accessing and exchanging elements in arrays, and printing arrays. Figure 8-6 shows a typical array, named `scores`, and its values.

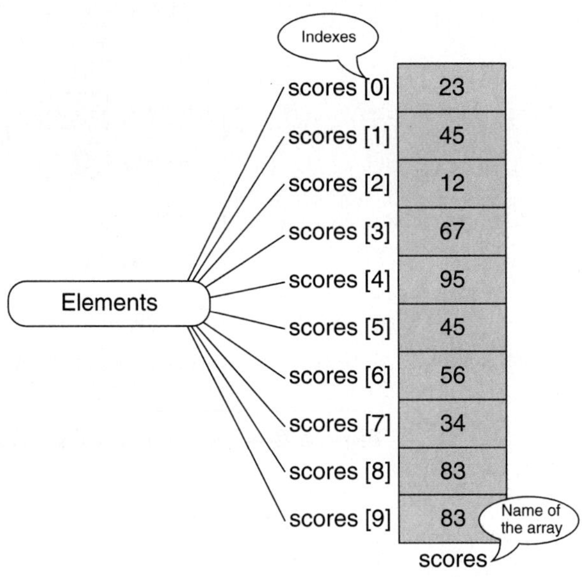

Figure 8-6 The *scores* array

DECLARATION AND DEFINITION

An array must be declared and defined before it can be used. **Declaration and definition** tell the compiler the name of the array, the type of each element, and the size or number of elements in the array. The size of the array is a constant and must have a value at compilation time. Figure 8-7 shows three different array declarations: one for integers, one for characters, and one for floating-point numbers.

ACCESSING ELEMENTS IN ARRAYS

C++ uses an **index** to **access** individual elements in an array. The index must be an integral value or an expression that evaluates to an integral value. The simplest form for accessing an element is a numeric constant. For example, given the `scores` array in Figure 8-6, we could access the first element as follows:

```
scores[0]
```

Typically, however, the index is a variable or an expression. Thus, to process all the elements in `scores`, a loop similar to the following code would be used:

```
for (i = 0; i < 9; i++)
     scores[i] … ;
```

How does C++ know where an individual element is located in memory? In `scores`, for example, there are nine elements. How does it find just one? The answer is simple. The array's name is a symbolic reference for the address to the first byte of the

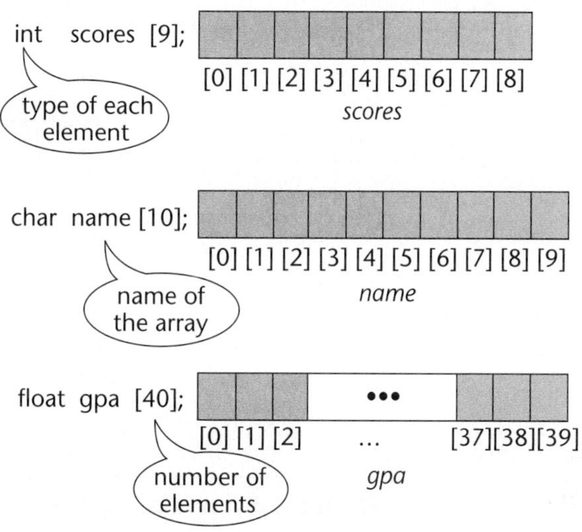

Figure 8-7 Declaring and defining arrays

array. Thus, when we use the array's name, we are actually referring to the first byte of the array. The index represents an offset from the beginning of the array to the element being referred to. With these two pieces of data, C++ can calculate the address of any element in the array using the following simple formula:

```
address = array address + (sizeof (element) * index)
```

For example, assume that `scores` is stored in memory at location 10,000. Since `scores` is an integer, the size of one element is the size of an integer. Assuming an integer size of two, the address of the element at index 3 is

```
element address = 10,000 + 2 * 3 = 10,006
```

This formula also works for index location 0. When the index is 0, the product of the element size and the index is 0: the address is therefore the array address, which is the address of the fist element (index 0).

STORING VALUES IN ARRAYS

Declaration and definition only reserve space for the elements in the array. No values will be stored. If we want to store values in the array, we must either initialize the elements, read values from the keyboard, or assign values to each individual element.

Initialization

Initialization of all elements in an array can be done at the time of declaration and definition, just as with variables. For each element in the array we provide a value. The only difference is that the values must be enclosed in braces and, if there is more than one, separated by commas. It is a compile error to specify more values than there are elements in the array.

Figure 8-8 contains four examples of array initialization. The coding in the first example, a simple array declaration of five integers, is typical of the way array initialization is coded. When the array is completely initialized, it is not necessary to specify the size of the array; this case is seen in the second example. Nevertheless, it is good

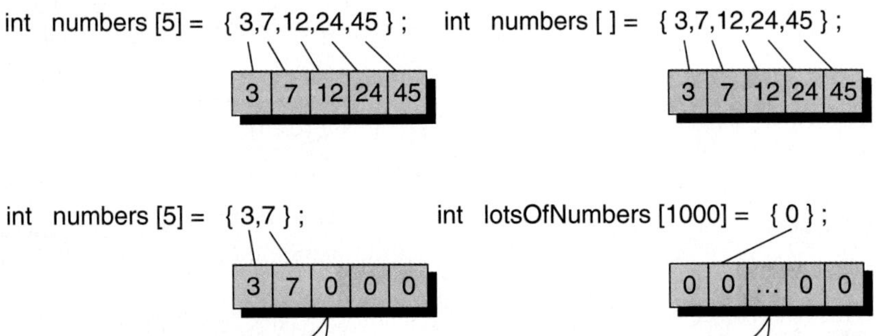

Figure 8-8 Initializing arrays

practice to define the size explicitly because doing so allows the compiler to do some checking and also provides good documentation.

If the number of values provided is less than the number of elements in the array, the unassigned elements are filled with zeros, as in the third example in Figure 8-8. We can use this rule to easily initialize an array to all zeros by supplying just the first zero value, as shown in the last example in Figure 8-8.

Inputting Values

Another way to fill the array is to read the values from the keyboard or a file. This method of **inputting values** can be done using a loop. When the array is going to be completely filled, the most appropriate loop is the *for* loop because the number of elements is fixed and known. A typical *for* loop to fill an array is shown below.

```
for (i = 0; i < 9; i++)
    cin >> scores [i];
```

Several concepts need to be studied in this simple statement. First, we start the index, `i`, at 0. Since there are nine elements in the array, we must load the values from index locations 0 through 8. The limit test, therefore, is set at `i` < 9, which conveniently is the number of elements in the array.

Finally, when there is a possibility that all the elements are not going to be filled, then one of the event-controlled loops (*while* or *do...while*) should be used. Which one you use would depend on the application.

Assigning Values

Individual elements can be assigned values using the assignment operator. Any value that reduces to the proper type can be assigned to an individual array element. A simple assignment statement for `scores` is seen below.

```
scores [4] = 23;
```

Note that you cannot assign one array to another array, even if they match fully in type and size. You have to copy arrays at the individual element level. For example, to copy an array of 25 integers to a second array of 25 integers, you could use a loop, as shown in the next example.

```
for (i = 0; i < 25; i++)
    holdScores [i] = scores [i];
```

If the values of an array follow a pattern, we can use a loop to assign values. For example, the following loop assigns a value that is twice the index number to array `scores`.

```
for (i = 0; i < 9; i++)
    scores [i] = i * 2;
```

For another example, the following code assigns the odd numbers 1 through 17 to the elements of `scores`.

```
for (i = 0; i < 9; i++)
    scores [i] = (i * 2) + 1;
```

Exchanging Values

A common application is to **exchange** the contents of two elements. We will use this operation later in the chapter when we begin sorting arrays. When you exchange variables, you swap the values of elements without knowing what's in them.

For example, imagine we want to swap `numbers[3]` and `numbers[1]` in Figure 8-8. A common beginner's mistake would be simply to assign each element to the other, as shown below.

```
numbers [3] = numbers [1];
numbers [1] = numbers [3];
```

Although this code looks as if it will do the job, if we trace the code carefully we find that it only does half the job. `Numbers[1]` is moved to `numbers[3]`, but that's all that happens; the second part isn't done. The result is that both elements have the same value. Figure 8-9 traces the steps.

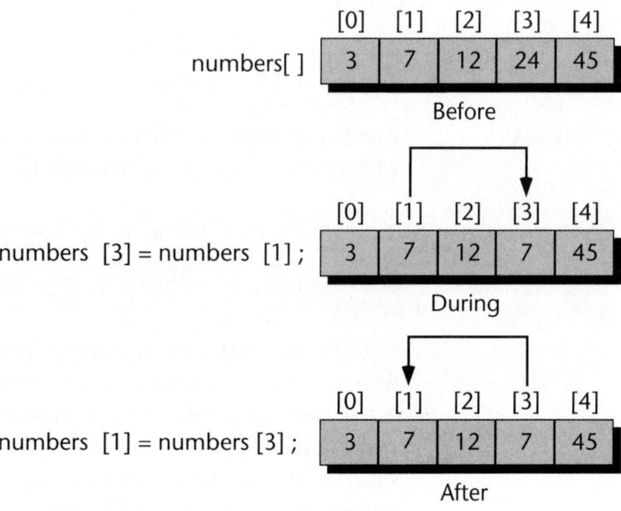

Figure 8-9 Exchanging scores—the wrong way

What we see in Figure 8-9 is that the original value of `numbers[3]` is destroyed before we can move it. The solution is to use a temporary variable to store the value in `numbers[3]` before moving the data from `numbers[1]`.

```
temp          = numbers [3];
numbers [3]   = numbers [1];
numbers [1]   = temp;
```

This technique is demonstrated in Figure 8-10.

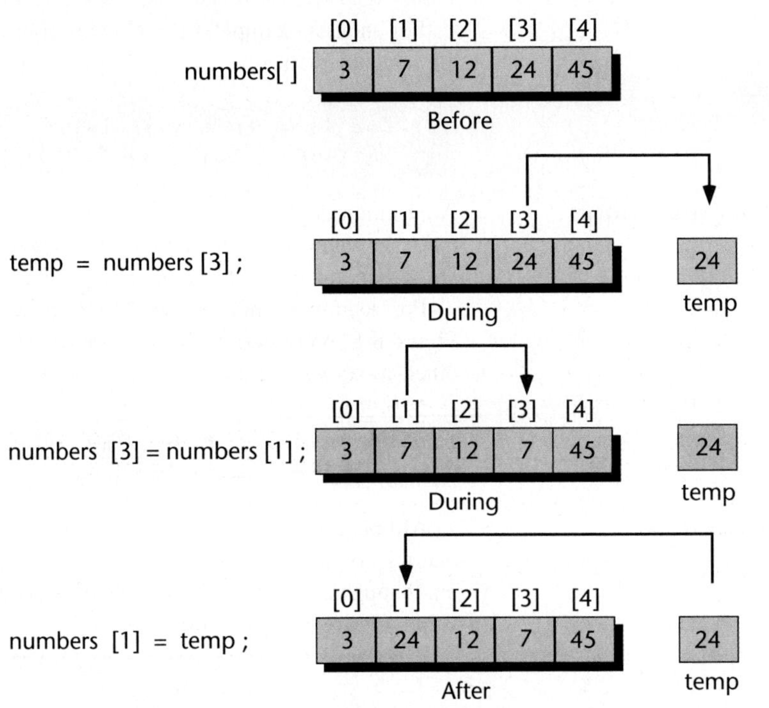

Figure 8-10 Exchanging scores with temporary variable

Outputting Values

Another common application is printing the contents of an array. This is easily done with a *for* loop, as shown in the following code.

```
for (i = 0; i < 9; i++)
    cout << scores[i];
cout << endl;
```

In this example, all the data are printed on one line. After the *for* loop completes, a final *cout* statement advances to the next line. But what if we had 100 values to be printed? In that case, they couldn't all fit on one line. Given a relatively small number width, however, we could put 10 on a line and use 10 lines to print all the data. This rather common situation is easily handled by adding a counter to track the number of elements we have printed on one line. This logic is used in Program 8-1.

Program 8-1 Print 10 numbers per line

```
// A program fragment
   int numPrinted = 0;
   for (int i = 0; i < cSIZE; i++)
      {
       cout << setw(3) << list[i];
       if (numPrinted < 9)
         numPrinted++;
       else
         {
          cout << endl;
          numPrinted = 0;
         } // else
      } // for
```

PRECEDENCE OF INDEX OPERATORS

References to elements in arrays are postfix expressions whose precedence can be found on the table on the inside cover of this book. By looking at the precedence table, we see that array references have a priority of 17, which is very high. What is not apparent from the table, however, is that the opening and closing brackets are actually operators. They create a postfix expression from a primary expression. With a little thought, you should recognize that this is exactly as it must be: When you are indexing an array element in an expression, the value must be determined immediately. Of course, you can override the normal precedence with parentheses, but such an approach is very rarely used.

Referring to the original array in Figure 8-10, what will be the result of the following code?

```
numbers[3] = numbers[4] + 15;
```

In this case, `numbers[4]` has a higher precedence than the addition operator (17 versus 12), so it is evaluated first. The result is then

```
numbers[3]  =  45  +  15;
```

After this statement has been executed, `numbers[3]` has been changed from 24 to 60.

INDEX RANGE CHECKING

The C++ language does not check the boundary of an array, so it is the programmer's job to ensure that all references to indexed elements are valid and within the range of the array. This is called **index range checking**. If you use an invalid index in an expression, you will get unpredictable results. (The results are unpredictable because you have no way of knowing the value of the indexed reference.)

On the other hand, if you use an invalid index in an assignment, you will be destroying some undetermined portion of your program. Usually, but not always, your program will continue to run and either produce unpredictable results or eventually abort.

An example of a common out-of-range index is seen in the code used to fill an array from the keyboard. For this example, we have reproduced the code we used to fill the `scores` array earlier, only this time we have intentionally made a common mistake. Can you spot it?

```
for (i = 1; i <= 9; i++)
   cin >> scores[i];
```

When dealing with array processing, be very careful at the beginning and end of the array. A careful examination of the preceding code discloses that we erroneously started at 1 instead of 0. So we fix it as shown below, only to find that it still doesn't work!

```
for (i = 0; i <= 9; i++)
   cin scores[i];
```

The moral of this example is to examine your logic. If you made one mistake, you may well have made two. Although we corrected the error for initialization (the beginning of the array), there is still an error at the other end. If you can't identify it, check the original code, shown on page 350.

The result of both versions of this error is that the data stored in memory after the *scores* array is erroneously destroyed. In the first version of the error, the first element of the array was not initialized.

The problems created by unmanaged indexes are among the most difficult to solve, even with today's powerful programming workbenches. So you want to plan your array logic carefully and fully test it.

Example: Squares Array

Let's write a program that uses arrays. Program 8-2 uses a *for* loop to initialize each element in an array to the square of the index value, and then prints the array.

Program 8-2 Squares array

```
/* Initialize array with square of index and print it.
      Written by:
      Date:
*/
#include <iostream>
#include <iomanip>
using namespace std;

const int cARY_SIZE = 5;

int main ()
{
   int sqrAry[cARY_SIZE];
   for (int i = 0; i < cARY_SIZE; i++)
      sqrAry[i] = i * i;

   cout << "Element\tSquare\n";
   cout << "=======\t======\n";
   for (int i = 0; i < cARY_SIZE; i++)
      {
       cout << setw(5) << i << "\t";
       cout << setw(5) << sqrAry[i] << endl;
      } // for i
   return 0;
}  // main
```

Program 8-2 Squares array *(continued)*

```
Results:
Element Square
======= ======
   0       0
   1       1
   2       4
   3       9
   4      16
```

Example: Read and Print Reversed

As another example of an array program, let's read a series of numbers from the keyboard and print them in reverse order; that is, if we read 1 2 3 4, we want to print them 4 3 2 1. With a little thought, it should be obvious that we must read all of the numbers before we can begin printing them. This definitely sounds like a problem for an array. In Program 8-3, we read up to 50 integers and then print them reversed, 10 to a line.

Program 8-3 Print input reversed

```
/* Read a number series and print it reversed.
      Written by:
      Date:
*/
#include <iostream>
#include <iomanip>
using namespace std;

int main ()
{
   int numbers[50];

   cout << "You may enter up to 50 integers:\n";
   cout << "How many would you like to enter? ";
   int readNum;
   cin  >> readNum;

   if (readNum > 50)
      readNum = 50;

   // Fill the array
   cout << "\nEnter your numbers: \n";
   for (int i = 0; i < readNum; i++)
       cin >> numbers[i];

   // Print the array
   cout << "\nYour numbers reversed are: \n";
   int numPrinted = 0;
   for (int i = readNum - 1; i >= 0; i--)
      {
       cout << setw(3) << numbers[i];
```

Program 8-3 Print input reversed (*continued*)

```
          if (numPrinted < 9)
              numPrinted++;
          else
             {
              printf("\n");
              numPrinted = 0;
             } // else
         } // for
    return 0;
}  // main
```

```
Results:
You may enter up to 50 integers:
How many would you like to enter? 12

Enter your numbers:
1 2 3 4 5 6 7 8 9 10 11 12

Your numbers reversed are:
 12 11 10  9  8  7  6  5  4  3
  2  1
```

Program 8-3 Analysis First, note how we validate the number of integers to be read. If the user requests more than 50, we simply set `readNum` to 50. This ensures that we will not run off the end of the array.

This is an interesting loop because we start at the end and work to the front. While many arrays are processed from the beginning, it is often necessary to process from the end. You will see more in the sorting functions later in the chapter.

Finally, note that we incorporate the logic from Program 8-1 on page 353 to print 10 numbers per line. Had we made Program 8-1 a function, we could have reused the code rather than repeating it.

8-3 ARRAYS AND FUNCTIONS

To process arrays in a large program, you have to be able to pass them to functions. You can do this either by **passing individual elements** or by **passing the whole** array. In this section, we discuss first how to pass individual elements and then how to pass the whole array.

PASSING INDIVIDUAL ELEMENTS

Individual elements can be passed to a function like any ordinary variable. As long as the array element type matches the function parameter type, it can be passed. Of course, it will be passed as a value parameter, which means that the function cannot change the value of the element in the calling function.

Assume that we have a function, `print_square`, that receives an integer and prints its square on the system console. Using the array, `base`, we can loop through the array, passing each element in turn to `print_square`. This program is shown in Figure 8-11.

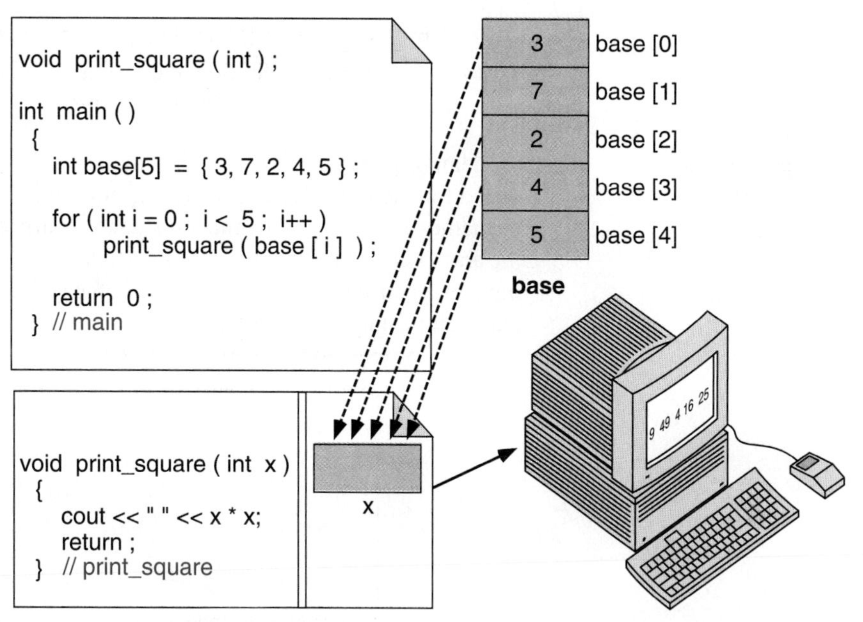

Figure 8-11 Passing individual elements

Note how only one element is passed at a time by using the indexed expression, `base[i]`. Since the value of this expression is a single integer, it matches the formal parameter type in `print_square`. As far as `print_square` is concerned, it doesn't "know" or "care" that the value it is working with came from an array.

Also note that in this example we have coded the function prototype without a name for the formal parameter. In this case, the name would not contribute to the documentation. We have also used the more traditional underscore separator to separate the words in the function name.

PASSING THE WHOLE ARRAY

If we want the function to operate on the whole array, we must pass the whole array. Here we see another situation in which C++ does not pass values to a function. It would use a lot of memory and time to pass large arrays around every time we wanted to use one in a function. For example, if an array containing 20,000 elements were passed by value to a function, another 20,000 elements would have to be allocated in the function and each element would have to be copied from one array to the other. So, instead of passing the whole array, C++ passes the address of the array.

In C++, the name of an array is a primary expression whose value is the address of the first element in the array. Since indexed references are simply calculated addresses, all we need to refer to any of the elements in the array is the address of the array. Because the name of the array is in fact its address, passing the array name, as opposed to a single element, allows the called function to refer to the array back in the calling function.

How do you pass the whole array? In the calling function, you simply use the array name as the actual parameter. In the called function, you must declare that the corresponding formal parameter is an array. You do not, however, need to specify the number of elements in the array. Since the array is actually defined elsewhere, all that is important is that the compiler knows it's an array.

In summary, there are two rules associated with passing the whole array to a function:

1. The function must be called by passing only the name of the array.
2. In the function definition, the formal parameter must be an array type; the size of the array does not need to be specified.

Passing Arrays as Constants

To demonstrate the concept of passing arrays as constants, we look at an example that uses a function to calculate the average of the integers in an array. In this case, we pass the name of the array to the function, and it returns the average as a real number. Because the array will not be changed by the called function, we can ensure its integrity by passing it as a constant. We do this by using the type modifier, **const**, in the function header parameter list as shown in Figure 8-12.

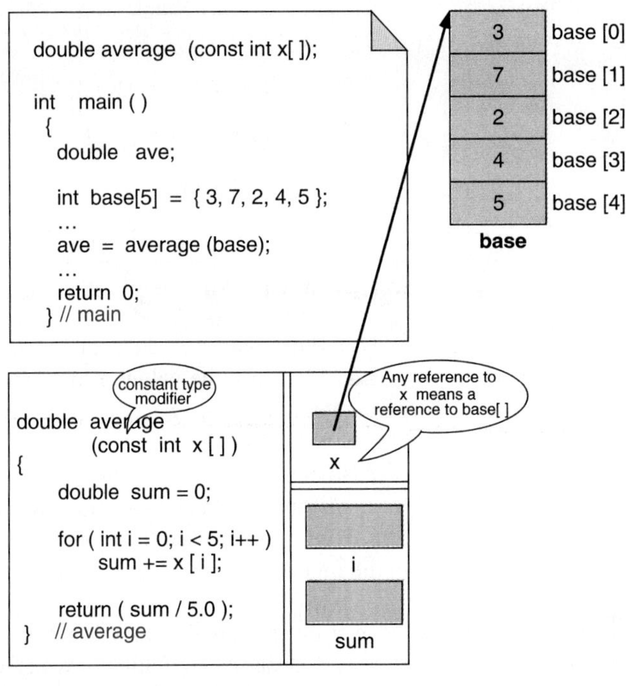

Figure 8-12 Passing arrays—*average*

What actually is passed in Figure 8-12 is the address of the array, `base`, as seen in the actual parameter. In the parameter list for `average`, we indicate that we are receiving an array by coding the array brackets, as shown below (note also the *const* modifier):

```
const int x []
```

The array, renamed `x`, is available in `average` and can be used in any expression or statement that does not modify the contents of the array.

Passing Arrays for Updating

We can let a function change the value of the array elements by passing the array name without the constant modifier. For example, in Figure 8-13, each element in `base` is multiplied by two. In this example, because we do not use the constant type modifier, we are telling the compiler that the array can be changed. Note that in addition to the array parameter, there is a local variable in the called function that is used to "walk" through the array.

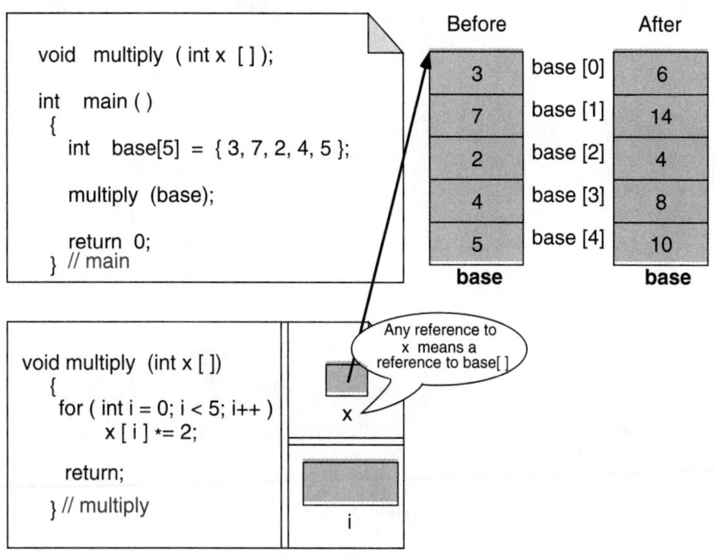

Figure 8-13 Changing values in arrays

8-4 ARRAY APPLICATIONS

In this section we discuss three common array applications.

FREQUENCY ARRAYS

A **frequency array** shows the number of elements with an identical value found in a series of numbers. For example, suppose we have taken a sample of 100 values between 0 and 19. We want to know how many of the values are 0, how many are 1, how many are 2, and so forth up through 19.

We can read these numbers into an array called `numbers`. We then create an array of 20 elements that will show the frequency of each number in the series. This design is shown in Figure 8-14.

With the data structure shown in Figure 8-14 in mind, how do we write the application? Since we know that there are exactly 100 elements, we can use a *for* loop to examine each value in the array. But how can we relate the value in `numbers` to a location in the frequency?

One way to do it is to assign the value from the data array to an index and then use the index to access the frequency array. The code for this technique is shown below.

```
f = numbers[i];
frequency [f]++;
```

Since an index is an expression, however, we can simply use the value from our data array as the index for the frequency array. This concept is shown in the following

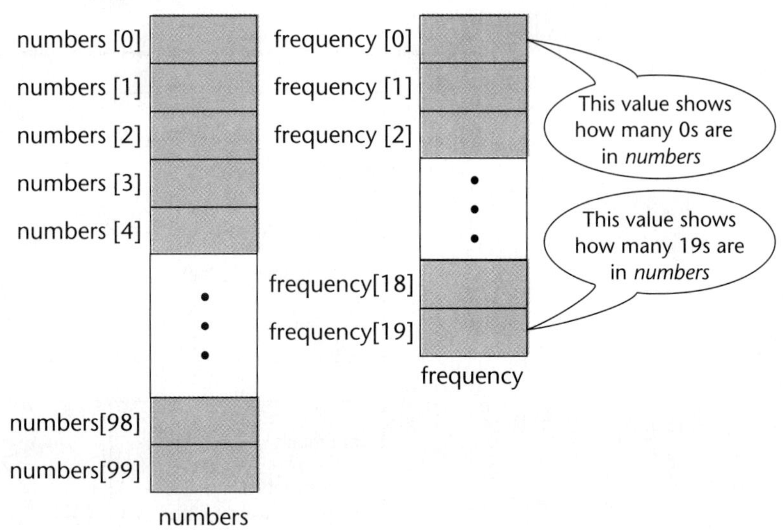

Figure 8-14 Frequency array

example in which the value of `numbers[i]` is determined first, and that value is then used to index into `frequency`.

```
frequency [numbers [i]]++;
```

The complete function is shown in Program 8-4 as `makeFrequency`. The function first initializes the frequency array and then scans the data array to count the number of occurrences of each value.

There is a potentially serious problem with this function. Can you see what it is? Think about our discussion of what happens if the index gets out of range (see page 338). What if one of the numbers in our data is greater than 19? We will be destroying some other part of our program! To protect against this possibility, each data value should be tested to make sure that it is within the indexing range of *frequency*.

HISTOGRAMS

A **histogram** is a pictorial representation of a frequency array. Instead of printing the values of the elements to show the frequency of each number, we can print a histogram in the form of a bar chart. For example, Figure 8-15 is a histogram for a set of numbers in the range 0…19. In this example, asterisks (*) are used to build the bar. Each asterisk represents one occurrence of the data value.

Let's write a program that builds a frequency array for data values in the range 0…19 and then prints their histogram. The data are read from a file. To provide flexibility, the `getData` function may only partially fill the array. The function that loads it also guards against too much data. The design for the program is shown in Figure 8-16, and the code used is shown in Program 8-4.

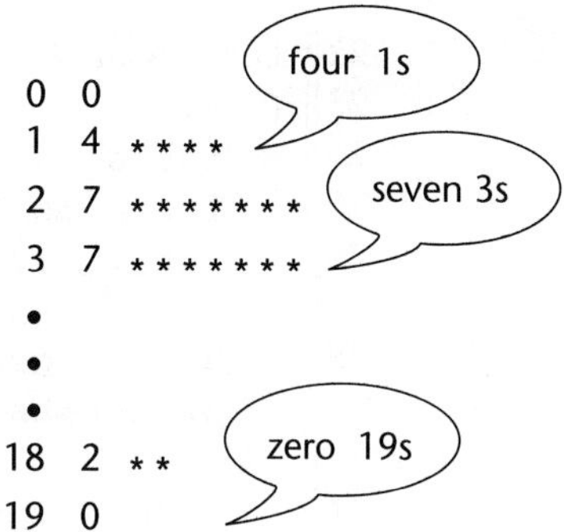

Figure 8-15 Frequency histogram

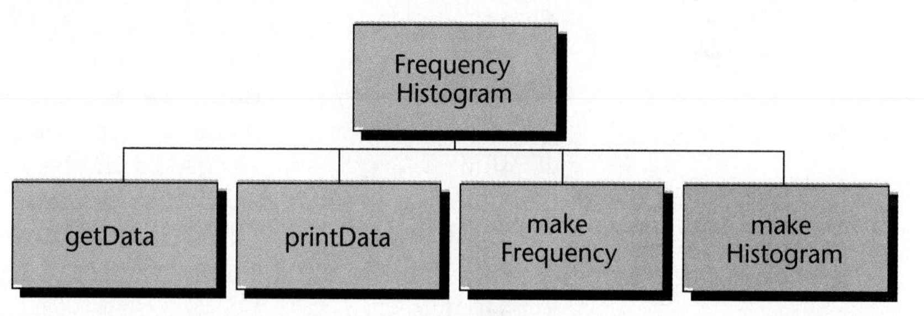

Figure 8-16 Histogram program design

Program 8-4 Frequency and histogram

```
/* Read data from a file into an array.
   Build frequency array & print the data with histogram.
      Written by:
      Date:
*/
#include <iostream>
#include <iomanip>
#include <fstream>
using namespace std;

const int cMAX_ELMNTS  = 100;
const int cANLYS_RANGE =  19;

   int getData (int  numbers[], int size, int range);

   void printData     (const int numbers[], int size,
                       int lineSize);
   void makeFrequency (int numbers[], int size,
                       int frequency[], int range);
   void makeHistogram (int frequency[], int range);

```

Program 8-4 Frequency and histogram *(continued)*

```
int main ()
{
   int size;
   int nums[cMAX_ELMNTS];
   int frequency[cANLYS_RANGE + 1];

   size = getData (nums, cMAX_ELMNTS, cANLYS_RANGE);
   printData (nums, size, 10);

   makeFrequency(nums,size,frequency,cANLYS_RANGE);
   makeHistogram(frequency, cANLYS_RANGE);
   return 0;
} // main
/* ================== getData ==================
   Read data from file into array. The array
   does not have to be completely filled.
      Pre   data is an empty array
            size is maximum elements in array
            range is highest value that can be accepted
      Post  Array is filled--Return number of elements
*/
int getData (int data[], int size, int range)
{
   ifstream  fsData;
   fsData.open("histogrm.dat");
   if (!fsData)
      cerr << "Error opening file\a\a\n", exit (100);

   int dataIn;
   int loader = 0;
   while (loader < size
       && (fsData >> dataIn))
      if (dataIn >= 0 && dataIn <= range)
         data[loader++] = dataIn;
      else
         cout << "Data point " << dataIn
              << " invalid. Ignored. \n";

// Test to see what stopped while
   if (loader == size && (fsData >> dataIn))
      // More data in file
     cout << "\nToo much data. Process what read.\n";
   return loader;
} // getData
/* ================== printData ==================
   Print the data as a two-dimensional array.
      Pre   data: a filled array
            size: size of array to be printed
            lineSize: max elements printed on a line
```

Program 8-4 Frequency and histogram ***(continued)***

```
      Post  The data have been printed
*/
void printData (const int data[], int size, int lineSize)
{
   cout << endl << endl;
   for (int i = 0, numPrinted = 0; i < size; i++)
      {
       numPrinted++;
       cout << setw(3) << data[i];
       if (numPrinted >= lineSize)
          {
           cout << endl;
           numPrinted = 0;
          } // if
      } // for
   cout << endl << endl;
   return;
} // printData
/* ================ makeFrequency =================
   Analyze the data in nums and build their frequency
   distribution.
      Pre    nums: array of data for analysis
             size: size of array containing data
             frequency: accumulation array
             range: maximum value of data
      Post   Frequency array has been built
*/
void makeFrequency (int nums[],       int size,
                    int frequency[], int range)
{
   // First initialize the frequency array
   for (int i = 0; i <= range; i++)
      frequency [i] = 0;

   // Scan numbers and build frequency array
   for (int i = 0; i < size; i++)
      frequency [nums [i]]++;
   return;
} // makeFrequency
/* ================ makeHistogram =================
   Print a histogram representing analyzed data.
      Pre   freq contains value count
            range max data value & max array index
      Post  histogram has been printed
*/
void makeHistogram (int freq[], int range)
{
   for (int i = 0; i <= range; i++)
      {
```

Program 8-4 Frequency and histogram *(continued)*

```
       cout << setw(3) << i << setw(3) << freq[i];
       for (int j = 1; j <= freq[i]; j++)
           cout << "*";
       cout << endl;
      } // for i
   return;
} // makeHistogram
// ================ End of Program =================
```

```
Results:
Data point 20 invalid. Ignored.
Data point 25 invalid. Ignored.

  1  2  3  4  5  6  7  8  7 10
  2 12 13 13 15 16 17 18 17  7
  3  4  6  8 10  2  4  6  8 10
  4  3  5  7  1  3  7  7 11 13
  5 10 11 12 13 16 18 11 12  7
  6  1  2  2  3  3  3  4  4  4
  7  7  8  7  6  5  4  1  2  2
  8 11 11 13 13 13 17 17  7  7
 13 17 17 15 15

  0  0
  1  4 ****
  2  7 *******
  3  7 *******
  4  8 ********
  5  4 ****
  6  5 *****
  7 12 ************
  8  5 *****
  9  0
 10  4 ****
 11  5 *****
 12  3 ***
 13  8 ********
 14  0
 15  3 ***
 16  2 **
 17  6 ******
 18  2 **
 19  0
```

RANDOM NUMBER PERMUTATIONS

A random number permutation is a set of random numbers in which no numbers are repeated. For example, given a random number permutation of 10 numbers, the values from 0 to 9 would all be included with no duplicates.

We saw how to generate a set of random numbers in Chapter 4. To generate a permutation, we need to eliminate the duplicates. Borrowing from the histogram concept in the previous section, we can solve the problem most efficiently by using two arrays. The first array contains the random numbers. The second array contains a logical value that indicates whether or not the number represented by its index has been placed in the random number array. This design is shown in Figure 8-17.

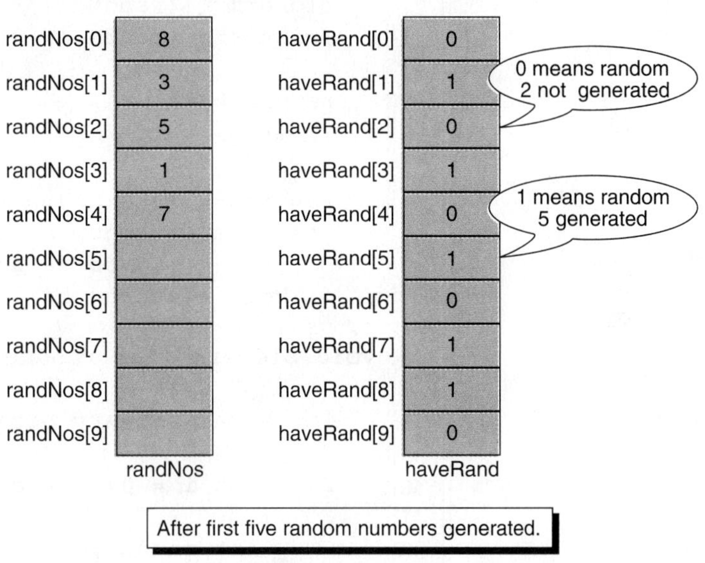

Figure 8-17 Design for random number permutations

As you study Figure 8-17, note that only the first five random numbers have been placed in the permutation. For each random number in the random number array, its corresponding location in the have-random array is set to 1. Those locations representing numbers that have not yet been generated are still set to 0. The implementation of the design is shown in Program 8-5.

Program 8-5 Generate a permutation

```
/* Generate a random number permutation.
      Written by:
      Date:
*/
#include <iostream>
#include <iomanip>
#include <cstdlib>
using namespace std;

const int cAry_Size = 20;

void bldPerm   (int randNos[]);
void printData (int data[], int size, int lineSize);

int main ()
```

Program 8-5 **Generate a permutation (*continued*)**

```
{
   int randNos [cAry_Size];

   cout << "Begin Random Permutation Generation\n";

   bldPerm    (randNos);
   printData (randNos, cAry_Size, 10);

   return 0;
}  // main

/* ==================== bldPerm ====================
   Generate a random number permutation in array.
      Pre   randNos is array to receive permutations
      Post  randNos filled
*/
void bldPerm (int randNos[])
{
   int haveRand[cAry_Size] = {0};

   for (int i = 0; i < cAry_Size; i++)
       {
        int randNo;
        do
          {
           randNo = rand() % cAry_Size;
          } while (haveRand[randNo] == 1);
        haveRand[randNo] = 1;
        randNos[i] = randNo;
       } // for
   return;
}  // bldPerm
/* =================== printData ===================
   Prints the data as a two-dimensional array.
      Pre  data: a filled array
                last: index to last element to be printed
              lineSize: number of elements printed on a line
      Post  the data have been printed
*/
void printData (int data[], int size, int lineSize)
{
   printf("\n");
   for (int i = 0, numPrinted = 0; i < size; i++)
       {
        numPrinted++;
        cout << setw(3) << data[i];
        if (numPrinted >= lineSize)
           {
            cout << endl;
```

Program 8-5 Generate a permutation (*continued*)

```
               numPrinted = 0;
             } // if
        } // for
     cout << endl;
     return;
  } // printData
```

```
Results:
Begin Random Permutation Generation

  18 13 15 11  7 10 19 12  6  9
   4  0  5  3 17 14  2 16  1  8
```

8-5 SORTING

One of the most common applications in computer science is **sorting**, which is the process through which data are arranged according to their values. We are surrounded by data. If the data were not ordered, it would take us hours and hours to find a single piece of information. Imagine the difficulty of finding someone's telephone number in a telephone book that was not ordered!

In this chapter, we introduce three sorting algorithms, which are the foundations for faster and more efficient algorithms taught in advanced courses: the selection sort, bubble sort, and insertion sort. In each section, we first introduce the basic concept, then use the idea in an example, and finally develop the code for the algorithm.

One programming concept common to the sorting algorithms we discuss in this section is the swapping of data between two elements in a list. You may find it helpful to review our discussion of this concept on page 351 before continuing on in this section.

SELECTION SORT

In the **selection sort**, the list is divided into two sublists, sorted and unsorted, which are divided by an imaginary wall. We find the smallest element from the unsorted sublist and swap it with the element at the beginning of the unsorted data. After each selection and swapping, the imaginary wall between the two sublists moves one element ahead, increasing the number of sorted elements and decreasing the number of unsorted ones. Each time we move one element from the unsorted sublist to the sorted sublist, we say that we have completed a **sort pass**. A list of n elements requires $n - 1$ passes to completely rearrange the data. The selection sort is presented graphically in Figure 8-18.

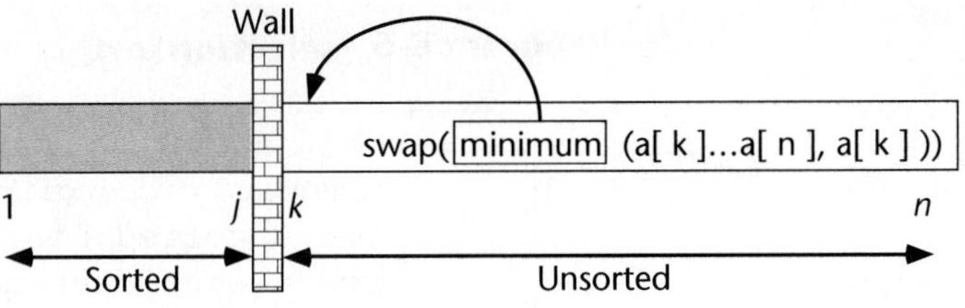

Figure 8-18 Selection sort concept

Figure 8-19 traces a set of six integers as we sort them. It shows how the wall between the sorted and unsorted sublists moves in each pass. As you study the figure, you will see that the array is sorted after five passes, which is one less than the number of elements in the array. Thus, if we use a loop to control the sorting, our loop will have one less iteration than the number of elements in the array.

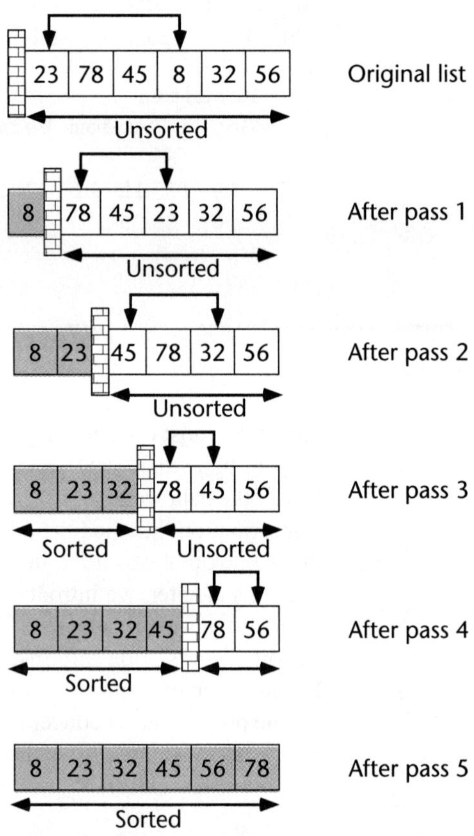

Figure 8-19 Selection sort example

SELECTION SORT ALGORITHM

The selection sort algorithm (Program 8-6) is rather straightforward. Starting with the first item in the list, the algorithm calls `exchangeSmallest` (Program 8-7) to examine the unsorted items in the list for the smallest element. In each pass, `exchange-Smallest` "selects" the smallest element and exchanges it with the first unsorted element. It then returns to `selectionSort`, which repeats the process until the list is completely sorted.

Program 8-6 selectionSort

```
/* Sorts by selecting smallest element in unsorted portion
   of array and exchanging it with element at the beginning
   of the unsorted list.
      Pre   list must contain at least one item
            last contains index to last element
      Post  list sorted smallest to largest
```

Program 8-6 selectionSort *(continued)*

```
*/
void selectionSort (int list[], int last)
{
   for (int current = 0; current < last; current++)
        exchangeSmallest (list, current, last);
   return;
} // selectionSort
```

Program 8-7 exchangeSmallest

```
/* Given array of integers, place smallest element into
   position in array.
      Pre   list: must contain at least one element
            current: beginning of unsorted portion
            last: last element--Must be > current
      Post  smallest moved to beginning of unsorted
*/
void exchangeSmallest (int list[], int current, int last)
{
   int smallest = current;
   for (int walker = current + 1; walker <= last; walker++)
      if (list[walker] < list[smallest])
           smallest = walker;

   // Smallest selected: exchange with current element
   int tempData    = list[current];
   list[current]   = list[smallest];
   list[smallest]  = tempData;
   return;
} // exchangeSmallest
```

Program 8-7 Analysis In this algorithm we see two elements that are common to all three sorts discussed in this section. First, each algorithm makes use of a subfunction either to determine the proper location of the data or to identify and exchange two elements. Each call of the subfunction is a sort pass.

Second, each time we want to move data, we must use a temporary storage area. This technique is found in every sort algorithm except those that use two sorting areas. In the selection sort, the temporary area is used to exchange the two elements.

BUBBLE SORT

In the **bubble sort** method, the list is divided into two sublists: sorted and unsorted. The smallest element is *bubbled* from the unsorted sublist and moved to the sorted sublist. After the smallest element has been moved to the sorted list, the wall moves one element ahead, increasing the number of sorted elements and decreasing the number of unsorted ones. Each time an element moves from the unsorted sublist to the sorted sublist, one sort pass is completed (Figure 8-20). Given a list of n elements, the bubble sort requires up to $n - 1$ passes to sort the data.

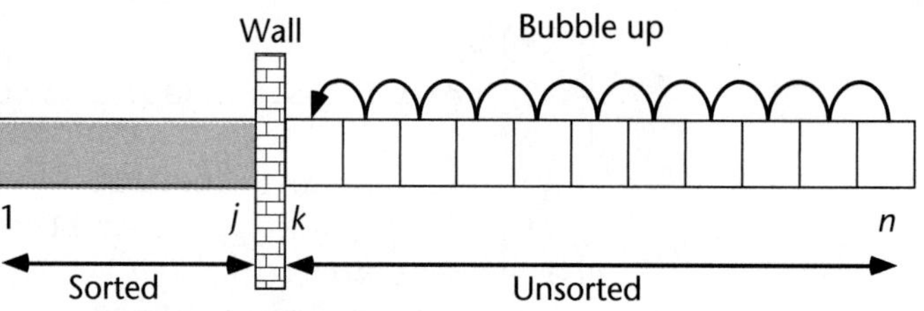

Figure 8-20 Bubble sort concept

Figure 8-21 shows how the wall moves one element in each pass. Looking at the first pass, we start with 56 and compare it to 32. Since 56 is not less than 32, it is not moved and we step down one element. No exchanges take place until we compare 45 to 8. Since 8 is less than 45, the two elements are exchanged and we step down one element. Because 8 was moved down, it is now compared to 78 and these two elements are exchanged. Finally, 8 is compared to 23 and exchanged. This series of exchanges places 8 in the first location, and the wall is moved up one position.

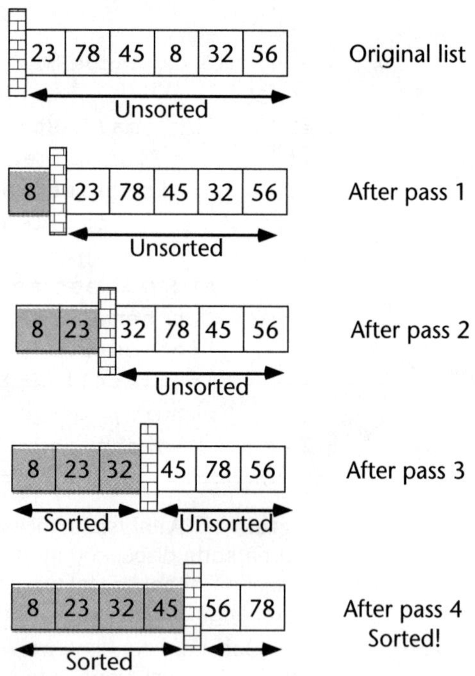

Figure 8-21 Bubble sort example

The bubble sort was originally written to "bubble up" the highest element in the list. From an efficiency point of view, it makes no difference whether the high element is bubbled or the low element is bubbled. From a consistency point of view, however, it makes comparisons between the sorts easier if all three of them work in the same manner. For that reason, we have chosen to bubble the lowest value in each pass.

BUBBLE SORT ALGORITHM

Like the selection sort algorithm, the bubble sort algorithm is quite simple. In each pass through the data, controlled by a *for* loop, the lowest element is *bubbled* to the beginning of the unsorted segment of the array. The bubbling process is actually accomplished in the called function, `bubbleUp`.

Each time it is called, `bubbleUp` makes one pass through the data. When it finds two elements out of sequence, it exchanges them. It then continues with the next element. This process allows the smallest element to be bubbled to the beginning of the array while at the same time adjacent elements along the way are being rearranged. The `bubbleSort` program is shown in Program 8-8, and `bubbleUp` is shown in Program 8-9.

Program 8-8 bubbleSort

```
/* Sort list using bubble sort. Adjacent elements are
   compared and exchanged until list is completely ordered.
      Pre  The list must contain at least one item
           last is index to last element in list
      Post List sorted low to high
*/
void bubbleSort (int list [], int last)
{
    for(int current = 0; current < last; current++)
       bubbleUp (list, current, last);
   return;
} // bubbleSort
```

Program 8-9 bubbleUp

```
/* Move the lowest element in unsorted portion of an
   array to the current element in the unsorted portion.
      Pre  list must contain at least one element
           current is start of unsorted data
           last is end of the unsorted data
      Post Array segment rearranged so that lowest
           element at beginning of unsorted portion
*/
```

Program 8-9 bubbleUp *(continued)*

```
void bubbleUp (int list[], int current, int last)
{
   for (int walker = last; walker > current; walker--)
      if (list[walker]  < list[walker - 1])
        {
         int temp            = list[walker];
         list[walker]        = list[walker - 1];
         list[walker - 1] = temp;
         } // if
   return;
} // bubbleUp
```

Program 8-9 Analysis If the data being sorted are already in sequence, `bubbleSort` will still go through the array element by element. One common modification is to stop the sort if there are no exchanges in `bubbleUp`. This change would require that `bubbleUp` return a "sorted" flag. You will encounter this modification in the practice sets at the end of the chapter.

INSERTION SORT

The **insertion sort** algorithm is one of the most common sorting techniques used by card players. Each card a player picks up is inserted into the proper place in his or her hand to maintain a particular sequence. (As an aside, card sorting is an example of a sort that uses two pieces of data to sort: suit and rank.)

In the insertion sort, as in the other two sorting algorithms we have discussed in this chapter, the list is divided into two parts: sorted and unsorted. In each pass, the first element of the unsorted sublist is picked up, transferred to the sorted sublist, and inserted at the appropriate place. Note that a list of n elements will take at most $n - 1$ passes to sort the data (Figure 8-22).

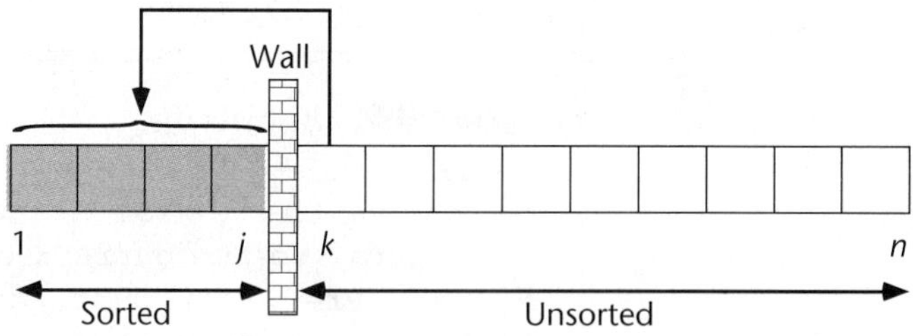

Figure 8-22 Insertion sort concept

Figure 8-23 traces the insertion sort through our list of six numbers. Each pass moves the wall as an element is removed from the unsorted sublist and inserted into the sorted sublist.

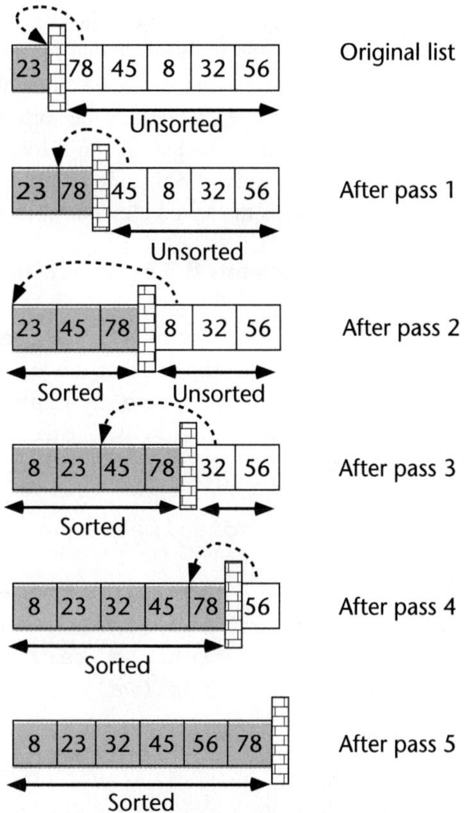

Figure 8-23 Insertion sort example

INSERTION SORT ALGORITHM

The design of the insertion sort follows the same pattern we saw in both the selection sort and the bubble sort—the sort function calls a subfunction for each sort pass. The called function then inserts the first element from the unsorted list into its proper position relative to the rest of the data in the sorted list. Program 8-10 shows the insertion sort.

Program 8-10 insertionSort

```
/* Sort list using Insertion Sort. The list is divided
   into sorted and unsorted list. With each pass, first
   element in unsorted list is inserted into sorted list.
      Pre   List must contain at least one element
            last is index to last element in the list
      Post  List has been rearranged
*/
void insertionSort (int list[], int last)
{
   for (int current = 1; current <= last; current++)
      insertOne(list, current);
   return;
} // insertionSort
```

Note how the exchange is worked in this sort. Before the loop starts, `insertOne` (Program 8-11) puts the data from the current element into a holding area. This is the first step in the exchange. It then looks for the correct position to place the element by starting with the largest element in the sorted list and working toward the beginning. As it searches, it spreads the sorted portion of the list by shifting each element one position higher in the list. When it locates the correct position, therefore, the data have already been moved right one position and the current location is "empty," so the sort simply places the saved element in its proper location, completing the exchange.

Program 8-11 insertOne

```
/* Sorts current element in unsorted list into its proper
   location in sorted portion of the list--one sort pass.
      Pre   list must contain at least one element
            current is beginning of unsorted list
      Post  next element in its proper location
*/
void insertOne (int list[], int current)
{
   bool located = false;
   int  temp    = list[current];
   int  walker;
   for (walker = current - 1; walker >= 0 && !located;)
   {
      if (temp < list[walker])
         {
          list[walker + 1] = list[walker];
          walker--;
         } // if
      else
         located = true;
   } // for loop
   list [walker + 1] = temp;
   return;
} // insertOne
```

INSERTION SORT REPROGRAMMED

In all three sorts, we have used two functions: one to control the sort phase loop and one to control the reordering of data. We did this to emphasize the sort operation; however, it is not the way you would write the sort in the field. Program 8-12 rewrites the insertion sort as it would normally be programmed.

Program 8-12 Reprogrammed insertion sort

```
/* Test driver for insertion sort.
      Written by:
      Date:
*/
#include <iostream>
#include <iomanip>
using namespace std;
```

Program 8-12 **Reprogrammed insertion sort (*continued*)**

```

#define cMAX_ARY_SIZE 15

void insertionSort (int list[], int last);

int main ()
{
   int ary[cMAX_ARY_SIZE] = { 89, 72,  3, 15, 21,
                              57, 61, 44, 19, 98,
                               5, 77, 39, 59, 61 };

   cout << "Unsorted array: ";
   for (int i = 0; i < cMAX_ARY_SIZE; i++)
         cout << setw(3) << ary[i];

   insertionSort (ary, cMAX_ARY_SIZE - 1);

   cout << "\nSorted array:   ";
   for (int i = 0; i < cMAX_ARY_SIZE; i++)
         cout << setw(3) << ary[i];
   cout << endl;
   return 0;
}  // main

/* ================ insertionSort =================
   Sort list using Insertion Sort. The list is divided
   into sorted and unsorted list. With each pass, first
   element in unsorted list is inserted into sorted list.
      Pre   list must contain at least one element
            last contains index to last element in list
      Post  list has been rearranged
*/
void insertionSort (int list[], int last)
{

   for (int current = 1; current <= last; current++)
      {
       int walker;
       int located = false;
       int temp     = list[current];
       for (walker = current - 1; walker >= 0 && !located;)
          {
           if (temp < list[walker])
              {
               list[walker + 1] = list[walker];
               walker--;
              } // if
           else
               located = true;
```

Program 8-12 Reprogrammed insertion sort (*continued*)

```
            } // for loop
         list [walker + 1] = temp;
        } // for
    return;
} // insertionSort
```

```
Results:
Unsorted:  89 72  3 15 21 57 61 44 19 98  5 77 39 59 61
Sorted  :   3  5 15 19 21 39 44 57 59 61 61 72 77 89 98
```

Program 8-12 Analysis As you can see, we simply copied the statements from `insertOne` into the *for* loop, replacing the function call. Of greater interest is our code for the test driver. We began by creating and printing an array. Then, after calling the insertion sort function, we reprinted the array to verify that the sort worked. When you write functions that are used in other programs, you need to write a test driver to verify that they work.

SORT CONCLUSIONS

In this section, we have covered three classic sorts. With the exception of the insertion sort, they are not generally implemented in production systems. The insertion sort is used as a subfunction in both Quicksort and Singleton's variation, Quickersort, which are considered the best general-purpose sorts.

Historically, however, these three sorts are the foundation of the improved and faster sorting methods that you will study in a data structures course. The selection sort is the foundation of a sorting method called the heap sort; the bubble sort is the foundation for Quicksort and Quickersort; and the insertion sort is the foundation of a sorting method called Shell Sort.

8-6 SEARCHING

Another common operation in computer science is **searching**, which is the process used to find the location of a target among a list of objects. In the case of an array, searching means that given a value, we want to find the location (index) of the first element in the array that contains that value. The search concept is illustrated in Figure 8-24.

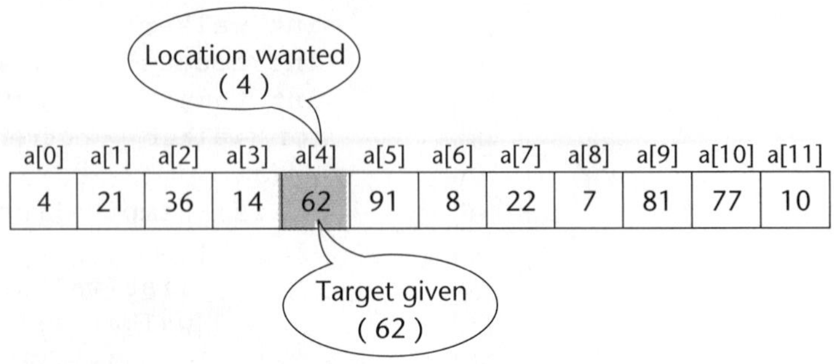

Figure 8-24 Search concept

The algorithm used to search a list depends to a large extent on the structure of the list. Since our structure is currently limited to arrays, we will study searches that work with arrays.

There are two basic searches for arrays: the sequential search and the binary search. The sequential search can be used to locate an item in any array, whereas the binary search requires the list to be sorted.

SEQUENTIAL SEARCH

The **sequential search** is used if the list being searched is not ordered. Generally, you would use this technique only for small lists or lists that are not searched often. In other cases, the best approach is to first sort the list and then search it using the binary search discussed later.

In the sequential search, we start searching for the target from the beginning of the list, and we continue until either we find the target or we are sure that it is not in the list (because we reach the end of the list). In Figure 8-25, we trace the steps to find the value 62. We first check the data at index 0, and, then at 1, 2, and 3 before finding the 62 in the fifth element (index 4).

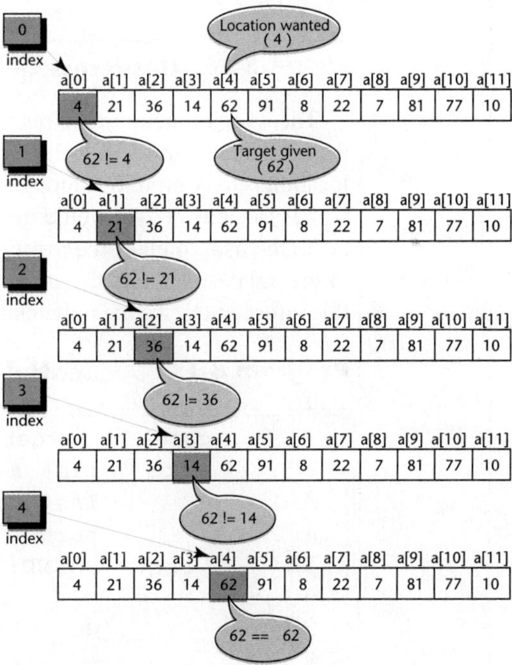

Figure 8-25 Locating data in an unordered list

What if the target we were seeking was not in the list? In that case, we would have to examine each element until we reached the end of the list. Figure 8-26 traces the search for a target of 72 to show an example of how this works.

Now we'll write the sequential search function. A search function needs to tell the calling function two things: Did it find the data it was looking for? If it did, what is the index at which the data were found?

But a function can return only one value. For search functions, we use the return value to designate whether we found the target or not. To "return" the index location where the data were found, we will use pass by reference.

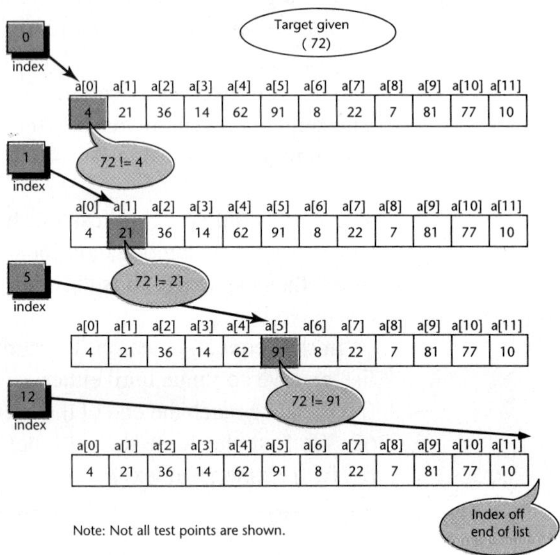

Figure 8-26 Unsuccessful search in an unordered list

The search function requires four parameters: the list we are searching, the index to the last element in the list, the target, and the address where the found element's index location is to be stored. Although we could write the function without passing the index to the last element, that would mean the search would have to know how many elements are in the list. To make the function as flexible as possible, therefore, we pass the index of the last data value in the array. This is also a good structured design technique. With this information, we are now ready to write the algorithm (Program 8-13).

Program 8-13 Sequential search

```
/* Locate the target in an unordered list of size elements.
       Pre   list must contain at least one item
             last is index to last element in list
             target contains data to be located
       Post  FOUND: matching index stored in locn
                    return true
             NOT FOUND: last stored in locn
                        return false
*/
bool seqSearch (int  list[], int  last, int  target,
                int& locn)
{
   int looker = 0;
   while (looker < last && target != list[looker])
      looker++;
   locn = looker;
   return (target == list[looker]);
} // seqSearch
```

Program 8-13 Analysis Program 8-13 is relatively simple, but it does merit some discussion. First, why did we use a *while* statement? Even though we know the limits of the array, it is still an event-controlled loop. We search until we find what we are looking for or reach the end of the list. Finding something is an event, so we use an event loop.

Next, note that there are two tests in the limit expression of the loop. We have coded the test for the end of the array first. In this case, it doesn't make any difference which test is first from an execution point of view, but in other search loops it might. It is good practice to always code the limit test first because it doesn't use an indexed value and is therefore safer. A typical call to the search would look like the statement shown in the next example.

```
found = seqSearch (stuAry, lastStu, stuID, locn);
```

Notice how succinct the function in Program 8-13 is. In fact, there are more lines of documentation than there are lines of code. The entire search is contained in one *while* statement. So why write the function at all? Why not just put the one line of code wherever it is needed? The answer lies in the structured programming concepts that each function should do only one thing and that code should be **reusable**, if possible. By isolating the search process in its own function, we separate it from the process that needs the search. This makes the code reusable in other parts of the program and portable to other programs that require a searching function.

One final point: This function assumes that the list is not ordered. If the list was ordered, we could improve the search slightly when the data we were looking for were not in the list. We will leave this improvement for a problem at the end of the chapter.

BINARY SEARCH

The sequential search algorithm is very slow. If we have an array of one million elements, we must do one million comparisons in the worst case. If the array is not sorted, this is the only solution. If the array is sorted, however, we can use a more efficient algorithm called the **binary search**. Generally speaking, programmers use a binary search when a list starts to become large. We suggest that you consider binary searches when a list contains more than 16 elements.

The binary search starts by testing the data in the element at the middle of the array. This determines if the target is in the first half or the second half of the list. If it is in the first half, there is no need to check the second half any more. If it is in the second half, there is no need to test the first half any more. In other words, we eliminate half the list from further consideration. We repeat this process until we find the target or satisfy ourselves that it is not in the list.

To find the middle of the list, we need three variables: one to identify the beginning of the list, one to identify the middle of the list, and one to identify the end of the list. We will analyze two cases: (1) the target is in the list and (2) the target is not in the list.

Target Found

Figure 8-27 shows how we find 22 in a sorted array. We descriptively call our three indexes `first`, `mid`, and `last`. Given `first` as 0 and `last` as 11, we can calculate mid as shown in the next example:[1]

```
mid = (first + last) / 2;
```

[1]This formula does not work if the number of elements in the array is greater than half MAX_INT. In this case, the correct formula is: `mid = first + ( last - first ) / 2`.

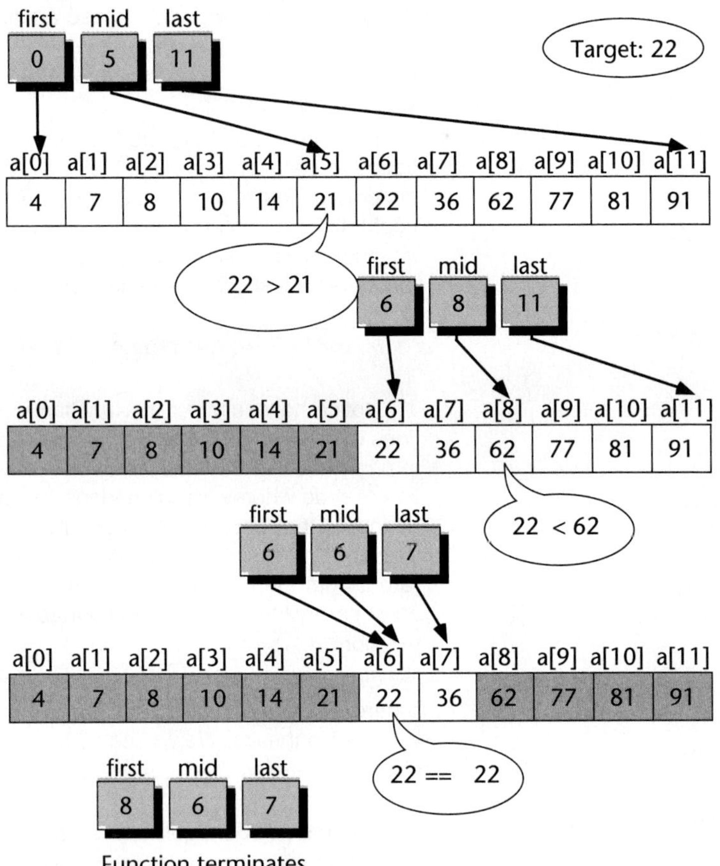

Figure 8-27 Binary search example

Since the index `mid` is an integer, the result will be the integral value of the quotient; that is, it truncates rather than rounds the calculation. Given the data in Figure 8-27, `mid` becomes 5 as a result of the first calculation.

```
mid = (0 + 11) / 2 = 11 / 2 = 5
```

At index location 5, we discover that the target is greater than the list value (22 > 21). We can therefore eliminate the array locations 0 through 5. (Note that `mid` is automatically eliminated.) To narrow our search, we assign `mid + 1` to `first` and repeat the search. The next loop calculates `mid` with the new value for `first` and determines that the midpoint is now 8.

```
mid = (6 + 11) / 2 = 17 / 2 = 8
```

Again we test the target to the value at `mid`, and this time we discover that the target is less than the list value (22 < 62). This time we adjust the ends of the list by setting `last` to `mid – 1` and recalculate `mid`. This effectively eliminates elements 8 through 11 from consideration. We have now arrived at index location 6, whose value matches our target. This stops the search (see Figure 8-27).

Target Not Found

A more interesting case is when the target is not in the list. We must construct our search algorithm so that it stops when we have checked all possible locations. This is done in the binary search by testing for `first` and `last` crossing; that is, we are done when `first` becomes greater than `last`. Thus, only two conditions terminate the binary search algorithm: Either the target is found or `first` becomes larger than `last`. Let us demonstrate this situation with an example. Imagine we want to find 11 in our binary search array. This situation is shown in Figure 8-28.

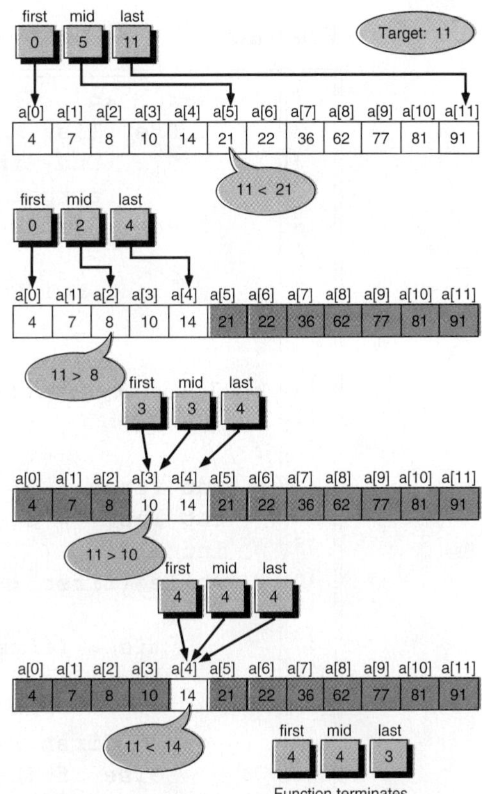

Figure 8-28 Unsuccessful binary search example

In this example, the loop continues to narrow the range as we saw in the successful search until we are examining the data at index locations 3 and 4. These settings of `first` and `last` set the `mid` index to 3.

```
mid = (3 + 4) / 2 = 7 / 2 = 3
```

The test at index location 3 indicates that the target is greater than the list value, so we set `first` to `mid + 1` or 4. We now test the data at location 4 and discover that 11 < 14.

```
mid = (4 + 4) / 2 = 8/ 2 = 4
```

At this point, what we have discovered is that the target should be between two adjacent values; in other words, it is not in the list. We see this algorithmically because `last` is set to `mid – 1`, which makes `first` greater than `last`, the signal that the value we are looking for is not in the list.

Program 8-14 contains the implementation of the binary search algorithm we have been describing. Similar to the design used for the sequential search, the first three parameters describe the list and the target we are looking for, and the last parameter contains the alias into which we place the located index. One point worth noting: When we terminate the loop with a not-found condition, the index returned is unpredictable—that is, it may indicate the node greater than or less than the value in `target`.

Program 8-14 Binary search

```
/* Search an ordered list using binary search.
      Pre  list must contain at least one element
           end--index to the largest element in list
           target is value of element being sought
      Post  FOUND--locn = index to target
                   return true
            NOT FOUND--locn = element < or > target
                       return false
*/
bool binarySearch (int  list[], int end, int target,
                   int& locn)
{
   int first = 0;
   int last  = end;
   int mid;
   while (first <= last)
      {
       mid = (first + last) / 2;
       if (target > list[mid])
          // look in upper half
          first = mid + 1;
       else if (target < list[mid])
          // look in lower half
          last = mid - 1;
       else
          // found equal: force exit
          first = last + 1;
      } // end while
   locn = mid;
   return target == list [mid];
}  // binarySearch
```

8-7 TWO-DIMENSIONAL ARRAYS

The arrays we have discussed so far are known as **one-dimensional arrays** because the data are organized linearly in only one direction. Many applications require that data be stored in more than one dimension. One common example is a table, which is an array that consists of rows and columns. Figure 8-29 shows a table, which is commonly called a **two-dimensional array**.

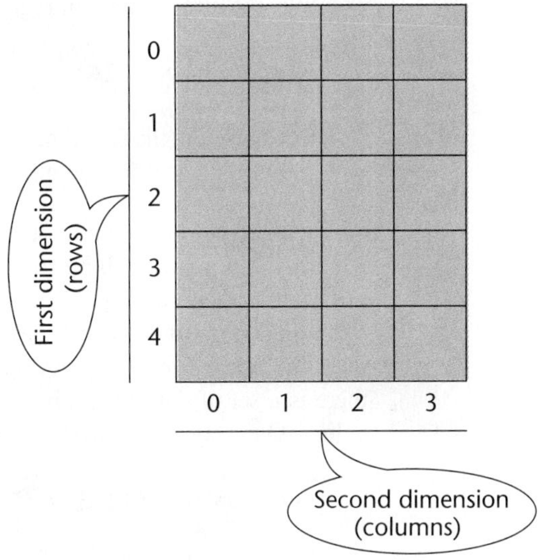

Figure 8-29 Two-dimensional array

Although a two-dimensional array is exactly what is shown by Figure 8-29, C++ looks at it in a different way. It considers the two-dimensional array to be an array of arrays. In other words, a two-dimensional array in C++ is an array of one-dimensional arrays. This concept is shown in Figure 8-30.

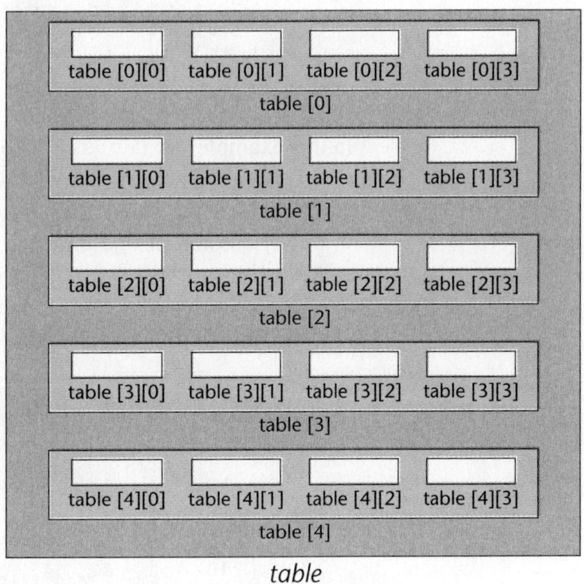

Figure 8-30 Array of arrays

DECLARING AND DEFINING TWO-DIMENSIONAL ARRAYS

Like one-dimensional arrays, two-dimensional arrays must be declared and defined before being used. Declaration and definition tell the compiler the name of the array, the type of each element, and the size of each dimension. As we saw with the one-dimensional array, the size of the array is a constant and must have a value at compilation time. For example, the array shown in Figure 8-30 can be declared and defined as follows:

```
int table[5][4];
```

By convention, the first dimension specifies the number of **rows** in the array. The second dimension specifies the number of **columns** in each row.

Initialization

As we noted before, declaration and definition only reserve memory for the elements in the array. No values will be stored. If we don't initialize the array, the contents are unpredictable. Generally speaking, all arrays should be initialized.

Initialization of the array elements can be done when the array is defined. As with one-dimensional arrays, the values must be enclosed in braces. This time, however, there is a set of data for each dimension in the array. So for `table`, we will need 20 values. One way to initialize it is shown below.

```
int table[5][4] =
    {0,1,2,3,10,11,\
     12,13,20,21,22,23,30,31,32,33,40,41,42,43};
```

It is highly recommended, however, that you nest the data in braces to show the exact nature of the array. For example, array `table` is better initialized as shown below.

```
int table [5][4] =
    {
     { 0, 1, 2, 3 },
     { 10, 11, 12, 13},
     { 20, 21, 22, 23},
     { 30, 31, 32, 33},
     { 40, 41, 42, 43}
    };
```

In this example, we define each row as a one-dimensional array of four elements enclosed in braces. The array of five rows also has its set of braces. Note that there are commas between the elements in the rows and also commas between the rows.

In our discussion of one-dimensional arrays, we said that if the array is completely initialized with supplied values, it is not necessary to specify the size of the array. This concept carries forward to multidimensional arrays, except that only the first dimension can be omitted. All others must be specified. The format is shown below.

```
int table [ ][4] =
    {
     { 0, 1, 2, 3},
     { 10, 11, 12, 13 },
     { 20, 21, 22, 23 },
     { 30, 31, 32, 33 },
     { 40, 41, 42, 43 }
    };
```

To initialize the whole array to zeros, we specify only the first value, as shown next.

```
int table [5][4] = {0};
```

Inputting Values

Another way to fill up the values is to read them from the keyboard. For a two-dimensional array this usually requires nested *for* loops. If the array is an *n* by *m* array, the first loop varies the row from 0 to $n - 1$. The second loop varies the column from 0 to $m - 1$. The code to fill the array in Figure 8-30 is shown below.

```
for (int row = 0; row < 5; row++)
    for (int column = 0; column < 4; column++)
          cin >> table[row][column]);
```

When the program runs, we enter the 20 values for the elements, and they are stored in the appropriate locations.

Outputting Values

We can also print the value of the elements one by one using two nested loops. Again, the first loop controls the printing of the rows, and the second loop controls the printing of the columns. To print the table in its table format, a new line is printed at the end of each row. The code to print Figure 8-30 is shown below.

```
for (int row = 0; row < 5; row++)
    {
     for (int column = 0; column < 4; column++)
         cout << setw(8) << table[row][column]);
     cout << endl;
    }
```

Accessing Values

Individual elements can be initialized using the assignment operator.

```
table [2] [0] = 23;
table [0] [1] = table [3][2] + 15;
```

Let us assume that we want to initialize our 5 × 4 array as shown below.

```
00    01    02    03
10    11    12    13
20    21    22    23
30    31    32    33
40    41    42    43
```

One way to do this would be to code the values by hand. However, it is much more interesting to examine the pattern and then assign values to the elements in the array using an algorithm. Do you see any patterns? One is that the value in each element increases by 1 from its predecessor in the row. Another is that the first element in each row is the row index times 10. With these two patterns, we should be able to write nested loops to fill the array. The code to initialize the patterns for the following array is given in Program 8-15.

```
int table [cMAX_ROWS][cMAX_COLUMNS];
```

Program 8-15 Fill two-dimensional array

```
/* This function fills an array such that each array
   element contains a number that, when viewed as a
   two-digit integer, the first digit is the row number
   and the second digit is the column number.
      Pre   table is array in memory
            numRows is number of rows in array
      Post  array has been initialized
*/
void fillArray (int table[][cMAX_COLS], int numRows)
{
   for (int row = 0; row < numRows; row++)
      {
       table [row][0] = row * 10;
       for (int col = 1; col < cMAX_COLS; col++)
         table[row][col] = table[row][col - 1] + 1;
      } // for
} // fillArray
```

Memory Layout

As discussed earlier, the indexes in the definition of a two-dimensional array represent rows and columns. This format maps to the way the data are laid out in memory. If we were to consider memory as a row of bytes with the lowest address on the left and the highest address on the right, then an array would be placed in memory with the first element to the left and the last element to the right. Similarly, if the array is a two-dimensional array, then the first dimension is a row of elements that are stored to the left. This is known as "row-major" storage and is shown in Figure 8-31.[2]

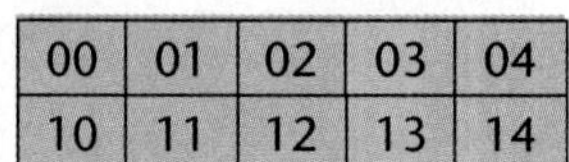

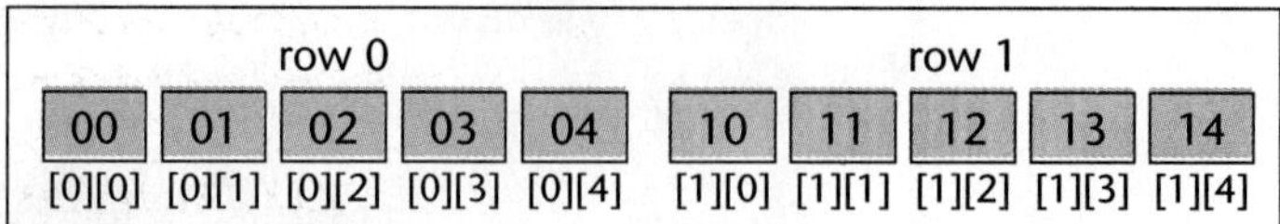

Figure 8-31 Memory layout

Memory Example: Map One Array to Another

Program 8-16 further demonstrates how data are laid out in memory. The program converts a two-dimensional array to a one-dimensional array

[2]At least one language, FORTRAN, reverses the placement of data values in memory. It stores data by columns.

Program 8-16 Convert table to one-dimensional array

```
1  /* This program changes a two-dimensional array to the
2     corresponding one-dimensional array.
3        Written by:
4        Date:
5  */
6  #include <iostream>
7  #include <iomanip>
8  using namespace std;
9
10 const int cROWS = 2;
11 const int cCOLS = 5;
12
13 int main ()
14 {
15    int table [cROWS] [cCOLS] =
16         {
17          { 00, 01, 02, 03, 04 },
18          { 10, 11, 12, 13, 14 }
19         };
20    int line [cROWS * cCOLS];
21
22    for (int row = 0; row < cROWS; row++)
23       for (int column = 0; column < cCOLS; column++)
24         line[row * cCOLS + column] = table[row][column];
25
26    cout << setfill ('0');
27    for (int row = 0; row < cROWS * cCOLS; row++)
28       cout << setw(2) << line[row] << " ";
29    return 0;
30 } // main
```

```
Results:
00  01  02  03  04  10  11  12  13  14
```

Program 8-16 Analysis In Program 8-16 we use nested *for* loops to make the conversion. The first loop controls the table rows, and the second loop controls the columns within each row. Since we know how many elements are in each row of the two-dimensional array, we can map it to the one-dimensional array by simply multiplying the row index by the number of elements in each row. When we are in row 0, we multiply the number of elements in one row (designated by the constant, COLS) by the row number (0) and add the result to the column. This maps the elements in the two-dimensional array to the beginning of the receiving array. When we are in row 1, we add the number of elements in one row times the row (1) to the current column, which maps the elements to the next set (in this case, 5...9). To generalize, we add the product of the row and the number of elements in a row to the column to determine the receiving location.

Study the technique we used to define the number of elements in the rows and columns (see statements 10 and 11). Note how they are used not only to define the arrays, but also to control the loop execution. To get a better understanding of the differences, copy this program and then run it with different row-column sizes. (You will have to change the initialization also. You might want to consider initializing the values by assignments within *for* loops.)

Finally, study the *for* loops carefully. Note how we defined the loop variables in each statement. This code proves that the initialization definition in the *for* statement is local to only the statement itself. If they weren't, then we would get a duplicate variable definition compile error when we defined `row` in statement 27.

PASSING A TWO-DIMENSIONAL ARRAY TO A FUNCTION

With two-dimensional arrays, there are three choices for passing parts of the array to a function. First, we can pass individual elements. We saw how to do that in "Passing Individual Elements" on page 356. Second, we can pass a row of the array. This would be similar to passing an array, as we saw in "Passing the Whole Array" on page 357. Finally, we could pass the whole array.

Passing a Row

The second case, **passing a row of the array**, is rather interesting. We pass a whole row by indexing the array name with only the row number. Referring to Figure 8-32, we see that a row is four integers. When we pass the row, therefore, the receiving function

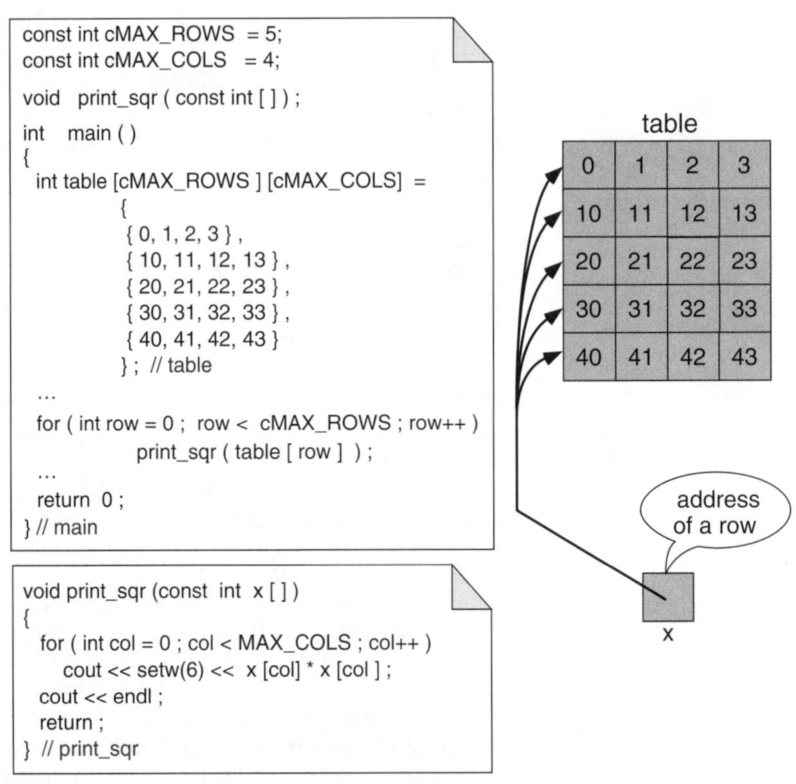

Figure 8-32 Passing a row

receives a one-dimensional array of four integers. The *for* loop in `print_sqr` prints the square of each of the four elements. After printing all the values, the function advances to the next line on the console and returns. The *for* loop in *main* calls `print_sqr` five times so that the final result is a table of the values squared shown on the monitor.

Note that we have defined the array dimensions as memory constants. This allows us to symbolically refer to the limits of the array in both the array definition and the *for* loops. Now, if we need to change the size of the array, all that is necessary is to change the constant values and recompile the program.

Passing the Whole Array

When we pass a two-dimensional array to a function, we use the array name as the actual parameter just as we did with one-dimensional arrays. The formal parameter in the called function header, however, must indicate that the array has two dimensions. The rules for declaring the array in the function are:

1. The function must be called by passing only the array name.
2. The size of the *second* dimension required.

The following code demonstrates how pass a two-dimensional array to a function (`average`) and how we declare in a function header.

```
ave = average (table);
...
double average (table [ ][cMAX_COLS])
{
   ...
}  // average
```

Note that again we do not have to specify the number of rows. It is necessary, however, to specify the size of the second dimension, so we specified the number of columns in the second dimension (`cMAX_COLS`). In summary, to pass two-dimensional arrays to functions,

1. The function must be called by passing only the array name.
2. In the function definition, the formal parameter is a two-dimensional array, with the size of the *second* dimension required.

For example, we can use a function to calculate the average of the integers in an array. In this case, we pass the name of the array to the function as shown in Figure 8-33.

ARRAY EXAMPLE

Now we can write a program that fills the left-to-right diagonal of a square matrix (a two-dimensional array with an equal number of rows and columns) with 0s, the lower left triangle with –1s, and the upper right triangle with +1s.The program code is shown in Program 8-17. The output of the program, assuming a six-by-six matrix, is shown in Figure 8-34.

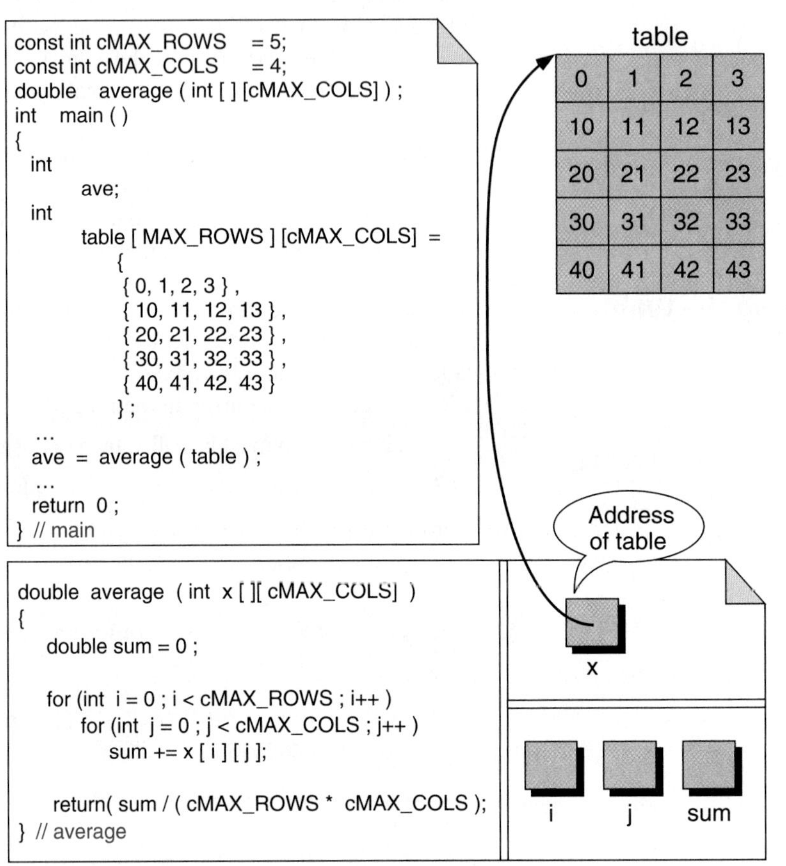

const int cMAX_ROWS = 5;
const int cMAX_COLS = 4;
double average (int [ ] [cMAX_COLS]) ;
int main ( )
{
int
ave;
int
table [MAX_ROWS] [cMAX_COLS] =
{
{ 0, 1, 2, 3 } ,
{ 10, 11, 12, 13 } ,
{ 20, 21, 22, 23 } ,
{ 30, 31, 32, 33 } ,
{ 40, 41, 42, 43 }
} ;
...
ave = average (table) ;
...
return 0 ;
} // main
table
0 1 2 3
10 11 12 13
20 21 22 23
30 31 32 33
40 41 42 43
Address of table
double average (int x [ ][cMAX_COLS])
{
double sum = 0 ;
for (int i = 0 ; i < cMAX_ROWS ; i++)
for (int j = 0 ; j < cMAX_COLS ; j++)
sum += x [i] [j];
return(sum / (cMAX_ROWS * cMAX_COLS);
} // average
x
i
j
sum

Figure 8-33 Calculate average of integers in array

Program 8-17 Fill matrix

```
/* This program fills the diagonal of a matrix (square
   array) with 0, the lower left triangle with -1 and the
   upper right triangle with 1.
      Written by:
      Date:
*/
#include <iostream>
#include <iomanip>
using namespace std;

int main ()
{
   int table [6][6];

   for (int row = 0; row < 6; row++)
      for (int column = 0; column < 6; column++)
         if (row == column)
            table [row][column] = 0;
```

Program 8-17 Fill matrix *(continued)*

```
            else if (row > column)
               table [row][column] = -1;
            else
               table [row][column] = 1;

      for (int row = 0; row < 6; row++)
         {
          for (int column = 0; column < 6; column++)
               cout << setw(4) << table[row][column];
          cout << endl;
         } // for row
      return 0;
   }  // main
```

Program 8-17 Analysis This is a rather simple pattern problem similar to many we saw in Chapter 6. The only difference is that now we are creating the pattern in array elements. Since there are two dimensions, we use two loops to control the pattern. If the row equals the column, we assign 0 to the element. If the row is greater than the column, meaning we are in the lower half of the matrix, we assign –1. And if the row is less than the column, then we are in the upper half of the matrix and we assign +1.

0	1	1	1	1	1
-1	0	1	1	1	1
-1	-1	0	1	1	1
-1	-1	-1	0	1	1
-1	-1	-1	-1	0	1
-1	-1	-1	-1	-1	0

Figure 8-34 Example of filled matrix

8-8 MULTIDIMENSIONAL ARRAYS

Multidimensional arrays can have three, four, or more dimensions. Figure 8-35 shows an array of three dimensions. Note the terminology used to describe the array. The first dimension is called a **plane**, which consists of rows and columns. Arrays of four or more dimensions can be created and used, but they are difficult to draw.

Although a **three-dimensional array** is exactly what is shown in Figure 8-35, the C++ language looks at it in a different way. C++ takes the three-dimensional array to be an array of two-dimensional arrays, and it considers the two-dimensional array to be an array of one-dimensional arrays. In other words, a three-dimensional array in C++ is an array of arrays of arrays. This concept also holds true for arrays of more than three dimensions. The C++ view of a three-dimensional array is illustrated in Figure 8-36.

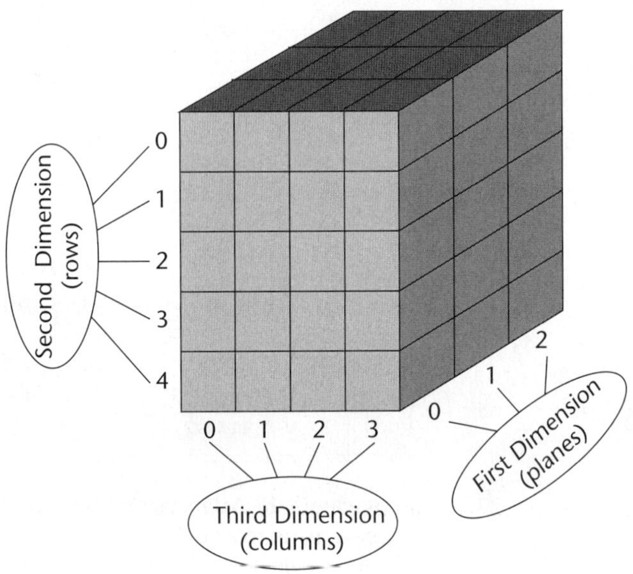

Figure 8-35 A three-dimensional array (3 × 5 × 4)

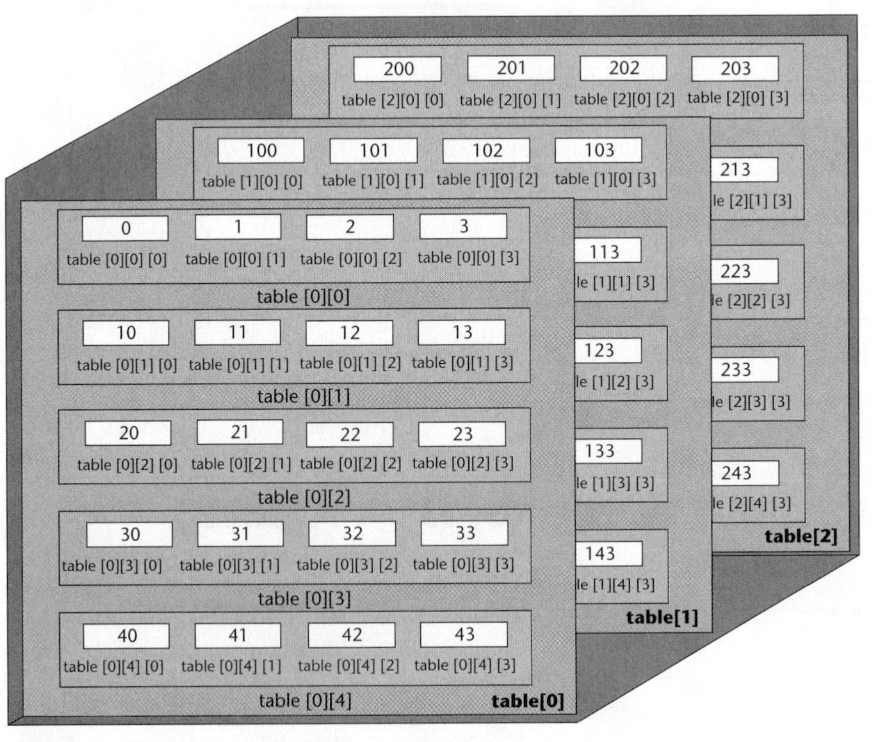

Figure 8-36 C++ view of three-dimensional array

DECLARING AND DEFINING MULTI-DIMENSIONAL ARRAYS

Like one-dimensional arrays, multidimensional arrays must be declared and defined before being used. Declaration and definition tell the compiler the name of the array, the type of each element, and the size of each dimension. The size of the array is a constant and must have a value at compilation time. The three-dimensional array shown in Figure 8-36 can be declared and defined as follows:

```
int table [3][5][4];
```

Initialization

As we said earlier, declaration and definition only reserve space for the elements in the array. No values will be stored in the array. If we want to store values, we must either initialize the elements, read values from the keyboard, or assign values to each individual element.

The initialization of multidimensional arrays relies on a simple extension of the concept used for initializing a two-dimensional array (see page 384). For the three-dimensional array, we nest each plane in a set of braces. For each plane, we bracket the rows as we did for the two-dimensional array. If you group the data by plane and row as we have done in Figure 8-37, the reader will be able to visualize the array with ease. We have added comments to make it even easier to read the values.

```
int table[3][5][4] =
      {
       { // Plane 0
         {0, 1, 2, 3},                // Row 0
         {10, 11, 12, 13} ,           // Row 1
         {20, 21, 22, 23},            // Row 2
         {30, 31, 32, 33},            // Row 3
         {40, 41, 42, 43}             // Row 4
       },
       { // Plane 1
         {100, 101, 102, 103},        // Row 0
         {110, 111, 112, 113},        // Row 1
         {120, 121, 122, 123},        // Row 2
         {130, 131, 132, 133},        // Row 3
         {140, 141, 142, 143}         // Row 4
       },
       { // Plane 2
         {200, 201, 202, 203},        // Row 0
         {210, 211, 212, 213},        // Row 1
         {220, 221, 222, 223},        // Row 2
         {230, 231, 232, 233},        // Row 3
         {240, 241, 242, 243}         // Row 4
       }
      }; // table
```

Figure 8-37 Initializing a three-dimensional array

As we saw previously, the plane's size, and only the plane's size, does not have to be specified when we use explicit initialization. The size of all dimensions after the first must be explicitly stated.

Of course, if we want to initialize all the elements to 0, we can simply initialize only the first element to 0 and let the compiler generate the code to initialize the rest of the array to 0s.

```
int table [3][5][4] = {0};
```

8-9 PROGRAMMING EXAMPLE—CALCULATE ROW AND COLUMN AVERAGES

This programming example contains many of the programming techniques used in array problems. It contains three arrays: a two-dimensional array of integers, and two one-dimensional arrays of averages, one for rows and one for columns. When you are working with a large program with many different data structures, in this case three arrays, it often helps to draw a picture of the arrays. You can then see how the different arrays work together to solve the problem. A picture of the array structure and their relationships is shown in Figure 8 38.

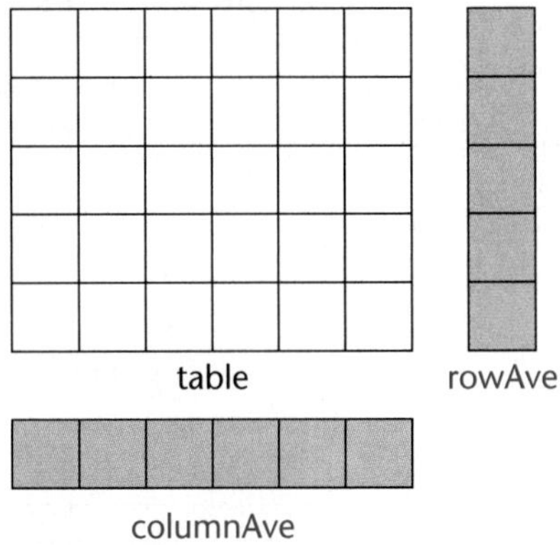

Figure 8-38 Data structures for calculate row-column averages

The program first requests the user to provide data for a two-dimensional array. Once the array has been filled, the program calculates the average of each row and places it in a parallel array of row averages. It then calculates the average for each column and places it in an array of column averages. Note that although we have represented the column-average array horizontally and the row-average array vertically, they are both one-dimensional arrays.

When all the calculations are complete, the program calls a function to print the array with the row averages at the end of each row and the column averages at the bottom of each column. The structure chart for the program is shown in Figure 8-39.

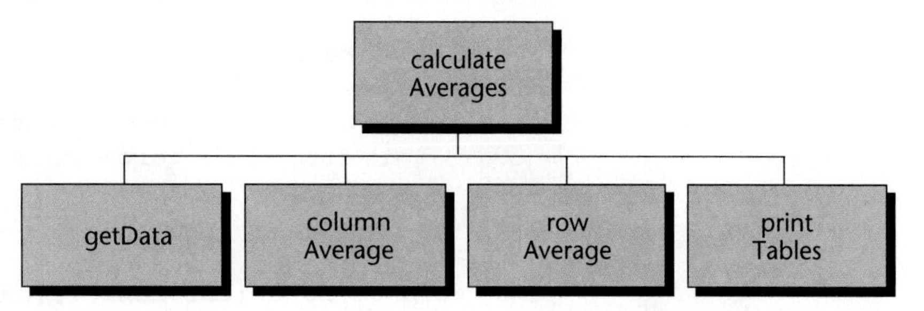

Figure 8-39 Calculate row-column average design

Program 8-18 contains the code.

Program 8-18 Calculate row and column averages

```
/* This program reads values of a two-dimensional array
   from the keyboard and creates two one-dimensional
   arrays, which are the averages of rows and columns.
      Written by:
      Date:
*/
#include <iostream>
#include <iomanip>
using namespace std;

const int cMAX_ROWS = 5;
const int cMAX_COLS = 6;

void getData       (int   table[][cMAX_COLS]);
void columnAverage (const int   table[][cMAX_COLS],
                    float colAvrg []);
void rowAverage    (const int   table[][cMAX_COLS],
                    float rowAvrg []);
void printTables   (const int   table[][cMAX_COLS],
                    const float rowAvrg[],
                    const float colAvrg[]);

int main ( )
{
   int table [cMAX_ROWS][cMAX_COLS];

   float rowAve [cMAX_ROWS]    = { 0 };
   float columnAve [cMAX_COLS] = { 0 };

// Statements
   getData       (table);
   columnAverage (table, columnAve);
   rowAverage    (table, rowAve);
   printTables   (table, rowAve, columnAve);

```

Program 8-18 Calculate row and column averages *(continued)*

```
   return 0;
} // main
/* ================== getData ==================
   This function receives data for two-dimensional array.
     Pre    table is array to be filled with integers
     Post   The array is filled
*/
void getData (int table[][cMAX_COLS])
{
   for (int row = 0; row < cMAX_ROWS; row++)
      for (int col = 0; col < cMAX_COLS; col++)
         {
          cout << "Enter integer and key <return>: ";
          cin >> table[row][col];
         } // for col
   return;
} // getData
/* ================= columnAverage =================
   This function calculates the average for each column.
      Pre   table filled with integer values
      Post  Average calculated and in average array
*/
void columnAverage (const int   table [][cMAX_COLS],
                               float colAvrg[])
{
   for (int col = 0; col < cMAX_COLS; col++)
      {
       for (int row = 0; row < cMAX_ROWS; row++)
          colAvrg [col] += table [row] [col];
       colAvrg [col] /=  cMAX_ROWS;
      } // for
   return;
} // columnAverage
/* ================== rowAverage ==================
   This function calculates the row averages for a table.
      Pre  table has been filled with values
     Post Averages calculated & in the average array
*/
void rowAverage (const int   table[][cMAX_COLS],
                            float rowAvrg [])
{
   for (int row = 0; row < cMAX_ROWS; row++)
      {
       for (int col = 0; col < cMAX_COLS; col++)
          rowAvrg[row] += table [row] [col];
       rowAvrg [row] /=  cMAX_COLS;
      } // for row
   return;
}  // rowAverage
```

Program 8-18 Calculate row and column averages *(continued)*

```
/* ================== printTables ==================
   Print data table, with average of rows at end of each
   row and average of columns below each column.
      Pre   each table has been filled with its data
      Post  the tables have been printed
*/
void printTables (const int   table[][cMAX_COLS],
                  const float rowAvrg[],
                  const float colAvrg[])
{
   cout.setf (ios::fixed);
   cout << setprecision (2);
   for (int row = 0; row < cMAX_ROWS; row++)
      {
       for (int col = 0; col < cMAX_COLS; col++)
          cout << setw(6) << table[row][col];
       cout << "   | " << rowAvrg [row] << endl;
      } // for row

   cout << "------------------------------------\n";
   for (int col = 0; col < cMAX_COLS; col++)
     cout << setw(6) << colAvrg[col];
   return;
} // printTables
// ================ End of Program =================
```

```
Results:
    10    12    14    16    18    20   |  15.00
    22    24    26    28    30    23   |  25.50
    25    27    29    31    33    35   |  30.00
    39    41    43    45    47    49   |  44.00
    51    53    55    57    59    61   |  56.00
---------------------------------------
 29.40 31.40 33.40 35.40 37.40 37.60
```

8-10 SOFTWARE ENGINEERING AND PROGRAMMING STYLE

In this section, we discuss two basic concepts: testing and algorithm efficiency. To be effective, testing must be clearly thought out. We provide some concepts for testing array algorithms by studying sorting and searching. We then continue the algorithm efficiency discussion started in Chapter 6 by studying sort and search algorithms as case studies.

TESTING SORTS

As your programs become more complex, you must spend more time creating test data that will completely validate them. In this section, we examine some techniques for testing sorts.

In general, four tests should be conducted: (1) sort a list of random values; (2) sort a list that is already in sequence; (3) sort a list that is in reverse order; and (4) sort a nearly ordered list, such as one in which every tenth item is one position out of sequence. Table 8-1 contains a summary of the tests that you should conduct and some sample test data to show the points.

Test case	Sample data
Random data	5 23 7 78 22 6 19 33 51 11 93 31
Nearly ordered	5 6 7 21 19 22 23 31 29 33 51 93
Ordered – ascending	5 6 7 11 19 22 23 31 33 51 78 93
Ordered – descending	93 78 51 33 31 23 22 19 11 7 6 5

Table 8-1 Recommended sort test cases

TESTING SEARCHES

When testing the sequential search, only four tests are required. Three deal with finding an element in the table—find the first, last, and any element in the middle. The fourth test deals with trying to find an element that is not in the list—look for any value that is not in the middle of the list.

The binary search requires the four tests discussed above, plus three more. Since it uses an ordered list, you should try to find a target lower than the first element in the list and another target greater than the last element. Finally, you should find two elements that are in adjacent array locations, such as list[0] and list[1]. The reason for this test is that the binary search includes logic that divides by two. An error could result in being able to find only even-numbered or only odd-numbered elements. Testing for adjacent locations ensures that such an error won't happen. These test cases are seen in Table 8-2.

Expected results	Index	Test	Search
found	0	target == list[0]	all
found	1	target == list[1]	binary only
found	$n - 1$	target == list[$n - 1$]	all
found	$0 < i < n - 1$	target == list[i]	all
not found	0	target < list[0]	binary only
not found	$n - 1$	target > list[$n - 1$]	all
not found	$0 < i < n - 1$	target != list[i]	binary only

Table 8-2 Test cases for searches

ANALYZING SORT ALGORITHMS

We have developed three sort algorithms. We examine each of them in this section.

Bubble Sort Analysis

The bubble sort essentially contains the block of code shown below. For simplicity, we have combined the first statement from `bubbleSort` with the loop from `bubbleUp`.

```
for (int current = 0; current <= last; current++)
   for (int walker = last; walker > current; walker--)
      if (list[walker] < list[walker - 1])
         exchange (walker, walker - 1);
```

To determine the relative efficiency, we analyze the two *for* statements. The first *for*, the outer loop, examines each entry in the sort array. It will therefore loop $n - 1$ times.

The inner loop starts at the end of the array and works its way toward the current node as established by the outer loop. The first time it is called, it examines $n - 1$ elements; the second time, $n - 2$ elements; and so forth, until it examines only one element. The average number of elements examined, therefore, is determined as shown below.

$$(n-1) + (n-2) + \cdots + 2 + 1 = n\frac{(n-1)}{2}$$

This is the nested dependent loop. On the average, therefore, each iteration of the outer loop will call the inner loop $(n - 1)/2$ times. The combination of the two loops is therefore

$$n\left(\frac{n-1}{2}\right) = \frac{1}{2}(n^2 - n)$$

Discarding the coefficient and selecting the larger factor, we see that the dominant factor in the bubble sort is n^2, which in big-O notation would be stated as $O(n^2)$ (see "Software Engineering" in Chapter 6).

The efficiency of the bubble sort is $O(n^2)$.

Selection Sort Analysis

Now let's examine the efficiency of the selection sort shown in Program 8-6 on page 368. Its essential, pivotal logic is shown in the next example.

```
for (int current = 0; current < last; current++)
    {
     for (int walker = current+1; walker <= last; walker++)
        if (list[walker] < list[smallest])
            smallest = walker;
    }
```

This algorithm strongly resembles the bubble sort algorithm discussed above. Its first loop looks at every element in the array from the first element (current = 0) to the one just before the last. The inner loop moves from the current element, as determined by `walker`, to the end of the list. This is similar to the bubble sort except that it works from the lower portion of the array toward the end. Using the same analysis, we see that it will test $n((n - 1)/2)$ elements, which means that the selection sort is also $O(n^2)$.

The efficiency of the selection sort is $O(n^2)$.

Insertion Sort Analysis

The last sort we covered was the insertion sort, introduced on page 373. The nucleus of its logic is shown below.

```
for (int current = 1; current <= last; current++)
    for (int walker = current - 1; walker >= 0 && !located;)
        if (temp < list[walker])
            {
             list[walker + 1] = list[walker];
             walker--;
            }
```

Does the pattern look familiar? It should. Again, we have the same basic nested *for* loop logic that we saw in the bubble sort and the selection sort. The outer loop is executed n times and the inner loop is executed $(n - 1)/2$ times, giving us $O(n^2)$.

The efficiency of the insertion sort is $O(n^2)$.

As we have demonstrated, all three of these sorts are $O(n^2)$, which means that they should be used only for small lists or lists that are nearly ordered. You will eventually study sorts that are $O(n\log n)$, which is much more efficient for large lists.

ANALYZING SEARCH ALGORITHMS

All of the sort algorithms we have discussed so far involve nested loops. We now turn our attention to two algorithms that have only one loop: the sequential search and the binary search. Recall that a search is used when we want to find something in an array or other list structure. The `target` is a value obtained from some external source.

Sequential Search

The basic loop for the sequential search is shown below.

```
while (looker < last && target != list[looker])
      looker++;
```

This is a classic example of a linear algorithm. In fact, in some of the literature, this search is known as a **linear search.** Since the algorithm is linear, its efficiency is $O(n)$.

The efficiency of the sequential search is $O(n)$.

Binary Search

The binary search locates an item by repeatedly dividing the list in half. Its loop is

```
while (first <= last)
    {
     mid = (first + last) / 2;
     if (target > list[mid])
        first = mid + 1;
     else if (target < list[mid])
        last = mid - 1;
     else
        first = last + 1;
    } // while
```

This is obviously a loop that divides, and it is therefore a logarithmic loop. This makes the efficiency $O(\log_2 n)$, which you should recognize as one of the more efficient of all the measures.

The efficiency of the binary search is $O(\log_2 n)$.

Comparing the sequential search and binary search, we see that, disregarding the time required to order the list, the binary search is obviously better for a list of any significant size (see Table 8-3). For this reason, the binary search is recommended for all but the smallest of lists—say, lists with fewer than 16 elements.

The big-O concept is generally concerned with only the largest factor. This tends to significantly distort the efficiency of the sequential search in that it is always the worst case. If the search is always successful, it turns out that the efficiency of the sequential search is $1/2\ n$. We include the average in Table 8-3 for comparison. (The average for the binary search is only one less than the maximum, so it is less interesting.)

Size	Binary	Sequential (average)	Sequential (worst case)
16	4	8	16
50	6	25	50
256	8	128	256
1,000	10	500	1,000
10,000	14	5,000	10,000
100,000	17	50,000	100,000
1,000,000	20	500,000	1,000,000

Table 8-3 Comparison of binary and sequential searches

8-11 TIPS AND COMMON PROGRAMMING ERRORS

1. In an array declared as `array[n]`, the index goes from 0 (not 1) to $n - 1$ (not to n).
2. Three things are needed to declare and define an array: its name, type, and size.
3. The elements of arrays are not initialized automatically. You must initialize them if you want them to start with known values.
4. To initialize all elements in an array to zero, all you have to do is initialize the first element to zero.
5. To exchange the value of two elements in an array, you need a temporary variable.
6. You cannot copy all elements of one array into another with an assignment statement. Instead, you must use a loop.
7. To pass the whole array to a function, you only use the name of the array as an actual parameter.
8. The most common logic error associated with arrays is an invalid index. An invalid index used with an assignment operator either causes the program to fail immediately or destroys data or code in another part of the program and causes it to fail later.
9. Invalid indexes are often created by invalid coding in a *for* statement. For example, given an array of 10 elements, the following *for* statement logic error results in an index value of 10 being used. Although it loops 10 times, the indexes are 1 through 10, not 0 through 9.

```
for (int i = 1; i <= 10; i++)
```

10. Another cause of invalid indexes is an uninitialized index. Make sure your indexes are always properly initialized.
11. When initializing an array when it is defined, it is a compile error to provide more initializers than there are elements.
12. It is a compile error to leave out the index operators in an assignment statement, as shown below in the next example.

```
float costAry[20];
...
costAry = quantity * price;
```

13. It is a compile error to leave out the index operators in a *cin* statement, as shown below.

```
float costAry[20];
...
cin >> costAry                    // Invalid
cin >> costAry[0]);               // correct code
```

14. It is a compile error to omit the array size in the parameter declaration for any array dimension other than the first.

8-12 KEY TERMS

accessing values
array
binary search
brackets
bubble sort
column
const
data structure
declaration and definition (of array)
exchange
frequency array
histogram
index
index range checking
initialization
inputting values
insertion sort
linear search
loops
multidimensional array
one-dimensional array
passing array rows to a function
passing individual elements
passing the whole array
plane
reusable code
row
search
selection sort
sequential search
sort pass
sorting
subscript
three-dimensional array
two-dimensional array

8-13 SUMMARY

- A one-dimensional array is a fixed sequence of elements of the same type.
- We use indexes in C++ to show the position of the elements in an array.
- An array must be declared and defined before being used. Declaration and definition tell the compiler the name of the array, the type of each element, and the size of the array.
- Initialization of all elements of an array can be done at the time of the declaration and definition.
- If a one-dimensional array is completely initialized when it is declared, it is not necessary to specify the size, but it is recommended.
- When an array is partially initialized, the rest of the elements are assigned to zero.
- We can fill the elements of an array by using a loop to read the values from the keyboard.
- We can access the individual elements of an array using the array name and the index. Accessing is done for two purposes: inspecting the value of the element or storing a new value in the element.
- We can output the values of an array using a loop.
- An array reference is a postfix expression with the opening and closing brackets as operators.
- C++ does not do boundary checking on the elements of an array.

- We can pass an individual element of an array to a function. In this case, the value of the element will be passed to the function.
- We can also pass the whole array to a function. In this case, only the address of the array will be passed. When this happens, the function can change the value of the elements in the array.
- A frequency array is an array whose elements show the number of occurrences of data values in another array.
- A histogram is a pictorial representation of a frequency array.
- A two-dimensional array is a representation of a table with rows and columns.
- We can pass one single element, a row, or the whole array to a function.
- A multidimensional array is an extension of a two-dimensional array to three, four, or more dimensions.
- An array can be sorted using a sorting algorithm.
- The selection sort divides the array into sorted and unsorted sublists. In each pass, the algorithm chooses the smallest element from the unsorted sublist and swaps it with the element at the beginning of the unsorted sublist.
- The bubble sort divides the array into sorted and unsorted sublists. In each pass, the algorithm bubbles the smallest element from the unsorted list into the sorted sublist.
- The insertion sort divides the array into sorted and unsorted sublists. In each pass, the algorithm inserts the first element from the unsorted list into the appropriate place in the sorted sublist.
- Searching is the process of finding the location of a target among a list of objects.
- The sequential search starts at the beginning of the array and searches until it finds the data or hits the end of the list. The data may be ordered or unordered.
- A binary search is a much faster searching algorithm. In the binary search, each test removes half of the list from further analysis. The data must be ordered.

8-14 PRACTICE SETS

REVIEW QUESTIONS

1. The type of all elements in an array must be the same.

a. True

b. False

2. Any expression that evaluates to an integral value may be used as an index.

a. True

b. False

3. When an array is defined, C++ automatically sets the value of its elements to zero.

a. True

b. False

4. When an array is passed to a function, C++ uses pass by reference.

a. True

b. False

5. Because of its efficiency, the binary search is the best search for any array, regardless of its size and order.

a. True

b. False

6. The selection, insertion, and bubble sort are all $O(n^2)$ sorts.

a. True

b. False

7. A(n) ____________ is an integral value used to access an element in an array.

a. Constant

b. Number

c. Element

d. Variable

e. Index

8. Which of the following array initialization statements is valid?
   a. int ary{ } = {1, 2, 3, 4};
   b. int ary[ ] = [1, 2, 3, 4];
   c. int ary[ ] = {1, 2, 3, 4};
   d. int ary{4}= [1, 2, 3, 4];
   e. int ary[4] = [1, 2, 3, 4];
9. Which of the following statements assigns the value stored in *x* to the first element on an array, *ary*?
   a. ary = x;
   b. ary = x[0];
   c. ary = x[1];
   d. ary[0] = x;
   e. ary[1] = x;
10. Which of the following statements concerning passing array elements is true?
   a. Arrays cannot be passed to functions because their structure is too complex.
   b. It is not possible to pass just a row of a two-dimensional array to a function.
   c. Only the size of the first dimension is needed when a two-dimensional array is declared in a parameter list.
   d. When an array is passed to a function, it is always passed by reference (only its address is passed).
   e. When a two-dimensional array is passed to a function, the size of the second dimension must be passed as a value parameter.
11. The process through which data are arranged according to their values is known as
   a. arranging
   b. searching
   c. listing
   d. sorting
   e. parsing
12. The ____________ sort finds the smallest element from the unsorted sublist and swaps it with the element at the beginning of the unsorted data.
   a. bubble
   b. quick
   c. exchange
   d. selection
   e. insertion
13. The ____________ search locates the target item by starting at the beginning and moving toward the end of the list.
   a. ascending
   b. selection
   c. binary
   d. sequential
   e. bubble
14. Which of the following statements about a sequential search is false?
   a. Any array can be searched using the sequential search.
   b. If the target is not found, every element in the list is tested.
   c. The efficiency of the sequential search is $O(n)$.
   d. The list must be sorted.
   e. The sequential search is generally recommended only for small lists.
15. Which of the following statements about two-dimensional arrays is true?
   a. A two-dimensional array can be thought of as an array of one-dimensional arrays.
   b. Only the size of the second dimension needs to be declared when the array is used as a parameter.
   c. Two different types can be stored in a two-dimensional array.
   d. The first dimension is known as the column dimension.
   e. When passed to a function, the size of the second dimension must be passed as a value parameter.

EXERCISES

16. What would be printed by the following program?

```
#include <iostream>
using namespace std;
int main ()
{
  int list [10] = {0};

   for (int i = 0; i < 5;  i++)
     list [2 *  i + 1] =  i  + 2;
   for (int i = 0; i < 10;  i++)
      cout << list[i] << endl;
  return 0;
} // main
```

17. What would be printed by the following program?

```
#include <iostream>
using namespace std;
int main ()
{
  int list [10] = {2, 1, 2, 1, 1,
                   2, 3, 2, 1, 2};
  cout << list[2] << endl;
  cout << list[list [2]] << endl;
  cout << list[list [2] + list [3]]
       << endl;
  cout << list[list [list [2]]]
       << endl;
  return 0;
} // main
```

18. What would be printed by the following program?

```
#include <iostream>
using namespace std;
int main ()
{
   int i;
   int list[10] = {2, 1, 2, 4, 1,
                   2, 0, 2, 1, 2};
   int line [10];
   for (i = 0; i < 10; i++)
      line [i] = list [9 - i];
   for (i = 0; i < 10; i++)
      cout << line[i] << " ";
   cout << endl;
   return 0;
} // main
```

19. An array contains the elements shown below. The first two elements have been sorted using a selection sort. What would be the value of the elements in the array after three more passes of the selection sort algorithm?

   7 8 26 44 13 23 98 57

20. An array contains the elements shown below. The first two elements have been sorted using a bubble sort. What would be the value of the elements in the array after three more passes of the bubble sort algorithm? Use the version of bubble sort that starts from the end and bubbles the smallest element.

   7 8 26 44 13 23 57 98

21. An array contains the elements shown below. The first two elements have been sorted using an insertion sort. What would be the value of the elements in the array after three more passes of the insertion sort algorithm?

   3 13 7 26 44 23 98 57

22. We have the following array:

   47 3 21 32 56 92

   After two passes of a sorting algorithm, the array has been rearranged as shown below.

   3 21 47 32 56 92

   Which sorting algorithm is being used (selection, bubble, or insertion)? Defend your answer.

23. We have the following array:

   80 72 66 44 21 33

   After two passes of a sorting algorithm, the array has been rearranged as shown below.

   21 33 80 72 66 44

   Which sorting algorithm is being used (selection, bubble, or insertion)? Defend your answer.

24. We have the following array:

   47 3 66 32 56 92

   After two passes of a sorting algorithm, the array has been rearranged as shown below.

   3 47 66 32 56 92

   Which sorting algorithm is being used (selection, bubble, or insertion)? Defend your answer.

25. An array contains the elements shown below. Using the binary search algorithm, trace the steps followed to find 88. At each loop iteration, including the last, show the contents of `first`, `last`, and `mid`.

   8 13 17 26 44 56 88 97

26. An array contains the elements shown below. Using the binary search algorithm, trace the steps followed to find 20. At each loop iteration, including the last, show the contents of `first`, `last`, and `mid`.

   8 13 17 26 44 56 88 97

27. Both the selection and bubble sorts exchange elements. The insertion sort does not. Explain how the insertion sort rearranges the data without exchanges.

PROBLEMS

28. We have two arrays, *A* and *B*, each of 10 integers. Write a function that tests if every element of array *A* is equal to its corresponding element in array *B*. In other words, the function must check if A[0] is equal to B[0], A[1] is equal to B[1], and so forth.

29. Write a function that reverses the elements of an array so that the last element becomes the first, the second from the last becomes the second, and so forth. The function is to reverse the elements in place—that is, without using another array. (It is permissible to use a variable to hold an element temporarily.)

30. Write a function that creates a two-dimensional matrix representing the Pascal triangle. In a Pascal triangle, each element is the sum of the element directly above it and the element to the left of the element directly above it (if any). A Pascal triangle of size 7 is shown below.

```
1
1   1
1   2   1
1   3   3   1
1   4   6   4   1
1   5   10  10  5   1
1   6   15  20  15  6   1
```

In the above example, `element` [0][0] is set to 1. Then `element` [0][1] is set to the sum of `element[0][-1]` + `element[0][0]`. Since there is no index for –1, your program must recognize that you are in column 0 and simply bring down the number above the current element. The `element[1][1]` then becomes the sum of `element[0][0]` + `element[0][1]`. Generalizing the algorithm gives the following pseudocode:

```
1. Set first element in matrix to 1
2. loop through rows and columns
     starting with row 1
3.   if col = 0
4.        assign cell[row -]1][0]
              to current
5.   else
6.        assign cell[row - 1][col - 1]
              + cell[row - 1][col]
              to current
```

Your function must be able to create a Pascal triangle of any size.

31. An international standard book number (ISBN) is used to uniquely identify a book. It is made of 10 digits, as shown in Figure 8-40. Write a function that tests an ISBN to see if it is valid. For an ISBN number to be valid, the weighted sum of the 10 digits must be evenly divisible by 11. The tenth digit may be x, which indicates 10.

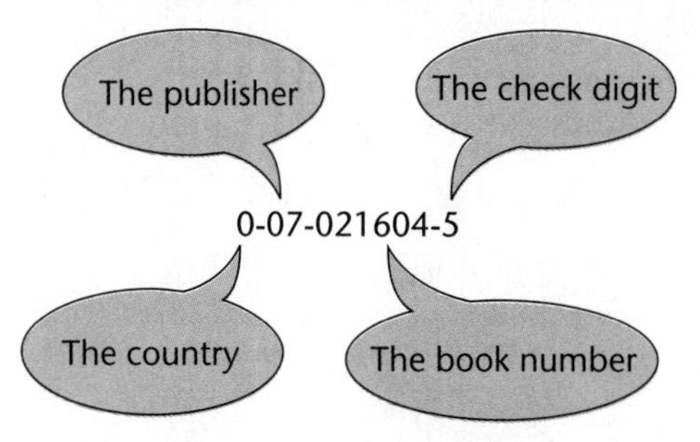

Figure 8-40 ISBN number (Problem 31)

To determine the weighted sum, the value of each position is multiplied by its relative position, starting from the right, and the sum of the products is determined. The calculation of the weighted sum for the ISBN shown above is seen in Table 8-4.

Code	Weight	Weighted value
0	10	0
0	9	0
7	8	56
0	7	0
2	6	12
1	5	5
6	4	24
0	3	0
4	2	8
5	1	5
Weighted Sum: 110		

Table 8-4 Weighted sum calculation for Problem 31

Since the weighted sum modulus 11 is zero, the ISBN number is valid. Test your function with the above example, the ISBN number for this text, and 0-07-201604-5 (an invalid ISBN—the fourth and fifth digits are reversed).

32. Another technique that can be used to validate the ISBN in Problem 31 is to calculate the sum of the sums modulus 11. The sum of the sums is calculated by adding each digit to the sum of the previous digits as shown in Table 8-5.

Code	Sum of digits	Sum of sums
0	0	0
0	0	0
7	7	7
0	7	14
2	9	23
1	10	33
6	16	49
0	16	65
4	20	85
5	25	110

Table 8-5 Sums of sums calculation for Problem 32

Rewrite the function to use the sum-of-the-sums method.

33. Write a function that copies a one-dimensional array of n elements into a two-dimensional array of k rows and j columns. The rows and columns must be valid factors of the number of elements in the one-dimensional array; that is, $k * j = n$.

34. Write a program that creates an array of 150 random integers in the range 1 to 200 (see Chapter 4 for a discussion of random numbers) and then, using the sequential search, searches the array 200 times using randomly generated targets in the same range. At the end of the program, display the following statistics:

a. The number of searches completed.

b. The number of successful searches.

c. The percentage of successful searches.

d. The average number of tests per search.

To determine the average tests per search, you must count the number of loops for each search target. Each successful search will loop between 1 and 150 times; each unsuccessful search will loop exactly 150 times. The average is the sum of all the loop counts divided by the number of searches (200).

35. Repeat Problem 34 using the binary search.

36. The sequential search assumes that a list is unordered. If it is used when the list is in fact ordered, the search can be terminated with the target not found whenever the target is less than the current element. Modify Program 8-13 on page 378 to incorporate this logic.

37. Repeat Problem 34 using the modified search you created in Problem 36.

38. Modify the bubble sort to stop as soon as the list is sorted. (See discussion in "Program 8-9 Analysis" on page 372).

39. Modify the selection sort function to count the number of exchanges needed to order an array of 50 random numbers (see Chapter 4 for a discussion of random numbers). Display the array before and after the sort. At the end of the program, display the total exchanges needed to sort the array.

40. Repeat Problem 39 using the bubble sort. Hint: Modify `bubbleUp` to return the count of the exchanges. Then, in `bubbleSort`, add the returned count to an accumulator.

41. Program 8-4 on page 361 builds a frequency array and its histogram. If there is an invalid data point in the input, it is displayed and ignored. Modify the program to make the `frequency` array one element larger than the data range and use the last element of the array as a count of numbers not in the specified range.

42. Write a program that fills the right-to-left diagonal of a square matrix with 0s, the lower right triangle with –1s, and the upper left triangle with +1s. The output of the program, assuming a 6×6 matrix, is shown in Figure 8-41.

1	1	1	1	1	0
1	1	1	1	0	-1
1	1	1	0	-1	-1
1	1	0	-1	-1	-1
1	0	-1	-1	-1	-1
0	-1	-1	-1	-1	-1

Figure 8-41 6 X 6 matrix for Problem 42

PROJECTS

43. Write a C++ program that simulates a guessing game. On each turn, you choose among nine possible guesses. As many as five guesses may be made

in a turn. For each turn, the program will generate a random number between 1 and 36. Each correct guess will be rewarded with points based on how many of your current points you risked.

A game board divides the numbers into rows and columns as shown in Figure 8-42. This board provides the basis for your guesses.

LOW	01	02	03
	04	05	06
	07	08	09
	10	11	12
MEDIUM	13	14	15
	16	17	18
	19	20	21
	22	23	24
HIGH	25	26	27
	28	29	30
	31	32	33
	34	35	36
	LEFT	CENTER	RIGHT

Figure 8-42 The guessing game board

You can guess whether the random number is even or odd. In this case, you get one point for each point risked when you guess right. You can guess whether the number is low (1–12), medium (13–24), or high (25–36). In this case, you get two points for each point risked. You can also guess left, center, or right as shown in Figure 8-42. In this case, you get two points for each point risked when your guess is correct. Finally, you can guess a specific number between 0 and 36. In this case, you get 36 points for each point risked when your guess is correct.

To make the game more interesting, each round allows up to five guesses. It may turn out that none of the five is correct; or any number up to all five may be correct. The program stops when the player quits or when the player is out of points.

The program first asks the number of points the user wants to start with, as shown below.

```
How many points would you like? 2000
```

It then prints the guess menu and allows up to five guesses, as shown next.

```
Guesses Choices
  O   Odd
  E   Even
  L   Low
  M   Med
  H   High
  F   Left
  C   Center
  R   Right
  N   Number

How many guesses would you like?  5

Guess 1   :
Enter your choice: L
Points at risk? 20

Guess 2   :
Enter your choice: H
Points at risk? 15

Guess 3   :
Enter your choice: N
Enter your number: 18
Points at risk? 20

Guess 4   :
Enter your choice: O
Points at risk? 120

Guess 5   :
Enter your choice: L
Points at risk? 10
```

After all guesses have been made, the program generates the random number and displays the following message:

```
My number is:    31
```

The program then prints the situation of the player.

```
Previous Points:   2000
```

Guess	Type	Number	Amount	Win or Lose
1	L		20	–20
2	H		15	+30
3	N	18	20	–20
4	O		120	+120
5	L		10	+20

```
You won 140 points in this turn.
Your new balance is : 2140 points
Do you want to play again (Y or N)? Y
```

Some special rules: The minimum amount risked on a guess is zero. The maximum is the player's current balance. You need to verify that at no time are the points risked more than the player's current balance. Any combinations of guesses are allowed on a round as long as the total does not exceed the player's balance.

Some hints: You must use at least four arrays, each of five elements. The arrays hold the guess information for the *kind of guess*, *chosen number* (in case the player chooses a number), *amount of the guess*, and *points won or lost*.

Run your program twice, first with 2,000 points and then with 500 points. Each run is to exercise each guess option at least twice.

44. Write a program to keep records and perform statistical analysis for a class of students. The class may have up to 40 students. There are five quizzes during the term. Each student is identified by a four-digit student number.

The program is to print the student scores and calculate and print the statistics for each quiz. The output is in the same order as the input; no sorting is needed. The input is to be read from a text file. The output from the program should be similar to the following:

Student	Quiz 1	Quiz 2	Quiz 3	Quiz 4	Quiz 5
1234	78	83	87	91	86
2134	67	77	84	82	79
3124	77	89	93	87	71
High Score	78	89	93	91	86
Low Score	67	77	84	82	71
Average	73.4	83.0	88.2	86.6	78.6

Use one- and two-dimensional arrays only. Test your program with the quiz data in Table 8-6.

Student	Quiz 1	Quiz 2	Quiz 3	Quiz 4	Quiz 5
1234	052	007	100	078	034
2134	090	036	090	077	030
3124	100	045	020	090	070
4532	011	017	081	032	077
5678	020	012	045	078	034
6134	034	080	055	078	045
7874	060	100	056	078	078
8026	070	010	066	078	056
9893	034	009	077	078	020
1947	045	040	088	078	055
2877	055	050	099	078	080
3189	022	070	100	078	077
4602	089	050	091	078	060
5405	011	011	000	078	010
6999	000	098	089	078	020

Table 8-6 Data for Project 44

45. Rework Project 44 creating statistics for each student. Print the students' high, low, and average scores to the right of Quiz 5. Provide appropriate column headings.

46. Program 8-4 on page 361 builds a frequency array. In the discussion of the algorithm, it was noted that there is a potential problem if any of the data are invalid.

Write a program that uses the random number generator, *rand*, to generate 100 numbers between 1 and 22. The array is then to be passed to a modified version of Program 8-4 that will count the number of values between 0 and 19. Add a 21st element in the array to count all numbers not in the valid range (0 to 19).

Print the input data in a 20 × 5 array—that is, 20 numbers in 5 rows—and then print the frequency diagram with a heading of the numbers as shown below.

--0- --1- --2- --3- --4- --5- --6- ... -18- -19- Invalid

47. Modify the program you wrote in Project 46 to include a histogram printout of the data. Its format should be similar to Figure 8-15.

48. Using the data from Project 44, build a two-dimensional array of students. Then write a search function that uses the sequential search to find a student in the array and prints his or her scores, average score, and grade based on an absolute scale (90% is A, 80% is B, 70% is C, 60% is D, less than 60% is F). After each printout, give the user the opportunity to continue or stop.

49. Modify the program you wrote in Project 48 to sort the two-dimensional array of students. Then rewrite the search function to use a binary search.

50. Write a program that sorts a 50-element array using the selection sort, the bubble sort, and the insertion sort. Each sort is to be executed twice.

a. For the first sort, fill the array with random numbers between 1 and 1,000.

b. For the second sort, create a nearly ordered list by exchanging every tenth element with its predecessor (9 and 10, 19 and 20, etc.).

c. Each sort (selection, bubble, insertion) is to sort the same data. For each sort, count the number of comparisons necessary to order the list.

d. After each sort execution, print the unsorted data followed by the sort data in 5 × 10 matrixes (5 rows of 10 numbers each). After the sorted data, print the number of comparisons and the number of moves required to order the data. Provide appropriate headings for each printout.

e. To make sure your statistics are as accurate as possible, you must analyze each loop limit condition test and each selection statement in your sort functions. The best way to count them is with a comma expression, as shown below. Use similar code for the selection statements.

```
while ((count++, a) && (count++, b))
```

f. Analyze the heuristics you generated and write a few lines concerning what you discovered about these sorts. Put your comments in a box (asterisks) after the program documentation at the beginning of your program.

51. Write a program to compute the arithmetic mean (average), median, and mode for up to 50 test scores. The data are contained in a text file. The program is also to print a histogram of the scores.

The program should start with a function to read the data file and fill the array. Note that there may be fewer than 50 scores. This will require that the read function return the index of the last element in the array.

To determine the average, write a function similar to that shown in Figure 8-12 on page 358. To determine the median, you must first sort the array. The median is the score in the middle of the range. This can be determined by selecting the score at *last*/2 if *last* is an even index and by averaging the scores at the floor and ceiling of *last*/2 if *last* is odd. The mode is the score that occurs the most often. It can be determined as a by-product of building the histogram. After building the frequency array, use it to determine which score occurred the most. (Note that two scores can occur the same number of times.)

Pointers 9

Every computer has addressable memory locations. In previous chapters, all of our data manipulations, whether for inspection or alteration, used memory location addresses symbolically. In other words, we assigned identifiers to data and then manipulated the data using the identifiers.

For a more direct approach we could use the data addresses directly, but that would mean giving up the ease and flexibility of symbolic names. Fortunately, C++ has the capability to work with addresses symbolically—using pointers.

Pointers have many uses in C++. Besides offering a very efficient method of accessing data, they provide efficient techniques for manipulating data in arrays, they are used in functions for reference parameters, and they are the basis for dynamic allocations of memory.

This chapter begins with a thorough discussion of the basic concepts of pointers. Then two basic applications of pointers—pointers with arrays and pointers with dynamic memory—are explored, as well as the natural affinity between pointers and arrays that stems in part from the fact that an array name is a pointer constant. After discussing the use of pointers with arrays, we examine dynamic memory, one of the most powerful aspects of most modern computer languages. Dynamic memory uses pointers exclusively to access data.

Figure 9-1 contains a summary of the derived types.

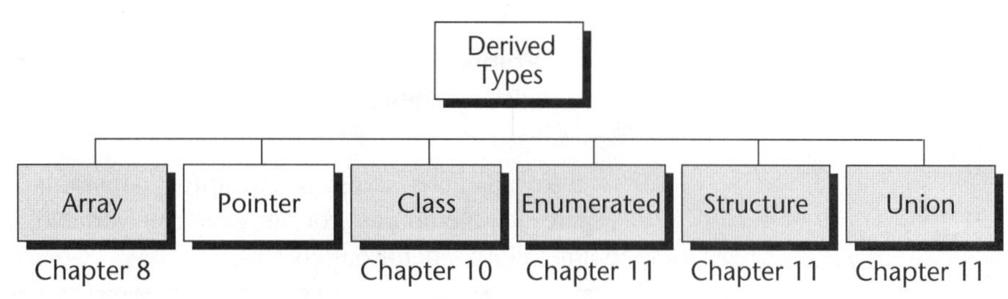

Figure 9-1 Derived types

9-1 CONCEPTS

A **pointer** is a derived data type; that is, it is a data type built from one of the standard types. Its value may be any of the addresses available in the computer for storing and accessing data. Pointers are built on the basic concept of pointer constants. To understand and use pointers, you must first understand this concept.

POINTER CONSTANTS

We'll begin our discussion of pointers by comparing character constants and pointer constants. As you know, we can have a character constant, such as any letter of the alphabet, that is drawn from a universe of all characters. In most computers, this universe is ASCII. A character constant can become a value and be stored in a variable. Although the character constant is unnamed, the variable has a name that is declared in the program. This concept is illustrated in Figure 9-2.

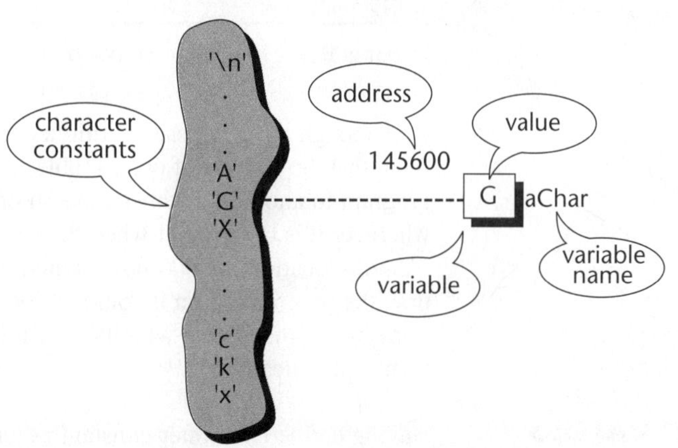

Figure 9-2 Character constants and variables

In Figure 9-2, there is a character variable, `aChar`. At this point, `aChar` contains the value 'G' that was drawn from the universe of character constants. The variable `aChar` has an address as well as a name. The name is created by the programmer; the address is the relative location of the variable with respect to the program's memory space. Assume that we have a computer that has only one megabyte of memory (2^{20} bytes).

Assume also that the computer has chosen the memory location 145600 as the byte to store this variable. This gives us the picture we see in Figure 9-2.

> **Pointer constants, drawn from the set of addresses for a computer, exist by themselves. We cannot change them; we can only use them.**

Like character constants, **pointer constants** cannot be changed. As shown in Figure 9-3, the address for our character variable, `aChar`, was drawn from the set of pointer constants for our computer.

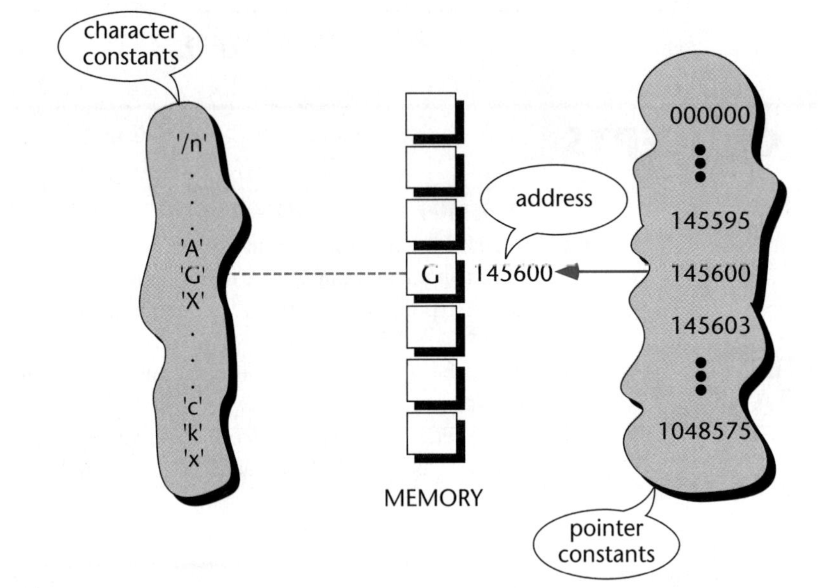

Figure 9-3 Pointer constants

Although the addresses within a computer cannot change, it is important to understand that the address of our variable, `aChar`, can and will change from one run of our program to another. Today's modern operating systems can put a program in memory wherever it is convenient when the program is started. Thus, while `aChar` is stored at memory location 145600 now, which is a constant for the duration of the run, the next time the program is run it could be located at 876050. Even though addresses are constant, we cannot know what they will be, and therefore it is still necessary to refer to them symbolically.

POINTER VALUES

Having defined a pointer constant as an address in memory, we now turn our attention to saving this address. If we have a pointer constant, we should be able to save its value if we can somehow identify it.

The **address operator (&)** provides a pointer constant to any named location in memory. Any time we need a pointer value, therefore, all we must do is use the address operator. In the Precedence Table (see the inside cover of this book), the address operator is one of the unary operators (precedence 15). The following code shows the address operator used with `aChar`.

```
&aChar
```

Let's write a program that defines two character variables and prints their addresses as pointers. Depending on the operating system, this program may print different numbers each time you run it, as we explained earlier. The addresses will also be different in different computers. However, most of the time, the computer allocates two adjacent memory locations because we define the two variables one after the other. If you are at your computer, take a moment to code and run the program in Figure 9-4 to demonstrate the concept of address constants.

When the ampersand (&) is used as a prefix to a variable name, it means "address" of variable. When it is used as a suffix to a type, it means reference parameter.

```
// This program prints character addresses
#include <iostream>
using namespace std;
int main ()
{
  char a;
  char b;

  cout << &a << &b ;
  return 0 ;
} // main
```

a 142300
b 142301

Figure 9-4 Print character addresses

The situation changes slightly when integers are involved. In most computers, integers occupy either 2 or 4 bytes. Let us assume that we are working on a system with 4-byte integers, which means that each integer variable occupies four memory locations. Which of these memory locations is used to find the address of the variable? In C++ the location of the first byte is used as the memory address. For characters, there is only 1 byte, so its location is the address; for integers, the address is the first byte of 4 (see Figure 9-5).

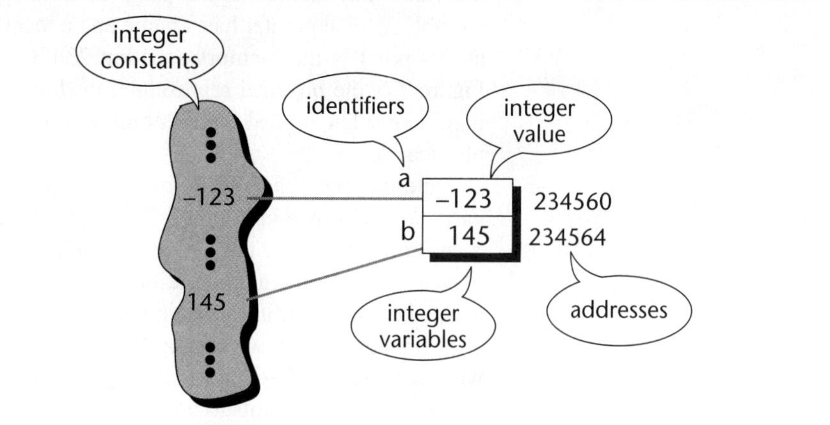

Figure 9-5 Integer constants and variables

The same system applies to floating-point and other data types. The address of a variable is the address of the first byte occupied by that variable.

> **The address of a variable is the address of the first byte occupied by that variable.**

9-2 POINTER VARIABLES

If we have pointer constants and pointer values, then we can also have pointer variables. Thus, we can store the address of a variable into another variable, which is called a **pointer variable**. This concept is illustrated in Figure 9-6.

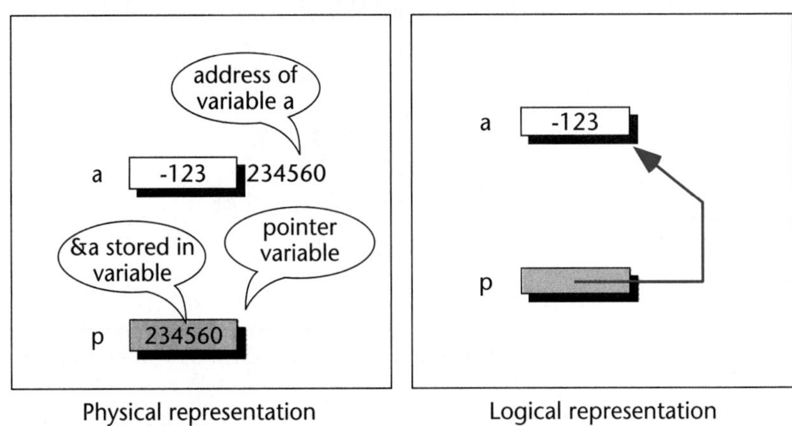

Figure 9-6 Pointer variable

We must distinguish between a variable and its value. Figure 9-6 details the differences. In this figure, we see a variable, a, with its value, -123. The variable a is found at location 234560 in memory. Although the variable's name and location are constant, the value may change as the program executes. In this figure, there is also a pointer variable, p. The pointer has a name and a location, both of which are constant. Its value at this point is the memory location 234560. This means that p is pointing to a. In Figure 9-6, the physical representation shows how the data and pointer variables exist in memory. The logical representation shows the relationship between them without the physical details.

Note that we can even store a variable's address in two or more different pointer variables, as shown in Figure 9-7. In this figure, there is a variable, a, and two pointers, p and q. Each pointer has a name and a location, both of which are constant. The value of p and q is the memory location 234560, which means that both p and q are pointing to a. There is no limit to the number of pointer variables that can point to a variable.

A final thought: If we have a pointer variable, but we don't want it to point anywhere, what is its value? C++ provides a special null constant, NULL, that can be used to set a pointer so that it points to nothing. The value of the NULL constant is 0. You may use either 0 or NULL to initialize a pointer does not contain an address. Similarly, when testing a pointer to determine if it is not active, you may test for either 0 or NULL.

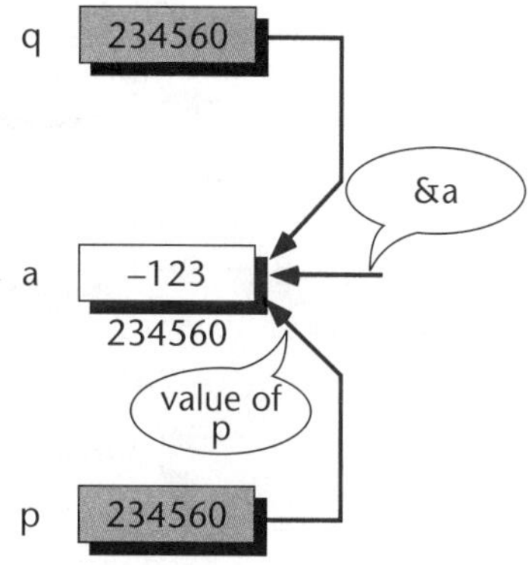

Figure 9-7 Multiple pointers to a variable

9-3 ACCESSING VARIABLES THROUGH POINTERS

THE INDIRECTION OPERATOR

Now that we have a variable and a pointer to the variable, how can we relate the two—that is, how can we use the pointer? Once again, C++ has an operator for this purpose. Right below the address operator in the unary portion of the Precedence Table, you will find the **indirection operator (*)**. When you dereference a pointer, you are using its value to reference (address) another variable. The indirection operator is a unary operator whose operand must be a pointer value. The result is an expression that can be used to access the pointed variable for the purpose of inspection or alteration. To access a through the pointer p, you simply code *p. The indirection operator is shown below.

```
*p
```

Let us assume that we want to add 1 to the variable, a. We could do this with any of the following statements, assuming that the pointer, p, were properly initialized (p = &a).

```
a++;    a = a + 1;    *p = *p + 1;    ++(*p)    (*p)++;
```

In the last example, (*p)++, the parentheses are necessary. The postfix increment has a priority of 16 in the Precedence Table, while indirection, which is a unary operator, has a priority of 15. The parentheses therefore force the dereference to take place before the addition so that we add to the data variable and not to the pointer. If the parentheses were not there, we would add to the pointer first, which would change the address. In the prefix increment example, the parentheses are not necessary but clarify the intent of the instruction and make it more readable.

Figure 9-8 expands the discussion. Let's assume that the variable x is pointed to by two pointers, p and q. As the figure shows, the expressions x, *p, *q all are expressions that allow the variable to be either inspected or changed. When used in the right-hand side of the assignment operator, they can only inspect (copy). When used in the left-hand side of the assignment operator, they alter the value of x.

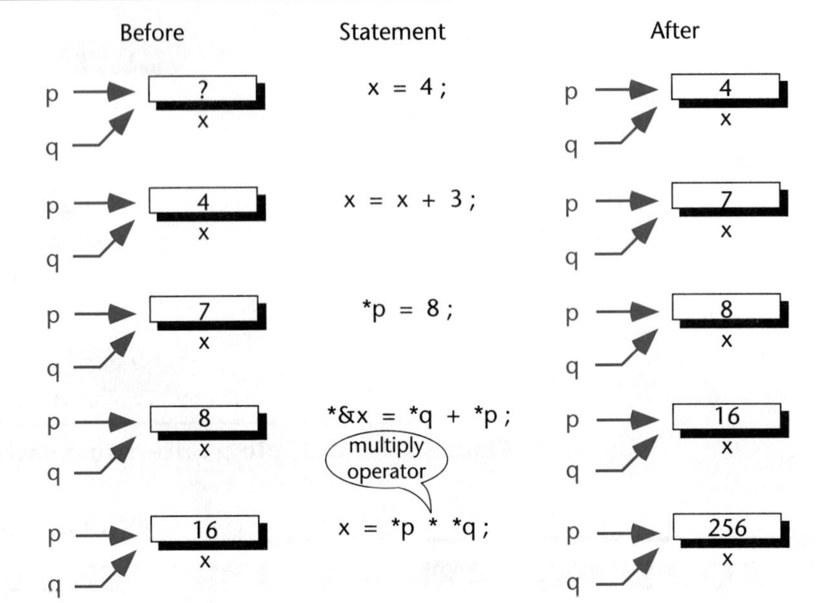

Figure 9-8 Accessing variables through pointers

The indirection and address operators are the inverse of each other, and when they are combined in an expression, such as `*&x`, they cancel each other. Let's break down the expression and examine it. These two unary operators are evaluated from the right. The first expression is therefore `&x`, the address of `x`, which as we have seen, is a pointer value. The second expression, `*(&x)`, dereferences the pointer constant, giving the variable (`x`) itself. Therefore, the operators effectively cancel each other (see Figure 9-9). Note that we would never code the expression `*&a` in a production program; we use it in Figure 9-8 for illustration only.

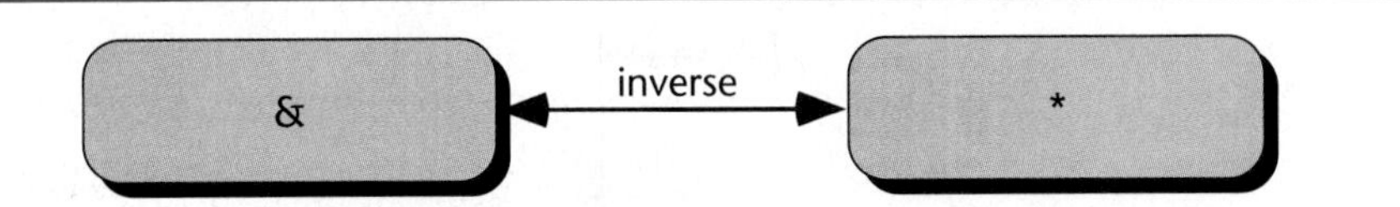

Figure 9-9 Address and indirection operators

9-4 POINTER DECLARATION AND DEFINITION

As shown in Figure 9-10, we use the indirection operator to define and declare pointer variables. Used in this way, it is really not an operator but rather a compiler syntactical notation. Making it the same token as the operator makes it easier to remember.

Figure 9-11 shows how we declare different pointer variables. Their corresponding data variables are shown for comparison. Note that in each case, the pointer is declared to be of a given type. Thus, `p` is a pointer to characters, `q` is a pointer to integers, and `r` is a pointer to floating-point variables.

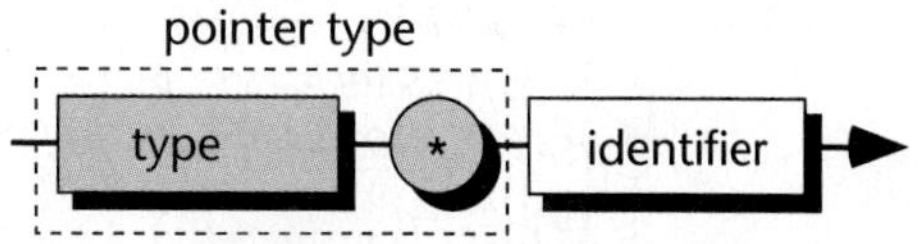

Figure 9-10 Pointer variable declaration

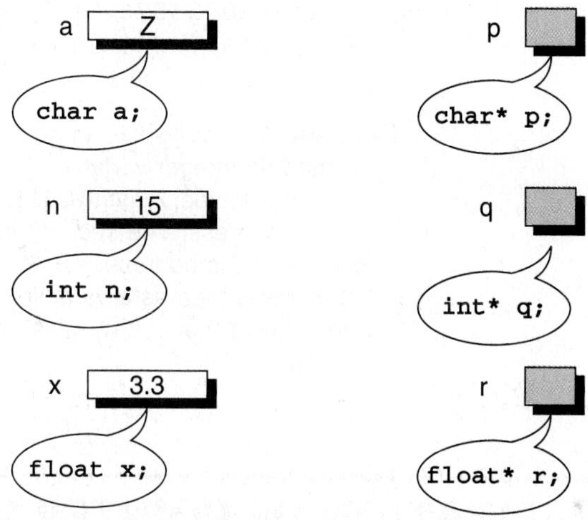

Figure 9-11 Declaring pointer variables

Program 9-1 stores the address of a variable in a pointer and then prints the data using the variable value and a pointer.

Program 9-1 Demonstrate use of pointers

```
/* Demonstrate pointer use.
      Written by:
      Date:
*/
#include <iostream>
using namespace std;

int main ()
{
   int  a;
   int* p;


   a = 14;
   p = &a;

```

a 14
135760
p 135760

Program 9-1 Demonstrate use of pointers *(continued)*

```
   cout << a << " " << &a << endl;
   cout << p << " " << *p << " " << a << endl;

   return 0;
} // main
```

```
Results:
14 0x00135760
0x00135760 14 14
```

Program 9-1 Analysis Program 9-1 requires a little explanation. First, we have defined an integer variable, `a`, and a pointer to integer, to which we assign `a`'s address. We then print twice. The first print displays the contents of the variable `a` and its address. The second print uses the pointer, `p`. It prints the pointer value containing the address of `a`, followed by the contents of `a`, first referenced as a pointer and then as a variable. This demonstrates two ways to access the data. We suggest that you run this program for yourself (remember that you will get a different address).

9-5 INITIALIZATION OF POINTER VARIABLES

Recall that the C++ language does not, in general, initialize variables. Thus, when we start our program, all of our uninitialized variables have unknown values in them. (The operating system often clears memory when it loads a program, but you can't count on this.)

The same thing is true for pointers. When the program starts, the pointers each have some unknown memory address in them. More precisely, they each have an unknown value that will be interpreted as a memory location. Most likely, the value will not be valid for the computer you are using, or if it is, will not be valid for the memory you have been allocated. If the address does not exist, you will get an immediate run-time error. If it is a valid address, you often, but unfortunately not always, get a run-time error. (It is better to get the error when you use the invalid pointer than to have the program produce invalid results.)

One of the most common causes of errors in programming, by novices and professionals alike, is uninitialized pointers. Such errors can be very difficult to debug because the effect of the error is often delayed until later in the program execution. Figure 9-12 shows both an uninitialized variable and an uninitialized pointer.

As with variables, it is possible to initialize pointers when they are declared and defined. Note that the data variable must be defined before the pointer variable. For example, if we have an integer variable, `x`, and a pointer to integer, `p`, then to set `p` to point to `x` at declaration time, we can code it as shown in Figure 9-13.

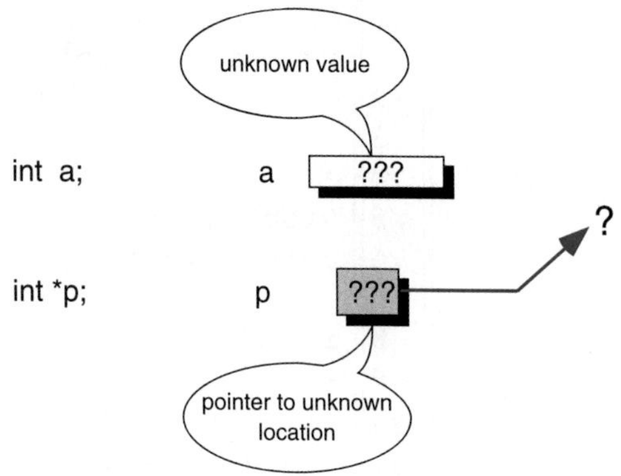

Figure 9-12 Uninitialized pointers

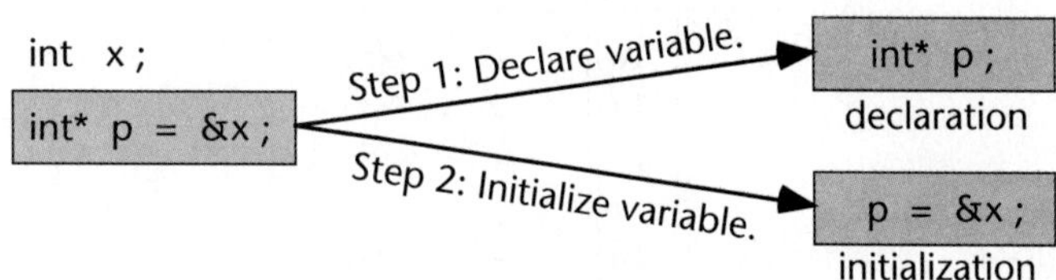

Figure 9-13 Initializing pointer variables

As shown in Figure 9-13, the initialization involves two different steps. First, the variable is declared. Second, the assignment statement to initialize it is generated. Some style experts suggest that you should not use an initializer in this way.[1] Their argument is that it saves no code; that is, that the initializer statement is required either as a part of the declaration and initialization or as a separately coded statement in the statement section of the function. While this was true in the C language, it is much less important in C++ where we tend to put the variable definitions near the statements that use them.

We can also set a pointer to 0 or to NULL, either during definition or during execution. The following statement demonstrates how we could define a pointer with an initial null value:

```
int* p = 0;
```

If you dereference `p` when it is null, you will most likely get a run-time error because 0 is not a valid user address. The type of error you get will depend on the system you are using.

EXAMPLE: FUN WITH POINTERS

Now let's write a program and have some fun with pointers. Our code is shown in Program 9-2. Do not try to figure out why this program is doing what it is doing; there is no reason. Rather, just try to trace the different variables and pointers as we change them.

[1]For example, see C++ *Elements of Style* by Steve Oualline (Mountain View, CA: M&T Books, 1982).

Program 9-2 Fun with pointers

```
1  /* Fun with pointers
2        Written by:
3        Date:
4  */
5  #include <iostream>
6  using namespace std;
7
8  int main ()
9  {
10    int  a = 6;
11    int  b = 2;
12    int  c;
13    int* p = &b;
14    int* q;
15    int* r;

16    q = p;
17    r = &c;
18

19    p  = &a;
20    *q = 8;
21    *r = *p;


22    *r = a + *q + *&c;
23
24    cout << a << " " << b
25         << " " << c << endl;
26    cout << *p  << " " << *q
27         << " " << *r  << endl;
28    return 0;
29 } // main
```

```
Results:
6 8 20
6 8 20
```

Program 9-2 Analysis We begin the program by initializing `a` and `b` and pointer `p`.

1. The first thing the program does is to initialize the other two pointers. After statement 17, both `p` and `q` point to `b`, and `r` points to `c`.
2. Statement 19 assigns the address of `a` to `p`. All three pointers then point to different variables. Using the indirection operator in statement 20, we dereference `q` (`*q`), and assign `b` the value 8. All variables then contain data.
3. Statement 21 demonstrates that both operands can be dereferenced when it assigns the contents of `a (*p)` to `c (*r)`.

4. In statement 22, we use three different formats to sum the values in the variables: a variable name, a dereferenced pointer, and a dereferenced address operator. Using the figures in the program, trace these statements carefully to assure yourself that you understand how they work.

EXAMPLE: ADD TWO NUMBERS

This example shows how we can use pointers to add two numbers. It explores the concept of using pointers to manipulate, in this case add, data. A graphic representation of the variables is shown in Figure 9-14. The code is given in Program 9-3.

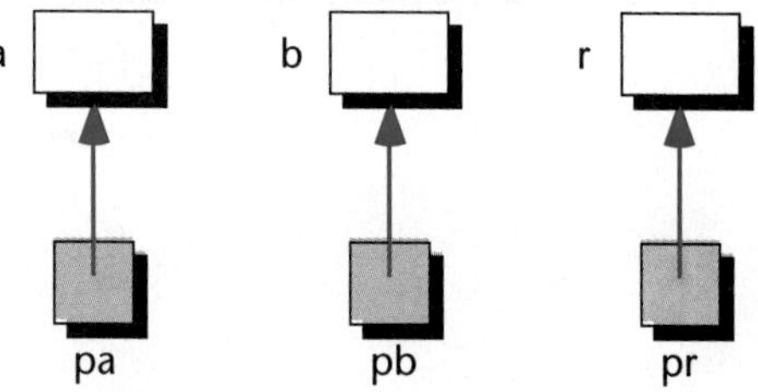

Figure 9-14 Add two numbers using pointers

Program 9-3 Add two numbers using pointers

```
/* This program adds two numbers using pointers, to
   demonstrate the concept of pointers.
      Written by:
      Date:
*/
#include <iostream>
using namespace std;

int main ()
{
   int  a;
   int  b;
   int  r;
   int* pa = &a;
   int* pb = &b;
   int* pr = &r;

   cout << "\nEnter the first number: ";
   cin  >> *pa;
   cout << "\nEnter the second number: ";
   cin  >> *pb;

   *pr = *pa + *pb;

   cout << endl;
   cout << *pa << " + " << *pb << " is " << *pr << endl;
   return 0;
}  // main
```

Program 9-3 Analysis While Program 9-3 uses rather straightforward logic, there is one syntactical notation to watch carefully, especially if you have programmed in C. Note that in statements 19 and 21, we must dereference the pointer when we read using the *cin* function; *cin* always needs the variable that is to be filled, not its address.

EXAMPLE: POINTER FLEXIBILITY

This example shows how we can use the same pointer to print the value of different variables. The variables and their pointer are shown in Figure 9-15, and the code is given in Program 9-4.

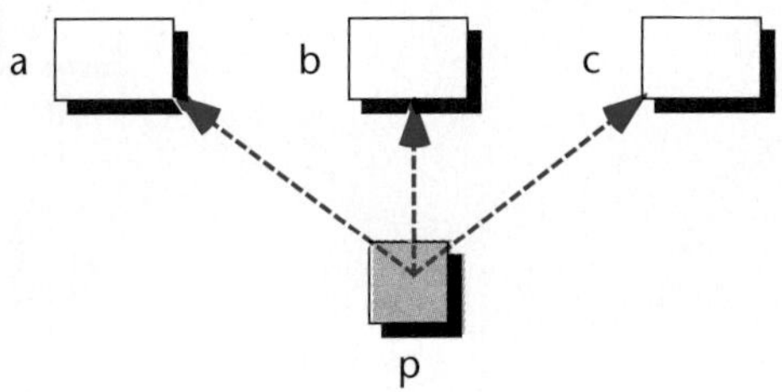

Figure 9-15 Demonstrate pointer flexibility

Program 9-4 Using one pointer for many variables

```
/* This program shows how the same pointer can point to
   different data variables in different statements.
      Written by:
      Date:
*/
#include <iostream>
#include <iomanip>
using namespace std;

int main ( )
{
   int  a;
   int  b;
   int  c;
   int* p;

   cout << "Enter three numbers and key return: ";
   cin  >> a >> b >> c;

   p = &a;
   cout << setw(3) << *p << endl;
   p = &b;
   cout << setw(3) << *p << endl;
   p = &c;
   cout << setw(3) << *p << endl;
   return 0;
}  // main
```

EXAMPLE: MULTIPLE POINTERS FOR ONE VARIABLE

This example shows how we can use different pointers to print the value of the same variable. The variable and its pointers are shown in Figure 9-16, and the code is given in Program 9-5.

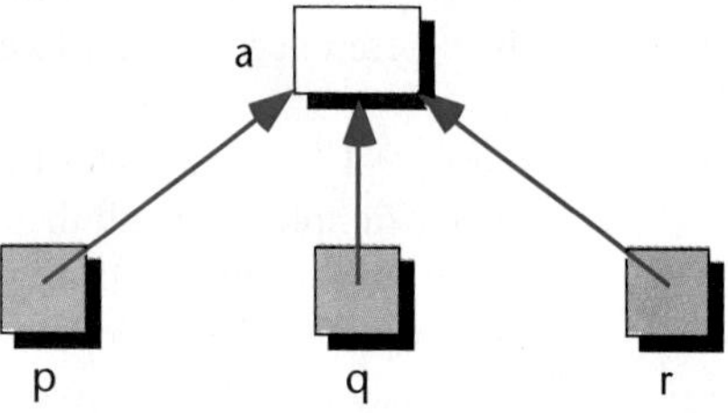

Figure 9-16 Using one variable with many pointers

Program 9-5 Using one variable with many pointers

```
/* This program shows how we can use different pointers
   to point to the same data variable.
      Written by:
      Date:
*/
#include <iostream>
using namespace std;

int main ()
{
   int  a;
   int* p = &a;
   int* q = &a;
   int* r = &a;

   cout << "Enter a number: ";
   cin  >> a;

   cout << *p << endl;
   cout << *q << endl;
   cout << *r << endl;

   return 0;
} // main
```

9-6 POINTERS AND FUNCTIONS

One of the most useful application of pointers is in functions. When we discussed functions earlier, we saw that C++ provides two ways to pass parameters to functions: pass by value and pass by reference. Furthermore, we saw that when we passed by reference, C++ passes the address of the parameter variable, and the parameter name becomes an alias for the variable. Any changes made using the alias name resulted in a change to the original value.

Now that we have studied pointers, we can add an alternative to pass by reference: pass a pointer and use it to change the original variable. The difference between pass by reference and passing pointers is that with pointers an alias is not created—we must use the dereference operator to effect the change.

POINTERS AS FORMAL PARAMETERS

Figure 9-17 demonstrates the three parameter formats with an exchange example. In all three examples, we call the exchange function, passing it two variables whose contents are to be exchanged. In Figure 9-17a, we use the pass by value method. The data are exchanged in the called function, but nothing changes in the calling program. This obviously unworkable solution is illustrated in Figure 9-17a.

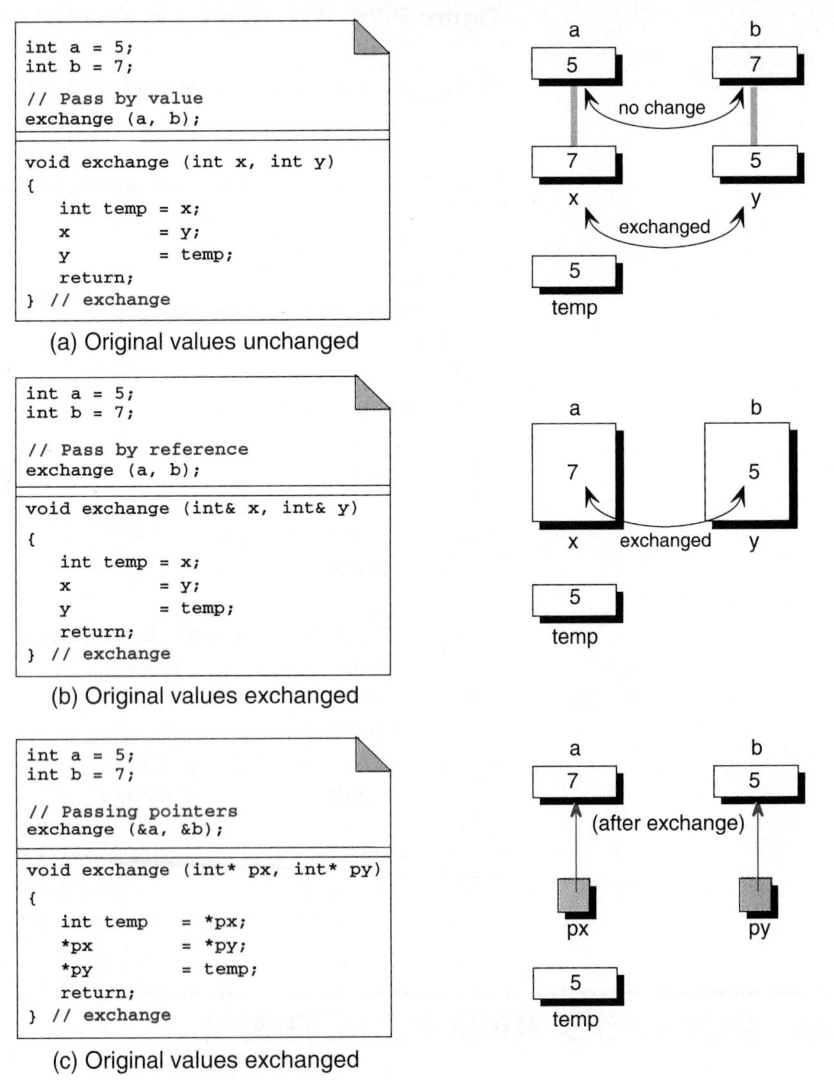

Figure 9-17 Exchanging values

The second example uses pass by reference. In this case, the values are exchanged using the alias names in the called function, as shown in Figure 9-17b.

Finally, we can pass pointers to the values. Once we have a pointer to a variable, it doesn't make any difference if it is local to the active function, if it is defined in *main,* or even if it is a global variable—we can change it. The important thing to remember, however, is that the pointer is not an alias; we need to dereference it to refer to the data it is pointing to.

In summary, when we must send back more than one value from a function, we have two choices: pass by reference or pointers. Both accomplish the same result: changing the values in the calling function's scope. Pass by reference is an easier, more natural way to work, however, and we recommend it over passing pointers.

FUNCTIONS RETURNING POINTERS

Nothing prevents a function from returning a pointer to the calling function. In fact, as we shall see, it is quite common for functions to return pointers.

As an example, let us write a rather trivial function to determine the smaller of two numbers. In this case, what we need is a pointer to the smaller of two variables, `a` and `b`. Since we are looking for a pointer, we pass two pointers to the function, which uses a conditional expression to determine which value is smaller. Once we know the smaller value, we can return the address of its location as a pointer. The return value is then placed in the calling function's pointer, `p`, so that after the call it points to either `a` or `b` based on its values. Both the code and a diagram of the variables and pointers are shown in Figure 9-18.

```
int* smaller ( int*, int* ) ;
int main ( )
{
  int  a ;
  int  b ;
  int  *p ;
  ...
  cin >> a >> b;
  p = smaller ( &a, &b );
  ...
} // main
```

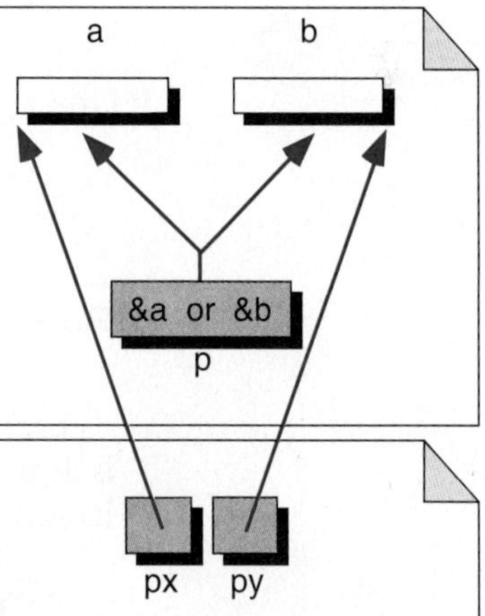

```
int*  smaller  (int*  px, int*  py )
{
  return  ( *px < *py ? px : py ) ;
} // smaller
```


Figure 9-18 Functions returning pointers

When you return a pointer, it must point to data in the calling function or higher level functions. It is an error to return a pointer to a local variable in the called function because when the function terminates, its memory may be used by other parts of the program. Although a simple program might not "notice" the error because the space was not reused, a large program would either get the wrong answer or fail when the memory being referenced by the pointer was changed.

It is a serious error to return a pointer to a local variable.

9-7 POINTERS TO POINTERS

So far, the pointers we have been using have pointed directly to data. It is possible—and often with advanced data structures necessary—to use pointers that point to other pointers. For instance, we can have a pointer pointing to a pointer to an integer. An example of this two-level indirection is shown in Figure 9-19. There is no limit as to how many levels of indirection you can use; however, in practice it seldom goes beyond two levels.

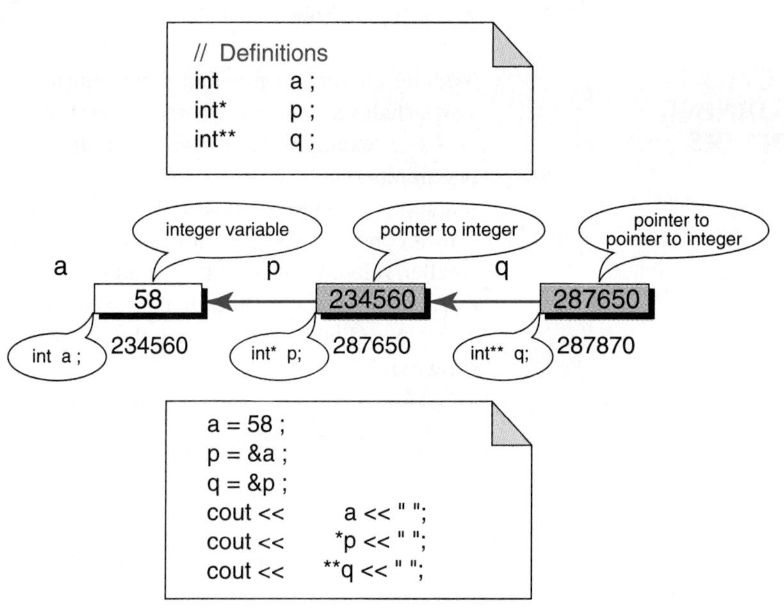

Figure 9-19 Pointers to pointers

Each level of **pointer indirection** requires a separate indirection operator when it is dereferenced. In Figure 9-19, to refer to `a` using the pointer `p`, we have to dereference it once, as shown in the following example.

```
*p
```

To refer to `a` using the pointer `q`, we have to dereference it twice because there are two levels of indirection (pointers) involved. In other words, `q` is a pointer to a pointer to an integer. The double dereference is shown below.

```
**q
```

Let's look at how we used these concepts in the C++ code fragment in Figure 9-19. All three references in the *cout* statements refer to the variable `a`. The first print statement prints the value of `a` directly; the second uses the pointer `p`; the third uses the pointer `q`. The result is that the value 58 prints three times, as shown below.

```
58   58   58
```

POINTER-TO-POINTER EXAMPLE

The last example in this section shows how we can use different pointers with pointers to pointers and pointers to pointers to pointers to read a value into the same variable. A graphic representation of the variables is shown in Figure 9-20.

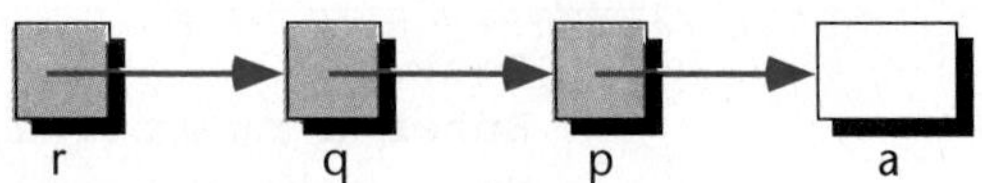

Figure 9-20 Using pointers to pointers

The code is given in Program 9-6.

Program 9-6 Using pointers to pointers

```
/* Show how pointer to pointer can be used by different
   input functions to read data to the same variable.
      Written by:
      Date:
*/
#include <iostream>
using namespace std;

int main ()
{
   int    a;
   int*   p;
   int**  q;
   int*** r;

   p = &a;
   q = &p;
   r = &q;

   cout << "Enter a number: ";
   cin  >> a;
   cout << "Your number is: " << a << endl;

   cout << "\nEnter a number: ";
   cin  >> *p;
   cout << "Your number is: " << a << endl;

   cout << "\nEnter a number: ";
   cin  >> **q;
   cout << "Your number is: " << a << endl;

   cout << "\nEnter a number: ";
   cin  >> ***r;
   cout << "Your number is: " << a << endl;
   cout << "That's all folks!";
```

Program 9-6 Using pointers to pointers *(continued)*

```
   return 0;
} // main
```

```
Results:
Enter a number: 1
Your number is: 1

Enter a number: 2
Your number is: 2

Enter a number: 3
Your number is: 3

Enter a number: 4
Your number is: 4
That's all folks!
```

Program 9-6 Analysis In each successive read, we use a higher level of indirection. In the print statements, however, we always use the integer variable, a, to prove that the reads were successful. Note once again that for each read we fully dereference the pointer so that the *cin* function receives the variable to be filled, not its address.

9-8 COMPATIBILITY

It is important to recognize that pointers have a type associated with them. They are not just pointer types, but rather are pointers to a *specific* type, such as integer. Each pointer therefore takes on the attributes of the type to which it refers in addition to its own attributes. This is demonstrated by Program 9-7, which prints the size of a pointer and what it refers to.

Program 9-7 Demonstrate size of pointers

```
/* Demonstrate size of pointers.
      Written by:
      Date:
*/
#include <iostream>
using namespace std;

int main ()
{
   char  c;
   char* pc;
   int   sizeofc      = sizeof(c);
   int   sizeofpc     = sizeof(pc);
   int   sizeofStarpc = sizeof(*pc);
```

Program 9-7 Demonstrate size of pointers *(continued)*

```

    int  a;
    int* pa;
    int  sizeofa       = sizeof(a);
    int  sizeofpa      = sizeof(pa);
    int  sizeofStarpa  = sizeof(*pa);

    double  x;
    double* px;
    int     sizeofx      = sizeof(x);
    int     sizeofpx     = sizeof(px);
    int     sizeofStarpx = sizeof(*px);

    cout << "sizeof(c): "   << sizeofc      << " | ";
    cout << "sizeof(pc): "  << sizeofpc     << " | ";
    cout << "sizeof(*pc): " << sizeofStarpc << endl;

    cout << "sizeof(a): "   << sizeofa      << " | ";
    cout << "sizeof(pa): "  << sizeofpa     << " | ";
    cout << "sizeof(*pa): " << sizeofStarpa << endl;

    cout << "sizeof(x): "   << sizeofx      << " | ";
    cout << "sizeof(px): "  << sizeofpx     << " | ";
    cout << "sizeof(*px): " << sizeofStarpx << endl;

    return 0;
} // main
```

```
Results:
sizeof(c): 1 | sizeof(pc): 4 | sizeof(*pc): 1
sizeof(a): 4 | sizeof(pa): 4 | sizeof(*pa): 4
sizeof(x): 8 | sizeof(px): 4 | sizeof(*px): 8
```

Program 9-7 Analysis What does this code tell us? First, note that the variables `a`, `c`, and `x` are never assigned values. This means that the sizes are independent of whatever value may be in a variable. In other words, the sizes are dependent on the type and not its values. Now look at the size of the pointers. It is 4 in all cases, which is the size of an address in the computer on which this program was run. This makes sense because all computers today have over 32,767 bytes, which is the maximum address that could be stored in 2 bytes. But note what happens when we print the size of the type that the pointer is referring to: The size is the same as the data size! This means that in addition to the size of the pointer, the system also knows the size of whatever the pointer is pointing to. To confirm this, look at the size of the pointer, `px`, and what it is pointing to when dereferenced `(*px)`.

COMPATIBILITY AND THE *void* POINTER

With one exception, it is invalid to assign a pointer of one type to a pointer of another type, even though the values in both cases are memory addresses and would therefore seem to be fully compatible. Although the addresses may be compatible because they are drawn from the same set, what is not compatible is the underlying data type of the referenced object. In C++, we can't use the assignment operator with pointers to different types; if we try to, we get a compile error.

The exception to the rule is the *void* pointer. The *void* pointer, known as the universal or generic pointer, can be used with any pointer, and any pointer can be assigned to a *void* pointer. However, since a void pointer has no object type, it cannot be dereferenced. A *void* pointer is created as shown below.

```
void* pVoid;
```

CASTING POINTERS

It is possible to make an explicit assignment between incompatible pointer types by using a cast, just as it is possible to cast an integer to a float. For example, to cast a character pointer, p, to point to an integer (a), you could cast it as shown below.

```
int   a;
char* p;

p = static_cast<char*> (&a);
```

In this case, however, it is *user beware!* Unless you cast all operations that used p, you would most likely end up creating serious errors. In fact, we will say that, with only a few exceptions such as the *void* pointer and casting for reading files (discussed in Chapter 16), you should never cast a pointer. The following assignments are all valid, but they are extremely dangerous and must be used with a very carefully thought-out design.

```
void* pVoid;
char* pChar;
int*  pInt;

pVoid  = pChar;
pInt   = pVoid;
pInt   = static_cast<int*> (pChar);
```

Let's construct an example in which we have two variables: one integer and one character. The character has one pointer associated with it; the integer has two, one a second-level pointer. These variables and their pointers are shown in Figure 9-21.

Without casting the assignment, we cannot make the character pointer point to the integer value. For example, it is invalid and will result in a compile error to store the address of a in pc.

Even when the pointers are associated with the same type, as seen in the integer pointers and examples in Figure 9-21, any assignment made must be at the correct level. It is an error to assign the address of a, even though it is an integer, to ppa. This is because ppa is a pointer to a pointer to an integer; its type is pointer to pointer, not pointer to integer. Therefore, it can only be assigned the address of a pointer to an integer. As shown in Figure 9-22, pointer types must match.

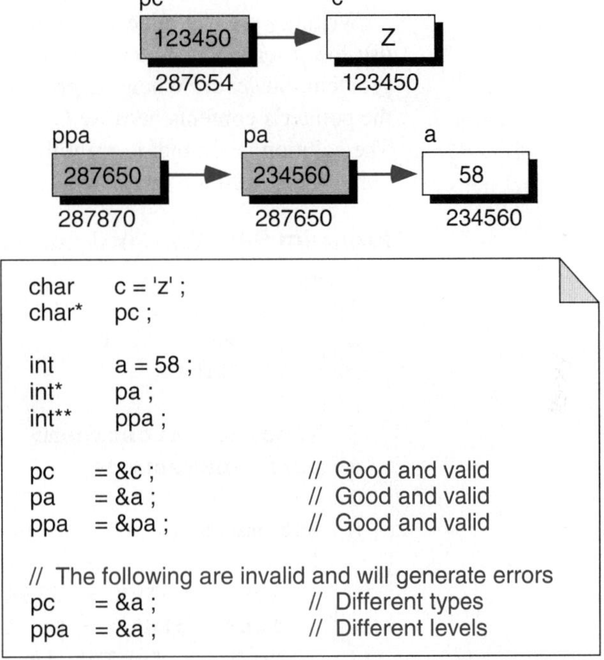

Figure 9-21 Pointer compatibility

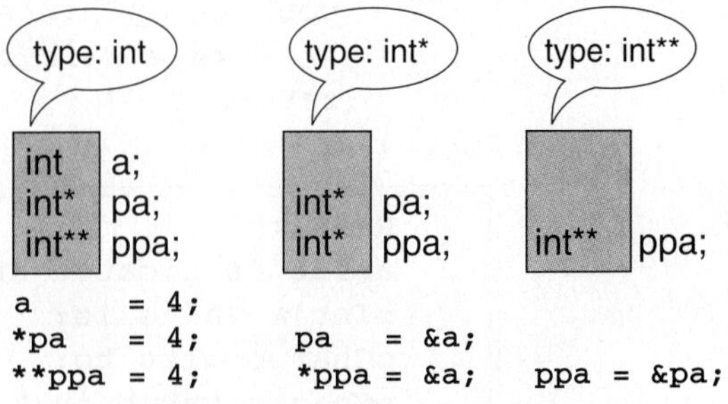

Figure 9-22 Pointer types must match

9-9 READING AND WRITING POINTER VALUES

In general, there is no reason to read pointer values and there is little reason to write them. Occasionally, especially in the absence of a debugger,[2] we use them to print out the contents of a pointer to help solve a program error.

[2]A debugger is a special compiler feature that allows us to examine, among other things, the contents of variables during the execution of a program. It is common in most compilers today.

The extraction operator (>>) is overloaded for pointers; however, the implementation is system dependent. We do not recommend using it to read addresses.

Writing a pointer value is a standard procedure supported by all compilers. We simply use the insertion operator to print the address. The character type presents a minor problem, however. When we print a pointer to character, it prints a string rather than the pointer's contents because C-style strings are defined using pointers to character.[3] The solution is simple; to print the address in a character pointer, we cast it to a *void* pointer. Program 9-8 demonstrates writing pointer values.

Program 9-8 Demonstrate writing pointer values

```
1  /* Demonstrate writing pointer values
2        Written by:
3        Date:
4  */
5  #include <iostream>
6  using namespace std;
7
8  int main ()
9  {
10    int   anInt = 1234;
11    int*  pInt  = &anInt;
12    cout << "anInt is located at:   " << &anInt << endl;
13    cout << "pInt's value is:       " << pInt   << endl;
14
15    char* pChar = "Hello";         // Pointer to C-string
16    cout << "pChar points to:       " << pChar  << endl;
17    cout << "pChar's value is:      "
18         << static_cast<void*> (pChar) << endl;
19    return 0;
20 }  // main
```

```
Results
anInt is located at:    0xbffffb20
pInt's value is:        0xbffffb20
pChar points to:        Hello
pChar's value is:       0x001cde5e
```

Program 9-8 Analysis To prove that we print the pointer's value, we first display the address of `anInt` in statement 12. Then we print `pInt`. The output verifies that `pInt` contains the address of `anInt`.

9-10 LVALUE AND RVALUE

In C++, an expression is either an lvalue or an rvalue. Every expression has a value, but the value in an expression (after evaluation) can be used in two different ways.

[3]We discuss C-style strings in Chapter 14.

1. An **lvalue** expression must be used whenever the object is receiving a value—that is, when it is being modified.
2. An **rvalue** expression can be used to supply a value for further use—that is, it can be used to examine or copy its value.

How can you identify when an expression is an lvalue and when it is an rvalue? Fortunately, only seven types of expressions are lvalue expressions. They are shown in Table 9-1.

	Expression type[a]	Comments
1.	identifier	Variable identifier
2.	expression[...]	Array indexing
3.	(expression)	Expression must already be lvalue
4.	*expression	Dereferenced expression
5.	expression.name	Structure selection
6.	expression->name	Structure indirect selection
7.	function call	If function uses *return* by reference

[a]The shaded expressions have not yet been covered in this book

Table 9-1 lvalue expressions

For example, the following are lvalue expressions:

```
a = ...     a[5] = ...     (a) = ...     *p = ...
```

All expressions that are not lvalue expressions are rvalues. The following are some examples of rvalue expressions:

```
5        a + 2        a * 6        a[2] + 3        a++
```

Note that even if an expression is an lvalue, if it is used as part of a larger expression in which the operators create only rvalue expressions, then the whole expression is an rvalue. For example, `a[2]` is an lvalue, but when it is used in the expression `a[2] + 3`, the whole expression is an rvalue, not an lvalue. Similarly, in the expression `a++`, a is an lvalue, whereas the whole expression `(a++)` is an rvalue.

Why do we concern ourselves with lvalues and rvalues? The reason is that some operators need an lvalue as their operand. If we use one of these operators and use an rvalue in place of the operand, we get a compile error. Fortunately, only a few operators need an lvalue expression as an operand. They are listed in Table 9-2.

Type of expression	Examples
Address operator	&score
Postfix increment/decrement	x++ y--
Prefix increment/decrement	++x --y
Assignment (left operand)	x = 1 y += 3 etc.

Table 9-2 Operators that require lvalue expressions

Table 9-3 contains several examples of invalid expressions that create syntax errors if an rvalue is used when an lvalue is needed.

Expression	Problem
a + 2 = 6;	a + 2 is an rvalue and cannot be the left operand in an assignment; it is a temporary value that does not have an address; there is no place to store 6.
&(a + 2);	a + 2 is an rvalue and the address operator needs an lvalue; rvalues are temporary values and do not have addresses.
&4;	Same as above (4 is an rvalue).
(a+2)++; ++(a +2);	Postfix and prefix operators require lvalues; (a + 2) is an rvalue.

Table 9-3 Invalid rvalue expressions

One final thought: A variable name can assume the role of either an lvalue or an rvalue depending on how it is used in an expression. In the following expression, a is an lvalue because it is on the left of the assignment and b is an rvalue because it is on the right of the assignment.

```
a = b
```

9-11 POINTER APPLICATIONS

In this section we demonstrate two ways we can use pointers when calling functions.

CONVERT SECONDS TO HOURS

We begin with a simple function that converts time in seconds to hours, minutes, and seconds. While the function is simple, it does require three address parameters to return the values. The code is shown in Program 9-9.

Program 9-9 Convert seconds to hours, minutes, and seconds

```
/* =================== secToHours ===================
   Given time in seconds, convert it to hours, minutes,
   and seconds.
      Pre    time in seconds
             addresses of hours, minutes, seconds
      Post   hours, minutes, seconds calculated
      Return error indicator--1 success, 0 bad time
*/
int secToHours (long  time,     int* hours,
                      int*  minutes, int* seconds)
{
   long localTime = time;
   *seconds   = localTime % 60;
   localTime = localTime / 60;
   *minutes   = localTime % 60;
```

Program 9-9 Convert seconds to hours, minutes, and seconds (*continued*)

```
    *hours     = localTime / 60;

    if (*hours > 24)
       return 0;
    else
       return 1;
} // secToHours
```

Program 9-9 Analysis The first question you might ask when reading this simple function is "Why define a local variable for the time?" In this short function, it really wasn't necessary. However, a good programmer does not change a value parameter within the function, because its original value maybe needed later. We have seen times when "later" turned out to be a maintenance change and hours were spent debugging the error when the wrong value was computed.

> **Create local variables when a value parameter will be changed within a function so that the original value will always be available for processing.**

Another important design point: If you need to send back two values from a called function, *do not pass one back through a pointer and return the other.* Either use the return for some other reason, such as a status flag, or make the return *void*. Keeping your design consistent—in this case by using a consistent method of returning the values—makes your programs easier to understand and is an example of the KISS principle.

> **When several values need to be sent back to the calling function, use address parameters for all of them. Do not return one value and use address parameters for the others.**

QUADRATIC EQUATIONS

Let's look at a typical program design that reads, processes, and prints data. This is a processing cycle that is common to many, many programs. Figure 9-23 shows its structure chart.

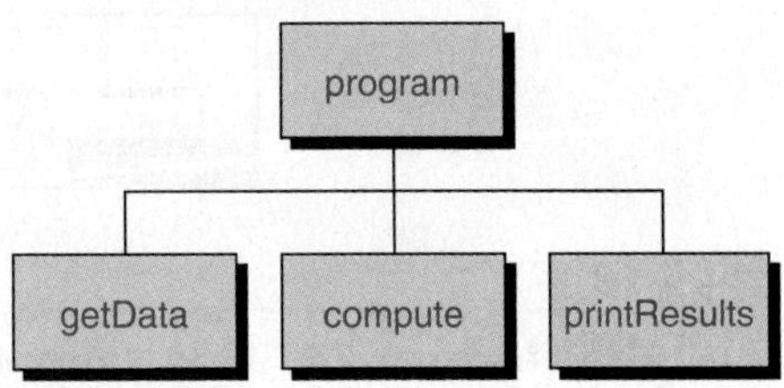

Figure 9-23 A common program design

To demonstrate the universality of this design, let's compute the real roots for a quadratic equation. Recall that a quadratic equation has the form

$$ax^2 + bx + c = 0$$

Four possible situations can occur when you solve for the roots in a quadratic equation. First, it is an error if both `a` and `b` are 0: There is no solution. Second, if `a` is 0 and `b` is not 0, there is only one root:

$$x = \frac{-c}{b}$$

Third, if $b^2 - 4ac$ is 0 or positive, there are two, possibly equal, roots derived from the following equation:

$$x = \frac{-b \pm \sqrt{b^2 - 4ac}}{2a}$$

Finally, if $b^2 - 4ac$ is negative, the roots are imaginary.

Figure 9-24 diagrams the interaction of the variables and pointers for Program 9-10. In this short program, we use pointers to pass data from a read function, pass both values and pointers to a compute function, and finally pass the values to a print function.

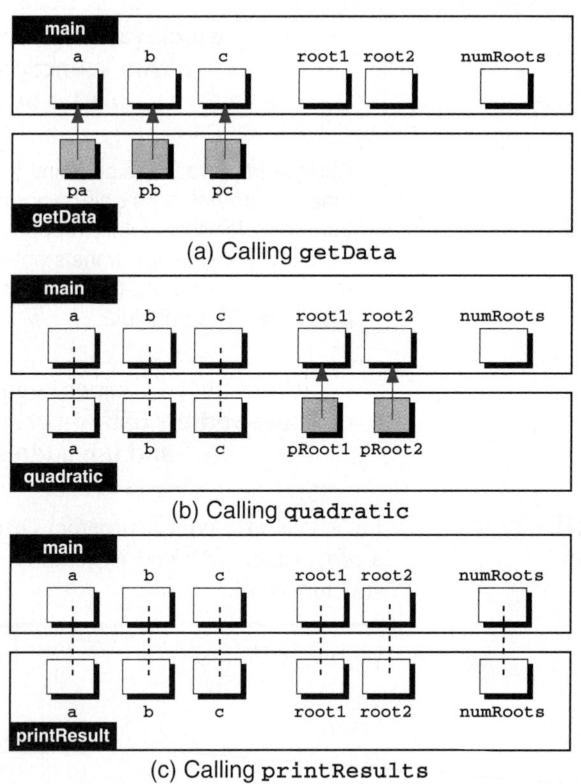

Figure 9-24 Using pointers as parameters

Program 9-10 Quadratic roots

```
/* Test driver for quadratic function.
      Written by:
      Date:
*/
#include <iostream>
#include <cmath>
using namespace std;

void getData      (int*    a,      int* b, int* c);
int  quadratic    (int     a,      int  b, int  c,
                   double* pRoot1, double* pRoot2);
void printResults (int     numRoots,
                   int     a,      int  b, int  c,
                   double  root1,  double root2);

int main ()
{
   cout << "Solve quadratic equations.\n\n";
   char again = 'Y';
   while (again == 'Y' || again == 'y')
      {
       int    a;
       int    b;
       int    c;
       getData (&a, &b, &c);

       double root1;
       double root2;
       int numRoots = quadratic (a, b, c, &root1, &root2);
       printResults (numRoots, a, b, c, root1, root2);

       cout << "\nDo you have another equation (Y/N): ";
       cin  >> again;
      } // while
   cout << "\nThank you.\n";
   return 0;
} // main

/* ================== getData =================
   Read coefficients for quadratic equation.
      Pre   a, b, and c contains addresses
      Post  data read into addresses in main
*/
void getData   (int* a, int* b, int* c)
{
   cout << "Please enter coefficients a, b, & c: ";
   cin  >> *a >> *b >> *c;
   return;
} // getData
```

Program 9-10 Quadratic roots (*continued*)

```
/* ================== quadratic ==================
   Compute the roots for a quadratic equation.
      Pre   a, b, & c are the coefficients
            pRoot1 & pRoot2 are variable pointers
      Post  roots computed, stored in calling function
      Return   2 two roots,
               1 one root,
               0 imaginary roots
              -1 not quadratic coefficients.
*/
int quadratic (int     a, int  b, int c,
                     double* pRoot1, double* pRoot2)
{
   int result;


   if (a == 0 && b == 0)
      result = -1;
   else
      if (a == 0)
         {
          *pRoot1 = -c / (double) b;
          result = 1;
         } // a == 0
      else
         {
          double discriminant =  b * b  - (4 * a * c);
          if (discriminant >= 0)
             {
              double root    = sqrt(discriminant);
              *pRoot1 = (-b + root) / (2 * a);
              *pRoot2 = (-b - root) / (2 * a);
              result  = 2;
             } // if >= 0
          else
              result = 0;
         } // else
   return result;
}  // quadratic

/* ================ printResults ================
   Prints the factors for the quadratic equation.
      Pre   numRoots contains 0, 1, 2
            a, b, c contains original coefficients
            root1 and root2 contains roots
      Post  roots have been printed
*/
```

Program 9-10 Quadratic roots (*continued*)

```
void printResults  (int    numRoots,
                    int    a,      int    b, int c,
                    double root1,  double root2)
{
   cout << "Your equation: " << a << "x**2 + "
        << b  << "x + " << c << endl;
   switch (numRoots)
      {
       case 2:  cout << "Roots are: "  << root1
                      << " & " << root2 << endl;
                break;
       case 1:  cout << "Only one root: "
                      <<  root1 << endl;
                break;
       case 0:  cout << "Roots are imaginary.\n";
                break;
       default: cout << "Invalid coefficients\n";
                break;
      } // switch
   return;
} // printResults
// ================ End of Program ==================
```

```
Results:
Solve quadratic equations.

Please enter the coefficients a, b, & c: 2 4 2
Your equation: 2x**2 + 4x + 2
Roots are: -1 & -1

Do you have another equation (Y/N): y
Please enter the coefficients a, b, & c: 0 4 2
Your equation: 0x**2 + 4x + 2
Only one root: -0.5

Do you have another equation (Y/N): y
Please enter the coefficients a, b, & c: 2 2 2
Your equation: 2x**2 + 2x + 2
Roots are imaginary.

Do you have another equation (Y/N): y
Please enter the coefficients a, b, & c: 0 0 2
Your equation: 0x**2 + 0x + 2
Invalid coefficients

Do you have another equation (Y/N): y
Please enter coefficients a, b, & c: 1 -5 6
Your equation: 1x**2 + -5x + 6
Roots are:  3 &  2
```

Program 9-10 Quadratic roots (*continued*)

```
Do you have another equation (Y/N): n

Thank you.
```

Program 9-10 Analysis This problem has many interesting points. The function `main` is a test driver—that is, code that will not be put into production. Therefore, we code much of the test logic in `main` rather than providing separate functions for it.

The variables in these examples are either integers or pointers to integers. Parameters that receive something from `main` are integers whose values will be filled when the call is made. Those that send data back to `main` are pointers to integer that will be filled with the addresses of the corresponding variables in `main`. As a general rule, if a value will be changed, it must be passed as a pointer. If it will not be changed, it should be passed as a value. This protects data from accidental destruction.

In `quadratic`, note the extensive testing to make sure that the coefficients are valid. To ensure valid code, they are all necessary. Look at how we calculated the square root of the discriminant separately (statement 80). Since square root is a complex function, it is more efficient to call it just once and save the value for later use. Note also that the function has only one *return* statement. This is proper structured code, although many professional programmers would simply return at statements 68, 73, 83, and 86.

Study our test data carefully. Note that this set of test data executes every line of code in the program. Designing test data that completely validates a function is not an easy task. Ensuring that all code has been executed is even more difficult and tedious. One way to make sure that all code has been tested is to use your debugger to set a break point at every statement and then clear them as the program executes. When all break points have been cleared, you know every instruction has been executed.

Executing every line of code does not ensure that the function has no bugs, however. With large programs, it is virtually impossible to test every possible combination of data. One of the advantages of structured programming is that by breaking the program down into separate functions, we can test it better.

This program has a potential problem. Do you see it? Hint: What if the user enters invalid data, such as a character rather than a number? There is no error checking in `getData`. If this were a production program, it would contain code to check for errors. It would then return a status flag to indicate if `getData` was successful or not.

9-12 ARRAYS AND POINTERS

There is a very close relationship between arrays and pointers. The name of an array is a pointer constant to the first element. Because the array's name is a pointer constant, its value cannot be changed. Figure 9-25 shows an array with the array name as a pointer constant.

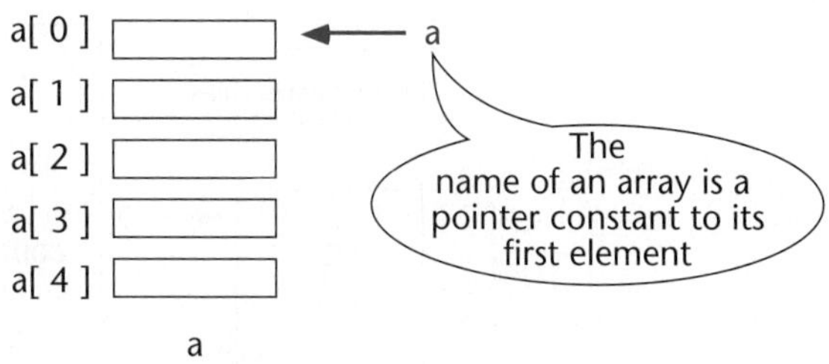

Figure 9-25 Pointers to arrays

Since the array name is a pointer constant to the first element, the address of the first element and the name of the array both represent the same location in memory. We can, therefore, use the array name anywhere we can use a pointer, as long as it is being used as an rvalue. Specifically, this means that we can use it with the indirection operator. When we dereference an array name, we are dereferencing the first element of the array; that is, we are referring to array[0]. Note, however, that when the array name is dereferenced, it is referring only to the first element, not the whole array.

> `a` ←same→ `&a[0]`
>
> `a` is a pointer only to the first element not the whole array.

Prove this to yourself by writing a program with the code block shown below. The block prints the address of the first element of the array (`&a[0]`) and the array name, which is a pointer constant.

```
{ // Demonstrate array name is a pointer constant
  int a [5];
  cout << "Address of a[0]: " << &a[0]
       << "Name as pointer: " << a  << endl;
}
```

The values printed by this code will be addresses in your computer. The first printed address (the address of the first element in the array) and the second printed address (the array pointer) will be the same, proving our point.

A simple variation on this code is to print the value in the first element of the array using both a pointer and an index. This code is demonstrated in Figure 9-26. Note that the same value, 2, is printed in both cases, again proving our point that the array name is a pointer constant to the beginning of the array.

Now we'll explore another point. If the name of an array is really a pointer, let's see if we can store this pointer in a pointer variable and use it in the same way we use the name of the array. The program that demonstrates this is shown in Figure 9-27.

Right after we define and initialize the array, we define a pointer and initialize it to point to the first element of the array by assigning the array name. Note especially that the array name is unqualified; that is, there is no address operator or index specification. We then print the first element in the array, first using an index notation and then pointer notation.

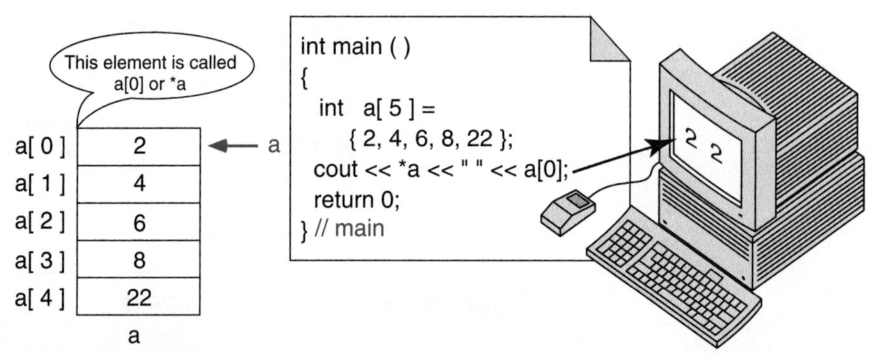

Figure 9-26 Dereference of array name

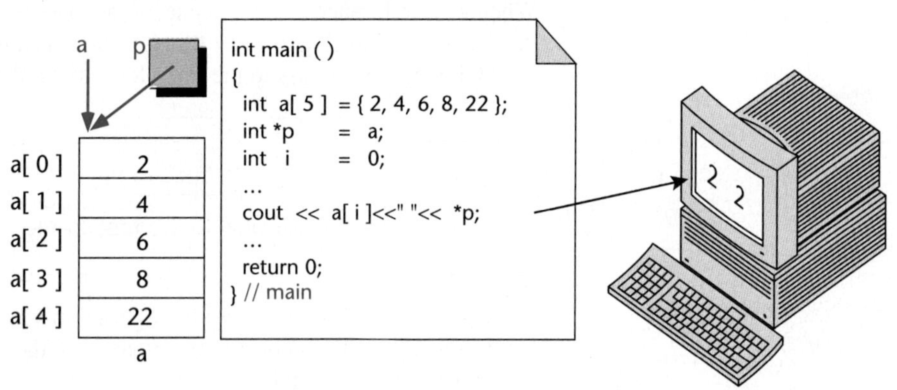

Figure 9-27 Array names as pointers

Let's look at another example that explores the close relationship between an array and a pointer. We store the address of the second element of the array in a pointer variable. Now we can use two different names to access each element. This does not mean that we have two arrays; rather, it shows that a single array can be accessed through different pointers.

> **To access an array, any pointer to the first element can be used instead of the name of the array.**

Figure 9-28 demonstrates the use of multiple names for an array to reference different locations at the same time. First, we have the array name. We then create a pointer to integer and set it to the second element of the array (`a[1]`). Now, even though it is a pointer, we can use it as an array name and index it to point to different elements in the array. We demonstrate this by printing the first two elements using first the array name and then the pointer. Note especially that, when a pointer is not referencing the first element of an array, it can have a negative offset. This is shown in the reference to `p[-1]`. (Offsets are discussed in the next section.)

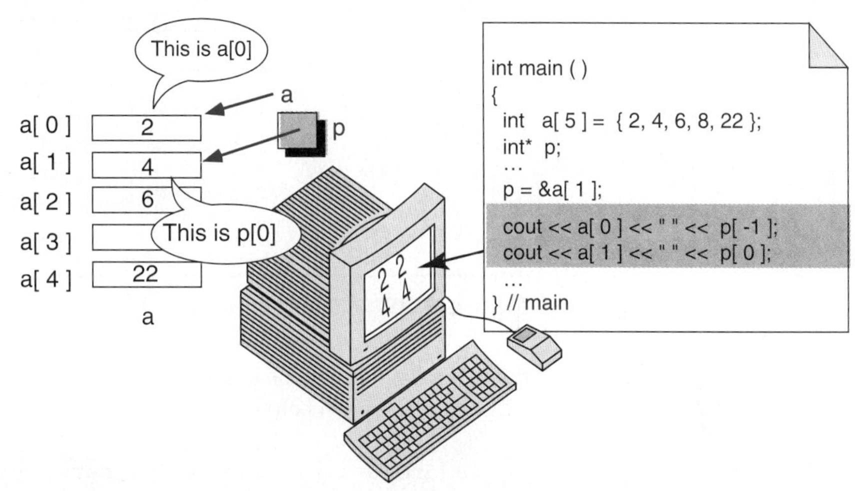

Figure 9-28 Multiple array pointers

9-13 POINTER ARITHMETIC AND ARRAYS

Besides indexing, there is another powerful method of moving through an array: **pointer arithmetic**. Pointer arithmetic offers a restricted set of arithmetic operators for manipulating the addresses in pointers. Pointer arithmetic is especially powerful when we want to move through an array from element to element, such as when we are searching an array sequentially.

POINTERS AND ONE-DIMENSIONAL ARRAYS

If we have an array, `a`, then `a` is a constant pointing to the first element and `a + 1` is a constant pointing to the second element. Again, if we have a pointer, `p`, pointing to the second element of an array (see Figure 9-28), then `p - 1` is a a pointer to the previous (first) element and `p + 1` is a pointer to the next (third) element. Furthermore, given `a`, `a + 2` is the address two elements from `a` and `a + 3` is the address three elements from `a`. We can generalize the notation, therefore, as follows:

> **Given pointer, *p*, *p* ± *n* is a pointer to the value *n* elements away.**

It does not matter how `a` and `p` are defined or initialized; as long as they are pointing to one of the elements of the array, we can add or subtract to get the address of the other elements of the array. This concept is portrayed in Figure 9-29.

The meaning of adding or subtracting here is different from normal arithmetic. When you add an integer *n* to a pointer value, you will get a value that corresponds to another index location *n elements away*. In other words, *n* is an **offset** from the original pointer. To determine the new value, C++ must know the size of one element. The size of the element is determined by the type of the pointer. This is one of the prime reasons that pointers of different types cannot be assigned to each other.

If the offset is 1, then C++ can simply add or subtract one element size from the current pointer value. This may make the access more efficient than the corresponding index notation. If the offset is more than 1, C++ must compute the offset by multiplying

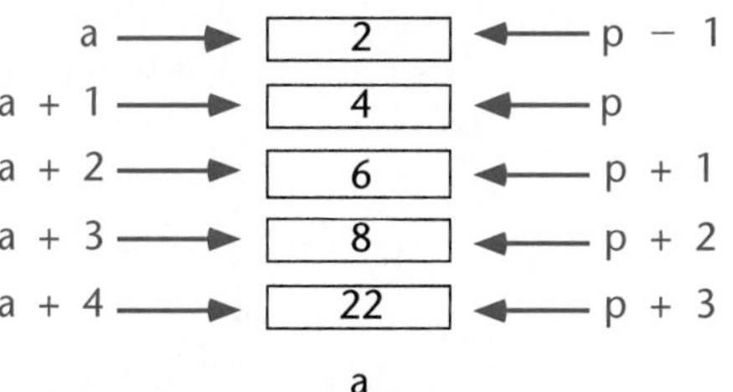

Figure 9-29 Pointer arithmetic

the offset by the size of one array element and adding it to the pointer value. This calculation is shown below.

```
address = pointer + (offset * size of element)
```

Depending on the hardware, the multiplication in this formula can make it less efficient than simply adding 1, and the efficiency advantage of pointer arithmetic over indexing may be lost.

We see the result of pointer arithmetic on different-sized elements in Figure 9-30. For *char*, which is usually implemented as one byte, adding 1 moves us to the next memory address (101). Assuming that integers are four bytes `(b)`, adding 1 moves us four bytes in memory (104). Finally, assuming the size of float is six bytes `(c)`, adding 1 moves us six bytes in memory (106). In other words, `a + 1` means different things in different situations.

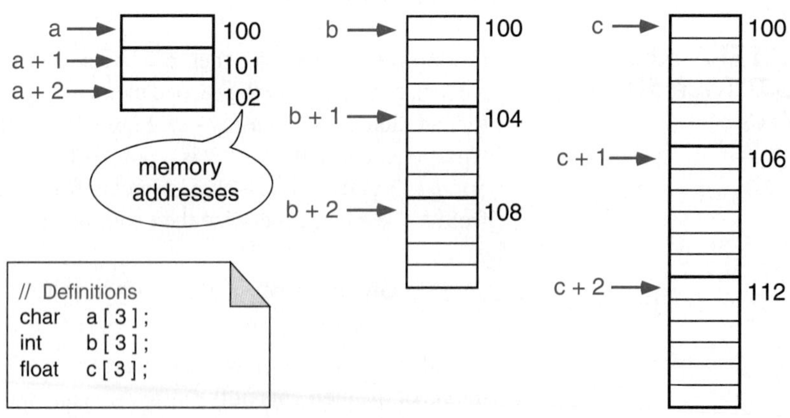

Figure 9-30 Pointer arithmetic and different types

We've shown how to get the address of an array element using a pointer and an offset; now let's look at how we can use that value. We have two choices: First, we can assign it to another pointer. This is a rather elementary operation that uses the assignment operator, as shown below.

```
p = aryName + 5;
```

Second, we can use it with the indirection operator to access or change the value of the element we are pointing to. This possibility is demonstrated in Figure 9-31.

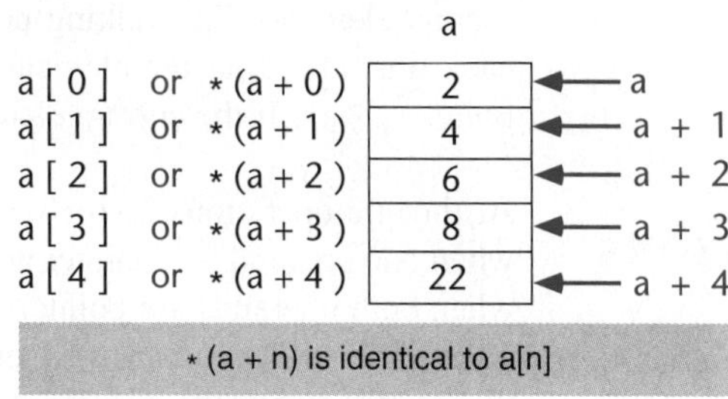

Figure 9-31 Dereferencing array pointers

To practice, let's use pointers to find the smallest number among five integers stored in an array. Figure 9-32 tracks the code as it works its way through the array.

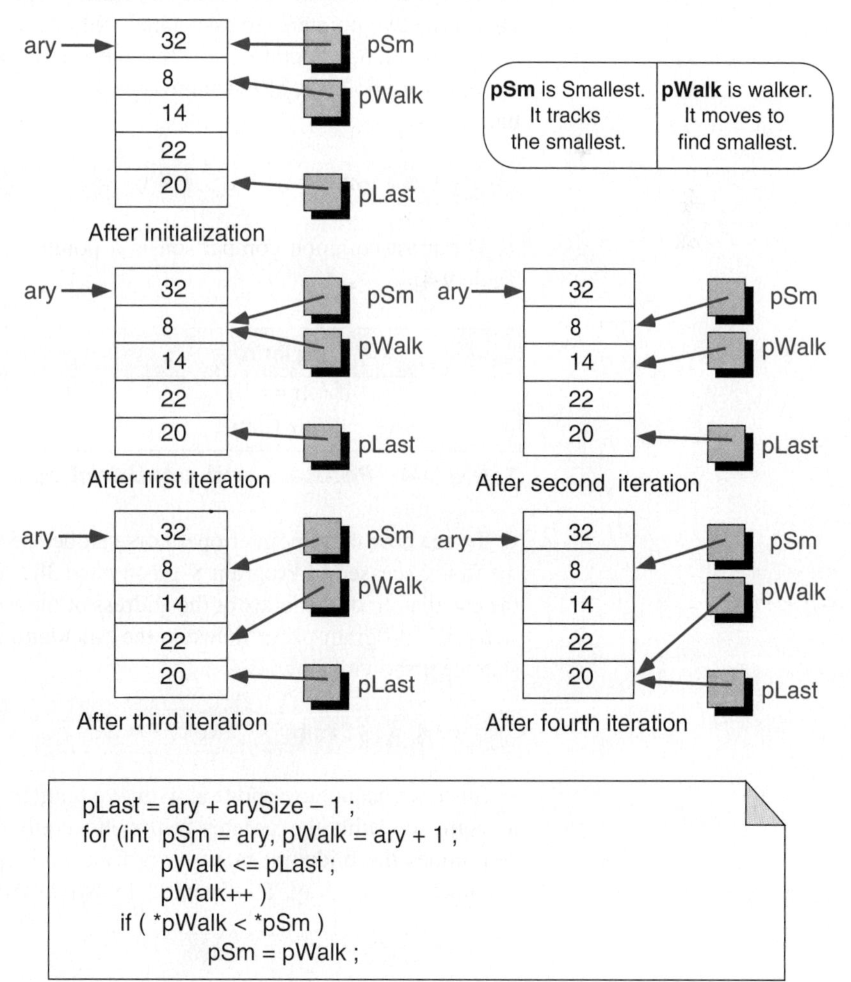

Figure 9-32 Find smallest

We start with the smallest pointer (pSm) set to the first element of the array. The function's job is to see if any of the remaining elements are smaller. Since we know that the first element is not smaller than itself, we set the walking pointer (pWalk) to the second element. The walking pointer then advances through the remaining elements, each time checking the element it is currently looking at against the smallest to that point, (pSm). If the current element is smaller, its location is assigned to pSm.

POINTERS AND OTHER OPERATORS

Arithmetic operations involving pointers are very limited. Addition can be used only when one operand is a pointer and the other is an integer. Subtraction can be used only when both operands are pointers or when the first operand is a pointer and the second operand is an integer, such as an array index. You can also manipulate a pointer with the postfix and unary increment and decrement operators. All of the following pointer arithmetic operations are valid:

```
p + 5    5 + p    p - 5    p1 - p2    p++    --p
```

When one pointer is subtracted from another, the result is an index representing the number of elements between the two pointers. Note, however, that the result is meaningful only if the two pointers are associated with the same array structure.

The relational operators (such as less than and equal) are allowed only if both operands are pointers of the same type. Two pointer relational expressions are shown below.

```
p1 >= p2          p1 != p2
```

The most common comparison is a pointer and the NULL constant, as shown in Table 9-4.

Long form	Short form
if (ptr == 0)	if (!ptr)
if (ptr != 0)	if (ptr)

Table 9-4 Pointers and relational operators

To see how these pointer operators can be used, consider the binary search program we first discussed in Program 8-14 on page 382. Recall that the binary search requires the calculation of the index or the address of the entry in the middle of a table. When we wrote the program using indexes, the calculation of the midpoint was done with the statement shown below.

```
mid = (first + last) / 2;
```

Since we cannot use addition with two pointers, this formula will not work. We need to come up with the pointer arithmetic equivalent. There is another formula that determines the midpoint in an array by calculating the number of elements from the beginning of the array. This method, known as the offset method, is shown below.

```
mid = first + (last - first) / 2;
```

The offset calculation also works with pointers. The subtraction of the first pointer from the last pointer gives us the number of elements in the array. The offset from the beginning of the array is determined by dividing the number of elements in the array by 2. We can then add the offset to the pointer for the beginning of the list to arrive at the midpoint. The pointer code is shown below.

```
midPtr = firstPtr + (lastPtr - firstPtr) / 2;
```

The pointer implementation of the binary search is shown in Program 9-11.

Program 9-11 Pointers and the binary search

```
1  /* Search an ordered list using binary search.
2     Pre  list: must contain at least one element
3          endPtr: pointer to largest element in list
4          target: is the value of element being sought
5     Post FOUND: locnPtr pointer to target element
6                 return true (found)
7        NOT FOUND: locnPtr = element below|above target
8                 return false (not found)
9  */
10 bool binarySearch (int list[ ], int*  endPtr,
11                    int target,  int** locnPtr)
12 {
13    int* midPtr;
14
15    int* firstPtr = list;
16    int* lastPtr = endPtr;
17    while (firstPtr <= lastPtr)
18       {
19        midPtr = firstPtr + (lastPtr - firstPtr) / 2;
20        if (target > *midPtr)
21           // look in upper half
22           firstPtr = midPtr + 1;
23        else if (target < *midPtr)
24              // look in lower half
25              lastPtr = midPtr - 1;
26        else
27              // found equal: force exit
28              firstPtr = lastPtr + 1;
29       } // end while
30    *locnPtr = midPtr;
31    return (target == *midPtr);
32 } // binarySearch
```

Program 9-11 Analysis Although the code in this function is relatively simple, the coding for `locnPtr` merits some discussion. In the calling function, `locnPtr` is a pointer to the found location. To store the pointer in `locnPtr`, therefore, we need to pass a pointer to a pointer to an integer (see statement 11). To correspond to this type, the calling function must pass the address of its location pointer.

In addition to demonstrating the subtraction of two pointers, Program 9-11 also shows the use of a relational operator with two pointers (see statement 17).

POINTERS AND TWO-DIMENSIONAL ARRAYS

The first thing to notice about two-dimensional arrays is that, just as in a one-dimensional array, the name of the array is a pointer constant to the first element of the array. In this case, however, the first element *is another array!* Assume that we have a two-dimensional array of integers. When we dereference the array name, we don't get one integer, we get an array of integers. In other words, the dereference of the array name of a two-dimensional array is a pointer to a one-dimensional array. Figure 9-33 contains a two-dimensional array and a code fragment to print the array.

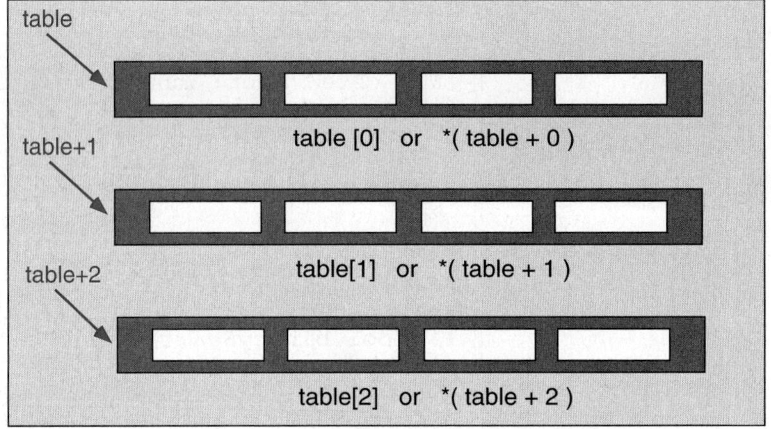

int table[3][4] ;

```
for ( int i = 0; i < 3; i++ )
   {
    for ( int j = 0; j < 4; j++ )
        int cout << setw(6)
                 << *(*(table + i ) + j ) ;
    cout << endl ;
   } // for i
```

Print table

Figure 9-33 Pointers to two-dimensional arrays

Each element in the figure is shown in both index and pointer notation. Note that `table[0]` refers to an array of four integer values. The equivalent pointer notation is the dereference of the array name plus zero, `*(table + 0)`, which also refers to an array of four integers.

```
table[0]  is identical to  *(table + 0)
```

To demonstrate pointer manipulation with a two-dimensional array, let's print the table in Figure 9-33. To print the array requires nested *for* loops. For multidimensional arrays, however, there is no simple pointer notation. To refer to a row, we dereference the array pointer, which gives us a pointer to a row. To refer to an individual element, therefore, we dereference the row pointer. This double dereference is shown below.

```
*(*(table))
```

The above expression refers only to the first element of the first row. To step through all the elements, we need to add two offsets, one for the row and one for the element within the row. We use loop counters, `i` and `j`, as the offsets. This is the same logic we saw when we printed a two-dimensional array using indexes. To print an element, we use the array name, `table`, and adjust it with the loop indexes. This gives us the relatively complex expression shown below.

```
*(*(table + i) + j)
```

This pointer notation is equivalent to the index syntax, `table[i][j]`. With multidimensional arrays, the pointer arithmetic has no efficiency advantage over indexing. Because the pointer notation for multidimensional arrays is so complex and there is no efficiency advantage, most programmers find it easier to use the index notation.

9-14 PASSING AN ARRAY TO A FUNCTION

Since the name of an array is actually a pointer to the first element, we can send the array name to a function for processing. When we pass the array, we do not use the address operator. Remember, the array name is a pointer constant, so the name is already the address of the first element in the array. A typical call would look like the following:

```
doIt (aryName);
```

The called program can declare the array in one of two ways. First, it can use the traditional array notation. This format has the advantage of telling the user very clearly that the program is dealing with an array rather than a single pointer. This is an advantage from a structured programming and human engineering point of view.

```
int doIt (int ary [ ]);
```

You can also declare the array in the prototype statement as a simple pointer. The disadvantage to this format is that, while technically correct, it actually masks the data structure (array). Note that for one-dimensional arrays, a simple pointer as shown in the following example is the code of choice with professional programmers.

```
int doIt (int* arySalary);
```

If you choose to code this way, it is advisable to use a good, descriptive name for the parameter to minimize any reader confusion. The function documentation should also indicate clearly that an array is being passed.

Note, however, that if you are passing a multidimensional array, you must use the array syntax in the header declaration and definition. The compiler needs to know the size of the dimensions after the first to calculate the offset for pointer arithmetic. Thus, to receive a three-dimensional array, you would use the following declaration in the function's header statement:

```
float doIt (int bigAry[ ] [12] [5]);
```

To see how it works, let's write a program that calls a function to multiply each element of a one-dimensional array by two. The program's variables are shown in Figure 9-34, and the code is given in Program 9-12.

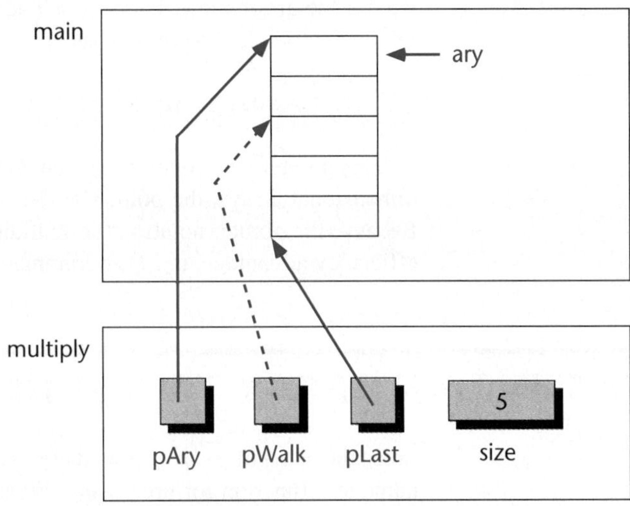

Figure 9-34 Variables for multiplying array elements by two

Program 9-12 Multiply array elements by two

```
/* Read integers from keyboard & print them multiplied by 2.
      Written by:
      Date:
*/
#include <iostream>
#include <iomanip>
using namespace std;

const short cSIZE = 5;

void multiply (int* pAry, int cSIZE);

int main ()
{
   int  ary [cSIZE];

   int* pLast = ary + cSIZE - 1;
   for (int* pWalk = ary; pWalk <= pLast; pWalk++)
      {
       cout << "Please enter an integer: ";
       cin  >> *pWalk;
      } // for pWalk

   multiply (ary, cSIZE);

```

Program 9-12 Multiply array elements by two *(continued)*

```
   cout << "Doubled size is: \n";
   for (int* pWalk = ary; pWalk <= pLast; pWalk++)
       cout << setw(4) << *pWalk << endl;
   return 0;
}  // main
/* ================== multiply ===================
   Multiply elements in an array by 2.
      Pre  pAry is pointer to full array
           size indicates number of elements in array
      Post Values in array doubled
*/
void multiply (int* pAry, int  size)
{
   int* pLast = pAry + size - 1;
   for (int* pWalk = pAry; pWalk <= pLast; pWalk++)
       *pWalk = *pWalk * 2;
    return;
}  // multiply
```

Program 9-12 Analysis There are several points of interest in this program. First, we have declared the array in the prototype using the more common pointer notation but have given it a name that indicates it is a pointer to an array (`pAry`).

In the multiply function, we use a separate pointer (`pWalk`) to walk through the list. We could have used `pAry`, since it was not being used other than to identify the beginning of the array. All too often, however, this type of "shortcut" saves a line or two of code only to create hours of debugging when the program is changed later. As a general rule, do not use formal parameters as variables unless their intent is to change a value in the calling program. This rule is especially important when the parameter is a pointer, as in this case.

Finally, note that we have passed the size of the array to the multiply function. We still need to know how much data we need to process, and we use the size to calculate the address of the last element in the list. As a variation on the limit test, however, we could have passed a pointer to the last element of the array, `&ary[SIZE-1]`. This would save the calculation of `pLast`. From a style and efficiency point of view, neither method has an advantage over the other. The structure and needs of other parts of the program usually dictate which method is used.

9-15 MEMORY ALLOCATION FUNCTIONS

One of the most serious limitations of the first high-level programming languages, FORTRAN and COBOL, is that their data structures are always fully defined at compile time. If they use an array that can vary greatly in size, the programmer must guess what will be the largest array ever needed. Of course, in keeping with Murphy's law that "what can go wrong, will!" their best guess is never big enough. Modern languages, such as C++, do not have this limitation because they have the capability to allocate memory at execution. This feature is known as *dynamic memory allocation.*

We therefore have two choices when we want to reserve memory locations for an object: static allocation and dynamic allocation. **Static memory allocation** requires that the declaration and definition of memory be fully specified in the source program. The number of bytes reserved cannot be changed during run time. Static allocation is the technique we have used in this book to this point. It works fine as long as you know exactly what your data requirements are.

Dynamic memory allocation uses predefined operators to allocate and release memory for data while the program is running. This approach effectively postpones the data definition to run time. To use dynamic memory allocation, the programmer must use either standard data types or already must have declared any derived types. Figure 9-35 shows the characteristics of memory allocation.

Understanding Complicated Declarations

To help you read and understand complicated declarations, we have developed the **right-left rule**. Using this rule to interpret a declaration, you start with the identifier in the center of a declaration and "read" the declaration by alternatively going right and then left until all entities have been read. The basic concept is shown below.

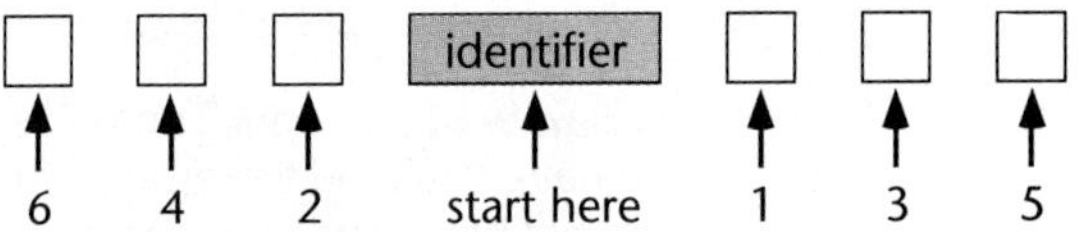

Consider the simple declaration

int x;

This is read as "x is □ an integer."[a]

```
int    x    □ ;
 ↑     ↑    ↑
 2     0    1
```

Since there is nothing on the right, we simply go left.

Now consider the example of a pointer declaration. This example is read as "p is □ a pointer □ to integer."

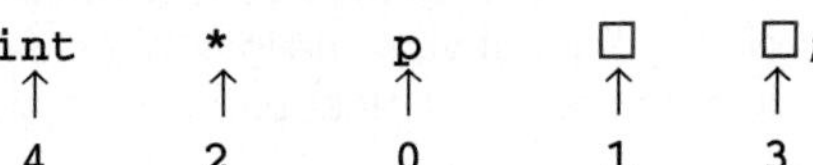

Note that we keep going right even when there is nothing there until all the entities on the left have been exhausted.

[a]The box (□) is just a place holder to show that there is no entity to be considered. Simply ignore it when you read each declaration.

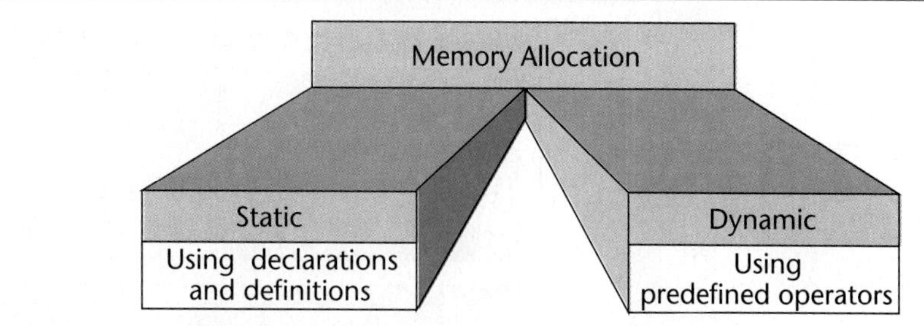

Figure 9-35 Memory allocation

MEMORY ALLOCATION

C++ uses two memory operators: *new* is used to allocate space from dynamic memory, and *delete* is used to return it for reuse, as shown in Figure 9-36.

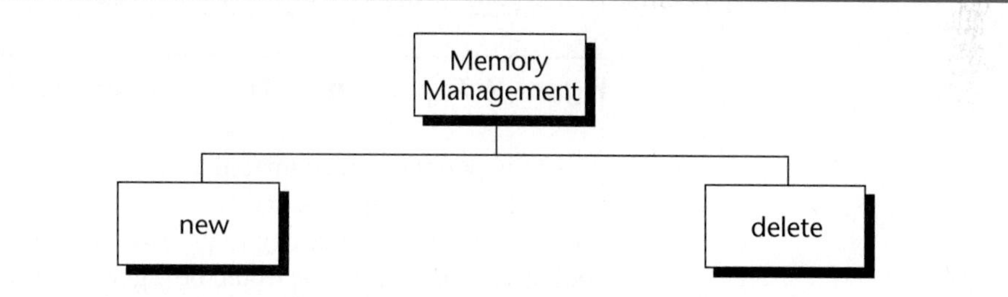

Figure 9-36 Memory management functions

To help you understand how dynamic memory allocation works, we will examine how memory is used. Conceptually, we can say that memory is divided into program memory and data memory. Program memory consists of the memory used for *main* and all called functions. Data memory consists of permanent definitions, such as global data and constants, local definitions, and dynamic data memory. Exactly how C++ handles these different needs is a function of the operating system and the compiler writer's skills. We can, however, generalize the concepts.

It should be obvious that *main* must be in memory at all times. Beyond *main,* each called function needs to be in memory only while it or any of its called functions are active. As a practical matter, most systems keep all functions in memory while the program is running.

Although the program code for a function may be in memory at all times, the local variables for the function are available only when it is active. Furthermore, it is possible for more than one version of the function to be active at a time. (See the discussion of recursion in Chapter 6.) In this case, multiple copies of the local variables will be allocated, although only one copy of the function is present. The memory facility for these capabilities is known as the **stack memory**.

In addition to the stack, there is a memory allocation known as the heap. **Heap memory** is unused memory allocated to the program and available to be assigned during its execution. It is the memory pool from which memory is allocated when requested by the memory allocation functions. This conceptual view of memory is shown in Figure 9-37.

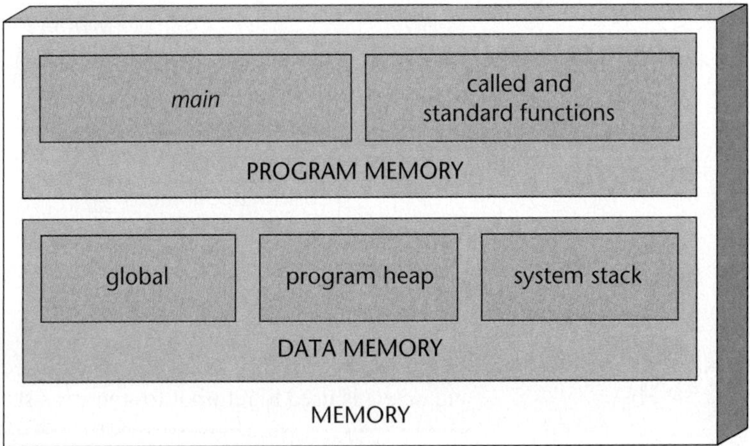

Figure 9-37 A conceptual view of memory

It is important to recognize that this is a conceptual view of memory. As we said before, how it is implemented is up to the software engineers who design the system. For example, there is nothing to prevent the stack and the heap from sharing the same pool of memory. In fact, it would be a good design concept to have them do so.

Dynamic Variable Allocation (*new*)

The ***new*** operator, found in the *new* library, allocates dynamic memory large enough to store the type being allocated and returns its address as a pointer. The allocated memory can only be referenced through a pointer. Also, the memory is not initialized. You should therefore assume that it will contain garbage and initialize it as required by your program.

The operator *new* is a unary operator; its operand is the object type for the memory being allocated. Since the compiler knows the size of all types, standard and derived, it knows the amount of space needed by the object's type. The following example allocates memory for an integer and assigns its address to the pointer.

```
int* ptr;

ptr = new int;
```

An attempt to allocate dynamic memory when there is not sufficient memory available is known as **overflow**. If there is not enough dynamic memory for an object, C++ throws an exception (aborts the program). In Chapter 14, "Exception Handling," we discuss how to intercept memory overflow in a program.

You can refer to dynamic memory only through a pointer.

Exactly what action should be taken when memory overflow is encountered depends on the specific application. If there is a possibility that memory will be released by another portion of the program, the memory request can be held. Generally, however, it is necessary to terminate the program. Figure 9-38 shows a typical *new* allocation. In this example, we are allocating one integer object. If the memory is allocated successfully, `ptr` contains a value (address). If the memory allocation is not successful (`ptr` contains NULL), there is no memory and we exit the program with error code 100.

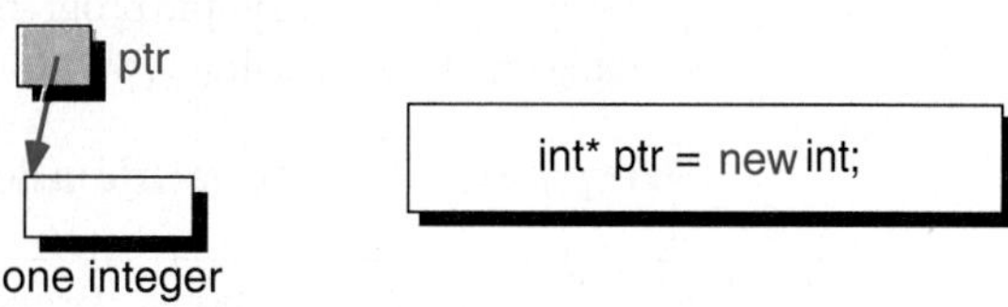

Figure 9-38 ***new* memory allocation for a single data item**

Dynamic Array Allocation (*new[ ]*)

Dynamic memory allocation for most objects is simple and straightforward, as shown above. When we must allocate memory for an array, however, we must also specify how many elements we need to allocate. We do this by suffixing the object's type with the number of elements required. For example, to allocate an array of 50 floating-point numbers, we would include the size [50] after the type, as shown below. For a one-dimensional array, the number of elements can be either a constant or a variable. For multidimensional arrays, all dimensions after the first must be specified with a constant size.

```
float* pSalesAry;

pSalesAry = new float[50];
```

The ability to allocate dynamic memory for arrays eliminates one of the most troublesome programming aspects for arrays: how big to make the array. Programmers no longer have to guess at the size only to find out that it was either too big, a waste of memory, or too small, an error that causes the program to terminate. The dynamic memory allocation of an array of 200 integers is shown in Figure 9-39.

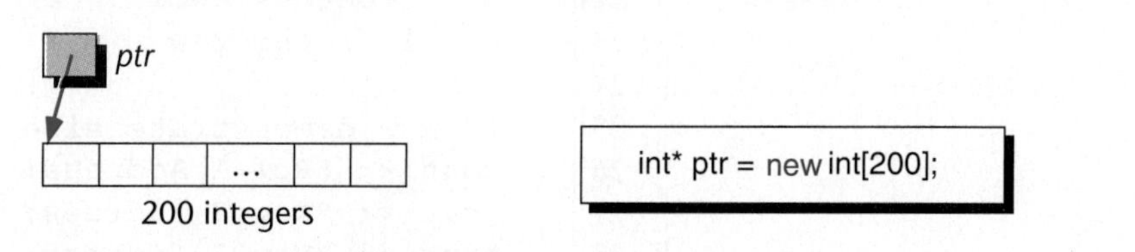

Figure 9-39 Memory allocation for an array

Now let's look at how we would allocate a two-dimensional array of integers with a variable number of rows, each containing 12 columns. Such a structure might be used to analyze the sales for a product line over a 12-month period. If we knew exactly how many items we were going to analyze each time we ran our program, we could simply create an array in static memory. However, if in one run we want to analyze 50 items and in the next run we want to analyze 20 items, dynamic arrays are the solution. Assuming that we read the number of items from the keyboard when we start the program, we could code the memory allocation as shown on the next example.

```
int** ptr;

ptr = new int[numItems][12];
```

Note that the number of items is a variable, while the number of months for each item (columns) is a constant 12. We examine the case where neither dimension is known in the next section.

Program 9-13 is a simple program that dynamically allocates a two dimensional array of integers. There are three rows of four columns each.

Program 9-13 Dynamic allocation of two-dimensional array

```
/* Demonstrate dynamic two-dimensional creating the
   array and printing the element addresses.
      Written by:
      Date:
*/
#include <iostream>
#include <new>
using namespace std;

const int cNumCols = 4;

int main ()
{
    int numRows = 3;
    int (*p2dAry)[cNumCols] = new int[numRows][cNumCols];

    // Now print array addresses
    for (int row = 0; row < numRows; row++)
        {
         for (int col = 0; col < cNumCols; col++)
             cout << &p2dAry[row][col] << " ";
         cout << endl;
        } // for row

    // Now demonstrate size of each row
    cout << "Row 1 Address: " << p2dAry     << endl;
    cout << "Row 2 Address: " << p2dAry + 1 << endl;
    cout << "Row 3 Address: " << p2dAry + 2 << endl;
    return 0;
} // main
```

```
Results:
0x80499d0 0x80499d4 0x80499d8 0x80499dc
0x80499e0 0x80499e4 0x80499e8 0x80499ec
0x80499f0 0x80499f4 0x80499f8 0x80499fc
Row 1 Address: 0x80499d0
Row 2 Address: 0x80499e0
Row 1 Address: 0x80499f0
```

Program 9-13 Analysis: The code that defines the array is not intuitive. It must be carefully studied. The name of an array, `p2dAry`, is a pointer to the first element of the array. In this case, the first element of the array is an array of four elements. The parentheses around the name create a pointer to an array of four integers. Assuming an integer size of 4 bytes, each row is 16 bytes long.

Because the first dimension of a multidimensional array is not required when the program is compiled, we can make the first dimension (numRows) a variable. The second, and any subsequent dimensions, however must be known. For this reason we made the number of columns a memory constant.

To verify the array, we print the address of each element. The addresses are printed in hexadecimal; by studying the results, you can see that each address is four larger than its predecessor. Finally, to demonstrate that the first row consists of four integers, we use pointer arithmetic to print the address of each row. In this case, each address is 16 bytes larger.

Initialization of Dynamic Memory

Only allocations for standard data types can be initialized with the *new* operator. Initialization for derived types must be programmed. To initialize a standard type, we enclose the initializer in parentheses after the type. To initialize the dynamic memory integer we allocated earlier to the value 39, we would write the following code:

```
int* ptr;

ptr = new int(39);
```

Releasing Memory (*delete*)

When dynamic memory locations are no longer needed, they should be released using the ***delete*** operator, which is also found in the *new* library. Delete is a unary operator. Its operand is a pointer that was previously used to dynamically allocate memory using the *new* operator. It is an error to delete memory that was not allocated with the *new* operator or to refer to memory after it has been released. The statement to delete our pointer to integer is shown below.

```
delete ptr;
```

To delete a dynamic array, we place brackets after the delete operator as shown below. It is an error to use the delete operator without brackets to delete an array.

```
delete [] ptr;
```

Figure 9-40 shows two delete examples. The first one releases a single element, allocated back to dynamic memory. In the second example, the 200 elements were previously allocated. When we *delete* the pointer in this case, all 200 elements are released. You should note two things in this figure. First, it is not the pointers that are being released but rather what they point to. Second, to release a dynamic memory array, you need only release the pointer once. It is an error to attempt to release each element individually.

Releasing memory does not change the value in a pointer. It still contains the address in the heap. It is a *logic* error to use the pointer after memory has been released. Your program may continue to run, but the data may be destroyed if the memory area is allocated for another use. This logic error is very difficult to trace in your program. We suggest that immediately after you free memory you also clear the pointer by setting it to NULL.

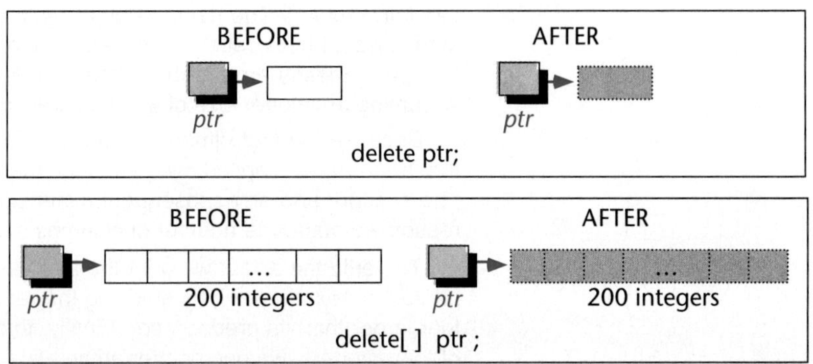

Figure 9-40 Freeing memory

One final thought: Be sure to free memory when it is no longer needed. It is not necessary, however, to clear memory at the end of the program. The operating system will release all memory when the program terminates.

Memory allocated by *new* must be released with *delete,* and memory allocated by *new*[...] must be released with *delete*[ ]

9-16 ARRAY OF POINTERS

Another useful structure that uses arrays and pointers is an array of pointers. This structure is especially helpful when the size of the data in the array is variable.

Table 9-5 is an example of a two-dimensional array in which only one row (1) is full. The rest of the rows contain from one to four elements. This array is also known as a "ragged array" because the right elements in each row may be empty, giving it an uneven (ragged) right border.

32	18	12	24			
13	11	16	12	42	19	14
22						
13	13	14				
11	18					

Table 9-5 A ragged array

Using a two-dimensional array to store these numbers would waste a lot of memory. The solution in this case is to create five one-dimensional arrays that are joined through an array of pointers. One implementation of this concept is shown in Figure 9-41 along with the statements needed to allocate the arrays in the heap. Note that `table` is a

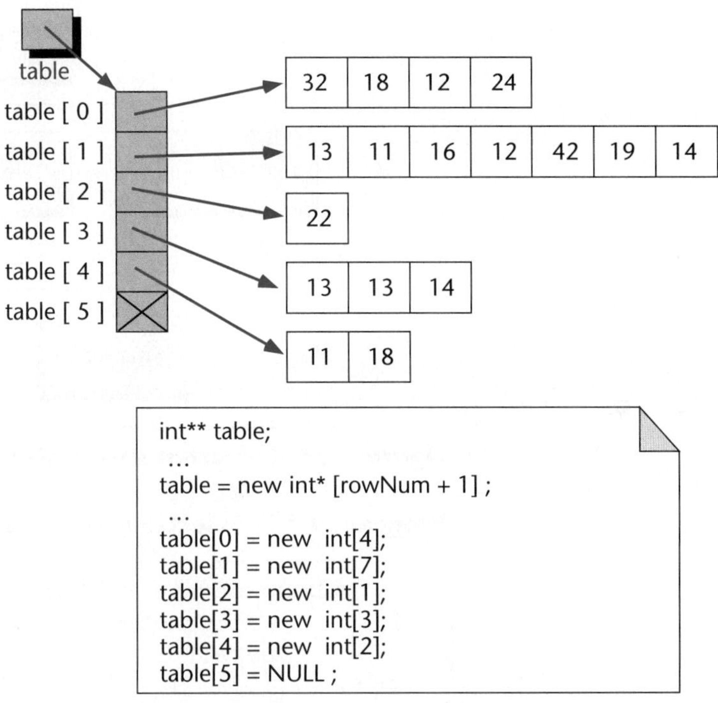

Figure 9-41 A ragged array

pointer to a pointer to an integer and must be declared as shown in Figure 9-41, not as an array.

Program 9-16 on page 466 demonstrates the concept in a complete program. We will see other variations on this data structure in the next few chapters.

9-17 PROGRAMMING APPLICATION

This section contains two applications. The first is a rewrite of the selection sort using pointers. The second uses dynamic arrays.

SELECTION SORT REVISITED

Let's revisit the selection sort we developed in Chapter 8. Using pointers, we can improve it in several ways. First, and perhaps most important, it is structured. The structure chart is shown in Figure 9-42.

Note that in Figure 9-42, *main* contains no detailed code. It simply calls the three functions that will get the job done. First, `getData` reads data from the keyboard and puts them into an array. Then `selectSort` calls two functions to sort the data. Finally, `printData` displays the result. The complete algorithm is found in Program 9-14.

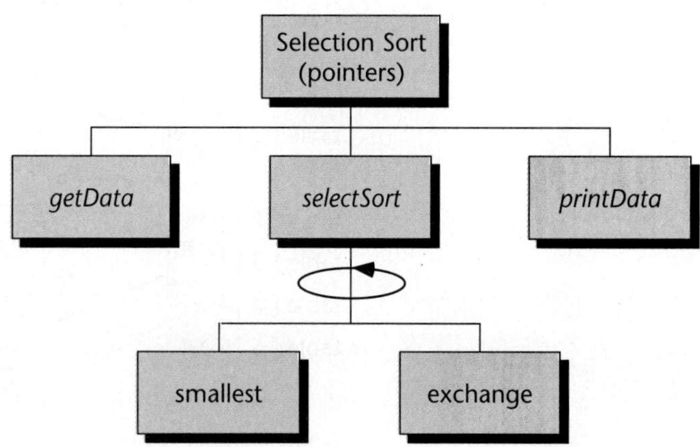

Figure 9-42 Selection sort with pointers

Program 9-14 Selection sort revisited

```
/* Demonstrate pointers with selection sort.
      Written by:
      Date:
*/
#include <iostream>
#include <iomanip>
using namespace std;

const int cSIZE = 25;

int* getData    (int* pAry,    int  arySize);
void selectSort (int* pAry,    int* last);
void printData  (int* pAry,    int* last);
int* smallest   (int* pAry,    int* pLast);
void exchange   (int* current, int* smallest);

int main ()
{
   int  ary[cSIZE];
   int* pLast = getData (ary, cSIZE);
   selectSort (ary, pLast);
   printData  (ary, pLast);

   return 0;
} // main
/* ================== getData ==================
   Reads data from keyboard and places in sort array.
   Pre   pAry is a pointer to an array to be filled
         arySize is integer for maximum array size
   Post  Array filled. Returns last element address
*/
int* getData (int* pAry, int  arySize)
```

Program 9-14 Selection sort revisited *(continued)*

```
{
   int readCnt = 0;
   int* pFill = pAry;

   cout << "\nPlease enter first number: ";
   do
      {
       cin  >> *pFill;
       if (cin.good())
          {
           pFill++;
           readCnt++;
           cout << "Enter next number or <EOF>: ";
          } // if
      } while (cin.good() && readCnt < arySize);

   cout << "\n\n" << readCnt << " numbers read.\n";
   return (--pFill);
} // getData
/* =================== selectSort ==================
   Sort by selecting smallest element in unsorted part
   of the array and exchanging it with element at the
   beginning of the unsorted list.
   Pre  array must contain at least one item
        pLast is pointer to last element in array
   Post The array rearranged smallest to largest
*/
void selectSort (int* pAry, int* pLast)
{
   for (int* pWalker = pAry; pWalker < pLast; pWalker++)
      {
       int* pSmallest = smallest (pWalker, pLast);
       exchange (pWalker, pSmallest);
      } // for
   return;
} // selectSort
/* ================== smallest =================
   Find smallest element starting at current pointer.
   Pre   pAry points to first unsorted element
   Post  smallest element identified and returned
*/
int* smallest (int* pAry, int* pLast)
{
   int* pSmallest = pAry;
   for (int* pLooker = pAry + 1;
        pLooker <= pLast;
        pLooker++)
      if (*pLooker < *pSmallest)
          pSmallest = pLooker;
```

Program 9-14 Selection sort revisited *(continued)*

```
   return pSmallest;
} // smallest
/* ================== exchange ================
   Given pointers to two array elements, exchange them
   Pre  p1 & p2 are pointers to values to be exchanged
   Post The exchange is completed
*/
void exchange (int* p1, int* p2)
{
   int temp  =  *p1;
       *p1   =  *p2;
       *p2   =  temp;

   return;
} // exchange
/* ================== printData ==================
   Given a pointer to an array, print the data.
   Pre  pAry points to the array to be filled
        pLast identifies last element in the array
   Post The data have been printed.
*/
void printData (int* pAry, int* pLast)
{
   int  nmbrPrt;
   int* pPrint;

   cout << "\nYour data sorted are: \n";
   for (pPrint = pAry, nmbrPrt = 0;
        pPrint <= pLast;
        nmbrPrt++, pPrint++)
      cout << setw(2) << nmbrPrt
           << setw(4) << *pPrint << endl;
   cout << "\nEnd of List\n";
   return;
} // PrintData
// ================= End of Program ===============
```

Program 9-14 Analysis Here are a few other points you should note as you study this algorithm.

1. We have used pointers and pointer arithmetic in all functions.
2. `getData` fills the array. Since the pointer, `pFill`, is always one ahead of the read, when we reach the end of file it is pointing to an empty element. Therefore, when we return it, we subtract 1.
3. `selectSort` advances through the array using a *for* statement. For each iteration, it selects the smallest element in the unsorted portion of the array and exchanges it with the first element in the unsorted portion of the array. Each loop, therefore, examines a smaller number of unordered elements. We stop at the element just

before the last one because `smallest` always tests the first element and at least one element after the first one. When we are at the element just before the last, therefore, we are also testing the last element.

4. Look at the style used to code the *for* statement in both `smallest` and `print-Data`. Long *for* statements are more readable if you put each expression on a separate line.

DYNAMIC ARRAY

This **dynamic array** program creates a dynamic table that can store a ragged array. The column and the width of the array are tailored to the needs of the user. The program starts by asking the user for the number of rows that must be stored. After allocating the row pointers, it asks for the number of entries in each row. The table is then filled with data supplied by the user from the keyboard. To demonstrate the applications that could be used with this type of structure, we then determine the minimum, maximum, and average of each row of data. The design is shown in Figure 9-43.

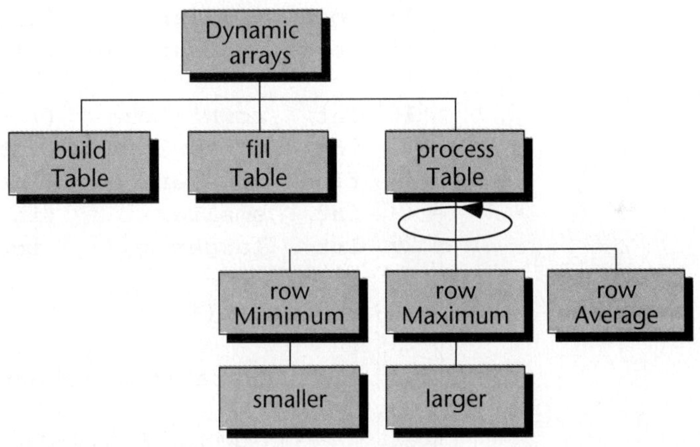

Figure 9-43 Dynamic array structure chart

The data structure is shown in Figure 9-44. The table pointer points to the first pointer in an array of pointers. Each array pointer points to a second array of integers, the first element of which is the number of elements in the list. All arrays are allocated out of the heap, giving us a structure that is limited only by the computer's memory.

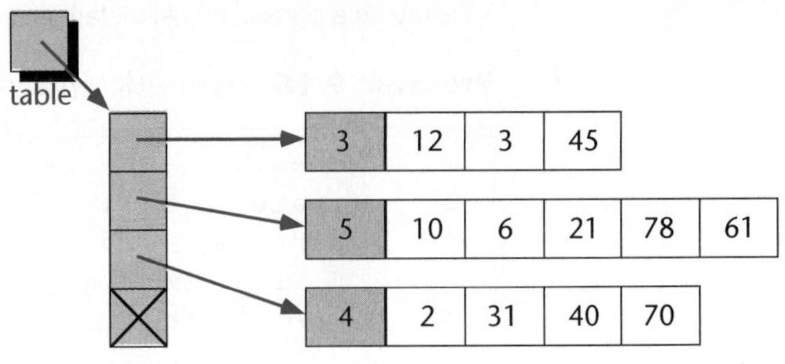

Figure 9-44 Ragged array structure

The complete set of programs to build and fill the table and some sample applications are shown in Programs 9-15 through 9-23.

Program 9-15 Dynamic arrays: *main*

```
/* Demonstrate concept of storing arrays in the heap.
   Program builds and manipulates a variable number of
   ragged arrays. It then calculates minimum, maximum,
   and average of the numbers in the arrays.
      Written by:
      Date:
*/
#include <iostream>
#include <climits>
using namespace std;

int** buildTable   (void);
void  fillTable    (int** table);
void  processTable (int** table);

int   rowMinimum   (int*  rowPtr);
int   rowMaximum   (int*  rowPtr);
float rowAverage   (int*  rowPtr);
int   smaller      (int   first, int second);
int   larger       (int   first, int second);

int main ()
{
   int** table = buildTable();

   fillTable    (table);
   processTable (table);
   return 0;
}  // main
```

Program 9-15 Analysis The `mainline` in Program 9-15 is a classic example of a well-written `main` function. It contains only one variable, the pointer to the array. There are only three functions, each of which uses the array. The function `build-Table` returns the address of the array, and the other two functions uses the array as a parameter. All detail processing is done in subfunctions.

Program 9-16 Dynamic arrays: *buildTable*

```
/* ================== buildTable ===================
   Create backbone of the table by creating an array of
   pointers, each pointing to an array of integers.
      Pre   Nothing
      Post  It returns a pointer pointing to the table
*/
int** buildTable ()
{
```

Program 9-16 Dynamic arrays: *buildTable* (continued)

```
9      cout << "\nEnter the number of rows in the table: ";
10     int rowNum;
11     cin  >> rowNum;
12 
13     int** table;
14     table = new int* [rowNum + 1];
15 
16     int row;
17     for (row = 0; row < rowNum; row++)
18        {
19         int   colNum;
20         cout << "Enter number of integers in row "
21              << row + 1 << ": ";
22         cin  >> colNum;
23         table[row]     = new int [colNum + 1];
24         table[row][0]  = colNum;
25        } // for
26     table[row] = 0;
27     return table;
28  } // buildTable
```

Program 9-16 Analysis We begin Program 9-16 by asking the user how many rows of data need to be entered. Using the *new* operator, statement 14 allocates the memory for an array of pointers plus one extra pointer at the end. The *for* loop in statement 17 then allocates the array for each row, storing its address in the table (see statement 23). Thus, each entry in the allocated table points to an array of integers. The number of elements in each row is stored in the first row element by statement 24.

Program 9-17 Dynamic arrays: *fillTable*

```
/* ================== fillTable ====================
   This function fills the rows.
      Pre   An array of pointers
      Post  The filled-up table
*/
void fillTable (int** table)
{
   cout << "\n ==============================";
   cout << "\n Now we fill the table.\n";
   cout << "\n For each row enter the data";
   cout << "\n and press return: ";
   cout << "\n ==============================\n";

   int row = 0;
   while (table[row] != NULL)
   {
    cout << "\n row " << row + 1
         << " (" << table[row][0] << " integers) =====> ";
```

Program 9-17 Dynamic arrays: *fillTable (continued)*

```
     for (int column = 1; column <= table[row][0]; column++)
          cin >> table[row][column];
      row++;
     } // while
   return;
}// fillTable
```

Program 9-17 Analysis To fill the rows, Program 9-17 requires a *while* statement to loop through the array pointers and a *for* statement to enter the data. We use the *while* statement because the pointer array is designed with a NULL pointer at the end and we use it to indicate that we are at the end of the array. We use the *for* statement for filling the row because the user has already told us how many elements are in each row.

Program 9-18 Dynamic arrays: *processTable*

```
/* ================== processTable ==================
   Process the table to create the statistics.
      Pre  Table
      Post Statistics (min, max, and average) for rows
*/
void processTable (int** table)
{
int   row = 0;
int   rowMin;
int   rowMax;
float rowAve;

   while (table[row] != 0)
       {
         rowMin = rowMinimum (table[row]);
         rowMax = rowMaximum (table[row]);
         rowAve = rowAverage (table[row]);
         cout << "\n\nStatistics for row " << row + 1;
         cout << "\nThe minimum: " << rowMin;
         cout << "\nThe maximum: " << rowMax;
         cout << "\nThe average: " << rowAve;
         row++;
       } // while
   return;
} // processTable
```

Program 9-18 Analysis The function `processTable` calls three functions to show how you could use a dynamic structure such as this. Many more functions could be used. What is important for you to remember from this example is the structure, which you will be able to use in future applications. Programs 9-19 through 9-23 contain the code for the three called functions.

Program 9-19 Dynamic arrays: find *rowMinimum*

```
/* ==================== rowMinimum ====================
   Calculates the minimum of the data in a row.
      Pre   A pointer to the row
      Post  Returns the minimum for that row
*/
int rowMinimum (int* rowPtr)
{
   int rowMin = INT_MAX;
   for (int column = 1; column <= *rowPtr; column++)
      rowMin = smaller (rowMin, *(rowPtr + column));
   return rowMin;
} //rowMinimum
```

Program 9-20 Dynamic arrays: find *rowMaximum*

```
/* =================== rowMaximum ===================
   Calculates the maximum of the data in a row.
      Pre   A pointer to the row
      Post  Returns the maximum for that row
*/
int rowMaximum (int* rowPtr)
{
   int rowMax = INT_MIN;
   for (int column = 1; column <= *rowPtr; column++)
      rowMax = larger  (rowMax, *(rowPtr + column));
   return rowMax;
} // rowMaximum
```

Program 9-21 Dynamic arrays: find *rowAverage*

```
/* ==================== rowAverage ====================
   This function calculates the average of the data in a row.
      Pre   A pointer to the row
      Post  Returns the average for that row
*/
float  rowAverage (int* rowPtr)
{
   float  total = 0;
   for (int column = 1; column <= *rowPtr; column++)
      total += *(rowPtr + column);

   float  rowAve;
   rowAve = total / *rowPtr;
   return rowAve;
} //rowAverage
```

Program 9-22 Dynamic arrays: find *smaller*

```
/* =================== smaller ====================
   This function returns the smaller of two numbers.
      Pre   two numbers
      Post  Returns the smaller
*/
int  smaller (int first, int second)
{
   return (first < second ? first : second);
} // smaller
```

Program 9-23 Dynamic arrays: find *larger*

```
/*  =================== larger ===================
   This function returns the larger of two numbers.
      Pre   two numbers
      Post  Returns the larger
*/
int  larger  (int first, int second)
{
   return (first > second ? first : second);
} // larger
```

9-18 SOFTWARE ENGINEERING AND PROGRAMMING STYLE

Programs that use pointers must be designed carefully to ensure that they work correctly and efficiently. Not only must great care be taken in the program design, but the data structures that are inherent with pointer applications must also be carefully considered. The design of such data structures is beyond the scope of this text, but we will discuss the design of the pointers.

Before we discuss specific aspects of pointer applications, we offer a word of caution: Remember the KISS principle (Keep It Short and Simple). The complexity of pointers grows exponentially as you move from single references to double references to triple references. In other words, the complexity of a statement that uses a double dereference is twice as complex as a single dereference, and a triple dereference is eight times more complex than a single dereference. In pointer applications, simplicity is truly a virtue.

POINTERS AND FUNCTION CALLS

When you need to change a value, use pass by reference if possible. If you must pass a pointer, then try to pass a pointer to the ultimate object to be referenced—that is, to the data variable rather than to a pointer to data. When the pointer refers to the data variable, it is a single dereference.

Despite everything we do to avoid it, there will be times when we have to pass a pointer to a pointer. When a function opens a file whose file pointer is in the calling function, we must pass a pointer to the pointer to the file table. In Figure 9-39 on page 457, we allocated a dynamic array of 200 integers. If an allocation like this is performed in a subfunction, then it must receive a pointer to the pointer to the array in memory so that it can store the address of the array.

Use value parameters when possible.

POINTERS AND ARRAYS

When you combine pointers and arrays, the complexity again increases very quickly. This is especially true when the array is multidimensional. Whenever possible, therefore, rather than passing a multidimensional array, pass just one row. This reduces the complexity significantly because the function is now dealing with a one-dimensional array. Not only are the references easier to work with, but it allows simple pointer arithmetic, which is usually more efficient.

When it is necessary to work with a two-dimensional array, use index notation rather than pointer notation. Index notation is much simpler to work with, and there is no difference in efficiency. To verify the soundness of this recommendation, consider the following equivalent expressions. Which one would you rather find in a strange program?

```
*(*(ary + i) + j)     or     a[i][j]
```

ARRAY INDEX COMMUTATIVITY

Commutativity is a principle in mathematics that says the results of an expression do not depend on the order in which the factors are evaluated. For example, `a + b` is identical to `b + a`. Pointer addition is commutative; subtraction is not. Thus, the following two expressions are identical:

```
a + i is the same as i + a
```

but

```
a - i is an error
```

However, we also know that `a + i` is identical to `a[i]`. Similarly, `i + a` would be equivalent to `i[a]`. Therefore, using the principle of commutativity, we see that

```
a[i] is identical to i[a].
```

A word of caution: This principle works in C++ because of the pointer concept and pointer arithmetic. Do not try this in another language!

DYNAMIC MEMORY: THEORY VERSUS PRACTICE

Do not get carried away with dynamic memory. The programming complexity of dynamically managing memory is very high. What you will often find, therefore, is that memory is not fully reused. To test your system, run Program 9-24.

Program 9-24 Testing memory reuse

```
/* This program tests the reuseability of dynamic memory.
      Written by:
      Date:
*/
#include <iostream>
using namespace std;

int main ()
{
   char* ptr1 = new char[16];
   cout << "Memory allocated at 1: " << &ptr1 << endl;

   char* ptr2 = new char[16];
   cout << "Memory allocated at 2: " << &ptr2 << endl;

   delete[] ptr1;

   char* ptr3 = new char[16];
   cout << "Memory allocated at 3: " << &ptr3 << endl;
   return 0;
} // main
```

Program 9-24 Testing memory reuse *(continued)*

```
Results in Personal Computer:
Memory allocated at 1: 0x244da350
Memory allocated at 2: 0x244da34c
Memory allocated at 3: 0x244da348

Results in UNIX system:
Memory allocated at 1: 0xbfffe344
Memory allocated at 2: 0xbfffe340
Memory allocated at 3: 0xbfffe33c
```

Program 9-24 Analysis First look at the logic of this simple program. We allocate an array of 16 characters twice and then delete the first. This means that the first array is now theoretically available for reuse. We then allocate a third array of 16 characters.

If the memory management is doing its job, the first 16 bytes should be allocated in the third allocation. In systems used for this test, the results were the same—the memory was not reused.

9-19 TIPS AND COMMON PROGRAMMING ERRORS

1. The address of a memory location is a pointer constant and cannot be changed.
2. Only an address (pointer constant) can be stored in a pointer variable.
3. Remember the concept of compatibility. Do not store the address of a data variable of one type into a pointer variable of another type. In other words, a variable of pointer to *int* can only store the address of an *int* variable, and a variable of pointer to *char* can only store the address of a *char* variable.
4. The value of a data variable cannot be assigned to a pointer variable. In other words, the following code creates an error:

```
int* p;
int  a;
p = a;                                      // ERROR
```

5. You must not use a pointer variable before it has been assigned the address of a variable. In other words, the following lines create an error unless *p* is assigned an address:

```
int* p;
x   = *p;                                   // ERROR
*p =  x;                                    // ERROR
```

6. A pointer variable cannot be used to refer to a nonexistent pointed variable. For example, the following lines create an error because *p* exists, but **p* does not exist until it is assigned an address (variable).

```
int* p;
cin >> *p;
```

7. Do not dereference a pointer variable of type *void* *.
8. Remember that the declaration for a pointer variable allocates memory only for the pointer variable, not for the variable to which it is pointing.
9. The address operator (&) can only be used with an lvalue.
10. A function that uses addresses as parameters needs a pointer to data as a formal parameter; the actual parameter in the function call must be a pointer value (address).
11. If you want a called function to change the value of a variable in the calling function, you must either pass the address of that variable or use pass by reference.
12. When multiple definitions are used in one statement—a practice we do not recommend—the pointer token is recognized only with one variable. Therefore, in the following definition, only the first variable is a pointer to an integer; the rest are integers.

```
int* ptrA, ptrB, ptrC;
```

13. It is a compile error to initialize a pointer to a numeric constant.
14. Similarly, it is a compile error to assign an address to any variable other than a pointer.

```
int* ptr = 59;
```

```
int x = &y;                        // ERROR
```

15. It is a compile error to assign a pointer of one type to a pointer of another type without a cast. (Exception: If one pointer is a *void* pointer, it is permitted.)
16. It is a common compile error to pass values when addresses are required in actual parameters. Remember to use the address operator when passing identifiers to functions to simulate pass by reference.
17. It is a compile error to use a pointer before it has been initialized. It is an error because a pointer to *void* is not pointing to typed data.
18. It is a logic error to dereference a pointer whose value is NULL.
19. If `ary` is an array, then

```
ary     is the same as     &ary[0]
```

20. If `ary` is the name of an array, then

```
ary[i]  is the same as  *(ary + i)
```

21. Remember that we usually pass the name of an array as a pointer value to a function that needs to access the elements of the array.
22. Remember that

```
int* a[5];     is different from     int (*a)[5];
```

23. The most common pointer error is referencing a nonexistent element in an array. This is especially easy to do with pointer arithmetic.

24. It is an error to use pointer arithmetic with a pointer that does not reference an array.
25. It is a logic error to use subtraction on two pointers that are referencing different arrays.
26. It is a compile error to subtract a pointer from an index.
27. It is a compile error to attempt to modify the name of an array using pointer arithmetic, such as `table` in the following statements.

```
table++;          // Error: table is constant
table = …;        // Error: table is constant
```

28. It is a compile error to assign the return value from *new* to anything other than a pointer.
29. It is a logic error to set a pointer to the heap to NULL before the memory has been released.
30. It is a compile error to use pointer arithmetic with multiply, divide, or modulo operators.

9-20 KEY TERMS

address operator (&)
delete
dynamic array
dynamic memory allocation
heap memory
indirection operator (*)
lvalue
new
offset
overflow
pointer
pointer arithmetic
pointer constant
pointer indirection
pointer variable
right-left rule
rvalue
stack memory
static memory allocation

9-21 SUMMARY

- Every computer has addressable memory locations.
- A pointer is a derived data type consisting of addresses available in the computer.
- A pointer constant is an address that exists by itself. We cannot change it—we can only use it.
- The address operator (&) makes a pointer value from a pointer constant. To get the address of a variable, we simply use this operator in front of the variable name.
- The address operator can only be used in front of an lvalue. The result is an rvalue.
- A pointer variable is a variable that can store an address.
- The indirection operator (*) accesses a variable through a pointer containing its address.
- The indirection operator can only be used in front of a pointer value.
- Pointer variables can be initialized just like data variables. The initializer must be the address of a previously defined variable or another pointer variable.
- A pointer can be defined to point to other pointer variables (pointers to pointers).
- The value of a pointer variable can be stored in another variable if they are compatible—that is, if they are of the same type.
- One of the most useful applications of pointers is in functions.
- We can simulate pass by reference in a function by using pointers.

- When passing a pointer, we pass the address of the variable to the called function and use the indirection operator to access the variable.
- A function can also return a pointer value.
- There is a close relationship between arrays and pointers. The name of an array is a pointer constant to the first element of the array.
- The name of an array and the address of the first element in the array represent the same thing: an rvalue pointer.
- The name of an array is a pointer only to the first element, not the whole array.
- A pointer variable to the first element of an array can be used anywhere the name of the array is permitted, such as with an index.
- In pointer arithmetic, if `ptr` is pointing to a specific element in an array, `ptr + n` is the pointer value `n` elements away.
- The following two expressions are exactly the same when `ary` is the name of an array and `n` is an integer:

```
*(ary + n)    or    ary[n]
```

- The name of a two-dimensional array is a pointer to a one-dimensional array—the first row.
- In a multidimensional array, the following two expressions are equivalent.

```
*(*(a + i) + j)    or    a[i][j]
```

- There are many ways we can pass an array to a function. One way is to pass the name of the array as a pointer.
- A ragged array—that is, an array of pointers—can be used to save space when not all rows of the array are full.
- The memory in a computer can be divided into program memory and data memory. Data memory can be partitioned into global area, heap, and stack.
- Static allocation of memory requires that the declaration and definition of memory be fully specified at compilation time.
- Dynamic allocation of memory uses two predefined memory allocation operators: *new* and *delete*.
- To read and interpret a complex declaration, we can use the right-left rule.

9-22 PRACTICE SETS

REVIEW QUESTIONS

1. Pointer constants are drawn from the set of addresses for a computer.

   a. True

   b. False

2. Pointers are declared using the address operator as a token.

   a. True

   b. False

3. The underlying type of a pointer is address.

   a. True

   b. False

4. An rvalue expression can be used only to supply a value.

   a. True

   b. False

5. Which of the following statements about pointers is false?

   a. Pointers are built on the standard type, address.

   b. Pointers are machine addresses.

   c. Pointers are derived data types.

   d. Pointers can be defined variables.

   e. Pointers can be constants.

6. The __________ operator is used with a pointer to dereference the address contained in the pointer.

   a. Address (`&`)

   b. Pointer (`^`)

   c. Assignment (`=`)

   d. Selection (`->`)

   e. Indirection (`*`)

7. Which of the following statements will not add 1 to a variable?
   a. a++;
   b. *p = *p + 1;
   c. a += 1;
   d. *p++;
   e. a = a + 1;
8. Which of the following defines a pointer variable to an integer?
   a. int &ptr;
   b. int** ptr;
   c. int &&ptr;
   d. int ^ptr;
   e. int* ptr;
9. Which of the following defines and initializes a pointer to the address of `x`?
   a. int* ptr = *x;
   b. int &ptr = *x;
   c. int* ptr = ^x;
   d. int &ptr = ^x;
   e. int* ptr = &x;
10. *Pointers to pointers* is a term used to describe
    a. Any pointer that points to a variable.
    b. Any two pointers that point to the same variable.
    c. Any two pointers that point to variables of the same type.
    d. Pointers used as formal parameters in a function header.
    e. Pointers whose contents are the address of another pointer.
11. Given the following definitions, which answer points to the value stored in `x`?

```
int     x;
int*    p = &x;
int** pp = &p;
```

    a. p
    b. *pp
    c. pp
    d. **pp
    e. &p
12. Given the definitions shown below, which answer is not valid?

```
int      i;
float    f;
int*     pd;
float*   pf;
```

    a. i = 5;
    b. pf = &f;
    c. f = 5;
    d. pd = pf;
    e. pd = &i;
13. Which of the following statements about pointer compatibility is true?
    a. Because all pointers are addresses, pointers of different types can be assigned without a cast.
    b. If pointers of different types are assigned, C++ uses an implicit cast.
    c. It is possible to cast a pointer to integer as a pointer to float.
    d. When a pointer is cast, C++ automatically reformats the data to reflect the correct type.
    e. When a void pointer is dereferenced, it must be cast.
14. Which of the following operators does not require an lvalue as its operand?
    a. Address operator (`&total`)
    b. Assignment (`x = ...`)
    c. Indirection (`*ptr`)
    d. Postfix increment (`x++`)
    e. Prefix increment (`++x`)
15. Given a pointer to an array element, `ptr`, `ptr - 5` is a pointer to the value 5 elements toward the beginning of the array.
    a. True
    b. False
16. Adding 1 to a pointer always increases the address stored in it by 1 byte.
    a. True
    b. False
17. The parameter declaration `int* a` can be used to declare an array of integers passed to a function.
    a. True
    b. False

18. Dynamically allocated memory can only be referred to through pointers.
    a. True
    b. False
19. Which of the following statements about pointers and arrays is true?
    a. The following expressions are identical when `ary` is an array: `*ary` and `&ary[0]`.
    b. The following expressions are identical when `ary` is an array: `*ary` and `*ary[0]`.
    c. The name of an array can be used with the indirection operator to reference data.
    d. The name of the array is a pointer variable.
    e. The only way to reference data in an array is with the index operator.
20. Which of the following statements about pointer arithmetic is true?
    a. Any arithmetic operator can be used to change the value of a pointer.
    b. Given a pointer `ptr`, `ptr + n` is a pointer to the value *n* elements away.
    c. Pointer arithmetic is a short-hand notation that changes the value that a pointer is referencing.
    d. Pointer arithmetic is valid only with pointers to arithmetic variables, such as pointer to integer.
    e. Pointer arithmetic is valid only with the name of the array.
21. Which of the following defines a two-dimensional array of integers?
    a. int ary
    b. int ary[ ][SIZE2]
    c. int* ary
    d. int* ary[ ][SIZE2]
    e. int* ary[SIZE2]
22. Which of the following statements about memory allocation is true?
    a. Allocated memory can be referred to only through pointers; it does not have its own identifier.
    b. It is an error to dereference a pointer to allocated memory after the memory has been released.
    c. It is an error to free memory with a pointer to other than the first element of an allocated array.
    d. Memory should be freed as soon as it is no longer needed.
    e. To ensure that it is released, allocated memory should be freed before the program ends.
23. Which of the following statements about ragged arrays is false?
    a. Ragged arrays are two-dimensional arrays in which the right elements of a row may be empty.
    b. Ragged arrays can be implemented using an array of pointers to one-dimensional arrays.
    c. Ragged arrays can only be used with arrays of integers.
    d. Ragged arrays implemented as an array of pointers save memory.
    e. Ragged arrays implemented as an array of pointers can be created in dynamic memory.

EXERCISES

24. Declare and define the following:
    a. A pointer variable `pi` pointing to an integer.
    b. A pointer variable ppi pointing to a pointer to an integer.
    c. A pointer variable pf pointing to a float.
    d. A pointer variable `ppc` pointing to a pointer to a character.
25. If `a` is declared as integer, which of the following statements is true and which is false?
    a. The expressions `*&a` and `a` are the same.
    b. The expressions *&a and &*a are the same.
26. Given the following declarations

```
int     x;
double  d;
int*    p;
double  q;
```

    which of the following expressions are not allowed?

    a. p = &x;　　b. p = &d;
    c. q = &x;　　d. q = &d;
    e. p = x;
27. Given the following declarations

```
int    a =  5;
int    b =  7;
int*   p = &a;
int*   q = &b;
```

    what is the value of each of the following expressions?

    a. ++a　　b. ++(*p)
    c. --(*q)　　d. --b

28. What is the error (if any) in each of the following expressions?

    a. int a = 5;

    b. int* p = 5;

    c. int a;
    int* p = &a;

    d. int a;
    int** q = &a;

29. Which of the following program segments is valid? Describe each error in the invalid statements.

    a. int* p;
    cin >> p;

    b. int* p;
    cin >> *p;

    c. int* p;
    cin >> &p;

    d. int a;
    int* p = &a;
    cin >> p;

30. Which of the following program segments has a logical error in it?

    a. int** p;
    int* q;
    q = &p;

    b. int** p;
    int* q;
    p = &q;

    c. int** p;
    int** q;
    p = &q;

    d. char c = 'A';
    char** p;
    char* q;
    q = & c;
    cout << *p;

31. Given the following declaration
    int* p;**
    what is the type of each of the following expressions?

    a. p
    b. *p
    c. **p
    d. ***p

32. If p is a name of a variable, which of the following expressions is an lvalue and which one is an rvalue? Explain.

    a. p
    b. *p
    c. p + 2
    d. *p + 2

33. If p and q are variable names and a is an array, which of the following expressions are not syntactically correct because they violate the rules concerning lvalues and rvalues?

    a. *p = *p + 2;

    b. &p = &a[0];

    c. q = &(p + 2);

    d. a[5] = 5;

34. Write a function prototype statement for a function named `calc` that returns *void* and contains a reference parameter to an integer, x, and a pointer parameter to a long double, y.

35. Write a function prototype statement for a function named `spin` that returns a pointer to an integer and contains a reference parameter to an integer, x, and a pointer parameter to the address of a long double, py.

36. Assuming all variables are integer and all pointers are typed appropriately, show the final values of the variables a and b in Figure 9-45 after the following assignments:

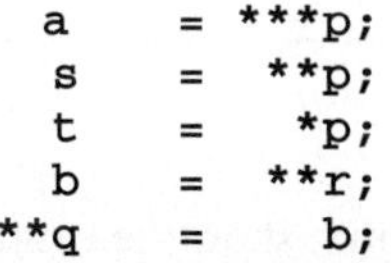

```
  a   = ***p;
  s   =  **p;
  t   =   *p;
  b   =  **r;
**q   =    b;
```

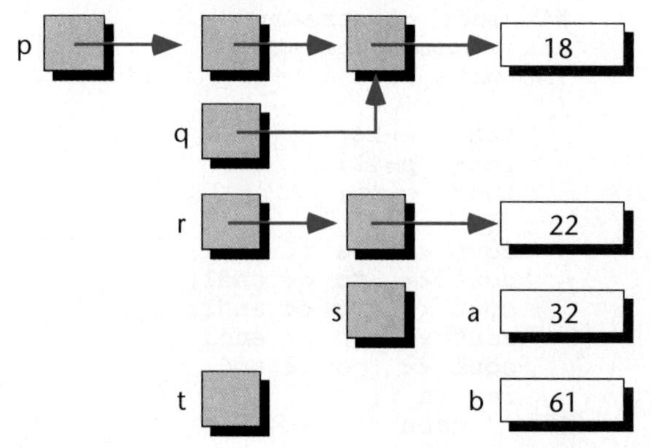

Figure 9-45 Exercise 36

37. Assuming all variables are integer, and all pointers are typed appropriately, show the final values of the variables in Figure 9-46 after the following assignments:

```
 t  =  **p;
 b  = ***q;
*t  =    c;
 v  =    r;
 w  =   *s;
 a  =  **v
*u  =   *w
```

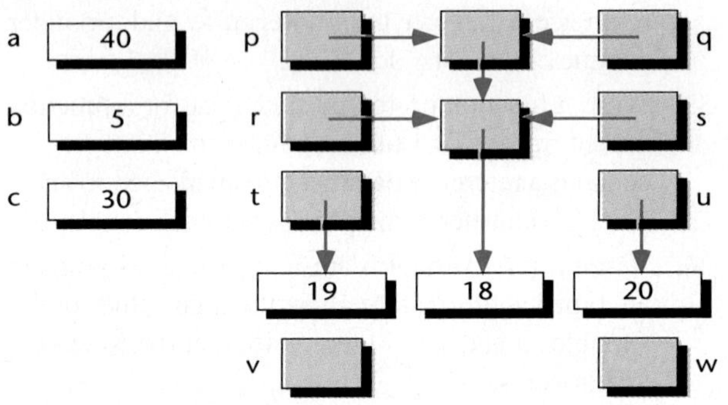

Figure 9-46 Exercise 37

38. In the program that follows, show the configuration of all the variables and the output.

```
#include <iostream>
using namespace std;
int main ()
{
    int   a=14;
    int*  p=&2;
    int** q=&p;

    cout <<   a << endl;
    cout <<  *p << endl;
    cout << **q << endl;
    cout <<   p << endl;
    cout <<   q << endl;
    return 0;
}   // main
```

39. Rewrite each of the following expressions by replacing the index operator ([...]) with the indirection operator (*):

a. tax[6] **b.** score[7]
c. num[4] **d.** prices[9]

40. Rewrite each of the following expressions by replacing the indirection operator (*) with the index operator ([...]). Each identifier refers to an array.

a. *(tax + 4)

b. *(score + 2)

c. *(number + 0)

d. *prices

41. Imagine we have the following declarations:

```
int  ary[10];
int* p = &ary[3];
```

Show how you can access the sixth element of `ary` using the pointer `p`.

42. Given the following declaration

```
float ary[200];
```

write the prototype declaration for a function named `fun` that can manipulate a one-dimensional array of floating-point numbers, `ary`. Provide an additional parameter, a pointer to the last element in the array. Code a call to the function.

43. Show what would be printed from the following block:

```
{
 int num[5] = {3, 4, 6, 2, 1};
 int* p   = num;
 int* q   = num + 2;
 int* r   = &num[1];
 cout << setw(3) << num[2]
      << setw(3) << *(num + 2)
      << endl;
 cout << setw(3) << *p
      << setw(3) << *(p + 1)
      << endl;
 cout << setw(3) << *q
      << setw(3) << *(q + 1)
      << endl;
 cout << setw(3) << *r
      << setw(3) << *(r + 1)
      << endl;
 return 0;
}
```

44. Show what would be printed from the following block:

```
{
    void printOne   (int* );
    void printTwo   (int* );
    void printThree (int* );
    int num [5] = {3 , 4 , 6 , 2 , 1};
    printOne   (num);
    printTwo   (num + 2);
    printThree (&num [2]);
    return 0;
}
void printOne (int* x)
{
 cout << x[2] << endl;
 return;
}

void printTwo (int* x)
{
 cout << x[2] << endl;
 return;
}

void printThree (int* x)
{
 cout <<* x << endl;
 return;
}
```

45. Given the following declaration

```
int table [4][5];
```

write the prototype declaration for a function named `fun` that can accept the whole array using a pointer. Write the statement that calls this function.

46. Given the following declaration

```
int table [4][5];
```

write the prototype declaration for a function named `torture` that accepts one row of an array at a time.

47. Draw pictures to show the memory configuration for each of the following declarations:

a. int* x [5]; **b.** int (*x) [5];

48. Show what would be printed from the following block:

```
{
    int x [2][3] =
            {
             { 4  , 5 , 2 },
             { 7 ,  6 , 9 }
            };
    int (*p) [3]  = &x [1];
    int (*q) [3]  =  x;
    cout << (*p)[0] << (*p)[1]
         << (*p)[2] << endl
    cout << *q[0] << *q[1] << endl;
}
```

49. Show what would be printed from the following block:

```
{
void fun (int (*p) [3]);

    int x [2][3] =
            {
             { 4  , 5 , 2 },
             { 7 ,  6 , 9 }
            };

    fun (x);
    fun (x + 1);
} // block
void fun (int  (*p)[3])
{
 cout << (*p)[0] << (*p)[1]
      <<  (*p)[2] << endl;
 return;
} // fun
```

50. Given the following declarations and definitions

```
int num[26] = {23, 3, 5, 7, 4, -1, 6 };
int* n = num;
int  i = 2;
int  j = 4;
```

show the value of the following expressions:

a. n

b. *n

c. *n + 1

d. *(n + 1)

e. *n + j

f. *&i

51. Given the following declarations and definitions

```
char a[20] = {'z', 'x', 'm', 's', 'e',
              'h'};
char* pa  = a;
int   i   = 2;
int   j   = 4;
int*  pi  = &i;
```

show the value of the following expressions:

a. *(pa + j)

b. *(pa + *pi)

52. Given the following declaration and definition

```
int data[15] = {5, 2, 3, 4, 1, 3, 7, 2,
                4, 3, 2, 9, 12};
```

show the value of the following expressions:

a. data + 4

b. *(data + 4)

c. *data + 4

d. *(data + (*data + 2))

53. Given the following declarations and definitions

```
int  i  = 2;
int  j  = 4;
int* pi = &i;
int* pj = &j;
```

show the value of the following expressions:

a. *&j

b. *&*&j

c. *&pi

d. **&pj

e. &**&pi

f. &i + 8

54. Given the following declarations and definitions

```
char a[20] = {'z', 'x', 'm', 's', 'e',
              'h'};
int i = 2;
int j = 4;
```

write pointer expressions that evaluate to the same value as each of the following:

a. a[0]

b. a[5]

c. The address of the element just before a[0]

d. The address of the last element in *a*

e. The address of the element just after the last element in *a*

f. The next element after a[3]

g. The next element after a[12]

h. The next element after a[j]

55. Given the following declarations and definitions

```
int num[10] = {23, 3, 5, 7, 4, -1
               6, 12, 10, -23};
int i = 2;
int j = 4;
```

write index expressions that evaluate to the same value as each of the following:

a. *(num + 2)

b. *(num + j)

c. *(num + i + j)

d. *(num + i) + *(num + j)

e. *(num + *(num + 1))

56. Given the following declaration and definition

```
int num[2000] = {23, 3, 5, 7, 4, -1, 6};
```

write two pointer expressions for the address of num[0].

57. Given the following declarations and definitions

```
int num[26] = {23, 3, 5, 7, 4, -1, 6};
int  i = 2;
int  j = 4;
int* n = num;
```

write the equivalent expressions in index notation.

a. n

b. *n

c. *n + 1

d. *(n + 1)

e. *(n + j)

58. Given the following declarations and definitions

```
int num[26] = {23, 3, 5, 7, 4, -1, 6};
int* pn;
```

write a test to check whether `pn` points beyond the end of `num`.

59. Given the following prototype for `mushem` and the declarations and definitions shown below

```
int mushem (int* x, int* y);
int  i  = 2;
int  j  = 4;
int* pi = &i;
int* pj = &j;
```

indicate whether each of the following calls to `mushem` is valid:

a. i = mushem (2, 10);

b. j = mushem (i, j);

c. j = mushem (&i, &j);

d. mushem (pi, pj);

e. i = mushem (pi, &j);

60. What is the output from the following program?

```
#include <iostream>
using namespace std;
int fun  (int*, int, int*);
int main ()
{
    int a     = 4;
    int b     = 17;
    int c[5]  = {9, 14, 3, 15, 6};
```

```
    a = fun(&a, b, c);
    cout << "2. " << a << " "
         << b    << " "
         << c[0]  << " "
         << c[1]  << " "
         << c[2]  << " "
         << c[3]  << " "
         << c[4]  << endl;
    return 0;
 } // main

int fun (int* px,
         int  y,
         int* pz)
{
    int  a = 5;
    int* p;

    cout << "1. " << *px << " " << y
         << " "   << *pz << endl;
    for (p = pz; p < pz + 5; ++p)
       *p = a + *p;
    return (*px + *pz + y);
} // fun
```

61. What is the output from the following program?

```
 #include <iostream>
 using namespace std;
 int sun (int*, int, int*);
 int main ()
 {
    int  a    = 4;
    int  b    = 17;
    int  c[5] = {9, 14, 3, 15, 6};
    int* pc   = c;
    a = sun(pc, a, &b);
    cout << "2. " << a << " "
         << b    << " "
         << c[0]  << " "
         << c[1]  << " "
         << c[2]  << " "
         << c[3]  << " "
         << c[4]  << endl;
    return 0;
 } // main

int sun (int* px,
         int  y,
         int* pz)
{
    int  i = 5;
    cout << "1. " << *px << " " << y
         << " "   << *pz << endl;
    for  (int* p = px; p < px + 5; p++)
       *p = y + *p;
    *px = 2 * i;
    return (*pz + *px + y);
} // sun
```

PROBLEMS

62. Write a function that converts a Julian date to a month and day. A Julian date consists of a year and the day of the year relative to January 1. For example, day 41 is February 10. The month and day are to be stored in integer variables whose addresses are passed as parameters. The function is to handle leap years. (For a discussion of the calculation of a leap year, see Project 57 on page 224.) If there is an error in a parameter, such as a day greater than 366, the function is to return 0. Otherwise, it returns a positive number.

63. Modify Program 9-3 on page 423 to include subtraction, multiplication, division, and remainder.

64. Write a function that receives a floating-point number representing the change from a purchase. The function is to pass back the breakdown of the change in dollar bills, half-dollars, quarters, dimes, nickels, and pennies.

65. Write a function that given the time in seconds passes back the time in hours, minutes, seconds, and a character indicating A.M. (`a`) or P.M. (`p`). If the number of seconds is more than 24 hours, the function is to return false as an error indicator.

66. Write a function that receives a floating-point number and sends back the integer and fraction parts.

67. Write a function that receives two integers and passes back the greatest common divisor and the least common multiple. The calculation of the greatest common divisor can be done using Euclid's method of repetitively dividing one number by the other and using the remainder (modulo). When the remainder is zero, the divisor has been found. For example, the greatest common divisor of 247 and 39 is 13 as shown in Table 9-6.

Factor	Factor	Modulo
247	39	13
39	13	0

Table 9-6 gcd for 247 and 39

Once you know the greatest common divisor (*gcd*), the least common multiple (*lcm*) is determined as shown in the following formula.

$$lcm = \frac{(\text{factor1} * \text{factor2})}{gcd}$$

68. We have two arrays, *A* and *B*, each containing 10 integers. Write a function that checks if every element of array *A* is equal to its corresponding element in array *B*. In other words, the function must check if *A[0]* is equal to *B[0]*, *A[1]* is equal to *B[1]*, and so on. The function must accept only two pointer values and return an integer—zero for equal and not zero for unequal.

69. Generalize the function in Problem 68 to include the number of elements to be compared as a parameter.

70. Write a function that reverses the elements of an array in place. In other words, the last element must become the first, the second from last must become the second, and so on. The function must accept only one pointer value and return *void*.

71. Write a function that creates a ragged array representing the Pascal triangle. In a Pascal triangle, each element is the sum of the element directly above it and the element to the left of the element directly above it (if any). A Pascal triangle of size 7 is shown below.

```
1
1   1
1   2   1
1   3   3   1
1   4   6   4   1
1   5  10  10   5   1
1   6  15  20  15   6   1
```

Your function must be able to create the triangle of any size. The function should accept an integer representing the size of the triangle and return a pointer to the array it created.

72. Write a function that tests an International Standard Book Number (ISBN) to see if it is valid. The ISBN is used to define a book uniquely. It is made of 10 digits, as shown in Figure 9-47. For an ISBN number to be valid, the weighted sum of the 10 digits must be evenly divisible by 11. The tenth digit may be x, which indicates 10. (If you are not familiar with the algorithm for the weighted sum, see Chapter 8, Project 31, on 407.)

The function must accept a pointer value (the name of the array) and return an integer—zero for invalid and nonzero for valid.

73. Write a function that copies a one-dimensional array of n elements into a two-dimensional array of j rows and k columns. The resulting array is to be placed in the heap. The data are to be inserted into the array in row order; that is, the first j items are to be placed in row 0, the second j items in row 1, and so forth until all rows have been filled.

If j and k are not factors of n—that is, if n ≠ j * k—the function returns a null pointer. Otherwise, it returns the pointer to the two-dimensional array. The input array and j, k, and n are to be passed as parameters.

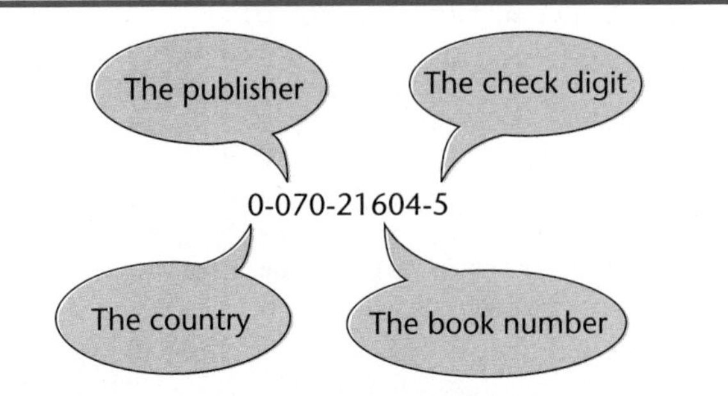

Figure 9-47 ISBN number format for Problem 49

74. Given the following declaration and definition

```
int num[20];
```

and using only pointer notation, write a *for* loop to read integer values from the keyboard to fill the array.

75. Given the following declaration and definition

```
char a[40];
```

and using only pointer notation, write a *for* loop to read characters from the keyboard to fill the array.

76. Given the following declaration and definition

```
char   a[6] = {'z', 'x', 'm', 's',
               'e', 'h'};
```

and using only pointer notation, write a loop to rotate all values in a to the right (toward the end) by one element.

77. Repeat Problem 76, with the rotation one element to the left.

78. Write a function named addem with two call-by-reference integer parameters. The function is to add 2 to the first parameter and 5 to the second parameter. Test the function by calling it with the values of 17 and 25.

PROJECTS

79. Write a program that creates the structure shown in Figure 9-48 and then reads an integer into variable `a` and prints it using each pointer in turn. That is, the program must read an integer into variable `a` and print it using `p, q, r, s, t, u,` and `v`.

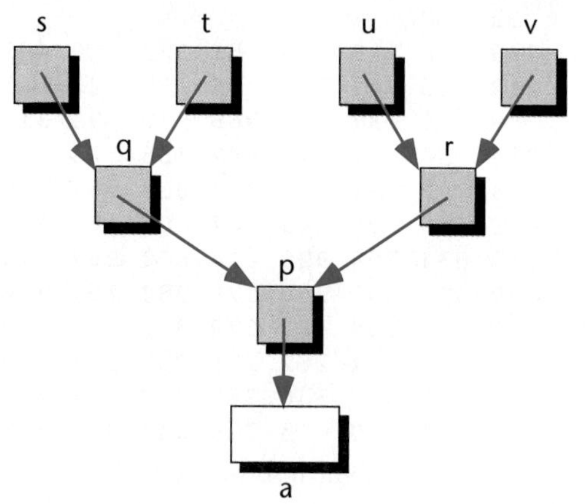

Figure 9-48 Structure for Project 79

80. Write a program that creates the structure shown in Figure 9-49. It then reads data into `a, b,` and `c` using the pointers `p, q,` and `r`.

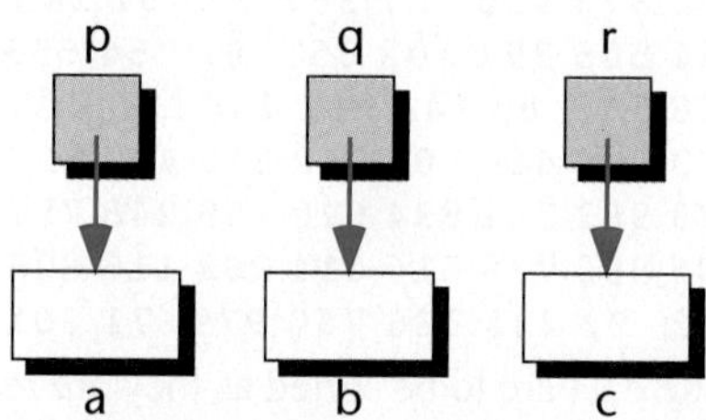

Figure 9-49 Data structure for Project 80

After the data have been read, the program reassigns the pointers so that `p` points to `c, q` points to `a,` and `r` points to `b`. After making the reassignments, it prints the variables using the pointers. For each variable, print both its contents and its address.

81. Write a program that creates the structure shown in Figure 9-50 and reads data into `a` and `b` using the pointers `x` and `y`.

    The program then multiplies the value of `a` by `b` and stores the result in `c` using the pointers `x, y,` and `z`. Finally it prints all three variables using the pointers `x, y,` and `z`.

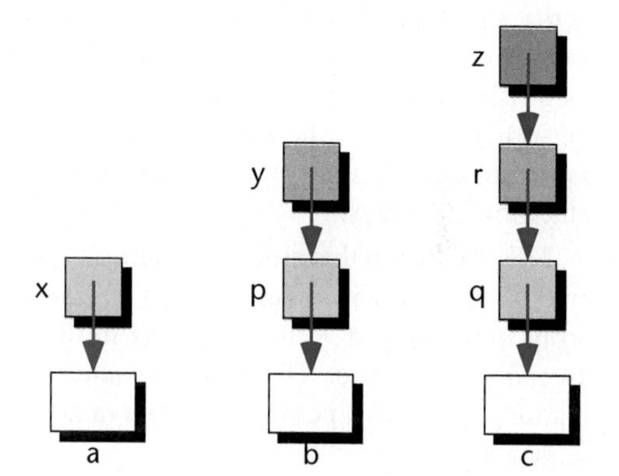

Figure 9-50 Data structure for Project 81

82. Write an exploratory program to study pointers. In this program, prompt the user to enter a character, an integer, a long integer, and a float. The program then calls a print function that accepts a void pointer as its only parameter and prints the address of the pointer followed by the data, first as a character, then as an integer, a long integer, and a float. Since void pointers have no type, you will need to cast the pointer appropriately in each of your print statements.

    A proposed output format is shown below. It is the result of calling the print function with a pointer to integer. You will most likely get different results.

```
Printing int 123
Printing data at location: 01D70C44
Data as char :
Data as int  :      123
Data as long :  8069185
Data as float:     0.00
```

    Call the print function for each of the user inputs.

Using the addresses that you printed, build a memory map of the variables as they existed in your program. Then, by analyzing the results of the printout, write a short explanation of what happened when your program ran. To fully understand the results, you may have to refer to your system documentation to determine the physical memory sizes of the various types.

83. Write a program that will read 10 integers from the keyboard and place them in an array. The program then will sort the array into ascending and descending order and print the sorted lists. The program must not change the original array or create any other integer arrays.

The solution to this problem requires two pointer arrays, as shown in Figure 9-51. The first pointer array is rearranged so that it points to the data in ascending sequence. The second pointer array is rearranged to that it points to the data in descending sequence.

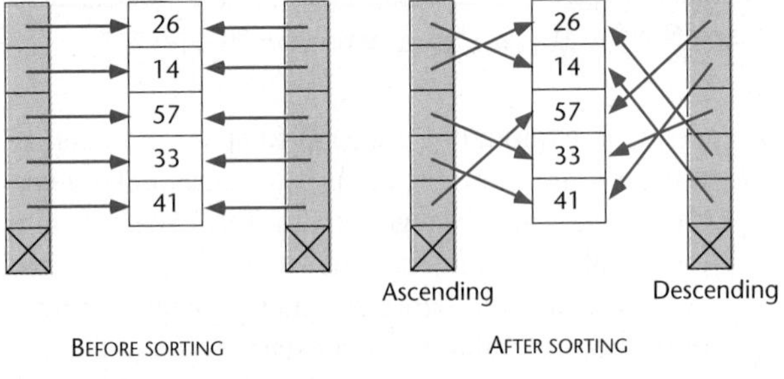

Figure 9-51 Structure for Project 60

Your output should be formatted with the three arrays printed as a vertical list next to each other, as shown in Table 9-7.

Ascending	Original	Descending
14	26	57
26	14	41
33	57	33
41	33	26
57	41	14

Table 9-7 Output format for Project 60

84. Write a program that creates a two-dimensional array in the heap and then analyzes it to determine the minimum, maximum, and average of each column.

The data are to be read from a file. The first two elements are the number of rows in the array and the number of columns in each row. The file data for the array follow. Data for a 12×8 array are shown.

```
 12   8
838 758 113 515  51 627  10 419
212  86 749 767  84  60 225 543
 89 183 137 566 966 978 495 311
367  54  31 145 882 736 524 505
394 102 851  67 754 653 561  96
628 188  85 143 967 406 165 403
562 834 353 920 444 803 962 318
422 327 457 945 479 983 751 894
670 259 248 757 629 306 606 990
738 516 414 262 116 825 181 134
343  22 233 536 760 979  71 201
336  61 160   5 729 644 475 993
```

85. Rewrite the straight insertion sort from Chapter 8 (Program 8-10 on page 373) using pointer arithmetic. The data to be sorted are to be read from a file. The array is to be dynamically allocated in the heap after reading the file to determine the number of elements. While reading the data, print them 10 integers to a line. Use the following test data:

```
838 758 113 515  51 627  10 419 212  86
749 767  84  60 225 543  89 183 137 566
966 978 495 311 367  54  31 145 882 736
524 505 394 102 851  67 754 653 561  96
628 188  85 143 967 406 165 403 562 834
353 920 444 803 962 318 422 327 457 945
479 983 751 894 670 259 248 757 629 306
606 990 738 516 414 262 116 825 181 134
343  22 233 536 760 979  71 201 336  61
```

The data are to be sorted as they are read into the array. *Do not fill the array and then sort the data.* After the array has been sorted, print the data again using the same format you used for the unsorted data.

86. Write a program to answer inquiries about student data. Using a menu-driven user interface, provide the capability to print out the scores, average, or grade for a student. A fourth menu option is to provide all information about a given student. All array functions are to receive the array as a pointer and use pointer arithmetic.

The data in Table 9-1 are to be stored in a two-dimensional array.

Student	Quiz 1	Quiz 2	Quiz 3	Quiz 4	Quiz 5
1234	052	007	100	078	034
1947	045	040	088	078	055
2134	090	036	090	077	030
2877	055	050	099	078	080
3124	100	045	020	090	070
3189	022	070	100	078	077
4532	011	017	081	032	077
4602	089	050	091	078	060
5405	011	011	000	078	010
5678	020	012	045	078	034
6134	034	080	055	078	045
6999	000	098	089	078	020
7874	060	100	056	078	078
8026	070	010	066	078	056
9893	034	009	077	078	020

Table 9-1 Student data for Project 86

87. Contract bridge is a popular card game played by millions of people throughout the world. It began in the 1920s as a variation of an old English card game, whist. In bridge, the entire deck is dealt to four players named North, South, East, and West. In tournament bridge, teams of players (North-South versus East-West) compete with other players using the same hands (sets of 13 cards). Today it is common for large tournaments to use computer-generated hands. Write a program to shuffle and deal the hands for one game.

    To simulate the bridge deck, use an array of 52 integers initialized from 1 to 52. To shuffle the deck, loop through the array exchanging the current card element with a random element (use the random number generator discussed in Chapter 4). After the deck has been shuffled, print the hands in four columns using the player's position as a heading. Use the following interpretation for the cards' suits:

1 to 13	Clubs
14 to 26	Diamonds
27 to 39	Hearts
40 to 52	Spades

    To determine the rank of the card, use its number modulo 13. The interpretation of the rank is: 1 is an ace, 2 through 10 have their value, 11 is a jack, 12 is a queen, and 0 is a king (interpreted as 13).

88. Modify Project 87 to sort each hand by suit (clubs lowest and spades highest), and within suit, by rank after the shuffle. Hint: After shuffling the deck, consider the first 13 cards the hand for North, the next 13 cards the hand for East, and so forth. Then use a function to sort each hand in turn.

Chapter 10

Classes

The pluses in the name C++ designate classes. Classes are a combination of data and functions joined together to form a type. However, they are more than just a type because they also provide the capability to build high-quality software that follows the principles of software engineering.

In this chapter, we introduce the basic concepts of classes. After presenting some of the general principles, we explain how to define a class object consisting of data and functions, including automatically invoked functions known as constructors and destructors. After discussing several examples of simple classes, we conclude with a programming example that demonstrates how a class can be built. Figure 10-1 summarizes the derived types covered in the text and the chapters in which they are covered. Classes are the subject of this chapter.

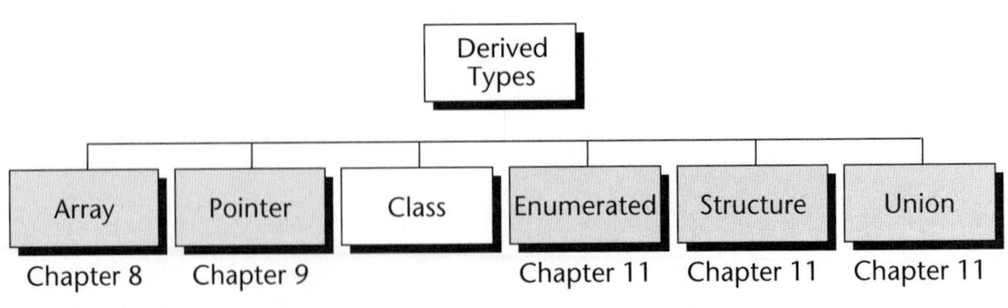

Figure 10-1 Derived types

10-1 BASIC CLASS CONCEPTS

Recall from Chapter 2 that a type is a set of values and a set of operations that can be applied on the values. The standard types are predefined with a fixed set of operations, such as the arithmetic operators for integer and floating-point numbers. We have also seen two derived types, array and pointer, which have a very limited set of built-in operators. We now begin our study of the third derived type, class, which allows us not only to define a type but also to define the operations that are necessary to manipulate it.

For example, consider a class we call `Fraction`. Within the fraction class, there are some data, specifically an integer called `numerator` and an integer called `denominator`. We also include operations, such as add and subtract, in our fraction class. These operations are defined by functions, which are also known as **methods**. For each operation, we write a function that handles the specific data manipulation. For the fraction class we need functions to add, subtract, multiply, and divide fractions, as well as to compare and print them.

By combining the data and operations into an object, we implement one of the basic principles of structured programming: **data hiding**. The data in the class, the numerator and denominator in our fraction, are physically located inside the class object and therefore can be hidden from the application program. This means that they cannot be directly referenced; that is, they cannot be accessed or changed except by functions (methods) that are a part of the class.

Data hiding is important, because when we create a data type we need to ensure its integrity. Thus, we **encapsulate** the data structure and the data operations inside the class and allow access only through controlled methods.

ACCESS SPECIFIERS

How data members within a class are accessed is determined by **access specifiers**. There are three access specifiers that can be used with either the class member data or the member functions (methods). We discuss the first two, private and public access specifiers, next. The third one, the protected access specifier, will be discussed when we study inheritance in Chapter 12. The access specifiers are seen in Figure 10-2.

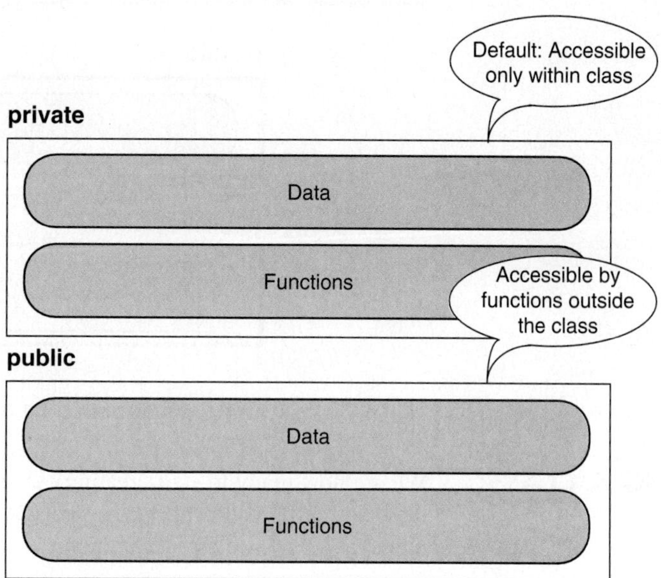

Figure 10-2 Class access specifiers

Private

When data are declared ***private***, they can be accessed only by functions within the class; that is, they cannot be accessed by functions outside of the class. We have already discussed the concept of protecting the data through data hiding. This is done by declaring that the data in the class are private.

Functions can also be declared *private*. When a function is declared *private*, it can be called only by other member functions. For example, in our fraction class, a function to simplify a fraction would be declared *private*. It would be needed whenever we use the fraction in a computation, but it is not needed outside of the class itself. Therefore, we would declare it to be a *private* function, usable only by other functions that are part of the class.

By default, data and functions in a class are *private*. We recommend, however, that you specifically declare them as *private* by using the *private* access specifier, even when such a declaration is not necessary. The extra effort provides good documentation and can prevent errors later when the class is modified.

Public

When data or functions within a class must be directly referenced outside of the class, they are declared to be ***public***. For example, the function to add two fractions must be declared *public* so that it can be called from outside the class.

While public access can technically be declared for data as well as functions, the principle of data hiding dictates that it be used only for functions. Data are generally declared *private*. When they need to be accessed, they are accessed through *public* functions. If necessary, however, it is possible to make data directly accessible by declaring them to be *public*.

In general, we recommend that you code *private* members first and *public* members last. This is good practice for two reasons: First, grouping all class members of one access type together simply makes it easier to read and understand the class. Second, once an access is specified, then all members that follow it have the same access until a new access is specified. By declaring the *private* members first, you are less apt to make an error in your access specifications.

Assuming that a class has only *public* functions and no public data members, a program can access the data only through the *public* functions. This concept is illustrated in Figure 10-3.

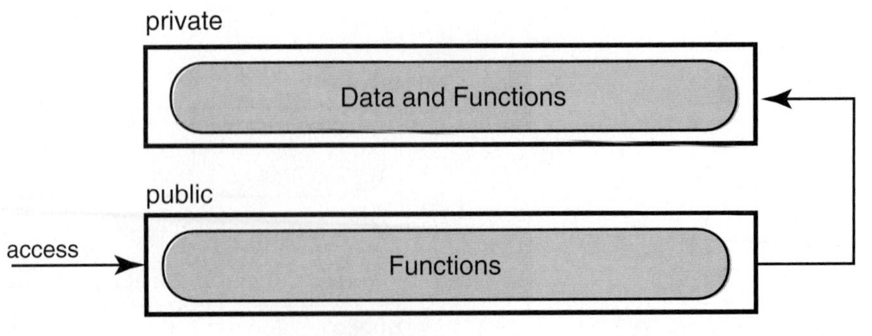

Figure 10-3 Accessing data in a class

CREATING A CLASS

We are now ready to start creating our fraction class. Classes must be declared before they can be used. Recall that a declaration describes the type without allocating any memory for it. A class declaration is nothing more than a skeleton that describes the members of the class. As with any declaration, only the skeleton is created. Names for both the data and functions are created. We still need to write the functions; space for the data will be allocated when an object is created using the class.

Declaring a Class

To declare a fraction class, we use the keyword ***class*** followed by its name, `Fraction`. This follows the same format we use for all data types. The members of the class are then declared in a block. As a practice, we first declare the private members and then the public members. For now, we include only two methods in the class, one to store the fraction data in the class and one to print the fraction. The code is given in Program 10-1.

Program 10-1 Declaration for the fraction class

```
class Fraction
{
   private:
        int numerator;
        int denominator;
   public:
        void store (int numer, int denom);
        void print () const;
}; // Fraction
```

Program 10-1 Analysis The name of the class is `Fraction`. The class name immediately follows the keyword class at the beginning of the class declaration. The body of the class, enclosed in braces, contains first the private members and then the public members. While the keyword *private* is not necessary, we highly recommend that you use it to ensure that all readers clearly understand the access specifications.

Within the private section, we have declared two integers, the numerator and the denominator. These declarations are coded just as any variable declaration, with the type first, followed by the identifier, and terminated with a semicolon. Since this is a class declaration, it is not possible to assign initial values to the data when the variables are being declared. We will see how to initialize them later.

Pay close attention to the semicolon at the end of the class declaration. It is a compile error to omit it.

Following the private section, we code the public access methods by coding prototype statements for their functions. These prototype statements are just like any function's prototype and all of the normal rules apply. Note that we have included the identifiers for the formal parameters; this is good style and provides good documentation. We have also declared the print function constant; we discuss the reason for this when we talk about accessor functions in Section 10-4.

Finally, let's discuss the name of the class. It would be more natural to call the class `fraction`. As a general practice, however, we do not use global identifiers that are common words, because they may conflict with other identifiers either in the system or in the application. To avoid such a conflict, we capitalize the first letter of a class name, thus ensuring that it is unique. The leading capital letter also helps us to recognize class names when we see them.

We recommend that class identifiers start with an uppercase letter to ensure uniqueness and to help identify the type as a class.

Scope

C++ uses identifiers to define entities, such as variables and functions, much the way we do to identify ourselves. In both situations, however, we need more than one level of identification to clarify exactly whom we refer to when we use an identifier. For example, we may have two people named George in an organization. If one of them is George Brown and he other is George Gonzales, we can easily qualify which one we are referring by adding the family name.

Similarly, in C++, we can use the same identifier in two classes within a program. Within each class, we simply use to the identifier when we need to refer to it. But, when we refer to the identifier outside the class, we need to qualify the identifier with the class name. That is, we add the class name to make it unique. We code the class name first, followed by a double colon (::) and then the member name as shown in the next example.

```
class_name :: member_name
```

The double colon is known as the **scope resolution operator**. It is used when an identifier that we refer to is not within the current scope. For example, consider the print function within our fraction class. We use a prototype declaration in the fraction class to declare its format. The function definition, however, is out of scope because it is defined outside of the class. Therefore, we need to use the class name and the scope resolution operator to specify that print belongs to the fraction class. This concept is shown in Figure 10-4.

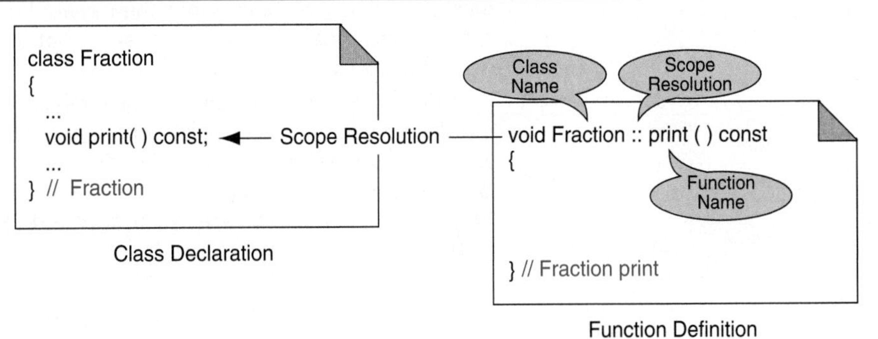

Figure 10-4 Scope resolution operator

Inside the fraction class, the print function is within scope, so it can be referred to using only print. Outside the class, as when it is defined, it must be qualified to establish that it is part of the fraction class and not a stand-alone print function for some other purpose.

Thinking back to Chapter 7, we used the scope resolution operator to access data members of the system class, *ios*. For example, we used `ios::showpoint`, in which *showpoint* is an identifier of a variable in the *ios* class.

Now that we have discussed the scope operator, we are ready to write the definition for the functions in the fraction class.

Fraction :: store

The store function in the fraction class receives two parameters, the numerator and the denominator, and stores them in their corresponding variables within the class. This function is shown in Program 10-2.

Program 10-2 Fraction store function

```
1  /* ================ Fraction :: store ================
2     Store the numerator and denominator in the fraction
3     class.
4         Pre   numer and denom contain the numerator
5               and denominator respectively
6         Post  data stored
7  */
8  void Fraction :: store (int numer, int denom)
9  {
10    numerator   = numer;
11    denominator = denom;
12    return;
13 } // Fraction store
```

Program 10-2 Analysis If you examine the fraction store function carefully, you will note two significant differences between it and any function you would write that is not a member of a class. First, statement 8 defines the function store to be a member of the fraction class by qualifying its scope to `Fraction`. The second difference is much more subtle because it centers around something that is missing. Look at the code carefully and see if you can see what is not there!

We use two variables, numerator and denominator. These variables are declared in the fraction class. Because they are private, they can be referenced only by other members of the class—in this case, the store function. We do not need to define them again, however. In fact, it would be an error to define them within the store function.

Returning to the scope operator, we would be more precise if we referred to them using the scope operator; for example, if we referred to them as `Fraction::numerator`. However, because there is no ambiguity, we can simplify our code by not using it.

Fraction :: print

Now let's write the function that prints the fraction. Because the variables we require to print the fraction are already declared and stored in the class, we do not need any additional information to print the fraction. All we need to know is what fraction we are referring to; therefore, the print function has no parameters. It is shown in Program 10-3.

Program 10-3 Fraction print function

```
/* ================= Fraction :: print ===============
   Prints the numerator and denominator as a fraction.
       Pre   fraction class must contain data
       Post  data printed
*/
void Fraction :: print () const
{
   cout << numerator << "/" << denominator;
   return;
} // Fraction print
```

Program 10-3 Analysis Note the keyword *const* at the end of the function header. This use of constant makes the function a **constant function**. Constant functions cannot change the state of the invoking object, that is the object that calls the function. We use constant functions to ensure that functions do not accidently change an object.

10-2 CLASS OBJECTS

In the previous section, we declared a class and defined two of its member functions (`store` and `print`). We have not defined any objects of type fraction. In this section we discuss how to create and use **class objects**.

INSTANTIATION

Defining an object of a class type is called **instantiation**. When we instantiate an object, we create an **instance** of the class. Each instance of a class is known as an **object**. Just as we can have as many integers as we need in a program, we can also have as many class objects as we need once we have declared the class and defined its functions.

Because the declaration of a class creates a type, we can use the class identifier just as we use any of the standard types. To define an integer object (variable), we simply state the type and the name of the object as follows:

```
int          quantity;
```

Similarly, once we have created a fraction type, we can define a fraction object.

```
Fraction   fr;
```

While the definition of these two objects is identical, how we use them is significantly different. The integer `quantity` is a variable that we can manipulate directly in our program. We can assign it a value using the assignment operator, or we can test its magnitude in a selection statement. We can assign `quantity` a value and we can test that value because the integer type has been given operators that perform these operations.

The defined fraction, `fr`, on the other hand, is an object that consists of two integers. These two integers are encapsulated within the object and cannot be directly referenced. To assign a value to the fraction, we must use the `store` function. If we wanted to test if one fraction were indeed larger than another fraction, we would have to write a compare function and make it a member of the fraction class.

ACCESSING OBJECT MEMBERS

As a type, a class is a model or blueprint from which objects can be created. Implicit in this design is the fact that each object has its own members. The data members are specific to each object; the system allocates[1] memory for all data items in an object when it is instantiated. On the other hand, the member functions are shared between objects; there is only one set of them. However, because each function can be called by only one object at a time, they are treated as members of each object. Member access, therefore, refers to accessing members of a specific object, be it a variable or a member function. As with all C++ types, an object must be defined (instantiated) before it can be accessed.

[1]In Chapter 11 we will discuss static members, which are the exception to this rule.

To refer to members within an object, we use the **member operator**, which is simply a period (.). The general format for member access is the object identifier, dot, member identifier.

```
objectID.memberID
```

For example, after we instantiate a fraction object, we can call the print function of the fraction using a member operator as shown below.

```
Fraction fr;
fr1.print();
```

Similarly, we can access the store function for the fraction object using

```
fr.store(5, 19);
```

Data members are also accessed using the member operator, but they can be accessed only when they are public. As we discussed previously, data members of a class are usually private to ensure their integrity. Within our fraction class, we can use `fr.numerator` and `fr.denominator`. For example, when we develop the add fraction function later in the chapter, we use the member operator to refer to the numerator and denominator of the fractions being added (see Program 10-20 on page 522).

New C++ programmers are often uncertain of when to use the scope resolution operator and when to use the member operator. To refer to the fraction print and store functions, we could actually use both operators as shown in the next example.

```
fr.Fraction::print();
fr.Fraction::store(5, 19);
```

We don't need the scope resolution operator in this case, however, because there is no ambiguity. It is clear that `fr` is an object of the fraction class and that `print` is a member of the class, so it is redundant to use both operators.

Use the scope resolution operator to refer to a specific class type and use the member operator to refer to data or functions within an instantiated class object.

USING CLASSES

Let's write a simple program to demonstrate the use of our fraction class. This program reads the numerator and denominator from the keyboard, stores them in a fraction object, and then prints the fraction.

First, we create a header file for the fraction class in Program 10-4.

Program 10-4 Fraction class header file

```
/* Header file for simple fraction class.
      Written by:
      Date:
*/
// Class Declarations
class Fraction
```

Program 10-4 Fraction class header file *(continued)*

```
{
  private:
      int numerator;
      int denominator;
  public:
     void store (int numer, int denom);
     void print () const;
}; // class Fraction

/* ================= Fraction :: store ===============
   Store the numerator and denominator in the fraction
   object.
      Pre    numer and denom contain the numerator and
             denominator respectively
      Post   data stored
*/
void Fraction :: store (int numer, int denom)
{
   numerator   = numer;
   denominator = denom;
   return;
} // Fraction store

/* ================ Fraction :: print ================
   Prints the numerator and denominator as a fraction.
      Pre   fraction object must contain data
      Post  data printed
*/
void Fraction :: print () const
{
   cout << numerator << "/" << denominator;
   return;
} // Fraction print
   // =========== End Fraction Functions ============
```

After we create the class header file, we are ready to write the application program. Its code is given in Program 10-5. Note that the header file created in Program 10-4 is called out in statement 8 of Program 10-5.

Program 10-5 Fraction class program

```
1  /* Create and use a simple fraction class.
2        Written by:
3        Date:
4  */
5  #include <iostream>
6  using namespace std;
7
8  #include "p10-04.h"
```

Program 10-5 Fraction class program *(continued)*

```
// Prototype Declarations
void getData (int& numer, int& denom);

int main ()
{
   cout << "This program creates a fraction\n\n";

   int numer;
   int denom;
   getData  (numer, denom);

   Fraction fr;
   fr.store (numer, denom);

   cout << "\nYour fraction contains: ";
   fr.print ();

   cout << "\n\nThank you for using fractions\n";
   return 0;
} // main

/* ================== getData ==================
   Reads the numerator and denominator from the keyboard.
     Pre    numer and denom contain the numerator and
            denominator respectively
     Post   data stored
*/
void getData (int& numer, int& denom)
{
   cout << "Please enter the numerator:   ";
   cin  >>  numer;

   cout << "Please enter the denominator: ";
   cin  >>  denom;
   return;
} // getData
```

```
Results
This program creates a fraction

Please enter the numerator:   19
Please enter the denominator: 51
Your fraction contains: 19/51

Thank you for using fractions
```

Program 10-5 Analysis In the header file (Program 10-4), we declare the fraction class and define its two functions. To use the fraction class in Program 10-5, we include the header file in statement 8. Note that we must use quotes, rather than pointed brackets, because it is a user-created header file.

The only new code in the program is found in the member references in *main*. Statement 22 uses the store function for the fraction; statement 25 uses the print function. Both of them use the member operator to identify the function that is to be used. Note also how we pass the data to be stored as parameters just as you would with any function that requires parameters.

In summary, a class is a declaration of data and the operations that can be performed on the data. The data are encapsulated in the class. The functions are associated with the class through function headers and scope specifications. Each instantiation of a class results in a separate object that has its own data but uses the common functions. A complete representation of a class with its functions and objects is shown in Figure 10-5.

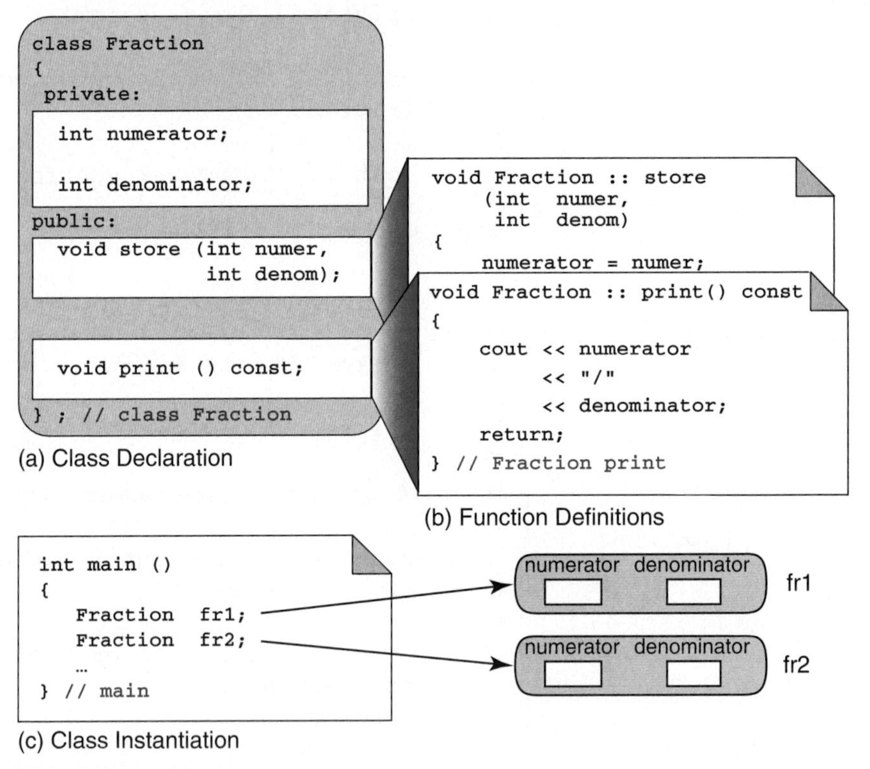

Figure 10-5 Class objects

THE *this* POINTER

When we call a class member function, it automatically contains a hidden pointer known as *this*. The ***this* pointer** contains the address of the invoking (host) object so that it can refer to data and other functions in the class. The *this* pointer has the following characteristics.

1. It is a constant pointer, which means that we cannot change its contents.
2. Most of the time it is used implicitly—that is, it is hidden.

3. We can use it explicitly when we need to access the current host object. As a pointer, it must be dereferenced as shown in the following examples that use the fraction class.

```
*this.numerator      *this.store(2, 5)
```

The first example references the numerator of the current object and the second example stores the fraction `2/5` in the current object. We logically diagram the operation of the *this* pointer as it would be found in the fraction print function in Figure 10-6.

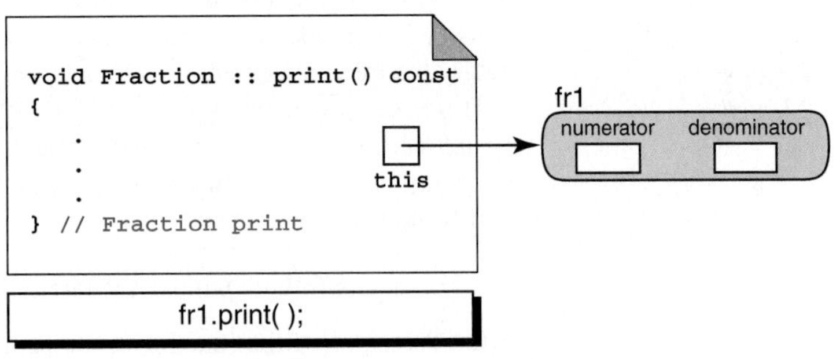

Figure 10-6 The *this* pointer

10-3 MANAGER FUNCTIONS

A class can contain three types of functions: manager functions, mutator functions, and accessor functions. In this section we discuss manager functions, which create, copy, or destroy objects; mutators and accessor functions are discussed in the next section. The **manager functions** are constructors, copy constructors, and destructors. They are shown in Figure 10-7.

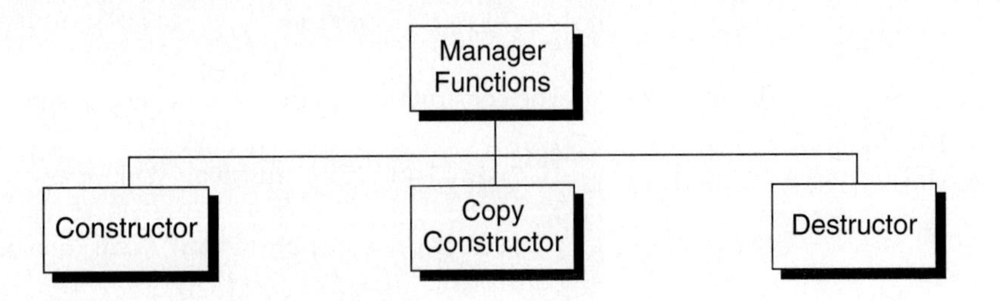

Figure 10-7 Manager functions

CONSTRUCTORS

Constructors are special member functions that are called when an instance of a class is created. Whenever an object is instantiated, a constructor is called.

A class may have more than one constructor. Each constructor initializes data members differently and each object, when instantiated, calls the appropriate constructors. Furthermore, a sophisticated constructor can ensure that only valid data are stored in the data members. For example, a constructor could ensure that a denominator is not zero or that the hour in a time class is not greater than 24.

A constructor is called every time an object is instantiated.

Constructors have three uses. First, a constructor initializes class data members when required. The data members of the class cannot be initialized in the class declaration because each created object has its own variables and must to be initialized with values required by the object being created.

Second, constructors can be used to validate data and thus make the program more robust. For example, in our fraction class, we have not normalized the fraction[2]. We will modify the fraction constructors in Section 10-5 to include normalizing the fractions.

Third, a constructor must be used to allocate memory for an object. Because data variables are encapsulated within the object, they are under the complete and sole control of the object. When data need to be stored in dynamic memory, the memory allocation must be done by the object.

Format

All constructors follow two basic rules:

1. The name of the function is the name of the class. Thus, the constructor for the fraction class must be called `Fraction`.
2. The function must have no return type, even void.

The name of a constructor is the same as the name of the class and it may not have a return type.

The basic format for a constructor is

```
className (parameter list);                  // Declaration

className :: className (parametr list)       // Definition
{
   ...
} // className
```

The constructor for our Fraction class is shown in the next example.

```
Fraction (int numem, int denom);             // Declaration

Fraction :: Fraction (int numem, int denom)
{
   ...
} // Fraction
```

Overloaded Constructors

By definition, a constructor must have the same name as the class. When we need multiple constructors, we implement them as overloaded functions. For our fraction class, we use three constructors. The first, also known as a **default constructor**,[3] has no parameters. It is used whenever an object is instantiated with a value of zero.

---

[2]We add the code to normalize them when we discuss invariants in Section 10-5.

[3]We discuss default constructors more fully on page 504.

```
Fraction :: Fraction ()
{
   numerator   = 0;
   denominator = 1;
}  // Fraction default constructor
```

The second constructor allows us to create a fraction with an integral value. It requires only one parameter, the numerator.

```
Fraction :: Fraction (int numen)
{
   numerator   = numen;
   denominator = 1;
}  // Fraction constructor
```

The third initializes the fraction by setting the numerator and denominator to values passed as parameters.

```
Fraction :: Fraction (int numen, int denum)
{
   numerator   = numen;
   denominator = denom;
}  // Fraction initialization constructor
```

Calling A Constructor

As we said before, a constructor is called when an object is instantiated. This is an automatic call that occurs whenever an object is defined in a program. The following code instantiates three objects using each of the constructors defined above.

```
Fraction fr1;                          // Default
Fraction fr2 (3);                      // Initialize integral
Fraction fr3 (3, 4);                   // Initialize fraction
```

Note that a constructor is a special function; it is not called like other functions nor do we use the member operator. The definition of the object automatically calls the appropriate overloaded constructor. However, if any values are required, we pass them as a parameter list enclosed in parentheses. The first object, `fr1`, uses the default constructor. Because it has no values, the parentheses are not used. As a matter of fact, it is an error to call the default constructor using parentheses.

```
Fraction fr1;                                        // Correct
Fraction fr1();                                      // Error
```

The second object `fr2`, calls the second constructor. Only one value is passed to the constructor. The value stored in this case is integral 3 with a denominator of 1.

The third object, fr3, is a typical fraction value with both a numerator and a denominator. Program 10-6 shows our Fraction class with three constructors added.

Program 10-6 Fraction class declarations

```
/* Fraction Class Declarations
      Written by:
      Date:
*/
```

Program 10-6 Fraction class declarations (*continued*)

```
class Fraction
{
  private:
     int numerator;
     int denominator;
  public:
          Fraction ( );
          Fraction (int numer);
          Fraction (int numer, int denom);
     void store (int numer, int denom);
     void print () const;
}; // Fraction
/* ==============  Fraction :: Fraction =========
   Default constructor for Fraction class.
   Initializes fraction to zero.
      Pre   none
      Post  fraction object initialized to 0
*/
Fraction :: Fraction ()
{
  numerator   = 0;
  denominator = 1;
} // constructor
/* ==============  Fraction :: Fraction ==========
   Constructor for Fraction class.
   Initializes fraction to values in parameter list.
      Pre   numen contains numerator value
      Post  fraction object initialized
*/
Fraction :: Fraction (int numen)
{
  numerator   = numen;
  denominator = 1;
} // Fraction constructor
/* ============== Fraction :: Fraction ==============
   Initialization constructor for Fraction class
   Initializes fraction to values in parameter list.
      Pre  numen and denom contain fraction values
      Post fraction object initialized
*/
Fraction :: Fraction (int numen, int denom)
{
  numerator   = numen;
  denominator = denom;
} // constructor
```

Program 10-7 is a test driver for the fraction class. It defines three fraction variables, each with a different initialization list, and then prints the contents of each variable. Each of the constructors is tested in the program.

Program 10-7 Fraction class test driver

```
/* Demonstrate use of Fraction initializer constructor.
      Written by:
      Date:
*/
#include <iostream>
using namespace std;

#include "p10-06.h"                              // Fraction class
#include "p10-03.h"                              // print function

int main ()
{
   Fraction fr1;
   cout << "fr1 contains: ";
   fr1.print ();
   cout << endl;

   Fraction fr2 (4);
   cout << "fr2 contains: ";
   fr2.print ();
   cout << endl;

   Fraction fr3 (5, 8);
   cout << "fr3 contains: ";
   fr3.print ();
   cout << endl;
   return 0;
} // main
```

```
Results
fr1 contains: 0/1
fr2 contains: 4/1
fr3 contains: 5/8
```

Figure 10-8 shows the three objects after they are created in Program 10-7.

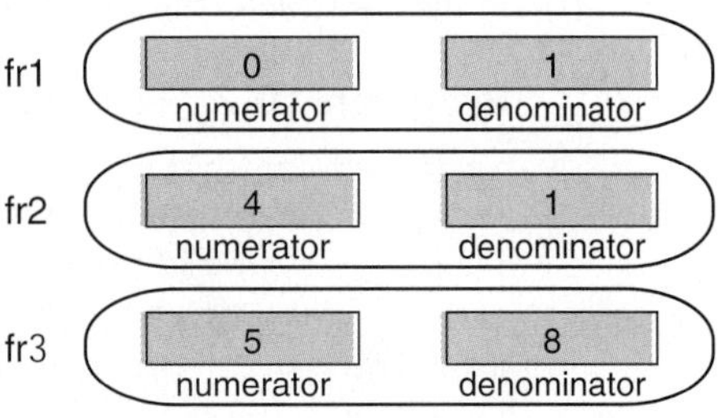

Figure 10-8 Fractions created by Program 10-7

One last point: Every class must have at least one constructor. Constructors are essential to the creation of objects; without a constructor, an object cannot be created. However, this statement does not mean that we must always define a constructor; constructors can also be provided by the compiler.

> **A class must have at least one constructor, either defined by the program or by the compiler.**

Default Constructor

A **default constructor** is a constructor that can be called without any arguments. The first fraction constructor in Program 10-6 is a default constructor. Whenever we call a constructor without arguments, we are calling a default constructor. In other words, whenever we instantiate an object as shown in statement 13 in Program 10-7, we are calling the default constructor.

> **The default constructor is called whenever an object is crated without passing any arguments.**

The default constructor is either defined by the programmer or the system.

1. If the programmer doesn't provide any constructors, the compiler provides a default constructor, which is very primitive and does nothing.
2. If we provide any type of constructor, then the compiler doesn't provide a default constructor. This means that if we define a nondefault constructor, such as any of the previous constructors or even a copy constructor discussed in the next section, then the class is left without a default constructor.

> **If we define any type of constructor, we must also define a default constructor if it is needed.**

Let's look at two examples, one that works and one that doesn't. In the first example, we define a class named `fun`, without any constructors. In this case, we can create an object using the system-defined default constructor and have no problems.

```
Class Fun
{
   ...                                          // No Constructor
}; // Fun
int main ()
{
   Fun fun;                                     // No errors
   ...
}  // main
```

In the second case, Program 10-8, we define a constructor that requires one parameter. Because we define one constructor, the system does not define a default constructor and we get an error when the compiler parses the second class definition (`Funny2`).

Program 10-8 Demonstrate no default constructor error

```
/* Demonstrate error--no default constructor.
      Written by:
      Date:
*/
#include <iostream>
using namespace std;

class Funny
{
  private:
     int num;
  public:
     Funny (int x);                          // A constructor
}; // Funny
Funny :: Funny (int x)
{
  num = x;
} // Initializtion Constructor

int main ()
{
  Funny funny1 (10);                      // Constructor called
  Funny funny2;          // Error: no default constructor
  return 0;
} // main
```

```
Results
Error: function call '[Funny].Funny()' does not match
'Funny::Funny(int)'
'Funny::Funny(const Funny &)'
temptest.cpp line 23    Funny funny2;
// Error. There is no default constructor
```

When we try to create the second object, `funny2`, we get an error because we did not provide a default constructor and the system did not do it because we define one constructor.

A programmer-defined constructor can also be used as a default constructor if all of the arguments have default values. For example, the constructor

```
Fraction :: Fraction (int numen = 0, int denom = 1)
{
   numerator   = numen;
   denominator = denom;
}  // Fraction default constructor
```

can be used as the default constructor. However, in this case we cannot have another default constructor because default constructors cannot be overloaded.

There is only one default constructor; it cannot be overloaded.

In general, C++ authorities recommend that we include a default constructor in a class declaration even if it does not appear to be needed. On the other hand, especially with classes that are placed in a library for general use, we can prevent the use of default constructors by defining a non-default constructor and no default constructor. In this case, anyone using the class and trying to define a default constructor will receive an error message.

COPY CONSTRUCTOR

Throughout the execution of a program, class objects are being created and destroyed. For example, when we pass an object to a function by value, a local copy of the object is created. In this case, the constructor needs to copy the data in the passed object to the invoking object. A **copy constructor** is a function that is called whenever a copy of an existing instance needs to be created.

The following code demonstrates how to write the declaration and definition of a copy constructor for our fraction class.

```
Fraction (const Fraction& fr);                  // Declaration

Fraction :: Fraction (const Fraction& fr) // Definition
{
   numerator   = fr.numerator;
   denominator = fr.denominator;
}  // Fraction copy constructor
```

Note that we pass a constant of the existing object to the function by reference. We pass the existing object by reference, not by value, to avoid creating an extra copy. We pass the existing object as a constant, because we do not want the function to be able to change the state of the object being passed—that is, to be able to change the value of its data members.

Calling Copy Constructor

As with all constructors, the copy constructor is called automatically when we define a class object using an existing instance of the object as a parameter as shown in the following code:

```
Fraction fr1;

Fraction fr2 (fr1);
```

Bitwise versus Logical Copy Constructors

There are two types of copy constructors. The first performs a simple variable-by-variable assignment copy of all of the components of an object. This is sometimes known as a **bitwise copy** because the object's contents are simply copied bit by bit from the original object to the new object.

The second type of copy constructor comes into play when there are complex objects, such as pointers, within an object. We refer to this constructor as a **logical copy** because it makes a true copy of the structure, including its dynamic structures if necessary. The difference between the two types of copy constructors is illustrated in Figure 10-9.

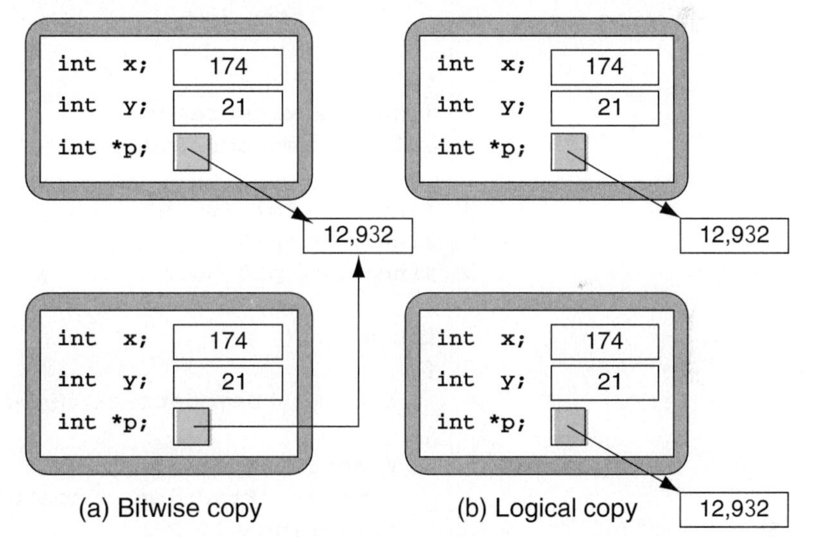

Figure 10-9 Bitwise and logical copies

As you study Figure 10-9, note that the values of all of the variables, including the pointer values, are the same. In the bitwise copy in Figure 10-9a, however, there is only one variable with both the original and new objects pointing to it. If either object changes the variable's value, therefore, the value will be changed for both objects. Now compare the results of the logical copy in Figure 10-9b. In the logical copy, we not only copy the values but we also create a new dynamic-member variable for the pointer.

Program 10-9 defines the copy constructor for the fraction class.

Program 10-9 Define copy constructor for fraction class

```
/* Copy constructor for Fraction class.
Pre    copyFrom exists and has values to be copied
Post   new object created and data copied
*/
Fraction :: Fraction (const Fraction& copyFrom)
{
```

Program 10-9 Define copy constructor for fraction class *(continued)*

```
// Statements
   numerator   = copyFrom.numerator;
   denominator = copyFrom.denominator;
} // Copy constructor
```

Program 10-10 is a test driver for the fraction copy constructor. Note that it includes the previously defined header files for the class.

Program 10-10 Fraction copy constructor execution

```
/* Demonstrate use of copy constructor.
      Written by:
      Date:
*/
#include <iostream>
using namespace std;

#include "p10-06.h"      // Basic class declaration
#include "p10-03.h"      // Print class member
#include "p10-09.h"      // Copy constructor

int main ()
{
   cout << "Demonstrate bitwise copy of a fraction\n";

   Fraction fr1 (19, 32);
   cout << "Fraction 1 contains: ";
   fr1.print ();

   Fraction fr2 (fr1);
   cout << "\nFraction 2 contains: ";
   fr2.print ();
   return 0;
} // main
```

```
Results
Demonstrate bitwise copy of a fraction
Fraction 1 contains: 19/32
Fraction 2 contains: 19/32
```

Default Copy Constructor

If we do not define a copy constructor, the system provides a bitwise one. However, in this case, the system does not care if we have defined 10 other constructors; it just checks to see if we have defined a copy constructor. This means that there is always one copy constructor, either defined by us or by the system. Again, we recommend that you always define the copy constructor rather than leaving it to the system.

> There is always one copy constructor available in a class.

There are three different situations in which a copy constructor is used: (1) when an object is instantiated using another object as a parameter, (2) when an object is passed by value to a function, and (3) when an object is returned from a function.

Instantiated Objects When a class object is explicitly passed as a parameter during instantiation, a copy constructor is called.

Passed Objects When an object is passed to a function by value, a local copy must be created. To create the local object, the copy constructor is called.

Returned Objects When an object is returned from a function, it must be copied to a receiving object or inserted in an expression.

Passing Objects by Reference

When we need to pass an object to a function, we can either pass it by value or by reference. When we pass an object by value, a temporary local instance is created. Depending on the complexity of the object, considerable overhead may be involved in copying the member data. Therefore, we recommend that all class objects be passed by reference. For data integrity, we also recommend that it be passed as a constant whenever the called function is not supposed to change the object. The following example shows how we pass an instance of the Fraction class to a function as a constant.

```
int fun (const Fraction& fr);
```

Always pass objects to a function by reference; when the object cannot be changed, pass it as a constant.

Returning Objects

The rule for returning objects from a function is opposite of the passing them to an object. We recommend that objects be returned by value; that is, do not return referenced objects. The reason is that when a referenced object is created in the called function, that reference ceases to exist when the function terminates.

Always return objects by value.

Explicit Call To Constructors

So far we have called constructors implicitly. We requested an object to be created and the system calls the appropriate constructors for us. In all of these creations, the object created had a name.

We can also create an **anonymous object** by calling a constructor **explicitly** (just as we call an ordinary function). In this case, we create an anonymous object. This is very useful, when, for example, we need to return an object from a function. The object to be returned does not need any name. The following shows the idea:

```
Fraction fun (int x)
{
   ...
   return Fraction (2, x);
}  // fun
```

DESTRUCTORS

Destructors are the opposite of constructors. They come into play when an object dies, either because it is no longer in scope or because it has been deleted.

Format

The name of the destructor is the name of the class preceded by a tilde (~). Like a constructor, a destructor cannot have a return type. However, unlike a constructor, the argument list of a destructor must be empty. This means that we cannot overload a destructor. A class can have one and only one destructor.

> **A class can have one, and only one, destructor.**

The following shows how we write a destructor for our fraction class:

```
Fraction :: ~Fraction ()
{

} // Fraction destructor
```

Note that the destructor for our Fraction class is very simple. We do not need to do anything. However, if we have a class that uses dynamic memory allocation, we need to release memory in the destructor. We show how to do it in the next chapter when we use classes involving memory allocations.

Default Destructor

If we do not provide a destructor for our class, the system provides one for us. In this case, it is called a default destructor. A default destructor is very primitive and does nothing. It is provided because the C++ compiler is looking for a destructor when the object ceases to exist. If we need a more sophisticated destructor, we need to write it ourselves. Note that the default destructor guarantees that we always have one destructor.

Explicit Call of Destructor

Like a constructor, a destructor can also be called explicitly, but it is very rare. It is done in some very special occasions that are beyond the scope of this book.

10-4 MUTATORS AND ACCESSORS

In the previous section we discussed the first class function type, manager functions. In this section we discuss the other two, mutators and accessors.

MUTATOR FUNCTIONS

A **mutator** is a function that can change the state of a **host object**, that is of the object that invokes it. For example, the store function we defined in Program 10-2 on page 493 is a mutator function. We call the store function as follows:

```
fr1.store (4, 7);
```

In this call, the store function actually changes the value of the numerator in `fr1` to 4 and the value of denominator to 7. Note that the mutators must always have a return type, even if it is only *void*. The only functions in a class that are defined and declared without a return value are manager functions—that is, constructors, copy constructors, and destructors.

ACCESSOR FUNCTIONS

An **accessor** is a function that cannot change the state of its invoking object. An accessor is called either for its side effects, such as to print, or for its return value. The print function in our fraction class is an example of an accessor that is used for its side effect. Like mutators, accessors must always have a return type.

To ensure that an accessor does not change the state of the host object, we make the function itself constant by adding the keyword *const* at the end of the declaration and definition as we did in Program 10-3 on page 493 and repeated in the following code.

```
void print () const;                              // Declaration

void Fraction :: print () const                   // Definition
{
   ...
}  // Fraction print
```

10-5 CLASS INVARIANTS

Classes should be **invariant**. Simply stated, this means that two or more instances of a class that represent the same value must have the same data members. Another way of stating this principle is that a class enforces uniqueness of representation so that different instances with the same value are identical. By definition, the standard types in C++ are invariant.

If we have two integer variables, `a` and `b`, and assign the first one the constant 5 and the second one the constant 10/2, both integers holds the value 5 in memory; they are invariant objects. But, because our fraction class is not normalized, we can have two fraction, `fr1` and `fr2` that represent the same fraction, but are different objects; that is, their states are different. Figure 10-10 shows this problem.

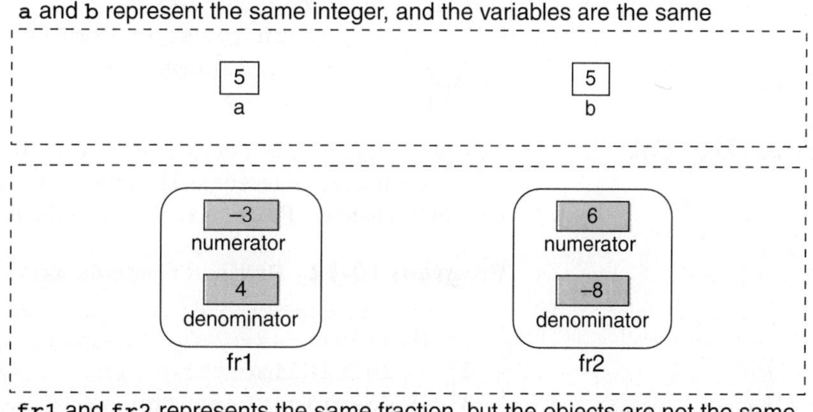

Figure 10-10 Class invariants

The two fractions, `-3/4` and `6/-8` have the same value; in their normalized form they both represent the fraction `-3/4`. In other words, we have two objects that represent the same fraction. We need to fix this flaw in our Fraction class.

GREATEST COMMON DIVISOR

The first function we need determines the **greatest common divisor** between two numbers. We can write it recursively using the formula shown in Figure 10-11.

$$\gcd(x, y) = \begin{bmatrix} x & \text{if } y = 0 \\ \gcd(y,\ x \bmod y) & \text{otherwise} \end{bmatrix}$$

Figure 10-11 Greatest common divisor

In Program 10-11 we use a recursive function to determine the greatest common divisor. As shown in Figure 10-11, the base case occurs when `x` is zero. In the general case, we recursively call the function, substituting `y` for the first parameter and making the second parameter the remainder of `x/y(x mod y)`. This approach is known as Euclid's algorithm.

Program 10-11 Greatest common divisor

```
/* Determine the greatest common divisor of two numbers.
      Pre  Given two integers
      Post GCD returned
*/
int Fraction:: greatestComDiv (int n1, int n2)
{
   // Base case
   if (n2 == 0)
      return n1;
   else
   // General case
      return greatestComDiv (n2, n1 % n2);
} // greatestComDiv
```

CONSTRUCTOR

Now we change the fraction constructor with two arguments (see Program 10-6) to normalize the fraction it receives. The other constructors and the copy constructor do not need to be changed. Program 10-12 shows the revised constructor.

Program 10-12 Revised fraction constructor

```
/* ============= Fraction :: Fraction =============
   Initializes fraction to values in parameter list
   ensuring that the fraction is normalized.
      Pre  numen and denom contain fraction values
      Post fraction object initialized
*/
Fraction:: Fraction (int numer, int denom)
{
   if (denom == 0)
      {
       cout << "Error: denominator is zero" << endl;
       exit (100);
```

Program 10-12 Revised fraction constructor (*continued*)

```
      } // Zero denom
   if (denom < 0)
      // Ensure that any negative is in numerator
      {
       denom = -denom;
       numer = -numer;
      } // demon < 0
   int gcd = greatestComDiv (abs(numer), abs(denom));
   numer = numer / gcd;
   denom = denom / gcd;

   numerator = numer;
   denomiator = denom;
} // Constructor
```

CHANGING STORE FUNCTION

The store function (see Program 10-2 on page 493) changes the state of the object. To ensure that a fraction is always stored in its normalized form, we need to ensure that any function that changes the state of the objects maintains normalization. The store function is one of them. We do this by explicitly calling the constructor to store the changed values. This technique ensures that we change the fraction values only through the constructor that guarantees that the fraction is normalized. Program 10-13 shows the revised code for store function.

Program 10-13 Revised store fraction function

```
/* ================= Fraction :: store ===============
   Store the numerator and denominator in the fraction
   class. Calls constructor to ensure normalization.
       Pre   numer and denom contain the numerator
             and denominator respectively
       Post  data stored
*/
void Fraction :: store (int numer, int denom)
{
   *this = Fraction (numer, denom);
   return;
} // Fraction store
```

REVISED FRACTION CLASS

We have made several changes to the fraction class. Let's combine them into one header file. The revised fraction class is shown in Program 10-14.

Program 10-14 Revised fraction class declarations

```
/* Fraction Class Declarations
      Written by:
      Date:
*/
class Fraction
```

Program 10-14 Revised fraction class declarations (*continued*)

```
{
   private:
      int numerator;
      int denominator;
      int greatestComDiv (int n1, int n2);
   public:
            Fraction ( );
            Fraction (int numer);
            Fraction (int numer, int denom);
            Fraction (const Fraction& copyFrom);
           ~Fraction () { }
      void store    (int numer, int denom);
      void print    ( ) const;
}; // Fraction
/* ==============  Fraction :: Fraction =========
   Constructor for Fraction class.
   Initializes fraction to zero.
      Pre   none
      Post  fraction object initialized to 0
*/
Fraction :: Fraction ()
{
   numerator   = 0;
   denominator = 1;
} // constructor
/* ==============  Fraction :: Fraction ==========
   Default constructor for Fraction class
   Initializes fraction to values in parameter list.
      Pre   numen contains numerator value
      Post  fraction object initialized
*/
Fraction :: Fraction (int numen)
{
   numerator   = numen;
   denominator = 1;
} // Fraction constructor
/* ==============  Fraction :: Fraction ==============
   Initializes fraction to values in parameter list
   ensuring that the fraction is normalized.
      Pre  numen and denom contain fraction values
      Post fraction object initialized
*/
Fraction:: Fraction (int numer, int denom)
{
   if (denom == 0)
      {
       cout << "Error: denominator is zero" << endl;
       exit (100);
      } // zero denom
```

Program 10-14 Revised fraction class declarations (*continued*)

```
   if (denom < 0)
      // Ensure that any negative is in numerator
      {
       denom = -denom;
       numer = -numer;
      } // denom < 0
   int gcd = greatestComDiv (abs(numer), abs(denom));
   numer = numer / gcd;
   denom = denom / gcd;

   numerator   = numer;
   denominator = denom;
} // Constructor
/* =================== copyFrom ===================
   Copy constructor for Fraction class.
     Pre   copyFrom exists and has values to be copied
     Post  new object created and data copied
*/
Fraction :: Fraction (const Fraction& copyFrom)
{
// Statements
   numerator   = copyFrom.numerator;
   denominator = copyFrom.denominator;
} // Copy constructor
/* ================= Fraction :: store ==============
   Store the numerator and denominator in the fraction
   class. Calls constructor to ensure normalization.
        Pre   numer and denom contain the numerator
              and denominator respectively
        Post  data stored
*/
void Fraction :: store (int numer, int denom)
{
   *this = Fraction (numer, denom);
   return;
} // Fraction store
/* ================= Fraction :: print ==============
   Prints the numerator and denominator as a fraction.
        Pre   fraction class must contain data
        Post  data printed
*/
void Fraction :: print () const
{
   cout << numerator << "/" << denominator;
   return;
} // Fraction print
/* ================= greatestComDiv =================
   Determine the greatest common divisor of two numbers.
      Pre  Given two integers
```

Program 10-14 Revised fraction class declarations (*continued*)

```
        Post GCD returned
*/
int Fraction:: greatestComDiv (int n1, int n2)
{
// Base case
   if (n2 == 0)
      return n1;
   else
       // General case
      return greatestComDiv (n2, n1 % n2);
} // greatestComDiv
```

Program 10-15 tests the revised class with several fractions. The first three test cases envoke the three different constructors. The last test case verifies that the fraction 4/-8 is normalized.

Program 10-15 Test driver for revised class

```
/* Demonstrate use of Fraction initializer constructor.
      Written by:
      Date:
*/
#include <iostream>
using namespace std;

#include "p10-14.h"                          // Fraction class

int main ()
{
   Fraction fr1;
   cout << "fr1 contains: ";
   fr1.print ();
   cout << endl;

   Fraction fr2 (4);
   cout << "fr2 contains: ";
   fr2.print ();
   cout << endl;

   Fraction fr3 (5, 8);
   cout << "fr3 contains: ";
   fr3.print ();
   cout << endl;

   Fraction fr4;
   cout << "fr4 contains: ";
   fr4.store (4, -8);
```

Program 10-15 Test driver for revised class (*continued*)

```
    fr4.print ();
    cout << endl;
    return 0;
} // main
```

```
Results
fr1 contains: 0/1
fr2 contains: 4/1
fr3 contains: 5/8
fr4 contains: -1/2                    // It has been normalized
```

10-6 COMPLEX CLASS FUNCTIONS

So far, our fraction class is very simple. It requires one print function, one store functions, three constructors, a copy constructor, and one destructor. In this section, we develop several class functions that deal with multiple class objects. If the function operates on one class object, we call it a unary class function. If it operates on two class objects, we refer to it as a binary class function.

UNARY CLASS FUNCTIONS

Like a unary operator, a **unary class function** uses only one instance of the class. While a unary class function may have parameters, none of the parameters can be an instance of its class. It can operate only on the data for the invoking object that is referenced in the call. For example, when we call print as shown below

```
fr1.print () const;
```

the value in the `fr1` fraction is printed. Since there are no parameters, it is obvious that the only the host object `fr1` is involved.

The Increment Function

We have already seen one unary class function: print. In this section, we develop a second one, increment, which adds 1 to a fraction. To add 1 to a fraction, we simply replace the numerator by the sum of the numerator and the denominator. The denominator remains unchanged. The prototype declaration for the increment function is

```
void increment ();
```

Program 10-16 contains the changes to the fraction header file.

Program 10-16 Fraction header file for increment

```
/* ============== Fraction :: increment ==============
   Add one to the fraction.
      Pre   numer and denom contain the numerator and
            denominator respectively
      Post  One added
*/
void Fraction :: increment ()
```

Program 10-16 Fraction header file for increment *(continued)*

```
{
   numerator += denominator;
   return;
} // Fraction increment
```

Program 10-17 contains an example of how the increment fraction function would be called from a program. Note that incrementing a normalized fraction creates a new normalized fraction; there is no need to call the constructor here.

Program 10-17 Increment fraction execution

```
1  /* Demonstrate the use of unary increment fraction.
2        Written by:
3        Date:
4  */
5  #include <iostream>
6  using namespace std;
7
8  #include "p10-14.h"              // Class declaration
9  #include "p10-16.h"              // Increment function
10
11 int main ()
12 {
13    Fraction fr (19, 51);
14    cout << "The fraction contains: ";
15    fr.print ();
16
17    cout << "\nIncrementing fraction.";
18    fr.increment ();
19
20    cout << "\nThe fraction contains: ";
21    fr.print ();
22    cout << endl;
23    return 0;
24 } // main
```

```
Results
The fraction contains: 19/51
Incrementing fraction.
The fraction contains: 70/51
```

Program 10-17 Analysis In Program 10-17, we create an initialized fraction (statement 13), then print it, increment it, and print it again. The results are shown at the end of the program.

BINARY CLASS FUNCTIONS

Often we need more than one object in a function. For example, when we add two fractions, we need two objects, which makes it a **binary class function**.

There are two formats for a binary class function. In the first, one of the objects is the host and the other object is a parameter. This is similar to the format for the complex binary add operator (+=) that we studied in Chapter 3. We discuss this format in the `addTo` function. In the second binary class function, both class objects are parameters.

addTo Function

The `addTo` function is a binary class function that adds two fractions and places the result in the host fraction. As we said above, it is the equivalent of the complex add (+=) expression. For example, given fractions `fr1` and `fr2`, we can add them as shown in Figure 10-12.

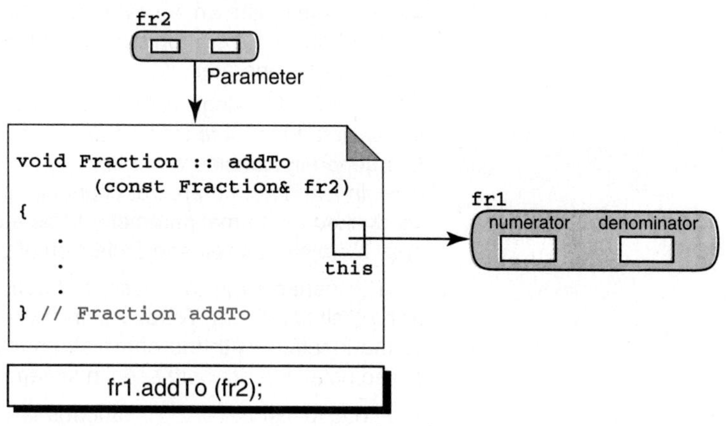

Figure 10-12 Add two fractions

Adding two fractions is relatively straightforward. We multiply the numerator of the first fraction by the second fraction's denominator and add the product to the numerator of the second fraction multiplied by the first fraction's denominator. The denominator is the product of the two denominators. The formula is shown below.

$$\frac{(\text{numerator1} \times \text{denominator2}) + (\text{numerator2} \times \text{denominator1})}{\text{denominator1} \times \text{denominator2}}$$

The addTo declaration, included in the fraction header file, is

```
void addTo (const Fraction& fr2);
```

The header file for the function is seen in Program 10-18.

Program 10-18 Fraction header file for *addTo*

```
/* Add two fractions.
       Pre   fractions contain values.
       Post  sum stored in calling fraction
*/
void Fraction :: addTo (const Fraction& fr2)
{
  numerator =
       (numerator      * fr2.denominator)
```

Program 10-18 Fraction header file for *addTo (continued)*

```
 9        + (fr2.numerator * denominator);
10     denominator *= fr2.denominator;
11     *this = Fraction (numerator, denominator);
12     return;
13  } // Fraction addTo
```

Program 10-18 Analysis Study this function carefully. It contains a very important concept that allows us to easily ensure that the results are normalized. In statement 11, we create an anonymous fraction, which uses the constructor to normalize the results. The anonymous fraction is then assigned to the current object using the *this* operator.

The rest of the logic used here is relatively simple, but the notation bears some discussion. First, note that we are passing the fraction as a reference parameter. It is generally considered better to pass classes as reference parameters; however, in `addTo`, we are not changing anything in the second fraction. Therefore, we declare the formal parameter to be a constant. This allows us the efficiency of pass by reference with the protection of pass by value.

The variables in the class that calls the function are referenced by simply using their identifiers. To refer to the parameter variables, however, we must qualify the identifier with the parameter's class identifier and the member operator. These notations are both seen in statements 8 and 9.

The code to test the `addTo` function is seen in Program 10-19.

Program 10-19 *addTo* function execution

```
/* Demonstrate the addTo function.
      Written by:
      Date:
*/
#include <iostream>
using namespace std;

#include "p10-14.h"      // Basic class declaration
#include "p10-18.h"      // addTo function

int main ()
{
   Fraction fr1 (1, 5);
   fr1.print ();
   cout << " + ";
   Fraction fr2 (3, 5);
   fr2.print ();

   fr1.addTo (fr2);

   cout << " is ";
   fr1.print ();
   cout << endl;
   return 0;
} // main
```

Program 10-19 ***addTo* function execution *(continued)***

```
Results
First Run
   1/5 + 3/5 is 4/5
Second Run
   1/5 + 3/-10 is -1/10
```

Program 10-19 Analysis To test the function, we ran the program twice. The first run used two fractions with the same denominator. Its results are seen in the first test results. Then we ran the program with fractions whose denominators were different. In the second example, the results after the addition is `-1/10`.

Add Fractions (Friend Function)

In the second binary format, both objects are parameters; there is no host object. The called function receives two class objects, such as two fractions, and usually returns a temporary class object that can be assigned to an object by the calling function. The add fraction function uses this format. A sample is shown below.

```
fr = add (fr1, fr2);
```

Our add fraction function must be a member of the fraction class. If it is not, then it can't access any of the private members of the class. But, in the above statement, what fraction is it associated with? The answer is none of them.

We now have a dilemma. To reference the private members of a class, a function must be associated with a class. On the other hand, when a function is associated with a class, it cannot be called except as a member of the class.

Functions that are members of a class can only be called through objects of that class. They cannot be called independently.

This means that our add fraction function can only be called using the notation shown below

```
fr = fr.add (fr2, fr3);
```

which references three objects, not just two.

Another possible solution would be to make the data public, but this violates the principle of data hiding. To solve this dilemma, C++ has available another type of function, the **friend function**. If a function is a friend of a class, it can have access to all members of the class, even the private ones. Note, however, that a function can only be declared a friend by the class itself. That is, a function cannot unilaterally declare itself to be a friend of a class. If it could, it would be violating the privacy principle of data hiding.

Friend functions are *not* members of a class. Rather, they are associated with the class and are given special privileges: They can access the private members of the class as though they were members. This means that they can refer to the private data and call any private functions. When a function is declared to be a friend, it is called as any other nonmember function.

Friend functions are not members of a class, but are associated with it.

To declare that a function is a friend of a class, its prototype declaration within the class is prefixed with the keyword *friend*. When the function is written, the keyword is not used. The prototype declaration for add fraction is shown in the following example.

```
class fraction
   {
    private:
    ...
    public:
      friend Fraction add (const Fraction& fr1,
                           const Fraction& fr2);
      ...
   }; // class fraction
```

We are now ready to write the binary class function to add two fractions and return the sum. The sum is stored in a locally declared fraction that automatically gets deleted by the compiler when it is returned. For example, given two fractions, `fr1` and `fr2`, the call in Figure 10-13 returns their sum and stores it in `fr3`. (We will see in the next chapter how to create an operator function that assigns the result to `fr3`. For now, we are concerned only with the concept that the add fraction function returns a fraction.)

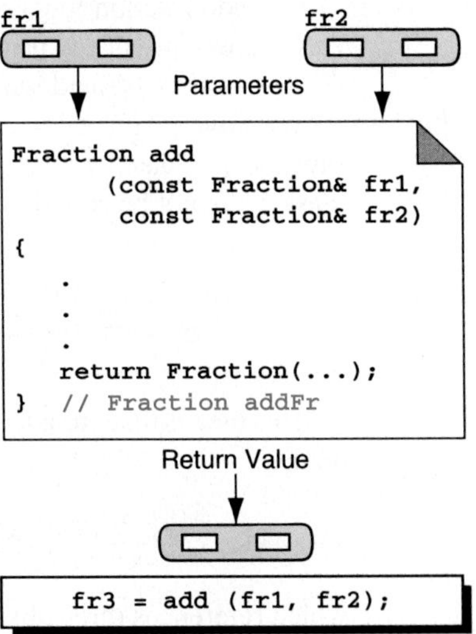

Figure 10-13 Add and return fraction value

The add fraction header file is seen in Program 10-20.

Program 10-20 Add fraction

```
/* Add two fractions and return sum.
      Pre   fractions contain values
      Post  sum returned
*/
Fraction add (const Fraction& fr1, const Fraction& fr2)
{
```

Program 10-20 Add fraction *(continued)*

```
   int numen = (fr1.numerator    * fr2.denominator)
             + (fr2.numerator    * fr1.denominator);
   int denom =  fr1.denominator * fr2.denominator;
   return Fraction (numen, denom);
} // friend Fraction addFr
```

Program 10-21 contains a demonstration of the add fraction function.

Program 10-21 Add fraction execution

```
/* Demonstrate add fraction.
      Written by:
      Date:
*/
#include <iostream>
using namespace std;

#include "p10-14.h"      // Basic class declaration
#include "p10-20.h"      // add fraction

int main ()
{
   Fraction fr1 (1, 5);
   Fraction fr2 (3, 5);
   Fraction fr3;
   fr3 = add (fr1, fr2);
   fr1.print ();
   cout << " + ";
   fr2.print ();

   cout << " is ";
   fr3.print ();
   cout << endl;
   return 0;
} // main
```

```
Results
First Run
   1/5 + 3/5 is 4/5
Second Run
   1/5 + 3/10 is 1/2
```

COMPARING FRACTIONS

In object-oriented programming, each class that has comparable values needs a function to compare objects. In the fraction class, the fraction is always normalized; that is, the greatest common divisor of the numerator and denominator is one. In this case, comparing two fractions is easy: The numerators must be equal and the denominators must be equal as shown in the following code.

```
bool Fraction :: compareTo (const Fraction& fr) const
{
   return ((numerator   == fr.numerator)
        && denominator == fr.denominator));
}  // Fraction compareTo
```

10-7 PROGRAMMING APPLICATIONS

In this section we present two applications: an account class and a time class.

ACCOUNT CLASS

The account class has one field, balance, and three methods: get balance, deposit, and withdraw. It is shown in Program 10-22.

Program 10-22 **An account class**

```
/* Maintain a bank account balance using deposit and
   withdraw methods.
      Written by:
      Date:
*/

#include <iostream>
#include <iomanip>
using namespace std;

class Account
{
   private:
   double balance;

   public:
           Account   ();               // Constructor
     void  getBalance() const;
     void  deposit   (double amount);
     void  withdraw  (double amount);
}; // Account

/* ============ Account :: constructor ===========
   Creates an Account and sets balance to 0.0.
      Pre   Account object is being created
      Post  Account created with 0 balance
*/
Account :: Account ()
{
   balance = 0.0;
} // Account default constructor

/* ============ Account :: getBalance ===========
   Prints account balance.
```

Program 10-22 An account class (*continued*)

```
        Pre   Account has been created
        Post  Balance printed
*/
void Account :: getBalance () const
{
   cout << "Your account balance is: "
        << setw(5) << balance << endl;
   return;
} // Account getBalance

/* ============= Account :: deposit ============
   Adds deposit amount to balance
        Pre   Account has been created
        Post  Balance updated
*/
void Account :: deposit (double amount)
{
   balance += amount;
   return;
} // Account deposit

/* ============= Account :: withdraw ============
   Subtracts withdrawal amount from balance
        Pre   Account has been created
        Post  Balance updated
*/
void Account :: withdraw (double amount)
{
   balance -= amount;
   return;
} // Account withdrawal
   // ============ End Account Functions =============

int main ()
{
   Account ac;

   ac.getBalance ();
   ac.deposit    (100.0);
   ac.getBalance ();
   ac.withdraw   ( 50.0);
   ac.getBalance ();
   return 0;
} // main
```

```
Results
Your account balance is:     0
Your account balance is:   100
Your account balance is:    50
```

TIME CLASS

While time functionality is included in the *ctime* library, it is a simple and intuitive example that we can adapt to a class. The design of our time class is shown in Figure 10-14. This figure uses UML, which is described in the software engineering section in this chapter, beginning on page 530.

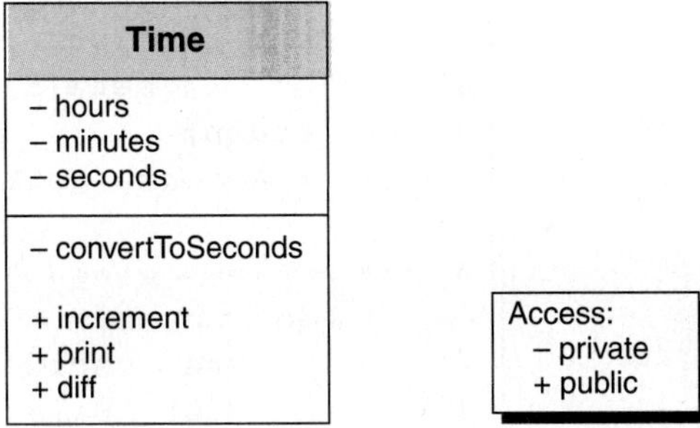

Figure 10-14 Time class design

As can be seen in the design, there are three private data members and one private methods. Note that in Program 10-23, we create a private constructor. This is somewhat unusual, but we don't want the functions that convert seconds to time to be available outside of the class. The rest of the code is rather straightforward.

Program 10-23 Time class

```
/* Time Class.
      Written by:
      Date:
*/
class Time
{
   private:
      unsigned short hours;
      unsigned short minutes;
      unsigned short seconds;

      long   convertToSeconds () const;
             Time(long s);         // Private constructor
   public:
             Time (unsigned short hourIn = 0,
                   unsigned short minIn  = 0,
                   unsigned short secIn  = 0);
             void  increment ();
             void  print () const;
      friend Time  diff (const Time& tStart,
                         const Time& tEnd);
}; // Time

// =============== Time constructor ===============
```

Program 10-23 Time class (*continued*)

```
Time :: Time (long secIn)
{
   // A day is 86400 seconds
   seconds = (secIn % 86400) % 60;
   minutes = (secIn / 60 )   % 60;
   hours   = ((secIn / 60 )   / 60) % 24;
} // Time constructor
// =============== Time constructor ===============
Time :: Time (unsigned short hourIn,
                 unsigned short minIn,
                 unsigned short secIn)
{
   if (hourIn > 23 || minIn > 59 || secIn > 59)
      {
       cout << "Error" << endl;
       exit (100);
      } // if
   seconds = secIn;
   minutes = minIn;
   hours   = hourIn;
} // Time constructor
/* =============== print ===============
   Prints time in format hh:mm:ss.
      Pre  Nothing
      Post Time printed
*/
void Time :: print ( ) const
{
   cout.fill('0');
   cout << setw(2) << hours   << ":"
        << setw(2) << minutes << ":"
        << setw(2) << seconds;
   cout.fill(' ');
} // print
/* =============== convertToSeconds ===============
   Returns time in seconds.
      Pre  Nothing
      Post Returns time in seconds
*/
long Time :: convertToSeconds () const
{
   return ( hours * 3600 + minutes * 60 + seconds);
} // convertToSeconds
/* =============== increment ===============
   Adds one second to the time object.
      Pre  Nothing
      Post Time incremented
*/
void Time :: increment ()
```

Program 10-23 **Time class (*continued*)**

```
{
   long s = convertToSeconds () + 1 ;
   *this = Time (s);
} // increment
/* =============== diff ===============
   Calculate the time difference between two
   time objects.
     Pre   tStart is beginnning time, tEnd is end time
     Post  Returns difference in Time object
*/
Time diff (const Time& tStart, const Time& tEnd)
{
   long sec = tStart.convertToSeconds()
            - tEnd.convertToSeconds ();
   if (sec < 0)
       sec = -sec;
   return Time (sec);
} // diff
```

The time class test driver and its execution results are found in Program 10-24.

Program 10-24 **Time class test driver**

```
/* Test driver for Time class.
      Written by:
      Date:
*/
#include <iostream>
#include <iomanip>
#include <cstdlib>
using namespace std ;

#include "p10-23.h"

int main ()
{
   Time t1;
   cout << "Time null        : ";
   t1.print();
   cout << "\n";
   t1.increment();
   cout << "Time 00:00:00 + 1: ";
   t1.print();
   cout << "\n";

   Time t2 (23, 59 , 59);
   t2.increment();
   cout << "Time 23:59:59 + 1: ";
   t2.print();
```

Program 10-24 Time class test driver (*continued*)

```
   cout << "\n";

   Time t3 (4 , 12, 16);
   cout << "\nTime ";
   t3.print ();
   cout << " - ";

   Time t4 (2 , 10 , 8);
   t4.print ();
   cout << " is ";

   Time timePass;
   timePass = diff(t3, t4);
   timePass.print();
   cout << "\n";
   return 0;
} // main
```

```
Results
Time null          : 00:00:00
Time 00:00:00 + 1: 00:00:01
Time 23:59:59 + 1: 24:00:00

Time 04:12:16 - 02:10:08 is 02:02:08
```

10-8 SOFTWARE ENGINEERING AND PROGRAMMING STYLE

The **Unified Modeling Language (UML)** is a graphical language used for Object-Oriented Analysis and Design. Through UML we can specify, visualize, construct, and document software and hardware systems using standard graphical notations. UML provides five different levels of abstraction, called views, as shown in Figure 10-15.

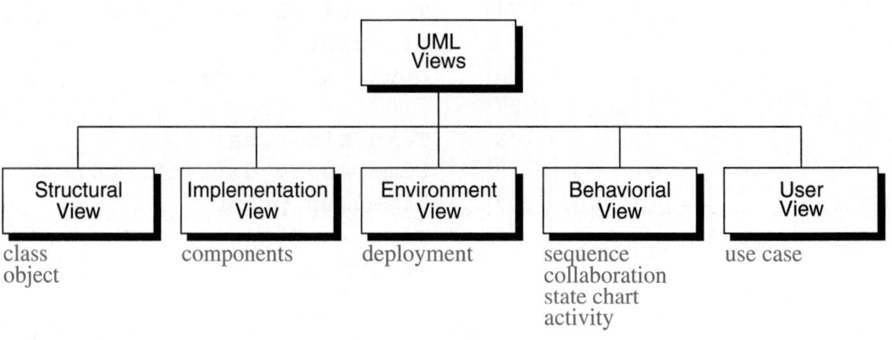

Figure 10-15 UML views

As shown in Figure 10-15, the five views are:

- The **structural view**, which shows the static structure of the system. It contains *class* and *object* diagrams.
- The **implementation view**, which shows the organization of software components and their relationships. It contains *component* diagrams.
- The **environment view**, which shows the configuration of elements and hardware components. It contains *deployment* diagrams.
- The **behavioral view**, which shows how the system behaves. It contains *sequence, collaboration, state chart,* and *activity* diagrams.
- The **user view**, which shows the interaction of the user with the system. It contains *use case* diagrams.

We only discuss the structural view of UML in this section. The structural view uses two groups of diagrams: classes and objects

UML: CLASS DIAGRAMS

A **class diagram** is a description of a set of objects with common features, such as attributes and operations. A class diagram is used to model a set of entities or concepts. In UML, a class is represented by a rectangle, known as a container, that documents the name of the class. By convention, the name of the class starts with an uppercase letter. If the name consists of multiple words, each word starts with an uppercase letter with no space between them. Examples are *Fraction, BankAccount,* and *UtilityVehicle.*

Basic Class Diagrams

There are three basic class diagrams: concrete classes, abstract classes, and templates.

Concrete Classes We represent concrete classes with bold class names. Additionally, in rectangles below the name, we can document the class attributes and operations. Figure 10-16 shows the four different representations of a concrete class diagram.

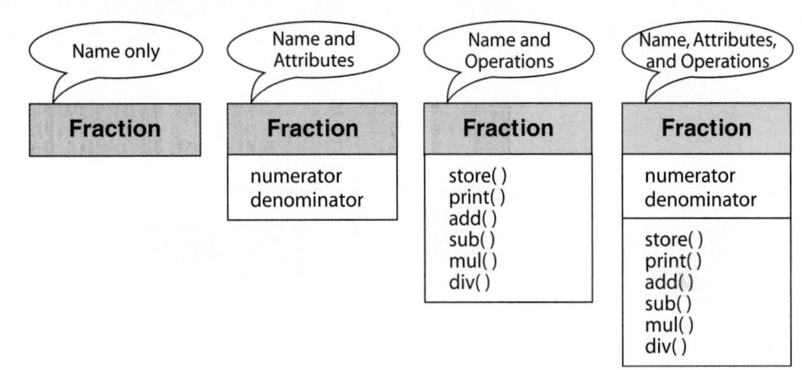

Figure 10-16 Class diagrams

Most of the time, we use just the basic notation, which contains only the class name. However, as shown in Figure 10-16, we can extend the notation by adding attributes (fields) or operations (methods), or both. Note that the attribute and operation compartments are optional, but the name compartment is mandatory in a class diagram.

The name compartment is mandatory in a class diagram.

We can add even more details to a class diagram. For example, we can show the attribute types for variables and the argument types for operations. We can also add the access type for each operation. We use a minus sign to denote a private attribute or operation, a plus sign to denote a public attribute or operation, and a pound sign to denote a protected attribute or operation. Figure 10-17 shows the Fraction class with more detail.

Abstract Class An abstract class follows the notation for a concrete class with the exception that its name is in italic type. Figure 10-18 represents the abstract class, *Employee*.

Class Template A class template diagram has the same basic format used for concrete and abstract classes. The template parametrized type is shown in an offset rectangle, drawn with dashed lines, to the right and above the class name. The type is then defined for each method. In Figure 10-19, note that the types are *protected* while some are parameterized and some are standard types.

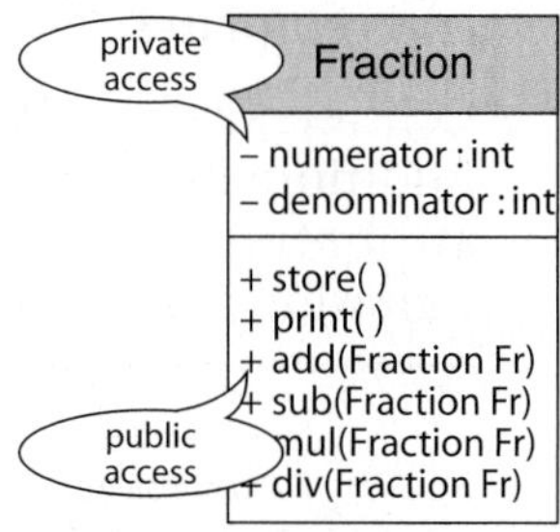

Figure 10-17 Expanded class diagram

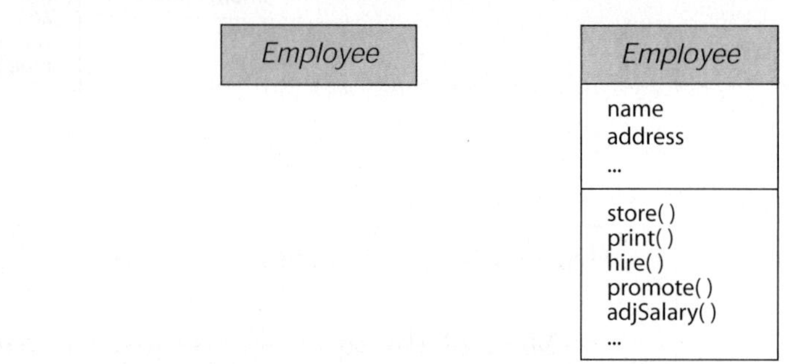

Figure 10-18 An abstract class

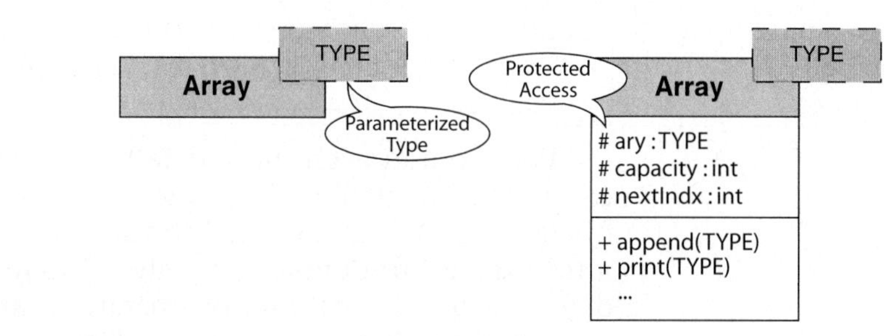

Figure 10-19 Class template diagrams

RELATIONSHIPS BETWEEN CLASSES

In object-oriented programming, classes (or the object instantiated from classes) are related to each other. UML distinguishes four types of relationship: association, composition, aggregation, and generalization (inheritance). Relationships are indicated by solid lines between the classes.

Association An object-oriented system may use classes that are associated (related) to each other. To show **association**, UML draws a solid lines between classes. The association can be labelled to show the nature of the relationship. When the label is used, an arrow-head is usually added to show the direction in which the association label is interpreted.

Figure 10-20 shows two classes, Customer and Account, and the association between them. The association label is "has" and the direction of interpretation is from the Customer class to the Account class.

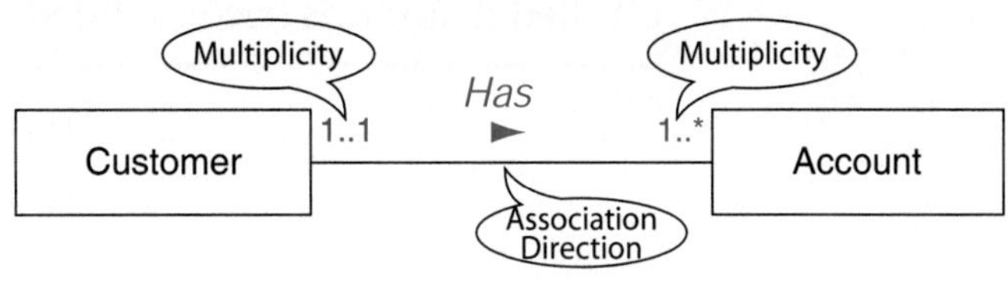

Figure 10-20 **Class association**

We can also show the multiplicity of the association. The multiplicity is shown as a range of numbers; for example 1..5 means one to five instances of one type can be associated with a specified number of instances of another type. To show only one instance, we use 1..1 and to show an unlimited maximum, we use 0..*. The asterisks here mean unlimited. The association multiplicity can be simplified: A multiplicity of 1..1 can be simplified to 1 and a multiplicity of 0..* can be simplified to *. In Figure 10-20, the multiplicity indicates that a customer has one or more accounts.

Aggregation An **aggregation** notation shows that an instance of a class may include instances of another class. For example, a class named TimeStamp, may include an instance of a class named Time and an instance of another class named Date. To show the aggregation, UML uses an unfilled diamond on the line at the aggregation class. For example, Figure 10-21 shows the aggregation relationship between the TimeStamp class and Date and Time classes. Note that here we use the multiplicity one on the component classes, not the aggregating class.

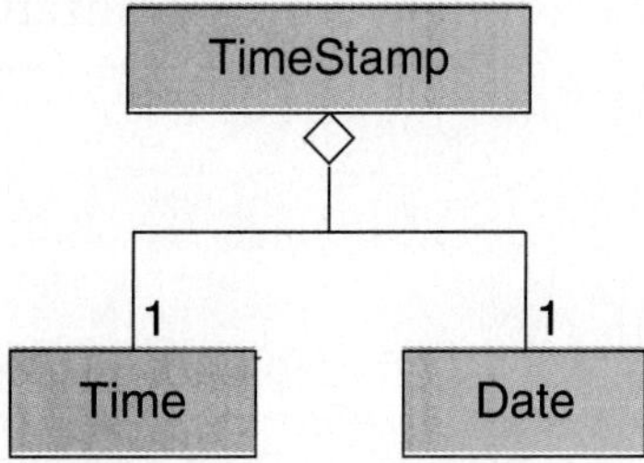

Figure 10-21 **Aggregation**

Composition **Composition** relation is almost the same as the aggregation relation; there is only one difference. In aggregation, the part can exist without the whole. In composition, there is a stronger relationship between the whole and the parts. When the whole is created, the parts are also created; when the whole ends, the parts also ends. In other words, there is a coincident lifetime, as it is sometimes called.

In Figure 10-21, we show the relationship between the car and its two components, body and engine, as a composition relationship. If we do not want this type of independency, we use a composition relationship as shown in Figure 10-22. The only difference is that the unfilled diamonds become filled.

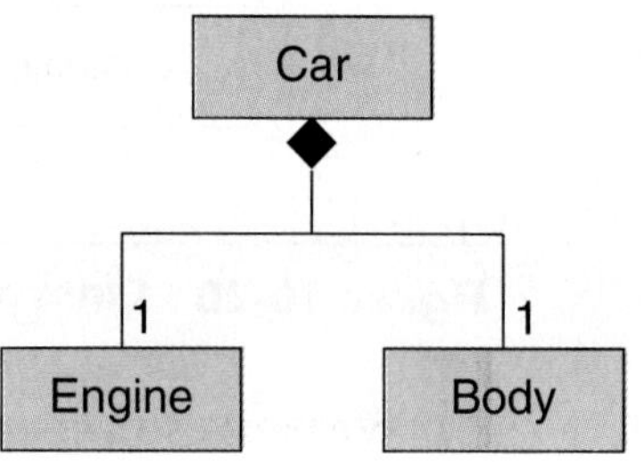

Figure 10-22 Composition

Generalization Two classes can be related by **generalization**. In this case, the first class, called the base class, is a generalization of the second class, called the derived class; conversely, the second class is a more specific definition of the first class. Generalization is mostly implemented through inheritance. When a class inherits from another class, the derived class inherits some of the attributes and operations of the base class. In ULM, generation is shown as the solid line between the classes, with an unfilled triangle arrowhead associated with the more general class.

The generalization is sometimes called "is a" relationship because the instance of a more specific object "is an" object of the more general class. For example, a car is a specific type of vehicle. A truck is also a type of vehicle. We can show the relationship among a vehicle, a car and a truck as shown in Figure 10-23. Note that we do not show multiplicity for generalization, because it is always one to one.

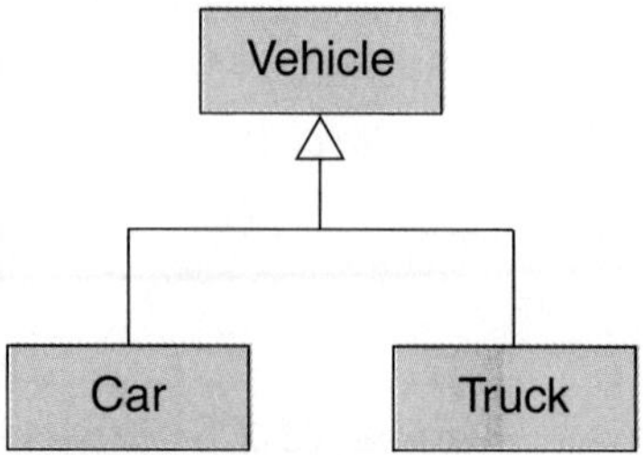

Figure 10-23 Generalization diagram

UML: OBJECTS

An object is an instance of a class. The diagram for an object is, therefore, related to the diagram of a class for which it is an instance.

Like a class diagram, an **object diagram** can be basic or extensive. In its simplest form, an object diagram has only the name compartment, which contains the name of the object, a colon and the name of the class.

Additionally, the diagram can contain an attribute compartment. Figure 10-24 shows two diagrams for an object of type Fraction.

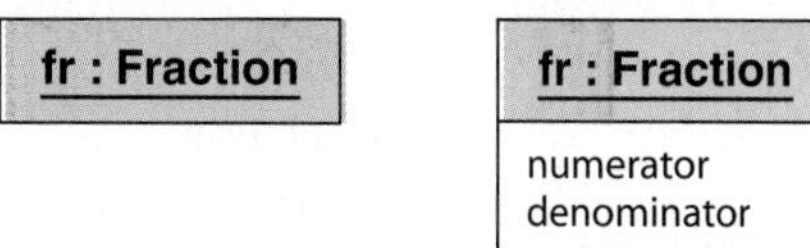

Figure 10-24 Object diagram

10-9 TIPS AND COMMON PROGRAMMING ERRORS

1. It is a compilation error to omit the semicolon at the end of a class definition.
2. It is a compilation error to initialize data variables when defined in a class declaration.
3. It is a compilation error to access a private member outside the class.
4. Remember that class declaration allocates no memory space for variables—they must be defined and initialized by constructors.
5. Declaring data members public within a class goes against the principle of data hiding.
6. It is a compilation error to declare any return value (even *void*) for a constructor or destructor.
7. It is a compilation error to declare parameters for a destructor.
8. Constructors must have the same name as the class to which they belong.
9. The destructor's name must be the same as the class except that it is preceded by a tilde (~).
10. We can have more than one constructor, but only one copy constructor and only one destructor.
11. A default constructor is the one that does not need any arguments.
12. A default constructor is created by the system when we don't provide any constructors.
13. A default copy constructor is created by the system if the program does not provide one.
14. A default destructor is created by the system if the program does not provide one.
15. An accessor function should be defined as a constant function.
16. The *this* pointer is a constant. We cannot modify it. It is illegal to store a pointer address in it.
17. Classes should be design to guarantee uniqueness of representation, as in our fraction class.

10-10 KEY TERMS

access specifier
accessor
aggregation
anonymous object
association
behavioral view
binary class function
bitwise copy
class
class diagram
class invariant
class object
composition
const
constructor
copy constructor
data hiding
default constructor
default copy constructor
default destructor
destructor
encapsulation
environment view
explicit constructor call
friend function
generalization
greatest common divisor
host object
implementation view
instance
instantiation
logical copy
manager function
member operator
method
mutator
object
object diagram
private
public
scope resolution operator (::)
structural view
this pointer
unary class function
user view
Unified Modeling Language (UML)

10-11 SUMMARY

- Combining data and operations in an object is a form of the data hiding principle of structure programming.
- The functions and operations through which the hidden data in an object can be accessed are referred to as methods.
- There are three access specifiers: *private, protected,* and *public.*
- Private data can be accessed only by functions within the class. Private functions can be called by other functions inside the class.
- Public functions can be called by other functions outside the class. However, all referenced data and functions must be within the class scope. Class scope is specified by the class name and the member operator. For example, the `fr1` fraction print function is referenced as `fr1.print()`.
- To declare a class, we use the keyword *class* followed by the class name. The members of the class are then coded in a block—first the private members and then the public members.
- The scope resolution operator (::) has a very high precedence (17).
- To define a function as a member of a class, we use the scope resolution operator.
- To access the class members, we use the member operator (the dot).
- Defining an object of a class type is called instantiation.
- Instances of a class are called objects.
- Constructors are special member functions that are called when an instance of a class is created.
- A constructor cannot have a return type, not even *void*.
- The copy constructor is used when we instantiate with an object, when we need a temporary object in an expression, when an object is passed by value, and when an object is returned from a function.
- Destructors are special member functions that are called when an instance of a class is destroyed—that is, when it ceases to exist.
- A destructor cannot have a return type, not even *void.* It cannot have any parameter except *void.*

- A unary class function uses only one instance of the class. It does not have any parameters of the class type.
- A binary class function uses two instances of the class. If only one of the instances is passed to the function, the function can be implemented as member function. If both of the instances are passed as parameters, then the function is better implemented as *friend* function.
- Functions in a class can be divided into three categories: manager, mutator, and accessor.
- Manager functions create, copy, or destroy objects. The manager functions are constructors, copy constructors, and destructors.
- A mutator function can change the state of the invoking object.
- An accessor function cannot change the state of the invoking object; it is normally defined as a constant function.
- Classes should be invariants; two instances of a class with the same value should have the same representation.
- The Unified Modeling Language (UML) is a graphical language used for Object-Oriented Analysis and Design.
- UML defines five views: structural, implementation, environment, behavioral, and user.
- The structural view includes class and object diagrams.
- A class diagram can contain three compartments: name, data, operation. The name compartment is mandatory.
- An object diagram can contain three compartments: name, data, operation. The name compartment is mandatory and the name must be underlined and include the name of the class, a colon, and the name of the object.
- Classes in UML can have four types of relationships: association, composition, aggregation, and generalization.

10-12 PRACTICE SETS

REVIEW QUESTIONS

1. A class definition needs a semicolon at the end.
   a. True
   b. False
2. We can initialize data variables in a class declaration.
   a. True
   b. False
3. The name of a constructor must be different from the name of the class to which it belongs.
   a. True
   b. False
4. The name of a destructor must be the same as the name of the class to which it belongs.
   a. True
   b. False
5. A programmer can change the value of *this* pointer.
   a. True
   b. False
6. A constructor return type can be ______.
   a. An integer
   b. A float
   c. An object of the same type as the class it belongs to
   d. None of the above
7. A unary class function can have ______ instance(s) of the class.
   a. No
   b. One
   c. Two
8. A binary class function has ______ instance(s) of the class.
   a. One
   b. Two
   c. No
9. Public functions can be called by ______.
   a. only functions inside the class
   b. only function outside the class
   c. both functions inside and outside the class.
10. To access a class member, we use the ______ operator.
   a. Dot (.)
   b. Pound (#)
   c. Asterisk (*)
   d. Scope resolution (: :)

11. Private data in a class can accessed by ______.
    a. Only other private data in the class
    b. Only public data in the class
    c. Only public functions in the class
    d. Both public and private functions in the class
    e. Only functions outside the class
12. A destructor can have ______ parameter(s).
    a. No
    b. One
    c. More than one
13. A member in a *struct* is ______ by default.
    a. Private
    b. Public
14. A member in a *class* is ______ by default.
    a. Private
    b. Public

EXERCISES

15. Find the error(s) in the following class declaration:
```
class Fun
{
 private:
    ... ;
    ... ;
 public:
    ... ;
}
```
16. Find the error(s) in the following class declaration:
```
class Fun
{
 private:
    ... ;
 public:
   int Fun (int x);
};
```
17. Find the error(s) in the following class declaration:
```
class Fun
{
   private:
    ... ;
   public:
     ~Fun (int x);
};
```
18. Find the error(s) in the following class declaration:
```
class Fun
{
 private:
     ... ;
 public:
     void ~Fun (void);
};
```
19. Find the logical error(s) in the following class declaration:
```
class Fun
{
 private:
     ... ;
     Fun (void);
 public:
     ... ;
};
```
20. Find the logical error(s) in the following class declaration:
```
class Fun
{
 private:
     ... ;
     ~ Fun (void);
 public:
     ... ;
};
```
21. Find the logical error(s) in the following class declaration:
```
class Fun
{
 private:
     ... ;
 public:
     ... ;
 private:
     ... ;
};
```
22. What is logically wrong with the following class declaration?
```
class Fun
{
 private:
     ... ;
 public:
     int x;
};
```

23. Is x private or public in this declaration? Explain your answer.

```
class Fun
{
 int x;
};
```

24. Is x private or public in this declaration? Explain your answer.

```
class Fun
{
 int x;
 private:
 int y;
};
```

25. Is x private or public in this declaration? Explain your answer.

```
class Fun
{
 int x;
 public:
 int y;
};
```

26. Find the error(s) in the following definition:

```
void Fun :: Fun (...)
{
    ... ;
}
```

27. Find the error(s) in the following definition:

```
void Fun :: ~Fun (void)
{
    ... ;
}
```

28. Find the error(s) in the following definition:

```
Fun :: ~ Fun (int x)
{
    ... ;
}
```

PROBLEMS

29. Write a binary member function to subtract one fraction from another. The function should simulate the subtract/assign operator (`fr1 -= fr2`) and should return *void*. Hint: Study Program 10-18, "Fraction header file for addTo," on page 519.

30. Write a binary member function to multiply two fractions. The function should simulate the multiply/assign operator (`fr1 *= fr2`) and should return *void*.

31. Write a binary member function to divide two fractions. The function should simulate the divide/assign operator (`fr1 /= fr2`) and should return *void*.

32. Write a binary *friend* function to subtract one fraction from another. The function should simulate the minus operator (`fr1 - fr2`) and should return a fraction.

33. Write a binary friend function to multiply two fractions. The function should simulate the multiply operator (`fr1 * fr2`) and should return a fraction.

34. Write a binary friend function to divide two fractions. The function should simulate the divide operator (`fr1 / fr2`) and should return a fraction.

35. Write a binary friend function to determine if two fractions are equal. The function should simulate the equal operator (`fr1 == fr2`) and should return a boolean value.

36. Write a binary *friend* function to check if one fraction is greater than the other. The function should simulate the greater-than operator (`fr1 > fr2`) and should return a boolean value.

37. Write a binary friend function to check if one fraction is smaller than the other. The function should simulate the less-than operator (`fr1 < fr2`) and should return a boolean value.

38. Write a print function that prints a fraction as an integral value plus the fraction. For example, given the fraction 7/2, it prints 3 1/2. If the integral is 0, print only the fractional part.

39. Modify the fraction class by adding a display "In function x" (where *x* is the name of the function) for each of the constructors, destructors, and member functions of the class. Then write a simple program that creates, stores, and prints the class as well as calling functions that receive it as a value parameter and return it. Analyze the output so that you fully understand the role of these functions in a class's operation.

PROJECTS

40. Define a class called `Array`. The class simulates a dynamic array of integers. The class should have two data members. The first data member is the length of the array—that is, the number of elements in it. The second data member is a pointer to an array that holds the data values.

The array should have two private member functions: one that extends the array when an element is added and one that contracts it when an element is deleted.

It should have the following public functions:

a. It should have one constructor that initializes the pointer to 0.

b. It should have one logical copy constructor that copies an array.

c. It should have one destructor that destroys the array. The destructor must delete the dynamic memory array.

d. It should have one function that appends one integer at the end of the array.

e. It should have one function that chops the array by deleting the last element.

f. It should have one function that prints the values in the array.

All functions should return a boolean value: *true* for success and *false* for error.

41. Declare and define a class for a complex number. A complex number in mathematics is defined as x + y, where *x* defines the real part of the number and *y* is the imaginary part. Write functions to simulate the operators (+=, -=, *=, /=, +, -, *, /). Use the following formulas:

```
add:      x3 = x1 + x2        y3 = y1 + y2
subtract: x3 = x1 - x2        y3 = y1 - y2
multiply: x3 = x1 * x2 - y1 * y2
          y3 = x1 * y2 + y1 * x2
divide:   x3 = (x1 * x2 + y1 + y2) /
               (x1² + y1²)
          y3 = (y1 * x2 - x1 * y2) /
               (x2² + y2²)
```

42. Declare and define a class for a set of integers. A set is a collection of data without repetition or ordering. The class should have only two private data members: a pointer to a dynamically allocated array of integers and an integer that holds the size of the set. It should have the following methods:

a. A constructor to create an empty set.

b. A copy constructor.

c. A destructor.

d. A function to add an element to the set. It must check for duplicates.

e. A function to remove an element from the set.

f. A function to count the number of elements in the set.

g. A binary friend function to determine the intersection of two sets. An intersection of two sets is another set with all elements common to the two sets.

h. A binary friend function to determine the union of two sets. A union of two sets is another set that contains all elements that are in either set or in both. Remember, the union set can have no duplicates.

i. A binary friend function to determine the difference of two sets. A difference of two sets is another set that has all elements that are in the first set but not in the second.

j. A function that determines if an element is in a set. It should return *true* if the element is present and *false* if it is not.

11 More Class Features and Other Types

In Chapter 10, we discussed the basic components of classes. Now we look at more C++ features that are used primarily with classes. Continuing our development of the fraction class, we begin with a discussion of inline functions, which provide an efficient way to implement small functions, and initialization lists. We then examine one of the more important C++ features: overloaded functions and operators. After discussing three more class features—static members, classes and pointers, and arrays of objects—we conclude with a discussion of four constructs inherited from the C Language: structure, union, enumerated type, and type definition.

Figure 11-1 places these topics in context with the other derived types.

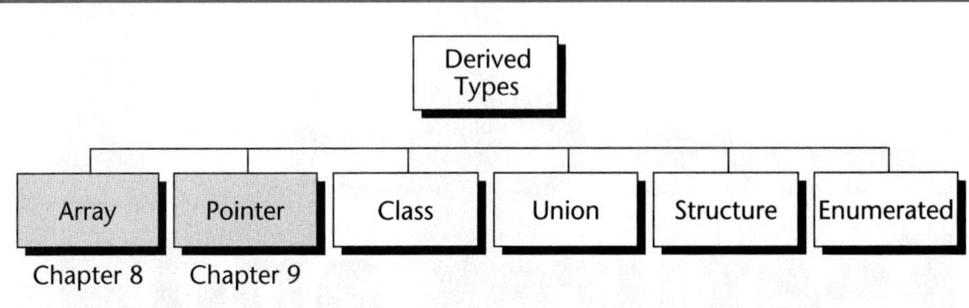

Figure 11-1 Derived types

11-1 INLINE FUNCTIONS

When a function, such as *main*, calls another function, control moves from the calling function to the called function. The calling function is temporarily suspended, and all of its local variables are protected so that they cannot be changed. When the called function returns, control reverts to the calling function. This process involves a lot of overhead, in the form of special code to protect the local variables and to transfer and restore control. This overhead tends to slow down a program. To enable programmers to make their programs more efficient, C++ has a feature known as **inline functions**. In an inline function, rather than transferring control to a called function, the called function's code replaces the call in the calling function. This substitution of replicated code in place of the call is made by the compiler. The function arguments are substituted for the called function's parameters.

> **Inline functions are used to improve the efficiency of a program.**

There are situations in which an inline function should not be used. For example, a large function called from many different points in a program may excessively increase the size of the program. As another example, a recursive function should not be designated inline. Because there are situations in which it is not appropriate, the designation of a function as inline is only a recommendation to the compiler and may be ignored. So when should a function be declared inline? Whenever the code is small, such as a function that contains only one or two simple statements—for example, a function that returns the count of the number of positive numbers in an array.

An inline recommendation can be made explicitly or implicitly. Class functions can be either explicit or implicit. Nonmember functions are always defined explicitly; we discuss them first.

NONMEMBER INLINE FUNCTIONS

An explicit recommendation is made by simply adding the function specifier *inline* to its prototype declaration, as shown in the following example. The inline designation does not appear in the function definition.

```
// Prototype Declarations
inline void doIt (int num);

void doIt (int num)
{
   // Function Definition
   ...
}  // doIt
```

INLINE MEMBER FUNCTIONS

Inline member functions can be explicit or implicit.

Explicit Inline Definition

When a class function is explicitly defined outside the class declaration, the function declaration in the class must contain the *inline* function specifier, which is placed at the beginning of the prototype declaration. Program 11-1 shows how we could specify the Fraction print function from Chapter 10 as an **explicit *inline* function.**

Program 11-1 Declaring an explicit inline function

```
class Fraction
{
   private:
      int numerator;
      int denominator;
   public:
      inline void print () const;
}; // Class Fraction
/* ================ Fraction::print ================
   Prints the numerator and denominator as a fraction.
      Pre  fraction class must contain data
      Post data printed.
*/
void Fraction :: print () const
{
   cout << numerator << "/" << denominator;
   return;
} // Fraction print
```

Implicit Inline Definition

An inline function can be defined in a class by coding it in the class declaration itself. In this case, no function declaration is needed, and the function is defined without the function specifier *inline.* Program 11-2 shows how the print function would be defined using an **implicit** definition.

Program 11-2 Defining an implicit inline function

```
class Fraction
{
   private:
      int numerator;
      int denominator;
```

Program 11-2 Defining an implicit inline function (*continued*)

```
6     public:
7        ...
8        void print () const
9        {cout << numerator << "/" << denominator; return;}
10  } ; // Class Fraction
```

Program 11-2 Analysis Note that we have not included all of the function documentation and formatting in this case. Because inline functions are small and simple, and because they are enclosed within the class declaration, they do not need all of the standard documentation used with global functions. Often in practice the function header (statement 8) and the function body (statement 9) are written on one line.

11-2 INITIALIZATION LIST

In Chapter 10, we used the assignment operator in the constructor function to initialize the members in a class object. They can also be initialized using a constructor initialization list. In an **initialization list**, the initialization values are associated with the object variables after the function header. Figure 11-2 shows how initialization can be done with the assignment operator and with an initialization list.

```
Fraction::Fraction (int num,
                    int denom)
{
   numerator   = num;
   denominator = denom;
   ...
}  // Fraction Constructor
```

(a) Using the assignment operator

```
Fraction::Fraction (int num,
                    int denom)
   : numerator   (num),
     denominator (denom)
{
   ...
}  // Fraction Constructor
```

(b) Using the initialization list

Figure 11-2 Using initialization lists

There are two parts to an initialization list:

1. A colon that separates the function header from the initialization values.
2. A set of variables, `numerator` and `denominator` in Figure 11-2, followed by their corresponding initialization values enclosed in parentheses. The member names are separated from each other with commas.

Referring to Figure 11-2, we see that the initialization list replaces the two assignment operators. Note also that there may be other code required in the constructor. If there is, it is unaffected by the initialization list and would be used in both approaches.

From the application's point of view, both the assignment initialization and the list initialization are the same. We simply put the initialization values in parentheses after the object definition, as follows:

```
Fraction fr (1, 2);
```

While our example shows both member variables being initialized through the initialization list, initializing both is not required in this case. We could have initialized only one of the variables, such as the denominator. In later chapters, we will discuss other cases in which the use of initialization lists is mandatory.

11-3 OVERLOADING

Overloading is the definition of two or more functions or operators within the same scope using the same identifier. We discussed overloading for nonmember function in Chapter 4 and used overloaded constructors in Chapter 10. In this section, we extend the concept to overloading operators as member functions.

OPERATOR OVERLOADING

In Chapter 10, we wrote three functions to increment and add fractions. Their prototype statements are shown below.

```
       void     increment ();
       void     addTo      (const Fraction& fr2);
friend Fraction add        (const Fraction& fr2,
                            const Fraction& fr3);
```

While these functions work well, they present an unnatural coding syntax. To add two fractions, for example, we used the function call syntax with the values as parameters, rather than the more natural `a + b` syntax. Table 11-1 shows the function syntax and the arithmetic syntax that we would naturally prefer.

Operation	Function syntax	Arithmetic syntax
Increment	fr1.increment( )	++fr1;
Add to	fr1.addTo (fr2)	fr1 += fr2
Add	add (fr2, fr3)	fr2 + fr3

Table 11-1 Comparison of function and arithmetic syntax

Overloading Member Operators

Because we have already written these operations as functions, let's start by converting them to overloaded operators. To convert our functions to overloaded operators, all we must do is change the function name to the keyword *operator* followed by the operator we want to use. With the exception of the prefix and postfix increments, nothing else in the function is changed. The prefix and postfix increments require that we also return the fraction object.

Prefix Increment and Decrement Operators The prototype for the overloaded prefix increment is

```
Fraction& operator++ ();                          // prefix
```

Program 11-3 implements the increment as a prefix-increment operator; that is, it overloads the unary increment operator, which means that the object is incremented before (pre) the expression's value is determined. It is the equivalent of `++a`. Because we need to return the fraction value, we have added fraction as a return type.

Program 11-3 Prefix increment overloaded operator

```
1 /* Add one to the fraction.
2        Pre   nothing
3        Post  One added
4 */
5 Fraction& Fraction :: operator++ ()
6 {
7    numerator += denominator;
8    return (*this);
9 } // Fraction increment (++)
```

Program 11-3 Analysis Compare this program to Program 10-16 on page 517. There are two changes: the header (statement 5) is changed to add a return type and to overload the operator, and return (statement 8) is changed to return the *this* pointer.

Postfix Increment and Decrement Operators To create a postfix increment or decrement, the code is more complex. Remember that these operators require that the value of the expression be the value before the increment. To do this, we must first save the value, then increment it, then return the original value.

As we start to write the code, another problem immediately surfaces. The same operator is used for both the prefix and postfix increment. How do we tell the compiler that this time we want the postfix operation.

The answer is not intuitive. If the overloaded operator's definition doesn't have a parameter list, then the function is a unary increment or decrement, which means that it is a prefix operator. On the other hand, if an integer parameter is specified in the parameter list, then the function is a postfix operator, which means that the object is incremented after the value is determined. Note, however, that the parameter type is simply a compiler directing convention: There is no way to pass a parameter; the type is ignored by the compiler. The prototype for the postfix increment is

```
const Fraction operator++ (int);                    // postfix
```

As with the prefix increment, we add a return type. The resulting postfix function is shown in Program 11-4.

Program 11-4 Postfix increment overloaded operator

```
/* Add one to the fraction using postfix design.

       Pre   nothing
       Post  One added
*/
const Fraction Fraction :: operator++ (int)
{
// Save value for return
   const Fraction saveObject(*this);   // Call copy constr
```

Program 11-4 Postfix increment overloaded operator (*continued*)

```
    numerator += denominator;
    return saveObject;
} // Fraction (++)increment
```

Program 11-4 Analysis There are three points that need to be noted in this function. First, we have included an integer type as a parameter but did not give it a name. This convention tells C++ that we are overloading the postfix, as opposed to the prefix, increment. It's just one of those esoteric rules that you have to memorize.

Second, we have made the return type a constant in the header statement. We do this to prevent users from adding one twice, as shown in the following statement.

```
fr++++
```

Third, to save the original value of the fraction, we use the *this* operator to store it in an object we call `saveObject`. Then, after the increment, we return the original value.

Add/Assign Operator Let's look at the code to overload the binary add/assign operator (+=). This would be the equivalent of the `addTo` function. Because this function requires two fraction objects, it must have a parameter that specifies the fraction is to be added to the current object. The declaration is shown below.

```
void operator+= (const Fraction& fr2);
```

The function definition uses exactly the same code as we saw in the `addTo` function (see Program 10-18, "Fraction header file for addTo" on page 519). Only the function header changes, as shown below.

```
void Fraction :: operator+= (const Fraction& fr2)
{
  // Same code as Program 10-18
} // Fraction add/assign operator (+=)
```

Overloading Friend Functions

Friend functions can be overloaded also.

Binary Add Operator As a final example, let's look at the code to implement the binary add operator. This is the equivalent of `add` in Program 10-20, Add fraction on page 522, which was implemented as a friend function. It requires two parameters representing the two fractions that are to be added. It returns a new fraction object that contains the sum. The declaration is shown below. Note that it is implemented as a friend function.

```
friend Fraction operator+ (const Fraction& fr2,
                           const Fraction& fr3);
```

Once again, the code is identical to the `add` function. The function definition format is shown in the following example.

```
Fraction operator+ (const Fraction& fr2,
                    const Fraction& fr3)
{
  // Same code as Program 10-20
} // Fraction add operator (+)
```

Overloading Assignment Operators

The assignment operator is used when we copy an object on the right side of the operator to the object on the left side as shown in the next example.

```
fr1 = fr2
```

We have been able to use the assignment operator without overloading it because the C++ compiler provides a default assignment operator for us. However, the default operator is a bitwise, not a logical, operator. For a discussion of the difference, see "Bitwise versus Logical Copy Constructors" on page 507.

> **C++ provides a bitwise overloaded assignment operator if we don't overload it ourselves.**

Whenever the class uses dynamic memory for data members, the bitwise copy does not work; we must use a logical copy. Program 11-5 demonstrates the code for overloading the assignment operator using our fraction class. Although this function is not needed for the fraction class, it is included to show the syntax.

Program 11-5 Overloaded assignment operator

```
1  /* Overload assignment operator for fraction class
2         Pre  Nothing
3         Post Logical copy of fraction
4  */
5  Fraction& Fraction :: operator= (const Fraction& fr)
6  {
7     numerator   = fr.numerator;
8     denominator = fr.denominator;
9     return *this;
10 }  // operator=
```

Program 11-5 Analysis Note that the return type in statement 5 is a reference. This allows us to chain assignments as shown in the following example.

```
fr1 = fr2 = fr3;
```

We need to understand the difference between an assignment operator and a copy constructor. The copy constructor is called when a class object is created and initialized with an existing object or when an object is passed to a function by value. The assignment operator is called when the left-hand side and the right-hand side of an assignment statement are both objects of the same class.

> **The assignment operator is different from the copy constructor.**

There is a commonality among the assignment operator, the copy constructor, and the destructor. When we need to write one, we need to write all of them. That is, if we need a logical copy because we are using dynamic memory, then we need a logical assignment and a destructor to recycle memory when the object is destroyed.

> **When we need to write a copy constructor, we also need to write an assignment operator and a destructor.**

Overloading Cast Operators (Type Conversion)

We often need to convert a standard type to an object or an object to a standard type. We discuss how to write these conversions in this section.

From Standard Type to Object Type Conversion from a standard type to an object is done with a constructor. We wrote one for our fraction class when we overloaded the constructor with one integer parameter (see Overloaded Constructors on page 500). This is an implicit use of the constructor. Using this type of implicit conversion, we can also call the constructor to create a temporary object and then pass it to a function as shown in the next example. In this example, we first convert 45 to a fraction (45/1) through an implicit constructor call and then add it to `fr1` and store the results in `fr1`

```
fr1.addTo (45);
```

Explicit Constructors The use of implicit constructor calls can create problems. To prevent implicit conversions—that is, to force the programmer to call the constructor explicitly—C++ provides an *explicit* constructor modifier. When a constructor is declared *explicit*, the compiler never uses it for implicit conversions. The *explicit* modifier is added only to the prototype statement as shown in the next example. It is not coded in the function definition.

```
explicit Fraction (int numer);
```

From Object Type to Other Type If we need to convert from a class object to another type, either standard or user-defined, we must write a **conversion operator** for the source type. The format of an conversion operator is:

```
operator TYPE () const;
```

in which the following rules apply.

1. TYPE defines the type to which we are converting.
2. There may not be any arguments.
3. It is normally declared *const* to support constant invoking objects.
4. No return type can be declared because the converted data are automatically returned.

It would seem a natural conversion to convert a fraction to a floating-point number. This conversion would be done with a float conversion operator as shown in Program 11-6.

Program 11-6 Float conversion operator

```
/* Convert fraction to float type.
      Pre  Nothing
      Post numerator / denominator returned
*/
Fraction :: operator float () const
{
   return (numerator / denominator);
} // operator float
```

Once we have written the conversion operator, we can print a fraction as a float value as shown in the next example. Of course, to print it as a fraction we would still use the fraction print function.

```
Fraction fr (5, 4);
cout << fr << endl;                              // Prints 1.25
```

Using Overloaded Operators

The primary purpose of **operator overloading** is to enable us to write code in a more natural style. For example, to add 1 to a fraction, we can use the equivalent of the increment operator, as shown below.

```
++fr1;
```

It is possible, however, to code the increment using the function identifier. For example, we can also code the increment as shown below.

```
fr1.operator++ ();
```

Similarly, we can use the function identifier for the add operators, as shown below.

```
fr2 += fr1;                fr2.operator+= (fr1);
fr3 = fr1 + fr2;           fr3 = operator+ (fr1, fr2);
```

Overloaded Operator Limitations and Restrictions

There are seven rules that we must follow when we overload an operator. When selecting an operator to overload, you must carefully consider the following rules:

1. With the exception of five operators that can't be overloaded, only the standard C++ operators found in the operator precedence table can be overloaded. The prohibited operators are:
   a. The member operator (`.`)
   b. The pointer to member operator (`.*`)
   c. The scope resolution operator (`::`)
   d. The conditional expression operator (`? :`)
   e. The sizeof operator (`sizeof (int)`)
2. Overloading does not change the precedence of the operator. The best example of this is the *iostream* operators << and >>. These are actually bitwise operators and have a very low priority (2). The iostream operators, therefore, have the

same low priority, although we would certainly like to make them higher. This means we have to be very careful when combining them with operators or we might get invalid results.

3. Overloading does not change the associativity of the operator.
4. Overloading does not change the commutativity of the operator. For example, the + operator is commutative (`a + b` is the same as `b + a`), while the minus operator is not (`a - b` is not the same as `b - a`).
5. Overloading does not change the *arity* of the operator.[1] If the standard definition of an operator is unary, then the overloaded definition must be unary. If the standard definition is binary, then the overloaded definition must be binary. If it is both a unary and a binary operator, it may be overloaded as unary, binary, or both.
6. The [bracket] and (parentheses) operators can be overloaded only as member operators. They cannot be implemented as nonmember operators.
7. Only objects in a class scope can be overloaded, either as a member operator or as a nonmember operator. It is not possible to overload an operator unless it is associated with a class. This means that an overloaded operator must contain a user-defined type as a parameter, either implicitly (via the *this* parameter) or explicitly.

Note that when we selected our `Fraction` operators, we abided by these rules. If you don't follow the rules, then the code most likely won't work and if it does work, it will be so confusing that the operators will be used incorrectly.

Beside the C++ rules, consider human engineering factors when you select an operator to be overloaded. The closer the operation of the overloaded operator to the original operator, the more intuitive it will be to use. In our fraction class, we used the established arithmetic operators for addition. We could have used any operators, but selecting the greater-than operator would have made things confusing.

FINAL FRACTION CLASS HEADER

At this point we have completed our development of the fraction class. As a summary, we include the complete fraction header and a short program that tests the newly added features. The header file is shown in Program 11-7.

Program 11-7 Revised fraction class declarations

```
/* Fraction Class Declarations
      Written by:
      Date:
*/
class Fraction
{
   private:
      int numerator;
      int denominator;
      int greatestComDiv (int n1, int n2);
   public:
             Fraction ( );
             Fraction (      int numer);
             Fraction (      int numer, int denom);
```

[1] Arity is the number of operands associated with an operator.

Program 11-7 Revised fraction class declarations (*continued*)

```
            Fraction (const Fraction& copyFrom);
           ~Fraction ( ) { }

          void      store (int numer, int denom);
   inline void      print () const;
   const  Fraction& operator++ ();         // Prefix  ++
   const  Fraction& operator++ (int);      // Postfix ++
          Fraction& operator=  (const Fraction& fr);
          void      operator+= (const Fraction& fr2);
                    operator   float () const;
}; // Fraction
/* =============  Fraction :: Fraction ===========
   Constructor for Fraction class.
   Initializes fraction to zero.
       Pre   none
       Post  fraction object initialized to 0
*/
Fraction :: Fraction ()
{
   numerator   = 0;
   denominator = 1;
} // constructor
/* =============  Fraction :: Fraction ===========
   Default constructor for Fraction class
   Initializes fraction to values in parameter list.
       Pre   numen contains numerator value
       Post  fraction object initialized
*/
Fraction :: Fraction (int numen)
{
   numerator   = numen;
   denominator = 1;
} // Fraction constructor
/* =============  Fraction :: Fraction =============
   Initializes fraction to values in parameter list
   ensuring that the fraction is normalized.
       Pre  numen and denom contain fraction values
       Post fraction object initialized
*/
Fraction:: Fraction (int numer, int denom)
{
   if (denom == 0)
      {
       cout << "Error: denominator is zero" << endl;
       exit (100);
      } // zero denom
   if (denom < 0)
      // Ensure that any negative is in numerator
      {
```

Program 11-7 Revised fraction class declarations (*continued*)

```
        denom = -denom;
        numer = -numer;
       } // demon < 0
   int gcd = greatestComDiv (abs(numer), abs(denom));
   numer = numer / gcd;
   denom = denom / gcd;

   numerator   = numer;
   denominator = denom;
} // Constructor
/* ==================== copyFrom ====================
   Copy constructor for Fraction class.
     Pre   copyFrom exists and has values to be copied
     Post  new object created and data copied
*/
Fraction :: Fraction (const Fraction& copyFrom)
{
// Statements
   numerator   = copyFrom.numerator;
   denominator = copyFrom.denominator;
} // Copy constructor
/* ================ Fraction :: store ===============
   Store the numerator and denominator in the fraction
   class. Calls constructor to ensure normalization.
       Pre   numer and denom contain the numerator
             and denominator respectively
       Post  data stored
*/
void Fraction :: store (int numer, int denom)
{
   *this = Fraction (numer, denom);
   return;
} // Fraction store
/* ================ Fraction :: print ===============
   Prints the numerator and denominator as a fraction.
       Pre   fraction class must contain data
       Post  data printed
*/
void Fraction :: print () const
{
   cout << numerator << "/" << denominator;
   return;
} // Fraction print
/* ================= ++operator =================
   Add one to the fraction.
       Pre   nothing
       Post  One added
*/
const Fraction& Fraction :: operator++ ()
```

Program 11-7 Revised fraction class declarations (*continued*)

```
{
   numerator += denominator;
   return (*this);
} // Fraction increment (++)
/* ================= operator++ =================
    Add one to the fraction using postfix design.

        Pre   nothing
        Post  One added
*/
const Fraction& Fraction :: operator++ (int)
{
// Save value for return
   const Fraction saveObject(*this);  // Call copy constr
   numerator += denominator;
   return saveObject;
} // Fraction (++)increment
/* ================= operator= =================
    Overload assignment operator for fraction class
       Pre  Nothing
       Post Logical copy of fraction
*/
Fraction& Fraction :: operator= (const Fraction& fr)
{
   numerator   = fr.numerator;
   denominator = fr.denominator;
   return *this;
} // operator=
/* ================ operator float ================
    Convert fraction to float type.
       Pre  Nothing
       Post numerator / denominator returned
*/
Fraction :: operator float () const
{
   return (numerator / denominator);
} // operator float
/* ================= operator+= =================
   Add two fractions.
        Pre   fractions contain values.
        Post  sum stored in calling fraction
*/
void Fraction :: operator+= (const Fraction& fr2)
{
   numerator =
         (numerator     * fr2.denominator)
       + (fr2.numerator * denominator);
   denominator *= fr2.denominator;
   *this = Fraction (numerator, denominator);
```

Program 11-7 Revised fraction class declarations (*continued*)

```
   return;
} // Fraction add/assign operator (+=)
Fraction :: operator float () const
{
   return (static_cast<float>(numerator) / denominator);
} // operator float
/* ================= greatestComDiv =================
   Determine the greatest common divisor of two numbers.
      Pre  Given two integers
      Post GCD returned
*/
intFraction::GreatestComDiv (int nl, int n2)
}
   // Base case
   if (n2 == 0)
      return n1;
   else
       // General case
      return greatestComDiv (n2, n1 % n2);
} // greatestComDiv
```

Program 11-8 is a test driver for the final fraction class.

Program 11-8 Add fraction execution

```
/* Demonstrate add fraction.
      Written by:
      Date:
*/
#include <iostream>
using namespace std;

#include "p11-07.h"          // Basic class declaration

int main ()
{
   Fraction fr1 (1, 5);
   Fraction fr2;
   fr2 = fr1++;
   cout << "Postfix Increment:\nOriginal fr1: ";
   fr1.print ();
   cout << " Expression Value: ";
   fr2.print ();
   cout << " Incremented fr1: ";
   fr1.print ();
   cout << endl;

   fr1.store (1, 5);
   fr2 = ++fr1;
```

Program 11-8 Add fraction execution *(continued)*

```
    cout << "\nPrefix Increment:\nOriginal fr1: ";
    fr1.print ();
    cout << " Expression Value: ";
    fr2.print ();
    cout << " Incremented fr1: ";
    fr1.print ();
    cout << endl;

    Fraction fr3 = fr2 = fr1 = 1;
    cout << "\nConversion & Assignment:\nOriginal fr1: ";
    fr1.print ();
    cout << "  fr2: ";
     fr2.print ();
    cout << "  fr3: ";
    fr3.print ();
    cout << endl;

    fr3.store (5, -10);
    cout << "\nConversion to Float:\nConverted value of ";
    fr3.print ();
    cout << " is ";
    cout << fr3 << endl;
    return 0;
}   // main
```

```
Results
Postfix Increment:
Original fr1: 6/5 Expression Value: 1/5 Incremented fr1: 6/5

Prefix Increment:
Original fr1: 6/5 Expression Value: 6/5 Incremented fr1: 6/5

Conversion & Assignment:
Original fr1: 1/1  fr2: 1/1  fr3: 1/1

Conversion to Float:
Converted value of -1/2 is -0.5
```

11-4 STATIC MEMBERS

All data and functions declared within a class are members of that class. Class members can be either instance members or static members. An **instance member** is associated with a specified instance of the object. Each occurrence of the class has its own data instance members with their own values. By default, class members are instance members.

> By default, a class member is an instance member.

A **static member** is associated with the class itself and not with any specific occurrence of the class. In other words, only one instance of a static class member exists. This means that regardless of how many instances of a class are created, there is only one set of static members that are shared by all instances. Because they must be accessible by the entire program, static members must be defined in global space. However, they can be declared either *public* or *private*. Assuming they are public, they can be directly referenced outside the class by using the scope operator as shown in the next example.

```
className :: staticMemberName
```

All of the classes we have discussed so far have contained only instance members. Returning to our fraction class, when a fraction object is instantiated, it contains all data members and a *this* pointer to the object being created.

STATIC DATA MEMBERS

A class data member should be declared static only when it applies to the class itself; that is, the same value is shared by all instances. A static data member does not belong to individual instances of class objects. In other words, only class metadata should be declared static. One excellent use is to encapsulate general class data, such as an employee wage table or a table of tax rates. Another example is a counter of the number of occurrences of an class within the execution of the program. Figure 11-3 depicts this usage of a static member.

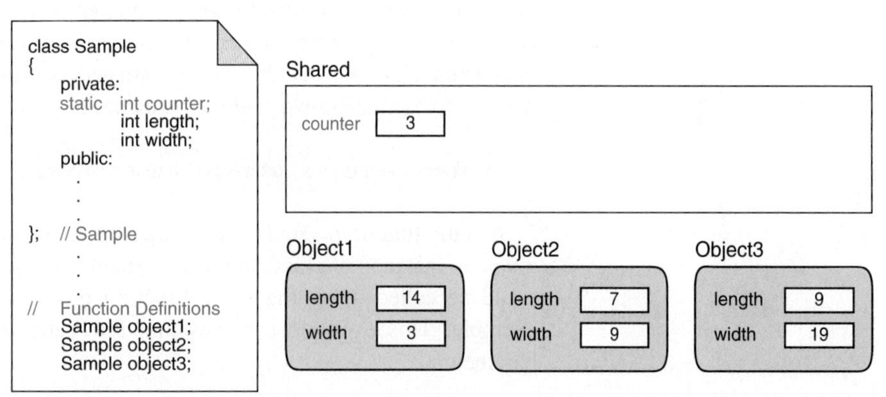

Figure 11-3 Class members

As shown in Figure 11-3, a data member is declared static by using the *static* type modifier. As mentioned previously, they can be either *public* or *private*.

> **Static data members are instance independent.**

Defining and Initializing Static Data

While static data members are declared within the class, they must be defined and initialized outside the class in the global area of the program. The definition must use the scope operator, but it cannot use the static type modifier. The general format of a static variable initialization is:

```
type className :: staticVariableName = value
```

The definition must follow the class declaration and be in the global area of the program. Because there can be only one instance of a static variable, it cannot be defined again, even in a different scope such as *main*. The definition of the counter in Figure 11-3 is shown in the next example.

```
int Sample :: counter = 0;
```

Other Static Members

In addition to explicitly declared static data members, there are two implicit static members, enumeration and type definition, which we discuss later in this chapter. While they are declared within the class, they are class-wide members and must be accessed using the scope operator when used outside the class scope.

> **There are three static data members:**
> - **explicit static data members**
> - **enumerated members**
> - **type defined members**

STATIC FUNCTION MEMBERS

Functions within a class can also be designated static. If they are not static, they are by default instance functions.

A static member function can be *public* or *private*. If *private*, it cannot access the static members when called outside the class. If *public*, it can be used to access the static member anywhere. Returning to our counter example, we can reference and change the counter from anywhere within the class. However, if we want to reference or change it outside the class, we can do so only with a static function. To reference a static function we use the format shown in the next example.

```
className :: staticFunctionName (…)
```

A static function can also be referenced using an instance of the class. For example, given an instance of class `Sample`, named `mySample`, a function to print the counter could be called using the static function or the class instance as shown in the next example. This example assumes that the static function, `printCounter`, has no parameters.

```
Sample :: printCounter()   or   mySample.printCounter()
```

STATIC MEMBER DEMONSTRATION

To demonstrate static members, Program 11-9 creates a class with a static counter and then displays the counter as class objects are created and destroyed.

Program 11-9 Demonstration of static members

```
/* Demonstration of static members.
      Written by:
      Date:
*/
#include <iostream>
#include <iomanip>
using namespace std;
```

Program 11-9 Demonstration of static members (*continued*)

```

class StaticDemo
{
   private:
   static int counter;                     // Static data

   public:
          StaticDemo ();                   // Constructor
         ~StaticDemo ();                   // Destructor
   static void printCount ();          // Static function
}; // StaticDemo

/* ============ StaticDemo constructor ============
   Adds one to instance counter when object created.
      Pre  Object being instantiated
      Post Static counter incremented by one
*/
StaticDemo :: StaticDemo ()
{
   counter++;
} // StaticDemo constructor

/* ============ StaticDemo destructor ============
   Subtracts one from instance counter when object
   is destroyed.
      Pre  Object being destroyed
      Post Static counter decremented by one
*/
StaticDemo :: ~StaticDemo ()
{
// Statements
   counter--;
   cout << "In destructor: counter: " << counter << endl;
} // StaticDemo destructor


/* ============ StaticDemo :: printCount ============
   Prints contents of class data members.
      Pre  Object has been instantiated
      Post data printed
*/
void StaticDemo :: printCount ()
{
   cout << "counter: "  << counter << endl;
   return;
} // printCount

```

Program 11-9 Demonstration of static members (*continued*)

```
55 // Static Members
56 int StaticDemo :: counter = 0;        // initialization
57
58 int main ()
59 {
60    cout << "Start static demonstration.\n";
61
62    StaticDemo a1;
63    cout << "After first instantiation:  ";
64    a1.printCount ();
65
66    StaticDemo a2;
67    cout << "After second instantiation: ";
68    StaticDemo :: printCount ();
69
70    cout << "Terminating demonstration\n";
71    return 0;
72 } // main
```

```
Results
Start static demonstration.
After first instantiation:  counter: 1
After second instantiation: counter: 2
Terminating demonstration
In destructor: counter: 1
In destructor: counter: 0
```

Program 11-9 Analysis While the concept is somewhat complex, the program is quite simple. The static member is defined in statement 12 and initialized in statement 56. After each object is instantiated, the count is displayed. Then, as the program terminates, the destructor displays the counter again. Be sure to note how we use two different ways to call the print counter function (statements 64 and 68).

11-5 FRIEND CLASSES

A class can grant ***friend*** status to a nonmember function or to another class. We have already discussed **friend functions** in Chapter 10—see "Add Fractions (Friend Function)" on page 521). We discuss class friendship in this section

A class can grant *friend* status to another class. In this case, all member functions of the class granted friendship have unrestricted access to the members of the class granting the friendship. Class friendship is not reciprocal; the member functions of the class granting friendship cannot access the members of the **friend class**. We grant class friendship in the prototype declarations of the granting class as shown in the next example.

```
class First
{
  private:
     ...
     friend class Second;
     ...
} // First
```

An example of class friendship is two or more class objects need to communicate with each other. For example, a linked list[2] is a combination of structures called nodes linked together with pointers. In a linked list we have two classes, list and node. The member functions of the list class object need to access the members of the node class, so the node class grants friendship to the list class. Friendship declarations for the node class are shown in Program 17-5, "Node Class Declaration and Constructor" on page 832.

11-6 CLASSES AND POINTERS

Classes and pointers, both derived data types, can be interact with each other. A class can have a pointer as data member and a pointer can point to a class object. We explore theses issues here.

CLASS CONTAINING POINTERS

An example of a pointer found in a class is a class that uses dynamic memory. Whenever we allocate memory we use a pointer. To demonstrate this usage of pointers in a class, we create a student class that uses a dynamically allocated array to store the students scores. The array is implemented dynamically using a pointer to integer. The design is shown in Figure 11-4.

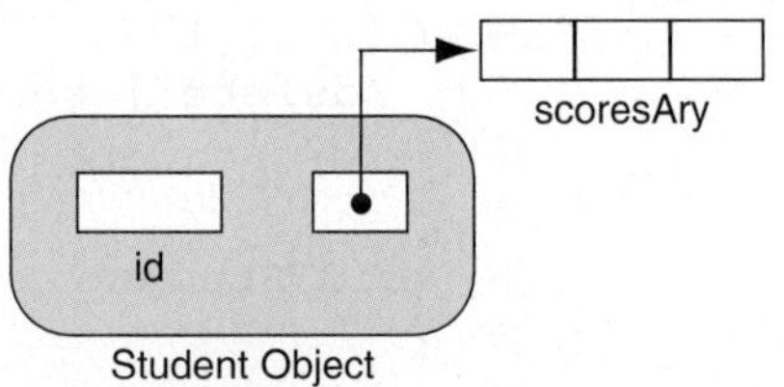

Figure 11-4 Student class object

Program 11-10 implements the student class.

Program 11-10 Demonstrate pointers in a class

```
/* Demonstrate pointer in a class
      Written by:
      Date:
*/
#include <iostream>
#include <iomanip>
```

[2]We discuss linked lists in Chapter 17.

Program 11-10 Demonstrate pointers in a class *(continued)*

```
using namespace std;

class Student
{
   private:
       long id;
       int* scoresAry;

   public:
           Student (long id);          // Default constr
           ~Student ();
         void print() const;
}; // Student

Student :: Student (long idIn) : scoresAry (0)
{
   id = idIn;
   scoresAry = new int [5];
   cout << "Enter scores for student " << id << endl;
   for (int i = 0; i < 5; i++)
        {
         cout << "Enter score " << i + 1 << ": ";
         cin >> scoresAry[i];
        } // for
}  // Student constructor

Student :: ~Student ()
{
   delete[] scoresAry;
}  // Student destructor

void Student :: print () const
{
   float sum = 0.0;
   for (int i = 0; i < 5; i++)
        {
         sum += scoresAry[i];
        } // for
   float average = sum / 5;
   cout << "Average score: " << average << endl;
}  // Student print

int main ()
{
   Student std1 (12121);
   std1.print();
   return 0;
}  // main
```

Program 11-10 Demonstrate pointers in a class (*continued)*

```
// Results
Enter scores for student 12121
Enter score 1: 15
Enter score 2: 12
Enter score 3: 7
Enter score 4: 9
Enter score 5: 14
Average score: 11.4
```

Program 11-10 Analysis There are two important concepts in this short program. First, in the constructor we dynamically allocate memory for the array. For integrity, we use an initialization list in the constructor to initialize the pointer `scoresAry` to 0 (see statement 21). This is a good programming technique for classes that use dynamic memory. Also, note that we release the array memory in the destructor. It's important to release memory so that dynamic memory doesn't become fragmented.

POINTERS TO OBJECTS

We can also have pointers to other objects in a class. In Chapter 12, we study an advanced class concept that requires pointers to objects. In this section we discuss how to use pointers to objects to reference object members.

Using *New* Operator with Objects

When we use the *new* operator with a standard type, we just provide the type in the statement. When we use a class object, however, we need to call the constructor explicitly to instantiation the object in the heap. In the following example, we provide initialization lists to establish the values for the allocated memory. The first allocates an integer and sets its value to 4. In the second example, we create a fraction and set its value to 3/4.

```
int*       intPtr = new int (4);
Fraction* frPtr   = new Fraction (3, 4);
```

Accessing Members

To access the member of the class through a pointer, we need to use the member operator (dot). However, first we need to reference the pointed object, which requires that we use the indirection operator (*).

```
*frPtr
```

Given a pointer to the object, we can refer to any public member of the fraction class through the member operator, the dot. The next example shows how we use it to store a fraction or print it.

```
(*frPtr).store (2, 5)      (*frPtr).print()
```

Note that the parentheses around `*frPtr` are absolutely necessary. They are required because the precedence priority of the member operator is higher than the priority of the indirection operator. If you do not use the parentheses, it is interpreted as

```
*frPtr.print()     is interpreted as     *(frPtr.print())
```

which is not what we want.

Selection Operator

Fortunately, there is another operator that eliminates the problems with pointers to objects—the selection operator (->). The following examples are equivalents.

```
(*frPtr.)print()          frPtr->print()
```

The following example demonstrates the two operators discussed in this section.

```
Fraction* frPtr = new Fraction (3, 4);

(*frPtr).print ();                     // Member operator
frPtr -> print ();                     // Selection operator
```

11-7 ARRAY OF OBJECTS

If a class is a type, we should be able to create an array of objects of that type. For example, we can create an array of fractions by using the object of fraction class as shown below:

```
Fraction fractionAry [10];
```

This statement creates an array of 10 elements, each of which is an object of type fraction. When we declare and define an array of *n* elements, the complier calls the default constructor of the class *n* times to create *n* objects.

INITIALIZATION OF OBJECTS

When we create an array of objects, we are allowed to call only the default constructor; the compiler does not allow us to call a constructor with arguments. This means that we cannot initialize objects using a constructor with arguments.

> **We are only allowed to call the default constructor when we create an array of objects.**

There are, however, two ways to initialize the members of the array: We can initialize them through a default constructor that assigns values to data members or by using anonymous objects.

Default Constructor

We can define the default constructor with default values. Remember, however, that this technique must support objects that are not in an array as well as objects in an array. For example, given a rectangle array with *private* members for the length and width area, we could create a default constructor that initializes the member variables to 0.

```
Rectangle :: Rectangle ( )
{
   length = 0;
   width  = 0;
}  // Rectangle constructor
```

All objects instantiated without values will use this default constructor, which sets their data members set to 0. Objects initialized using the overridden constructor will be initialized with the supplied values.

Initializing with Anonymous Objects

Another way to initialize the objects is to use anonymous objects. This technique uses an initialization list that contains anonymous objects. The anonymous objects use an initialization constructor to assign the values. The following example calls the initialization constructor to store values in two of the three array objects; the third object is assigned values only through the default constructor.

```
Rectangle ary[3] = {Rectangle(1, 2), Rectangle(3, 4)};
```

Note that this is the same as initializing an array of two integers. Instead of using integer values, we are using the a constructor that creates a temporary anonymous object and assigns it to the corresponding array object.

ACCESSING OBJECTS

We can access the objects in an array of objects the way we access the elements of array of standard types. To demonstrate the concept, we create a rectangle class. The class contains three *private* data members: the length, width, and area. There are four public methods: a constructor, a destructor, print, and store. The constructor provides initializers to set the rectangle to a null state when an object is instantiated without any initial values. We define a null rectangle as a point; that is, with the length of the sides and the area set to zero.

Program 11-11 demonstrates the techniques developed in this section, including loops that access and print individual array object data members by calling the class print function.

Program 11-11 Demonstrate array of class objects

```
/* Demonstrate array of class objects
      Written by:
      Date:
*/
#include <iostream>
using namespace std;

class Rectangle
{
   private:
      int  length;
      int  width;
      int  area;

   public:
         Rectangle (int len = 0, int wid = 0);
        ~Rectangle () {}
     void print () const;
     void store (int len, int area);
}; // Rectangle
// ============= Rectangle Constructor ============
Rectangle :: Rectangle (int len, int wid)
{
   length = len;
   width  = wid;
   area   = length * width;
```

Program 11-11 Demonstrate array of class objects (*continued*)

```
}  // Rectangle constructor
/* ================ Rectangle Print ================
   Print members of rectangle object
      Pre  Nothing
      Post Length, width, and area printed
*/
void Rectangle :: print () const
{
   cout << "Length: " << length << " Width: " << width
        << " Area: "  << area   << endl;
} // Rectangle print
/* ================ Rectangle Store ================
   Stores length and width; calculates and stores area.
      Pre  Nothing
      Post Length, width, and area stored
*/
void Rectangle :: store (int len, int wid)
{
   length = len;
   width  = wid;
   area   = length * width;
} // Rectangle constructor

int main ()
{
   // Initialize and print using anonymous objects
   Rectangle rectAry1[3] =  {Rectangle(1, 2),
                             Rectangle(2, 3)};
   cout << "\nPrinting Rectangle Array #1\n";
   for (int i = 0; i < 3; i++)
       {
        cout << "Rectangle " << i << ": ";
        rectAry1[i].print();
       } // for

   // Initialize and print using store method
   Rectangle rectAry2[2];
   rectAry2[0].store(10, 11);
   rectAry2[1].store(12, 13);
   cout << "\nPrinting Rectangle Array #2\n";
   for (int i = 0; i < 2; i++)
       {
        cout << "Rectangle " << i << ": ";
        rectAry2[i].print();
       } // for
   return 0;
} // main
```

Program 11-11 Demonstrate array of class objects (*continued*)

```
Results
Printing Rectangle Array #1
Rectangle 0: Length: 1 Width: 2 Area: 2
Rectangle 1: Length: 2 Width: 3 Area: 6
Rectangle 2: Length: 0 Width: 0 Area: 0

Printing Rectangle Array #2
Rectangle 0: Length: 10 Width: 11 Area: 110
Rectangle 1: Length: 12 Width: 13 Area: 156
```

Program 11-11 Analysis There is an important design concept in this program: We define a null rectangle. While we could have crated a null rectangle with uninitialized values by providing a constructor with no parameters, doing so could lead to problems when it is used. It is a better design to define a null state for an object.

We could also have written it so that the user always had to initialize the rectangle by not including a default constructor. This would break a basic C++ array design concept, however. Recall that when an array is created with fewer initializers than elements, the uninitialized elements are set to a null state. By providing a default constructor that initializes the rectangle to a null state, we are consistent with the basic C++ array design. We demonstrate this concept in the first array definition (statement 53).

11-8 STRUCTURE

Structure, a construct inherited from the C language, behaves exactly like a class with one exception: Data members in a structure are *public* by default; they are *private* by default in a class. With this understanding, structure and class are synonymous terms. In other words, a structure can do whatever a class can do and vice versa.

> **The class and structure constructs are identical with one exception:**
> **Members in a structure are *public* by default**
> **whereas they are *private* by default in a class**

The structure keyword is *struct*. Figure 11-5 shows the declaration for a class and for a structure. For the class, we use the keyword *class*; for the structure, we use the keyword ***struct***.

To prove that structure and class are synonymous, take a working program that contains a class and make one change: change the keyword *class* to *struct*. When you run the program, you will get identical results. Of course, this assumes that you have followed our recommendation and explicitly coded *public* and *private* members in the class declaration.

Now consider the declarations in Figure 11-6. In this case, are the two objects identical?

```class Sample```
```{```
```   private:```
```   ...```
```   private:```
```   ...```
```}; // Sample```
	```struct Sample```
	```{```
	``` private:```
	``` ...```
	``` private:```
	``` ...```
	```}; // Sample```

Figure 11-5 Class and structure declarations

```class Sample```
```{```
```   int x;```
```   int y;```
```   ...```
```   void print();```
```}; // Sample```
	```struct Sample```
	```{```
	``` int x;```
	``` int y;```
	``` ...```
	``` void print();```
	```}; // Sample```

Figure 11-6 Private versus public defaults

The answer is no! The integers and print function in the class are *private*. The integers and print function in the structure are *public*. This emphasizes the one difference between the two constructs: Members are *private* by default in a class; they are *public* by default in a structure.

STRUCTURE APPLICATION

Given that we have two virtually identical constructs, when should we use structure? In the C language, the structure was required to create a type that holds members of different types. For example, if we need a structure to hold characters, integers, and floating-point numbers in the C language, we must use a structure. Structures are used in C to pass data aggregations to a function, to build arrays that contain different types, and to read and write binary files (see Chapter 16).

Basically, we would use structure in a C++ program for the same reasons. As long as the data are public and no functions need to be encapsulated into the structure, we can use the structure construct. However, if we want to hide the data by encapsulating them in a structure or if we want to include functions to process data as a part of the structure, then we should use a class.

> **Use structures only for simple constructs that do not require data protection or specialized functions.**

INITIALIZATION

A structure can be initialized. The rules for structure initialization are similar to the rules for array initialization: (1) the initializers are enclosed in braces and separated by commas and (2) the initializers must match their corresponding types in the structure declaration.

Figure 11-7 shows two examples of structure initialization. In the first example, there is an initializer for each field. Note how initializers are mapped to the structure in sequence. The second example demonstrates what happens when not all fields are initialized. As with arrays, when one or more initializers are missing, the structure elements will be assigned null values—0 for integers and floating-point numbers and '\0' for characters.

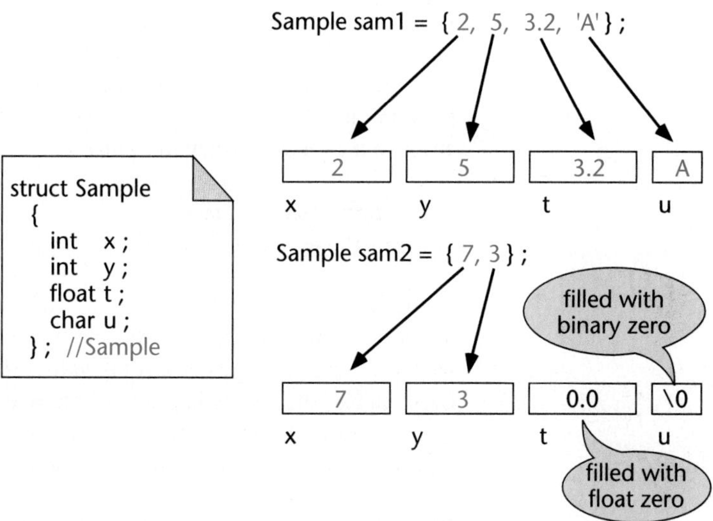

Figure 11-7 Initializing structures

SUMMARY

In summary, there is virtually no difference between a class and a structure. Classes are better suited to objects that require data protection and specialized functions to process the data. Structures are better suited to simple, public objects that do not need the protection provided by private data members

11-9 UNIONS

The ***union*** is a construct that allows memory to be shared by different types of data. This redefinition can be as simple as redeclaring an integer as four characters or as complex as redeclaring an entire structure. For example, we know that a short integer is 2 bytes and that each byte is a character. Therefore, we could process a short integer as a number or as two characters.

The union follows the same format syntax as the structure. In fact, with the exception of the keywords *struct* and *union,* the formats are the same. Figure 11-8 shows how we declare a union that can be used as either a short integer or as two characters.

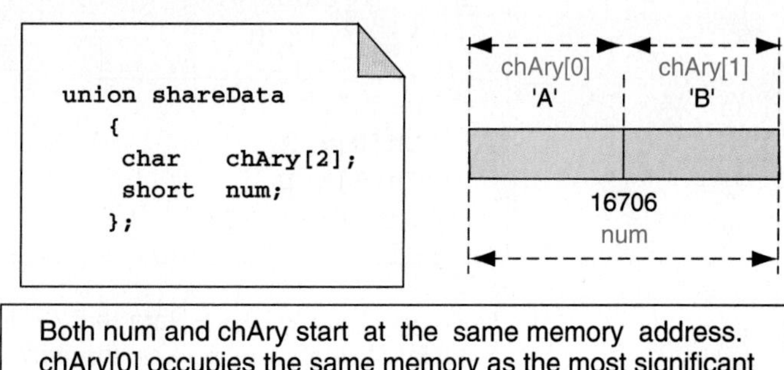

Figure 11-8 Unions

REFERENCING UNIONS

The rules for referencing a union are identical to those for structures. To reference individual fields within the union, we use the member (dot) operator. Each reference must be fully qualified from the beginning of the structure to the element being referenced. This includes the name of the union itself. When a union is being referenced through a pointer, the selection operator (arrow) can be used. The following are both valid references to the unions shown in Figure 11-8.

```
shareData.num
shareData.chAry[0]
```

INITIALIZERS

While ANSI/ISO C++ permits unions to be initialized, only the first type declared in the *union* can be initialized when the variable is defined. The other types can only be initialized by assigning values or reading values into the *union*. When initializing a *union*, you must enclose the values in a set of braces, even if there is only one value.

Program 11-12 demonstrates unions in a program. It uses the structure in Figure 11-8 to print a variable, first as a number and then as two characters.

Program 11-12 Demonstrate effect of union

```
/* Demonstrate union of short integer and two characters.
      Written by:
      Date:
*/
#include <iostream>
using namespace std;

union shareData
   {
    char   chAry[2];
    short  num;
   }; // shareData

int main ()
{
   shareData data = {'A', 'B'};
   cout << "Ch[0]: " << data.chAry[0] << endl;
   cout << "Ch[1]: " << data.chAry[1] << endl;
   cout << "Short: " << data.num      << endl;
   return 0;
} // main
```

```
Results:
Ch[0]: A
Ch[1]: B
Short: 16706
```

Program 11-12 Analysis Note that we initialize `data` using characters to make it easier to verify the results, the initializers are assigned to the first format in a *union*. To prove to yourself that A and B are in fact 16706, however, you will need to either analyze the bit pattern of the two values or run the program. Don't be surprised, however, if you get a different number on your computer. If you do, it means that you have a "little-endian" computer (see the box "Big- and Little-Endian Computers").

Big- and Little-Endian Computers

Computer hardware can be physically designed to store the most significant byte of a number at either the left end of the number (big-endian) or at the right end of the number (little-endian), as shown below.

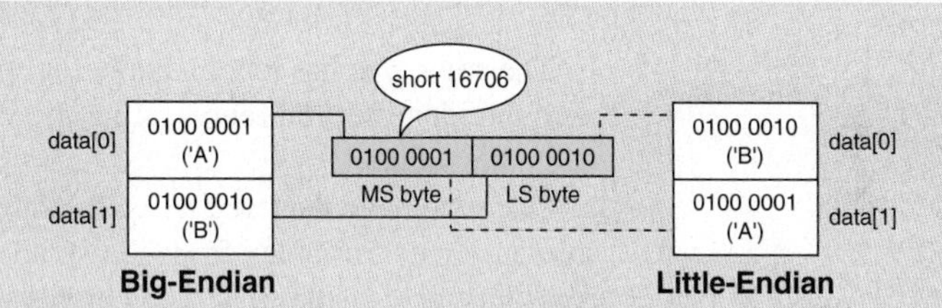

If we consider memory as an array of bytes, then a computer that uses big-endian stores the most significant byte—that is, the larger portion of the number (16,000 in the above example—at the beginning of the array. This is shown in the example on the left. Note that `data[0]` is 'A' and `data[1]` is 'B'.

In a little-endian computer, the most significant byte is stored on the right. This example is seen on the right in the above example. This time, `data[0]` contains 'B' and `data[1]` contains 'A.' If you want to know if your computer is big- or little-endian, then run Program 11-12 and check out the results.

11-10 ENUMERATED TYPES

The **enumerated type** is a user-defined type based on the standard integer type. In an enumerated type, each integer value is given an identifier called an **enumeration constant**. We can thus use the enumerated constants as symbolic names, which makes our programs much more readable.

Recall from Chapter 2 (see page 33) that a type is a set of values and a set of operations that can be applied on those values. Each type also has an identifier or name. For example, the standard type *int* has an identifier (*int*), a set of values (-∞. . . +∞), and a set of operations (such as add and multiply). While the system defines the names, values, and operations for standard types, we must define them for types we create.[3]

DECLARING AN ENUMERATED TYPE

To declare an enumerated type, therefore, we must declare its identifier and its values Because it is derived from the integer type, its operations are the same as for integers. The syntax for declaring an enumerated type is:

```
enum typeName {identifier list};
```

[3]When the defined type directly translates into a standard type, as with the enumerated type, the standard types may be automatically defined.

The keyword, ***enum***, is followed by an identifier and a set of enumeration constants enclosed in a set of braces. The statement is terminated with a semicolon. The enumeration identifiers are also known as the enumeration list.

Each enumeration identifier is assigned an integer value. If we do not explicitly assign the values, the compiler assigns the first identifiers the value 0, the second identifier the value 1, the third identifier the value 2, and so on until all of the identifiers have a value. For example, consider an enumerated type for colors as defined in the next statement. Note that for enumeration identifiers, we use uppercase alphabetic characters.

```
enum color {RED, BLUE, GREEN, WHITE};
```

The color type has four and only four possible values. The range of the values is 0 . . 3, with the identifier red representing the value 0, blue the value 1, green the value 2, and white the value 3.

Once we have declared an enumerated type, we can create variables from it just as we can create variables from the standard types. In fact, C++ allows the enumerated constants, or variables that hold enumerated constants, to be used anywhere that integers can be used. The following example defines three variables for our color type.

```
color productColor;
color skyColor;
color flagColor;
```

ASSIGNING VALUES TO ENUMERATED TYPES

After an enumerated type has been declared and defined, we can store values in its variables. Remember, however, that an enumerated variable can hold only declared values for the type. The following example defines a color variable and uses it in several statements.

```
color x;
color y;
color z;

x = BLUE;
y = WHITE;
z = PURPLE;                        // Error. There is no purple.
```

Similarly, once a variable has been defined and assigned a value, we can store its value in another variable of the same type. Given the previous example, the following statements are valid.

```
x = y;
z = y;
```

ENUMERATION TYPE CONVERSION

Enumerated types can be implicitly and explicitly cast. The compiler implicitly casts an enumerated type to an integer as required. However, it is a compile error to implicitly cast an integer to an enumerated type. The following example demonstrates valid and invalid implicit casts.

```
int   x;
color y;
x = BLUE;                               // Valid. x contains 1
y = 2;                                  // Compiler error
```

However, we can explicitly cast an integer to an enumerated type. To assign y the value blue in the previous example, we could use the code in the next example.

```
color y;
y = static_cast<color>2;          // Valid. y contains blue
```

INITIALIZING ENUMERATED CONSTANTS

While the compiler automatically assigns values to enumerated types starting with 0, we can override it and assign our own values. For example, to set up an enumerated type for the months of the year, we could use the following declaration.

```
enum months
{JAN,FEB,MAR,APR,MAY,JUN,JUL,AUG,SEP,OCT,NOV,DEC};

months dateMonth;
```

While this declaration works, it could be confusing because JAN is assigned the value 0, FEB the value 1, and so forth until dec, which is 11. To make JAN start with 1, we could use the following declaration.

```
ENUM MONTHS {JAN =  1, FEB, MAR, APR, MAY, JUN,
                       JUL, AUG, SEP, OCT, NOV, DEC;
```

Note that we don't have to assign initializers to every value. If we omit the initializers, the compiler assigns the next value by adding 1. To initialize the months, therefore, we simply assign the value for JAN. The rest will be automatically assigned by the compiler.

C++ also allows us to assign duplicate values to identifiers. For example, we could assign similar colors identical values as shown in the next example.

```
enum color {RED,    ROSE = 0, CRIMSON = 0, SCARLET = 0,
            BLUE,   AQUA = 1, NAVY    = 1,
            GREEN,  JADE = 2, WHITE};
```

To emphasize the point, even though ROSE has the same value as RED in myColor, the two types are different and cannot be used together unless one of them is cast.

ANONYMOUS ENUMERATION: CONSTANTS

If we create an enumerated type without a name, it is an anonymous enumerated type. Because the identifiers in enumerated types are constants, enumerated types are a convenient way to declare constants. As a matter of fact, C++ prefers enumerated constants to integral constants. For example, to assign names to common punctuation characters, we would use the following code.

```
enum (space = ' ', comma ',', colon = ':', ...);
```

As another example, to declare the constants on and off, we could use the following code.

```
enum {OFF, ON};
```

The identifier OFF is a constant with a value of 0; ON is a value of 1. As an aside, we coded OFF first because we wanted it to have a connotation of false. Similarly, ON has a connotation of true.

11-11 THE TYPE DEFINITION (*typedef*)

The **type definition** statement creates a new name for an existing type. A carryover from the C language, the type definition construct, ***typedef***, was originally used to name a programmer-defined type. Once created, the type could then be used anywhere a type is permitted. We discuss its syntax and use it briefly in this section. The format for the type definition is shown in Figure 11-9.

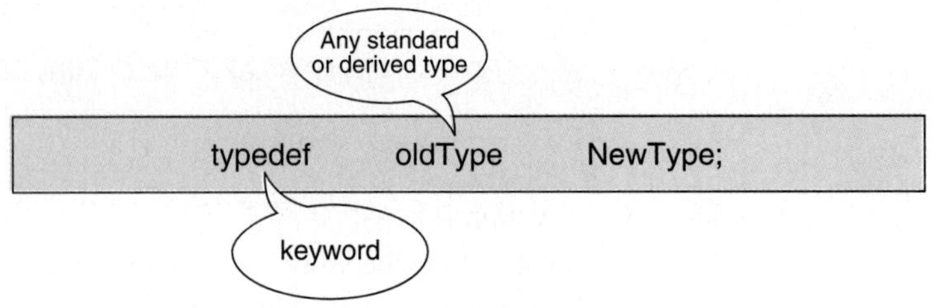

Figure 11-9 **Typed definition format**

We can use the type definition with any type. For example, we can redefine *int* to `Integer` with the statement shown below, although we would never recommend this.

```
typedef int Integer;
```

Note how we code the *typedef* identifier: the first character is uppercase. This alerts the reader that there is something unusual about the type. This is the same style we use with classes and is consistent because type definitions are classes.

The typedef is different from any other derived type. It does not create a new type; it just renames a type that already exists.

> The *typedef* command does not create a new type.
> It just creates an alias, that is, a new name, for an existing type.

typedef AND PORTABLE PROGRAMS

A good use of the type definition is to create portable programs. For example, in network programming we need two data types: a device address, which must be exactly 32 bits, and a port address, which must be exactly 16 bits. In a network program, we could declare these two data types as shown in the next example.

```
long  machineAddr;
short portAddr;
```

While this works in many computers, it does not guarantee that the size of *long* is always 32 bits and that the size of *short* is always 16 bits. Remember, we need exactly 32 bits and 16 bits for sending data over the Internet.

To solve this problem, network programmers create a header that contains the following two type definitions along with other definitions they may need.

```
typedef long  int32;
typedef short int16;
```

Having created two Internet compatible types, we now can use them for the machine and port addresses in all of our programs. If we must move our programs to a computer that uses a different physical size for *short* and *long*, we change the type definition in the header file to the appropriate types in the new computer and compile the programs. In other words, we simply change the header file, not all of our programs.

typedef AND ARRAY DECLARATIONS

Another common use of the *typedef* statement is to create a simple type that can be used to replace a complex declaration as shown in the next example.

```
typedef Fraction* pFraction;
...
pFraction aryFraction[12];
```

There are those, however, who discourage the use of this technique because, as often implemented, it hides the structure. For example, in the above definition, is `aryFraction` an array of objects or an array of pointers to objects? The answer, of course, is the latter, although we have to trace the code back to the type definition to determine which it is. On the other hand, the following definition is clearly understood because the code directly contains the pointer reference.

```
pFraction* aryFraction[12];
```

11-12 PROGRAMMING APPLICATIONS

In this chapter we present an example of a class that uses several concepts we discussed in the last two chapters.

ELEVATOR DESIGN

For a class application, we present a program that simulates an elevator. The elevator serves floors from zero (the basement) to the top floor. It is a very old elevator and is not automatic. When people get in the elevator, they enter their desired floor number. Several numbers can be requested at a time. After all numbers have been entered, the door is closed by pressing the close door button (the return key).

Each time the door closes, the elevator checks to see if there are any floors in the current direction (up or down) that need to be serviced. If there are, it services these floors first, starting with the closest one to the current floor. If there are no floors requiring stops in the current direction, it checks the opposite direction, again servicing the floor closest to the current floor. If the elevator is not moving (direction `STOP;` see below), it services up requests before down requests.

Each time the elevator arrives at a floor, new passengers can get on and request a floor. The new requests are added to the ones still pending, and the elevator again evaluates which floor will be processed next.

The structure for this program is shown in Figure 11-10. The elevator is represented as a structure with three fields: the current floor, a pointer to an array of buttons, and the current direction of the elevator. The button values are `IN,` meaning the floor has been requested, and `OUT,` meaning the floor has not been requested. After a floor has been serviced, the button is reset. The direction values are `UP, DOWN,` and `STOP.`

The elevator design can be shown two different ways. Figure 11-11 shows a structure chart for the program.

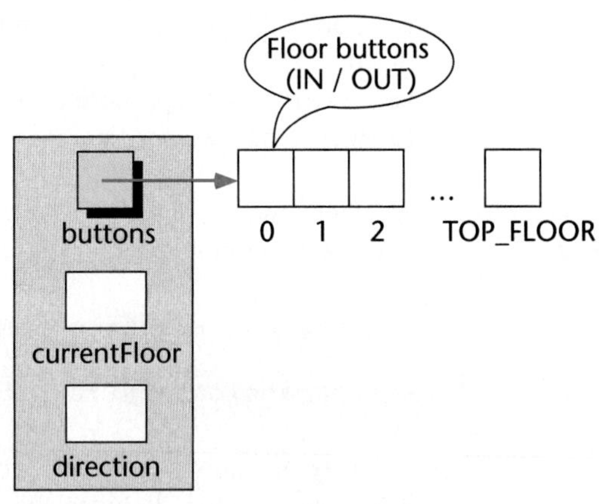

Figure 11-10 **Elevator structure**

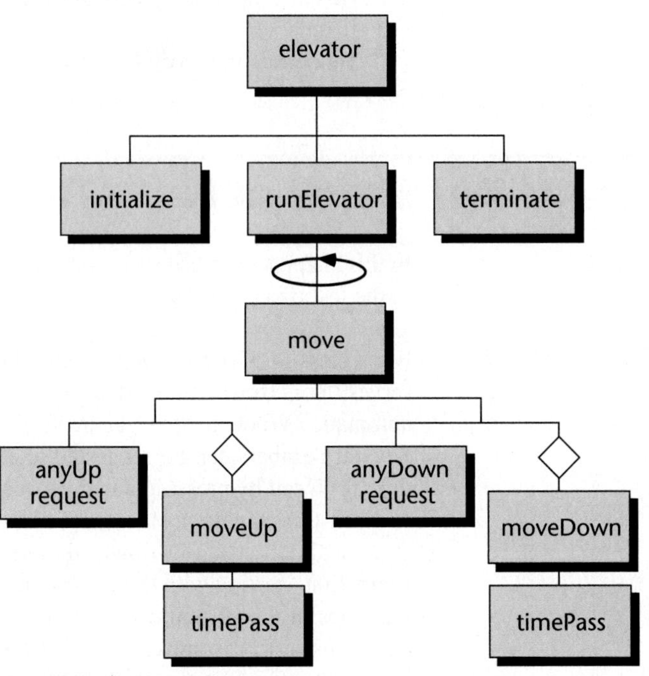

Figure 11-11 **Elevator structure chart**

In Figure 11-12 we use a state diagram to describe the elevator operation. A state diagram is a design technique that is often used with real-time systems to show how a system moves from one state to another. An elevator can be in one of three states: moving up, moving down, or stopped. Each of these states is represented by a circle in the diagram. To move from one state to another, a change must occur in the elevator environment. For example, to change from the stop state to the up state, a button must be pressed. This is reflected on the line between stop and up as `anyUp`.

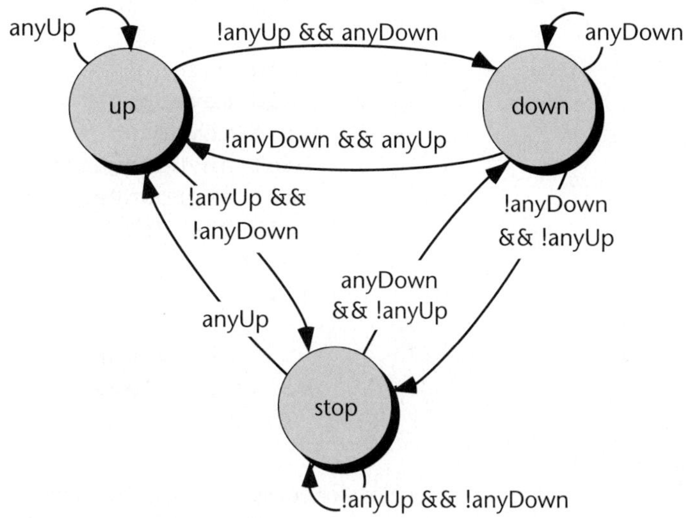

Figure 11-12 Elevator states

ELEVATOR CLASS

Now that we have examined the problem, let's look at the code.

Class Definition

We begin by examining the elevator class in Program 11-13. The elevator structure (Figure 11-10) shows that there are only three variables required for the problem: the current floor, an array of button flags that indicate whether or not a floor has been requested, and the elevator's current direction. These elements are found in Program 11-13 in the private area of the class (statements 14, 15, and 16). The buttons array and the direction are implemented using enumerated types, which are also defined in the private section of the class for scope data protection.

There are only three public functions: the constructor, the destructor, and the function that runs the elevator. All of the other functions are private.

Program 11-13 Elevator class structure

```
1  /* Elevator class structure
2        Written by:
3        Date:
4  */
5  const int TOP_FLOOR = 8;
6  const int DELAY_FACTOR = 10000;
7  
8  class Elevator
9  {
10    private:
11       enum BUTTONS    {OUT, IN};
12       enum DIRECTION {DOWN, STOP, UP};
13 
14       BUTTONS*   buttons;
15       int        currentFloor;
16       DIRECTION direction;
```

Program 11-13 Elevator class structure *(continued)*

```
     void move          ();
     void moveUp        ();
     void moveDown      ();
     bool anyUpRequest   () const;
     bool anyDownRequest () const;
     void timePass       (int time) const;

   public:
          Elevator    ();
         ~Elevator    ();
     void  runElevator ();
}; // Class Elevator
```

Elevator Constructor and Destructor

The elevator constructor and destructor are shown in Program 11-14. The constructor allocates memory for the button array and initializes the current floor to 1. The destructor deletes the button array.

Program 11-14 Elevator *constructor* and *destructor*

```
/* ================== Constructor ====================
   This function dynamically allocates memory locations
   for the buttons and initializes the current floor to 1
   to show that the elevator is parked at the first floor.
      Pre  Nothing
      Post Elevator created, all buttons are reset, and
        elevator is parked at first floor (not basement)
*/
Elevator :: Elevator () : buttons (0)
{
   buttons = (BUTTONS*) new(BUTTONS[TOP_FLOOR + 1]);

   for (int i = 0; i <= TOP_FLOOR; i++)
      buttons[i]   = OUT;
   currentFloor    = 1;
   direction       = STOP;
} // constructor

/* ================== Destructor ====================
   Release the memory occupied by buttons.
   Pre    The elevator
   Post   The memory is released
*/
Elevator :: ~Elevator ()
{
// Statements
   delete [ ]buttons;
} // destructor
```

Run Elevator

The heart of the program is runElevator (see Program 11-15). It contains the most difficult logic in the program. Before we discuss the logic, however, study the way we handled the user messages; they are all coded as constants at the beginning of the function. By placing them at the beginning and using good descriptive names, we were able to unclutter the code and make it more readable.

The elevator design requires that several floors can be requested at the same time. This is very realistic; during the busy periods, many users get on the elevator at the same time, and all need to request a floor. This requires that we have a loop (statements 33 to 53) to read and set the requested floors. It reads floors until a newline is detected.

The outer loop, starting at statement 29, moves the elevator one floor at a time until the simulation is complete. Because this is a simulation, we request that the user enter a Q when the simulation is complete.

Program 11-15 runElevator

```
1  /* ================ runElevator ==================
2     This function simulates the operation of the elevator.
3        Pre  The elevator structure has been initialized
4        Post The simulation is complete
5  */
6  void Elevator :: runElevator ()
7  {
8  // Message Constants
9     const char* INSTRUCTION1 =
10       "\n\nThis elevator goes from basement (0) to floor ";
11    const char* INSTRUCTION2 =
12       "\nType floors & press return key to start";
13    const char* INSTRUCTION3 =
14       "\nIf no new floors, just press return key.";
15    const char* INSTRUCTION4 =
16      "\nTo quit, enter <Q> \n\nPlease enter floors: ";
17    const char* INVALID_FLOOR = " not a valid floor.\n";
18    const char* CURRENT_FLOOR = "\aAlready on Floor ";
19    const char* INVALID_IP =
20              "\n\aInvalid Input. Please re-enter: ";
21    const char* NEXT_FLOOR =
22             "\n\nPlease enter next floors or <Q>: ";
23
24    cout << INSTRUCTION1 << TOP_FLOOR
25         << INSTRUCTION2 << INSTRUCTION3
26         << INSTRUCTION4;
27
28    char  aCh = toupper( cin.get () );
29    while (aCh != 'Q')
30       {
31        int   floor;
32
33        do
34           {
35            if (isdigit(aCh))
36               {
```

Program 11-15 runElevator (*continued*)

```
                    // Convert digit to decimal
                    floor = (aCh - '0');
                    if (floor < 0 || floor > TOP_FLOOR)
                    cout << "\n\a" << floor << INVALID_FLOOR;
                    else
                        if (floor == currentFloor)
                           cout << CURRENT_FLOOR << floor;
                        else
                            buttons[floor] = IN;
                  } // if digit
                else
                    if (!isspace(aCh) && aCh != 'Q')
                        cout << INVALID_IP;
                if (aCh != '\n')
                    // Read next floor
                    aCh = toupper( cin.get () );
              } while ( aCh != '\n' && aCh != 'Q');
         if (aCh != 'Q')
             move ( );
         cout << NEXT_FLOOR;
         aCh = toupper( cin.get () );
       } // while
    return;
} // runElevator
```

Move Elevator

There are three functions required to move the elevator: `move`, `moveUp`, and `moveDown`. The function `move` (Program 11-16) begins by determining the current direction of the elevator. If it is going up, it first checks to see if there are any requests for a higher floor, and if there are, it calls a function to move the elevator up. Only after all of the up requests have been processed does it start down. Similarly, if the current direction is down, it first tests to see if there are lower floors requested and processes them before checking for higher floors.

Program 11-16 Elevator: *move*

```
/* ==================== move =====================
   Moves the elevator to a requested floor. It stops
   the elevator after responding to one request.
      Pre    The elevator
      Post   The elevator has been moved. While it is
             moving, the floors are called out
*/
void Elevator :: move ()
{
   bool anyUp    = anyUpRequest   ( );
   bool anyDown = anyDownRequest ( );

   if (direction == UP)
      {
```

Program 11-16 Elevator: *move (continued)*

```
          if (!anyUp && anyDown)
              direction = DOWN;
          else
              if (!anyUp && !anyDown)
                  direction = STOP;
        } // UP

    else if (direction == DOWN)
        {
          if (!anyDown && anyUp)
              direction = UP;
          else
              if (!anyDown && !anyUp)
                  direction = STOP;
        } // DOWN

    else if (direction == STOP)
        {
          if (anyUp)
              direction = UP;
          else
              if (anyDown)
                  direction = DOWN;
        } // STOP

    if (direction == UP)
        moveUp ( );
    else
        if (direction == DOWN)
            moveDown ( );
        else
            cout << "\n***** NO BUTTON PRESSED ***** ";
    return;
} // move
```

The `moveUp` function (Program 11-17) and the `moveDown` function (Program 11-18) simply pass some time and display appropriate messages.

Program 11-17 Elevator: *moveUp*

```
/* ==================== moveUp =====================
   This function simulates the movement of the elevator
   when it is going up.
      Pre   The elevator
      Post  The up simulation is displayed on the screen
*/
void  Elevator :: moveUp ()
{
   cout << "\nThe door is being closed..."
```

Program 11-17 Elevator: *moveUp (continued)*

```
          << "\nWe are going up.";
   currentFloor++;
   while (buttons[currentFloor] != IN)
     {
      timePass (2);
      cout << "\nPassing floor " << currentFloor << endl;
      timePass (2);
      currentFloor++;
     } // while

   buttons[currentFloor] = OUT;
   cout << "\nThe door is  being opened...\n"
      << "\n ***** FLOOR " << currentFloor << " *****\n";
   timePass( 4 );
   return;
} // moveUp
```

Program 11-18 Elevator: *moveDown*

```
/* ================== moveDown ====================
   This function simulates the movement of the elevator
   when it is going down.
      Pre   The elevator
      Post down simulation displayed on the screen
*/
void Elevator::moveDown ()
{
   cout << "\nThe door is being closed..."
        << "\nWe are going down";
   currentFloor--;
   while (buttons[currentFloor] != IN)
     {
      timePass (2);
      cout << "\nPassing floor " << currentFloor << endl;
      timePass (2);
      currentFloor--;
     } // while
   buttons[currentFloor] = OUT;
   cout << "\nThe door is being opened...\n"
      << "\n ***** FLOOR " << currentFloor << " *****\n";
   timePass (4);
   return;
} // moveDown
```

Status Functions

There are three minor functions. One checks to see if there are any requests for higher floors (`anyUpRequest`—Program 11-19). Another checks for lower floors (`anyDownRequest`—Program 11-20). The last function (`timePass`—Program 11-21) simply passes time to simulate the moving of the elevator.

Program 11-19 Elevator: *anyUpRequest*

```
/* =================== anyUpRequest ===================
   This function checks to see if any request is for
   a floor above the current floor.
    Pre  The elevator
    Post returns true if button above current floor pushed
         returns false otherwise
*/
bool Elevator :: anyUpRequest () const
{
   bool isAny = false;

   for (int check = currentFloor;
        check <= TOP_FLOOR && !isAny;
        check++ )
           isAny = (buttons[check] == IN);
   return isAny;
} // anyUpRequest
```

Program 11-20 Elevator: *anyDownRequest*

```
/* ================ anyDownRequest =================
   This function checks to see if any request is for
   a floor below the current floor.
     Pre  The elevator
     Post returns true if button below current floor pushed
        returns false otherwise
*/
bool Elevator :: anyDownRequest () const
{
   bool isAny = false;

   for (int check = currentFloor;
            check >=  0 && !isAny;
            check--)
           isAny = (buttons[check] == IN);
   return isAny;
} // anyDownRequest
```

Program 11-21 Elevator: *timePass*

```
/* ================== timePass =====================
   This function simulates the concept of passing time by
   executing an empty for-loop.
      Pre  The time to be passed (number of moments)
      Post Time has passed
*/
void Elevator :: timePass  (int time) const
```

Program 11-21 Elevator: *timePass (continued)*

```
{
  for (long i = 0; i < (time * DELAY_FACTOR); i++)
     ;
  return;
} // timePass
```

Main

The function *main* (Program 11-22) is a three-line function that calls `runElevator`, displays an end message, and returns.

Program 11-22 Elevator: *main*

```
/* This program simulates the operation of an elevator.
      Written by:
      Date:
*/
#include <iostream>
#include <cstdlib>
#include <cctype>
using namespace std;

#include "elevClas.h"

int main ()
{
Elevator elevator;

   elevator.runElevator ();
   cout << "\nThank you for using Elevator Simulator\n";
   return 0;
} // main
```

11-13 SOFTWARE ENGINEERING AND PROGRAMMING STYLE

In this chapter we discuss two important aspects of program design: function coupling and data hiding.

COUPLING

In Chapter 4, we discussed a concept known as functional cohesion, a measure of how closely related the processes are within a function. A related topic, coupling, is a measure of how tightly two functions are bound to each other. The more tightly coupled they are, the less independent they are. Since our objective is to make the modules as independent as possible, we want them to be loosely coupled.

There are several reasons why loose coupling is desirable.

1. Independent—that is, loosely coupled—functions are more likely to be reusable.
2. Loosely coupled functions are less likely to create errors in related functions; conversely, the tighter the coupling, the higher the probability that an error in one function will generate an error in a related function.
3. Maintenance modifications—that is, modifications required to implement new user requirements—are easier and less apt to create errors with loosely coupled functions.

In his book on designing structured systems, Page-Jones describes five types of coupling. We review them here. For an in-depth discussion of the concept, refer to Chapter 5 in his book, *The Practical Guide to Structured Systems Design.*[4]

Data Coupling

Data coupling passes only the minimum required data from the calling function to the called function. All required data are passed as parameters, and no extra data are passed. This is the best form of coupling and should be used whenever possible.

When you are writing simple functions that work on only one task, the coupling naturally tends to be data coupling. Consider, for example, the function `exchange` in the selection sort in Program 9-14 on page 462. This function exchanges two integers. It receives pointers to the two integers it is to exchange and nothing else. It makes no references to any data outside the function, except through the parameter pointers. This function uses data coupling and is highly reusable.

> **Functions in well-structured programs are highly cohesive and loosely coupled.**

We could have fallen into the trap of passing extra parameters by passing the array and the index locations of the two integers. The function would have worked just as well, but the coupling would not have been

[4]Meilir Page-Jones, *The Practical Guide to Structured Systems Design,* Yourdon Press Computing Series (Englewood Cliffs, NJ: Prentice-Hall, 1988).

as loose. Now it requires an array of integers instead of just integers. Furthermore, we could have made the coupling even tighter had we referred to the maximum size of the array using the precompiler declaration SIZE. At this point, it is highly questionable whether the function could be used in another program.

Stamp Coupling

Functions are **stamp coupled** if the parameters are composite objects such as arrays or structures. Most of the functions in the selection sort in Chapter 9 (see page 462) use stamp coupling because they pass the array. (Although it could be argued that we are passing only a pointer to the array, the intent is to modify the array. We are, therefore, passing the array for the purposes of this discussion.)

You should now be arguing, "But we have to pass the array!" Yes, that is true. Stamp coupling is not bad in and of itself, and is often necessary. The danger with stamp coupling is that often it is just too easy to send a structure when all the data in the structure are not required. When extra data are sent, we begin to open the door for errors and undesired side effects.

Consider the time stamp described in Chapter 10 in Figure 10-14 (page 526). This structure contains two nested structures, `date` and `time`. If we were to use these data—for example, to print the date in a report heading—and passed the whole structure, we would be sending too much data! In addition, if we were to pass the structure by reference rather than by value, we would risk the possibility of an error in one function's accidentally changing the data in the structure and causing a second error. The correct solution is to pass only the data that are needed and then only by value when possible.

Stamp coupling should pass only the data needed.

A common practice to reduce the number of parameters required for a function is to create a structure that contains all the data the function needs and pass them. Page-Jones refers to this as *bundling*. It is a common practice, but it is not a good practice for three reasons:

1. Maintenance is made more difficult because it is more difficult to trace data through a program.
2. Extra data can be passed. For example, a bundled structure is created for a series of related functions, but not all of them use all the data. The temptation is just too great to pass the structure even though only one or two of the members are needed.
3. The semantics of the structure are often artificial, making the program more difficult to read and understand.

Avoid bundling unrelated data just to reduce the number of parameters being passed between functions.

Control Coupling

Control coupling is the passing of flags that may be used to direct the logic flow of a function. It closely resembles data coupling except that a flag is being passed rather than data.

In C++, flags are often returned from a function rather than being passed as parameters, but the intent and usage are the same. For example, consider the logic involved with reading an input file to its end. When the input file reaches the end, a special end-of-file flag is set. You can then test it with an end-of-file function. An example of a flag being passed in a function you might write is the user-selected option in the menu function of an interactive program. This flag directs the entire flow of the program. The option is a special type of flag known as a data flag. It is data entered by the user, and at the same time it is a flag intended to direct the flow of the program.

Properly used, control coupling is a necessary and valid method of communicating between two functions. Like stamp coupling, however, it can be misused. Properly used, it communicates status: The end of the file has been reached. The search value was found.

Poor flag usage is usually an indication of poor program design—for example, dividing a process between two or more independent functions. Flags used to communicate horizontally across several functions in the structure chart are often an indication of poor design. Action flags (as opposed to status flags) requiring the receiving function to perform some special processing are also highly suspect. An example of an action flag is a flag that directs a customer's purchase not to be approved rather than simply reporting that the credit limit has been exceeded or that no payment was received last month.

Control coupling should be used only to pass status.

Global Coupling

Global coupling uses global variables to communicate between two, or usually more, functions. Page-Jones calls it *common coupling*. With all that we have said about not using global variables, it should not come as a surprise that this is not a good coupling technique. In fact, it should *never* be used.

There are several reasons why you should never use global coupling. We will cite only the "big three":

1. Global coupling makes it virtually impossible to determine which modules are communicating with each other. When a change needs to be made to a program, therefore, it is not possible to evaluate and isolate the impact of the change. This often causes functions that were not changed to suddenly fail.

2. Global coupling tightly binds a function to the program. This means that it cannot be easily transported to another program.

3. Global coupling leads to multiple flag meanings. This problem is often made worse by using generic flag names, such as f1, f2, ..., f21. (Twenty-one flags in a single program is not an exaggeration.

We know of one assembly program that had more flags than that. In fact, it had one flag that was used solely to indicate that another flag had been set, but was now turned off; in other words, a flag that returned the status of a flag!)

The danger here should be obvious. If a flag can be used globally to communicate between two functions, it is highly probable that at some point this flag could be erroneously changed by a third function that used it for another purpose.

Avoid global coupling within a program.

Content Coupling

The last type of coupling is very difficult, but not impossible, to use in C++. **Content coupling** occurs when one function refers directly to the data or statements in another function. This concept breaks all the tenets of structured programming.

***Never* use content coupling.**

Referring to the data in another function requires that the data be made externally visible outside the function, which is impossible in C++. The only thing in C++ that allows a situation even remotely close to this is global variables. Since we have stressed the dangers of global variables before, we will simply state here that they should not be used for communication within one compile unit.

DATA HIDING

We have previously discussed the concept of global and local variables. In the discussion, we pointed out that anything placed before *main* was said to be in the global part of the program. With the exception of data that must be visible to functions in other compile units, no data should be placed in this section.

One of the principles of structured programming states that the internal data structure should be hidden from the user's view. The two terms you usually hear are *data hiding* and *data encapsulation.* Both of these principles have as their objective protecting data from accidental destruction by parts of a program that don't need access to the data. In other words, if a part of your program doesn't need data to do its job, it shouldn't be able to *see* the data.

Programming Standard:
Do not place any variables in the global area of a program.

Any variables placed in the global area of your program—that is, before *main*—can be used and changed by every part of your program. This is in direct conflict with the structured programming principles of data hiding and data encapsulation.

SUMMARY

We have described five different ways that two functions can communicate. The first three are all valid and useful, although not without some dangers. These communication techniques also provide data hiding. Data coupling is universally accepted and provides the loosest communication between two functions. Stamp and control coupling present some dangers that must be recognized. When using stamp coupling, do not pass more data than are required. Keep control coupling narrow—that is, between only two functions. The last two, global and content coupling, are to be avoided at all times. They do not protect the data.

11-14 TIPS AND COMMON PROGRAMMING ERRORS

1. Do not use an inline function if it is large or if it is called from several places in the program.
2. Do not use an inline function if it is called recursively.
3. Do not forget the colon between the header of a constructor and the initialization list.
4. Do not initialize members in an initialization list using the assignment operator (=).
5. Functions are overloaded only if there is a difference in their parameter lists: The return type does not distinguish between two overloaded functions.
6. Use overloaded operators wisely. Do not overload an operator for a purpose that is not logically related to the original purpose of the operator. For example, do not use the + operator for incrementing; use ++.
7. When selecting an operator to be overloaded, consider the precedence of the operator. Overloading does not change the operator's precedence.
8. It is a good practice to write and debug a function and then change it to an overloaded operator.
9. Be aware that a static member is shared among all objects of a class.
10. Remember that a static data member can only be initialized in the global section of the program.
11. Remember that only a class can grant friendship to a function or another class.
12. Don't forget the semicolon at the end of the structure declarations, unions, and enumerated types.
13. Remember that the members of a class are private by default whereas the member of a structure are public by default.
14. Because the member operator has a higher precedence than the indirection operator, parentheses are required to reference a member with a pointer.

```
(*ptr).mem
```

15. The selection operator (->) is one token. Do not put a space between its symbols (between – and >).

16. Use the index operator to access a member in an array of classes or structure objects. For example, the correct expression to access a member named `mem` in an array of named `ary` is

```
ary[i].mem
```

17. A union can store only one of its members at a time. You must always keep track of the available member. In other words, storing one data type in a union and accessing another data type is a logic error and may be a serious run-time error.
18. It is a compile error to initialize a union with data that do not match the type of the first member.
19. Remember that a *typedef* cannot create a new type; it only creates a new name for an existing type.

11-15 KEY TERMS

content coupling
control coupling
data coupling
enum
enumerated type
enumeration constant
explicit *inline* function
friend
friend class
friend function
global coupling
implicit inline function
initialization list
inline function
instance member
operator overloading
overloading
stamp coupling
static member
struct
structure
type definition
typedef
union

11-16 SUMMARY

- C++ contains a construct known as an inline function. In an inline function, rather than transferring control to a called function, the called function's code replaces the call in the calling function. Inline functions are used to improve the efficiency of a program.
- In a class, we can have either explicit or implicit inline functions. The explicit inline function is defined outside the class declaration. The implicit inline function is defined inside the class declaration.
- We can use the initialization list to initialize the members of a class.
- There are two parts to an initialization list: a colon that separates the function header from the initialization list and a set of member names followed by their corresponding values enclosed in parentheses. The member names are separated by commas.
- Function overloading is the definition of two or more functions with the same name but different parameter lists.
- Operator overloading is a mechanism that allows us to apply standard operators (such as +, *, and <<) to class objects. This can be done by writing operator functions and redefining the corresponding operator.
- There are five operators that cannot be overloaded: the member operator (`.`), the selection operator (`->`), the scope resolution operator (`::`), the conditional expression operator (`?:`), and the sizeof operator (`sizeof(`type`)`).

- Overloading does not change the precedence, associativity, or commutativity of the operator.
- By default a class member is an instance member.
- A static member is an instance-independent member of a class.
- There are three entities that act as static members in a class: explicit static members, enumerated types, and type defined members.
- A public static data member or function can be called using the class name and the scope resolution operator.
- An object can contain a pointer and a pointer can point to an object.
- We can have an array of objects and an object can also contain an array.
- A class can grant friendship to a function or another class.
- An enumerated type is built on the standard type, integer.
- In an enumerated type, each identifier is given an integer value.
- A structure is a construct inherited from C that is identical to a class with one exception; the members in a structure are *public* by default, the members in the class are *private* by default.
- A *union* is a construct that allows a portion of memory to be used by different types of data.
- In software engineering, coupling is the measure of how tightly two functions are bound to each other.
- Computer science has identified five types of coupling: data, stamp, control, global, and content.
- Functions in a well-structured program are loosely coupled.
- Data coupling means passing only the data needed.
- Stamp coupling means passing data in a structure.
- Control coupling means passing only control status.
- Global coupling should be avoided.
- Never use control coupling.
- Good program design can be measured by three principles: modules must be independent, modules must be loosely coupled, and each module must do a single job.

11-17 PRACTICE SETS

REVIEW QUESTIONS

1. An inline function can be called recursively.
   a. True
   b. False
2. To initialize members in a initialization list, we can use the assignment operator (=).
   a. True
   b. False
3. Overloading is the definition of a two or more classes with the same name.
   a. True
   b. False
4. Which of the following operators cannot be overloaded?
   a. Multiplication (*)
   b. Addition (+)
   c. Scope resolution (::)
   d. All can be overloaded
5. An integer value can be assigned to only one enumeration constant in an enumerated type.
   a. True
   b. False
6. A structure is used to declare a type containing multiple fields.
   a. True
   b. False
7. The selection operator is used with a pointer to access individual fields in a structure.
   a. True
   b. False
8. Which of the following is not a derived type?
   a. Arrays
   b. Float
   c. Union
   d. Enumerated
   e. Pointers

9. The ______ can be used to create a new type that can be used anywhere a type is permitted.
   a. Array
   b. Record type
   c. Structure (*struct*)
   d. Type definition
   e. Both a structure and a type definition
10. The enumerated type (*enum*) is derived from the ______ type.
   a. Character
   b. Integer
   c. Boolean
   d. Structured
   e. Floating-point
11. Which of the following statements about enumerated types is true?
   a. Declaring an enumerated type automatically creates a variable.
   b. Declaring an enumerated variable without a tag creates an enumerated type.
   c. Enumerated types cannot be used in a type definition.
   d. The enumerated values are automatically assigned constant values unless otherwise directed.
   e. The identifiers in an enumerated type are enumeration variables.
12. Given a pointer, `ptr`, to a structure, `stu`, containing a field `name`, which of the following statements correctly references `name`?
   a. `ptr.name`
   b. `ptr->name`
   c. `ptr.stu.name`
   d. `ptr->stu->name`
   e. `ptr->stu.name`
13. A(n) ______ is a construct that allows a portion of memory to be shared by different types of data.
   a. array
   b. union
   c. field
   d. variable
   e. struct

EXERCISES

14. Identify any errors in the following operator overloading:

```
void operator+  (int x, int y)
{
  ... ;
}
```

15. Given that `Fun` is the name of a class, identify any errors in the following operator overloading:

```
void Fun ::  operator?:
             (int x, int y, int z)
{
  ... ;
}
```

16. Given that `Fun` is the name of a class, identify any errors in the following operator overloading:

```
void Fun ::  operator+ (int x, int y)
{
  ... ;
}
```

17. Given that `Fun` is the name of a class, identify any errors in the following operator overloading:

```
void void operator+
           (const Fun& fun, int x)
{
  ... ;
}
```

18. Given that `Fun` is the name of a class, identify any errors in the following operator overloading:

```
Fun Fun :: operator+ (const Fun& fun,
             const Fun& fun)
{
  ... ;
}
```

19. Given that `Fun` is the name of a class, identify any errors in the following operator overloading:

```
void Fun :: operator[]
             (const Fun& fun, int x)
{
  ... ;
}
```

20. Given that `Fun` is the name of a class, identify any errors in the following operator overloading:

```
void Fun :: operator()
             (const Fun& fun, int x)
{
  ... ;
}
```

21. Given that `Fun` is the name of a class, identify any errors in the following operator overloading:

```
void Fun :: operator[]
                (const Fun& fun , int x)
{
  ... ;
}
```

22. Given that `Fun` is the name of a class, identify any errors in the following operator overloading:

```
void Fun :: operator+ ()
{
  ... ;
}
```

23. Given that `Fun` is the name of a class, identify any errors in the following operator overloading:

```
void Fun :: operator. ()
{
  ... ;
}
```

24. Given that `Fun` is the name of a class, identify any errors in the following operator overloading:

```
void Fun :: operator, ()
{
  ... ;
}
```

25. Given that `Fun` is the name of a class, what is the difference between the two overloaded operators shown below? Can they both be present in the `Fun` class?

```
void Fun :: operator+= (const Fun& fun)
{
  ... ;
}
void Fun :: operator+= (int x)
{
  ... ;
}
```

26. Assume that `x, y,` and `z` are objects defined in the same class. Also assume that the +=, +, ++, ( ), [ ], – (unary minus), <, ==, and && are overloaded. Write the equivalent of the following expressions in the functional format as described in "Using Overloaded Operators" on page 550:

   a. x += y

   b. z = x + y

   c. z++

   d. x(5)

   e. x[3]

   f. –x

   g. x < y

   h. x== y

   i. x && y

27. Assume that `x, y,` and `z` are objects defined in the same class. Also assume that the +=, +, ++, ( ), [ ], – (unary minus), <, ==, and && are overloaded. Write the equivalent of the following functions using the corresponding operators:

   a. operator&& (y, z)

   b. operator== (y, z)

   c. y.operator+= (x)

   d. z.operator++( );

   e. x.operator[ ](6)

   f. x.operator– ( )

   g. operator< (y, x)

   h. x.operator( ) (4)

   i. operator+ (y, z)

28. Declare a class for an inventory item consisting of four fields: part number (integer), reorder point (integer), number of items currently on hand (integer), and unit price (float).

29. Declare an array of 12 elements. Each element is a class object with three data members. The first member contains the month in numeric form (1 to 12). The second member contains an array of 31 floating-point numbers for the daily sales. The third member shows the number of days in the month. Code a variable for the array and initialize it in the definition. Then write one statement that uses each of the three variables.

30. Imagine we have the following declaration:

```
enum  CHOICE { ONE = 1, TWO = 2};
union U_TYPE
    {
     char choice1;
     int  choice2;
    };

struct S_TYPE
    {
     float   fixedBefore;
     CHOICE choice;
     U_TYPE flexible;
     float   fixedAfter;
    };
```

Draw a schematic diagram for S_TYPE.

31. Using the declaration of S_TYPE (declared in Exercise 30), show what will be printed from the following program segment. (Assume that the S_TYPE declaration is global.)

```
#include <iostream>
using namespace std;
int main ()
{
 S_TYPE  s;
 S_TYPE  *ps;

 s.fixedBefore = 23.34;
 s.choice = ONE;
 s.flexible.choice1 = 'B';
 s.fixedAfter = 12.45;
 ps = &s;
 cout << endl << ps->fixedAfter;
 cout << endl << ps-
 >flexible.choice1;
 cout << endl << s.fixedBefore;
 return 0;
}
```

PROBLEMS

32. Overload the -= operator for the fraction class. The operator should be a binary member function. It should return void.
33. Overload the *= operator for the fraction class. The operator should be a binary member function. It should return void.
34. Overload the /= operator for the fraction class. The operator should be a binary member function. It should return void.
35. Overload the - operator for the fraction class. The operator should be a binary *friend* function. It should return a fraction.
36. Overload the * operator for the fraction class. The operator should be a binary *friend* function. It should return a fraction.
37. Overload the / operator for the fraction class. The operator should be a binary *friend* function. It should return a fraction.
38. Overload the == operator for the fraction class. The operator should be a binary *friend* function. It should return a Boolean value.
39. Overload the < operator for the fraction class. The operator should be a binary *friend* function. It should return a Boolean value.
40. Overload the > operator for the fraction class. The operator should be a binary *friend* function. It should return a Boolean value.
41. Overload the += operator for the fraction class to add an integer to a fraction.
42. Overload the unary operator – (minus sign) to change the sign of a fraction.
43. Overload the && as the binary friend operator for the fraction class to determine if neither of the fractions is zero. It should return boolean.
44. Overload the || as the binary operator for the fraction class to determine if at least one of the fractions is not zero.
45. Overload the () operator for the fraction class to extract the integral part of a fraction. It should return an integer. For example, if the fraction is 18/5, it returns 3.
46. Overload the [] operator for the fraction class to extract the fractional part of a fraction. It should return a fraction. For example, if the fraction is 18/5, it returns 3/5.
47. Write an implicit inline function for the constructor of fraction class.
48. Write an explicit inline function for the constructor of fraction class.
49. Write an implicit inline function for the destructor of fraction class.
50. Write an explicit inline function for the destructor of fraction class.
51. Create a class called Bills. The data members of the class are a structure with six data members: the minimum number of $100, $50, $20, $10, $5, and $1 bills needed to total a dollar value. Write a constructor that accepts an amount in dollars, and stores the bill values and a print function can prints the value of the dollar members.

PROJECTS

52. Redesign the time class created in Chapter 10 on page 526 using the following overloaded operators:
    - **a.** Use ++ for increment.
    - **b.** Use the == operator for comparison.
53. Redesign the Complex class created in Chapter 10 (Project 41 on page 540) using overloaded operators. Use +=, -+, *=, /=, +, -, *, /.

54. Redesign the `Set` class created in Chapter 10 (Project 42 on page 540) using the following overloaded operators:

   a. Use += to add an element to the set.

   b. Use –= to remove an element from the set.

   c. Use the && operator for intersection.

   d. Use the || operator for union.

   e. Use the – for difference.

   f. Use the [ ] operator to check if an integer is in the set.

55. Write a program to keep records and perform statistical analysis for a class of students. For each student you will have a four-digit ID, four quizzes, and one examination. The student data are to be stored in an array of student structures. Provide for up to 50 students.

   The input is read from a text file. Each line in the file contains a student ID; four quiz scores, and one examination score, in order. If a quiz or examination was not taken, the score is 0. The student ID, the quiz scores, and the examination score are all separated from each other by one or more spaces. A newline ends the data for one student. The number of lines in this file is the same as the number of students.

   The output consists of a listing of the students in the order they are read from the file—no sorting is required. Print each student on a separate line with an appropriate caption for each column. After the last student, print the highest, lowest, and average score for each quiz and the examination. In determining the lowest score, do not consider 0 scores. A suggested report layout is shown in Figure 11-13.

DATA

ID	Quiz 1	Quiz 2	Quiz 3	Quiz 4	Exam
1234	23	19	22	23	89
4321	0	23	21	18	76
1717	21	22	18	19	91

STATISTICS

	23	25	23	25	96
	17	15	12	18	53
	21.3	20.1	19.8	21.1	81.3

Figure 11-13 Sample output for Project 55

The data for the project are shown in Table 11-2.

ID	Quiz 1	Quiz 2	Quiz 3	Quiz 4	Exam
1234	052	007	100	078	034
2134	090	036	090	077	030
3124	100	045	020	090	070
4532	011	017	081	032	077
5678	020	012	045	078	034
6134	034	080	055	078	045
7874	060	100	056	078	078
8026	070	010	066	078	056
9893	034	009	077	078	020
1947	045	040	088	078	055
2877	055	050	099	078	080
3189	082	080	100	078	077
4602	089	050	091	078	060
5405	011	011	000	078	010
6999	000	098	089	078	020

Table 11-2 Data for Project 55

56. Rework Project 55 to report the average quiz score, total quizzes score, and total score for each student. Then assign a grade based on an absolute scale of 90% for A, 80% for B, 70% for C, and 60% for D. Any score below 60% is an F. There are 500 total points available. Print the student data to the right of the input data. At the end of the report, print the number of students who earned each grade, A to F.

57. Write a program that uses an array of student objects to answer inquiries. Using a menu-driven user interface, provide inquiries that report a student's scores, average, or grade based on an absolute scale (90% A, 80% B, etc.). A fourth menu option provides all data for a requested student. To create the array, load the data from Project 55.

58. Using a sort of your choice, modify Project 55 to sort the data on `Student ID`.

12 Inheritance and Aggregation

Chapters 10 and 11 provided you with a basic understanding of classes; now we look at relationships between classes. We begin with a discussion of inheritance, which is a powerful capability in C++. In discussing inheritance, we use two simple examples to demonstrate the capabilities and construction of derived classes to extend the capabilities of an existing class. Included in our discussion of inheritance are the concepts of abstract classes, polymorphism, and dynamic binding. The chapter concludes with a discussion of aggregation, which includes other class objects as data members.

12-1 INHERITANCE

What really makes classes powerful, as we will discuss in this section, is the ability to extend a class so that it creates a new class while at the same time retaining the basic characteristics of the original. This concept of extending a class is known as **inheritance**. To carry the concept even further, a derived class not only has all of the capabilities of the original class, but it may also take on new attributes and methods of its own. Thus, the derived class becomes more powerful than the original.

Inheritance is an *is-a* relation. A derived class *is-a* base class with more detail added. Inheritance allows us to define a hierarchy of classes in which each layer defines an object with more details.

BASIC CONCEPTS

To set the stage for the discussions that follow, let's look at a simple example. At the same time, we will use the example to define the terminology commonly used when referring to inherited objects.

We are all familiar with polygons: two-dimensional objects that can have three or more sides. Simple examples of polygons are the triangle, square, and rectangle.

Every polygon has two basic attributes: area and perimeter. The area of a polygon is a measure of the space within the borders of the polygon; its perimeter is the sum of all of its sides. Figure 12-1 shows three simple polygons.

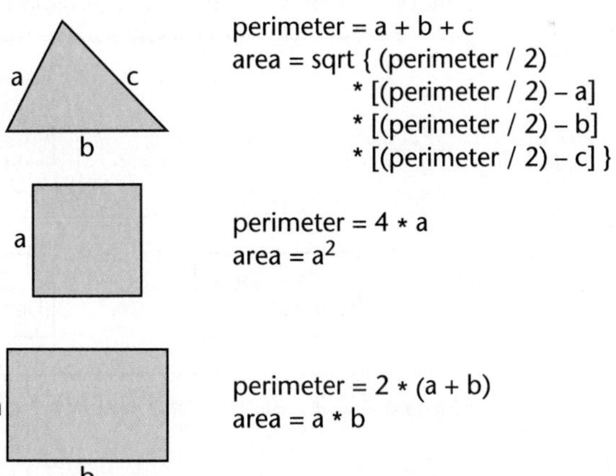

Figure 12-1 Simple polygons

With this information, we are ready to create a polygon class. It needs two attributes: area and perimeter. It also needs two methods. In addition to constructors and destructors, it needs functions to print the area and the perimeter. The polygon class is shown in Program 12-1.

Program 12-1 Declaration for the polygon class

```
class Polygons
{
  protected:
      double area;
```

Program 12-1 Declaration for the polygon class (*continued*)

```
      double perimeter;

      void printArea () const;
      void printPeri () const;
}; // Class Polygons
```

Program 12-1 Analysis So that `area` and `perimeter` are available when they are inherited, they need to be in an inheritance type known as *protected*. We explain inheritance types in the next section.

Base and Derived Classes

Our polygon class is known as a **base class** because it contains all of the common attributes and functions that form the basis for the derivation of other classes. Even though polygons all have areas and perimeters, however, each different type of polygon uses different calculations to determine these values. For example, the calculation for the area of a triangle is different from the calculation for the area of a rectangle. What we need, therefore, is to define new classes for the different polygons. Each of these new classes is known as a **derived class** because it has access to the attributes and functions in the base class while having its own attributes and functions to process data.

For example, we declare a derived class, triangle, that needs three sides as attributes and two functions, one to calculate the area and one to calculate the perimeter. The relationship between the base class and its derived classes is shown in Figure 12-2.

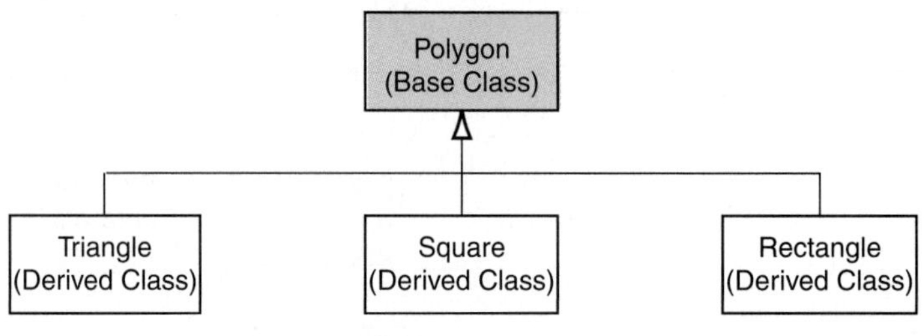

Figure 12-2 Base and derived classes

In our polygon example, each derived class has only one base class. This situation is known as **simple inheritance**. It is also possible for a derived class to inherit data and functions from multiple classes, in which case it is known as **multiple inheritance**. Multiple inheritance is discussed later in the chapter. The code for triangle, square, and rectangle is given in Program 12-2. Note that the base class is related to the derived class through the derived-class operator (`:`) in the derived-class header.

Program 12-2 Derived polygon classes

```
class Triangle : public Polygons
{
   private:
      double sideA;
      double sideB;
      double sideC;
```

Program 12-2 Derived polygon classes (*continued*)

```
7
8          void calcArea ();
9          void calcPeri ();
10   }; // Class Triangle
11   class Square : public Polygons
12   {
13      private:
14          double side;
15
16          void calcArea ();
17          void calcPeri ();
18   }; // Class Square
19   class Rectangle : public Polygons
20   {
21      private:
22          double sideA;
23          double sideB;
24
25          void calcArea ();
26          void calcPeri ();
27   }; // Class Rectangle
```

Inheritance Syntax

Let's look at the derived class declaration carefully. To declare a derived class, we specify the keyword *class* followed by the class name. This is the standard syntax to create a new class. To relate it to the base class and make it a derived class, we use a colon (:) followed by the inheritance type and the name of the base class. The inheritance type can be *public*, *protected*, or *private*. We discuss the meaning of the different classes in the next section. The syntactical format for a derived class is shown below. Three examples of this format appear in Program 12-2 (statements 1, 11, and 19).

```
class derivedClassID : inheritance_type baseClassID
```

Once a derived class has been declared, it is a known type that can be used whenever it is in scope. Thus, to define an instance of our polygon objects, we would use the following code:

```
Triangle      triangle;
Square        square;
Rectangle     rectangle;
```

Inheritance Rules

Because the derived classes can access the data and methods in the base class, they are said to have inherited them. A copy of the base class object is created (inherited) and then extended with the new object elements required by the derived class. Figure 12-3 shows the inheritance for our triangle and rectangle examples.

As you study Figure 12-3, look for examples of the following inheritance rules:

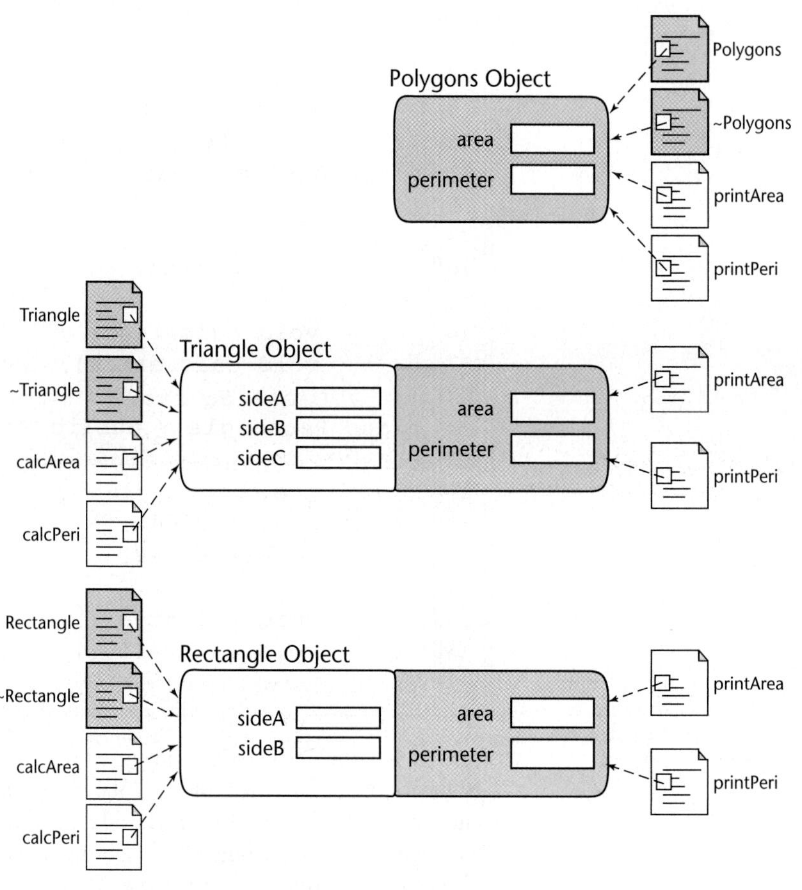

Figure 12-3 Inheritance

1. All data members of the base object are inherited.
2. All function members of the base object are inherited, except:
   a. Constructors
   b. Destructors
   c. Nonmember functions
   d. Assignment operator
   e. Virtual methods (discussed later)

In Figure 12-3, we see that both the `area` and `perimeter` are inherited. This follows rule 1. When we examine the function prototypes, however, we see that only the two print functions are inherited; the constructor and destructor are not. This follows rule 2. There are no friend functions or assignment operators, so these are not shown.

Constructors, destructors, nonmember functions, assignment operators, and virtual methods are not inherited in a derived class. If needed, they must be created.

12-2 PRIVATE, PROTECTED, PUBLIC

To protect data and functions in a class when it is used with inheritance, they must be given an inheritance classification. In this section, we explain how these three inheritance types work.

> **The combination of the base class access type and the inheritance type determines if and how the base class data and functions can be accessed by the derived class.**

To see how the base class access is combined with the inheritance access types, refer to Table 12-1.

Inheritance type	Base access type	Derived access type
private	private	inherited but inaccessible
	protected	private
	public	private
protected	private	inherited but inaccessible
	protected	protected
	public	protected
public	private	inherited but inaccessible
	protected	protected
	public	public

Table 12-1 Inherited access rules

PRIVATE INHERITANCE TYPE

When the inheritance is **private**, the access to inherited data and methods is highly limited. The *private* data and methods in the base class are inaccessible in the derived class. However, the derived class can use public methods of the base class to access them if necessary. The *protected* and *public* data and methods become *private*.

By extension, a second level of *private* inheritance would make all members of the original class inaccessible because they would be *private* after the first inheritance. In effect, this prevents classes using *private* inheritance from being inherited more than once.

Private is the default inheritance type. Therefore, to make the triangle class private, we can either omit the inheritance type or explicitly code it as private. We prefer the latter approach as shown below.

```
class Triangle : private Polygons
{
 …
}; // Triangle
```

PROTECTED INHERITANCE TYPE

When the inheritance is ***protected***, the access to inherited data and methods is again limited. The *private* data and methods in the base class become inaccessible. The *protected* and *public* members become protected. To make the inheritance protected in our triangle class, we would use the code shown in the next example.

```
class Triangle : protected Polygons
{
 ...
}; // Triangle
```

PUBLIC INHERITANCE TYPE

When inheritance is ***public***, the access to inherited data and methods is less limited than the two previous situations. The data and methods that have *private* access in the base class are still inaccessible in the derived class. However, the access of the *protected* and *public* members is preserved; the *protected* access remains protected and the *public* access remains public. To make the inheritance *public* in our triangle class, we would use the code shown in the next example.

```
class Triangle : public Polygons
{
 ...
}; // Triangle
```

INHERITANCE EXAMPLE

In Figure 12-4, we have four classes, a base class, Fruit, and three derived classes, Apple, Banana, and Orange. The three derived types inherit from Fruit. Given the access types class Fruit, we can determine the access types in Apple, Banana, and Orange.

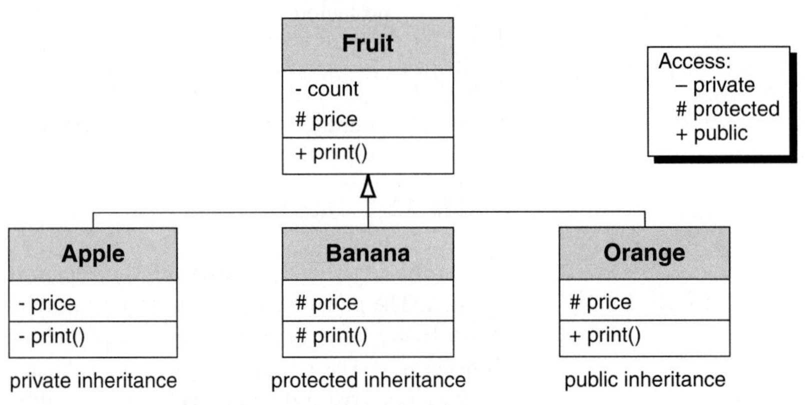

Figure 12-4 Inheritance example

POLYGON-TRIANGLE IMPLEMENTATION

Now let's write a program that uses inheritance. To demonstrate the concept, we first develop the polygon class and the triangle class. Then we write a short implementation to demonstrate their operation.

The Polygon Base Class

The polygon base class is very simple. It defines the two class variable members and uses only default constructors and destructors; and there are only two functions: `printArea` and `printPeri`. Program 12-3 gives the code.

Program 12-3 Implement triangle class

```
class Polygons
{
   protected:
      double area;
```

Program 12-3 Implement triangle class *(continued)*

```
      double perimeter;
   public:
         Polygons   () {};
        ~Polygons   () {};
   void printArea () const;
   void printPeri () const;
}; // Class Polygons

/* ============== Polygons :: printArea ==============
   Prints the area of a polygon.
      Pre   area calculated & stored in area
      Post  area printed
*/
void Polygons :: printArea () const
{
   cout << "The area of your polygon is "
        << area << endl;
   return;
}  // Polygons printArea
/* =============== Polygons :: printPeri =============
   Prints the perimeter of a polygon.
      Pre   polygon perimeter calculated and stored
      Post  perimeter printed
*/
void Polygons :: printPeri () const
{
   cout << "The perimeter of your polygon is "
        << perimeter << endl;
   return;
}//Polygons printPeri
```

The Triangle Class

Now that we have built the base class, we are ready to define the triangle derived class. While both classes would ordinarily be put into the same header file, we show them separately.

The triangle class inherits the polygon base class's data variables and its two print functions. In addition to the members found in the polygon class, the triangle has three side data members and two *private* methods. Additionally, we overload the constructor to verify that the sides are valid. To be a valid, the sum of any two sides must be greater than the third. If they are not, we abort the program.[1]

---

[1]In Chapter 15, we learn how to pass the error back to the calling function. For now, we *exit* the program.

The triangle class definition is shown in Program 12-4.

Program 12-4 ***Triangle*** **class definition**

```
class Triangle : public Polygons
{
   private:
       double sideA;
       double sideB;
       double sideC;

       void calcArea ();
       void halfPeri ();

   public:
       // initialization constructor
       Triangle (double sideAIn, double sideBIn,
                 double sideCIn);
}; // Class Triangle
/* ============ Triangle :: Triangle =============
   Initialization constructor for triangle class.
   Stores sides. Calculates area and perimeter.
       Pre   Given sideA, sideB, and sideC
       Post  data stored; area & perimeter calculated
*/
Triangle :: Triangle (double sideAIn,
                      double sideBIn,
                      double sideCIn)
{
   // Verify sides are valid
   if  ( ((sideAIn + sideBIn) <= sideCIn)
     ||  ((sideBIn + sideCIn) <= sideAIn)
     ||  ((sideCIn + sideAIn) <= sideBIn) )
       {
        cout << "Invalid Triangle\n";
        exit (100);
       } // if
   // Valid Triangle
   sideA = sideAIn;
   sideB = sideBIn;
   sideC = sideCIn;

   halfPeri();
   calcArea();
   return ;
} // Triangle initialization constructor
/* ============= Triangle :: calcArea ============
   Calculates triangle area & stores in base class area.
      Pre  sideA, sideB, sideC, & perimeter available
      Post  area calculated and stored
*/
```

Program 12-4 *Triangle* class definition *(continued)*

```
void Triangle :: calcArea ()
{
   double halfPeri = perimeter / 2;
   area = (  halfPeri
          * (halfPeri - sideA)
          * (halfPeri - sideB)
          * (halfPeri - sideC) );
   area = sqrt(area);
   return;
} // Triangle calcArea
/* ============= Triangle :: halfPeri ============
   Calculates perimeter & stores in base class area.
      Pre   sideA, sideB, & sideC available
      Post  perimeter calculated and stored
*/
void Triangle :: halfPeri ()
{
   perimeter = sideA + sideB + sideC;
   return;
} // Triangle halfPeri
```

Program 12-4 Analysis It is important to understand what needs to be done in a derived class and what doesn't need to be done. First, we have to provide any necessary constructors and destructors because they can't be inherited. For triangle, we need only the initialization constructor.

The functions to calculate the perimeter and area of the polygon are not provided in the base class. Therefore, we must write them for each derived class. Conversely, the base class does provide the functions to print the perimeter and area of the polygon, so we don't have to write them. They are inherited.

In the constructor, we calculate the perimeter before we calculate the area because the calculation of the area requires that we know the perimeter. While we could recalculate the perimeter when we calculate the area, this would not be efficient programming.

Polygon Implementation

Now that we have created a polygon class and a derived triangle class, let's put them in a simple program. In this program, we assume that the polygon class has been defined in a header file that we include. The code is shown in Program 12-5.

Program 12-5 A polygon–triangle implementation

```
/* Demonstrate use of inheritance.
      Written by:
      Date:
*/
#include <iostream>
#include <cmath>
#include <cstdlib>
using namespace std;
#include "p12-03.h"                          // Polygon class
```

Program 12-5 A polygon–triangle implementation *(continued)*

```
10 #include "p12-04.h"                          // Triangle class
11
12 int main ()
13 {
14    cout << "Start Polygon Demonstration\n\n";
15    Triangle tri (3, 4, 5);
16    tri.printPeri();
17    tri.printArea();
18    cout << "\nEnd Polygon Demonstration\n";
19    return 0 ;
20 } // main
```

```
Results
Start Polygon Demonstration

The perimeter of your polygon is 12
The area of your polygon is 6

End Polygon Demonstration
```

Program 12-5 Analysis As is typical with class objects, most of the work is done in the classes themselves. When we define the triangle (statement 15), we pass to it the triangle's side lengths. These data are then stored in the triangle derived class by the constructor. Once the data have been stored, the constructor then calls the functions to calculate and store the perimeter and area of the triangle. All of this work is done in the class itself, however, and all that our program sees is that we define a triangle and then print its area and perimeter.

To test for an invalid triangle, try sides 2, 3, and 6.

OVERRIDING INHERITED ACCESS SPECIFIERS

There are situations in which we need to **override** the default access types that we inherit from a class. For example, consider the two classes in Figure 12-5.

```
class B
{
   protected:
      int datum;
   public:
      void print();
      ...
}; // B
```

```
class D : private B
{
   protected:
      using B :: datum;


      ...
}; // D
```

Figure 12-5 Class and structure declarations

Because of the inheritance rules, `datum` and `print` are inherited as *private*. If we want to inherit `datum` as *protected*, we can override it with a *using* statement and the scope resolution operator as shown in the next example.

```
protected:
   using B :: datum;
```

12-3 MANAGER FUNCTIONS UNDER INHERITANCE

As we mentioned before, the constructor and destructor manager functions are not inherited in the derived class. We need to define these functions. This presents some issues that we discuss in this section.

CONSTRUCTORS

A derived object is made up of two parts: the part inherited from the base class and the new members that extend the base class. While constructors are not inherited, C++ requires that a base class constructor be called, either implicitly by the system or explicitly by us. This means that a derived class constructor must have code to call the base class constructor first, and then whatever code is needed to initialize the derived class members. The base class constructor must be called in the initialization list of the derived class constructor as shown in the following example.

```
Derived :: Derived (parameters) : BaseClass (parameters)
{
   ...
} // Derived Class
```

Given that constructors can be default or initialization, there are four possible cases: default derived and base class constructors, derived initialization constructor and default base constructor, base class initialization with default derived constructor, or base class and derived class initialization.

Default Derived and Base Class Constructors

This case occurs when both the derived and base class constructors are defaulted, that is, created by the system. We do not need to do anything here. However, it is sometimes necessary to write an explicit default constructor.

Derived Initialization Constructor and Default Base Constructor

Because the base class constructor is a default constructor, it is called implicitly. We don't need to do anything. The triangle class is an example of this case. Because the polygon class uses a default constructor, we didn't need to include it in header for the derived constructor. The system implicitly generates a call to the base class. (See Program 12-4, statement 22, on page 604.)

Note that the base class constructor is called first. After the base class constructor has been executed, the code in the derived class constructor is executed.

Base Class Initialization with Default Derived Constructor

This is the first case that requires an explicit call to the base class constructor through the initialization list. We must code the default constructor and pass the required data in the initialization list. This case is more of a theoretical situation; while it may occur, it is rare. The next example demonstrates this case.

```
Derived :: Derived   (parameters)
         : BaseClass (baseclass parameters)
{
   ...
} // Derived
```

In this example, an argument is required by the base class. When an object of the derived class is initialized, the argument list is passed to the derived class and it is then passed to the base class.

Base Class and Derived Class Initialization

When both classes require initialization, the base class is initialized first, then the derived class. Program 12-6 contains an example of this case in statements 43 and 73. The basic format is shown in the next example.

```
Derived::Derived (parameters):Base(baseclass parameters)
{
   ...                            // Derived Part Initialization
} // Derived
```

COPY CONSTRUCTORS

The same situation exists for the copy constructor. We need to ensure that when we use a copy constructor for the derived class, the copy constructor for the base class is called. That is, the base class constructor must be explicitly called by us or implicitly called by the system. The format is shown in the next example.

```
Derived :: Derived (const Derived& derivedObject)
                   : BaseClass (derivedObject)
{
   ...
} // Derived
```

Again, we can have four different situations. They exactly parallel the analysis for the default constructors and are not repeated here.

DESTRUCTORS

While constructors must ensure that the base case is executed before the derived case, the opposite is true for destructors. With a little thought, it is apparent that this is logical. Consider the analogy of building a house. First the foundation (base class) is built. Then the house (derived case) is constructed on the foundation. When we destroy the house, we must first raze the house, then dig up the foundation.

Fortunately, this is not a problem. Because there is only one destructor for a class, we simply write the derived class to take care of its cleanup. Then, when our destructor is done, the system automatically calls the base destructor so that it can do its work.

EMPLOYEE CLASS EXAMPLE

Now let's write a more realistic, although still simple, example. In the employee program that follows, we have three classes. The employee base class has all of the data that apply to all employees, in this simplified example only the employee ID. A derived salary class then has the data that pertain only to salaried employees, while a derived hourly class contains data that apply only to hourly employees. The design of the classes is shown in Figure 12-6.

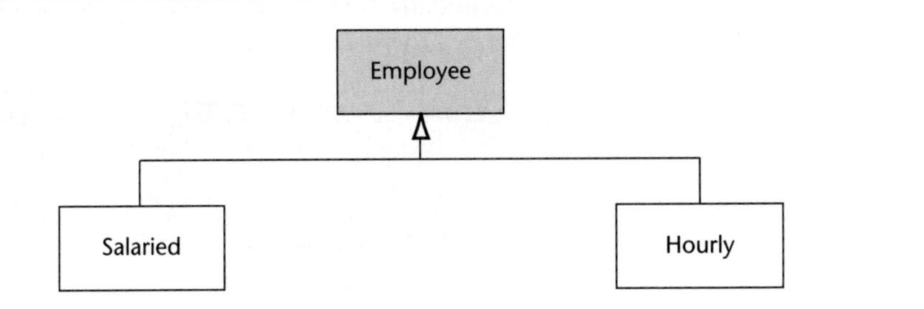

Figure 12-6 Employee class design

When a derived class constructor is executed, it must first execute the constructor for the base class. This is logical. Some of the data that are established when the derived class is created belong in the base class and some of them belong in the derived class. Because the derived class may need to use the base class data even in its constructor, these data must be in place before the derived class is constructed. To pass data from a derived class to the base class, we use the explicit base class initialization through a base-member initialization list. The employee class definitions are shown in Program 12-6.

Program 12-6 Employee class definitions

```
/* Demonstrate use of inherited constructors.
      Written by:
      Date:
*/
// Class Declarations
class Employee
{
   protected:
      int id;

   public:
       Employee (int idIn);
      ~Employee ();
}; // Employee

// ============= Employee constructor ==============
   Employee :: Employee (int idIn)
{
   id = idIn;
   cout << "Base constr for Employee : "
        << idIn << endl;

}  // Employee constructor
// ============== Employee destructor ===============
Employee :: ~Employee ()
{
   cout << "Base destr  for Employee : "
        << id << endl;
}  // Employee Destructor

// ================ SalaryEmp Class =================
class SalaryEmp : public Employee
{
   private:
      int  salary;

   public:
       SalaryEmp (int idIn, int   salaryIn);
      ~SalaryEmp ();
}; // SalaryEmp
```

Program 12-6 Employee class definitions *(continued)*

```
// ============= SalaryEmp constructor ==============
SalaryEmp :: SalaryEmp (int idIn, int salaryIn)
             : Employee (idIn)
{
   salary = salaryIn;
   cout << "Derv constr for SalaryEmp: "
        << id << " Salary: " << salary << endl;
} // SalaryEmp constructor

// ============= SalaryEmp destructor ==============
SalaryEmp :: ~SalaryEmp ()
{
   cout << "Derv destr  for SalaryEmp: "
        << id << endl;
} // SalaryEmp destructor

// =============== HourlyEmp Class ==================
class HourlyEmp : public Employee
{
   private:
      float  payRate;
      float  hours;

   public:
       HourlyEmp (int   idIn,
                  float payRateIn, float hoursIn);
      ~HourlyEmp ();
}; // HourlyEmp Class

// ============= HourlyEmp constructor ==============
HourlyEmp :: HourlyEmp (int idIn,
                      float payRateIn, float hoursIn)
             : Employee (idIn)
{
   payRate = payRateIn;                      //Derived data
   hours   = hoursIn;
   cout << "Derv destr for HourlyEmp: "
        << id           << " Pay Rate: " << payRate
        << " Hours: " << hours         << endl;
} // HourlyEmp constructor

// ============= HourlyEmp destructor ==============
HourlyEmp :: ~HourlyEmp ()
{
   cout << "Derv destr for HourlyEmp: "
        << id << endl;
} // HourlyEmp destructor
// ============== End Employee classes ============
```

Program 12-6 Analysis To demonstrate that the constructors and destructors are working correctly, we have included print statements in their functions. These statements would not be part of the production coding, however. To make the employee id number accessible in the derived classes, we also had to make it protected in the base class.

As you may have noticed, these classes have no mutator or accessor functions because we use them just to show the order the constructors and destructors are called. We would need to add many other functions to make the class usable.

EMPLOYEE CLASS PROGRAM

To demonstrate how the base and derived class initiators and destructors work, we use the employee class in a simple program. This program contains one salaried and one hourly employee definition. As the class objects are created and destroyed, we print out a message (see Program 12-6). The output from the program is shown at the end of Program 12-7.

Program 12-7 Run employee demonstration

```
/* Demonstrate use of inherited constructors with a
   base-member initialization list.
      Written by:
      Date:

*/
#include <iostream>
using namespace std;

#include "p12-09.h"

int main ()
{
   SalaryEmp  slryEmp (1234, 43000);
   HourlyEmp  hrlyEmp (5678, 15.76, 40);

   return 0 ;
} // main
```

```
Results
Base constr for Employee : 1234
Derv constr for SalaryEmp: 1234 Salary: 43000
Base constr for Employee : 5678
Derv constr for HourlyEmp: 5678 Pay Rate: 15.76 Hours: 40
Derv destr  for HourlyEmp: 5678
Base destr  for Employee : 5678
Derv destr  for SalaryEmp: 1234
Base destr  for Employee : 1234
```

Program 12-7 Analysis The first thing you may have noticed about this program is that *main* contains only class definitions; there is no application code. Because we are interested only in demonstrating the constructor and destructor execution sequences, we do not include any application code.

So, where does all of the output come from? To answer this question, remember what happens when we create a class object. The very definition of the class objects create the first four lines of output. As each constructor is executed in turn, it displays a message. This clearly shows that the base class constructors are executed first, followed by the derived class constructors.

The last four lines come from the program termination. As the program terminates, the object destructors are executed. In this case, the destructors are executed in reverse order: The derived class destructors are executed first and the base class destructors are executed last.

12-4 OVERRIDING MEMBER FUNCTIONS

A derived class inherits all the member variables and member functions from the base class. However, sometimes a derived class needs to change the implementation (code) of a member function without changing the parameter list. This can be done by redefining the member function in the derived class. To redefine a member function, we redeclare it in the derived class and then rewrite the function. In this case, the function is **overridden** in the derived class.

OVERRIDDEN METHOD EXAMPLE

Let's write a simple class to demonstrate the concept. In this example, the derived class needs to print data in the base class as well as its own data.

The base class contains one integer and one function that prints the member data. When we print from the base class, the print function identifies itself as belonging to the base class. In the derived class, we rewrite the print function and include a message that identifies itself as the derived print class.

In the derived class, we need to print the base class's member data (`datum`). However, because it is *private*, it is inaccessible in the derived class. This means that we cannot directly print its value. But, we can use the base class print function because it is *public*. To print both data values, we use the following code.

```
void Derived :: print () const
{
  Base::print( );                  // Print Base class data
  cout << "Datum in Derived Class is: "
       << derivedDatum << endl;
} // Derived:: print
```

The print function in the derived class has the same name and definition as the base class; both have no return value and their parameter lists are *void*. This makes it an overridden function.

When we override a function in the derived class, the function in the base class is not lost; we can still access it using the derived class object. For example, we can still access the print function in the above example if we use the scope resolution operator.

```
Derived dObject;
dObject.Base :: print();
```

We demonstrate these overriding function concepts in Program 12-8.

Program 12-8 Overridden print function

```
/* Demonstrate overridden function.
      Written by:
      Date:
*/
#include <iostream>
using namespace std;

class BaseClass
{
   private:
      int datum;

   public:
           BaseClass  (int datumIn);
      void print      () const;
}; // BaseClass
// ============= BaseClass :: Baseclass =============
BaseClass :: BaseClass (int datumIn)
{
   datum = datumIn;
} // BaseClass constructor
/* ============== BaseClass :: print ================
   Base class print function.
      Pre  Nothing
      Post Data in base class printed
*/
void BaseClass :: print () const
{
// Statements
   cout << "**Datum in Base Class is:   " << datum << endl;
   return;
} // BaseClass :: print
// ================= Derived Class =================
class Derived : public BaseClass
{
   private:
      int derivedDatum;

   public:
           Derived (int baseDatum, int datumIn);
      void print   () const;
}; // Derived
// ============== Derived :: Derived ===============
Derived :: Derived (int baseDatum, int datumIn)
        : BaseClass (baseDatum)    // Call base constr
{
   derivedDatum = datumIn;
} // Drived constructor
```

Program 12-8 Overridden print function (*continued*)

```
49 /* ================ Derived :: print ================
50    Derived class print function.
51       Pre  Nothing
52       Post Data in derived class printed
53 */
54 void Derived :: print () const
55 {
56    BaseClass::print( );         // Print inherited data
57    cout << "**Datum in Derived Class is: "
58         << derivedDatum << endl;
59    return;
60 } // Derived:: print
61
62 int main ()
63 {
64    BaseClass baseObj (1);
65    Derived   derObj  (12, 13);
66
67    cout << "Using print in base class: \n";
68    baseObj.print ();
69
70    cout << "\nUsing print in derived class: \n";
71    derObj.print  ();
72
73    return 0 ;
74 } // main
```

```
Results:
Using print in base class:
**Datum in Base Class is:    1

Using print in derived class:
**Datum in Base Class is:    12
**Datum in Derived Class is: 13
```

Program 12-8 Analysis There are two functions that need to be studied carefully. First, look at the code in the derived class constructor starting at statement 44. Note that it receives two pieces of data: one for the base class and one for the derived class. To pass the data to the derived class, we call its constructor in the initialization list and pass it `baseDatum`. The derived class data is initialized in statement 47.

Now study the derived class print function carefully. Note that in statement 56, we explicitly call the base class print function, which prints the data in the base class. We then print the data in the derived class. This proves that both functions are accessible and executable.

OVERRIDING VERSUS OVERLOADING

Overriding is different from overloading. In overloading, two functions have the same name but different parameter lists. In overriding, the functions have the same name and the same parameter list.

12-5 POLYMORPHISM

Polymorphism is such a powerful feature of object-oriented programming that we need to spend some time on the subject even in an introductory course. Polymorphism[2] is the ability to write several versions of a function, each in a separate class. Then, when we call it, the function appropriate for the object being referenced is executed.

We use the same concept in our everyday language. We use one verb (function) to mean different things. For example, we say "open" meaning to open a door, a jar, or a book; which one is determined by the context. Similarly, in C++, we can call `printArea` to print the area of a triangle or the area of the rectangle.

For polymorphism to work, we need three conditions. First, we need to have a hierarchy of inherited classes. Second, the functions need to be virtual. And third, we need to use pointers or references to objects. Polymorphism needs all three: inheritance, **virtual functions**, and pointers or references. We explore these conditions one by one. Before we discuss them, however, we need to talk about a related issue, static versus dynamic binding.

STATIC BINDING

Assume that we have a base class named appropriately, `BaseClass`, and a derived class named `DervClass` that is inherited from `BaseClass`. Each contains a print function.

In *main*, we create a pointer to the base class and call it `objPtr`. We then allocate memory for a base class object using *new* and store the address in the object pointer. After calling the print function, we create another object, this time of derived class type, and store it in the same pointer. Note that the pointer is defined as a base type, but the allocation is for a derived class. The results are shown in Program 12-9.

Program 12-9 Demonstrate static binding problem

```
/* Demonstrate Static Binding
      Written by:
      Date:
*/
#include <iostream>
using namespace std;

class BaseClass
{
   public:
   void print() const {cout << "Base class object\n";}
}; // BaseClass

class DervClass: public BaseClass
{
   public:
   void print() const {cout << "Derived class object\n";}
}; // DervClass
```

[2]Literally, *many forms*.

Program 12-9 Demonstrate static binding problem (*continued*)

```

int main ()
{
   BaseClass* objPtr = new BaseClass ();
   objPtr->print ();
   delete objPtr;                               // Release memory

   objPtr = new DervClass ();                  // Reallocate object
   objPtr->print ();
   return 0;
} // main
```

```
Results
Base class object
Base class object
```

When we run the program, we see that the message "Base class object" is printed two times although the second assignment points to an object of type `DervClass`. The reason is that the complier *statically* resolves the question of which function to call. When we create a pointer of type `BaseClass`, no matter what object we point it to, the compiler calls the function associated with the pointer type, BaseClass. This is called **static binding**. The function is bound to the pointer at compile time, although the object to which it points, which is dynamically allocated by the *new* operator, is created during run time. This situation is shown in Figure 12-7.

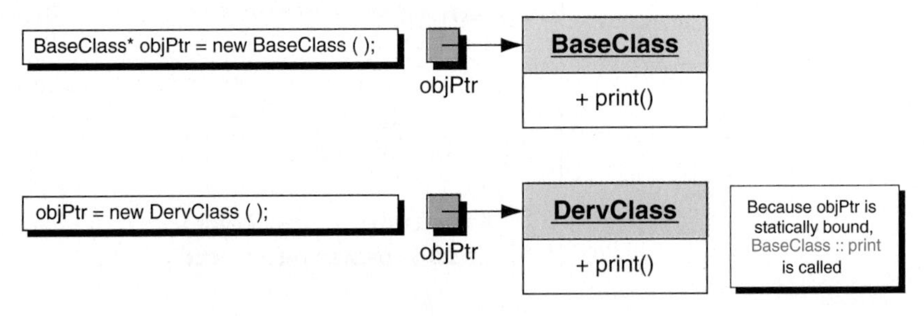

Figure 12-7 Static function binding

DYNAMIC BINDING AND VIRTUAL FUNCTIONS

The solution to this problem is to use dynamic binding. In **dynamic**, or **late**, **binding**, the pointer is not associated with the object until the program is run. In other words, we tell the compiler to delay binding until the program is run.

To create dynamic binding we use virtual functions. A virtual function tells the compiler to bind a function with an object during the run time, not with the pointer defined during compilation time. Program 12-10 changes the print functions in Program 12-9 to virtual.

Program 12-10 uses polymorphism. We called the print function two times. The first time it prints the base-class message. The second time, it prints the derived-class message. Figure 12-8 shows this concept.

Program 12-10 Demonstrate dynamic binding solution

```
/* Demonstrate dynamic binding
      Written by:
      Date:
*/
#include <iostream>
using namespace std;

class BaseClass
{
   public:
      virtual void print() const
                   {cout << "Base class object\n";}
}; // BaseClass

class DervClass: public BaseClass
{
   public:
      virtual void print() const
                  {cout << "Derived class object\n";}
}; // DervClass

int main ()
{
   BaseClass* objPtr = new BaseClass ();
   objPtr->print ();
   delete objPtr;                        // Release memory

   objPtr = new DervClass ();
   objPtr->print ();
   return 0;
} // main
```

```
Results
Base class object
Derived class object
```

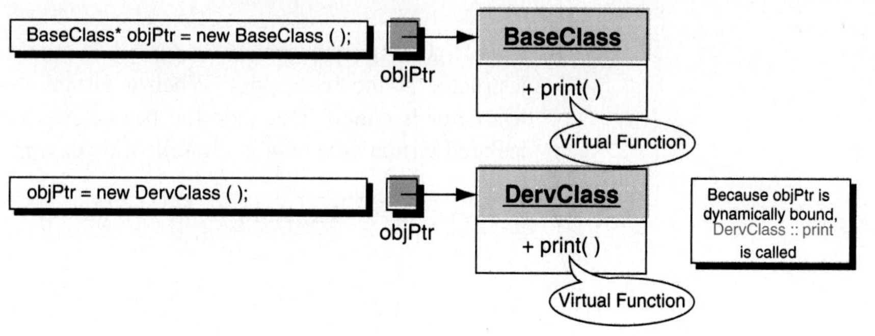

Figure 12-8 Dynamic binding through polymorphism

Virtual Destructors

Recall that a virtual function is redefined with the same name in the base and derived class. Because the constructors and destructors have different names in the base and derived class—the names of the constructor and destructor are the name of the class—it appears that we cannot use virtual constructors and destructors. This is partially true; we cannot have virtual constructors. On the other hand, we can create virtual destructors.

The primary use of a **virtual destructor** is to ensure that dynamic memory allocated in a derived class is properly deleted when the object is destroyed. For example, if we dynamically allocate memory for base class members and for derived class members, we need to ensure that a derived class destructor is available and is called first when a derived object is destroyed.

To visualize the problem, consider the example of a base class that dynamically allocates an array of integers. Its derived class allocates a dynamic array of floating-point numbers. When the base class pointer is used to point to a derived class object, it can see only the base class members. When the object is deleted, only the base class array is deleted, resulting in a memory leak for the derived class. This example is diagrammed in Figure 12-9. The problem is corrected by forcing polymorphism through a virtual destructor.

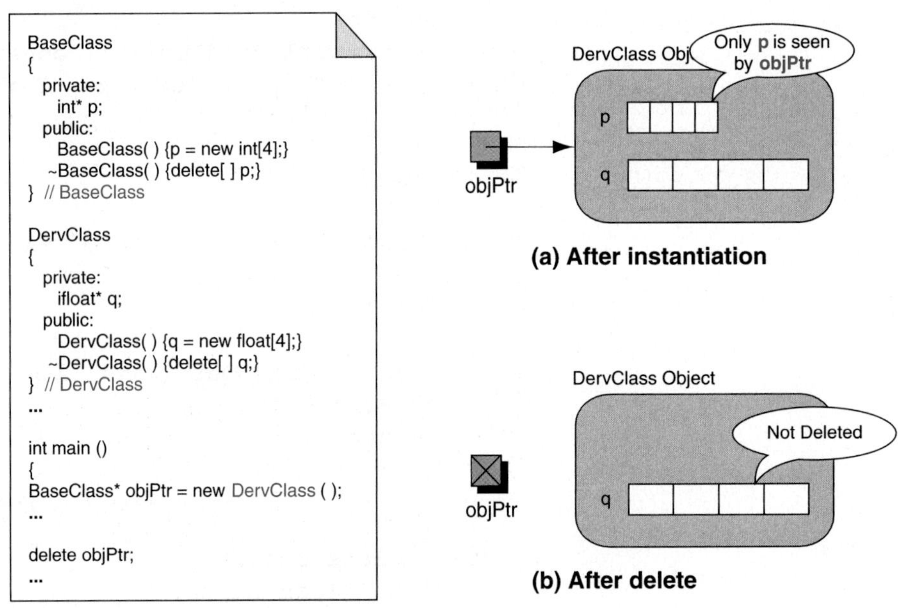
BaseClass
{
private:
int* p;
public:
BaseClass( ) {p = new int[4];}
~BaseClass( ) {delete[ ] p;}
} // BaseClass
DervClass
{
private:
ifloat* q;
public:
DervClass( ) {q = new float[4];}
~DervClass( ) {delete[ ] q;}
} // DervClass
...
int main ()
{
BaseClass* objPtr = new DervClass ( );
...
delete objPtr;
...
DervClass Obj
Only p is seen by objPtr
p
q
objPtr
(a) After instantiation
DervClass Object
Not Deleted
q
objPtr
(b) After delete

Figure 12-9 Virtual destructors

Destructor polymorphism is forced by the compiler when we declare a virtual destructor in the base class. When a virtual destruct is declared, the derived class destructor is called first, then the base class destructor. The base class destructor is declared virtual as shown in the following example.

```
virtual ~BaseClass () {...};
```

12-6 PURE VIRTUAL FUNCTIONS: ABSTRACT CLASSES

The virtual functions that we discussed in "Dynamic Binding and Virtual Functions" on page 616 do not force the overriding of a function; virtual functions are for the purpose of polymorphism. However, there are occasions that we want to force the derived class to override (redefine) a function. This is particularly true if we expect our program to grow and new derived classes to be added. For example, consider our polygon class. When we designed our polygon base class, we used only three derived classes: triangle, rectangle, and square. What if in the future we want more polygons? To do so, we need to define a model in the base class and let the derived classes follow the model. In the base class, we can define the minimum number of functions and the format (argument list) that is needed for each derived class to include. We can use pure virtual functions, discussed next.

PURE VIRTUAL FUNCTION

Whereas a virtual function can have executable code in the base class, a pure virtual function can have no code. It is simply a declaration of a function that must be overridden in each derived class.

A base class function is declared as **pure virtual** for two reasons. First, we cannot anticipate actions that the derived class might need. For example, in the polygon class, we have two calculation methods: calculate area and calculate perimeter. Different polygons have different calculations for these values. Rather than try to define them all, we can just declare a pure virtual function and let the derived classes override it with a concrete function.

Second, we want to force every derived class to redefine the function. The compiler generates an error if a virtual function is not replaced by a concrete function in the derived class. Every derived class has to define its own version of a pure virtual function without changing the signature—that is, the return type and the parameter list. In other words, we provide a model in the pure virtual function and the implementation is left to the derived class.

A virtual function is declared to be pure by assigning it the value zero. This is a convention; as such, it is a syntactical rule that must be memorized. The following code shows the format for declaring a virtual function.

```
virtual return_type indentifier (parameter list) = 0;
```

ABSTRACT CLASSES

An **abstract class** is a class that has at least one pure virtual function. An abstract class is just a model for all derived classes and cannot be instantiated. We cannot have an object of an abstract class because the virtual functions cannot be called. An abstract class has many uses:

1. It allows polymorphism.
2. It can define concrete members that can be inherited in derived classes and that do not have to be redefined.
3. It provides a model for the pure virtual functions that must be redefined in the derived class.

> **An abstract class combines the idea of inheritance, polymorphism, and modeling.**

To show how it works, let us rewrite our polygons classes changing the polygon base class to an abstract class. The design is shown in Figure 12-10. Note that the name of an abstract class in ULM notation is in italic.

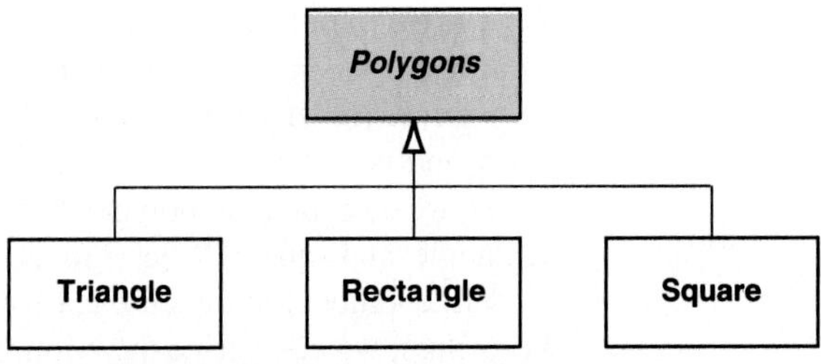

Figure 12-10 Abstract polygon class design

The following programs show how we change our polygons class to an abstract class. We have also extended it to include a rectangle class and a square class.

Note that we even have defined an inline constructor, and an inline destructor for our polygons class (statements 9 and 10) although no object is created from this class. The reason is that the derived classes need to call this constructors and destructor to instantiate and destroy their own objects.

The rewritten polygon class is shown in Program 12-11.

Program 12-11 Abstract class for polygons

```
1  class Polygons
2  {
3     protected:
4                 double area;
5                 double perimeter;
6        virtual void calcArea () = 0;
7        virtual void calcPeri () = 0;
8     public:
9               Polygons  () { }
10             ~Polygons  () { }
11         void printArea () const;
12         void printPeri () const;
13 }; // Class Polygons
14 /* ============= Polygons :: printArea =============
15    Prints the area of a polygon.
16        Pre   area calculated & stored in area
17        Post  area printed
18 */
19 void Polygons :: printArea () const
20 {
21    cout.setf (ios::fixed, ios :: floatfield);
22    cout.precision(1);
23    cout << "Area of polygon:      " << setw (5)
24         << area << endl;
25    return;
```

Program 12-11 Abstract class for polygons (*continued*)

```
} // Polygons printArea

/* ============= Polygons :: printPeri ===========
   Prints the perimeter of a polygon.
        Pre   polygon perimeter calculated and stored
        Post  perimeter printed
*/
void Polygons :: printPeri () const
{
   cout.setf (ios::fixed, ios :: floatfield);
   cout.precision(1);
   cout << "Perimeter of polygon: " << setw (5)
         << perimeter << endl;
   return;
} // Polygons printPeri
```

The abstract class for triangle is shown in Program 12-12.

Program 12-12 Abstract class for triangle

```
class Triangle : public Polygons
{
   private:
                double sideA;
                double sideB;
                double sideC;

       virtual void calcArea ();
       virtual void calcPeri ();

   public:
        Triangle (double sideAIn, double sideBIn,
                    double sideCIn);
}; // Class Triangle
/* ============ Triangle :: Triangle =============
   Initializating/default constructor for triangle class.
   Stores sides. Calculates area and perimeter.
       Pre   Given sideA, sideB, and sideC (default 0)
       Post  data stored; area & perimeter calculated
*/
Triangle :: Triangle (double sideAIn, double sideBIn,
                           double sideCIn)
{
   // Verify sides are valid
   if  ( ((sideAIn + sideBIn) <= sideCIn)
     ||  ((sideBIn + sideCIn) <= sideAIn)
     ||  ((sideCIn + sideAIn) <= sideBIn) )
        {
```

Program 12-12 Abstract class for triangle (*continued*)

```
          cout << "Invalid Triangle\n";
          exit (100);
         } // if
   // Valid Triangle
   sideA = sideAIn;
   sideB = sideBIn;
   sideC = sideCIn;
   calcPeri();
   calcArea();
   return;
} // Triangle constructor
/* ============= Triangle :: calcArea ============
   Calculates triangle area & stores in base class area.
       Pre   sideA, sideB, sideC, & perimeter available
       Post  area calculated and stored
*/
void Triangle :: calcArea ()
{
   double halfPeri = perimeter / 2;
   area = (  halfPeri
           * (halfPeri - sideA)
           * (halfPeri - sideB)
           * (halfPeri - sideC) );
   area = sqrt(area);
   return;
} // Triangle calcArea
/* ============= Triangle :: calcPeri ============
   Calculates perimeter & stores in base class area.
       Pre   sideA, sideB, & sideC available
       Post  perimeter calculated and stored
*/
void Triangle :: calcPeri ()
{
   perimeter = sideA + sideB + sideC;
   return;
} // Triangle calcPeri
```

Program 12-13 contains the derived rectangle class.

Program 12-13 Abstract class for rectangle

```
class Rectangle : public Polygons
{
   private:
               double sideA;
               double sideB;
       virtual void calcArea ();
       virtual void calcPeri ();

```

Program 12-13 Abstract class for rectangle (*continued*)

```
   public:
        Rectangle (double sideAIn, double sideBIn);
}; // Class Triangle
/* =========== Rectangle ::  Rectangle ============
   Initializing/default constructor for Rectangle class.
   Stores sides. Calculates area and perimeter.
        Pre   Given sideA and sideB (default 0)
        Post  data stored; area & perimeter calculated
*/
Rectangle :: Rectangle (double sideAIn,
                        double sideBIn)
{
   sideA = sideAIn;
   sideB = sideBIn;
   calcPeri();
   calcArea();
   return;
} // Rectangle constructor
/* ============= Triangle :: calcArea ============
   Calculates triangle area & stores in base class area.
        Pre   sideA, sideB, sideC, & perimeter available
        Post  area calculated and stored
*/
void Rectangle :: calcArea ()
{
   area = sideA * sideB;
   return;
} // Rectangle calcArea
/* ============= Triangle :: calcPeri ============
   Calculates perimeter & stores in base class area.
        Pre   sideA and sideB available
        Post  perimeter calculated and stored
*/
void Rectangle :: calcPeri ()
{
   perimeter = 2 * (sideA + sideB);
   return;
} // Rectangle calcPeri
```

Program 12-14 contains the square class.

Program 12-14 Abstract Class for Square

```
class Square : public Polygons
{
   private:
               double side;
      virtual void calcArea ();
      virtual void calcPeri ();
```

Program 12-14 Abstract Class for Square (*continued*)

```

   public:
       Square (double sideIn);
}; // Class Square

/* ============== Square ::  Square  ===============
   Initialization constructor for Square class.
   Stores sides. Calculates area and perimeter.
       Pre   Given side
       Post  data stored; area & perimeter calculated
*/
Square :: Square (double sideIn)
{
   side = sideIn;
   calcPeri();
   calcArea();
   return;
}  // Square constructor
/* =============== Square :: calcArea ==============
   Calculates Square area & stores in base class area.
       Pre   side
       Post  area calculated and stored
*/
void Square :: calcArea ()
{
   area = side * side;
   return;
}  // Square calcArea
/* =============== Square :: calcPeri ==============
   Calculates perimeter & stores in base class area.
       Pre   side
       Post  perimeter calculated and stored
*/
void Square :: calcPeri ()
{
   perimeter = 4 * side;
   return;
}  // Square calcPeri
```

Program 12-15 is a test driver to verify the polygon abstract class.

Program 12-15 Demonstrate abstract class

```
/* Demonstrate use of abstract classes.
      Written by:
      Date:
*/
#include <iostream>
#include <cmath>
```

Program 12-15 Demonstrate abstract class (*continued*)

```
#include <iomanip>
#include <cstdlib>
using namespace std;
#include "p12-11.h"                     // Polygon class
#include "p12-12.h"                     // Triangle class
#include "p12-13.h"                     // Rectangle class
#include "p12-14.h"                     // Square class

int main ()
{
   cout << "Start Polygon Demonstration\n\n";

   Triangle tri (2, 3, 4);
   tri.printPeri();
   tri.printArea();

   Rectangle rec (3, 4);
   rec.printPeri();
   rec.printArea();

   Square sqr (3);
   sqr.printPeri();
   sqr.printArea();
   cout << "\nEnd Polygon Demonstration\n";
   return 0;
} // main
// ================= End of Program =================
```

```
Results
Start Polygon Demonstration

Perimeter of polygon:   9.0
Area of polygon:        2.9
Perimeter of polygon:  14.0
Area of polygon:       12.0
Perimeter of polygon:  12.0
Area of polygon:        9.0

End Polygon Demonstration
```

12-7 TYPE CONVERSION IN HIERARCHICAL CLASSES

We have learned that we can convert a standard data type to another standard data type using either implicit or explicit casting (static casting). We have also learned that we can convert a pointer to a standard data type to a pointer to another standard data type. However, in this case casting needs to be explicit.

Now we want to expand the concept to objects and pointer to objects. It is obvious that casting an object of one type to an object of another type does not make sense unless we have function in both classes to do the conversion or there is a relationship between the two classes. In this section, we discuss casting of objects (or pointer to objects) when the classes form a hierarchy (base and derived classes).

Hierarchical class objects can be upcast or downcast. **Upcasting** occurs when a derived-class object is converted to a base-class object; **downcasting** occurs when a base-class object is converted to a derived-class object.

Because objects and pointers are handled differently, we have four distinct cases: upcasting objects, downcasting objects, upcasting pointers to objects, and downcasting pointers to objects. We first discuss casting objects and then casting pointers to objects.

CASTING OBJECTS

In this section we discuss object upcasting and downcasting.

Upcasting

Just as an automobile is a special type of vehicle, a derived class object is a special type of its base class object. This means that we can assign a derived class object to a base type object. In this case, we can either use an implicit or an explicit (static) cast; it does not make any difference. Implicit casts occur when we assign a derived class object to a base class object or when we pass a derived class object to a function that expects a base class object. Figure 12-11 demonstrates implicit upcasting.

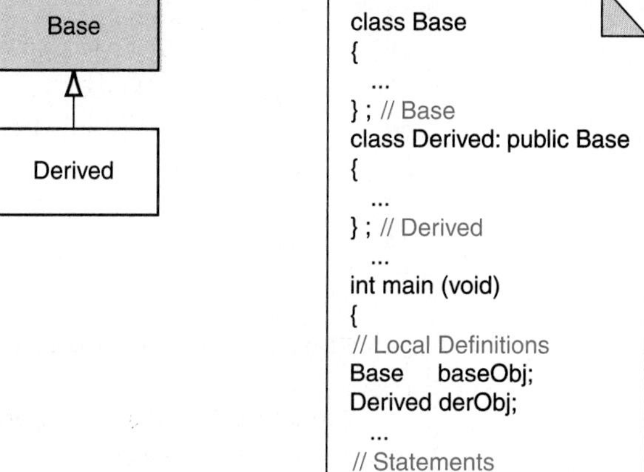


```
class Base
{
  ...
} ; // Base
class Derived: public Base
{
  ...
} ; // Derived
  ...
int main (void)
{
// Local Definitions
Base    baseObj;
Derived derObj;
  ...
// Statements
  baseObj = derObj;
  ...
} // main
```

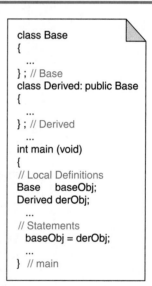

Figure 12-11 Upcasting objects

While upcasting of objects is permitted, we need to recognize that whenever we convert a derived class object to base class object, only the base class data members are copied. The derived class data members cannot be copied because they are not declared in the base class object. This is sometimes referred to as **slicing**.

Program 12-16 demonstrates upcasting. We display the contents of the base class before and after the assignment to show its effect.

Program 12-16 Implicit class conversion

```
/* Demonstrate implicit class conversion.
      Written by:
      Date:
*/
#include <iostream>
using namespace std;

class Base
{
   protected:
      int baseData;
   public:
         Base  (int baseIn);
   void print () const;
}; // Base

Base :: Base (int baseIn)
{
    baseData = baseIn;
}  // Base constructor
void Base :: print () const
{
   cout << "Value of baseData in class Base is: "
        << baseData << endl;
   return;
}  // Base :: print
class Derived: public Base
{
   protected:
      int derivedData;
   public:
         Derived (int baseIn, int derivedIn);
   void print    () const;
}; // Derived

Derived :: Derived (int baseIn, int derivedIn)
         : Base (baseIn)
{
   derivedData = derivedIn;
}  // Derived constructor
void Derived :: print () const
{
   cout << "Value of baseData "    << baseData    << endl;
   cout << "Value of derivedData " << derivedData << endl;
}  // Derived :: print

int main ()
{
   cout << "Before assign: ";
```

Program 12-16 Implicit class conversion (*continued*)

```
   Base    baseObj (1);
   baseObj.print ();

   Derived derObj  (3, 5 );
   baseObj = derObj;
   cout << "After assign:  ";
   baseObj.print ();
   return 0;
} // main
```

```
Results
Before assign: Value of baseData in class Base is: 1
After assign:  Value of baseData in class Base is: 3
```

Downcasting

Downcasting of objects is not allowed in C++. With a little thought, the reason should be obvious. Downcasting converts a base class object to a derived class object. A derived class object normally has more data members than the base class. This means that the system needs to add these extra data members and initialize them using its own discretion. This is something we do not want in programming.

CASTING POINTERS TO OBJECTS

Casting pointers to objects is allowed in both directions: upcasting and downcasting. However, the mechanism that handles upcasting is totally different than the mechanism that handles downcasting.

Upcasting

Upcasting pointers to objects is very straightforward. It can be done explicitly, as shown in Figure 12-12.

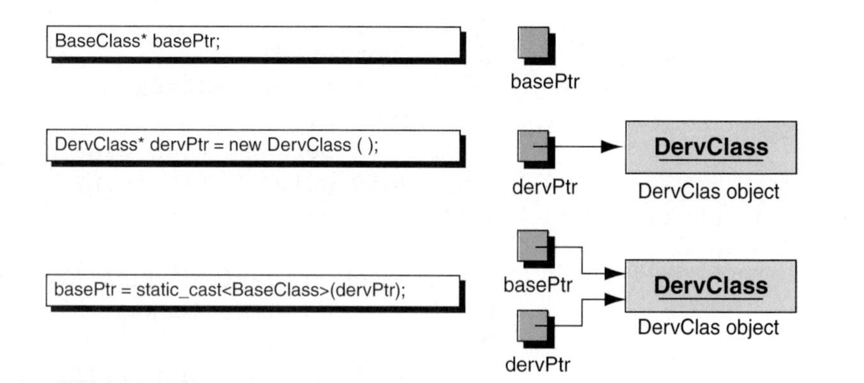

Figure 12-12 Upcasting objects

Downcasting

Downcasting pointers to objects is possible, but it needs a different approach; it must be done using dynamic casting. **Dynamic casting**, like dynamic binding is done during run time, not compilation time. The following example shows the syntax for dynamic casting:

```
dynamic_cast<type> (data)
```

However, dynamic casting has two design considerations. First, dynamic casting can be done only with polymorphic classes—that is, classes using virtual functions. Second, dynamic casting can be valid or invalid.

Valid Dynamic Downcasting Dynamic downcasting is valid only when the base-class pointer is *already* pointing to a derived class object. This cast is shown in Figure 12-13.

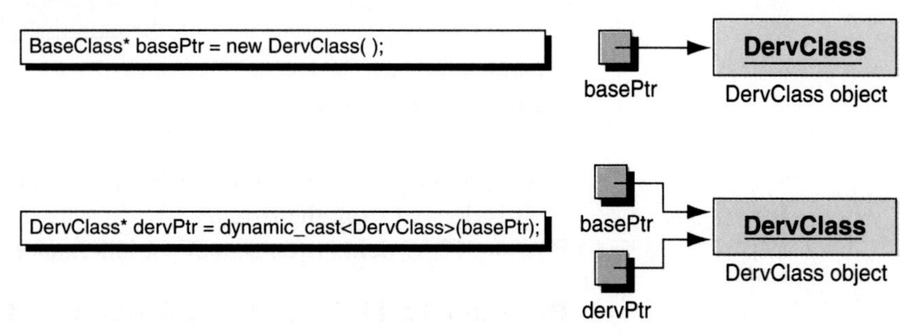

Figure 12-13 **Valid downcasting**

Invalid Dynamic Downcasting On the other hand, we cannot downcast to a pointer that is pointing to a derived class. The reason behind this restriction is similar to the reason we cannot downcast an object: The base class does not contain the members added by the derived class. In this case, the cast returns a null pointer value (0). We can then test the pointer to ensure that it is valid before we use it. Figure 12-14 shows invalid down casting.

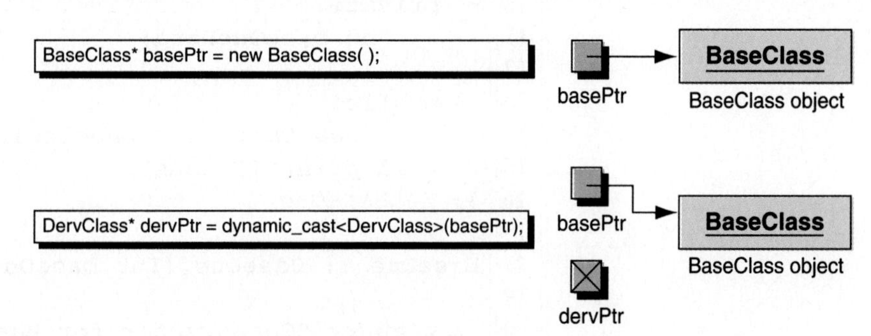

Figure 12-14 **Invalid downcasting**

12-8 MULTIPLE INHERITANCE

All of our previous examples have used only one base class. Multiple inheritance provides the capability for a derived class to draw from two or more base classes. In Figure 12-15, the derived class inherits from both base classes.

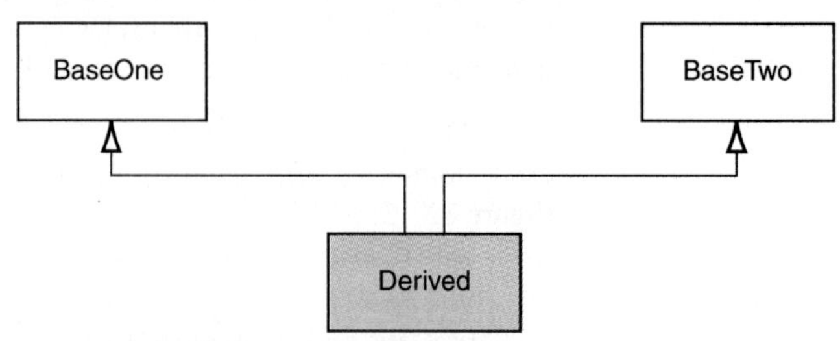

Figure 12-15 Multiple inheritance

One common example of multiple inheritance is the C++ file library. The *iostream* class is derived from the *istream* and *ostream* classes (See Figure J-1 in Appendix J). Program 12-17 demonstrates multiple inheritance.

Program 12-17 Multiple inheritance demonstration

```
/* Demonstrate multiple inheritance.
      Written by:
      Date:
*/
#include <iostream>
using namespace std;

class BaseOne
{
   private:
      int baseOneData;

   public:
        BaseOne  (int baseOneIn);
   void print () const;
}; // BaseOne

BaseOne :: BaseOne (int baseOneIn)
{
   cout << "Constructor for BaseOne called " << endl;
   baseOneData = baseOneIn;
}  // BaseOne constructor

void BaseOne:: print () const
{
   cout << baseOneData << endl;
}  // BaseOne :: print

class BaseTwo
{
   private:
      int baseTwoData;

```

Program 12-17 Multiple inheritance demonstration (*continued*)

```
   public:
        BaseTwo (int baseTwoIn);
   void print () const;
}; // BaseTwo

BaseTwo :: BaseTwo (int baseTwoIn)
{
   cout << "Constructor for BaseTwo called " << endl;
   baseTwoData = baseTwoIn;
} // BaseTwo constructor

void BaseTwo :: print () const
{
   cout << baseTwoData << endl;
} // BaseTwo :: print

class MultiInherit: public BaseOne, public BaseTwo
{
   private:
      int multiData;

   public:
      MultiInherit (int baseOneIn, int baseTwoIn,
                       int multiIn);
   void print () const;
}; // MultiInherit

MultiInherit :: MultiInherit (int baseOneIn,
                                  int baseTwoIn,
                                  int multiIn)
             : BaseOne (baseOneIn), BaseTwo (baseTwoIn)
{
   cout << "Constructor for MultiInherit called" << endl;
   multiData = multiIn;
} // MultiInherit constructor

void MultiInherit :: print () const
{
   BaseOne :: print ();
   BaseTwo :: print ();
   cout << multiData << endl;
} // MultiInherit :: print

int main ()
{
   MultiInherit multi (1, 2, 12);
   multi.print ();
   return 0;
} // main
```

Program 12-17 Multiple inheritance demonstration (*continued*)

```
Results
Constructor for BaseOne called
Constructor for BaseTwo called
Constructor for MultiInherit called
1
2
12
```

12-9 AGGREGATION

Inheritance, which is an *is-a* relationship, is different from aggregation, which is a ***has-a*** relationship. Whereas the inheritance relationship is between two different class objects, **aggregation** is the inclusion of objects within an object. These differences are shown in Figure 12-16.

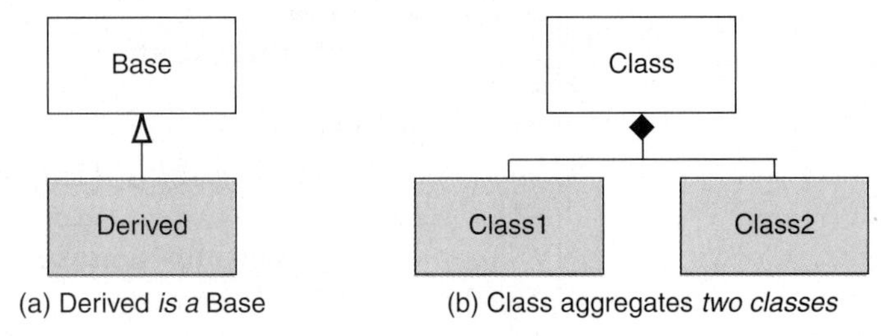

Figure 12-16 Aggregation

EXAMPLE: STUDENT CLASS

As an example of aggregation, we design a student class that contains the following data members: student id, units attempted, grade points earned, and date of birth. The design is shown in Figure 12-17.

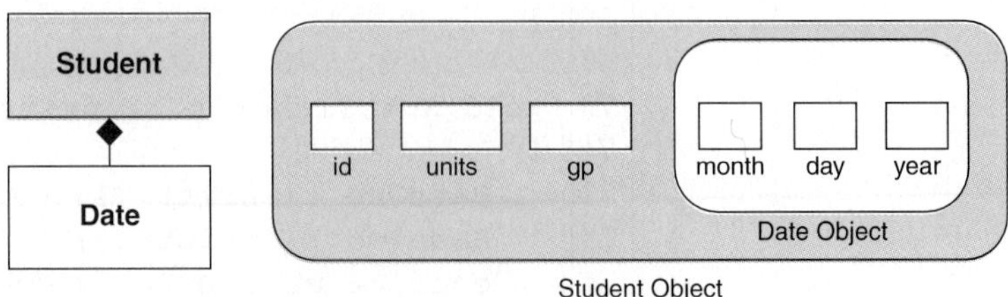

Figure 12-17 Student class

To include the date class within the student class, we declare it as shown in the following example.

```
class Student
{
   private:
      Date dob;                      // object of type Date
      ...
}; // Student
```

In the student constructor, we initialize the date-of-birth *object* (dob) in an initialization list. Compare this to the way we relate the derived and base classes in inheritance: In inheritance the base class, not an object, is referenced; that is, we call the constructor of the base class. These differences are shown in Figure 12-18.

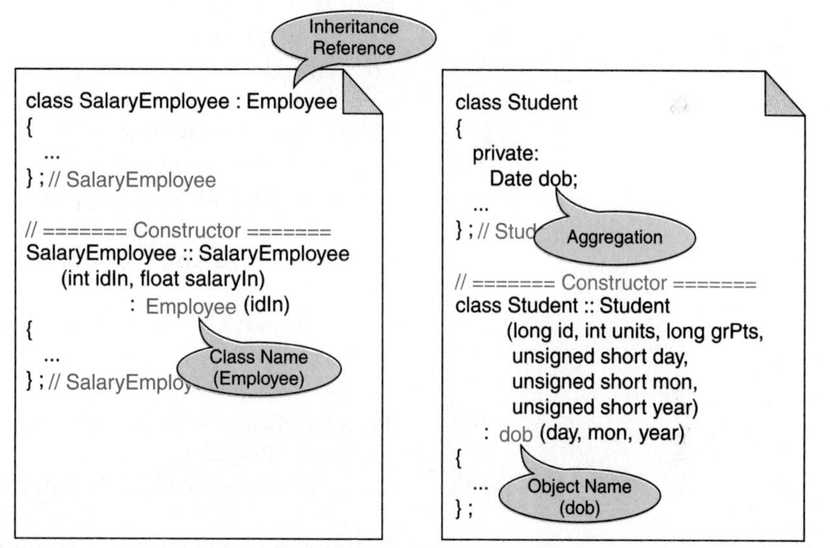

Figure 12-18 Instantiating an object

Program 12-18 declares the date class.

Program 12-18 Date class declaration

```
class Date
{
   private:
      unsigned short day;
      unsigned short month;
      unsigned short year;
      bool validate (unsigned short day,
                     unsigned short mon) const;
   public:
      Date (unsigned short day,
            unsigned short mon,
            unsigned short year);
      void print () const;
}; // Class Date
```

Program 12-18 Date class declaration (*continued*)

```
Date  :: Date (unsigned short dayIn,
               unsigned short monIn,
               unsigned short yearIn)
{
   if (!validate (dayIn, monIn))
      {
       cout << "Not a valid date" << endl;
       exit (100);
      } // if
   day   = dayIn;
   month = monIn;
   year  = yearIn;
} // Constructor
/* ================= Date :: print =================
   Print Date members.
      Pre  Nothing
      Post Members printed
*/
void Date :: print () const
{
   cout << month << "/" << day << "/" << year << endl;
} // Date
/* ================= Date :: validate ================
   Ensure that month and day are valid
      Pre  Nothing
      Post Date valid or program aborted
*/
bool Date :: validate (unsigned short dayIn,
                       unsigned short monIn) const
{
   int months [12] = {31, 29, 31, 30, 31, 30,
                      31, 31, 30, 31, 30, 31};

   return ((monIn <= 12) && (dayIn <= months [monIn + 1]));
} // validate
```

Program 12-19 declares the student class.

Program 12-19 Student class declaration

```
class Student
{
   private:
       long  id;
       int   units;
       int   grPts;
       Date  dob;

   public:
```

Program 12-19 Student class declaration (*continued*)

```
      Student (long  idIn, int unitsIn,
                int   grPts,
                unsigned short day,
                unsigned short mon,
                unsigned short year);
      void print () const;
}; // Class Student
Student :: Student (long  idIn, int unitsIn, int grPtsIn,
                    unsigned short dayIn,
                    unsigned short monIn,
                    unsigned short yearIn)
        : dob (dayIn, monIn, yearIn)
{
   id    = idIn;
   units = unitsIn;
   grPts =  grPtsIn;
}  // Constructor
/* ============== Student :: print  =============
   Prints Student date including date of birth
      Pre  Nothing
      Post Data printed
*/
void Student :: print () const
{
   cout << "Student: "   << id
        << " Units:  "   << units
        << "\nGr Pts:  " << setw (4) << grPts
        << " Birth Date: ";
   dob.print();
   cout << endl;
}  // Student
```

Program 12-20 is a test driver to validate the student and date classes.

Program 12-20 Demonstrate student and date classes

```
/* Demonstrate use of student classes.
      Written by:
      Date:
*/
#include <iostream>
#include <iomanip>
#include <cstdlib>
using namespace std;

#include "p12-18.h"                          // Student Class
#include "p12-19.h"                          // Date Class

int main ()
```

Program 12-20 Demonstrate student and date classes (*continued*)

```
{
   cout << "Start Student  Demonstration\n\n";
   Student st1 (1234, 15, 48, 12, 7, 1981);
   st1.print();
   cout << "End Student Demonstration\n";
   return 0 ;
} // main
```

```
Results
Start Student  Demonstration

Student: 1234 Units: 15
Gr Pts:  48   Birth Date: 7/12/1981

End Student Demonstration
```

AGGREGATION VERSUS COMPOSITION

Although the terms aggregation and **composition** are sometimes used interchangeably, we distinguish between them. In aggregation, the contained object, `dob` in the previous example, is an independent object that can exist without the container, the student object. In composition, on the other hand, the contained object cannot exist without the container object. Composition can be accomplished using **nested classes**—that is, the declaration of one class inside of another. We avoid this complex construct in this text.

12-10 SOFTWARE ENGINEERING AND PROGRAMMING STYLE

We've come a long way since the "Greeting" program in Chapter 2. Along the way we've talked a lot about designing programs. In this chapter, we formalize some of the concepts and principles that we've discussed throughout the text—that is, the principles that define good programs.

PROGRAM DESIGN CONCEPTS

You will study many different analysis and design tools as you advance in computer science. Since this text deals primarily with program analysis and design, we discuss here the primary tool we have used throughout the text: the structure chart.

The overriding premise of good design is that the program is modular; that is, it is well structured. This is the *sine qua non* of good programming. A program's degree of good design can be measured by two principles: Its modules are independent—that is, their implementation is hidden from the user—and they have a single purpose.

INFORMATION HIDING

Information hiding is the principle of program design in which the data structure and functional implementation are screened from the user. Modules are independent when their communication is only through well-defined parameters and their implementation is hidden from the user. The purpose of the function should be defined in its inputs and outputs, and the user should not need to know how it is implemented or how its data are structured. Pressman states it well when he says:

> **Hiding implies that effective modularity can be achieved by defining a set of independent modules that communicate with one another only that information necessary to achieve software function. … Hiding defines and enforces access constraints to both procedural detail within a module and any local data structure used by the module.**[3]

The concept of information hiding is the basis of the object-oriented design, programming, and database movements gaining popularity today. When you study data structures, you will encounter another technique used for information hiding called the abstract data type.

COHESION

The most common weakness of function design is the combining of related processes into one primitive function. In Chapter 4, we discussed the concept that each module (function) should do only one thing. This principle of structured programming is known as cohesion. **Cohesion,** first discussed by Larry Constantine in the 1960s,[4] is a measure of how closely the processes in a function are related.

---

[3]Roger S. Pressman, *Software Engineering: A Practitioner's Approach* (2nd ed.), McGraw-Hill Series in Software Engineering and Technology (New York: McGraw-Hill, 1982), p. 228.

[4]E. N. Yourdon and L. L. Constantine, *Structured Design* (Englewood Cliffs, NJ: Yourdon Press [Prentice Hall], 1978).

There are three primary reasons why we are concerned with cohesion. The first and most important is *accuracy*. The more cohesive a function is, the simpler it is. The simpler it is, the easier it is to write and the fewer errors it will have.

This is closely related to the second reason for high cohesion: **maintainability**. If a function is easy to understand, it is easy to change. This means that the job can be done faster and with fewer errors.

Finally, cohesive modules are more *reusable*. Reusability is also closely related to the concepts of accuracy and maintainability. Existing functions have stood the test of time and have been tempered in the heat of use. They are more likely to be error-free, and they certainly are easier and faster to develop.

Cohesion is most applicable to the primitive functions in a program—those that are at the bottom of the structure chart—and least applicable to the controlling functions that appear above the lowest level. This does not mean, however, that cohesion can be ignored at the higher levels. To make the point with an absurd example, you wouldn't write a program to manage your checkbook and maintain your daily calendar. Even though both of these processes are related to things you do, they are so unrelated that you wouldn't put them in the same program. The same concept applies in a program. For example, at the lower levels of your program, you shouldn't combine functions that read data with functions that print a report.

The seven levels of cohesion are mapped out in Figure 12-19.

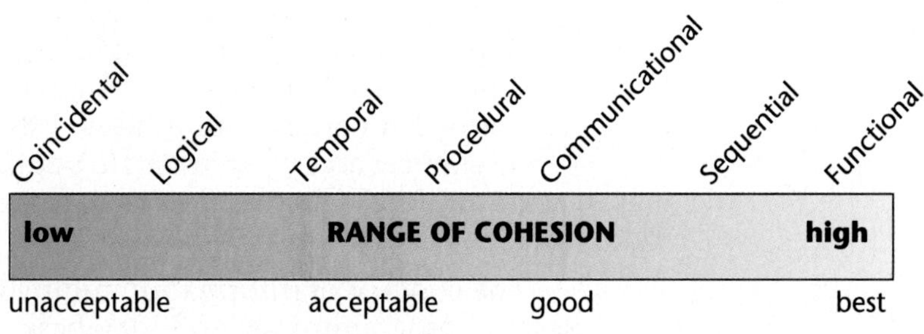

Figure 12-19 Types of cohesion

Functional Cohesion

Functional cohesion modules contain only one process. This is the highest level of cohesion and the level that we should hold up as a model. Using the example of printing a report, the report function should call three lower-level functions: one to get the data, one to format and print the report header, and one to format and print the data. This design is shown in Figure 12-20. The print report heading function is optional because it is called only when a new page is started.

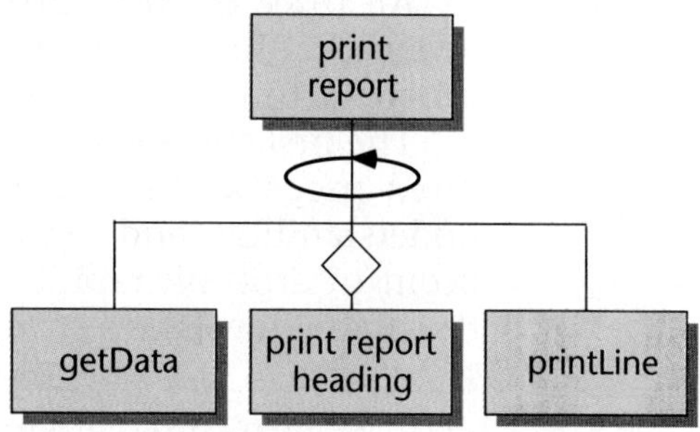

Figure 12-20 Example of functional cohesion

Sequential Cohesion

A **sequential cohesion** module contains two or more related tasks that are closely tied together, usually with the output of one flowing as input to the other. An example of sequential cohesion is seen in the calculations for a sale. The design for this function might be as follows:

1. Extend item prices
2. Sum items
3. Calculate sales tax
4. Calculate total

In this example, the first process multiplies the quantity purchased by the price. The extended prices are used by the process that calculates the sum of the purchased items. This sum is then used to calculate the sales tax, which is finally added to the sum to get the sale total. In each case, the output of one process was used as the input of the next process.

Although it is quite common to find the detail code for these processes combined into a single function, this approach makes the function more complex and less reusable. On the other hand, reusability would be a concern only if the same or similar calculations were being made in different parts of one program.

Communicational Cohesion

Communicational cohesion combines processes that work on the same data. It is natural to have communicational cohesion in the higher modules in a program, but you should never find it at the primitive level. For example, consider a function that reads an inventory file, prints the current status of the parts, and then checks to see if any parts need to be ordered. The pseudocode for this process is shown in Algorithm 12-1.

Algorithm 12-1 Process inventory pseudocode

```
1 While not end of file
  1 read a record
  2 print report
  3 check reorder point
```

All three of these processes use the same data. If they are calls to lower-level functions, they are acceptable. If the detail code is in the function, however, the design is unacceptable.

The first three levels of cohesion are all considered to be good structured programming principles. Beyond this point, however, ease of understanding and implementation, maintainability, and accuracy begin to drop off rapidly. The next two levels should be used only at the higher levels of a structure chart, and then only rarely.

> Well-structured programs are highly cohesive and loosely coupled.

Procedural Cohesion

The fourth level, **procedural cohesion,** combines unrelated processes that are linked by a control flow. (This differs from sequential cohesion, in which data flow from one process to the next.) As an example, consider the main line of a program that builds and processes a list. Algorithm 12-2 gives an example of a procedural flow.

Algorithm 12-2 Process list pseudocode

```
Open files.
Initialize work areas.
Create list.
Print menu.
while not stop
   get user's response
   if locate ...
   if insert ...
   if delete ...
   print menu
clean up
Close files
```

A much better approach would be to have only three function calls in *main:* initialize, process, and end. Not only is this easier to understand, but it also simplifies the communication.

Temporal Cohesion

The fifth level, **temporal cohesion,** is acceptable only over a limited range of processes. It combines unrelated processes that always occur together. Two temporally cohesive functions are initialization and end of job. They are acceptable as temporal cohesive processes because they are used only once in the program and because they are never portable. Recognize, however, that they should still contain calls to functionally cohesive primitive functions whenever practical.

Logical and Coincidental Cohesion

The last two levels of cohesion are seldom found in programs today. **Logical cohesion** combines processes that are related only by the entity that controls them. A function that conditionally opened different sets of files based on a flag passed as a parameter would be logically cohesive. Finally, **coincidental cohesion** combines processes that are unrelated. Coincidental cohesion exists only in theory. We have never seen a productional program that contained coincidental cohesion.

SUMMARY

We have discussed two design concepts in this chapter: information hiding and cohesion. Cohesion describes the relationship among processes within a function. Keep functions as highly cohesive as possible. When designing a program, pay attention to the levels of cohesion. It is much easier to design high cohesion into a program than it is to program it in. For more information about these concepts, refer to *The Practical Guide to Structured Systems Design*[5] by Meilir Page-Jones.

12-11 TIPS AND COMMON PROGRAMMING ERRORS

1. Constructors, destructors, nonmember functions, and assignment operators are not inherited in a derived class; they must be redefined.
2. Each inheritance type (*private*, *protected*, *public*) has its own inheritance rule with respect to members with different access type (*private*, *protected*, *public*).
3. The constructor of a base class is called before the constructor of a derived class.
4. The destructor of a derived class is called before the destructor of a base class.
5. A constructor for a derived class must, explicitly or implicitly, call the constructor for the base class. The call to the base class constructor should be in the initialization list section of the derived class.
6. A destructor for a derived class implicitly calls the destructor for a base class; we cannot code this call.
7. Note that overriding a member function is different from overloading it. In overriding, the list of the argument and the return type must be the same; in overloading, the argument list must be different.
8. Polymorphism needs three conditions to be effective: virtual functions, pointers or references to objects, and dynamic binding.
9. A virtual function does not force a function to be redefined in the derived class: the pure virtual function does.
10. If a class has even one pure virtual function, it is an abstract class and cannot be instantiated.
11. We can explicitly or implicitly upcast an object. However, some of the data members in the derived object are lost. We cannot downcast an object.
12. We can upcast or downcast a pointer to an object. Downcasting, however, must be done dynamically.
13. In aggregation, the constructor for the container class must initialize the contained object in the initialization list.

---

[5]Ibid. Meilir Page Jones, *The Practical Guide to Structured Systems Design*, 2nd ed. (Chap. 6) Englewood Cliffs, New Jersey: Prentice Hall, 1988.

12-12 KEY TERMS

abstract class
aggregation
base class
cohesion
coincidental cohesion
communicational cohesion
composition
derived class
downcasting
dynamic binding
dynamic casting
functional cohesion
has-a relationship
information hiding
inheritance
is-a relationship
late binding
logical cohesion
maintainability
multiple inheritance
nested classes
override
overriding inheritance access
overriding member functions
polymorphism
private inheritance
procedural cohesion
protected inheritance
public inheritance
pure virtual function
sequential cohesion
simple inheritance
static binding
temporal cohesion
upcasting
virtual destructor
virtual function

12-13 SUMMARY

- In C++, the concept of extending a class is known as inheritance.
- In C++, a derived class inherits all members of its base class; it can also add members of its own.
- Inheritance is an *is-a* relation; the derived class object *is a* base class object.
- There are three inheritance types in C++: *private*, *protected*, and *public*. The default is *public*.
- The following rules govern inheritance: All data members of the base class object are inherited in the derived class; all function members of the base class object, except constructors, the destructor, friend functions, virtual functions, and the assignment operator, are inherited in the derived class.
- In a *private* inheritance, the private members of the base class become inaccessible in the derived class. The protected and public members become *private*.
- In *protected* inheritance, the private members of the base class become inaccessible in the derived class. The protected and public members become *protected.*
- In a *public* inheritance, the private members of the base class become inaccessible in the derived class. However, the protected members remain *protected* and the public members remain *public.*
- A derived class can override a member function defined in the base class. Overriding is different than overloading.
- Constructors, copy constructors, destructors, assignment operators, and virtual functions are not inherited; they need to be redefined in the derived class.
- A derived class constructor must call the base class constructor, either explicitly or implicitly, in the initialization process.
- The base class destructor is implicitly called in the derived class constructor by the system; the programmer cannot call it explicitly.
- A base class constructor is called before the derived class constructor; a base class destructor is called after the derived class constructor.
- Dynamic binding is the mechanism that allows a function to be bound to an object during run time. Dynamic binding is done through virtual functions.
- Polymorphism is the concept of using the same name for different functions. Polymorphism can be accomplished through dynamic binding, virtual functions, and using pointer or references to objects.
- A pure virtual function forces a function to be redefined in the derived class.

- A class with one or more pure virtual functions is called an abstract class. An abstract class is a model for derived classes. No object can be instantiated from an abstract class because there is no definition for the virtual functions in the class; they need to be redefined in the derived classes.
- A derived class object can be cast to a base class object (upcasting) either explicitly or implicitly; a base class object cannot be cast to a derived class object (downcasting).
- A pointer to a derived class object can be cast to a pointer to a base class object (downcasting) using either static or dynamic casting; a pointer to a base class object can be cast to a pointer to a derived class object (upcasting) using only dynamic casting.
- C++ allows multiple inheritance.
- An aggregation is a *has-a* relation in which an object of a class contains object(s) from other classes.
- The principle of data cohesion specifies that each module must do only one job.
- There are seven types of cohesion. Only the first three (functional, sequential, and communicational) should be used for low-level functions. The last two (logical and coincidental) should never be used. Procedural and temporal cohesion are sometimes acceptable but should be avoided.

12-14 PRACTICE SETS

REVIEW QUESTIONS

1. Constructors are inherited by derived classes.
   a. True
   b. False
2. Destructors are inherited by derived classes.
   a. True
   b. False
3. In private inheritance, the private members of the base class become ____ in the derived class.
   a. inaccessible
   b. private
   c. protected
   d. public
4. In private inheritance, the protected members of the base class become ____ in the derived class.
   a. inaccessible
   b. private
   c. protected
   d. public
5. In private inheritance, the public members of the base class become ____ in the derived class.
   a. inaccessible
   b. private
   c. protected
   d. public
6. In protected inheritance, the private members of the base class become ____ in the derived class.
   a. inaccessible
   b. private
   c. protected
   d. public
7. In protected inheritance, the protected members of the base class become ____ in the derived class.
   a. inaccessible
   b. private
   c. protected
   d. public
8. In protected inheritance, the public members of the base class become ____ in the derived class.
   a. inaccessible
   b. private
   c. protected
   d. public
9. In public inheritance, the private members of the base class become ____ in the derived class.
   a. inaccessible
   b. private
   c. protected
   d. public

10. In public inheritance, the protected members of the base class become ____ in the derived class.
    a. inaccessible
    b. private
    c. protected
    d. public
11. In public inheritance, the public members of the base class become ____ in the derived class.
    a. inaccessible
    b. private
    c. protected
    d. public
12. What is the difference between a virtual function and a regular function?
13. What is the difference between a virtual function and a pure virtual function?
14. Can a derived class have a pure virtual function? Explain why or why not.
15. Can a constructor be a virtual function? Explain why or why not.
16. Can a destructor be a virtual function? Explain why or why not.
17. Can an abstract class have a constructor or destructor although no object is created from an abstract class? Explain why or why not.
18. To force a derived class to redefine a function, we need to declare that function as a ____ function.
19. Can a class inherit from two abstract class? Explain why or why not.
20. Can we assign an object of a derived class to an object of a base class? Explain why or why not.
21. Can we assign an object of a base class to an object of a derived class? Explain why or why not.
22. Can polymorphism be used without pointers or references? Explain why or why not.
23. If you want to achieve polymorphism, you need to pass an object to a function by ____ or ____.
24. In static binding, the association between a pointer and a function is determined during ____.
25. In dynamic binding, the association between a pointer and a function is determined during ____.
26. If a cast is not valid, the dynamic cast returns a ____ pointer; if it is valid, it returns a ____ pointer.
27. A derived class constructor (or copy constructor) must call the base class constructor in the ____.
28. A derived class constructor code is executed ____ the base class constructor code; a derived class destructor code is executed ____ the base class destructor code.

EXERCISES

29. What is the type of inheritance in the following class?

```
Class Fun
{
  ... ;
};
Class Funny : Fun
{
  ... ;
};
```

30. Identify the error(s) in the following code:

```
Class Fun
{
   int  x;
};
Class Funny : private Fun
{
   Funny (int x) {x = 5}
};
```

31. Identify the error(s) in the following code:

```
Class Fun
{
   public:
      int  x;
};
Class Funny : public Fun
{
   Funny (int x) {x = 5}
};
```

32. Identify the error(s) in the following code:

```
Class Fun
{
   protected:
      int  x;
} ;
Class Funny : public Fun
{
   Funny (int x) {x = 5}
};
```

33. Identify the error(s) in the following code:

```
Class Fun
{
   private:
     int x;
   protected:
     int y ;
   public:
     int z;
};
Class Funny : public Fun
{
   private:
     int u;
   protected:
     int v;
   public:
     int w;
};
int main (void)
{
     Fun   fun;
     Funny funny;
     fun.x  = 1;
     fun.y    = 2;
     fun.z    = 3;
     funny.x = 11;
     funny.y = 12;
     funny.z = 13;
     funny.u = 14;
     funny.v = 15;
     funny.w = 16;
}
```

34. Given the declarations shown below, how many data elements are contained in an object of type Sun? How many total elements are in Sunny?

```
Class Sun
{
   private:
     int x;
    public:
     int z;
};

Class Sunny : public Fun
{
      private:
        int u;
      protected:
        int v;
      public:
        int w;
};
```

35. If A is the base class and B is the derived class from A, find any errors in the following code.

```
A a;
B b;
b = a;
```

36. If A is the base class and B is the derived class from A, find any errors in the following code.

```
A a;
B b;
a = b;
```

37. If A is the base class and B is the derived class from A, find any errors in the following code.

```
A* a;
B* b;
a = b;
```

38. If A is the base class and B is the derived class from A, find any errors in the following code.

```
A* a;
B* b;
b = a;
```

39. If A is the base class and B is the derived class from A, find any errors in the following code.

```
A* a = new A ();
B* b = a;
```

40. If A is the base class and B is the derived class from A, find any errors in the following code.

```
A* a = new B ();
B* b = a;
```

PROBLEMS

41. Write the constructor and destructor definitions for the class Fun and Funny.

```
Fun
{
   private:
     int  x;
   protected:
     int  y ;
   public:
     Fun (int n, int m);
     ~Fun (void);
 } ;
Funny : public Fun
{
   private:
     int u ;
   protected:
     int v;
   public:
    Funny (int n, int m, int p, int q);
     ~Funny (void);
};
```

42. Write a copy constructor for class `Fun` and `Funny` in Problem 41.

43. Class C is inherited from class B and B is inherited from A. Write the default explicit constructors for A, B, and C.

44. Class B is inherited from A. A uses a dynamic pointer. B inherits that dynamic pointer and uses another dynamic pointer. Write a constructor and destructor for both A and B.

PROJECTS

45. Redefine the employee class definition in Figure 12-6 by making the Employee class, the Salaried class, and the Hourly class abstract. Then create two classes, PartTime and FullTime, under the Salary and Hourly classes. Add the following information about an employee:

    a. Data of Birth (using a Date class)

    b. Date of Hiring (using a Date class)

    c. Number of people in the family

    d. Add the health plan for the full-time employees (include at least the following data members: deduction, provider, and family coverage [yes/no]).

46. Write the declarations and definitions for the geometric classes defined in Figure 12-21. Use the following hints:

    a. Define Shape, Two-Dimensional and Three-Dimensional as abstract classes.

    b. Define PI (π) as static class member in the Shape class.

    c. Define area calculation and print functions as pure virtual functions in the Shape class.

    d. Use public inheritance.

    e. Define all data or member functions common to two-dimensional shapes in the Two-dimensional class. Do the same for all common data or member functions for the three-dimensional shape.

47. Define an abstract class called Length that defines the length of an object in milimeters. Then define two classes inherited from Length, called MetricLength and EnglishLength. The MetricLength has methods that provide the length of the object in millimeters, centimeters, and meters. The EnglishLength has methods that provide the length of the object in inches, feet, and yards.

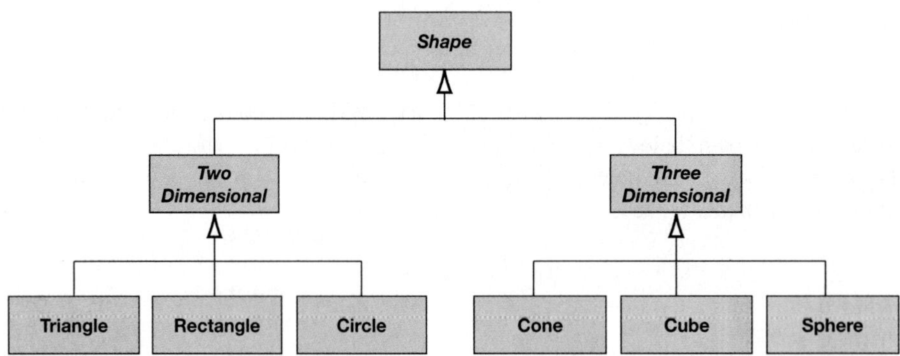

Figure 12-21 Design for Project 46

48. Define a card class that uses two objects hand and deck (aggregate). The class should allow us to play poker. Use the following tips:

Card class:

a. Use an enumeration for the rank of a card (Two, Three, ..., Ten, Jack, Queen, King, Ace).

b. Use an enumeration for the suit of a card (Clubs, Diamonds, Hearts, Spades).

c. Use a default constructor, an initializing constructor, a copy constructor, and destructor for the Card class.

d. Use accessor functions to access the rank or suit of a card.

e. Overload the << operator to print the rank and the suit of a card.

Hand Class:

a. Use a constructor that accepts a dynamically allocated array of cards (5 by default).

b. Use a destructor to delete the cards in a hand.

c. Use a function to display the contents of the hand by calling one of a set of boolean print functions pair, twoPair, threeOfKind, straight, flush, fullHouse, fourOfKind, straightFlush, and royalFlush.

Deck Class:

a. Use a constructor.

b. Use a function to shuffle the deck.

c. Use a function to deal.

d. Use an array to stores cards.

13 Templates

In C++, **templates** are a model of a function or a class that can be used to generate functions or classes. During the compilation, C++ uses the template to generate functions and classes. For example, given a **function template**, one, two, or more concrete functions can be generated in the program. Similarly, given a **class template**, one, two, or more concrete classes can be generated from it. This concept is shown in Figure 13-1.

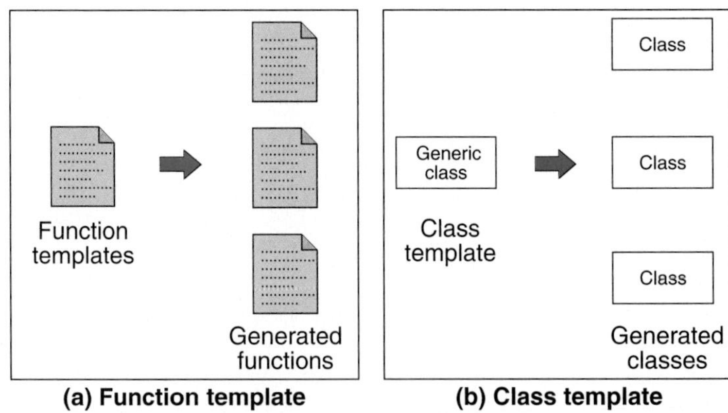

Figure 13-1 Basic template concepts

Templates provide a major implementation for code reusability. From one template, different functions and classes can be easily created. For example, while all functions created from a function template must have the same interface—that is, must have the same number of arguments and return, their argument types and return value are usually different. Similarly, all classes created with a class template have the same design, but their data members and function arguments may be different. In this chapter, we explore the use of templates.

13-1 FUNCTION TEMPLATES

A basic program concept is that a function applies actions to one or more objects or data types and may create and return one data type. In other words, a function can be defined by the:

- Actions that are applied
- Data that are involved

For example, a function that returns the larger of two integers applies logic to find the larger of two integers passed as arguments. Given such a function, however, if we need to find the larger of two long integers, we need to write a second function. Similarly, if we need to find the larger of two floats, we need to write a third function. Figure 13-2 shows this situation.

```
int max (int x, int y)
{
  return (x > y) ? x : y;
} // max
```

(a) Integer max

```
float max (float x, float y)
{
  return (x > y) ? x : y;
} // max
```

(c) Float max

```
long max (long x, long y)
{
  return (x > y) ? x : y;
} // max
```

(b) Long max

```
double max (double x, double y)
{
  return (x > y) ? x : y;
} // max
```

(d) Double max

Figure 13-2 Multiple `max` functions

In C++ we can increase productivity by writing one generic function using a template. The compiler can then use the generic function to create different functions based on the need of the application program. Program 13-1 shows such a generic function.

Program 13-1 `max` template

```
/* Create max function template
      Written by:
      Date:
*/
template <class TYPE>
TYPE max (TYPE x, TYPE y)
{
   return (x > y) ? x : y;
} // max template
```

In this template definition, `TYPE` is a **generic type** that will be replaced when the function is created. Based on the need of the application program, the compiler produces the appropriate function code and inserts it into the program. Note that the word `class`, as used in the template header, means that we are declaring a generic type that will be used in the function; it is not a class declaration as used previously.

To use function templates, we need to understand the difference between a function and a function template. Functions, by their design, are made to process different sets of data. Each time a function is called, a new set of data must be provided and different results are produced. To describe a function's operation, we can say that it creates only **one level of generalization**—one function with different sets of data.

A function template, on the other hand, creates **two levels of generalization**. During the compilation, the template can create several functions, each with different argument types. The generated functions, at run time, then process a different set of data each time they are called.

> **A function template can create multiple functions, each with potentially different arguments and return types.**

The differences between a function and a function template are summarized in Figure 13-3.

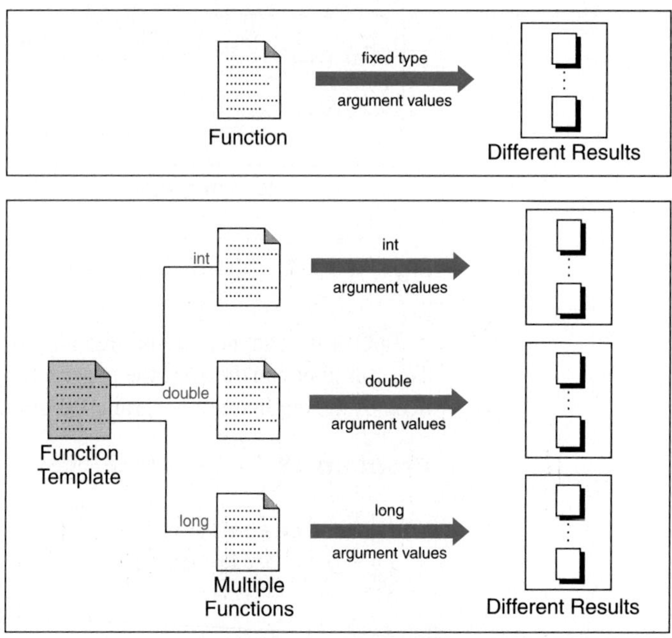

Figure 13-3 Function template operation

Let's see how we can use this generic function to create a set of different functions. Program 13-2 creates pairs of random integers, long integers, floating-point numbers, and doubles and then displays the larger of each.

Program 13-2 Demonstrate function templates

```
/* Demonstrate function templates
      Written by:
      Date:
*/
#include <iostream>
#include <iomanip>
#include <cstdlib>
using namespace std;

/* ==================== max ====================
   This template compares two elements and returns
   the larger.
      pre  x and y are the values to be compared
      post larger value returned
*/
template <class TYPE>
TYPE max (TYPE x, TYPE y)
{
    return (x > y ) ? x : y;
} // max template

int main ()
{
   int i1      = rand();
   int i2      = rand();
   cout << "Given "       << setw(5) << i1
        << " and "        << setw(5) << i2   << ": "
        << max(i1, i2)    << " is larger\n";
   float f1    = rand() / 3.3;
   float f2    = rand() * 6.7;
   cout << "\nGiven "     << setw(5) << f1
        << " and "        << setw(5) << f2   << ": "
        << max(f1, f2)    << " is larger\n";
   return 0;
} // main
```

```
Results
Given 16838 and  5758: 16838 is larger

Given 3064.55 and 117350: 117350 is larger
```

Program 13-2 Analysis As you study this simple program, note that there are no functions other than `main` and the template `max`. Without the template, we would have had to create four different functions, as shown in Figure 13-4. While we prefer the term "generated function," the functions created by the function template are also known as **instances** of the template.

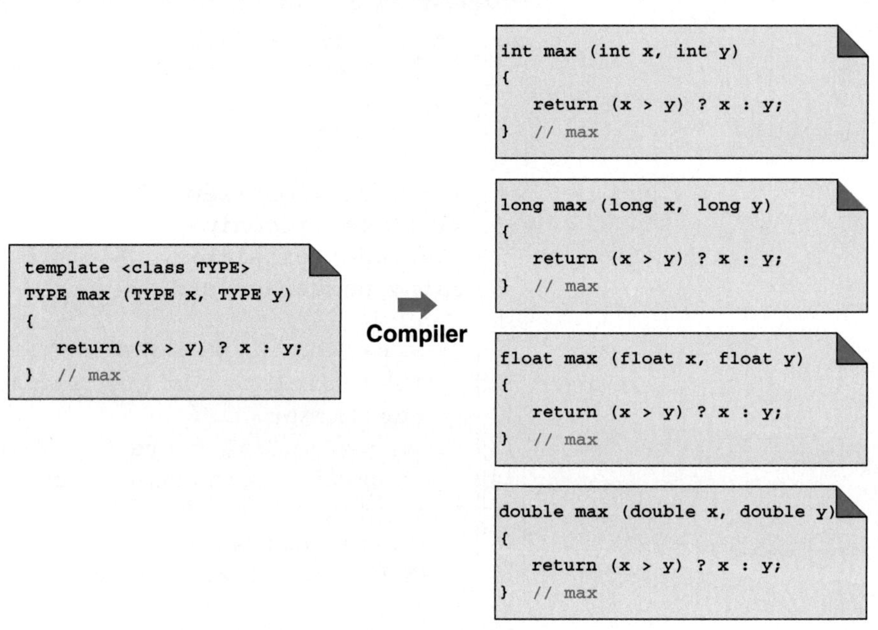

template <class TYPE>
TYPE max (TYPE x, TYPE y)
{
return (x > y) ? x : y;
} // max
Compiler
int max (int x, int y)
{
return (x > y) ? x : y;
} // max
long max (long x, long y)
{
return (x > y) ? x : y;
} // max
float max (float x, float y)
{
return (x > y) ? x : y;
} // max
double max (double x, double y)
{
return (x > y) ? x : y;
} // max

Figure 13-4 Generated functions

TEMPLATE FORMAT

A function template begins with a **template prefix** that provides the generic parameters, enclosed in a set of pointed brackets, used in the template. The presence of the template prefix tells the compiler that the code that follows is a template. Its format is shown in the next example:

```
template <class TYPE>
```

in which *class* is a keyword and `TYPE` is the name of the generic parameter that will be replaced during generation with a concrete parameter. Do not confuse the keyword *class* with class declarations; the keywords are identical, but the meanings are different. For example, Figure 13-4 represents a function template and its generated functions, not a class. The function template code immediately follows the template prefix.

> **Function templates allow us to write a single function for a whole family of similar functions.**

Study Figure 13-4 carefully. Note that the template parameters are different than normal parameters. Although they can contain standard types, they generally contain one or more generic types. When the functions are generated, the compiler first replaces the template parameter types with the concrete types required by a call. This substitution creates a function, with the correct types matching the calling function. When the call is made, the corresponding parameters are replaced by the actual data as in any function call. This function generation and call are shown in Figure 13-5.

Function templates may be coded in the global area at the beginning of the program. They should be placed after the library include statements so that the libraries are available for their use. We also recommend that they be identified by a comment. Figure 13-6 shows this technique.

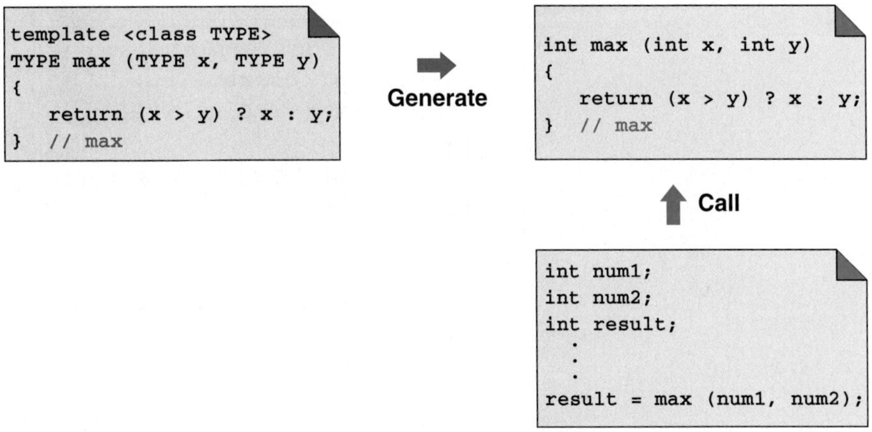

```
template <class TYPE>
TYPE max (TYPE x, TYPE y)
{
   return (x > y) ? x : y;
}  // max
```

Generate

```
int max (int x, int y)
{
   return (x > y) ? x : y;
}  // max
```

Call

```
int num1;
int num2;
int result;
   .
   .
   .
result = max (num1, num2);
```

Figure 13-5 Function template generation

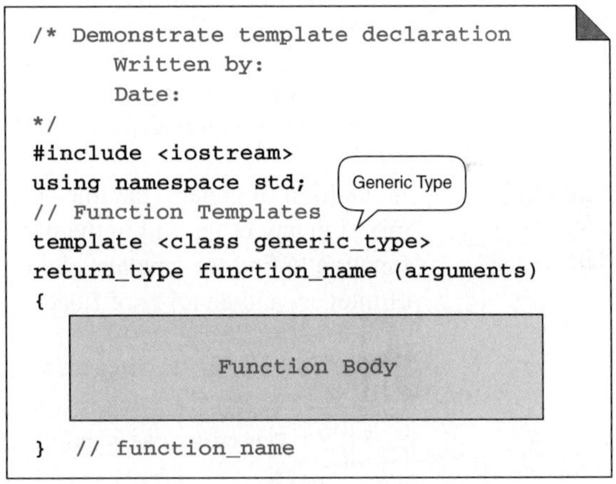

```
/* Demonstrate template declaration
      Written by:
      Date:
*/
#include <iostream>
using namespace std;
// Function Templates
template <class generic_type>
return_type function_name (arguments)
{
            Function Body
}  // function_name
```

Generic Type

Figure 13-6 Function declaration

As an alternative, especially when they are used in several programs, function templates can be included in a header file. In this case, the supporting library files should be included in the file along with the templates.

OVERLOADING FUNCTION TEMPLATES

There are times when a function template will not work. Perhaps the most common situations occur when one or more of the arguments is a pointer or the relational operators are not defined for the object. For example, we cannot use the max template to compare two objects when the selection operator (`? :`) is not defined for them.

In these situations, the solution is to write an overloaded function that handles the specific types. For example, to create a `max` function that compares two fractions, we simply overload it as shown in Program 13-3. Note that the overloaded function is not a function template.

Program 13-3 Overloading `max` for fractions

```
// Function template
template <class TYPE>
TYPE max (TYPE x, TYPE y)
{
   return (x > y) ? x : y;
} // max

//  Overload max for Fractions
Fraction max (Fraction fr1, Fraction fr2)
{
   if (fr1.compare(fr2) > 0)
      return fr1;
   else
      return fr2;
} // max Fraction
```

Program 13-3 Analysis Obviously, the header file for the `Fraction` class will need to be included in the program. Because the Fraction class has a compare function, we use it to determine which fraction is larger. Once again, while `max` is a function template, `Fraction max` is not. It is a concrete function that overrides the max functions for the `Fraction` class.

MIXED ARGUMENT TYPES

In addition to generic parameter types, we can use standard types. They can be intermixed in any order within the parameter list. In Program 13-4, we create a generalized function to find the smallest element in an array. To test it, we create and print an array of integers and an array of floats.

Program 13-4 Using mixed argument types

```
/* Demonstrate mixed argument types--generic and stan-
dard
      Written by:
      Date:
*/
#include <iostream>
using namespace std;

template<class TYPE>
TYPE smallest  (TYPE arr[] , int size)
{
   TYPE smallestValue = arr[0];
   for (int index = 0; index < size; index++)
       {
        if (arr[index] < smallestValue)
             smallestValue = arr[index];
   } // for
   return smallestValue;
} // smallest

```

Program 13-4 Using mixed argument types (*continued*)

```
int main ()
{
   // Test template with array of integers
   int   arr1[4] = {8, 2, 45, 67};
   cout << "Smallest integer value is: ";
   cout << smallest (arr1, 4) << endl;

   // Now test with array of floats
   float arr2[5] = {3.5, 5.6, 1.22, 78.4 , 6.0};
   cout << "Smallest float value is  : ";
   cout << smallest (arr2 , 5) << endl;
   return 0;
}  // main
```

```
Results
Smallest integer value is: 2
Smallest float value is  : 1.22
```

MULTIPLE GENERIC ARGUMENT TYPES

The argument types in a function template do not have to be the same generic type. In the next program, we create a template for a simple sequential search of an array that contains structured elements. Because we don't know in advance the format of the structure or of the key, we use generic types for them. The size of the array must be in integer, so we use a standard parameter type for it. We use a header file for the search template. It is shown in Program 13-5.

Program 13-5 Search Structure Header File

```
/* Template header file for search structure.
      Written by:
      Date:
*/
template<class TYPE, class KEY>
int search (TYPE arr[], KEY key, int size)
{
   int index = 0;
   while ( index < size )
      {
       if (key != arr[index].key)
           index++;
       else
           return index;
      } // while
   return -1;
}  // search Template
```

To test the template, we create a program that contains two structures. The first structure uses an integer key; the second structure uses a character key. The structures are shown in Figure 13-7.

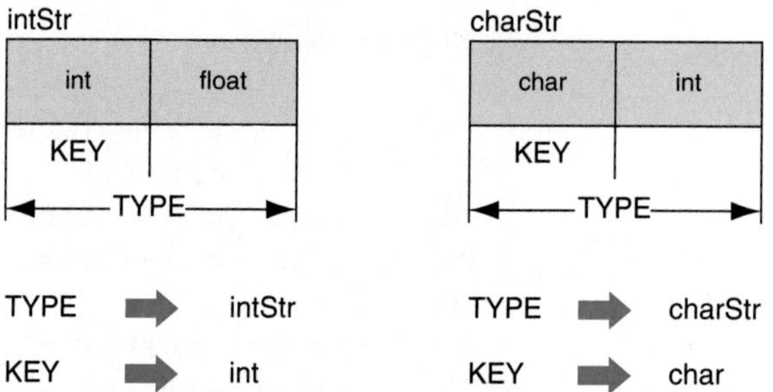

Figure 13-7 Structure design for search template

We then search each array to demonstrate that the template generated valid functions. Program 13-6 contains the code and the program results.

Program 13-6 Using multiple generic keys

```
/* Demonstrate multiple generic keys
      Written by:
      Date:
*/
#include <iostream>
using namespace std;

#include "p13-05.h"

// Structures
struct  intStr
{
     int   key;
     float data;
}; // intStr

struct charStr
{
   char key;
   int  data;
}; // charStr

int main ()
{
   intStr   arr1[3] = { { 2, 4.5}, {6,   1.1},
                        { 9, 11.2} };
   charStr  arr2[2] = { {'A', 45}, {'N', 678} };

   // Calling  search for the first array
   int locn1 = search (arr1, 9, 3);
```

Program 13-6 Using multiple generic keys (*continued*)

```
   if (locn1 >= 0)
       cout << "Data: " << arr1[locn1].data
            << " found at location " << locn1 << endl;
   else
       cout << "Data not found" << endl;

   // Calling search for the second array
   int locn2 = search (arr2,  'A',  2);
   if (locn2 >= 0)
        cout << "Data: " << arr2[locn2].data
             << " found at location " << locn2 << endl;
   else
        cout << "Data not found" << endl;
   return 0;
} // main
```

```
Results
Data: 11.2 found at location 2
Data: 45 found at location 0
```

FUNCTION TEMPLATES VERSUS OTHER SOLUTIONS

A reasonable question to ask is, "Why use function templates when we can do the same job with function overloading or macros?" We investigate the differences in the next two sections.

Function Templates versus Overloading

When we write overloaded functions, we must code the function for each usage. On the other hand, when we write a function template, we code the function only once, making much better use of a programmer's time. Figure 13-4 on page 652 demonstrates this efficient use of programmer time. The template automatically creates an instance of the function for each different calling type. To do the same job with function overloading, we would have to write the function four times, as shown in Figure 13-4.

Function Templates versus Macros

Program 13-7 contains a macro that generates the `max` function automatically for each different type usage. However, consider the following points:

1. It is easier to make a mistake when coding a macro. Furthermore, the compiler may not catch it. For example, if we accidently mix types, as in the third example in Program 13-7, the mistake is undetected.
2. It is more difficult to debug macros because they are handled by the preprocessor. What we see in the listing is not what C++ is looking at.
3. On the other hand, macros are more efficient because they are compiled inline rather than being a function call.

Program 13-7 Function templates versus macros

```
/* This program uses a macro to write the max
   function.
      Written by:
      Date:
```

Program 13-7 Function templates versus macros (*continued*)

```
*/
#define MAX(x, y) (((x) > (y)) ? (x) : (y))

#include <iostream>
using namespace std;

int main ()
{
   cout << "Begin macro tests\n";
   cout << "Test1: " << MAX (1, 4)     << endl;
   cout << "Test2: " << MAX ('A', 'B') << endl;
   cout << "Test3: " << MAX (4, 'A')   << endl;
   cout << "End of macro tests\n";
} // main
```

```
Results
Begin macro tests
Test1: 4
Test2: B
Test3: 65
End of macro tests
```

13-2 CLASS TEMPLATES

The basic use for a class is to create a model for a group of objects that have the same attribute types (variables) and use the same operations (functions). By definition, the functions in a class must accept the same argument types and must return the same data type. As we saw with function templates, however, there are occasions when we need to have not only one class, but several classes in which the objects of each class behave the same while their attributes are of different types. For example, if we were to create a generalized array type using a class structure, we would need to define several different classes: one for an array of integers, one for an array of floats, and so on. This is the purpose of the class template. Figure 13-8 demonstrates the concept of class templates.

CLASS TEMPLATE SYNTAX

The general syntax of a class template closely follows the syntax for the function template. The class declaration is immediately preceded by a template prefix that specifies the generic types to be associated with the class. The class then uses these generic types to complete its declaration. Program 13-8 contains a simple class template declaration with only one generic type, `TYPE`.

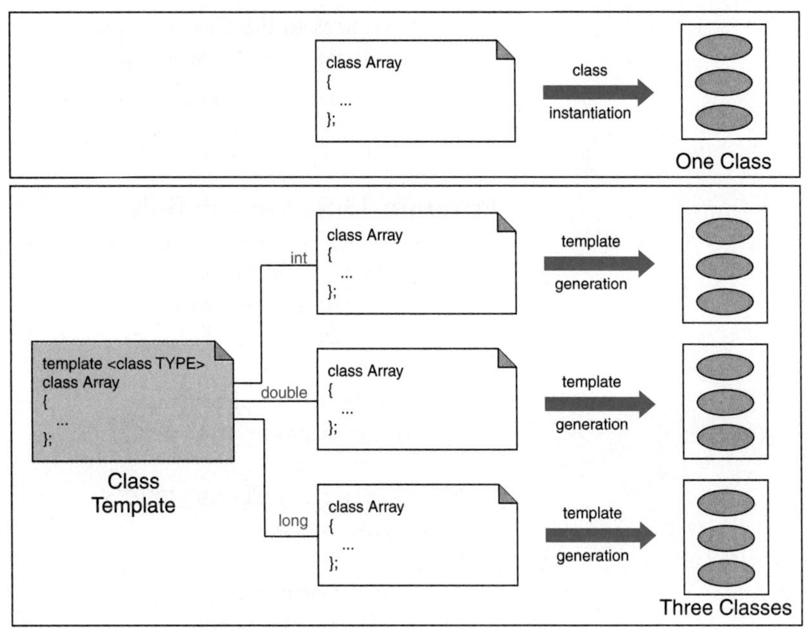

Figure 13-8 Class template operation

Program 13-8 Class template syntax

```
template <class TYPE>
class Array
{
   protected:
      TYPE* ary;
      int   capacity;
      int   nextUnusedIndex;

   public:
      ...
}; // class Array
```

DEFINING THE CLASS

The generation of a class with a template follows the rules for any class, with five differences:

1. The parameterized types can be used in declaring data members.
2. The parameterized types can be used in declaring function members.

3. All functions must be defined using the template prefix.
4. References to the class in scope definitions, such as in function headers, must include the parameterized types.
5. Class instantiations must include concrete types.

These points are shown in Program 13-9.

Program 13-9 Class definition

```
1  /* Class definition
2        Written by:
3        Date:
4  */
5  #include <iostream>
6  using namespace std;
7
8  template <class TYPE>
9  class Array
10 {
11    protected:
12       TYPE* ary;                        // Parameterized
13       int   capacity;
14       int   nextUnusedIndex;
15
16    public:
17          Array  (int size);             // Constructor
18    void append (TYPE data);             // Parameterized
19 } ; // Array
20 // ================== constructor ==================
21 template<class TYPE>
22 Array<TYPE> :: Array (int size)
23 {
24    ...
25 } // constructor
26 // =================== append =====================
27 template <class TYPE>
28 Array<TYPE> :: append (TYPE data)
29 {
30    ...
31 } // append
```

Program 13-9 Analysis Carefully study the use of the template parameter, `TYPE`, in this program. It appears first in the template prefix in statement 8. It is then used in the declaration of the array in statement 12. When instantiated, the concrete type will replace the generic type in this statement, creating an array of the specified type.

In statement 18, `TYPE` is used to specify that the generic type is passed to the function. Again, this type will be substituted with a concrete type when the class is instantiated.

When we define the constructor method in statement 22, we must first code the template prefix as required by rule 3. The template prefix is coded in statement 21. `Array` appears twice in the function header. Before the scope operator (`::`), we need the class name. The class name includes the template parameter to qualify it. Thus, we have, `Array<TYPE>`. After the scope operator, we need the function header. Because it is the function name, it doesn't use the template parameter. It must match its prototype in statement 17.

Statement 27 again repeats the template prefix. The function header in statement 28 uses `TYPE` twice. Because it is part of the class name, it must be used when the class is specified before the scope operator. It is then required in the parameter list and will be replaced by a concrete type when the function is instantiated.

INSTANTIATION OF OBJECTS

After we have defined the class template, we can instantiate objects. Remember, however, that the compiler replaces the parameterized type with the concrete type that we specified. For example, Program 13-10 shows how we tell the compiler to first generate a concrete class replacing the parameterized type with integer and then generate another concrete class with a replacement type of float.

Program 13-10 Using class templates

```
int main ()
{
// Local Definitions
   Array <int>   intary   (...);
   Array <float> floatary(...);
    ...
} // main
```

ARRAY CLASS

To demonstrate the concept, we complete the definition of the array class seen in the previous two program segments. It is similar to the array structure defined in the C++ standard template library, but it has more features. The array objects can be of any type (including string types, discussed in Chapter 14). It includes methods to check if the array; object is full, append to the array, find the index of an element containing specified data, and several others to maintain and process the array.

Planning ahead, we use protected data items in the array class because we will use it as the base class for another array class later in the chapter. The class structure is shown in Program 13-11.

Program 13-11 Header file for array class

```
/* Declaration and definition of generic array class.
      Written by:
      Date:
*/
template<class TYPE>
class Array
{
   protected:
      TYPE* ary;                  // Pointer to the array
      int   capacity;
```

Program 13-11 Header file for array class (*continued*)

```
      int   nextUnusedIndex;

   public:
              Array       (int size);  // Constructor
      int  getCapacity () const;
      int  getUnused   () const;
      bool isFull      () const;
      void append      (TYPE data);
      int  find        (TYPE data) const;
      TYPE retrieve    (int index) const;
      void change      (int index, TYPE data);
}; // Array

// ================== constructor ==================
template<class TYPE>
Array<TYPE> :: Array (int size)
{
   capacity        = size;
   nextUnusedIndex = 0;
   ary             = new TYPE [capacity];
} // constructor
/* ================== getCapacity ==================
   Retrieve and return size of the array.
      Pre  nothing
      Post capacity returned
*/
template<class TYPE>
int Array<TYPE> :: getCapacity () const
{
   return capacity;
} // getCapacity
/* =================== getUnused ===================
   Return number of empty cells in array.
      Pre  nothing
      Post number of empty cells returned
*/
template<class TYPE>
int Array<TYPE> :: getUnused () const
{
   return (capacity - nextUnusedIndex);
} // getUnused
/* =================== isFull ====================
   Return boolean true if array full, false if not.
      Pre  nothing
      Post full status returned
*/
template<class TYPE>
bool  Array<TYPE> :: isFull() const
{
```

Program 13-11 Header file for array class (*continued*)

```
   return (nextUnusedIndex == capacity);
} // isFull
/* ==================== append =====================
   Insert new data in first empty cell in array.
      Pre  array is not full
      Post data inserted or program aborted
*/
template<class TYPE>
void   Array<TYPE> :: append( TYPE data)
{
   if (capacity > nextUnusedIndex)
      {
       ary[nextUnusedIndex] = data;
       nextUnusedIndex++;
      } // if
   else
      {
       cout << "Error 100: Array overflow";
       exit (100);
      } // else
} // append

/* ====================== find =====================
   Search for data in array and return index
   location or -1 if not found.
      Pre   data contains value to be located
      Post  index location or -1 returned
*/
template<class TYPE>
int  Array<TYPE> :: find (TYPE data) const
{
   int  index = 0;
   bool found = false;
   while (!found && index < nextUnusedIndex)
      {
       if (ary[index] == data)
           found = true;
       else
           index++;
      } // while
   if (found)
       return index;
   else
       return -1;
} // find
/* =================== retrieve ==================
   Return value in specified index location.
      Pre  index location is valid
      Post data returned or program aborted.
```

Program 13-11 Header file for array class (*continued*)

```
*/
template<class TYPE>
TYPE  Array<TYPE> :: retrieve (int index) const
{
   if (index < 0 || index >= nextUnusedIndex)
      {
       cout << "Error 101: index out of range";
       exit (101);
      } // else
   return ary[index];
} // retrieve
/* =================== change ===================
   Insert data in specified index location.
      Pre  index location must be valid
           data contains new value to be inserted
      Post data inserted or program aborted
*/
template<class TYPE>
void  Array<TYPE> :: change (int index, TYPE data)
{
   if (index < 0 || index >= nextUnusedIndex)
      {
       cout << "Error 102: index out of range";
       exit (102);
      } // else
     ary[index] = data;
} // change
```

Program 12-13 Analysis Most of the code in this program is straightforward. One question that might be asked, however, is, "Why do we abort the program when we find an error?" The reason is that the errors are programmer errors and not user errors. In general, programs should validate data and allow users to correct any errors. Program logic errors, however, cannot be corrected during a run. In Chapter 15, "Exception Handling," we discuss how programmers can intercept these types of errors and provide application solutions to them.

To validate the array class, we write a test driver that exercises each of the methods in the class. It creates two arrays: the first for integers and the second for floating-point numbers. The code is seen in Program 13-12.

Program 13-12 Demonstrate array class

```
/* Test driver to test array class.
      Written by:
      Date:
*/
#include <iostream>
#include <cstdlib>
using namespace std;

```

Program 13-12 Demonstrate array class (*continued*)

```
#include "p13-11.h"

int main ()
{
   // Build two arrays
   Array<int>   intary   (30);
   Array<float> floatary (20);

   for (int i = 0; i < 20; i++)
       {
        intary.append   (i * 100);
        floatary.append (i * 3.14);
       } // for

   cout << "Testing int array:\n";
   cout << "Capacity of array is:       "
        << intary.getCapacity() << endl;
   cout << "Value 400 is at location:  "
        << intary.find (400) << endl;
   cout << "Changing value at location 5 to 999\n";
   intary.change (5, 999);
   cout << "Value at location 5 is:    "
        << intary.retrieve(5) << endl;
   cout << "Checking full status:      "
        << intary.isFull()    << endl;

   cout << "\nTesting float  array:\n";
   cout << "Unused cells in array:     "
        << floatary.getUnused() << endl;
   cout << "Value 6.28 is at location: "
        << floatary.find (6.28) << endl;
   cout << "Changing value at location 5 to -12.80\n";
   floatary.change(5, -12.80);
   cout << "Value at location 5 is:    "
        << floatary.retrieve (5) << endl;
   cout << "Checking full status:      "
        << floatary.isFull()    << endl;

   return 0;
}  // main
```

```
Results
Testing int array:
Capacity of array is:      30
Value 400 is at location:  4
Changing value at location 5 to 999
Value at location 5 is:    999
Checking full status:      0
```

Program 13-12 Demonstrate array class (*continued*)

```
Testing float  array:
Unused cells in array:     0
Value 6.28 is at location: 2
Changing value at location 5 to -12.80
Value at location 5 is:    -12.8
Checking full status:      1
```

Program 13-12 Analysis While we have tested every method in the class, we have not tested the error conditions in the class. None of the tests for invalid indexes has been exercised. More testing is required to completely validate the class.

SPECIALIZED MEMBER FUNCTIONS

As with function templates, there will be occasions when the template does not support a specific need. With function templates, we wrote an overloaded function. With classes, we write specialized class templates. Unlike overloaded functions, however, the whole class must be rewritten with the type specified.

Specialized classes must follow the following rules:

1. The class must be rewritten.
2. The template statement for the specialized class has no parameters between the pointed brackets.
3. The specific type(s) must be declared in the class statement.

CLASS TEMPLATE INHERITANCE

When a class is inherited from a class template, the derived class is also a class template. Before we demonstrate inheritance, however, let's review the basic inheritance rules:

1. All data members of the base class template are inherited.
2. All functions of the base type are inherited except for the constructors, destructors, nonmember functions, and the assignment operator.

This means that to write a derived class template, we need to redefine the constructors, destructors, any nonmember functions, and, if necessary, the assignment operator.

You may also want to review the inheritance access rules. They are covered in Table 12-1 on page 601.

To demonstrate how inheritance from a template class works, we create a derived class, manageable array (`MArray`). Objects of the manageable array are the same as the array class, with two extra features: (1) the size of the array is increased by 10 elements automatically whenever we exceed the current capacity, and (2) the array can be copied into another array.

These two changes require that we redefine the append function and add a copy function. The resulting code is shown in Program 13-13.

Program 13-13 MArray class inheritance header file

```
/* Create a derived class from the class template, Array.
   The new template automatically extends the array when
   it overflows and provides a copy method.
      Written by:
      Date:
*/
#include "p13-11.h"
```

Program 13-13 MArray class inheritance header file (*continued*)

```
template<class TYPE>
class MArray : public Array<TYPE>
{
  public:
       MArray (int size);            // Constructor
     void append (TYPE data);
     void copy   (const MArray <TYPE>& toBeCopied);
}; // MArray

template<class TYPE>
MArray<TYPE> :: MArray (int size) : Array<TYPE> (size)
{

} // constructor
/* ==================== append ===================
  Insert new data in first empty cell in array.
  If array is full, extends it by 10 elements.
     Pre  data contains new values to be inserted
     Post data inserted; array extended if needed
*/
template<class TYPE>
void    MArray<TYPE> :: append (TYPE data)
{
  if (capacity == nextUnusedIndex)
   {
    TYPE *temp = ary;
    capacity += 10;
    ary = new TYPE [capacity];
    for (int index = 0; index < nextUnusedIndex; index++)
         ary[index] = temp [index];
    delete [] temp;
   } // if
  ary[nextUnusedIndex] = data;
  nextUnusedIndex++;
} // append
/* ==================== copy =====================
  Copies array (toBeCopied) to this array class.
  Any data in this class's array is lost.
     Pre  toBeCopied is an MArray class
     Post data copied to array
*/
template<class TYPE>
void MArray<TYPE> :: copy (const MArray<TYPE>& toBeCopied)
{
  if (capacity !=  toBeCopied.capacity)
     {
      delete [] ary;
      ary  = new TYPE [toBeCopied.capacity];
```

Program 13-13 MArray class inheritance header file (*continued*)

```
        } // if
    capacity = toBeCopied.capacity;
    nextUnusedIndex = toBeCopied.nextUnusedIndex;
    for (int index = 0; index < nextUnusedIndex; index++)
         ary [index] = toBeCopied.ary[index];
} // copy
```

Program 13-13 The constructor definition (statement 19) requires some explanation. The first thing that looks strange is that there is no code in the function body. Recall, however, that the base class constructor initializes the *protected* variables in the class. We must call it from our derived class and at the same time pass on the array size. This is done with the initialization list after the colon.

To test the derived class, we use the test driver in Program 13-14. Note that only the new functions need to be tested.

Program 13-14 Test driver for MArray class

```
/* Driver program to validate MArray class.
      Written by:
      Date:
*/
#include <iostream>
#include <cstdlib>
using namespace std;

#include "p13-13.h"

int main ()
{
   // Bulid int array
   MArray<int>  intMAry (10);

   for (int i = 0; i < 10; i++)
        intMAry.append (i * 100);

   cout << "Testing int array:\n";
   cout << "Capacity of array is:      "
        << intMAry.getCapacity() << endl;
   cout << "Appending 999 to array.\n";
   intMAry.append (999);
   cout << "Capacity of array is:      "
        << intMAry.getCapacity() << endl;
   cout << "Value at location 10 is:   "
        << intMAry.retrieve(10)  << endl;

   cout << "Copy to new array class\n";
   MArray<int> newIntMAry (5);
   newIntMAry.copy (intMAry);

```

Program 13-14 Test driver for MArray class (*continued*)

```
   cout << "Capacity of newarray is:   "
        << newIntMAry.getCapacity ()<< endl;
   cout << "Value at location 10 is:   "
        << newIntMAry.retrieve (10)  << endl;

   return 0;
} // main
```

```
Results
Testing int array:
Capacity of array is:      10
Appending 999 to array.
Capacity of array is:      20
Value at location 10 is:   999
Copy to new array class
Capacity of newarray is:   20
Value at location 10 is:   999
```

13-3 SOFTWARE ENGINEERING AND PROGRAMMING STYLE

In this section we discuss three conceptual design concepts: atomic and composite data, structures, and abstract data types.

ATOMIC AND COMPOSITE DATA

Atomic data are data that we choose to consider as a single, nondecomposable entity. For example, the integer 4562 may be considered as a single integer value. Of course, you can decompose it into digits, but the decomposed digits will not have the same characteristics of the original integer; they will be four one-digit integers in the range 0 to 9.

An **atomic data type** is a set of atomic data having identical properties. These properties distinguish one atomic data type from another. Atomic data types are defined by a set of values and a set of operations that act on the values.

Atomic Data Type

1. A set of values
2. A set of operations on values

For example, we can define the following atomic data types:

```
int
    VALUES:     -∞, …, -2, -1, 0, 1, 2, …, ∞
    OPERATIONS: *, +, -, %, /, ++, --, …
float
    VALUES:     -∞, …, 0.0, …, ∞
    OPERATIONS: *, +, -, /, …
char
    VALUES:     \0, …, 'A', 'B', …, 'a', 'b', …,\127
    OPERATIONS: +, -, …
```

The opposite of atomic data is **composite data.** Composite data can be broken into subfields that have meaning. As an example of a composite data item, consider your telephone number. There are actually three different parts to a telephone number. First, there is the area code. Next, there is a prefix consisting of three digits, and then the number after the prefix, consisting of four digits. (Years ago the prefixes were names, such as DAvenport and CYpress, rather than numbers.)

DATA STRUCTURE

A **data structure** is a collection of elements and the relationships among them. Data structures can be nested—that is, we can have a data structure that consists of other data structures.

Data Structure

1. A combination of elements, each of which is either an atomic type or another data structure
2. A set of associations or relationships (structure) involving the combined elements

For example, we can define the two structures, *array* and *class,* as shown in Table 13-1.

array	class
1. A homogeneous combination of data structures	1. A heterogeneous combination of data structures
2. Position association	2. No association
3. No user-defined operations	3. Methods

Table 13-1 Two structures

Most of the programming languages support several data structures. In addition, modern programming languages allow programmers to create new data structures that are not available in the language they are using. In C++, this is done with a *struct* or a *class*.

ABSTRACT DATA TYPE

Generally speaking, programmers' capabilities are determined by the tools in their tool kits. These tools are acquired by education and experience. Your knowledge of C++ is one of your tools. As you continue your studies with subjects such as data structures, file management, and systems analysis, your tools will increase. Abstract data types are another tool to be added to your tool kit.

Looking back when programming began, there were no abstract data types. If we wanted to read a file, we wrote the code to read the file device. It did not take programmers long to realize that they were writing the same code over and over again, so they created what is known today as an ADT. This enabled programmers to write a code to read a file and then place the code in a library for other programmers to use.

This concept is found in C++ today. For example, the string class is an abstract data type. It defines a template class that can read and write strings of different character sizes.

With an abstract data type, the user is not concerned with *how* the task is done but rather with *what* it can do. In other words, the ADT consists of a set of prototype definitions that allow the programmer to use the functions while hiding the implementation. This generalization of operations with unspecified implementations is known as abstraction. We abstract the essence of the process and leave the implementation details hidden.

The concept of abstraction means:

- **We know *what* a data type can do.**
- ***How* it is done is hidden.**

Consider the concept of a list. There are at least three data structures that will support a list. We can use an array, a linked list, or a file. If we place the list in an abstract data type, the user should not be aware of the structure we use. As long as data can be inserted and retrieved, it should make no difference how we store the data. Figure 13-9 shows several structures that might be used to hold a list.

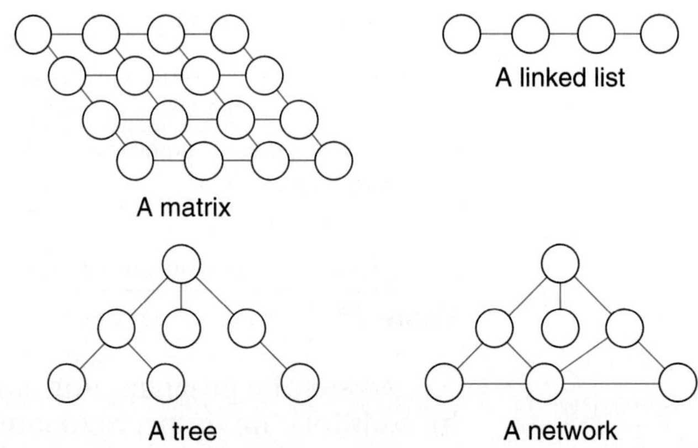

Figure 13-9 Some structures

Let us now formally define an abstract data type. An **abstract data type** is a data declaration packaged together with the operations that are allowed on the data type. In other words, we *encapsulate* the data and the operations on data and we *hide* their implementation from the user.

> **Abstract Data Type**
>
> 1. Declaration of data
> 2. Declaration of operations

The abstract data type definition implies two attributes for ADTs:

1. *The structures are opaque.* We can use them without knowing how they are implemented.
2. *The operations are opaque.* We know what they will do; we don't know how they will do it.

We cannot overstress the importance of hiding the implementation. For example, the programmer should not have to know the data structure to use the ADT. This is a common fault in many implementations that keeps the ADT from being fully portable to other applications. Fortunately, C++ has a very powerful mechanism—templates—that allows us to create ADTs.

A MODEL FOR AN ABSTRACT DATA TYPE

The abstract data type model is illustrated in Figure 13-10. The model is represented by the area with an irregular outline. Inside the model there are two different aspects of the model: the data structure and the operational functions. Both are entirely contained in the model and are not within the user's scope. However, the data structure is available to all the ADTs operations as needed, and an operation may call on other functions to accomplish its task. In other words, the data structure and the functions are within scope of each other.

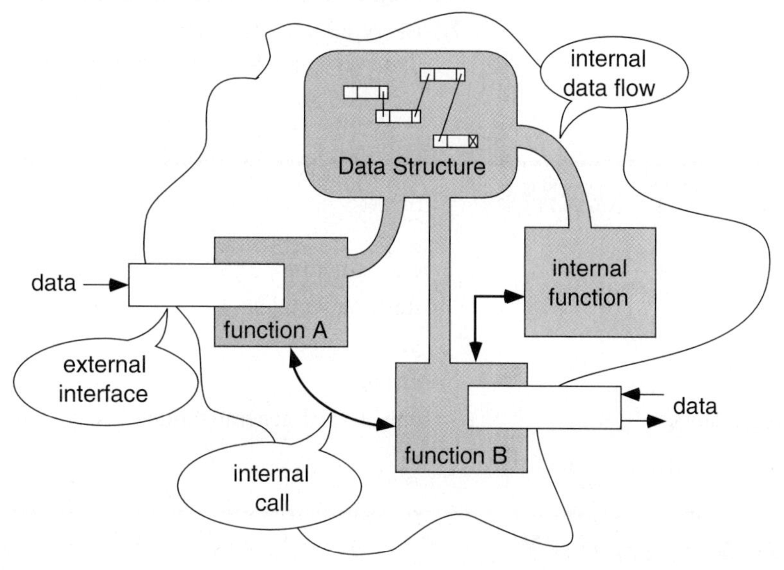

Figure 13-10 Abstract data type model

Data flow in and out of the ADT through the operation headers drawn as rectangles partially in and partially out of the model outline. For each operation header there is a function. For instance, in a linked list ADT (see Chapter 17), there would be operations such as insert, remove, and search. There could also be an operation to return the number of nodes in the linked list or perhaps the data in the last node in the list. In C++, these operations would be defined as prototype header declarations that are visible to the user. They are the only things the user must know to use the ADT.

ADTs AND TEMPLATES

C++ implements the ADT concept using templates. As we saw in this chapter, we can define a class template to be used to generate a set of classes. For example, once a list template has been created, it can be used to create a list of any type, such as a list of integers or a list of floating-point numbers.

13-4 TIPS AND COMMON PROGRAMMING ERRORS

1. It is an error to define a function template without the template prefix.
2. It is an error to define a class template without the template prefix.
3. Compilers need to see the definition for a function template before the call. The solution is to insert the definition at the global area or in a header file.
4. Compilers need to see the definition for a class template before the call. The solution is to insert the definition at the global area or in a header file.
5. It is an error to reference a template class without specifying the type.

6. A class inherited from a template is a template.
7. Every member function in a class template is a function template. This means that every member function must use the template prefix.

13-5 KEY TERMS

abstract data type
atomic data
atomic data type
class template
composite data
data structure
function template
generic type
instances
one level of generalization
template
template prefix
two levels of generalization

13-6 SUMMARY

- A function template is useful when we need a set of functions all having the same logic (code), but each requiring a different data type.
- A function creates one level of generalization; a function template creates two levels of generalization.
- In C++, we can use function templates to generate a set of actual functions, each with different argument(s) type or return type.
- To create a function template, we need to use a template prefix in the format

```
template<class TYPE>
```

  in which the word class actually means *type* and `TYPE` stands for the generic type.
- The type or types defined in the prefix are used in the function template header definition as generic types.
- If all of the functions needed in a program cannot be generated by one template, we can overload the template.
- We can mix generic types with standard types in a function template.
- We can have more than one generic type in a function template.
- A class template is useful when we need several sets of objects, in which the object in each set use different data types.
- A class creates a set of objects; a class template creates several sets of objects.
- In C++, we can use a class template to create a set of actual classes, each with different data types.
- The syntax for a class template closely follows the syntax for a function template.
- To create a class template, we need to use a template prefix in the format

```
template<class TYPE>
```

  in which the word *class* actually means *type* and `TYPE` stands for the generic type.
- The class uses generic types to complete its declaration.
- In class declaration, the data and function members can be declared using generic types.
- All member functions in a class template must be defined as function templates.
- Reference to a class must include either a generic type or a concrete type.
- After the class has been declared or defined, we can instantiate objects. However, we must specify a concrete type to replace each generic type.
- As with function templates, we can have specialized class templates.
- A derived class can be inherited from a template class. The rules for inheritance are the same as those for concrete classes.

13-7 PRACTICE SETS

REVIEW QUESTIONS

1. How many levels of generalization does a regular function provide?
2. How many levels of generalization does a generic function provide?
3. Can we define one function template to be used either to sort or search an array? Explain your answer.
4. Can we define one function template to find either the maximum or the minimum of two integers? Explain your answer.
5. Can we use two generic types in a function template to find the maximum between two data types (an integer and a float)? Explain your answer.
6. Which technique is more efficient—using a function template or overloading a function? Explain your answer.
7. Can function templates free us from using overloading functions in all situations? Explain your answer.
8. Which technique is more reliable—using a function template or a macro? Explain your answer.
9. Can a function template free us from using a macro in all situations? Explain your answer.
10. Can a generic type be used more than once in a function template? Provide an example.
11. Can more than one generic type be used in a function template? Provide an example.
12. Can a generic type be used only as a return type in a function template? Provide an example.
13. Can we have a class template `Arrays`, in which the size of the array is a generic type? Explain your answer.
14. Can we use a macro instead of a class template? Explain your answer.
15. Can we use overloaded functions in a concrete class to do the same job as a class template? Explain your answer.

EXERCISES

16. Find errors (if any) in the following function template:

```
void fun (T  x)
{
  ...
}
```

17. Find errors (if any) in the following function template:

```
template(class T)
void fun (T  x)
{
  ...
}
```

18. Find errors (if any) in the following function template:

```
template<class T>
void fun (int  x)
{
  ...
}
```

19. Find errors (if any) in the following function template:

```
template<class T, U>
void fun (T  x , U y)
{
  ...
}
```

20. Find errors (if any) in the following function template:

```
template<class T>
T fun (int  x)
{
  ...
}
```

21. Find errors (if any) in the following function template:

```
template<class T, class U>
Z  fun (T  x , U y)
{
  ...
}
```

22. Find errors (if any) in the following class template:

```
template<class T>
class Sample
{
  ...
public:
    Sample<T>   ();
};
```

23. Find errors (if any) in the following class template:

```
template<class T>
class Sample
{
  ...
public:
Sample ();
};
Template<class T>
Sample::Sample () : {}
```

PROBLEMS

24. Define a function template that adds two numeric data types and returns the result.
25. Define a function template that swaps two numeric data types.
26. Define a function template that returns the absolute value of a number.
27. Define a function template that returns the sum of an array of numbers. The function must use two arguments: the type of array (generic) and the size of the array *(int)*.
28. Define a function template that reverses an array of numbers. The function must use two arguments: the type of array (generic) and the size of the array *(int)*.
29. Define a function template that finds the largest element in an array of numbers. The function must use two arguments: the type of array (generic) and the size of the array *(int)*. The function can use the `max` function we defined in this chapter.
30. Write a test driver to test the `max` function template defined in the chapter using character types.
31. Write a test driver to test the `smallest` function template defined in the chapter using an array of doubles.
32. Write a test program to test the search function template defined in the chapter using an array of structures in which the key is an integer (id) and the data are another structure of one integer (age) and one float-point value (salary).

PROJECTS

33. Write a test driver to test the array template class defined in the chapter using Fraction type (see Chapter 11). Note that you may need to overload some of the relational operators for the Fraction class.
34. Rewrite bubble sort function (Chapter 8) using generic type so that the function can sort any array of numeric type (*int*, *long*, *float*, and *double*). Test your function with four different arrays.
35. Rewrite insertion sort function (Chapter 8) using generic type so that the function can sort any array of numeric type (*int*, *long*, *float*, and *double*). Test your function with four different arrays.
36. Rewrite binary search function (Chapter 8) using generic type so that the function can search any array of numeric type (*int*, *long*, *float*, and *double*). Test your function with four different arrays.
37. Rewrite calculate row and column average program (Chapter 8) using a generic type so that the program can create averages for any numeric data type (*int*, *long*, *float*, and *double*).
38. Rewrite history and frequency program (Chapter 8) using a generic type so that the program can create history and frequency diagrams for any numeric data type (*int*, *long*, *float*, and *double*).
39. Write a derived class template, `EArray <TYPE, ENUM>`, inherited from the array class presented in the chapter, that accepts enumerated type as the index. For example, we can have an instance Sales that shows the sales amount for each day of the week, as shown in the following example.

```
Sales[MON] = 2200.00
```

40. Write a template class, `Set`, that implements a set. A set is an unordered collection of zero or more elements with no duplicates. The public functions are to be:
    - **a.** Constructor
    - **b.** Destructor
    - **c.** Add an element
    - **d.** Delete an element
    - **e.** List the elements
    - **f.** Intersection. An intersection of two sets is another set that contains the common elements from the two sets.
    - **g.** Union. A union of two sets is another set that contains the elements in either the first set or the second.
    - **h.** Difference. The difference of two sets is another set that contains the elements belonging to the first set, but not the second.

14 Strings

It is impossible to write a well-structured and human-engineered program without using strings. Although you probably weren't aware of it, even your first C++ program that you wrote while studying Chapter 2 used strings, and you have been using them ever since.

Whereas some languages, such as Pascal and Ada, provide intrinsic string types, C++ implements them as a class. In addition, C++ programmers can use the string library inherited from the C Language, although we recommend that the string class be used.

In this chapter, we first consider how strings are defined and stored in general, and then we explore the string class as well as the standard string functions that are available from the C Language.

14-1 STRING CONCEPTS

In general, a **string** is a series of characters treated as a unit. Computer science has long recognized the importance of strings, but it has not adapted a standard for their implementation. Thus, a string created in Pascal is different from a string created in C++.

Virtually all string implementations treat a string as a **variable-length** piece of data. Consider, for example, one of the most common of all strings: a name. Names—whether of people, textbooks, automobiles, or whatever—by their very nature vary in length.

Given that we have data that can vary in size, how do we accommodate them in our programs? We can store them either in fixed-length objects or in variable-length objects, as shown in Figure 14-1.

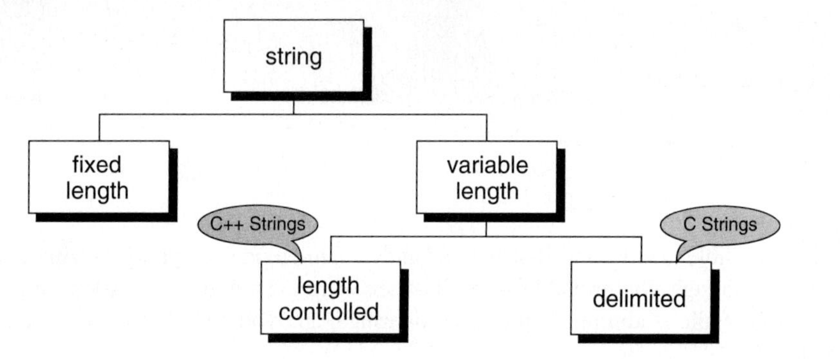

Figure 14-1 String taxonomy

FIXED-LENGTH STRINGS

A fixed length string is implemented as an array of characters. When implementing a **fixed-length string** format, we must first decide what size to make the variable. If we make it too small, we are unable to store all the data; if we make it too big, we waste memory.

Another problem associated with storing variable data in a fixed-length data structure is how to tell the data from the nondata. A common solution is to add nondata characters, such as spaces, at the end of the data. Note that in this case the character selected to represent the nondata value cannot be used as data.

VARIABLE-LENGTH STRINGS

A much preferred solution is to create a structure that can expand and contract to accommodate the data. Thus, to store a person's name that consists of only one letter, the structure would provide only enough storage for one character.[1] To store a person's name that consists of 30 characters, the structure would be expanded to provide storage for 30 characters.

Such flexibility does not come without a cost, however. There must be some way to tell when you get to the end of the data. Two common techniques are to use length-controlled strings and delimited strings.

[1]The shortest name that we are aware of is O. To accommodate the computers of credit card and other companies, however, Mr. O was compelled to legally change his name to Oh.

Length-Controlled Strings

Length-controlled strings add a count that specifies the number of characters in the string. Generally, the count is a single byte, which provides for strings of up to 255 characters. This count is then used by the string manipulation functions to determine the actual length of the data. This is the structure design used in the C++ string class.

Delimited Strings

Another technique used to identify the end of the string is a **delimiter**. You are already familiar with the concept of delimiters, although you probably don't recognize them as such. In English, each sentence, which is a variable-length string, ends with a delimiter—the period. Commas, semicolons, colons, and dashes are other common delimiters found in English.

The main disadvantage of the delimiter is that it eliminates one character from being used for data. Since this leaves 127 different characters (255 if we use Extended ASCII or EBCDIC) available, however, this is not a major problem. The most common delimiter is the ASCII null character, which is the first character in the ASCII character sequence (\0). This is the technique used by the C Language implementation.

Figure 14-2 shows fixed-length, length-controlled, and **delimited strings** in memory.

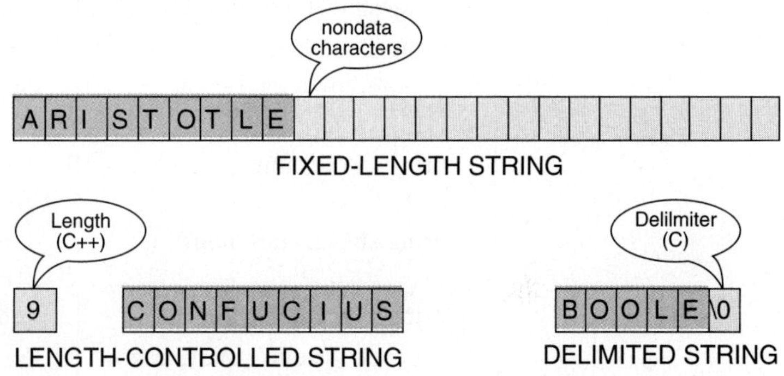

Figure 14-2 String formats

14-2 C++ STRINGS

A **C++ string** is a sequence of characters implemented as a length-controlled string object. This means that a C++ string is an instantiation of the string class.

String characters are usually selected only from the printable ASCII character set. There is nothing, however, that prevents any ASCII character from being used in a string. In fact, it is quite common to use formatting characters, such as tabs, in strings.

The C++ name for the string class is `basic_string`. Within the basic string class is a type definition for the type `string`, which equates the two. In this chapter, we simplify the terminology by using only the type defined string, which is the normal use. Included in the class is also an extensive set of methods to manipulate and process them.

THE STRING CLASS

The C++ standard defines the *string* type. An object instantiated of this type is a length-controlled string. Figure 14-3 shows the representation of a C++ string object named `str1`. We can refer to individual characters in the string using index notation.

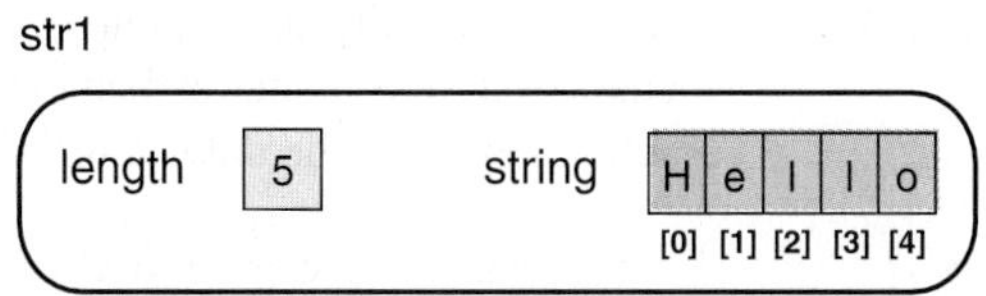

Figure 14-3 A C++ string

As a class, *string* has a rich set of constructors. The default constructor creates an empty string; because it is empty, the string length is set to zero. A set of constructors creates a C++ string from a C-language string,[2] from characters, from other strings, or from portions of another string. The constructors are summarized in Table 14-1.

Constructor format	Operation
string s1;	Default constructor (empty string)
string s2 ("Hello World");	Initialization constructor using C string
string s3 (n, 'c');	Initialization constructor using *n* identical characters
string s4 (s2);	Copy constructor
string s5 (s2, num);	Copy constructor that copies `num` characters from beginning of string
string s6 (s2, start, num)	Copy constructor that copies `num` characters from index location `start` in string `s2`
string s7 ("Hello", num);	Same as s5, but with C string
string s8 ("Hello", start, num);	Same as s6, but with C string

Table 14-1 String constructors

The `s6` and `s8` constructors in Table 14-1 use an index location, `start`. Note that even though we can use indexes, we can't use one that is after the end of the string. When we do, the string class throws an out of range exception (see Chapter 17). However, the character count, `num`, can go beyond the last index location. As a matter of fact, a large character count is often used to specify a range after the last character.

As you study the function formats in Table 14-1, note that none allows a single character as an argument. While `s3` may appear to, it is actually a string of *n* characters. Using this format to obtain a string of one character works, but it is easier to use a string literal of only one character.

[2]We provide an overview of C-language strings later in the chapter. At this point, all you need to remember is that C strings are nil delimited as shown in Figure 14-2.

Program 14-1 demonstrates the string class constructors.

Program 14-1 Demonstrate string constructors

```
/* Demonstrate string constructors.
      Written by:
      Date:
*/
#include <iostream>
#include <iomanip>
#include <string>
using namespace std;

int main ()
{
   string s1;
   string s2 ("Hello World");
   string s3 (s2);
   string s4 (5, 'A');
   string s5 (s2, 6);
   string s6 ("Hello", 2);
   string s7 ("Hello", 3, 25);

   cout << "Value of s1: " << s1 << endl;
   cout << "Value of s2: " << s2 << endl;
   cout << "Value of s3: " << s3 << endl;
   cout << "Value of s4: " << s4 << endl;
   cout << "Value of s5: " << s5 << endl;
   cout << "Value of s6: " << s6 << endl;
   cout << "Value of s7: " << s7 << endl;
   return 0;
} // main
```

```
Results
Value of s1:
Value of s2: Hello World
Value of s3: Hello World
Value of s4: AAAAA
Value of s5: World
Value of s6: He
Value of s7: lo
```

Program 14-1 Analysis We begin by defining a string (`s1`) with no initializers. The result is a null string. When we print it, nothing prints because there are no data. The second definition copies a literal string to a C++ string. We then create a third string using the copy constructor and the new C++ string (`s2`).

The fourth definition creates a string of five `A'`s. The fifth definition creates a string from a string literal by copying the first two characters only. The next definition copies string `s3` starting at location 6. Finally, the last definition copies nine characters from a string literal starting at location 3. Note that the number of characters is larger than the characters in the string. This is not an error.

14-3 C++ STRING INPUT/OUTPUT

The *string* class is overloaded for the insertion and extraction operators. This means that we can read a string just like any other variable.

STRING OUTPUT (<<)

String output is provided by the overloaded insertion operator (<<), which is overloaded in the string class. Shown below are two examples for writing the string `month`.

```
cout << month;     or     fsOut << month;
```

STRING INPUT(<<)

There are two ways to read C++ strings: using the extraction operator (>>) and the get line function.

String Extraction Operator

Reading strings in some languages, such as Pascal, requires that you read each character individually and assign it to the next position in the string. In C++, this task is much easier: You simply use the extraction operator (>>), which is overloaded for string objects, and let it do all the work. First, it skips any leading whitespace. Then it extracts all contiguous non-whitespace characters. When it finds any whitespace character it stops. The terminating whitespace character is left in the input stream.

The extraction operator can be used to read data from the keyboard (*cin* stream) or from a file using an open file stream. For example, to read a value into the string object, `month`, you could simply write one of the statements shown below.

```
cin >> month;     or     fsIn >> month;
```

One more point: After skipping leading whitespace, the extraction operator stops at the *first* whitespace character it finds. If it is in the middle of a phrase, such as *Hello World,* it stops at the space before *World,* not after it.

> **The extraction operator stops at whitespace.**
> **To read a string with spaces, we must use *getline.***

The *getline* Function

The ***getline* function** extracts text from an input stream and makes a string out of it. When text is read with *getline,* the text is placed in the receiving string and the terminating character, usually a newline, is deleted. The getline function is defined in the string header file.

> **The string input/output operators and functions are defined in the string header file, not the I/O stream header file.**

The *getline* function can have two or three parameters. The first parameter specifies the input stream. The second parameter specifies the string object where the data are to be stored. The third parameter specifies the terminating character, which defaults to the newline character is none is specified. Figure 14-4 shows how it works, first with the default delimiter and then with a semicolon specified as the default.

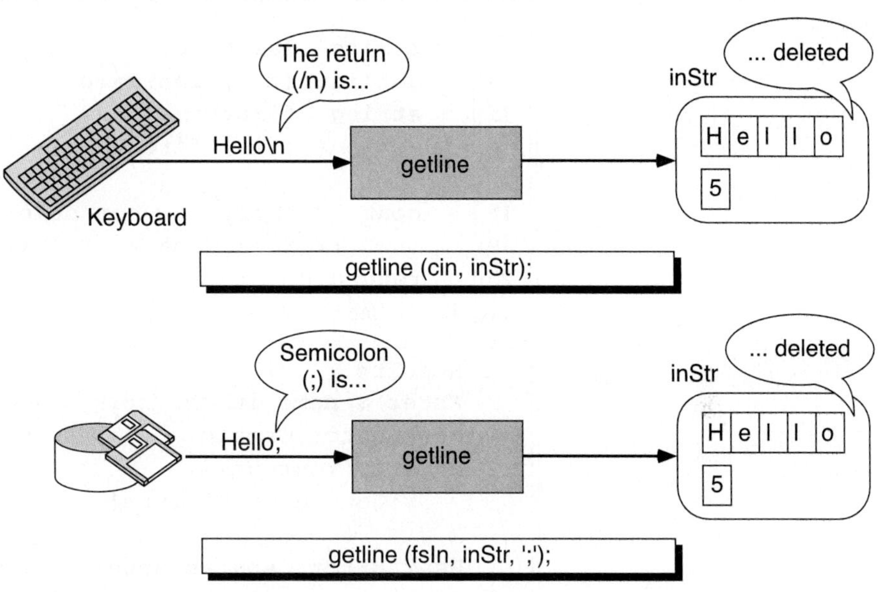

Figure 14-4 ***getline*** **function**

There is a big difference between reading a string with the extraction operator (>>) and reading the same line with *getline*: When data are read with the extraction operator, the reads stops with the first whitespace. When data are read with *getline*, however, all characters, including whitespace, are read into the string until the terminating character is found. Note that the getline function is a stand-alone function and does not need the member operator (.) as discussed in Section 14-5.

> **The getline function is overloaded to work with two or three arguments.**

Now let's write a simple program that uses *getline*. In Program 14-2, we use it to read a name string in which the first and last names are separated by a comma. We then print the name.

Program 14-2 Demonstrate *getline* operation

```
/* Demonstrate the use of getline in a program.
      Written by:
      Date:
*/
#include <iostream>
#include <iomanip>
#include <string>
using namespace std;

int main ()
{
   cout << "Enter a name in the form <last,first>: \n";
```

Program 14-2 Demonstrate *getline* operation *(continued)*

```
13      string  lastName;
14      getline (cin, lastName, ',');
15      string  firstName;
16      getline (cin, firstName);
17
18      cout << "Here is your name:\n\t|"
19           << firstName << ' ' << lastName << "|\n";
20      return 0;
21   }  // main
```

```
Results:
Enter a name in the form <last,first>:
Washington,George
Here is your name:
     |George Washington|

User Error: spaces after comma
Enter a name in the form <last,first>:
Washington,    George
Here is your name:
     |    George Washington|
```

Program 14-2 Analysis There are two things to look for in Program 14-2. First, while the user enters only one line, we read the data with two separate *getline* functions. We do this because we want to reformat the data into two separate fields: a first name and a last name. The first read (see statement 14) reads the last name. It terminates when a comma is encountered. The terminating character, the comma, is discarded. The second *getline* (statement 16) then reads the rest of the line, terminating when it reads a newline character. Since we didn't specify the terminating character in the second call, the default newline was used.

Second, note that the *getline* function reads white space characters. In fact, it will read all characters except the terminating character—the comma in the first call and the newline in the second call. We include a second test case in which the user makes a common mistake and types spaces after the comma. These leading spaces are then read by *getline*.

ASSIGNMENT OPERATOR

The assignment operator has been overloaded for three source types:

1. The value of a C++ string
2. The value of a C string
3. A single character

Program 14-3 demonstrates the assignment of one string to another.

Program 14-3 Demonstrate string assignment

```
/* Demonstrate string assignment.
      Written by:
      Date:
*/
#include <iostream>
#include <string>
using namespace std;

int main ()
{
   string str1 ("String 1");
   string str2;
   string str3;
   string str4;
   string str5 = "String 5";

   cout << "String 1: " << str1 << endl;
   str2 = str1;
   cout << "String 2: " << str2 << endl;
   str3 = "Hello";
   cout << "String 3: " << str3 << endl;
   str4 = 'A';
   cout << "String 4: " << str4 << endl;
   cout << "String 5: " << str5 << endl;
   return 0;
} // main
```

```
Results:
String 1: String 1
String 2: String 1
String 3: Hello
String 4: A
String 5: String 5
```

The assignment operator can also be used to initialize a string as shown in the next example. This format provides only for string assignment, however; it is not supported for a single character.

```
string s1 = "Hello";
string s2 = 'a';                          // Error: Not allowed
```

C++ STRING EXAMPLES

The rest of this section contains examples to demonstrate the use of the string functions discussed so far.

Read Words

We can take advantage of the fact that C++ stops at whitespace when it reads strings to parse words. Program 14-4 reads and prints words until it reaches the end of the file.

Program 14-4 Parse words

```
/* Demonstrate the use of getline to parse words.
      Written by:
      Date:
*/
#include <iostream>
#include <iomanip>
#include <string>
using namespace std;

int main ()
{
   cout << "Enter some text and I'll parse it into words. \n";

   string strIn;
   while (cin >> strIn)
      cout << strIn << endl;
   cout << "End of demonstration\n";
   return 0;
} // main
```

```
Results:
Enter some text and I'll parse it into words.
Now is the time
Now
is
the
time
For all good students
For
all
good
students
^dEnd of demonstration
```

Program 14-4 Analysis In many languages, this would be a complex program. We are able to write it in C++ with a one-statement loop. Note that we don't have any special logic for end of file. This is because the extraction operator returns false when it detects the end of file, thus terminating our loop.

Typewriter Program

Program 14-5 plays the role of a line-at-a-time typewriter. In other words, it accepts text, line by line, from the keyboard and writes it to a text file. The program stops when it detects an end of file.

Program 14-5 Typewriter program

```
1  /* Creates a text file from keyboard input.
2        Written by:
3        Date:
4  */
5  #include <iostream>
6  #include <fstream>
7  #include <cstdlib>
8  #include <string>
9  using namespace std;
10
11 int main ()
12 {
13    ofstream fsOut;
14
15    cout << "Begin file copy. Enter your text.\n"
16         << "<EOF> to stop.\n";
17
18    fsOut.open ("prog14-5.txt");
19    if (!fsOut)
20       {
21        cerr << "\aCould not open output file.\n\a";
22        exit (100);
23       } // if
24
25    string str;
26    while (getline(cin, str))
27       fsOut << str << endl;
28    fsOut << str << endl;               //Write last line
29    fsOut.close();
30
31    cout << "\nEnd file copy\n";
32    return 0;
33 }  // main
```

Program 14-5 Analysis This program reads data from the keyboard and writes it to a file. We use *getline* (see statement 26) to read the data. As long as some data, even a newline, is entered, the program continues. When the user keys end-of-file, the *getline* expression becomes false and the loop terminates.

Add Left Margin

Program 14-6 reads text from a file, line by line, and adds two blanks (spaces) at the beginning of each line before writing it to a new file. In other words, it shifts each line two characters to the right.

Program 14-6 Add left margin

```
/* Typewriter program: adds two spaces to the left
   margin and writes line to file.
      Written by:
      Date:
*/
#include <iostream>
#include <fstream>
#include <cstdlib>
#include <string>
using namespace std;

int main ()
{
   ifstream fsIn;
   ofstream fsOut;

   cout << "Begin file copy and shift.\n";

   fsIn.open ("prog14-5.txt");
   if (!fsIn)
      {
       cerr << "\aCould not open input file.\n\a";
       exit (100);
      } // if

   fsOut.open ("prog14-6.out");
   if (!fsOut)
      {
       cerr << "\aCould not open output file.\n\a";
       exit (101);
      } // if

   string str;
   int    lineCount = 0;
   while (getline (fsIn, str))
      {
       fsOut << "  " << str << endl;
       lineCount++;
} // while
   fsIn.close();
   fsOut.close();
   cout << "End of file shift. "
        << lineCount << " lines written\n";
   return 0;
} // main
```

Print File Double-Spaced

Program 14-7 reads a single-spaced text from a file and prints the text double-spaced. In other words, it inserts a blank line after each line. In this program, we direct the output to the standard output file, *cout*, which is usually the monitor. To get the output to a printer, you would need to redirect the output or assign *cout* to the printer.

Program 14-7 Print file double-spaced

```
/* Print text file double-spaced.
      Written by:
      Date:
*/
#include <iostream>
#include <fstream>
#include <cstdlib>
#include <string>
using namespace std;

int main ()
{
   ifstream fsTextIn;

   fsTextIn.open ("prog14-5.txt");
   if (!fsTextIn)
      {
       cout << "\aCould not open input file.\n\a";
       exit (100);
      } // if open

   string str;
   while (getline (fsTextIn, str))
      cout << str << endl << endl;
   fsTextIn.close();
   return 0;
}  // main
```

14-4 ARRAYS OF STRINGS

Strings can be used in an array. Consider, for example, the need to store the days of the week in their textual format. Each entry in the array is a day of the week. In this way, each string is independent, but at the same time, they are grouped together through the array. In other words, although each string is independent, we can pass them as a group to a function by passing only the name of the array. Program 14-8 demonstrates this structure.

Program 14-8 Print days of the week

```
/* This program demonstrates an array of strings.
      Written by:
      Date:
*/
```

Program 14-8 Print days of the week *(continued)*

```
#include <iostream>
#include <string>
using namespace std;

int main ()
{
   string daysAry[7];

   daysAry[0] = "Sunday";
   daysAry[1] = "Monday";
   daysAry[2] = "Tuesday";
   daysAry[3] = "Wednesday";
   daysAry[4] = "Thursday";
   daysAry[5] = "Friday";
   daysAry[6] = "Saturday";

   cout << "\nThe days of the week\n";
   for (int daysIndex = 0; daysIndex < 7; daysIndex++)
      cout << daysAry[daysIndex] << endl;
   return 0;
} // main
```

14-5 STRING MANIPULATION FUNCTIONS

The C++ string class provides a rich set of string functions (methods) that can be used to manipulate strings. These functions make it easier for us to write programs.

All of the string methods, which are found in the string library (<string>), are used with the string object and the member operator (`.`) followed by the function name as shown in the following format. Depending on the function, the parameter list may be void or may require one or more values.

```
object.function (…)
```

Before discussing string methods, let's discuss a string concept common to many of the string methods, the substring. A **substring** is a contiguous set of characters within a string. It is identified by a start position and a length. This concept is shown in Figure 14-5.

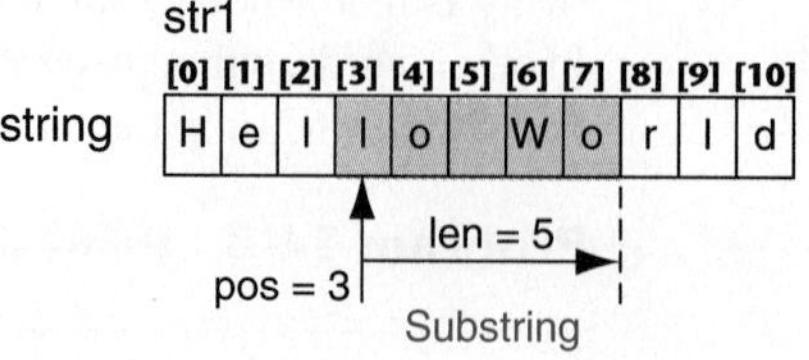

Figure 14-5 Substring concept

In many of the functions in this section, we refer to a substring with a position (`pos`) and length (`len`). When the position is omitted, it is assumed to be the beginning of the string (position 0). When the length is missing, it is assumed to be the maximum size for the string length, which is defined as the `npos` constant in the string class.

STRING LENGTH (*length* and *size*)

The ***length*** function returns the length of a string, which is defined as the number of characters in the string. If the string is empty, it returns zero. The *size* function is identical to *length*; either may be used. Examples of how they are used are shown below.

```
len = str1.length();
len = str1.size();
```

STRING COMPARE

To compare string objects, we can use the compare operators or the ***compare* method** found in the string library. In general, we use the operators whenever we need a boolean result, such as in a *while* or *if* statement; we use the *compare* method when we need a ternary answer (less-than zero, zero, or greater-than zero), such as when searching or sorting. In either case, the comparison can be between two string objects or between a string object and a C string. Comparing a string object and a character is not permitted. When two C strings are to be compared, they require a different set of functions (described later in the chapter). The string compare operation is illustrated in Figure 14-6.

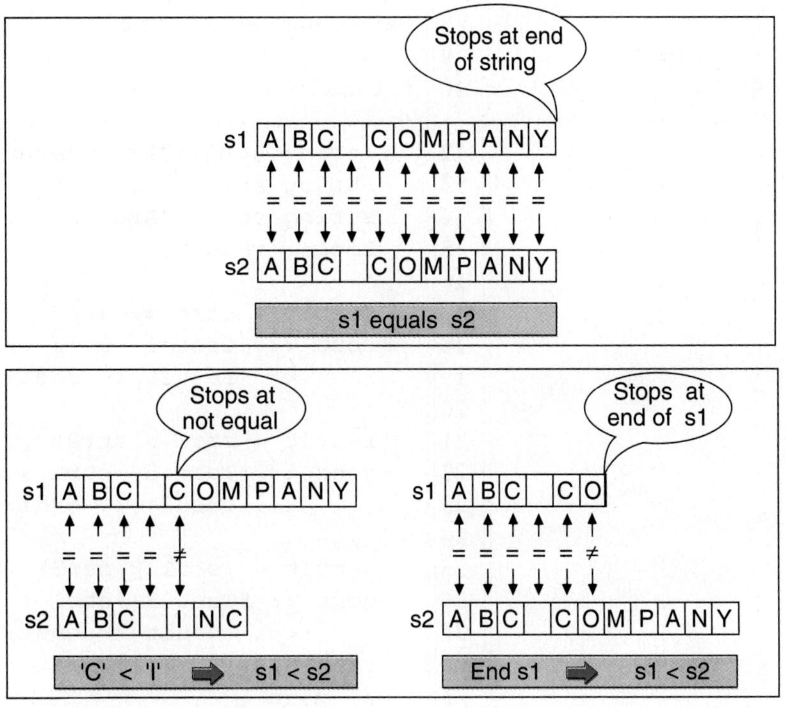

Figure 14-6 String compares

Strings are compared beginning with the first (left-most) character and comparing characters until unequal characters are found or until the end of the strings is reached. If unequal characters are found, the strings are unequal. Greater-than and less-than comparisons are determined by comparing the value of the unequal characters. If the end of the string is reached, the strings are equal.

String Relational Operators

All of the relational operators are overloaded for the string class. They return a boolean value—true or false. Given string objects, `str1` and `str2`, the following comparisons are valid.

```
str1 == str2    str1 <  str2    str1 >  str2
str1 != str2    str1 <= str2    str1 >= str2
```

Either `str1` or `str2`, but not both, can be a C string. Program 14-9 demonstrates string relational operators.

Program 14-9 Relational operators for strings

```
/* Relational operators for string comparisons.
      Written by:
      Date:
*/
#include <iostream>
#include <iomanip>
#include <string>
using namespace std;

int main ()
{
   string str1 ("ABC Company");
   string str2 ("ABC Co");
   string str3 ("ABC Inc");
   bool   result;

   result = str1 == str2;
   cout << "Test 1--str1 == str2:      "
        <<  result << endl;

   result = str1 > str2;
   cout << "Test 2--str1 >  str2:      "
        <<  result << endl;

   result = (str1 < str3);
   cout << "Test 3--str1 <  str2:      "
        <<  result << endl;
   return 0;
}  // main
```

```
Results
Test 1--str1 == str2:     0
Test 2--str1 >  str2:     1
Test 3--str1 <  str2:     1
```

String Compare Method

When using the comparison operators, the result is a boolean—true or false. When using the *compare* method, the results are a negative number (less than), 0 (equal), or a positive number (greater than). Some of the basic formats for the *compare* method are

```
str1.compare(str2);
str1.compare(pos1, len1, str2);
str1.compare(pos1, len1, str2, pos2, len2);
```

where `str1` must be a C++ string object, `pos1` and `len1` define the substring in `str1`, and `pos2` and `len2` define the substring in `str2`. The second string can be a C string. Program 14-10 demonstrates the use of the relational operators and the compare method in a simple program.

Program 14-10 Comparing strings using *compare*

```
/* Demonstrate string comparisons using compare.
      Written by:
      Date:
*/
#include <iostream>
#include <iomanip>
#include <string>
using namespace std;

int main ()
{
   string str1 ("ABC Company");
   string str2 ("ABC Co");
   string str3 ("ABC Inc");
   int    result;

   cout << "Compare Method Test 1. "
        << "Should return greater than\n";
   result = str1.compare(str2);
   cout << "**str1.compare(str2) is: "
        << result << endl;

   cout << "\nCompare Method Test 2. "
           "Should return equal\n";
   result = str1.compare(0, 6, str2);
   cout << "**str1.compare(0, 6, str2) is: "
        << result << endl;

   cout << "\nCompare Method Test 3. "
           "Should return less than\n";
   result = str2.compare(4, 2, str1, 4, string::npos);
   cout << "**str2.compare(4, 2, str1, 4, npos) is: "
        << result << endl;
   return 0;
}  // main
```

Program 14-10 Comparing strings using *compare* (*continued*)

```
Results
Compare Method Test 1. Should return greater than
**str1.compare(str2) is: 1

Compare Method Test 2. Should return equal
**str1.compare(0, 6, str2) is: 0

Compare Method Test 3. Should return less than
**str2.compare(4, 2, str1, 4, npos) is: -1
```

CONCATENATING AND APPENDING

A common string operation is the joining of two strings to make one long string. This operation, called *concatenate* or *append*, places the contents of one string at the end of another. As with string *compare*, we can append two string objects or a C string to a string object.

Concatenation

The first way to join two strings is with the plus operator (+). Think of it as "adding" two strings. As with addition, the result must be placed in a string object to be saved. The following example demonstrates the plus operator with a string object and a C string.

```
str1 + str2
```

Append

There are two ways to append strings in C++. First, we can use the overloaded plus-assign operator (+=) as shown in the following example in which the second string is appended to the end of the first string.

```
str1 += str2;
```

The second way to append two strings is to use the string class method, *append*. It works the same way as the overloaded operator; the second string is appended to the end of the first string. The use of the *string* method is shown in the next example.

```
str1.append(str2);
str1.append(str2, pos2, len2);
```

Figure 14-7 shows the results using the plus-assign operator and the string method.

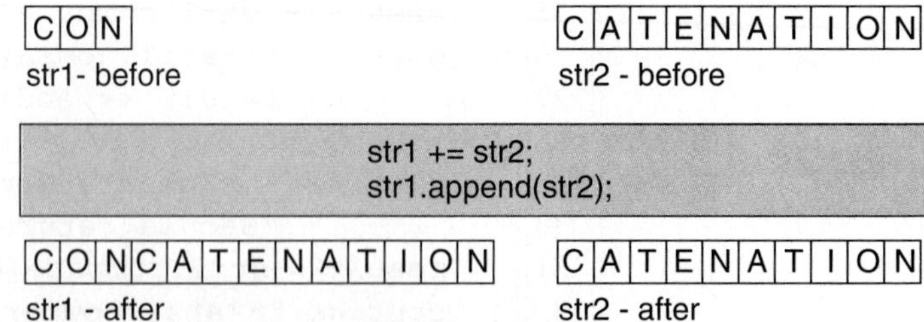

Figure 14-7 String append

Program 14-11 demonstrates the use of operators and the *append* method to concatenate strings.

Program 14-11 **Concatenating and appending strings**

```
/* Demonstrate string concatenation.
      Written by:
      Date:
*/
#include <iostream>
#include <string>
using namespace std;

int main ()
{
   cout << "Begin concatenation demonstration:\n";

   string str1 = "This is ";
   string str2 = "a string";
   string str3;

   str3 = str1 + str2;
   cout << str3 << endl;

   cout << "\nBegin append demonstration:\n";
   cout << "Append using the += operator: ";
   str1 += str2;
   cout << str1 << endl;

   str1.append(str2, 1, string::npos);
   cout << "Append method:  " << str1 << endl;

   str3.append(5, '!');
   cout << "Append characters:  " << str3 << endl;

   cout << "End of concatenation demonstation\n";
   return 0;
}  // main
```

```
Results
Begin concatenation demonstration:
This is a string

Begin append demonstration:
Append using the += operator: This is a string
Append method:  This is a string string
Append characters:  This is a string!!!!!
End of concatenation demonstation
```

EXTRACTING A SUBSTRING

We can create a new string using the substring method to extract part of a string. The basic formats for the substring extraction method are

```
str1.substr();
str1.substr(pos1);
str1.substr(pos1, len1);
```

where `pos1` is the start position in the string and `len1` is the number of characters to be extracted. If no start position is specified, it defaults to the beginning of the string (`0`); if no length is specified, it defaults to `npos`. When the length is specified, the start position must be specified also.

Program 14-12 demonstrates the substring operation.

Program 14-12 Demonstrate string extraction

```
/* Demonstrate string extraction.
      Written by:
      Date:
*/
#include <iostream>
#include <string>
using namespace std;

int main ()
{
   cout << "Begin substring extraction demonstration:\n";

   string str1 = "Concatenation";
   string str2;

   cout << "str1 contains: " << str1      << endl;
   cout << "str2 contains: " << str2      << endl;
   cout << "                0123456789012" << endl;

   str2 = str1.substr();
   cout << "str2 change 1: " << str2 << endl;

   str2 = str1.substr(5, 3);
   cout << "str2 change 2: " << str2 << endl;

   str2 = str1.substr(5);
   cout << "str2 change 3: " << str2 << endl;

   cout << "End of extraction demonstration\n";
   return 0;
} // main
```

```
Results
Begin substring extraction demonstration:
str1 contains: Concatenation
```

Program 14-12 Demonstrate string extraction (*continued*)

```
str2 contains:
                0123456789012
str2 change 1: Concatenation
str2 change 2: ten
str2 change 3: tenation
End of extraction demonstration
```

Program 14-12 Analysis There is only one small point in this demonstration. It is not an error to request that more characters be extracted than are available. This fact is demonstrated in statement 26. The default for the number of characters is the size of the string, which is obviously greater than the substring starting at position 5. The result is the substring from position 5 to the end of the string.

SEARCHING FOR A SUBSTRING

Sometimes we need to know if a substring is in a string. If a match is found, we also want to know where it is; that is, we want to know its offset from the beginning of the string. The string class provides two *find* methods for locating substrings.

Searching Forwards: The *find* Method

The ***find* method** can be used to search for a substring anywhere in a string starting at the beginning of the string. Its basic format is

```
where = str1.find (str2, pos1);
```

where `str1` is the string to be searched; `str2` is an instance of a string object, a C string, or a character to be located; and `pos1` is the start position in `str1`. If the start position is not given, the default is 0.

To locate the first occurrence in a string, we call *find* without a start position. It returns the index location within the string for the substring it located. A typical statement to locate the first occurrence is shown in the next example.

```
where = str.find("ten");
```

In this example, we are searching for the substring `ten`, which is coded as a string literal (C string). If the substring is found, its location is stored in `where`. If it is not found, it stores `npos`. To determine if the find was successful, we must test the return value as shown in the next example.

```
if (where != string::npos)                  // Test for success
   // Found processing
else
   // Not found processing
```

To find the second, third, or last occurrence of a substring, we must use a loop. Using the index of a successful *find*, we can locate the next occurrence of the substring by starting at the previous location plus one. When the *find* is no longer successful, the previous location represents the last occurrence of the substring. The basic statement is shown in the next example.

```
where = str.find("cat", where + 1)
```

Search Backwards: The *rfind* Method

The ***rfind* method** can be used to search for a substring starting at the end of a string and searching toward the beginning of the string. Its basic function format is

```
where = str1.rfind (str2, pos1);
```

where `str2` is an instance of a string object, a C string, or a character to be located, and `pos1` is the start position in `str1`. If the start position is not given, the default is the maximum string length (`npos`).

Program 14-13 demonstrates the usage of the substring extraction methods.

Program 14-13 Demonstrate extraction methods

```
/* Demonstrate the extraction methods.
      Written by:
      Date:
*/
#include <iostream>
#include <string>
using namespace std;

int main ()
{
   cout << "Begin find demonstration:\n";
   string str1 = "ccccatenatttt";
   cout << "str1 contains:  " << str1      << endl;
   cout << "                0123456789012" << endl;

   int    where;
   where = str1.find("ten");
   cout << "\"ten\" at:                " << where << endl;

   where = str1.rfind("tin");
   if (where != string::npos)
      cout << "\"tin\" at:             " << where << endl;
   else
      cout << "\"tin\" not at:         " << where << endl;
   cout << "End of find demonstration\n";
   return 0;
}  // main
```

```
Results
Begin find demonstration:
str1 contains:  ccccatenatttt
                0123456789012
"ten" at:           5
"tin" not at:       -1
End of find demonstation
```

SEARCHING FOR CHARACTERS

C++ provides a powerful capability to search for characters in a string. The search set, consisting of one or more characters, is specified in a string. In a character search, each character in a string is matched to the character as specified by the requirements of the particular method being used. When a matching character is located, its index position is returned.

One example of character searching involves parsing a string into tokens. We can use a set of characters—such as comma, period, and space—to locate words and then extract them for processing. Four character search methods are provided: **find_first_of**, **find_last_of**, **find_first_not_of**, and **find_last_not_of**.

Character Search Forward

Forward searches can locate the first character that matches the set or the first character that doesn't match the set.

Find First Matching Character To find the first occurrence of a character in the set, we use the find first method. In this search, the first character in the string that matches any of the characters in the set terminates the search. The function returns the position of the matching character; if no matching characters are found, it returns the maximum size of the string (npos).

The basic format of the function is

```
whereFwd = str1.find_first_of(str2, pos1);
```

where str1 is the string object to be searched, str2 is a string object, a C string, or a character containing the match set, and pos1 is the starting index location in str1. It returns the index location of the first matching character. If the starting index location is omitted, the search begins at the first character; that is, it defaults to 0.

Figure 14-8 demonstrates the find first method results. In this example, we are looking for the first character that contains an 'L', 'M', or 'N'. The find skips over the 'C' and 'O' because they don't match and stops at the third character, index location 2, because it does match.

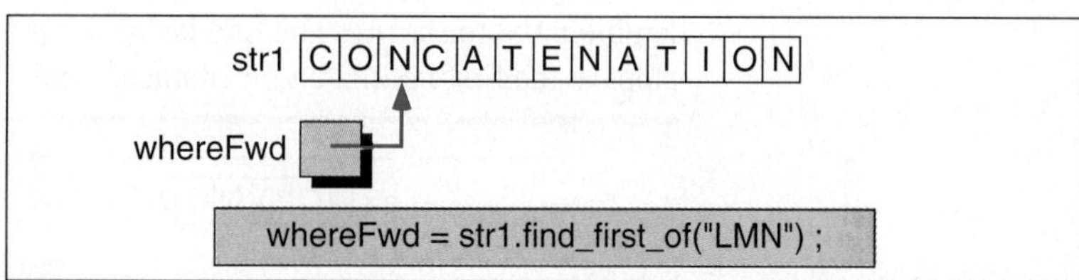

Figure 14-8 Find first

Find First Nonmatching Character Sometimes, we are not interested in the delimiter, but rather in the substring between the delimiters. In this case, we need to find the first character that does not match the set. The basic format of the find-first-not function is

```
whereFwd = str1.find_first_not_of(str2, pos1);
```

where str1 is the string object to be searched, str2 is a string object, a C string, or a character containing the set of characters to be skipped, and pos1 is the starting index location in `str1`. It returns the index location of the first matching character. If the starting index location is omitted, the search begins at the first character; that is, it defaults to 0.

Figure 14-9 demonstrates the find-first-not method results. In this example, we are looking for the first character that doesn't contain a punctuation delimiter (space, ',' ';' ':' '.', or '!'. Starting at position 3, the find skips over the comma and space because they do match and stops at the 'd' character, index location 5 because it doesn't match.

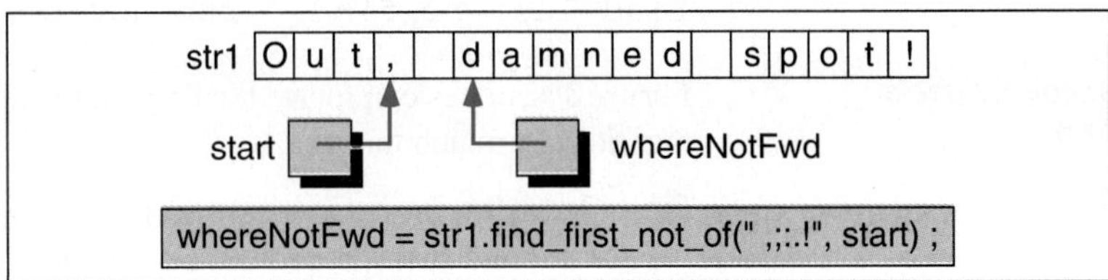

Figure 14-9 Find first not

Character Search Backwards

We can also search for a character in a string starting at the end of the target string. Once again, there are two methods that can be used: one to find the first matching character and one to find the first nonmatching character. These methods parallel the find forwards methods in everything but the direction of the search. Starting at the end of the string, they search toward the beginning of the string stopping at the first matching character for a find last or the first nonmatching character for a not-find last. If the start position is not specified, it defaults to the end of the string (`npos`).

The format for the backwards find character searches are shown in the next example.

```
whereBack    = str1.find_last_of     (str2, pos1);
whereNotBack = str1.find_last_not_of (str2, pos1);
```

In Figure 14-10, both find methods start at the end of the string and search toward the beginning of the string. The find last stops at the 'C' in position 3, while the not-find last stops at the first nonmatching character, the 'T' in position 9.

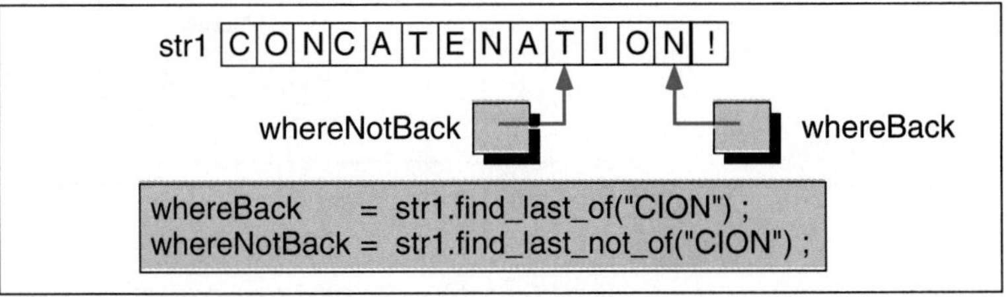

Figure 14-10 Find last

To demonstrate the character methods, let's write a program that tokenizes a line into words. To locate a word, we must find its first and last characters. We use the find-first and find-not-first functions to locate the word. Once its start and end positions are known, we can use the substring function to extract and print it. While this would be a difficult program in many languages, the character functions make it easy in C++. The code and results are shown in Program 14-14.

Program 14-14 Parse and print words

```
/* Parse and print words.
      Written by:
      Date:
*/
#include <iostream>
#include <iomanip>
#include <string>
using namespace std ;

int main ()
{
   // Macbeth, Act V, Scene I
   string lines = "Out, damned spot! out, I say! One; two:"
                  "why then, 'tis time to do 't.";
   string  delimiters = " ,;:.!/";

   unsigned int end;
   unsigned int start =
             lines.find_first_not_of (delimiters);
   while (start != string::npos)
      {
      end = lines.find_first_of (delimiters, start + 1);
      cout << lines.substr (start , end - start) << endl;
      start = lines.find_first_not_of (delimiters, end + 1);
}  // while
   return 0 ;
}  // main
```

```
Results
Out
damned
spot
...
to
do
't
```

ACCESS AND MODIFY CHARACTERS

C++ provides two additional methods for working with characters. The *at* method can be used to access a character in a string. The index notation (brackets) can be used to access and modify a character in a string.

The *at* Function

When using the *at* function, the index location is passed as a parameter. The *at* function tests for an invalid index and may abort the program if it is out of range. Its format us shown in the following example.

```
oneChar = str.at(where);
```

Index Notation

When using index notation, the location is enclosed in brackets. Because it doesn't require a function call, the index notation is more efficient; however, bracket access does not check for a out-of-range error. Its format is shown in the following example.

```
oneChar = str[where];
```

Program 14-15 demonstrates the index notation. It reads text from the keyboard, line by line, and prints only the lines that start with uppercase letters. Because the input and output will be interleaved, as shown in the results section of the program, we identify the output by inserting two asterisks before each line as we write it.

Program 14-15 Print selected sentences

```
/* Echo keyboard input that begins with a capital letter.
      Written by:
      Date:
*/
#include <string>
#include <iostream>
using namespace std;

int main ()
{
   cout << "Echo keyboard capitals. Begin input.\n\n";

   string str;
   while (getline (cin, str))
      if (isupper (str[0]))
          cout << "**" << str << endl;
   cout << "End of input.\n";
   return 0;
} // main
```

```
Results:
Echo keyboard capitals. Begin input.

Now is the time
**Now is the time
for all good students
to come to the aid
of their school.
Amen
**Amen
End of input.
```

STRING INSERTION

The C++ string class has several methods that allow us to insert a character, a character a specified number of times, a string, or a substring at a specific position in a string object. The basic format of the ***insert* method** is

```
str1.insert(pos1, str2);
str1.insert(pos1, str2, pos2, len2);
str1.insert(pos1, numchar, char);
```

where `str1` is a string class, `pos1` is the insertion index position in the string, `str2` is a character, a C string, or another string object, and len2 is either the number of characters to be inserted when `str2` is a character, or the length of the string to be inserted when `str2` is a string. When a character is being inserted, the second argument is the number of times the character is to be inserted (`numchar`) and the third argument is the character to be inserted (`char`). The *insert* method returns the modified string.

Program 14-16 demonstrates all of the insert methods. Note that the last example assigns the returned value to a new string and prints it to verify that the string is returned.

Program 14-16 Demonstrate string insertion

```
/* Demonstrate insertion into a string object.
      Written by:
      Date:
*/
#include <string>
#include <iostream>
using namespace std;

int main ()
{
   int    where;
   string str1 = "This is string";
   string str2 = "This is a new string ojbect";
   string str3;

   cout << "str1 at start:       " << str1 << endl;

   where = str1.find_last_of('s');
   str1.insert(where, "a ");
   cout << "str1 after insert 1: " << str1 << endl;

   str1.insert(where + 2, str2, 10, 4);
   cout << "str1 after insert 2: " << str1 << endl;

   str3 = str1.insert(str1.length(), 3, '!');
   cout << "str1 after insert 3: " << str1 << endl;
   cout << "str3 after assign:   " << str3 << endl;

   cout << "End of demonstration.\n";
   return 0;
}  // main
```

Program 14-16 Demonstrate string insertion (*continued*)

```
Results:
str1 at start:         This is string
str1 after insert 1: This is a string
str1 after insert 2: This is a new string
str1 after insert 3: This is a new string!!!
str3 after assign:    This is a new string!!!
End of demonstration.
```

REPLACE STRING

The string class provides several methods to replace all[3] or part of a string with another string. We describe the two more common ones.

The basic formats for the ***replace* method** are

```
str1.replace(pos1, len1, str2);
str1.replace(pos1, len1, str2, pos2, len2);
```

where `pos1` is the start position of the characters in `str1` to be replaced, `num1` is the number of characters to be replaced, and `str2` is the replacement value. The replacement string value can be a string object or a C string. It can be the same size as the string being replaced, or it can be smaller or larger; the string length is adjusted as required. When `pos2` and `len2` are included (second format), they specify the length of the second string. If `pos2` is used without `len2`, the length of the second string starts at `pos2` and goes to the end of the string. Unlike many of the other string methods, it may not be a single character.

In Program 14-17 we use three examples to demonstrate string replacement. The first replaces a substring with a C string. The second replaces a substring with a string object. The third replaces the entire string with a C string.

Program 14-17 Demonstrate string replacement

```
/* Demonstrate string replacement.
      Written by:
      Date:
*/
#include <string>
#include <iostream>
using namespace std;

int main ()
{
   string str1 = "This is one string";
   string str2 = "This is another string";
   string str3;

   cout << "str1 at start:            " << str1 << endl;
   str3 = str1;

```

[3]While the *replace* method can be used to replace the entire string, the assignment operator is easier and faster.

Program 14-17 Demonstrate string replacement (*continued*)

```
   str1.replace(8, 3, "a different");
   cout << "str1 after replace 1: " << str1 << endl;

   str1 = str3;
   str1.replace(8, 3, str2, 8, 7);
   cout << "str1 after replace 2: " << str1 << endl;

   str1 = str3;
   str1.replace(0, str1.length(), "A new string");
   cout << "str1 after replace 3: " << str1 << endl;

   cout << "End of demonstration.\n";
   return 0;
}  // main
```

```
Results:
str1 at start:         This is one string
str1 after replace 1: This is a different string
str1 after replace 2: This is another string
str1 after replace 3: A new string
End of demonstration.
```

ERASE STRING

The string class contains two methods to erase all or part of a string. The ***erase* method** can be used to erase the entire string or to erase from a specific index position. When specifying the start position, we can also specify the number of characters to be erased. Its format is

```
str.erase(pos, num);
str.clear();
```

where `pos` is the start position and `num` is the number of characters to be erased. The method returns a temporary string containing the value after the characters are deleted.

The default value for the start position is 0; the default value for the number of characters is the size of the string. This means that if no parameters are specified, the entire string is deleted. It also makes it easy to delete from a start position to the end of the string by specifying only the start position.

A second method, *clear*, erases the entire contents of the string. It takes no arguments and does not return a value.[4]

Program 14-18 demonstrates the *erase* and *clear* methods.

Program 14-18 Demonstrate erase and clear

```
/* Demonstrate erase string.
      Written by:
      Date:
*/
#include <string>
```

[4]The *clear* method calls *erase* with default values.

Program 14-18 Demonstrate erase and clear (*continued*)

```
#include <iostream>
using namespace std;

int main ()
{
   string str1 = "This is one string";
   string str2 = "This is another string";
   string str3;

   cout << "str1 at start:      " << str1 << endl;
   str3 = str1;

   str1.erase();
   cout << "str1 after erase 1: " << str1 << endl;

   str1 = str3;
   str1.erase(8, 4);
   cout << "str1 after erase 2: " << str1 << endl;

   str1 = str3;
   str1.clear();
   cout << "str1 after clear  : " << str1 << endl;

   cout << "End of demonstration.\n";
   return 0;
} // main
```

```
Results:
str1 at start:      This is one string
str1 after erase 1:
str1 after erase 2: This is string
str1 after clear  :
End of demonstration.
```

SWAP STRINGS

A common processes in programming is swapping the contents of two variables. The string class provides a method to swap two string objects. Its format is

```
swap (str1, str2);
```

where `str1` and `str2` are the string to be exchanged. Program 14-19 demonstrates the ***swap* method**.

Program 14-19 Demonstrate swap string

```
/* Demonstrate swap string.
      Written by:
      Date:
*/
```

Program 14-19 Demonstrate swap string (*continued*)

```
#include <string>
#include <iostream>
using namespace std;

int main ()
{
   string str1 = "A short string";
   string str2 = "A longer string object";

   cout << "str1 at start:    " << str1 << endl;
   cout << "str2 at start:    " << str2 << endl;

   swap(str1, str2);

   cout << "str1 after swap: " << str1 << endl;
   cout << "str2 after swap: " << str2 << endl;

   cout << "End of demonstration.\n";
   return 0;
} // main
```

```
Results:
str1 at start:   A short string
str2 at start:   A longer string object
str1 after swap: A longer string object
str2 after swap: A short string
End of demonstration.
```

CONVERT TO C STRING

The last string method we discuss converts a string object to a C string. It returns a character pointer constant. Its format is

```
char* cString = str.c_str();
```

14-6 A PROGRAMMING EXAMPLE: MORSE CODE

Morse code, patented by Samuel F. B. Morse in 1837, is the language that was used to send messages by telegraph from the middle of the nineteenth century until the advent of the modern telephone and today's computer-controlled communications systems. In Morse code, each letter in the alphabet is represented by a series of dots and dashes, as shown in Table 14-2.

Our implementation of Morse code uses a class. The class contains two public methods: one to encode (convert) a line of text to Morse code and one to decode (convert) Morse code to a line of text. These functions call on a private function for the actual conversions. The private function uses a two-dimensional array of strings in which each

Letter	Code	Letter	Code	Letter	Code	Letter	Code
A	.-	H	....	O	---	V	...-
B	-...	I	..	P	.--.	W	.--
C	-.-.	J	.---	Q	--.-	X	-..-
D	-..	K	-.-	R	.-.	Y	-.--
E	.	L	.-..	S	...	Z	--..
F	..-.	M	--	T	-		
G	--.	N	-.	U	..-		

Table 14-2 Morse code

element has two strings: one containing English characters and one containing the corresponding Morse code. The array structure is shown in Figure 14-11.

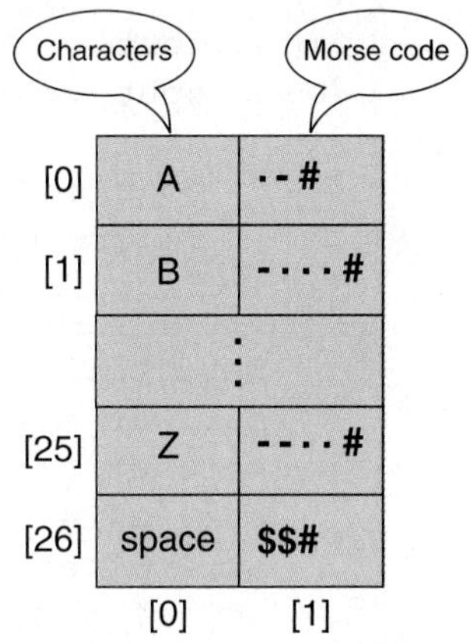

Figure 14-11 Character to Morse code structure

Each column has 27 strings. Each string in the first column contains one English letter (uppercase). Each string in the second column contains the corresponding Morse code for the English letter.

The implementation uses a menu-driven program that includes the Morse code class. The menu, shown in Figure 14-12, has three options: encode English to Morse code, decode Morse code to English, and quit.

```
        M E N U
    E         encode

    D         decode

    Q         quit
Enter your option and press the return key.
```

Figure 14-12 Morse code menu

If the encode or decode function detects an error, such as an invalid character or an invalid Morse code sequence, it returns an error message. In a production program, we would use the exception handler (see Chapter 15).

The class header file is shown in Program 14-20.

Program 14-20 Morse code: *class* header file

```
/* This header file contains the code for the Morse
   code class.
      Written by:
      Date:
*/
using namespace std;

class Morse
{
   private:
      bool convert (string& str1, int col,
                    string& str2);

   public:
      string encode (string& inStr);
      string decode (string& inStr);

}; // class Morse

// ================= encode =================
/* Transforms character data to Morse Code
      Pre:  inStr contains data to transform to Morse
      Post: data encoded and returned in outStr
            --or- error message returned in outStr
*/
string Morse::encode (string& inStr)
{
   string s1;
   string s2;
   string outStr = "";
   bool   error  = false;
   int    curr   = 0;

   while ( curr < inStr.length() && !error )
      {
       s1     = toupper(inStr[curr]);
       error  = !convert (s1, 0, s2);
       outStr += s2;
       curr++;
      } // while
   if (!error)
```

Program 14-20 Morse code: *class* header file (*continued*)

```
         return (outStr);
      else
         return ("Invalid Character in Code\n");
   } // encode
   // ================== decode ==================
   /* Transforms Morse Code data to character string
         Pre:   inStr contains data to transform to string
         Post:  data has been encoded and placed in outStr
                --or- error message returned in outStr
   */
   string  Morse::decode (string& inStr)
   {
      string s1;
      string s2;
      string outStr = "";
      bool   error  = false;
      int    curr   = 0;
      int    index;

      while (curr < inStr.length () && !error )
         {
          index = inStr.find ("#", curr);
          s1= inStr.substr (curr, index - curr + 1 );
          error  = !convert (s1, 1, s2);
          outStr +=  s2;
          curr   = index + 1;
        } // while
      if (!error)
          return (outStr);
      else
          return ("Invalid Morse Code\n");
   } // decode
   // ================== convert ==================
   /* Looks up code in table and converts to opposite format
          Pre:  s1 is string being converted
                s2 is output string
                col is code: 0 for character to Morse
                             1 for Morse to character
         Post: converted output in calling program area (s2)
   */
   bool Morse :: convert (string& s1, int col, string&  s2)
   {
      string encDec[27][2] =
         {
            { "A", ".-#" },
            { "B", "-...#" },
            { "C", "-.-.#" },
            { "D", "-..#" },
            { "E", ".#" },
```

Program 14-20 Morse code: *class* header file (*continued*)

```
91              { "F", "..-.#" },
92              { "G", "--.#" },
93              { "H", "....#" },
94              { "I", "..#" },
95              { "J", ".---#" },
96              { "K", "-.-#" },
97              { "L", ".-..#" },
98              { "M", "--#" },
99              { "N", "-.#" },
100             { "O", "---#" },
101             { "P", ".--.#" },
102             { "Q", "--.-#" },
103             { "R", ".-.#" },
104             { "S", "...#" },
105             { "T", "-#" },
106             { "U", "..-#" },
107             { "V", "...-#" },
108             { "W", ".--#" },
109             { "X", "-..-#" },
110             { "Y", "-.--#" },
111             { "Z", "--..#" },
112             { " ", "$$#" }
113          }; // endDec
114
115      bool found = false;
116      int  i;
117      for (i = 0; i < 27 && !found; i++)
118          found = ( s1 == (encDec [i][col]) );
119
120      if (found)
121          s2 = encDec [i - 1] [(col + 1) % 2];
122      else
123          s2 ="";
124      return found;
125  }  // convert
```

Program 14-20 Analysis This is a very simple class. There are no constructors or destructors, just three application methods. The encode and decode functions are rather basic code. Note how we use the return value from the convert function to determine if the conversion worked. If any problems were encountered, we return an error message.

The `convert` function does the actual conversion. Note, however, how it is designed to handle the conversion both from English to Morse and Morse to English. The only difference between the two conversions is which column we want to use. We pass the column to be used for the search as a parameter. Once we have located the correct string, we use the formula shown below to pick up the matching string (see statement 122).

```
(col + 1) % 2
```

If we are searching on the English letters in column 0, then the modulus of the column (0 + 1) is column 1, which contains the matching Morse code string. Conversely, if we are searching Morse code using the string in column 1, then the modulus of the column (1 + 1) is column 0, which contains the English letter.

We use a simple test driver to validate the Morse code class. It contains a loop to read a user option and then either encode or decode user input. The test driver is shown in Program 14-21.

Program 14-21 Test driver for Morse code class

```
/* Convert English to Morse code and Morse code to English.
      Written by
      Date
*/
#include <iostream>
#include <cstdlib>
#include <string>
using namespace std;

#include "p14-20.h"

#define   FLUSH while (cin.get() != '\n')

char   menu        (void);
string getInput    (void);
void   printOutput (string&, string&);

int main ()
{
   string  inStr;
   string  outStr;
   bool    done = false;
   char    option;
   Morse   mCode;       }// Object of type Morse class

   while (!done)
       {
        option = menu ();
        switch (option)
            {
             case 'E' :  inStr = getInput ();
                         outStr = mCode.encode (inStr);
                         printOutput (inStr, outStr);
                         break;
             case 'D' :  inStr = getInput ();
                         outStr = mCode.decode (inStr);
                         printOutput(inStr, outStr);
                         break;
```

Program 14-21 Test driver for Morse code class (*continued*)

```
            default   :  done = true;
           }// switch
        }// while
} // main
```

Program 14-21 Analysis The function *main* is rather straightforward. Although it could be argued that the *switch* should be in a subfunction, we place it here because it controls the entire program. One noteworthy point is the default condition. We test for only two options: encode and decode. If it is neither, then we assume quit. We can do this because we validate the option in `menu` (Program 14-22) At this point in the program, therefore, option can be one of only three values. We test for two and default the third.

The menu program is shown in Program 14-22.

Program 14-22 Morse code: *menu*

```
/* Display menu of choices and return selected character.
      Pre  nothing
      Post returns validated option code
*/
char menu ()
{
   bool validData;
   char option;

   cout << "\t\t\tM E N U \n";
   cout << "\t\tE)  encode \n";
   cout << "\t\tD)  decode \n";
   cout << "\t\tQ)  quit \n";

   do
      {
       cout << "\nEnter option: press return key: ";
       cin  >> option;
       FLUSH;
       option = toupper (option);
      if (option == 'E' || option == 'D' || option == 'Q')
         validData = true;
       else
         {
          validData = false;
         cout << "\aEnter only one of the options\n";
          cout << "\tE, D, or Q\n";
         }// else
      } while (!validData);
   return option;
}    // main
```

Program 14-22 Analysis The menu function shown in this program displays the options and reads the user's choice. It then validates the choice and, if the choice is invalid, displays an error message and asks for the option again. Although it is always good design to validate the user input, it must be validated in the correct place. Since `menu` is communicating with the user, this is the logical place to do the validation. Note that as the option is read it is converted to uppercase. Not only does this make the validation simpler, but it also simplifies the *switch* statement in *main.* Whenever you have a single character code, convert it to uppercase or lowercase for processing in the program. Finally, note that to prevent any problems created by extraneous user input, we flush the input stream after each option is read.

Program 14-23 reads a string, which may be either a line of text to be converted to code or a line of code to be converted to text.

Program 14-23 Morse code: *get input*

```
/* Reads input string to be encoded or decoded.
      Pre  nothing
      Post input string returned
*/
string getInput ()
{
   string inStr;
   cout << "\nPlease enter line of text to be coded: \n";
   getline (cin, inStr);
   return inStr;
} // getInput
```

The code to print the output of this program is shown in Program 14-24.

Program 14-24 Morse code: print output

```
/* Print the input and the transformed output
      Pre  inStr contains the input data
      Post outStr contains the transformed string
*/
void printOutput (string& inStr, string& outStr)
{
   cout << "\nThe information entered was: \n  ";
   cout << inStr << endl;
   cout << "The transformed information is: \n  ";
   cout << outStr << endl << endl;
   return;
} // printOutput
```

14-7 C STRINGS

A **C string** is a variable-length array of characters that is delimited by the null character (`\0`). In this section we briefly describe the more common C strings found in the C string (`<cstring>`) header file.[5]

BASIC C-STRING CONCEPTS

Because strings are variable-length structures, we must provide enough room for the maximum-length string that will be stored plus *one* for *the delimiter*. It is possible that the structure will not be filled, so an array may have the null character in the middle. In this case, we treat the part of the array from the beginning to the null character as the string and ignore the rest. This situation is shown in Figure 14-13.

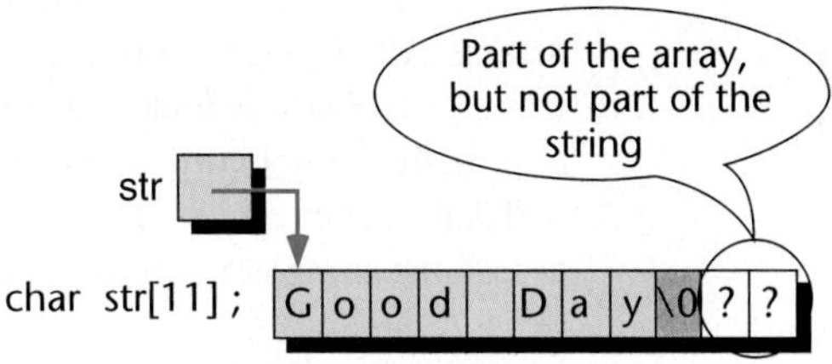

Figure 14-13 Strings in arrays

Initializing Strings

We can initialize a string by assigning a value to it when it is defined. The following example creates an 11-byte array and fills the first 9 positions with the string value "Good Day" and a delimiter.

```
char str[11] = "Good Day";
```

An alternate string declaration technique defines the string as a character pointer and assigns a value to it. In this case, the size of the string is automatically set to the size of the string. Its format is shown below.

```
char* str = "Good Day";
```

Strings and the Assignment Operator

Since the string is an array, the name of the string is a pointer constant. As a pointer constant, it is an rvalue and therefore cannot be used as the left operand of the assignment operator. This is one of the most common errors in writing a program that uses C strings; fortunately, it is a compile error, so we must correct the code to run it. The next example shows two common string assignment errors.

```
char str1[11] = "Hello";
char str2[11];
str2 = str1;                          // Compile error
str1 = "Hello";                       // Compile error
```

[5]For a complete discussion of C strings, we suggest you refer to a C Language text, such as our companion text to this book.

Although we could write a loop to assign characters individually, there is a better way. C++ includes `<cstring>`, a rich library of functions to manipulate C strings. We discuss them later in this section.

> We cannot use the assignment operator to copy C strings.
> We must use the *strcpy* function.

C STRING INPUT/OUTPUT

This section discusses how to read and write C strings.

Reading Strings

There are two ways to read strings. We can read strings with the extraction operator (>>) or we can use a special string-only function, *getline*.

Extraction Operator Reading strings with the extraction operator is simple and natural. All we need to know are the rules. First, the extraction operator skips any leading whitespace. Once it finds a character, it reads until it finds whitespace, putting each character in the array in order. When it finds a whitespace character, it stores the string with a null delimiter character. The whitespace character is left in the input stream. For example, to read the string `month`, we could simply write one of the statements shown below.

```
cin >> month;            or    fsIn >> month;
```

Our only concern is to make sure that the array is large enough to store all the data. If it isn't, then whatever follows the array in memory will be destroyed. For this reason, it is usually wise to make sure you don't exceed the length of the data. Assuming that `month` has been defined as

```
char  month[10];
```

we can protect against the user's entering too much data by setting the width with the set-width manipulator. The modified statement is shown below.

```
cin  >> setw(10) >> month;
```

One more point: After skipping leading whitespace, the extraction operator stops at the *first* whitespace character it finds. If it is in the middle of a phrase, such as *Hello World,* it stops at the space before *World,* leaving the rest of the characters in the input stream.

> Always use set width when reading C strings.

Read String—*getline( )* The ***getline*** function extracts text from an input stream and makes a null-terminated string out of it.

The *getline* function has three parameters. The first parameter specifies the string area into which the string is to be read. The second parameter specifies the maximum number of characters that are to be transferred, including the generated string delimiter character. The best way to specify it, therefore, is with the *sizeof* operator, so you know you always have the correct size. Finally, the third parameter specifies an optional terminating character; if it is not included, *getline* stops when it finds a newline in the input stream. An example of each is shown below.

```
cin.getline  (inArea, sizeof(inArea));        //Stop at \n
fsIn.getline (inArea, sizeof(inArea), ';');  //Stop at ;
```

Writing Strings

String output is provided by the insertion operator (<<). Shown below are two examples for writing the string month.

```
cout << month;     or     fsOut << month;
```

There are two options of interest when you write strings: justification and width. The width sets the *minimum* print area for the string in the output. Within the print width, the string can be justified left (the default) or right. To set the justification, we use the left and right ios flags, as shown in the following two examples. (For a complete discussion of justification and ios flags, see Chapter 7.) In the following code, the first example writes a right-justified string to the standard output unit, and the second example writes the same example left-justified to a file.

```
cout.setf (ios::right, ios::adjustfield);
cout "|" << setw(30) << "This is a string" << "|\n";

Output:
          |                  This is a string|


fsOut.setf (ios::left, ios::adjustfield);
fsOut "|" << setw(30) << "This is a string" << "|\n";

Output:
          |This is a string                  |
```

THE C-STRING FUNCTION LIBRARY

This section describes the more commonly used string functions found in the C string library (*cstring*).

String Length (*strlen*)

The ***strlen*** **function** returns the length of a string, specified as the number of characters in the string excluding the null character. If the string is empty, it returns zero. The format statement is shown below.

```
length = strlen (const char* cStr);
```

String Copy

There are two string copy functions. The first, ***strcpy***, copies the contents of one string to another string. The second, ***strncpy***, also copies the contents of one string to another, but it sets a maximum number of characters that can be moved. For this reason, it is a safer function.

strcpy This basic copy function copies the contents of the from-string, including the null character, to the to-string. Its format is

```
strcpy (toStr, fromStr);
```

where `toStr` is a pointer to the array that is to receive the string and `fromStr` is the string being copied. The string copy function also returns the new string's address, which may be stored or discarded.

If the from-string is longer than the to-string array, the data in memory after the to-string array are destroyed. This is obviously a program error.

strncpy Many of the problems associated with unequal string-array sizes can be controlled with *strncpy*, string-number copy. This function contains a size parameter that specifies the *maximum* number of characters that can be moved at a time, as shown in the statement below.

```
strncpy  (toString, fromString, size);
```

In this function, `size` specifies the maximum number of characters that can be moved. If the sending string is longer than `size`, the copy stops after *size* bytes have been copied. In this case, the destination variable will not be a valid string: it will not have a delimiter. On the other hand, the data following the destination variable will be intact, assuming the size was properly specified. If this is a concern, you can easily test for a short copy and repair the string with the following statements:

```
if(*(s1 + (sizeof (s1) - 1)))             // if not null char
   *(s1 + (sizeof (s1) - 1)) = '\0';
```

An even simpler solution is to move one less character than the maximum and then automatically place a null character in the last position. The code for this solution is shown below.

```
strncpy(s1, s2, sizeof(s1) - 1);
*(s1 + (sizeof (s1) - 1)) = '\0';
```

String Compare

Similar to the situation for string copy functions, there are two string compare functions. The first, ***strcmp***, compares two strings until unequal characters are found or until the end of the strings is reached. The second, ***strncmp***, compares until unequal characters are found, a specified number of characters have been tested, or until the end of a string is reached.

Both functions return an integer to indicate the results of the compare. Unfortunately, the results returned do not map well to the true-false logical values that we see in the *if...else* statement, so you will need to memorize a new set of rules:

1. If the two strings are equal, the return value is *zero*. Two strings are considered equal if they are the same length and all characters in the same relative positions are identical.
2. If the first parameter is less than the second parameter, the return value is *less than zero*. A string, `s1`, is less than another string, `s2`, if, when comparing character by character, (a) the `s1` character is less than the `s2` character or (b) the end of `s1` is reached and `s2` is not at its end.

3. If the first parameter is greater than the second parameter, the return value is *greater than zero*. A string, `s1`, is greater than another string, `s2`, if, when comparing character by character, (a) the `s1` character is greater than the `s2` character or (b) `s1` is not at its end and the end of `s2` is reached.

Note that the not-equal values are specified as a range. If the first parameter is less than the second parameter, the value can be any negative value. Likewise, if the first parameter is greater than the second parameter, the value can be any positive number. This is different from other situations, such as end of file, where we can count on one given value being returned.

strcmp The format statement for string compare (*strcmp*) is shown below.

```
result = strcmp (str1, str2);
```

Since the equal return value is 0, to test for equality in a selection statement we must test the return value, `result`, from the string compare. For example, to compare two strings for equal, we must write the statement as follows.

```
if (strcmp(str1, str2) == 0)
   // strings are equal
else
   // strings are not equal
```

The following statement tests whether the first string is less than the second string:

```
if (strcmp (string1, string2) < 0)
   // string1 is less than string2
```

To test for `string1` greater than `string2`, use the following statement:

```
if (strcmp (string1, string2) > 0)
   // string1 is greater than string2
```

We can also test for greater than or equal to with the following statement:

```
if (strcmp (string1, string2) >= 0)
   // string1 is greater than or equal to string2
```

strncmp The string number compare tests two strings for a specified maximum number of characters (`size`). The format for *strncmp* is shown below.

```
result = strncmp (str1, str2, size);
```

In this function, `size` specifies the maximum number of characters to be compared in the first string. The *strncmp* compare logic is the same as for *strcmp*, except for the length limit.

String Concatenate

The string concatenate (***strcat*** and ***strncat***) functions append one string to the end of a second string. Both functions return the address pointer to the destination string. The size of the destination string array is assumed to be large enough to hold the resulting string. If it isn't, the data at the end of the string array will be destroyed. The results are unpredictable if the strings overlap.

strcat The format statement for string concatenation is shown below.

```
strcat (str1, str2);
```

In this function, `str2` is copied to the end of `str1` beginning with `str1`'s delimiter. That is, the delimiter is replaced with the first character of `str2`. The delimiter from `str2` is copied to the resulting string to ensure that a valid string results. The length of the resulting string is the sum of the length of `str1` plus the length of `str2`.

strncat The format statement for *strncat* is shown below.

```
strncat (str1, str2, size);
```

If the length of `str2` is less than `size`, then the call works the same as the basic string concatenation described above. However, if the length of `str2` is greater than `size`, then only the number of characters specified by `size` are copied and a null character is appended at the end.

Searching for Characters

Sometimes we want to know if a given character is contained in a string. If it is, we also want to know where it is; that is, we want a pointer to the located character.[6] Two functions search for a character in a string. The first, string character (*strchr*), searches for the first occurrence from the beginning of the string. The second, string rear character (*strrchr*), searches for the first occurrence beginning at the end and working toward the beginning.

In either case, if the character is located, the function returns a pointer to it. If the character is not in the string, the function returns a null pointer. The formats for these two functions are shown below.

```
newStrPtr = strchr  (str, ch);
newStrPtr = strrchr (str, ch);
```

Searching for a Substring

If we can locate a character in a string, we should be able to locate a string in a string. We can, but only from the beginning of the string. There is no function to locate a substring starting at the rear. The function used to locate a string in a string is named ***strstr***. This function also returns a pointer to the beginning of the substring in the string. Its format is shown in the next example.

```
newStrtr = strstr  (str, subStr);
```

Searching for Characters in a String

Programmers quite often must locate one of a set of characters in a string. C++ provides two functions to do this. The first, *strspn*, locates the first character that does *not* match the string set. The second, *strcspn*, locates the first character that is in the set.

[6]Remember that C++ uses indexes (integrals) whereas C uses pointers to characters.

strspn String span searches the string, spanning characters that are in the set and stopping at the first character that is not in the set. It returns the number of characters that matched those in the set. If no characters match those in the set, it returns zero. The format is seen below.

```
numChars =  strspn (str1, charSet);
```

strcspn The second function, string complement span (*strcspn*), stops at the first character that matches one of the characters in the set. If none of the characters in the string matches the set, it returns the length of the string.

Searching for Tokens (*strtok*)

The string token function, ***strtok***, is used to locate substrings, called tokens, in a string. Its most common use is to parse a string into tokens, much as a compiler parses lines of code. Depending on how it is called, it either locates the first or the next token in a string. Its format is shown below.

```
charPtr = strtok (str1, delimiters);
```

The first parameter is the string that is being parsed; the second parameter is a set of delimiters that are to be used to parse the first string. If the first parameter contains an address, then *strtok* starts at that address, which is assumed to be the beginning of the string. It first skips over all leading delimiter characters. If all the characters in the string are delimiters, then it terminates and returns a null pointer. When it finds a nondelimiter character, it changes its search and skips over all characters that are not in the set; that is, it searches until it finds a delimiter. When a delimiter is found, it is changed to a null character ('\0'), which turns the token just parsed into a string.

If the first parameter is a null pointer, *strtok* assumes that it has already parsed part of the string and begins looking at the end of the previous string token for the next delimiter. When a delimiter is located, it again changes the delimiter to a null character marking the end of the token and returns a pointer to the new token string.

CONVERTING C STRINGS TO C++ STRINGS

A C string can be easily copied to a C++ string by assigning it to the C++ string or by using the C string as the copy constructor value. The following examples demonstrate these two techniques.

```
char* cStr = "Hello";
string str1;
cStr = cStr;                         // Assignment
string str2 (cStr);                  // In copy constructor
```

14-8 COMPARISON BETWEEN C AND C++ STRINGS

Table 14-3 shows the similarities and differences between C and C++ string formats and usage.

Action	C++ string	C string
Input	<< getline	<< getline
Output	>>	>>
Copy	=	strcpy strncpy
Compare	relational operators compare	strcmp strncmp
Concatenation	+ += append	strcat strncat
Extraction	substr	strstr
Search for Substring	find rfind	strstr
Search for Character	find rfind	strchr strrchr
Search for Character in Set	find_first_of find_last_of	strspn
Search for Character not in Set	find_first_not_of find_last_not_of	strcspn
Access Character	at [ ]	strchr [ ]
Insert	Insert	
Erase	erase clear	
Swap	swap	
Convert to Other Format	c_str	assign or copy constructor

Table 14-3 Comparison between C and C++ strings

14-9 SOFTWARE ENGINEERING AND PROGRAMMING STYLE

In Chapter 11, we examined the software engineering principle known as coupling—how two functions communicate. In Chapter12, we examined the principle of cohesion as it relates to designing functions. In this chapter, we discuss the program design process so that you will be able to design better programs.

PAYROLL CASE STUDY

To provide a discussion focus, we use a payroll program as a case study. Although our example is rather simple, it does contain all the elements involved in designing a program. A description of the payroll program is provided in Figure 14-14.

Payroll Case Study

1. Requirements:

   Given employees and their hours worked, compute net pay and record all payroll data for subsequent processing, such as W-2 statements. Prepare paychecks and a payroll ledger.

   Maintain data on a sequential payroll file.

2. Provide for the following nonstatutory deductions:
   a. Health plan
   b. United Way
   c. Union dues

3. The payroll data are:
   a. Employee number
   b. Pay rate
   c. Union member flag
   d. United Way contribution

4. Maintain the following year-to-date totals:
   a. Earnings
   b. FICA taxes
   c. SDI taxes
   d. Federal withholding
   e. State withholding
   f. Health plan fees
   g. United Way donations
   h. Union dues

5. Algorithms
   a. Gross Pay = (Reg Hours * Rate) + (OT Hours * Rate * 1.5)
   b. FICA Taxes = (Gross Pay * FICA Rate) if less than MaxFICA
   c. SDI Taxes = (Gross Pay * SDI Rate) if less than Max SDI
   d. Taxable Earnings = (Gross Pay – (Exemptions * Exemption Rate))
   e. Federal Taxes = (Taxable Earnings * Federal TaxRate)
   f. State Taxes = (Taxable Earnings * State Tax Rate)
   g. Net Pay = Gross Pay – (FICA Taxes + SDI Taxes + Taxable Earnings + Federal Taxes + State Taxes + Health Fee + United Way Donation + Union Dues)

Figure 14-14 Requirements for case study

PROGRAM DESIGN STEPS

There are seven basic steps used to develop a program:

1. Determine requirements.
2. Determine data structures.
3. Build structure charts.
4. Create test cases.
5. Write and unit test programs.
6. Test system.
7. Implement system in production.

Our interest here is only in the third step—building the structure charts. A few general comments are in order, however. The second and third steps are often reversed or done concurrently. Which one is done first is not of major consequence as long as both steps are done before the fourth step.

Many programmers think that test cases should be built after a program has been written. Good programmers know better. The process of creating test cases based on the requirements (step 1) and your design (steps 2 and 3) helps you understand the problem better. You will even find occasions when you change your design based on what you learned creating test cases.

This does not mean that you will be done with creating test cases at step 4; that is just where you start. You will develop more test cases *while you are writing the program,* and you will create still more as you conduct unit testing.

STRUCTURE CHART DESIGN

A good program starts with a good design, as reflected in the **structure chart**. By now you should have progressed to the point where you are designing your programs before you start coding; that is, you are creating your structure chart first.

One tool used in designing the structure chart is known as **transform analysis**. Transform analysis is a design technique that identifies the processes in a program as input, process, and output and then organizes them around one or more processes that convert inputs to outputs. These conversion processes are known as the **central transforms**. Having determined the first-cut design, you repeat the process, decomposing the identified modules into subtasks using transform analysis.

This is a good design technique to use for a program that reads, processes, and writes data, which covers the majority of programs. Although transform analysis is usually used in conjunction with another tool known as a data flow diagram, you can use it independently.

Good programs start with a good structure chart design.

Recognize, however, that transform analysis is an approach to the design of a program. It is not a cookbook that leads to the same results every time. Different programmers using the same steps will arrive at different designs.

There are six steps used to design a structure chart:

1. Determine program modules.
2. Classify modules.
3. Construct preliminary structure chart.
4. Decompose modules.
5. Complete structure chart.
6. Validate design.

Determine Modules

The first step in program design is to identify the processes that the program will use. This is usually done by reviewing the program specification and identifying the tasks it needs to accomplish. A review of our payroll case identifies the following tasks (the numbers in parentheses refer to the case study description):

1. Read hours worked (1)
2. Compute pay (1)
3. Maintain payroll master file (1)
4. Prepare paychecks (1)
5. Prepare payroll ledger (1)
6. Calculate nonstatutory deductions (2)
7. Calculate year-to-date totals (4)
8. Calculate gross pay (5)
9. Calculate taxes (5)

Remember the rule that each module is to do only one thing. You might be tempted to start with a module to prepare output instead of prepare paychecks and prepare payroll ledger. And in fact, you may well end up with an intermediate module that combines the preparation of all reports. But at this point, we want to keep different things separate as much as possible. On the other hand, experience indicates that to have separate modules for calculating FICA taxes, SDI taxes, federal taxes, and state taxes is unnecessary.

Classify Modules

In transform analysis, we are looking for the central transforms—that is, the module(s) that turn inputs into outputs. To identify these transforms, we classify each identified task, which now represents a module in the structure chart, as afferent, efferent, or transform. A module is **afferent** if its processing is directed toward the central transform. Another way of looking at this concept is to say that the module is a gatherer of data. **Efferent** modules direct data away from the central processing or toward the outputs of the program. (One way to remember is input comes before output and *a* comes before *e;* therefore, afferent is input and efferent is output.) A **transform** module is balanced; that is, it has data flowing both in and out. The concepts of afferent, efferent, and transform are shown in Figure 14-15.

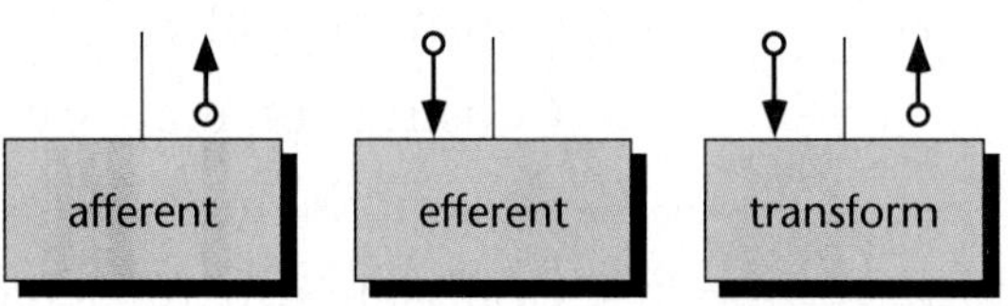

Figure 14-15 Afferent, efferent, and transform modules

Table 14-4 classifies each of the modules identified above as afferent, efferent, or transform.

Module	Afferent	Efferent	Transform
Read hours worked	✓		
Compute pay			✓
Maintain payroll master file	✓	✓	
Prepare paychecks		✓	
Prepare payroll ledger		✓	
Calculate nonstatutory deductions			✓
Calculate year-to-date totals			✓
Calculate gross pay			✓
Calculate taxes			✓

Table 14-4 Classified payroll modules

We have two comments about this classification. Note that "maintain payroll master file" is classified as both input and output. This is because it is a master file. We will have to read it to get the employee personnel and history data, and then we will have to write the updated data after they have been calculated. Therefore, it is really two modules—one to read the master and one to write the master.

Second, there are many transform modules. This will result in a large fan out, which is not desirable. Fan out is the number of submodules emanating from a module. We will have to reduce the fan out later.

Construct Structure Chart

At this point, you are ready to construct the first-cut structure chart. Transform analysis structure charts are organized with inputs on the left, transforms in the center, and outputs on the right. This organization is seen in Figure 14-16.

For the first-cut structure chart, place all afferent modules below the input block, all transform modules below the process block, and all

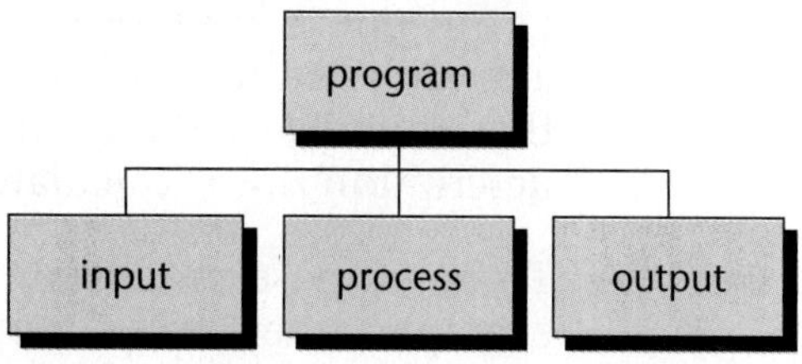

Figure 14-16 **Basic structure chart organization**

efferent modules below the output block. In this process, analyze each module to determine if it has to be called before or after the other processes at the same level. Those that must be called first are placed on the left, and those that must be called last are placed on the right. The resulting structure chart is shown in Figure 14-17.

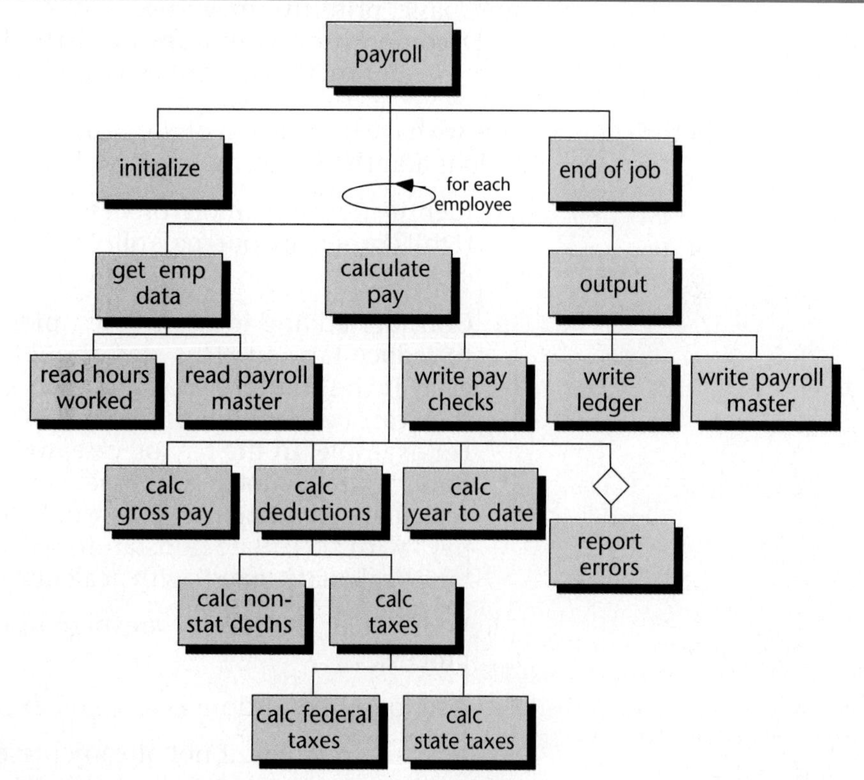

Figure 14-17 **First-cut structure chart**

Up to this point, we have been almost algorithmic; that is, we have exercised little judgment. We now need to analyze the preliminary structure chart to see if it makes sense. We do this by asking a simple question: "What do we mean by ..." For example, "What do we mean by compute pay?" The answer is that we must take hours worked and multiply them by the pay rate, also considering overtime and so forth. Or, to put it another way, we compute gross pay. But this is already a module in the structure chart, so these two modules are the same. We therefore delete the module "compute pay," since it is a less specific description than "calculate gross pay."

Decompose Modules

To decompose modules we look at the cohesion of each module. For example, when we ask what we mean by "calculate taxes," the answer is calculate federal taxes and calculate state taxes. Since we are dealing with two different entities (things), the cohesion of this module is communicational—it uses the gross pay and payroll data to calculate the different taxes.

When we find that a module is doing more than one thing, or that it is so complex that it is difficult to understand, then we need to consider breaking the module into submodules. This refinement of the modules was named *stepwise refinement* by Niklaus Wirth, the creator of Pascal.[7] It refines the processes in a module until each module is at its most basic, primitive meaning.

Decomposition continues until the lowest levels in our structure chart are all functionally cohesive and easily understood.

Complete Structure Chart

Now we have the nucleus of the structure chart complete, and all we have to do is add the finishing touches. These steps are almost mechanical:

1. Identify any common processes with a crosshatch in the lower right corner. In our payroll case, there aren't any common processes.
2. Consider adding intermediate (middle-level) modules if necessary to reduce fan out. This step should not be done arbitrarily, however. If the modules next to each other have a common entity, they can be combined. If they don't, they should be left separate. For example, in the payroll case, we have combined "calculate nonstatutory deductions" and "calculate taxes" into one module called "calculate deductions." We would not combine "calculate gross pay" with "calculate nonstatutory deductions," nor would we combine "calculate taxes" with "calculate year-to-date deductions."
3. Verify that the names are descriptive and meaningful for their processes.
4. Add loops, conditional calls, and exclusive *or* designators.
5. Add I/O modules, if not already present.
6. Add initialization and end-of-job modules.
7. Add error routines (if necessary).
8. Add data flows and flags as required.

[7]Niklaus Wirth, "Program Development by Stepwise Refinement," *Communications of the ACM,* Vol. 14, no. 4 (April 1971).

The completed design for the payroll case study is shown in Figure 14-18.

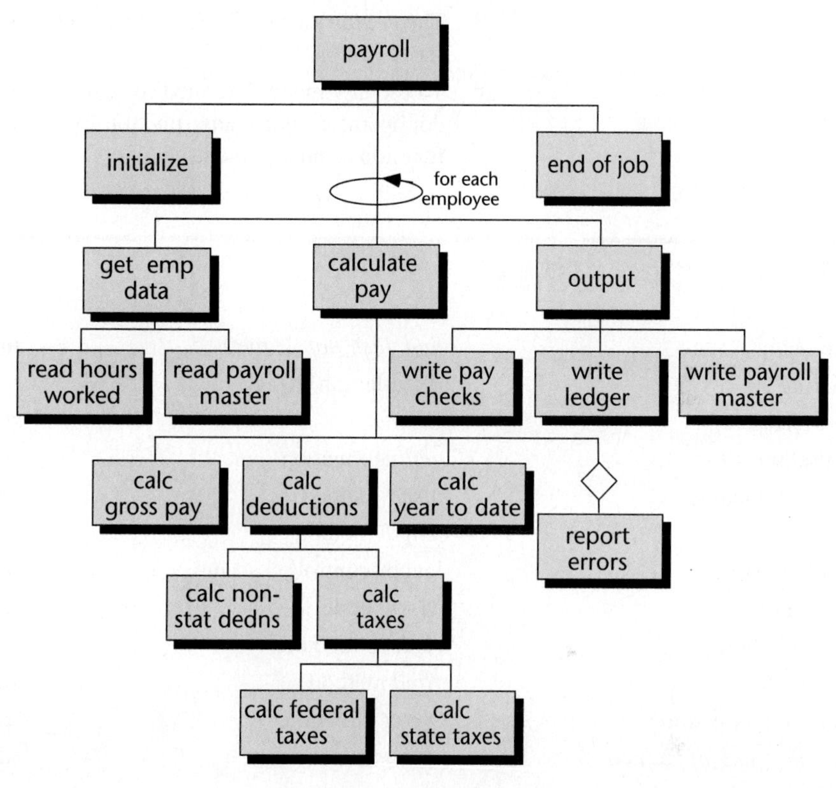

Figure 14-18 Final payroll structure chart

Validate the Design

At this point you are ready to validate the design with a structured walk-through. Before you convene the review board, however, you should review your design once more by repeating all the design steps, especially the functional decomposition step.

14-10 TIPS AND COMMON PROGRAMMING ERRORS

1. The header file `<string>` is required when using C++ strings; the header file `<cstring>` is needed when using C strings.
2. C++ strings are length strings; C strings are null-character delimited.
3. A C++ string is an object; a C string is a pointer to a character.
4. A string literal is a C string, not a C++ string.
5. We cannot read whitespaces using the extraction operator (<<); we need to use the *getline* function.
6. We can use the assignment operator to copy a C++ string to another, but we need to use the *strcpy* function to copy a C string to another.

7. To create a C++ string, we use the class string; to create a C string, we allocate an array of characters.
8. The index values in a C++ or C string start from 0, not 1.
9. The *getline* method for C++ string has a different format than the *getline* function for C strings.
10. To use any method defined for C++ string, we need to use the string object and dot operator; to use any function for C string, we need to pass the pointer to the function as an argument.

14-11 KEY TERMS

afferent
C string
C++ string
central transform
compare method
delimiter
delimiter string
efferent
erase method
find method
find_first_of method
find_last_not_of method
find_last_of method
find_last_not_of method
fixed-length string
getline
getline function
insert method
length method
length-controlled string
Morse code
replace method
rfind method
strcat function
strcmp function
strcpy function
string
strlen function
strncat function
strncmp function
strncpy function
strstr function
strtok function
structure chart
substring
swap method
transform
transform analysis
variable-length string

14-12 SUMMARY

- Strings can be fixed length or variable length.
- A variable-length string can be controlled by a length or a delimiter.
- C++ strings are length controlled.
- C strings are delimiter controlled.
- A C++ string is an object of *string* class.
- A C string is an array character that uses the null character '\0' as the delimiter.
- We can initialize a C++ string:
  a. With an initializer when we define it.
  b. With the assignment operator.
  c. With the string copy constructors.
- A C string identifier is a pointer constant to the first element in the string.
- The insertion (<<) and extraction (>>) operators can be used to write and read C++ and C strings.
- The *getline* function is used to read a C++ or a C string, but with different format.
- Individual characters in a C++ or C string can be accessed and modified using an index inside brackets.
- We can find the length of a C++ string using *length* method; we can find the length of a C string using *strlen* function.
- We copy a C++ string using the assignment operator or the copy constructor; we copy a C string using *strcpy* or *strncpy* function.
- We concatenate a C++ string with another C++ string using the overloaded operators (+, +=) or *append* method; we concatenate a C string with another C string using the *strcat* or *strncat* function.

- We compare a C++ string with another C++ string using the overloaded relational operators or the *compare* method; we compare a C string with another C string using the *strcmp* or *strncmp* function.
- We extract a substring from a C++ string using *substr* method; we extract a substring from a C string using the *strstr* function.
- We search for a substring in a C++ string using *find* (forward search) and *rfind* (backward search); we search for a substring in a C string using *strstr* (forward search) function.
- We search a C++ string to find the occurrence of a character belonging to a set of characters using *find_first_of* (forward search) or *find_last_of* (backward) method; we search a C string to find the occurrence of a character belonging to a set of characters using *strcspn* (forward search).
- We search a C++ string to find the occurrence of a character not belonging to a set of characters using *find_first_not_of* (forward search) or *find_last_not_of* (backward) method; we search a C string to find the occurrence of a character not belonging to a set of characters using *strspn* (forward search) function.
- We insert a substring into a C++ string using the *insert* method.
- We replace a substring with another substring in a C++ string using the *replace* method.
- We swap two C++ strings using the *swap* method.
- We erase a C++ string using the *erase* method.
- We tokenize a C string using *strtok* function.
- A C++ string can be converted to a C string using *c_str* method; a C string can be converted to a C++ string using the assignment operator or a copy constructor.
- There are seven steps in the design of a program:
  a. Determine requirements
  b. Determine data structures
  c. Build structure charts
  d. Create test cases
  e. Write and unit test programs
  f. Test system
  g. Implement system in production
- Transform analysis is a design technique that identifies the processes in a program as input, process, and output and then organizes them around one or more processes that convert inputs to outputs.
- There are six steps in designing a structure chart:
  a. Determine program modules
  b. Classify modules
  c. Construct preliminary structure chart
  d. Decompose modules
  e. Complete structure chart
  f. Validate design
- Program modules are classified as afferent (processing directed toward central transform), efferent (processing directed away from central processing), or process (module is balanced with data flowing both in and out).
- Stepwise refinement refines the processes in a module until each module is at its most basic, primitive state.
- The last step in program design is to validate the design.

14-13 PRACTICE SETS

REVIEW QUESTIONS

1. The two basic techniques for storing a stream of characters are fixed-length strings and variable-length strings.
   a. True
   b. False
2. A variable-length string can be controlled by a delimiter to a length.
   a. True
   b. False
3. What is the difference between a C++ strings and C strings?
4. C strings are length controlled.
   a. True
   b. False
5. C++ strings are delimiter controlled.
   a. True
   b. False
6. The standard defines a C string as a class object.
   a. True
   b. False

7. The standard defines a C++ string as a class object.
   a. True
   b. False
8. A literal string is a ____ string.
   a. C++
   b. C
9. Can we use the assignment operator to copy a C++ string into another C++ string?
10. Can we use the assignment operator to copy a C string into another C string?
11. Can we use the relational operators to compare two C++ strings?
12. Can we use the relational operators to compare two C strings?
13. To find the length of a C++ string, we use ____ method; to use the length of a C string, we use ____ function.
14. To copy a C++ string, we use ____; to copy a C string, we use ____ function.
15. To concatenate C++ strings, we use the ____ operators or the ____ method; to concatenate C strings, we use the ____ function.
16. To compare C++ strings, we use ____ method; to compare C strings we use ____ function.
17. To extract a substring from a C++ string, we use ____ method; to extract a substring from a C string, we use ____.
18. To search for a substring in a C++ string, we use ____ method; to search for a substring in a C string, we use ____ function.
19. To search a C++ string for a character in a set, we use ____ methods; to search a C string for a character in a set, we use ____ functions.
20. To insert a substring into a C++ string, we use the ____ method; to insert a substring into a C++ string, we use the ____ function.
21. To replace a substring with another substring in a C++ string, we use ____ method.
22. To swap two C++ strings, we use the ____ method.
23. To erase a C++ string, we use ____ method.
24. To tokenize a C string, we use the ____ function;
25. A C++ string can be converted to a C string using ____ method; a C string can be converted to a C++ string using ____.

EXERCISES

26. What would be printed from the following block?

```
{
   string s1 ("Hello!");
   s1.erase (4, 1);
   cout << s1 << endl;
}
```

27. What would be printed from the following block?

```
{
   string s1 ("Good Morning!");
   s1.replace (5,7, "Evening", 0, 7);
   cout << s1 << endl;
}
```

28. What would be printed from the following block?

```
{
   string s1 ("Hello World!");
   string s2 = s1.substr (6, 2);
   cout << s1 << endl;
   cout << s2 << endl;
}
```

29. What would be printed from the following block?

```
{
   boolean b;
   string s1 ("Hello");
   string s2 ("Hello!");
   b = (s1 == s2);
   cout << b << endl;
}
```

30. What would be printed from the following block?

```
{
   string s1 = "Hello";
   string s2 = "Hello!";
   int i = s1.compare (0, 3, s2, 0, 3);
   cout << i << endl;
}
```

31. What would be printed from the following block?

```
{
   string s1 ("Hello");
   string s2 (s1);
   string s3 = s1 + " " + s2;
   cout << s3 << endl;
}
```

32. What would be printed from the following block?

```
{
  string s1 ("Hello");
  s1.erase (4, 1);
  cout << s1 << endl;
}
```

33. What would be printed from the following block?

```
{
  string s1 = " The C++ Standard";
  int i = s1.find ("C", 0);
  int j = s1.rfind ("C", 0);
  cout << i  << j << endl;
}
```

34. Find the value of `*x`, `*(x+1)`, and `*(x+4)` for the following declaration:
char* x = "The life is beautiful";

35. What is the error in the following program block?

```
{
 char* x;
 cin >> x;
}
```

36. What would be printed from the following program block?

```
{
 char  s1[50] = "xyzt";
 char* s2 = "uabefgnpanm";
 char* s3;
 char* s4;
 char* s5;
 char* s6;
 s3 =  s1;
 s4 =  s2;
 strcat (s1, s2);
 s5 = strchr(s1, 'y');
 s6 = strrchr(s2, 'n');
 cout << s3 << endl;
 cout << s4 << endl;
 cout << s5 << endl;
 cout << s6 << endl;
}
```

37. What would be printed from the following program block?

```
{
  char* s1 = "abefgnpanm";
  char* s2 = "ab";
  char* s3 = "pan";
  char* s4 = "bef";
  char* s5 = "panam";
  int d1;
  int d2;
  int d3;
  int d4;
  d1 = strspn (s1, s2);
  d2 = strspn (s1, s3);
  d3 = strcspn (s1, s4);
  d4 = strcspn (s1, s5);
  cout << d1 << endl;
  cout << d2 << endl;
  cout << d3 << endl;
  cout << d4 << endl;
}
```

38. What would be printed from the following program block?

```
{
  char* a[5] =
  {"GOOD","BAD","UGLY","WICKED","NICE"};
  cout << a[0] << endl;
  cout << *(a + 2) << endl;
  cout << *(a[2] + 2) << endl;
  cout << a[3] << endl;
  cout << a[2] << endl;
  cout << a[4] << endl;
  cout << *(a[3] + 2) << endl;
  cout << *(*(a + 4) + 3) << endl;
}
```

39. If *str* is a C++ string, write a code fragment to print the length of *str*.

40. If *str1* and *str2* are C++ strings, write a code fragment to copy *str1* into *str2*.

41. If *str1* and *str2* are C++ strings, write a code fragment to compare the first eight characters of *str1* with the last eight characters of *str2*.
42. If *str1* and *str2* are C++ strings, write a code fragment to append characters 5 to 9 of *str1* at the end of *str2*.
43. If *str* is a C++ strings, write a code fragment to extract the last six characters of *str*.
44. If *str1* and *str2* are C++ strings, write a code fragment to find the first occurrence of the first four characters of *str1* in *str2*.
45. If *str1* and *str2* are C++ strings, write a code fragment to find the second occurrence of the first four characters of *str1* in *str2*.
46. If *str1* and *str2* are C++ strings, write a code fragment to find the last occurrence of the first four characters of *str1* in *str2*.
47. If *str1* and *str2* are C++ strings, write a code fragment to find, in *str2*, the first occurrence of any characters in *str1*.
48. If *str1* and *str2* are C++ strings, write a code fragment to find, in *str2*, the last occurrence of any characters in *str1*.
49. If *str1* and *str2* are C++ strings, write a code fragment to find, in *str2*, the first occurrence of any characters that are not *str1*.
50. If *str1* and *str2* are C++ strings, write a code fragment to find, in *str2*, the last occurrence of any characters that are not *str1*.

PROBLEMS

51. Write a function that accepts a C++ string (by reference) and deletes the last character.
52. Write a function that accepts a C string (a pointer) and deletes the last character by moving the null character one position to the left.
53. Write a function that accepts a C++ string (by reference) and deletes the first character.
54. Write a function that accepts a C string (a pointer) and deletes the first character.
55. Write a function that accepts a C++ string (by reference) and deletes all the trailing spaces at the end of the string.
56. Write a function that accepts a C++ string (by reference) and deletes all the leading spaces. It returns the new string.
57. Write a function that returns the number of times a character is found in a C++ string. The function has two parameters. The first parameter is a reference to a string. The second parameter is the character to be counted.
58. Write a function that given a string, an empty string as an output area, and the width of the output area, centers the string in the output area. The function is to return *true* if the formatting is successful and *false* if any errors, such as string length greater than width, are found.
59. A string is a palindrome if it can be read forward and backward with the same meaning. Capitalization and spacing are ignored. For example, *anna* and *go dog* are palindromes. Write a function that accepts a C++ string and returns *true* if the string is a palindrome or *false* if it is not. Test your function with the following two palindromes and at least one case that is not a palindrome.

```
Madam, I'm Adam
Able was I ere I saw Elba
```

60. Today's spelling checkers do much more than simply test for correctly spelled words. They also verify common punctuation. For example, a period must be followed by only one space. Write a program that reads a text file and removes any extra spaces after a period, comma, semicolon, or colon. Write the corrected text to a new file.

PROJECTS

61. Write a program that converts a C++ string representing a number in Roman numeral form to decimal form. The symbols used in the Roman numeral system and their equivalents are given below:

```
I    1
V    5
X    10
L    50
C    100
D    500
M    1000
```

For example, the following are Roman numbers: XII (12), CII (102); XL (40).

The rules for converting a Roman number to a decimal number are as follows:

a. Set the value of the decimal number to zero.

b. Scan the string containing the Roman character from left to right. If the character is not one of the symbols in the numeral symbol set, the program must print an error message and terminate. Otherwise, continue with the following steps. (Note that there is no equivalent to zero in Roman numerals.)
   - If the next character is the last character, add the value of the current character to the decimal value.
   - If the value of the current character is greater than or equal to the value of the next character, add the value of the current character to the decimal value.
   - If the value of the current character is less than the next character, subtract the value of the current character from the decimal value.

Solve this project using parallel arrays. Do not solve it using a *switch* statement.

62. Rework Project 61 to convert a decimal number to a Roman numeral.

63. Write a program that simulates the search-and-replace operation in a text editor. The program is to have only three function calls in *main*. The first function prompts the user to type a string of fewer than 80 characters. It then prompts the user to type the search-substring of 10 or fewer characters. Finally, it prompts the user to type the replace-substring of 10 or fewer characters.

    The second call is the search-and-replace function, which replaces all occurrences of the search-substring with the replace-substring and creates a new string. If no occurrences are found, it returns the original string. Theoretically, the new string could be 800 characters long (80 identical characters replaced by 10 characters each). The search-and-replace function returns the address of the new string.

    After the search-and-replace function returns, a print function prints the resulting string as a series of 80 character lines. It performs word-wrap because a line can end only at a space. If there is no space in 80 characters, then print 79 characters and a hyphen and continue on the next line.

    Write each called function using good structured programming techniques. Each function is expected to call subfunctions as necessary.

    Run the program at least three times:

    a. First, run it with no substitutions in the original input.
    b. Second, run it with two or more substitutions.
    c. Finally, run it with substitutions that cause the output to be at least three lines, one of which requires a hyphen.

64. Write a program that "speaks" pig latin. Words in pig latin are taken from English. To form a word in pig latin, the first letter of an English word beginning with a consonant is removed and then is suffixed at the end of the word, adding the letters *ay*. Words that begin with a vowel are simply suffixed with *ay*. Thus, in pig latin, the word *pig latin* is "igpay-atinlay."

    Your program is to read a sentence at a time using *getline*. It is to parse the words into strings. As words are parsed, they are to be converted to pig latin and printed.

65. Write a program that provides antonyms to common words. An antonym is a word with the opposite meaning. For example, the antonym of happy is sad.

    The data structure is to be patterned after the Morse code program on page 707. Given a word, the program is to look for the word on both sides of the structure and, if found, report the antonym. If the word is not found, the program is to display an appropriate message.

    The program is to use an interactive user interface. The words are to be read from a dictionary file. Use your dictionary to provide at least 30 antonyms, including at least one from each letter in the alphabet.

    Test your program by finding the antonyms for the first word, last word, and a word somewhere in the middle on both sides of the structure. Include in your test data at least three words that are not found, one less than the first word on the left, one in the middle somewhere, and one greater than the last word on the right side.

66. The Morse code program in this chapter is a public example of a cryptographic system. We can apply the same techniques to encoding and decoding any message. For example, we can substitute the letter Z for the letter A, the letter Y for the letter B, and so forth to create the following simple encoded message:

```
NZWZN, R ZN ZWZN
MADAM, I AM ADAM
```

Write a program that encodes and decodes messages using any user-supplied code. To make it more difficult to read, spaces and the common punctuation characters are to be included in the code. The code is to be read from a text file to build the encode/decode array. The user is then given a menu of choices to encode, decode, or enter a new code from the keyboard.

Test your program with the following code and message and with the complete alphabet entered in its encoded sequence so that it prints out in alphabetical order.

```
(English)
  ABCDEFGHIJKLMNOPQRSTUVWXYZ .,?!;
(Code)
  ?Q.W,EMRNTBXYUV!ICO PZA;SDLFKGJH
(Coded Message)
    WNWLSVPLM, LN G
```

67. Write a program that parses a text file into words and counts the number of occurrences of each word. Allow for up to 100 different words. After the list has been built, sort and print it.

68. Modify the program you wrote in Project 67 to eliminate common words such as *the*, *a*, *an*, *and*, *for*, and *of*. You may add other common words to the list.

15 Exception Handling

One of the fundamental aspects of programming is error handling. A program needs a facility to handle potential error and abnormal conditions. Programming does not end with writing code that executes and creates a result; a robust program must handle errors in a user-friendly manner.

Several types of errors can occur when we run a program. Some occur when the user enters bad data. Some, such as a disk read error, occur when the hardware fails. Some occur when a programming error, such as a bad pointer, causes the program to fail.

We can categorize error handling based on the nature of error. For example, invalid user input is not a serious problem and provision can be included in the code to prompt the user to re-enter the data. On the other hand, a disk read or write failure is a non-recoverable error. In between, there are some errors that can be recovered if they are handled appropriately.

The exceptional handling mechanism we discuss in this chapter separates the code that discovers an error from the code that handles it.

15-1 HANDLING ERRORS

In general, we have two options to handle errors, especially those detected by the system: (1) include code in the program to intercept and handle the error, or (2) let the system handle it—that is, ignore it. Assuming we decide to handle the error, we can handle the error in the code that detects the error—the traditional approach—or we can use the C++ exception handling design that separates the detection and handling of errors.

TRADITIONAL ERROR HANDLING

Traditional error handling uses the return value from a function to communicate status. If the function is successful, it returns `0` to indicate that there were no errors. If an error occurs, the function returns a unique number to identify the error. This is true even for *main*, only in this case the error code is interpreted by the operating system. Programming languages that do not support exception handling must use the traditional approach. Program 15-1 shows an example of the traditional approach that prevents division by zero.

Program 15-1 Traditional error logic

```
/* Demonstrate simple error handling logic.
      Written by:
      Date:
*/
#include <iostream>
#include <cstdlib>
using namespace std;

int main ()
{
   cout << "Enter the dividend: ";
   double dividend;
   cin  >> dividend;
   cout << "Enter the divisor:  ";
   double divisor;
   cin  >> divisor;

   if (divisor == 0)
      {
       cout << "**Error 100: divisor 0\n";
       exit (100);        // Tell OS program failed
      } // if

   double quotient = dividend / divisor;
   cout << "Quotient is: " << quotient << endl;
   return 0;
}  // main
```

```
Results:
Enter the dividend: 7
Enter the divisor:  0
**Error 100: divisor 0
```

USING THE EXCEPTION HANDLING MECHANISM

A better way of handling errors is to use the exception handling mechanism of C++. An **exception** is an event that signals the occurrence of an error. C++ allows us to separate the code that may generate the event (error) from the code that handles it. The error detection logic is coded in a special construct called the ***try* statement**; the error handling logic is coded in another construct called the ***catch* statement**. In this design, the *try* statement throws an exception that is caught by the *catch* statement. In using exception handling, the error can be thrown and caught in the same function or different functions—that is, in a hierarchy of function calls.

We throw an exception using a typed object. The typed object can be a standard type, such as an integer or floating-point variable, or a class instance. In the first part of this chapter, we use standard type objects to throw an exception; later we use classes.

Handling the Exception Where it Occurs

We can catch an exception in the same function that throws it. For example, we can catch and handle a divide-by-zero error in *main* using *try* and *catch* statements, as shown in Figure 15-1.

```
try
  {
    Code that contains logic to throw an exception
  } // try
catch (error type)
  {
    Exception handler
  } // catch
```

Figure 15-1 The *try* and *catch* statements

Try Statement The *try* statement allows us to encapsulate the codes that may create an exception. It is designed as a compound statement; the braces are required even if it is only one statement. When an error, such as divide by zero, is detected, the *try* statement transfers control to the *catch* statement by throwing an exception. If no error is detected, the *try* statement executes normally and the *catch* statement is ignored.

Throw Statement The ***throw* statement** inside the *try* statement raises an exception by throwing a variable or an object to the *catch* statement. In Program 15-2, the throw statement throws the divisor, which is type *double*, but it could throw any type.

Catch Statement The catch statement is an **exception handler** that receives the object raised by the *throw* statement. It contains whatever logic is necessary to handle the exception. Once again, it is a compound statement and the braces are required. If no *catch* statement is provided when an exception is thrown, the program aborts. The *catch* statement requires an object whose type matches the type of the variable or object thrown in the *try* statement.

Program 15-2 shows how we guard against the divide-by-zero error in Program 15-1 by throwing an exception in a *try* statement and handling it in a *catch* statement.

Program 15-2 Catch divide by zero

```
1  /*      Demonstrate simple error handling logic.
2          Written by:
3          Date:
4  */
5  #include <iostream>
6  #include <cstdlib>
7  using namespace std;
8  int main ()
9  {
10    cout << "Enter the dividend: ";
11    double dividend;
12    cin  >> dividend;
13    cout << "Enter the divisor:  ";
14    double divisor;
15    cin  >> divisor;
16
17    try
18       {
19        if (divisor == 0.00)
20            throw divisor;
21        double quotient = dividend / divisor;
22        cout << "Quotient is: " << quotient << endl;
23       } // try
24
25    catch (double& error)
26       {
27        cout << "**Error 100: divisor 0\n";
28        exit (100);
29       } // catch
30    return 0;
31 } // main
```

Program 15-2 Analysis Study statement 25 carefully. Note that we pass the error type by reference. While it is not necessary in this simple program, it is required when we create error classes later in the chapter. For consistency and so that we don't forget it when it's necessary, we make a habit of passing the error type by reference.

We didn't use `error` in the *catch* statement. While it is required, it doesn't need to be referenced. On the other hand, there is nothing that prevents us from using its value in the *catch* statement logic. For example, the value could be used to further analyze an error.

Propagating Exception

While Program 15-2 demonstrates the basic exception handling concept, it is more common for the error to occur in a called function and be caught in the calling function. Figure 15-2 demonstrates this design.

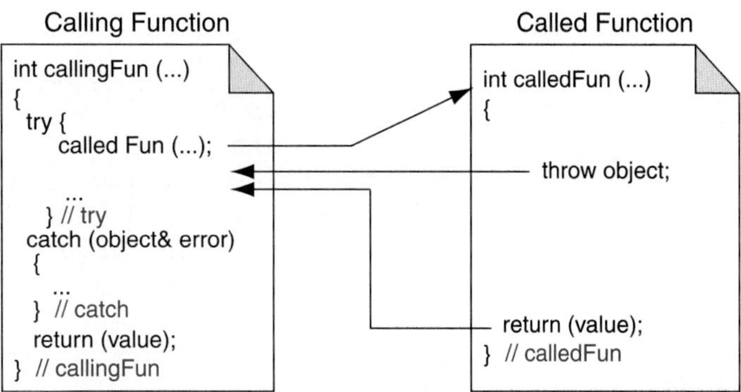

Figure 15-2 Throwing an exception in a separate function

To continue with our example, if we write the quotient processing as a function, we can **throw an exception** in the function, but handle it in the calling function, *main*. Program 15-3 implements this solution.

Program 15-3 Divide with exception handling

```
/* A simple exception handling example.
      Written by:
      Date:
*/
#include <iostream>
#include <cstdlib>
using namespace std;

double divide (double quot, double dvsr);

int main ()
{
   cout << "Enter the dividend: ";
   double dividend;
   cin  >> dividend;
   cout << "Enter the divisor:  ";
   double divisor;
   cin  >> divisor;

   try
      {
       double quotient = divide (dividend, divisor);
       cout << "Quotient is:  " << quotient << endl;
      } // try

   catch (double& error)
      {
       cout << "**Error 100: divisor 0\n";
       exit (100);
```

Program 15-3 Divide with exception handling (*continued*)

```
      } // catch
   cout << "End of Exception Handling Test\n";
   return 0;
} // main
/* ==================== divide ====================
   Divides the dividend by the divisor and returns
   the quotient as a double.
      Pre  dvnd and dvsr are defined and valid
      Post quotient of dvnd / dvsr returned
           or error thrown
*/
double divide (double dvnd, double dvsr)
{
   if (dvsr == 0)
        throw dvsr;
   return dvnd / dvsr;
} // divide
```

```
Results
Run 1:
   Enter the dividend: 7
   Enter the divisor:  0
   **Error 100: divisor 0

Run 2:
   Enter the dividend: 7
   Enter the divisor:  3
   Quotient is:    2.33333
   End of Exception Handling Test
```

Program 15-3 Analysis While this is a simple example, we would like to make four points. First, the exception handler must specify the type of data that are returned by the called function when it raises an exception. The type does not need a name, but it cannot be *void*. Second, the handler must return a value of the type specified in the exception handler. Third, while this program terminates when an error occurs, it could continue. Finally, the *catch* statement is skipped when no exception is thrown.

Re-Throwing an Exception

Sometimes the exception handler cannot completely handle the exception. When this happens, it handles as much as it can and then **re-throws the exception** to the higher level function that called it. Figure 15-3 traces a flow through three levels of exceptions.

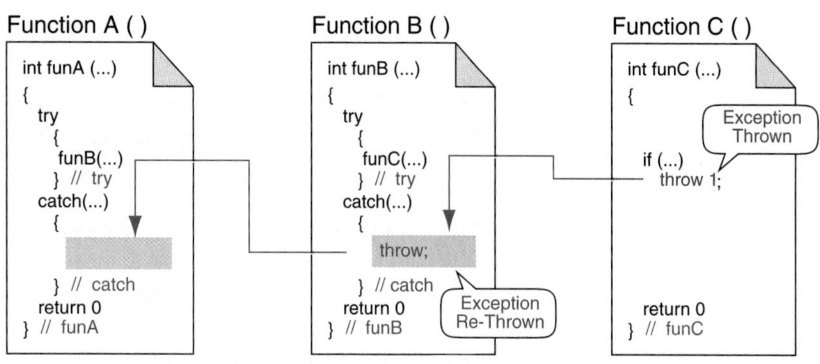

Figure 15-3 Re-throwing an exception

The ***re-throw* statement** is the same as the *throw* statement but without an object identifier. If a *throw* statement has an object identifier, it throws a new exception. If it doesn't, it re-throws the previous exception.

> A re-throw statement uses *throw* without an object identifier.

MULTIPLE ERRORS

In Program 15-3 there was only one type of error, division by zero. A function can test for different types of errors and throw different results depending on the error. The calling function includes a series of *catch* statements, one for each error. Note, however, that there can be no other code between the *try* and the first *catch* statements or between *catch* statements. An an example, let's modify the divide function again to test for division by 0 and division by a negative number. Program 15-4 demonstrates this logic.

Program 15-4 Throwing multiple errors

```
/* Throwing multiple errors. This program tests for
   divide by zero and divide by a negative number.
      Written by:
      Date:
*/
#include <iostream>
#include <cstdlib>
using namespace std;

double divide (double dividend, double divisor);

int main ()
{
   cout << "Enter the dividend: ";
   double dividend;
   cin  >> dividend;
   cout << "Enter the divisor:  ";
   double divisor;
   cin  >> divisor;

```

Program 15-4 Throwing multiple errors (*continued*)

```
   try
      {
       double quotient = divide (dividend, divisor);
       cout << "Quotient is : " << quotient << endl;
      } // try

   catch (float& zeroError)
      {
       cout << "**Error 100: divisor 0\n";
       exit (100);
      } // DivByZero

   catch (double& negError)
      {
       cout << "**Error 101: negative divisor\n";
       exit (101);
      } // DivByNeg

   cout << "End of Exception Handling Test\n";
   return 0;
} // main
/* ===================== divide =====================
   Divides the dividend by the divisor and returns
   the quotient as a double.
      Pre  dvnd and dvsr are defined and valid
      Post quotient of dvnd / dvsr returned
           or error thrown
*/
double divide (double dvnd, double dvsr)
{
   float  zeroError = 0;
   double negError  = -1;

   if (dvsr == 0)
       throw zeroError;
   if (dvsr < 0)
      throw negError;
   return dvnd / dvsr;
} // divide
```

```
Results
Run 1:
   Enter the dividend: 10
   Enter the divisor:  0
   **Error 100: divisor 0
Run 2:
   Enter the dividend: 10
   Enter the divisor:  -1
   **Error 101: negative divisor
```

Program 15-4 Analysis The logic is the same as the previous programs, except that we are using more than one error handler. Note, however, that each error must have a different type. We made `zeroError` type *float* and `negError` type *double*.

GENERIC HANDLER

Sometimes we cannot determine all of the errors that may occur or do not need to provide unique handlers for each error. If an error occurs for which there is no handler, the system terminates the program, possibly ungracefully. To prevent system aborts, we can include a generic handler in the program to terminate the program gracefully. This can be done by a *catch* statement that uses ellipses (**...**) as the argument. Figure 15-4 contains a generic exception handler.

```
try
  {
   ...
  }
catch (Object1& e1)
  {
   ...
  }
catch (Object2& e2)
  {
   ...
  }
catch (...)
  {
   ...           // Code for handling generic error
  }
```

Figure 15-4 Generic exception handler

Multiple *catch* statements use the flow design we saw in the *switch* statement. When an exception is thrown, the exception handler first tries to match the exception with the first *catch* statement. If it matches, the exception is handled and the remaining *catch* statements are skipped. If the exception thrown does not match the first *catch* statement, the exception handler tries the second *catch* statement. If it has the matching type, it is executed and any remaining *catch* statements are skipped. This logic continues until either a matching type is found, a **generic *catch* statement** is found, or all *catch* statements have been tested. The generic catch statement acts like the *default* case statement in a *switch*. But, note that unlike the *switch* statement, there is no need for a *break* statement. One and only one of the *catch* statements can be executed. The other difference between the *switch default* case and the generic exception handler is that the generic exception handler must be last.

15-2 EXCEPTION HANDLING CLASSES

The standard type error handlers described in the previous section work well in simple situations. For more complex error handling, especially for generalized software functions, error classes provide a more powerful and elegant solution.

Error classes allow us to categorize errors and create a hierarchy of classes. Each class represents one type of error. This design allows us to include an error message for each type in the appropriate class and throw different objects for different errors. Then, using polymorphism, we can create a "generic" handler that provides different logic and error messages for each situation. This means that we can use only one *catch* statement to handle multiple errors—that is, every error in the hierarchy. Furthermore, if error messages are printed in virtual functions, we can write only one *catch* statement that catches different exceptions by using a reference to the object.

CLASS HIERARCHY

Figure 15-5 contains the design for a hierarchy of divide errors.

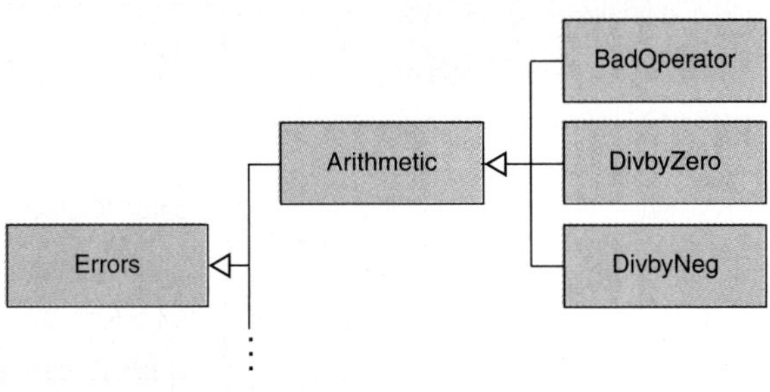

Figure 15-5 Error class design

Error Class Declaration

We begin the implementation of our error class by declaring a hierarchy of classes using virtual message printers. Program 15-5 declares the five classes shown in Figure 15-5.

Program 15-5 Error class declaration

```
/* Declaration for Error class.
      Written by:
      Date
*/
using namespace std;
class Error
{
   public:
   virtual void printMessage ()
       {cout << "**Error: type Error\n";}
}; // Error
class Arithmetic: public Error
{
   public:
   virtual void printMessage ()
       {cout << "**Error: type Arithmetic\n";}
}; // Arithmetic
class DivbyZero: public Arithmetic
{
   public:
   virtual void printMessage ()
     {cout << "**Error: 100 divisor 0\n";}
}; // DivbyZero
```

Program 15-5 Error class declaration (*continued*)

```
class DivbyNeg: public Arithmetic
{
   public:
   virtual void printMessage ()
     {cout << "**Error: 101 negative divisor\n";}
}; // DivbyZero
class BadOperator: public Arithmetic
{
   public:
   virtual void printMessage ()
     {cout << "**Error: 102 invalid operator\n";}
};// BadOperator
```

To test the Error class, we first write a generalized math function that adds, subtracts, multiplies, and divides. It contains three error checking conditions: divide by zero, divide by a negative number, and invalid operator. If any of these errors is detected, it throws the appropriate error in the `Error` class. Program 15-6 contains the implemented code. Note that it is also a header file.

Program 15-6 Generalized math function

```
/* A generalized math function that adds, subtracts
   subtracts, multiplies, and divides.
      Written by:
      Date
*/
double math (char oper, double data1, double data2)
{
   double result;
      switch (oper)
         {
          case '+': result = data1 + data2;
                    break;
          case '-': result = data1 - data2;
                    break;
          case '*': result = data1 * data2;
                    break;
          case '/': if (data2 == 0 )
                        throw DivbyZero ();
                    if (data2 < 0 )
                        throw DivbyNeg ();
                    result = data1 / data2 ;
                    break;
          default:  throw BadOperator () ;
                    break;
         } // switch
   return result;
}  // math
```

Program 15-6 Analysis One subtle point needs explanation in this program. In statements 19, 21, and 24, we instantiate an anonymous object by explicitly calling the constructor for the error class.

We are now ready to write a test driver. Both the error class and math header files are included in our program. The error hierarchy can be used any time we need one of the errors defined in the hierarchy.

In the test driver, we see one of the major benefits of using an error class: There is only one *catch* statement. Because the error class uses virtual print message functions, we just call the print function and it prints the appropriate message. We do lose one capability, however; while we can assign unique error numbers to the messages, we have only one return value, 100. Program 15-7 contains the test driver and test results from four runs.

Program 15-7 Test driver for math errors

```
/* Test driver for arithmetic Error class & math function
      Written by:
      Date:
*/
#include <iostream>
#include <cstdlib>
using namespace std;

#include "p15-05.h"             // Error class hierarchy
#include "p15-06.h"             // Math function
#define FLUSH while (cin.get() != '\n')

int main ()
{
   cout << "Begin Error class demonstration\n";

   cout << "Enter the first data:  " ;
   double data1;
   cin >> data1;
   cout << "Enter the second data: " ;
   double data2;
   cin >> data2;
   cout << "Enter the operator:    " ;
   char oper;
   cin  >> oper;
   FLUSH;

   try
      {
       double result = math (oper, data1, data2);
       cout << "result: "<< result << endl;
      } // try

   catch (Error& error)
      {
```

Program 15-7 Test driver for math errors (*continued*)

```
        error.printMessage() ;
        exit 100;
      } // catch
    cout << "Normal end of demonstration\n";
    return 0;
} // main
```

```
Results:
Run 1:
   Begin Error class demonstration
   Enter the first data:  12
   Enter the second data: 6
   Enter the operator:    *
   result: 72
   Normal end of demonstration
Run 2:
   Begin Error class demonstration
   Enter the first data:  12
   Enter the second data: 0
   Enter the operator:    /
   **Error: 100 divisor 0
Run 3:
   Begin Error class demonstration
   Enter the first data:  12
   Enter the second data: -5
   Enter the operator:    /
   **Error: 101 negative divisor
Run 4:
   Begin Error class demonstration
   Enter the first data:  12
   Enter the second data: -5
   Enter operator:        ?
   **Error: 102 invalid operator
```

15-3 EXCEPTION SPECIFICATION

So far, all of our functions have been allowed to throw any type of exception. There may be situations, however, where we need to limit—or prevent entirely—what types of exceptions can be thrown. To control what exceptions a function is allowed to throw, we can add an **exception specification** to the declaration and definition of the function. There are three types of exception specifications, as shown in Figure 15-6.

When we limit the exceptions that can be thrown from a function, any attempt to throw an unauthorized exception results in a call to a special system function, ***unexpected***, that aborts the program. Within limits, we can control the execution of the unexpected function. We describe how this is done at the end of this section.

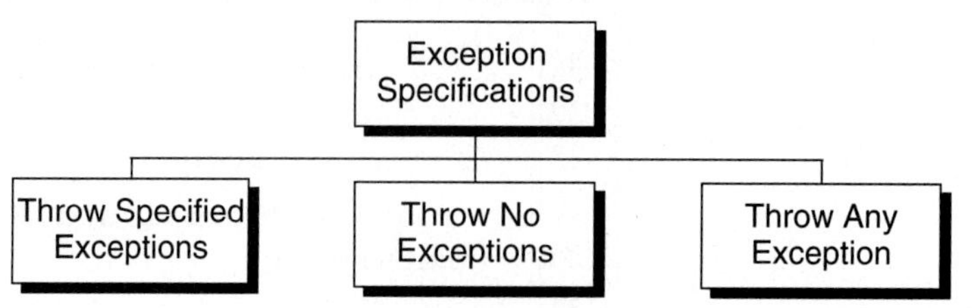

Figure 15-6 Exception specifications

THROW SPECIFIED EXCEPTIONS

To limit the exceptions that can be thrown, we use a **some-exception specification**. To specify some exceptions, we list them after the function header in the function declaration and in the function definition. In the next example, we limit the exceptions in our `doIt` function to divide by zero and divide by a negative number only. If we use an exception specification clause with a list of exceptions (separated by comma), then the function throws those exception. This is shown below:

```
// Prototype Declaration
void doIt(...) throw (DivbyZero, DivbyNeg);

// Function Definition
void doIt(...) throw (DivbyZero, DivbyNeg)
{
...
} // doIt
```

When we specify an exception, all exceptions derived from it are included. In the following example, we limit the exceptions only to those found in the arithmetic class. Because divide by zero, divide by a negative number, and bad arithmetic operator are derived from the arithmetic class, they are automatically included.

```
// Prototype Declaration
void doIt(...) throw (Arithmetic);

// Function Definition
void doIt(...) throw (Arithmetic)
{
...
} // doIt
```

THROW NO EXCEPTIONS

To prevent any exception from being thrown, we add a **no-exception specification**; that is, we add a *throw* with an empty exception list. This code is shown in the next example.

```
// Prototype Declaration
void doIt(...) throw ();

// Function Definition
void doIt(...) throw ()
{
...
} // doIt
```

THROW ANY EXCEPTION

Any exception is the default. When we don't code an exception specification in the function header, any exception can be thrown.

THE *unexpected* EXCEPTION

If a function encounters an exception that is not part of its exception specification, then the exception handler calls the *unexpected ()* library function. The *unexpected* function calls, by default, another function called ***terminate()***, which by default calls the ***abort()*** function to abort the program.

This chain of actions can be undesirable because the *abort* function terminates the program ungracefully. As an example, a program can be terminated without calling the destructor for instantiated objects. It is possible, therefore, that some dynamic memory allocation will not be released.

We can change this chain of events by either changing the default behavior of the unexpected function or the default behavior of the *terminate* function.

Changing Default for *unexpected*

We can change the default value of the unexpected function by calling the ***set_unexpected*** function. As a parameter to the *set_unexpected* function, we can define the name of a handler function that we write. In other words, we can write a handler function to be used when the program terminates unexpectedly. The name of our function is a pointer to that function. (Pointers to functions are covered in Appendix M.) The next example shows how to change the *unexpected* function to call `myTerminateHandler`. This call should be made at the beginning of the program.

```
set_unexpected (myTerminateHandler);
```

Changing Default for *terminate*

We can change the default value of the *terminate* function by calling another system function called ***set_terminate*** *()*.When we call *set_terminate*, we pass the name of a handler function as the argument as described in the discussion of the *set_unexpected* function.

abort* versus *exit

There is a very important point that we need to discuss here. A program can be terminated abnormally by using one of the two system functions: *abort* or ***exit***. The *abort* function is very undesirable because it does not terminate gracefully. No files are closed and only cryptic system messages, if any, are displayed. On the other hand, the *exit* function terminates gracefully.

15-4 EXCEPTIONS IN CLASSES

The exceptional handling process can be complicated when it applies to **classes**. In particular, we need to pay attention to two issues: exceptions in constructors and exceptions in destructors.

To understand these issues, we need to understand the lifetime of an object. In C++, an object is instantiated when the constructor completes its tasks and returns. An object is destroyed when the destructor is called, not when it returns. In other words, the lifetime of an object is between the end of the constructor and the beginning of the destructor.

Now what happens if a constructor is terminated abnormally at the middle of its execution? The object is never instantiated. When the object is not instantiated, it cannot be destroyed. This means that if a constructor terminates abnormally, the destructor is never called. Although constructor failure doesn't always cause problems, there are situations when it does—for example, when during creation it dynamically allocates memory. In this case, the destructor is not called and memory is not released.

EXCEPTIONS IN CONSTRUCTORS

There are many design issues involved when an exception needs to be thrown during constructor execution. Just to discuss one, a constructor of a derived class needs to first call the constructor of the base class. When the base class constructor completes, the derived class constructor continues. If the base class constructor completes successfully, but the derived object fails, the constructor fails and the destructor not called.

There is no clear-cut solution to this problem and different C++ experts offer different opinions. In our opinion, the constructor must handle critical exceptions, such as memory allocation, unless the program is going to be terminated. Even when it terminates, however, it should be done gracefully.

C++ even allows us to call the try function with the initialization list, which means that the *try* statement can catch exceptions even in the creation of base objects. This is done by placing the constructor's body in a *try* statement, as shown in Program 15-8.

Program 15-8 Constructor exception handler

```
1  /* Sample constructor to demonstrate exception handling
2        Pre  Nothing
3        Post Object instantiated
4  */
5  Derived::Derived (...)
6     try : Base (...)
7        {
8          // Constructor's code
9        } // Derived constructor
10    catch (...)
11       {
12         // Release memory
13       } // catch statement
```

Program 15-8 Analysis Study statement 6 carefully. This *try* statement calls the base class constructor (`Base`). If the constructor fails, control is transferred to the `catch` statement, which deletes the allocated memory before continuing.

EXCEPTIONS IN DESTRUCTORS

Virtually everyone agrees that a destructor should not throw any exceptions. To understand why, consider the following scenario. Imagine an exception happens somewhere in the program and handling the exception involves a call to a destructor. If, during the execution of the destructor, it fails and throws an exception, the system immediately terminates the program. In this case, the handler cannot finish its job. To prevent the destructor from throwing any exceptions, we add an exception specification as shown in the next example.

```
// Prototype Declaration
      ~MyClass() throw ();
// Destructor Definition
MyClass::~MyClass() throw ()
{
...
} // MyClass destructor
```

15-5 STANDARD EXCEPTIONS

In addition to the programmer-designed exceptions described in the previous section, standard C++ functions have their own exception handling logic. We can catch them if their calls are placed within a *try* statement.

C++ defines an exception class, `std::exception`. It is found in the *exception* library file. Included in the exception class, or derived from it, are seven types of exceptions. Two of them, **logic error** and **run-time error**, have derived types. The standard exceptions are shown in Figure 15-7.

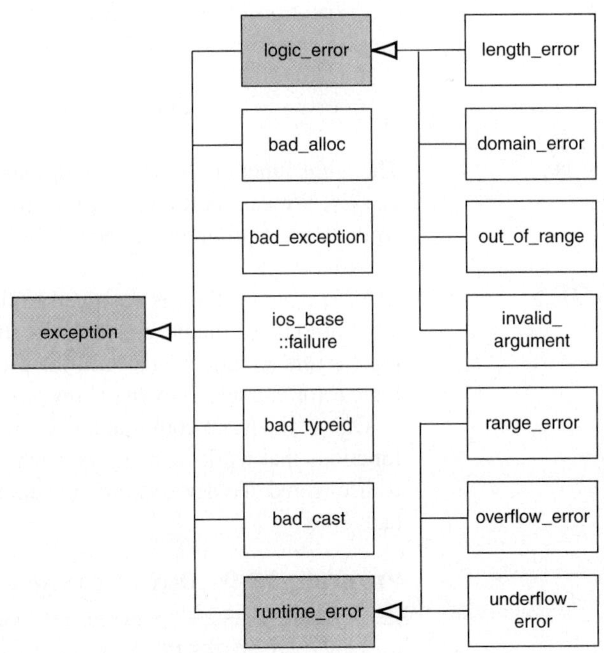

Figure 15-7 Standard exceptions

Table 15-1 contains a summary of the standard exceptions with their class types and an explanation of each. In the following sections we demonstrate three standard exception conditions.

Exception	Explanation
Logic Errors - domain_error - invalid_argument - length_error - out_of_range	Errors in the internal logic of the program. - function argument is invalid - invalid argument in C++ standard function - object's length exceeds maximum allowable length - reference to array element out of range
bad_alloc	*new* cannot allocate memory.
bad_exception	Exception doesn't match any *catch*
ios_base::failure	Error in processing external file
bad_typeid	Error in *typeid*
bad_cast	Failure in a dynamic cast
Run-time Error - range_error - overflow_error - underflow_error	Errors beyond the scope of the program. - error in standard template library (STL) container - overflow in standard template library (STL) container - underflow in standard template library (STL) container

Table 15-1 Standard exceptions

Sometimes the cause of an error is not obvious. To help explain what caused an error, the exception class has a public virtual method called *what* that returns a C-string message explaining the error. Its format is shown in the following example.

```
cout << "Error: " << err.what() << endl;
```

The *what* function is virtual and, using polymorphism, it is overridden in its derived classes. We can therefore call it even if we access it through a base class. We demonstrate it in the programs in the following sections.

LOGIC ERRORS

The *logic_error* class is designed to throw errors, such as an invalid argument, in the internal logic of the program. While the compiler catches and flags many errors, some logic errors are not caught until the program is executed. C++ has defined four derived logic error classes. They are shown in Table 15-1.

One of the more common logic errors is the out-of-range exception. In those system functions that work with arrays, such as the *string* class, it is thrown when a bad index is discovered. To demonstrate this exception, Program 15-9 calls the *at* function with a bad index.

Program 15-9 Out-of-range exception

```
/* Demonstrate out of range exception.
      Written by:
      Date:
*/
#include <iostream>
#include <string>
#include <iomanip>
#include <exception>
using namespace std;

```

Program 15-9 Out-of-range exception (*continued*)

```
11 int main ()
12 {
13 string s1 ("This is the string") ;
14
15    cout << "Testing out_of_range exception\n";
16    try
17       {
18        cout << "s1(125) contains: "
19               << s1.at(125) << endl;
20       } // try
21
22    catch (exception& err)
23       {
24        cout << err.what() << endl;
25       } // catch
26    cout << "End of exceptions tests\n";
27    return 0;
28 }  // main
```

```
Results
Testing out_of_range exception
**basic_string::at index out of range
End of exceptions tests
```

Program 15-9 Analysis Study this example carefully. As you examine the include statements, note that the exception class is needed. The error is thrown in the substring function. This can be verified by looking at the output. We use the *what* function to print an explanation of the error in statement 24. The printed message shows that the exception was thrown in the string class *at* function.

MEMORY ALLOCATION FAILURE

While today's large-memory computers reduce the risk of running out of memory, it can still happen. If a program without a test for memory allocation runs out of memory, it aborts without any messages. Therefore, even when the probability is low, all programs should allocate memory in an appropriate *try* statement as shown in Program 15-10.

Program 15-10 Test for memory allocation exception

```
/* Demonstrate memory allocation exception handling.
      Written by:
      Date:
*/
#include <iostream>
#include <new>
using namespace std;

int main ()
{
   cout << "Demonstrate memory allocation failure\n";
   try
```

Program 15-10 Test for memory allocation exception (*continued*)

```
        {
         double* Arr = new double [100000000000];
         cout << "Memory allocated successfully\n";
        } // try

    catch (exception& err)
        {
        cout << "**Error 100: Program out of memory\n**"
             << err.what() << endl ;
        } // catch

    cout << "End of exceptions tests\n";
    return 0;
}  // main
```

```
Results
Demonstrate memory allocation failure
**Error 100: Program out of memory
**bad_alloc
End of exceptions tests
```

Program 15-10 Analysis Note that we have included the *new* library to catch this exception.

I/O (FILE) EXCEPTIONS

Another common set of errors center around file input and output. In Program 15-11, we demonstrate the code for catching a file open error.

Program 15-11 Demonstrate file open error

```
/* Demonstrate standard exception handling for file open
   error.
      Written by:
      Date:
*/
#include <iostream>
#include <fstream>
#include <stdexcept>
using namespace std;

int main ()
{
   ifstream noSuchFile;
   noSuchFile.exceptions(ios::badbit|ios::failbit);

   cout << "Testing open error\n";
   try
       {
        noSuchFile.open ("notThere", ios::in);
```

Program 15-11 Demonstrate file open error (*continued*)

```
20          cout << "File 'NotThere' successfully opened\a\n";
21          } // try
22
23       catch (exception& err)
24          {
25           cout << "Error opening file 'NotThere'\n**"
26                << err.what() << endl;
27          } // catch
28       cout << "End of exceptions tests\n";
29       return 0;
30    }  // main
```

```
Results
Testing open error
Error opening file 'NotThere'
**ios_base failure in clear
End of exceptions tests
```

Program 15-11 Analysis First note the code in statement 14. This code tells the file system that we want to test for errors. If statement is not there, the traditional method for testing for open failure must be used; the open function returns a null value.

In the *catch* statement, we specify that we are looking for *ios* errors. Note that the scope operator must be used to correctly locate the failure exceptional handler. We also give it an identifier, `err`, so that we can print out the error message thrown by the I/O function. Because it will not be meaningful to the user, however, we also include our own error message.

We have demonstrated three of the more common system exceptions. The others are very difficult to demonstrate in a simple program. When they are needed in a program, however, their implementation follows the example shown in this section. Testing them can be a challenge.

ADDING NEW CLASSES TO THE STANDARD EXCEPTION CLASS

In the previous sections, we created a set of classes to handle arithmetic exceptions. We can combine these classes with the standard exception classes. We do this by using the exception class as a base class to our arithmetic class. This allows us to use the exception class reference to catch all of our exceptions. The design is shown in Figure 15-8.

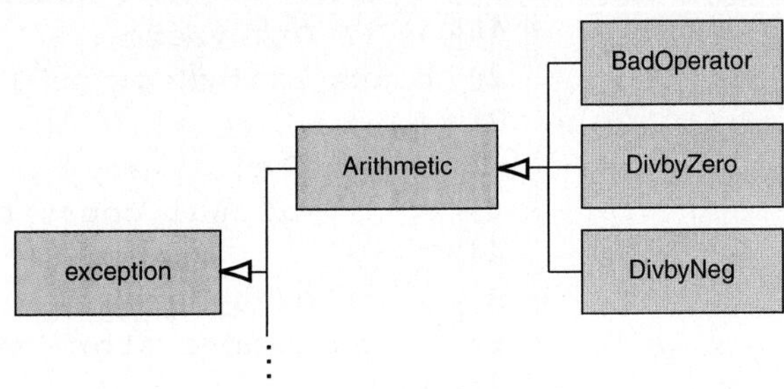

Figure 15-8 Adding errors to standard error class

To effect this change, we modify Program 15-5 to associate the arithmetic class with the system exception class. There are several changes that need to be made:

1. The Error class is no longer needed. We deleted it from the header file.
2. The arithmetic class needs to be changed to reflect the system's exception file as its base class (not the Error class).
3. Rather than printing our own messages, we now use the system *what* function by overriding it and then returning the message we want to print. The code is shown in the following statement.

```
virtual const char* what () const throw ()
          {return "**Error: type Arithmatic\n";}
```

4. There are no changes in the math function.
5. In the test driver, we must change the *catch* statement to use the system *what* function.

Program 15-12 contains the revised error class declaration. Program 15-13 contains the revised test driver.

Program 15-12 Revised error class declaration

```
/* Declaration for Error class.
       Written by:
       Date
*/
#include <exception>
using namespace std;

class Arithmetic: public exception
{
   public:
      virtual const char* what () const throw ()
                {return "**Error: type Arithmetic\n";}
}; // Arithmetic
class DivbyZero: public Arithmetic
{
   public:
      virtual const char* what () const throw ()
                {return "**Error: 100 divisor 0\n";}
}; // DivbyZero
class DivbyNeg: public Arithmetic
{
   public:
      virtual const char* what () const throw ()
            {return "**Error: 101 negative divisor\n";}
}; // DivbyZero
class BadOperator: public Arithmetic
{
```

Program 15-12 Revised error class declaration (*continued*)

```
   public:
      virtual const char* what () const throw ()
           {return "**Error: 102 invalid operator\n";}
};// BadOperator
```

Program 15-13 Revised test driver for math errors

```
/* Test driver for arithmetic Error class & math function
       Written by:
       Date:
*/
#include <iostream>
#include <cstdlib>
using namespace std;

#include "p15-12.h"          // Error class hierarchy
#include "p15-06.h"          // Math function
#define FLUSH while (cin.get() != '\n')

int main ()
{
   cout << "Begin Error class demonstration\n";

   cout << "Enter the first data:  " ;
   double data1;
   cin >> data1;
   cout << "Enter the second data: " ;
   double data2;
   cin >> data2;
   cout << "Enter the operator:    " ;
   char oper;
   cin  >> oper;
   FLUSH;

   try
      {
       double result = math (oper, data1, data2);
       cout << "result: "<< result << endl;
      } // try

   catch (exception& error)
      {
       cout << error.what();
       exit (100);
      } // catch
   cout << "Normal end of demonstration\n";
   return 0;
}  // main
```

Program 15-13 Revised test driver for math errors (*continued*)

```
Results:
Run 1:
   Begin Error class demonstration
   Enter the first data:  12
   Enter the second data: 6
   Enter the operator:    *
   result: 72
   Normal end of demonstration
Run 2:
   Begin Error class demonstration
   Enter the first data:  12
   Enter the second data: 0
   Enter the operator:    /
   **Error: 100 divisor 0
Run 3:
   Begin Error class demonstration
   Enter the first data:  12
   Enter the second data: -5
   Enter the operator:    /
   **Error: 101 negative divisor
Run 4:
   Begin Error class demonstration
   Enter the first data:  12
   Enter the second data: -5
   Enter operator:        ?
   **Error: 102 invalid operator
```

15-6 SOFTWARE ENGINEERING AND PROGRAMMING STYLE

In Chapter 1, we discussed some general testing concepts. At that time we stressed two points: Development of a test plan begins with the design of the program, and it takes multiple test cases to fully validate a program. In this section we talk about techniques for testing and debugging a program.

During unit or whitebox testing, programs may fail to complete successfully or they may produce incorrect output. Programs that fail during execution require detailed analysis of the code to correct them. Programs that produce invalid output require detailed analysis of the program logic. Invalid output is more difficult to detect and requires a good test plan and a knowledge of the program requirements.

CORRECTING PROGRAM FAILURES

A program that fails to complete must first be analyzed to determine exactly where it failed. Partial output may provide a clue to the location of the failure. This is especially true in programs that follow the basic input, process, output design common in data processing. Using the program design documentation, analyze the output to determine what phase of the program failed. Was all of the input read? Was the data processing complete? If output processing had started but is not complete, what function was executing when the program terminated?

There are two tools that can help with this phase of the code analysis: a debugger and display statements.

Code Debuggers

Most compilers today have a built-in debugging facility. Debuggers allow the programmer to step through a program statement by statement or function by function. At any given statement in a program, the programmer can then analyze the current data values to determine the cause of the program failure.

While their technical operation varies from compiler to compiler, debuggers have a general set of capabilities that include the following. Refer to the documentation for your compiler for specifics on these capabilities.

Break Points A break point identifies a statement that suspends the program run pending some action by the programmer at the terminal.

Data Display At any point in the execution, the data in scope to the current statement are displayed. Some compilers allow the programmer to change the data before resuming execution.

Stack Display Whenever a function call is executed, the return information and other data are placed in a system call stack. By examining the stack display, the active functions can be traced.

Step-by-Step Execution When the program execution is suspended, the programmer can execute statements one at a time. At any time, the program run can be continued, in which case it runs to the next break point or until the end of the program.

Function Execution When in a step-by-step operation, a function can be executed by either stepping into the function or stepping over the function.

When a function is stepped into, the function executes in a step-by-step operation. At the end of the function, the step-by-step operation continues after the return to the calling function.

At any point during the step-by-step execution of a function, the step-by-step operation can be terminated, which executes all of the remaining statements and returns to the calling function. The step-by-step operation then resumes in the calling function.

When a function is stepped over, the function runs to completion with the step-by-step operation resuming when the function returns to the calling statement.

Program Termination During execution, the program can be terminated through a debug command. This capability is used to terminate loops or to kill the execution so that the program can be modified for further testing.

MANUAL DEBUGGING

When a debugger is not available, programmers use displays to trace a program's execution. These displays generally show the current function and any data that may be of interest. Program 15-14 demonstrates a common display technique.

Program 15-14 Demonstrate program debugging displays

```
/* Demonstrate Debugging messages
      Written by:
      Date:
*/
#include <iostream>
using namespace std;

void fun1 (int& parm1, char& parm2);
int  fun2 (int  parm1, char  parm2);

int main ()
{
   cout << "Begin debugging messages demonstration\n";

   int  value1;
   char value2;
   fun1 (value1, value2);

   int prod = fun2 (value1, value2);

   cout << "End debugging messages demonstration\n";
   return 0;
} // main

```

Program 15-14 Demonstrate program debugging displays (*contin-*

```
/* ===================== fun1 =====================
   This function reads two values.
      Pre  nothing
      Post parm1 &parm2 read
*/
void fun1 (int& parm1, char& parm2)
{
   cout << "**Entered fun1\n";

   cout << "Enter an integer value: ";
   cin  >> parm1;
   cout << "Enter a character value: ";
   cin  >> parm2;

   cout << "**Leaving fun1: parm1 is " << parm1
        << " parm2 is '" << parm2 << "'\n";
   return;
} // fun1
/* ===================== fun2 =====================
   Multiplies parm1 and parm2 and returns product.
      Pre  parm1 and parm2 have been read
      Post product calculated and returned
*/
int  fun2 (int  parm1, char  parm2)
{
   cout << "**Entered fun2\n";

   int prod = parm1 * parm2;

   cout << "**Leaving fun2: parm1 is " << parm1
        << " parm2 is '" << parm2 << "' "
        << " prod is " << prod << endl;
   return prod;
} // fun2
```

```
Results
Begin debugging messages demonstration
**Entered fun1
Enter an integer value: 5
Enter a character value: a
**Leaving fun1: parm1 is 5 parm2 is 'a'
**Entered fun2: parm1 is 5 parm2 is 'a'
**Leaving fun2: parm1 is 5 parm2 is 'a'  prod is 485
End debugging messages demonstration
```

Program 15-14 Analysis The points of interest in this demonstration are all styles. As we enter a function, we display a message. As we leave a function, we display another message. If the program fails, we know exactly where we are in the program.

When using debugging messages, be sure to somehow distinguish them from any program messages. Each debugging message starts with two asterisks.

Also note how we display data inside of each function. This allows us to trace the data values from function to function.

There is one major problem with these display messages. They cannot be in the program when it goes into production. This means that we have to locate and delete them when the debugging is complete. It also means that we have to add them back when we need to change the program.

This problem is easily solved with conditional compilation directives. For more information on conditional compilations, refer to Section G-3 in Appendix G. Program 15-15 repeats Program 15-14 using conditional compilation directives.

Program 15-15 Demonstrate conditional compilation displays

```
/* Demonstrate Debugging messages
      Written by:
      Date:
*/
#include <iostream>
using namespace std;

#define DEBUG 0                  // Set 1 to debug

void fun1 (int& parm1, char& parm2);
int  fun2 (int  parm1, char  parm2);

int main ()
{
   cout << "Begin debugging messages demonstration\n";

   int  value1;
   char value2;
   fun1 (value1, value2);

   int prod = fun2 (value1, value2);

   cout << "End debugging messages demonstration\n";
   return 0;
} // main

/* ==================== fun1 ====================
   This function reads two values.
      Pre  nothing
      Post parm1 &parm2 read
```

Program 15-15 Demonstrate conditional compilation displays (*continued*)

```
*/
void fun1 (int& parm1, char& parm2)
{
#if DEBUG
   cout << "**Entered fun1\n";
#endif

   cout << "Enter an integer value: ";
   cin  >> parm1;
   cout << "Enter a character value: ";
   cin  >> parm2;

#if DEBUG
   cout << "**Leaving fun1: parm1 is " << parm1
        << " parm2 is '" << parm2 << "'\n";
#endif
   return;
} // fun1
/* ====================== fun2 ======================
   Multiplies parm1 and parm2 and returns product.
      Pre  parm1 and parm2 have been read
      Post product calculated and returned
*/
int  fun2 (int  parm1, char  parm2)
{
#if DEBUG
   cout << "**Entered fun2\n";
#endif

   int prod = parm1 * parm2;

#if DEBUG
   cout << "**Leaving fun2: parm1 is " << parm1
        << " parm2 is '" << parm2 << "' "
        << " prod is " << prod << endl;
#endif
   return prod;
} // fun2
```

TEST DRIVERS

When working on a large project, it is not unusual for a programmer to write only part of a system. Often, this entails writing classes or generalized functions that are not complete programs in themselves. In these cases, in addition to developing the code, it is also necessary to write a program that will not be placed into production. Its only purpose is to test the code that will be placed in header files or libraries. This nonproduction code is known as a test driver. We have several examples throughout the chapters. The first is found in Program 6-12, "Print calendar month," on page 250.

CORRECTING INVALID OUTPUT

When the program runs successfully but does not produce the expected results, a different approach is required. The first step in this debugging process is to compare the program requirements statement to the program design. Each program algorithm must be compared to the program requirements to determine what caused the erroneous output.

If the requirements algorithms and the program code appear to be correct, then the program can be run using the debugger. In this case, the analysis must concentrate on the code implementation of the algorithmic requirements. Often the error will be found in the precedence of a complex arithmetic statement. Other times it will be that old nemesis—the invalid pointer. This type of error can be very difficult to debug and there are no general rules or short cuts to solve the problem.

One technique that programmers often use to solve these types of problems is to use the "buddy system." In the buddy system, another program is enlisted to help solve the problem. The first step in the process is for the authoring programmer to explain the approach and implementation to the buddy. Often the problem is solved by simply explaining it. Other times, the solution is not found until the two programmers have worked for several hours tracing the data through the program.

15-7 TIPS AND COMMON PROGRAMMING ERRORS

1. There can be no code between a *try* and a *catch* statement(s).
2. There can be no code between a list of *catch* statements.
3. There cannot be more than one generic *catch* statement in a function.
4. The generic *catch* statement must be the only *catch* statement or the last in the list of *catch* statements.
5. The *throw* statement can only be used in a *catch* statement to rethrow an exception; it cannot be used with an object.
6. A re-thrown exception cannot be caught in the same function.
7. A function without an exception specification is allowed to throw all exceptions.
8. To prevent a function from throwing exceptions, we use the no-exception specification after the function parameter list in the function header.
9. To limit the exceptions that a function can throw, we list the allowable exceptions in the function header.
10. Exception specifications must be included in both the function declaration and the function definition.
11. The base class must be accessed by reference when polymorphism is used in one single *catch* statement to catch several different exceptions
12. We recommend that *try* and *catch* statements be written in a class constructor rather than in a calling function.
13. We recommend that destructors be written using the no-exception specification.

15-8 KEY TERMS

abort function
any-exception specification
catch statement
exception
exception class
exception handler
exception specification
exit function
generic *catch* statement
logic error
no-exception specification
re-throw statement
re-throwing an exception
run-time error
set_terminate function
set _unexpected function
some-exception specification
terminate function
throw statement
throwing an exception
try statement
unexpected function

15-9 SUMMARY

- In traditional error handling, the error handling code is included in the code that detects errors.
- In the C++ exception handling constructs, we separate the error handling code from the potential error generating code.
- An exception is an object that signals an error in a program.
- Exceptions can be created by the system or by an application program.
- An exception can either be caught in the function that throws it or in the function that directly or indirectly calls it.
- The *throw* statement is used to throw an exception.
- Two statements, *try* and *catch*, are used to handle exceptions.
- If an exception handler cannot completely handle the exception, it can re-throw it.
- To re-throw an exception, we use the *throw* statement without an object.
- To catch any type of exception, we use a generic *catch* statement.
- Instead of using standard types to throw exceptions, we can use an object (an instance of a class).
- A better way to handle exceptions is to design a hierarchy of classes.
- A function can choose to catch no exceptions, a specified list of exceptions, or any exceptions by using an exception specification.
- To catch exceptions in a constructor, we recommend that the *try* and *catch* statements be coded in the constructor itself, not in the calling function.
- We recommend that no exception be allowed in the destructor; it should be coded with the no exceptions specification.
- When an exception is not caught by an exception handler, the *unexpected* function is called. This function calls the *terminate* function by default. The *terminate* function calls the *abort* function by default.
- We can modify the default behavior of *unexpected* function to use our exception processing function.
- We can modify the default behavior of *terminate* function in a program.
- A program can be terminated either by an *exit* function or an *abort* function.
- The *abort* function does not call destructors to destroy objects; the *exit* function does.
- In addition to the programmer-designed exceptions, C++ defines a hierarchy of classes to handle exceptions. At the root of this hierarchy is the *exception* class defined in the `<exception>` header file.
- Program errors can cause a program to fail or to produce invalid output. In either case, the program must be analyzed to determine the cause of the failure.
- Code debuggers offer a rich set of tools to help debug a program.
- Manual debugging involves placing strategic display statements throughout a program to determine where it fails.
- Invalid program output requires that the program requirements be analyzed in addition to the program logic.

15-10 PRACTICE SETS

REVIEW QUESTIONS

1. Explain the difference between the traditional way of handling errors and using the exceptional handler in C++.
2. Can an exception be handled only in the current function? Explain your answer.
3. Can an exception be handled only in the calling function? Explain your answer.
4. Discuss the difference between throwing an exception and re-throwing an exception.
5. The criteria of choosing an exception handler (*catch* statement) is based on the ______ (type or value) of data thrown?
6. A re-thrown statement uses ______without ______.
7. Explain the use of polymorphism in designing exception handling classes.
8. What is a generic *catch* statement?
9. All C++ standard exception-handling classes are derived (directly or indirectly) from a class named ______.
10. What is an exception specification?
11. List three types of exceptions that a function can specify.
12. Name the four classes under the *logic_error* class.
13. Name the three classes under the *runtime_error* class.
14. If the *new* operator cannot allocate memory, some compilers throw an object of type ______.
15. If a file cannot be opened or closes, some compilers throw an object of type ______.
16. If a reference to an array object is invalid, some compilers throw an object of type ______.

EXERCISES

17. Find errors, if any, in the following code segments:

```
int main()
{
   catch (exception& e)
      {
         ...
      }
   return 0;
}
```

18. Find errors, if any, in the following code segments:

```
int main()
{
   try
      {
         ...
      }
   return 0;
}
```

19. Find errors, if any, in the following code segments:

```
int main()
{
   catch (...)
      {
         ...
      }
   try
      {
         ...
      }
   return 0;
}
```

20. Find errors, if any, in the following code segments:

```
int main()
{
   try
      {
         ...
      }
   catch (...)
      {
       throw exception ();
      }
   return 0;
}
```

21. Find errors, if any, in the following code segments:

```
void  fun ()
{
   throw exception;
}
```

22. Find errors, if any, in the following code segments:

```
class x  { };
void  fun () throw ()
 {
    throw x ();
    ...
 }
```

23. Find errors, if any, in the following code segments:

```
class x  { };
void  fun () throw (x)
 {
    throw y ();
    ...
 }
```

24. Find errors, if any, in the following code segments:

```
class x   { };
class y   { };
class z   { };
void  fun () throw (x, y)
{
    throw z ();
    ...
}
```

25. Find errors, if any, in the following code segments:

```
class x   { };
class y   { };
class z   { };
void  fun ()
{
   throw z ();
   ...
}
```

PROBLEMS

26. Write a function that allocates memory for a single data type passed as a parameter. The function uses the *new* operator and returns a pointer to the allocated memory. The function, however, catches and handles any exceptions detected during allocation.

27. Write a function that allocates memory for an array given the type of the array and its size as parameters. The function uses the *new* operator and returns a pointer to the allocated memory. The function, however, catches and handles any exceptions detected during allocation.

28. Write a function that handles divide by zero and divide by a negative number internally, allowing the user to correct the error, but throws a bad operator exception to the calling function (see Program 15-7).

29. Write a program that handles an unexpected exception by changing the default behavior of the *unexpected* function. Use the *set_unexpected* function as the first line in your program using your own handler. The minimum code in the handler displays an error message and calls the *exit* function to gracefully terminate the program.

30. Write a program that prevents the ungraceful termination of your program by changing the default behavior of the *terminate* function. Use the *set_terminate* function as the first line in your program using your own handler. The minimum code in the handler displays an error message and calls the *exit* function to gracefully terminate the program.

PROJECTS

31. Rewrite only those methods or operators in the Fraction class (Chapter 10) that can be affected by divide by zero error. Include code to catch the divide-by-zero error and handle it properly.

32. Rewrite only those methods or operators in the Array class (Chapter 13) that can be affected by out of index error. Include the appropriate exception class from standard library exception classes.

33. Investigate the use of the *domain_error*, *length_error*, *out_of_range*, and *invalid_argument* exception classes and write a program to test them.

34. Investigate the use of *range_error*, *underflow_error*, and *overflow_error* exception classes and write a program to test them.

35. Investigate the use of *bad_cast* and *bad_typeid* exception classes and write a program to test them.

36. Investigate the use of *bad_exception* exception class and write a program to test it.

37. Write a program that randomly catches exceptions. The program generates a random number with the value of 0, 1, or 2. If the value is 0, the program does not catch any exception. If the value is 1, the program catches only a specified list of exceptions. If the value is 2, the program catches all of the exceptions.

16 Advanced I/O Concepts

In Chapter 7, we discussed the basic input / output system in C++. We introduced streams, discussed formatting text files, and showed how to use manipulators.

In this chapter, we explore the advanced input / output features that are available in C++. We begin with a short discussion of the stream class hierarchy. Then, we discuss binary files and how we can access them randomly, how to convert a text file to a binary file and vice versa, and at the end of the chapter, we show how to use string streams; that is, how to read from a string as though it were a file and to write to string as though it were a file.

16-1 INPUT/OUTPUT CLASSES

As we learned in Chapter 7, input / output in C++ is based on streams. Streams are objects of stream classes. Figure 16-1 shows a simplified hierarchy of stream classes used in C++. We say "simplified" because the figure shows only the relations among classes. The details, such as which classes are concrete, which classes are templates, and which classes use virtual functions, are not shown. All we need to know about the I/O classes is their relationship, not their details.

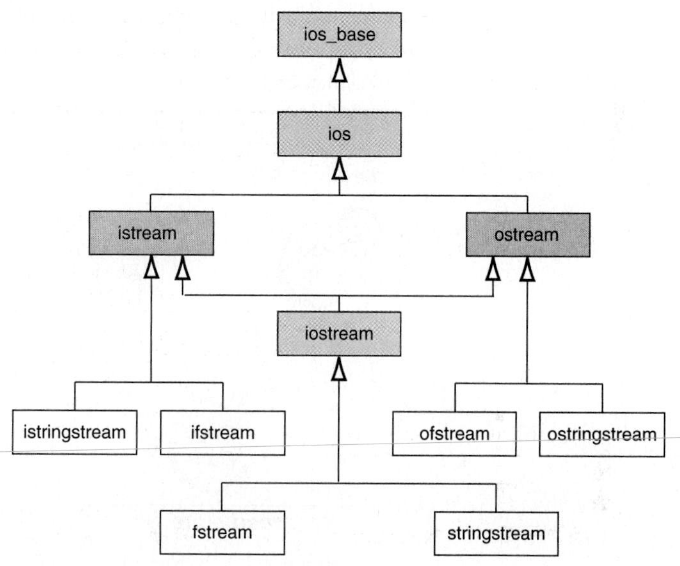

Figure 16-1 Input/output classes

The following list provides a very short functional definition of each class.

- *ios_base*: This class keeps track of the stream state and has function for formatting.
- *ios*: This class tests and sets the stream state. It is a parameterized class. Examples are shown in the next section.
- *istream*: Used to allow sequential or random input access to disk and standard input files. The standard input streams are defined here.
- *ostream*: Used to allow sequential or random output access to disk and standard output files. The standard output and error streams are defined here.
- *iostream*: Used to allow sequential or random input/output access to disk and standard input files.
- *ifstream*: Defines the functions that read from a file.
- *ofstream*: Defines the functions that write to a file.
- *fstream*: Defines the functions that read and write to a file.
- *istringstream*: Defines the functions that read from a string.
- *ostringstream*: Defines the functions that write to a string.
- *stringstream*: Defines the functions that read and write to a string.

16-2 FILE STATES

An opened file is in a read state, a write state, or an error state.

A file must be in the **read state** to read from it and in the **write state** to write to it. If we try to read from a file in the write state, an error occurs. Likewise, if we try to write to a file in the read state, an error occurs. The **error state** is the result of a logical error, such as reading from a file in the write state, or a physical error, such as an unreadable disk file. When a file is in an error state, we cannot read from it or write to it.

It is possible to open a file for both reading and writing. This is sometimes referred to as opening a file for **update**. Even when the file is opened for update, however, it can still be in only one of the states at a time. These states and their potential error conditions are shown in Figure 16-2.

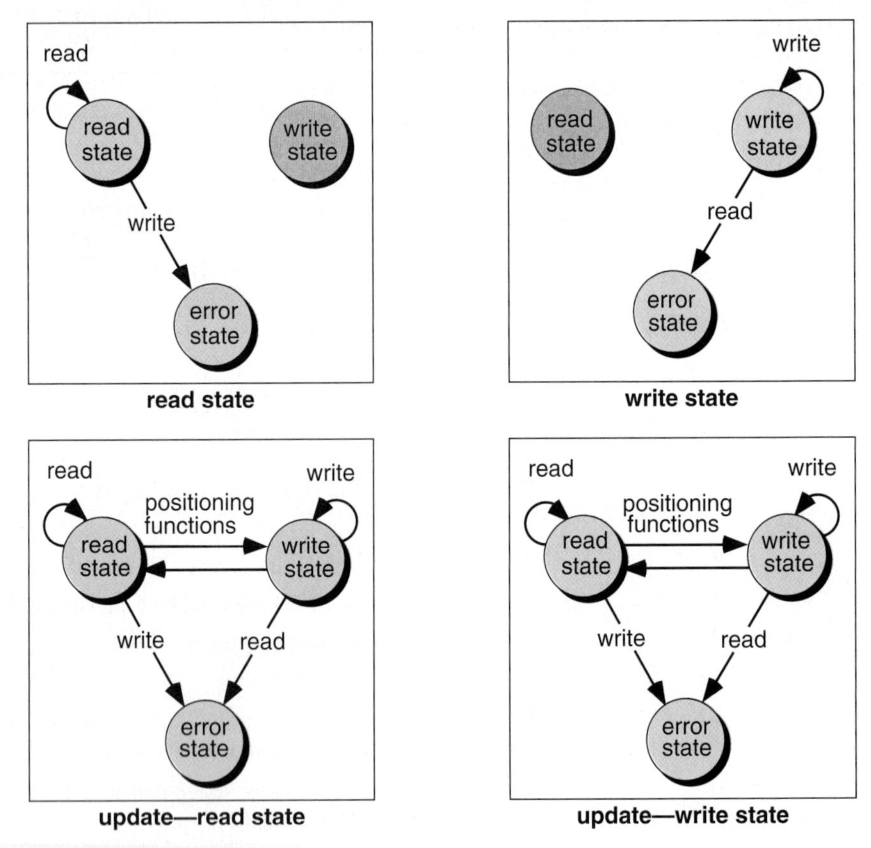

Figure 16-2 File states

Study this figure carefully. If a state is shaded, that state is not available for the indicated file operation. Notice that in the read mode, only two states are possible: read and error. The file will stay in the read state as long as you use only read functions, as indicated by the looping arrow in the read-state circle. However, if you try to write when the file is in the read state, the state changes to the error state. Once the file is in an error state, any subsequent attempt to read it will result in an error.

Now look at the update read and write states in Figure 16-2. During updating, the file can be in either the read or the write state. To move from one to the other we must use one of the positioning functions[1] as indicated by the arrows between the read state and write state. If we try to write after a read without repositioning, the file will be in the error state. The error can be cleared by the clear function, which we discussed in Chapter 7.

OPENING FILES IN READ STATE

To open a file in read state, we create a stream object of type *ifstream*. An object of type *ifstream* always opens for the read state as the default.

```
ifstream fsIn;
...
fsIn.open ("file1");
```

Figure 16-3 shows a **file** opened in the read state. The data are represented by the shaded rectangle. The boxed triangle indicates the end of the file. The current position within the file is maintained by a file marker that is not shown in the figure. When a file is opened in the read state, the file marker is positioned to begin reading data from the beginning of the file. If the file doesn't exist, the file object is in the error state.

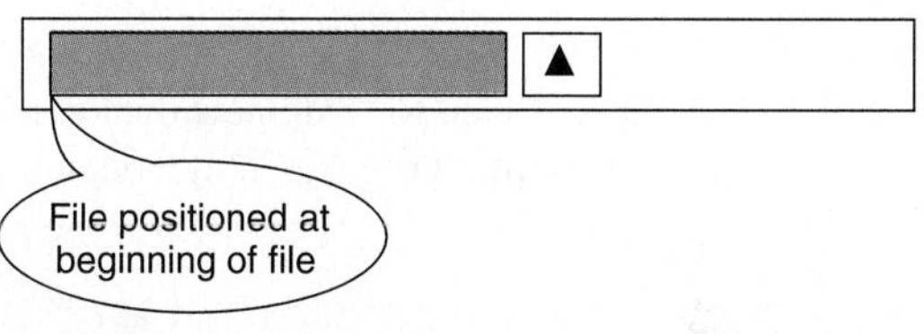

Figure 16-3 Open file in read state

In Figure 16-3, the file marker is positioned at the beginning of the file. When we read from the file, the file marker moves ahead—that is, toward the end of the file.

OPENING FILES IN WRITE STATE

We open a file in write state for two different purposes: to write a new file—that is, to write data at the beginning of the file—or to append data at the end of an existing file.

Create New File

To create a new file, we use the *ofstream* stream object. An *ofstream* object always opens in the write state with the file marker positioned at the beginning of the file. The following statements show the format.

```
ofstream fsOut;
...
fsOut.open ("file1");
```

Figure 16-4 shows a file opened in the write state. As we write to the file, the file marker moves ahead with the end of file marker. If the file exists, the current data are deleted; if it doesn't exist, a new file is created.

---

[1]We discuss the positioning functions on page 782.

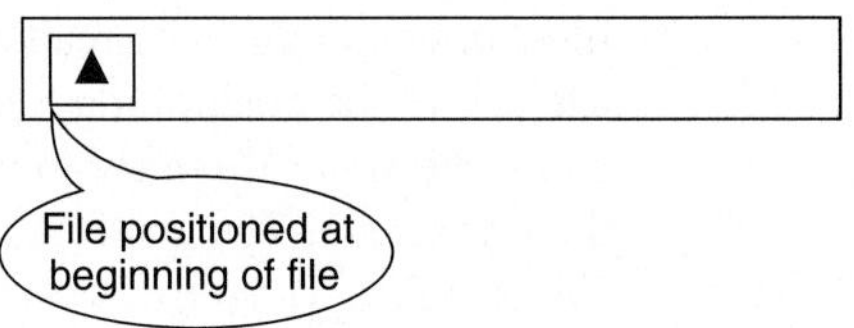

Figure 16-4 File open in write state

Append File

We can also write at the end of the file. This is called **append**. To append a file we need to define to a second open argument that sets the output and append input/output system (ios) flags. We did not need to use ios flags in the previous two examples because the defaults were correct for the file state we needed. Append, on the other hand, needs two flags: one for output and one for append. The two flags need to be bitwise or'd because together they constitute only one argument for the open function.

```
ofstream fsOut;
...
fsOut.open ("file1", ios :: out | ios :: app);
```

Figure 16-5 shows a file opened for appending. If the file exists, the file marker is positioned to write new data at the end; if the file doesn't exist, the file marker is positioned to write data at the beginning of a new file.

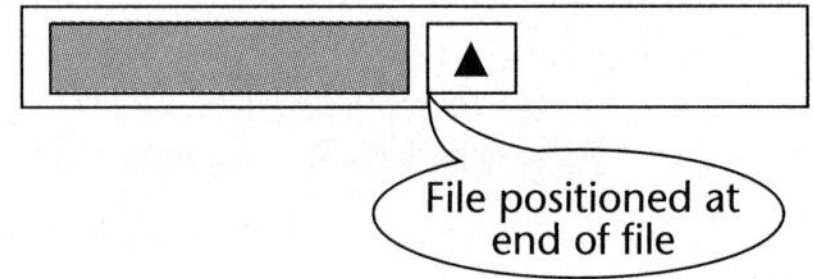

Figure 16-5 File open in write/append state

Open Files For Updating

When we open a file for updating—that is, for both reading and writing—we use the *fstream* object. An object of type *fstream* opens for both input and output by default so we don't need to specify the ios flags. The following example opens a file in the update state.

```
fstream fsUpDate;
...
fsUpDate.open ("file1");
```

I/O SYSTEM FLAGS

There are several input/output system (ios) flags that are used to define the state of a file. We have already demonstrated two of them. Table 16-1 summarizes them.

When used in an open statement, the ios flags are the second argument. Their basic format is shown in the following example.

```
file_stream.open (file_id, ios_flags)
```

Flag	Explanation
ios :: in	Input state; default for input file.
ios :: out	Output state; default for output file.
ios :: app	Append output state.
ios :: ate	Position file marker at end of the file.
ios :: trunc	Delete all data from an existing file when it is opened.
ios :: binary	Binary file; default is text file.

Table 16-1 Input/output system flags

Input Flag

The input flag (`ios :: in`) is used to explicitly open the file in the read state. Because it is the default for opening a file in the read state, it is not often used. It is needed, however, when we include other flags.

Output Flag

The output flag (`ios :: out`) is used to explicitly open a file in the write state. It is needed when we include other flags, such as when we open in the append mode.

Append Flag

The append flag (`ios :: app`) is used to open a file in the append mode. Because there is no default file open for append, it always needs to be explicitly coded with the output flag. We demonstrated this code in the previous section.

At End Flag

The at-end flag (`ios :: ate`—pronounced "at end") opens the file and positions the file marker at the end of the file.

Truncate Flag

The truncate flag (`ios :: trunc`) opens a file and deletes all of its data; that is, it truncates the file. It is used to destroy an existing file, but keeps its name. Note that output files default flags are `ios::out | ios::trunc`.

Binary Flag

By default, a file is open for text data. If we want to open it for binary data, we need to use the binary flag (`ios :: binary`). We discuss text and binary data in the next section.

TESTING IF A FILE IS OPEN

To verify that a file is currently open and connected to a stream, we use the *is_open* function. This function returns a Boolean value that can be tested in an *if* statement as shown in the following code.

```
if ( fs.is_open() )
{
...
} // if open
```

OPEN AND OVERLOADED CONSTRUCTORS

All stream classes have an overloaded constructor to open a file when the stream is instantiated. This coding technique saves the call to the open function as shown in the next example. While we don't show any, ios flags can be used.

```
// Traditional Open              // Constructor Open
ifstream fsIn;                   ifstream fsIn ("file1");
...                              ...
fsIn.open ("file1");
```

16-3 TEXT AND BINARY FILES

There are two broad classes of files: **text files** and **binary files**. In text files, all data are stored as graphic characters, which must be converted to internal formats when read into the memory. For example, integral data must be converted to the appropriate numeric characters; character data, on the other hand, do not need to be converted. Text files are also organized around lines, each of which ends with a new line character (`\n`). At the end of the file, there is a special marker called **end-of-file**.

The major characteristics of text files are:

1. All data in a text file are human-readable graphic characters
2. Each line of data ends with a newline character.
3. There is a special character called end-of-file (EOF) at the end of the file.

Binary files, on the other hand, store data in their internal computer format. This means that an *int* in C++ is stored in its binary format, usually 4 bytes in a PC; a character is stored in its ASCII format, usually 1 byte; and so forth. There are no lines in a binary file but there is an end-of-file marker.

The major characteristics of text files are:

1. Data are stored in the same format as they are stored in memory.
2. There are no lines or a new line characters
3. There is an end-of-file marker.

Figure 16-6 shows how two data items are stored in a text file (which uses 8-bit ASCII code) and in a binary file.

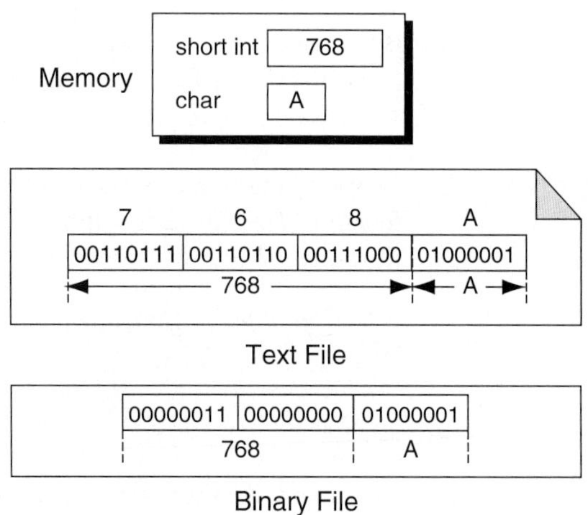

Figure 16-6 Binary and text files

In the text file, the number 768 is stored as three numeric characters. The character A is stored as one character. At the end, there is an end-of-file marker that is not shown because its representation depends on the implementation.

In the binary file, the number 768 is stored in 2 bytes, which assumes that the *short int* type has a size of 2 bytes. The character A is stored as 1 byte. At the end of the file there is an end-of-file marker, again its format is implementation dependent. In a binary file, negative numbers are stored in the two's complement format, the same way they are stored in memory.[2]

16-4 STANDARD LIBRARY FUNCTIONS FOR FILES

There are seven categories of standard file library functions, as shown in Figure 16-7. We have already discussed five of them: open and close, character input and output, formatted input and output, and file status (in Chapter 7); and line input (in Chapter 13). We discuss the last two, block input and output and file positioning, in this section.

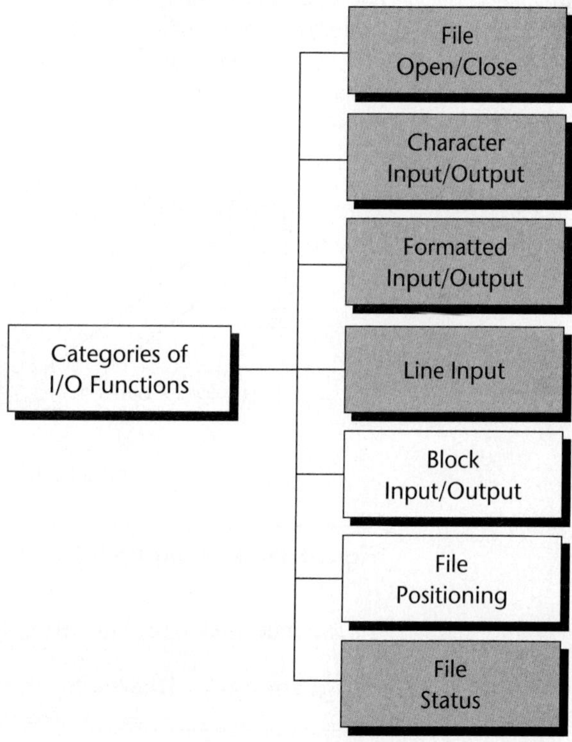

Figure 16-7 Types of standard input/output functions

BLOCK INPUT/OUTPUT FUNCTIONS

The block input and output functions are used to read and write data to binary files. As we discussed previously, when we read and write binary files, the data are transferred just as they are found in memory. That is, there are no format conversions. This means that with the exception of character data, you cannot "see" the data in a binary file; they look like hieroglyphics. If you have ever accidentally opened a binary file in a text editor, you have seen these strange results.

The block read function is file read (*read*). The block write function is file write (*write*). They are discussed next.

[2]For more information on the two's complement format, see Appendix D, "Numbering Systems."

File Read (*read*)

The function ***read***, whose prototype is shown below, reads a specified number of bytes from a binary file and places them into memory at the specified location.

```
istream& read (char* buffer, int size);
```

The *read* function expects a pointer to the input area, `buffer` in the above prototype statement. The buffer is usually a structure because binary files are most often used to store structured records. However, the design gives us the flexibility to read any type of data, from a character to a complex record structure, or even a multidimensional array. This flexibility comes at the cost of slightly more complex coding, however. Whenever we read a file, we must cast the address of the buffer area to a character pointer.

The next element, `size`, specifies how many bytes of data are to be read. Figure 16-8 shows an example of a file read that inputs data into an array of integers. Because we don't know how many bytes are in an integer, we multiply the number of integers to be read (3) by the size of an integer. Assuming that an integer is 4 bytes, this gives us 12 bytes to be read. When *read* is called, then, it transfers the next 3 integers (12 bytes) from the file to the array, `inArea`.

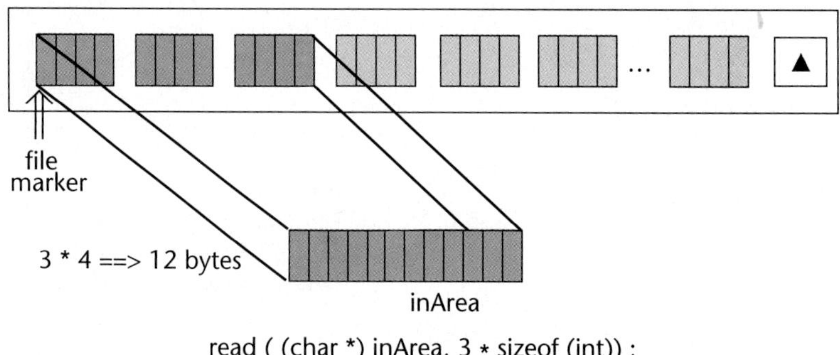

Figure 16-8 ***read*** **operation**

The code used to read the file is shown in Program 16-1.

Program 16-1 Read file of integers

```
/* Read a file of integers, three integers at a time,
   into an array and then print them.
      Written by:
      Date:
*/
#include <iostream>
#include <fstream>
#include <cstdlib>
using namespace std;

```

Program 16-1 Read file of integers *(continued)*

```
11 int main ()
12 {
13    ifstream fsIn;
14    fsIn.open("P16-01.dat", ios::binary | ios::in);
15    if (!fsIn)
16       {
17        cerr << "Input file open failure\a\n";
18        exit (100);
19       } // open error
20
21    int intAry[3];
22    while (fsIn.read((char *) intAry, 3 * sizeof(int)))
23       {
24        int numRead;
25        numRead = fsIn.gcount() / sizeof (int);
26
27        // process array
28        for (int i = 0; i < numRead; i++)
29           cout << intAry[i] << "   ";
30        cout << endl;
31       } // while
32 } // main
```

Program 16-1 Analysis The loop limit test in statement 22 tests the status of the file to determine if it is good. In this simple program, we assume that if it is not, we have reached the end of the file. A more complete program would test to verify that we had actually reached the end of file and did not have some other failure condition.

Because we are reading 3 integers at a time, a question we may wish to answer is, "How many did we read in the last read?" We may have read 1, 2, or 3. We can tell by using another file stream function, get count (*gcount*). Get count returns the number of characters read. In statement 25, we get the count and then divide it by the size of 1 integer. The result, `numRead`, is then used to control the print *for* loop.

Read Structure

Now let's look at a more common use of *read*—reading structures (records). Assume that we have defined a structure that stores data about students. Given the type of data that must be stored about students, we would expect the structure to contain some string data and also other data, such as integers or floating-point numbers. One advantage of block input/output functions is that they can transfer these data one structure (record) at a time. A second advantage is that the data do not have to be formatted. Figure 16-9 shows the operation of *read* when a structure is being read.

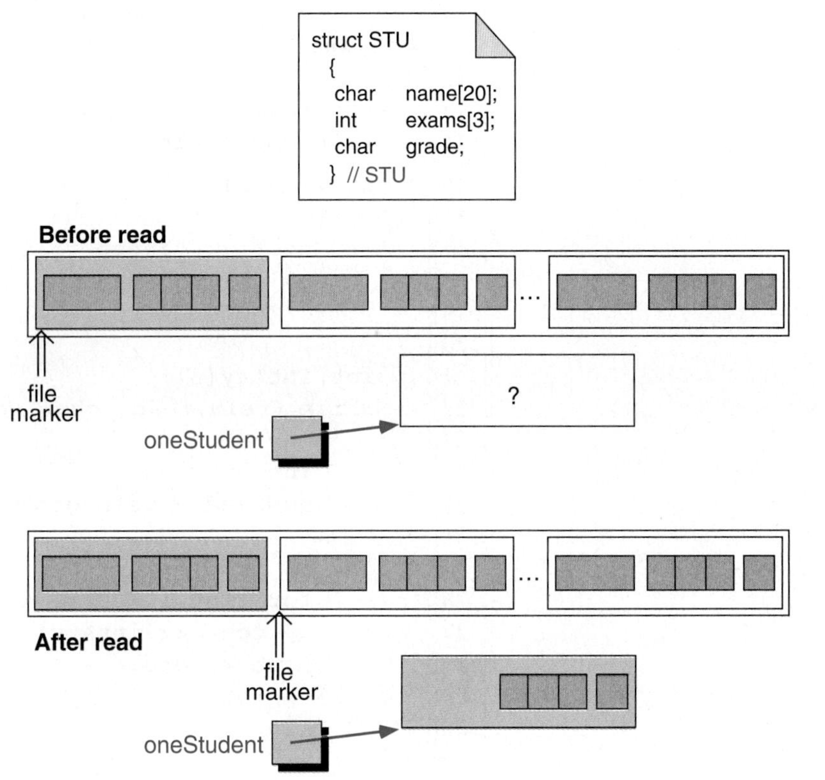

Figure 16-9 Reading a structure

We can use the code shown in Program 16-2 to read the file.

Program 16-2 Read student file

```
/* Reads one student's data from a file.
      Pre   stuFile is opened for reading
      Post  stu data structure filled
            returns true if successful/false if not
*/
bool readStudent  (STU&       oneStudent,
                   ifstream& fsStudent)
{
   fsStudent.read((char *) &oneStudent, sizeof(STU));
   bool ioResult = fsStudent.good();
   return ioResult;
} // readStudent
```

Program 16-2 Analysis Different companies have different standards. One company with which we are familiar has a standard that programs shall have only one read and one write statement for each file. The standard was created to make it easier to make changes to the programs. Program 16-2 is a typical implementation of this standard. One difficulty with this type of function, however, is that it is impossible to generalize the steps that are to be taken for various input results, such as error handling and end of file. Therefore, we pass the I/O result back to the calling function for analysis and action.

File Write (*write*)

The function ***write***, whose prototype is shown below, writes a specified number of items to a binary file.

```
ofstream& write (const char* buffer, int size);
```

The parameters for file write correspond exactly to the parameters for the file read function, including the requirement to cast the address of the input area as a pointer to character.

Functionally, *write* copies `size` bytes from the buffer to the file. Figure 16-10 shows the write operation that parallels the read operation shown in Figure 16-8.

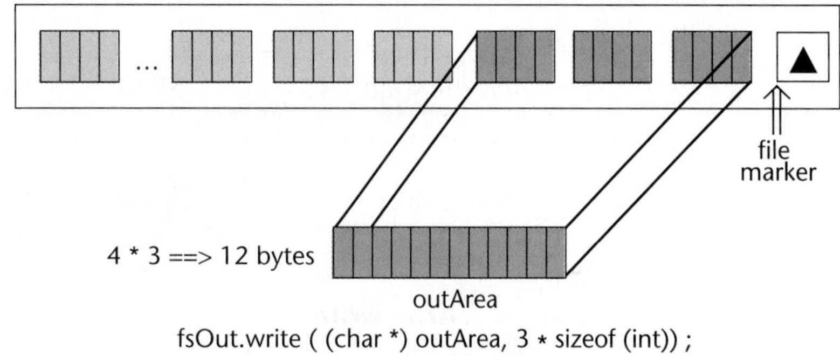

Figure 16-10 ***write*** **operation**

Assuming that we are writing a simple file, Program 16-3 shows a function that we could use to write a structure. It is diagrammed in Figure 16-11.

Program 16-3 Write structured data

```
/* Writes one student's record to a binary file.
      Pre   aStudent has been filled
            fileOut is open for writing
      Post  aStudent written to fileOut
*/
void writeStudent (STU&      aStudent,
                   ofstream& fsStuOut)
{
   fsStuOut.write ((char*) &aStudent, sizeof(STU));
   if (!fsStuOut.good())
       {
        cout << "\aError 100 writing student file\a\n";
         exit (100);
       } // if
   return;
} // writeStudent
```

Program 16-3 Analysis Contrast the function in this program with the function we wrote to read data (Program 16-2). Although it is not possible to generalize on the action to be taken if data are not read, it is possible to do so with write errors. If the program cannot write data, it must be aborted. Therefore, we put the error checking and action in the write function itself.

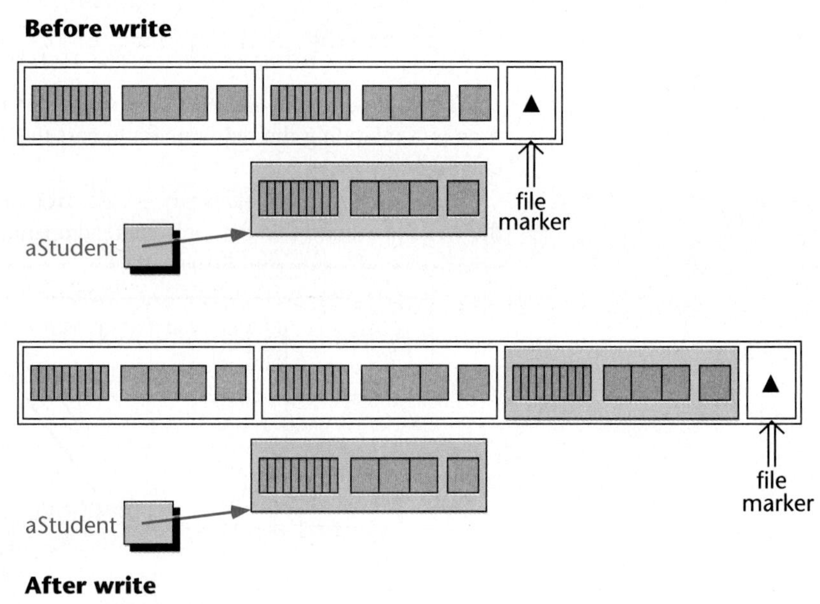

Figure 16-11 Writing a structure

POSITIONING FUNCTIONS

There are two uses for positioning functions. First, to randomly process data in disk files (you cannot process tape files randomly), you have to position the file to read the desired data. Second, you can use the positioning functions to change a file's state. Thus, if you have been writing a file, you can change to a read state after you use one of the positioning functions. It is not necessary to change states after positioning a file, but it is allowed.

We discuss two file position functions: tell location and file seek.

Current Location

The ***tellg*** and ***tellp*** functions "tell" you the current position of the file marker in the file, relative to the beginning of the file. Recall that C++ considers files as streams of data structured as individual characters or bytes. Therefore, it measures the position in the file by the number of bytes, relative to zero, from the beginning of the file. Thus, when the file position indicator is at the beginning of the file, the tell functions return 0. If the file position indicator is at the second byte of the file, the tell functions return 1, representing the position 1 byte offset from the beginning of the file. While the file position indicator measures the current location of the file in integral bytes, the return value is not an integer type. Rather, C++ creates a special type, known as *streampos* (stream position), into which it stores the results. The actual value is hidden from the application program and can only be used with the position functions described below.

C++ provides two different tell functions, one for input (*tellg*—tell get) and one for output (*tellp*—tell put). A typical statement for each is shown next. Note that location must be defined as a type *streampos*.

```
streampos location;

location = fsIn.tellg();
location = fsOut.tellp();
```

The operation of the tell function is shown graphically in Figure 16-12.

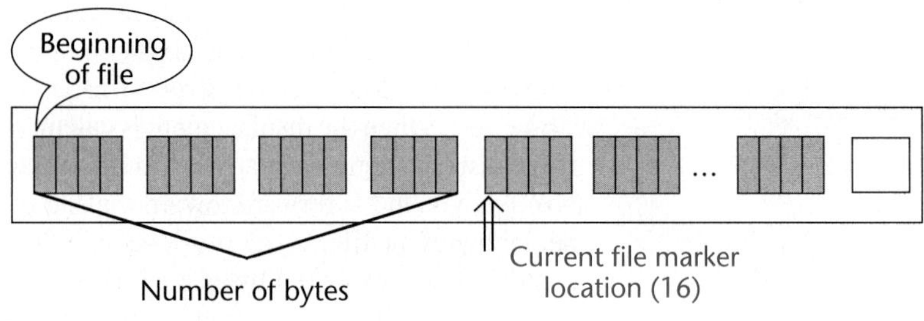

Figure 16-12 ***tell* operation**

The primary purpose of *tellg* and *tellp* is to provide a data address (offset) that can be used in a file seek. It is especially useful when you are dealing with text files in which you cannot calculate the position of data.

Set Position

The ***seekg*** and ***seekp*** functions position the file location indicator at a specified byte position in a file. The function gets its name from the disk positioning operation, seek. Seek moves the access arm on a disk to a position in the file for reading or writing. Since this is exactly the purpose of file seek, it is an appropriate name.

As we saw with tell, there are two seek functions: *seekg* is used to seek a location on an input file, and *seekp* is used to seek a location on an output file. Their prototype declarations are shown below.

```
istream& seekg (long offset, ios::seek_dir wherefrom);
ostream& seekp (long offset, ios::seek_dir wherefrom);
```

The first parameter is a long integer that specifies the number of bytes the position indicator must move absolutely or relatively. To help you understand what we mean by absolutely or relatively, we first discuss the second parameter, `wherefrom`.

C++ provides three enumerated constants that can be used to specify the starting point (`wherefrom`) of the seek. They are shown below.

```
enum seek_dir {beg, cur, end);
```

When wherefrom is ios::beg, then the offset is measured absolutely from the beginning of the file. This is the most common use of file seek. You get the same result if you use the seek function without the wherefrom parameter (both functions are overloaded with wherefrom set to beginning automatically). Thus, to set the file indicator to byte 100 on a file, you would use one of the following two statements:

```
fsStreamName.seekg(99L);
fsStreamName.seekg(99L,ios::beg);
```

If you are puzzling over the first parameter in the preceding statements, remember that the file position is relative to zero and must be a long integer. Actually, the compiler is "smart enough" to convert an integer value to long integer, but it is more efficient if you specify the correct type, especially with literals.

Now let's look at the wherefrom option, ios::cur. If wherefrom is ios::cur, then the displacement is calculated relatively from the current file position. If the displacement is negative, you move back toward the beginning of the file. If it is positive, you move forward toward the end of the file. It is an error to move beyond the beginning of the file. If you move beyond the end of the file, the file is extended, but the contents of the extended bytes are unknown. Whenever you extend the file, there is always the possibility of running out of space, which would be an error.

To move to the next record in a structured file, you must advance into the file the number of bytes in the file's data structure. In the following examples, the first entry advances one integer while the second entry advances the number of bytes in one student structure (*STU*).

```
fsBinFile.seekg(sizeof(int), ios::cur);
fsStuFile.seekg(sizeof(STU), ios::cur);
```

Finally, if wherefrom is ios::end, you will position the file location indicator relative to the end of the file. If the offset is negative, you will move backward toward the beginning of the file; if it is positive, you will extend the file. This technique can be used to write a new record at the end of the file. Simply position the file at the end with wherefrom set to ios::end and a displacement of zero, as shown below, and then write the new record.

```
fsStuOut.seekp(0L, ios::end);
```

Figure 16-13 shows the effect of *seekg* in different situations. Each of the examples is also valid with *seekp.*

The file seek is intended primarily for use with binary files, although it does have limited functionality with text files. You can position a text file to the beginning using *seekg* or *seekp* with a zero offset from the beginning of the file (ios::beg). To position a text file at the end, you can use *seekg* or *seekp* with a zero offset and a wherefrom of ios::end, as we showed previously.

You cannot use file seek to move to the middle of a text file unless you have used *tellg* or *tellp* to record the location. The reasons for this have to do with control codes, newlines, vertical tabs and other nuisances of text files. However, if you have recorded a location using *tellg* or *tellp* and you want to go back to that position, you can seek as shown on the next page, using *seekg* or *seekp* as appropriate.

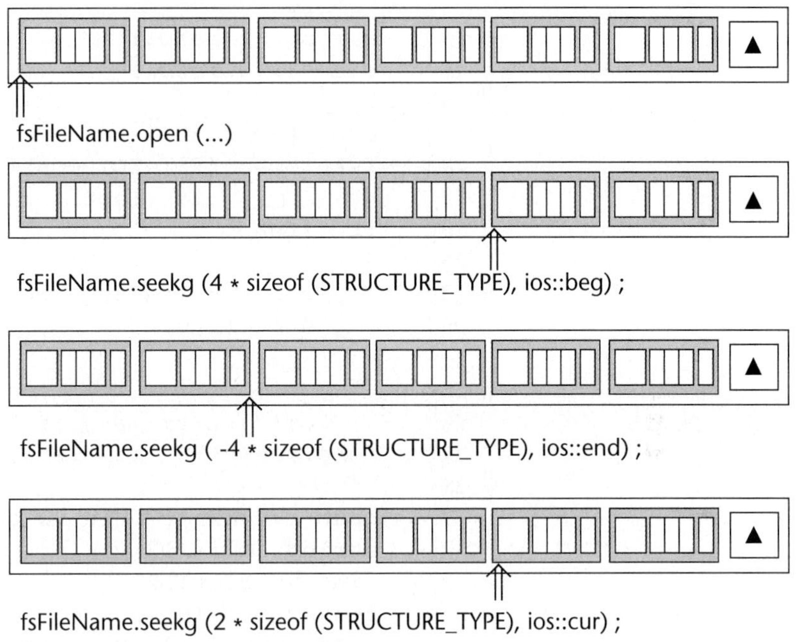
fsFileName.open (...)
fsFileName.seekg (4 * sizeof (STRUCTURE_TYPE), ios::beg) ;
fsFileName.seekg (-4 * sizeof (STRUCTURE_TYPE), ios::end) ;
fsFileName.seekg (2 * sizeof (STRUCTURE_TYPE), ios::cur) ;

Figure 16-13 ***seek*** **operation**

```
fsFileName.seekg(tell_location, ios::beg);
fsFileName.seekp(tell_location, ios::beg);
```

Note that since *tell* returns a position relative to the beginning of the file, you must use the beginning of the file stream (ios::beg) when you reposition the file.

BLOCK I/O EXAMPLE: APPEND FILES

Now let's look at a program that reads and writes binary files. Suppose that we have two copies of files with integer data. Perhaps one file represents data from one week and the other file represents data for a second week. We want to combine both files into a single file. The most efficient way to do this is to append the data from one file to the end of the other file. This logic is evident in Program 16-4.

Program 16-4 Append binary files

```
/* This program appends two binary files of integers.
      Written by:
      Date:
*/
#include <iostream>
#include <fstream>
#include <cstdlib>
using namespace std;

int main ()
{
   cout << "\nThis program appends two files.\n";
   cout << "Please enter file ID of primary file: ";
```

Program 16-4 Append binary files (*continued*)

```
   string  fileID1;
   cin  >> fileID1;

   ofstream fsAp;
   fsAp.open (fileID1.c_str(),
              ios::out | ios::app | ios::binary);
   if (!fsAp)
      {
       cout << "\aCan't open " << fileID1 << endl;
       exit (100);
      } // if

   // Position primary file at end
   fsAp.seekp (0, ios::end);

   cout << "Enter file ID of the second file:     ";
   string  fileID2;
   cin  >> fileID2;
   ifstream fsIn;
   fsIn.open (fileID2.c_str(),
              ios::in | ios:: binary);
   if (!fsIn)
      {
       cout << "\aCan't open " << fileID2 << endl;
       exit (110);
      } // end

   long apndCnt = 0;
   int  data;
   while (fsIn.read ((char *)&data, sizeof(int)))
      {
       fsAp.write ((char *)&data, sizeof(int));
       apndCnt++;
      } // while

   // Test for read failure rather than eof
   if (!fsIn.eof())
      {
       cout << "\aRead Error 120. No output.\n";
       exit (120);
      } // if
   fsAp.close ();
   fsIn.close ();

   cout << "Append complete:  "
        << apndCnt << " appended to file\n";
   return 0;
} // main
```

Program 16-4 Analysis The first thing to notice about this program is the way the files are defined. Because we are going to write the data at the end of the first file, its file type is output (*ofstream*). The second file, on the other hand, is going to be read, so its file type is input (*ifstream*). After the first file is opened, we use a seek to place the file marker at the end of the file (see statement 27).

Now look at the way the external file names are handled. Under the assumption that this program would be used to append different files at different times, we asked the user to enter the file names. This technique provides maximum flexibility for generalized programs.

The heart of the program is contained in statements 43 through 47. As long as the read is successful, we keep going. When we reach end of file, *read* returns false and the loop terminates. We now have another problem, however. We don't know if the read terminated at end of file or because of a read error. We therefore use the *eof* function to make sure we read to the end of the file.

The program concludes with a printed message that contains the number of records appended to the file.

16-5 CONVERTING FILE TYPES

A rather common but somewhat trivial problem is to convert a text file to a binary file and vice versa. There are no standard functions for these tasks, so you must write a program to make the conversion. We describe file conversion logic in this section.

CREATING A BINARY FILE FROM A TEXT FILE

To create a binary file, you usually start with data provided by the user. Since the user is providing the data, they will be in human readable form—that is, in text form. If only a small amount of initial data are required, they are often read from a keyboard. When there is a lot of data, however, it is easier for the user to enter the data with a text editor, and then the program can read the text file and create the binary file.

For the program to read the text file, either you must use the extraction operator (>>) to read the data into a variable and then assign the variable to the structure or you can have the data read directly into the structure. At the end of each line, the structure is written to the binary file. This process is repeated until the text file has been completely converted to the binary structure. The structure chart for this program is given in Figure 16-14.

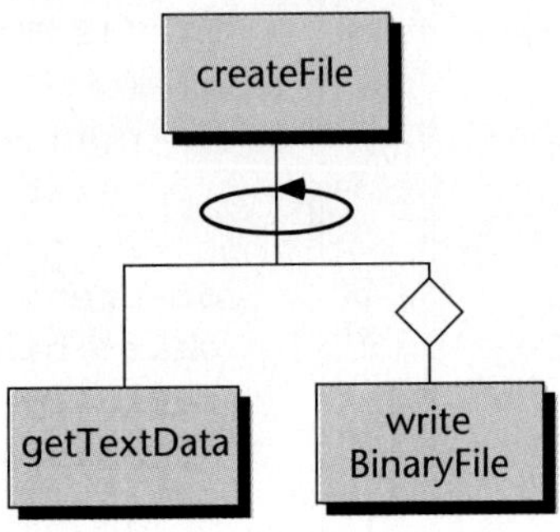

Figure 16-14 Create binary file structure chart

Let's assume that we want to convert student data to a binary file. The data consist of a student's name, three exam scores, and a final grade. In the text file version, each separate field is separated by one or more whitespace characters and each student's data are stored on a separate line. The create file program is shown in Program 16-5.

Program 16-5 Text to binary student file

```
/* Reads student text file and creates binary file.
      Written by:
      Date:
*/
#include <iostream>
#include <fstream>
#include <cstdlib>
#include <string>
using namespace std;

// Global Declarations
struct STU
   {
    char   name[20];
    int    exams[3];
    char   grade;
   }; // STU

bool getData      (ifstream& fsText, STU& aStudent);
void writeBinFile (STU& aStudent,   ofstream& fsStu);

int main ()
{
   cout << "\nBegin Student Binary File Creation\n";

   flush (cout);

   ifstream fsText;
   char* textFileID = "p16-05.txt";
   fsText.open (textFileID);
   if (!fsText)
      {
      cout << "\nCannot open " << textFileID << endl;
       exit (100);
      } // if
   ofstream fsBinary;
   char* binFileID  = "p16-05.bin";
   fsBinary.open(binFileID, ios::out | ios::binary);
   if (!fsBinary)
      {
       cout << "\nCannot open " << binFileID << endl;
       exit (101);
      } // if

```

Program 16-5 Text to binary student file *(continued)*

```
   STU aStudent;
   while (getData (fsText, aStudent))
       writeBinFile (aStudent, fsBinary);

   fsText.close();
   fsBinary.close();

   cout << "\n\nFile creation complete\n";

   return 0;
} // main
/* ================== getData ==================
   This function reads the text file.
      Pre   fsText opened for reading
      Post  data read and file status returned
*/
bool getData  (ifstream& fsText, STU& aStu)
{
   // Read name
   fsText.unsetf (ios::skipws);
   for (int i = 0; i < 20; i++)
        fsText >> aStu.name[i];
   if (fsText.good())              // Test for EOF
      {
       fsText.setf (ios::skipws);
       fsText >> aStu.exams[0]  >> aStu.exams[1]
              >> aStu.exams[2]  >> aStu.grade;
       while (fsText.get() != '\n')
           ;
      } // if
   return (fsText.good());
} // getDat
/* =============== writeBinFile ===============
   Writes the student data to a binary file.
      Pre   fsBinary opened as a binary output file
            aStudent is complete
      Post  Record written
*/
void writeBinFile    (STU&        aStudent,
                      ofstream&  fsBinary)
{
   fsBinary.write ((char *) &aStudent,  sizeof(STU));
   if (!fsBinary)
      {
       cout << "Can't write student file. Exiting\n";
       exit (110);
      } // if
   return;
} // writeBinFile
```

Program 16-5 Analysis There are a few noteworthy points in this program. First, note how we specified the external file names as strings. This makes it easy to change the file names if and when necessary and also allows us to identify the file by name if the open fails. Also, the program starts and ends with a message that identifies what program is running and that it has successfully completed. This is a good programming technique and is a standard requirement in many organizations.

The *while* loop is controlled by the results of the `getData` function call. To understand how it works, therefore, we first look at `getData`. We read the data with the input extraction operator. At the end of the function, we return the current file status. When end of file is detected, the result of the good test is false and we return *false*.

Now that you have seen that the `getData` function returns either *true* or *false* based on the result of testing good, you should understand how the *while* in statement 46 works. It simply loops until an end of file is detected—that is, until *false* is returned.

CREATING A TEXT FILE FROM A BINARY FILE

There are two situations in which you would want to convert a binary file to a text file. The first is when you want to display the data for people to read, as discussed below. The second is when it is necessary to export the data to a system that can't read the binary file. This would occur, for example, if the word sizes for integers and floats were different on the two different hardware systems. As long as all lines are formatted the same and they use the same ASCII code, text files are portable.

An interesting problem is to create a report of the data in the binary file. You must read the binary file and write the data as a text file, but there is much more to it than that. First, the report needs a name, so there must be a title on each page. The title should include the report date and a page number. To make the report meaningful, each column should have a column caption. Finally, there should be an end-of-report message as the last line of the report so that the user knows that all data have been reported.

To put a title on the top of each page, we need a way to tell when a page is full. This is generally done by counting the number of lines on a page and when the count exceeds the maximum, skipping to the next page. Good structured programming requires that the heading logic be in a separate function. The design for printing the student data is shown in Figure 16-15.

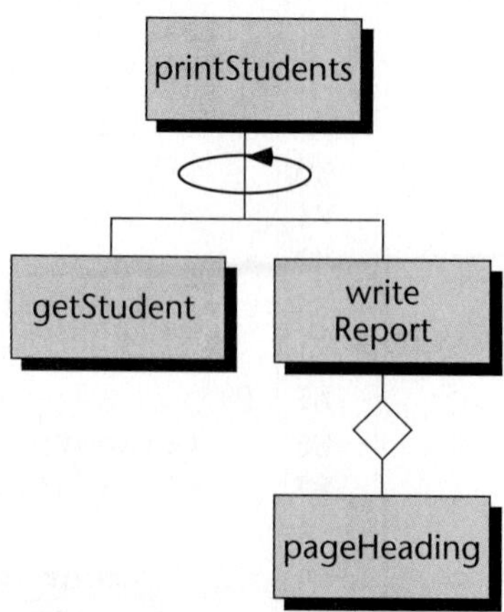

Figure 16-15 Design for print student data

We will write the data to a file so that it can be sent to the printer when we want a hard copy.

One final point before we look at the program. In the print functions, we use a type modifier known as the *static* storage class (see statements 92 and 118 in Program 16-6). When a variable is defined as *static* in a function, it is initialized only the first time the function is called. After that, its value will be retained between calls. This useful C++ feature reduces the need to pass parameters just to retain a local variable. The program is shown in Program 16-6.

Program 16-6 Print student data

```
1  /* Reads a binary file of student data and prints it.
2         Written by:
3         Date:
4  */
5  #include <iostream>
6  #include <fstream>
7  #include <iomanip>
8  #include <cstdlib>
9  #include <string>
10 using namespace std;
11 
12 const int  MAX_LINES_PER_PAGE =  50;
13 const char FORM_FEED          = '\f';
14 
15 struct STU
16    {
17     char   name[20];
18     int    exams[3];
19     char   grade;
20    }; // STU
21 
22 STU getData (istream& fsStu);
23 
24 void writeReport (STU& aStu, ofstream& fsReport);
25 void pageHeaders (ofstream& fsReport);
26 
27 int main ()
28 {
29    cout << "\nBegin Student Report Creation\n ";
30 
31    char* stuFileID = "p16-05.bin";
32    ifstream fsStu;
33    fsStu.open(stuFileID, ios::in | ios::binary);
34    if (!fsStu)
35       {
36        cout << "\nCannot open " << stuFileID << endl;
37        exit (200);
38       } // if !fsStu
39 
40    char* rptFileID = "p16-06.rpt";
```

Program 16-6 Print student data *(continued)*

```
   ofstream fsReport;
   fsReport.open (rptFileID);
   if (!fsReport)
      {
       cout << "\nCannot open " << rptFileID << endl;
       exit (201);
      } // if !fsReport

   STU  aStu;
   aStu = getData (fsStu);
   while (!fsStu.eof())
      {
       writeReport (aStu, fsReport);
       aStu = getData (fsStu);
      } // while

   fsReport << "\n\nEnd of Report\n";

   fsStu.close();
   fsReport.close();

   cout << "\n\nEnd Student Report Creation\n";

   return 0;
} // main
/* ================= getData ==================
   This function reads the student binary file.
      Pre   fsStu is opened for reading
      Post  one student record read and returned
*/
STU getData (istream& fsStu)
{
   STU  aStu;

   fsStu.read((char*) &aStu, sizeof(STU));
   if (!fsStu)
      if (!fsStu.eof())
         {
         cout << "\n\aError reading student file\n";
          exit (210);
         } // !fsStu
   return aStu;
} // getData
/* ================= writeReport ==================
   This function writes the student report to a text file.
      Pre   fsReport is opened as a text output file
            aStu is complete
      Post  Report line written--with page headers
*/
```

Program 16-6 Print student data *(continued)*

```
void writeReport (STU& aStu, ofstream&  fsReport)
{
   static int lineCount = MAX_LINES_PER_PAGE + 1;

   if (++lineCount > MAX_LINES_PER_PAGE)
      {
       pageHeaders  (fsReport);
       line count = 1;
      } // if

   fsReport.setf (ios::left);
   fsReport << setw(25) << aStu.name;

   fsReport.unsetf (ios::left);
   fsReport << setw(4)  << aStu.exams[0]
            << setw(4)  << aStu.exams[1]
            << setw(4)  << aStu.exams[2]
            << " "      << aStu.grade
            << endl;
   return;
} // writeBinaryFile
/* ================== pageHeaders ==================
   Writes the page headers for the student report.
      Pre   fsReport is opened as a text output file
      Post  Report headers and captions written
*/
void pageHeaders (ofstream& fsReport)
{
   static int pageNo = 0;

   pageNo++;
   fsReport << FORM_FEED;
   fsReport.setf (ios::left);
   fsReport << setw(31) << "Student Report";

   fsReport.unsetf (ios::left);
   fsReport << "Page"  << setw(4) << pageNo << endl;

   fsReport.setf (ios::left);
   fsReport << setw(27) << "Student Name"
            << setw(10) << "Exams"
                        << "Gr\n\n";
   return;
} // pageHeaders
```

Program 16-6 Print student data *(continued)*

```
Report Output:
Student Report                    Page   1
Student Name                    Exams     Gr

Adams, John                     84  92  95 A
Madison, James                  83  80  87 B
Washington, George              74  71  86 C

End of Report
```

Program 16-6 Analysis While this program is rather simple, there are a few things to call to your attention.

First, we have declared the maximum number of lines per page as a constant. This makes it easy to change it should it become necessary. It also makes it easy to set the print logic so that it will print the header the first time through the function.

This leads us to the second point of note. The logic for `pageHeaders` will cause the first page to be blank. That is, we issue a page form feed before any data have been written. This is standard in production programs, but you may want to change it so that the first page is not wasted. In this case, you will have to call the `pageHeaders` function before you start the file reading to write the first headings, change the initialization of the line count in line 92 to 0, and move the form feed write from the `pageHeaders` function to just before line 96.

The file is read using look-ahead logic. At statement 50, we read the first record of the file. This logic allows us to use the *eof* function to control the *while* loop. At the end of the loop, we read the file again. Although this loop closely resembles a post-test loop, there is one difference. If the file were empty, a post-test loop would fail. By reading the first record of the file before the loop, we ensure that we can process any file condition using the simplest possible logic.

Note the way we handle the report title and line captions in `pageHeaders`. Many programmers simply try to code them as one long string. This works, but it takes a lot of hit and miss to get it right. Our technique simply adds the widths from the data write and uses them for the widths in the caption prints. There may still be a little manual adjustment, but it is a much simpler approach.

16-6 STRING STREAMS

The formatting capabilities found in text files are very powerful. To extend their use, C++ defined three I/O classes—***istringstream***, ***ostringstream***, and ***stringstream***. These streams allows us to connect streams and strings so that we can *read* a string and store its data in a set of variables or *write* a set of variables to a string. These classes are shown in Figure 16-1 on page 771.

Generally, we use these stream methods when we process text data from a file one line at a time. After reading the line, we can parse the data into variables using *istringstream*. Similarly, if we want to completely format a line of text before writing it to a file or to the monitor, we use *ostringstream*. We show the operation of these methods in Figure 16-16.

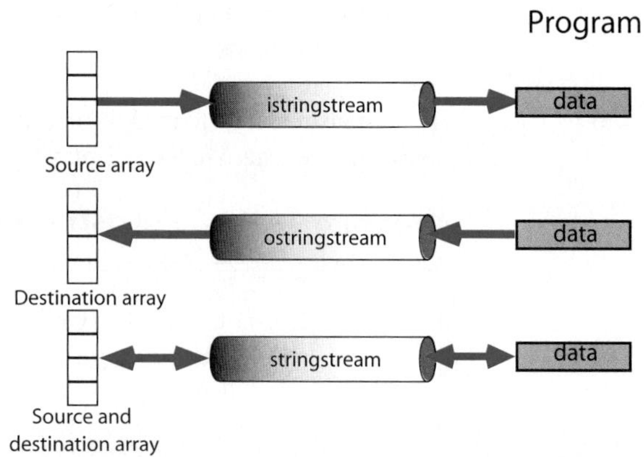

Figure 16-16 ***Stringstream* objects**

WRITING TO A STRING

Program 16-7 demonstrates how we write to a string. After using stream string to format data in a string, we use the *str* function to extract and print the string.

Program 16-7 Demonstrating writing to a string

```
/* This program demonstrates the operation of the
   ostringstream function.
      Written by:
      Date:
*/
#include <sstream>
#include <iostream>
#include <iomanip>
#include <string>
using namespace std;

int main ()
{
   cout << "Begin ostringstream demonstration\n";
   ostringstream ssOut;

   ssOut << setw(4) << 23
         << setw(4) << 'a'
         << setw (8) << 23.6 << endl;
   cout << ssOut.str ();
   cout << "End of ostringstream demonstration\n";
   return 0;
} // main
```

```
Results:
Begin ostringstream demonstration
  23   a    23.6
End of ostringstream demonstration
```

Program 16-7 Analysis Note how we used manipulators to format the output. This demonstrates that the full functionality of text formatting is available in the string stream functions.

READING FROM A STRING

To demonstrate how to read from a string, we create one in memory and then string stream to extract the data. We then display the results. The code is shown in Program 16-8.

Program 16-8 Demonstrate reading from a string

```
   /*Demonstrate the use of string string to extract
    data from a string.
       Written by:
       Date:
*/
#include <sstream>
#include <iostream>
#include <string>
using namespace std;

int main ()
{
   string s = "22 A 34.2";
   istringstream ssIn (s);

   int i;
   ssIn >> i;
   char charA;
   ssIn >> charA;
   float fNum;
   ssIn >> fNum;

   cout << i     << " "
        << charA << " "
        << fNum  << endl;
   return 0;
}  // main
```

```
Results
22 A 34.2
```

16-7 FILE PROGRAM EXAMPLES

In this section, we give examples of programs for handling two common file applications. The first example uses the file positioning functions to randomly process the data in a file. The second example merges two files.

RANDOM FILE ACCESSING

Program 16-9 demonstrates the concept of randomly accessing data in a file. We begin by creating a binary file of integers. Each integer is the square of the data's position in the file, relative to 1. After the file has been created, we print it in sequence, starting at the beginning of the file. We then print it in a random sequence using *seekg* and a random number generator.

Program 16-9 Random file application

```
/* Shows some of the function applications we have
   learned in this chapter. The program first creates a
   binary file of integers. It then prints the file,
   first sequentially and then randomly using rand().
      Written by:
      Date:
*/
#include <iostream>
#include <fstream>
#include <iomanip>
#include <cstdlib>

void buildFile   (fstream& fsData);
void printFile   (fstream& fsData);
void randomPrint (fstream& fsData);

int main ()
{
   cout << "Begin seek program\n\n";
   fstream fsData;
   buildFile   (fsData);
   printFile   (fsData);
   randomPrint (fsData);
   cout << "\nEnd seek program\n";
   return 0;
}  // main
```

Program 16-9 Analysis: ***main*** The *main* function simply calls three functions in order. The first function passes the file stream, the only variable declared in *main*, by reference because the file is opened in `buildFile`. While the other two calls do not change the stream, we still pass by reference so that we don't have to copy the stream with each call.

The `buildFile` function in Program 16-10 simply creates a file with 10 records. Each record consists of a single integer, which is the square of the ordinal record number relative to 1 (not 0).

Program 16-10 **Random file: *buildFile***

```
1  /* =================== buildFile ===================
2     Creates a disk file that we can process randomly.
3        Pre   Nothing
4        Post  File has been built
5  */
6  void buildFile (fstream& fsData)
7  {
8     fsData.open ("p15-07.dat", ios :: in  | ios::out
9                           | ios::trunc | ios::binary);
10    if (!fsData)
11       {
12       cerr << "\a\nError opening file for writing.\n";
13        exit (100);
14       } // if open
15
16    for (int i = 1; i <= 10; i++)
17       {
18        int data;
19        data = i * i;
20        fsData. write((char*) &data, sizeof(int));
21       } // for
22    return;
23 } // buildFile
```

Program 16-10 Analysis: `buildFile` The file is opened with the ios flags set for both input and output (see statement 8) so that we can first write to it and then later in the program read it. We also introduce a new flag, `ios::trunc`. This flag deletes (truncates) any existing data in a file when the file is opened. It is most often used when a file is opened for both reading and writing and the file is to be written first. The final flag, `ios::binary`, specifies that we want data written to the file in the binary (internal) formats.

The `printFile` function in Program 16-11 reads the file sequentially starting at the beginning (record zero).

Program 16-11 **Random file: sequential print**

```
/* ================== printFile ==================
   Prints the file starting at the first record.
      Pre   fsData is an open file
      Post  The file has been printed
*/
void printFile (fstream& fsData)
{
   cout << "\nFile contents in sequential order.\n";
   fsData.seekg (0L, ios::beg);

```

Program 16-11 Random file: sequential print (*continued*)

```
   int data;
   int recNum = 0;
   while (fsData.read((char*) &data, sizeof(int)))
       cout << "Record " << recNum++
            <<  setw(4)  << data     << endl;
   fsData.clear();
   return;
} // printFile
```

Program 16-11 Analysis This is not a very robust function because we assume that when we stop we have, in fact, detected end of file. A better design would at least add an end of file test after the *while* loop.

Because of the possibility that the file input/output status fail flag will be set in the read loop, we clear the file status at the end of the function so that the next function will be able to read it.

Program 16-12 randomly prints the file using the random number generator to determine which value to read. Because random number generators may duplicate numbers, some values may be printed more than once.

Program 16-12 Random file: *randomPrint*

```
/* ================== randomPrint ==================
   This function randomly prints the file. Some values
   may be printed twice, depending on the random
   numbers generated.
      Pre   fsdata is an open file
      Post  Ten random records have been printed
*/
void randomPrint (fstream& fsData)
{
   cout << "\n\nFile contents in random sequence.\n";

   int data;
   int randSeek;
   for (int i = 0; i < 10; i++)
      {
        randSeek =    (rand () % 10);
        fsData.seekg (sizeof(int) * randSeek, ios::beg);
        fsData.read   ((char*) &data, sizeof(int));

        cout << "Record " << setw(4) << randSeek
             << " ==> "   << setw(4) << data
             << endl;
      } // for
   fsData.close();
   return;
} // randomPrint
```

Program 16-12 Analysis: `randomPrint` The `randomPrint` function is more interesting. We use a *for* loop to print 10 records. Within the loop, we use a random number generator to determine which record we will read next. Since there are 10 records in the file, we set the random number to modulo 10, which gives us potential record numbers from 0 to 9. This corresponds exactly with the file on disk, which occupies record positions 0 to 9.

MERGE FILES

In "Block I/O Example: Append Files" on page 785 we discussed the concept of combining two files by appending the data. Another useful way to combine data is by means of the file merge. When you **merge** data from two files, the result is one file with the data ordered in key sequence. To do this, we must completely read two input files, which are both ordered in key sequence, and create a new output file. This concept is shown in Figure 16-17.

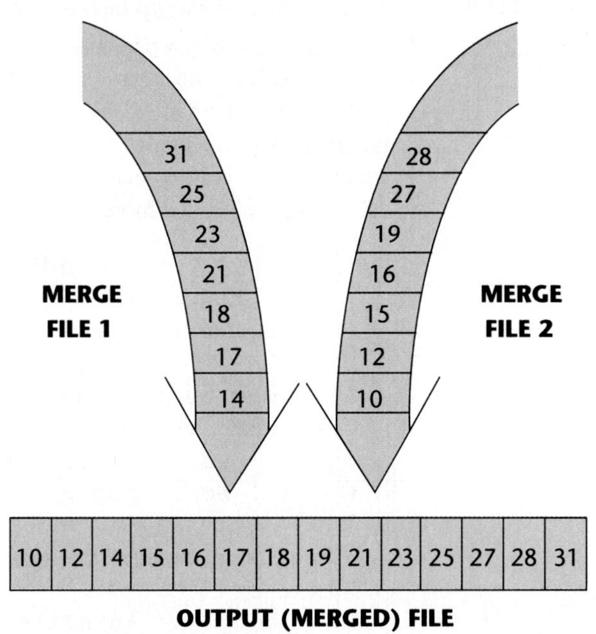

Figure 16-17 File merge concept

The merge files pseudocode is shown in Algorithm 16-1. The design is rather simple. We start by reading a record from each merge file. We then compare the keys of the two files and write the smaller to the merge output file, read the next record from the file whose record was written, and continue the loop.

Algorithm 16-1 Pseudocode for merging two files

```
This program merges two files.
1 input (File1, Rec1)
2 input (File2, Rec2)
3 HighSentinel = high-value
4 while (not eof(File1)) OR (not eof(File2))
  4.1 if Rec1.Key <= Rec2.Key then
      1  output (File3, Rec1)
```

Algorithm 16-1 Pseudocode for merging two files *(continued)*

```
        2  input  (File1, Rec1)
        3  if eof(File1)
           1  Rec1.Key = HighSentinel
   4.2 else
        1  output (File3, Rec2)
        2  input  (File2, Rec2)
        3  if eof(File2)
           1  Rec2.Key = HighSentinel

END Merge
```

The difficult part of the merge design is the end-of-file logic. One of the merge files will end first, but you never know which one. To simplify the end-of-file processing, this design introduces a concept known as a sentinel. A sentinel is a guard; in our merge algorithm, the sentinel guards the end of file. The sentinel has the property that its value is larger than any possible key. For the sentinel value, we use MAX_INT, which is found in the <climits> header file. The merge code is shown in Program 16-13.

Program 16-13 Merge two files

```
/* This program merges two files.
      Written by:
      Date:
*/
#include <iostream>
#include <fstream>
#include <cstdlib>
#include <climits>
using namespace std;

struct STU_DATA
    {
     char  name[26];
     int   id;
     char  grade;
    };

int main ()
{
   cout << "Begin merge demonstration\n";

   ifstream fsM1;
   char fs1ID[] = "p1611M1.bin";
   fsM1.open (fs1ID, ios::in | ios::binary);
   if (!fsM1)
       {
        cerr << "\aError opening " << fs1ID << endl;
        exit (100);
       } // !fsM1
```

Program 16-13 Merge two files *(continued)*

```
   ifstream fsM2;
   char fs2ID[] = "p1611M2.bin";
   fsM2.open (fs2ID, ios::in | ios::binary);
   if (!fsM2)
      {
       cerr << "\aError opening " << fs2ID << endl;
       exit (101);
      } // !fsM2
   ofstream fsOut;
   char fsOutID[] = "p1611M3.bin";
   fsOut.open (fsOutID, ios::out | ios::binary);
   if (!fsOut)
      {
       cerr << "\aError opening " << fsOutID << endl;
       exit (102);
      } // !fsOut

   STU_DATA recM1;
   STU_DATA recM2;
   fsM1.read ((char*) &recM1, sizeof(STU_DATA));
   fsM2.read ((char*) &recM2, sizeof(STU_DATA));

   while (!fsM1.eof() || !fsM2.eof())
      {
       int  sentinel   = INT_MAX;
       if (recM1.id <=  recM2.id)
          {
           fsOut.write ((char*) &recM1, sizeof(STU_DATA));
           fsM1.read  ((char*) &recM1, sizeof(STU_DATA));
           if (fsM1.eof())
               recM1.id = sentinel;
          } // if
       else
          {
           fsOut.write ((char*) &recM2, sizeof(STU_DATA));
           fsM2.read  ((char*) &recM2, sizeof(STU_DATA));
           if (fsM2.eof())
               recM2.id = sentinel;
          } // else
      } // while
   fsM1.close ();
   fsM2.close ();
   fsOut.close ();
   cout << "End merge demonstration\n";
   return 0;
} // Merge
```

Program 16-13 Analysis We have written this simple program without any subfunctions because it is so simple.

Programs that involve the comparison of data from two files require that the first record from both files be read before any comparisons can be made. This is sometimes called "priming the files." The reads that prime the files are coded before the main *while* loop. Since duplicate read statements are required in the loop, you might wonder why we didn't use a *do...while*. The reason is that the program would fail if both files were empty. As we coded it, the program works only if both files contain data.

Study the logic at statements 59 and 66 carefully. These statements implement the sentinel concept. When a file reaches its end, we set the key in the record area for the file to the sentinel value. This ensures that all the data on the other file will compare low and be written to the output file.

The most difficult statement in this simple program is the *while* statement. We need to keep looping as long as either of the files is not at the end of file. The most straightforward way to code this is as we coded it in statement 51. Another common way to code it is shown below.

```
(!(fpM1.eof() && fpM2.eof()))
```

You can use De Morgan's Rule on page 179 to prove to yourself that these two statements are identical.

16-8 SOFTWARE ENGINEERING AND PROGRAMMING STYLE

In every file environment, there must be some means of keeping the file current. Data are not static; they are constantly changing, and these changes need to be reflected in their files. The function that keeps files current is known as **updating.** To complete our discussion of files, we discuss some of the software engineering design considerations for file updating. For this discussion, we use as our example a student binary file similar to the ones we have discussed in the chapter.

UPDATE FILES

There are three specific files associated with an update program. First, there is the permanent data file, which is called the master file. The **master file** contains the most current computer data for an application.

The second file, the **transaction file,** contains changes to be applied to the master file. There are three basic types of changes in all file updates (note that there may be other changes, too, depending on the application). *Add transactions* contain data about a new student to be added in the master file. *Delete transactions* identify students that are to be deleted from the file. *Change transactions* contain revisions to specific student records in the file.

To process any of these transactions, we need a key. A **key** is one or more fields that uniquely identify the data in the file. For example, in the student file, the key would be student ID. In an employee file, the key would be Social Security number.

The third file needed in an update program is an **error report file.** Most update processes contain at least one error in the data. When an error occurs, it must be reported to the user. The *error report* contains a listing of all errors discovered during the update process and is presented to the user for corrective action.

There are two types of file updates: batch and online. In a **batch update,** changes are collected over time and then all changes are applied to the file at once. In an **online update,** the user is directly connected to the computer and the changes are processed one at a time, often as the change occurs.

SEQUENTIAL FILE UPDATE

For our discussion, we assume a batch, sequential file environment. A **sequential file** is a file that must be processed serially, starting at the beginning. It does not have any random processing capabilities. The sequential master file has the additional attribute that it is ordered on the key.

In a sequential file update, there are actually two copies of the master file: the old master and the new master. We use two because whenever a sequential file is changed, it must be entirely recreated—even if only one student's score on one exam is being changed.

Figure 16-18 contains an environment chart for a sequential file update. This chart shows the four files discussed above. Note that we use the tape symbol for the files because it is the classic symbol for sequential files, but sequential files can just as easily be stored on a disk. After the update program completes, the new master file is sent to off-line storage, where it is kept until it is needed again. When the file is to be updated, the master file is retrieved from the offline storage and used as the old master.

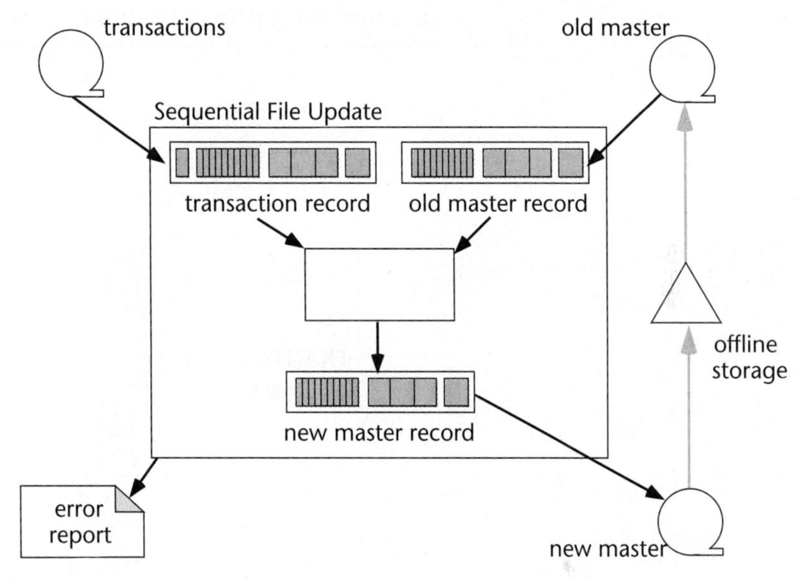

Figure 16-18 Sequential file update environment

Generally, there are at least three copies of a master file retained in offline storage in case it becomes necessary to regenerate an unreadable file. This retention cycle is known as the grandparent system because there are always three generations of the file available: the grandparent, the parent, and the child.

THE UPDATE PROGRAM DESIGN

Several years ago, a computer scientist named Barry Dwyer published an update algorithm in *Communications of the ACM* that was so elegant it has become a classic.[3] We have adapted his algorithm for our discussion.

Since a sequential master file is ordered on a key and since it must be processed serially, the transaction file must also be ordered on the same key. The update process requires that we match the keys on the transaction and master file and, assuming that there are no errors, take one of the following three actions:

1. If the transaction file key is less than the master file key, add the transaction to the new master.
2. If the transaction file key is equal to the master file key, either (a) change the contents of the master file data if the transaction is

[3]Barry Dwyer, "One More Time—How to Update a Master File," *Communications of the ACM*, Vol. 24, no. 1 (January 1981): 3–8.

a revise transaction, or (b) remove the data from the master file if the transaction is a delete.

3. If the transaction file key is greater than the master file key, write the old master file record to the new master file.

This updating process is illustrated in Figure 16-19.

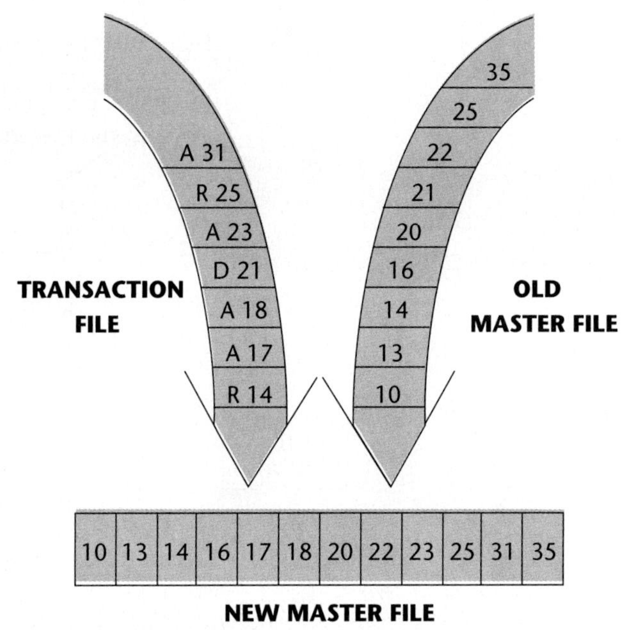

Figure 16-19 File updating example

In the transaction file, the transaction codes are A for add, D for delete, and R for revise. The process begins by matching the keys for the first record on each file. In this case,

```
14 > 10
```

so rule 3 is used and we write the *old* master record to the new master record. We then match 14 and 13, which results in 13 being written to the new master. In the next match, we have

```
14 == 14
```

so according to rule 2(a), we use the data in the transaction file to change the data in the master file. However, we do not write the new master file at this time. There may be more transactions that match the master file, and we need to process them, too.

After writing 16 to the new master, we have the following situation:

```
17 < 20
```

According to rule 1, we must add 17 to the new master file. We do this by copying the transaction to the new master file, but again we don't write it yet. There may be some revision transactions to this newly added record, and we must be able to process them. For example, this capability is needed when a new student registers and adds classes on the same day. The computer has to be able to add the new student and then process the class registrations in the same batch run. We will write the new master for 17 when we read transaction 18.

The processing continues until we read the delete transaction, at which time we have the following situation:

```
21 == 21
```

and since the transaction is a delete, according to rule 2(b), we need to drop 21 from the new master file. To do this, we simply read the next master record and transaction record without writing the new master. The processing continues in a similar fashion until all records on both files have been processed.

UPDATE ERRORS

Two general classes of errors can occur in an update program. First, the user can submit bad data, such as a grade that is not A, B, C, D, or F. For our discussion, we are going to assume that there are no data errors. Detecting data errors is the subject of data validation and has been discussed in Chapter 6.

The second class of errors is file errors. File errors occur when the data on the transaction file are not in synchronization with the data on the master file. Three different situations can occur, as follows:

1. An add transaction matches a record with the same key on the master file. Master files do not allow duplicate data to be present. When the key on an add transaction matches a key on the master file, therefore, we reject the transaction as invalid and report it on the error report.
2. A revise transaction's key does not match a record on the master file. In this case, we are trying to change data that don't exist. This is also a file error and must be reported on the error report.
3. A delete transaction's key does not match a record on the master file. In this case, we are trying to delete data that don't exist and we must also report this situation as an error.

UPDATE STRUCTURE CHART

The structure chart for the sequential file update is shown in Figure 16-20. In this structure chart, `Process` contains the updating function.

UPDATE LOGIC

`Initialization` is a function that opens the files and otherwise prepares the environment for processing. `End of Job` is a function that closes the files and displays any end-of-job messages. The mainline processing is done in `Process`.

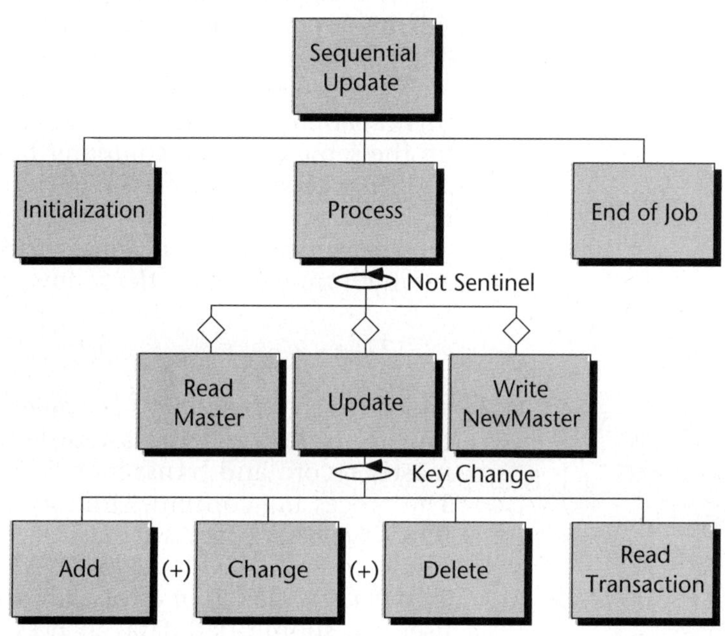

Figure 16-20 Update structure chart

Although it is beyond the scope of this discussion to develop the complete set of update functions, it is important that you understand the mainline logic found in `Process`. Its pseudocode is shown in Algorithm 16-2.

ALGORITHM 16-2 Pseudocode for sequential file update

```
1 read first record from transaction file
2 read first record from old master file
3 select next entity to be processed
4 while current entity not sentinel
  1  if current entity equal to old master entity
     1  copy old master to new master work area
     2  read old master file
  2  end if
  3  if current entity equal to transaction entity
     1  update new master work area
  4  end if
  5  if current entity equal to new master entity
     1  write new master file
  6  end if
  7  select next entity to be processed
5 end while
```

Let's look at the update logic in a little more detail. The first three statements contain initialization logic for `Process`. The driving force behind the update logic is that in each *while* loop, we process all the data for one student (entity). To determine which student we need to process next, we compare the key of the transaction file with the key of the master file and select the smaller. This logic is seen in statement 3 and again in statement 4.7.

Before we can compare the keys, however, we must read the first record in each file. This is known as "priming the files" and is seen in statements 1 and 2.

The *while* statement in Algorithm 16-2 contains the driving logic for the entire program. It is built on a very simple principle: As long as there are data in either the transaction file or the master file, we continue to loop. When a file has been completely read, we set its key to a sentinel value. When both files are at their end, therefore, both of their keys will be sentinels. Then when we select the next student to be processed, it will be a sentinel, which is the event that terminates the *while* loop.

Three major processing functions take place in the *while* loop. First, we determine if the student on the old master file needs to be processed. If it does, we move it to the new master output area and read the next student from the old master file. The key on the old master can match the current key in two situations: There is a change or delete transaction for the current student.

The second major process handles transactions that match the current student. It calls a function that determines the type of transaction being processed (add, change, or delete) and handles it accordingly. If it is an add, it moves the new student's data to the new master area. If it is a change, it updates the data in the new master area. And if it is a delete, it clears the key in the new master area so that the record will not be written. To handle multiple transactions in the update function, it reads the next transaction and continues if its key matches the current student.

The last major process writes the new master when appropriate. If the current student matches the key in the new master file area, then the record needs to be written to the file. This will be the case unless a delete transaction was processed.

SUMMARY

In this section we looked at a very important algorithm, the classic sequential file update, and discussed its mainline logic flow.

The elegance of Dwyer's algorithm, as seen in Algorithm 16-2, lies in the determination of the current student and the separation of the update process into three distinct functions: read the old master, update the current student, and write the new master. After studying the concept of the current student carefully and making sure you understand how it controls the three major processes in the loop, you should be able to develop the other functions in the update program.

Note that there is only one read transaction function. Because its function is to read a valid transaction, it contains all of the simple data validation logic to determine if the data are correct. It does not perform any file errors; they are handled in the update function. If any errors are found, it writes the transaction to an error report and reads the next transaction. When the read transaction file returns to the calling function, it has either read a valid transaction or found the end of the file.

16-9 TIPS AND COMMON PROGRAMMING ERRORS

Refer to the Tips and Common Programming Errors section in Chapter 7. Many of those tips apply to binary files as well.

1. Remember to open a file before using it.
2. You can create a file for writing; however, for you to read a file, it must already exist.
3. An open file can be in one of the three states: read, write, or error. If you want to switch from read to write or from write to read you must use one of the file positioning functions.
4. When you open a file for writing using `ios::out` mode, you must close it and open it for reading (`ios::in` mode) if you want to read from it. To avoid this problem, open the file in the `ios::in | ios::out mode`.
5. Do not open a file in `ios::out` mode when you want to preserve the contents of the file. The `ios::out` mode erases the contents of the file.
6. If you want to append to an existing file, use `ios :: out | ios :: app`.
7. Remember that, in general, you cannot print the contents of a binary file. It must be converted to a text file first.
8. The first parameter of the *read* and *write* functions is a pointer to the I/O area.
9. The second parameter of the *read* and *write* functions is the number of bytes to be read or written.
10. The *gcount* and *pcount* functions return the number of *elements* read or written, not the number of *bytes* read or written.
11. Remember that *stream.eof( )* does not look ahead. It returns *true* only if an attempt is made to read and the end of file is found before any data.
12. The first parameter in a seek function is the number of *bytes*, not the number of *elements*.
13. When the second parameter in the seek function is `ios::end`, the first parameter should normally be a negative long integer to access a byte in the file. If it is positive, it is referring to a byte after the end of file.
14. To add an element at the end of the file, you use the seek function with the first parameter set to zero and the second parameter set to the value of `ios::end`.
15. Remember that every time you use the *read* or *write* function, it automatically advances the file position indicator toward the end of the file the number of bytes read or written.
16. It is good practice to close all files before terminating a program.
17. It is a compile error to refer to a file with its external file name rather than the stream object attached to it.
18. It is a logic error to refer to a file before it is opened.
19. It is a logic error to open a file for reading when it doesn't exist. This is usually an error in the external file name in the open statement.
20. It is a logic error to attempt to read from a file in the write state and vice versa.
21. Opening an output disk file will fail if the disk is full.

22. Opening an existing file in write mode deletes the file. If your input file disappears, check your open modes.
23. It is a logic error to use seek functions to place the file marker before the first byte of a file.

16-10 KEY TERMS

append
batch update
binary file
end-of-file marker
error report file
error state
file
istringstream
key
master file
merge
online update
ostringstream
read
read state
seekg
seekp
sequential file
stringstream
tellg
tellp
text file
transaction file
update file
updating
write
write state

16-11 SUMMARY

- A file is a collection of related data in an auxiliary storage device.
- A stored stream of 0s and 1s can be interpreted as either a text or a binary file.
- A text file is a file of characters.
- A binary file is a collection of related data stored in the internal format of the computer.
- A file is always in one of the following states: read, write, or error.
- The *read* function reads a specified number of bytes from a binary file.
- The *write* function writes a specified number of bytes into a binary file.
- The *tell* functions return the current position of the file position indicator relative to the beginning of the file.
- The *eof* function checks for end of file.
- The *error* function is used to check the error status of a file.
- The *clear* function is used to clear an error.
- The process that keeps files current is known as updating.
- The seek functions position the file position indicator to the specified location.
- Seek can be relative to the beginning or the end of the file or to the current position in the file.
- The *istringstream* connects an input stream to a string.
- The *ostringstream* connects an output stream to a string.
- The *stringstream* connects an input/output string to a stream.
- There are three files associated with an update program: the master file, the transaction file, and the error report file.
- A sequential file is a file that must be processed serially starting at the beginning. It does not have any random processing capabilities.

16-12 PRACTICE SETS

REVIEW QUESTIONS

1. A file can be read only if it is opened in the input state.
   a. True
   b. False
2. Binary files are read using the block input/output function *read.*
   a. True
   b. False
3. Using *seekg* or *seekp* to position a file beyond the current end of file places the file in an error state.
   a. True
   b. False
4. To merge two files, you can use the merge function found in the standard input/output library.
   a. True
   b. False
5. The ______ results when a failure occurs during an open or during either a read or write operation.
   a. Error state
   b. Update state
   c. Fail state
   d. Write state
   e. Read state
6. If a file in the input mode is written to, then the following occurs:
   a. The file is placed in an error state regardless of the file mode.
   b. The file is placed in an error state unless it was opened in the update write mode (`w+b`).
   c. The file state is automatically switched if the file is opened for updating.
   d. The program is aborted regardless of how the file was opened.
   e. The program is aborted unless the file was opened for updating.
7. The ______ function can be used to position a file at the beginning for writing.
   a. close
   b. seekg
   c. eof
   d. tellg
   e. seekp
8. A ______ is one or more fields that uniquely identify the data in a file.
   a. field
   b. structure
   c. identifier
   d. transaction
   e. key
9. Which of the following statements about sequential file updating is false?
   a. Add, change, and delete transactions are used to update the file.
   b. Sequential files are often updated in an online environment.
   c. Sequential files contain structures (records) with a key to identify the data.
   d. The file must be processed starting at the beginning.
   e. The file must be entirely re-created when it is updated.

EXERCISES

10. Explain the difference between the following pairs ios settings :
    a. (ios :: in | ios :: binary) and (ios :: in | ios :: out | ios :: trunc | ios :: binary)
    b. (ios :: out | ios :: binary) and (ios :: in | ios :: out | ios :: binary)
    c. (ios :: app | ios :: binary) and (ios :: in | ios :: out | ios :: app | ios :: binary)
11. Find the error(s) in the following code. (Assume the PAY_REC type has been properly defined.)

```
PAY_REC payRec;
ofstream fs;
fs.open ("Payroll", ios :: out
    | ios :: binary);
fs.read ((char *) &payRec,
    sizeof (payRec));
```

12. Given the following declarations

```
ofstream fs ;
char s[20] ;
```

find any errors in each of the following lines:

a. fs.read(s);

b. fs.read(s, 20);

c. read(s, 20);

d. read(fs, s, 20);

e. fs.read(20, s);

13. Given the following declarations

```
ofstream fs ;
char s[20] ;
```

find any errors in each of the following lines:

a. tellp (fs);

b. fs.tellp (1);

c. seekp (0, 20L, fs);

d. fs.seekp (14, beg);

e. seekp (fs, 5, end);

14. What would be printed from the following program? Draw a picture of the file with the file marker to explain your answer.

```
#include <iostream>
#include <fstream>
using namespace std;
int main ()
 {
  char       c;
  streampos pos;
  fstream    fs;
  fs. open("SAMPLE5.DAT", ios ::
       in |ios :: out);
  for (c = 'A'; c <= 'E'; c++)
      fs.write ((char*) &c ,
      sizeof (char));
  pos = fs.tellg ();
  cout << "Position of the file"
        " marker: " << pos
      << endl;
  return 0;
 }
```

15. What would be printed from the following program? Draw a picture of the file with the file marker to explain your answer.

```
#include <iostream>
#include <fstream>
using namespace std;
int main ()
{
 char    c;
 fstream fs;
 fs. open( "SAMPLE6.DAT", ios ::
     out | ios :: in );
 for (c = 'A'; c<= 'E'; c++)
      fs.write((char*) &c,
      sizeof (char));
 fs.seekg(2, ios :: beg);
 fs.read((char*)&c, 1);
 cout << c << endl;
 return 0;
}
```

16. What would be printed from the following program? Draw a picture of the file with the file marker to explain your answer.

```
#include <iostream>
#include <fstream>
using namespace std;
int main ()
{
 char    c;
 fstream fs;
 fs. open( "SAMPLE7.DAT", ios ::
     out | ios :: in);
 for ( c = 'A'; c <= 'E'; c++ )
      fs.write( (char*)&c ,
      sizeof ( char ) );
 fs.seekg (-1, ios :: end );
 fs.read( (char*) &c, 1 );
 cout << c << endl ;
 return 0;
}
```

17. What would be printed from the following program? Draw a picture of the file with the file marker to explain your answer.

```
#include <iostream>
#include <fstream>
using namespace std;
int main ()
{
 char    c;
 char    d;
 fstream  fs;
 fs. open("SAMPLE8.DAT", ios ::
     out | ios:: in);
 for (c = 'A'; c <= 'E'; c++)
      fs.write((char*)&c,
      sizeof (char));
 fs.seekg(0, ios :: beg);
 fs.read((char*) &d, 1);
 cout << d  << endl;
 return 0;
}
```

18. What would be printed from the following program? Draw a picture of the file with the file marker to explain your answer.

```
#include <iostream>
#include <fstream>
using namespace std;
int main ( )
{
 char     c;
 fstream  fs;
 fs.open("SAMPLE9.DAT", ios ::
     out | ios :: in);
 for (c = 'A'; c <= 'L'; c++)
        fs.write((char*)&c ,
        sizeof (char));
 fs.seekg (-3, ios :: end);
 fs.read((char*) &c, 1);
 cout << c << endl;
 return 0;
}
```

19. What would be printed from the following program? Draw a picture of the file with the file marker to explain your answer.

```
#include <iostream>
#include <fstream>
using namespace std;
int main ( )
{
 char c;
 fstream  fs;
 fs.open( "SAMPLE10.DAT",
     ios :: out|ios:: in);
 for ( c = 'A'; c <= 'L'; c++ )
         fs.write( (char*)&c ,
         sizeof ( char ) );
 fs.seekg( -1 , ios :: end );
 fs.read( (char*) &c, 1 );
 cout << c << endl;
 fs.seekg (-1, ios :: end);
 fs.read( (char*) &c, 1 );
 cout << c << endl ;
 return 0;
}
```

20. What would be printed from the following program? Draw a picture of the file with the file marker to explain your answer.

```
#include <iostream>
#include <fstream>
using namespace std;
int main ()
{
 fstream  fs;
 fs.open("SAMPLE11.DAT",
    ios :: out  |ios:: in);
 char c;
 for (c = 'A'; c <= 'L'; c++)
       fs.write((char*)&c,
       sizeof (char));
 fs.seekg (-3 , ios :: end);
 fs.read((char*) &c, 1);
 cout << c << endl;
 c = '?';
 fs.seekp (0, ios :: cur);
 fs.write ((char*)&c,
    sizeof (char));
 fs.seekg (-1, ios:: cur);
 fs.read( (char*) &c, 1);
 cout << c << endl;
 return 0;
}
```

21. What would be printed from the following program? Draw a picture of the file with the file marker to explain your answer.

```
#include <iostream>
#include <fstream>
using namespace std;
int main ()
{
 fstream  fs;
 fs.open("SAMPLE12.DAT",
    ios :: out | ios :: in);
 for (char c = 'A'; c <= 'L'; c++)
       fs.write((char*)&c,
       sizeof (char));
 fs.seekg (-3, ios :: end);
 c = '?';
 fs.write ((char*)&c,
 sizeof (char));
 fs.seekg (0, ios::beg);
 fs.read((char*) &c, 1);
 while (!fs.eof())
    {
     cout << c;
     fs.read((char*) &c, 1);
    } // while
  cout << endl;
 return 0;
}
```

22. What would be printed from the following program? Draw a picture of the file with the file marker to explain your answer.

```
#include <iostream>
#include <fstream>
using namespace std;
int main ()
{
 fstream  fs;
 fs.open("SAMPLE13.DAT",
    ios :: out  |ios:: in);
 for (int i = 1; i <= 10; i++)
      fs.write((char*)&i,
      sizeof (int));
 fs.seekg (-3 * sizeof (int),
    ios :: end);
 fs.read((char*) &i, sizeof(int));
 cout << i << endl;
 return 0;
}
```

23. What would be printed from the following program? Draw a picture of the file with the file marker to explain your answer.

```
#include <iostream>
#include <fstream>
using namespace std;
int main ()
{
 fstream  fs;
 fs.open("SAMPLE14.DAT",
    ios :: out | ios :: in);
 for (int i = 1 ; i <= 10 ; i++)
      fs.write((char*)&i,
      sizeof (int));
 int i = 100;
 fs.seekp(-3 * sizeof (int),
    ios :: end);
 fs.write((char*)&i, sizeof (int));
 fs.write((char*)&i, sizeof (int));
 fs.seekg(-2 * sizeof (int),
    ios :: cur);
 fs.read ((char*) &i, sizeof (int));
 cout << i << endl;
 fs.read ((char*) &i, sizeof (int));
 cout << i << endl;
 fs.read ((char*) &i, sizeof (int));
 cout << i << endl;
 return 0;
}
```

24. What would be printed from the following program? Draw a picture of the file with the file marker to explain your answer.

```
#include <iostream>
#include <fstream>
using namespace std;
int main ()
{
 int      i;
 int      j;
 fstream  fs;
 fstream  temp;
 fs.open  ("SAMPLE15.DAT",
    ios :: out  | ios :: in);
 temp.open("TEMP.DAT", ios ::
    out | ios :: in | ios :: trunc);
 for (int i = 1; i <= 10 ; i++)
      fs.write((char*)&i,
      sizeof (int));
 for (int j = 1; j <= 10; j++)
     {
      fs.seekg  (-j * sizeof (int),
         ios :: end);
      fs.read   ((char*) &i,
        sizeof (int));
      temp.write ((char*)&i,
        sizeof (int));
     } // for j
 temp.seekg (0, ios :: beg);
 temp.read ((char*)&i, sizeof (int));
 while (!temp.eof())
     {
      cout << i << " ";
      temp.read((char*) &i,
         sizeof (int));
     } // while
 cout << endl;
 return 0;
}
```

PROBLEMS

25. Write a function that copies the contents of a binary file of integers to a second file. The function must accept reference parameters to stream objects and return a boolean (false representing a processing error and true indicating successful completion).

26. Write a function that prints a specified number of records from the beginning of a file. The function is to accept two parameters. The first is a reference parameter to a binary file of structure type `STR`. The second is an integer that specifies the number of records to be printed (inclusive). The structure type is shown below:

```
struct STR
   {
    int   i;
    float f;
   } ;
```

If any errors occur, such as fewer records in the file than specified, it should return false. Otherwise, it returns true.

27. Write a function that compares two files and returns *true* if the files are identical and *false* if their contents vary. The functions should receive reference parameters to stream objects associated to two opened files and compare them byte by byte.
28. Write a function that returns the number of records in a binary file.
29. Write a function that prints the last integer in a binary file of integers.
30. Write a function that physically removes all items with a specified key value (key) from a binary file of structure STR. You may use a temporary file. The file may contain more than one record with the delete value. The key value to be removed is to be entered from the keyboard.

```
struct STR
   {
    int  key;
    char c;
   } ;
```

31. Write a function that appends one binary file at the end of another.
32. Write a function that, given a binary file, copies the odd items (items 1, 3, 5, ..., *n*) to a second binary file and the even items (items 2, 4, 6, ..., *n*) to a third binary file.
33. Write a function that reads items from a binary file and copies them to a dynamically allocated array. The function must first find the size of the binary file to allocate the array.
34. Write a function that takes a binary file of long integers and appends a new long integer at the end that is the sum of all integers in the original file.

PROJECTS

35. A company has two small warehouses. The list of the products in each warehouse is kept in a text file (InvFile1 and InvFile2) with each line representing information about one product. The manager wants to have only one list showing information about all products in both warehouses. Therefore, the two text files must be combined into one single text file (OutFile). Write a program to merge the files and print the results. Create a record structure containing a part number, quantity on hand, and price. Each merge file is to contain at least ten records.
36. Write a program that will copy information from the two text files (InvFile1 and InvFile2) to two binary files (BinFile1 and BinFile2). After creating the binary files, merge them to produce a combined binary file. After the combined binary file has been created, create a report file that can be printed. The report file is to contain page headers with an appropriate title and page numbers. The structure for the files is shown below.

```
struct INV_REC
   {
    char  partNo[5];
    char  partName[15];
    int   qtyOnHand;
   };
```

37. A company keeps a list of parts that it purchases, with a line of information for each part that gives the part's unique code, name, and codes for three suppliers that provide that particular part. This list is kept in a binary file and is sorted in ascending order according to the supplier's code.

    Each record in the part file is made up of a part's code, name, and the codes for three suppliers. The part's code is an integer; the name is a string with a maximum length of 10 characters; and each supplier's code is an integer. Note that not all parts have three suppliers. If there are fewer than three suppliers, a special supplier code of 0000 is used to indicate "no supplier."

    The company also keeps a list of its suppliers, with a line of information for each supplier, that gives the supplier's unique code, name, and address. This list is also kept in a binary file, which is sorted in ascending order according to the supplier's code.

    Each record in the supplier file is made up of a supplier's code, name, and address. The supplier's code is an integer, the name is a string with a maximum length of 10 characters, and the address has a maximum length of 25 characters.

    Write a program that enables the user to enter a part's unique code on the monitor and receive a list of three suppliers. If the code is found, the program prints the names and addresses of the three suppliers. If the code is not found, it prints a message to tell the user that the code is not in the file. After each inquiry, the program is to give the user the option to quit.

    Format the output with the first line showing the data for the part and the following lines showing data for the suppliers, indented one tab.

Sample data for the files are shown in Table 16-2 and Table 16-3. You will first have to write a file conversion program to create the binary files. We suggest that you create a text file version of each file with your text editor and then read it to create the binary version.

Part code	Part name	Supl 1	Supl 2	Supl 3
1000	Pen	5010	5007	5012
1001	Pencil	5006	5008	0000
1002	Paper	5001	5000	5003
1003	Ball pen	5013	5009	5014
1004	Folder	5009	5007	5002
1005	Pointer	5012	5006	5005
1006	Mouse	5012	0000	0000
1007	Monitor	5000	5002	5007

Table 16-2 Project 37 part file

Supplier code	Supplier name	Supplier address
5000	John Marcus	2322 Glen Place
5001	Steve Chu	1435 Main Avenue
5002	David White	2345 Steve Drive
5003	Bryan Walljasper	780 Rose Mary Street
5004	Andrew Tse	P. O. Box 7600
5005	Joanne Brown	1411 Donnybrook Sq
5006	Lucy Nguyen	2345 Saint Mary Road
5007	Fred West	11 Duarte Road
5008	Dennis Andrews	14 California Avenue
5009	Leo Washington	134234 San Rosa Place
5010	Frankie South	12234 North Justin St
5011	Amanda Trapp	1345 South Bush Circle
5012	Dave Lightfoot	222 George Territory Dr
5013	Danna Mayor	11 George Bush Street
5014	Robert Hurley	14 Republican Alley

Table 16-3 Project 37 supplier file

To read a record on the files, you must determine its position on the file. To do this, subtract 1000 from the `PartCode` for the part file and 5000 from the `SupplierCode` for the supplier file. Then use *seekg* to position the file for reading.

38. Write a program that builds a histogram (see Chapter 8) using a randomly accessed disk file. The program begins by creating a new file of 20 integers. Each integer is to represent the accumulator for its relative position: the first for the number 0, the second for the number 1, and so forth until the last for the number 19. Next, the program uses the random number generator to create 100 random numbers in the range 0…19. As each random number is generated, it is displayed in a 10 × 10 matrix (10 lines of 10 numbers each) and added to its accumulator on the disk using the seek function. After the random numbers have been generated, the file is read sequentially and a histogram displayed.

39. Your stockbroker has an online inquiry system that allows you to check the price of stocks using your personal computer. Simulate this system as described below.

Each stock is assigned a unique integral number in the range 1000…5000. They are stored on the disk so that stock 1000 is stored in location 0, stock 1001 in location 1, stock 2010 in location 1010, and so forth. To calculate the disk address for a requested stock, your program subtracts 1000 from the stock number and uses the result as the address in the file. (This is actually a simplified version of a concept known as "hashing" that you will learn when you study data structures.)

The data for each stock are described as follows:

```
structure
 stock key       short integer
 stock name      string[21]
 stock symbol    string[6]
 current price   floating-point
    number
 YTD High        floating-point
    number
 YTD Low         floating-point
    number
 Price-Earning
    Ratio        short integer
 (YTD: Year to Date)
```

Using data from your local newspaper, create a binary file of at least 20 stocks. Then write a menu-driven system that allows the user to request data on any individual stock.

In addition, provide a capability to get a report of up to 20 stocks at one time. When this option is requested, open a temporary work file and write the requested stocks to the file. After the last stock has been entered, read the file (without closing it) and prepare the report.

40. Rework Project 37 using a class for the inventory file and a class for the supplier file. Provide overloaded operators for reading (>>), searching (==), and printing (<<) each file.

17 Linked Lists

We have now covered all the basic material traditionally found in an introduction to programming text. In this last chapter, we turn our attention to a concept that is so pervasive in computer science that it should be studied by all programming students—the linked list.

To this point, the only structure you have studied that can be used to internally store significant amounts of data is the array. While the array can be a very efficient storage structure, especially for retrieving data, it is not well suited to data that are constantly changing. Inserting and deleting data from an array can be very slow.

The linked list, on the other hand, is very efficient when data have to be changed. Its limitation is that it takes longer to locate one element of the list. Nevertheless, the linked list is the basis on which many efficient structures are built, and you will study them in other courses if you continue to study programming. We present the linked list here as an introduction to those data structures.

17-1 LINKED LIST STRUCTURE

A **linked list** is an ordered collection of data in which each element contains the address of the next element; that is, each element contains two parts: *data* and *link.* The data part holds the useful information, the data to be processed. The **link** is used to ***chain*** the data together. It contains a pointer that identifies the next node in the list. Each linked list also requires a special pointer variable that points to the first entry. This special pointer that points to the element at the beginning of the list is called a **head pointer**; we name it `pHead`.

Figure 17-1 shows a linked list, named `pHead`, containing four nodes. The link in each node, except the last, points to its successor. The link in the last node contains a 0 pointer, indicating the end of the list. We define an **empty linked list** to be a single pointer having the value of 0. Figure 17-1 also shows an example of an empty linked list.

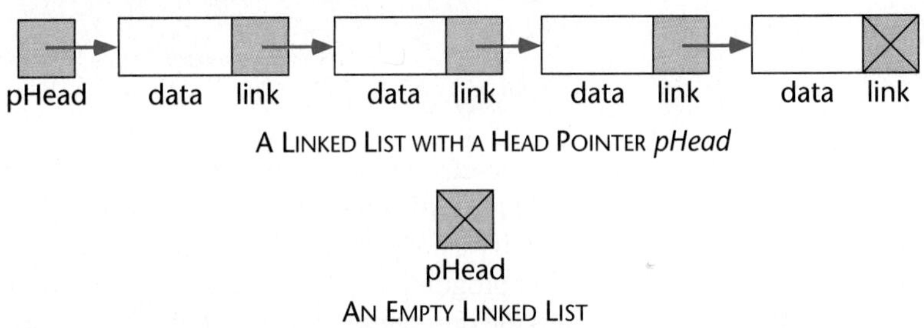

Figure 17-1 A linked list

NODES

A **node** in a linked list is a structure or a class that has at least two items. One of them is a data field; the other is a pointer that contains the address of the next node in the sequence. Figure 17-2 shows three nodes. The first node contains a single field, `number`, and a link. The second node contains three data fields—a `name`, `ID`, and grade points `(grdPts)`—and a link. The third node is the one we recommend. The fields are defined in their own structure, which is then put into the definition of a node structure or class. The one common element in all examples is a link field.

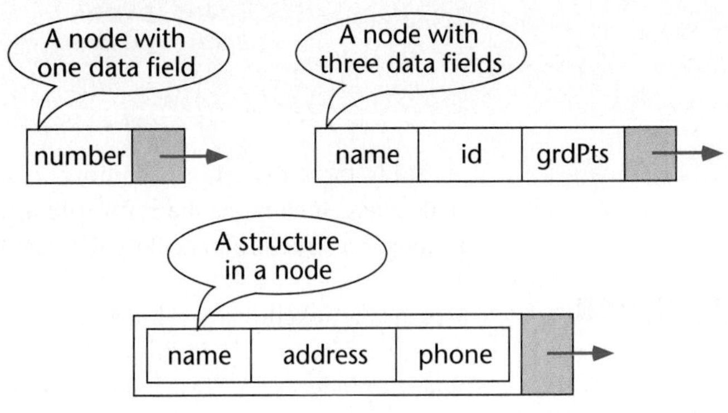

Figure 17-2 Nodes

The nodes in a linked list are called **self-referential** because each instance of a node contains a pointer to another instance of the same type.

When you study data structures, you will see that the nodes can become quite complex with several pointers. We will limit our discussion to nodes that contain data and only one link field.

DECLARATIONS FOR A LINKED LIST

Our design for a link list uses two classes: one for the nodes and one for the list.

Node Class

The following example shows the code for a generic linked list. Note that the sections shown with an ellipsis (...) must be filled in for the particular application being created.

```
class Node
  {
   private:
      int   key;
      ...                             // Other Data Fields
      Node* link;
  }; // Node
```

The data include all attributes needed to satisfy the application. We include a key field for those functions that require searching by key. A **key** is one or more fields that identify a node or otherwise control its use. The key type defined above is an integer. In your program, you have to use either one of the standard types or create a type for it. To test the programs in this chapter we have used a node with only an integer key; no other data have been included.

List Class

This list class contains the variables and methods required to maintain and process the list nodes. As explained in the following sections, at least three variables are required. The first, `pHead`, identifies the location of the first node in the list. The other two, a predecessor pointer (`pPre`) and a current node pointer (`pCur`) are used by the class methods to process the list. The list class design is outlined in the following code.

```
class List
   {
    private:
       Node* pHead;
       Node* pPre;
       Node* pCur;
    ...
   }; // List
```

Study these two classes carefully. Note that the list class contains references to the node class. It contains the infrastructure, data and methods, for the list. The node class is simply a structure to declare the data that are used in the list.

LINK LIST ORDER

Because a linked list is a linear structure, it always has an order. Generally, the list is sequenced by its key. In this case, the key in each node in the list is equal to or greater than its predecessor. New data added to the list must therefore be placed at the correct location relative to the data already in the list. Most of the examples in this chapter assume a key-sequenced list.

On the other hand, a list can also be ordered chronologically. When a list is chronologically ordered, new data are added at the beginning or the end of the list.

POINTERS TO LINKED LISTS

One of the attributes of a linked list is that it is not stored contiguously. When data are stored in an array, we know from the array structure where the list begins, and the successor to each element is simply the next element in the array. In a linked list, however, there is no physical relationship between the nodes.

Because there isn't a physical relationship between the nodes, we need some way to distinguish the beginning of the list—that is, to identify the first logical node in the list. This pointer is the special pointer mentioned earlier, the head pointer, which points to the node at the head of the list (see Figure 17-1).

A linked list must always have a head pointer. If you lose it, you lose your entire list because the access to the list in dynamic memory is only through this head pointer. Depending on how you are going to use the head pointer, you may have several other pointers as well. For example, if you are going to search a linked list, you will undoubtedly have a pointer (`pCur`) to the location where you found the data you were looking for. In many structures, programming efficiencies will result if there is a pointer to the last node in the list as well as a head pointer. This *last* pointer, also known as a *tail* or *rear* pointer, is often named either `pLast`, for pointer to `last`, or `pRear`, for pointer to rear.

17-2 BASIC LINKED LIST FUNCTIONS

To work with a linked list, we need some basic operations that manipulate the nodes. For example, we need functions to add a node and to delete a node. We also need a function to find a requested node. Once we have these basic functions, we can build an object that will process any linked list.

ADD A NODE

There are four steps required to **add a node** to a linked list.

1. Allocate memory for the new node.
2. Determine the insertion point—that is, the position within the list where the new data are to be placed. To identify the insertion position, you need to know only the new node's logical predecessor (`pPre`).
3. Point the new node to its successor.
4. Point the predecessor to the new node.

As outlined in step 2, to insert a node into a list we need to know the location of the node that precedes the new node (`pPre`). This pointer can be in one of two states: It can contain the address of a node or it can be 0. A linked list and its pointers are shown in Figure 17-3.

If the predecessor is 0, then we are adding either to an empty list or at the beginning of the list. If it is not 0, then we are adding somewhere after the first node—that is, in the middle of the list—or we are adding at the end of the list. Let's discuss each of these situations in turn.

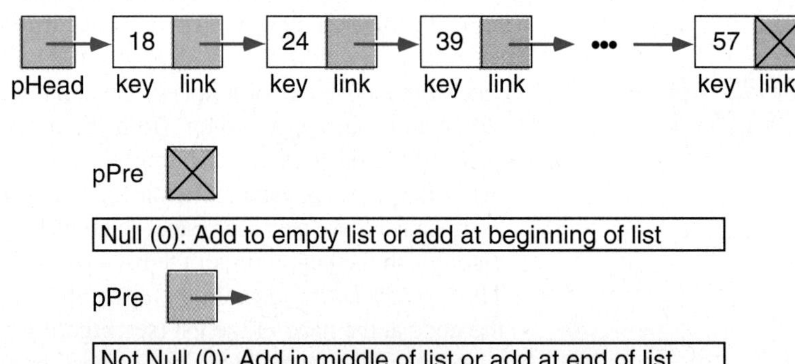

Figure 17-3 Pointer combinations for add

Add to Empty List

When the head pointer contains the value 0, the list is empty. This situation is shown in Figure 17-4. All that is necessary to add a node to an empty list is to point the list head pointer to the address of the new node and make sure that its link field is 0. We could use 0 to set the link field of the new node, but we will use the value contained in the list head pointer. The reason for this will become apparent in the next section.

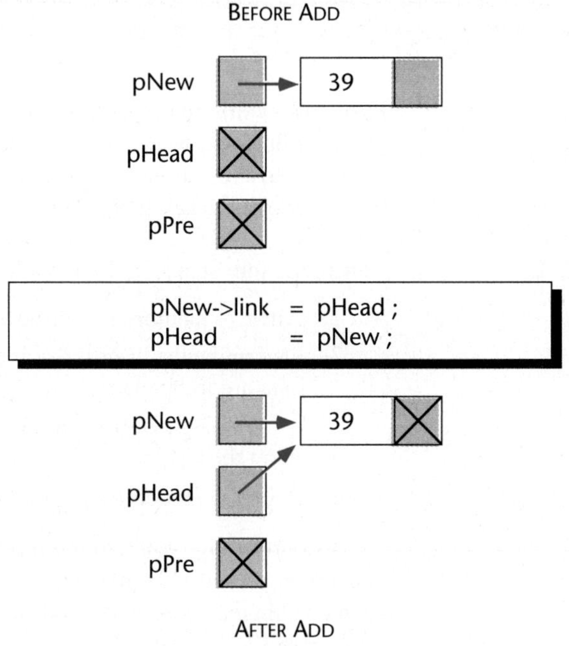

Figure 17-4 Add node to empty list

The statements used to insert a node into an empty list are shown below.

```
pNew->link = pHead;     // set link to 0
pHead      = pNew;      // point list to first node
```

Add at Beginning

Adding at the beginning of the list occurs anytime we need to insert a node before the first node of the list. We determine that we are adding at the beginning of the list by testing the predecessor pointer (`pPre`). If it is 0 there is no predecessor, so we know we are at the beginning of the list.

To insert a node at the beginning of the list we simply point the new node to the first node of the list and then set the head pointer (`pHead`) to point to the new first node. We know the address of the new node—now how can we find the address of the first node currently in the list so we can point the new node to it? The answer is simple: The first node's address is stored in the head pointer (`pHead`). The statements used to insert at the beginning of the list are shown below.

```
pNew->link  = pHead;
pHead       = pNew;
```

If you compare these two statements to the statements given above for inserting into an empty list, you will see that they are the same. Logically, inserting into an empty list is the same as inserting at the beginning of a list. We can therefore use the same logic to cover both situations. Adding at the beginning of the list is shown in Figure 17-5.

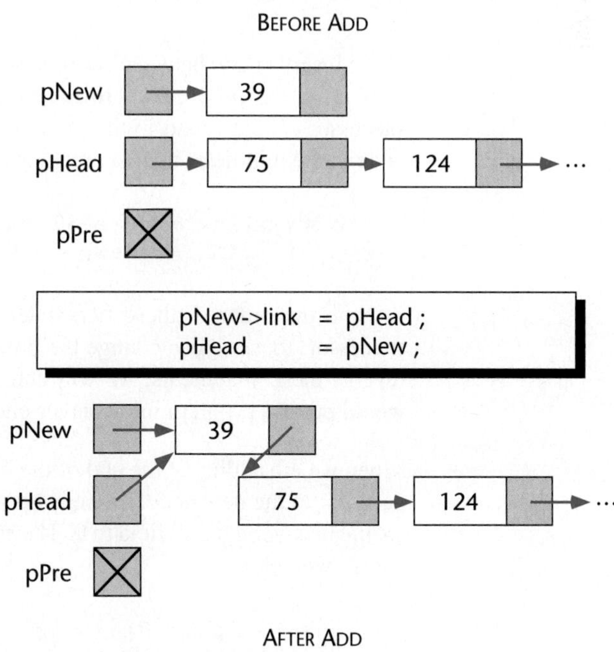

Figure 17-5 Add node at beginning

Add in Middle

When we add a node anywhere in the middle of the list, the predecessor (`pPre`) is not 0. This case is illustrated in Figure 17-6.

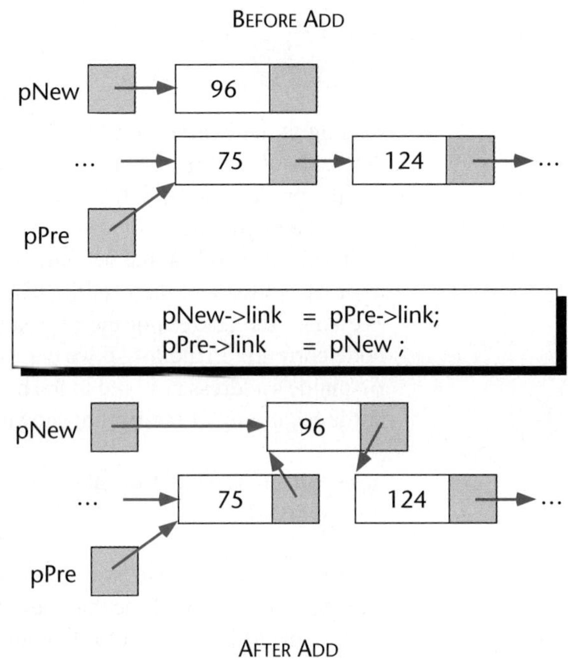

Figure 17-6 Add node in middle

To insert a node between two nodes, we must point the new node to its successor and then point the predecessor to the new node. Again, the address of the new node's successor can be found in the predecessor's link field. The statements used to insert a node in the middle of the list are shown below.

```
pNew->link = pPre->link;
pPre->link = pNew;
```

Note the order of these two statements. We must first point the new node to its successor; then we can change the predecessor pointer to point to the new node. If we reverse these statements, we will end up with the new node pointing to itself, which would put our program into a never-ending loop when we process the list.

Add at End

When we are adding at the end of the list, the only thing we have to do is point the predecessor to the new node. There is no successor to point to. It is necessary, however, to set the new node's link field to 0. The statements used to insert a node at the end of a list are shown below.

```
pNew->link = 0;
pPre->link = pNew;
```

Rather than using special logic in the function for inserting at the end, however, we can take advantage of the existing linked list structure. We know that the last node in the list will have a 0 `link` pointer. If we use this pointer rather than a constant, then the code becomes exactly the same as the code for inserting in the middle of the list. The revised code is shown below. Compare it to the code for adding a node in the middle, shown previously.

```
pNew->link = pPre->link;
pPre->link = pNew;
```

Figure 17-7 shows the logic for adding a node at the end of a linked list.

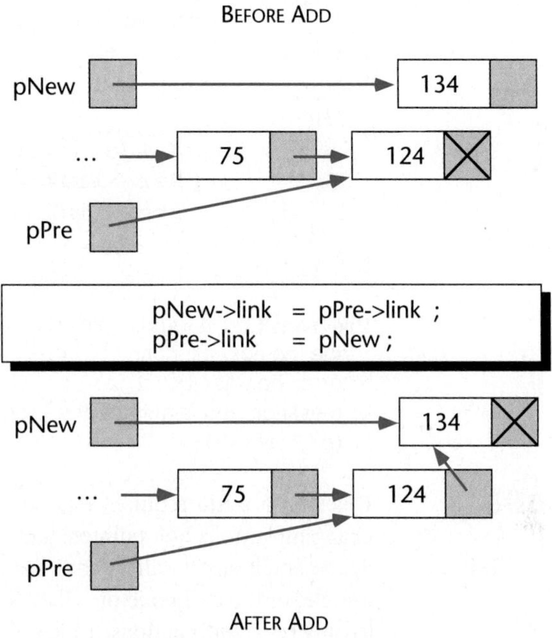

Figure 17-7 Add node at end

Add Node Logic

Now let's put it all together. Given the head pointer (`pHead`), the predecessor (`pPre`), and the data to be inserted (item), we must allocate memory for the new node (*new*) and adjust the link pointers. The code is shown in Program 17-1.

Program 17-1 Add a node

```
// Insert a node into a linked list.
   Node* pNew;
   try
      {
       pNew   = new NODE;
      } // try
   catch (bad_alloc& err)
      {
       cout << "Error 100: Memory overflow in addNode"
             << err.what() << endl;
       exit (100);
      } // catch
```

Program 17-1 Add a node (continued)

```

    pNew->data = item;

    if (pPre == 0)
       {
        // Adding before first node or to empty list
        pNew->link   = pHead;
        pHead        = pNew;
       } // if
    else
       {
        // Adding in middle or at end
        pNew->link = pPre->link;
        pPre->link = pNew;
      } // else
```

Program 17-1 Analysis We have discussed all the logic in this function except for the memory allocation. To test for an **overflow** error we use the system exception error handler (`bad_alloc`). If overflow occurred, we display an appropriate message and terminate the program. We also display the system error message (`err.what`).

DELETE A NODE

Deleting a node requires that we logically remove the node from the linked list by changing various link pointers and then physically deleting the node from the heap. The delete situations parallel those for add. We can delete the first node, any node in the middle, or the end node of a list. As we will demonstrate, these three situations reduce to only two combinations: Delete the first node and delete any other node.

To logically delete a node, we must first locate the node itself (identified by `pCur`) and its predecessor (identified by `pPre`). We will discuss location concepts shortly. Once the node to be deleted has been located, we can simply change its predecessor's link field to point to the deleted node's successor. We then recycle the node using *delete*. We must be alert to the possibility that we are deleting the only node in a list. Deleting the only node results in an empty list, so we must be careful that in this case the head pointer is set to 0.

Delete First Node

When we delete the first node, we must reset the head pointer to point to the first node's successor and then recycle (*delete*) the deleted node. We can tell we are deleting the first node by testing the predecessor (`pPre`). If the predecessor is 0, we are deleting the first node. This situation is diagrammed in Figure 17-8.

The statements used to delete the first node are shown below.

```
pHead = pCur->link;
delete (pCur);
```

Note that this logic also handles the situation when we are deleting the only node in the list. If the first node is the only node, then its link field is 0. Since we move its link field (0) to the head pointer, the result is by definition an empty list.

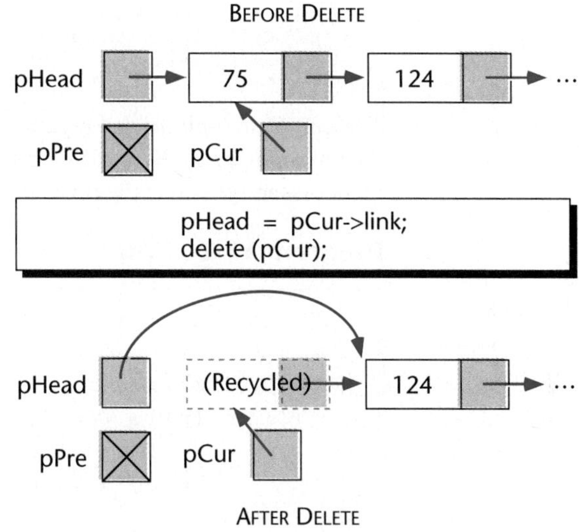

Figure 17-8 Delete first node

General Delete Case

We call deleting any node other than the first a general case since the same logic handles deleting a node in the middle of the list and deleting a node at the end of the list. For both of these cases, we simply point the predecessor node, identified by `pPre`, to the successor of the node being deleted. The node being deleted is identified by the current node pointer, `pCur`. Its successor is therefore `pCur->link`.

Deleting the last node is handled automatically. When the node being deleted is the last node of the list, its 0 pointer is moved to the predecessor's link field, making the predecessor the new logical end of the list. After the pointers have been adjusted, the current node is recycled. The general case is shown in Figure 17-9.

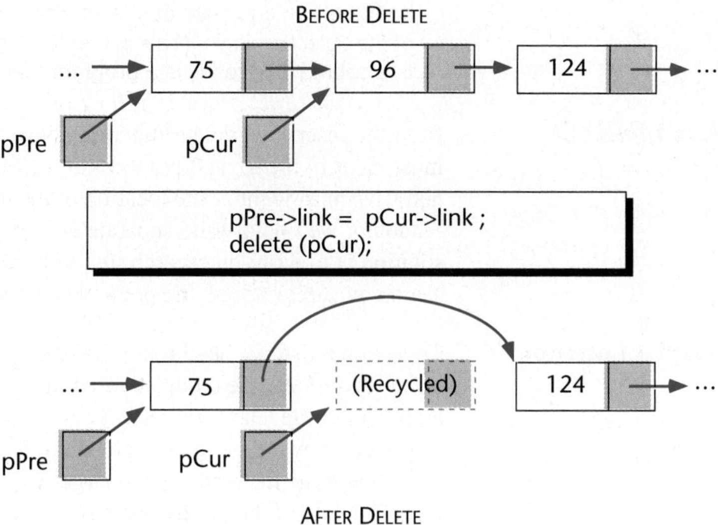

Figure 17-9 Delete—general case

The delete general case statements are shown below.

```
pPre->link = pCur->link;
delete (pCur);
```

Logic to Delete a Node

The complete logic to delete a node is shown in the code fragment in Program 17-2. Given a pointer to the head of the list, the node to be deleted, and the delete node's predecessor, we delete the node and recycle its memory.

Program 17-2 Delete a node

```
// Delete a node from a linked list.

// Statements
    if (pPre == 0)
       // Deleting first node
       pHead = pCur->link;
   else
       // Deleting other nodes
       pPre->link = pCur->link;

   delete (pCur);
```

Program 17-2 Analysis Three points about this function merit discussion. The first and most important is that the node to be deleted must be identified before this function is called. The logic assumes that the predecessor and current pointers are properly set. If they aren't, the code will most likely fail—and even if it doesn't fail, the data will be wrong. (It is better for a program to fail than for it to report invalid results.)

Second, when we discussed the individual logic cases above, we placed the recycle statement *(delete)* after each link pointer assignment. In the implementation, we moved it to the end of the function. When the same statements appear in both the true and false blocks of a selection statement, they should be moved out of the selection logic. (This is the same concept as factoring common expressions in algebra.) The result is a program that is smaller and easier to maintain.

SEARCH LINKED LIST

Both the insert and delete functions have to search the linked list. To add a node, we must identify the logical predecessor of the new node in its key sequence. To delete a node, we must identify the location of the node to be deleted and its logical predecessor. Although we could write separate search functions for add and delete, the traditional solution is to write one search that will satisfy both requirements. This means that our search must return both the predecessor and the current (found) locations.

Basic Search Concept

To search a list, we need a key field. For simple lists, the key and the data can be the same field. For more complex structures, we use a separate key field (see the code example in "Node Class" on page 820).

Given a key target, the search attempts to locate the requested node in the linked list. If a node in the list matches the target value, the search returns true; if no key matches, it returns false. The predecessor and current pointers are set according to the rules in Table 17-1. Each of these conditions is also diagrammed in Figure 17-10.

Condition	*pPre*	*pCur*	Return
target < first node	0	first node	false
target == first node	0	first node	true
first < target < last	largest node < target	first node > target	false
target == middle node	node's predecessor	equal node	true
target == last node	last's predecessor	last node	true
target > last node	last node	0	false

Table 17-1 Linear list search results

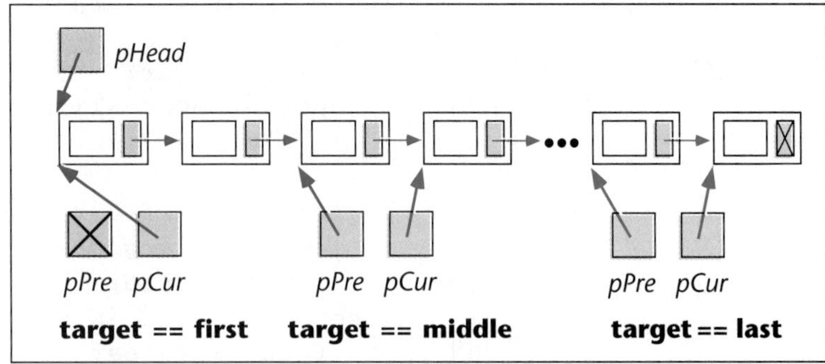

SUCCESSFUL SEARCHES (RETURN *true*)

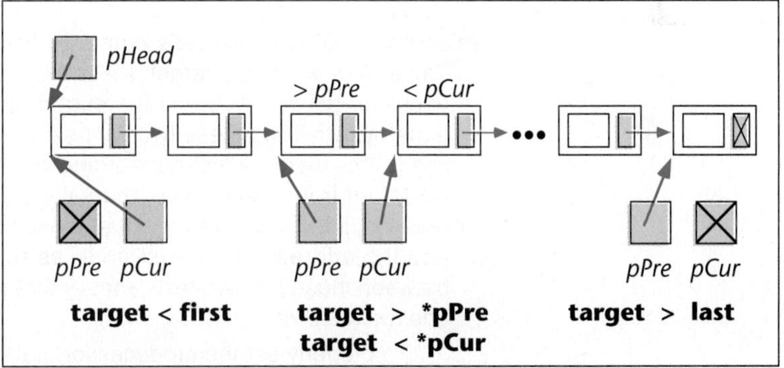

UNSUCCESSFUL SEARCHES (RETURN *false*)

Figure 17-10 Search results

The Search Function

Because the linked list is in key sequence, we use a modified version of the sequential search. Knuth[1] calls this search "sequential search in ordered table." We simply call it an ordered sequential search.

We start at the beginning and search the list sequentially until the target value is no longer greater than the current node's key. At this point, the target value is either less than or equal to the current node's key, while the predecessor is pointing to the node immediately before the current node. We now use the current node pointer (`pCur`) to

[1]Donald E. Knuth. *The Art of Computer Programming, Second Edition, Volume 3, Sorting and Searching.* (Reading, MA: Addison-Wesley, 1998), Algorithm T, p. 398.

test for equal and set the return to *true* if the target value is equal to the list value or *false* if it is less (it cannot be greater). We then terminate the search. The logic is seen in Program 17-3.

Program 17-3 Search linked list

```
1  // Search nodes in a linked list.
2     pPre = 0;
3     pCur = pHead;
4  
5     // Search until target <= list data key
6     while (pCur && target > pCur->data.key)
7        {
8         pPre = pCur;
9         pCur = pCur->link;
10       } // while
11 
12    // Determine if target found
13    if (pCur && target == pCur->data.key)
14        found = true;
15    else
16        found = false;
17    return found;
```

Program 17-3 Analysis Let's compare the algorithm to the conditions shown in Table 17-1. When the target is less than the first node, we must set the logical predecessor (`pPre`) to 0 and the current location (`pCur`) to the first node. This is done by initializing these two variables in statements 2 and 3. Because the target key is less than the first node's key, we don't execute the *while* statement. When we return from the function, the values are therefore properly set. For the same reasons, if the target key is equal to the first argument, we return a 0 predecessor and the address of the first node as the current location. The only difference between these first two test cases is that the first one returns *false* and the second one returns *true*.

To properly set the predecessor in the rest of the cases, we must have it one step behind the current pointer as we search the list. This is done by assigning the current pointer to the predecessor in statement 8 during each loop iteration. We then advance the current pointer and test the loop limit condition again. When the loop terminates, therefore, the predecessor is pointing to the node just before the current pointer. The only exception is when the target key is greater than the last key. In this case, the predecessor is pointing to the last node and the current location is 0, which means that the search key is greater than the last node in the list. Use Figure 17-10 and Table 17-1 to verify that you understand this logic.

TRAVERSING LINKED LISTS

There are two basic models for processing the data in a list. First, we can search for a specific element in the list and then process only the data in that element. This is the general model for online user interaction where the application requires that only one element be retrieved for reporting or updating. The second model, the **list traversal**, requires that all of the data in the list be processed.

Algorithms that traverse a list start at the first node and examine each node in succession until the last node has been processed. Several different types of functions use list traversal logic. In addition to printing the list, we could count the number of nodes in the list, total a numeric field in the node, or calculate the average of a field. In fact, any application that requires processing the entire list uses a traversal. Figure 17-11 is a graphic representation of a linked list traversal.

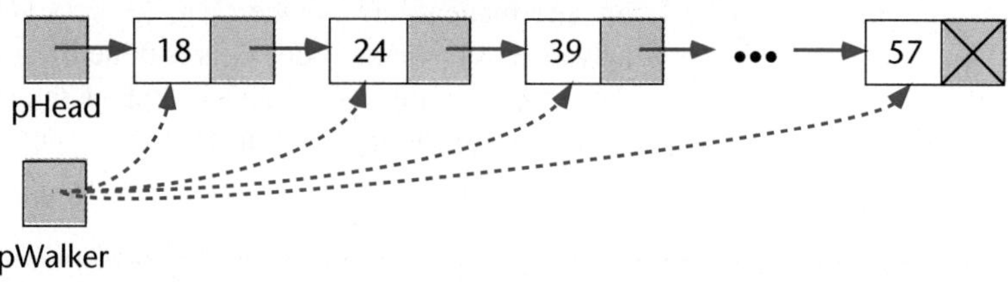

Figure 17-11 Linked list traversal

The basic logic to traverse a linked list is found in the pseudocode shown below. It incorporates two concepts. First, an event loop is used to guard against overrunning the end of the list. Second, after processing the current node, the looping pointer is advanced to the next element.

```
traverse (list)
1 Set pointer to the first node in list
2 while (not end of the list)
   1 process (current node)
   2 set pointer to next node
   3 end while
end traverse
```

Program 17-4 is a simple implementation of the traversal algorithm. It shows the basic logic used to print a linked list.

Program 17-4 Traverse linked list and print data

```
1 // Traverse a linked list
2    NODE* pWalker = pHead;
3    cout << "\nList contains:\n";
4
5    while (pWalker)
6       {
7        cout << setw(3) << pWalker->data.key << endl;
8        pWalker = pWalker->link;
9       } // while
```

The code in statement 5 is the most common form of pointer evaluation for a linked list. Study it carefully. C++ guarantees that the evaluation of a 0 pointer will be *false* and all other pointer values will evaluate to *true*. This expression is therefore equivalent to

```
while (pWalker != 0)
```

where `pWalker` is read as pointer to current node.

The other important piece of code in the traversal is in statement 8.

```
pWalker = pWalker->link;
```

This statement advances us through the list. If we forget it, our program will end up in a permanent loop. Since `pWalker` points to the current node, we must change it to advance to the next node. This is done by simply assigning the link field to `pWalker`. When we finally arrive at the end of the list, `link` is 0, which, when assigned to `pWalker`, terminates the *while* loop.

17-3 LINKED LIST DESIGN

Now that we have explained the basic operation of a linked list, we are ready to create a linked list object. Our basic linked list consists of two related objects: the list itself and the nodes in the list plus a third class, known as an iterator, that we use to traverse the list. While there are other designs that can be used to solve the problem, this approach is truer to the principles of object-oriented design.

THE NODE CLASS

The node class contains the node data and a link pointer to the next logical node. Recall from Chapter 11 that when two objects are related, one must be declared as a friend of the other. Because both the list and iterator classes must access the data in the node class, the node class declares them as friend classes. We code the node class first as shown in Program 17-5.

Program 17-5 Node class declaration and constructor

```
/* Node class declaration.
      Written by:
      Date:
*/
class Node
{
   private:
      int   key;
      Node* link;

      friend class List;
      friend class ListIterator;

      Node (int);            // constructor
}; // class Node

/* Node class constructor
      Pre  dataIn contains data to be stored
      Post dataIn stored in data--link set to 0
*/
Node :: Node (int dataIn)
{
```

Program 17-5 Node class declaration and constructor *(continued)*

```
   key  = dataIn;
   link = 0;
} // Node constructor
```

Program 17-5 Analysis The node class requires a constructor to set its data variable to the value passed to it and the link variable to 0 when a node is created. To hide the implementation of the linked list from the application, we declare the constructor private. This means that only the node's friends can call it; it cannot be called directly by the application.

THE LIST CLASS

Now that we have created the node class, we are ready to create the list class. The list must have a data structure, which is the node object, several local variables to store information about its state, and several functions to control its operation. For this example, we are keeping the design at a minimum, with only three variables, three private functions, and four public functions. The design is shown in Program 17-6.

Program 17-6 List class declaration

```
/* List class declaration.
      Written by:
      Date:
*/
class List
{
   private:
       Node* pHead;
       Node* pPre;          // pCur's predecessor
       Node* pCur;          // Current position in list

   friend class ListIterator;

   // Prototypes for private functions
   bool  addNode      (int item);
   void  deleteNode ();
   bool  searchList (int argument);

   public:
   // Prototypes for public functions
         List ();                           // constructor
        ~List ();                           // destructor
   int   addToList       (int dataIn);
   bool  deleteFromList (int key);
}; // class List
```

It is important to understand the relationship between these two objects. The list class controls all of the linked list updating. Its head pointer identifies the logical beginning of the linked list in the node class object when it is processed, such as for searching or traversing. Its functions insert data into the list and delete data from the list. On the other hand, the node class contains all of the data. These structural interrelationships are illustrated in Figure 17-12.

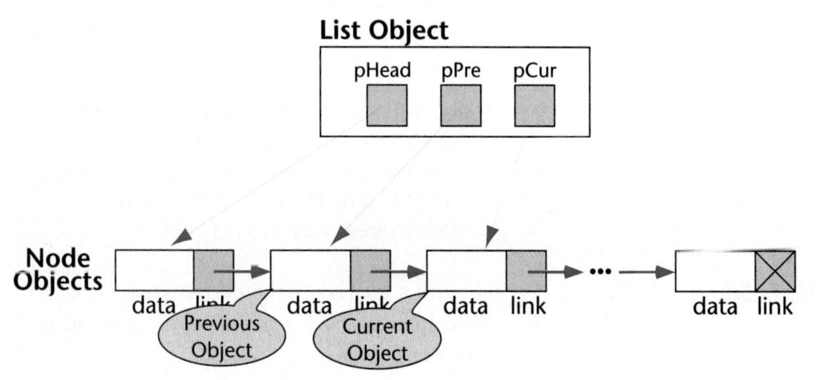

Figure 17-12 List and node interrelationships

List Constructor

The `List` constructor initializes the list's three pointer variables to 0. The code is given in Program 17-7.

Program 17-7 List constructor

```
/* Initializes linked list object.
     Pre   List object is being created by application
     Post  pointers set to 0
*/
List :: List ()
{
// Statements
   pHead = 0;
   pPre  = 0;
   pCur  = 0;
} // List constructor
```

Add to List

To insert a node into the list requires two add functions. The first is a public function that the user calls passing the data to be inserted. The second is a private function that physically creates a node and inserts the data.

Public: `addToList` We are now ready to write the public function to add a node to the list.The user passes the data to be inserted into the list as a parameter. The function then uses the private search function (see Program 17-12 on page 838) to locate the proper insertion point in the list and another private function to complete the insertion.

When data are being added to a list, we must make a decision regarding duplicate keys. Some lists allow duplicate data, while others do not. We assume that duplicate data are not allowed. If the search finds that the data are already in the list, therefore, it returns an error code (1). A second error condition arises when dynamic memory is full. In this case, we return a different error code (2). If the insertion is successful, then we return no error (0).

The `addToList` design is shown in Figure 17-13. The function code found in Program 17-8 is rather straightforward.

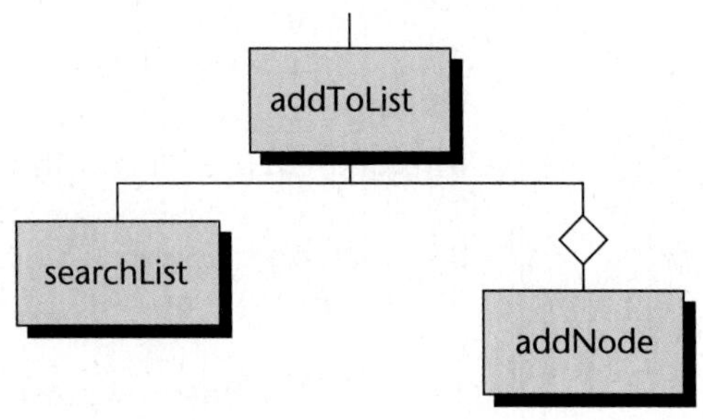

Figure 17-13 Design for `addToList`

Program 17-8 `addToList` **function**

```
/* This function adds data to the linked list.
      Pre    item contains data to be inserted
      Post   Data have been inserted in key sequence
      Return 0 if insertion successful
             1 if duplicate data
             2 if dynamic memory full
*/
int List :: addToList (int item)
{
   int success = 0;       // Default is sucessful
   if (searchList (item))
      success = 1;        // Found duplicate data
   else
      if (addNode (item) == false)
         success = 2;  // Memory overflow
   return success;
} // List addToList
```

Private: `addNode` On page 821, we presented the four steps required to insert a node into a linked list. For review:

1. Allocate memory for the new node.
2. Determine the insertion point.
3. Point the new node to its successor.
4. Point the predecessor to the new node.

These steps are seen in the `addNode` function shown in Program 17-9. With the exception of the error handling and return values, the code is identical to Program 17-1.

Program 17-9 `addNode` **function**

```
/* Private function that inserts node into linked list.
      Pre   addToList has set the pPre pointer to
            the insertion point
```

Program 17-9 `addNode` **function (*continued*)**

```
        Post  data have been inserted
*/
bool List :: addNode (int item)
{
   Node* pNew;
   try
       {
        pNew  = new Node (item);
       } // try
   catch (bad_alloc& err)
       {
        return false;
       } // catch

   if (pPre == 0)
       {
        // Adding before first node or to empty list
        pNew->link  = pHead;
        pHead       = pNew;
       } // if pPre == 0
   else
       {
        // Adding in middle or at end
        pNew->link = pPre->link;
        pPre->link = pNew;
      } // else
   return true;
} // List addNode
```

Delete from List

Deleting a node from a linked list also requires a public and a private function.

Public: `deleteFromList` The design to delete a node is straightforward: Given the key of the node to be removed, we search the list to set the current pointer in the list object to the delete location and then call the private delete function to do the physical deletion. The design is shown in Figure 17-14, and the code is given in Program 17-10.

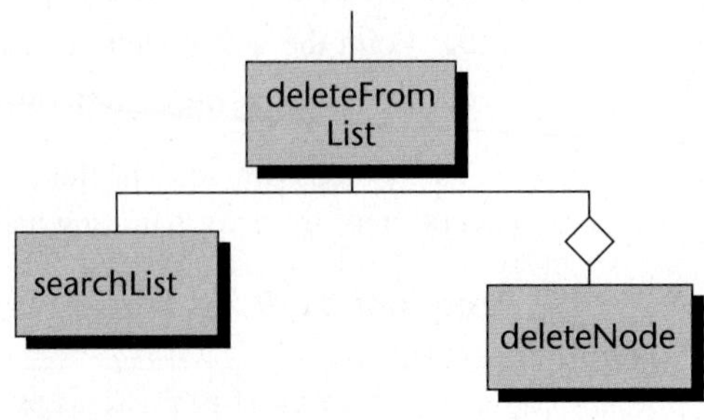

Figure 17-14 Design for *deleteFromList*

Program 17-10 Delete node from list

```
/* This function deletes a node from the linked list.
      Pre    key identifies data to be deleted
      Post   if found, the node has been deleted
      Return boolean: true if found, false if not
*/
bool List :: deleteFromList (int key)
{
   if (searchList (key))
      {
       deleteNode ();
       return true;
      } // if found
   else
      return false;                            // Not found
} // List deleteFromList
```

Program 17-10 Analysis The only possible error that we might encounter when deleting a node from a list is that the data to be deleted are not there. We therefore return a Boolean: *true* if we found and deleted the data, *false* if the data could not be found.

Private: `deleteNode` Once the deletion location is known, the code to delete a node from a linked list is very simple. All we have to do is determine if we are deleting the first node in the list, in which case the head pointer must be updated, or deleting some other node, in which case the predecessor's link field must be updated. After the delete, we also have to recycle the node's memory. The code, shown in Program 17-11, follows the design we created in Program 17-2 on page 828.

Program 17-11 Delete a node

```
/* Delete a node from a linked list.
      Pre    deleteFromList has set predecessor and
             current pointers
      Post   node deleted and recycled
*/
void List :: deleteNode ()
{
   if (pPre == 0)
      // Deleting first node
      pHead = pCur->link;
   else
      // Deleting other nodes
      pPre->link = pCur->link;
   delete (pCur);
   return;
} // List deleteNode
```

List Search

When we created the list class in Program 17-6 on page 833, we gave it three private variables: a pointer to the first node (`pHead`) and two search pointers, one to the current node (`pCur`) and one to its predecessor (`pPre`). To search the nodes in the class, we use the predecessor and current pointers in the list object. Note that in our simple example, there is no key, only data. The complete class search implementation is shown in Program 17-12. Compare it to the general linked-list search function shown in Program 17-3 on page 830.

Program 17-12 Search linked list class

```
/* Search nodes associated with list class.
      Pre   list exists
      Post  returns boolean true  if found
                                 false if not found
*/
bool List :: searchList (int target)
{
   pPre = 0;
   pCur = pHead;

   // Search until target <= list data
   while (pCur && target > pCur->key)
      {
       pPre = pCur;
       pCur = pCur->link;
      } // while
   // Determine if target found
   return (pCur && target == pCur->key);
} // List searchList
```

Program 17-12 Analysis The most important point to note in this function is how we use the predecessor and current pointers. First, they are found in the list object. Therefore, they are available to all functions that have access to the private variables in the class.

When we are adding data to the list, the predecessor must be set to the logical predecessor to the new data. Assuming that the data are not already in the list, that is exactly what this search does. It stops when the target is no longer greater than the current pointer, leaving the predecessor pointer pointing to the node with the largest data less than the new data.

Now look at how the search works when we use it to find the node to be deleted. In this case, the search stops when we locate the data. At the same time, the predecessor pointer is pointing to the node immediately before the delete node, which is what we must know for a delete.

List Destructor

The last function is the destructor. If the application creates the list object in the heap, then when it is deleted we must make sure that any nodes still in the list are also deleted. Therefore, we write a destructor function, as shown in Program 17-13.

Program 17-13 List destructor

```
/* Delete nodes remaining in list before it is destroyed.
      Pre   object being destroyed
      Post  all nodes deleted from dynamic memory
*/
List :: ~List ()
{
   Node* pTemp;
   Node* pDelete = pHead;
   while (pDelete)
      {
       pTemp   = pDelete->link;
       delete  (pDelete);
       pDelete = pTemp;
      } // while
} // List destructor
```

THE CLASS ITERATOR

To process the entire list, we must provide the traversal logic presented in Program 17-4 on page 831. When the implementation of the data structure is hidden in the node class, however, the application does not have access to the predecessor, current, and next pointers. Furthermore, when we are inside the list class where we can access the pointers, we have no access to the data—the class doesn't know what the application data look like. This presents us with a dilemma: Outside the node we don't know how the data structure works, and inside the list we don't know how the data are formatted.

Fortunately, there is a solution—the **class iterator**. An iterator object has the ability to start at the beginning of the list and "visit" each node in turn. In other words, it provides the capability to iterate (loop) through the data structure. Figure 17-15 demonstrates the relationships among the list class, node class, and iterator class.

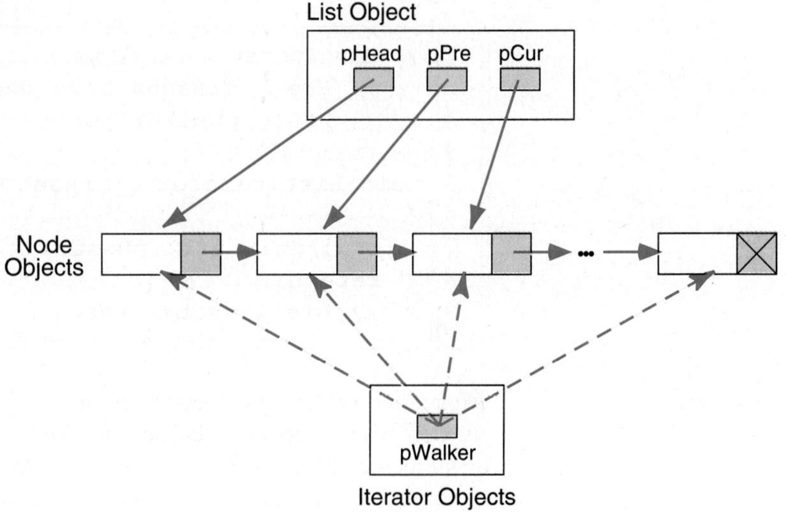

Figure 17-15 Iterator, list, and node objects

A typical iterator has four processes that it must perform:

1. Set the processing to start at the first element of the list.
2. Determine if the current element contains data or is 0.
3. Access the data at the current position.
4. Advance the list to the next element.

The design of the class iterator is shown in Program 17-14.

Program 17-14 Iterator class design

```
// =============== class ListIterator ===============
class ListIterator
{
   private:
      Node *pWalker;

   public:
         void  reset       (List& pList);
         int   operator*   ( ) const;
         bool  operator!   ( ) const;
   const Node* operator++ (int);
}; // ListIterator
```

Reset Iterator

Iteration requires the ability to set the processing to the beginning of the list. This is the same as opening a file. C++ provides this capability with a reset function. This function receives one parameter, a pointer to the list class, sets the walker pointer to the beginning of the list, and returns nothing. The code for the reset function is shown in Program 17-15.

Program 17-15 Code for start iterator

```
/* ListIterator reset sets iterator to start processing.
      Pre   classes have been defined
      Post  pWalker points to first node of list
*/
void ListIterator :: reset (List& list)
{
   pWalker = list.pHead;
   return;
}  // ListIterator reset
```

Advance List

After a node has been processed, the application must advance to the next node. If the list were in an array, we would advance the list by adding 1 to the current index, usually using the postfix increment operator (++). We have chosen to override this operator, therefore, to advance through the list. The advance iterator function is shown in Program 17-16.

Program 17-16 Code for advance iterator

```
1  /* ListIterator operator++ advances node pointer 1 element
2        Pre    classes have been defined
3        Post  pWalker points to next node in linked list
4  */
5  const Node* ListIterator :: operator++ (int)
6  {
7     if (pWalker)
8        pWalker = pWalker->link;
9     return pWalker;
10 }  // ListIterator operator++
```

Program 17-16 Analysis In this code, two points merit discussion. First, note how we guard against the application program's trying to advance beyond the end of the list. If `pWalker` is null, the application is trying to advance beyond the end of the list, which is a logic error. In this case, we simply return the current contents of `pWalker`, which are a null pointer. The calling function must then test the return value to verify a successful delete.

Second, study statement 5 carefully. It is reproduced below.

```
const Node* ListIterator :: operator++ (int)
```

What is unusual about this statement? While it is a function definition header, the parameter does not have an identifier. Therefore, we can not use the parameter in the function. In fact, the integer parameter type is there for only one reason: To tell the compiler that this operator overloads the postfix increment, not the prefix increment. This is one of those rather obscure C++ syntax rules that are so difficult to remember. For more discussion, see "Postfix Increment and Decrement Operators" on page 546.

End of List

As the application advances through the list, it eventually gets to the end of the list. As we have seen, the end of a linked list is identified by a 0 pointer, which must be checked in each loop iteration. Because this 0 test is usually done with the *not* operator, we overload it to represent the null iterator. The code for end of list is shown in Program 17-17.

Program 17-17 Code for end of list

```
/* ListIterator operator! determines if pWalker is
   pointing to a valid node.
      Pre     classes have been defined
      Return true if pWalker points to valid node
             false if pWalker 0
*/
bool ListIterator :: operator! () const
{
   return pWalker != 0;
}  // ListIterator operator!
```

Access Node Data

To retrieve the data from the list, we use the dereference operator (*). Because our list class contains integer data, the dereference operator is designed to return an integer. If the data were in a structure, we would return the structure type. The code for accessing the data is presented in Program 17-18.

Program 17-18 Code for accessing node data

```
/* ListIterator operator* returns data in current node.
     Pre    classes have been defined
     Return data (integer)
*/
int ListIterator :: operator* () const
{
   if (!pWalker)
      {
       cout << "\a**ERR 105: Invalid list reference";
       exit (105);
      } // if
   return pWalker->key;
} // ListIterator operator*
```

Program 17-18 Analysis Once again, note how we guard against the application program's trying to access data when `pWalker` is 0. In the advance and dereference functions, we must guard against the function's being called when `pWalker` is invalid. We therefore check to make sure that `pWalker` is valid before using it and abort the program if it isn't.

17-4 PROGRAMMING EXAMPLE—LINKED LIST AVERAGE

We have now built the class objects needed to insert data into a linked list. In this section, we turn our attention to using the linked list class with a program that builds a linked list and then traverses it to compute the average of the nodes in the list. Since this is a test driver,[2] we simply generate 100 random numbers and insert them into the list. Once the linked list has been built, we print the list and then compute the average of the data and print it. The program design is shown in Figure 17-16.

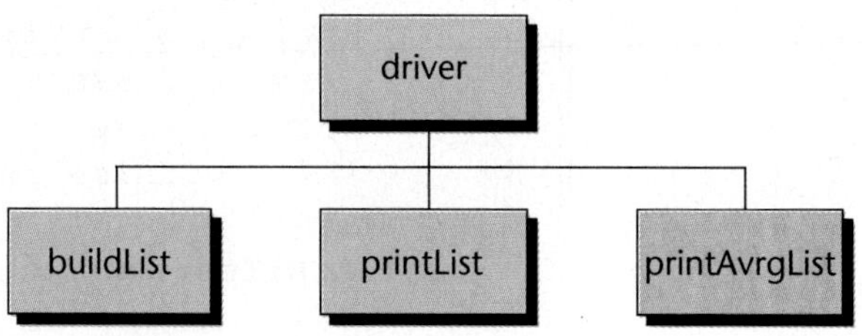

Figure 17-16 Design for linked list average

[2]A test driver is a program that is used to test generalized software as opposed to a program that solves a user problem.

Program 17-19 was built using the linked list class. To support linked lists, we put the linked list class, declarations, and functions in a user header file, `ListClas.h` (see statement 13). The global definitions and *main* are also shown in Program 17-19.

Program 17-19 Average driver with global definitions

```
1  /* Test driver to validate List class. It generates 100
2     random numbers in the range 1 to 500 and inserts them
3     into a linked list. After the list is built, it
4     prints the list and the average of its data.
5        Written by:
6        Date:
7  */
8  #include <iostream>
9  #include <iomanip>
10 #include <cstdlib>
11 using namespace std;
12 
13 #include "ListClas.h"
14 
15 // Prototype Declarations
16 void buildList       (List& list);
17 void printAvrgList   (List& list);
18 void printList       (List& list);
19 
20 // Global Constants
21 const int LIST_SIZE = 100;
22 const int LINE_SIZE =  10;
23 
24 int main ()
25 {
26    cout << "Begin List test driver\n\n";
27 
28    List list;
29    buildList      (list);
30    printList      (list);
31    printAvrgList (list);
32 
33    cout << "\nEnd List test driver\n";
34    return 0;
35 } // main
```

Program 17-19 Analysis The *main* function in our test driver consists of only three function calls: the first to build the list, the second to print it, and the third to calculate and print the average. As a good programming practice, we also include a start and end program print statement.

BUILD LINKED LIST

So that we don't have to enter 100 numbers from the keyboard, we build the list by generating 100 random numbers inserting them into the linked list. As shown in

Program 17-8 on page 835, the addToList function returns one of three success indicators. If the data are inserted successfully, it returns 0. If the data to be inserted match data already in the list, it does not insert the data and returns 1. Finally, if dynamic memory is full, it returns 2. Our buildList function tests to make sure the data were inserted successfully, and if they weren't, it takes appropriate action. The code is shown in Program 17-20.

Program 17-20 Build linked list

```
/* ================== buildList ==================
   Creates linked list of 100 random numbers.
      Pre  list is an empty list object
      Post list has been filled
*/
void buildList (List& list)
{
   srand (997);

   int  datum;
   int  result;
   for (int looper = 0; looper < LIST_SIZE; looper++)
      {
       datum  = rand() % 500 + 1;
       result = list.addToList (datum);
       if (result == 1)
         cerr << "Duplicate data: " << datum << endl;
       else if (result == 2)
          {
           cerr << "\a\aERR 200: Memory Overflow\n";
           exit (200);
          } // else if
      } // for looper
   return;
} // buildList
```

PRINT LIST

The function used to print the list and the function used to print the list average both use the list iterator. The first call to the iterator class sets its walker pointer to the beginning of the list. We then loop as long as we have a node to print. Because our data consist of only integers, we print up to 10 integers on one line. Before printing the data, therefore, we test to see if the line is full. Note that we use a global constant to control the number of values in a line, which makes the program very flexible.

To print the data, we use the dereference operator with the iterator. While this appears to be a standard pointer dereference, it is not. The list iterator class overloads the dereference operator. In this case, the operator invokes a list iterator function that returns the data at the current position in the list, which is then printed.

After we have printed the data, we again use an overloaded operator, this time the postfix increment (++). Once again, this looks like standard pointer arithmetic, but it actually invokes a list iterator function that advances the pointer to the next node in the list. The print logic can be seen in Program 17-21.

Program 17-21 Print linked list

```
1  /* ================== printList ==================
2     Given a linked list of integers, print the data
3     ten integers to a line.
4        Pre   list has been created
5        Post  data in list printed
6  */
7  void printList (List& list)
8  {
9     ListIterator listWalker;
10    listWalker.reset(list);
11
12    int lineCount = 0;
13    while (!listWalker)
14       {
15        if (lineCount == LINE_SIZE)
16           {
17            cout << endl;
18            lineCount = 1;
19           } // if lineCount
20        else
21           lineCount++;
22        cout << setw(5) << *listWalker;
23        listWalker++;
24       } // while
25    cout << endl;
26    return;
27 }  // printList
```

Program 17-21 Analysis Carefully study the *while* loop, which begins with statement 13. Now compare it to the traditional linked list logic shown next.

```
pWalker = pHead;
while (pWalker != 0)
   {
    ...
    ...
    pWalker = pWalker->link;
   } // while pWalker
```

The logic is identical, but the notation is significantly different. The important point in this function is how we use the iterator. To set the starting point in the loop, we use `listWalker.reset()`. The loop is controlled by testing the iterator for a non-0 value using the not operator(!) in statement 13. Then, to access the data in the loop, we use the dereference operator with the iterator variable in statement 22. Finally, to advance the node pointer, we use the increment operator (see statement 23).

PRINT LIST AVERAGE

The last function in our linked list driver uses the iterator class to add all of the values in the linked list. After it has processed all of the data, it computes the average and prints it. The code is shown in Program 17-22.

Program 17-22 Print linked list average with results

```
/* ================ printAvrgList ================
   Given a linked list of integers, print the average
   of all data.
      Pre   list has been created
      Post  average printed
*/
void printAvrgList (List& list)
{
   ListIterator listWalker;
   listWalker.reset(list);

   int count = 0;
   int sum   = 0;
   while (!listWalker)
      {
       sum += *listWalker;
       count++;
       listWalker++;
      } // while

   float avrg;
   if (count)
      avrg = (float)sum / count;
   else
      avrg = 0;
   cout << "\nTotal value: " << sum
        << "\n        for  " << count << " items."
        << "\nAverage is:  " << avrg  << endl;
   return;
} // printAvrgList
```

```
Results:
Begin List test driver

Duplicate data: 202
Duplicate data: 421
Duplicate data: 310
Duplicate data: 44
Duplicate data: 378
Duplicate data: 421
Duplicate data: 247
Duplicate data: 104
Duplicate data: 180
Duplicate data: 375
    5   11   14   17   23   32   34   37   44   49
   56   62   72   73   76   78   80   87   98  100
  104  108  111  127  134  158  170  174  180  183
  196  198  202  203  227  235  246  247  255  259
  262  264  265  272  273  275  277  296  304  305
```

Program 17-22 Print linked list average with results *(continued)*

```
    306  310  322  323  331  332  335  337  341  343
    348  362  364  365  366  370  371  375  378  379
    382  383  388  392  400  408  412  421  434  436
    438  442  447  458  460  463  464  479  487  489

   Total value: 23199
          for   90 items.
   Average is:  257.767

   End List test driver
```

Program 17-22 Analysis This program is rather simple. More interesting than the program itself, however, are the results at the end of the program. Recall that as we built the list, we rejected any data that duplicated data already in the list. We see that of the 100 random numbers we generated, only 90 were inserted into the list. The duplicates are shown in the result.

From the duplicate rejections, it is obvious that the numbers were being generated in a random fashion. When we print the list, however, we note that the data are now in sequence. This is because the list class builds the list in key sequence, which for our simple example is the same as the data sequence.

As a final note, we used the global constant that controls the list size to test the program. Rather than laboriously adding 90 numbers to compute the average, we ran the program with only 10 random numbers. This made it easy to validate that the list iterator was indeed processing all of the data for our average.

17-5 SOFTWARE ENGINEERING AND PROGRAMMING STYLE

In this chapter, we discuss a general software engineering topic, quality, which can be applied to any topic, including classes. You will find no one who would even consider minimizing software quality—at least publicly. Everyone wants the best software available, and to listen to the creators of systems on the market, their systems are all perfect. Yet, as software users, we often feel that quality software is a contradiction in terms. We all have our favorite software products, but not one of them is without a wart or two.

Since you are now learning how to be one of those software creators, you need to be aware of the basic concepts of software quality. In this section, we discuss some of the attributes of a quality product and how to go about achieving quality.

QUALITY DEFINED

Quality software is defined as:

> **Software that satisfies the users' explicit and implicit requirements, is well documented, meets the operating standards of the organization, and runs efficiently on the hardware for which it was developed**

Every one of these attributes of good software falls squarely on you, the system designer and programmer. Note that we place on you the burden of satisfying not only the users' explicit requirements but also their implicit needs. Often users don't fully know what they need. In such a case, it is your job to determine their implicit requirements, which are hidden in the background. This is a formidable task indeed.

Of course, it is also your job to document the software. If you are lucky, you will have a technical writer to help, but even if you do, the final product is still your responsibility. And as an analyst and programmer, you are expected to know the standards of your organization and to implement them properly.

Finally, it is your program, so you are responsible for its efficiency. This means that you are expected to use appropriate and efficient algorithms. This was the focus of our discussion in Chapters 6 and 8 when we talked about analyzing algorithms and the big-O theory.

But quality software is not just a vague concept. If we want to attain it, we have to be able to measure it. Whenever possible, these measurements should be quantitative; that is, they should be numerically measurable. For example, if an organization is serious about quality, it should be able to tell you the number of errors (bugs) per thousand lines of code and the mean time between failures for every software system it maintains. These are measurable statistics.

On the other hand, some of the measurements may be qualitative, meaning that they cannot be measured numerically. Flexibility and testability are examples of qualitative software measurements. Being qualitative does not necessarily mean that they can't be measured, but rather that they rely on someone's judgment in some way.

QUALITY FACTORS

Software quality can be divided into three broad measures, or **quality factors**: operability, maintainability, and transferability. Each of these measures can be further broken down, as shown in Figure 17-17.

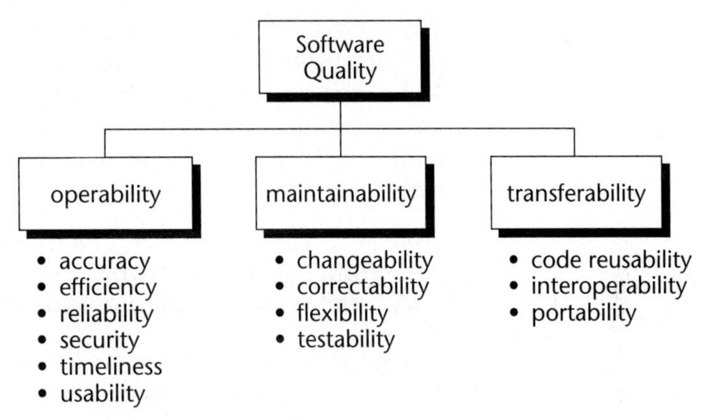

Figure 17-17 Software quality

Operability

Operability refers to the basic operation of a system. The first thing a user notices about a system is its "look and feel." This means, especially for an online, interactive system, how easy and intuitive it is to use. Does it fit well into the operating system it is running under? For example, if it is running in a windows environment, its pull-down and pop-up menus should work the same way the operating system's menus do. In short, operability answers the question, "How does it drive?"

But these factors are subjective; they are not measurable. So let's look at the factors that comprise operability. They are listed alphabetically.

Accuracy A system that is not accurate is worse than no system at all. Most workers would rather rely on intuition and experience than on a system that they know gives false and misleading information.

Any system that you develop, therefore, must be thoroughly tested, both by you (whitebox) and by a systems test engineer and the user (blackbox). If you get the opportunity, take a course on software testing. There are many "tricks of the trade" that will help you.

Accuracy can be measured by such metrics as mean time between failures, number of bugs per thousand lines of code, and number of user requests for change.

Efficiency Efficiency is, by and large, a subjective term. In some cases the user will specify a performance standard, such as that a real-time response must be received within 1 second, 95% of the time. This is certainly measurable.

Reliability Reliability is really the sum of the other factors. If users count on the system to get their job done and are confident in it, then it is most likely reliable. On the other hand, some measures speak directly to a system's reliability, most notably, mean time between failures.

Security How secure a system is refers to how easy it is for unauthorized persons to get at systems data. Although this is a subjective area, there are checklists that assist in assessing the system's security. For example, does the system have and require passwords to identify users?

Timeliness Does the system deliver its output in a timely fashion? For online systems, does the response time satisfy the users' requirements? For batch systems, are the reports delivered in a timely fashion? It is also possible, if the system has good auditability, to determine if the data in the system are timely; that is, are data recorded within a reasonable time after the activity that creates them takes place?

Usability This is another area that is highly subjective. The best measure of usability is to watch the users and see if they are using the system. User interviews will often reveal problems with the usability of a system.

Maintainability

Maintainability refers to keeping a system up-to-date and running correctly. Many systems require regular changes, not because they were poorly implemented but because of changes in external factors. For example, the payroll system for a company must be changed yearly, if not more often, to meet changes in government laws and regulations.

Changeability How easy it is to change a system is a subjective factor. Experienced project leaders, however, are able to estimate how long a requested change will take. If it takes too long, it may well be because the system is difficult to change. This is especially true of older systems.

There are software measurement tools in the field today that can estimate a program's complexity and structure. They should be used regularly, and if a program's complexity is high, it is a good candidate for rewriting. Programs that have been changed many times over the years have often lost their structured focus and are difficult to change. They also should be rewritten.

Correctability One measure of correctability is mean time to recovery, which is the measure of how long it takes to get a program back in operation when it fails. Although this is a reactive definition, there are currently no predictors of how long it will take to correct a program after it fails.

Flexibility Users are constantly requesting changes in systems. This qualitative attribute attempts to measure how easy it is to make these changes. If a program must be completely rewritten to effect a change, it is not flexible. Fortunately, this factor became less of a problem with the advent of structured programming.

Testability You might think that this would be a highly subjective area, but a test engineer actually has a checklist of factors that can be used to assess a program's testability.

Transferability

Transferability refers to the ability to move data and/or a system from one platform to another and to reuse code. In many situations, it is not an important factor. On the other hand, if you are writing generalized software, it can be critical.

Code Reusability If functions are written so that they can be reused in different programs and on different projects, then they are highly reusable. Good programmers build libraries of reusable functions that they can use when they need to solve a similar problem.

Interoperability This factor addresses the capability of sending data to other systems. In today's highly integrated systems, it is a desirable attribute. In fact, it has become so important that operating systems now support the ability to move data between systems, such as between a word processor and a spreadsheet.

Portability Portability addresses the ability to move software from one hardware platform to another; for example, from a Macintosh to a Windows environment or from an IBM mainframe to a VAX environment.

THE QUALITY CIRCLE

The first and most important point to recognize about quality is that it must be designed into a system. It can't be added as an afterthought. Attention to quality begins at step 1, determining the user requirements, and continues throughout the life of the system. Since quality is a continuous concept that, like a circle, never ends, we refer to it as the **quality circle.**

There are six steps to quality software: quality tools, technical reviews, formal testing, change control, standards, and measurement and reporting. These steps are shown graphically in Figure 17-18.

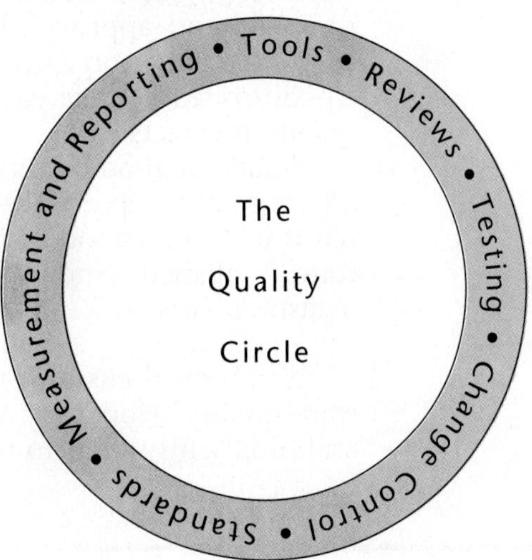

Figure 17-18 The quality circle

While no one can deny that quality begins with the software engineers assigned to the team, these professionals need quality tools to develop a quality product. Fortunately, today's development tools are excellent. A whole suite of quality tools known as computer-aided software engineering (CASE) guides software development through requirements, design, programming and testing, and into production. For the programmer there are workstations that not only assist in writing the program but also in testing and debugging. For example, it is possible to track tests through a program and then determine which statements were executed and which were not. Tools such as this are invaluable for whitebox testing.

Another major step in quality software is the technical review. These reviews should be conducted at every step in the development process, including requirements, design, programming, and testing. A typical program review begins after the programmer has designed the data structures and structure chart for a program. A design review board consisting of the systems analyst, test engineer, user representative, and one or two peers is then convened. Note that no one from management is allowed to attend a technical review. During the review, the programmer explains the approach and discusses interfaces to other programs while the reviewers ask questions and make suggestions.

Quality also requires formal testing. Formal testing assures that programs work together as a system and meet the defined requirements. After the programmer has completed unit testing, the program is turned over to another software engineer for integration and system testing. For a small project, this is most likely the systems analyst and/or the user. For a large project, there is usually a separate testing team.

Large systems take months and sometimes years to develop. It is only natural that over extended periods of time, changes to the requirements and design will be necessary. To ensure quality, each change should be reviewed and approved by a change control board. The impact of a requested change on each program must be assessed and properly planned. Uncontrolled change causes schedule and budget overruns and poor-quality products.

Finally, a good quality environment measures all aspects of quality and regularly reports the results. Without measurement, you cannot tell if quality is good or bad, improving or deteriorating. At the same time, published standards provide the yardstick for many of the quality measurements.

CONCLUSION

In this short discussion, we have only introduced the concept of software quality. Hopefully you will consider these points as you design and program systems in the future.

17-6 TIPS AND COMMON PROGRAMMING ERRORS

1. The link field in the last node of a linked list must always have a 0 value.
2. Memory must be allocated for a node before you add the node to a linked list.
3. It is a logic error to forget to delete memory after you delete a node. The memory is lost for the rest of the program's execution.

4. You must create an empty linked list (by assigning 0 to the head pointer) before using the functions introduced in this chapter.
5. Remember that a 0 link means there is no pointer; therefore, you cannot use it to dereference another node (or any other object). For example, the following code creates a run-time error because when the loop terminates, the value of `pCur` is 0:

```
while (pCur != 0)
    {
     ...
     ...
     pCur = pCur->link;
    }
cout << pCur->data.member_name;          // ERROR
```

6. It is a logic error to allocate a node in the heap and not test for overflow.
7. It is a logic error to refer to a node after its memory has been released with *delete*.
8. It is a logic error to set a pointer to 0 before the node has been deleted. The node is irretrievably lost.
9. It is a logic error to delete a node from a linked list without verifying that the node contains the target of the delete.
10. It is a logic error to fail to set the head pointer to the new node when a node is added before the first node in a linked list. The new node is irretrievably lost.
11. It is a logic error to update the link field in the predecessor to a new node before pointing the new node to its logical successor. This error will result in a never-ending loop the next time the list is traversed, and the rest of the list is lost.
12. It is a logic error to fail to set the link field in the last node to 0. This will result in the next traversal's running off the end of the list.
13. It is a potential logic error to use the node pointer in a linked list search before testing it for a 0 pointer. In the following statement, the Boolean operands must be reversed to prevent an invalid memory access.

```
while (pCur->data.key < target && pCur != 0)
```

17-7 KEY TERMS

add node
chain
class iterator
delete node
empty linked list
head pointer
key
link
linked list
list traversal
maintainability
node
operability
overflow
quality circle
quality factor
self-referential structure
transferability

17-8 SUMMARY

- A linked list is a collection of nodes in which each element contains the address of the next node.
- The link in each node, except the last, points to its successor.
- An empty linked list can be defined as a single pointer having the value of 0.
- A node in a linked list is a structure with at least two fields: one data field and one link field.
- A node in a linked list is self-referential because it contains a pointer to another structure of its type.
- To add a node to a linked list, we must allocate memory locations for the new node, determine the insertion location, point the new node to its successor, and point the predecessor pointer to the new node.
- To process the nodes in a linked list, we use three pointer variables: `pPre`, `pCur`, and `pWalker`.
- Traversing a linked list means going through a linked list, node by node, and processing each node—for example, counting the number of nodes, printing the contents of nodes, and summing the values of some fields.
- Traversing a linked list can be in full or in part. For example, we can print the value of the *n*th node in a linked list if we traverse the first $n - 1$ nodes.
- There are four different cases when we add a node: adding to an empty list, adding at the beginning, adding at the middle, and adding at the end of the list.
- Deleting a node means removing a node from the list. There are two general cases when we delete a node: deleting the first node and deleting any other node.
- Before using functions to add or delete a node, we need to use another primitive function to find the location of the action.
- Two upper-level functions were introduced in this chapter: `addToList` and `deleteFromList`. These functions use the add, delete, and search primitive functions to actually insert a node into or remove a node from a linked list.
- To design a linked list, we have defined three classes: node class, list class, and iterator class.
- The node class contains the node data and a link pointer to the next node.
- The list class contains the `pHead`, `pPre`, and `pCur` pointers.
- The iterator class contains the `pWalker` pointer that allows us to traverse the linked list.
- In software engineering, quality factors are the attributes that a piece of software must have to be considered quality software.
- Quality factors are defined as operability, maintainability, and transferability.
- One of the most important points about the quality of software is that quality must be designed into the system; it cannot be added as an afterthought.

17-9 PRACTICE SETS

REVIEW QUESTIONS

1. Each element in a linked list must contain data and a link field.
   a. True
   b. False
2. All linked lists require a head pointer to identify the beginning of the list.
   a. True
   b. False
3. The first step in adding a node to a linked list is to allocate memory for the new node.
   a. True
   b. False
4. For efficiency, searching a linked list should use the binary search.
   a. True
   b. False

5. A(n) __________ is an ordered collection of data in which each element contains the location of the next element.
   a. Array
   b. Node
   c. File
   d. Structure
   e. Linked list
6. Which of the following statements about linked lists is false?
   a. A linked list is an ordered collection of data.
   b. Each node in a linked list must contain at least one pointer.
   c. Nodes in a linked list must be structures.
   d. The link field in a linked list always points to a successor.
   e. The sequence of a link list is controlled by the link fields.
7. A(n) __________ identifies the first logical node in a linked list.
   a. Array identifier
   b. Head pointer
   c. List identifier
   d. Structure variable identifier
   e. Structure tag
8. Which of the following is not a step in adding a node to a linked list?
   a. Allocate memory for the new node
   b. Determine the insertion point
   c. Point the new node to the successor
   d. Point the predecessor to the new node
   e. Traverse the list
9. Which of the following statements about linked list deletes is false?
   a. Deletion of a node from the middle of the list requires that its predecessor be changed.
   b. Deletion of the first node requires that the head pointer be changed.
   c. Deletion of the rear node requires a separate test to set the predecessor's link to 0.
   d. Deletion physically removes a node from the list.
   e. The deleted node must be recycled.

EXERCISES

10. Imagine we have the linked list shown in Figure 17-19. Show what will happen if we apply the following statement to this linked list:

```
pHead = pHead -> link;
```

What is the problem with using this kind of statement? Does it justify the need for the two walking pointers (pPre and pCur) that we introduced in the text?

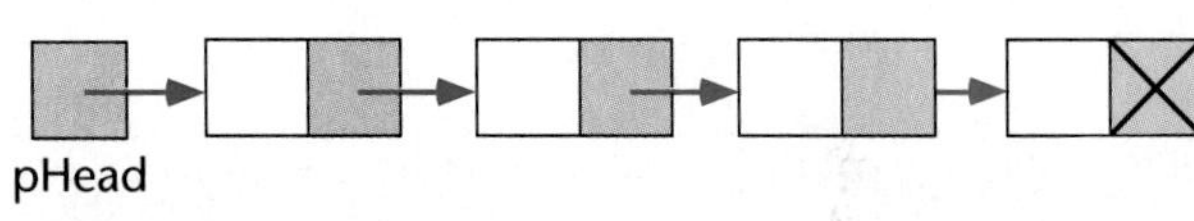

Figure 17-19 Linked list for Exercise 10

11. Imagine we have the linked list shown in Figure 17-20. As discussed in "Search Linked List" on page 828, the search must be able to pass back both the location of the predecessor (pPre) and the location of the current (pCur) node based on search criteria.

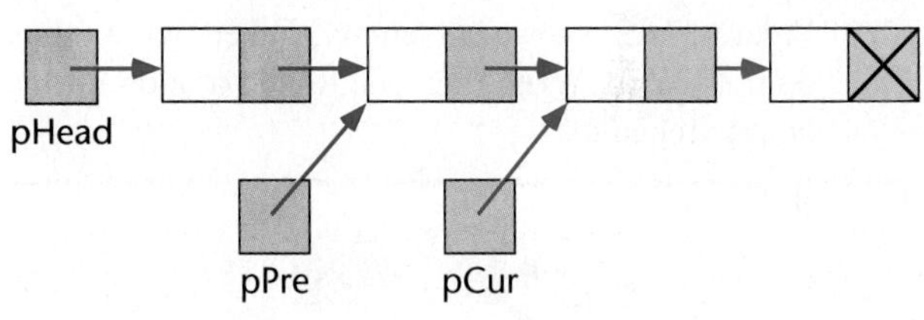

Figure 17-20 Linked list for Exercise 11

The following code to set pPre and pCur contains a common error. Determine what it is and how it should be corrected. (Hint: What are the contents of these pointers at the beginning of the search?)

```
pCur = pCur -> link;
pPre = pPre -> link;
```

12. Imagine we have a dummy node at the beginning of a linked list. The dummy node does not carry any data. It is not the first data node; it is an empty node. Figure 17-21 shows a linked list with a dummy node. Write the code to delete the first node (the node after the dummy node) in the linked list.

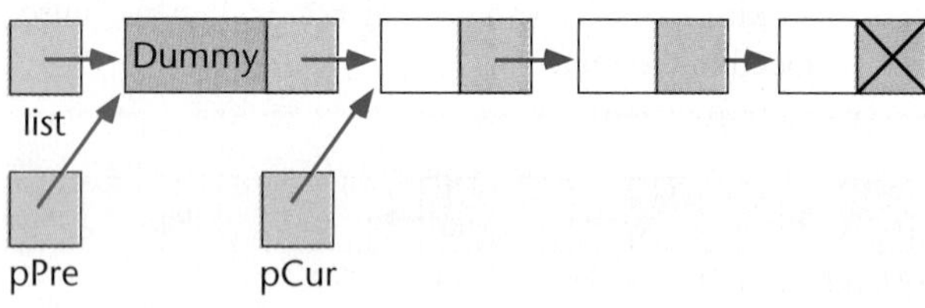

Figure 17-21 Linked list for Exercise 12

13. Write the code to delete a node in the middle of a linked list with the dummy node (see Exercise 12). Compare this answer with your answer to Exercise 12. Are they the same? What do you conclude? Does the dummy node simplify the operation on a linked list? How?
14. Figure 17-22 shows an empty linked list with a dummy node. Write the code to add a node to this empty linked list.

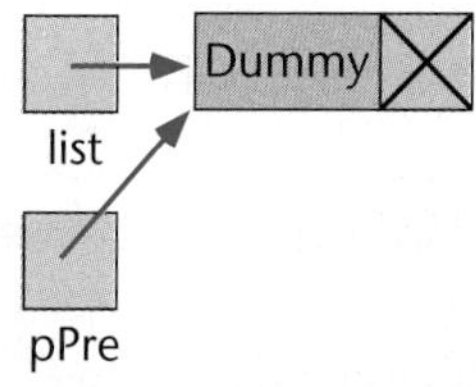

Figure 17-22 Linked list for Exercise 14

15. Write the statements to add a node in the middle of a linked list with the dummy node (see Exercise 12). Compare this answer with your answer to Exercise 14 Are they the same? What do you conclude? Does the dummy node simplify the operation on a linked list? How?
16. Imagine we have the two linked lists shown in Figure 17-23. What would happen if we applied the following statement to these two lists?

```
list1 = list2;
```

17. Show what would happen if we applied the following statements to the two lists in Exercise 16.

```
temp = list1;
```

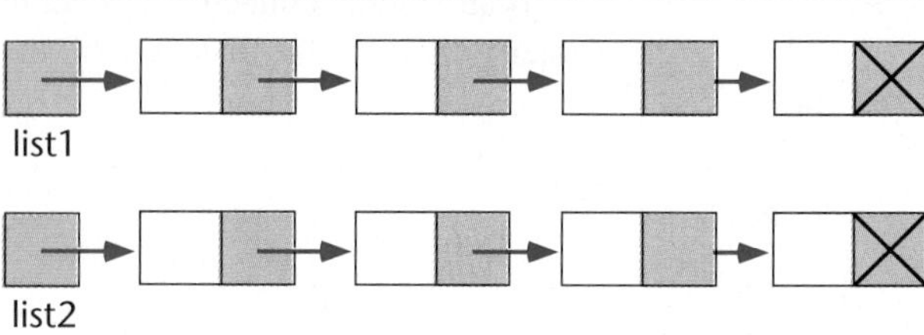

Figure 17-23 Linked lists for Exercise 16

```
while ( temp -> link != 0 )
    temp = temp -> link;
temp->link = list2;
```

18. Imagine we have the linked list shown in Figure 17-24. What would happen if we applied the following statements to this list?

```
temp = list;
while (temp -> link != 0)
    temp = temp -> link;
temp->link = list;
```

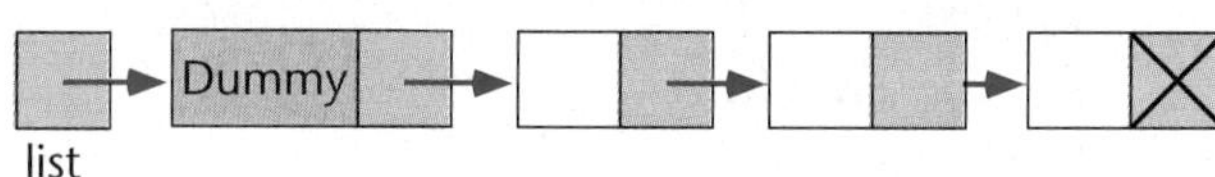

Figure 17-24 Linked list for Exercise 18

PROBLEMS

19. Write a program that reads a list of integers from the keyboard, creates a linked list from them, and prints the result.
20. Write a function that accepts the linked list from problem 19, traverses it, and returns the data in the node with the minimum key value.
21. Write a function that traverses the linked list from Problem 19 and deletes all nodes whose keys are negative.
22. Write a function that traverses the linked list from Problem 19 and deletes any node that immediately follows a node with a negative key.
23. Write a function that traverses the linked list from Problem 19 and deletes any node that is immediately preceded by a node with a negative key.
24. Write a program that creates a two-dimensional linked list. The nodes in the first column contain only two pointers, as shown in Figure 17-25. The left pointer points to the next row. The right pointer points to the data in the row.

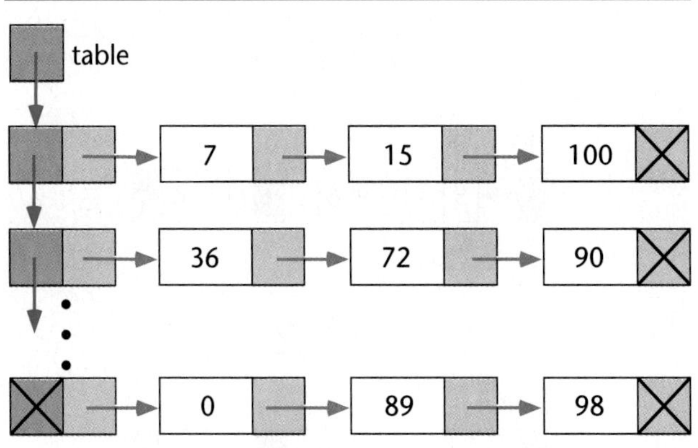

Figure 17-25 Linked list structure for Problem 24

25. We can simplify most of the algorithms in this chapter using a linked list with a dummy node at the beginning as shown in Figure 17-26.

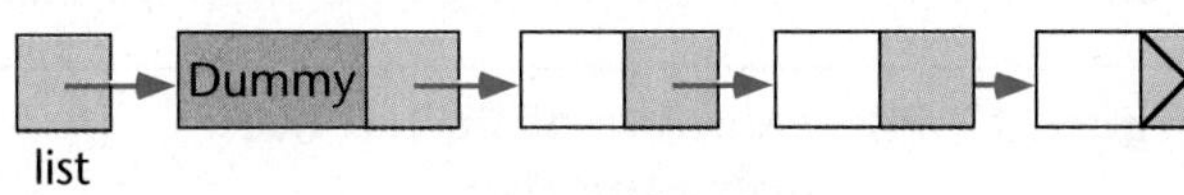

Figure 17-26 Linked list for Problem 25

Rewrite the function `addNode` (see Program 17-1 on page 825) using a linked list with a dummy node.

26. Rewrite the function `deleteNode` (see Program 17-2 on page 828) using a linked list with a dummy node.
27. Rewrite the function `searchList` (see Program 17-3 on page 830) using a linked list with a dummy node.
28. Write a function that returns a pointer to the last node in a linked list.
29. Write a function that appends two linked lists together.
30. Write a function that appends a linked list to itself.
31. Write a function that swaps (exchanges) two nodes in a linked list. The nodes are identified by number and are passed as parameters. If the exchange is successful, the function is to return true. If it encounters an error, such as an invalid node number, it returns false.

PROJECTS

32. Write a program that builds a linked list of 100 random numbers. After the list is built, display it on the monitor.
33. Write a program that reads a file and builds a linked list. After the list is built, display it on the monitor. You may use any appropriate data structure, but it is to have a key field and data. Two possibilities are a list of your favorite CDs or your friends' telephone numbers.
34. Modify the program you wrote in Project 33. After the file has been created, the program is to present the user with a menu to insert new data, remove existing data, or print a list of all data.
35. Write a program to read a list of students from a file and create a linked list. Each entry in the linked list is to have the student's name, a pointer to the next student, and a pointer to a linked list of scores. There may be up to four scores for each student. A picture of the structure is shown in Figure 17-27.

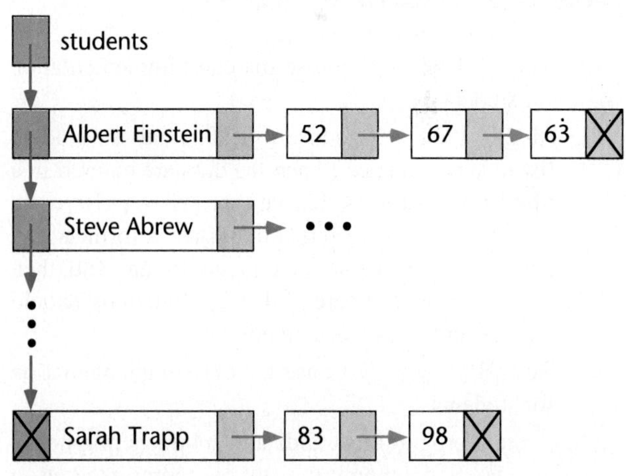

Figure 17-27 Data structure for Project 35

The program is to initialize the student list by reading the students' names from the text file and creating null scores lists. It then loops through the list, prompting the user to enter the scores for each student. The scores prompt is to include the name of the student.

After all scores have been entered, the program is to print the scores for each student along with the score total and average score. The average is to include only those scores present.

The data for each student are shown in Table 17-2.

Student name	Score 1	Score 2	Score 3	Score 4
Albert Einstein	52	67	63	
Steve Abrew	90	86	90	93
David Nagasake	100	85	93	89
Mike Black	81	87	81	85
Andrew Dijkstra	90	82	95	87
Joanne Nguyen	84	80	95	91
Chris Walljasper	86	100	96	89
Fred Albert	70	68		
Dennis Dudley	74	79	77	81
Leo Rice	95			
Fred Flintstone	73	81	78	74
Frances Dupre	82	76	79	
Dave Light	89	76	91	83
Hua Tran	91	81	87	94
Sarah Trapp	83	98		

Table 17-2 Data for Project 35

36. Rework Project 35 to use the class implementation for students.

37. Modify Project 35 to insert the data into the student list in key sequence. Since the data are entered in a first name–last name format, you will have to write a special `compare` function that reformats the name into last name–first name format and then does a string compare. All other functions should work as previously described.

38. Rework Project 37 to use the class implementation for students.

39. Write a program that adds and subtracts polynomials. Each polynomial is to be represented as a linked list. The first node in the list represents the first term in the polynomial, the second node represents the second term, and so forth.

Each node contains three fields. The first field is the term's coefficient. The second field is the term's power, and the third field is a pointer to the next term. For example, consider the polynomials shown in Figure 17-28. The first term in the first polynomial has a coefficient of 5 and an exponent of 4, which is interpreted as $5x^4$.

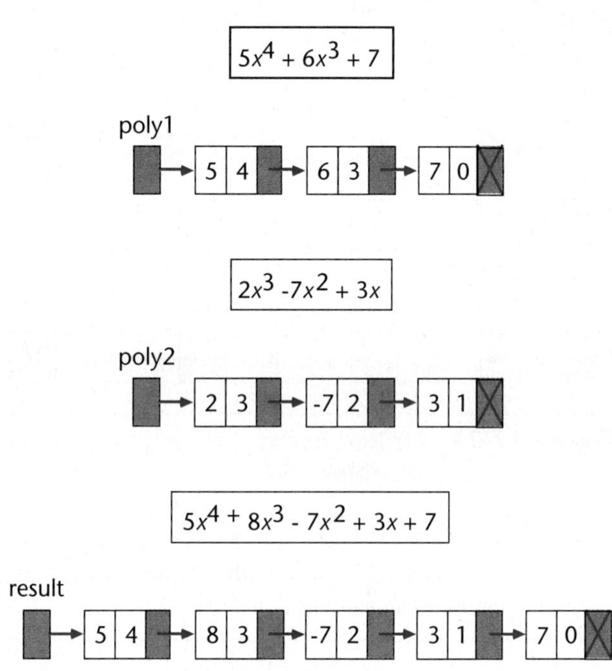

Figure 17-28 Example of linked list polynomials

The rules for the addition of polynomials are as follows:

a. If the powers are equal, the coefficients are algebraically added.

b. If the powers are unequal, the term with the higher power is inserted in the new polynomial.

c. If the exponent is 0, it represents x^0, which is 1. The value of the term is therefore the value of the coefficient.

d. If the result of adding the coefficients results in 0, the term is dropped. (Zero times anything is zero.)

A polynomial is represented by a series of lines, each of which has two integers. The first integer represents the coefficient; the second integer represents the exponent. Thus, the first polynomial in Figure 17-28 would be

```
5    4
6    3
7    0
```

To add two polynomials, the program reads the coefficients and exponents for each polynomial and places them into a linked list. The input can be read from separate files or entered from the keyboard with appropriate user prompts. After the polynomials have been stored, they are added and the results are placed in a third linked list.

The polynomials are added using an operational merge process. An operational merge combines the two lists while performing one or more operations—in our case, addition. To add, we take one term from each of the polynomials and compare the exponents. If the two exponents are equal, the coefficients are added to create a new coefficient. If the coefficient is 0, the term is dropped; if it is not 0, it is appended to the linked list for the resulting polynomial. If one of the exponents is larger than the other, the corresponding term is immediately placed into the new linked list, and the term with smaller exponent is held to be compared with the next term from the other list. If one list ends before the other, the extra data in the longer list is simply copied to the list for the new polynomial.

After the polynomials have been added, delete any node whose coefficient is 0. Then print the two input polynomials and their sum by traversing the linked lists and displaying them as sets of numbers. Be sure to label each polynomial.

Test your program with the two polynomials shown in Table 17-3.

Polynomial 1		Polynomial 2	
Coefficient	**Exponent**	**Coefficient**	**Exponent**
7	9	–7	9
2	6	2	8
3	5	–5	7
4	4	2	4
2	3	2	3
6	2	9	2
6	0	–7	1

Table 17-3 Text data for Project 39

40. Redesign the linked list class discussed in this chapter using overloaded operators for the functions shown in Table 17-4

Function	Program	Operator
addToList	Program 17-8	+
deleteFromList	Program 17-10	–
searchList	Program 17-12	==

Table 17-4 Overloaded operators for Project 40

41. Rework Project 39 to create a `Polynomial` class. The `Polynomial` class is to use the `List` class defined in the text (see "The List Class" on page 833).

A

ASCII Tables

ASCII is the abbreviation for the American Standard Code for Information Interchange. Table A-1 of this appendix indicates the decimal, hexadecimal, octal, and graphic ASCII codes with an English interpretation, if appropriate. Table A-2 gives a hexadecimal matrix of all ASCII values.

Decimal	Hex	Octal	Symbol	Interpretation
0	00	00	NUL	NULL value
1	01	01	SOH	Start of heading
2	02	02	STX	Start of text
3	03	03	ETX	End of text
4	04	04	EOT	End of transmission
5	05	05	ENQ	Enquiry
6	06	06	ACK	Acknowledgment
7	07	07	BEL	Ring bell
8	08	10	BS	Backspace
9	09	11	HT	Horizontal tab
10	0A	12	LF	Line feed
11	0B	13	VT	Vertical tab
12	0C	14	FF	Form feed
13	0D	15	CR	Carriage return
14	0E	16	SO	Shift out
15	0F	17	SI	Shift in

Table A-1 Full ASCII table

Decimal	Hex	Octal	Symbol	Interpretation
16	10	20	DLE	Data link escape
17	11	21	DC1	Device control 1
18	12	22	DC2	Device control 2
19	13	23	DC3	Device control 3
20	14	24	DC4	Device control 4
21	15	25	NAK	Negative acknowledgment
22	16	26	SYN	Synchronous idle
23	17	27	ETB	End of transmission block
24	18	30	CAN	Cancel
25	19	31	EM	End of medium
26	1A	32	SUB	Substitute
27	1B	33	ESC	Escape
28	1C	34	FS	File separator
29	1D	35	GS	Group separator
30	1E	36	RS	Record separator
31	1F	37	US	Unit separator
32	20	40	SP	Space
33	21	41	!	
34	22	42	"	Double quote
35	23	43	#	
36	24	44	$	
37	25	45	%	
38	26	46	&	
39	27	47	'	Apostrophe
40	28	50	(	
41	29	51	)	
42	2A	52	*	
43	2B	53	+	
44	2C	54	,	Comma
45	2D	55	–	Minus
46	2E	56	.	
47	2F	57	/	
48	30	60	0	
49	31	61	1	
50	32	62	2	
51	33	63	3	
52	34	64	4	
53	35	65	5	
54	36	66	6	
55	37	67	7	

Table A-1 Full ASCII table *(continued)*

Decimal	Hex	Octal	Symbol	Interpretation
56	38	70	8	
57	39	71	9	
58	3A	72	:	Colon
59	3B	73	;	Semicolon
60	3C	74	<	
61	3D	75	=	
62	3E	76	>	
63	3F	77	?	
64	40	100	@	
65	41	101	A	
66	42	102	B	
67	43	103	C	
68	44	104	D	
69	45	105	E	
70	46	106	F	
71	47	107	G	
72	48	110	H	
73	49	111	I	
74	4A	112	J	
75	4B	113	K	
76	4C	114	L	
77	4D	115	M	
78	4E	116	N	
79	4F	117	O	
80	50	120	P	
81	51	121	Q	
82	52	122	R	
83	53	123	S	
84	54	124	T	
85	55	125	U	
86	56	126	V	
87	57	127	W	
88	58	130	X	
89	59	131	Y	
90	5A	132	Z	
91	5B	133	[	Open bracket
92	5C	134	\	Backslash
93	5D	135	]	Close bracket
94	5E	136	^	Caret
95	5F	137	_	Underscore

Table A-1 Full ASCII table *(continued)*

Decimal	Hex	Octal	Symbol	Interpretation
96	60	140	`	Grave accent
97	61	141	a	
98	62	142	b	
99	63	143	c	
100	64	144	d	
101	65	145	e	
102	66	146	f	
103	67	147	g	
104	68	150	h	
105	69	151	i	
106	6A	152	j	
107	6B	153	k	
108	6C	154	l	
109	6D	155	m	
110	6E	156	n	
111	6F	157	o	
112	70	160	p	
113	71	161	q	
114	72	162	r	
115	73	163	s	
116	74	164	t	
117	75	165	u	
118	76	166	v	
119	77	167	w	
120	78	170	x	
121	79	171	y	
122	7A	172	z	
123	7B	173	{	Open brace
124	7C	174			Bar
125	7D	175	}	Close brace
126	7E	176	~	Tilde
127	7F	177	DEL	Delete

Table A-1 Full ASCII table *(continued)*

Right / Left	0	1	2	3	4	5	6	7	8	9	A	B	C	D	E	F
0	NUL	SOH	STX	ETX	EOT	ENQ	ACK	BEL	BS	HT	LF	VT	FF	CR	SO	SI
1	DLE	DC1	DC2	DC3	DC4	NAK	SYN	ETB	CAN	EM	SUB	ESC	FS	GS	RS	US
2	SP	!	"	#	$	%	&	´	(	)	*	+	,	–	.	/
3	0	1	2	3	4	5	6	7	8	9	:	;	<	=	>	?
4	@	A	B	C	D	E	F	G	H	I	J	K	L	M	N	O
5	P	Q	R	S	T	U	V	W	X	Y	Z	[	\	]	^	_
6	`	a	b	c	d	e	f	g	h	i	j	k	l	m	n	o
7	p	q	r	s	t	u	v	w	x	y	z	{	|	}	~	DEL

Table A-2 Short ASCII table (hexadecimal)

B

Reserved Words

C++ language contains several key or reserved words that cannot be used for functions, variables, or named constants. They are shown below.

and	double	not_eq	throw
and_eq	dynamic_cast	operator	true
asm	else	or	try
auto	enum	or_eq	typedef
bitand	explicit	private	typeid
bitor	extern	protected	typename
bool	false	public	union
break	float	register	unsigned
case	for	reinterpret_cast	using
catch	friend	return	virtual
char	goto	short	void
class	if	signed	volatile
compl	inline	sizeof	wchar_t
const	int	static	while
const_cast	long	static_cast	xor
continue	mutable	struct	xor_eq
default	namespace	switch	
delete	new	template	
do	not	this	

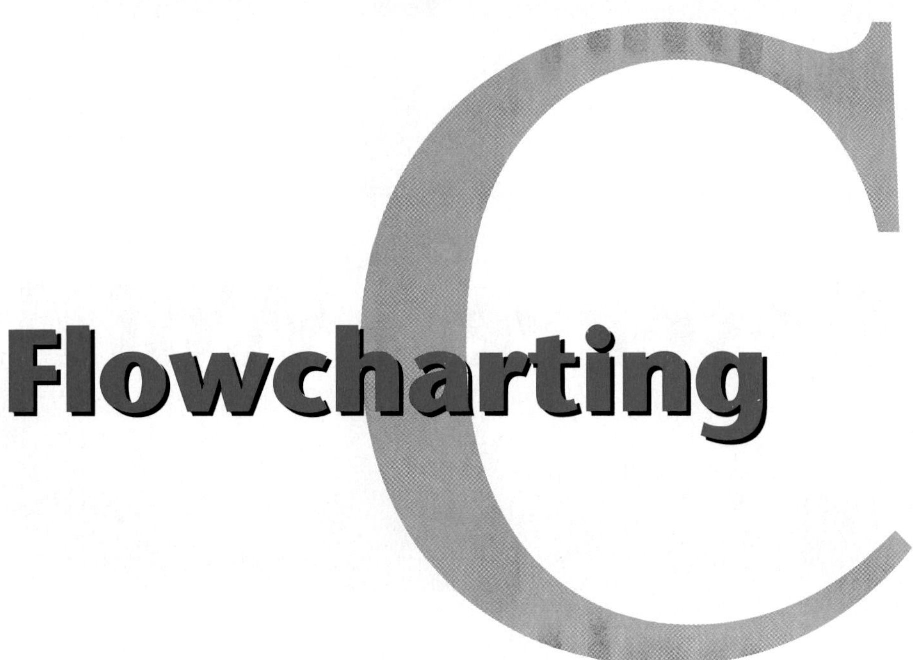

Flowcharting

A flowchart is a tool that is used to show the logic flow of a program. Although it is generally considered a computer programming tool, it can and has been used for many other purposes.

In a programming environment, a flowchart can be used to design a complete program or just a part of a program. Depending on the language being used to write a program, the parts can be called such things as procedures (Pascal), functions (C++), or paragraphs (COBOL). We will use the general term *algorithm* to indicate any part of a program that needs to be designed.

The primary purpose of a flowchart is to show the design of an algorithm. At the same time, it frees the programmer from the syntax and details of a programming language while allowing him or her to concentrate on the details of the problem to be solved.

A flowchart gives a pictorial representation of an algorithm. This is in contrast to another programming design tool, pseudocode, that provides a textual design solution. Both tools have their advantages, but a flowchart has the pictorial power that other tools lack. With flowcharting, a picture really can be worth a thousand words. A new student of computer science must learn how to think about an algorithm before writing it, and a pictorial representation—a flowchart—is just the tool for this kind of thinking.

C-1 AUXILIARY SYMBOLS

A flowchart is a combination of symbols. Some symbols are used to enhance the readability or functionality of the flowchart but are not used directly to show instructions or commands. Such symbols show the start and stop points, the order and sequence of actions, and how one part of a flowchart is connected to another. These auxiliary symbols are shown in Figure C-1.

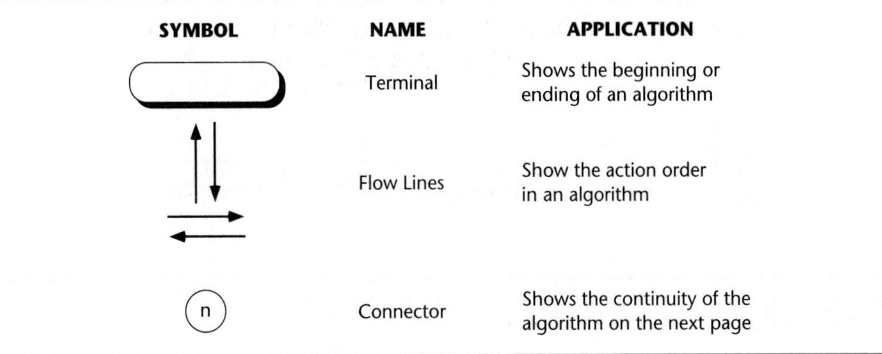

SYMBOL
NAME
APPLICATION
Terminal
Shows the beginning or ending of an algorithm
Flow Lines
Show the action order in an algorithm
n
Connector
Shows the continuity of the algorithm on the next page

Figure C-1 Auxiliary symbols

An oval is used to show the beginning or ending of an algorithm. When it is used to show the beginning of an algorithm, we write the word START inside the oval. When it is used to show the ending of an algorithm, we write the word STOP in the oval.

One of the first rules of structured programming is that each algorithm should have only one entry point and one exit. This means that a good structured flowchart should have one and only one START, and one and only one STOP. Beside the STOP and START, ovals should be aligned to show clearly the flow of the actions in an algorithm. For example, a flowchart for a program that does nothing is shown in Figure C-2. This program starts and stops without doing anything.

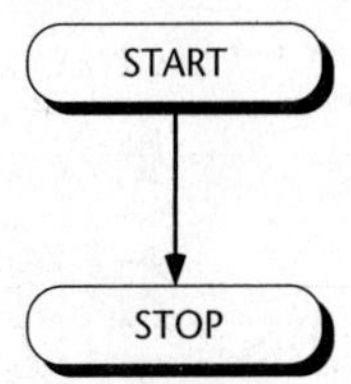

Figure C-2 Use of the oval symbol

FLOW LINES

Flow lines are used to show the order or sequence of actions in a program. They connect symbols. Usually a symbol has some entering and some leaving lines. The START oval has only one leaving line. The STOP oval has only one entering line. We have already shown the use of flow lines in Figure C-2. We will show other flows in the examples that follow.

CONNECTORS

We use only one symbol, a circle with a number in it, to show connectivity. It is used when we reach the end of the page, but our flowchart is not finished. At the bottom of the page we use a connector to show that the logic flow is continued at the top of the next page. The number in the connector can be a simple serial number or it can be a combination of a page and symbol in the form page.number. Figure C-3 shows an off-page connector.

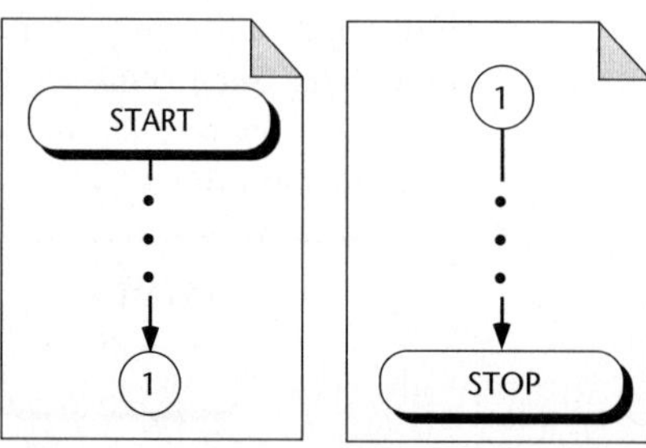

Figure C-3 Use of connectors

C-2 MAIN SYMBOLS

Main symbols are used to show the instructions or actions needed to solve the problem presented in the algorithm. With these symbols it is possible to represent all five structured programming constructs: *sequence*, *decision*, *while*, *for*, and *do…while*.

SEQUENCE

Sequence statements simply represent a series of actions that must continue in a linear order. Although the actions represented in the sequence symbol may be very complex, such as an input or output operation, the logic flow must enter the symbol at the top and flow out at the bottom. Sequence symbols do not allow any decisions or flow changes within the symbol.

There are four sequence symbols: assignment, input/output, module call, and compound statement. They are shown in Figure C-4.

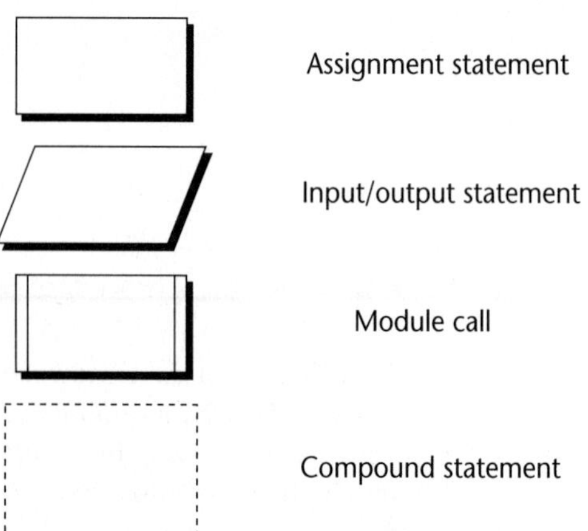

Figure C-4 Sequence symbols

Null Statement

It is worth noting that *do nothing* is a valid statement. It is commonly referred to as a null statement. The null statement is considered a sequence statement since it cannot change the flow direction of a program. There is no symbol for a null statement. It is simply a flow line. Figure C-2 on page 867 contains an example of a null statement.

Assignment Statement

The assignment statement is shown using a rectangle. Within the assignment symbol the assignment operator is shown as a left-pointing arrow. At the right side of the arrow is an expression whose value must be stored in the variable at the left side. Figure C-5 shows an assignment statement.

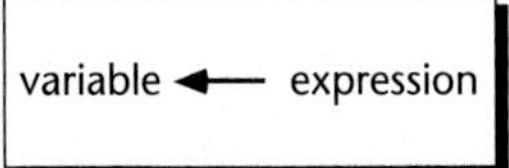

Figure C-5 The assignment statement

Input/Output Statement

A parallelogram is used to show any input or output, such as reading from a keyboard or writing on the system console. For example, an algorithm that reads the value of two variables from the keyboard and then writes their values on the screen in reverse order is shown in Figure C-6.

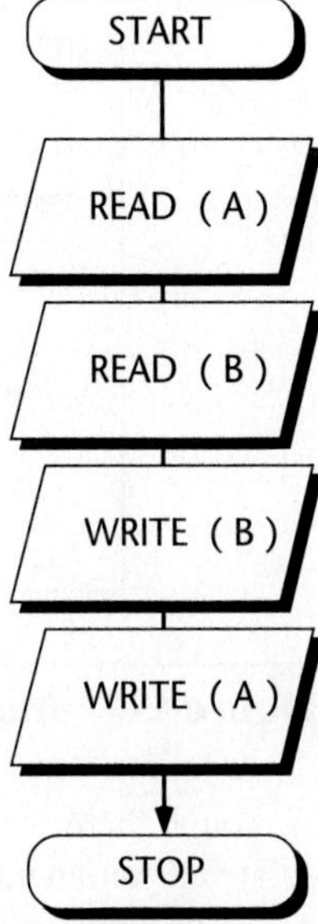

Figure C-6 Read and write statements

Module-Call Statement

The symbol used for calling a module is a rectangle with two vertical bars inside. The flowchart for the called module must be somewhere else. In other words, each time you see a module call statement, look for another flowchart with the module name.

C++ Programmer's Note The module-call symbol is used only for a void function. Functions that return values are shown in the assignment statement.

To show how a module call is used in a program, let's design the flowchart (see Figure C-7) for a program that calculates and prints the average of three numbers. There are two things to note in this example. First, the flowchart for the called module (AVRG) does not begin with START. Rather, it shows the name of the module and the parameter list. Also, the exit oval contains RETURN, indicating that it is not the end of the program, but rather a return from a called module.

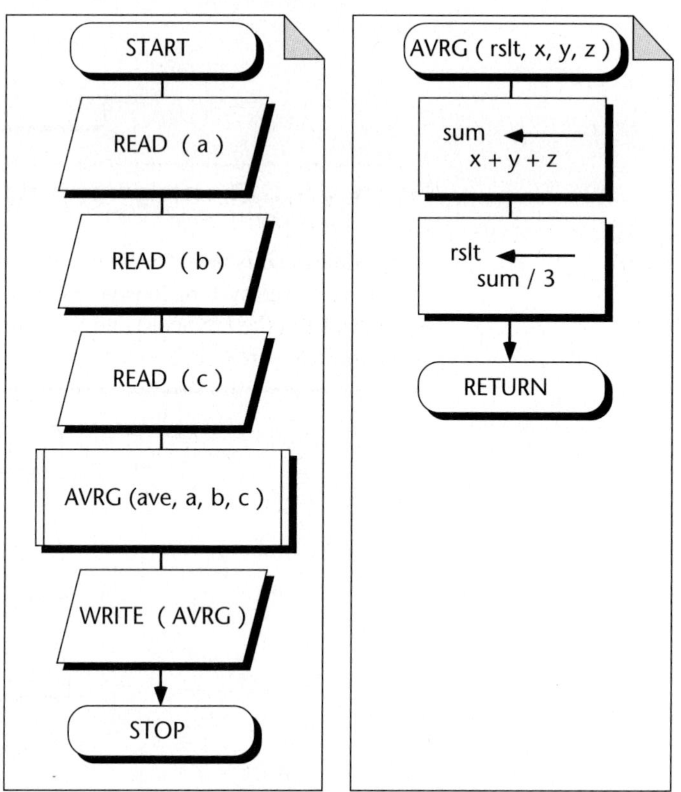

Figure C-7 Module-call example

Compound Statement

Although there is no actual symbol used to indicate a compound statement, we encapsulate all statements that make up a compound statement in a broken-line rectangle. In a C++ program, compound statements are used to represent a block of code, code that is enclosed in braces. (An example of a compound statement is seen in Figure C-9 on page 872.)

SELECTION STATEMENTS

Unlike the sequence statements, selection statements can cause the flow of the program to change. They allow the execution of selected statements and the skipping of other statements. There are two selection statements in structured programming: two-way and multiway selection.

Two-Way Selection

The two-way symbol is the diamond. When it is used to represent an *if...else* statement, the true condition logic is shown as the right leg of the logic flow and the false condition, if present, is shown on the left leg of the logic flow. With the *if...else*, there must always be two logic flows, although often one of them is null. (Remember that the null statement is represented by a flow line; there is no symbol for a null statement.) Finally, the statement ends with a connector where the true and false flows join. In this case, the connector has nothing in it.

Although you will often see decisions drawn with the flow from the bottom of the diamond, this is not good style. Even when one of the flows is null, it still must flow from the left or right sides of the diamond.

Figure C-8 shows the use of the decision symbol in the *if...else* statement. As pointed out above, there are always two branches. On each branch, we are allowed to have one and only one statement. Of course, the statement in each branch can be either a null statement or a compound statement. But only one statement is allowed in each branch; not less, not more. Also remember that the whole figure is only one statement, not two or three; it is one *if...else* statement.

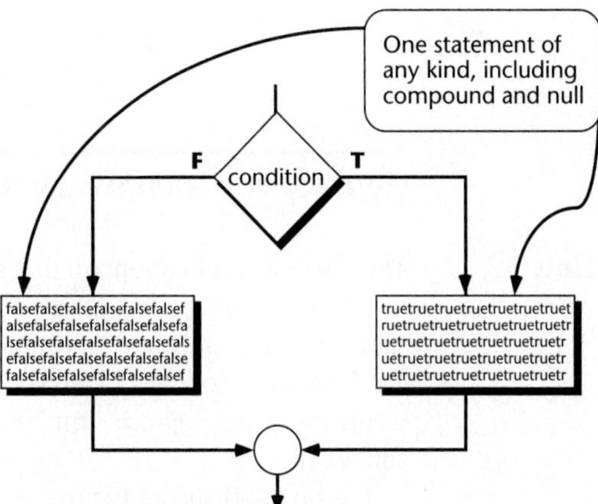

Figure C-8 ***if ... else* statement**

Let's design an algorithm that reads an integer. If the integer's value is greater than 10, it subtracts 10 and writes the original number and the result. If the value is less than 10, it does nothing. The flowchart for this program is shown in Figure C-9.

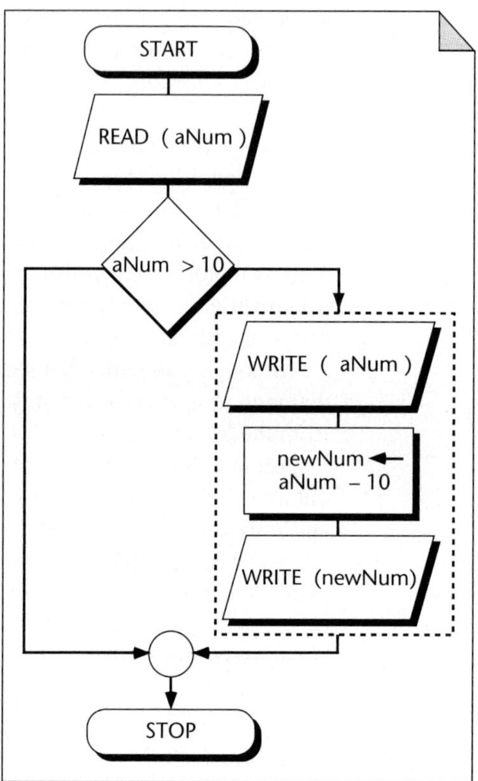

Figure C-9 Example: Read and subtract 10

Multiway Selection

The second application of the selection symbol used with structured programming is multiway selection. C++'s implementation of multiway selection is the *switch* statement. Actually, the multiway selection statement is nothing more than a shorthand notation for the *if...else* statement. If a language does not have a *switch* statement, the same logic is implemented using nested *if...else* statements or the *else if* construct.

Figure C-10 shows the use of the *switch* statement. As you can see, we can have as many branches as we need. On each branch, we are allowed to have one, and only one, statement. Of course, the statement in each branch can be either a null statement or a compound statement. But remember that only one statement in each branch is allowed; not less, not more. Also remember that the whole figure is only one statement, not two or three; it is one *switch* statement. (These rules should sound familiar. Remember that the *switch* statement is nothing but a shorthand form of *if...else,* so the rules are the same for both.)

Now we'll design an algorithm for a program that reads one character representing a letter grade and prints the corresponding grade point average (GPA). Figure C-11 shows this design.

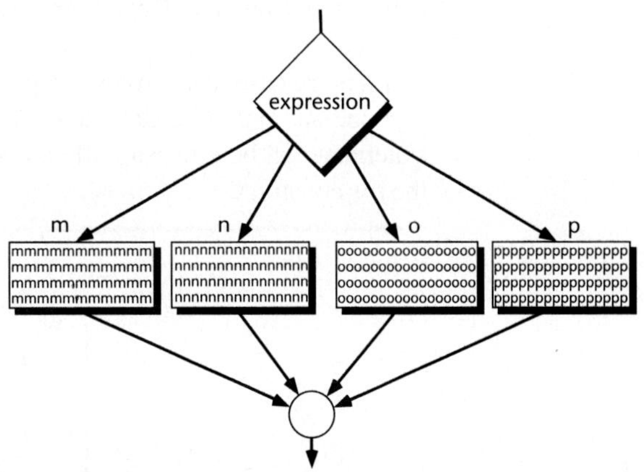

Figure C-10 Multiway selection statement

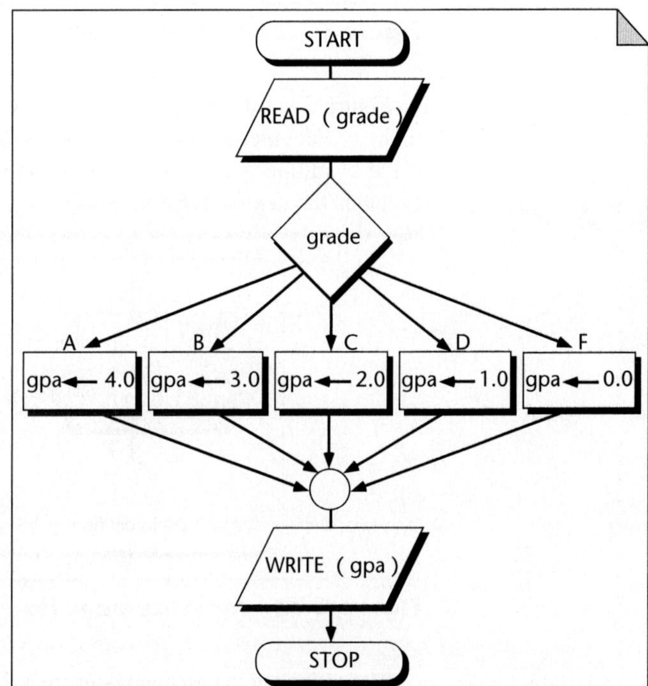

Figure C-11 Example: Calculate grade point average

LOOPING STATEMENTS

There are three looping statements: *for*, *while*, and *do...while.*

for Statement

The *for* statement is a counter-controlled loop. It is actually a complex statement that has three parts, any of which can be null: (1) the loop initialization, which normally sets the loop counter; (2) the limit test; and (3) the end-of-loop action statements, which usually increment a counter. Since the *for* statement is a pretest loop, it is possible that the loop may not be executed. If the limit test is false at the start, the body of the *for* statement is skipped.

As is the case in all structured programming constructs, the body of the loop can contain one and only one statement. As is the case with the other constructs also, this one statement can be either a null statement or a compound statement. Figure C-12 shows the *for* construct.

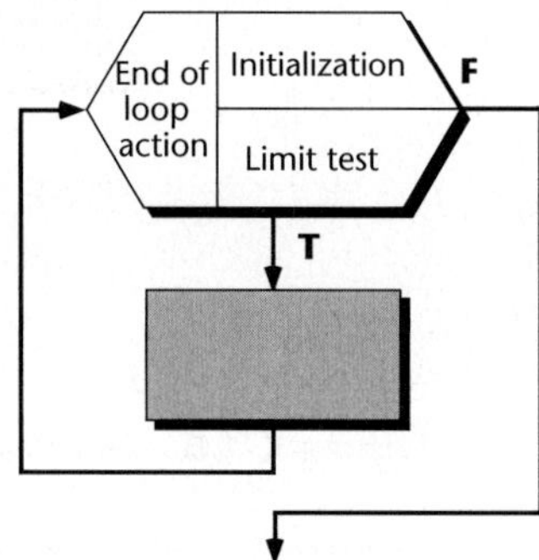

Figure C-12 ***for*** **statement**

Figure C-13 shows the flow of actions when the program enters the loop for the first time. The counter is initialized, the condition is tested, and the program enters the loop if the condition is true. If the condition is false, the program does not enter the loop; it executes the next statement, if any.

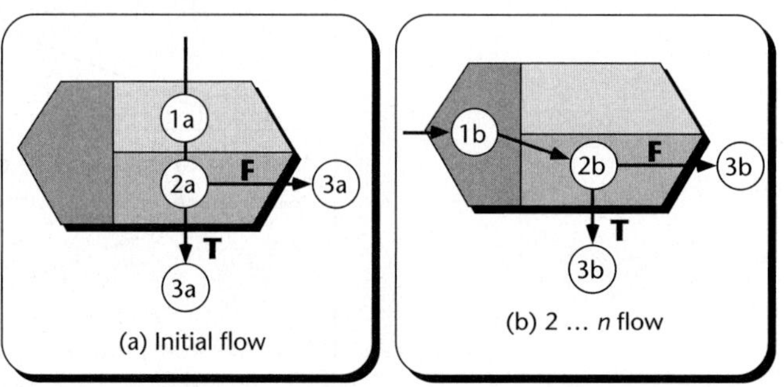

Figure C-13 ***for*** **statement flow**

The actions of the *for* statement are rather complex. Let's trace them through the figure. When the statement is entered for the first time, the initialization (1a) is performed. The limit test (2a) is then checked (remember, *for* is a pretest construct), and if the limit test is true, the body of the statement is entered (3a—true). This flow is seen in Figure C-13a.

Figure C-13b shows the logic flow at the end of each loop. Note that first the end-of-loop action (1b), usually an increment or decrement of the loop counter, is executed; then the limit condition is tested (2b). If the limit test is true, the loop continues for at least one more time (3b—true). If the limit has been reached, the loop terminates (3b—false). Obviously, only one of the two branches can be taken in one loop.

Let's design an algorithm that will read 20 numbers and print their sum. Since the number of times is known in advance, *for* is an excellent choice for the looping construct. The design for this program is shown in Figure C-14.

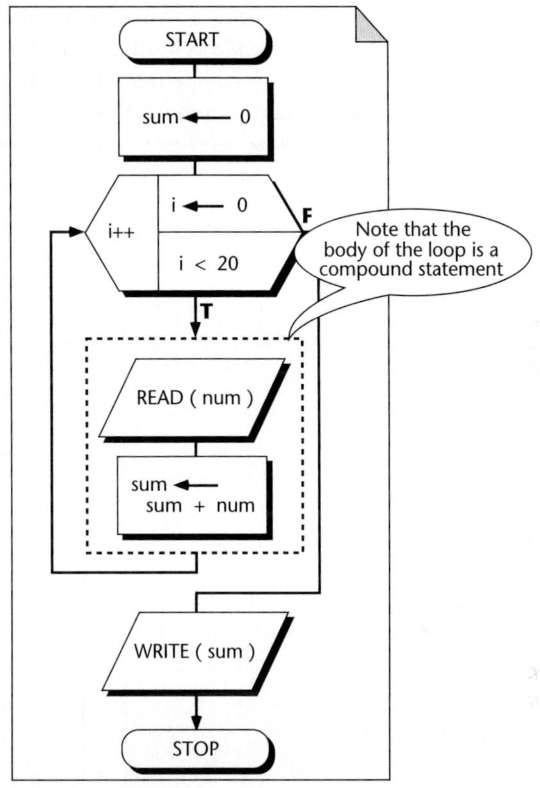

Figure C-14 Example: Read 20 numbers

while Statement

The second looping construct is the *while* statement. The major difference between the *for* and *while* loops is that the *while* loop is not a counting loop. Both are pretest loops; this means that, like the *for,* the body of the *while* loop may never be executed.

We use the same basic symbol for the *while* loop, but since there is only a limit test, the internal divisions are not necessary. Figure C-15 shows the basic format of the *while* statement.

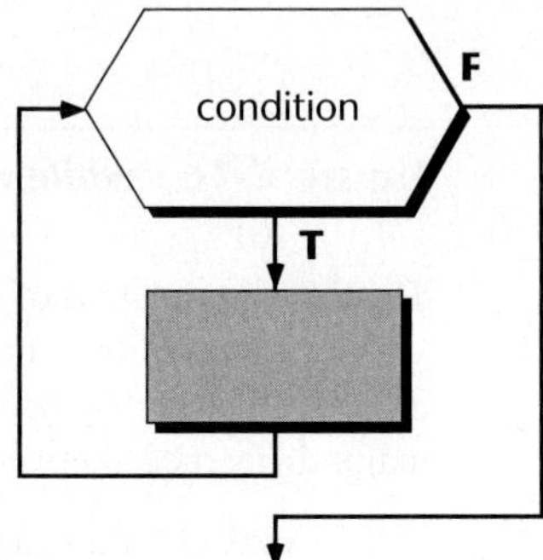

Figure C-15 *while* statement

Let's design another program that reads numbers from the keyboard and prints their total. This time, we don't know how many numbers we may be reading. All we know is that all the numbers are positive. We can therefore signal the end of the numbers by having the user key –1.

Since we don't know how many times we must loop, we need a construct other than *for*. The *while* is well designed for this type of logic. The program flow is shown in Figure C-16. Note that in this design, the first number is read *before* the loop. This is known as "priming the loop" and is common in pretest loops.

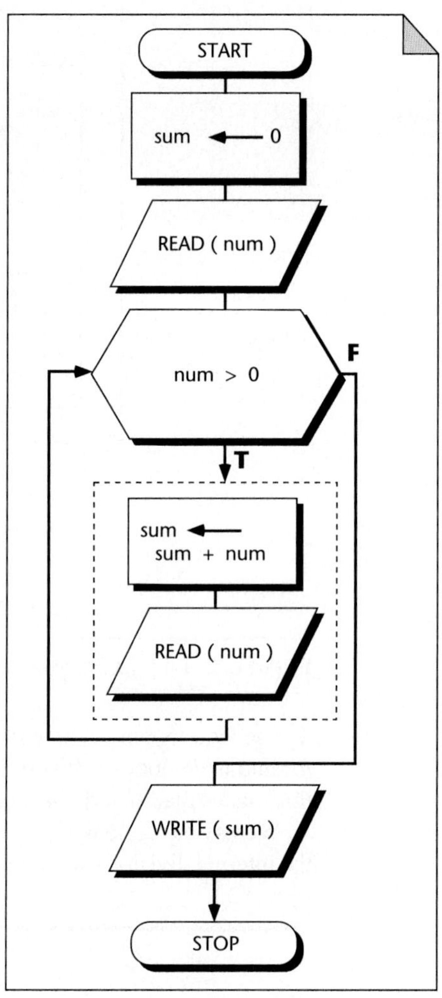

Figure C-16 *while* read and total

do...while Statement

The third application of the loop symbol is the *do...while* statement.

Because of the inherent differences between the *for* and *while* loops and the *do...while* loop, the *do...while* must be used differently in a flowchart. There are two major differences between the *while* and the *do...while*.

1. A *while* loop is a pre-test loop. The *do...while* loop is a post-test loop.
2. The body of a *while* loop may never be executed. The body of a *do...while* loop is always executed at least once.

Figure C-17 shows the use of the *do...while* statement. Note that in this statement, the condition is tested at the end of the loop.

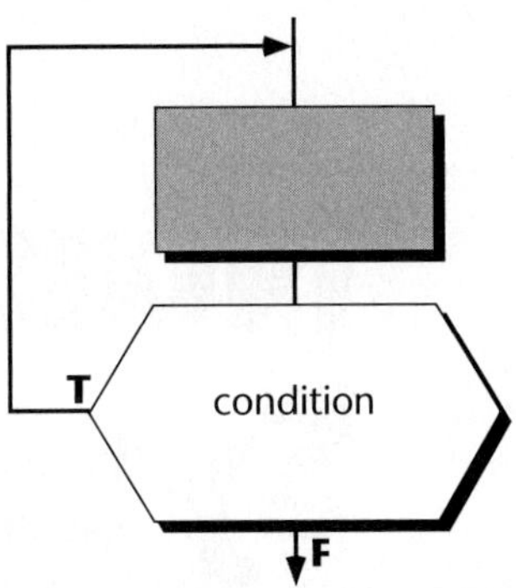

Figure C-17 *do...while* statement

Let's design an algorithm that reads and processes a number. In this algorithm, the number must be between 1 and 5. To make the program robust, we use a *do...while* loop that forces the user to enter a valid number. This is a common technique for validating user input. Note that as in previous looping constructs, there can be only one statement in the *do...while* loop. For that reason, the prompt and read are enclosed in a compound symbol. The algorithm is shown in Figure C-18.

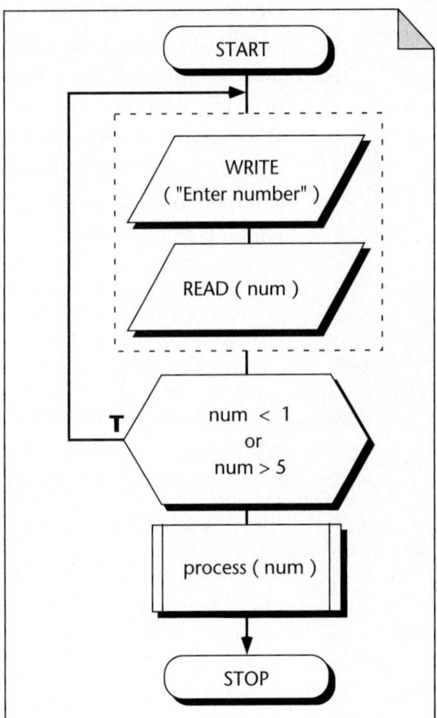

Figure C-18 Example: Input validation with *do...while*

D Numbering Systems

Today, the whole world uses the decimal number system developed by Arabian mathematicians in the eighth century. We acknowledge their contribution to numbers when we refer to our decimal system as using Arabic numerals.

Decimal numbers were not always commonly used. The first people to use a decimal numbering system were the ancient Egyptians. The Babylonians improved on the Egyptian system by making the positions in the numbering systems meaningful, but instead of using decimals, the Babylonians used a sexagesimal (base 60) numbering system. Whereas our decimal system has 10 values in its graphic representations, a sexagesimal system has 60. We still see remnants of the Babylonians' sexagesimal system in our measurement of time, which is based on 60 minutes to an hour, and in the division of circles, which contain 360°.

D-1 COMPUTER NUMBERING SYSTEMS

There are four different numbering systems used in computer programming. The computer itself uses a binary system. In a binary system, there are only two values for each number position, 0 and 1. Programmers use two different shorthand notations to represent binary numbers: octal and hexadecimal. And of course, programmers also use the decimal system. Since all these systems are used in C++, a basic understanding of each is required for you to fully understand the language.

DECIMAL NUMBERS

We all readily understand the decimal numbering system. In fact, we have used it so much that it is basically intuitive. But do you really understand why the second position in the decimal system is tens and the third position is hundreds? The answer lies in the powers of the base to the system, which in decimal is 10. Thus, the first position is 10 raised to the power zero, the second position is 10 raised to the power one, and the third position is 10 raised to the power two. Figure D-1 shows the relationship between the powers and the number 243.

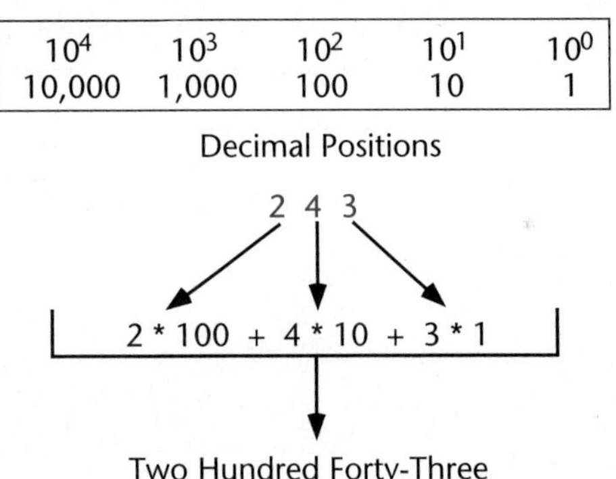

Figure D-1 Positions in the decimal numbering system

BINARY NUMBERS

Whereas the decimal system is based on 10, the binary system is based on 2. There are only two digits in binary, 0 and 1. Binary digits are known as bits, which is an acronym created from *B*inary dig*IT*.

Figure D-2 shows the powers table for a binary system and the value 243 in binary. In the position table, each position is double the previous position. Again, this is because the base of the system is two. You should memorize the binary powers to at least 2^{10}.

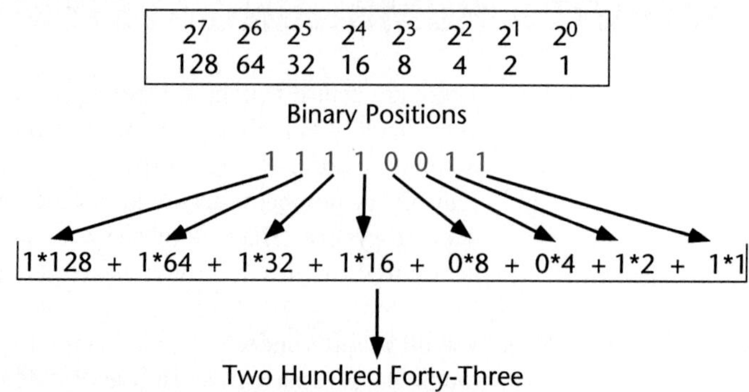

Figure D-2 Positions in the binary numbering system

OCTAL NUMBERS

The base of the octal system is eight. This means that there are eight different symbols: 0, 1, 2, 3, 4, 5, 6, and 7. Although octal is not commonly used in modern computer systems, you should still be sure you understand it because it is supported by C++. The octal numbering system is shown in Figure D-3. Again, the number represented is 243.

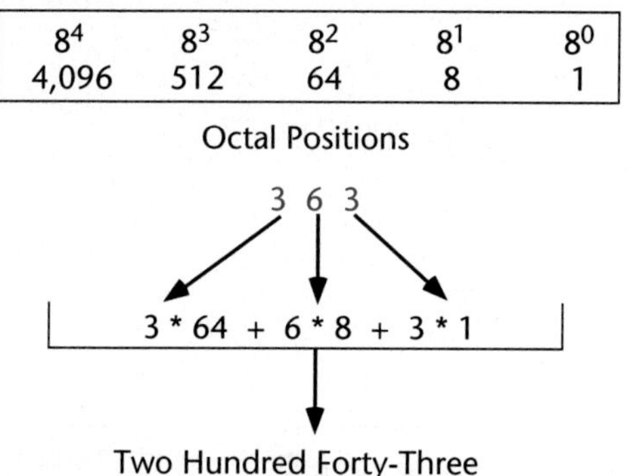

Figure D-3 Positions in the octal numbering system

HEXADECIMAL NUMBERS

The hexadecimal system is based on 16 (*hexadec* is Greek for 16). This means that there are 16 symbols: 0, 1, 2, 3, 4, 5, 6, 7, 8, 9, A, B, C, D, E, and F. Since the base is 16, each positional value is 16 times the previous one. This is illustrated in Figure D-4.

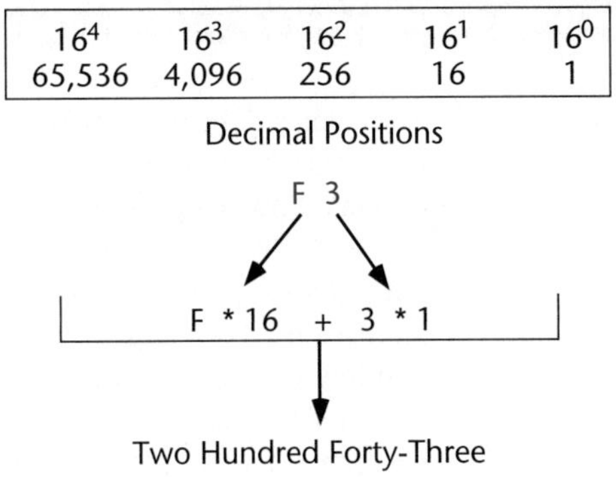

16^4	16^3	16^2	16^1	16^0
65,536	4,096	256	16	1

Figure D-4 Positions in the hexadecimal numbering system

Look carefully at the binary, octal, and hexadecimal numbering systems in Table D-1. Do you see that some of the values are duplicated? This is because octal and hexadecimal are simply shorthand notations for binary. Rather than represent a number as a large string of 0s and 1s, it is therefore possible to use either octal or hexadecimal.

Decimal	Binary	Octal	Hexadecimal
0	0000	0	0
1	0001	1	1
2	0010	2	2
3	0011	3	3
4	0100	4	4
5	0101	5	5
6	0110	6	6
7	0111	7	7
8	1000	10	8
9	1001	11	9
10	1010	12	A
11	1011	13	B
12	1100	14	C
13	1101	15	D
14	1110	16	E
15	1111	17	F
16	10000	20	10

Table D-1 Decimal, binary, octal, and hexadecimal table

D-2 INTEGER TRANSFORMATIONS

Since you will be working in all four numbering systems when you program in C++, you must learn how to convert to and from binary to the other formats. If you understand the concepts shown in the previous section, you will find it easy to do the conversions.

BINARY TO DECIMAL

Let's start by converting a number from binary to decimal. Refer to Figure D-5 for this discussion. To convert from binary to decimal, you start with the binary number and multiply each binary digit by its value from the binary positions table in Figure D-2. Since each binary bit can be only 0 or 1, the result will be either a 0 or the value of the position. After multiplying all the digits, add the results. This conversion is shown in Figure D-5.

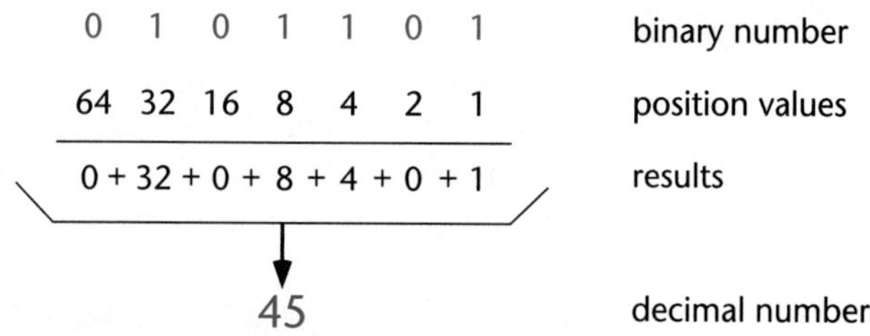

Figure D-5 Binary to decimal conversion

DECIMAL TO BINARY

To convert from decimal to binary, we use repetitive division. The original number, 45 in the example, is divided by 2. The remainder (1) becomes the first binary digit, and the second digit is determined by dividing the quotient (22) by 2. Again the remainder (0) becomes the binary digit and the quotient is divided by 2 to determine the next position. This process continues until the quotient is 0. This conversion is shown in Figure D-6.

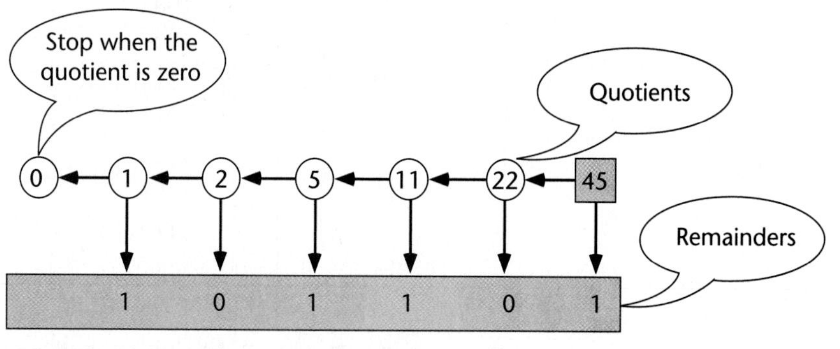

Figure D-6 Decimal to binary conversion

BINARY TO OCTAL OR HEXADECIMAL

The previous section showed a mathematical way to convert from binary to decimal. Converting from binary to octal and hexadecimal is done by grouping binary digits into groups of three for octal and groups of four for hexadecimal. Do you see why we use these groupings? Table D-1 shows the bit configurations for the binary, octal, hexadecimal, and decimal representations of the numbers 1 to 16.

Now, if we have a large binary number, we can easily change it to a hexadecimal using the above information. We divide the number into 4-bit sections (from the right). Then to each section, we assign the appropriate hexadecimal digit. This concept is shown in Figure D-7.

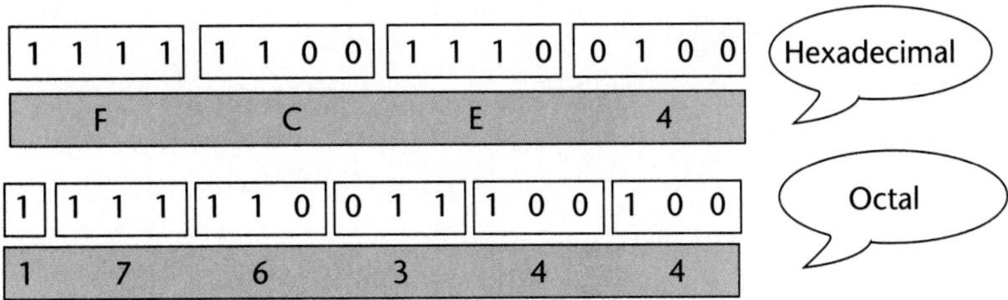

Figure D-7 Converting a large binary number

If we have a large binary number, we can easily change it to an octal number using the same concept. Divide the number into 3-bit sections (from the right). Then to each section, assign the appropriate octal digit. This is also shown in Figure D-7.

D-3 STORING INTEGERS

Sometimes when you print out integer values, you get a surprising result. What you thought was a positive number may be printed as a negative number. In another case, what you expected to be a small number turns out to be very large. If you understand how numbers are stored in the computer, you may still be surprised, but you will understand what happened and therefore be able to debug your program easier and faster. So let's study how integers are stored. We will first look at unsigned integers and then at signed integers. In all cases, we assume that the size of an integer is 2 bytes (16 bits).

UNSIGNED INTEGERS

Storing unsigned integers is a straightforward process. The number is changed to the corresponding binary form, and the binary representation is stored. For example, an unsigned integer can be stored as a number from 0 to 65535 as shown in Figure D-8.

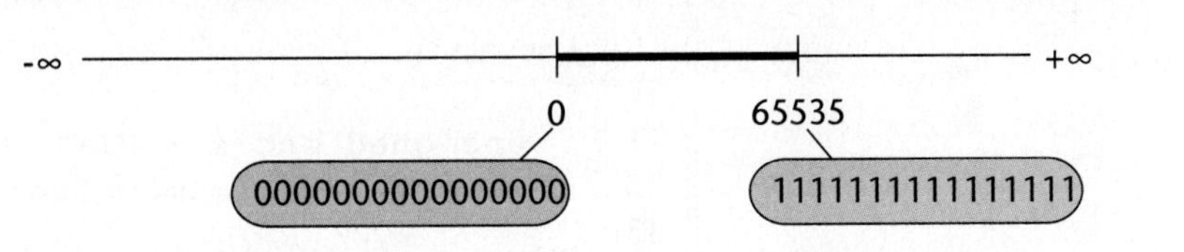

Figure D-8 Storing integers

Figure D-8 also shows the range of an integer stored in a 16-bit word. Another way to show the range is with a circle. In this case, 0 is placed at the top of the circle and the values are placed around the circle clockwise until the maximum value is adjacent to the first value, 0. This format is seen in Figure D-9.

In Figure D-9, the number after 65,535 is 0! Why? Part of the reason is that 65,536 requires 17 bits to store its value and all we have is 16 bits. The reason the value is 0 is

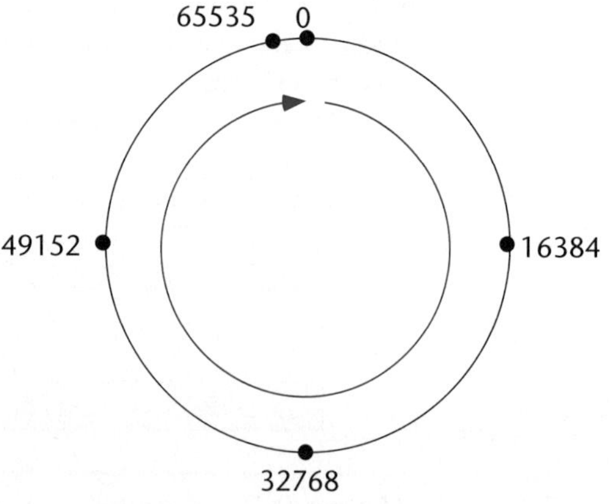

Figure D-9 Range of integer values

that we start over at the beginning of the circle. Another way to look at it is that storing numbers is a modulo process. The number to be stored is represented as modulus the maximum number that can be stored + 1, in this case 65,536. This relationship is shown below.

```
65,535 + 1 → 65,536 % 65,536 → 0
```

Program D-1 demonstrates this concept. Note that you may get a different maximum value depending on the size of an integer in your system.

Program D-1 Demonstrate integer numbers

```
/* Demonstrate circular nature of unsigned integer numbers.
      Written by:
      Date:
*/
#include <iostream>
#include <climits>
using namespace std;

int main ()
{
   unsigned int x = UINT_MAX;
   cout << "Maximum value:        " << x << endl;

   x++;
   cout << "Maximum value + 1:    " << x << endl;

   x++;
   cout << "Maximum value + 1:    " << x << endl;

   return 0;
}  // main

```

Program D-1 Demonstrate integer numbers *(continued)*

```
Results:
   Maximum value:        65535
   Maximum value + 1:    0
   Maximum value + 1:    1
```

SIGNED INTEGERS

Storing signed integers is different from storing unsigned integers because we must consider the sign bit. There are three methods used to store signed integers in a computer: sign and magnitude, one's complement, and two's complement.

Sign and Magnitude

Storing an integer in the sign-and-magnitude format uses 1 bit to represent the sign (0 for positive, 1 for negative), which means only 15 bits are left over to represent the absolute value of the number. Therefore, the maximum positive value is one-half of the unsigned value.

Aside from the magnitude of the number that we can store, there are two significant differences between the sign and magnitude and unsigned numbers. First, we can now store negative numbers. Second, there are two zero values: a plus zero and a minus zero (see Figure D-10). Since this method is not used to store values in today's computers, we leave further discussions to those information areas in which it is used, such as communications systems.

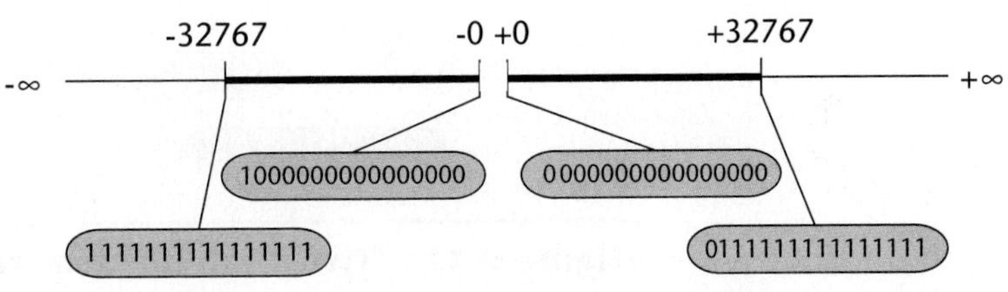

Figure D-10 Sign-and-magnitude bit configurations

One's Complement

The one's complement differs from the sign and magnitude in two ways. First, negative numbers are stored in their complemented format. Second, the sign bit, zero for positive and one for negative, is propagated from the sign bit to the most significant bit of the value. Like the sign and magnitude, the one's complement has two zero values—plus and minus. Figure D-11 shows the configurations for one's complement values.

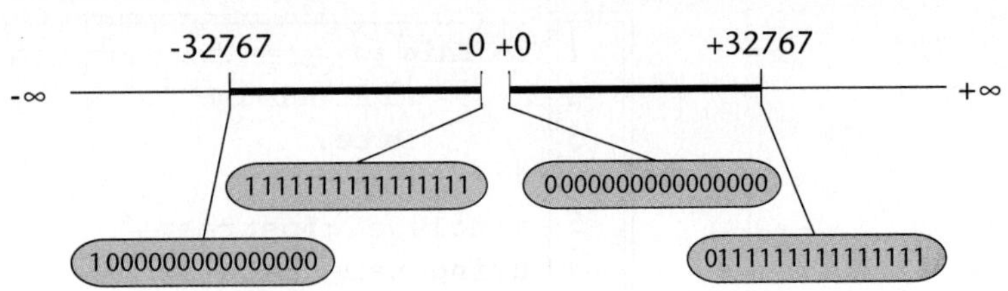

Figure D-11 One's complement format

Let's look at each of these differences in turn. To complement a bit, you simply reverse it as in the one's complement unary operator (~). If it is a zero, it becomes a one;

if it is a one, it becomes a zero. This is seen in the following example in which we complement +10. After complementing the value, the sign is propagated as shown below.

```
+10  →  0000000000001010
-10  →  1111111111110101
```

Like the sign and magnitude, the one's complement is not used to store data in general-purpose computers. We therefore defer any further discussion to those areas where it is used.

Two's Complement

In this method, like the one's complement, all the bits change when the sign of the number changes. So the whole number, not just the most significant bit, will take part in the negation process. However, we have only one zero.

In this way, our integer variable can store numbers from –32,768 up to +32,767. Note that because zero belongs to the domain of positive numbers, although it is considered neither positive nor negative, the absolute value of the maximum integer is one less than the absolute value of the minimum integer. This range is shown in Figure D-12.

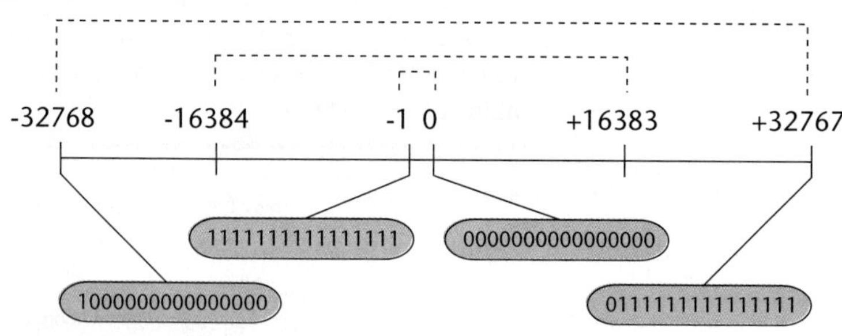

Figure D-12 Two's complement range

As Figure D-12 shows, there is symmetry between the positive and negative numbers. However, if you complement a positive number using the one's complement operator (~), you will not get the negative number with the same absolute value. The absolute value will be one more. In a symmetrical manner, if you complement a negative number, you will get a positive number whose absolute value is one less. This concept is demonstrated in Program D-2.

Program D-2 Demonstration of two's complement

```
/* This program demonstrates the two's complement values.
      Written by:
      Date:
*/
#include <iostream>
using namespace std;

int main ()
{
   int a = +13422;
   int b = -768;
```

Program D-2 Demonstration of two's complement *(continued)*

```
    int ca = ~ a;
    int cb = ~ b;
    cout << "Complement of " << a << " is " << ca << endl;
    cout << "Complement of " << b << " is " << cb << endl;
    return 0;
} // main
```

```
Results:
Complement of  13422 is -13423
Complement of   -768 is    767
```

With a little thought, you should recognize that 0 and –1 are the complement of each other. Likewise, +32767 and –32768 are the complement of each other. These facts are apparent from the bit pattern of the number. The range of integers in two's complement format are shown in Figure D-13.

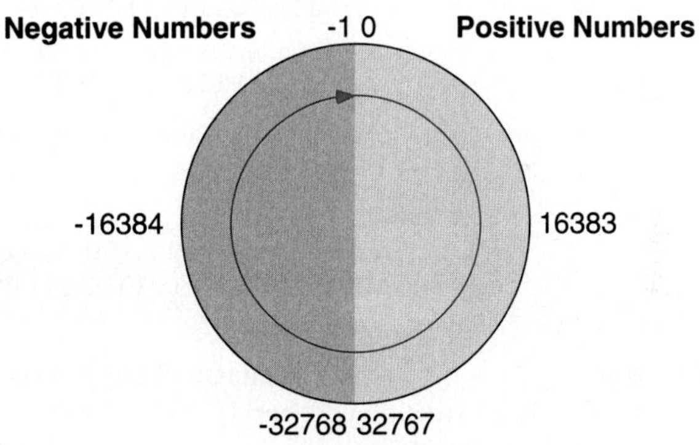

Figure D-13 Range of two's complement values

Converting to Two's Complement

To change a decimal number to its two's complement form, follow these steps:

1. Ignore the sign.
2. Change the absolute value of the number to binary form.
3. Add extra zeros at the left of the number to make the number of bits the same as the size of the integer.
4. If the number is positive, stop; if the number is negative:
   a. Complement the number (change 0 to 1 and 1 to 0).
   b. Add 1 to the number.

For example, let's change +76 to its two's complement.
Step 1: The absolute value is 76.
Step 2: 76 in binary is 1001100.
Step 3: Add extra zeros to make the number 16-bits long.

```
0000000001001100
```

Step 4: The sign was positive, so the two's complement is

```
0000000001001100
```

As another example, let us change –77 to its two's complement.
Step 1: The absolute value is 77.
Step 2: 77 in binary is 1001101.
Step 3: We add extra zeros to make the number 16-bits long.

```
0000000001001101
```

Step 4: The sign was negative, so the two's complement can be obtained using the following two steps:

a. We complement the number.

```
1111111110110010
```

b. We add 1 to the number.

```
1111111110110010+
               1
________________
1111111110110011
```

Did you notice that the two numbers (+76 and –77) are complements of each other? As we said before

```
+76   →   0000000001001100
–77   →   1111111110110011
```

Two's Complement Addition

One of the advantages of the two's complement method is that it makes addition and subtraction very easy.

To add two numbers, just add individual bits.

```
   7      0000000000000111
+ 10    + 0000000000001010
  17      0000000000010001
```

As shown in the next example, the addition works even if one of the numbers is negative.

```
   7           7   0000000000000111
 -10      + (-10)  1111111111110110
  -3          -3   1111111111111101
```

If there is a carry from the most significant digit into the sign, an overflow has occurred and the result is invalid. For example, if we add 10 to 32,767, we get an invalid result, as shown below.

```
+ 32767    0111111111111111
+    10    0000000000001010
- 32759    1000000000001001
```

What is the value of 1000000000001001 in binary? To understand what happens, refer to Figure D-13 on page 887. First, note that 32,767 is at the bottom of the circle. When we add 10, we move clockwise ten positions, which puts us in the negative portion of the number range. The value at that position is –32,759. Now you should understand why sometimes you get strange output when you print numbers.

Two's Complement Subtraction

Surprisingly, subtraction is also very easy. To subtract a number from another number, we take the two's complement of the subtrahend and then add the numbers as shown below.

```
  7        7      0000000000000111
-10    +(-10)     1111111111110110
 -3       -3      1111111111111101
```

D-4 EXCESS SYSTEM

Another representation that allows you to store both positive and negative numbers in a computer is called the **excess system**. In this system, it is easy to transform a number from decimal to binary, and vice versa. However, operations on the numbers are very complicated. The only application in use today is in storing the exponential value of a fraction. This is discussed in the next section.

In an Excess conversion, a positive number, called the magic number, is used in the conversion process. The magic number is normally (2^{N-1}) or (2^{N-1}–1), where N is the bit allocation. For example, if N is 8, the magic number is either 128 or 127. In the first case, we call the representation Excess_128, and in the second case, it is Excess_127.

REPRESENTATION

To represent a number in Excess, use the following procedure:

1. Add the magic number to the integer.
2. Change the result to binary and add 0s so that there is a total of N bits.

Example Represent –25 in Excess_127 using an 8-bit allocation.

Solution First add 127 to –25 and get 102. This number in binary is 1100110. Add 1 bit to make it 8 bits in length. The representation is 01100110.

INTERPRETATION

To interpret a number in Excess, use the following procedure:

1. Change the number to decimal.
2. Subtract the magic number from the integer.

Example Interpret 11111110 if the representation is Excess_127.

Solution First change the number to decimal. It is 254. Then subtract 127 from the number. The result is decimal 127.

D-5 FLOATING-POINT REPRESENTATION

To represent a **floating-point number** (a number containing an integer and a fraction), the number is divided into two parts: the integer and the fraction. For example, the floating-point number 14.234 has an integer of 14 and a fraction of 0.234.

CONVERTING TO BINARY

To convert a floating-point number to binary, use the following procedure:

1. Convert the integer part to binary.
2. Convert the fraction to binary.
3. Put a decimal point between the two parts.

Converting the Integer Part

This procedure is the same as that presented in "Decimal to Binary" on page 882.

Converting the Fraction Part

To convert a fraction to binary, use repetitive multiplication. For example, to convert 0.125 to binary, multiply the fraction by 2; the result is 0.250. The integer part of the result (0) is extracted and becomes the leftmost binary digit. Now multiply by 2 the fraction part (0.250) of the result to get 0.50. Again, the integer part of the result (0) is extracted and becomes the next binary digit. This process continues until the fraction part becomes 0 or you reach the limit of the number of bits you can use (Figure D-14).

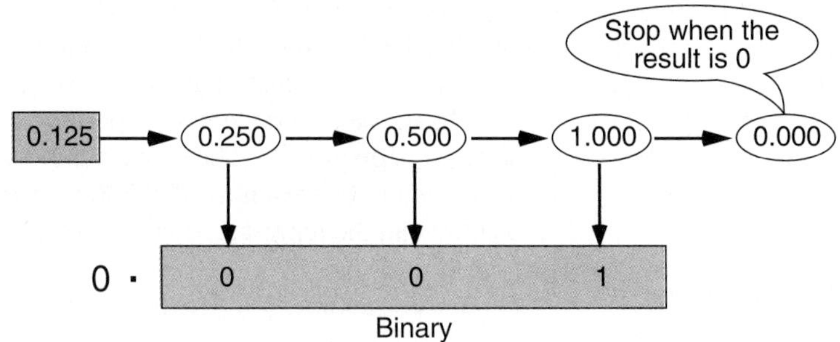

Figure D-14 Changing fractions to binary

Example Transform the fraction 0.875 to binary.

Solution Write the fraction at the left corner. Multiply the number continuously by 2 and extract the integer part as the binary digit. Stop when the number is 0.0.

Fraction	0.875	→	1.750	→	1.50	→	1.0	→	0.0
			↓		↓		↓		
Binary:	0		1		1		1		

Example Transform the fraction 0.4 to a binary of 6 bits.

Solution Write the fraction at the left corner. Multiply the number continuously by 2 and extract the integer part as the binary digit. In this case, you can never get the exact binary representation because the original fraction reappears. However, you can continue until you get 6 bits.

Fraction	0.4	→	0.8	→	1.6	→	1.2	→	0.4	→	0.8	→	1.6
			↓		↓		↓		↓		↓		↓
Binary:	0		0		1		1		0		0		1

NORMALIZATION

To represent the number 71.3125 (+1000111.0101), store the sign, all of the bits, and the position of the decimal point in memory. Although this is possible, it makes operations on numbers difficult. You need a standard representation for floating-point numbers. The solution is **normalization**, the moving of the decimal point so that there is only one 1 to the left of the decimal point.

```
1 . xxxxxxxxxxxxxxxxxx
```

To indicate the original value of the number, multiply the number by 2^e, where e is the number of bits that the decimal points moved: positive for left movement, negative for right movement. A positive or negative sign is then added depending on the sign of the original number. Table D-2 shows examples of normalization.

Original Number	Move	Normalized	
+1010001.11001	← 6	$+2^{6}$	× 1.01000111001
−111.000011	← 2	-2^{2}	× 1.11000011
+0.00000111001	6 →	$+2^{-6}$	× 1.11001
−0.001110011	3 →	-2^{-3}	× 1.110011

Table D-2 Examples of normalization

SIGN, EXPONENT, AND MANTISSA

After a number is normalized, you store only three pieces of information about the number: sign, exponent, and mantissa (the bits to the right of the decimal point). For example, +1000111.0101 becomes

	+	2^{6}	×	1.0001110101
Sign:	+	Exponent: 6		Mantissa: 0001110101

Note that the 1 to the left of the decimal point is not stored; it is understood.

Sign

The sign of the number can be stored using 1 bit (0 or 1).

Exponent

The exponent (power of 2) defines the movement of the decimal point. Note that the power can be negative or positive. Excess representation is the method used to store the exponent. The number of bits allocated (N) defines the range of numbers that a computer can store.

Mantissa

The **mantissa** is the binary number to the right of the decimal point. It defines the precision of the number. The mantissa is stored as an unsigned integer.

IEEE STANDARDS

The Institute of Electrical and Electronics Engineers (IEEE) has defined three standards for storing floating-point numbers; two are used to store numbers in memory (single precision and double precision). These formats are shown in Figure D-15. Note that the number inside the boxes is the number of bits for each field.

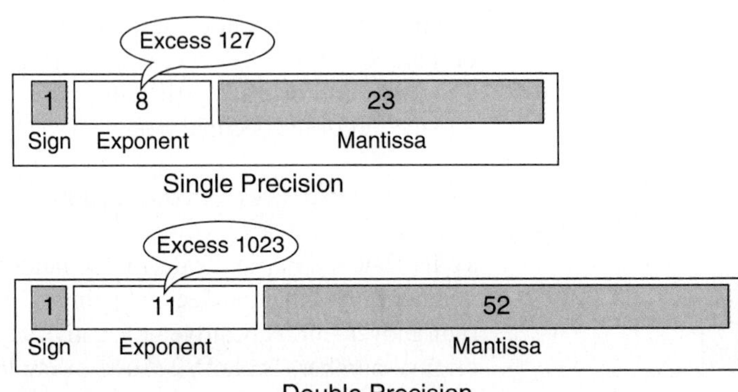

Figure D-15 IEEE standards for floating-point representation

Single-Precision Representation

The procedure for storing a normalized floating-point number in memory using **single-precision format** is as follows:

1. Store the sign as 0 (positive) or 1 (negative).
2. Store the exponent (power of 2) as Excess_127.
3. Store the mantissa as an unsigned integer.

Example Show the representation of the normalized number

$+ \quad 2^6 \quad \times \quad 1.01000111001$

Solution The sign is positive, and it is represented as 0. The exponent is 6. In Excess_127 representation, add 127 to it and get 133. In binary, this is 10000101. The mantissa is 01000111001. When you increase the bit length to 23, you get 01000111001000000000000. Note that you cannot ignore the 0 on the left because this is a fraction. Ignoring that 0 is the same as multiplying the number by 2. Note that you add extra 0s on the right side (not the left) because it is a fraction. Adding 0s to the right side of a fraction does not change the fraction, but adding 0s to the left means dividing the number by a power of 2. The number in memory is a 32-bit number as shown next:

sign	exponent	mantissa
0	**10000101**	01000111001000000000000

Table D-3 shows more examples of floating-point representation.

Number	Sign	Exponent	Mantissa
$-2^2 \times 1.11000011$	1	10000001	11000011000000000000000
$+2^{-6} \times 1.11001$	0	01111001	11001000000000000000000
$-2^{-3} \times 1.110011$	1	01111100	11001100000000000000000

Table D-3 Examples of floating-point representation

Floating-Point Interpretation for Single Precision

The following procedure interprets a 32-bit floating-point number stored in memory.

1. Use the leftmost bit as the sign.
2. Change the next 8 bits to decimal and subtract 127 from it. This is the exponent.
3. Add 1 and a decimal point to the next 23 bits. You can ignore any extra 0s at the right.
4. Move the decimal point to the correct position using the value of the exponent.
5. Change the whole part to decimal.
6. Change the fraction part to decimal.
7. Combine the whole and the fraction parts.

Example Interpret the following 32-bit floating-point number

```
1 01111100  11001100000000000000000
```

Solution The leftmost bit is the sign (–). The next 8 bits are 01111100. This is 124 in decimal. If you subtract 127 from it, you get the exponent –3. The next 23 bits are the mantissa. If you ignore the extra 0s, you get 110011. After you add 1 to the left of the decimal point, the normalized number in binary is:

$$-2^{-3} \times 1.110011$$

E

Standard Libraries

E-1 HEADER FILES

C++ contains a rich set of header files that are used to provide functionality and standard definitions for programs. With the approval of the C++ standard, many of the library header files changed slightly. In general, the ".h" suffix was dropped from all files, although many compilers still allow it. C-style files included in the standard are prefixed with the letter "C." The previous and standard names are shown in Table E-1.

Previous	Standard
assert.h	cassert
ctype.h	cctype
float.h	cfloat
limit.h	climit
stddef.h	cstddef
stdlib.h	cstdlib
math.h	cmath
string.h	cstring
fstream.h	fstream
iomanip.h	iomanip
iostream.h	iostream
	string
	sstream

Table E-1 Renamed header files

E-2 CLIMITS

The limits file contains the minimum and maximum values for internal types. As indicated by its name, its concept and use was inherited from the C language. Its contents are shown in Table E-2.

Meaning	Identifier	16-bit word[a]	32-bit word[a]
bits in a char	CHAR_BIT	Varies: May be 8, 16, or 24 bits	
short char minimum	SCHAR_MIN	–128	–128
short char maximum	SCHAR_MAX	127	127
unsigned char maximum	UCHAR_MAX	255	255
char minimum	CHAR_MIN	–128	–128
char maximum	CHAR_MAX	127	127
short int minimum	SHRT_MIN	–32,768	–32,768
short int maximum	SHRT_MAX	32,767	32,767
unsigned short maximum	USHRT_MAX	65,535	65,535
int minimum	**INT_MIN**	-32,768	-2,147,483,648
int maximum	**INT_MAX**	32,767	2,147,483,647

[a]Libraries contain unformatted numbers (no commas), often expressed in hexadecimal.

Table E-2 Contents of <climits>

Meaning	Identifier	16-bit word[a]	32-bit word[a]
unsigned int maximum	**UINT_MAX**	65,535	4,294,967,295
long minimum	**LONG_MIN**	-2,147,483,648	-2,147,483,648
long maximum	**LONG_MAX**	2,147,483,647	2,147,483,647
unsigned long maxim	**ULONG_MAX**	4,294,967,295	4,294,967,295

[a]Libraries contain unformatted numbers (no commas), often expressed in hexadecimal.

Table E-2 Contents of <climits> (*continued*)

E-3 CFLOAT

The float library, also inherited from the C language, contains the minimum and maximum values for floating-point numbers.

Meaning	Identifier	Typical Value)
digits of precision	FLT_DIG	6
	DBL_DIG	15
	LDBL_DIG	15
size of mantissa	FLT_MANT_DIG	24
	DBL_MANT_DIG	53
	LDBL_MANT_DIG	53
largest integer for negative exponent (float radix)	FLT_MIN_EXP	–125
	DBL_MIN_EXP	–1021
	LDBL_MIN_EXP	–1021
largest integer for negative exponent (base 10)	FLT_MIN_10_EXP	–37
	DBL_MIN_10_EXP	–308
	LDBL_MIN_10_EXP	–308
largest integer for positive exponent (float radix)	FLT_MAX_EXP	128
	DBL_MAX_EXP	1024
	LDBL_MAX_EXP	1024
largest integer for positive exponent (base 10)	FLT_MAX_10_EXP	38
	DBL_MAX_10_EXP	308
	LDBL_MAX_10_EXP	308
largest possible real number	FLT_MAX	3.40282e+38
	DBL_MAX	1.79769e+308
	LDBL_MAX	1.79769e+308
smallest possible real number	FLT_MIN	1.17549e-38
	DBL_MIN	2.22507e-308
	LDBL_MIN	2.22507e-308
smallest possible fraction	FLT_EPSILON	1.19209e-07
	DBL_EPSILON	2.22045e-16
	LDBL_EPSILON	2.22045e-16

Table E-3 Contents of <cfloat>

Program E-1 can be used to determine the values of your system.

Program E-1 Determine size of floating-point values

```
/* This program dispslays the values of floating-point numbers in CW.
      Written by:
      Date:
*/
#include <iostream>
#include <iomanip>
#include <cfloat>
using namespace std;

int main ()
{
   cout << "Digits of Precision:\n";
   cout << "float:      " << setw(10) << FLT_DIG  << endl;
   cout << "double:     " << setw(10) << DBL_DIG  << endl;
   cout << "long dbl:   " << setw(10) << LDBL_DIG << endl;

   cout << "\nSize of Mantissa:\n";
   cout << "float    :  " << setw(10) << FLT_MANT_DIG  << endl;
   cout << "double   :  " << setw(10) << DBL_MANT_DIG  << endl;
   cout << "long dbl:   " << setw(10) << LDBL_MANT_DIG << endl;

   cout << "\nLargest Integer for Negative Exponent (Float Radix):\n";
   cout << "float    :  " << setw(10) << FLT_MIN_EXP  << endl;
   cout << "double   :  " << setw(10) << DBL_MIN_EXP  << endl;
   cout << "long dbl:   " << setw(10) << LDBL_MIN_EXP << endl;

   cout << "\nLargest Integer for Negative Exponent (Base 10):\n";
   cout << "float    :  " << setw(10) << FLT_MIN_10_EXP  << endl;
   cout << "double   :  " << setw(10) << DBL_MIN_10_EXP  << endl;
   cout << "long dbl:   " << setw(10) << LDBL_MIN_10_EXP << endl;

   cout << "\nLargest Integer for Positive Exponent (Float Radix):\n";
   cout << "float    :  " << setw(10) << FLT_MAX_EXP  << endl;
   cout << "double   :  " << setw(10) << DBL_MAX_EXP  << endl;
   cout << "long dbl:   " << setw(10) << LDBL_MAX_EXP << endl;

   cout << "\nLargest Integer for Positive Exponent (Base 10):\n";
   cout << "float    :  " << setw(10) << FLT_MAX_10_EXP  << endl;
   cout << "double   :  " << setw(10) << DBL_MAX_10_EXP  << endl;
   cout << "long dbl:   " << setw(10) << LDBL_MAX_10_EXP << endl;

   cout << "\nLargest Possible Real Number:\n";
   cout << "float    :  " << setw(10) << FLT_MAX  << endl;
   cout << "double   :  " << setw(10) << DBL_MAX  << endl;
   cout << "long dbl:   " << setw(10) << LDBL_MAX << endl;
```

Program E-1 Determine size of floating-point values (*continued*)

```
  cout << "\nSmallest Possible Real Number:\n";
  cout << "float    :  " << setw(10) << FLT_MIN  << endl;
  cout << "double   :  " << setw(10) << DBL_MIN  << endl;
  cout << "long dbl:   " << setw(10) << LDBL_MIN << endl;

  cout << "\nSmallest Possible Fraction:\n";
  cout << "float    :  " << setw(10) << FLT_EPSILON  << endl;
  cout << "double   :  " << setw(10) << DBL_EPSILON  << endl;
  cout << "long dbl:   " << setw(10) << LDBL_EPSILON << endl;
  return 0;
} // main
```

F Function Prototypes

F-1 FUNCTION INDEX

In this appendix, we list most of the standard functions found in the C++ language. We have grouped them by library so that related functions are grouped together. The functions are listed alphabetically in the table for your convenience. Note that not all functions are covered in the text and that there are functions that are not covered in this appendix.

Function / page	Library	Function / page	Library	Function / page	Library
abort page 905	cstdlib	fwrite page 902	cstdio	realloc page 905	cstdlib
abs page 905	cstdlib	gcount page 904	iostream	remove page 903	cstdio
acos page 901	cmath	get page 904	iostream	rename page 903	cstdio
asctime page 906	ctime	getc page 902	cstdio	resetiosflags page 904	iomanip
asin page 901	cmath	getchar page 902	cstdio	rewind page 902	cstdio
atan page 901	cmath	getline page 904	iostream	scanf page 902	cstdio
atan2 page 901	cmath	gets page 903	cstdio	seekg page 904	iostream
atexit page 905	cstdlib	gmtime page 906	ctime	seekp page 904	iostream
atof page 905	cstdlib	good page 903	iostream	setf page 903	iostream
atoi page 905	cstdlib	hex page 904	iostream	setfill page 904	iomanip
atol page 905	cstdlib	ignore page 904	iostream	setiosflags page 904	iomanip
bad page 903	iostream	isalnum page 901	cctype	setprecision page 904	iomanip
calloc page 905	cstdlib	isalpha page 901	cctype	setw page 904	iomanip
ceil page 901	cmath	iscntrl page 901	cctype	sin page 902	cmath
clear page 903	iostream	isdigit page 901	cctype	sinh page 902	cmath
clearerr page 902	cstdio	isgraph page 901	cctype	sprintf page 902	cstdio
clock page 906	ctime	islower page 901	cctype	sqrt page 902	cmath
close page 903	fstream	isprint page 901	cctype	srand page 905	cstdlib
cos page 901	cmath	ispunct page 901	cctype	sscanf page 902	cstdio
cosh page 901	cmath	isspace page 901	cctype	strcat page 905	cstring
ctime page 906	ctime	isupper page 901	cctype	strchr page 906	cstring
dec page 904	iostream	isxdigit page 901	cctype	strcmp page 906	cstring
difftime page 906	ctime	labs page 905	cstdlib	strcpy page 905	cstring
div page 905	cstdlib	ldexp page 902	cmath	strcspn page 906	cstring
endl page 904	iostream	ldiv page 905	cstdlib	strlen page 906	cstring
eof page 903	iostream	localtime page 906	ctime	strncat page 905	cstring
exit page 905	cstdlib	log page 902	cmath	strncmp page 906	cstring
exp page 901	cmath	log10 page 902	cmath	strncpy page 905	cstring
fabs page 901	cmath	malloc page 905	cstdlib	strpbrk page 906	cstring
fail page 903	iostream	memchr page 906	cstring	strrchr page 906	cstring
fclose page 902	cstdio	memcmp page 906	cstring	strspn page 906	cstring
feof page 902	cstdio	memcpy page 905	cstring	strstr page 906	cstring
ferror page 902	cstdio	memmove page 905	cstring	strtod page 905	cstdlib
fgetc page 902	cstdio	mktime page 906	ctime	strtol page 905	cstdlib
fgets page 903	cstdio	modf page 902	cmath	strtoul page 905	cstdlib
fill page 903	iostream	oct page 904	iostream	system page 905	cstdlib
flags page 903	iostream	open page 903	fstream	tan page 902	cmath
floor page 901	cmath	pcount page 904	iostream	tanh page 902	cmath
flush page 904	iostream	peek page 904	iostream	tellg page 904	iostream
fmod page 901	cmath	pow page 902	cmath	tellp page 904	iostream
fopen page 902	cstdio	precision page 903	iostream	ctime page 906	ctime

Function / page		Library	Function / page		Library	Function / page		Library
fprintf	page 902	cstdio	printf	page 902	cstdio	tmpfile	page 903	cstdio
fputc	page 902	cstdio	put	page 904	iostream	tmpnam	page 903	cstdio
fputs	page 903	cstdio	putback	page 904	iostream	tolower	page 901	cctype
fread	page 902	cstdio	putc	page 902	cstdio	toupper	page 901	cctype
free	page 905	cstdlib	putchar	page 902	cstdio	ungetc	page 902	cstdio
frexp	page 901	cmath	puts	page 903	cstdio	unsetf	page 903	iostream
fscanf	page 902	cstdio	rand	page 905	cstdlib	width	page 903	iostream
fseek	page 902	cstdio	rdstate	page 903	iostream	write	page 903	iostream
ftell	page 902	cstdio	read	page 903	iostream	ws	page 904	iostream

F-2 CHARACTER LIBRARY

The following functions are found in <cctype>.

isalnum	int	isalnum (int a_char);
isalpha	int	isalpha (int a_char);
iscntrl	int	iscntrl (int a_char);
isdigit	int	isdigit (int a_char);
isgraph	int	isgraph (int a_char);
islower	int	islower (int a_char);
isprint	int	isprint (int a_char);
ispunct	int	ispunct (int a_char);
isspace	int	isspace (int a_char);
isupper	int	isupper (int a_char);
isxdigit	int	isxdigit (int a_char);
tolower	int	tolower (int a_char);
toupper	int	toupper (int a_char);

F-3 CMATH LIBRARY

The following functions are found in <cmath>.

acos	double	acos (double number);
asin	double	asin (double number);
atan	double	atan (double number);
atan2	double	atan2 (double number1, double number2);
ceil	double	ceil (double number);
cos	double	cos (double number);
cosh	double	cosh (double number);
exp	double	exp (double number);
fabs	double	fabs (double number);
floor	double	floor (double number);
fmod	double	fmod (double number1, double number2);
frexp	double	frexp (double number, int* exp);

ldexp	double	ldexp (double number, int* exp);
log	double	log (double number);
log10	double	log10 (double number);
modf	double	modf (double number, double* divisor);
pow	double	pow (double number1, double number2);
sqrt	double	sqrt (double number);
sin	double	sin (double number);
sinh	double	sinh (double number);
tan	double	tan (double number);
tanh	double	tanh (double number);

F-4 TRADITIONAL C I/O LIBRARY

We have divided the traditional C input/output library <ccstdio> by the type of data being read.

GENERAL I/O

Input/output functions that apply to all files.

clearerr	void	clearerr (FILE *fp);
fclose	int	fclose (FILE *fp);
feof	int	feof (FILE *fp);
ferror	int	ferror (FILE *fp);
fopen	FILE	*fopen (const char *extn_name, const char *file_mode);

FORMATTED I/O

Input/output functions that convert text data to/from internal memory formats.

fprintf	int	fprintf (FILE *fileOut, const char *format_string, …);
printf	int	printf (const char *format_string, …);
sprintf	int	sprintf (char * to_loc, const char *format_string, …);
fscanf	int	fscanf (FILE *fileIn, const char *format_string, …);
scanf	int	scanf (const char *format_string, …);
sscanf	int	sscanf (const char *from_loc, const char *format_string, …);

CHARACTER I/O

Input/output functions that read and write one character at a time.

fgetc	int	fgetc (FILE *fp);
fputc	int	fputc (int, FILE *fp);
getc	int	getc (FILE *fp);
getchar	int	getchar (void);
putc	int	putc (int, FILE *fp);
putchar	int	putchar (int char_out);
ungetc	int	ungetc (int char_out, FILE *fp);

FILE I/O

Input/output functions for binary files.

fread	size_t	fread (void *in_area, size_t size, size_t count, FILE *fp);
fwrite	size_t	fwrite (const void *out_data, size_t size, size_t count, FILE *fp);
fseek	int	fseek (FILE *fp, long offset, int from_loc);
ftell	long	ftell (FILE *fp);
rewind	void	rewind (FILE *fp);

CSTRING I/O

Input/output functions that read and write strings.

gets	char	*gets (char *cstring);
puts	int	puts (const char *cstring);
fgets	char	*fgets (char *cstring, int size, FILE *fp);
fputs	int	fputs (const char *cstring, FILE *fp);

SYSTEM FILE CONTROL

System commands that create and delete files on the disk.

tmpnam	char	*tmpnam (char *fp);
tmpfile	FILE	*tmpfile (void);
remove	int	remove (const char *file_name);
rename	int	rename (const char *old_name, const char *new_name);

F-5 C++ I/O LIBRARY

The following functions are found only in C++. For a complete discussion of the C++ class library design, refer to Appendix K on page 937.

GENERAL

close	void	fstream :: close (void);
close	void	ifstream :: close (void);
close	void	ofstream :: close (void);
open	void	fstream :: open (const char *fs_ID, int mode);
open	void	ifstream :: open (const char *fs_ID, int mode);
open	void	ofstream :: open (const char *fs_ID, int mode);

FILE STATUS

bad	int	ios :: bad (void);
fail	int	ios :: fail (void);
eof	int	ios :: eof (void);
flags	long	ios :: flags (void);
flags	long	ios :: flags (long new_flag);
good	int	ios :: good (void);
setf	long	ios :: setf (long new_flag);
setf	long	ios :: setf (long new_flag, long mask);
unsetf	long	ios :: unsetf (long flag);
rdstate	int	ios :: rdstate (void);
clear	int	ios :: clear (int = ios :: goodbit);

OUTPUT FORMATTING

fill	int	ios :: fill (char fill_char);
precision	int	ios :: precision (void);
precision	int	ios :: precision (int new_precision);
width	int	ios :: width (void);
width	int	ios :: width (int new_width);

BLOCK I/O

read	istream&	read (char *data);
read	istream&	read (signed char *buffer, int size);
read	istream&	read (unsigned char *buffer, int size);
write	ostream&	write (const char *buffer, int size);
write	ostream&	write (const signed char *buffer, int size);
write	ostream&	write (const unsigned char *buffer, int size);

tellg	streampos	istream :: tellg (void);
tellp	streampos	ostream :: tellp (void);
seekg	istream&	istream :: seekg (streampos position);
seekg	istream&	istream :: seekg (long offset, seek_dir where_from);
seekp	ostream&	ostream :: seekp (streampos position);
seekp	ostream&	ostream :: seekp (long offset, seek_dir where_from);

CHARACTER I/O

get	istream&	istream :: get (char& character);
get	istream&	istream :: get (signed char& character);
get	istream&	istream :: get (unsigned char& character);
put	ostream&	ostream :: put (char character);
put	ostream&	ostream :: put (signed char character);
put	ostream&	ostream :: put (unsigned char character);
peek	int	istream :: peek (void);
putback	istream&	istream :: putback (char character);

LINE I/O

get	istream&	istream :: get (char *buffer, int n, char stop = '\n');
get	istream&	istream :: get (signed char *buffer, int n, char stop = '\n');
get	istream&	istream :: get (unsigned char *buffer, int n, char stop = '\n');
getline	istream&	istream :: getline (char *buffer, int n, char delimiter = '\n');
getline	istream&	istream :: getline (signed char *buffer, int n, char delimiter = '\n');
getline	istream&	istream :: getline (unsigned char *buffer, int n, char delimiter = '\n');

MISCELLANEOUS I/O

gcount	int	istream :: gcount (void);
pcount	int	ostream :: pcount (void);
ignore	istream&	ignore (int count = 1, int stop = EOF);
flush	ostream&	ostream :: flush (void);

MANIPULATORS

This section lists the manipulators that can be used with the input/output classes. They are not function prototypes—they just show the usage format.

oct	oct
dec	dec
hex	hex
ws	ws
endl	endl
flush	flush
setfill	setfill (fill_char)
setw	setw (width)
setprecision	setprecision (size)
setiosflags	setiosflags (flags)
resetiosflags	resetiosflags (flags)

F-6 STANDARD LIBRARY

The following functions are found in <cstdlib>.

CMATH FUNCTIONS

The following cmath functions are found in <cstdlib>.

abs	int	abs (int number);
div	div_t	div (int numerator, int divisor);
labs	long	labs (long number);
ldiv	ldiv_t	ldiv (long numerator, long divisor);
rand	int	rand (void);
srand	void	srand (unsigned seed);

MEMORY FUNCTIONS

The following functions are for memory allocation.

calloc	void	*calloc (size_t num_elements, size_t element_size);
free	void	free (void *);
malloc	void	*malloc (size_t num_bytes);
realloc	void	*realloc (void *stge_ptr, size_t element_size);

PROGRAM CONTROL

The following functions control the program flow.

exit	void	exit (int exit_code);
abort	void	abort (void);
atexit	int	atexit (void (* function_name) (void));

SYSTEM COMMUNICATION

The following function communicates with the operating system.

system	int	system (const char *system_command);

CONVERSION FUNCTIONS

The following functions convert data from one type to another.

atof	double	atof (const char *real_num);
atoi	int	atoi (const char *real_num);
atol	long	atol (const char *real_num);
strtod	double	strtod (const char *str, char **next_str);
strtol	long	strtol (const char *str, char **next_str, int base);
strtoul	unsigned long	strtoul (const char *str, char **next_str, int base);

F-7 CSTRING LIBRARY

The following functions are found in <cstring>.

COPYING DATA

The following functions all copy strings or memory.

memcpy	void	*memcpy (void *to_mem, const void *fr_mem, size_t bytes);
memmove	void	*memmove (void *to_mem, const void *fr_mem, size_t bytes);
strcpy	char	*strcpy (char *to_str, const char *fr_str);
strncpy	char	*strncpy (char *to_str, const char *fr_str, size_t bytes);
strcat	char	*strcat (char *to_str, const char *fr_str);
strncat	char	*strncat (char *to_str, const char *fr_str, size_t bytes);

COMPARING DATA

The following functions all compare strings or memory.

memchr	void	*memchr (const void *mem, int a_char, size_t bytes);
memcmp	int	memcmp (const void *mem1, const void *mem2, size_t bytes);
strchr	char	*strchr (const char *str, int a_char);
strrchr	char	*strrchr (const char *str, int a_char);
strcmp	int	strcmp (const char *str1, const char *str2);
strncmp	int	strncmp (const char *str1, const char *str2, size_t bytes);
strpbrk	char	*strpbrk (const char *str1, const char *str2);
strstr	char	*strstr (const char *str1, const char *str2);

CSTRING LENGTHS

The following functions return the length of strings or substrings.

strlen	size_t	strlen (const char *str);
strspn	size_t	strspn (const char *str1, const char *str2);
strcspn	size_t	strcspn (const char *str1, const char *str2);

F-8 TIME

The following functions are found in <ctime>.

clock	clock_t	clock (void);
difftime	double	difftime (time_t time_start, time_t time_end);
mktime	time_t	mktime (struct tm *cal_time);
ctime	time_t	ctime (time_t *num_time);
asctime	char	*asctime (const struct tm *cal_time);
ctime	char	*ctime (const time_t *num_time);
gmtime	struct tm	*gmtime (const time_t *num_time);
localtime	struct tm	*localtime (const time_t *num_time);

G Preprocessor Directives

A C++ compiler is made of two functional parts: a preprocessor and a translator. The preprocessor uses programmer-supplied commands to prepare the source program for compilation. The translator converts the C++ statements into machine code that it places in an object module. Depending on the compiler design, the preprocessor and translator can work together or the preprocessor can create a separate version of the source program, which is then read by the translator. This is the design shown in Figure G-1.

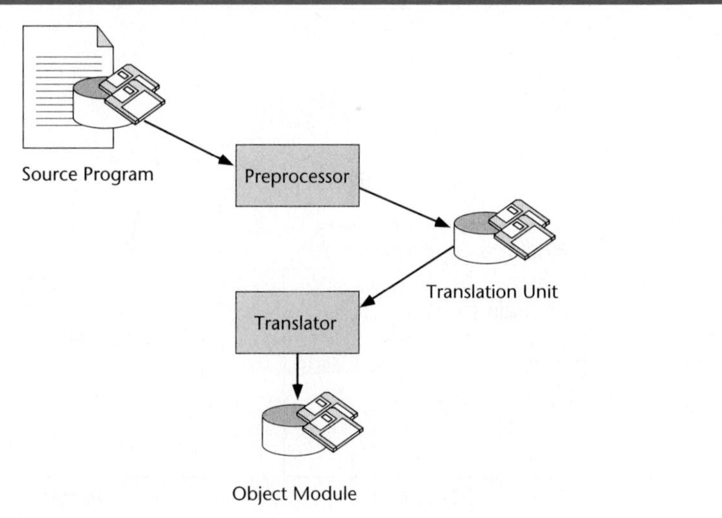

Figure G-1 Compiler environment

The preprocessor can be thought of as a smart editor. Like a smart editor, it inserts, includes, excludes, and replaces text based on commands supplied by the programmer. In this case, however, the commands are made a permanent part of the source program.

All preprocessor commands start with a pound sign (#). Some of the traditional compilers require the pound sign to be in the first column. ANSI C++ specifies that it can be anywhere on the line. In addition, preprocessor commands can be placed anywhere in the source program.

The preprocessor performs three different functions. First, as we have seen ever since our first program, it is used to specify which header files are to be included in the program. Second, it is used for macro definition, which gives us the capability to create macros for use in our program. The FLUSH statement is a simple macro definition. Finally, it can be used to conditionally include or exclude code from the program.

G-1 FILE INCLUSION

The first and most common job of a preprocessor is to copy the contents of files into programs. The files are usually header files that contain prototype statements and data declarations for the program, but they can contain any valid C++ statement.

The preprocessor command is *#include* and it has two different types of operands. The first directs the preprocessor to include header files from the system library. This form places the library name in pointed brackets, as shown below and in Figure G-2.

```
#include <iostream>
```

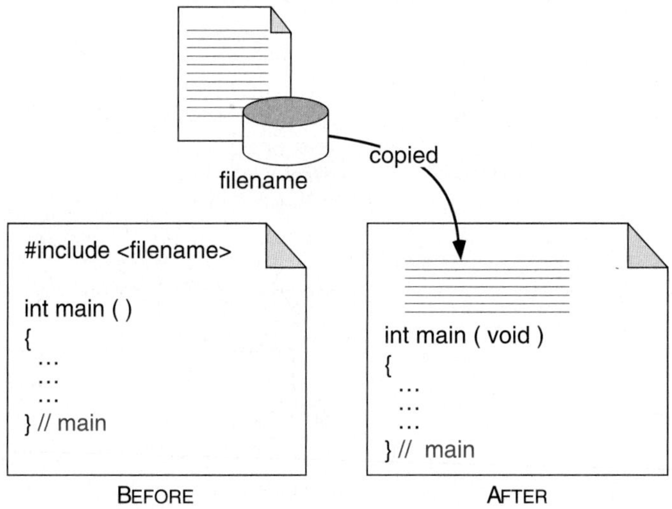

Figure G-2 Include directive

In the second form, the preprocessor looks for the header files in the library that holds the source code. This format is shown below. (ANSII/ISO C++ has changed the standard to format the header files without the *.h* extension; however, we recommend that you continue using it until you are sure your compiler has been upgraded to the new standard.)

```
#include "filename.h"
```

G-2 MACRO DEFINITION

The second preprocessor function is macro definition. A macro is formal syntax that can be used to generate statements for use in a program. For the C++ language, the macro generates C++ statements.

There are two different macro formats: simple and parameterized. Both use the command format shown below.

```
#define name token(s)
```

Tokens are text that is used to specify the format of the resulting statement and are considered to be the macro body.

Once defined, a macro may be used until it is undefined (deleted). When the preprocessor encounters the name of a macro within the program, it generates the appropriate C++ statements as specified by the macro definition using the tokens specified in the definition body. The tokens can be straightforward C++ code or complex parameterized statements.

SIMPLE COMMANDS

Simple commands are so named because they have no parameters. This does not mean that the code is simple, however; it means that the macro code can be used without modification. For example, each of the following macros is simple.

```
#define SIZE   9
#define TRUE   1
#define OF_MSG "Error 304: Heap overflow. Call programmer."
#define LIMIT  (234)
#define FLUSH  while (cin.get(aCh) && aCh != '\n')
```

It is a traditional standard that the names of macros be coded in uppercase to warn the reader that they are macros. There is no syntactical requirement that they be uppercase, however. Figure G-3 shows two examples of simple macros. The first uses macros to define the dimensions of an array. The second uses a macro to define an error code.

```
#define ROWS 5
#define COLS 4

#define  OFMsg "Err 201: Stack Overflow\n"

int main ( )
{
 int  ary[ ROWS ][ COLS ] ;
 ...
 cout << OFMsg ;
 ...
} //  main
```

BEFORE

```
int main ( )
{
 int  ary[ 5 ][ 4 ] ;
 ...
 cout << "Err 201: Stack Overflow\n" ;
 ...
} //  main
```

AFTER

Figure G-3 Define substitution

There are some points you should remember about macro expansion. First, macro expansion does not require an assignment operator. Everything following the macro name is simply treated as text to be substituted for the macro name by the preprocessor. If you include an assignment operator, it will be included in your generated code. Second, preprocessor commands are not terminated by semicolons. If you place a semicolon at the end of the statement, it will be included in the expanded code. Both of these situations are common errors. Table G-1 shows examples of the errors that they can generate.

Code	Result
Example 1	
`#define   SIZE = 9;`	
...	...
`a = SIZE;`	`a = = 9;;`
Example 2	
`#define LIMIT 9;`	
...	...
`for ( i = 0; i < LIMIT; i++ )`	`for ( i = 0; i < 9;; i++ )`
...	...

Table G-1 Examples of define substitution errors

In the first example, the intent is to assign SIZE to the variable a. Since an assignment operator is included, however, the result is an expression that tests a for 9. This is a valid statement and no error is generated, but no code is generated either.

The first example contains a second error, the semicolon at the end. In this case, this also results in valid code, a null statement, which will not cause a compile error. These types of errors can be difficult to locate, especially when you consider that you normally do not see the expanded code.

In the second example, the macro expansion does result in a compile error. In this case, the semicolon creates too many expressions in the *for* statement.

PARAMETERIZED MACRO

Often the macro you want to generate must contain variable data. In this case, you indicate the variable data through parameters. This capability is very powerful.

To include parameters in the macro, the opening parenthesis must be placed immediately at the end of the macro name; that is, there can be no whitespace between the macro name and the opening parenthesis of the parameter list. If there is a space, the opening parenthesis is considered part of the token body and the macro is assumed to be simple.

The identifiers inside the parentheses are formal parameters (as in a function) and are replaced with actual parameters during the expansion. However, the replacement of formal parameters with actual parameters in macro expansion works differently than the substitution in a function. In a function, the formal parameters are replaced with the *value* of actual parameters. In macro expansion, only the token text is replaced. In other words, the actual parameters are replaced by the formal parameters textually. The form is shown below.

```
#define   name( par1, par2, …) replacement-tokens
```

Note that the parameters are separated by commas. The name of each parameter must be unique within the macro.

The parameterized macro expansion takes place in two steps:

1. The actual parameters in the macro are associated with the formal parameters in the macro definition (command).
2. A copy of the macro body, with the actual parameters substituted for the formal parameters, replaces the macro statement.

This substitution is demonstrated in Figure G-4.

Remember that the preprocessor operates much like an editor. This means there is no checking that the expanded statement is valid. Because a macro expansion is a textual substitution instead of a value substitution, it is possible to generate erroneous, but syntactically valid, code. For example, consider the following macro that sometimes generates what you want and sometimes gives very different results.

```
#define PRODUCT( x, y )     x * y
```

In the following example, the result is as you would expect and want.

```
z = PRODUCT ( a, b );
```

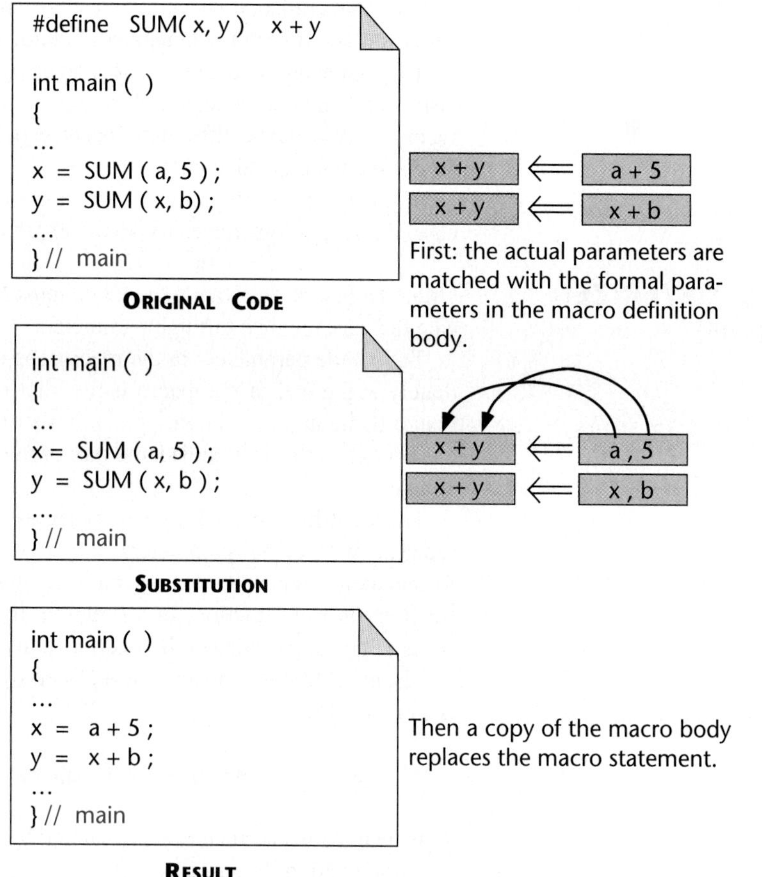
#define SUM(x, y) x + y
int main ( )
{
...
x = SUM (a, 5) ;
y = SUM (x, b) ;
...
} // main
ORIGINAL CODE
x + y
a + 5
x + y
x + b
First: the actual parameters are matched with the formal parameters in the macro definition body.
int main ( )
{
...
x = SUM (a, 5) ;
y = SUM (x, b) ;
...
} // main
SUBSTITUTION
x + y
a , 5
x + y
x , b
int main ( )
{
...
x = a + 5 ;
y = x + b ;
...
} // main
Then a copy of the macro body replaces the macro statement.
RESULT

Figure G-4 Macro parameters

The resulting code is

```
z = a * b;
```

Now, however, watch what happens when the same macro is used in the following statement:

```
z =  PRODUCT ( a + 1, b + 2 );
```

After expansion, we have the following code:

```
z = a + 1 * b + 2;
```

which is undoubtedly not what is wanted. Because of the rules of precedence, this expression becomes, in effect,

```
z = a + b + 2;
```

For this reason, always enclose the format parameters for the replacement tokens in parentheses. The correct code for PRODUCT then becomes

```
#define PRODUCT( a, b )     ( a ) * ( b )
```

which results in the correct expansion, as shown below.

```
z = ( a + 1 ) * ( b + 2 );
```

NESTED MACROS

It is possible to nest macros. C++ handles nested macros by simply rescanning a line after macro expansion. Therefore, if an expansion results in a new statement with a macro, the second macro will be properly expanded. For example, consider the macros shown below.

```
#define PRODUCT( a, b ) ( a ) * ( b )
#define SQUARE( a )   PRODUCT( a, a )
```

The expansion of

```
x = SQUARE ( 5 );
```

results in the following expansion:

```
x = PRODUCT( 5, 5 );
```

which after rescanning becomes

```
x = ( 5 ) * ( 5 );
```

Note, however, that the macro expansion will not rescan and reexpand a macro that appears in its own definition.

Finally, note that this rescanning may result in unexpected code. For example, consider the following preprocessor commands:

```
#define SIZE   S
#define S      10
```

The preprocessor first scans the text for SIZE and changes it to *S*. It then scans the text and changes *S* to 10. This situation is illustrated in Figure G-5.

```
#define SIZE S
#define S    10

int main ( )
{
...
if (length < SIZE )
...
} // main
```

ORIGINAL CODE

```
int main ( )
{
...
if ( length < S )
...
} // main
```

FIRST MACRO SCAN

```
int main ( )
{
...
if ( length < 10 )
...
} // main
```

SECOND MACRO SCAN

Figure G-5 Example of macro rescanning

MACRO STATEMENT CONTINUATION

Macros must be coded on a single line. If the macro is too long to fit on a line, you must use a continuation token. The continuation token is a backslash (\) followed immediately by a newline. If there is any whitespace between the backslash and the newline, then it is not a continuation token and the code will most likely generate an error. An example of a macro continuation is used in Program G-1.

Program G-1 Example of string directive

```
/* This program tests string directives.
      Written by:
      Date:
*/
#include <iostream>
using namespace std;

#define PRINT_INT(a) \
   cout << "Variable '" #a "' contains: " << a << endl

```

Program G-1 Example of string directive *(continued)*

```
int main ()
{
   int legalAge = 21;

   PRINT_INT (legalAge);

   return 0;
} // main
```

```
Results:
   Variable 'legalAge' contains: 21
```

STRING COMMAND (#)

The string command (#) is used to create text enclosed in quotes. This use of the pound sign must not be confused with the preprocessor command token. In this case, the pound sign appears in front of the formal parameter in the replacement section. The result is the use of the actual parameter as a string. This macro command operator is also used in Program G-1.

MERGE COMMAND (##)

Occasionally, it may be necessary to write macros that generate new tokens. With the merge command operator, two tokens are combined. For example, imagine we want to create `A1`, `B3`, and `Z8` in our program. This can be done easily with the following macro definition:

```
#define FORM(T, N)  T##N
```

Now, if we use the following code:

```
int   FORM (A, 1) = 1;
float FORM (B, 3) = 1.1;
char  FORM (Z, 8) = 'A';
```

we get

```
int   A1 = 1;
float B3 = 1.1;
char  Z8 = 'A';
```

UNDEFINE COMMAND

Once defined, a macro name cannot be redefined to change its value. Any attempt to do so will result in a compile error.

It is possible to delete the definition of a macro with the *#undef* command. This command terminates the definition of a macro command. Once a macro has been undefined, it can then be redefined with a new value as shown below.

```
#define  SIZE 20
...
#undef   SIZE
#define  SIZE 40
```

G-3 CONDITIONAL COMPILATION

The third use of the preprocessor is to conditionally include or exclude code from the program. For an application programmer, there are two common uses of this capability: inserting debugging logic in a program and commenting out code. The conditional compilation commands are defined in Table G-2.

Command	Meaning
#if	If expression: when true, following code included.
#endif	End of if expression: terminates included statements.
#else	Specifies alternate code to be included when expression is false.
#elif	Else-if: specifies alternate condition for including text when previous conditional statement is false.
#ifdef	If defined: include following statements when a macro name is defined by *#define*.
#ifndef	If not defined: include the following statements when a macro name is *not* defined.

Table G-2 Conditional compilation commands

IF...ELSE COMMANDS

The precompiler *if...else...endif* commands work just like their C++ counterparts, with two exceptions. First, the expression does not have to be enclosed in parentheses. Using parentheses is permitted, however, and it is a wise thing to do. Second, you do not have to block (use braces) multiple lines of code. All statements from the beginning of the conditional *if* command to its matching *endif* command are included. The format of the conditional *if* command is shown in Figure G-6.

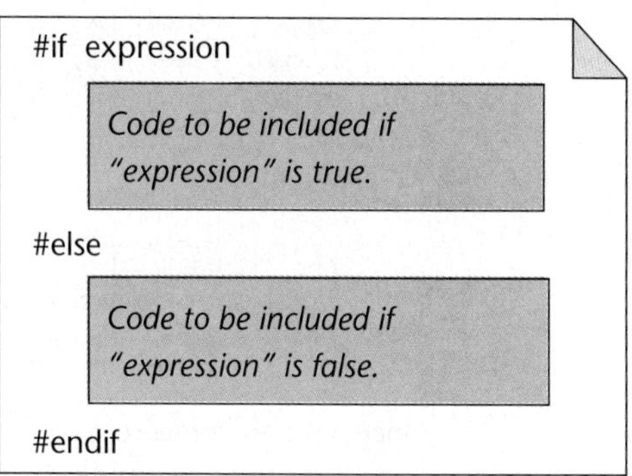

Figure G-6 Conditional *if* command

When the conditional expression is true, the statements that follow are included in the program to be compiled. If the condition is false, they are not included. Note that the conditional *if* command must be terminated by a conditional *#endif* command. If you leave out a matching *#endif,* then all of your program that follows will be part of the conditional compilation! As shown in Figure G-6, you can also use an *else* command. In this case, when the *#if* expression is false, the code following the *#else* is sent to the compilation.

Program G-2 contains an example of a conditional *if* command that you might use while debugging a program. In this example, we are tracing a variable as it changes in different functions in a program. When we are in debugging mode, as determined by DEBUG being set to 1, we will print the contents of the variable at key locations in the program. Since other variables may be displayed for debugging purposes also, we use the PRINT_INT defined macro we described earlier to print the value in the variables.

Program G-2 Debug example

```
#define DEBUG 0
#define PRINT_INT(a) \
   cout << "Variable '" #a "' contains: " << a << endl
   ...
   int totalScore = 0;
   ...
#if (DEBUG)
   PRINT_INT (totalScore);
#endif
```

CONDITIONAL MULTIWAY SELECTION

When we need a multiway decision, we use the fourth directive, *#elif.* For example, if you are writing a software application that has to run at multiple locations, you have to define unique code depending on the location you are compiling for. Each installation needs unique report headings and perhaps other unique code. One way to do this is shown in Program G-3.

Program G-3 Conditional multiway selection

```
#define DENVER  0
#define PHOENIX 0
#define SANJOSE 1
#define SEATTLE 0
...
#if (DENVER)
   // Denver unique initialization
   #include "Denver.h"
#elif (PHOENIX)
   // Phoenix unique initialization
   #include "Phoenix.h"
#elif (SANJOSE)
   // San Jose unique initialization
   #include "SanJose.h"
#else
   // Seattle unique initialization
   #include "Seattle.h"
#endif
```

Program G-3 Analysis First we create a unique header file for each installation. Then, using conditional commands, we select which include file to use based on defined flags for each site. In this example, we have selected San Jose, so only its code is included in the program.

EXCLUDING CODE

Often when working on a large program, we find that we want to "comment out" some code while we concentrate on a troublesome block of code. If there are comments in the code being excluded, using the comment token to exclude code can be difficult. (Remember, comments cannot be nested.) An easy way to exclude the code is with an *#if* command, as shown in Figure G-7. In this example, all the code for *locate part* is excluded from the compile. Note that we have used a very simple form of the conditional if, *#if 0*. Since we want to temporarily drop the shaded code, we simply set the condition to false (0).

```
// Locate part
   ...
   ...
   // Part not found
   ...
   ...
   // Wrong part found
   ...
// Process part
   ...
```

```
#if 0
// Locate part
   ...
   ...
   // Part not found
   ...
   ...
   // Wrong part found
   ...
#endif
// Process part
   ...
```

Figure G-7 Blocking out code

IF DEFINED (*ifdef/ifndef*)

The if-defined commands allow us to set conditional compilations based on whether or not a name has been *previously* defined in the compile unit. Its operation is illustrated in Figure G-8. While there are many uses for this command, it is most commonly used to prevent multiple definitions for the same name.

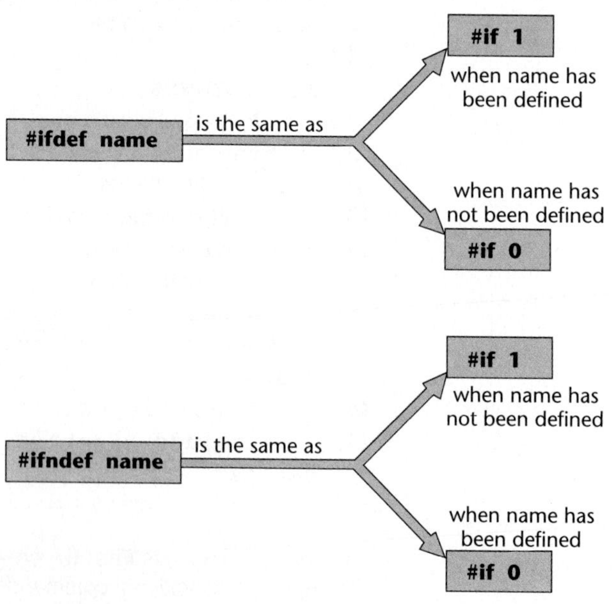

Figure G-8 The *#ifdef* and *#ifndef* commands

For example, assume that you are including several different application header files, many of which are also used separately. If one of the header files gets included multiple times, then there will be compilation errors. The solution is to use conditional compilation macros that prevent the code from being included in the program more than once. The concept is seen in the following block of code that used the *ifndef* to block an include.

```
#ifndef MSGa
  #define MSGa
  #include "PG-04B.h"
#endif
```

Note that we use the same *end-if* command (*#endif*).

G-4 PREVENTING DUPLICATE LIBRARY INCLUDES

In a project environment where many application libraries are used, we must guard against including a library more than once. This occurs when separate header files have to include a common library. For example, in Program G-4, the common functions (Program G-5 and Program G-6) both are designed to display a message when they are called. This would not be a problem, however, except that Program G-6 is called from both the mainline program and from Program G-5. Because both of them are including Program G-6, it will be included twice, resulting in compile errors.

The solution is relatively simple. By creating a defined constant, we are able to prevent the library from being included a second time (see statements 1 and 2 in Program G-5 and Program G-6).

Program G-4 Demonstrate conditional include

```
/* PG-04.cp  Demonstrate multiple includes.
      Written by:
      Date:
*/
#include <iostream>
using namespace std;

#include "PG-05.h"    // Contains include for PG-06.h
#include "PG-06.h"

int main ()
{
  cout << "Begin mainline PG-04.cp\n";

  printMsgA ("mainline");
  printMsgB ("mainline");

  cout << "End mainline PG-04.cp\n";
  return 0;
} // main
```

Program G-4 Demonstrate conditional include *(continued)*

```
Results:
Begin mainline PG-04.cp
**PG-05 called from: mainline
**PG-06 called from: PG-05
**PG-06 called from: mainline
End mainline PG-04.cp
```

Program G-5 First include file for Program G-4

```
#ifndef MSGa
#define MSGa
#include "PG-06.h"

const char* MSG_A = "**PG-05 called from: ";

void printMsgA (const char* from)
{
cout << MSG_A << from << endl;
printMsgB ("PG-05");
return;
} // printMsgA
#endif
```

Program G-6 Second include file for Program G-4

```
#ifndef MSGb
#define MSGb

const char* MSG_B = "**PG-06 called from: ";

void printMsgB (const char* from)
{
cout << MSG_B << from << endl;
return;
} // printMsgB
#endif
```

H

Bitwise Operators

The C++ language is a proper language for system programming because it contains operators that can manipulate data at the bit level. For example, the Internet requires that bits be manipulated to create addresses for subnets and supernets.

There are two categories of **bitwise operators** available in C++ that let you operate on data at the bit level: logical bitwise operators and shift bitwise operators. The logical operators look at data as individual bits to be manipulated. The shift operators, on the other hand, may treat the data as signed or unsigned integers at the discretion of the software engineer who designs the system. This decision is often predicated on the hardware for which the compiler is being written. In other words, ANSI has not specified an absolute standard in this area. For this reason, the shift operators should be used cautiously. *They may make the code nonportable!*

H-1 LOGICAL BITWISE OPERATORS

Four operators manipulate the bits logically: *bitwise and* (&), *bitwise inclusive or* (|), *bitwise exclusive or* (^), and *one's complement* (~). The first three are binary expressions; the one's complement is a unary expression.

BITWISE *and* OPERATOR

The ***bitwise and*** (&) is a binary operator that requires two integral operands (character or integer). It does a bit-by-bit comparison between the two operands. The result of the comparison is one only when both bits are one; it is zero otherwise. Table H-1 shows the result of bit-by-bit comparison.

First Operand Bit	Second Operand Bit	Result
0	0	0
0	1	0
1	0	0
1	1	1

Table H-1 ***and*** **truth table**

FORCING TO ZERO

One of the applications of the *bitwise and* operator is ***forcing*** selected bits in a field **to zero**. This is done by building a mask for the second operand. A ***mask*** is a variable or constant that contains a bit configuration used to control the setting of bits in a bitwise operation. Any bit location that is to be zero in the result is set to zero in the mask; any bit location that is to be unchanged in the results is set to one in the mask. Therefore, the rules for constructing an *and* mask are:

1. To force a location to zero, use a zero bit.
2. To leave a location unchanged, use a one bit.

To understand why these rules work, refer to Table H-1. The mask bit is the second bit. Note how when it is a zero, the result is always zero. When it is a one, the result is always the same as the first bit. In other words, any bit *and* zero is zero; any bit *and* one is unchanged.

The second operand in bitwise operators is called a mask.

For example, assume that we want to turn off the five leftmost bits of a number stored as an 8-bit integer. The mask should start with 5 zero bits to turn off the first 5 bits and then contain 3 one bits to leave the last 3 unchanged. The *and* mask is seen in the following example:

```
number   XXXXXXXX  &
mask     00000111
         --------
result   00000XXX
```

As you can see from this example, the job of forcing bits to zero (or turning them off) is done by the zeros in the mask operand. The power to force a zero is in the hand of zeros in the second operand.

BITWISE INCLUSIVE *or* OPERATOR

The ***bitwise inclusive or*** is a binary operator (|) that requires two integral operands (character or integer). It does a bit-by-bit comparison between the two operands. The result of the comparison is zero if both operands are zero; it is one otherwise. Table H-2 shows the result of bit-by-bit comparison.

First bit	Second bit	Result
0	0	0
0	1	1
1	0	1
1	1	1

Table H-2 Inclusive *or* truth table

FORCING TO ONE

One common application of *bit inclusive or* is ***forcing*** selected bits in a field to one. To understand this, refer to Table H-2. Note that if either bit is a one, then the result is a one. To force a bit on, therefore, all that you need to do is to construct a mask with the desired one bit set on. This guarantees that the result will have a one bit in that location. The rules for constructing an *or* mask are:

1. To force a location to one, use a one bit.
2. To leave a location unchanged, use a zero bit.

For example, assume that we need to turn on the 5 leftmost bits in a field stored as an 8-bit integer. This requires that the leftmost bits of the mask be set to one and the remaining bits be set to zero. The mask is shown below.

```
number          XXXXXXXX    |
mask            11111000
                --------
result          11111XXX
```

As you can see from this example, the job of forcing a bit to one (on) is done by the ones in the mask operand.

BITWISE EXCLUSIVE *or* OPERATOR

The ***bitwise exclusive or*** is a binary operator (^) that requires two integral operands (character or integer). It does a bit-by-bit comparison between the two operands. The result of the comparison is one only if one of the operands is one and the other is zero; it is zero if both operands' bits are zero or one—that is, if they are both the same. Table H-3 shows the result of bit-by-bit comparison.

First bit	Second bit	Result
0	0	0
0	1	1
1	0	1
1	1	0

Table H-3 *Exclusive or* truth table

FORCING A CHANGE

One of the applications of bitwise exclusive *or* is ***forcing*** selected bits in a field **to change**—that is, to change zeros to ones and ones to zeros. This is sometimes called "flipping bits." To understand flipping bits, refer to Table H-3. The resulting bit is one when one bit is a zero and the other is a one; if both bits are zero or both are one, the result is zero. To force a bit to change, therefore, the forcing bit in the mask is set to one; bits that are to be unchanged are set to zero. The rules for constructing an *exclusive or* mask are:

1. To force a location to change, use a one bit.
2. To leave a location unchanged, use a zero bit.

For example, assume that we want to change the 5 leftmost bits of a number stored as an 8-bit integer. We code the mask with five ones and three zeros as shown below. (Y indicates a changed bit.)

```
number          XXXXXXXX     ^
mask            11111000
                --------
result          YYYYYXXX
```

As you can see from this example, the job of forcing a bit to change is done by the ones in the masking operand.

ONE'S COMPLEMENT OPERATOR

The ***one's complement*** is a unary operator (~) applied to an integral value (character or integer). It complements the bits in the operand; that is, it reverses the bit value. The result is one when the original bit is zero; it is zero when the original bit is one. Table H-4 shows the result of the *one's complement.*

Original bit	Result
0	1
1	0

Table H-4 One's complement truth table

H-2 SHIFT OPERATORS

The shift operators move bits to the left or the right. When applied to unsigned numbers, these operators are implementation independent. However, they must be used with caution when used with signed numbers. ANSI C++ leaves the implementation up to the compiler writer; there is no standard. Therefore, code that shifts signed numbers may not be portable to other platforms.

BITWISE SHIFT LEFT OPERATOR

The *bitwise **shift left*** is a binary operator (<<) that requires two integral operands (character or integer). The first operand is the value to be shifted. The second operand specifies the number of bits to be shifted.

Shifting binary numbers is just like shifting decimal numbers. If we have an eight-digit decimal number and we shift it three places to the left, then the leftmost three digits are lost and three zero digits are added on the right. The binary shift operation is seen in Figure H-1.

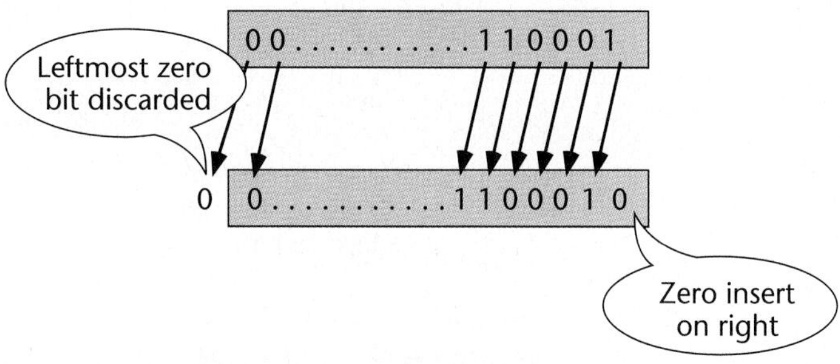

Figure H-1 ***Shift left*** **operation**

MULTIPLYING BY TWO

Let's start with something we know: decimal numbers. When we shift a decimal number one position to the left and insert a zero on the right, we are in effect multiplying by 10. If we shift it two places, we are multiplying by 100. If we shift it three places, we are multiplying by 1000. But what is actually taking place is that we are multiplying by a power of 10: in our examples, 10^1, 10^2, and 10^3.

Applying the same principle to binary numbers, the left shift operator multiplies by a power of two. If we shift a binary number two places to the left, we are multiplying by four (2^2). If we shift it three places, we are multiplying by eight (2^3). Table H-5 shows the multiplication pattern used with bit shifting.

Shift value (m)	Multiplies by (2^m)	Shift operator
1	2	<< 1
2	4	<< 2
3	8	<< 3
4	16	<< 4
...	...	...
n	2^n	<< *n*

Table H-5 Multiply by shift

BITWISE SHIFT RIGHT OPERATOR

The ***bitwise shift right*** is a binary operator (>>) that requires two integral operands (character or integer). The first operand is the value to be shifted. The second operand specifies the number of bits to be shifted.

When bits are shifted right, the bits at the rightmost end are deleted. What is shifted in on the left, however, depends on the type and the implementation. If the type is unsigned, then the standard calls for zero bits to be shifted in. If the type is signed, however, the implementation may either shift in zeros or copies of the leftmost bit. Since the implementation is left to the system programmer, any function that shifts signed values may not be portable. The shift right operation is diagrammed in Figure H-2.

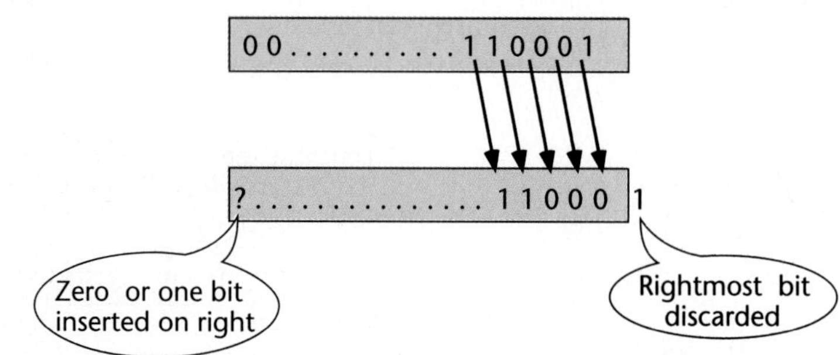

Figure H-2 ***Shift right*** **operation**

DIVIDING BY TWO

Shift right is the opposite of shift left; divide is the opposite of multiply. It is reasonable to assume, therefore, that shifting right has the effect of dividing by a power of two. Table H-6 shows the shift operator values for division.

Shift value (m)	Divides by (2^m)	Shift operator
1	2	>> 1
2	4	>> 2
3	8	>> 3
4	16	>> 4
…	…	…
n	2^n	>> *n*

Table H-6 Divide by shift

I
Manipulators

One of the most common and most repetitive aspects of programming is input and output (I/O). In the early days of computers, programmers spent a lot of time writing I/O functions. It didn't take long before they realized that if these functions were standardized they would save a lot of time and drudgery.

While C++ provides a robust set of functions for I/O, there are still times when we must spin our wheels formatting text for presentation. Fortunately, C++ also provides a facility—manipulators—that allows us to write the format code once and save it for future use.

In this appendix, we first explain how the standard manipulators work and then demonstrate how you can write your own.

I-1 INTRODUCTION

Whenever we use the insertion operator (<<), we are calling the stream function operator and passing data in the form of an argument list to it. For example, consider the statement to print the number 5.

```
cout << 5;
```

When we print 5, we are calling the overloaded insertion operator and passing it the integer 5. It is the same as

```
cout.operator<< (5);
```

This is properly interpreted as the object *cout* being instantiated and the public insertion operator being called to print the parameter data on the monitor. Figure I-1 graphically represents printing the integer 5 with the overloaded insertion operator.

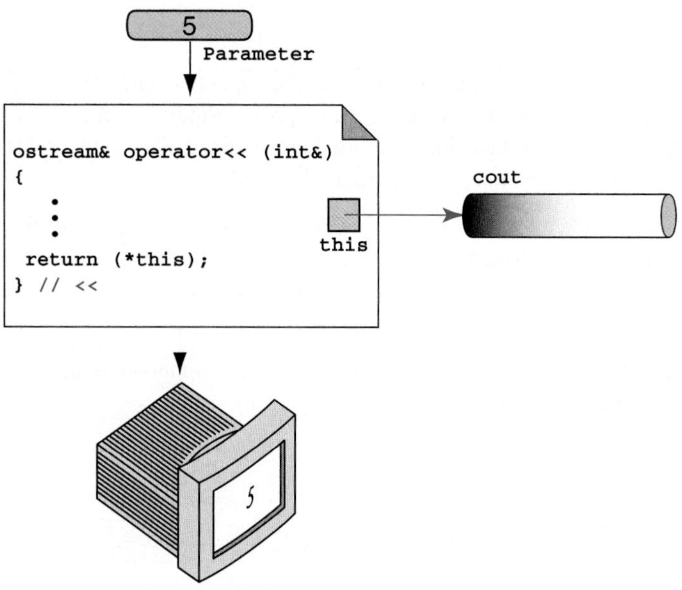

Figure I-1 The insertion operator

The insertion and extraction operators are overloaded for several data types. This enables us to use the following statement when `data` is any of the integer or floating-point types.

```
cout << data;
```

I-2 MANIPULATORS WITH NO ARGUMENTS

As an example of a manipulator with no arguments, let's examine *endl*. This manipulator takes a stream object, which is pointed to by the *this* pointer, and adds a newline character to it. It is effectively

```
ostream& operator<< (endl);
```

But this presents a problem: *endl* is not a data type. It is not an integer, character, float, or any derived type that is overloaded for the insertion operator. As a matter of fact, it is an action, not data. It adds the newline to the end of the stream object. Our problem, therefore, is that the insertion operator is not overloaded to accept an action as an argument. Furthermore, even if it were overloaded to accept the insert newline action, it would not be generalized. We would have to overload it for every possible action that a user might need.

By design, the insertion operator is overloaded to accept a pointer to a function (see Appendix M) that accepts an object of type *ostream*& and returns an object of type *ostream*. The prototype is shown below.

```
ostream& operator<< (ostream& (*f)(ostream&));
```

This overloaded function accepts a pointer to a function that can perform any required action, such as inserting a newline in the output stream. To work properly, the function must accept an object of type *ostream* and return an object of type *ostream*. Returning an *ostream* object is required so that the manipulator can be used in a chained series. This concept is shown graphically in Figure I-2.

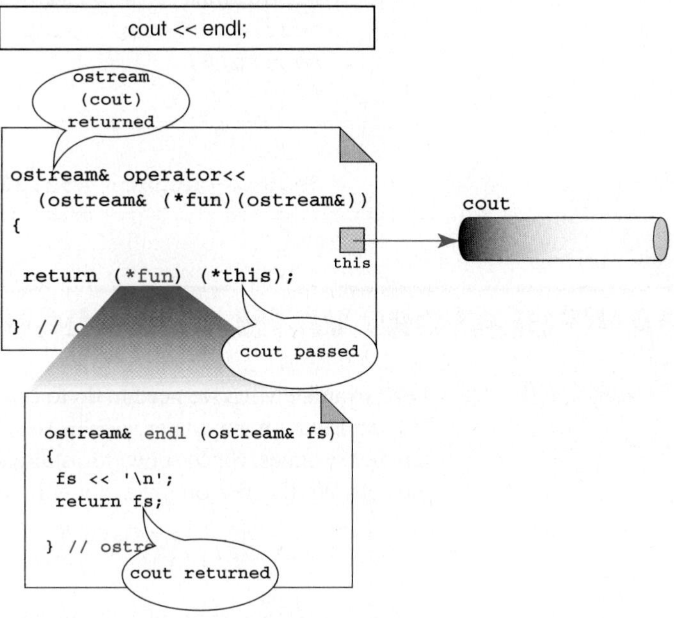

Figure I-2 Overloaded extraction operator

Now let's write a simple manipulator, `dec5p2`, that automatically sets the flags to display floating-point numbers in a width of five characters with two decimal places. The code is shown in Program I-1. It also contains a short test driver to verify the code.

Program I-1 dec5p2 manipulator

```
/* Test driver to verify dec5p2 manipulator
      Written by:
      Date:
*/
#include <iostream>
#include <iomanip>
using namespace std;

/* Manipulator to print 5.2 floating-point numbers.
      Pre  the file stream is open
      Post width and precision flags set
*/
ostream& dec5p2 (ostream& fs)
{
 fs.setf      (ios :: fixed);
 fs.width     (5);
 fs.precision (2);
 return fs;
} // ostream dec5p2

int main ()
{
   float num = 452.323457;
   cout << "dec5p2 output: " << dec5p2 << num << endl;
   return 0;
} // main
```

```
Results
   dec5p2 output: 452.32
```

I-3 MANIPULATORS WITH ONE ARGUMENT

Let's examine what we need to do to create a manipulator with one argument. Imagine that we need a manipulator such as set width (*setw*) or one to ring the bell a specified number of times. Since set width is already included in C++, let's write one that rings the bell. We'll call it `bell`, and it will be used as shown below.

```
cout << bell (3)
```

Once again, we are faced with a problem: The function call operators (the parentheses) have a higher precedence than the insertion operator (<<). This means that if we write a bell function call, the call will be executed first and its return value becomes the data to be written to the output stream. In other words, its effect is shown in the following statement in which the function call is executed first.

```
cout << ( bell(3) );
```

One solution is to write our bell function as a member function of the *fstream* class. However, this is not practical because it requires that we modify the system library every time we want to add a new manipulator.

The practical solution requires that we write two functions. The first is our bell function that has only one parameter, the number of times to ring the bell. Because it has the *this* pointer to identify its object, *cout*, it can call a second function that overloads the insertion operator and also writes to the output stream. It has a prototype as shown below.

```
ostream& ringBell (ostream& fs, int count);
```

Our problem now is to somehow associate the functions with the correct operator in the library. Unfortunately, the solution to this problem lies in a concept known as the Standard Template Library (STL), which is beyond the scope of this text. You will study the STL if you take an advanced C++ class. (It is included in this text as Appendix O.) Until then, you will have to limit your manipulators to those without parameters.

J Classes Related to Input and Output

This appendix documents the input/output classes (see Figure J-1). Each class is described and the prototype declarations for each method used in the text is shown.

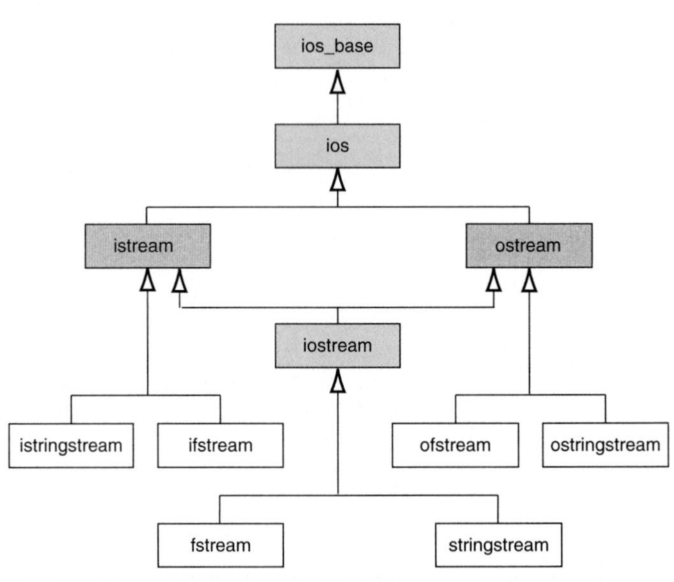

Figure J-1 ios class and derived classes

This discussion is not intended to be comprehensive. There are many more classes than the ones we discuss.

J-1 ios CLASS

The ios class is the base class for all C++ input and output. It provides the data members and methods to manage stream objects in the classes derived from it as shown below:

- Error-state flags
- Mode flags
- Seek flags
- Format flags
- Format parameters

ERROR-STATE FLAGS

Input/output error status is stored in a data member with three flags, as shown in Table J-1.

Flag	Description
bad	I/O: operation invalid
fail	I/O: transmission error
eof	Input: end of file detected

Table J-1 Error-state flags

Given this design, the user can check or clear these flags using the following methods:

```
streamobj.good   ();
streamobj.eof    ();
streamobj.fail   ();
streamobj.bad    ();
streamobj.rdstate();
streamobj.clear  (...);
```

IOS FLAGS

The ios class also handles the mode of a stream object. There are six ios flags, as described in Table J-2. These flags can be set only by the open method defined in the inherited classes.

Mode	Description
ios::in	input mode (default for istream)
ios::out	output mode (default for ostream)
ios::ate	file marker positioned at end
ios::app	append mode
ios::trunc	delete data in existing file
ios::binary	binary mode (default is text)

Table J-2 Mode flags

SEEK FLAGS

The ios class contains a set of seek flags that are used by the inherited classes to determine how the seek operates (see Table J-3). These flags are used by the *seekg* and *seekp* methods.

Flag	Description
beg	I/O: seek from beginning of file
cur	I/O: seek from current file position
end	I/O: seek from end of file

Table J-3 Seek flags

FORMAT FLAGS

Fifteen flags are used to designate the data formats for input (only *skipws*) and output. They are listed in Table J-4.

Flag	Description
skipws	input: skip leading whitespace characters
left	output: left justification
right	output: right justification
internal	output: fill char fill after sign or base
dec	output: display integer value in decimal
oct	output: display integer value in octal
hex	output: display integer value in hex
showbase	output: display base indicator octal (0) or hex (0X)
showpoint	output: display decimal on floating-point values, even zero
uppercase	output: display hex base indicator and value in uppercase display scientific notation E in uppercase
showpos	output: display plus (+) for positive numbers
scientific	output: display floating-point values in exponential format
fixed	output: display floating-point values in fixed point format
unitdef	output: flush data immediately
stdio	output: allows use of C and C++ output in same stream

Table J-4 Format flags

The ios class provides the following five methods that can be used to test or store data in the format flags:

```
streamobj.flags  ();                  // get flags
streamobj.flags  (...);               // set flags
streamobj.setf   (...);               // set masks
streamobj.setf   (..., ...);          // set flags
streamobj.unsef  (...);               // unset flags
```

FORMAT PARAMETERS

The ios base class also contains three variable members that are used to format output: width, fill, and precision. They are described in Table J-5.

Variable	Description
width	output: length of display area in characters
fill	output: padding character for nondata positions
precision	output: number of digits after decimal point

Table J-5 ios variable members

To store settings in these members, the ios class provides the three methods shown below, all of which are fully discussed in the text.

```
streamobj.width     ();                   // get width
streamobj.width     (...);                // set width
streamobj.fill      (...);                // get fill
streamobj.fill      (..., ...);           // set fill
streamobj.precision (...);                // unset flags
```

J-2 CLASSES INHERITED FROM ios

This section describes the two classes directly derived from the ios class: the input stream (*istream*) and output stream (*ostream*).

INPUT STREAM

The input stream class (*istream*) is derived from the ios class. It contains functions and operators for extracting data from an input stream, along with several member data and methods to handle input operations. Most of the methods shown below are covered in the text.

```
istreamobj.operator>>(...);
istreamobj.gcount();
istreamobj.get   (...);
istreamobj.getline(...);:
istreamobj.ignore(...);:
istreamobj.peek  (...);:
istreamobj.putback(...);:
istreamobj.read  (...);:
istreamobj.seekg (...);:
istreamobj.tellg ();
```

OUTPUT STREAM

The output stream class (*ostream*) is derived from the ios class. It contains functions and operators for inserting data into an output stream, along with several member data and methods to handle output operations. Most of the methods shown below are covered in the text.

```
ostreamobj.operator<<(...);
ostreamobj.pcount();
ostreamobj.put   (...);
ostreamobj.write (...);
ostreamobj.seekp (...);
ostreamobj.tellp ();
```

J-3 CLASSES INHERITED FROM *istream* AND *ostream*

In this section, we describe the input file stream, output file stream, and input /output file stream.

INPUT FILE STREAM

The input file stream (*ifstream*) is designed to process stream objects that are associated in input files. It inherits the properties from both *istream* and *ios*. The primary functions supported by *ifstream,* as seen in this text, are to open and close input streams. Their prototype declarations follow.

```
ifstreamobj.open (...);
ifstreamobj.close();
```

INPUT/OUTPUT STREAM

The input /output stream (*iostream*) is derived from both *istream* and *ostream* (see Figure J-1 on page 932). It is designed to allow the instantiation of stream objects for both input and output and is the most common stream included in your programs. It contains no data members or methods of its own. It is simply used as a convenience.

OUTPUT FILE STREAM

The output file stream (*ofstream*) is designed to process stream objects that are associated with output files. It inherits the properties from both *ostream* and *ios*. The primary functions supported by *ofstream,* as seen in this text, are to open and close output streams. Their prototype declarations are shown below.

```
ofstreamobj.open (...);
ofstreamobj.close();
```

I/O STRING STREAMS

The *istringstream* and *ostringstream* streams allows us to connect streams and strings so that we can *read* a string and store its data in a set of variables or *write* a set of variables to a string. The *istringstream* stream is derived from *istream*; it is automatically opened for reading a string. The *ostringstream* stream is derived from *ostream*; it is automatically opened for writing a string.

J-4 CLASSES INHERITED FROM *iostream*

In this section, we describe input and output streams.

FILE STREAM

The file stream (*fstream*) is derived from the iostream class, and through it the *istream*, *ostream*, and *ios* classes. It is used primarily for stream objects that process files opened for both input and output. The open and close methods are shown below.

```
fstreamobj.open  (...);
fstreamobj.close ();
```

STRING STREAM

The *stringstream* stream allows us to connect streams and strings so that we can *read* and *write* a set of variables to a string. It conains one method that converts a string class object to a C string.

```
stringobj.str();
```

K C Language I/O

Whereas C++ uses objects and methods to handle input and output, traditional C uses functions. It is reasonable to expect, therefore, that there are material differences between the two. That is not to say, however, that there are not times when you will want to use traditional C stream input/output in a C++ program. For that reason, we provide a brief description of it in this appendix.

All traditional C I/O functions are contained in the standard I/O library, <cstdio>. You will have to include this library in any program that uses traditional I/O.

The C input and output functions covered in this appendix can be categorized as shown in Figure K-1.

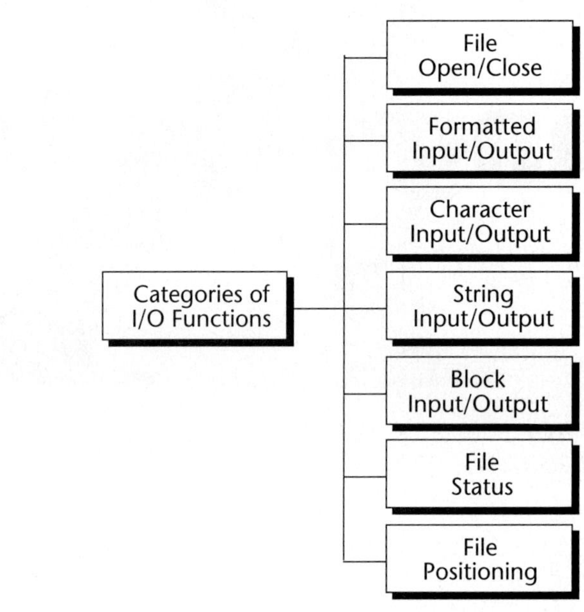

Figure K-1 Types of standard input/output functions

K-1 STANDARD LIBRARY INPUT/OUTPUT FUNCTIONS

The C standard library contains several different **input/output functions**. They are grouped into seven different categories, as shown in Figure K-1. Before introducing them, we must discuss a few basic concepts.

FILES AND STREAMS IN C

C uses the concept of streams for its files. A **stream** is a sequence of elements in time. Only one stream element, the current one, is available at a time. In other words, the computer looks at input and output data, whether from a physical device such as keyboard or from files resident on a secondary storage, as a stream of characters or bytes.

FILE TABLE

Since files exist separately from the computer and our programs, we must have some way to connect them; we must create a linkage between the external file and its usage in our program. In C, this linkage is known as a **file table**. We define a file by using a standard **FILE** type, which has been created for us in the standard input/output library. The format for the file type is shown below.

```
FILE *filename
```

STANDARD C FILES

The C language automatically defines three **standard file streams**, called **standard input**, **standard output**, and **standard error**. These three files are associated with two physical files: the keyboard and the monitor. The file tables that point to these file streams are defined in the standard input/output header file (<cstdio>) and are referred to as ***stdin***, ***stdout***, and ***stderr***, respectively (Figure K-2). Standard input is associated with the user's primary input file, usually the keyboard. Standard output and standard error are both usually assigned to the user's monitor, but can be individually directed to a printer if one is available. You may use these files without defining them as long as you include the proper header file (<cstdio>).

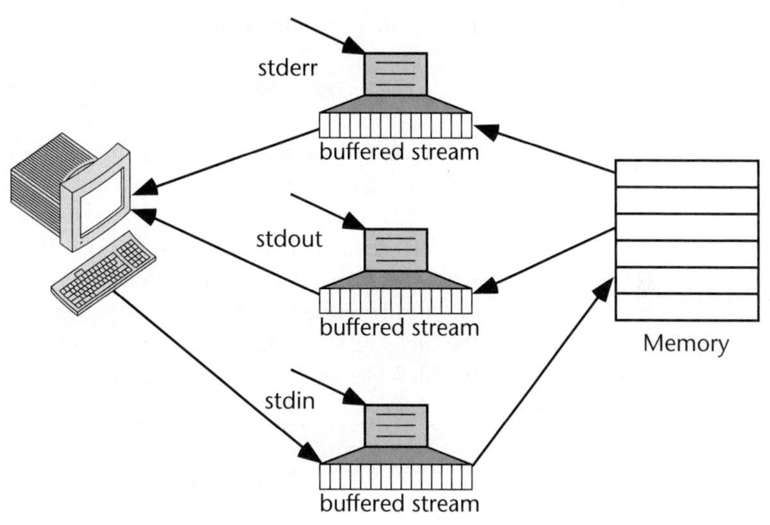

Figure K-2 Standard files

USER FILES

Using the FILE type, you can define any external files you need, as shown in Figure K-3.

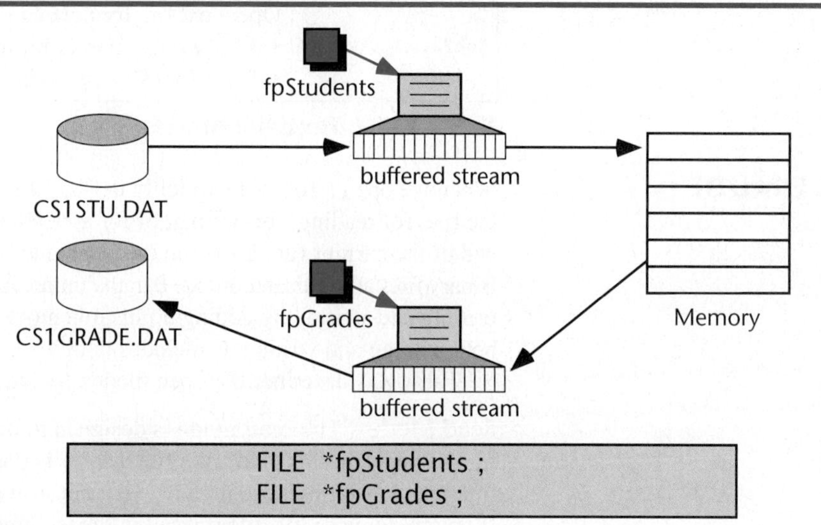

Figure K-3 User files

K-2 FILE OPEN AND CLOSE

Like C++, C uses open and close functions to process files.

FILE OPEN (*fopen*)

The function that prepares a file for processing is *fopen*. To open a file, you need to specify the file name and its mode, as shown below.

```
file_pointer = fopen("filename", "mode");
```

When a file is successfully opened, a pointer to the file table is returned. If the open fails, a null pointer is returned. We can therefore use the file pointer to determine if the open was successful.

The file name is the same as in C++. It is the name of the file on the disk, complete with its path name. It can be passed to the open either as a string constant or as a variable.

The **file mode** is a little more complex. It is a string that tells C how you intend to use the file: Are you going to read an existing file, write a new file, or both read and write the file? The mode codes are shown in Table K-1.

Mode	Meaning
"r" "rb" "r+b"	Open file for reading. • if file exists, marker positioned at beginning • if file doesn't exist, error returned
"w" "wb" "w+b"	Open text file for writing • if file exists, it is emptied • if file doesn't exist, it is created
"a" "ab" "a+b"	Open text file for append • if file exists, marker positioned at end • if file doesn't exist, it is created

Table K-1 Text file modes

FILE MODE

When we open a file, we explicitly define its mode. The mode shows how we will use the file: for reading, for writing, or for appending, which means adding new data at the end of the current file. Each file can be opened in either a text mode or a binary mode. Binary files are indicated by the *b* in the mode. Additionally, files can be opened for both reading and writing by adding a plus token (+) to the mode. When a file is opened for both reading and writing, C includes both read and write functions.

Table K-1 describes the open modes.

Read Mode The **read mode** is designed to open an existing file for reading. When a file is opened in this mode, the file marker is positioned at the beginning of the file (the first byte). The file must already exist; not: if it does not, NULL is returned as an error. If you try to write to a file opened in the read mode, you will get an error message.

Write Mode The **write mode** is designed to open a file for writing. If the file doesn't exist, it is created. If it already exists, it is opened and all its data are deleted; that is, it assumes the characteristics of an empty file. In either case, the file marker is positioned at the beginning. It is an error to try to read from a file opened in write mode.

Append Mode The **append mode** is designed to open an existing file for writing. Instead of writing from the beginning of the file, however, the writing starts after the last byte; that is, data are *appended* at the end of the file. If the file doesn't exist, it is created and opened. In this case, the writing will start at the beginning of the file; the result will be logically the same as opening a new file for writing. If you try to read a file opened for write append, you will get an error message.

FILE CLOSE (*fclose*)

When a file is not needed any more, it should be closed to free system resources, such as buffer space. A file is closed using the *fclose* function, as shown below.

```
fpTemps = fopen ("TEMPS.DAT", "w");
...
fclose(fpTemps);
```

K-3 FORMATTED INPUT/OUTPUT FUNCTIONS

There are several traditional C functions that are used to format data. The input functions (*scanf* and *fscanf*) format data by converting text input to internal formats, such as integers and floating-point numbers. The output functions (*printf* and *fprintf*) do the reverse: They convert data from the internal machine formats to text data. A third set of format functions convert strings to internal formats (*sscanf*) and internal formats to strings (*sprintf*).

We begin with a basic discussion of the input format function (*scanf*) and output format (*printf*) and then discuss a concept used by all of the formatting functions, the format string.

INPUT FORMATTING

The ***scanf*** and ***fscanf*** functions read text data and convert the data to the types specified by a format string (see below). The only difference between them is that *scanf* reads data from the standard input unit (the keyboard by default) and *fscanf* reads the input from a file specified by the first parameter. This file can be the standard input unit (*stdin*). These functions have the following formats:

```
scanf ("format string", address list)
fscanf(fp, "format string", address list)
```

where *fp* is the address of a file that has been defined as type FILE *, *"format string"* is a string containing formatting instructions, and the address list specifies the address where the data are to be stored after they have been formatted. There must be a comma separating the format string from the address list. If there is more than one address, the addresses are separated from each other by commas.

There must be a variable address in the address list for every field specification in the format string that requires data. If there isn't, the result is "unpredictable and undefined." The input format concept is seen in Figure K-4.

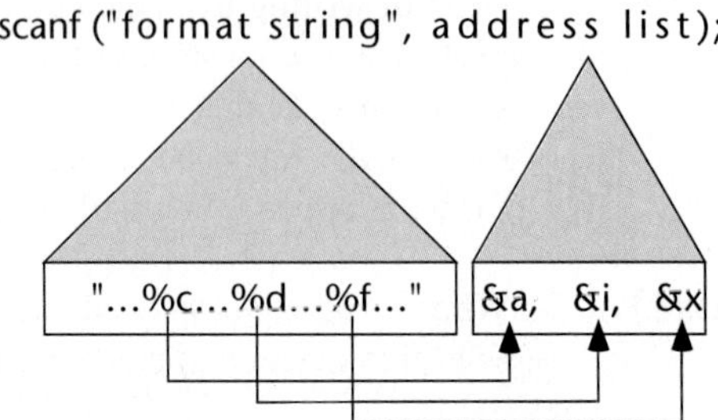

Figure K-4 Formatting input

The conversion operation processes input characters until:

1. End of file is reached.
2. An inappropriate character is encountered.
3. The number of characters read is equal to an explicitly specified maximum field width.

OUTPUT FORMATTING

The output formatting functions display output in human-readable form under the control of a format string, as described in the following sections. These functions have the following formats:

```
printf  ("format string", value list)
fprintf (fp, "format string", value list)
```

where *fp* is the address of a file that has been defined as type FILE *, *"format string"* is a string containing formatting instructions, and the value list specifies the data values to be formatted. Whereas the address list is required for inputting data, it is possible to display data with no values. When values are present, there must be a comma separating the format string from the value list and the values from each other. The output format is shown in Figure K-5.

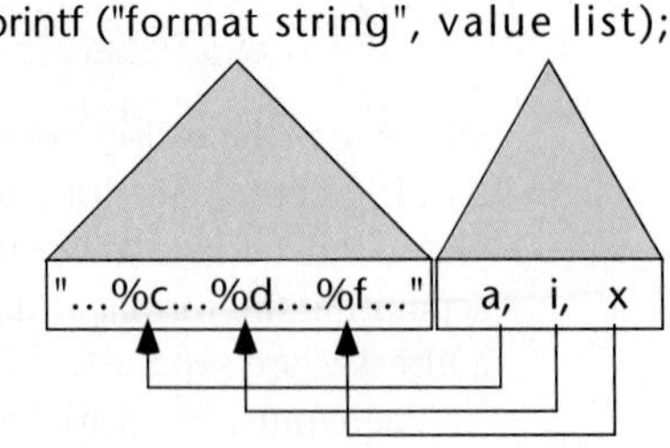

Figure K-5 Output formatting

FORMAT STRING

The primary purpose of the format string is to describe how data are to be formatted when read or written. It consists of three types of data, which may be repeated: whitespace, text characters, and the most important of the three, the field specification, which describes how the data are to be formatted as they are read or written.

Whitespace

Whitespace in the format string is handled differently for input and output. In an input function, one or more whitespaces in the format string cause zero, one, or more whitespaces in the input stream to be read and discarded. Thus, any sequence of consecutive whitespace characters in the format string will match any sequence of consecutive whitespace characters, possibly of different length, in the input stream.

Whitespace in an output function is simply copied to the output stream. Thus, a space character will be placed in the output stream for every space character in the format string. Likewise, tabs in the format string will be copied to the output stream. Note that this is not a good idea, however, because you can't see tabs in the format string. It is better to use the tab escape character (\t) so that the reader can see the tabs.

Text

Any text character other than a whitespace in an input format string must match exactly the next character of the input stream. If it does not match, a conflict occurs that causes the operation to be terminated. Text characters in an output format string are copied to the output stream. They are usually used to display messages to the user or to label data being output.

Field Specification

The **field specification** consists of a percent character (%), a conversion code, and other formatting instructions. With one exception, each format specification must have a matching variable in the parameter list that follows the format string. The type in the field specification and the type of the variable must match.

Field specifications can have up to six elements, as shown in Figure K-6. (Note that for input there are only five; precision is not used.) The first element is a field specification token (%). The last element is the conversion code. Both of these elements are required; the other elements are optional. Generally, the meaning and usage of each element is the same for both input and output. The exceptions are noted in the following discussion.

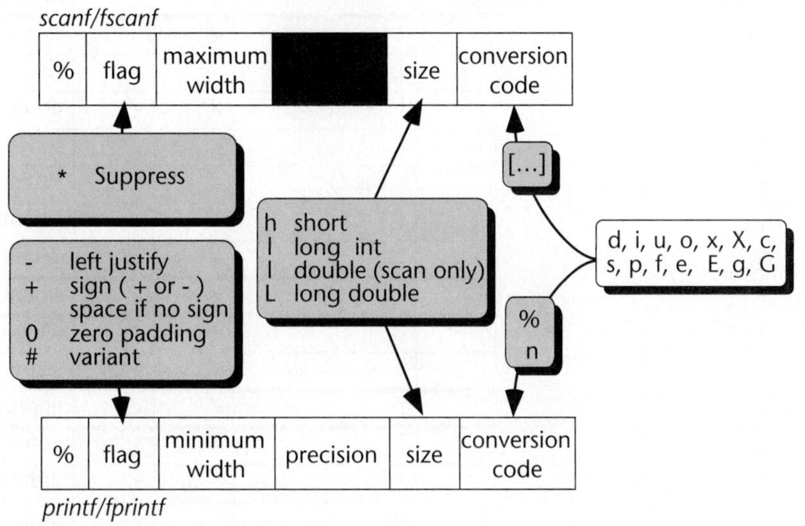

Figure K-6 Field specification

Conversion Codes

The **conversion code** specifies the type of data that are being formatted. For input, it specifies the type of variable into which the data are formatted. For output, it specifies the type of data in the variable associated with the specification. *It is the programmer's* *responsibility to ensure that the data are of the right type.* If they are not, strange output may result.

In this section, the integer (i and d), octal (o), hexadecimal (x), the scientific formatting codes (e and g), the number (n), and the percent sign (%) codes are discussed. Table K-2 discusses the codes.

Size	Codes[a]	scanf	printf	Usage
	d	✓	✓	signed decimal number
h	d	✓	✓	decimal stored as short
l	d	✓	✓	decimal stored as long
	i[b]	✓	✓	integer: decimal octal (lead digit zero) hexadecimal (lead 0x | 0X)
h	i	✓	✓	short integer (see above)
l	i	✓	✓	long integer (see above)
	o	✓	✓	integer in octal format
h	o	✓	✓	short int in octal format
l	o	✓	✓	long integer in octal format
	x X	✓	✓	int hex (x: a…f; X: A…F)
h	x X	✓	✓	short hex (x: a…f; X: A…F)
l	x X	✓	✓	long hex (x: a…f; X: A…F)
	u	✓	✓	unsigned decimal
h	u	✓	✓	unsigned stored as short
l	u	✓	✓	unsigned stored as long
	f	✓		float—standard notation
	f		✓	float or double
l	f	✓	✓[c]	double
L	f	✓	✓	long double
	e,E,g,G	✓		scientific notation float
	e,E,g,G		✓	scientific float/double
l	e,E,g,G	✓		scientific double(
L	e,E,g,G	✓	✓	scientific long double(
	c	✓	✓	character
	s	✓	✓	string
	p	✓	✓	address (machine dependent)
	[…]	✓		edit set
	n		✓	number of characters output
h	n		✓	number of characters output
l	n		✓	number of characters output
	%		✓	to print percent sign (%)

[a]With size specification

[b]i and d have the same meaning in output specifications

[c]ISO Standard provides for lf on output

Table K-2 Input and Output Conversion Codes

Decimal (d) Decimal is the standard conversion code for all integers. It is much safer than the integer code covered next.

Integer (i) When the integer code (i) is used for input, the digits in the input stream are interpreted as follows:

1. If the number starts with 0x or 0X, it is interpreted as hexadecimal.
2. If the number starts with 0 other than 0x and 0X, it is interpreted as octal.
3. If the number starts with a digit other than 0, it is a decimal number.

Octal and Hexadecimal The octal (o) and hexadecimal (x or X) conversion codes perform unsigned conversion. For octal, the only valid input digits are 0…7. For hexadecimal input, the valid digits are 0…9, a…f, and A…F. For output, the number will be formatted in either octal or hexadecimal as indicated by the conversion code. The alpha hexadecimal codes will be printed in lowercase if the x code is used and in uppercase for the X code.

Floating Point (e, E, g, G) There are two floating-point format codes for scientific notation. In scientific notation, the significand and exponent are specified separately. These forms are shown below.

$$123e03 \rightarrow 123*10^{3} \qquad 123e\text{-}03 \rightarrow 123*10^{-3}$$

All of the following numbers are in scientific notation:

```
3e     -1.0e-3     0.1+e1     2e2
```

When the *e* and *g* format codes are used for input, they work just like the floating-point (f) code. With output, the *e* code displays numbers using scientific notation; the *g* code will use either the standard floating-point format or the scientific format, whichever results in a smaller display. E and G print the "e" in scientific notation as a capital letter.

Count (n) If you want to verify the number of characters output, you can do so by specifying the *n* code. This code identifies a matching variable into which *printf* is to place the count of the characters output. If the code is prefaced with an *h*, the matching variable must be a *short*; if it is *l*, the variable must be *long*. Since the *printf* places the results in the variable, its address must be used in the parameter list. In the following example, *count* is a *short integer* that is to receive the number of characters written (note the address operator).

```
printf( "%d %8.2f %d %hn", i, x, j, &count ) ;
```

Percent (%) The percent sign as a conversion code is used to output a percent sign. For example, assume that *grade* contains a student's score expressed as a percentage. The following statement could then be used to print the grade in the format 93.5%.

```
printf( "%4.1f%%", grade ) ;
```

The String Conversion Code (%s) The conversion code for a string is *s*. The *scanf* function then does all the work. First, it skips any leading whitespace. Once it finds a character, it reads until it finds whitespace, putting each character in the array in order. When it finds a trailing whitespace character, it ends the string with a null character. The whitespace character is left in the input stream. To delete the whitespace from the input stream, use a space in the format string before the next conversion code. An address operator is not required for a string because a string's name is automatically an address (pointer constant).

The Edit Set Conversion Code (%[...]) The **edit set** conversion specification consists of the open bracket ([), followed by the edit characters, and terminated by the close bracket (]). The characters in the edit set identify the valid characters, known as the **scanset**, that are to be allowed in the string. All characters except the close bracket can be included in the set.

Edited conversion reads the input stream as a string. Each character read by *scanf* is compared against the edit set. If the character just read is in the edit set, it is placed in the string and the scan continues. The first character that does not match the scan set stops the read. The nonmatching character remains in the input stream for the next read operation. If the first character read is not in the edit set, the *scanf* terminates and a null string is returned.

A major difference between the edit set and the string conversion code (%s) is that the edit set does not skip leading whitespace. Leading whitespace is either put into the string being read when the edit set contains the corresponding whitespace character, or stops the conversion if it is not.

In addition to reading a character that is not in the edit set, there are two other terminating conditions. First, the read will stop if an end of file is detected. Second, the read will stop if a field width specification is included and the maximum number of characters has been read.

Always use a width in the field specification when reading strings.

Flag The **flag** is the first field specification modifier. Its usage is different for input and output. For input there is only one flag (*). It means "do not store the data" and is the one exception to the rule that all field specifications must have a matching variable in the parameter list. This flag is very helpful for discarding leading material. The input function will read but not convert the data and store the results. It will stop with the next whitespace.

```
%*d
```

For output, the flag interpretation is much more extensive. The codes and their meanings are:

1. **Justification**: Normally output is **right-justified**. This means that if the print width (see "**Field Width**") is larger than required, the data will appear in the right side of the print area. This is fine for numeric output, but it is not what is wanted all of the time. To reverse the justification, set the flag to minus (–).
2. **Sign**: Numeric data are normally **signed** only if they are negative. Some applications require that a plus sign be printed if the number is positive. Using a plus (+) for a flag causes positive numbers to print with a plus sign prefix and negative numbers to print with the standard minus sign prefix.

3. **Space**: A **space flag** causes a leading space to be printed if there is no sign printed. This can help alignment when you print positive numbers unsigned. (Remember, negative numbers are always signed.)
4. **Leading zero padding**: If your application requires that leading zeros be printed, then you use a zero (0) flag. This is known as **leading zero padding**.
5. **Variant Flag**: The **variant flag** (#) changes the conversion code for printing numbers. Most of these conversions are special situations that you will seldom use. They are shown in Table K-3.

Conversion code	Interpretation
o	Begin number with a zero (octal)
x	Begin number with 0x (hexadecimal)
X	Begin number with 0X (hexadecimal)
e f E	Include decimal point in number
g G	Include decimal point in number Retain trailing zeros in fractional part

Table K-3 Numeric variant flag (#) interpretation

Field Width The meaning of the **field width** is conceptually the same for input and output, but in the opposite direction. For input data, it specifies the maximum width of the input (in characters). This allows you to break out a code that may be stored in the input without spaces. Consider what happens when you are reading a Social Security number from a file and the number has no formatting; it is just nine digits in a row, followed by a space. You could read it into three variables, thus allowing you to format it with dashes in your output, with the following format specifications:

```
scanf("%3d%2d%4d…", &ssn1, &ssn2, &ssn3, … );
```

Note that the width is a maximum. If there are less data than required, the scan terminates. What determines the end of the data depends on the type of data, but generally whitespace will terminate most scans.

For output specifications, the width provides the minimum output width. However, if the data are *wider* than the specified width, *C will print all the data*. Thus, the output width is the minimum area provided.

Precision The **precision** is specified as a period followed by an integer. It has meaning only for output fields, and it is an error to use it for input. Precision can control the following:

1. The minimum number of digits for integers. If the number has fewer significant digits than the precision specified, leading zeros will be printed.
2. The number of digits after the decimal point in float.
3. The number of significant digits in g and G.

Size The **size** specification is a modifier for the conversion code. Used in combination, they allow you to specify that the associated variable is, for example, a long double (Lf). The size codes with their associated conversion codes are explained in Table K-2.

K-4 CHARACTER INPUT/OUTPUT FUNCTIONS

Character input and functions read one character at the time from a text stream.

getchar

The *getchar* function reads the next character from the standard input stream and returns its value. The only things that stop it are the end of file or a read error. If the end of file condition results, or if an error is detected, *getchar* returns EOF. It is the programmer's responsibility to determine if some condition other than end of file has stopped the reading. The prototype statement for *getchar* follows.

```
int getchar ( void ) ;
```

Note that the return type is integer and not character as you might expect. This is because EOF is defined as an integer in the standard definition <cstddef> and other header files. There is another reason for this: ANSI C guarantees that the EOF flag is not a character. This is true regardless of what character set it is using—ASCII, EBCDIC, or whatever. If you examine the control characters in ASCII—you will find none for end of file. Traditionally EOF is defined as –1, but this is not prescribed by ANSI. An individual implementation could therefore choose a different value.

putchar

The *putchar* function writes one character to the standard output unit. If any error occurs during the write operation, it returns EOF. This may sound somewhat unusual since EOF is normally thought of as an input file consideration, but in this case it simply means that the character couldn't be written. The prototype statement for *putchar* is shown below.

```
int putchar ( int out_char ) ;
```

Again, the type is integer. There is an interesting result with *putchar:* It returns the character it wrote!

getc AND *fgetc*

The ***getc*** and ***fgetc*** functions read the next character from the file stream and convert it to an integer format. If the read detects an end of file, both functions return EOF. EOF is also returned if any error occurs. The prototype functions are shown below.

```
int  getc( FILE *fpIn ) ;
int fgetc( FILE *fpIn ) ;
```

Examples of *getc* and *fgetc* are shown below.

```
nextChar = getc ( fpMyFile ) ;
nextChar = fgetc ( fpMyFile ) ;
```

putc AND *fputc*

The ***putc*** and ***fputc*** functions write the character parameter to the file stream specified. For *fputc*, the first parameter is the character to be written and the second parameter is the file. If the character is successfully written, the function returns it. If any error occurs, it returns EOF. The prototype functions are shown below.

```
int  putc( int oneChar, FILE *fpOut ) ;
int fputc( int oneChar, FILE *fpOut ) ;
```

Examples are shown below.

```
putc  ( oneChar, fpMyFile ) ;
fputc ( oneChar, fpMyFile ) ;
```

Note that we have discarded the return value. Although you may occasionally find a use for it, it is almost universally discarded.

You may be wondering why there are two different read and write functions that are virtually identical. The answer lies in the history of the C language and is beyond the scope of this text.

K-5 STRING INPUT/OUTPUT FUNCTIONS

Two sets of C functions, *gets/fgets* and *puts/fputs*, are used to read and write strings.

READ STRING (*gets/fgets*)

The ***gets*** and ***fgets*** functions, which parallel *getline* in C++, take a line (terminated by a newline) from the input stream and make a null-terminated string out of it. For this reason, they are sometimes called line-to-string input functions.

The prototype statements for get string are shown below.

```
char *gets  ( char *strPtr ) ;
char *fgets ( char *strPtr, int size, FILE *fp ) ;
```

Figure K-7 shows the concept. As you can see, the two functions do not work the same. The *gets* function converts the return (newline character) to the end-of-string character (\0), while the *fgets* puts it in the string and appends an end-of-string delimiter.

The *gets* function reads from the standard input file stream; *fgets* reads the file stream specified by the file pointer (`fp`). Both accept a string pointer and return the same pointer if the input is successful. If there are any input problems, such as detecting end of file before reading any data, they return NULL. If no data were read, the input area is unchanged. If an error occurs after some data have been read, the contents of the read-in area cannot be determined. There may or may not be a valid null character for the current string.

Note that since no size is specified in *gets*, it will read data until it finds a newline or until the end of file. If a newline is read, it is discarded and replaced with a null character.

The *fgets* function requires two additional parameters: one specifying the array size that is available to receive the data and the other a file pointer (`fp`) that identifies the input file. The function can be used with the keyboard by specifying the *stdin* file

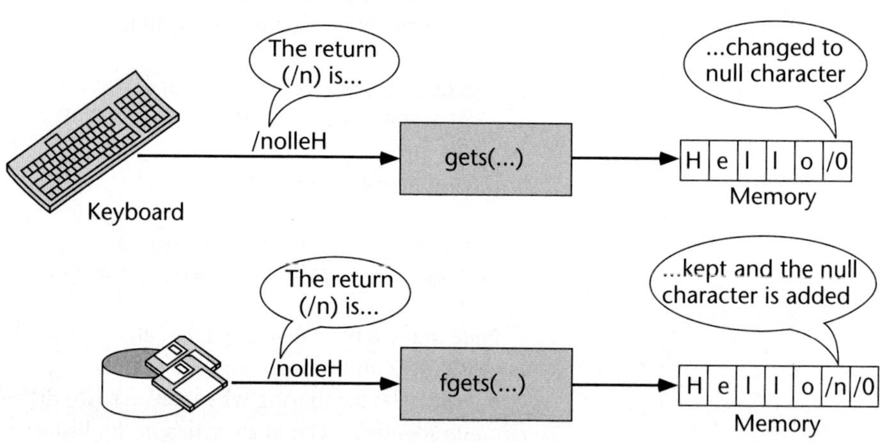

Figure K-7 ***gets* and *fgets* functions**

pointer. In addition to newline and end of file, the reading will stop when *size – 1* characters have been read.

Since there is no length checking with *gets*, we recommend that you never use it in a program. Should a user enter too much data, your program will destroy the data after the string input area and the program will not run correctly. Rather, use *fgets* and specify the standard input file pointer (*stdin*).

> **Always make sure you have defined enough memory for *gets*.**

WRITE STRING (*puts*/*fputs*)

The ***puts*** and ***fputs*** functions, which do not have a counterpart in C++, take a null-terminated string from memory and write it to a file as a line. For this reason, they are sometimes called string-to-line output functions.

Figure K-8 shows how *puts* and *fputs* work. Both functions change the string to a line. The null character is replaced with a newline in *puts*; it is dropped in *fputs*. When you consider that *puts* is writing to the standard output unit, usually a display, this is entirely logical. On the other hand, *fputs* is assumed to be writing to a file where newlines are not necessarily required. It is the programmer's responsibility to make sure the newline is present at the appropriate place. Note how the newline is handled in these two functions, then compare their use of the newline to the *gets* and *fgets* functions. Note that the output functions treat the newline the opposite of the input functions.

The prototypes for these functions are shown below.

```
int puts   ( const char *strPtr ) ;
int fputs  ( const char *strPtr, FILE *fp ) ;
```

The string pointed to by *strPtr* is written to the indicated file as explained above. If the write is successful, it returns a non-negative integer; if there are any transmission errors, it returns EOF. Note that the absence of a null character to terminate the string is not an error; however, it will most likely cause your program to fail.

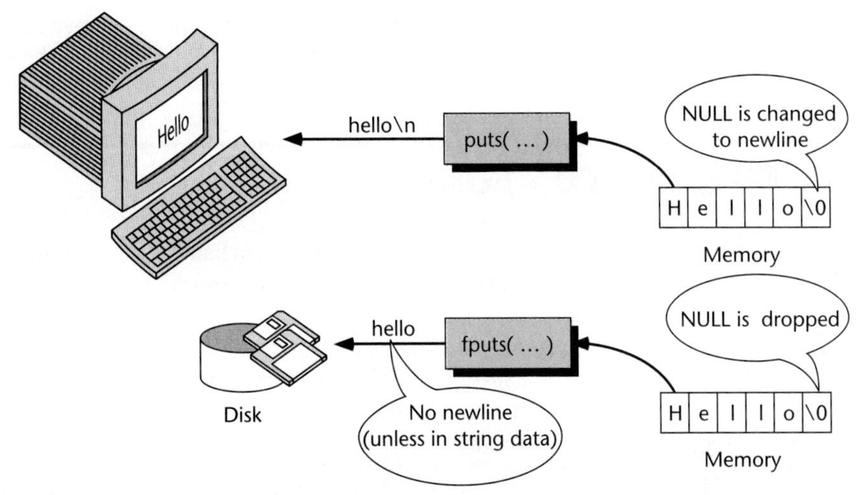

Figure K-8 ***puts*** **and** ***fputs*** **operations**

K-6 BLOCK INPUT/OUTPUT FUNCTIONS

The block input and output functions are used to read and write data to binary files. There are two C block input/output functions: *fread* and *fwrite*. These functions parallel the C++ *read* and *write* functions.

FILE READ (*fread*)

The function ***fread***, whose prototype is shown below, reads a specified number of bytes from a binary file and places them into memory at the specified location.

```
int fread ( void *pInArea,
            int   elementSize,
            int   count,
            FILE *fp ) ;
```

The first parameter, `pInArea`, is a pointer to the input area in memory. Note that a generic (void) pointer is used. This allows any pointer type to be passed to the function. The next two elements, `elementSize` and `count`, are multiplied to determine how much data are to be transferred. The size is normally specified using the *sizeof* operator, and the count is normally 1 when writing structures. The last parameter is the file pointer of an open file. A file read returns the number of items read.

FILE WRITE (*fwrite*)

The function ***fwrite***, whose prototype is shown below, writes a specified number of items to a binary file.

```
int fwrite ( void *pOutArea,
             int   elementSize,
             int   count,
             FILE *fp ) ;
```

The parameters for file write correspond exactly to the parameters for the file read function. Functionally, *fwrite* copies `elementSize * count` bytes from the address specified by `pOutArea` to the file. It returns the number of items written.

K-7 FILE STATUS FUNCTIONS

C provides three functions to handle file status questions: test end of file (*feof*), test error (*ferror*), and clear error (*clearerr*).

TEST EOF (*feof*)

The *feof* function is used to check if the end of file has been reached. If the file is at the end—that is, if all data have been read—the function returns *true* (nonzero). If end of file has not been reached, *false* (zero) is returned. The prototype declaration is shown below.

```
int feof ( FILE  *stream ) ;
```

TEST ERROR (*ferror*)

Test error (***ferror***) is used to check the error status of the file. Errors can be created for many reasons, ranging from bad physical media (disk or tape) to illogical operations, such as trying to read a file in the write state. The *ferror* function returns *true* (nonzero) if an error has occurred. It returns *false* (zero) if no error has occurred. The prototype is shown below.

```
int ferror ( FILE *stream ) ;
```

Note, however, that testing for an error does not reset the error condition. Once a file enters the error state, it can only return to a read or write state by calling clear error (see below).

CLEAR ERROR (*clearerr*)

When an error occurs, the subsequent calls to *ferror* return nonzero until the error status of the file is reset. The function ***clearerr*** is used for this purpose. Its prototype is given below

```
void clearerr ( FILE *stream ) ;
```

Note, however, that even though you have cleared the error, you have not necessarily cured the problem. You may find that the next read or write returns you to the error state.

K-8 POSITIONING FUNCTIONS

There are two uses for positioning functions. First, for randomly processing data in disk files (you cannot process tape files randomly), you must position the file to read the desired data. Second, you can use the positioning functions to change a file's state. Thus, if you have been writing a file, you can change to a read state after you use one of the positioning functions. It is not necessary to change states after positioning a file, but it is allowed.

We will discuss two file position functions: tell location and file seek.

CURRENT LOCATION (*ftell*)

The *ftell* function is used with both input and output files. It is equivalent to the combination of *tellg* and *tellp* in C++. The prototype declaration for *ftell* is shown below.

```
long int ftell( FILE *stream ) ;
```

Note that *ftell* returns a long integer. This is necessary because many files have more than 32,767 bytes, which is the maximum integer value on many computers.

SET POSITION (*fseek*)

The *fseek* function is used with both input and output files. It is the equivalent of *seekg* and *seekp* in one function. Its prototype declaration is shown below

```
int fseek( FILE *stream, long offset, int wherefrom );
```

The first parameter is a pointer to an open file. Since the seek is used with both reading and writing files, the file state can be either read or write. The second parameter is a signed integer that specifies the number of bytes the position indicator must move absolutely or relatively. To help you understand what we mean by absolutely or relatively, we will first discuss the third parameter, `wherefrom`.

C provides three named constants that can be used to specify the starting point (`wherefrom`) of the seek. They are shown below.

```
#define SEEK_SET 0
#define SEEK_CUR 1
#define SEEK_END 2
```

When `wherefrom` is SEEK_SET (0), then the offset is measured absolutely from the beginning of the file. This is the most common use of file seek.

K-9 SUMMARY OF C I/O FUNCTIONS

Table K-4 lists the common C input/output functions discussed in this appendix and their corresponding C++ functions.

C++ function	C equivalent		
`file_stream.open(...)`	`fopen(...)`		
`file_stream.close(...)`	`fclose(...)`		
`<<`	`printf(...)`		`fprintf(...)`
`>>`	`scanf(...)`		`fscanf(...)`
`file_stream.get(...)`	`getchar(...)`	`getc(...)`	`fgetc(...)`
`file_stream.put(...)`	`putchar(...)`	`putc(...)`	`fputc(...)`
`fs.getline(...)   <<`	`gets(...)`		`fgets(...)`
`>>`	`puts(...)`		`fputs(...)`
`file_stream.read(...)`	`fread(...)`		
`file_stream.write(...)`	`fwrite(...)`		
`file_stream.tellg(...)` `file_stream.tellp(...)`	`ftell(...)`		

Table K-4 C++ and C input/output functions

C++ function	C equivalent
`file_stream.seekg(…)` `file_stream.seekp(…)`	`fseek(…)`

`file_stream.bad()`
`file_stream.fail()`
`file_stream.good()`
	`ferror(…)`

`file_stream.setf` `file_stream.unsetf`	
`file_stream.rdstate(…)`	
`file_stream.flag(…)`	

`file_stream.fill(…)`
`file_stream.precision(…)`
`file_stream.width(…)`	

`file_stream.clear(…)`	`clearerr(…)`
`file_stream.gcount` `file_stream.pcount`	

Table K-4 C++ and C input/output functions *(continued)*

L
Command-Line Arguments

All the programs we have written have *main* coded with no parameters. But *main* is a function called by the operating system, and as a function it may have parameters. When *main* has parameters, they are known as **command-line arguments**.

Command-line arguments are parameters to *main* when the program starts. They allow the user to specify additional information when the program is invoked. For instance, if you write a program to append two files, rather than specifying the names of the files as constants in the code, the user could supply them when the program starts. Thus, a UNIX user might execute the program with the command line shown below.

```
$apndfile file1 file2
```

As the programmer, you design the parameter lists for functions you write. When you use system functions, such as *srand,* you follow the parameter design set up by the language specification. Command-line arguments are a little like both programmer-designed and system parameters. As the programmer, you have control over the names of the parameters, but their type and format are predefined for the language.

The function *main* can be defined either with no argument (*void*) or with two arguments, one an integer and the other an array of pointers to *char* (strings) that represent user-determined values to be passed to *main.* The number of elements in the array is stored in the first argument. The pointers to the user values are stored in the array. The two different formats are shown in Figure L-1.

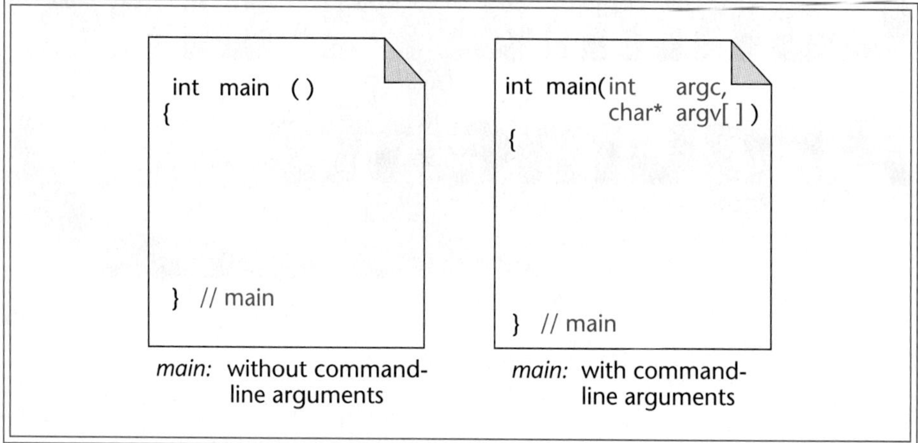
int main ()
{
} // main
main: without command-line arguments
int main(int argc,
char* argv[ ])
{
} // main
main: with command-line arguments

Figure L-1 Arguments to *main*

Although the names of the arguments are your choice, traditionally they are called ***argc*** (argument count) and ***argv*** (argument vector). This data structure design, with six string pointers in the vector, is shown in Figure L-2.

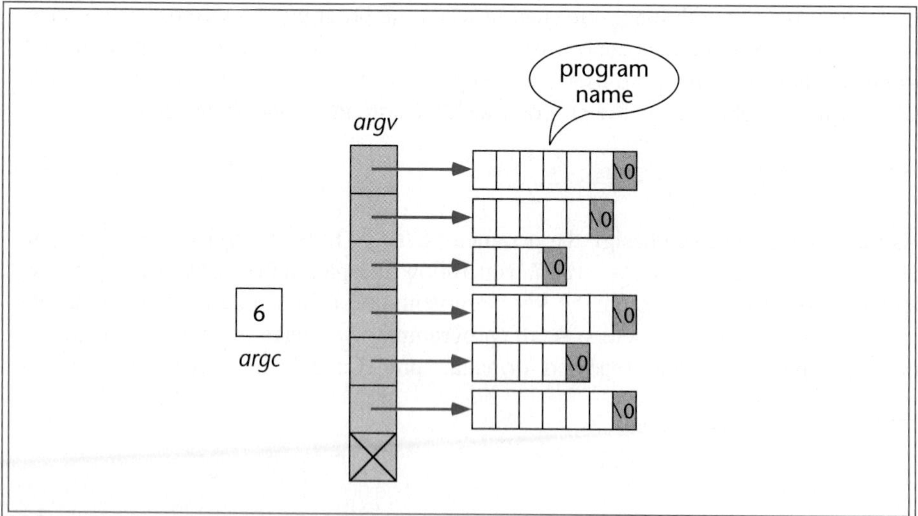
program name
argv
6
argc
\0
\0
\0
\0
\0
\0

Figure L-2 *argc* and *argv*

The first argument, *argc,* defines the number of elements in the array identified in the second argument. The value for this argument is not entered from the keyboard; it is provided automatically by the system.

There are several different types of elements in the *argv* array. The first element points to the name of the program (its file name). It is provided automatically by the system. The last element contains NULL and may be used to identify the end of the list. The rest of the elements contain pointers to the user-entered string values.

As an example of command-line arguments, let's revisit Program 16-4, "Append binary files," on page 785. Command-line arguments are often used with utility programs like this. Rather than have the user respond to prompts, the file names are entered as user values when the program is run. The modified code is seen in Program L-1.

Program L-1 **Command-line arguments to append two files**

```
/* This program appends two binary files of integers.
     Written by:
     Date:
*/
#include <iostream>
#include <fstream>
using namespace std;

int main (int   argc, char* argv[])
{
   cout << "\nThis program appends two files.\n";
   if (argc != 3)
      {
       printf("\aTwo file names required\n");
        exit(100);
      } // if

   ofstream fsAp;
   fsAp.open (argv[1], ios::out | ios::app |
ios::binary);
   if (!fsAp)
      {
       cout << "\aCan't open " << argv[1] << endl;
       exit (100);
      } // if

   // Position primary file at end
   fsAp.seekp (0, ios::end);

   ifstream fsIn;
   fsIn.open (argv[2],  ios::in | ios:: binary);
   if (!fsIn)
      {
       cout << "\aCan't open " << argv[2] << endl;
       exit (110);
      } // if file at end

   long apndCnt = 0;
   int       data;
   while (fsIn.read ((char *)&data, sizeof(int)))
```

Program L-1 Command-line arguments to append two files *(continued)*

```
        {
         fsAp.write ((char *)&data, sizeof(int));
         apndCnt++;
        } // while

    // Test for read failure rather than eof
    if (!fsIn.eof())
        {
         cout << "\aRead Error 120. No output.\n";
         exit (120);
        } // if
    fsAp.close ();
    fsIn.close ();

    cout << "Append complete:  "
         << apndCnt << " appended to file\n";
    return 0;
} // main
```

Program L-1 Analysis To read the file names as command-line arguments, we added *argc* and *argv* as parameters to *main.* Then to guard against the common error of forgetting to use the file names when the program is executed, we tested to make sure three user values were read. (Remember, the file name is the first element, so we needed three elements—the program name and the name of the two files being merged.)

After changing the program to make sure that the correct user values were read, we deleted the user interface prompts and reads. Finally, we had to change all references to the file names to use the user values. To execute the file, the user would enter the following simple UNIX run-time command:

```
$apndfile file1 file2
```

M Pointers to Functions

Functions in your program occupy memory. The name of the function is a pointer constant to the first byte of memory. For example, imagine that you have four functions stored in memory: main, `fun`, `pun`, and `sun`. This relationship is shown graphically in Figure M-1. The name of each function is a pointer to its code in memory.

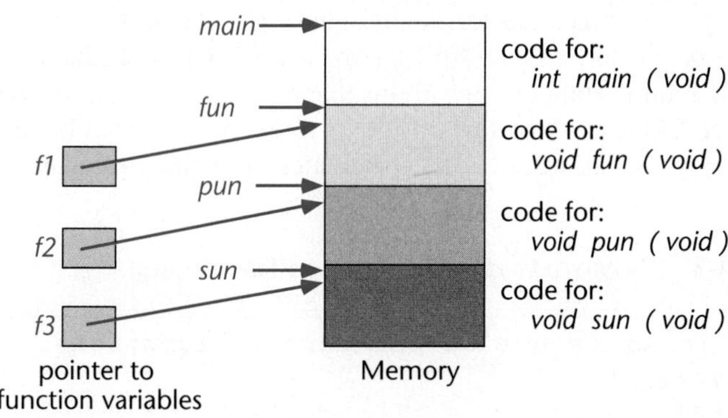

Figure M-1 Functions in memory

Just as we can with all other pointer types, we can define pointers to function variables and store the address of `fun`, `pun`, and `sun` in them. The syntax for declaring pointers to functions is different. To declare a pointer to a function, you code it as if it were a prototype definition, with the function name and its pointer token in parentheses. This format is shown in Figure M-2. The parentheses are important: without them, C++ would interpret the function return type as a pointer. Pointers to function variables are also shown in Figure M-2.

f1 is a pointer to a function with no parameters that returns *void*

```
...
// Local Declarations
void (*f1) ( void );
void (*f2) ( void );
void (*f3) ( void );
...
// Statements
...
f1 = fun ;
f2 = pun ;
f3 = sun ;
...
```

Figure M-2 Pointers to functions

Program M-1 shows how our three functions, `fun`, `pun`, and `sun`, can be executed when they are passed as a parameter. Analyze the prototype declaration for `strange` carefully. The parameter, `ptrToFunction`, is a pointer to a function that has no parameters and returns nothing. This means that `strange` expects to receive the address (a pointer) of the function that it is going to execute. To pass the function's address, we simply use its name as the parameter: The function name is a pointer constant.

Program M-1 Demonstrate pointers to functions

```
/* Demonstrate use of pointers to functions.
   Written by:
   Date:
*/
#include <iostream>
using namespace std;

void strange (void(*ptrToFunction)());
void fun ();
void pun ();
void sun ();

```

Program M-1 Demonstrate pointers to functions *(continued)*

```
int main ()
{
strange (fun);
strange (pun);
strange (sun);
return 0;
} // main
/* ================== strange ==================
   This function will call whatever function is passed
   to it by the calling function.
      Pre  ptrFun pointer to  function to be executed
      Post requested function has been executed
*/
void strange (void(*ptrToFunction)())
{
   (*ptrToFunction)();
   return;
}  // strange
/* ================== fun ==================
   Prints a simple message about fun.
      Pre  Nothing
      Post Message has been printed
*/
void fun ()
{
   cout << "Fun is being with good friends.\n";
   return;
}  // fun
/* ================== pun ==================
   Prints a simple message about pun.
      Pre  Nothing
      Post Message has been printed
*/
void pun ()
{
   cout << "Pun is a play on words.\n";
   return;
}  // pun
/* ================== sun ==================
   Prints a simple message about sun.
      Pre  Nothing
      Post Message has been printed
*/
void sun ()
```

Program M-1 Demonstrate pointers to functions *(continued)*

```
{
   cout << "Sun is a bright star.\n";
   return;
} // sun
```

```
Results:
Fun is being with good friends.
Pun is a play on words.
Sun is a bright star.
```

As a more practical example, consider the role of manipulators in the ios class libraries. In Appendix I we saw two manipulators, *endl* and `dec5p2`, that both used pointers to functions in their implementation.

N

Namespace

In this appendix we discuss the basic concepts for namespaces, as introduced in the C++ standard. Namespaces provide a technique for organizing and using names within a program and between programs.

N-1 BACKGROUND

Naming things and people can be difficult. Within our family, we can name different family members John, George, Ann, and Alice. Within the family, when we say Ann, everyone knows whom we are talking about. However, outside the family there are lots of people named Ann. When we need to refer to her outside the family, we may need to qualify her name; we need to say which Ann we are referring to because otherwise someone may think of another person named Ann.

One way to qualify which Ann we are referring to is to associate her with the family name. For example, we have two families, the Washingtons and the Nguyens, each with a family member named Ann. Inside the Washington family, everybody called Ann by her first name; inside the Nguyen family, everybody called Ann by her first name. Outside the family, they are known as "Washington, Ann" and "Nguyen, Ann." The comma that separates the last name from the first name can be called, ironically, a *family resolution operator*.

In programming, particularly large programs, we have the same situation. We need to name constants, variables, functions, and other objects within the program. But what happens as our program is combined with other programs written, either by ourselves, other project members, or by the system programmers? Some of the names may be used in more than one function or object. Now we are in trouble. If two program segments use the same name, such as *num*, to define an integer, when we refer to *num,* it is not clear to which one we are referring.

To solve the problem, C++ defines ***namespaces***. A namespace is a collection of names belonging to a group. For example, we can have two groups: G1 and G2. If we define a variable called *num* in each of the groups, we can refers to *num* inside G1 or *num* within G2 without any ambiguity. But if we need to refer to *num* outside their groups, we need to qualify the name with the *scope resolution operator* (: :). In other words, *num* in G1 is called `G1: :num` and *num* in G2 is called G2: :`num`.

Figure N-1 shows how C++ defines namespaces using a namespace statement.

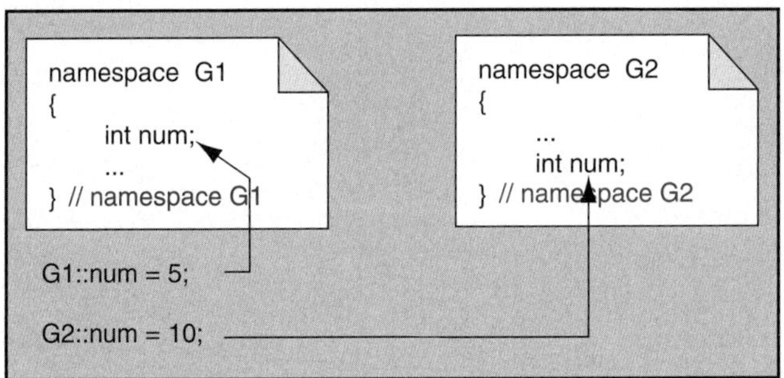

Figure N-1 Namespace and the scope resolution operator

To make the concept clear, let us write a very unusual program. Although we never recommend you to do so, we have written a program that uses the name `cout` two times. The first `cout` is the name of the name of a variable (with value 5). Because it does not use the scope resolution operator, its scope is local to *main* in our program. The second `cout` uses the scope resolution protocol that associates it with ***std***, a namespace that defines all names used in C++ library. When we use `cout`, the compiler knows that it should look that the declaration in our program; when we use `std::cout`, the program cannot find this full name (surname and first name) in our program, so it tries to look in the header files and find it in <iostream> header file. Program N-1 contains the code and results.

Program N-1 Demonstrate namespace scope

```
/* Demonstrate namespace scope.
      Written by:
      Date:
*/
#include <iostream>

int main ()
{
   int cout = 5;
   std::cout << cout << "\n";
   return 0;
}  // main
```

```
Result:
5
```

Program N-1 demonstrates that `cout` and `std::cout` are completely two different names.

> **The names `cout` and `std::cout` are two different names; one belongs to the global namespace, the other to *std* namespace.**

To investigate further, let's write a program that uses only `cout` as the name of output stream. This example is shown in Program N-2.

Program N-2 cout not in scope

```
/* Demonstrate not in scope error.
      Written by:
      Date:
*/
#include <iostream>

int main ()
{
   cout << "Hello\n";
   return 0 ;
}  // main
```

```
Results:
Error    : undefined identifier 'cout'
PnameSp-02.cpp line 9   cout << "Hello\n";
```

The program does not compile because the compiler is looking for the declaration for `cout` and can't find one. It neither finds it in the program nor in the *iostream* file. The *iostream* file uses `std::cout`, not just `cout`.

N-2 USING NAMES FROM NAMESPACES

To use names in a particular namespace, we have three choices: mention the full name, add a using directive, or add a using declaration.

FULL NAMES

Probably the most simple way to solve the problem is to use full names. Although this is simpler, it requires more keystrokes and makes the program longer. When we use full names, we add the namespace's family name, such as *std*, and the scope resolution operator to the name. Thus, `cout` becomes `std::cout`. Program N-3 shows this approach using the input and output file streams, *cin* and *cout*.

Program N-3 Using full names

```
/* Demonstrate using full names.
      Written by:
      Date:
*/
#include <iostream>

int main ()
{
   std::cout << "Enter an integer: ";
   int numIn;
   std::cin  >> numIn;
   std::cout << "You entered:      " << numIn << "\n";
   return 0;
} // main
```

```
Result:
Enter an integer: 5
You entered:      5
```

USING DIRECTIVE

The second solution adds what is called a **using directive**. It is usually placed in the global area of the program after the include statements. The format is shown below. It must end with a semicolon.

```
using namespace name_of_namespace;
```

When the compiler encounters a name without a declaration, it adds the name of namespace defined in the using directive to the name and then tries to find the declaration for the full name.

In Program N-4, we repeat Program N-3, this time using a namespace directive to direct the compiler to use the *std* namespace for any name that it cannot find.

Program N-4 Using namespace directive

```
/* Demonstrate using a namespace directive.
      Written by:
      Date:
*/
#include <iostream>
using namespace std;

int main ()
{
   cout << "Enter an integer: ";
   int numIn;
   cin  >> numIn;
   cout << "You entered:       " << numIn << "\n";
   return 0 ;
} // main
```

USING DECLARATION

The using directive method adds the name of the namespace to every name that the compiler cannot find. The third solution, the using declaration, limits the names that the compiler tries to resolve. It tells the compiler to add the namespace to only a selected number of names, not all. The format is shown below:

```
using name_of_the_namesapce::identifier;
```

When the compiler encounters a name that includes the identifier declared in using declaration, it adds the name of the namespace and tries again. For example, in Program N-5, we have added the two using namespace declarations to direct the compiler to add *std* only to *cin*, *cout*, and *endl*.

Program N-5 Using name declarations

```
/* Demonstrate using name declarations.
      Written by:
      Date:
*/
#include <iostream>
using std::cout;
using std::cin;
using std::endl;

int main ()
{
   cout << "Enter an integer: ";
   int numIn;
   cin  >> numIn;
   cout << "You entered:       " << numIn << "\n";
   return 0;
} // main
```

DIFFERENCE BETWEEN DIRECTIVE AND DECLARATION

A using declaration adds its names to a local scope; a using directive makes names available to the scope in which they are declared, usually the compile unit. Another major difference between namespace directives and declarations is the number of names included by the using statement. The directive adds all names within the namespace. The declaration adds only the specified names. In general, it is safer to use a declaration, especially when we use more than one namespace.

Let's look at an example. Assume that we have two namespaces: `purchasing` and `inventory`, as declared in Program N-6.[1] Both of them have two common names: `i` and `j`. We want to use `i` from `purchasing` and `j` from `inventory` 2. The compiler would generate errors if we used directives in this case. However, the declarations limit the variables that can be used and no errors are found. We instruct the compiler to use `purchasing::i` each time it finds an `i` and to use `inventory::j` each time it finds a `j`. Program N-6 shows this solution.

Program N-6 Using declarations for multiple namespaces

```
/* Demonstrate use of declarations for multiple namespaces.
      Written by:
      Date:
*/
#include <iostream>
using namespace std;

namespace purchasing
{
   int i;
   int j;
  // ...
}  // purchasing namespace

namespace inventory
{
  int i;
  int j;
  // ...
}  // inventory namespace

using purchasing::i;
using inventory::j;

int main ()
{
   i = 5 ;                                // purchasing::i
   cout << "Purchasing i is: " << purchasing::i << endl;

```

[1] We discuss the coding of application namespaces in the next section.

Program N-6 Using declarations for multiple namespaces (*continued*)

```
   j = 12;                                       // inventory::j
   cout << "Inventory j is: " << inventory::j << endl;
   return 0 ;
} // main
```

```
Results:
Purchasing i is: 5
Inventory  j is: 12
```

N-3 DECLARING NAMESPACES

We have informally shown how to declare namespaces. In this section, we formally introduce the topic and discuss some issues related to it.

DECLARATION

The following example shows the format for a namespace. It begins with the keyword *namespace*, followed by the an identifier, `nameSp`. The declarations to be included in the namespace are coded in a block. Note that there is no need for a semicolon at the end of the declaration.

```
namespace nameSp
{
   ...
}  // nameSp
```

The declarations within the block can be any valid name within a program, such as variable names, function names, and class names. The data names are declared using their types; the function names are declared using their prototypes.

EXTENSION

We can extend the declaration of a namespace after it has been declared. For example, if we have declare a namespace in a header file and we need to add more declarations to it without changing the header file, we can write a new declaration with the same name. The following example demonstrates the code.

```
#include <myDeclarations>
using namespace nameSp
...
namespace nameSp
{
   ...
}  // nameSp Extension
```

NESTING

We can define a namespace inside another namespace. In the next example, we declare two namespaces, `nameSp` and `nested`. As with all nested code, we recommend that the nested code be indented for readability.

```
namespace nameSp
{
   ...
   namespace nested
      {
       ...
      } // nested
}  // outer
```

When we refer to the names in a nested namespace, they must be qualified. In the previous example, if we declare that we are using namespace `nameSp`, we can refer to all declarations in it with or without qualification. However, to refer to `nested`, we must either qualify it with an the namespace name and a scope operator or use a namespace declaration or directive. We demonstrate these techniques in Program N-7.

Program N-7 Demonstrate nested namespaces

```
/* Demonstrate use of nested namespaces.
      Written by:
      Date
*/
#include <iostream>
using namespace std;

namespace numNames
{
   int i;

   namespace shrt
      {
       short shJ;
      } // namespace shrt

   namespace lng
   {
     long lnK;
   } // namespace lng
}  // numNames namespace
using namespace numNames;

int main ()
{
   i = 5;
   cout << "numNames::i is:           "
        << numNames::i << endl;

   shrt::shJ = 12;
   cout << "numNames::shrt::shJ is: "
        <<  numNames::shrt::shJ << endl;

   using lng::lnK;
```

Program N-7 Demonstrate nested namespaces (*continued*)

```
35     lnK = 12345;
36     cout << "numNames::shrt::lnK is: "
37          << numNames::lng::lnK << endl;
38     return 0 ;
39 } // main
```

```
Results:
numNames::i is:         5
numNames::shrt::shJ is: 12
numNames::shrt::lnK is: 12345
```

Program N-7 Analysis There are several points that we need to examine in this program. Let's begin by studying the namespace declaration (statement 8). We declare integer types at the first level; that is, under the `numNames` scope. We then use two nested namespace declarations, one for short integer and one for long integer. As you study the code, note that the print statements use the full name for all data references.

To make the namespace available, we include a using statement. It makes everything in the name space visible so in statement 26, we can directly refer to `i`. However, we cannot refer to the data in the short and long namespaces. To make `shJ` visible, we qualify its use in statement 30. Note that we don't need to use its full name `(numNames::shrt::shJ)` because the using in statement 22 makes it visible.

To make `lnK` visible, we use a namespace directive in statement 34. Again, we need only the nested namespace name; the first-level qualification is provided by statement 22.

N-4 NAMESPACE TYPES

We can have three types of namespaces as shown in Figure N-2.

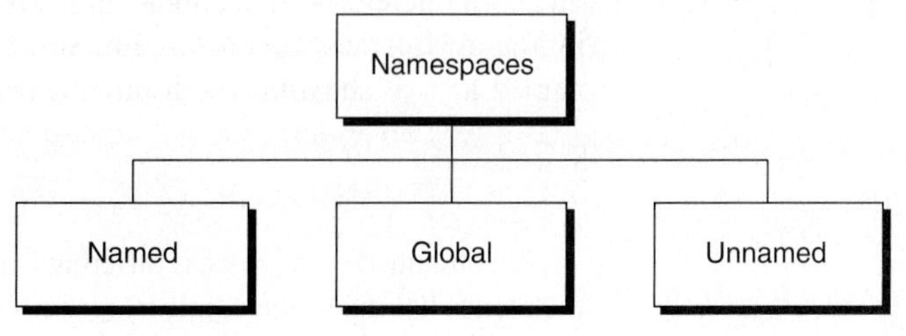

Figure N-2 Namespaces

NAMED NAMESPACE

We have used the named namespace throughout the text. We can declare it or we can reference a system library. The reference to the standard system namespace is shown in the following example.

```
using namespace std;
```

GLOBAL NAMESPACE

A global namespace is a default namespace when we use names in our programs that do not belong to any namespace. It is important to recognize, however, that being in the global namespace does not make it globally accessible. The normal rules for scope are still enforced.

Global namespace does not mean global scope

When we write a program and declare an integer named `amt`, it means that `amt` belongs to the global namespace. Using global namespace is fine when a program is small. When a program is made up of several include files, especially when they are written by different programmers, global namespaces often create problems because the same names used in different units may have different definitions and different intentions. In this case, it is advised to design and build namespaces.

UNNAMED NAMESPACE

Namespaces can be unnamed. When we declared a namespace without name, it is called an unnamed namespace. The following example contains an unnamed namespace.

```
namespace
{
    ...
}  // unnamed namespace
```

An unnamed namespace is unique within a translation unit. A **translation unit** is a separately compiled unit of code that can be linked with other compile units to form a program. The most common translation units are those supplied with the system and *included* in our programs. In a large project, locally written translation units may also be used.

Because unnamed namespaces are unique within a translation unit, every name declared in the unnamed namespace can be used only in the translation unit; they are inaccessible from other translation units. Unnamed namespaces deprecate—that is, they are intended to replace the *static*[2] type modifier for data and functions. When we use an unnamed namespace, every variable and function is static. Today, the recommendation is not to use static but rather to use unnamed namespaces.

The scope operator can be used with an unnamed namespace when it is necessary to qualify a reference. For example, given two variables with the same identifier, `amt`, one in a named namespace and one in an unnamed namespace, we would qualify the unnamed `amt` as shown in the following example.

```
::amt
```

The unnamed namespace is different from the global namespace. In a global namespace, the names belong to the whole program; in the unnamed namespace, the names are local to the translation unit.

An unnamed namespace is different from a global namespace.

[2]The use of *static* within a function is still valid.

O

Standard Template Library

The Standard Template Library (STL) is a collection of template classes and template functions that can be used to implement common data structures and their corresponding algorithms. It is included with ANSI/ISO implementations of C++.

STL has five components: containers, container adaptors, iterators, generic algorithms, and function objects.

O-1 CONTAINERS

Containers are objects that store a collection of other objects. There are two broad categories of containers: sequence containers and associative containers.

SEQUENCE CONTAINERS

A sequence container is an unsorted, linear collection of objects, all of the same type. The three standard sequence containers are vector, deque, and list.

vector

A vector is a sequence container that supports random access iterators. It is optimized for insertions and deletions at the end of the collection. Insertions and deletions anywhere else in the collection, such as the beginning or middle, take linear time. Storage management is handled automatically.

The vector template class declaration in Program O-1 has been simplified: We have omitted some details and several methods.

Program O-1 vector class

```
template <class T >
class vector
{
  public:
// =========== constructor and destructor ===========
      vector  ();                              // default
      vector  (size_type n, const T& t);
      vector  (input_iterator first,
               input_iterator last);
      vector  (const vector<T>& x);
      ~vector (void);

// ================= assignment =================
  vector<T>&  operator= (vector<T>&, x);
  void        assign    (input_iterator first,
                         input_operator last);
  void        assign    (size_type n, const T& t);

// =================  capacity =================
  size_type size     (void);     // check current size
  size_type max_size (void);    // check maximum size
  void      resize   (size_type n);
  bool      empty    (void);
  size_type capacity (void);

// =============== create iterators ===============
  iterator          begin   (void);  // forward
  iterator          end     (void);  // forward
  reverse_iterator  rbegin  (void);  // reverse
  reverse_iterator  rend    (void);  // reverse
```

Program O-1 vector class *(continued)*

```
// ================= element access =================
  reference front       (void);                    // first
  reference back        (void);                     // last
  reference operator[] (size_type n);             // middle
  reference at          (size_type n);            // middle

// ================= modifiers =================
  void      push_back   (const T& t);             // at back
  iterator  insert      (iterator i,            // at middle
                         const T& x);
  void      insert      (iterator i,            // at middle
                          size_type n,
                          constant T& x);
  void      insert      (iterator i,            // at middle
                          iterator start,
                          iterator end);
  void      pop_back    (void);                 // from back
  iterator  erase       (iterator postion); // from middle
  iterator  erase       (iterator start,            // range
                         iterator end);      // start...end
  void      swapnn      (vector<T>&, x);
  void      clear       (void);               // remove all
}                                                  // vector
```

Program O-2 contains the relational operators associated with the vector class.

Program O-2 vector class relational operators

```
// ============= relational operators =============
   bool operator==   (const vector <T>& x,
                      const vector <T>& y);
   bool operator!=   (const vector <T>& x,
                      const vector <T>& y);
   bool operator<    (const vector <T>& x,
                      const vector <T>& y);
   bool operator>    (const vector <T>& x,
                      const vector <T>& y);
   bool operator<=   (const vector <T>& x,
                      const vector <T>& y);
   bool operator>=   (const vector <T>& x,
                      const vector <T>& y);
```

deque

A deque is a sequenced container that supports random access iterators. It provides highly efficient insert and delete operations at the beginning or at the end of the data. Insert and delete at the middle require linear time. Thus, a deque is optimized for inserting and erasing elements at the beginning or at the end. Storage management is handled automatically.

Program O-3 contains a basic template class declaration for deque. We omit some of the details and methods for simplicity.

Program O-3 deque class

```
template <class T>
class deque
{
   public:
// ================= modifiers =================
          deque ();                                   // default
          deque (size_type n, const T& t);
          deque (input_iterator first,
                 input_iterator last);
          deque (const deque<T>& x);                  // copy
          ~deque (void);

// ================= assignment =================
   deque<T>&       operator= (deque<T>&, x);
   void            assign    (input_iterator first,
                              input_operator last);
   void            assign    (size_type n,   const T& t);

// ================= capacity =================
   size_type       size      (void);         // current size
   size_type       max_size  (void);
   void            resize    (size_type n);
   bool            empty     (void);

// ================= iterators =================
   iterator           begin  (void);              // forward
   iterator           end    (void);              // forward
   reverse_iterator   rbegin (void);              // reverse
   reverse_iterator   rend   (void);              // reverse

// ================= element access =================
   reference   front       (void);                // first
   reference   back        (void);                // last
   reference   operator[]  (size_type n);         // middle
   reference   at          (size_type n);         // middle

// ================= modifiers =================

   void        push_front (const T&    t);   // front
   void        push_back  (const T&    t);   // back
   iterator    insert     (iterator    i,    //  middle
                           const T&    x);
   void        insert     (iterator    i,
                           size_type   n,
                           constant T& x);
```

Program O-3 deque class *(continued)*

```
   void        insert     (iterator    i,
                           iterator    start,
                           iterator    end);

   void        pop_front(void);
   void        pop_back (void);
   iterator    erase     (iterator postion);// from middle
   iterator    erase     (iterator start,
                          iterator end);
   void        swap      (deque<T>&, x);
   void        clear();                      // removing all
}; // deque
```

The relational operators in Program O-4 are associated with the deque.

Program O-4 deque relational operators

```
// ============== relational operators ==============
   bool          operator== (const deque <T>& x,
                             const deque <T>& y);
   bool          operator!= (const deque <T>& x,
                             const deque <T>& y);
   bool          operator<  (const deque <T>& x,
                             const deque <T>& y);
   bool          operator>  (const deque <T>& x,
                             const deque <T>& y);
   bool          operator<= (const deque <T>& x,
                             const deque <T>& y);
   bool          operator>= (const deque <T>& x,
                             const deque <T>& y);
```

LIST

A list is a sequenced container that supports bidirectional iterators with constant time insert and delete operations anywhere in the list; however, it does not support random access to elements. Thus, a list is especially designed for sequential access. Storage management is handled automatically.

Program O-5 contains a simplified template class declaration for list, omitting the allocators for simplicity.

Program O-5 list class

```
template <class T >
class list
{
   public:
// =========== constructor and destructor ===========
                  list  ();
                  list  (size_type n,
                         const T& t);
                  list  (input_iterator first,
```

Program O-5 list class *(continued)*

```
                        input_iterator last);
                 list  (const list<T>& x);
                 ~list (void);

// ================= assignment ===============
  list <T>&      operator= (list<T>&, x);
  void           assign (input_iterator first,
                         input_operator last);
  void              assign (size_type n, const T& t);

// ================= capacity ================
  size_type      size     (void);        // current size
  size_type      max_size (void);        // maximum size
  void           resize   (size_type n);
  bool           empty    (void);

// ================= iterators ================
  iterator          begin  (void);          // forward
  iterator          end    (void);          // forward
  reverse_iterator  rbegin (void);          // backward
  reverse_iterator  rend   (void);          // backward

// ================= element access ================
  reference         front  (void);
  reference         back   (void);

// ================= modifiers ================
  void      push_front (const T& t);
  void      push_back  (const T& t);
  iterator  insert     (iterator i,            // middle
                        const T& x);
  void      insert     (iterator i,            // middle
                        size_type n,
                        constant T& x);
  void      insert     (iterator i,            // middle
                        iterator start,
                        iterator end);

  void      pop_front  (void);
  void      pop_back   (void);
  iterator  erase      (iterator postion);     // middle
  iterator  erase      (iterator start,
                        iterator end);
  void      swap       (list<T>& x);
  void      clear      (void);              // delete all
```

Program O-5 list class *(continued)*

```
//  ============ special list operations ============
   void        splice       (iterator postion,
                            list<T>& x);
   void        splice       (iterator postion,
                            list<T>& x,
                            terator i);
   void        splice       (iterator postion,
                            list<T>& x,
                            iterator first,
                            iterator last);
   void        remove       (const T& value);
   void        remove_if    (Predicate pred);
   void        unique       (BinaryPredicate binary_pred);
   void        merge        (list<T>& x);
   void        merge        (list<T>& x, Compare comp);
   void        sort         (Compare comp);
   void        reverse      (void);
}; list
```

The relational operators for the list class are shown in Program O-6.

Program O-6 list class relational operators

```
// ============== relational operators ==============
   bool  operator== (const list <T>& x, const list<T>& y);
   bool  operator!= (const list <T>& x, const list<T>& y);
   bool  operator<  (const list <T>& x, const list<T>& y);
   bool  operator>  (const list <T>& x, const list<T>& y);
   bool  operator<= (const list <T>& x, const list<T>& y);
   bool  operator>= (const list <T>& x, const list<T>& y);
```

ASSOCIATIVE CONTAINERS

An associative container is a collection of sorted objects that allows fast retrieval using a key. In each container, the key must be unique. There are four standard associative containers: *set*, *multiset*, *map*, and *multimap*.

set

A set is an associative container (Program O-7) that supports unique key and bidirectional iterators. It provides fast retrieval on keys. Only the key is stored in the container; there are no other data.

Program O-7 set class

```
template <class Key>
class set
{
public:
```

Program O-7 set class *(continued)*

```
// ============== constructor and destructor ============
                   set  ();
                   set  (input_iterator first,
                         input_iterator last);
                   set  (const set<Key>& x);     // copy
                   ~set (void);
// ================= assignment =================
  set<Key>&        operator= (set<Key>&, x);
  void             assign    (input_iterator first,
                              input_operator last);
  void             assign    (size_type n, const Key& t);

// ================= capacity =================
  size_type        size     (void);// current size
  size_type        max_size (void);
  bool             empty    (void);

// ================= iterators =================
  iterator          begin  (void);          // forward
  iterator          end    (void);          // forward
  reverse_iterator  rbegin (void);          // reverse
  reverse_iterator  rend   (void);          // reverse

// ================= modifiers =================
  pair <iterator, bool> insert (const value_type & x);

  iterator    insert (iterator i, const value_type & x);
  void        insert (InputIterator start,
                      InputIterator end);

  void          erase  (iterator postion);    // middle
  void          erase  (const Key& x);
  void          erase  (iterator start, iterator end);
  void          swap   (set<Key>&, x);
  void          clear  (void);// remove all

// ================= observers =================
  key_compare   key_comp   (void);
  value_compare value_comp (void);

// ============== special set operations ==============
  iterator      find        (const key_type& x);
  size_type     count       (const key_type& x);
  iterator      lower_bound (const key_type& x);
  iterator      upper_bound (const key_type& x);
  iterator      equal_range (const key_type& x);
}; // set
```

Program O-8 contains the relational operators for the set class.

Program O-8 Relational operators for set class

```
// ============== relational operators ===============
   bool          operator== (const set <Key>& x,
                             const set <Key>& y);
   bool          operator!= (const set <Key>& x,
                             const set <Key>& y);
   bool          operator<  (const set <Key>& x,
                             const set <Key>& y);
   bool          operator>  (const set <Key>& x,
                             const set <Key>& y);
   bool          operator<= (const set <Key>& x,
                             const set <Key>& y);
   bool          operator>= (const set <Key>& x,
                             const set <Key>& y);
```

multiset

A multiset, shown in Program O-9, is an associative container that supports duplicate keys and bidirectional iterators. It provides fast retrieval on key searches. As with the set, only the key is stored.

Program O-9 multiset class

```
template <class Key>
class multiset
{
   public:
// ============= constructor and destructor =============
              multiset  ();
              multiset  (input_iterator first,
                         input_iterator last);
              multiset  (const multiset<Key>& x);// copy
             ~multiset (void);

// ================= assignment =================
   multiset<Key>&    operator= (multiset<Key>&, x);
   void              assign    (input_iterator  first,
                                input_operator  last);
   void              assign    (size_type        n,
                                const Key&       t);

// ================= capacity =================
   size_type         size       (void);     // current size
   size_type         max_size   (void);
   bool              empty      (void);

// ================= iterators =================
   iterator          begin  (void);            // forward
   iterator          end    (void);            // forward
```

Program O-9 multiset class *(continued)*

```
   reverse_iterator rbegin (void);           // reverse
   reverse_iterator rend   (void);           // reverse

// ================= modifiers =================
   pair <iterator, bool> insert (const Key& x);

   iterator      insert    (iterator i, constant Key& x);
   void          insert    (InputIterator start,
                            InputIterator end);
   void          erase     (iterator postion);// middle
   void          erase     (const Key& x);
   void          erase     (iterator start, iterator end);
   void          swap      (multiset<Key>& x);
   void          clear     ();            // remove all

// ================= observers =================
   key_compare   key_comp   (void);
   value_compare value_comp (void);

// ================= special operations =================
   iterator      find               (const key_type& x);
   size_type     count              (const key_type& x);
   iterator      lower_bound        (const key_type& x);
   iterator      upper_bound        (const key_type& x);
   pair<iterator, iterator> equal_range (const key_type& x);
}; // multiset
```

Program O-10 contains the relational operators for the multiset class.

Program O-10 Relational operators for multiset

```
// ============== relational operators ================
   bool          operator== (const multiset <Key>& x,
                             const multiset<Key>& y);
   bool          operator!= (const multiset <Key>& x,
                             const multiset<Key>& y);
   bool          operator<  (const multiset <Key>& x,
                             const multiset<Key>& y);
   bool          operator>  (const multiset <Key>& x,
                             const multiset<Key>& y);
   bool          operator<= (const multiset <Key>& x,
                             const multiset<Key>& y);
   bool          operator>= (const multiset <Key>& x,
                             const multiset<Key>& y);
```

map

A map is an associative container (Program O-11) that supports unique key and bidirectional iterators. It provides fast retrieval of values of another type T based on the keys. The key is an index to the data in the container; the key is not stored.

Program O-11 map class

```
template <class Key, class T>
class map
{
  public:
// ============= constructor and destructor =============
                    map ();
                    map (input_iterator first,
                         input_iterator last);
                    map (const map<Key, T>& x); // copy
                    ~map (void);

// ================= assignment =================
  map<Key, T>&      operator= (map<Key, T>& x);

// ================= capacity =================
  size_type         size     (void);     // current size
  size_type         max_size (void);
  bool              empty    (void);

// ================= iterators =================
  iterator          begin    (void);     // forward
  iterator          end      (void);     // forward
  reverse_iterator  rbegin   (void);     // reverse
  reverse_iterator  rend     (void);     // reverse

// ================= element access =================
  T&          operator[](const key_type& k);

// ================= modifiers =================
  pair <iterator, bool> insert (const value_type& x);
  iterator    insert (iterator i, const value_type& x);
  void        insert (InputIterator start,
                      InputIterator end);

  void        erase  (iterator postion); // from middle
  size_type   erase  (const key-type& k);
  void        erase  (iterator start,
                      iterator end);
  void        swap   (map<Key, T>& x);
  void        clear  ();                 // remove all

// ================= observers =================
  key_compare    key_comp   (void);
  value_compare  value_comp (void);
```

Program O-11 map class *(continued)*

```
// =============== special map operations ===============
   iterator       find (const key_type& x);
   size_type      count (const key_type& x);
   iterator       lower_bound (const key_type& x);
   iterator       upper_bound (const key_type& x);
   pair <iterator, iterator> equal_range (const key_type& x);
}; // map
```

Program O-12 contains the relational operators for the map class.

Program O-12 Relational operators for map

```
// =============== relational operators ================
   bool        operator== (const map <Key, T>& x
                           const map <Key, T>& y
   bool        operator!= (const map <Key, T>& x
                           const map <Key, T>& y
   bool        operator<  (const map <Key, T>& x
                           const map <Key, T>& y
   bool        operator>  (const map <Key, T>& x
                           const map <Key, T>& y
   bool        operator<= (const map <Key, T>& x
                           const map <Key, T>& y
   bool        operator>= (const map <Key, T>& x
                           const map <Key, T>& y
```

multimap

A multimap is an associative container (Program O-13) that supports duplicate keys and bidirectional iterators. It provides for fast retrieval of the values of another type T based on keys. The key is an index.

Program O-13 multimap class

```
template <class Key, T>
class multimap
{
   public:
// ============ constructor and destructor ============
            multimap  ();
            multimap  (input_iterator first,
                       input_iterator last);
            multimap  (const multimap<Key, T>& x);// copy
            ~multimap (void);

// ================ assignment ================
   multimap<Key>&    operator= (multimap<Key, T>&, x);
   void              assign    (input_iterator first,
                                input_operator last);
   void              assign   (size_type n, const Key& t);
```

Program O-13 multimap class *(continued)*

```
// ================= capacity =================
   size_type         size     (void);     // current size
   size_type         max_size (void);
bool                 empty    (void);

// ================= iterators =================
   iterator          begin (void);             // forward
   iterator          end (void);               // forward
   reverse_iterator  rbegin (void);            // reverse
   reverse_iterator  rend (void);              // reverse

// ================= modifiers =================
  pair <iterator, bool>  insert (const key_value& x);
  iterator               insert (iterator   i,
                         constant key_value& x);
  void                   insert (InputIterator start,
                                InputIterator end);


   void       erase   (iterator postion);// from middle
   void       erase   (const key_value& x);
   void       erase   (iterator start,
                        iterator end);
   void       swap    (multimap<Key, T>& x);
   void       clear   ();                     // remove all

// ================= observers =================
   key_compare           key_comp    (void);
   value_compare         value_comp (void);

// ============= special multimap operations ===========
   iterator       find          (const key_type& x);
   size_type      count         (const key_type& x);
   iterator    lower_bound (const key_type& x);
   iterator    upper_bound (const key_type& x);
   pair<iterator, iterator> equal_range (const key_type& x);
}; // multimap
```

The relational operators for the multimap class are shown in Program O-14.

Program O-14 Relational operators for multimap

```
// =============== relational operators ===============
   bool        operator== (const multimap <Key, T>& x
                           const multimap <Key, T>& y
   bool        operator!= (const multimap <Key, T>& x
                           const multimap <Key, T>& y
   bool        operator<  (const multimap <Key, T>& x
                           const multimap <Key, T>& y
```

Program O-14 Relational operators for multimap (*continued*)

```
bool        operator>  (const multimap <Key, T>& x
                         const multimap <Key, T>& y
bool        operator<= (const multimap <Key, T>& x
                         const multimap <Key, T>& y
bool        operator>= (const multimap <Key, T>& x
                         const multimap <Key, T>& y
```

O-2 CONTAINER ADAPTORS

Programmers often need to use other objects, such as a stack, queue, or priority queue, whose interfaces are more limited than those of standard containers. For example, a stack object needs only four types of operations: *push, pop, top*, and *empty*. The STL contains template classes for stack, queue, and priority queue and has made them generic by allowing the programmer to choose the desired sequence container (*vector*, *deque*, or *list*). These generic classes are called *container adaptors*.

STACK

A stack is a sequenced object in which insertions and deletions both take place at one end, known as the top. STL defines a container adaptor that can be adapted to any container that supports *back*, *push_back,* and *pop_back* operations. Any of the three containers—list, vector, or deque—can be used. The default container is deque. The stack class is shown in Program O-15.

Program O-15 stack class

```
template <class T, class Container = deque <T> >
class stack
{
   protected:
   Container c;

   Public:
// ================= constructor =================
      stack (const Container& = Container ());

// ================= interfaces =================
   size_type        size  (void)
                          {return c.size ();}
   bool             empty (void)
                          {return c.empty ();}
   value_type&      top   (void)
                          {return c.back ();}
   void             push  (const value_type& x)
                          {c.push_back (x);}
   void             pop   (void)
                          {c.pop_back ();}
}; // stack
```

Relational Operators

The stack uses the same relational operators as those found in the containers—equal (==), not equal (!=), less than (<), less than or equal (<=), greater than (>), and greater than or equal (>=)—to compare two stacks.

QUEUE

A queue is a sequenced container in which insertion takes place at one end (the rear) and deletion takes place at the other end (the front). The STL defines a container adaptor that can be used with any container that supports *front*, *back*, *push_back*, and *pop_front*. The best candidates are *list* and *deque*; *vector* is not suitable because *pop_front* is not supported by a vector. The default is *deque*. The *queue* class is shown in Program O-16.

Program O-16 queue class

```
template <class T, class Container = deque <T>>
class queue
{
   protected:
   Container c;

   Public:
// ================= constructor =================
      queue (const Container& = Container ());

// ================= interfaces =================
   size_type          size   (void)
                             {return c.size ();}
   bool               empty  (void)
                             {return c.empty ();}
   value_type&        front  (void)
                             {return c.front ();}
   value_type&        back   (void)
                             {return c.back ();}
   void               push   (const value_type& x)
                             {c.push_back (x);}
   void               pop    (void)
                             {c.pop_front ();}
}; // queue
```

Relational Operators

The queue uses the same relational operators as those found in the containers—equal (==), not equal (!=), less than (<), less than or equal (<=), greater than (>), and greater than or equal (>=)—to compare two queues.

PRIORITY QUEUE

A priority queue is a queue in which the sequence is created in such a way that the element with the highest (or smallest) priority is at the front and the rest of the elements are arranged in priority sequence. Entries with equal priorities are processed in FIFO sequence.

The priority queue (Program O-17) can use any container that provides a random access iterator and *front*, *push_back*, and *pop_back* operations. The *vector* and *deque* are good candidates. List is not because it does not provide a random access iterator. The default is the vector. No relational operators are provided for priority queue objects.

Program O-17 priority_queue class

```
template <class T, class Container = vector<T> >
class priority_queue
{
   protected:
   Container c;
   Compare   comp;

   Public:
// ================= constructor =================
         priority_queue
                        (const Compare& x = Compare(),
                         const Container& = Container ());
         priority_queue (InputIterator first,
                         InputIterator last,
                         const Compare& x = Compare(),
                         const Container& = Container ());

//================= interfaces =================
   size_type        size  (void)
                          {return c.size ();}
   bool             empty (void)
                          {return c.empty ();}
   value_type&      top   (void)
                          {return c.front ();}
   void             push  (const value_type& x);
   void             pop   (void);
}; // priority_queue
```

O-3 ITERATORS

Iterators are objects that provide access to objects stored in a container. They work like regular pointers in C++. They can be used to store and retrieve objects in a container the same way a pointer accesses objects in C++. In this manner, iterators act as the connection between the generic algorithms and the containers. Provided that programmers use the correct iterator, they don't need to know how the objects are stored in the container.

STL defines five different iterators: *input, output*, *forward*, *bidirectional*, and *random access,* as shown in Figure O-1.

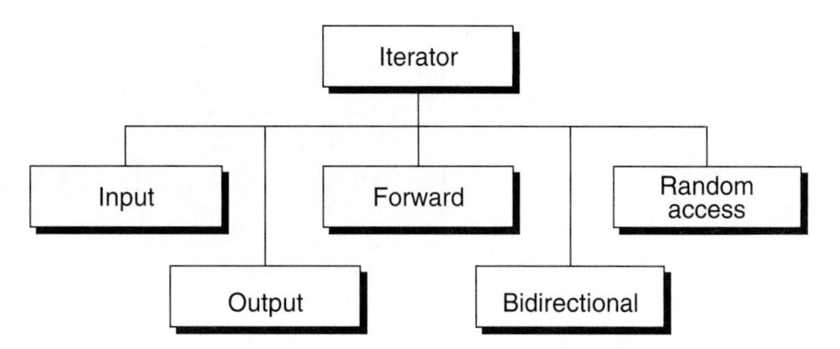

Figure O-1 Types of STL iterators

INPUT ITERATOR

An input iterator can be used only to retrieve a value from the input stream; it cannot be used to store a value. It can only move in the forward direction, retrieving the objects one by one. It cannot go backward and it cannot jump. Figure O-2 shows the concept of an input iterator in relation to an input stream.

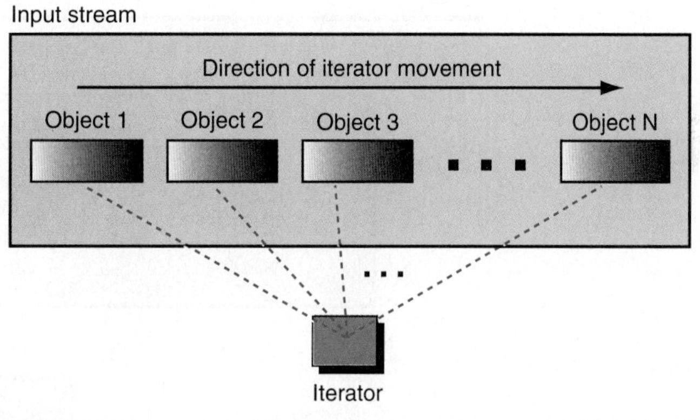

Figure O-2 STL input iterator

OUTPUT ITERATOR

An output iterator can be used only to store a value in an output stream; it cannot be used to retrieve a value. It only moves in the forward direction, storing the objects one by one. It cannot go backward and it cannot jump. Figure O-3 shows the concept of an output iterator in relation to an output stream.

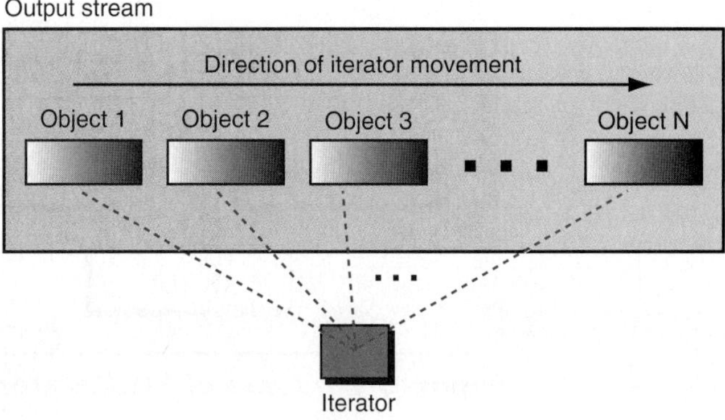

Figure O-3 STL output iterator

FORWARD ITERATOR

A forward iterator can be used to both retrieve and store a value. It can only move in the forward direction, visiting the objects one by one. It cannot go backward and it cannot jump. Figure O-4 shows the concept of a forward iterator in relation to a container.

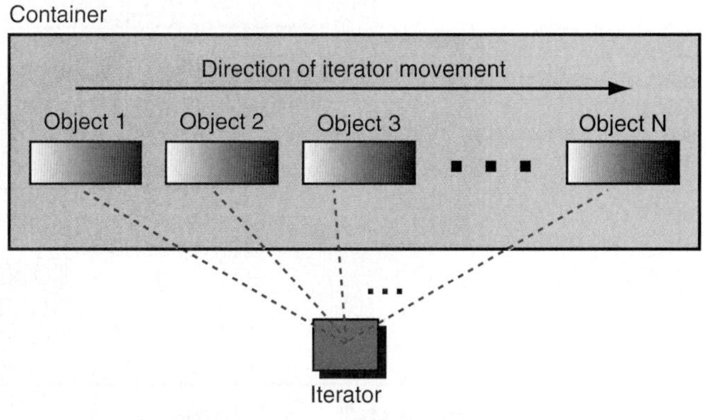

Figure O-4 STL forward iterator

BIDIRECTIONAL ITERATOR

A bidirectional iterator can be used to both retrieve and store values. Unlike the forward iterator, it moves backward and forward, one item at a time: It cannot jump. Figure O-5 shows the concept of a bidirectional iterator in relation to a container.

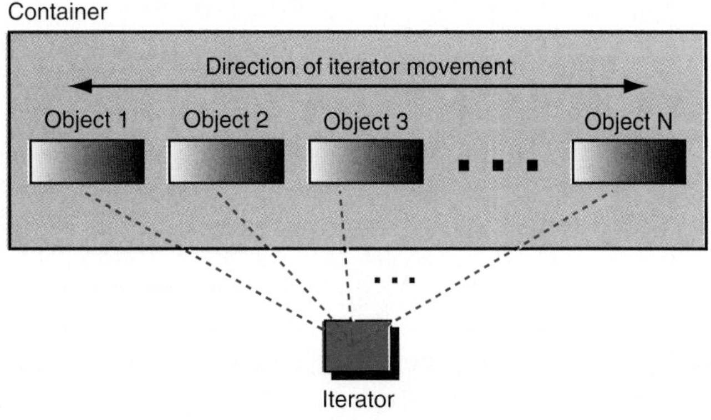

Figure O-5 STL bidirectional iterator

RANDOM ACCESS ITERATOR

A random access iterator is like a bidirectional operator with one extra capability, it can jump in both direction. Figure O-6 shows the concept of a random access iterator in relation to a container.

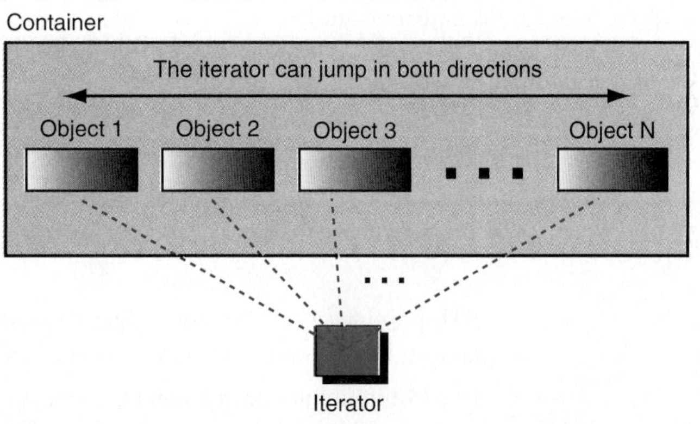

Figure O-6 STL random access iterator

HIERARCHICAL RELATION

There is a hierarchical relation between the iterators. Every forward iterator is also an input and an output iterator. Every bidirectional iterator is also a forward iterator. A random access iterator is also a bidirectional iterator. Figure O-7 shows the hierarchical relationship between five different iterators.

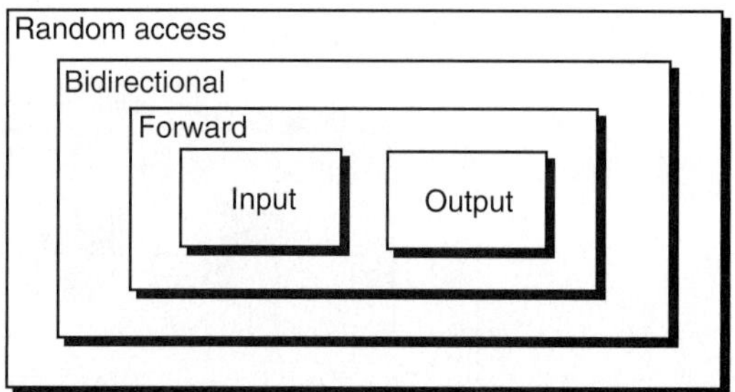

Figure O-7 Iterator hierarchical relationships

OPERATORS SUPPORTED BY ITERATORS

Each iterator can support different operators according to its type. Table O-1 shows the types of operators that can be supported by each iterator.

Iterator	Operator
Input	*, =, ++, ==, !=, ->
Output	*, =, ++
Forward	*, =, ++, ==, !=, ->
Bidirectional	*, =, ++, ==, !=, ->, --
Random access	*, =, ++, ==, !=, ->, --, +, -, <, >, <=, >=, []

Table O-1 Iterator operators

O-4 GENERIC ALGORITHMS

STL provides a set of generic algorithms, each of which can operate on a variety of containers. Generic algorithms are normally divided into the groups shown below:

- Minimum and maximum algorithms
- Numeric algorithms
- Nonmutating sequence algorithms
- Sorting algorithms
- Set operation on sorted structure
- Heap operation

O-5 FUNCTION OBJECTS

A function object encapsulates a function. STL uses this strategy to pass a function to a generic algorithm or to a method in a container without using the traditional pointers to functions. This design is accomplished by overloading the *operator()* in the corresponding class. A function object can be used in place of a function pointer. Table O-2 shows some of the function objects.

Category	Function	Example
Mathematical	plus<T>	plus <int>
	minus<T>	minus <float>
	multiplies<T>	multiplies <double>
	divides<T>	divides <int>
	modulus<T>	modulus <float>
Relational	equal_to<T>	equal_to <int>
	not_equal_to<T>	not_equal_to <float>
	greater<T>	greater <int>
	greater_equal<T>	greater_equal <string>
	less<T>	less <double>
	less_equal<T>	less_equal <int>
Logical	logical_not<T>	logical_not<bool>
	logical_and<T>	logical_and<bool>
	logical_or<T>	logical_or<bool>

Table O-2 STL encapsulated function objects

Glossary

A

absolute value: the magnitude of a number regardless of its sign.

abstract class: a class that contains at least one pure virtual function.

access specifier: the C++ class specification that designates the class members as private, protected, or public.

accessor: a function that cannot change the state of its invoking object.

accuracy: the quality factor that addresses the correctness of a system.

actual parameters: the parameters in the function calling statement that contain the values to be passed to the function. Contrast with *formal parameters*.

additive expression: the binary expression that includes the add and subtract operators.

address: the physical location in memory where data or program instructions are stored. See also *pointer*.

afferent: a module whose processing is directed toward the central transform; that is, a module that gathers data to be transmitted toward the central processing functions of a module.

aggregation: the declaration of a class type inside a class definition. In UML, the design notation that depicts aggregation.

algorithm: the logical steps necessary to solve a problem in a computer; a function or a part of a function.

algorithmics: the term created by Brassard and Bratley that refers to the study of techniques used to create efficient algorithms.

and: a logical operator with the property that the expression is true if and only if all of the operands are individually true.

anonymous object: an unnamed object created by an explicit call to a class constructor.

ANSI C++: the standard for the C++ language adopted by the American National Standards Institute.

append: in file processing, the mode that adds to the end of a file.

application software: computer software developed to support a specific user requirement. Contrast with *system software*.

arity: the number of operands associated with an operator. For example, a unary operator has one operand, a binary operator has two, and a ternary operator has three.

array: a fixed-sized, sequenced collection of elements of the same data type.

ascending sequence: a list order in which each element in the list has a key greater than or equal to its predecessors; *lexicographical order*.

ASCII: the American Standard Code for Information Interchange. An encoding scheme that defines control characters and graphic characters for the first 128 values in a byte.

assembler: system software that converts a source program into executable object code. See also *compiler*.

assembly language: A programming language in which there is a one-for-one correspondence between the symbolic instruction set of the language and the computer's machine language.

assignment expression: an expression containing the assignment operator (=) that results in the value of the expression being placed into the left operand.

association: the relationship between two independent classes. In UML, the notation that depicts the relationship between classes as a solid lines between classes.

associativity: the parsing direction used to evaluate an expression when all operators have an equal priority. See *left* and *right associativity*. See also *precedence*.

atomic data: data that cannot be meaningfully subdivided.
atomic data type: see *standard type*.
auto: the default storage class for a local variable.
auxiliary storage: any storage device outside main memory; permanent data storage; external storage.

B

base class: any class from which other classes are derived; also called parent class. See also *derived class* and *inheritance*.
batch update: an update process in which transactions are gathered over time for processing as a unit. Contrast with *online update.*
big-O notation: a measure of the efficiency of an algorithm in which only the dominant factor is considered.
binary a numbering system with base 2. The binary digits are 0 and 1.
binary class function: a member or friend function that operates on two instances of a class object. Contrast with *unary class function.*
binary expression: any expression containing one operator and two operands.
binary file: a collection of structured data stored in the internal format of the computer. Contrast with *text file.*
binary operator: an operator that requires two operands.
binary search: a search algorithm in which the search value is located by repeatedly dividing the list in half.
bit: acronym for Binary digIT. The basic storage unit in a computer with the capability of storing only the value 0 or 1.
bitwise copy: a copied object that is equal to the original object, bit by bit. Contrast with logical copy.
bitwise operator: any of the set of operators that operate on individual bits in a field.
blackbox testing: testing based on the system requirements rather than a knowledge of the workings of a program.
block: in C++, a group of statements enclosed in braces {...}.
block comment: a comment beginning with /* and ending with */ that can be used to identify a comment spanning multiple lines. See also *line comment.*
block scope: see *scope.*
body: the part of a function that contains the definitions and statements; all of a function except the header declaration. Contrast with *function header.*
***bool*:** the C++ boolean type: an integral type with value of *true* or *false*.
Boolean: a type whose only permitted value *is true* or *false*.
braces: the { and } symbols.
brackets: the [and] symbols.
bubble sort: a sort algorithm in which each pass through the data moves (bubbles) the lowest element to the beginning of the unsorted portion of the list.
buffer: (1) hardware, usually memory, used to synchronize the transfer of data to and from main memory; (2) memory used to hold data that have been read before they are processed or data that are waiting to be written.
buffered input/output: input or output that is temporarily stored in intermediate memory while being read or written.
buffered stream: C++ term for buffered input/output.
bug: a colloquial term used for any error in a piece of software.
byte: a unit of data, shorter than a word, usually consisting of eight bits.

C

call: the invocation of a module in which control is transferred from the current module, known as the calling module, to another module, known as the called module.
call by reference: a parameter passing technique in which the address, rather than the value, of a variable is passed to a function. See also *call by value.*
call by value: a parameter passing technique in which a value is passed to a function. See also *call by reference.*
called function: in a function call, the function that is the object of the call.
calling function: in a function call, the function that invokes the call.
cast: a C++ operator that changes the type of an expression.
ceiling: the smallest integral value greater than or equal to a number.
central processing unit (CPU): the part of a computer that executes instructions; that is, the part that interprets instructions. It is made of two components: a control unit and an arithmetic-logical unit.
central transform: the modules of a program that take input and convert it to output. See also *afferent* and *efferent.*
chaining: In I/O, using extraction or insertion operators, reading or printing more than one element of data in one statement. Assignment: the assignment of one value to multiple variables in one statement.
chained list: another term for *linked list.*
changeability: the quality factor that addresses the ease with which changes can be accurately made to a program.
char: the C++ type for character.

character: a member of the set of values that are used to represent data or control operations. See *ASCII.*

chronological list: a list that is organized by time; that is, in which the data are stored in the order in which they were received. See also *FIFO* and *LIFO*.

***cin*:** the C++ standard input stream object.

class: the combination of data and functions joined together to form a type.

class diagram: a set of UML notations that show classes and their relationships.

class invariant: a software engineering design concept stating that two or more instances of a class that represent the same value must have the same data members.

class iterator: see *iterator.*

class object: an instantiation of a class with its members.

class template: a parameterized declaration of a class that can be used to generate one, two, or more concrete classes.

client: see *client/server*

client/server: a computer system design in which two separate computers control the processing of the application, one providing the basic application computing (the client) and the other providing services, such as database access (the server).

close: the function that concludes the writing of a file by writing any pending data to the file and then making it unavailable for processing.

cohesion: the attribute of a module that describes how closely the processes within a module are related to each other.

coincidental cohesion: a design attribute that describes a module in which the processes within the module are totally unrelated. Considered an unacceptable design in structured programming.

command-line argument: in C++, a parameter passed to *main* during execution of the program.

comma expression: an expression that uses the comma operator.

comma operator: in C++, the operator that connects multiple expressions to be executed one after another.

comment: a textual explanation within code that contains explanatory notes to readers of the code.

communicational cohesion: The attribute of a module that describes how closely the processes in a module are related only in that they share the same data.

compilation error: any error detected during the translation of a source program into machine code.

compile: to translate a high-level language, such as C++, into machine language.

compiler: system software that converts a source program into executable object code; traditionally associated with high-level languages. See also *assembler.*

complement: in a logical expression, a change in the code syntax that makes a true expression false or a false expression true.

composite data: data that are built on other data structures; that is, data that can be broken down into discrete atomic elements.

composition: the inclusion of the definition of a class inside another class. In UML: the design notation that depicts composition.

compound statement: a sequence of statements enclosed in braces. See also *block*.

computer language: any of the syntactical languages used to write programs for computers, such as machine language, assembly language, C++, COBOL, and FORTRAN.

computer system: the set of computer components required for a complete system, consisting of at least an input device, an output device, memory central processing unit, and auxiliary storage.

const: a storage class that designates that a field's contents cannot be changed during the execution of the program.

constant: a data value that cannot change during the execution of the program. Contrast with *variable*.

constructor: a class member function that is called when an instance of a class is created or copied.

content coupling: the direct reference to the data in one module by statements in another module. The lowest form of coupling and one to be avoided.

control character: a nonprintable character value whose function is to perform some operation, such as form-feed, or that is used to indicate status, such as the start of a transmission.

control coupling: communication between functions in which flags are set by one module to control the actions of another.

control variable: in I/O, a system variable that provides formatting instructions. See also *I/O flag*.

conversion code: in C formatted input and output, the code in the format specification that identifies the data type.

copy constructor: a function that is called whenever a copy of an existing instance needs to be created.

correctability: the quality factor that addresses the ease with which errors in a module can be fixed.

counter-controlled loop: a looping technique in which the number of iterations is controlled by a count; in C++, the *for* statement. Contrast with *event-controlled loop*.

coupling: a measure of the interdependence between two separate functions. See also: *content coupling*, *control coupling*, *data coupling*, *global coupling*, and *stamp coupling*.

cout: the C++ standard output stream object.

CPU: central processing unit.

C++ standard library: see *standard library.*

D

dangling *else:* a code sequence in which there is no *else* statement for one of the *if* statements in a nested *if.*

data coupling: communication between modules in which only the required data are passed. Considered the best form of coupling.

data encapsulation: see *encapsulation.*

data hiding: the principle of structured programming in which data are available to a function only if it needs them to complete its processing; data not needed are "hidden" from view. See also *encapsulation* and *scope.*

data name: an identifier given to data in a program.

data member: any identified data object declared in a class.

data structure: the syntactical representation of data organized to show the relationship among the individual elements.

data type: a named set of values and operations defined to manipulate them, such as character and integer.

data validation: the process of verifying and validating data read from an external source.

declaration: in C++, the association of a name with an object, such as a type, variable, structure, or function. Contrast with *definition.*

default argument: a C++ formal parameter that contains an initializer to be used whenever an actual parameter is not supplied in the call.

default constructor: the constructor that is called without an argument.

default copy constructor: a copy constructor provided by the compiler when one is not explicitly coded.

default destructor: a destructor provided by the compiler when one is not explicitly coded.

default value: see *default argument.*

definition: in C++, the creation of physical objects or functions within a program. Contrast with *declaration.*

delimited string: a string terminated by a nondata character, such as the null character in C++.

delimiter: any token used to separate a series of data items.

De Morgan's rule: a rule used to complement a logical expression.

dereference: access of a data variable through a pointer containing its address.

dereference operator: in C++, the asterisk (*). Used to indicate that a pointer's contents (an address) are to be used to access the data stored at that address.

derived class: a class created from a base class through inheritance. The derived class has all of the capabilities as the base class and may also declare and define new data members and functions of its own.

derived type: a composite data type constructed from other types (array, structure, union, pointer, and enumerated type).

descending sequence: a list order in which each element in a list has a key less than or equal to its predecessor.

design error: an error built into the design of a system or program specification; that is, an error created during the design phase of a system or program.

destructor: a class member function that is called when an instance of a class is destroyed; that is, when it ceases to exist.

disk: an auxiliary storage medium used to store data and programs required for a computer.

disk drive: the auxiliary storage hardware device used to read and write to a disk.

diskette: a removable flexible disk, enclosed in a protective flexible or ridged cover, used to store data for a personal computer.

distributed computing: an environment that provides a seamless integration of computing functions between different servers and clients.

***double*:** the C++ type for double-precision floating-point type.

downcast: a cast that converts a base-class object to a derived-class object.

drive: an external storage device that can write and read data, such as the internal hard disk, a floppy disk, or a tape unit.

dynamic allocation: allocation of memory for storing data during the execution of a program. Contrast with *static allocation.*

dynamic array: An array whose memory is allocated at execution time.

dynamic binding: the binding of a pointer and an object during execution through the use of a virtual function.

dynamic casting: casting in which the type is determined during the execution of the program, as opposed to during the compilation. Contrast with *static casting.*

dynamic memory: memory whose use can change during the execution of the program; also known as the *heap*.

dynamic memory allocation: the assignment of data memory when requested during the execution of a program.

E

EBCDIC: Extended Binary Coded Decimal Interchange Code. The character set designed by IBM for its large computer systems. (Pronounced "ebb-see-dic.")

edit set: a list of characters used to validate characters during the formatted reading of a string.

efferent: a module whose processing is directed away from the central transform; that is, a module that predominately disposes data by reporting or writing to a file.

efficiency: the quality factor that addresses the optimum use of computer hardware or responsiveness to a user.

else-if: a style (as opposed to syntax) convention used to simulate a *switch* statement for a nonintegral expression. Each *if* statement in the series must evaluate the same variable.

empty list: a list that has been allocated but that contains no data. Also known as a null list.

encapsulation: the process of specifying data members and methods within a type so that their implementation is hidden from applications that use them; also known as *data hiding*.

end of file: the condition that occurs when a read operation attempts to read after it has processed the last piece of data.

***enum*:** the C++ keyword for an enumerated data type.

enumerated data type: an integral data type in which identifiers are assigned to specified or default values.

enumeration constant: an integer value in an enumerated data type.

environment view: in UML, a set of diagrams that show the configuration of elements and hardware components.

eof: end of file. In C++, an ios member function that indicate's a file is at the end.

error report file: in a file update program, the file that contains input errors to be reported to the user.

error state: one of three states that an open file may assume. An error state occurs when a program issues an impossible command, such as a read command while the file is in a write state, or when a physical device failure occurs. See also *read state, write state.*

error stream: in C++, the *ostream* instance (cerr) used to display errors; usually assigned to the screen.

escape character: in C++, the backslash (\) is used to indicate that the character that follows represents a control character.

escape sequence: any group of keystrokes or characters used to identify a control character.

event-controlled loop: a loop whose termination is predicated upon the occurrence of a specified event. Contrast with *counter-controlled loop*.

exclusive or: a logical operation in which the result is true when only one of the operands is true and not both.

exception class: defined in the exception library file, the class that defines the system errors.

exception handler: any *catch* statement that receives the object raised by the *throw* statement and determines the action to be taken when the error occurs.

exception specification: code added to a function header to control what exceptions a function is allowed to throw.

executable file: a file that contains program code in its executable form; the result of linking the source code object module with any required library modules.

explicit constructor: a constructor, designated by the modifier *explicit*, that cannot be implicitly called; a constructor that cannot be used for type conversion.

explicit constructor call: a call to a class constructor that creates an anonymous (unnamed) object.

explicit inline function: an inline function coded outside a class declaration.

explicit type conversion: the conversion of a value from one type to another through the cast operator. Contrast with *implicit type conversion*.

exponential efficiency: a category of algorithm efficiency in which the run time is a function of the power of the number of elements being processed, as in $O(n) = c^n$.

expression: a sequence of operators and operands that reduces to a single value.

expression statement: an expression terminated by a semicolon.

expression type: one of seven expression attributes that broadly describes an expression's format: *primary, postfix, unary, binary, ternary, assignment,* and *comma.*

extent: the attribute of a field that determines when it can be accessed within a source program. See also *temporal authority.*

extern: the storage class that exports the name of a field to the linker so that it can be used by other programs. Unless otherwise designated, global fields are automatically storage class *externs*.

extraction operator: the C++ operator (>>) that reads data from a file stream.

F

factorial efficiency: a measure of the efficiency of a module in which the run time is proportionate to the factorial of the number of elements, as in $O(n) = n!$.

fan out: an attribute of a module that describes the number of submodules it calls.

field: the smallest named unit of data that has meaning in describing information. A field may be either a variable or a constant.

field specification: a C subcomponent of the format string used to describe the formatting of data in the formatted input and output functions.

field width: in a field specification, the specification of the maximum input width or minimum output width for formatted data.

FIFO: First In, First Out.

file: a named collection of data stored on an auxiliary storage device. Compare with *list*.

file mode: a designation of a file's input and/or output capability; files may be opened for reading, writing, appending, or updating.

file state: the current mode of a file limited to read mode or write mode or an error mode, which allows neither read nor write.

file table: in C, the predefined standard structure, `FILE`, used to store the attributes of a file.

fixed-length string: a string whose size is constant regardless of the number of characters stored in it.

flag: an indicator used in a program to designate the presence or absence of a condition; *switch*.

flexibility: the quality factor that addresses the ease with which a program can be changed to meet user requirements.

***float*:** a single-precision floating-point type.

floating-point number: a number that contains both an integral and a fraction.

floor: the largest integral value that is equal to or less than a number.

flowchart: a program design tool in which standard graphical symbols are used to represent the logical flow of data through a function.

formal parameter: the parameter declaration in a function prototype used to describe the type of data to be processed by the function. Contrast with *actual parameter.*

format string: in C, the first parameter in a formatted input or output function used to describe the data to be read or written.

formatted input/output: in C, any of the standard library functions that can reformat data to and from text while they are being read or written.

frequency array: an array that contains the number of occurrences of a value or of a range of values. See also *histogram.*

friend class: a separately declared class that has access to another class, which has granted it friendship.

friend function: a function defined outside a class that is given access to the class's internal data members and functions.

front: when used to refer to a list: a pointer that identifies the first element.

function: a named block of code that performs a process within a program; an executable unit of code, consisting of a header and a body, that is designed to perform a task within the program.

function call: a statement that invokes another function.

functional cohesion: a module in which all of the processing is related to a single task. The highest level of cohesion.

function declaration: in C++, a prototype statement that describes a function's return type and formal parameters.

function definition: in C++, the implementation of a function declaration.

function header: in a function definition, that part of the function that supplies the return type, function identifier, and formal parameters. Contrast with *body.*

function member: a function defined in the scope of a class.

function overloading: the definition of two or more functions within the same scope using the same identifier with different argument lists.

function overriding: the redefinition of a function in a derived class using the same argument list and return type.

function template: a model of a function that can be used to generate one, two, or more concrete functions.

G

general purpose software: software that can be used for more than one application.

generic type: a type that can represent any of the other standard types.

global coupling: communication between different modules that uses data accessible to all modules in a program. Considered to be a very poor communications technique for intraprogram communication.

global declaration: the declaration and/or definition of a variable or function outside the boundaries of any function; that is, before *main* or between function definitions. Contrast with *local declaration.*

global variable: a variable defined in the global declaration section of a program; that is, defined outside a function block.

graphical user interface (GUI): a user interface that uses a windows environment to communicate with the user.

greatest common divisor: in mathematics, the largest integral number that contains the common factors of two other numbers.

H

hard copy: any computer output that is written to paper or other readable mediums such as microfiche. Contrast with *soft copy*.

hardware: any of the physical components of a computer system, such as the keyboard or a printer.

header declaration: that part of a function that contains the return type, function name, and parameter declarations.

header file: in C++, a file consisting of prototype statements and other declarations and placed in a library for shared use.

head pointer: a pointer that identifies the first element of a list.

heap: see *heap memory*.

heap memory: a pool of memory that can be used to dynamically allocate space for data while the program is running.

hexadecimal: a numbering system with base 16. Its digits are 0 1 2 3 4 5 6 7 8 9 A B C D E F.

high-level language: a (portable) programming language designed to allow the programmer to concentrate on the application rather than the structure of a particular computer or operating system.

histogram: a graphical representation of a frequency distribution. See also *frequency array*.

host object: the object that invokes a class method; the object pointed to by the *this* pointer.

I

identifier: the name of an object. In C++, identifiers can consist only of digits, letters, and the underscore.

implicit inline function: an inline function coded inside a class definition.

implicit type conversion: the automatic conversion of data from one type to another when required within a C++ program. Contrast with *explicit type conversion*.

implementation view: in UML, the diagram that shows the organization of software components and their relationships.

include: a preprocessor command that specifies a library file to be inserted into the program.

inclusive or: see *or*.

indentation: a coding style in which statements dependent on a previous statement, such as *if* or *while*, are coded in an indented block to show their relationship to the controlling statement.

index: the address of an element within an array. See also *subscript*.

index range checking: a feature available in some compilers that inserts code to ensure that all index references are within the array.

indirection operator: the operator (*) used to refer to the data through the address contained in a pointer; also known as the dereference operator.

indirect pointer: a pointer that locates the address of data through one or more other pointers; pointer to pointer.

infinite loop: a loop that does not terminate.

information hiding: a structured programming concept in which the data structure and the implementation of its operations are not known by the user.

inheritance: the ability to extend a class to create a new class while retaining the data objects and methods of the base class and adding new data objects and methods.

inheritance type: the attribute of a derived class (*public*, *protected*, or *private*) that determines the access method of the inherited members.

initialization: the process of assigning values to a variable at the beginning of a program or a function.

initialization constructor: the function invoked when a class is defined with initializers.

initialization list: the establishment of an object's values through the association of header argument values with an object's variables.

inline function: a function whose implementation code is used in place of a call.

I/O flag: any of a set of flags used to format input and output. Also known as input/output system (ios) flags.

input device: a device that provides data to be read by a program.

input stream: C++ term for any input to a program.

inquiry: a request for information from a program.

insertion operator: the C++ operator (<<) that receives data from a program and converts it to an external format to be inserted into an output object.

insertion sort: a sort algorithm in which the first element from the unsorted portion of the list is inserted into its proper position relative to the data in the sorted portion of the list.

instance: the object created when a class is defined. See also *instantiation*.

instance member: data or functions that are associated with each instance of a class object; the default member status of a class. Contrast with *static member*.

instantiation: the process of defining an occurrence of a class.
int: the C++ data type for an integer.
integer: an integral number; a number without a fractional part.
interoperability: the quality factor that addresses the ability of one system to exchange data with another.
iteration: a single execution of the statements in a loop.
iterator: a C++ object designed to move to the next element in a list with each call.

J

justification: the orientation of variable-length data in a fixed-length format through addition of space characters. The most common justifications are left, centered, and right.

K

key: one or more fields used to identify a record.
keyboard: an input device used for text or control data, that consists of alphanumeric keys and function keys.
keyboard file: in C, the standard input file (stdin).
keyword: any specified word that has a defined syntactical meaning to a compiler.
KISS: In this text, Keep It Short and Simple.

L

late binding: see *dynamic binding.*
leading zero flag: the C flag in the format string of a print statement indicating that numeric data are to be printed with leading zeros.
left associativity: the evaluation of an expression that parses from the left to the right. Contrast with *right associativity.*
left justification: the orientation of variable-length data in an output format such that trailing null values are inserted and the first data character is at the left end of the print area. Contrast with *right justification.*
length-controlled string: a variable-length string function in which the data are identified by a structural component containing the length of the data.
lexicographical order: a data order based on the dictionary. See also *ascending sequence*.
LIFO: Last In, First Out.
limit test: in a loop, the expression that determines if the loop will continue or stop. See also *terminating condition.*
line comment: a comment, beginning with //, that must be completed on one line.
linear efficiency: a measure of the efficiency of a module in which the run time is proportionate to the number of elements being processed, as in $O(n) = n$.
linear list: a list structure in which each element, except the last, has a unique successor.
linear loop: a loop whose execution is a function of the number of elements being processed. See also *linear efficiency.*
linear search: see *sequential search.*
link: in a list structure, the field that identifies the next element in the list; a sequence pointer in a linked list.
linked list: a linear list structure in which the ordering of the elements is determined by link fields.
linked list traversal: processing in which every element of a linked list is processed in order.
linker: the program by which an object module is joined with precompiled functions to form an executable program.
literal: an unnamed constant coded as a part of an expression.
list: an ordered set of data contained in *main* memory. Compare with *file.*
loader: the operating system function that fetches an executable program into memory for running.
local declaration: a variable or type declaration that is only visible to the block in which it is contained. Contrast with *global declaration.*
local definition: definitions within a function.
local variables: variables defined with a block.
logarithmic efficiency: a measure of the efficiency of a module in which the run time is proportionate to the log of the number of elements being processed, as in $O(n) = \log \underline{n}$.
logarithmic loop: a loop whose efficiency is a function of the log of the number of elements being processed. See also *logarithmic efficiency.*
logic error: an error in the design of a function or program that causes it to produce invalid output.
logical cohesion: a design attribute that describes a module in which the processing within the module is related only by the general type of processing being done. Considered unacceptable design in structured programming.
logical copy: a copy of an object in which dynamic data items are reallocated and their values copied. Contrast with *bitwise copy.*
logical data: data whose values can be only *true* or *false*. See *Boolean.*
logical error: a design error in a program that while satisfying the syntactical requirements of the compiler does not produce the desired results.

logical operator: one of the three operator, *and, or*, and *not*, that can be used to evaluate an expression as a logical value.

logical value: an expression value that evaluates to *true* or *false*.

***long double*:** a C++ data type whose precision may be greater than *float*.

***long integer*:** a C++ data type whose values may be greater than *int*.

loop: the construct used to repeat one or more statements in a program. The *while, for,* and *do...while* in C++.

loop control expression: the expression in a loop statement that determines if the loop will iterate or terminate.

loop update: the code within a loop statement or body that changes the environment such that the loop will eventually terminate.

lvalue: an expression attribute indicating that the expression can be used to access, modify, examine, or copy its data.

M

machine language: the instructions that are native to the central processor of a computer and are executable without assembly or compilation.

maintainability: a software engineering and quality attribute that refers to the ease with which a program can be changed or updated.

manager function: a function used in the creation, copying, or destruction of objects; constructors, copy constructors, and destructors.

manipulator: an input/output function that provides functionality to data being read or written.

mask: a variable or constant that contains a bit configuration used to control the setting of bits in a bitwise operation.

master file: a permanent file that contains the most current data regarding an application.

member function: a function created within the scope of a class.

member operator: the operator (dot) that is used to reference a member within an object.

memory: the main memory of a computer, consisting of random access memory (RAM) and read-only memory (ROM), used to store data and program instructions.

merge: to combine two or more sequential files into one sequential file based on a common key and structure format.

method: a function declared within a class scope.

module: a generic term for a function.

monitor: the visual display unit of a computer system, usually a video display device.

Morse code: the language patented by Samuel F. B. Morse in 1837 to send messages by telegraph.

multiplicative expression: the binary expression that includes the multiply, divide, and modulus operators.

multiplicity: in UML, the range of instances between two classes.

multiple inheritance: the capability for a derived class to draw from two or more base classes. Contrast with *simple inheritance.*

multidimensional array: an array whose elements consist of two or more arrays.

multiway selection: a selection statement that is capable of evaluating more than two alternatives. In C++, the *switch* statement. Contrast with *two-way selection.*

mutator: a function that can change the state of a host object.

N

namespace a collection of names belonging to a group.

natural language: any spoken language.

negative logic: an expression that begins with the negation operator (!).

nested class: the declaration of one class inside of another.

nested loop: a loop contained within another loop.

nested structure: a structure that contains other structures.

newline: the ASCII character that designates the end of a line of input or output.

node: in a data structure, an element that contains both data and structural elements used to process the list.

null character: the ASCII character with a zero value; also known as nil character.

null pointer: a pointer that contains an address value indicating no address is assigned to the pointer.

O

object: an entity that defines data and can access a set of processes to manipulate those data; in object oriented programming, any instantiation of a class.

object diagram: in UML, the notation, containing a name compartment and an attribute compartment, that depicts an object.

object file: the output of a compilation consisting of machine language instructions.

object-oriented programming: the design concept that centers around objects that contain (encapsulate) the data and the necessary functions to process the data.

object state: in Object Oriented Programming (OOP), the current state of an object represented by the value of its data members.

octal: a numbering system with a base of 8. The octal digits are 0 1 2 3 4 5 6 7.

offset: a measure of the number of elements before or after a predefined point in an array or file.

one-dimensional array: a simple array in which each element contains only one type value.

one's complement: the bitwise operator that reverses the value of bits in a variable; a 0 becomes a 1 and a 1 becomes a 0.

online update: an update process in which transactions are entered and processed by a user who has direct access to the system.

open: the function that locates and prepares a file for processing.

operability: the quality factor that addresses the ease with which a system can be used.

operand: an object in a statement on which an operation is performed. Contrast with *operator.*

operating system: the software that controls the computing environment and provides an interface to the user.

operator: the action symbol(s) in an expression. Contrast with *operand.*

operator overloading: the definition of two or more operators using the same operator token and same arity.

or: a logical operator with the property that if any of the operands is true, the expression is true.

ordered list: a list in which the elements are arranged so that the key values are placed in ascending or descending sequence.

output device: a device that can be written but not read.

output stream: In C++, a stream that can be used for output operations.

overflow: the condition that results when an attempt is made to insert data into a list and there is no room.

overloading: the C++ capability that associates multiple function definitions within the same scope with one function name or one operator.

P

parameter: a value passed to a function.

pass by reference: a function coupling technique in which the address of a field is passed to a function.

pass by value: a function coupling technique in which only a copy of the data is passed to a function.

plane: the first dimension in a multidimensional array.

pointer: a constant or variable that contains an address that can be used to access data.

pointer arithmetic: addition or subtraction in which a pointer's contents (an address) are changed by a multiple of the size of the data to which it is pointing.

pointer constant: a pointer whose contents cannot be changed.

pointer indirection: a data reference in which two or more pointers are used; that is, in which a pointer is used to point to a pointer that points to data.

pointer to function: a pointer that identifies the entry point to a function. It is used to pass a function's address as a parameter.

pointer variable: a variable declared or defined as a pointer; a variable whose contents are the address of another variable.

polynomic efficiency: a measure of the efficiency of a module in which the run time is proportionate to the number of elements raised to the highest factor in a polynomial, as in $O(n) = n^k$.

polymorphism: Polymorphism is the ability to write several versions of a function, each in a separate class related by inheritance. When called, the function appropriate for the object being referenced is executed.

portability: the quality factor that addresses the ease with which a system can be moved to other hardware environments.

postfix decrement: in C++, the operator that subtracts one from a variable after its value has been used in an expression.

postfix expression: an expression in which the operand(s) follow the operator.

postfix increment: in C++, the operator that adds one to a variable after its value has been used in an expression.

post-test loop: a loop in which the terminating condition is tested only after the execution of the loop statements. Contrast with *pretest loop.*

precedence: the priority assigned to an operator or group of operators that determines the order in which operators will be evaluated in an expression. See also *associativity.*

precision: the maximum number of integral digits, the number of significant digits or fractional digits in a floating-point number, or the maximum number of characters in a string.

prefix decrement: the operator that subtracts one from a variable before its value has been used in an expression.

preprocessor: the first phase of a C++ compilation in which the source statements are prepared for compilation and any necessary libraries are loaded.

preprocessor directives: commands to the C++ precompiler.

pretest loop: a loop in which the terminating condition is tested before the execution of the loop statements. Contrast with *post-test loop.*

primary expression: an expression consisting of only a single value (no operator); the highest-priority expression.

primary storage: computer storage that contains a running program and its data.
printable character: a character value that is associated with a print graphic.
printer: an output device that displays the output on paper.
private inheritance: the inheritance type in which data and methods in the base class are inaccessible in a derived class .
procedural cohesion: a module design in which the processing within the module is related by control flows. Considered acceptable design only at the higher levels of a program.
procedural programming: the design concept that centers around the rules or procedures for processing the data.
processing unit: short form of central processing unit.
program development: the system development activity in which requirement specifications are converted into executable programs.
program file: a file that contains an executable program.
program testing: the process that validates a program's operation and verifies that it meets its design requirements.
protected inheritance: the inheritance type in which *protected* and *public* members become protected in a derived class and any private members become inaccessable.
prototype statement: in C++, the declaration of a function that provides the return type and formal parameter types.
pseudocode: English-like statements that follow a loosely defined syntax and are used to convey the design of an algorithm or function.
pseudorandom numbers: a set of numbers with random qualities that can be repeatedly generated.
public inheritance: the inheritance type in which access of *protected* and *public* members is preserved in the derived type; *private* data are inaccessible, *protected* access remains protected and *public* access remains public.
pure virtual function: within an abstract class, a member function that must be overrided for each derived class.

Q

quadratic efficiency: a measure of the efficiency of a module in which the run time is proportionate to the number of elements squared. Quadratic efficiency is one of the polynomial efficiency, as in $O(n) = n^2$.
quadratic loop: a loop that consists of two or more loops, each of which has a linear efficiency, resulting in a loop with quadratic efficiency.
quality: see *software quality.*
query: inquiry.

R

random number: a number selected from a set in which all members have the same probability of being selected.
read mode: the attribute of a file that indicates that it is opened for input only.
read state: one of three states that an open file may assume. The state of a file during which only input operations may be performed. See also *error state, write state.*
realtime: processing in which updating takes place at the time the event occurs.
rear: when used to refer to a list: a pointer that identifies the last element.
record: see *structure.*
recursion: a repetitive process in which a function calls itself; the design of a function that allows it to call itself.
register: the storage class that requests that, if possible, a variable be allocated to a CPU register.
relational operator: one of six operators, such as equal and less than, that return a Boolean value based on the relationship between its two operands.
reliability: the quality factor that addresses the confidence or trust in a system's total operation.
***return*:** the C++ statement that causes execution of a function to terminate and control to be resumed by the calling function.
return code: the value sent back to the calling function by a called function.
reusability: the quality factor that addresses the ease with which software can be used in other programs.
reusable code: code that can be used by more than one process.
right associativity: the evaluation of an expression that parses from the right to the left. Contrast with *left associativity.*
right justification: the orientation of variable-length data in an output format such that leading spaces are inserted and the last data character is at the right end of the print area. Contrast with *left justification.*
right-left rule: a method of reading complex declarations that starts with the identifier and alternately reads right and left until the declaration has been fully read.
run-time error: any error encountered during the execution of a program that causes it to terminate abnormally.
rvalue: an expression attribute indicating that the expression can be used only to supply a value for an expression.

S

scope: an attribute of a variable that defines whether it is visible to or hidden from statements in a program. See also *temporal authority.*

scope resolution operator: the C++ operator (::) that relates an object to a class member.

search: the process that examines a list to locate one or more elements containing a designated value known as a search argument.

secondary storage: synonym for auxiliary storage.

security: the quality factor that addresses the ease or difficulty with which an unauthorized user can access data.

selection: see *selection statement.*

selection sort: the sort algorithm in which the smallest value in the unsorted portion of a list is selected and placed at the end of the sorted portion of the list.

selection statement: a statement that chooses between two or more alternatives. In C++, the *if...else* or *switch* statements.

self-referential structure: a structure that contains a pointer to itself.

sentinel: a flag that guards the end of a list or a file. The sentinel is usually the maximum value for a key field and cannot be a valid data value.

separate compilation: a capability within a programming language that allows parts of a program to be compiled independently and later assembled into an executable unit.

sequential cohesion: a module design in which the processing within the module flows such that the data from one process are used in the next process.

sequential file: a file structure in which data must be processed serially from the first entry in the file.

sequential search: a search technique used with a linear list in which the searching begins at the first element and continues until the value of an element equal to the value being sought is located, or until the end of the list is reached.

serial search: any search technique that starts at the beginning of the list and continues toward the end.

server: see *client/server.*

***short*:** the C++ type for short integer.

short integer: an integer format used for smaller numbers.

side effect: a change in a variable that results from the evaluation of an expression.

***signed*:** a type modifier indicating that a numeric value may be either positive or negative. Contrast with *unsigned*.

sign flag: the C flag value (+) in the conversion code of a print format string that indicates that positive numbers are to be printed with a plus sign.

simple inheritance: object design in which each derived class has only one base class. Contrast with *multiple inheritance*.

size: a C modifier (h, l, L) in the conversion code of a format string that modifies integer and float types.

slack bytes: inaccessible memory locations added between fields in a structure to force a hardware-required boundary alignment.

soft copy: computer output written to a nonpermanent display such as a monitor. Contrast with *hard copy.*

software: the application and system programs necessary for computer hardware to accomplish a task including their documentation and any required procedures.

software quality: an attribute of software that measures the user's total satisfaction with a system.

sort: the process that orders a list or file.

sort pass: one iteration of a sort algorithm during which all unsorted data are examined.

source file: the file that contains program statements written by a programmer before they are converted into machine language; the input file to an assembler or compiler.

space flag: the C flag value in the conversion code of a print format string indicating that positive numbers are to be printed with a leading space.

spatial authority: an attribute of a field that determines which functions within a program can refer to it or change its contents.

square brackets: the [and] symbols.

stack: a data structure in which data are logically accessible only from one end known as the top.

stack memory: in C++, the memory management facility that is used to store local variables while their function is active.

stamp coupling: the communication technique between modules in which data are passed as a structure; often results in unrequired data being passed.

standard error file: the file to which *cerr* is connected (the monitor by default).

standard input file: the file to which *cin* is connected (keyboard by default).

standard library: any of a collection of libraries containing functions required by the C++ standard provided by an implementation of the C++ language.

standard output file: the file to which *cout* is connected (monitor by default).

standard type: one of the intrinsic C++ types that are considered atomic; that is, that cannot be broken down (*void, char, int, float*).

statement: a syntactical construct in C++ that represents one operation in a function.

static: a storage class that designates (a) that a local field is to maintain its contents throughout the execution of a program (contrast with *auto*), or (b) that a global variable's name is not to be exported to the linker (contrast with *extern*).

static allocation: memory whose location is determined by the compiler and therefore preset before run time. Contrast with *dynamic allocation.*

static binding the binding of a function to an object is fixed during compilation.

static casting: the conversion of a standard data type to another standard data type using either implicit or explicit casting; casting done during the compilation of a program. Contrast with *dynamic casting*.

static memory: memory whose use can change during the execution of the program; also known as the *heap*.

static member: data or functions that are associated with the class object and not with instances of the class. Members are designated static with the keyword *static*.

static memory: memory whose use (e.g., for a variable) does not change during the running of a program.

stderr: the C standard error file.

stdin: the C standard input file.

stdout: the C standard output file.

stepwise refinement: a design methodology in which a system or program is developed from the top down; starting with the most inclusive, each module is decomposed and refined until the meaning of a component is intrinsically understood.

storage class: an attribute of a field that determines its spatial and temporal usage. See also *auto*, *extern*, *static*, *register.*

stream: the C++ abstraction of I/O, consisting of a sequence of characters divided into lines (text stream) or sequences of byte values representing data in their internal memory formats (binary stream).

string: in C++, the class used to store and manipulate string values; in C, a variable-length sequence of characters delimited by a null character.

string literal: a string constant enclosed in double quotes.

***struct*:** the C++ a user-defined type containing multiple fields.

structure: a named collection of fields grouped together for processing; *record.*

structure chart: a design and documentation tool that represents a program as a hierarchical flow of functions.

structural view: in UML, a set of diagrams that show the static structure of the system.

stub: in top-down program development, an incomplete function used to test the interface with higher-level functions in the program.

subfunction: in a program, any function that is called by another function; all functions other than *main* are functions.

subscript: an ordinal number that indicates the position of an element within an array. See also *index.*

suffix: a modifier to a numeric constant that indicates its type when used in an expression.

switch: see *flag*.

symbolic language: a computer language, one level above from machine language, in which there is a mnemonic identifier for each machine instruction and which has the capability of using symbolic data names.

syntax: the rules that define the usage of keywords and tokens within a language; the grammar of a language.

syntax error: an error detected during the compilation of a source program that breaks the syntactical rules of a compiler. See also *compilation error.*

system development life cycle: a model of the steps required to develop software that begins with the need for the software and concludes with its implementation.

system development software: any computer tool used to develop software, such as but not limited to compilers, debuggers, and documentation tools.

system software: any software whose primary purpose is to support the operation of the computing environment. Contrast with *application software*.

system support software: software used for non-application processing, such as system utilities.

T

tagged structure: a structure in which the structure is given an identifier that can be used to declare variables of the structure type.

tape storage: an auxiliary storage medium that stores data as a sequential file on a magnetic recording surface.

template: a model of a function or a class that can be used to generate functions or classes.

temporal authority: an attribute of a field that determines when a field is alive and active during the execution of a program.

temporal cohesion: a module design in which processes are combined because they all need to be processed in the same time sequence.

terminating condition: in a loop, the condition that stops a loop. See also *limit test.*

ternary expression: an expression that contains three operands; the conditional expression (?:) is the only ternary expression in C++.

test driver: a program used to test generalized software as opposed to a program that solves a user problem.

testability: an attribute of software that measures the ease with which the software can be tested as an operational system.

testing: see *program testing*, *blackbox testing*, or *whitebox testing*.

text editor: software that maintains text files, such as a word processor or a source program editor.

text file: a file in which all data are stored as characters. Contrast with *binary file*.

***this* pointer:** the specified pointer within a class member function that points to the invoking instance of the class.

timeliness: an attribute of software that measures responsiveness of a system to a user's time requirements.

time-sharing environment: an operating system concept in which more than one user has access to a computer at the same time.

token: in C++, a syntactical construct that represents an operation or a flag, such as the assignment token (=).

top-down design: a program design concept in which a design progresses through a decomposition of the functions, beginning with the top of the structure chart and working toward the lowest modules. See also *stepwise refinement*.

transaction file: a file containing relatively transient data to be used to change the contents of a master file.

transform analysis: an analytical process that creates a program design by classifying modules as input, process, or output.

transform module: the function in a program that takes input from the afferent modules and prepares it for processing by the efferent modules.

translation unit: a separately compiled unit of code that can be linked with other compile units to form a program.

translator: a generic term for any of the language conversion programs. See also *assembler* and *compiler*.

traversal: an algorithmic process in which each element in a structure is processed once and only once.

throwing an exception: when an error is detected in a program, the process of transferring the error handling to another part of the program.

transferability: the attribute of software quality that refers to the ease with which a program can be transferred from one hardware environment to another. In general, C++ is highly transferable.

transform analysis: a design technique that identifies the processes in a program as input, process, and output and then organizes them around one or more processes that convert inputs to outputs.

translator: software that convert source programs into machine language

two-dimensional array: an array in which each element contains a one-dimentional array. See also *multidimensional array*.

two-way selection: a selection statement that is capable of evaluating only two alternatives. In C++, the *if...else* statement. Contrast with *multiway selection*.

type: a set of values and a set of operations that can be applied on those values.

type cast: the C++ operator that explicitly changes the type of a data value.

type definition: a C++ construct (*typedef*) that creates a new type identifier from an existing type.

type qualifier: a C++ construct that modifies a type and its usage. The *const* construct is a type modifier that creates a constant.

U

UML: Unified Modeling Language. A graphical language used for Object-Oriented Analysis and Design.

unary class function: a function that can operate on only one instance of a class. Contrast with *binary class function*.

unary decrement: see *prefix decrement*.

unary expression: any of the C++ expressions that contain only one operand.

unary increment: see *prefix increment*.

unary minus: in C++, the operator that complements the value of an expression.

unary operator: an operator that requires only one operand.

unbuffered input/output: input or output that is transmitted directly to or from memory without the use of a buffer.

underflow: an event that occurs when an attempt is made to delete data from a data structure that is empty.

***union*:** C++ term for variable structure.

***unsigned*:** a type modifier indicating that a numeric value may be only positive. Contrast with *signed*.

upcast: a cast that converts a derived-class object to a base-class object.

update: (1) in array processing, the process that changes the contents of an element; (2) in file processing, a mode that allows a file to be both read and written.

user-defined function: any function written by the programmer, as opposed to a standard library function.

V

variable: a memory storage object that can be changed during the execution of a program. Contrast with *constant*.

variable length string: a character structure, such as the string class, that is not limited by its structure.

variable structure: a data structure in which two or more types of data may occupy the same positions within the structure. In C++, a *union*.

virtual function: a function bound to an object during the run time.

visibility: the temporal authority for a field that designates where in the program it can be accessed or changed; *scope*.

***void*:** the absence of data.

void functions: functions whose return value is void.

volatile: an attribute of a field that indicates that it may be accessed or changed by functions beyond the control of the compiler.

W

waterfall model: a system development life cycle in which each phase of development, such as requirement development and design, is completed before the next phase starts.

whitebox testing: program testing in which the internal design of the program is considered; also called clear box testing. Contrast with *blackbox testing.*

whitespace: in C++, the space, vertical and horizontal tabs, newline, and form-feed characters.

write mode: the attribute of a file indicating that it is opened for output only.

write state: one of three states that an open file can assume. A file in the write state can only be used for output. See also *error state, read state.*

Index

Symbols

A

D

E

F

J

K

L

P

Q

R

T

U

V

W

Y

Stream Flag	Set/Unset Flag	Input	Output	Manipulator
			✓	endl
Boolean alpha	stream.setf(ios::boolalpha) stream.unsetf(ios::boolalpha)	✓ ✓	✓ ✓	boolalpha noboolalpha
Decimal	stream.setf(ios::dec)	✓	✓	dec
Fixed Point	stream.setf(ios::fixed)	✓	✓	fixed
Hexadecimal	stream.setf(ios::hex)	✓	✓	hex
Internal	stream.setf(ios::internal)		✓	internal
Left Justify	stream.setf(ios::left)		✓	left
Octal	stream.setf(ios::oct)	✓	✓	oct
Right Justify	stream.setf(ios::right)		✓	right
Scientific	stream.setf(ios::scientific)	✓	✓	scientific
Show Base	stream.setf(ios::showbase) stream.unsetf(ios::showbase)		✓ ✓	showbase noshowbase
Show Point	stream.setf(ios::showpoint) stream.unsetf(ios::showpoint)		✓ ✓	showpoint noshowpoint
Show Position	stream.setf(ios::showpos) stream.unsetf(ios::showpos)		✓ ✓	showpos noshowpos
Skip Whitespace	stream.setf(ios::skipws) stream.unsetf(ios::skipws)	✓ ✓		skipws noskipws
Unit Buffer	stream.setf(ios::unitbuf)		✓	flush
Upper Case	stream.setf(ios::uppercase) stream.unsetf(ios::uppercase)		✓ ✓	uppercase nouppercase

Stream flags and manipulators (See Chapter 7)

Control Variable	Set with Function/Operator	Set with Manipulator
width	stream.width(number)	setw(n)
fill	stream.fill(character)	setfill(c)
precision	stream.precision(number)	setprecision(n)

Stream control variables and manipulators (See Chapter 7)

Status	Function	In/Out	Example	Action
Success	good()	Both	if (cin.good( ))	Continue
End of file	eof()	Input	if (cin.eof( ))	Terminate reading
Invalid data	fail()	Input	if (cin.fail( ))	Prompt user to reenter
Hardware failure	bad()	Both	if (cin.bad( ))	Gracefully terminate

File stream status (See Chapter 7)